Twentieth-Century
Literary Criticism

Guide to Gale Literary Criticism Series

For criticism on	Consult these Gale series
Authors now living or who died after December 31, 1999	*CONTEMPORARY LITERARY CRITICISM (CLC)*
Authors who died between 1900 and 1999	*TWENTIETH-CENTURY LITERARY CRITICISM (TCLC)*
Authors who died between 1800 and 1899	*NINETEENTH-CENTURY LITERATURE CRITICISM (NCLC)*
Authors who died between 1400 and 1799	*LITERATURE CRITICISM FROM 1400 TO 1800 (LC)* *SHAKESPEAREAN CRITICISM (SC)*
Authors who died before 1400	*CLASSICAL AND MEDIEVAL LITERATURE CRITICISM (CMLC)*
Authors of books for children and young adults	*CHILDREN'S LITERATURE REVIEW (CLR)*
Dramatists	*DRAMA CRITICISM (DC)*
Poets	*POETRY CRITICISM (PC)*
Short story writers	*SHORT STORY CRITICISM (SSC)*
Black writers of the past two hundred years	*BLACK LITERATURE CRITICISM (BLC)* *BLACK LITERATURE CRITICISM SUPPLEMENT (BLCS)*
Hispanic writers of the late nineteenth and twentieth centuries	*HISPANIC LITERATURE CRITICISM (HLC)* *HISPANIC LITERATURE CRITICISM SUPPLEMENT (HLCS)*
Native North American writers and orators of the eighteenth, nineteenth, and twentieth centuries	*NATIVE NORTH AMERICAN LITERATURE (NNAL)*
Major authors from the Renaissance to the present	*WORLD LITERATURE CRITICISM, 1500 TO THE PRESENT (WLC)* *WORLD LITERATURE CRITICISM SUPPLEMENT (WLCS)*

ISSN 0276-8178

Volume 100

Twentieth-Century Literary Criticism

**Criticism of the
Works of Novelists, Poets, Playwrights,
Short Story Writers, and Other Creative Writers
Who Lived between 1900 and 1999,
from the First Published Critical
Appraisals to Current Evaluations**

Jennifer Baise, Linda Pavlovski
Editors

Thomas Ligotti
Associate Editor

*Detroit
New York
San Francisco
London
Boston
Woodbridge, CT*

STAFF

Lynn M. Spampinato, Janet Witalec, *Managing Editors, Literature Product*
Kathy D. Darrow, *Product Liaison*
Jennifer Baise, Linda Pavlovski, *Editors*
Mark W. Scott, *Publisher, Literature Product*

Jenny Cromie, Thomas Ligotti, *Associate Editors*
Vince Cousino, *Assistant Editor*
Mary Ruby, Patti A. Tippett, *Technical Training Specialists*
Deborah J. Morad, Kathleen Lopez Nolan, *Managing Editors*
Susan M. Trosky, *Director, Literature Content*

Maria L. Franklin, *Permissions Manager*
Erin Bealmear, *Permissions Associate*

Victoria B. Cariappa, *Research Manager*
Tracie A. Richardson, *Project Coordinator*
Tamara C. Nott, *Research Associate*
Nicodemus Ford, Sarah Genik, Timothy Lehnerer, Ron Morelli, *Research Assistants*

Dorothy Maki, *Manufacturing Manager*
Stacy L. Melson, *Buyer*

Mary Beth Trimper, *Manager, Composition and Electronic Prepress*
Carolyn Roney, *Composition Specialist*

Michael Logusz, *Graphic Artist*
Randy Bassett, *Imaging Supervisor*
Robert Duncan, Dan Newell, *Imaging Specialists*
Pamela A. Reed, *Imaging Coordinator*
Kelly A. Quin, *Editor, Image and Multimedia Content*

Library of Congress Catalog Card Number 76-46132
ISBN 0-7876-4560-5
ISSN 0276-8178
Printed in the United States of America

10 9 8 7 6 5 4 3 2 1

Contents

Preface vii

Acknowledgments xi

Preface

Since its inception more than fifteen years ago, *Twentieth-Century Literary Criticism* (*TCLC*) has been purchased and used by nearly 10,000 school, public, and college or university libraries. *TCLC* has covered more than 500 authors, representing 58 nationalities and over 25,000 titles. No other reference source has surveyed the critical response to twentieth-century authors and literature as thoroughly as *TCLC*. In the words of one reviewer, "there is nothing comparable available." *TCLC* "is a gold mine of information—dates, pseudonyms, biographical information, and criticism from books and periodicals—which many librarians would have difficulty assembling on their own."

Scope of the Series

TCLC is designed to serve as an introduction to authors who died between 1900 and 1999 and to the most significant interpretations of these author's works. Volumes published from 1978 through 1999 included authors who died between 1900 and 1960. The great poets, novelists, short story writers, playwrights, and philosophers of the period are frequently studied in high school and college literature courses. In organizing and reprinting the vast amount of critical material written on these authors, *TCLC* helps students develop valuable insight into literary history, promotes a better understanding of the texts, and sparks ideas for papers and assignments. Each entry in *TCLC* presents a comprehensive survey on an author's career or an individual work of literature and provides the user with a multiplicity of interpretations and assessments. Such variety allows students to pursue their own interests; furthermore, it fosters an awareness that literature is dynamic and responsive to many different opinions.

Every fourth volume of *TCLC* is devoted to literary topics. These topics widen the focus of the series from the individual authors to such broader subjects as literary movements, prominent themes in twentieth-century literature, literary reaction to political and historical events, significant eras in literary history, prominent literary anniversaries, and the literatures of cultures that are often overlooked by English-speaking readers.

TCLC is designed as a companion series to Gale's *Contemporary Literary Criticism,* (*CLC*) which reprints commentary on authors who died after 1999. Because of the different time periods under consideration, there is no duplication of material between *CLC* and *TCLC*.

Organization of the Book

A *TCLC* entry consists of the following elements:

- The **Author Heading** cites the name under which the author most commonly wrote, followed by birth and death dates. Also located here are any name variations under which an author wrote, including transliterated forms for authors whose native languages use nonroman alphabets. If the author wrote consistently under a pseudonym, the pseudonym will be listed in the author heading and the author's actual name given in parenthesis on the first line of the biographical and critical information. Uncertain birth or death dates are indicated by question marks. Single-work entries are preceded by a heading that consists of the most common form of the title in English translation (if applicable) and the original date of composition.

- A **Portrait of the Author** is included when available.

- The **Introduction** contains background information that introduces the reader to the author, work, or topic that is the subject of the entry.

- The list of **Principal Works** is ordered chronologically by date of first publication and lists the most important works by the author. The genre and publication date of each work is given. In the case of foreign authors whose works have been translated into English, the English-language version of the title follows in brackets. Unless otherwise indicated, dramas are dated by first performance, not first publication.

■ Reprinted **Criticism** is arranged chronologically in each entry to provide a useful perspective on changes in critical evaluation over time. The critic's name and the date of composition or publication of the critical work are given at the beginning of each piece of criticism. Unsigned criticism is preceded by the title of the source in which it appeared. All titles by the author featured in the text are printed in boldface type. Footnotes are reprinted at the end of each essay or excerpt. In the case of excerpted criticism, only those footnotes that pertain to the excerpted texts are included.

■ A complete **Bibliographical Citation** of the original essay or book precedes each piece of criticism.

■ Critical essays are prefaced by brief **Annotations** explicating each piece.

■ An annotated bibliography of **Further Reading** appears at the end of each entry and suggests resources for additional study. In some cases, significant essays for which the editors could not obtain reprint rights are included here. Boxed material following the further reading list provides references to other biographical and critical sources on the author in series published by Gale.

Indexes

A **Cumulative Author Index** lists all of the authors that appear in a wide variety of reference sources published by the Gale Group, including *TCLC*. A complete list of these sources is found facing the first page of the Author Index. The index also includes birth and death dates and cross references between pseudonyms and actual names.

A **Cumulative Nationality Index** lists all authors featured in *TCLC* by nationality, followed by the number of the *TCLC* volume in which their entry appears.

A **Cumulative Topic Index** lists the literary themes and topics treated in the series as well as in *Classical and Medieval Literature Criticism, Literature Criticism from 1400 to 1800, Nineteenth-Century Literature Criticism,* and the *Contemporary Literary Criticism* Yearbook, which was discontinued in 1998.

An alphabetical **Title Index** accompanies each volume of *TCLC*. Listings of titles by authors covered in the given volume are followed by the author's name and the corresponding page numbers where the titles are discussed. English translations of foreign titles and variations of titles are cross-referenced to the title under which a work was originally published. Titles of novels, dramas, nonfiction books, and poetry, short story, or essay collections are printed in italics, while individual poems, short stories, and essays are printed in roman type within quotation marks.

In response to numerous suggestions from librarians, Gale also produces an annual paperbound edition of the *TCLC* cumulative title index. This annual cumulation, which alphabetically lists all titles reviewed in the series, is available to all customers. Additional copies of this index are available upon request. Librarians and patrons will welcome this separate index; it saves shelf space, is easy to use, and is recyclable upon receipt of the next edition.

Citing *Twentieth-Century Literary Criticism*

When writing papers, students who quote directly from any volume in the Literary Criticism Series may use the following general format to footnote reprinted criticism. The first example pertains to material drawn from periodicals, the second to material reprinted from books.

George Orwell, "Reflections on Gandhi," *Partisan Review* 6 (Winter 1949): 85-92; reprinted in *Twentieth-Century Literary Criticism,* vol. 59, ed. Jennifer Gariepy (Detroit: The Gale Group, 1995), 40-3.

William H. Slavick, "Going to School to DuBose Heyward," *The Harlem Renaissance Re-examined,* ed. Victor A. Kramer (AMS, 1987), 65- 91; reprinted in *Twentieth-Century Literary Criticism,* vol. 59, ed. Jennifer Gariepy (Detroit: The Gale Group, 1995), 94-105.

Suggestions are Welcome

Readers who wish to suggest new features, topics, or authors to appear in future volumes, or who have other suggestions or comments are cordially invited to call, write, or fax the Managing Editor:

Managing Editor, Literary Criticism Series
The Gale Group
27500 Drake Road
Farmington Hills, MI 48331-3535
1-800-347-4253 (GALE)
Fax: 248-699-8054

Acknowledgments

The editors wish to thank the copyright holders of the excerpted criticism included in this volume and the permissions managers of many book and magazine publishing companies for assisting us in securing reproduction rights. We are also grateful to the staffs of the Detroit Public Library, the Library of Congress, the University of Detroit Mercy Library, Wayne State University Purdy/Kresge Library Complex, and the University of Michigan Libraries for making their resources available to us. Following is a list of the copyright holders who have granted us permission to reproduce material in this volume of *TCLC*. Every effort has been made to trace copyright, but if omissions have been made, please let us know.

COPYRIGHTED EXCERPTS IN *TCLC*, VOLUME 100, WERE REPRODUCED FROM THE FOLLOWING PERIODICALS:

American Literature, v. 70, December, 1998. Copyright © 1998 by Duke University Press, Durham, NC. Reproduced by permission.—*American Quarterly,* v. 41, June 1989. © 1989. Reproduced by permission of The Johns Hopkins University Press.—*The American Scholar,* v. 46, Winter, 1976-77 for a review of "F.O. Matthiessen" by Kenneth S. Lynn. Copyright © 1976 by the United Chapters of the Phi Beta Kappa Society. Reproduced by permission of the author.—*Arizona Quarterly,* v. 48, Autumn, 1992, for "The 'Wholeness' of the Whale: Melville, Matthiessen, and the Semiotics of Critical Revisionism" by Marc Dolan. Copyright © 1992 by the Regents of the University of Arizona. Reproduced by permission of the publisher and the author.—*Contemporary Literature,* v. 31, Fall, 1990. Reproduced by permission.—*Critical Quarterly,* v. 37, Autumn, 1995. © 1995. Reproduced by permission of Blackwell Publishers.—*Journal of Popular Culture,* v. VIII, Spring, 1975. Reproduced by permission.—*The Kenyon Review,* v. VII, Spring, 1945. Copyright © 1945 by Kenyon College. All rights reserved. Reproduced by permission.—*Monthly Review,* February, 1983. Reproduced by permission.—*The New Criterion,* v. 7, June, 1989, for a review of "Politics and Art in the Criticism of F. O. Matthiessen" by James W. Tuttleton. Copyright © 1989 by The Foundation for Cultural Review. Reproduced by permission of the Estate of James W. Tuttleton.—*The New England Quarterly,* v. LX, June, 1987, for a review of "Criticism and Politics: F. O. Matthiessen and the Making of Henry James" by William E. Cain. Copyright © 1987 by *The New England Quarterly*. Reproduced by permission of the publisher and the author.—*Philosophy and Phenomenological Research,* v. 1, June, 1940; v. 1, September, 1940; v. XXXVI, December, 1975; v. XXXVI, June, 1976; v. LII, September, 1992. Copyright 1940, renewed 1968 by University of Buffalo. All reproduced by permission.—*Quarterly Journal of Speech,* v. 84, August, 1998, for "'The Responsibilities of the Critic': F. O. Matthiessen's Homosexual Palimpsest" by Charles E. Morris, III. Copyright © 1998 by the Speech Communication Association. Used by permission of Speech Communication Association and the author.—*The South Atlantic Quarterly,* v. 87, Spring, 1988. Copyright © 1988 by Duke University Press, Durham, NC. Reproduced by permission.—*Telos: A Quarterly Journal of Critical Thought,* Spring, 1970; Fall 1970; Fall, 1973. All reproduced by permission.

COPYRIGHTED EXCERPTS IN *TCLC*, VOLUME 100, WERE REPRODUCED FROM THE FOLLOWING BOOKS:

Arac, Jonathan. From *Critical Genealogies: Historical Situations for Postmodern Literary Studies.* Columbia University Press, 1987. Copyright © 1987 Columbia University Press, New York. All rights reserved. Reproduced by permission of the author.—Bergman, David. From *Gaiety Transfigured: Gay Self-Representation in American Literature.* The University of Wisconsin Press, 1991. Copyright © 1991 The Board of Regents of the University of Wisconsin System. All rights reserved. Reproduced by permission.—Brendon, Piers. From "Mrs. Pankhurst" in *Eminent Edwardians.* Houghton Mifflin Company, 1980. Copyright © 1979 by Piers Brendon. All rights reserved. Reproduced by permission.—Cadden, Michael. From "Engendering F. O. M.: The Private Life of American Renaissance" in *Engendering Men: The Question of Male Feminist Criticism.* Edited by Joseph A. Boone and Michael Cadden. Copyright © 1990. Reproduced by permission of Taylor & Francis, Inc./Routledge, Inc.—Gurwitsch, Aron. From *Studies in Phenomenology and Psychology.* Northwestern University Press, 1996. Copyright © 1966 by Northwestern University Press. Reproduced by permission.—Merleau-Ponty, Maurice. From "The Philosopher and His Shadow" in *Signs.* Edited by John Wild. Translated by Richard C. McCleary. Northwestern University Press, 1964. Copyright © 1964 by Northwestern University Press. Reproduced by permission.—Probst, Gerhard F. From "Alfred Neumann's and Erwin Piscator's Dramatization of Tolstoy's 'War and Peace' and the Role of Theater as a Contribution to America's War Efforts," in *Exile and Enlightenment.* Uwe Faulhaber, Jerry Glenn, Edward

PHOTOGRAPHS APPEARING IN *TCLC*, VOLUME 100, WERE RECEIVED FROM THE FOLLOWING SOURCES:

Edmund Husserl
1859-1938

(Full name Edmund Gustav Albrecht Husserl) German philosopher.

INTRODUCTION

Husserl was the founder of phenomenology, a philosophical method that seeks certainty about the existence of being and about the authenticity and reliability of knowing. He was a formative influence on twentieth-century thought and methodology, not only in philosophy as one of the progenitors of existentialism, structuralism, and postmodernism, but in literature, music, painting, psychology, and the physical sciences, where his concern for the reduction of investigation to the essential minimum, his identification of the act of perception and the thing perceived, and his postulation of the authority of subjective perception have become standard. Husserl refined phenomenology and its focus throughout his life, moving from a world-based contemplation of actual things and phenomena without presuppositions to a transcendental contemplation of *a priori* essentials to a philosophy of inter-subjective social relationship in the actual world.

BIOGRAPHICAL INFORMATION

Husserl was born in Prossnitz, Moravia. His early school career was not distinguished, but he did show aptitude in the sciences and went on to study astronomy, mathematics, physics, and philosophy at the universities of Leipzig, Berlin, and Vienna, where he received his doctorate in philosophy in 1882. A year later he began studying with the psychologist and philosopher Franz Brentano. Brentano's influence was of particular importance because he championed a psychology that described phenomena, rather than the organs deemed responsible for psychological conditions. With Brentano, too, Husserl studied logic and the British empiricists Locke, Hume, and Mill, and developed the belief that philosophy had to be a "strict and rigorous science." In 1886, with Brentano's recommendation, Husserl became a lecturer at the University of Halle. During his years there, until 1901, his shaping as a philosopher took place, and the fundamental content of his philosophy was formulated. His publication of a theory of arithmetic in 1891 was of particular significance to his thought because it elicited a critical response from the mathematician-philosopher Gotlob Frege, which turned Husserl away from psychologism and toward logic. His 1901 publication of the *Logische Untersuchungen* (*Logical Investigations*) was the first full, systematic presentation of phenomenol-

ogy, and it brought him recognition and esteem. That same year Husserl joined the faculty of the University of Goettingen, where he lectured on the works of other philosophers as well as phenomenology. He also wrote copiously but published only an article titled "Philosophie als strenge Wissenschaft" (1910; "Philosophy as Rigorous Science") and the first volume of his monumental *Jarbuch fuer Philosophie und Phaenomenologische Forschung* (11 vols., 1913-31; *Ideas: General Introduction to Pure Phenomenology*). From 1916 until 1928 Husserl was a full professor of philosophy at the University of Freiburg, where he remained until his retirement in 1928. During his Freiburg years, his reputation grew to international proportions: he lectured in London, was published in Japan, became a corresponding member of the Aristotelian Society, and was asked to contribute an entry on phenomenology to the *Encyclopedia Britannica*. During those years a number of important students gathered around him, including Martin Heidegger, whose work was strongly influenced by Husserl's even when it diverged from it. Husserl retired in 1928 but continued to work vigorously, lecturing in Amsterdam, Paris, Vienna, Prague, and within Germany. In 1933 he was invited to join the philosophy faculty of the University of Southern California, which he declined. After 1935 the Nazi government forbade Husserl, who had been born Jewish, though a convert to Lutheranism, to travel or to lecture. In 1938 one of his students, Herman Van Breda, learned that the Nazis were intending to burn Husserl's work. After Husserl's death in 1938, Van Breda managed, with the help of Husserl's widow, to smuggle all of his manuscripts (more than forty-thousand pages, many written in shorthand) out of Germany to safety in Belgium, where they were archived for transcription, publication, and research.

MAJOR WORKS

All of Husserl's writings considered together constitute a single work formulating and refining phenomenology. From *Logical Investigations,* "Philosophy as Rigorous Science," and the volumes of *Ideas,* through the *Meditations cartesiennes* (1931; *Cartesian Meditations*) and the later "Die Krisis der europaeischen Wissenschaften und die tranzendentale Phänomenologie" (1936; *The Crisis of European Sciences and Transcendental Phenomenology*), his work shows phenomenology as a philosophy whose ongoing project is to reconcile the Cartesian division between an objective, concrete reality and the subjective constructions of thought; to reestablish the observational methodology of Aristotle; to provide a reliable basis for attaining authentic knowledge; and by means of clarity of thinking and rigor of perception to provide for the ethical interaction between people necessary for the development of civilization and humane association. The last challenge Husserl felt keenly because of his belief that World War I had marked the end of validity and humanity for European thought. After the triumph of Nazism and what he saw as the mystification of thought, this project became even more urgent. Husserl maintained that the actualization of humanity depended upon the freedom of the mind. Establishing and exercising that freedom, as well as providing the description of fundamental human reality, he believed, were the tasks of phenomenology.

PRINCIPAL WORKS

Philosophie der Arithmetik: Psychologische und logische Untersuchungen [*The Philosophy of Arithmetic: Psychological and Logical Investigations*] (philosophy) 1891

Logische Untersuchungen [*Logical Investigations*] 2 vols. (philosophy) 1901

"Philosophie als strenge Wissenschaft" ["Philosophy as Rigorous Science"] (essay) 1910

Jarbuch fuer Philosophie und Phaenomenologische Forschung [*Ideas: General Introduction to Pure Phenomenology*] 11 vols. (philosophy) 1913-31

Transzendentale Phänomenologie [*Transcendental Phenomenology*] (philosophy) 1913

"Phänomenologie" ["Phenomenology"] (essay) 1929

Meditations cartesiennes: Introduction a la phenomenologie [*Cartesian Meditations: An Introduction to Phenomenology*] (philosophy) 1931

"Die Krisis der europaeischen Wissenschaften und die transzendentale Phänomenologie" [*The Crisis of European Science and Transcendental Phenomenology: An Introduction to Phenomenological Philosophy*] (philosophy) 1936

Erfahrung und Urteil [*Experience and Judgement*] (philosophy) 1936

CRITICISM

Gottlob Frege (review date 1894)

SOURCE: A review of Dr. E. Husserl's *Philosophy of Arithmetic,* in *Husserl: Expositions and Appraisals,* University of Notre Dame Press, 1977, pp. 314-24.

[*The following excerpt is a translation (by E. W. Kluge) of Frege's 1894 critical review of Husserl's* Philosophy of Arithmetic, *which played a significant role in causing Husserl to refocus the direction of his thought.*]

The author decides in the Introduction [of ***Philosophy of Arithmetic***] that for the time being he will consider (only) cardinal numbers (cardinalia), and thereupon launches into a discussion of multiplicity, plurality, totality, aggregate, collection, set. He uses these words as if they were essentially synonymous; the concept of a cardinal number[1] is supposed to be different from this. However, the logical relationship between multiplicity and number (p. 9) remains somewhat obscure. If one were to go by the words "The concept of number includes the same concrete phenomena as the concept of multiplicity, albeit only by way of the extensions of the concepts of its species, the numbers two, three, four, etc.," one might infer that they had the same extension. On the other hand, multiplicity is supposed to be more indeterminate and more general than number. The matter would probably be clearer if a sharper distinction were drawn between falling under a concept and subordination. Now the first thing he attempts to do is to give an analysis of the concept of multiplicity. Determinate numbers, as well as the generic concept of number which presupposes them, are then supposed to emerge from it by means of determinations. Thus we are first led down from the general to the particular, and then up again.

Totalities are wholes whose parts are collectively connected. We must be conscious of these parts as noticed in and by themselves. The collective connection consists neither in the contents' being simultaneously in the awareness, nor in their arising in the awareness one after another. Not even space, as all-inclusive form, is the ground of the unification. The connection consists (p. 43) in the unifying act itself. "But neither is it the case that over and above the act there exists a relational content which is distinct from it and is its creative result." Collective connection is a relation *sui generis*. Following J. St. Mill, the author then explains what is to be understood by "relation": namely that state of consciousness or that phenomenon (these expressions are supposed to coincide in the extension of their reference) in which the related contents—the bases of the relation—are contained (p. 70). He then distinguishes between primary and mental relations. Here only the latter concern us more closely. "If a unitary mental act is directed towards several contents, then with respect to it the contents are connected or related to one another. If we perform such an act, it would of course be futile for us to look for a relation or connection in the presentational content which it contains (unless over and above this, there is also a primary relation). The contents here are united only by the act, and consequently this unification can be noticed only by a special reflection on it" (p. 73). The difference-relation, whereby two contents are related to one another by means of an evident negative judgment, is also of this kind (p. 74). Sameness, on the other hand, is (p. 77) a primary relation. (According to this, complete coincidence, too, would be a primary relation, while its negation—difference itself—would be a mental one. I here miss a statement of the difference between the difference-relation and collective connection, where in the opinion of the author the latter, too, is a mental relation because perceptually no unification is noticeable in its presentational content.) When one is speaking of "unrelated" contents, the contents are merely thought "together", *i.e.* as a totality. "But by no means are they really unconnected, unrelated. On the contrary, they are connected by the mental act holding them together. It is only in the content of the latter that all noticeable unification is lacking" (p. 78). The conjunction 'and' fixes in a wholly appropriate manner the circumstance that given contents are connected in a collective manner (p. 81). "A presentation . . . falls under the concept of multiplicity insofar as it connects in a collective manner any contents which are noticed in and by themselves" (p. 82). (It appears that what is understood by "presentation" is an act.) "Multiplicity in general . . . is no more than something and something and something, etc.; or any one thing and any one thing and any one thing, etc.; or more briefly, one and one and one, etc." (p. 85). When we remove the indeterminateness which lies in the "etc.," we arrive at the numbers one and one; one, one and one; one, one, one and one; and so on. We can also arrive at these concepts directly, beginning with any concrete multiplicity whatever; for each one of them falls under one of these concepts, and under a determinate one at that (p. 87). To this end, we abstract from the particular constitution of the individual contents collected together in the multiplicity, retaining each one only insofar as it is a something or a one; and thus, with respect to the collective connection of the latter, we obtain the general form of multiplicity appropriate to the multiplicity under consideration, *i.e.* the appropriate number (p. 88). Along with this number-abstraction

goes a complete removal of restrictions placed on the content (p. 100). We cannot explain the general concept of number otherwise than by pointing to the similarity which all number-concepts have to one another (p. 88).

Having thus given a brief presentation of the basic thoughts of the first part, I now want to give a general characterization of this mode of consideration. We here have an attempt to provide a naive conception of number with a scientific justification. I call any opinion naive if according to it a number-statement is not an assertion about a concept or the extension of a concept; for upon the slightest reflection about number, one is led with a certain necessity to such conceptions. Now strictly speaking, an opinion is naive only as long as the difficulties facing it are unknown—which does not quite apply in the case of our author. The most naive opinion is that according to which a number is something like a heap, a swarm in which the things are contained lock, stock and barrel. Next comes the conception of a number as a property of a heap, aggregate, or whatever else one might call it. Thereby one feels the need for cleansing the objects of their particularities. The present attempt belongs to those which undertake this cleansing in the psychological wash-tub. This offers the advantage that in it, things acquire a most peculiar suppleness, no longer have as hard a spatial impact on each other and lose many bothersome particularities and differences. The mixture of psychology and logic that is now so popular provides good suds for this purpose. First of all, everything becomes presentation. The references of words are presentations. In the case of the word "number," for example, the aim is to exhibit the appropriate presentation and to describe its genesis and composition. Objects are presentations. Thus J. St. Mill, with the approval of the author, lets objects (whether physical or mental) enter into a state of consciousness and become constituents of this state (p. 70). But might not the moon, for example, be somewhat hard to digest for a state of consciousness? Since everything is now presentation, we can easily change the objects by now paying attention, now not. The latter is especially effective. We pay less attention to a property and it disappears. By thus letting one characteristic after another disappear, we obtain concepts that are increasingly more abstract. Therefore concepts, too, are presentations; only, they are less complete than objects; they still have those properties of objects which we have not abstracted. Inattention is an exceedingly effective logical power; whence, presumably, the absentmindedness of scholars. For example, let us suppose that in front of us there are sitting side by side a black and a white cat. We disregard their color: they become colorless but are still sitting side by side. We disregard their posture: they are no longer sitting, without, however, having assumed a different posture; but each one is still at its place. We disregard their location: they are without location, but still remain quite distinct. Thus from each one we have perhaps derived a general concept of a cat. Continued application of this process turns each object into a less and less substantial wraith. From each object we finally derive something which is completely without restrictions on its content; but the something derived from the one object nevertheless does differ from that derived from the other object, although it is not easy to say how. But wait! This last transition to a something does seem to be more difficult after all; at least the author talks (p. 86) about reflection on the mental act of presentation. But be that as it may, the result, at any rate, is the one just indicated. While in my opinion the bringing of an object under a concept is merely the recognition of a relation which previously already obtained, in the present case objects are essentially changed by this process, so that objects brought under the same concept become similar to one another. Perhaps the matter is to be understood thus, that for every object there arises a new presentation in which all determinations which do not occur in the concept are lacking. Hereby the difference between presentation and concept, between presenting and thinking, is blurred. Everything is shunted off into the subjective. But it is precisely because the boundary between the subjective and the objective is blurred, that conversely the subjective also acquires the appearance of the objective. For example, one talks of this or that presentation as if, separated from the presentor, it would let itself be observed in public. And yet, no-one has someone else's presentation but only his own, and no-one knows how far his presentation—*e.g.* that of red—agrees with that of someone else; for the peculiarity of the presentation which I associate with the word "red," I cannot state (so as to be able to compare it). One would have to have the presentations of the one as well as that of the other combined in one and the same consciousness; and one would have to be sure that they had not changed in the transfer. With thoughts, it is quite different: one and the same thought can be grasped by many people. The components of a thought, and even more so the things themselves, must be distinguished from the presentations which in the soul accompany the grasping of a thought and which someone has about these things. In combining under the word "presentation" both what is subjective and what is objective, one blurs the boundary between the two in such a way that now a presentation in the proper sense of the word is treated like something objective, and now something objective is treated like a presentation. Thus in the case of our author, totality (set, multiplicity) appears now as a presentation (pp. 15, 17, 24, 82), now as something objective (pp. 10, 11, 235). But isn't it really a very harmless pleasantry to call, for example, the moon a presentation? It is—as long as one does not imagine that one can change it as one likes, or produce it by psychological means. But this is all too easily the result.

Given the psychologico-logical mode of thought just characterized, it is easy to understand how the author judges about definitions. An example from elementary geometry may illustrate this. There, one usually gives this definition: "A right angle is an angle which is equal to its adjacent angle." The author would probably say to this, "The presentation of right-angledness is a simple one; hence it is a completely misguided undertaking to want to give a definition of it. In our presentation of right-angledness, there is nothing of the relation to another adjacent angle. True

enough; the concepts 'right angle' and 'angle which is equal to its adjacent angle' have the same extension; but it is not true that they have the same content. Instead of the content, it is the extension of the concept that has been defined. If the definition were correct, then every assertion of right-angledness, instead of applying to the concretely present pair of lines as such, would always apply only to its relation to another pair of lines. All I can admit is (p. 114) that in this equality with the adjacent angle we have a necessary and sufficient condition for right-angledness." The author judges in a similar way about the definition of equinumerosity by means of the concept of a univocal one-one correlation. "The simplest criterion for sameness of number is just that *the same* number results when counting the sets to be compared" (p. 115). Of course! The simplest way of testing whether or not something is a right angle is to use a protractor. The author forgets that this counting itself rests on a univocal one-one correlation, namely that between the numerals 1 to n and the objects of the set. Each of the two sets is to be counted. In this way, the situation is made more difficult than when we consider a relation which correlates the objects of the two sets with one another without numerals as intermediaries.

If words and combinations of words refer to presentations, then for any two of these only two cases are possible: either they designate the same presentation, or they designate different ones. In the first case, equating them by means of a definition is useless, "an obvious circle"; in the other, it is false. These are also the objections one of which the author raises regularly. Neither can a definition dissect the sense, for the dissected sense simply is not the original one. In the case of the word to be explained, either I already think clearly everything which I think in the case of the definiens—in which case we have the "obvious circle"—or the definiens has a more completely articulated sense—in which case I do not think the same thing in its case as I do in the case of the one to be explained: the definition is false. One would think that the definition would be unobjectionable at least in the case where the word to be explained does not yet have a sense, or where it is expressly asked that the sense be considered non-existent, so that the word acquires a sense only through this definition. But even in the latter case (p. 107), the author confutes the definition by reminding us of the distinctness of the presentations. Accordingly, in order to avoid all objections, one would probably have to create a new root-word and form a word out of it. A split here manifests itself between psychological logicians and mathematicians. The former are concerned with the sense of the words and with the presentations, which they do not distinguish from the sense; the latter, however, are concerned with the matter itself, with the reference of the words.[2] The reproach that it is not the concept but its extension which is being defined, really applies to all the definitions of mathematics. So far as the mathematician is concerned, the definition of a conic section as the line of intersection of a plane with a cone is no more and no less correct than that as a plane whose equation is given in Cartesian coordinates of the second degree. Which of these two—or even of other—definitions is selected depends entirely on the pragmatics of the situation, although these expressions neither have the same sense nor evoke the same presentations. By this I do not mean that a concept and the extension of a concept are one and the same; rather, coincidence of extension is a necessary and sufficient condition for the fact that between the concepts there obtains that relation which corresponds to that of sameness in the case of objects.[3] I here note that when I use the word "same" without further addition, I am using it in the sense of "not different," "coinciding," "identical." Psychological logicians lack all understanding of sameness, just as they lack all understanding of definitions. This relation cannot help but remain completely puzzling to them; for if words always designated presentations, one could never say "A is the same as B." For to be able to do that, one would already have to distinguish A from B, and then these would simply be different presentations. All the same, I do agree with the author in this, that Leibniz' explanation "Eadem sunt quorum unum potest substitui alteri salva veritate" does not deserve to be called a definition, although I hold this for different reasons. Since every definition is an equation, one cannot define equality itself. One could call Leibniz' explanation a principle which expresses the nature of the sameness-relation; and as such it is of fundamental importance. I am unable to acquire a taste for the author's explanation that (p. 108) "We simply say of any contents whatever that they are the same as one another, if there obtains sameness in the . . . characteristics which at that moment constitute the center of interest."

Let us now go into details! According to the author, a number-statement refers to the totality (the set, multiplicity) of objects counted (p. 185). Such a totality finds its wholly appropriate expression in the conjunction "and." Accordingly, one should expect that all number-statements have the form "A and B and C and . . . Q is *n*," or at least that they could be brought into such a form. But what is it that we get exactly to know through the proposition "Berlin and Dresden and Munich are three" or—and this is supposed to be the same thing—through "Berlin and Dresden and Munich are something and something and something"? Who would want to go to the trouble of asking, merely to receive such an answer? It is not even supposed to be said by this that Berlin is distinct from Dresden, the latter from Munich, and Munich from Berlin. In fact, in the second form at least there is contained neither the difference of Berlin from Dresden nor even their sameness. Surely it is peculiar that this form of number-predication almost never occurs in every-day life and that when it does occur, it is not intended as a statement of number. I find that there are really only two cases in which it is used: in the first case, together with the number-word "two", to express difference—"Rapeseed and rape are two (different things)"—in the other, together with the number-word "one" to express sameness—"I and the Father are one"—. This last example is particularly disastrous, for according to the author it should read, "are something and something" or "are two". In reality we do not ask "How many are Caesar and Pompei and London and Edinburgh?" or "How many are Great Britain and Ireland?" although I am curious as to what the author would answer to this. Instead, one asks, for example, "How many moons does Mars have?" or "What is the number of moons of Mars?" And from the answer "The number of moons of Mars is two" one gets to know something which is worth asking about. Thus we see that in the question as well as in the answer, there occurs a concept-word or a compound designation of a concept, rather than the "and" demanded by the author. How does the latter extricate himself from this difficulty? He says that the number belongs to the extension of the concept, *i.e.* to the totality. "It is only indirectly that one can perhaps say that the concept has the property that the number . . . belongs to its extension" (p. 189). Herewith everything I maintain has really been admitted: In a number-statement, something is predicated of a concept. I am not going to argue over whether the assertion applies directly to a concept and indirectly to its extension, or indirectly to the concept and directly to its extension; for given the one, the other also obtains. This much is certain, that neither the extension of a concept nor a totality are designated directly, but only a concept. Now if the author used the phrase "extension of a concept" in the same sense as I, then our opinions about the sense of a statement of number would scarely differ. This, of course, is not the case; for the extension of a concept is not a totality in the author's sense. A concept under which there falls only one object has just as determinate an extension as a concept under which there falls no object or a concept under which there fall infinitely many objects—where according to Mr. Husserl, there is no totality in any of these cases. The sense of the words "extension of the concept moon of Mars" is other than the sense of the words "Deimos and Phobos"; and if the proposition "The number of Deimos and Phobos is two" contains a thought at all, at any rate it contains one which differs from that of the proposition "The number of moons of Mars is two". Now, since one never uses a proposition of the latter form to make a statement of number, the author has missed the sense of such a statement.

Let us now consider the ostensible genesis of a totality somewhat more closely (pp. 77 ff.). I must confess that I have been unsuccessful in my attempt to form a totality in accordance with the instructions of the author. In the case of collective connections, the contents are merely supposed to be thought or presented together, without any relation or connection whatever being presented between them (p. 79). I am unable to do this. I cannot simultaneously represent to myself redness, the Moon and Napoleon, without presenting these to myself as connected; *e.g.* the redness of a burning village against which stands out the figure of Napoleon, illuminated by the Moon on the right. Whatever is simultaneously present to me, I present to myself as a whole; and I cannot disregard the connection without losing the whole. I suspect that in my soul there just isn't anything which the author calls "totality", "set", "multiplicity"; no presentation of parts whose union is not presented with them, although it does exist. Therefore it is not at all astonishing that Mr. Husserl himself later (p. 242) says of a set that it contains a configurative moment which characterizes it as a whole, as an organization. He talks of series (p. 235), swarms, chains, heaps as of peculiar kinds of sets. And no union is supposed to be noticeable in the presentation of a swarm? Or is this union present over and above the collective connection? In which case it would be irrelevant so far as the totality is concerned, and the "configurative moment" could not serve to distinguish kinds of sets. How does the author come to hold his opinion? Probably because he is looking for certain presentations as the references of words and word-complexes. Thus there ought to correspond a presentational whole even to the word-complex "redness and the Moon and Napoleon"; and since the mere "and" allegedly does not express a presentable relation or union at all, neither ought one to be presented. Add to this the following. If the union of the parts were also presented, almost all of our presentations would be totalities; e.g., that of a house as well as that of a swarm or heap. And hereby, surely, one notices only too easily that a number as a property of a house or of the presentation of a house would be absurd.

The author himself finds a difficulty in the abstraction which yields the general concept of totality (p. 84). "One must abstract completely . . . from the particularities of the individual contents collected together, at the same time, however, retaining their connection. This seems to involve a difficulty, if not a psychological impossibility. If we take this abstraction seriously, then of course the collective connection, rather than remaining behind as a conceptual extract, also disappears along with the particular contents. The solution lies at hand. To abstract from something merely means: not paying any particular attention to it."

The core of this exposition clearly lies in the word "particular." Inattention is a very strong lye which must not be applied in too concentrated a form, so as not to dissolve everything; but neither ought it to be used in too diluted a form, so that it may produce a sufficient change. Everything, then, depends on the proper degree of dilution, which is difficult to hit. I, at least, did not succeed in doing so.

Since in the end, the author himself really does admit that I am right after all—that in a number-statement there is contained an assertion about a concept—I need not consider his counterarguments in more detail. I only want to remark that he evidently has not grasped my distinction between a characteristic and a property. Given his logicopsychological mode of understanding, this is of course not surprising. Thus he comes to foist on me the opinion that what is at issue in the case of numberstatements is a determination, the definition of a concept (p. 185). Nothing was farther from my mind.

Three reefs spell danger for naive, and particularly for psychological, views of the nature of numbers. The first lies in the question, how the sameness of the units is to be reconciled with their distinguishability. The second consists in the numbers zero and one; and the third, in the large numbers. Let us ask how the author seeks to circumnavigate these reefs! In the case of the first, he adduces (p. 156) my words, "If we want to let a number arise by collecting different objects, then we obtain a heap in which the objects are contained with just those properties in which they differ; and this is not the number. On the other hand, if we want to form a number by collecting what is the same, the latter will always coalesce into one and we shall never arrive at a multiplicity." It is clear that I have used the word "same" in the sense of "not different." Therefore the author's charge that I confuse sameness with identity does not apply. Mr. Husserl tries to blunt this antithesis by means of his hazy sameness: "In a certain respect, sameness does obtain; in another, difference. . . . A difficulty, or better, an impossibility would obtain only if the expression 'collection of what is the same' (which is intended to describe the genesis of a number) demanded absolute sameness, as Frege mistakenly assumes" (pp. 164, 165). Well, if the sameness is not absolute, then the objects will differ in one or the other of the properties with which they enter into combination. Now with this, compare the following: "The sameness of the units, as it results from our psychological theory, is obviously an absolute one. Indeed, already the mere thought of an approximation is absurd, for what is at stake is the sameness of the contents insofar as they are contents" (p. 168). According to the author, a number consists of units (p. 149). He here understands by "unit" a "member of a concrete multiplicity insofar as number-abstraction is applied to the latter" or "a counted object as such." If we consider all of this together, we shall be hard pressed to get clear about the author's opinion. In the beginning, the objects are evidently distinct; then, by means of abstraction, they become absolutely the same with respect to one another, but for all that, this absolute sameness is supposed to obtain only insofar as they are contents. I should think that this sameness is very far indeed removed from being absolute. But be that as it may, the number consists of these units which are absolutely the same; and now there enters that impossibility which the author himself emphasizes. After all, one must assume that this abstraction, this bringing under the concept of something, effects a change; that the objects which are thought through the medium of this concept—these very units which are absolutely the same—are distinct from the original objects, for otherwise they would resemble one another no more than they did at the beginning and this abstraction would be useless. We must assume that it is only through being brought under the concept of a something that these units which are absolutely the same arise, whether they appear through a metamorphosis out of distinct objects or whether they appear in addition to these as new entities. Therefore one would think that in addition to the remaining objects there are also units, sets of units over the above sets of apples. This, however, the author most emphatically denies (p. 139). Number-abstraction simply has the wonderful and very fruitful property of making things absolutely the same as one another without altering them. Something like this is possible only in the psychological wash-tub. If the author really has avoided this first reef, then surely he has done so more by way of magic than by way of science.

Further, Mr. Husserl adduces (p. 156) my words "If we designate each of the objects to be counted by 1, this is a mistake because what differs receives the same sign. If we supply the 1 with differentiating strokes, it becomes useless for arithmetic." To this he makes the following comment (p. 165), "However, we commit this mistake with each application of a general name. When we call Tom, Dick, etc., each a human being, this is the same case as that of the 'faulty notation' in virtue of which when counting, we write 1 for each object to be counted." If we did designate Tom by "human being" and Dick likewise, we should indeed be committing that mistake. Fortunately, we do not do that. When we call Tom a human being, we are thereby saying that Tom falls under the concept human being; but we neither write nor say "human being" instead of "Tom." What would correspond to the proposition "Tom is a human being" would be "Tom is a 1." If we call A, B in the sense of assigning the proper name B to A, then of course everywhere we say "A" we can say "B"; but then we may not give this very name "B" to still another object. This unfortunate expression, "common name," is undoubtedly the cause of this confusion. This so-called common name—better called concept-word—has nothing directly to do with objects but refers to a concept. And perhaps objects do fall under this concept, although it may also be empty without the concept-word referring any less because of this. I have already explained this sufficiently in sec. 47 of my *Foundations of Arithmetic*. Surely it is obvious that anyone using the proposition "All human beings are mortal" does not want to say anything about a certain chief Akpanya, of whom he has perhaps never even heard.

According to the author, 5 + 5 = 10 means the same thing as "a set (any one, whatever it may be) falling under the concept five, and any other (why other?) set falling under the same concept yield, when combined, a set falling under the concept 10" (p. 202). To illustrate this to ourselves, we are to consider for example the fingers of the right hand as the first set, and a fountain-pen and the fingers of the right hand excluding the thumb as the other. It is possible that the author has here had Mr. Biermann as a teacher?[4]

We now proceed to the second reef, which consists in the numbers zero and one. The first way out is easily found. One says, "They aren't numbers at all." But now there arises the question "What, then, are they?" The author says, negative answers to the question "How many?" (p. 144) Answers like "Never" to the question "When?" "Not-many or 'no multiplicity' is not a particularization of manyness." Perhaps someone might even hit upon the idea that two is not yet a multiplicity but merely twoness (duality as opposed to multiplicity); that none, one and two, therefore, are the three negative answers to the question "How many?" In corroboration of this he would perhaps adduce the fact that two is the only even prime num-

ber. It is really asking a lot to want us to consider "one" a negative answer to the question "How many moons does the Earth have?" In the case of zero, the matter has more appearance of being correct. Exactly how are the answers "Never," "Nowhere," "Nothing" to the questions "When?" "Where?" "What?" to be understood? Obviously not as proper answers, but rather as refusals to answer, couched in the form of an answer. One says "I cannot give you a time, a place or an object of the kind wanted because there is none." According to this, an analogous reply to the question "How many?" would be "I cannot tell you such a number because there isn't one." Given my conception of the sense of a number-statement, this is what I should reply for example to the question "How many are Great Britain and Ireland?" I cannot regard either the answer "One" or the answer "Zero" as answers to the question "How many?" as synonymous with "There is no such number." How is it that there are here two negative replies? If to the question "Who was Romulus' predecessor on the throne of Rome?" one answers "No one," then one herewith denies that someone preceded Romulus. Therefore the negation belongs to the predicate, and its fusion with the grammatical subject—whence arises the appearance that "No one" designates a human being just as much as does "Romulus"—is logically incorrect. As is well known, the possibility of certain sophisms rests on this. One would think that such dangers also threaten with zero and one; but these are used just as are all other numbers, without special precautionary measures. Whence this difference? "Zero" is just as little a negative answer to the question "What is the number of Romulus' predecessors on the throne of Rome?" as "Two" would be. One does not thereby deny that there is such a number; rather, one names it. The author says, "To every unit there applies the number one" (p. 170) (presumably as a negative property!) and calls zero and one concepts (p. 145). Given this, one assumes that unit and one are concepts having the same extension. Or is it not the case that every one is a unit? Wherein do the thoughts of the two propositions "Tom is one" and "Tom is a unit" differ? To which one, then, does the number zero apply? Unnoticed and in concert with the author, we have again said "The number one!" There are here still many other puzzles left unresolved by the author, and I cannot admit that he has successfully avoided this reef.

We come to the third reef: the large numbers. If numbers are presentations, then the limited nature of our powers of presentation must also carry along with it a limitation of the domain of numbers. Thus the author states, "It is only under extremely favorable circumstances that we can still have a real presentation of a concrete multiplicity of about a dozen elements" (p. 214). Now, at this point he introduces figurative or symbolic presentations as means of giving information, and the whole second part deals with these. Nevertheless, the author is forced to admit that "Naturally, not even now, when dealing with pure signs, are we completely unbounded; but we no longer feel these bounds" (p. 274). The finitude of the domain of numbers is thereby admitted. If numbers are presentations which I or someone else must form, then there cannot be infinitely many numbers; and no symbolism can remove this limitation. According to the author (p. 215), a symbolic presentation is a presentation by means of signs which uniquely characterize what is to be presented. "For example, we have a real presentation of the external appearance of a house when we are actually looking at it; we have a symbolic presentation when someone is giving us the indirect characteristic: the corner house on such-and-such sides of such-and-such streets." This refers to the case where something objective is present of which I am to make a presentation to myself; and for that very reason, this explanation does not fit our case at all well. To be sure, one cannot help but assume that according to the author, numbers are presentations: results of mental processes or activities (pp. 24, 46). But where is what is objective: that of which a number is a presentation? What is it that here corresponds to the house in the example above? And yet it is precisely this object that is the connecting link between a real and a symbolic presentation; it is this that justifies our saying that the symbolic presentation appertains to the real one, and it is this that is uniquely characterized by the signs when we have a symbolic presentation. The confusion of the subjective with the objective, the fact that no clear distinction is ever made between expressions like "Moon" and "presentation of the Moon," all this diffuses such an impenetrable fog that the attempt to achieve clarity becomes hopeless. I can only say that I have acquired the following impression of the author's opinion: If I want to have a symbolic presentation where I do not have a real one, I *idealize* (p. 251) my powers of presentation; *i.e.*, I imagine or present to myself that I have a presentation which in fact I neither have nor can have; and what I thus imagine would be my symbolic presentation. So, for example, I can form a symbolic presentation by means of the sign "15," by presenting to myself that I am presenting to myself a set consisting of the elements of a set to which the number 10 belongs and the elements of a set to which the number 5 belongs, and then apply to this the procedure which according to the author produces the appropriate number. The presentations of the signs are incorporated into the symbolic presentations. "Here the sensible signs are not mere companions of the concepts, in the manner of linguistic signs. They participate in our symbolic constructions in a much more prominent manner—so much so, that they finally predominate over almost everything else" (p. 273, similarly p. 264). Herewith the author approaches very closely the opinions of Helmholtz and Kronecker. If this were correct, the numbers would change whenever we change the signs. We should have completely different numbers from the ancient Greeks and Romans. But would these symbolic presentations also have the properties which the real ones are supposed to have? Just as little, I think, as my presentation of a green meadow is green. Now, the author does of course note (p. 217) that a real presentation and a symbolic one belonging to it stand in a relation of logical equivalence. "Two concepts are logically equivalent if every object of the one is also an object of the other, and *vice versa.*" He explains that it is on the basis of this that symbolic presentations can "go proxy for" the corresponding real ones. Here the confusion of presentation and concept interferes with our understanding. If we confine ourselves to the example of the corner-house, we may presume that the "equivalence" is here supposed to consist in the fact that my real presentation and the symbolic one are referred to the same object (that very corner-house). Now, when can the latter "go proxy for" the former? Presumably, when I am talking about the corner-house itself, not about my presentation. In reading this book, I have been able to see how very difficult it is for the sun of truth to penetrate the fog which arises out of the confusion of psychology and logic. Happily, we here see the beginnings of such a penetration. It becomes overwhelmingly evident that our presentations matter very little here, but that instead it is the very thing of which we seek to make presentations to ourselves that is the subject of our concern, and that our assertions are about it. And expressions to this effect occur several times in the second part; which is the more remarkable, the less it really agrees with the author's whole mode of thought. We read (p. 214, bottom), "Even if we have not *really* given the concepts, at least we have given them in a *symbolic* way." Here, concepts appear as something objective, and the difference between real and symbolic concepts refers only to the way in which they are given. There is talk of *species* of the concept of number which are not accessible to us in any real sense (p. 265), and of *real* numbers, of numbers in themselves which are inaccessible to us in general (p. 295). We read (p. 254) about symbolic formations of numbers which belong to one and the same real number. Given the opinion of the author, one should expect "non-existent" instead of "real"; for if a number were a real presentation, in this case there would not be one. What are these "numbers in themselves" (p. 294), these "real numbers", if not objective numbers which are independent of our thinking; which exist even when they are not accessible to us (p. 296)? The author says (p. 295), "Any number whatever can be uniquely characterized . . . by means of diverse relations to other numbers, and each such characteristic provides a new symbolic presentation of this very number." Here the objective number "in itself" clearly plays the role of the corner-house in our example of the latter. It is not my presentation that is the number; rather, I form one or several presentations of one and the same number, or at least I try to do so. A pity that the author does not try to keep the expressions "A" and "presentation of A" clearly distinct. But if my presentation of a number is not that number itself, then the ground is herewith cut out from under the psychological mode of consideration insofar as the latter's aim is to investigate the nature of numbers. If I want to investigate a presentation, I have to keep it as unchanged as possible—which of course is difficult to do. On the other hand, if I want to investigate something objective, my presentations will have to conform as much as possible to the matter at hand, to the results of this investigation; in general, then, they have to change. It makes a tremendous difference to the mode of investigation whether the number-presentation is itself the object of the investigation, or whether it is merely a presentation of the real object. The author's procedure fits only the first case, whereas the last passages adduced above can only be interpreted as instances of the second. If a geographer were to read a work on oceanography in which the origin of the seas were explained psychologically, he would undoubtedly receive the impression that the very point at issue had been missed in a very peculiar way. I have the same impression of the present work. To be sure, the sea is something real and a number is not; but this does not prevent it from being something objective; and that is the important thing.

In reading this work, I was able to guage the devastation caused by the influx of psychology into logic; and I have here made it my task to present this damage in a clear light. The mistakes which I thought it my duty to show reflect less upon the author than they are the result of a widespread philosophical disease. My own, radically different position makes it difficult for me to do justice to his achievements, which I presume to lie in the area of psychology; and I should like to direct the attention of psychologists especially to Chapter XI, where the possibility of momentary conceptions of sets is discussed. But I consider myself insufficiently qualified to pass judgment in that area.

Notes

1. Henceforth I shall take 'cardinal' to be understood [Trans.]

2. On this point, please compare my essay "On Sense and Reference" in *Zeitschrift für Philosophie und Philosophische Kritik.*

3. For strictly speaking, the relation does not obtain in the case of concepts. Compare my essay "On Concept and Object" in *Vierteljahrsschrift für wiss. Philosophie* [16 (1892), pp. 192-205; Trans.].

4. Otto Biermann, Professor of Mathematics at the Deut. Techn. Hochsch. in Brünn; student of Weierstrass. [Trans.]

Dorion Cairns (essay date 1930)

SOURCE: "Mr. Hook's Impression of Phenomenology," in *The Journal of Philosophy,* Vol. XXVII, No. 15, July 17, 1930, pp. 393-96.

[In the following essay, Cairns challenges Hook's critique of Husserl.]

In the course of a recent article called "A Personal Impression of Contemporary German Philosophy" (this JORNAL, Vol. XXVII, No. 6, March 13, 1930, pp. 141-160) Mr. Sidney Hook says:

> Writers of the phenomenological school keep their eyes on the object, for that in a sense is what the phenomenological method is defined to be. Consequently they are the strongest analytical group in Germany and closest to the English and American school of neo-realism.

But latterly Husserl's school has abandoned the standpoint of "pure description" and invaded the field of ontology. For many years, its opponents had maintained that its so-called "presuppositionless analysis" was only a deceptive phrase which concealed many presuppositions about the nature of knowledge, logic, and consciousness with which it was operating. And now Heidegger has come forward, as one crowned by the master himself to reveal what these presuppositions are and where they lead. Husserl had originally attracted notice with his *Logische Untersuchungen,* a keen attack on all psychological interpretations of the idea of validity. He himself regarded this work as a preface to larger studies which would contain a new logic. But in his subsequent works, instead of a new logic, he presented a new psychology—or rather a logicized version of pre-Lockean psychology. The fundamental dogmas of this "new logic" are the belief in immediate knowledge, the conviction theory of evidence and the doctrine of *hypostatic* essences which these entail. These entities, maintains Husserl, are self-contained and autonomous, but are imbedded in the content of consciousness and recognized by an act of intellectual vision (*Wesenschau*). [p. 152.]

To begin with, let me point out that Husserl had already attracted notice through the publication of the first volume of his *Philosophie der Arithmetik* in 1891, nine years before the publication of the first volume of his *Logische Untersuchungen.* In the second place, the *Logische Untersuchungen* are not in the main an attack on psychological interpretations of the idea of validity. The first volume is called a *Prolegomena zur reinen Logik,* and the first nine of its ten chapters are indeed largely devoted to a refutation of the doctrine that logic should be based on psychology. But the second volume, published in 1901 and entitled *Untersuchungen zur Phänomenologie und Theorie der Erkenntnis*, contains six *Untersuchungen,* none of which is devoted to "an attack on . . . psychological interpretations of the idea of validity." The attack on psychologism is entirely prolegomenary, and occupies only about a fifth of the entire book.

"Keeping one's eyes on the object" is a bad definition of the phenomenological method. If it means "testing judgments by observed facts," it is too wide. If it means "restricting observation to the non-subjective," it is even more clearly false. For Husserl and his followers it is not the mere object, but the subjective act with its intentional correlate as such, which is the fundamental datum. Mere *Wesensanalyse* of objects is not what Husserl means by phenomenology. Incidentally, the emphasis on act-analysis, quite apart from profound metaphysical differences, would distinguish Husserl from the neo-realists.

If the recentness of Husserl's *Formale und transzendentale Logik* justified ignoring it, Mr. Hook would be justified in saying that Husserl's work published subsequently to the *Logische Untersuchungen* did not contain a new logic. Since the original publication of the *Logische Untersuchungen* and prior to 1929, there had been published, in addition to a revised edition of the *Logische Untersu-*

chungen, three philosophical contributions from Husserl's pen: in 1911 a fifty-page article on **"Philosophie als strenge Wissenschaft"** in 1913 the first book of the *Ideen zu einer reinen Phänomenologie und phänomenologischen Philosophie*—this first book of the *Ideen* bears the subtitle, *Allgemeine Einführung in die reine Phänomenologie*—and in 1928 his *Vorlesungen zur Phänomenologie des inneren Zeitbewusstseins*. The titles alone should show that Mr. Hook is wrong in intimating that any of these works pretends to offer a "new logic."

What is meant by saying Husserl presented a "logicized version of pre-Lockean psychology"? Were there not many different psychologies before Locke? Of which did Husserl present a "logicized" version? In explanation Mr. Hook states, as fundamental dogmas of this logicized psychology, "belief in immediate knowledge, the conviction theory of evidence and the doctrine of *hypostatic* essences." Of these three alleged dogmas, only the first is accepted by Husserl; the second and third are expressly rejected in his published writings.

Moreover, as Mr. Hook doubtless knows, the doctrine of immediate knowledge is expressly asserted in Locke's *Essay* (Bk. IV, ch. I, sec. 4, and especially Bk. IV, ch. II, sec. 1), and has had many non-phenomenologist adherents since Locke's day. How, then, does it earn for Husserl's doctrines the epithet, "pre-Lockean"?

Husserl is quite explicit in asserting that conviction is no indication of truth (*cf. Ideen,* Bk, I, sec. 136, p. 284). Indeed the phenomenological method is designed to lessen the danger of uncritically accepting as truths what are merely blind convictions. Immediate self-givenness of the object is for Husserl the source of all evidence (*cf. op. cit.*, secs. 142 et seq., pp. 296 ff.). Such intuition brings, not mere conviction, but rational insight.

It is true that, according to Husserl, essences are recognized in an act of intellectual vision (*Wesenschau*), though, of course, Husserl does not say we have such a vision every time we mean an essence—any more than we have a vision of a horse every time we mean a horse. *Wesenserschauung* is the act in which an essence is given "in person" (*cf. op. cit.*, secs., 3 and 4, pp. 10 ff.). An act which "intends" an essence is necessarily founded upon another act, wherein a particular exemplification of the aforesaid essense is intended (*cf. loc. cit.*). To say that Husserl maintains that essences are "imbedded in the content of consciousness" is, to say the least, misleading. We think most properly of the "content" of consciousness as being the immanent constituents of consciousness, the acts of seeing, hoping, remembering, etc., as contrasted with the generally transcendent objects, which are seen, hoped, remembered, etc. If "imbedded" is here equivalent to "exemplified," then essences are not, according to Husserl, "imbedded" *only* in the immanent content of consciousness; they are exemplified in every particular, in the outer world as well as in our minds (*cf. op. cit.*, sec. 2, pp. 8 f.). If, on the other hand, we take the phrase more literally, "imbedded in" may mean "being present as particular parts

of." But it were absurd to suppose that a universal essence could be a particular part of anything. The only plausible meaning which Mr. Hook's phrase can have, if what he says is true, is that, according to Husserl, particular objects of consciousness are exemplifications of essences. But what an infelicitous way of saying the obvious!

If the denial that an essence is reducible to its particular exemplifications, to parts of its exemplifications, to the class of its real or possible exemplifications, or the like, implied the doctrine of hypostatic essences, then Husserl's views would imply it. But he does not believe that essences are real or substantial (*cf. Logische Untersuchungen,* Bk. II, pt. I, *IIte Untersuchung,* passim.; also *Ideen,* I, sec. 22)—and that is what the doctrine of hypostatic essences properly means.

Husserl's ideal is a philosophy based on clear intuitions of essences, a philosophy which never goes beyond what is clearly given, but remains purely descriptive of that given. Neither he nor his closer followers feel it necessary to renounce that ideal in order to invade the field of ontology. The phenomenological ideal and the phenomenological method can and do govern their treatment of ontological problems. Some who have come under Husserl's influence—and in that sense are of his "school"—add speculation to phenomenological description, but to abandon the standpoint of pure description is to abandon the central principle of phenomenology. If only to keep our concepts clear, we ought not to call such speculative philosophers phenomenologists.

Mr. Hook's characterization of Heidegger as one crowned by the master himself to reveal what the presuppositions of phenomenology are and where they lead, is inexcusable, even as a bit of ironic rhetoric. True, Husserl has long recognized Heidegger's extraordinary capability and achievement, but the "master" is far from accepting or sponsoring all the pupil's views. In particular, Husserl would not take it, from Heidegger or anyone else, that phenomenology rests ultimately on any presuppositions whatsoever.

There remains a word to be said about the identification of phenomenology with psychology, a confusion indicated by Mr. Hook's epithet, "logicized psychology." Psychology deals with the actual nature of existent minds, the minds belonging to organisms in the physical world. Phenomenology deals with the necessary natures of acts, quite apart from the reality or unreality of their exemplifications (*cf. op. cit.,* **Einleitung,** pp. 2 f.). There are indeed important similarities between the two disciplines, but their differences are of at least equal significance.

Mr. Hook warns us at the beginning of his article that his "Personal Impression of Contemporary German Philosophy" is "a truer picture of the student impressed, his interests, prejudices, and mindset, than of the cause of his impressions, German philosophy." Even so, it is interesting to note that his impression of Husserl's phenomenology seems largely erroneous.

Marvin Farber (essay date 1930)

SOURCE: A review of *Recent Phenomenological Litera-ture,* in *The Journal of Philosophy,* Vol. XXVII, No. 13, June 19, 1930, pp. 337-47.

[*In the following excerpt, Farber illustrates the aim of phenomenology and the method Husserl uses in his phe-nomenological analysis of time-consciousness.*]

Undoubtedly the most prominent philosophical movement of present-day Germany is Phenomenology, of which Pro-fessor Husserl is the founder and leader. It is not a unified "school" in point of doctrine, but is due rather to the per-sonal teaching and influence of Husserl. The development of the school has been determined mainly, until recently, by the development of Husserl's own thought. Beginning as a disciple of Brentano, whose *Psychology from on Em-pirical Standpoint* has remained a permanent influence on him, Husserl elaborated his earliest philosophical stand-point in the **Philosophy of Arithmetic** (1891). Mathemati-cal interests naturally led over to problems concerning the foundations of logic, and to the publication in 1901 of the **Logical Investigations,** the first volume of which contains a repudiation and refutation of "Psychologism." This work represents a realistic-ontological manner of investigation, although Husserl later reinterpreted these investigations in the light of his systematically formulated phenomenologi-cal method, which leads on to the track of idealism. In its original version it is one of the great landmarks in the study of the foundations of logic. These investigations, and particularly those relating to "intentional" or meaning-ful experience, were extended by his studies of inner time-consciousness (1905-1910), which have recently been pub-lished under the title **Lectures on the Phenomenology of Time-Consciousness.**[1] The central theme of the lectures is "the temporal constitution of pure sense-data and the self-constitution of the 'phenomenological time' which is basic to such constitution." Following these studies a definite transition to idealism was made, as seen in the **Ideas con-cerning Pure Phenomenology** (1913), in which work much attention is devoted to method. The final period of Husserl's development has led to the formulation of an ab-solute system of philosophy, his *First Philosophy*. The di-versity of standpoints and interests among his disciples is due largely to their failure or refusal to develop along with him; and latterly some of the younger phenomenologists, such as Heidegger, have shown evidence of independence in starting out on new paths.

In keeping with the pretensions of a system of philosophy Husserl sought to establish the phenomenological method as an absolute or presuppositionless and certain method, which he introduces into his studies of time-consciousness. Whether this is a later addition is not stated, but that might well be the case, since the requirements of the later system are not involved on the purely descriptive level of con-sciousness. There are at least two senses in which the term "phenomenology" has been used: (1) In a narrower sense, as pure "eidetic" or essential psychology, or that discipline which had been sought formerly by the exponents of em-pirical psychology and theory of knowledge; (2) in a wider sense, as transcendental phenomenology or First Philoso-phy, in which all sciences are supposed to be rooted.[2] The lectures on inner time-consciousness obviously belong to the former, although the peculiarly fundamental nature of phenomenological time and Husserl's insistent use of his method of the "elimination of transcendences" give them direct significance for his First Philosophy.

In the introduction to the work on time-consciousness Husserl defines the problem of time as seen from his stand-point. It will perhaps be best to follow his account closely, since his method requires that one abandon the "natural" attitude, in which one's view is directed at or to the object as an independently existing thing. Although time is prob-ably the best known of all things, its adequate understand-ing is very difficult, and must include placing objective time and subjective time-consciousness in their proper re-lationship to one another and the explanation of how tem-poral objectivity, and hence individual objectivity in gen-eral, can be "constituted" in subjective time-consciousness. Husserl's purpose is the phenomenological analysis of time-consciousness, which requires the complete exclusion of all assumptions and convictions concerning objective time or transcendent existence. "Objectively" every expe-rience, as well as every real being, may have its place in the one and only objective time, which therefore includes the experience of the perception of time and the idea of time itself. It might be of interest to determine the objec-tive time of an experience, or to compare the estimates of time-intervals with real time intervals. But these are no problems for phenomenology. The real thing, the real world, is no phenomenological datum, and neither is world time, or the time of nature in the sense of natural science and also of psychology as the natural science of the psy-chical. Now it might appear to the reader, when Husserl speaks of the analysis of time-consciousness or of the tem-poral character of objects of perception, memory, and an-ticipation, as if he had already assumed objective time and then only studied the subjective conditions of the possibil-ity of time perception and of real knowledge of time. But what he professes to take over is not the existence of a world time, the existence of a thingish duration, and the like, but rather *appearing* time and appearing duration *as such*. These are regarded as being absolutely given, since doubting them would be meaningless: the external objects may or may not exist in truth, but the appearances them-selves are indubitable. An existing time is assumed in the realm of appearances, but that is not the time of the expe-riential world, it is the immanent time of the stream of consciousness. Thus there is an essential change from the contingent realm of transcendence to the "certain" realm of immanence. The evidence that we have for the fact that the consciousness of a tone or melody exhibits a succes-sion is given as an example of such inner certainty; it is such that all doubt or denial would appear meaningless. This is the basic distinguishing character of the phenom-enological field of description, to which Husserl attains by means of a systematic elaboration of the Cartesian method of doubt, which requires the elimination of all transcendent existence. Objective space and time, and with them the world of real things and occurrences, are all examples of transcendent entities which must be "eliminated" and "bracketed" if a descriptive science of pure immanence is to be realised.[3]

Beginning with the field of cognition as such, it is then the task of the phenomenologist to describe its content and trace the "constitution" of objectivity in it. Suppose that we look at a piece of chalk; we close and open our eyes. Then we have two perceptions, although we say that we see the same chalk twice. The contents of our experience are separated temporally, but there is no separation in the object, which persists as the same. Thus there is duration on the side of the object, and change in the phenomenon. The experienced content is "objectivated," and then "the object is constituted out of the material of the experienced contents through meaningful apprehension." But the object is not merely the sum or complex of these "contents," which do not enter into it at all; it is more than content and other than it. The objectivity belongs to "experience" and in fact to the unity of experience; expressed phenomenologically, "the objectivity is not constituted in the 'primary' contents (i.e., sensed contents), but rather in the characters of meaningful apprehension and in the laws which belong to the essence of these characters." It is thus clear that the ultimate purpose of the phenomenology of knowledge is to construct a theory of objectivity on the basis of cognitive immanence, a setting particularly favorable for idealism.

Husserl insists upon the distinction between the phenomenological (or epistemological) approach to the problem of time and the psychological approach. The epistemological question concerning the possibility of experience is answered by a study of the essence of experience; and similarly the problem of time leads back to a study of the "origin" of time—i.e., the primitive formations of time-consciousness. He is not interested in the psychological problem of the origin of time, or in the manner in which objective space and time perception arise in the human individual or species. For him the question of the empirical origin of time is indifferent; he is interested only in pure experiences with respect to their descriptive content and objective meaning. The phenomenologist does not fit the experiences into any "reality." He is concerned with reality only in so far as it is meant, perceived, or conceived. With regard to the problem of time this means that the *temporal experiences* interest the phenomenologist. That they are in turn contained in a world of things in which they have their empirical being and origin does not interest him; he knows nothing of that. On the other hand, it is important for him that "objective temporal" data are *meant* in these experiences. The description of the way in which cognitive acts mean this or that "objectivity," or, more specifically, the determination of the "*a priori* truths," which govern the "constitutive factors of objectivity," belong to the task of phenomenology. Husserl endeavors to delineate this *a priori* nature of time by investigating time-

consciousness and determining its essential structure, an investigation which takes account of the specific contents of temporal experience as well as the acts through which they arise. By the essential structure of time he means laws such as the following: that the fixed temporal order is a two-dimensional infinite series, that two different times can never be at the same time, that the relational nature of time is insymmetrical, that it is transitive, that to every time there belongs an earlier and a later stage, etc. What distinguishes these laws from the usual analyses of time is the context of pure consciousness in which they are elaborated, and what is here called "*a priori*" would ordinarily go by the name of "formal properties."

One of the most interesting and instructive features of the work is the exposition and critique of Brentano's theory of the origin of time. Both because of its intrinsic value and its usefulness as an introduction to the descriptive side of phenomenology it would be well worth while reproducing in detail. However, a brief statement of it will have to suffice for the present. Husserl's thorough-going and constructive critique of Brentano's theory shows his genius for making distinctions and adhering to them; and he is revealed at his best when he proceeds to concrete descriptive studies. Brentano believed that he had found an explanation of the origin of time in the occurrence of the "original associations" which are attached to all perceptions. That is to say, in any act of perception what is perceived remains present for a time, but not without modifying itself; in addition to changes in intensity and content, there is also the peculiar modification of being pushed back temporally. Thus every sensation of a tone, after the passing of the stimulus, awakens out of itself an idea which is similar and is determined temporally, and this makes possible the idea of a melody. This principle is then stated as a general law: a continuous series of ideas is naturally connected with every given idea, and in this series every idea reproduces the content of its predecessor—i.e., every new idea acquires the property of being past. Phantasy is therewith regarded as being productive, for it is held to create the factor of time in ideas. The origin of temporal ideas is thus referred to the domain of phantasy. The present sense-content of a given experience is caused by a stimulus, and if the stimulus disappears the sensation also disappears. But the sensation then becomes creative: it begets a phantasy-idea which is similar or nearly similar with respect to content, and is enriched by the temporal character. This idea awakens a new idea which is attached to it, and so on. The continuous series of such modifications is what Brentano means by "primitive" or "original" associations. In consistency with his theory he denies the perception of succession; we believe that we hear a melody and hence that we hear something past, but that is only an appearance which is due to the liveliness of the original association. The modifying temporal predicates he holds to be "unreal," only the determination of the "now" being real, and the real "now" becomes unreal in turn through a series of infinitesimal differences.

In his critique of Brentano's theory Husserl points out, as he never tires of doing, that it does not meet the requirements of a phenomenological analysis of time-consciousness. For although it deals with the immanent side of consciousness, it still operates with transcendent presuppositions, with existing temporal objects which "stimulate" us and "cause" sensations. He therefore regards it as another theory of the psychological origin of time. But Husserl recognizes that it contains parts of an epistemological theory of the conditions of the possibility of time-consciousness, for duration, succession, and changes are spoken of as "appearing." A "now" appears in a succession, and united with it is a "past." The unity of the consciousness comprising the present and past is a phenomenological datum. The question arises, whether the past really appears in consciousness by means of phantasy. Inspection shows that a distinction must be drawn between time as perceived and time as phantasied; the difference between the perception of a succession and the remembrance or phantasy of a perceived succession must be explained. Insisting upon an examination of all the factors involved in experience, Husserl finds still further defects in Brentano's analysis, for the latter does not distinguish between act and content, or between act, content of apprehension, and the apprehended object. To which of these factors is the element of time to be attributed? As a matter of fact, we do not merely discern the element of time in connection with the primary or sensed contents of experience, but also in connection with cognitive objects and acts. An analysis of time which is limited to one level of "constitution" is not adequate and fails to grasp the essence of time as a real succession.

A complete descriptive analysis of the process of experience and particularly of the acts of knowledge through which objects are given must therefore be undertaken for the foundation of an adequate theory of time. Husserl asks: How are we to explain the apprehension of transcendent time-objects, whether changing or changeless, and which are extended over a duration? Such objects are "constituted" in a manifold of immanent data and views, which occur as a succession. Is it possible to unite these successively occurring representative data in a present experience? An entirely new question arises therewith: How, along with the temporal objects, both immanent and transcendent, is time itself constituted, how are the duration and succession of objects constituted? These various avenues of description, which are here indicated briefly, and which require still further analysis, must be kept in view in the investigation, although all of these questions are closely related. It is evident that the perception of a temporal object has time, that the perception of duration presupposes the duration of perception, and that the perception of any time-form has its own time-form; and if we abstract from all transcendences, then only phenomenological time remains, which belongs to the irrefragable essence of perception. Husserl goes beyond description and reveals his metaphysical tendency when he states that "objective time is actually constituted phenomenologically" and that "it is there for us as an objectivity and as an element of an objectivity only through this constitution" (p.

384). It follows that a phenomenological analysis must take account of the constitution of time-objects.

It will be of interest to follow Husserl in a typical example of his descriptive analysis, which may be justified on grounds of description alone; stripped of some of its vocabulary there would be no suggestion of metaphysical implications. Suppose that a time-object, a tone, for example, is viewed as a pure sense-datum. It begins and stops, and the unity of the entire occurrence recedes into the ever more remote past. In the recession I still have a "hold" on it, I have it in retention; and as long as the retention lasts the tone has its own time, it is the same, its duration is the same. I can attend to its aspect of givenness. It and the duration which it fills are known in a continuity of "modes," in a "continuous stream"; one point, or one phase of this stream, is called "consciousness of the beginning tone," and in that the first time-point of the duration of the tone is known in the mode of the now. The tone is given—i.e., it is known now; and it is known as now as long as any one of its phases is known as now. But if any phase of time, with the exception of the beginning phase, is a present now, then a continuity of phases is known as "before," and the entire stretch of the time-duration from the beginning-point until the now-point is known as a past duration; but the remaining stretch of the duration is not yet known. At the close the end-point is itself known as a now-point, and the entire duration is known as past. "During" this whole stream of consciousness the one and the same tone is known as enduring, as enduring now. It was not known "before," in case it had not been expected; and it is "still known" for a time "afterwards" in retention, in which it can be fixated and remain as past. The entire stretch of the duration of the tone or "the" tone in its extension remains then as something "dead," with no creative point of the now to animate it; but it is continually modified and lapses back into "emptiness."

What has been described is the whole in which the immanent temporal object "appears" in a continuous stream, in which it is "given." However, to describe this mode is not the same as to describe the appearing time-duration itself. For the same tone with the duration belonging to it was not described but rather presupposed in the description. The same duration is a duration now being built up, and then becomes a "past" duration: it is still known and is formed anew "as it were" in memory. The tone which now sounds is the same tone which is viewed as past in a later stream of consciousness. The points of a time-duration remove themselves from my consciousness analogous to the way in which the points of a resting object in space are removed from me when "I remove myself from the object." The object keeps its place, and similarly the tone keeps its time, every time-point is changeless, but it flees to the remotenesses of consciousness, the distance from the creative now becomes ever greater. The tone itself is the same, but the tone "in the mode how" appears always as a different one.

There is much of a descriptive nature in Husserl's work which shows how the theory of knowledge may be enriched by the adoption of the phenomenological method in the narrower sense of pure descriptive psychology. The discussion of the difference between retention and reproduction, or between primary and secondary memory or phantasy (p. 404), completes the correction of Brentano's theory of time as based on phantasy, and again illustrates Husserl's skill in finding great complexity where others see only simplicity. In this respect phenomenology does extend the vision of philosophy. There is a difference, for example, between the modification of consciousness which transforms an original now into a reproduced now, and the modification which transforms either an original or reproduced now into a past now. The latter passes by continuous gradations into the past; whereas there can be no talk of a continuous transition from perception to phantasy, or from impression to reproduction. Perception is built up on the basis of sensation, and sensation, which functions in the presentation of an object, forms a continuum. Similarly, the phantasmas form a continuum for the representation of a phantasy-object. From the standpoint of reflective consciousness we appreceive when we view the contents of sensation, even though we may abstract from all transcendent apperception; the "flow of time" or duration is presented as a kind of objectivity. An instance of Husserl's readiness to pass from the order of knowledge to that of reality is seen when he states that "objectivity presupposes the consciousness of unity or identity" (p. 324). In strict keeping with the method of description he should have said that our knowledge or experience of objectivity presupposes the consciousness of unity or identity. The same tendency is illustrated in his discussion of the stages of the constitution of time and of temporal objects (p. 427 ff.).

Husserl finally divides the sphere of time-consciousness into three levels, which are called "stages of constitution": (1) The first stage is the perception of empirical objects in the usual sense, including the thing of the experience of an individual subject, the intersubjective identical thing and the thing of physics. (2) From the phenomenological point of view the object is taken as a phenomenon and attention is directed to the process of perception. All appearances and forms of consciousness have the properties of being now and receding into the past, properties which characterize all "subjective" time. Perception, memory, anticipation, phantasy, judgment, feeling, the will—in short everything that may be the object of reflection—appears in the same reflective time, and in fact in the same time in which the perceptual objects appear. The appearances are viewed as immanent unities in a "pre-empirical" time. (3) The third and last stage is that of the absolute stream of consciousness, which constitutes time. Subjective time is regarded as being constituted in an absolute "timeless" consciousness, which can not be an object of cognition. This absolute consciousness is supposed to be prior to all constitution. In other words, the phenomena which constitute time are different in principle from those which are formed in time. They are not individual objects or events, and therefore it can not be said that they are present or past.

Nevertheless, the absolute consciousness comes to givenness. Consider, for example, the appearance of a tone, and attend to the appearance as such. The tone-appearance has its duration, and presents itself as an immanent object. But that is not the ultimate consciousness. The immanent tone is a constituted phenomenon, for with each tonal now there is a series of tone-nuances, in which each now recedes as a past. The perception of the present and the memory of the past may be apprehended in a comprehensive now. In the ordinary experience of the consciousness of objects one regards the past from the point of view of the present. But it is possible to grasp the entire consciousness of objects as a now, or to view it in its togetherness as "at once." Time-consciousness of this kind can not in turn be made to be an object of consciousness, for that would assign to it a position in a process of subjective time. The flow of absolute time-consciousness has a permanent formal structure. This structure is determined by the law that a now is constituted by means of an impression, to which a series of retentions and a horizon of protentions or anticipations are attached. A continuity of appearances belonging to the stream of consciousness is ingredient in a now, but this stream is not something temporally "objective." It is, in short, "absolute subjectivity" (p. 429), which as the most fundamental principle of experience defines at the same time a necessary condition for *objects* of experience.

On the basis of this principle, the emergence of all objects, including transcendent objects and things, is to be explained. The principle that all possible objects are by themselves as they are for knowledge is a reasonable assumption for philosophy; but Husserl goes a step further when he implies that objects can only be "in" the system knowledge, and are in fact conditioned and formed by an absolute consciousness. There can be no doubt that he had this goal in view from the very start, when introducing the phenomenological method. That temporal things are constituted and are as such dependent upon an absolute subjectivity, and that, furthermore, spatial things are constituted similarly, since they are held to presuppose temporal constitution (p. 446), clearly indicate a standpoint of genetic, transcendental idealism, which no amount of descriptive material can conceal.

The *Lectures on Time-Consciousness* illustrate both the strength and the weakness of the phenomenological method. Even granting all of the alleged advantages of this method—namely, that it furnishes a certain or indubitable realm for investigation, and that it makes possible the exact delineation of the facts of knowledge as such, thus deepening our understanding of the problem of knowledge, it must be clear that dangers are incurred through the use of the method. Husserl's very language betrays his predisposition to treat the transcendent realm of existence, in which belief was suspended as a matter of method, as something reducible to pure consciousness. The very formulation of the problem of the constitution of objectivity in subjectivity indicates his metaphysical leaning. That the stream of experiences occurs in configurations, that cognitive contents are formed as unities amid multiplicity, may be taken as matters of fact, whether empirical or phenomenological. Furthermore, that they refer to objects "of" which they are appearances is recognized by Husserl: but the objects themselves are not "constituted" phenomenologically! The alleged constitution occurs only on the cognitive side, and it is sheer dogmatism to inject such a condition into the essence of objectivity. The phenomenological method is unable to restore the external world to its position of stability and independence, however far from "absoluteness" it may be in the natural view. The material realm of existence must be assumed for the world of experience, and no theory of reality can afford to dispense with it. That it is impossible to get outside of the field of nature, even a phenomenologist will have to admit. Even if this metempsychosis is permitted as a methodological expedient, assumptions which are similar in principle to those of the "natural" attitude must be made on the phenomenological level. For one thing there is the supposition of consciousness in general, with a fixed essential structure. Strictly speaking, Husserl must begin with solipsism in the use of his method, for the only indubitable sphere is that of individual consciousness—the "egological" sphere. Even then it is at once apparent that only the actual experience of the present moment is "certain." It would be better to speak of the present experience as *unavoidable*; and nothing of any significance follows from it without special assumptions. Husserl's transition to intersubjectivity is a cumbrous and difficult operation, and depends in the last analysis upon the assumption of a consciousness in general. The trust in memory introduces another group of assumptions of the "essential" uniformity of phenomenological "substances," which can not be explained away by an appeal to "essential insight" into the structure of knowledge. The use of logical principles in the course of phenomenological descriptions may also be mentioned. Surely they must be employed in the ordering of any data, phenomenological or otherwise. In short, the much-vaunted "presuppositionless" method assumes a great deal, and fails to reinstate the transcendent world except as a "constituted" world, a conclusion rendered plausible only by the ambiguous use of the concept of constitution and the tacit assumption of a subject-object limitation applied to all reality. The phenomenological method thus presents a strange appearance: for on the one hand, it enables us to extend the descriptive method to include all regions of pure consciousness, in the course of which the method is illustrated by truly admirable descriptions; and on the other hand, Husserl falls into the traditional error of supposing that pure consciousness may be the adequate source of all science and reality. It is to be hoped that the student of philosophy will not fail to recognize the positive advance Husserl has made in pure psychology and theory of knowledge, despite the tendency of the system to smother the method.

Notes

1. Edmund Husserl, *Vorlesungen zur Phänomenologie des inneren Zeitbewusstseins* herausgegeben von Martin Heidegger (Jahrbuch für Philosophie und phänomenologische Forschung, Vol. IX, Halle, 1928).

2. *Cf.* Farber, *Phenomenology as a Method and as a Philosophical Discipline* (University of Buffalo Studies, 1928).

3. Thus Husserl states (p. 482): "The phenomenology which I had in mind in the *Logical Investigations* was the phenomenology of experiences in the sense of what is given in inner consciousness, and that is a closed domain in any case."

Sidney Hook (essay date 1930)

SOURCE: "Husserl's Phenomenological Idealism," in *The Journal of Philosophy,* Vol. XXVII, No. 14, July 3, 1930, pp. 365-80.

[*In the following essay, Hook presents an expository critique of Husserl's "Phenomenological Idealism."*]

Husserl's *Formale und transzendentale Logik*[1] marks the end of the most promising movement in recent German philosophy. Starting as a reaction to the psychologized logic of the nineteenth century, it succeeded in reviving the logical realism which had been obscured by too much preoccupation with the empirical descriptions of knowing and gave a modernized version of the Platonic doctine of the autonomy of the purely logical or ideal realm of meanings. All of Husserl's earlier writings with the exception of the very first were not devoted to logic, but rather to prolegomena of logic. The only book on strict logic produced by a member of his school is Pfänder's *Logik.*[2] But this last is not very much different from an ordinary book on formal logic. It is an extended treatment of subjects similar to those taken up, say, in the first part of Joseph's or Keynes' texts; and since it defines logic as the science of *thoughts,* as a discipline whose task is to analyze "the essence of thoughts, their ultimate elements, their structure, kinds and mutual relations" (p. 30), it is questionable whether recent English logicians who usually take their point of departure from the "proposition" would regard it as very strict. The development of a pure formal logic, however, was not Husserl's intention. He had early come to the conclusion that that could best be accomplished by the arithmetization of mathematics. What he really aimed at doing was to elaborate a fundamental method for philosophy, distinct from the method of natural science, which would give insight into the way all the possible objects of possible conscious experience were organized and related to one another. This method of analysis would begin with whatever was given in the acts of consciousness, would extrude all reference to existence, strip off verbal and hypothetical associations dependent upon such reference and reach its conclusions by an intuition of the implication of the essences constituting the ideal nucleus of what we are conscious of. Now this method operated in its preparatory state, i.e., just before the final vision of eidetic relationships, with a logical scheme of its own. If this logic were itself made an object of phenomenological analysis, if it were asked, for example, what evidence have the alleged rules of logical evidence, logic would seem to be swallowed up again in some kind of descriptive psychology. This, together with the fact that Husserl insisted that essences were always given in consciousness, made those who believed in the autonomy of logic fear that empirical psychologism had been driven out in order to let a transcendental psychologism in.

There are others who felt that in a world where logic was so effectively in use, it was useless to try to save for logic more than a conditional autonomy, that the really important question was not whether logic was subordinate, but whether it was subordinate to ontology or transcendental psychology. Husserl was given a choice between some variety of Aristotelianism or some variety of Kantianism. The Catholic philosophers hailed him as a continuator of the Thomist tradition and tried to make it appear that the only difference between Aquinas and Husserl was that between their respective theocentric and egocentric orientation. The Neo-Kantians, especially Natorp, pointed out that Husserl's doctrines were not so far removed from their own if only he would less ambiguously admit that the act of mind involved in the intuition of essences was not a passive beholding, but in some sense a construction. In his ***Formale und transzendentale Logik*** which is supposed to be the definitive statement of his *standpoint,* Husserl examines the relation between formal logic, ontology, and phenomenology. If I have understood his book aright, it aligns him beyond any doubt with the tradition of German idealism and leaves as a landmark to his philosophical memory only his critique of sensationalistic naturalism and some positive, albeit strained, analyses of ambiguities in the fundamental categories of psychology.

The following summary and running commentary is intended as an exposition rather than as an immanent criticism, for it seems to me that the final position into which Husserl's thought develops is its own best criticism. In a writer so difficult to follow as Husserl repetitions are unavoidable and often desirable.

I

Husserl admits that by some incautious words in his earlier writings he had given a handle to some of his critics to raise the cry of "psychologism" against his analysis of pure logical meaning. The fault, however, lay mainly with them, for they had failed to take his distinction between natural and transcendental psychology seriously. To deepen and clarify this distinction is one of the purposes of the book. Ideal meanings or universals can not be explained as composite effects of experiences in space and time. Nor are they arbitrarily invented notational links between such experiences. Nor are they free constructions, postulates, fictions or what not of our *ordinary* consciousness. Any one of these views represents what Husserl means by psychologism and nominalism which sin against the light by not recognizing the *objectivity* of essences. But to say that

something is objective does not mean that it necessarily exists prior to and independent of any reference to some consciousness. That meanings are *given* in consciousness (and how else are they given?) does not preclude their being *produced* (*erzeugt*) in consciousness especially if we recognize different levels of consciousness. In what sense can we say that meaning is both an objective logical datum and a production? Husserl's answer reads ". . . it can not be denied that we are as exactly and originally certain of the characteristic of meaning of ideal objects given to us by our own evidential sense as we are of the real objects given in our sense experience. But on the other hand it can not be denied that those ideal objects are also produceable ends, final ends and means, and that they are what they are '*out of*' a more original creation. That does not at all mean that they are what they are *in* and *during* this original creation. To say that they are *in* this act of original generation [*ursprünglichen Erzeugung*] is to say that they are in it as a certain intentionality, as a form of conscious *spontaneous activity*. . . . *This mode of giveness in such original activity* is nothing else than *its own peculiar form of 'perception.'* Or in other words, this original productive activity is the '*evidence' for ideal* entities" (p. 150).

Whatever else this means, it means that the only difficulty we are faced with is to find out what kind of an idealist Husserl is. This is not a difficulty to be sneered at, for all of philosophic Germany has been trying for the last twenty-five years to make it out. It is not Platonic idealism, since Plato's Ideas were stored up in heaven and were the models, not the instruments, of demiurgic creation. It is not Berkleian idealism, since that is a theory of mentalism which denies on principle the objectivity of non-mental ideal meanings. It is not Kantian idealism, for Kant stopped where he should have begun; instead of asking how logic itself was possible and submitting the ideal laws of logic to transcendental analysis (230-231) he accepted the Aristotelian logic as something finished and self-justifying. As distinct from all these Husserl's idealism is phenomenological idealism. It asks for the certification of everything found in consciousness—even the objective meanings. It asks how are *meanings* in general possible? How is formal logic as such possible? What evidence have we that the laws of formal logic are what they are, that what we regard as a meaning really is a meaning and not nonsense? What is the relation between our sense of evidence and that which is evidenced? What is the most fundamental of all evidencing relationships? To put such questions as these to logic, Husserl calls putting transcendental questions. The method of transcendental cross-examination is the phenomenological method; the answers, the content of phenomenological idealism.

The status and function of this phenomenological idealism can be made clear if we remember that it is actually involved in the third thematic sphere of every science (152 ff). Anything that we "see" and which can be controlled by our normal superficial notions of evidence, can be made the subject of a science. Anything "seen" (i.e., intellectually understood) can, as a domain of possible experience, be organized in terms of immanent relationships. This is the first and original thematic level of science. We are never satisfied with a science no matter how complete until we subject it to criticism. When we subject any science to a criticism of the relations its results bear to the *method* of knowledge and reasoning followed in attaining them, when we examine the origin and place of the ideal meanings used by these methods and reveal the implicit theory of procedure which normatively controls empirical practice, and when, finally, we become conscious of the higher psychic acts of "drawing inferences" or "concluding"—then we are in the second thematic sphere of a science. But there is still another sphere in which a science may be discoursed about. This does not concern itself with scientific method or results, but rather with an analysis of the activity of the *konstituirende Subjectivität,* or transcendental Mind, as it goes from one phase of the inquiry to another. A science does not spring ready-made from the bowels of nature nor from the mind of one man. What appears independent in it is in some way related to our reason, what appears "given" has already been "taken," what seems "to have" meaning is already endowed with it, what is "clear" has already been "clarified." Now what is this *konstituirende Subjectivität* to which the apparently independent is related, which "takes," "posits," and "endows with meaning," which clarifies and synthesizes? What are its secret and original sources of relevance and evidence in general? That answer can only be given by a new *Kritik der Vernunft,* by a transcendental critique of knowledge which includes formal logic as well as science. It is what Kant's logical purpose would have been if he had thrown his psychology and implicit metaphysics overboard. Really critical idealism must become phenomenological idealism. It is the most fundamental and genuine of all sciences, for without it we can not even understand how analytic criticism can affect our ordinary every-day scientific procedure.

This, as I understand it, is the crux of Husserl's position and I shall now try to give some of the details of the argument.

II

Both science and logic, to be really understood, must be brought to reflective self-consciousness by a theory which accounts for their possibility. This is especially necessary, says Husserl, in a world in which faith in reason and method have lost ground in direct proportion to their practical efficacy. We seem to be living in a world which grows more unintelligible, the more we are able to do with it. Husserl's study falls into two parts. Part one is devoted to the relation between formal logic and pure mathematics and justifies the identification of both in a formal *mathesis universalis* or a "pure apophantic analysis." Pure logic and formal ontology are equivalent. Since they show a structural correlation throughout they may be regarded as different aspects of the same science (p. 98). Formal ontology is distinguished from material ontology in that the

central conception of the first is an analytic *a priori*; of the second, a synthetic *a priori*. Formal ontology is really the study of the realm of possibility; its correlative formal logic is the analysis of consistency. Part two of the book is devoted to the transition from a formal logic to a transcendental logic or *Wissenschaftslehre*. Transcendental logic is the study of the presuppositions which formal logic itself makes. It is here claimed that all the basic problems of meaning which are relevant to logic and science are problems, not of the natural self, but of a transcendental subject. In passing we may note the coincident belief of Weyl, influenced by Husserl, as well as by Brouwer, that the foundations of mathematics must be sought in a Fichtean ego.[3]

A. In his discussion of formal logic Husserl is under the disadvantage of trying both to defend logic from any connection with psychology and "real" ontology and at the same time preparing the ground for his own transcendental critique. Some of the arguments of the naturalists against the "purity" of logic which Husserl rejects in the first part reappear in modified form in the second. The argument will be easier to follow if it is remembered that Husserl is waging war on two fronts against enemies who are as much opposed to one another as they are to him, viz., naturalism and extreme analytic logical realism.

Pure apophantic analysis, or universal formal logic, is concerned only with themes arising from the quest of consistency. Every problem of consistency can be shown to be reducible to a problem of compossibility. The notion of material truth does not enter here and is replaced by the relations of "inclusion" or "exclusion" of the various parts of a possible whole (47 ff). The validity of an analytic argument depends upon the reference of its component judgment to an ideal form posited or intuited by the mind. Stated propositionally, two judgments are compatible when it is possible to make them integral elements of the unity of another clear judgment. We recognize this "unity and clarity" by our sense of immediate evidence. The evidence of the clarity of such a synthesizing judgment can not be derived from a knowledge of its certainty, for a great many things are certain which are by no means immediately evident. This evidence can only be given by a principle of intuition. But, says Husserl, arguing against a naturalistic realism, our intuition is not related to a "real ontology"; it does not reflect generic or invariant characters of the existing world. Criticizing Aristotle, he holds that these intuitions reflect the order of a formal ontology, of those antecedent *conditions* of existence won by insight into pure possibilities. Formal ontology must logically precede real ontology (p. 70). Choosing to ask what are the conditions of existence instead of what are the conditions of genuine possibility, Husserl declares Aristotle's conception of "first philosophy" to be inadequate. The former dissociates formal and real ontology only because he assumes it to be self-evidently true that a significant proposition which does not depend for its intelligibility upon reference to any particular member of a class, is independent of the existence of the class itself. "The problem of formal ontology," he writes, "is, what kind of *a priori* propositions can be made about the realm of 'something-in-general'" (*Etwas überhaupt* p. 132). In other words ultimate categories of logical predication can not be taken from this world of space, time, and man. From which world, then Husserl's answer is given in the section on transcendental logic.

But, as has already been said, Husserl prepares his answer by showing that formal logic and ontology, although irreducible to a real ontology, are not yet independent on their own account. He uses the formalists arguments against the existentialist position in order to save logic from vicious psychologism and then turns around and used the existentialist's arguments (in modified form) against the formalist—in order to prove that both the subject-matter and the form of thought are only differentiations in certain transcendental psychic *acts*. Psychologism, presumably, loses its sting when it becomes transcendental.

The gist of the argument against pure formalism, as I understand it, is as follows. Logical categories are distinguishable among themselves. That is to say, they are meanings. As meanings they have implications which give other meanings. Reflection on these meanings show that they are organized in specific ways statable in terms of categorial laws. These laws have formal ontological validity for the realm of everything-in-general. Everything-in-general, however, does not exclude, but must include individuals-in-particular; the things of this world must be part of the realm of possibility, since if they were impossible, they could not exist. Consequently, if categorial relations are valid distributively for everything in general they must be valid for the existences we have knowledge about, We have a right, then, to seek for the evidence of formal *a priori* relations in the perception of individuals. The *invariant* and *constant* relation in any act of perception might give us evidence of these formal *a priori* truths. We naïvely take these truths for granted without trying to analyze them out of our perception of individual things. But when the validity of any "supposedly valid" formal truth is questioned, can we continue in this naïveté? "In fact," claims Husserl, "the criticism of logical principles as the revelation of the presuppositions implicitly hidden in them will show that even for the evidence of formal universalizing, *die Kerne* [i.e., the residual elements of the *sachhaltige* or material *a priori*—S. H.*] are not altogether irrelevant" (pp. 189-190).

Believing this does not prevent him from believing that every possible judgment is already true or false at the time of its utterance, that truth and falsity belong to the essence of any judgment as such (p. 175). How these statements can be reconciled with the acceptance of Heidegger's idea of the omnipresence of a *Situationshorizont,* or meaning determining context, is probably a secret of the transcendental Ego. Husserl admits that every judgment presupposes a certain range of relevance which can not itself be exhaustively expressed in a logical premise or series of premises, but which makes the acceptance of certain logical premises as over against others intelligible. He admits

that this idea of relevance prescribes the sense and limits of those operations in intellectual inquiry which we later recognize as norms (177-178). He implies therefore that a proposition can not be referred to as intrinsically true or false, or necessarily "either true or false" before an "intentional analysis" reveals the field in which, and the purpose for which, it is to operate. Let me hasten to add, however, that for Husserl terms like context, intention, and relevance have no naturalistic connotation. Whereas for the naturalist, logical characters arise in regulated inference controlled by the structure of certain existential wholes, for Husserl they are necessarily posited by our Ego whose acts will appear as foreign to the naïve consciousness of the scientific psychologist as to that of the mathematical logician. Husserl denies that logical characters of implication can be traits of an existential mode of empirical inquiry, for these characters are already involved *in* the process of inquiry from the very outset. The naturalist's answer to this and every other charge of circlarity is that implication can be viewed as a limit of a probability relation, which is not taken as *a priori* certain, but as hypothetically valid, subject to whether or not it can adequately organize or handle the existential affairs in which it is applied (Peirce). And if the laws of logic apply to any and every subject-matter, then we know something about the nature of the world we live in and not merely something about our minds; we know that the world has an ontological order that becomes explicitly logical when it enters into inference. Refusing to accept this or any other naturalistic argument, and refusing to grant that formal logic can be intuitively certain of its own laws in any save a psychological sense, Husserl takes an extreme step. In order to get certainty in knowledge, he *identifies the act of knowledge with the subject-matter of knowledge.* Starting out with the admission that essences are transcendent to knowledge in order to explain the possibility of knowing what seems to be outside the act of knowing, he ends by converting what is transcendent into a pole of an immanent noetic relation. The whole realm of essences becomes Ego-centrically oriented. Husserl and his naturalistic opponents are one in the denial that logic is self-contained, one in their emphatic claim that formal analysis is incomplete without a theory of evidence and experience. But it is in the character of the experience invoked that all the difference lies. For despite Husserl's contention that phenomenology is *jenseits Naturalismus und Apriorismus,* experience in his philosophy is nothing if not, literally supernatural. His great positive merit in the eyes of one who disagrees with him is to show that one *must* choose some type of experience as a source and setting for formal logic.

In the *Logische Untersuchungen* Husserl had shown that every judgment, no matter what its modality, referred to an ideal content of meaning which conditioned the very possibility of significant utterance. "I doubt whether," "I am sure that," "It is questionable if," "It is impossible that," can not be completed as judgments unless the *what* which is intended to be doubted, certified, or denied has a possible ideal existence. Or, to put it a little differently, the possibility of *drawing* a judgment depends upon absence of contradiction in the connotative constituents of what is judged. We have already seen that Husserl believes both in the autonomy of meanings and their ego-centric reference. He can not stop with a *Gegenstandstheorie*. He holds that the ideal existence of the objects of meaning is itself conditioned by the unity of possible experience (p. 193 ff). The unity of possible experience is the primary basis of all judgment. It is the community of meanings and intentions in which everything stands in some objective relation to something else. What does not fall in the realm of this possible experience is nonsense. For example, "red + 1 = 3" may have the psychological and grammatical form of a judgment, but it lacks reference to an objective content in the domain of possible experience. It consequently has no meaning. Impossible of being either true or false, it is not a proposition. The letters and counters of symbolic logic can only be sensibly used because some experienced objective relation is presupposed to hold between them in some context (p. 195).

Opposed to this view is the doctrine which, before the publication of the *Ideen zu einer reinen Phänomenologie* etc., used to be identified as Husserl's own, viz., that formal logic has an apriority which involves no reference to *any* factual subject-matter. The laws of logic are the invariant rules of combination of whatever is formally possible. And so long as one does not raise questions as to the meaning, consistency, and application of logical rules, it is the easiest position to take. But Husserl insists upon raising these questions as if intent upon crushing the old logical Adam within himself. He uses three types of argument—all used by the hereditary enemy, the naturalists, before him—against the sharp disjunction between possibility and actuality. First, that behind this play of elaborating possibilities is the assumption of the *existence* of a world in space and time which serves logically as the base of operations and as the ultimate control of our excursions into the realm of possibility. We get our possible constructions by varying the details of a world already given. If the possible is not to be correlated in some way with the actual, how is it to be distinguished from the nonsensical? Second, wherever formal logic analyzes its fundamental concepts such as implication and validity, it can not avoid a theory of *evidence*, a theory of know*ing* or inner (*subjektiv gerichtete*) experience indissociable from the existence of human beings. This is not psychologizing logic. It is a reminder that if the laws of logic *must* be psychologically possible, the nature of mind—or some aspects of it—must be part of logical theory. The third argument is indicated rather than stated explicitly. Logic as a formal study of all possible worlds is necessarily applicable to this world and has a place in the series of positive sciences. To deny to logic the name of a positive science is to fall into the error of regarding our natural sciences as purely existential. Every science contains more than reference to what is actual. Every hypothesis before verification is a statement of possibility. The possibility is drawn from some other segment of existence regarded as relevant.

This sounds very much like a return to Aristotle and certainly reflects the influence of Geyser and the revived Thomist philosophy. The conversion of logic into a propodeutic of ontology (p. 256) and the interpretation of "pure form" and "pure matter" as *limiting concepts* of some concretion in discourse (p. 262) seem also to point to a modified Aristotelianism. But there are at least two considerations which indicate that Husserl is basically as far from Aristotle as any of the classical German idealists and that like them he is compelled to tie up the loose ends in his thinking by reverting to a "logical solipsism" distinguishable only in minor details from the early positions of Fichte and—*horror horrorum*—of Hegel. First, there is Husserl's retraction in the last appendix to the book of all the concessions made in earlier pages to a material ontological logic. For that is what the claim to have justified the traditional conception of formal logic as a logic of pure consistency means. He takes over the logistic conception that all laws of logic are tautologies (derived by negating a contradiction), and, instead of squarely facing the problem of a *test* for consistency, substitutes the equivalent idea of compossibility, as if compossibility any more than consistency were a matter of intuition and did not depend ultimately upon an exhibition of the structures, operations, meaning, complexes, or what not declared to be compossible. I can see no significant difference between Husserl's theory of consistency and that of Kant's. Second, and far more important as far as Husserl's distance from Aristotle is concerned, there is the whole conception of transcendental phenomenology, which is a deeper and more radical defence of the constitutive activity of consciousness.[4] To an examination of this doctrine we shall now turn.

B. The transition to what Husserl understands by transcendental phenomenology can best be given in his own words. "Every science has its field and works with a theory of this field. In this field it gathers its results. But it is the scientific reason which creates [schafft] these results and it is the experiencing reason which creates this field. That holds good for formal logic too, in its manifold levelled relations to existence and ultimately to any possible world, and to its theory of ordered powers of generality applicable to any special theories. Existence, theory, and reason do not come together by accident and they can not be presupposed to have accidentally fallen in together even out of an 'unconditioned universality and necessity.' This very necessity and universality must be investigated as that of the logically thinking subject—of *my* subject, for I can only submit to a logic which I myself have clearly thought through—of my subject, because for the time being we are not talking of any other reason but mine, of any other experience and theory but mine, and of any other existence save that manifested in my experience and which in some way must be intended in my field of consciousness if I am to produce theories by means of it. . . .

"Just as in daily life so in science (when it has not been misled by a 'realistic' theory of knowledge into misunderstanding its own activity), experience is the consciousness of being with the things themselves, of directly grasping and having them. But experience is not a hole in a space of consciousness through which a world existing antecedently to it shines through. Nor is it a mere taking over into consciousness of something which is foreign to consciousness. For how can I even sensibly say that this is so without 'seeing' it myself and therewith 'seeing,' experiencing, both consciousness and that which is foreign to it? And how can I conceive it as thinkable? . . ." (205-6). Not only is the *that* of any subject of discourse given in experience, but its *what*. Its modality and objective content can not be intelligibly taken out of experience. "Kein Sein und So-sein für mich, ob als Wirklichkeit oder Möglichkeit, es sei denn als *mir geltend*" (207).

Does not this prolegomena to a transcendental logic apparently contradict *some* of the positions Husserl took in his discussion of formal logic? Had it not been maintained that logical laws are invariant forms of all possibility? And was not my experience only *one* possibility among others and hence subject to laws of possible arrangement outside of it? Did not the doctrines of "truths in themselves," "truths forever and for every one," "invariance of meaning," taken over from Bolzano, set the criteria of what I can truly experience even before I can experience it? Husserl recognizes this apparent contradiction, but is undaunted by it. "Zuerst und allem Erkenklichen voran bin *Ich*,". he insists. All that has been said about necessary and universal criteria of validity has first been thought by a self. Everything is related to this self in specifically different ways. It is the "*intentionaler Urgrund*" of the given world and all its other selves; if not the generating matrix, at least the self-enclosed continuum, the indispensable referent of whatever is or may be conceived. Husserl is in deadly earnest with this position. The following passage seems wrung from him by the fear of being misunderstood "Whether easy or not, . . . whether it sounds monstrous or not, it is *the fundamental fact upon which I must stand* and from which as a philosopher I can not for one moment look away. To philosophical children it may appear as the eerie nook haunted by the ghosts of solipsism, psychologism, or relativism. But the real philosopher, instead of running away, prefers to illumine this dark corner" (p. 210).

The first step in the illumination is both inevitable and familiar. My every-day psychophysical self is distinguished from my transcendental ego, for which it is only an object of discourse. The self that the philosopher is, the *I* of his demonstration, is not identical with the self which someone else loves.[5] But since he can not believe that in being loved he is only loving himself, there is a strong temptation to believe in another transcendental ego which, although not identical with the loving psycho-physical self of another, is a close relative to it. But how can one transcendental ego admit the existence of, no less know, another transcendental ego? That seems to be impossible by definition. And the second step, very familiar in the history of German idealism, is taken. The first ego discovers that by some miraculous conception it is pregnant with other egos. Since the transcendental ego is *posited* by the

necessity of understanding pure logic, empirical considerations are declared to be useless and we are compelled of necessity to posit levels of consciousness and phases of development in the transcendental ego in order to derive some of those empirical considerations we pretended to ignore. By a play on words, an "intersubjective objectivity" of selves is created so that one can say that the existence of other selves is implied already by my own and yet that they are in no fundamental sense independent of my own. Out of a witches' cauldron of verbiage comes the conclusion "Alle Objektivität dies Sinnes ist konstitutiv zuruckbezogen auf das *erste Ich-fremde,* das in der Form des 'Anderen,' d.h. des nicht-Ich in der Form 'anderes Ich.'" Compared to this, Fichte is a model of lucidity. The bogey of solipsism, Husserl declares can be laid by a proper interpretation or exgesis (*Auslegung*) of the contents of my consciousness. Offhand one would say that given Husserl's definitions, this is just what he can not do, but he refers us for the details of this "novel" theory of *Einfühlung* to a forthcoming work.

By revealing the way in which the community of transcendental egos is organized we discover all the possible forms of intentional reference. This gives us the schemata of the *a priori* relationships with which the mind works and explains why the method of *Wesensforschung* can be effective. It is not the particular features of any object which the mind intuits that is important for transcendental analysis, but the way in which the mind operates through and upon objects. What the mind gets to know are the forms of its own *a priori* constitutive activity. But since from Husserl's own starting point nothing can be save as an object of mind and since the acts of mind can themselves become objects of mind, how justify the distinction between the particular content of consciousness and the *a priori* organizing activities of consciousness without introducing aspects of an empirical world? Object and act may be distinguished by regarding objects as a series of acts grown cold, but generically they are made of the same stuff and the mind must be just as active in positing itself into material for reflection as in reflecting on the manner in which it has already posited it. Even God, says Husserl, is a result of my consciousness, the end product of the milling of the subjective *a priori* (p. 222). There is no external world to be opposed to the activity of consciousness. When we speak of the real world we mean by it a constant presumption that our experience will continue to run in the same way. What right have we to "presume" this? Is it any more certain that the mind will continue to function in the same way than that the natural processes will always show the same pattern? The difficulties of induction and causality do not become any less acute if the world is sunk into consciousness and all the things of this world construed as objects of primal activities. In an effort to avoid the imputation that the traditional difficulties of subjective and critical idealism affect his own position, Husserl distinguishes sharply between transcendental phenomenological subjectivism and psychological subjectivism. The latter tries to build up the world on the basis of psychic elements given to the natural experiencing self or soul. But for phenomenological subjectivism, the natural self or souls as well as its elements are themselves *Weltbegriffe,* are intended as existing things, are themselves objects and problems of transcendent apperception (p. 223). But what Husserl fails to see is that if the logic which repudiates psychological subjectivism is sound, the same logic applies even more strongly to his own phenomenological idealism. It is easier to believe or, more conservatively, it is not more difficult to believe, that a table exists only when it is perceived than that 2 + 2 = 4 is true only because a mind—transcendental or Divine—becomes ultimately conscious of its activities.

Meanings for Husserl are ideal. But ideal meanings can not be accepted as spontaneously arising from nowhere or as subsisting forever with no essential relation to some kind of subsisting mind. Just as the existence of the real world is a problem which has to be solved by reference to the structure of the knowing mind, so the subsistence of logical meanings is a problem which must be solved by reference to the activity of a mind of still higher order (p. 234). Kant was "transcendentally naïve" in assuming logic to be something absolute and primary, in regarding it as something upon which philosophy could build. Instead of putting questions to it, instead of challenging its rational sovereignty and compelling it to seek refuge in a transcendental justification, he uncritically used it as the touchstone of his own attempted justifications of science and mathematics. "How is logic in general possible?" can only be answered by the investigations of transcendental phenomenology. But is the latter itself critical? Suppose someone asks, "How is the world of transcendental phenomenology in general possible?" That is a question, responds Husserl, which disappears in the insight that this world has a reality which follows from its very Idea, since it is the construction of a consciousness that can not be negated without assuming consciousness again (p. 237). Another disguised revival of the ontological proof.

The logic of the most ultimate phase of this most ultimate of disciplines is a personal logic, although what the *ich* and the *mich* means here can only be understood by the metaphysically blessed. The *a priori* is openly characterized as a solipsistic *a priori.* "Objective logic," we read, "*is for us a first but not the last logic.*" Husserl does not hesitate to call this personal and ultimate logic "*the only philosophy, the only genuine science.*" All being, all categorial determination is relative—and relative to transcendental subjectivity. Only this last is absolute "in sich and für sich," only *it* is free from presupposition and prejudice (p. 241), on the ground, that there is nothing unrelated to the transcendental ego, that there is nothing which controls *It.* It can only be described in the oxymoron of mystics. From this transcendental ego not only is the intersubjective objectivity of selves and all actual and possible worlds derived—or better, organized, since they are already contained in the ego—but it has an infinite capacity to reflect itself and its forms on many levels of self-consciousness. "The whole phenomenology is nothing else than the *scientific self-reflection of transcendental subjectivity,* a self re-

flection (*Selbstbesinnung*) which advances from the fact as such to the consciousness of the essential necessities and from that to the *Urlogos* from which all that is logical springs. All prejudices at this point necessarily fall away since they are themselves intentional forms set in their proper place in the consistent progress of self-consciousness. All *criticism* of logical knowledge . . . the criticism of knowledge in all types of science . . . is the *self-exposition* [Selbstauslegung] *of the transcendental function of reflecting subjectivity.* All objective being and all truth has its ground of being and knowledge in transcendental subjectivity . . ." (p. 242). Impartial evidence, or that which is absolutely grounded, can only be found here. The criteria of evidence in the particular sciences are relative and uncertain. They receive their credentials only when both the methods and results of the particular science in question can be fitted into a *summa philosophia.* Despite certain differences in detail, and despite Husserl's own denials, who can fail to recognize the Substance of the Hegelian Absolute spinning madly in its thematic web of self-consciousness? Every knot in the web is understood when it is construed in terms of a transcendental grammar. And the great mystery of the relation between the syntactical constructions of the Absolute and the grammar of our own broken speech dogs Husserl's analysis in the same way as it did all mystical emanationists before him.

To really develop a theory of evidence, according to Husserl, we must not content ourselves with our ordinary working rules of validity which naïvely imply something transcendent and normative, we must go on to ask under what conditions the material we are investigating lends itself to the use of evidence, we must make explicit those psychological acts and powers, e.g., comparison and recollection, involved in the process, and finally test our principle of inference in the light of the transcendental subject whose "ego-logical powers" they are. "The ultimate criticism of knowledge in which everything else is rooted is the transcendental self-criticism of phenomenological knowledge itself" (p. 255). Again Husserl asks us to wait for the details of this ultimate criticism.

III

If all this strikes the English reader as "romantic madness," it is well to remember that Husserl's doctrine *in its present form* is an original variant of classic German idealism and follows from the same refusal to accept the given and from the same illicit and half-hearted desire to deduce existence. A rationalism which seeks to make things intelligible by regarding them as the deposit of an anthropomorphic logic is indistinguishable from the extremest of magical romanticisms. Husserl would probably vehemently deny this relationship to Fichte or Hegel and point out that nowhere does he directly attempt to deduce the *existence* of things, that the phenomenological method is directed to the contents of *consciousness* and does not even raise the question of reality outside of it. But when we are told that the organizing forms of this method can be derived from the way our transcendental ego—in conjunction with other egos—functions, when we are told that the content of that consciousness is given with and within an ego-logical subject and that these are made explicit by an introspective exegesis, in what *essential* respect does it differ from Hegel's substantializing of the self-renewing activities of the Subject into an Absolute Whole? The only difference that Husserl's refusal to use the word "existence" makes, is that instead of the world and its history being the autobiography of God, as it was for Hegel, it is now more like the ordered dream of a sleeping God.

All this is the inevitable outcome of Husserl's logical method. Whitehead's last books show that he, too, using this method in part, is on the road to the same conclusions. Whoever claims that he can investigate essential relationships between ideas, or universals or essences, independent of ultimate reference to, or control by, existence, is driven on to define these ideas as possible objects of some consciousness in order to intelligibly distinguish them from that which has no character at all. But since whatever can be known must be an object of consciousness, the mere "having" of objects in consciousness (*Gegenstandsbewusstsein*) is taken to be the same as "knowing" them. Knowing, then, becomes the mind's consciousness of the presence of objects. And if all the possible objects of consciousness are defined as transcendental Mind or Divine Mind or the Community of Mind—real knowledge is given by the Mind thinking itself. It is easy to see that all the logical difficulties involved in the belief that there is something outside of mind to be known, and that this something has an intelligible order—which the resort to the standpoint of immanence was designed to solve—still remain as difficulties in logical or phenomenological idealism. If both my natural mind and the objects of my natural thinking are swallowed up in a great Mind in order to explain the possibility of natural knowledge and the logic of that knowledge, my mind and the things it knows can not be the same parts of that Mind even though they bear the same name. The search is renewed and turns into the torturous labor of jumping from one imagined level of Mind to another. My original mind and the little knowledge it has, although baptized by the same name, get separated and lost in this series of transcendental discoveries of one level of Mind in another, and probably never find one another again, since in the nomenclatural dusk each *is* the other and this other is something else.

Knowledge is a unified act. But it can not lose sight of the fundamental duality of the knower and the known involved in that act without making *specific* knowledge impossible. Boasting of his independence from all psychology, Husserl has fallen victim to a defective psychology of the knowledge relation. Our choice is not between a logic with psychology or a logic without psychology, but rather between a logic with good psychology and a logic with bad psychology. That, to my mind, is the moral of this exposition of Husserl.

Notes

1. This article is an extended review of Husserl's latest work in the tenth volume of the *Jahrbuch für Philosophie und phänomenologische Forschung*, Halle, 1929 (Max Niemeyer Verlag), pp. 1-298.

2. The second edition of which has appeared in 1929 at Halle (Max Niemeyer Verlag).

3. "For the ultimate analysis of the essence of judgment, content of judgment, object and character . . . we must derive our clues from men whose names one can not mention among mathematicians without provoking a pitying smile—Fichte, e.g., *Das Kontinuum,* 1918, p. 2. *Cf.* also pp. 70-71-72.

4. "Alles Seiende konstituiert in der Bewusstseinssubjektivitat," p. 205.

5. The illustration is mine.

V. J. McGill (essay date 1930)

SOURCE: "An Analysis of the Experience of Time," in *The Journal of Philosophy,* Vol. XXVII, No. 20, September 25, 1930, pp. 533-44.

[*In the following essay, McGill describes Husserl's phenomenological mapping of time in contrast to the models provided by Henri Bergson, J. M. E. McTaggart, and Bertrand Russell.*]

Bergson's discovery that the time of inner experience is radically different from the objective time of mechanics, the one being a free-moving undifferentiated unanalyzable stream, the other a fixed correlation of points of space with positions of moving bodies, has done a great deal to focus attention upon the uniqueness and originality of subjective time. The relativity theory, since it implied that the time calculations and measurements of various observers are unavoidably different, that therefore the position and motion of these observers goes to constitute the objective time of physics, also reinforced this interest. Idealists were quick to construe an argument for subjectivism and idealism, and Neo-Kantians, such as Cassirer, were quite as convinced that the acceptance of the new physics implied the Kantian Forms of Intuition.

In the "space-time interval," however, all subjective differences due to different observers seemed to be transcended. The result of the General Theory was a space-time continuum, from which subjective time had been banished quite as effectively as in the Newtonian physics which Bergson found so objectionable. Time in the new scheme presents many oddities due to its affiliation with space. Like the dimensions of space, it seems at first sight to be quite reversible, for no physical law, according to Eddington, distinguishes between future and past. There is perhaps one exception: the Second Law of Thermodynamics. This provides for an increase in the random element toward one end of the time-line and thus gives it direction and irreversibility. But for this important exception, the laws of physics would be indifferent to the distinction of future and past. Unfortunately the law in question is very doubtful and many authorities now deny the progressive increase of the random element. Thus no principle of physical science would seem to supply the necessary directionality of time, or to distinguish between past and future. But past and future are essential to time. Any series which did not admit a unique distinction between them would not be a time series. And if physical nature does not supply this distinction, it must, of necessity, arise in consciousness; i.e., the forms of apprehension, or the contents of these apprehensions, must be the source of temporal determinations. Certainly, in any case, it is not the increase of the random element which constitutes the distinction between past and future in consciousness. The distinctive nature of time is not a feature of the passage of nature, but due to the transcendental forms of apprehension.

If we consider the theories of time held by Russell and McTaggart we are led to the same conclusion. Mr. Russell holds that time is the difference, with respect to truth and falsity, between two propositions whose sole difference is that the one specifies the time, T, and the other the time, T'. Thus time exists when "my poker is hot at time T" is true and "my poker is hot at time T'" is false. All true propositions about change and temporal events, according to Mr. Russell, are *eternally* true, and the facts which correspond to them are changeless. That is to say, each fact of change is itself changeless. Propositions about temporal occurrences state relations of "before" and "after," but such relations exist permanently and if they hold at all, hold at all times. Thus "The Battle of Hastings occurred 748 years before The Battle of Waterloo" is true at all times, since at any point of time the same interval exists between the two events. Now if all propositions about temporal events take this form, it would seem to McTaggart, that change is banished from the world and the distinction between the actual present in contrast to its particular past and future, reduced to an illusion.

In criticizing Mr. Russell's theory he distinguishes between the two time-series. The A series is the constantly changing series of present moments with the dwindling future ahead and the growing past behind. The B series, on the other hand, is the series of before and after relations which bind all events together in a changeless concatenation. In the B series change is excluded, in the A series there is constant change. But this change can only be stated as a changeless fact and Mr. Russell evidently regards it as a sort of illusion. Mr. Russell's account of time, according to McTaggart, excludes the A series, all propositions about temporal events being assertions of constant relations of before and after. But if Mr. Russell rejects the A series, according to McTaggart, he has rejected time, for the A series is necessary for time if time is to include change. The B series alone, he holds, does not suffice to the constitution of time. It might indeed be the case that events are arranged in serial order, determined by asymmetry, transitivity, connexity, etc., but there would be nothing distinctively

temporal about such a series. The relations "before" and "after" themselves would have no temporal significance without a reference to the actual "now" which is constantly moving into the future through the changeless intervals of the B series. Thus in the above proposition: "The Battle of Hastings occurred 748 years before The Battle of Waterloo," the past tense of the verb is used, which demonstrates at once the essential dependence of "before" upon a reference to the actual "now." If the same proposition had been asserted a thousand years ago, the verb would necessarily have been in the future tense. From this follows the important phenomenological law, once expressed by G. E. Moore, that it is impossible to assert the same judgment about temporal events twice over, for each successive judgment will contain a reference to a different "now."

The consideration of the A and B series and the failure to understand the above law, leads McTaggart to a drastic conclusion. Both series, he holds, are necessary for the constitution of time, but show themselves on analysis, contradictory. In the A series an event is either present, past, or future, but if it has one of these time determinations it can not have either of the other. Thus if it is present it can not be either past or future. In the B series, on the other hand, every event is both future, present, and past. But an event can not be exclusively either present, past, or future and all three, and therefore nothing can exist in time. This argument involves a strangely obvious equivocation in the word, "present." In the A series the present is an absolute point of subjective time, the actual now, and is expressed by a proper name, "the present." In the B series the present is *any* event relative to the events which are before and after it. Here "the present" is not a proper name, but rather a relative term, a description. But this description, i.e., "the present" in this sense, is also dependent for its temporal significance, as has been shown, upon a reference to the present in the first sense, i.e., the actual "now."

McTaggart's argument does not disprove the reality of time, but serves to bring out its essential dependence upon the time-determinations of consciousness, for the actual "now" is not a quality of relation of natural objects, nor can it be reduced to the changeless concatenation of before and after relations. The determinations future, now, just now, and past arise only in consciousness. In "the passage of nature," there is no passage, but only the changeless spread of space-time intervals.

But McTaggart has advanced a more serious argument against time. Whatever is extended in time must have parts of parts to infinity. And all these parts of parts to infinity must have sufficient descriptions which determine them as parts of these parts and distinguishable from all the other parts. McTaggart argues that in the case of matter supposed to be extended in time, it is impossible to find a relation which would determine these parts by "determining correspondence," and that since matter *qua* in time must have parts, matter can not be in time. But that

McTaggart has proved the impossibility of selecting or determining relations in this case, seems now very doubtful. The discussion of Zermelo's principle of "selection" has indeed shown that such selecting relations can not be proved for these infinite cases, but what McTaggart needs for his argument is not that these relations in the case of matter *qua* in time are *doubtful,* but that they are impossible.

But after having proved, as he believed, the unreality of time, McTaggart was far too sophisticated to conclude that there is therefore no *experience* of time. If time is an illusion, it is at least a real illusion. The unreality of the temporal series, if it were a fact, would not make our experience of time a bit less real. McTaggart therefore defines the *C* series, a series which *seems* to have all the properties which are attributed to the real time series but does not, and can not, have them. Throughout the second volume of *The Nature of Existence,* he continues to analyze this *C* series in its various aspects and instances, and approaches, in so doing, the method of phenomenology. The phenomenological analysis of the experience of time, like McTaggart's account of the *C* series, is quite independent of the reality or unreality, or the nature of the transcendent time of physical objects. Its data are time apperceptions, i.e., immediate experiences, in which temporal experiences appear, together with the temporal contents of these experiences. Physical objects, being transcendent of consciousness, are excluded from the phenomenological analysis. Many of our experiences, to be sure, are directed upon the duration or succession of physical processes, but neither these processes nor the appearances of these processes appear as immanent objects in inner consciousness. The proof of this is seen in the fact that the sensational content which represents the appearance in consciousness may receive subjective determinations, may vary, in fact, while the appearance, or its object, remains the same, and conversely; while in the case of illusion or hallucination, the appearance or the object may be wanting altogether. Every such mental act directed upon transcendent physical objects has, to be sure, a sensational or imaginal core, but neither the one nor the other can be identified with any aspect or appearance of a physical object. The very possibility of the analysis of appearances or sense-data, and the obvious fact of error, presupposes the variation of sensational content while the sense-datum remains the same. It is no doubt these circumstances which lead Broad to announce the principle, so dangerous to his Sensum Theory, that there is no reason to suppose that sensa *must* have all the qualities which they *seem* to have. Specifically we may conclude that the sensed duration is never identical with the perceived, the objective, duration.

The phenomenological analysis of the inner consciousness of time is thus logically independent of any consideration of the objective physical order. It is concerned not with physical objects, but with a description of those intentional mental acts (according to their essences) in which physical processes, like the ringing of a bell, are meant or intended. It is also occupied, of course, with the immanent objects such as the tone (of the bell) in consciousness. It confines itself accordingly to mental experiences and their contents, and to whatever objects can be immediately known, and thus remains in the one field in which absolute knowledge can be certified.

Professor Husserl's lectures on this subject, which were first delivered at Göttingen in 1904-1905, but not published until the 1928 *Jahrbuch,* begin with the usual attack on empiricism, an attack in this case on empirical theories of time-perception. The theory that the objective duration and succession enter the mind through sensation and thus determine our perception of time is completely mistaken. The duration of sensation is not the same as the sensation of (or rather consciousness of) duration; the succession of sensations is not the same as the sensation of (or rather consciousness of) succession, and the temporal qualities of physical objects, if they have any, would not explain the consciousness of time. Nor can it be said, with Brentano, that the consciousness of duration is due to the presence in consciousness of sensations and images from previous sensations, for this would give us only the consciousness of an aggregate. It is, of course, significant that, as Professor Husserl remarks, Brentano is led by his psychological theory to regard the perception of succession or duration as an illusion caused by the liveliness of the original association. A similar debacle has also been observed in the non-phenomenological theories of Russell and McTaggart.

The source of all temporality in consciousness, according to Professor Husserl, is the original impression, which, arising in consciousness as the content of the present moment, sinks steadily into the past, every moment widening the interval between it and its origin, and so shifting by an inevitable sequence from the present, to the just present, then down the long corridor of the past; yet retaining always its fixed position in the series of impressions, yielding its place in the present moment to a new impression which it had foreshadowed, yet echoing throughout the subsequent moments, fading out and reverberating, and thus binding itself both to the future and to the past.

The original impression has the following characters: (1) It is the limit of a series of fading-out processes, but is not itself the fading out of any other object. That is, every fading-out or reverberation in consciousness has an impression as its source. Every original impression is likewise swept by the comet-like tail of the reverberations and fading-out processes of earlier impressions. (2) The original impression is not founded upon other elements of consciousness as is an imagination or a memory. On the one hand, it is the absolutely unmodified, the source of all other modifications of consciousness. On the other hand, it is logically dependent for existence upon the existence of a future impression and a past impression quite as much as these are dependent upon it. As the unmodified source of all modifications of consciousness, it is logically independent. As the present content in contrast to the future and the past, or as *before* or *after* other contents, it is logically dependent. (3) Each original impression is always displaced toward the past by a new impression and this by still another impression according to an *a priori* modification which is independent of the similarity or dissimilarity, continuity or discontinuity, of the sensuous content. Thus a tone sinks into the past whether it continues the same or changes or ceases. But through the steady overlapping of impressions, the effect in consciousness is always that of non-discreteness. (4) But a more important type of continuity is constituted by the essential fact that every impression means or intends the coming moment. And this meaning or intention or expectancy, which is called protention, is always partially fulfilled when the dawning moment becomes the actual present. The very essence of the impression requires that it mean or intend the coming moment, and be fulfilled in it, for an impression which did not realize itself in a new impression would not be an impression, a consciousness which came to an end without an experience of that end, an impossibility, a time which completed itself without there being a time beyond, and hence temporal objects beyond, an absurdity. In the ***Ideen zu einer reinen Phänomenologie und phänomenologischen Philosophie***, where this point is briefly discussed, the seeming implication of immortality for the two dimensional individual time series, is consciously avoided, as irrelevant to the phenomenological investigation under hand.

(5) Protention logically depends upon another character which is also essential to every original impression, namely, retention. Retention is a continual beholding of the "just now." That every preception has this feature is, of course, a phenomenological insight, a product of pure description. But it is also implied by the essential fact that the impression has duration and that the corresponding perception is simultaneous with this impression and passes over continuously into new perceptions. Also it is necessary for the explanation of the intentional continuity of consciousness, and of the nature of protention, for protention is dependent upon, and constituted specifically by, the retention of previous moments. Thus when we wake up suddenly without a retention of previous moments, the protention is also wanting (as something given in an act of apprehension), which explains our instant shock of ambiguity. But the protention is present, in such a case, nevertheless, as reflecting back upon the experience shows, and retention is also present and of both there is awareness, as the possibility of recovery through reflection shows. Only they are not known at the time by an act of apprehension. That retention of previous conscious moments is present in this most critical case is proved by our happy capacity, aided in memory, of linking the awakening consciousness with the previous states. For it will be shown that certainty on this point is only achieved through the corroboration of the memory of A by retentions of A. Retention, of course, is essentially different from memory. Retention of A demands the existence of A, while memory of A does not make this requirement. Memory, moreover, is an act which endures in time; retention, an act-character, a mere intentional aspect.

(6) It is thus a peculiarity of the original impression that it is always accompanied by retentions of previous moments of consciousness. Thus we have the series of original impressions: A, B, C, D . . . , which is the time-line of the immanent objects (tones, for example) in consciousness. But in contrast to this real temporal series, i.e., the series of original impressions (representing in the case of simple perception, the focal objects), there are the series of retentions of these impressions. Thus the retention of A, which we may symbolize as a, is simultaneous with B; a', the retention of the retention of A (i.e., the retention of a), will be simultaneous with C, and so on. Simultaneous with D we therefore have a simultaneous set of retentions, namely, a'', b', c and so on. By a law of temporal perspective, the further these retentions are removed from their source, the more their content is depleted. Yet in spite of this they serve to corroborate the memory of A, which otherwise has no evidence of any kind, by their backward glimpse, however indirect, at A itself. The elements simultaneous with D constitute a phase of temporal consciousness and it is interesting to note that a whole phase of consciousness requires a preceding and succeeding phase and has, in fact, many of the *a priori* characters which are possessed by the impressions within it. This is necessary for the unity and integration of a biography and for its *a priori* character as *one* biography.

(7) The original impression has also the essential character, which, of course, belongs also to consciousness in a complementary way, that it can be reproduced, "brought back" to consciousness after it is long past. Here consciousness possesses *a priori* the freedom to reproduce any experience (*Erlebnis*) of its past, independent of its nature, nor is it confined in memory to a chronological or any other fixed sequence of remembering. In other words, the past experience may be fixed upon freely and out of context (a fact which incidentally could never be exclusively explained by either association or the conditioned reflex). In remembering any such past experience, the remembered experience has necessarily the same protention, retention, and simultaneous environment as it had when present, and here, of course, the protention is rich and exhaustive. The mind is thus led on *passively* in the progressive recapitulation, of a past experience in the order in which it was originally lived through. In the original selection of the remembered experience, on the other hand, consciousness is *active*. In reproductive memory, since a past time is made present, a past "now" lived through as though it were the actual "now," there are necessarily two protentions, two retentions, and two fields of simultaneous objects, for the remembered object has its time determinations and associations in the past, while the memory, as an act in the actual "now," possesses quite different determinations which are only revealed by reflecting back upon it. It is, of course, quite possible to refer back to a past experience in what is called a signifying act, without reproducing it. In this case the past "now" with all its qualities and temporal determinations is not lived through again and this is by far the best way to bring to mind a past toothache. It is a pity that the theories of many New Realists cut them off from this mercy.

Professor Husserl's account of memory and retention shows a great advance over Bergson's rather mystical, and certainly mystifying, theory of our knowledge of the past. That the past should be contained in the present actually (and not merely intentionally) is certainly a contradiction, for a past and a present moment can not have the same position in time. A present act, on the other hand, can mean or intend a past event, or even reproduce it *anschaulich*, recapitulating the experience with all its sensuous or imaginal characters and all its temporal determinations. Also, through retention, it is possible in certain cases to verify a memory. Thus Professor Husserl's description of the past permits a certain corroboration of memory, without involving the contradiction or incomprehensibility of Bergson's theory. It also escapes the skepticism of the usual dualistic theory, according to which memory, never verifiable, must be accepted as a postulate, i.e., as a doctrine of blind faith. Professor Husserl's account of the myriad fading-out processes which float through consciousness at all times, in the twilight indistinctness of "primary awareness," and his doctrine of the temporal stream as opposed to the temporal objects which float upon it, also serve to separate out the true discernments of Bergson, and to bring to light those certain facts of inner consciousness, the misinterpretation of which has led him to his erroneous theories.

We have now finished a brief description of the time determinations of the original impression and of the other contents of consciousness which all arise from it. Every temporal object in consciousness is either (1) an impression disclosed in perception or (2) an impression disclosed by retention, or (3) an impression brought back to the mind by memory or some similar act, or (4) an impression protended (or anticipated) in the future. Thus the temporal determinations of the *original* impression, i.e., in the actual "now" phase, involves the time determinations of every other constituent of consciousness. The various laws of temporal experience established in this phenomenological investigation, it is interesting to note, are *a priori* and transcendental. Thus to take an example, there are the two *a priori* temporal modifications of the impression as it sinks into the past. First, it retains its identical position in the time series, i.e., relative to other impressions, but, secondly, with respect to the actual "now," it recedes steadily into the past, changing its position every instant. These two modifications are obviously independent of the qualitative change or constancy, the qualitative continuity or discontinuity, of the impressions themselves, and are, therefore, *a priori*.

An interesting illustration of the *a priori* and transcendental character of the time determinations we have been discussing is afforded by the case of time in fiction. Every time, if it is thought of as real time, must necessarily be conceived as a segment of the *one* time and hence as either simultaneous with, future to, or past to, the actual "now." Moreover, when, in reading a novel, we make the fictitious "now" present and live in this "now," protention, retention, and all the other necessary modifications occur,

in general, much as they do in memory, though the fictitious time we experience so vividly, corresponds to no objective time whatever.

So much for temporal objects. We must now return to the temporal stream in which their temporal nature is constituted. It has already been pointed out that the impression, and indeed every constituent of consciousness, fades out with other such reverberating processes into the dim indistinctness of the one temporal stream and that every actual "now" is swept by many reverberations of previous experiences, all uniform components of the one great echo from the past. This flow of reverberations or fading-out processes may be said to move in James's outer margin or fringe and to partake of the indeterminateness of that "twilight region," for the stream is not the object of attention, nor is it the object or content of an apprehensive act, and is thus not determined in consciousness, nor for consciousness, with respect to either quality or difference. Into the stream also enter the mental acts themselves as contrasted with their contents or objects. The auditory perception of the ringing of the bell intends primarily the transcendent process of the ringing of the bell and it also intends, in a different way, the immanent temporal object, the tone (of the bell) in consciousness, but in no sense does it intend itself. The perception and the same is true, of course, of memory, anticipation, etc., we live through, but do not experience as something intended. A mental act in the phase in which (as reflection assures us) it occurs, is not a mental object, but a strand of the flowing homogeneous stream. That is, there is no apprehension simultaneous with a mental act which intends it. An act of reflection, to be sure, may be directed upon a past perception, but when the perception becomes intended in such an act, it ceases to be a strand of the stream.

The temporal stream must be sharply distinguished from temporal objects, such as tones. The stream itself is timeless; the temporal objects are in time. They undergo time-modifications, being first future, then present, then past, but retaining always their fixed place in the temporal series of impressions. But only if the future, present, and past moments occupied by a temporal object are related to something outside time, is it possible for a temporal object to be first future, then present, then past, for all relations holding exclusively between moments of time are fixed and changeless. The timeless relatum here is the stream. By its intrinsic nature, its flow is even, uniform, and homogeneous, all strands of the stream being homogeneous with each other and with the one identical stream, and all flowing at the same uniform rate. It is by virtue of this uniform flowing stream of reverberations and mental acts that the impressions receive their temporal inflection of future, present, just present, and past, whereas it is by virtue of their before and after relations to each other, that they preserve their constant place in the time series. The existence of the stream is established by inspection of inner consciousness, but it is also necessary to any explanation of the time characters of temporal objects. Whatever the nature of temporal objects, whether they change or remain the same, vary continuously or discontinuously, etc., they must play their part against the uniform movement of the stream, and if they sink steadily into the past, it is only by virtue of the constant stream that they do so. But the temporal stream which constitutes the time movement of impressions is itself timeless as inspection shows, and reason prescribes, for were the stream itself made up of temporal objects, it would require another stream to constitute its temporality. And this second stream in turn could not be made up of temporal objects, for all the progressive time modifications of future, present, and past are not qualities of temporal objects, but determined by their relation to a background of uniform movement. Such a background is also presupposed in all measurement of time, however refined and ingenious, with whatever stars and clocks.

With a certain insistence, the question now arises, how, if the stream is never apprehended, can we know so much about it? The answer can only be that the stream knows itself with an awareness in which the difference between subject and object does not appear. That the reverberations and mental acts should be unconscious, is impossible, says Professor Husserl, for they are within the stream of consciousness. Moreover, every mental act such as a perception, possesses retention, which can only be retention of a *conscious* experience. We must therefore ascribe to reverberations and mental acts an immediate, primary awareness, which belongs, in fact, initially to all contents of consciousness. Thus in every perception we distinguish the passage of the perception itself, though our attention, or rather the intention of the act, is directed upon some transcendant object, such as a table. We observe the table, as we say, while time flows. But the primary awareness of the perception while we are perceiving the table, though it is certainly an awareness of a homogeneous uniform flow, is in other respects, *sui generis*. It does not make distinction with respect to quality and difference. We do not distinguish the character or nature of our perception of the table while we are perceiving the table. But in reflecting back upon the perception in question in an act of apprehension (an apperceptive act), what was "before" *sui generis* becomes articulate, what was unanalyzed and undistinguished is apprehended cognitively.

This particular analysis, though Professor Husserl does not carry it out explicitly, is nevertheless consistent with the general discussion in the ***Ideen***, sections 77-79, and provides, I think, the only possible explanation of our knowledge of the temporal stream. Our phenomenological knowledge of mental acts is attained in other reflective acts, which analyze what is given *sui generis* in the retention of the original act. That is, of every original act, *A,* there is a primary awareness, *sui generis*. In the succeeding moment there is a retention of *A,* and then, a retention of a retention of *A.* Simultaneous with a given retention of *A,* a reflective act may occur, which analyzes the nature of *A* as given *sui generis* in that retention of *A.* Were this not possible no knowledge of our experiences would be possible. The doctrine of retention is the only escape from a sweeping skepticism otherwise enforced by the fleeting character of all acts and their contents.

But how can it be said that the stream which moves is yet out of time? Does not movement presuppose temporality? The answer requires a preliminary understanding that we are here dealing with time as given to consciousness, not with time in some other sense, if indeed there is another sense. What is given to consciousness in primary awareness is not movement in the sense of a transit from place, or from moment to moment. What is given is *a sense of movement, a sense of uniform flow,* and this sense of movement is quite consistent with the non-temporality of the stream, i.e., for consciousness at the phase of consciousness in question. And this non-temporality of the stream in the actual present phase of consciousness does not contradict its temporality after this phase of consciousness has passed. A reflective act may be directed upon the undiscriminated contents, which forthwith cease to be stream, and through this reflective act, the original act is analyzed and given a place in the time series, which it did not have "before." The difficulty here is in saying that a mental act, as a strand in the stream, is *first* timeless, and *later,* through the reflective act, constituted as a temporal object. But this difficulty only appears if we assert an objective time, external to, and independent of, the time constituted by and in consciousness. But such a time, as we have seen, would be meaningless and impossible. All that is needed for the solution of this difficulty is the phenomenological structure of intentions in consciousness, by which we *refer* to such an external time.

This last analysis, for which Professor Husserl should not be held strictly accountable, illustrates the difficulty of discussing the time stream (*qua* stream) which by its very nature can not be known by an act of cognition or apprehension, but it also illustrates the necessary existence of this stream, inasmuch as the effort to seize it directly always seems to transform it into a temporal object, which presupposes again, a timeless stream as the necessary correlate of any temporal process. In any case it will be seen that the above analysis corrects the rather illogical theory of Bergson and the time-killing theories of Russell and McTaggart, at many points.

Theodore W. Adorno (essay date 1940)

SOURCE: "Husserl and the Problem of Idealism," in *The Journal of Philosophy*, Vol. XXXVII, No. 1, January 4, 1940, pp. 5-18.

[*In the following essay, Adorno examines the meaning of idealism in Husserl's thought, and the problems it poses with regard to thinking and knowing.*]

The merits of a philosopher, that is, his truly philosophical merits, not the merits he may have as a teacher or *Anreger,* should not be defined by the "results" he has achieved in his thinking. The idea that a philosopher must produce a fixed set of irrefutable findings, an idea which Husserl himself certainly would have shared, presupposes that all the tasks he sets for himself can actually be fulfilled, that there can be an answer to every question he raises. This assumption, however, is disputable. It is possible that there are philosophical tasks which, although arising necessarily in a coherent process of thinking, can *not* be fulfilled; thus, they lead to an impasse which is not the fault of the philosopher, nor an accident which can be accounted for only by the contingencies of the history of philosophy, but which has its roots in inherent antagonisms of the problem itself. It is in this connection that I wish to discuss the problem of idealism. One might define idealism here as a philosophy which tries to base such notions as reality or truth on an analysis of consciousness. It starts with the general assumption that in the last instance there can be established an identity between the object and the subject. It was the fate of idealistic philosophy that all the notions which it derived from the sphere of *Erlebnis* led to a dead-lock. That can be illustrated by the notion of givenness (*Gegebenheit*), the notion of immediate inner experience. In the last period of his development Husserl has critically and at length dealt with this notion. In his book, ***Formale und transzendentale Logik,*** he says: "Even here, that is, in the case of inner experience, where, in a way that must be described more precisely and discriminately, it is meaningful to say that the immanent datum really exists in the constitutive experience, it must be warned against the error of assuming that the datum qua object is fully constituted in this its real occurrence" (p. 251). On the other hand, it is quite obvious that no analyses of consciousness could dispense with the notion of givenness such as it occurs in Locke's theory of sensations. One must even concede that in a way the concept of the immediately given is much closer to the psychological operations and acts of the human mind than are the highly differentiated and mediated notions of Kant's transcendental synthesis or Husserl's theory of evidence as a process. The fact that such a notion as that of givenness can not be ultimately upheld is due not so much to the fact that it does not square with certain experiences; it leads into the difficulty described by Husserl because he assumes that the ultimate source of truth is the unity of consciousness. It is characteristic that the objections Husserl raises against any notion of givenness refer to the function of the given within that unity and to the relativity that any givenness necessarily assumes within the context of that unity. Clearly, such analyses as Husserl's criticism of givenness produce no results in the current sense of the word; Husserl is not able to replace the notion of givenness by a more adequate term, nor is he able to express theoretical hypotheses like the intentional process of evidence in terms of elementary facts illustrating such a process. The value of the whole procedure, however, may consist in its turning against the idealist presupposition of the ultimate identity of subject and object. It appears to me that Husserl's philosophy was precisely an attempt to destroy idealism from within, an attempt with the means of consciousness to break through the wall of transcendental analysis, while at the same time trying to carry such an analysis as far as possible. The few analyses here selected from Husserl's philosophy will illustrate this attempt on the part of Husserl to break out of the idealist tradition and the difficulties he encounters thereby because he never fully freed himself from the presuppositions of idealism.

I realize that such a phrase as that of the "inherent antagonism of the problem itself" may sound objectionable and that a method that dwells on the movement of notions, including the above-mentioned notion of givenness, has a touch of Hegelian speculation. This suspicion Husserl certainly would have shared, for he boasted of never having understood one sentence by Hegel and once, when discussing the fact that Hegel rejected the principle of contradiction, he referred to Hegel as one of those cases where it is hard to draw the distinction between a genius and lunacy. It seems to me all the more interesting that Husserl himself involuntarily gave an example of the Hegelian method. There was no other philosopher in his time in whose thought terms like "dynamics" or "process" played so small a rôle as in Husserl's, except for his last period. He used to interpret thinking not as action but as looking at things, that is, quietly facing them like pictures in a gallery. He did not want to interconnect thoughts by spiritual processes, but to detach them from each other as neatly and clearly as possible. From his mathematical beginnings to the very end he was concerned only with the justification of *vérités éternelles* , and for the passing phenomena he held all the contempt of the classical rationalist. In brief, he was the most static thinker of his period and it is this fact that brings him into so fundamental an opposition to Bergson, with whom he is often compared because of his concept of ideation or *Wesensschau,* which is often associated with Bergson's intuition. Still, his thought has developed in antithetic form, and by implication ends up with an antithesis to the whole sphere of thinking to which his philosophy itself belongs. Husserl started as a pupil of the Austrian philosopher, Franz Brentano, to whom he bore a certain similarity throughout his philosophical life. Brentano's philosophy was nourished from two sources: from the Aristotelian tradition of the Roman Catholic church and from English empiricism. He tried all his life to blend these sources into one coherent set of thoughts, that is to say, he tried to combine a strictly ontological objective apriorism with a largely psychological epistemology. This attempt in Brentano's case had from the very beginning a strongly anti-Kantian tendency. For Brentano, the *a priori* elements of truth were not constituted subjectively, but were of a strictly objective character, and the same point was maintained in his moral philosophy, particularly in his famous essay, *On the Origin of Moral Knowledge* (*Vom Ursprung sittlicher Erkenntnis*), where he tried to characterize the good in terms of right and wrong, i.e., in terms of the objective rightness of the love or hatred related to the idea in question. Paradoxical as it may sound, it is this representation of the objective nature of the *a priori* which makes him inclined to empiricist psychology. If the essences to which our knowledge is related are given objectively and not constituted by our process of thinking, the process of thinking loses its Kantian dignity and its compelling character: it can be treated on a strictly empirical basis. Brentano, however, did not satisfy himself with a lofty combination of dogmatism and scepticism versus criticism. He tried to unify the ontological and empirical trends of his thinking and it is this attempt of unification which probably made his influence so considerable upon a whole generation of Austrian thinkers. In order to convey this synthesis he took up an old scholastic concept which, so far as I know, had been developed for the first time by Duns Scotus. It is the concept of intentionality, aiming at certain psychical acts—"experiences"—which are characterized fundamentally as having a "meaning" which transcends them. In the introduction of this concept one may see a radical empiricist tendency tilting over into its opposite. For this view, the Humian doctrine that ideas are just somewhat weaker and modified impressions, is not tenable. When analyzing those experiences which classical empiricism calls "ideas," we are entitled to interpret them in terms of those experiences which they are *not,* namely, of impressions. Remaining on a strictly descriptive level, we can only say that they mean something which they are not themselves. E.g., if I now think of the toothache I had yesterday, then my present experience, that is, the act of thinking, is different from what it aims at, namely, the toothache; whereas, on the other hand, in a certain sense the toothache I had yesterday is mentally implied in my present act of thinking as its intentional object, without any reference to its transcendent reality or unreality. Intentionality became later one of the principal instruments of Husserl. He took over from his teacher Brentano the concept as well as the idea of the objective character of essences and a desire to combine a doctrine of objective essences with an analysis of subjective processes of thinking. Husserl started as a mathematician. The material of his thought was detached from the very beginning as much as possible from the relativity of subjective reflection, a material the objectivity of which stood beyond any possible doubt. Still, under Brentano's influence he tried to apply the psychological epistemology of his time to this realm and to give in his philosophy of arithmetic a psychological foundation for arithmetic. An antithetic motive in his thinking made itself felt for the first time when some of his mathematical critics made him aware of the necessary failure of such an attempt. It is significant that when speaking about it for the first time the Hegelian term *"Übergang"* (transition) creeps into Husserl's language: "As soon as the transition from the psychological interconnections of thinking to the logical unity of the content of thought (the unity of the theory) was to be made, no sufficient continuity and clarity could be achieved" (*Logische Untersuchungen*, Vol. I, Preface, p. vii). From this time on, Husserl tried to emancipate mathematics, and not only mathematics but logical validity as a whole, from psychological reflection and to justify it as a realm of its own. The tremendous influence Husserl had in his time is due to this attempt: an attempt to reconquer the objectivity of truth as against relativistic psychologism. One ought to know that during the early nineties in Germany no philosophy except Neo-Kantianism was accepted which did not declare itself as psychological. Why has Husserl's *Logische Untersuchungen* made this tremendous impression? The answer is this: the tendencies by

which he became an enemy of the psychologistic positivism of his time—which of course, is something very different from modern logical positivism—have their roots in positivism itself. Even in his mature period, in his *Ideas*, Husserl maintains "if by 'positivism' we are to mean the absolute unbiased grounding of all science, on what is positive, i.e., what can be primordially apprehended, then it is *we* who are the genuine positivists" (*Ideas*, transl. by Gibson, p. 86). That is to say, if he criticized the psychological approach to mathematics and hence to logic, his motive was not one of metaphysical speculation, but he found that when analyzing scientifically the nature of mathematical truth such as this truth is given in positive mathematical science, it could not possibly be reduced to the psychological acts of thinking related to those truths. When Husserl's philosophy emphasized more and more the concept of essence as against the notion of facts, the source for this emphasis is a scientific one. Husserl thought he was insisting upon facts themselves, namely, the "fact" of mathematical truths as ideal unities unrelated to any factual existence. These truths themselves have to be regarded as facts in the sense of something given which has to be accepted as it is and can not be modified by any explanatory hypotheses. If Husserl himself did not want primarily to save a higher world, whatever this may imply, nevertheless his philosophy became effective in the intellectual German post-War atmosphere as a method to reestablish some kind of hierarchy of values by means of positive science itself. What he actually wanted to show was that a truly scientific and enlightened method trained by mathematical procedure could not possibly content itself with the psychological method and had to look for a different justification. For him the psychological foundation of logic is hypothetical, speculative, and in a way even metaphysical.

His struggle against psychologism does not mean the reintroduction of dogmatic prejudices, but the freeing of critical reason from the prejudices contained in the naïve and uncritical religion of "facts" which he challenged in its psychological form. It is this element of Husserl's philosophy in which I see even today its "truth."

I attribute to this point such significance that I wish to show more concretely what actually went on and to reproduce the central argument of the first volume of the *Logische Untersuchungen*, although this volume compared with mature phenomenological philosophy shows Husserl *in statu pupillari*. This central argument is pointed against the assumption that the laws of formal logic as "laws of thinking" are identical with "natural laws" or the causal laws according to which the psychical processes of thing are interconnected. He insists that the causal norms, according to which actual thinking must proceed in such a way as to agree with the ideal norms of logic, are by no means identical with these ideal norms themselves (*cf. Logische Untersuchungen*, Vol. I, p. 68). "If a thinking being, a person, were constituted psychologically in such a way that he could not make contradictory judgments within a single trend of thought or could not draw any inference contradictory to the modi of the syllogism, this would by no means imply that the logical principles, such as the principle of contradiction, are natural laws by which this psychological constitution of the individual, who is not able to think otherwise than according to these laws, can possibly be explained." Husserl makes this clear by the example of an adding machine. "The set-up of the interconnection of the outstanding figures is by mechanical laws, 'laws of nature' regulated according to the meaning of the arithmetical principles postulated. Nobody, however, would refer to arithmetical instead of mechanical laws to explain the working of the machine physically." The realm of psychical acts with which Husserl here compares the machine can no more be derived from the realm of logical norms than the mechanical working of the adding machine can be explained by the mathematical rules according to which the figures appear. As Husserl says: "The psychologistic logicians disregard the essential and eternally unbridgeable differences between ideal law and real law, between normative regulation and causal regulation, between logical and real necessity, between logical reason and real reason [*logischer Grund und Realgrund*]. No thinkable gradation is able to mediate between the ideal and real" (*loc. cit.*). The impossibility of a psychological reduction of logical truth leads Husserl to a total severing of the real and the ideal because according to his view it is impossible to link them up without making assumptions which have no possible basis within the meanings of logical and mathematical principles themselves. It is possibly the most extreme χωρισμός which has ever been suggested since Plato—but rooted in a very severe concept of scientific truth which wants to keep pure mathematics free from every pollution by the empirical—even by thinking, inasmuch as thinking implies a psychological act.

Yet, Husserl could tolerate this sort of χωρισμός, this extreme and irreconcilable dualism of the real and the ideal, as little as any former philosopher. The second step of his antithetic development is the attempt to bring them together. Now obviously the only way in which the "real," the psychological reality of man, and the ideal, the absolute validity of logical and mathematical truth, are interconnected, is the very same principle which was rejected as a means of justification in the first volume of the *Logische Untersuchungen*, namely, the process of thinking. For the ideal truths are truths of thinking and of thinking only. There is no mathematical or logical proposition which could be conceived of otherwise than in terms of possible thought. On the other hand, thinking means human thinking and we know of no thought which would not presuppose actual psychical acts of thinking of actual living individuals. Hence, Husserl's philosophy in its next stage had to focus the nature of thinking itself in its ambiguity between the real and the ideal. Husserl has often been blamed for having reintroduced psychology in the second volume of the *Logische Untersuchungen*, which bears the subtitle *Untersuchungen zur Phaenomenologie und Theorie der Erkenntnis* (*Inquiries concerning the Phenomenology and Theory of Knowledge*). I do not want to decide the question whether Husserl actually has re-

lapsed into psychology. The second volume of the *Logische Untersuchungen* is the most difficult part of his work and there are long passages in it where even the most patient reader will find it very hard to establish an unambiguous meaning, particularly because in this book Husserl does not distinguish quite clearly between actual descriptions of the structure of thinking and terminological discussion, especially the disentangling of equivocations of some of the main terms of current epistemology. This may contribute considerably to the difficulty of deciding how far these analyses are actually psychological ones again. It occurs to me, however, that similar difficulties have been encountered by the Kantian philosophy, particularly in the deduction of the categories in the different versions of the first and second editions of the *Critique of Pure Reason*. It appears to me that the sphere of the factual and the sphere of thought are involved in such a way that any attempt to separate them altogether and to reduce the world to either of those principles is necessarily doomed to failure. It is most likely that the very abstraction which the contrast of the real and the ideal implies, is derivative to such a degree that we are not entitled to regard this abstraction as a basic principle which could be attributed to the nature of being itself. Whoever tries to reduce the world to either the factual or the essence, comes in some way or other into the position of Münchhausen, who tried to drag himself out of the swamp by his own pigtail. One must concede that Husserl, in his Münchhausen attempts to dispense with the factual altogether, while still treating the ideal as something given, as only the fact can be given, was faced by insurmountable difficulties. I shall not enter the labyrinth of the second volume of the *Logische Untersuchungen*. The most influential though most involved of these *Untersuchungen*, however, is the last, called *Elemente einer phänomenologischen Aufklärung der Erkenntnis* (*Elements of a Phenomenological Enlightenment of Knowledge*). It is actually supposed to provide that "bridge" between the ideal and the real. It tries to establish a method of knowledge, by which we should be able to be immediately aware of those logical objectivities or ideal units. This bridge, this method, by which we could "think" ideal realities (*Ideale Tatbestände*) that are not produced by us and still get their absolute validity into rational evidence, Husserl calls categorial intuition (*kategoriale Anschauung*). This notion which is fundamental to all later phenomenology, particularly that of Hedwig Conrad-Martius, Scheler, but by implication also Heidegger, and which later was called *Wesensschau*, intuition of essences, or, as Gibson translates it, "essential insight," was actually developed only in the last *Untersuchung* of the second volume. In Husserl's *Ideas* this notion is more or less taken for granted and treated only in the introductory and somewhat cryptic first chapter. Those who hear Husserl's name probably think first of all of this notion. It leads into the very center of the problem of idealism in Husserl's philosophy. It seems to me to be all the more advisable to dwell upon it since Husserl's so-called main work, the *Ideas,* is available in an English translation, whereas the *Logische Untersuchungen*, where the theory of categorial intuition is unfolded, has never been translated.

To be sure, Husserl was an exceedingly cautious man. The notion of categorial intuition which made him both famous and notorious as the renovator of metaphysical speculation, plays only a limited rôle in the last *Untersuchung* and after it has been introduced it becomes limited and revoked to such an extent that actually nothing of it is left. His whole theory of intuition was from the very beginning intended to be much more harmless than it actually proved to be. If there were alive in Husserl some authoritarian drives, the desire to vindicate for truth a superhuman objectivity which must merely be recognized, there was also the contrary alive in him, a very critical attitude with an almost exaggerated fear in committing himself to any truth which could not be regarded as eternal and absolutely certain. Husserl was the rationalist of irrationalism and the paradoxical quality about him is revealed by his theory of categorial intuition.

The paradoxical structure of a thinking that contents itself with a mere "finding" of truths as of something pre-given, derives in a certain sense from the nature of Husserl's logical absolutism in the first volume of the **Logische Untersuchungen**. One could say that the doctrine of categorial intuition is the necessary consequence of logical absolutism with respect to the thinking subject. Thus even in the first volume we can find a passage which in fact contains the whole doctrine: "May he be deceived by psychologistic arguments, who ever remains bound to the sphere of vague general considerations. The mere looking at [*Hinblick auf*] any of the logical principles, at its true meaning and the evidence by which it is apperceived as truth in itself, is apt to dispense with a remaining illusion" (**Logische Untersuchungen**, Vol. I, p. 64). It is the thesis of the theory of categorial intuition that "truths in themselves," ideal items as they are, pre-given objectively, become evident by "mere looking at them" (*blossem Hinblick*). These truths are called *Sachverhalte*. The difficulty of any translation of that term points in the direction of the difficulty of the problem itself. I translate it here by "item," this being the most abstract term available which does not carry in itself any implication as to the factual nature of the *Sachverhalte* in question. The literal meaning of the word "*Sachverhalt*," however, is relatedness of facts. What is meant by it here is actually something highly paradoxical. On the one hand, it means something like a fact inasmuch as it is something given, something which we do not build ourselves, something which we can not alter, something over which we have no power, in short, something which may remind you of the English phrase about stubborn facts. On the other hand, however, these *Sachverhalte* are nothing less than facts: they are merely ideal laws like the principles of mathematics. It does not matter for arithmetical rules after the model of which Husserl's notion of *Sachverhalt* is built, whether there are any real, "worldly" objects which can be counted according to these rules. They describe mere possibilities of such objects, the validity of which is by no means affected by the

reality to which they may be related. Husserl says: "The *Sachverhalt* is related to the more or less 'giving' act of becoming aware of it as the sensual object is related to sense perception. We feel impelled to go even so far as to say, the *Sachverhalt,* the purely logical ideal truth, is related to its intellectual perception as the sensual object to the sense perception" (**Logische Untersuchungen**, Vol. II, 2, p. 140). The rationalist Husserl wants by means of categorial intuition to vindicate for the *vérités de raison* that character of immediate givenness which appears to the positivist Husserl as the only legal source of knowledge. On the one hand, he assumes Bolzano's "propositions in themselves," that is, the pure unities of validity; on the other hand, he assumes the region of consciousness from which all possible justification of insight derives, the sphere of the given, of experience, of "*Erlebnis*." These two spheres are connected only by intentionality. The *vérités de raison* are "meant" symbolically, signified by actual experiences. Intention, according to Husserl, is apt to lead to the *vérités* as such without subjectivizing or relativizing them in the least. The being in itself of the *vérités* is supposed to "appear." They are not interpreted as being produced by subjective reflection or abstraction, but as something self-given and perceptible. However, they shall not be made to pay the penalty of being merely factual and contingent, a penalty which the "simple" sensual perception must always pay. Categorial intuition is the *deus ex machina* in Husserl's philosophy, by which it tries to reconcile the contradictory motives of his philosophy, namely, his desire to save the absolute objectivity of truth and his acceptance of an imperative need of positivistic justification.

Now, such a paradoxical achievement can not be expected from the notion of intentionality, from mere "meaning." For the notion of intentionality implies only that we can mean the objective essences in the stream of our consciousness; it implies nothing about their being. To mean something, to mean even ideal items such as arithmetical sentences, is certainly not identical with being evident. One can mean something wrong as well. Husserl, therefore, supplements intentionality by its "intuitive fulfillment" (*intuitive Erfüllung*). "A statement which first functions merely symbolically may later be followed by a more or less adequate intuition of what is meant by the statement. If this takes place, we experience a 'consciousness' of fulfillment *sui generis*. The act of pure meaning, pure intention, finds its *fulfillment* in the *representing* act of intuition as if the intention were actually directed toward some aim or design" (**Logische Untersuchungen**, Vol. II, 2, p. 32). The core of the whole doctrine of categorial intuition is the theory of fulfillment. Let us take an example which is not quite as abstract as most of Husserl's doctrines: "National Socialism and Fascism are not the only possible forms of government." This is an intention, that is to say, I make a sequence of those words by means of a single meaning. But there may be persons to whom this sentence, although they understand its meaning, is not evident. They will have to try to "fulfill" it by an intuition of its total meaning. Some of its elements, e.g., the governments mentioned in the sentence, may be "fulfilled" in the last analysis by sense perception. With other elements of the proposition, like "and," "not," "the only possible," this is not the case. Husserl is worried about these elements. But in his search for the objectivity of the truth of the proposition he rejects the idea that they might be functions of our own thinking. He wants them to be more than mere subjective elements. He attributes to the meaning of such terms a fulfillment *sui generis*. He says that they can be fulfilled by an intuition of their own, a nonsensual yet immediate awareness.

"The 'an' and the 'that,' the 'and' and the 'or,' the 'if' and the 'thus,' the 'all' and the 'non,' the 'something and nothing,' the forms of quantity, etc. all these are significant elements of propositions, but their objective correlates [*gegenständliche Korrelate*], if we are at all entitled to attribute to them such correlates, can not be found in the sphere of real objects, which means the same as in the sphere of objects of a possible sense perception" (**Logische Untersuchungen,** Vol. II, 2, p. 139). The concept of categorial intuition finds the following extreme formula: "If we ask, wherein do the categorial forms of intentions find their fulfillment if not in the perception of intuition in that narrower sense which we hinted at in speaking about sensibility [*Sinnlichkeit*], the answer is clearly prescribed to us by the above considerations. First of all, any representation of any example of a faithful proposition about a preceding perception puts it beyond doubt that actually *also the forms find their fulfillment,* just as we presupposed it as a matter of course." Or: "There must be an act, an experience which does to the categorial elements of intention the same services which is granted to the merely material elements of intention by simple sense perception" (*loc. cit.*, p. 142). Such acts which do the analogous service to words like "so" and "and," which is done to words like "green" or "red" when we have a sense perception of something green or red, induce Husserl to call the evidence of the whole sentence "categorial intuition." A statement can become evident only if not alone the material in it but the whole of its meaning can be fulfilled by perceptions. Husserl, strictly speaking, does not arrive at the categorial intuitions by a phenomenological method, he does not describe any actual acts of categorial intuition, but he deduces them in a somewhat hypothetical form. One could almost say, he derives them rather by a discussion of terms than by viewing any matter itself. Under the title of analysis of meanings, Husserl and some of his disciples display an odd confidence that they are able to find the truth by looking at the mere intentions of words. Though Husserl is always on the lookout for equivocations, he has here fallen victim to an equivocation himself: The term "categorial intuition" is ambiguous in itself. The character of immediacy which Husserl attributes to the awareness of the *Sachverhalt,* or the alleged ideal reality behind such terms as "so" and "and," is nothing but the immediacy of the act of actual judging. It may be formulated as follows: The judgment, viewed subjectively, is an act, an experience, and as such it is something immediately given. To judge or to become aware of a judged *Sachverhalt* is the same, or more

precisely, the second expression is a metaphorical circumscription of the first one. There is no second act of becoming aware of what one has judged in addition to the actual judging itself, unless of course one reflects on the judgment. Such a reflection, however, would necessarily transcend the "immediacy" of the actual act of judgment which for itself would become the *object* of such a reflection. That immediacy of judgment, however, is implied by Husserl's notion of becoming aware of the *Sachverhalt.* But to become aware of a *Sachverhalt* means for Husserl also to reassure oneself of the truth of the judgment. The equivocation within the term "giving act of becoming aware of something" (*loc. cit.*, p. 140), "*gebender Akt der Gewahrwerdung,*" is strictly this, (1) to become aware of a *Sachverhalt,* to achieve the synthesis of judgment, and (2) to bring the truth of this judgment to absolute evidence. None of the meanings of the expression, however, can possibly be interpreted as categorial intuition. The synthesis of judging is no categorial intuition because, according to Husserl, judgment in the sense of spontaneous thinking just requires its fulfillment by some sort of intuition. Reflection, however, being the necessary condition of that evidence which according to Husserl is guaranteed by categorial intuition, is as little intuitive as it is immediate. Reflection puts the *Sachverhalt* into relation with other *Sachverhalte:* its own result is a new categorization. Even if reflection in the last analysis would go back to sensual, perceptible elements, it would contain in itself qua reflection nonperceptible, conceptual forms. Husserl calls the mediate *immediate* because he believes in the datum: he wants to detach the mediate, that is, the *vérités de raison,* from the mere possibility of being fallacious. In turn he attributes to the immediate a generality and necessity which can be obtained only by mediation, by the progress of reflection.

One often speaks of the platonic realism of Husserl. This realism, of course, is accompanied in Husserl's writing by an extreme epistemological idealism: that is to say, the essences to which he attributes that sort of platonic reality are essences totally devoid of any relation to the real, to facts, to the world constituted within time and space. When closely observing Husserl's attempt to reconcile his quasi-platonic realism of essences with an idealist theory of thinking, one notices that he relapses into what might be called a naïve realism of logic. He hypostasizes the logical principles which are actually valid only in relation to thinking, just as if they were things of the second power. If they are things, however, thinking, directed toward them, degenerates into their merely passive reception. Husserl has thrown back the Kantian notion of the spontaneity of thinking to the level of mere passivity. To Husserl thinking is affected by the *vérités de raison* in a way rather analogous to that in which Kant thought of our senses as affected by transcendent things-in-themselves. Kant ran into difficulties with his notion of transcendent things-in-themselves while attempting to ground our experience on an exclusive analysis of the forms of consciousness. I hope to have shown that the difficulties into which Husserl runs by maintaining a kind of things-in-themselves of the second power, that is to say, his notion of truths independent of their subjective constitution and his reducing the thinking of those truths to a merely passive intuition, are not smaller than those encountered by Kant. In other words, the whole idea of categorial intuition, which had such extraordinary consequences not only in Germany, but for the whole of modern philosophy, is not actually a phenomenological discovery. The doctrine of categorial intuition is a *tour de force* for bringing together the analysis of consciousness and the being in itself of truth.

Why had Husserl to take refuge in such a *tour de force*? It may be worth while to point out that his whole philosophy is full of notions as paradoxical as that of categorial intuition; even in his last writings one finds notions such as that of the contingent *a priori*, or that of the *Eidos Ego*, which means a strictly individual, personal consciousness which is nevertheless supposed to be absolutely nonfactual, a pure essence, whilst not derived from any plurality of individual consciousnesses. These paradoxical notions definitely point in one direction. Husserl has set for himself a task which, in his terms, is insoluble. The paradoxical terms are but the expression of the insolubility of his problem. Roughly his problem may be stated as follows: he rebels against idealist thinking while attempting to break through the walls of idealism with purely idealist instruments, namely, by an exclusive analysis of the structure of thought and of consciousness. It is essential that Husserl, when turning against psychologism, attributes to this term a much broader meaning than what is usually understood by it. His attack upon psychologism is directed against any notion of a subject, however abstract it may be, that is derived from "worldly" existence and presupposes a "world." For him, even the Cartesian Ego is still a "bit of world" because it is gained by a process of limitation of our worldly experiences to the "undubitable" and not, as Husserl wants it, by "a changed attitude" which is concerned with the *sum cogitans* not as a reality, but as a mere possibility. If Kant speaks of "our" consciousness and if for him the functioning of the intellectual apparatus is bound to factual, real impressions, without which the categories are empty forms devoid of validity, then surely for Husserl, Kant would be a psychologist, too. Indeed, Husserl, in his last publication in the periodical *Philosophia*, has put the blame of psychologism on the whole history of the modern mind since the Renaissance. In other words, his attack was directed not only against positivism and empiricism, but against idealism, and his effect was largely that of an anti-idealist philosopher.

It became such an attack by the slogan "*Zu den Sachen*," "Back to the subject-matter itself," and the motive of his insistence upon notions such as intuition is in fact this anti-idealist desire of getting back to the materials themselves. He wants to destroy every hypothetical superstructure of the pure acts of thinking and meanings, every arbitrary construction which derives from systematical bias. His campaign is directed, if I may say so, against any philosophical ornamentation, against anything that does not belong to the matter itself. The spontaneity of the

mind which for the great systems of German idealism is the source of all truth, is for him mainly a source of speculative fallacy. He is anti-idealist in this specific sense.

But the slogan "*Zu den Sachen*" implies in Husserl's philosophy the greatest difficulties. He wants to go to the *Sachen* not merely for avoiding the fallacies of arbitrary conceptual construction, but for getting hold of an absolutely secure, unshakable, unchallengeable truth. This desire, however, to get hold of the Absolute and, in the last analysis, to deduce with an absolute stringency everything from one absolute point, is an idealist desire, dwelling in the refuge of an anti-idealist philosophy. Once attempting to build up a philosophy of the Absolute, he is thrown back to the same principle of the Ego, the spontaneity of which he has rejected. It is clear that the ultimate notions to which his philosophy resorts are idealistic ones. The principle of principles by which, according to Husserl, the matters themselves can be grasped, is in Husserl's own words the following: "that every primordial dator intuition is a source of authority [*Rechtsquelle*] for knowledge, that whatever presents itself in 'intuition' in primordial form (as it were in its bodily reality) is simply to be accepted as it gives itself out to be, though only within the limits in which it then presents itself" (*Ideas,* p. 92). Behind this principle there is nothing but the old idealist principle that the subjective data of our consciousness are the ultimate source of all knowledge, and that therefore any fundamental philosophical analysis must be an analysis of consciousness. On the other hand, the opposite pole to givenness, the pure notion, or what Husserl calls the essence, obtains its justification in Husserl by the same reduction to pure subjective consciousness, being freed from everything factual and contingent. The doctrine of essence which was regarded as the main anti-idealist stroke of Husserl's finally reveals itself as the summit of idealism: the pure essence, the objectivity of which seems to spurn any subjective constitution, is nothing but subjectivity in its abstractness, the pure function of thinking, the "I think" in the sense of the Kantian unity of consciousness.

Marvin Farber (essay date 1940)

SOURCE: "Edmund Husserl and the Background of his Philosophy," in *Philosophy and Phenomenological Research*, Vol. 1, No. 1, September, 1940, pp. 1-20.

[*In the following excerpt, Farber traces the precursors to and outlines the development of Husserl's philosophy.*]

Nothing in recent philosophy approaches the supreme confidence with which Husserl announced his triumphant beginning of a new science of philosophy, an "absolute" discipline achieved by means of an elaborately worked out method. It was advanced as the real positive outcome of the philosophical efforts of the centuries. In fact, all preceding philosophers were classified by him as either adumbrating or falling short of the ideals of phenomenology.

There is something majestic and heroic about the tone of Husserl. His is not an opinion hastily advanced. More than fifty years of consecutive reflection and hard work, resulting in numerous superb examples of descriptive analysis, have made it necessary to greet his claim with respect and to give his contentions a hearing. The thought and contributions of one of the most penetrating and thorough of the philosophers of the last century deserve more widespread attention than they have received. A thoroughgoing consideration of his philosophy is now made all the more necessary in view of the insistent claim that his philosophy is still unknown,[1] and the philosopher's own repeated assertion that he had been misunderstood. The fact that Husserl rarely answered his critics has made it more difficult for the general philosophical public to grasp the significance of his work. For the most part he went steadfastly on his way, regardless of opposition, which was largely based upon misunderstanding. The important publications which appeared near the close of his life include two replies to critics, the only elaborate ones published since his answer to Palagyi in 1903. It is now possible to examine and appraise the phenomenological philosophy with far greater assurance than has hitherto been the case, despite the fact that numerous manuscripts have never been published. These manuscripts contain an enormous amount of valuable material which will enrich and no doubt modify the understanding of phenomenological method. Thus the recent publication of Husserl's *Erfahrung und Urteil* was revealing, and added much to the understanding of his philosophy of logic. It is nevertheless reasonable to assert that enough of Husserl's writings have been published to provide a basis for a just appreciation of his philosophy and a point of departure for further fruitful work along phenomenological lines.

It is necessary to conduct the examination of this philosophy objectively, i.e., free from "standpoint" narrowness and from personal attachments. This means that one must be prepared to recognize the positive advance made by Husserl in philosophy and in outlying sciences such as psychology; and also that one must endeavor to ascertain whether all elements in his thought are consonant with his avowed precepts. Of particular interest is the final form of idealism represented by the later system of transcendental phenomenology, which reveals the limits as well as the merits of the subjective mode of philosophical procedure. The renewed attention to method in philosophy makes the examination of phenomenology pertinent; and the great development of logical theory makes it desirable to bring phenomenology into connection with it for possible mutual reactions. Particular attention must be devoted to his logical contributions. Their significance for the present is great in view of doubts and difficulties which are analogous to the problems of the period of the *Logical Investigations*.

Inasmuch as the riddle presented by Husserl's thought can best be solved by close adherence to its development, this paper will point out some of the early influences upon it and indicate its various stages. It will not be possible in the present account to do justice to all the influences: Husserl derived from the entire history of philosophy, and undoubtedly owed much indirectly to thinkers never explicitly mentioned by him. It will be sufficient for present purposes to call particular attention to that controversy for which Husserl has been most famous—the issue of the relationship of psychology and philosophy (in particular, logic)—and to indicate, in part by the mere mention of names, the most important effective influences upon his thought as acknowledged by himself.

I. PSYCHOLOGISM AND PHILOSOPHY IN THE 1880s

Prominent in philosophy at the close of the nineteenth century was a standpoint known as "psychologism." The philosophy of a given period has always been conditioned and influenced by the leading scientific ideas, particularly by those which were new. Thus rationalism in modern philosophy reflected the advances in the mathematical and physical sciences. In the period under consideration the rising science of psychology had a twofold significance for German philosophy: it suggested a sure way of solving perplexing problems of logic and theory of knowledge, and it afforded either a substitute or a supplement to the idealistic standpoint in philosophy. Psychologism had already been prominent in English philosophy, J. S. Mill having been a recent representative. In Germany, Wundt and Lipps may serve as examples. Natorp, Brentano, Stumpf, and later Frege are of particular importance, as providing the main historical background for Husserl. The reaction against psychologism was clearly illustrated in Natorp's early writings; and Schuppe and Volkelt, if only in a broad, programmatic manner, anticipated Husserl in the theory of knowledge, although they had no direct influence upon him. This is not to impugn Husserl's originality, for the systematic use to which he put the same motives resulted in their being recast radically.

Psychologism was an extreme point of view, and a reaction was inevitable. Natorp's review of Theodor Lipps' *Basic Facts of Mental Life*[2] is an early indication of such a reaction. Lipps regarded psychology as constituting the basis of philosophy, but Natorp expressed doubt as to the possibility of "basing" logic and the theory of knowledge upon psychology. Lipps considered such topics as the psychological ground of the principle of contradiction and the general function of concepts in knowledge. In his view, the genetic derivation of the basic laws of knowledge out of original facts of psychical life was identical with their "epistemological" foundation; the theory of knowledge was a branch of psychology. Everyone will concede to the author, Natorp remarked, that psychical facts are represented in the laws of knowledge, and that these facts, as psychical, are also an object of investigation for psychology. But it is not a matter of indifference whether it is psychical facts or psychology that is a presupposition of the theory of knowledge. Knowledge is admittedly only a psychical process, in the form of concepts and theories, or in general as consciousness. Even the truth of knowledge and the law of its truth as something objectively valid must be investigated by means of the consciousness which thinking beings have of it. The concepts and the truth of geometry are psychical facts in that sense, and yet Euclid's axioms are not regarded as psychological laws by anyone, nor does anyone suppose that its objective certainty depends upon the psychological understanding of geometrical presentation. Natorp merely emphasized the fact that the consciousness of truth is independent of all genetic explanation by means of general psychological connections, and called attention to the independence of an objective foundation of the principles of knowledge. The critique and the psychology of knowledge, in his view, require and condition each other. An indication of his point of view is given by his assertion that a law of knowledge is *a priori,* just as every law is *a priori* as opposed to that which is subject to the law.

Natorp's early reaction against psychologism is also expressed in a paper on the objective and the subjective foundation of knowledge,[3] in which he argued that there is either no logic, or it must build entirely on its own ground, and not borrow its foundations from any other science. Those that make logic to be a branch of psychology assume that psychology is the basic science, and that logic is at best an application of psychology. Natorp asserted that not only the meaning of logic but the meaning of all objective science is ignored and almost perverted into its opposite, if one makes the objective truth of knowledge to be dependent upon subjective experience. To base logic upon subjective grounds would be to annul it as an independent theory of the objective validity of knowledge. Hence Natorp was not only defending the rights of logic in the hitherto accepted sense of the term, but also the claim to objective validity that is made by all science, when he maintained that the objective validity must also be objectively founded. He formulated as a presupposition of objective science the precept that true scientific knowledge may depend only upon those laws which can be brought to certainty in the inner connection of science, and which are developed in a logical form, independently of all presuppositions that might be introduced from elsewhere. Thus all recourse to the knowing subject and its capacity for objective science is ruled out as completely foreign. Natorp was very clear in affirming that the objectivity of science requires the overcoming of subjectivity. His view of scientific truth is compatible, as far as it goes, with Husserl's later ideal of a rigorous science of philosophy, but it does not go so far as even to suggest the idea of a universal science, or of a "root-science" of philosophy. The object of Natorp's criticism was psychologism, however, and he succeeded in formulating the issue clearly. He pointed out that scientific truth, as illustrated in mathematical natural science, becomes certain to us on the basis of objective presuppositions, and he insisted upon the autonomy of such science. The mathematician and the physicist were not to look for the ground of the truth of their cognitions in psychology.

The expression "objective validity" was used to indicate independence of the subjective aspect of knowing. Its positive meaning was less clear to Natorp. The idea that there are objects outside of and independent of all subjectivity would be one answer; but Natorp believed that the "being-in-itself" of the object was itself a riddle, in conformity no doubt to his unresolved Kantianism. He held that the object's independence of the subjectivity of knowing could only be understood by means of an abstraction, for objects really are given to us only in the cognition that we have of them. Thus it would be necessary to abstract from the content of subjective experience. In Natorp's view, the true beginnings and bases of knowledge are final objective unities. In mathematics it is not the phenomena that are basic, but rather the fundamental abstractions, which are expressions of the unity of the determination of possible phenomena, such as point, line, straightness, and equality of magnitude. All of these involve the fundamental function of objectification, and the Kantian and Platonic "unity of the manifold." It is only in this way that the uniquely determined "phenomena" of science are possible. Natorp argued that there must be a determining and "positing" function, in order to make this positivity possible. In a later discussion[4] he undertook to see how the kind of foundation which he used was objective in the sense in which mathematical procedure is objective, and to show that formal logic must be based upon the logic of objective knowledge, or transcendental logic.

Another important idea of the time was the ideal of presuppositionlessness in philosophical procedure. This ideal was taken by Husserl in the *Logical Investigations* as an obvious requirement that is to be imposed upon epistemological investigation.

It is possible to point out the direct influences upon his thought at the beginning of his career. They were derived from a few sources to begin with, although Husserl was later to approach philosophers who were at first avoided or neglected. Natorp, Volkelt, Schuppe, and Rehmke may be singled out as representing the rising generation of idealists whose works were to be prominent in the philosophical literature of the coming decades. Their published writings were either closely read by Husserl, as in the case of Natorp, or they may be regarded as developments parallel to Husserl's, which responded to similar motives. The orientation to Kant's philosophy, always prominent in Germany, was to be of great significance for Husserl. Brentano, who is not easily classified, combined scholasticism and the philosophy of Aristotle with empiricism. He inaugurated a fruitful period of development in psychology, Stumpf being one of his earliest productive disciples. The modern development of symbolic logic, which was begun in England by Boole, was carried on in Germany by Schröder and Frege. These scholars may be cited as constituting most immediately the philosophical scene into which Husserl entered when he joined the faculty of the University of Halle in 1887. They represent a special section of the German philosophical world of the time, reflecting his early interests.

II. The Disciple of Brentano

"My teacher Brentano" was an expression frequently heard in Husserl's classroom. Intellectually his debt to Brentano was considerable in the early period; but it was the moral element and the personal example of Brentano which led him to choose philosophy as a lifework, and which constituted a lasting influence upon him. Husserl was a grateful student of Brentano, whom he accompanied, along with Stumpf on occasion, during vacation trips. He was not at the time prepared, however, to profit fully by such contact. The effectiveness of Brentano as a teacher is sufficiently shown by the number of noted scholars owing their start to him, Stumpf, Husserl, Meinong, Höfler, and Marty heading the list.

Husserl has left a revealing tribute to Brentano in his contribution to a Brentano memorial volume.[5] He attended Brentano's lectures for two years, from 1884 to 1886, after having completed his formal university studies, in which philosophy had been a minor subject. Brentano lectured on practical philosophy, elementary logic and its necessary reforms, and also on selected psychological and aesthetic questions. Husserl was then in doubt as to whether he would devote himself to philosophy or remain with mathematics, and Brentano's lectures decided his choice. Although he had been repeatedly advised by his friend Masaryk to study with Brentano, he relates that it was out of curiosity that he first attended the lectures, for Brentano was much discussed in Vienna at the time, admired by some, and reviled by others as a Jesuit in disguise. He was impressed from the beginning by the slender form with the mighty head. The expressive facial lines seemed not only to bespeak mental labor, but also deep mental struggles. Brentano impressed him as one who was always conscious of having a great mission. The language of the lectures was free from all artificiality and display of wit. The peculiar, soft, veiled tone of voice and the priestly gestures made him appear to be a seer of eternal truths and an announcer of another world. Husserl related that he did not long resist the power of this personality, despite all prejudices. It was from these lectures that he gained the conviction that philosophy is a field for earnest work which can be treated in the spirit of the most rigorous science, and this led him to choose philosophy as a lifework.

Brentano was most effective in the seminars, in which the following works were studied: Hume's *Enquiry Concerning Human Understanding* and *Principles of Morals,* Helmholtz's speech on "The Facts of Perception," and Du Bois-Reymond's "Limits of Natural Knowledge." He was at that time especially interested in questions of descriptive psychology, which he discussed with Husserl. In the lectures on elementary logic he treated the descriptive psychology of continua and took account of Bolzano's "Paradoxes of the Infinite," and also the differences between "intuitive and non-intuitive," "clear and unclear," "distinct and indistinct," "real and unreal," and "concrete and abstract" ideas. Other topics included the investigation of judgment and descriptive problems of phantasy. How great

an influence was due to Brentano is amply shown by Husserl's early writings as well as by later investigations in logic and the theory of knowledge. His indebtedness to Brentano was explicitly and gladly acknowledged. It is interesting to note that Brentano felt himself to be the creator of a *philosophia perennis,* although he did not remain fixed in his views and never really stood still. He required clarity and distinctness of fundamental concepts, and regarded the exact natural sciences as representing the ideal of an exact science of philosophy. This ideal was opposed to the tradition of German idealism, which was in his view a degeneration of philosophy.

Husserl carried on little correspondence with Brentano. In answer to a letter asking him to accept the dedication of the ***Philosophy of Arithmetic,*** Brentano expressed his warm thanks but warned against it, lest Husserl incur the animosity of his enemies. Husserl received no reply upon sending a copy of the book when it appeared. It was fourteen years later that Brentano first observed that the work had been dedicated to him, and he then heartily expressed his thanks. Husserl revered and understood his master too much to be sensitive to this incident. The independent development of the two men accounts for the small amount of correspondence between them.

Husserl saw Brentano in 1908 in Florence, when the latter was almost blind. He again felt like a timid beginner, and was inclined to listen rather than to speak. Once he was asked to speak, and was listened to without interruption. His account of the meaning of the phenomenological method of investigation and of his former conflict with psychologism did not lead to any agreement. Husserl stated that perhaps the fault was partly his own. He was inhibited by the inner conviction that Brentano, due to the firm structure of his concepts and arguments, was no longer adaptable enough to understand the need for the transformation of his fundamental ideas that Husserl had found himself compelled to make. Brentano continually lived in his world of ideas and in the completion of his philosophy, which he said had undergone a great development in the course of the decades. There lay about him an aura of transfiguration, as though he no longer belonged to this world, and as though he lived half in that higher world in which he believed so firmly. This last image sank most deeply into Husserl's mind.

This tribute from one great thinker to another reveals the degree of influence exerted personally upon Husserl by Brentano. The resemblance between the two men is striking. Husserl's acknowledgment that Brentano was a determining influence in his life is to be taken literally. He shared to a high degree the earnestness and lofty manner of Brentano, and also the disdain of humor and other lecture devices, which impressed him at the outset. Strongly characteristic also was his often expressed belief that he had created the foundation of the only valid philosophy. He too never stood still, and believed that his advances even in the last decade of his life were notable and far-reaching. The spirit of a "school" in which the master's beginnings would be developed further by young investigators was also illustrated in the phenomenological movement, although, to be sure, the elaborately developed method of the latter lifted it above the confines of a school in the usual sense. The portrait of Brentano is strangely familiar to those who have known Husserl personally; in depicting his teacher he has revealed himself.

III. HUSSERL'S FINAL JUDGMENT OF BRENTANO

Brentano is best known for his *Psychologie vom empirischen Stand punkt* (1874). The recent publication of his works by Kraus and Kastil[6] has made more clear the reasons for the extraordinary influence exercised by him. Husserl was indebted to Brentano for his interest in the concept of intentionality and the descriptive investigation of inner perception, and undoubtedly learned how to become a philosophical investigator by being shown concrete examples of descriptive analysis and how to recognize problems. It was inevitable that his development should run parallel to and overlap to some extent that of Brentano. Although it would also be easy to overdraw the amount of Husserl's indebtedness, it may be said that the study of the main elements of Brentano's thought is indispensable for the genetic understanding of phenomenology.

Brentano's judgment of Husserl's work a few years after the publication of the *Logical Investigations* has been made available by the publication of two letters written to Husserl in 1905,[7] in which he expressed his objections and misgivings concerning Husserl's work. He professed agreement with Husserl's criticism of psychologism, which he conceived to be essentially the Protagorean standpoint that man is the measure of all things. While admitting that Husserl's undertaking in pure logic was not sufficiently clear to him, he judged it to be impossible to assemble completely all truths following intuitively from concepts into a theoretical science of logic; and he was not disposed to give his approval to the attempt to delimit a theoretical science of truths which would exclude every empirical datum. Brentano's comments, although interesting in themselves, indicate his almost complete misunderstanding of Husserl's aim and work.

In the opinion of the editor, Professor O. Kraus, Husserl failed even to answer Brentano's "conclusive arguments," and Brentano's hope to turn him away from his errors was completely illusory. Kraus was particularly interested in undermining Husserl's claim to originality. Challenging the belief that the refutation of psychologism was due to the *Logical Investigations*, Kraus referred to Brentano's paper on evidence which he had incorporated in the text of the volume on *Truth and Evidence*. Brentano also opposed the conception of evidence as a feeling, an antipsychologistic point which had been credited to Husserl. By means of some passages from Brentano's *The Origin of the Knowledge of Right and Wrong (Ursprung sittlicher Erkenntnis,* 1889), Kraus attempted to establish Brentano's priority in opposing psychologism. Husserl's ideal objects and Meinong's "objectives" were traced by him to Brentano's introduction of the assumption of irreal "facts" (*Sachverhalte,* existents and non-existents).

All that this proves is that Brentano was a stimulating thinker who initiated many ideas which were developed further by gifted students. One can trace numerous ideas of phenomenology back to suggestions in Brentano's thought, but it would be absurd to overestimate such indebtedness to the extent of raising a claim of priority. From Kraus's point of view, the idea of irreal facts is hardly to the credit of Brentano, because the latter came to hold that only things, relia, or real essences can be thought, and irrealia such as being, non-being, fact, and truth are mere fictions.

In the *Logical Investigations*, Husserl called attention to defects in Brentano's theory of knowledge, pointing out the ambiguity of such expressions as "in consciousness" and "immanent in consciousness."[8] There can be no doubt about his indebtedness to Brentano for the concept of intentionality and the field for descriptive analysis opened up therewith. But it was his belief that Brentano nevertheless failed to grasp its real nature and to put it to philosophical use. As he expressed it near the close of his life, it was very late before he could correctly characterize reflectively the radically new kind of problems under the title of intentionality which were discovered in the *Logical Investigations*, in their universal significance for a genuine psychology and transcendental philosophy. He finally came to the understanding that his honored teacher Brentano to be sure sought a psychology of the phenomena of consciousness (intentional experiences), but had no notion, in the sense of carrying it through, of the real meaning and method of such a task.

Kraus's criticism neither impressed nor detained Husserl. Looking back upon his early period from the perspective of his final maturity, he wondered at his attachment to Brentano for so many years. In a state of self-deception that he now found difficult to understand, he had believed himself to be a collaborator of Brentano's philosophy, and especially his psychology. But, he pointed out, in his first work (the habilitation thesis of 1887, in part more fully developed in the *Philosophy of Arithmetic*) his whole mode of thought was already entirely different from that of Brentano. Taken formally, Brentano sought a psychology whose entire theme is "psychical phenomena," which, among other things, was defined as consciousness "of" something. And yet his psychology was anything but a science of intentionality, the real problems of intentionality were never revealed to him, he did not even see that no given experience of consciousness is to be described without the statement of the pertinent intentional object "as such" (e.g., that this table-perception is only to be described exactly if I describe this table *as what* and *just as* it is perceived). Of intentional implication, intentional modifications, problems of evidence, problems of constitution, etc., he had no idea. Although Brentano had striven to go beyond Neo-Scholasticism, he was unsuccessful; the writings of his old age were regarded as "distilled scholasticism" by Husserl. It was not possible that the latter could "borrow" ideas from a source in which they were not present. In a simple answer to such an extreme Brentanist as Kraus, one may readily grant every meaningful claim to Brentano's priority without in the least diminishing the stature of Husserl thereby. An unfortunate controversy will thus be reduced to its proper insignificance.

IV. HUSSERL'S DEVELOPMENT

Husserl's own special preparation included mathematics and psychology. His doctor's degree was taken in mathematics, his studies under Weierstrass giving him a firm basis for later logical work. In psychology he was interested primarily in the pure descriptive type of investigation, "empirical" in Brentano's sense. The fusion of these two apparently diverse streams of scholarship determined the setting for his career. The important changes in his development are to be explained to a large extent by difficulties encountered in integrating these elements. His inner feeling of uncertainty, at times reaching distressing proportions of intensity, reflected the conflict between a formal, "realistic" point of view, according to which all logical propositions are determinate in themselves, and the psychologistic method of accounting for logical forms and principles by means of the process of experience. Shortly before his death, he spoke of having gone through a period of flagging, similar to experiences undergone periodically earlier in life, during which he was unable to undertake any work. Such periods were followed by intense work and productivity.

It is possible to distinguish a number of different periods in Husserl's development with respect to the determining elements in his early training. These are, broadly speaking, the periods of psychologism, simple descriptive phenomenology (phenomenology in a narrow sense), and transcendental phenomenology.[9] From the point of view of the later transcendental phenomenology, the first two periods are simply stages of progress toward the realm of philosophy which only the phenomenological reduction makes accessible. Thus the *Logical Investigations* was characterized as a work of "Durchbruch" by Husserl. Therefore one may speak of the two major periods in his development as being pretranscendental and transcendental philosophy. The great progress recorded in the *Logical Investigations* was fully recognized shortly after the publication of that work, when he proclaimed phenomenology as an autonomous discipline. Being completely conscious of the important progress he had made, he was soon able to conceive the next step to be taken—the phenomenological reduction—which alone could provide adequate technique for the reflective descriptive analysis required for purposes of the theory of knowledge and philosophy in general.

Husserl himself believed that his development displayed an inner consistency despite the occurrence of epoch-making changes, which occasioned so much difficulty for his followers in the various periods. Those that failed to grasp or to endorse the periodical changes simply failed to participate in "the development." The epochal changes that occurred recall the philosophy of Schelling. The difference between the earlier and the later stages is striking; and yet Husserl spoke of the fundamental unity of his development. The early period was one of a gifted and well trained young scholar with a penchant for the most fundamental problems. The extent of his psychologism may be questioned, although he did defend the psychologistic thesis concerning the fundamental concepts of mathematics and logic. But in logic he knew very well how to apply the formal method, as seen in his papers on the "Calculus of Inference" (1891). Although he reacted against his early position and continued to change periodically, the chief results of each stage were always retained in the later work. It may well be that the perspective of his development is distorted somewhat by the emphasis placed upon the issue of psychologism, so that one may be led to underestimate the element of continuity. It should be noted for example, that the *Logical Investigations* made use of the **"Psychological Studies of Elementary Logic,"** belonging to his early period. Furthermore, although Frege has been credited with the demolition of the *Philosophy of Arithmetic* and with turning Husserl away from his early position, that contention cannot be sustained by the facts. Frege did indeed successfully point out inadequacies in that work, but he by no means discredited it as a whole; and the fact that Husserl's confidence in his work was not seriously shaken is shown by the frequent references to it in his later writings. Indeed, a close study of the *Philosophy of Arithmetic* brings to light some of Husserl's fundamental descriptive interests, and presents in a simple form types of problems which his later and more developed descriptive technique reveals in their proper complexity. If one reads all of Husserl's writings consecutively, one cannot but be impressed by the continuity of his development. But it would be absurd to disregard the great changes in Husserl's views (thus, e.g., the "phenomenological reduction" was not presented until 1913, in the *Ideas*, even though it was conceived and formulated some years earlier), or to discount his own repeated assertions concerning the important changes in his views.

Husserl made the following comments about his early period in a letter to the writer: "Concerning the inner connection of all of my writings, and consequently concerning my inner development, the new edition of the *Philosophen Lexikon* will give a correct account under my name in case the material prepared by Dr. Fink is accepted without change. External 'influences' are without significance. As a young beginner I naturally read much, including classics and contemporary literature of the 1870's to the 1890's. I liked the critical-skeptical point of view, since I myself did not see firm ground anywhere. I was always very far removed from Kantianism and German idealism. Only Natorp interested me, more for personal reasons, and I read thoroughly the first edition of his *Introduction to Psychology,* but not the enlarged second edition. I zealously read (especially as a student) Mill's *Logic* and later the work on Hamilton's philosophy. I have repeatedly studied the English empiricists and the principal writings of Leibniz (ed. by J. E. Erdmann), especially his mathematical-philosophical writings. I first got to know Schuppe after the *Logical Investigations* (1900-1901), when he could offer me nothing further. I never looked seriously at anything by Rehmke. Really, my course was already marked out by the *Philosophy of Arithmetic* (1891), and I could do nothing other than to proceed further." This statement is by no means complete, however. Husserl frequently spoke of James, whose *Principles of Psychology* was of lasting value for him. Lotze and Bolzano were of great importance for him: to Lotze he was indebted for his interpretation of Plato's theory of ideas, which determined all his further studies; and to Bolzano for his *Wissenschaftslehre,* which provided him with a first draft of a "pure logic" at a critical time in his development. Furthermore, no account of his intellectual relationships may omit mention of Twardowski, Marty and the other Brentanists, and also Avenarius and Dilthey.

Looking back upon his development near the close of his life,[10] Husserl emphasized the importance of the "correlative mode of procedure" that was illustrated in the *Logical Investigations*. This he traced back to the *Philosophy of Arithmetic,* with its "peculiar doubling in psychological and logical analyses," which were now seen to have an inner relationship. The unity of the *Prolegomena* and the six investigations, which was missed by contemporary critics, was due to the realization of the correlative nature of the descriptive analysis. It was first necessary to defend the objectivity of logical structures against all subjectivizing attempts, before proceeding to the epistemological preparation of the science of pure logic. Although a great advance over the *Philosophy of Arithmetic* had been made, the analysis of consciousness was mainly "noetic," which means that it was concerned more with the experiencing than with the "noematic" stratum of meaning belonging to each experience. The necessity and technique for a thoroughgoing two-sided analysis of consciousness was first made clear by the *Ideas*.

The "phenomenology" represented by the *Logical Investigations* makes use of immanent intuition alone, and does not pass beyond the sphere of intuitive self-givenness. That is the meaning of the precept, "Back to the things themselves": it meant the appeal to intuitive givenness. The second volume of the work illustrates this methodological principle by means of extensive concrete analyses. All of the insights of this work are apodictic insights of essence. The realm of ideas which is thus disclosed is finally referred back to the subjectivity of consciousness, which is the "primal field of everything *a priori.*" Of deciding importance in the universal investigation of consciousness is the insight that the immanent sphere is governed by essential laws.

It may well be true that no position held earlier was ever wholly wrong, so that the "correct" results of his investigations could always find their place in each successive systematic period. The genetic account of Husserl's thought is therefore the best way to explain the role of the

various divisions and aspects of his philosophy. All through his intellectual life the main motives of his philosophy can be traced out, until the last period, when it was maintained that only the "difficult" medium of phenomenological reduction, now intricately elaborated, can reveal the "unmotivated" and unconditioned basis of all philosophy and science.

Bearing in mind the element of continuity, it is helpful to distinguish several groups of writings, which will describe more exactly the three major periods already indicated. The arrangement will not be entirely chronological, in order to distinguish the psychological-epistemological writings from the formal. The content and method of the works are in question in this classification. Thus even though *Erfahrung und Urteil* derives from an earlier period, as Landgrebe points out, it also derives from a later period, which is what is in question. It therefore belongs with the latest logical writings. (1) There is the work resulting from the first period of mathematical training, the dissertation on the calculus of variations, **"Beiträge zur Variationsrechnung."**[11] (2) The attempt to establish a psychological foundation for logic and mathematics may be distinguished as a distinct stage in the early 1890's, although it runs parallel to investigations of a strictly logical nature. Husserl's studies from 1886 to 1895 were primarily in the field of mathematics and formal logic. This was the period of adherence to psychologism as a methodological position. It seemed to Husserl that the philosophy of mathematics was concerned with the psychological origin of the fundamental concepts of mathematics. In the course of his work on the *Philosophy of Arithmetic*, he devoted attention to what he called the "quasi-qualitative" or "figural" factors, which were called "Gestalt qualities" by von Ehrenfels. (3) *The Logical Investigations* consists of the main results of Husserl's intellectual labors in the 1890's. The various portions of it were written at different times, so that they had to be revised fully in order to give them unity. The critical portion of the first volume, which has been most widely read, consists of a critique and repudiation of psychologism; it had already been presented in lectures in 1895. The last chapter of that volume, on **"The Idea of a Pure Logic,"** was added later. It derived from Husserl's earlier mathematical-logical studies, which were discontinued after 1894, and advanced the idea of a formal ontology. It is noteworthy that the *Logical Investigations* register a distinct advance in the understanding of formal science, as well as a landmark in the development of the theory of knowledge, the subject-matter of which predominates in the work. In it phenomenology is characterized as a *descriptive psychology* designed to provide the clarification of the fundamental ideas of formal reasoning. This was especially unfortunate in that it was a factor preventing the correct understanding of the investigations. It was, however, evident to the careful reader that they presented *essential analyses.* In his subsequent correction of this error, Husserl pointed out the fact that all psychological apperception is excluded, that experiences belonging to real thinking beings are not in question. In other words, "descriptive psychology" was not meant to be understood in the usual sense, but, as was clearly pointed out in the first edition of this work, the method of investigation was intended to be free from all assumptions of psychology and metaphysics. (4) The published writings after the first edition of the *Logical Investigations* and up to the publication of the *Ideas* in 1913 may be included in one group, comprising all known writings up to the first published formulation of the phenomenological reduction. The second *Logical Survey* (a critical discussion of German logical publications at the close of the century), while containing material largely belonging to the preceding period, contains a correction of the conception of phenomenology as descriptive psychology. The *Lectures on the Consciousness of Inner Time* (1905-1910) and the *Logos* essay, **"Philosophy as a Rigorous Science"** (1910) illustrate respectively the nature of phenomenological description and the programmatic ideal of phenomenology as the most rigorous of all the sciences. In this period the clarifying function of phenomenology is assigned to an autonomous discipline which serves as the prelude to all other knowledge. Although the descriptive analysis of time-consciousness includes elements of a genetic and constitutive character, and extends the field for analysis, the reduction of all knowledge to pure consciousness is not defined systematically, either there or in the *Logos* essay. Phenomenology is now, in short, an autonomous region for investigation that is free from the assumptions of psychology, in keeping with the requirements of a presuppositionless philosophy. (5) The *Ideas* usher in a period of transcendental phenomenology, the method of phenomenological reduction being the way to philosophy. This work provided a systematic presentation of the new phenomenology. In it the phenenological is distinguished from the natural "attitude." The latter assumes the existence of the world, along with other normally made assumptions. The phenomenological attitude requires the suspension of all assumptions. The existence of the world, and of everything that is "posited," is "bracketed." The phenomena that remain are the subject-matter of phenomenology, which is defined as the science of pure transcendental consciousness. The discussion of *noesis* and *noema* is especially important in bringing to light some fundamental structures of experience, and as indicating a fruitful field for research. The "reduction" opens up a universal field for philosophical investigation which is free from all prejudgments and assumptions, hence its crucial methodological importance. Husserl is careful to distinguish eidetic reduction (proceeding from fact to essence) from transcendental reduction, according to which the phenomena are characterized as "irreal," and are not ordered in the "actual world." The method of phenomenological reduction is applied in order to achieve the presuppositionless field of philosophy in the consciousness of an individual ego to begin with, which involves the suspension of all beliefs in transcendent realities. Phenomenology now becomes the most fundamental science and the absolute ground of all knowledge. Husserl's aim to bring the *Logical Investigations* up to the level of the *Ideas* in a revised edition (1913-1921) was not realized completely, although some portions of it were altered radically in conformity to the greater clarity which he had

gained. The term "epochistic" aptly names this period. There need be no ambiguity in the use of this term. Other meanings of "epoché" than that of the *Ideas* must be pointed out explicitly. It signifies the way to the transcendental sphere, and its more detailed elaboration is provided by the *Cartesian Meditations*. This work deals with the problem of the experiencing of other minds through empathy, and introduces the concept of transcendental intersubjectivity, which is necessary for a complete constitutive phenomenology. (6) Although they properly come under the heading of transcendental phenomenology, it is desirable to list the latest logical writings separately. *The Formal and Transcendental Logic* (1929) is important not only in view of its marked excellence as a classic of logic, but also because it is the culmination of the lines of development of logic and transcendental phenomenology. The term "perspectivistic" calls attention to the attempt at a synthesis of the two traditionally divergent fields of interest with which Husserl's philosophical activity began, i.e., his original problem-statement, which involved psychology and epistemology as well as formal reasoning. The detailed examination of this work will enable the reader to judge the success of that synthesis. Included in it is a reinterpretation and evaluation of the *Logical Investigations* as viewed from the advanced level of transcendental phenomenology. The preparation and publication of Husserl's last logical studies, entitled *Experience and Judgment* (1939), finally makes possible the understanding of the phenomenological foundation of logic. It presents much needed material for his analysis of experience, and adds still more support to the claim to concrete investigations and results that has already been made with so much justification. This applies particularly to the analysis of "prepredicative experience" and the "origin-analyses" of logical concepts and forms.[12] Like the *Formal and Transcendental Logic,* this is a work of the greatest importance for logic, theory of knowledge, and psychology. It should be borne in mind that Husserl's opposition to psychologism by no means implied an opposition to psychology. On the contrary, not the least of his contributions has been to the field of psychology. (7) The last publications to appear, one before his death and the other posthumously, reveal his interest in extending the phenomenological method to an even greater scope than had heretofore been accomplished, to include reference to the history of science and philosophy, and to meet the problem of history confronting this method by means of the concept of "intentional history." . . .

V. TOWARD THE FUTURE

Husserl believed that he had been making great progress until the last, and that he had finally achieved complete clarity of understanding. Declassed by official Germany and deserted or ignored by most of the outstanding "Aryan" scholars in Germany who were influenced by him, he faced the future with an appeal to the judgment of eternity, with the serene consciousness of one who had accomplished much that is permanent. He wrote: "And we old people remain here. A singular turn of the times: it gives the philosopher—if it does not take away his breath—much to think of. But now: *cogito ergo sum,* i.e., I prove *sub specie aeterni* my right to live. And this, the *aeternitas* in general, cannot be touched by any earthly powers."

To be sure, Husserl had very few "followers" at the close of his life, from the point of view of the unreserved acceptance of his final philosophical efforts. But it would be a mistake to restrict the number of sincere representatives of the phenomenological philosophy to a few final adherents to it. The spirit of Husserl's work was one which forbade completion; his problems had a horizon that was forever open. If few students of philosophy could keep abreast of his progress, that was due to the paucity of his publications in relationship to the total output. But not only that; it must be admitted that most students of philosophy did not devote the necessary time to the study of phenomenology. It was thoroughly understood by few, although it was discussed by many. Husserl could not but feel alone under the circumstances; and this was accentuated by his status in the new Germany.

The period of Husserl's international effectiveness on a large scale has now begun, as shown by the systematically organized interest of scholars all over the world in the understanding and development of his philosophy. Husserl is destined to be a subject of discussion for a long time. It is the intention of those organized in the International Phenomenological Society to make phenomenology effective for further philosophical progress.

The phenomenological method forbids all prejudgments and dogmas. Its ideal is the elaboration of a descriptive philosophy by means of a *radical* method, proceeding with the greatest possible freedom from presuppositions. It is a scientific tendency in philosophy, and its constructive program gives great promise of positive results. That the phenomenological method has a wide range of application to the various fields of scholarship has already been shown by numerous studies, which are concerned with art, mathematics, law, social science, psychology, and psychiatry. Admittedly only a beginning has been made. On the other hand, the nominal adoption and misuse of the phenomenological method has already illustrated the dangers of mysticism, one-sided and hence misleading description, dogmatism, and agnosticism. Its competent critical mastery should keep the method free from such errors, and should provide a common basis for all scholars interested in the constructive program of philosophy as a rigorous science.

Notes

1. Cf. E. Fink, "Was will die Phänomenologie Edmund Husserls?" *Dis Tatwelt,* 1934, p. 15.

2. Cf. Paul Natorp, review of Lipps' *Grundtheteschen des Seelenlebens,* Bonn, 1883, in the *Göttingische gelehrte Anseigen,* 1885, pp. 190-232.

3. P. Natorp, "Uber objektive und subjektive Begründung der Erkenntnis" (Erster Aufsats), *Philosophische Monatshefte,* vol. XXIII, 1887, pp. 257-286. Husserl

refers to pp. 265 f. of this paper in the *Logical Investigations ,* for a supplement to his discussion of psychologism.

4. Cf. P. Natorp, "Quantität und Qualität in Begriff, Urteil und gegenständlicher Erkenntnis," *Philosophische Monatshefte,* vol. XXVII, 1891, pp. 1-32, 129-160. In his *Einleitung in die Psychologië nach kritischer Methode* (Freiburg i. B., 1888), Natorp set himself the task of making secure the bases of psychology by a preliminary investigation of its object and method.

5. Cf. Husserl's "Erinnerungen an Franz Brentano," Supplement II, pp. 153-167, in Oskar Kraus's *Franz Brentano, Zur Kenntnis seines Lebens und seiner Lehre* (Supplement I is by Carl Stumpf), München, 1919.

6. *Brentanos Gesammelte Philosophische Schriften,* edited by O. Kraus and A. Kastil, Leipsig, 1922-1930, 10 volumes.

7. Cf. Brentano, *Wahrheit und Evidenz,* edited by O. Kraus, Leipzig, 1930. The letters are in an appendix entitled "Concerning the Generality of Truth and the Fundamental Error of a Socalled Phenomenology."

8. *Logische Untersuchungen,* vol. II, part 1, p. 375. Cf. L. Landgrebe, "Husserls Phänomenologie und die Motive su ihrer Umbildung," *Revue internationale de Philosophie,* 1, 2 (1939), pp. 280ff

9. Cp. E. Fink's account in his introduction to Husserl's hitherto unpublished "Entwurf einer 'Vorrede' zu den 'Logischen Untersuchungen'" (1913), *Uit Tijdschrift Voor Philosophie,* I, 1 (1939), p. 107. Fink divides the development of Husserl's phenomenology—taken externally—into three phases, approximately corresponding to Husserl's periods of teaching in Halle, Göttingen, and Freiburg. Accordingly, the *Logical Investigations* and the *Ideas* are the culminating works of the first two periods. This classification is useful in calling attention to the trend in each period toward the achievement of a deeper and more general level of analysis. Looking backward, one can discern the inner unity of each phase.

10. Cf. *Philosophen Lexikon,* by E. Hauer, W. Ziegenfuss, and G. Jung, Berlin, 1937, pp. 447ff.

11. Cp. Illemann, *Husserls vor-phänomenologische Philosophie,* p. 70. Illemann is correct in pointing out the three periods of pure mathematics, prephenomenology, and pure or "epochistic" phenomenology, although it would be more in keeping with Husserl's own terminology to speak of phenomenology in two senses—simple descriptive and transcendental. Illemann makes the mistake of introducing criticism from the standpoint of the Driesch-Schingnitz school, while at the same time recognizing the incompleteness of the earlier periods. Cf. Becker's review of Illemann's book in the *Deutsche Literaturzeitung,* Feb. 4, 1934, in which Becker suggests the title of "perspectivistic phenomenology" for the fourth period.

12. Cf. *Erfahrung und Urteil,* §§ 5, 11, and 12 for the significance of the concept of "origin" or of "genesis" as conceived in the phenomenological method. Husserl's "genetic" statement of the problems of origin, as relating to logic, is not psychological in the usual sense. The term "genetic" refers to the production by which knowledge arises in its "origin-form" of self-givenness, a process which repeatedly yields the same cognition. The factual, historical process of meanings arising out of a definite historical subjectivity is not at all in question. Our world becomes an example for us, by means of which we study the structure and the origin of a possible world in general. The clarification of the origin of the predicative judgment is a fundamental task for the genealogy of logic in a transcendental sense. The aim is to investigate the contributions of the knowing reason to the construction of the world. In order to attain to the ultimate, original experiences, it is necessary to go back to the simplest units and to regard the world purely as the world of perception, abstracting from everything else. In this way the realm of nature as perceived by me is first obtained. Thus we may come to the most primitive building stones of logical contribution, out of which our world is built up. The systematic line of 'transcendental" inquiry of these logical studies is an illustration of such "origin-analysis."

Maximillian Beck (essay date 1941)

SOURCE: "The Last Phase of Husserl's Phenomenology: An Exposition and a Criticism," in *Philosophy and Phenomenological Research,* Vol. 1, No. 4, June, 1941, pp. 479-91.

[*In the following essay, Beck criticizes the direction Husserl takes in his last work, arguing that he abandons the methods and principles upon which he first founded phenomenology.*]

I. REPORT

1. *Concerning the foundations of modern times and its philosophy and science.* Husserl's last essay published before his death is entitled **"The Crisis of European Science and Transcendental Phenomenology: An Introduction to Phenomenological Philosophy."**[1]

To Husserl the crisis prevailing among mankind today seems to be basically a crisis caused by a self-misunderstanding of reason. This self-misunderstanding has brought about a crisis of the European sciences, has brought about skepticism, irrationalism, and, hence, the domination of inhumanity.[2] With the sacrifice of reason, however, mankind and modern European culture are in greater danger than ever before of complete destruction. For modern men and their culture are determined by a conscious opposition to the traditionalism of the Middle Ages which, in Husserl's opinion, were but blind and obedient.[3] On the other hand, mankind in modern times has been striving with all its power to mould its practical environs and itself autonomously by free reason and in accordance with its own insight.[4] For modern mankind, therefore, the sacrifice of reason is equivalent to the destruction of its basis and the stopping of all the sources of its strength.[5]

But it must be remembered that the essential being of man as an *animal rationale* is to exist freely under conditions determined by reason. And this fact alone can furnish a basis for the higher value of European culture. For universal unity and common consent are essential to reason. And this universal validity of reason as the very principle of modern European culture makes possible by the use of reason a Europeanization of non-European mankind. Free self-forming through universally valid reason is the *entelecheia* or the "innate" idea of the modern European. If he abandons the realization of his *entelecheia,* he will decay to an empirical-anthropological type like the Chinese or the Indian. Then the drama of the Europeanization of all the various races of mankind will have been but historical nonsense.[6]

2. *Self-misunderstanding of reason through the philosophy and the sciences of modern European times.* But upon what is this self-misunderstanding of reason based? It is, in the first place, based upon the fact that the concept of reason is bound to mathematics, the original meaning of which was lost long ago.

Modern philosophy and sciences presuppose laws of universal validity in the real world.[7] That means that these laws are founded on really existing relations of numbers and measures with regard to space and time, motion and shape. Sensual qualities as well are reduced to motions and shapes that can be calculated mathematically.[8]

But mathematics and especially its prototpe, the geometry of Euclid, were originally only an empirical way of measuring! This means that geometry, too, does not find mathematical objects in the real world but constructs them only by means of the imagination in order to govern nature practically and to fix it on a generally valid base by measuring it.[9]

Hence mathematical identities and invariabilities had, originally, only a mere methodological meaning. But the original methodological meaning, particularly that of Euclid's figures, has been misunderstood by modern science and philosophy as an objectively existing thing. Moreover, this creation of the imagination has been assumed to be the objective reality of the physical world.[10] (Husserl obviously came to that opinion through the attempt to justify modern mathematics which, in fact, is a practical method of calculating and of dominating nature.[11] Therefore he also abandons the meaning of objective knowledge within classical mathematics, particularly that of Euclid, because of its presumed practical meaning. Thus absurdities are eliminated which result from the opinion that a field of objective counterparts corresponds to modern and totally non-perceptible mathematics. It is to be remembered here that modern mathematics contradicts the ancient as well as itself, *if* understood as making assertions about reality. There are, for instance, various geometries.)

Also modern physics is but applied mathematics and its objects are likewise totally non-perceptible. Husserl denies that physics is a knowledge of an objective reality and stresses its practical meaning. Thus an intolerable dualism between sensuous and perceptible reality and the world we are living in on the one hand, and the totally abstract world of modern physics on the other hand is eliminated. This dualism becomes more intolerable because it declares that the sensible-perceptible world exists merely as appearance, while the non-perceptible world of physics is held to be objectively real.[12]

But speaking thus, we have already passed beyond the cause for the misunderstanding of mathematical reason.

The *second* misunderstanding of reason, according to Husserl, is the fact that an objectively existing reality is not only urged for mathematical objects but also for the world in which mathematical reason is applied. The second misunderstanding consists in the granting of objectivity to the world as independent of the subjectivity which produces it.[13] "World," "nature" would be cut off from a consciousness which produces them. They are held to be really existing, a "in sich abgeschlossene Körperwelt," "abgekapselt," *beyond the consciousness-appearances* which alone bring them forth to knowledge.[14] The senselessness of this proposition is not seen. It consists in speaking of an objective existence of things, beyond the appearances by which they manifest themselves to consciousness. Essential to a thing, according to Husserl, is its realization by means of "deshadings" (Abschattungen); it exists only by a certain succession of mere mental images (Bewusstseinserscheinungen).

Husserl also asserts that the geometrical figures of things and their motion are never given objectively in themselves, but only in the succession of their perspective appearances, relative to certain points of view. (Even God would be unable to see a thing, for instance a globe, as an absolute and complete figure without perspective, i.e., see its front and rear sides simultaneously.)[15]

The misunderstanding concerning the existence of things and the world as being beyond their consciousness-appearances involves fatal consequences, and finally leads to a radical skepticism. Through such a misunderstanding, reality is divided into two parts of completely different value: *On the one side* is the objective reality of physical things. This reality is held to reveal itself finally to progressive knowledge merely as a reality of figure and motions with regard to space and time. *On the other side* is the reality of the consciousness or of the soul, or subjectivity as a totality of that which does not exist in itself objectively but only "subjectively."

Furthermore, one tries to coördinate these two parts. Within the research field of a particular science, of psychology namely, one therefore ascribes reality to subjectivity, too. But that psychical reality (*res cogitans*), is subjected to physical research methods (*more geometrico*), ignoring any other conception of reality than the physical one (*res extensa*).[16]

Such a division into an objective real being and a "mere" subjective one leads to inherent contradictions. The mere recognition of an objective real entity, as recognition, belongs to the subjective sphere of the soul of consciousness.[17] When man began to develop a point of view of the physical world, he certainly expected to be able to advance gradually towards constant and objectively true reality, by separating the mere subjective from what is measurable and objectively determinable.[18]

But what had at first been held most firm and objective, was also by progressive research discovered to be subjective, so for instance, space, time, mass, causality.[19] Aside, however, from such a grasp of an objective reality beyond all subjectivity, there was no other meaning of scientific and philosophical knowledge in sight. That is why reason and science seem to be abandoned (Hume's skepticism).[20]

The separation of subjectivity from objective reality has still another consequence. Very important problems of high interest to man, namely questions about the sense and value of the world, of man's own being and the like, have been, from the very beginning, outside the sphere of scientific research. For these questions and their answers have their origin in special interests of man, in his subjectivity which is to be banned from the sphere of science. That is why objective science is condemned to lack all importance. And at the same time the antagonism between reality and reason is proclaimed.[21] For the aims and values of reality are degraded to illusions.

3. *The aims of Husserl's phenomenology.* Husserl entitles the essay under review here, **"Crisis of the European Sciences and *Transcendental Phenomenology."*** And he adds as subtitle, "An Introduction to Phenomenological Philosophy." For he believes that his phenomenology would be able to do away with the crisis of the European sciences. What is this phenomenology"?

It is, *first,* a foundation for reason and science which is in itself intelligible. For it discovers the ultimate origins of reason and science and uses them instead of blind tradition and the remnants of former real experience.[22]

Phenomenology, *secondly,* shows what is really meant when speaking of "true existence," "truth," "objective existence," "reality." It shows, furthermore, what is not meant by them, namely no existing thing, independent of thinking, tending toward it by means of *cogitationes*. For phenomenology discovers reason as a certain universal synthesis of cogitations by the agreement of which an objectively true entity is realized as one identical world reality, valid for all thinking beings.[23]

Thus it becomes clear why philosophy always wants to be systematic. And the true meaning of the endless progressive method of modern European science becomes clear too. For the idea of a philosophical system as well as the endless progress of science gives rise to a misunderstanding of the endless horizon and harmony of experience as corresponding to an endless reality which exists objectively in itself.[24]

Thirdly, however, phenomenology tries to discover that system of lawfulness and reason, by virtue of which universally valid norms and an accordant reality could be established for all men who agree with one another.[25] Thereby phenomenology unmasks scientific reason as derived from a preceding practical reason founded upon subjectivity.[26]

But the true meaning of reason unanimously agreeing with itself has to serve practical subjectivity. For the true meaning of reason is autonomy and freedom of self-determination. It is, furthermore, determination of the aims of universal mankind by means of free reason.[27] The old ideal of Greek philosophy radically reinforced, again became the decisive impulse of modern European philosophy and science: self-determination of man through knowledge of what is final truth. That, however, is recognizing subjectivity.[28] And that penetration of subjectivity which affects the meaning of an objective validity and reality, is just the origin of an "objectivity" which is mistaken as being scientific (*Wissenschaftlichkeit*).[29]

4. *The phenomenological method.* It is the method of a radical elimination ("Ausschaltung") of all assertions about reality or the method of suspension (like the "*epoché*" of the Greek skeptics). What does it mean?

Husserl emphasizes what essentially constitutes the "*epoché*" made by Descartes: Descartes, in order to get absolutely firm ground for philosophizing, starts his *Meditationes* by a methodical doubt as to the reality of all things. For they possibly could be mere dreams. By this very doubt, however, he discovers as self-evident and absolutely firm truth that this doubt itself, the "act" of this doubt as a way of thinking (*cogitatio*) cannot be merely dreamed. It is itself, it "exists," but what is thought does not exist? That the *cogitatum* exists only *as* thought, *qua cogitatum,* even if only dreamed.

To be sure, Descartes himself overhastily mistakes this self-evident *cogitatio* for the *cogitatio* of the real individual ego and asserts that the reality of this individual ego is insured by that methodological doubt. And he also mistakes the thought or *cogitatum qua cogitatum* for an integral part of this ego, as a psychical reality. Husserl, on the contrary, emphasizes that this empirical individual ego realizes its existence only through consciousness, together with the realization of certain external things, namely by a certain synthesis and succession of *cogitationes*. Therefore only these *cogitationes* are immediately self-evident. The reality of my individual ego is just as doubtful as the real-ity of the external physical world. Therefore the true radical doubt as represented by Husserl's own phenomenological method, consists in radical suspension ("*epoché*") from the maintenance of reality at all. The phenomenologist eliminates ("schaltet aus") the reality not only of the external world, but also of the phenomenologizing ego itself as really being individuality. Instead of participating in the maintenance of reality, the phenomenologist analyzes acts of such a maintaining. Instead of naïvely living in it, the phenomenologist makes it into an object of his research. The object of that research method, artificially gained through "*epoché*" and "Ausschaltung," is called by Husserl "transcendentally purified consciousness." It is the only original and immediately self-evident ground which Descartes sought.[30]

II. Notice

The incoherence of the following criticism may be explained by the author's intention of summarizing on this occasion not only some objections against the paper under review here but against all Husserl's later philosophy. As a young man I was freed by Husserl from the very same subjectivism to which I found him turning back in his later philosophy. This may explain the sharp tone of my criticism. But I want to emphasize the great gratitude which I owe to the author of the *Logische Untersuchungen* and that way of philosophizing which honestly tries to found all assertions only upon immediate experience. To be sure, the properly practiced phenomenological method and its theoretical explanation and justification must not be identical. Even the results of a properly practiced method can be different according to different theoretical presuppositions.

In my opinion Husserl eventually arrived at subjectivism because of his identification of consciousness and intentionality, as I tried to demonstrate in my *Psychologie*.[31] Lack of space makes it impossible even to hint at this discussion here.

III. Criticism

(1) Husserl's method claims to be an original beginning without any premises. But it assumes the rules of logic. It is not what it pretends to be, a mere description of *cogitata qua cogitata,* but it also requires the exercise of judgment, the drawing of conclusions and the use of reason. Certainly, it would be unable to make any assertion without, for instance, presupposing the validity of the law of identity.

Furthermore, it assumes many evidences of connections between general ideas—so, for instance, the evidence that every action, thought, or doubt is impossible without a subject who acts, thinks, or doubts. Husserl himself calls his inquiries "egological." Thus he also assumes an "ego" as subject of the "transcendentally purified consciousness" which, to be sure, is not the real and individual ego of Descartes. But also Husserl's general ego is not a *cogitatum qua cogitatum,* it is only an *a priori* accepted as a necessary premise of any thinking.

(2) Husserl is, furthermore, unable to eliminate, even methodologically, the transcendent existence of this ego. Even if the existence of this ego were eliminated in favor of an immanent subjectivity of phenomenological consciousness, it would yet be incomprehensible why the succession and teleology of the phenomena of consciousness are beyond the free will of all subjectivity.

In *Ideen zu einer reinen Phänomenologie* (p. 111, Husserl's *Jahrbuch,* Halle, 1913) Husserl supposed as "cause for the factualness of a corresponding constitutional consciousness" a creative God as transcendent to the world as well as to an absolute consciousness. But in the essay under review here, Husserl speaks of the "innate reason" or "entelecheia of a reasoning mankind."[32] But words like "innate" and "entelecheia" should not make us overlook the transcendence of these presuppositions of Husserl.

Mere factualness of a certain selection and succession of phenomena, present in consciousness, is not to be eliminated by eliminating the meaning of the objective reality of its synthesis. The stream of consciousness in which the conviction of the reality of an objective real world is formed lacks every reasonable necessity. It exists only insofar as it is present. It is only immediately self-evident that this stream of consciousness exists and is present. For it is evidently impossible to deny that I am conscious of certain phenomena (*cogitata qua cogitata*). But the immediate self-evidence of the existence of a certain consciousness is radically different from self-evidence by self-evident *reason.*

(3) One has to distinguish between the self-evidence of an immediate perception and self-evidence of an understanding through reasons. Only this self-evidence by means of reasonable understanding belongs to the sphere of reason. And the perceptive method employed by phenomenology completely lacks this reasonable understanding. It only shows what is conscious, how it is conscious, how one succeeds another and is connected to it. In short, it *states* only what is. Its immediate self-evident certainty is only a certainty of a knowledge of facts. But it does not show the *necessary reasons* for the connection of the conscious phenomena. And therefore it is quite wrong to suggest that the phenomenological method would be able to clarify and establish the self-understanding of reason. Finally, phenomenology, too, would only be a science of facts, a "positivistic" science—despite all methodological elimination of reality.

To be sure, Husserl strives toward the same end which Kant had already sought. He wants to show that reason is an autonomic organon of structures and functions of consciousness, a kind of psychical texture in which every one would necessarily have to think truth and world-reality, if he thought at all. Husserl, however, instead of showing the necessity of this psychical texture, arrives at the contrary of necessity. He speaks of a universal-causal-style,[33] just as one speaks of a classic or baroque style in the history of art. He identifies identical and irrelative objectivity with an intersubjective validity of measure.[34] He interprets ideas as invariable and unattainable poles, towards which experience, which is steadily completing and perfecting itself, tends.[35] But this kind of interpretation is typical of empiricism which completely fails to conceive reason and necessity.

(4) In fact, Husserl landed at the empirical way of philosophizing against which he had formerly fought fiercely. And he makes the same mistakes for which he himself reproached his nominalistic opponents in his first main work, **Logische Untersuchungen**, where he showed that universals were already supposed by those who argued against them. They maintain, for instance, that universals are founded upon the experience of many real things which are similar to one another. A universal may be derived if we abstract from them what is different in them. Husserl, however, objected correctly: If I did not already know the universal as the identical and not the different in similar things, I would not know either in what respect these things are different or from what things I have to abstract. Every similarity already presupposes the universal, in view of which things are similar to one another.

In his last essay Husserl himself makes the very mistakes typical of the nominalists. He is operating with concepts like "practice of improving," "approximation," "typical likeness," "repeating," and "custom." By these concepts he may explain how the identical and invariant meaning of geometrical figures results, although they do not objectively exist. But all these concepts assume just those determined figures as the identical and invariant goal and aim of these experiences of "improving," "approximating," "repeating," "custom," "typical likeness."[36] It is, for instance, impossible to aim at or approximate motion within a space if one does not know already where to aim and what to approximate. There is no aiming or approximating without an aim. Without distinct contents which may serve as a goal to prescribe where and in what direction a motion must occur, it is impossible to speak of fixed rules of motion or determined methods of governing them. These contents, however, are the geometrical figures.

(5) Moreover, I cannot admit that we are unable to have an adequate and complete intuition of geometrical figures simultaneously and without perspective distortion. In spite of all theories, it is a matter of fact that we perceive, for instance, rectangles and cubes rectangularly and not inclined, corresponding to their perspective distortion. We usually perceive the rectangles of our dwellings and furniture through their perspective appearance. To see perspective distortions requires of draftsmen and painters, as every one knows, very much practice and training.

(6) But these empirical facts of seeing the real thing *through* its distorting appearance do apply not only to geometrical figures but also to the real thing in itself. This penetrating character (*Mehrschichtigkeit*) of perceptual experiences radically contradicts Husserl's description. It is hardly true that the objective reality of an identical thing

means only a certain agreement of appearances succeeding one another in a continual stream of consciousness. Already in single separate appearances the thing manifests itself as certain and identical, visible through its various appearances. It manifests itself as different from both its single and its total appearances.

(7) According to Husserl particular peculiarities of the bodily thing are psychical, being generated by human subjectivity.[37] But every one distinguishes psychical and physical peculiarities as *qualities*. One cannot differentiate psychical and physical from one another just by applying them to a bodily thing or an individual ego. There are essential differences between psychical and physical, excluding *a priori,* for instance, the color red from becoming some time in the future an attribute of a psychical being, or joy from becoming an attribute of a bodily thing.

Just so, too, a bodily thing, for instance, a piece of sugar, does not mean only a formal objective reality or identity or an agreement of appearances. But every thing is also an entity determined as a certain essential *quid*. In short: the differences between a bodily thing and a psychical ego are determined long before all phenomena of realization. And the general essence of a thing disproves all research methods deriving the world of bodily things from human subjectivity as *a priori* contradictory.

(8) But that is not all. One cannot approve, it seems to me, of the fundamental assumption of Husserl's theory and method, namely that only the physical adumbrates itself by appearances, whereas the psychical does not. Husserl's entire theory of the immanent self-evidence of consciousness stands or falls with this thesis. But it falls! For the psychical adumbrates itself and appears in another psychical phenomenon. For instance, the psychical subject, namely I, as a certain individual essence[38] manifests itself in its acts in just the same way as an inanimate thing by its peculiarities. There is a very old and difficult science concerned with these phenomena; it is that of the practical psychologists, of the great poets and moralists, the theologians and philosophers, which is able to apprehend the constant psychical being through many different psychical phenomena. Husserl's assertion that the psychical does not adumbrate itself[39] is a mere theoretical invention, contradictory to experience.

(9) Husserl truly wants to describe the consciousness of an objective world reality. But his analysis contradicts the conviction of common sense and perverts it radically. Every one is convinced that everything must also have its reverse side; he knows it *a priori* through the evidence of the general character of a bodily thing as being extended within space. And because everyone knows it already, he also expects that when going around the bodily thing, he certainly will, as a matter of course, see the reverse side of it.

Husserl, however, turns that matter of fact into this: Through the continuity of agreeing experience concerning the adumbration of things I am always expecting a reverse side of a thing. If such an expectation is verified, it marks an agreement of experience which is meant by the objective reality of things, namely not a real thing independently existing from its experiences, but only that continuity and harmony of experiences.

It radically contradicts common sense to believe that subjectivity produces ("leistet") the world. Everyone is convinced that the world is pregiven in itself to all perception of it. Such a world produced by human subjectivity would not be called reality, objectivity, truth by common sense—but rather illusion, deception!

(10) It is true that a corporeal thing always appears to us as one-sided, fragmentary, and never at once complete. Husserl asserts it as necessarily founded in the essential nature of a material thing, as not really and objectively existing in itself, but only as a certain succession and synthesis of appearances to consciousness. But the fact that things become reality to us through a certain succession of one-sided appearances—the so-called adumbrations ("Abschattungen")—is by no means a proof for the subjectivity of things. It is only a necessary consequence of our own finiteness. Our intellect as body-bound is compelled to perceive corporeal things only from one point of view, namely that of our own body. And, therefore, we can of course see only those sides of a thing which it objectively turns towards our point of view. Just because the corporeal thing exists really and objectively in itself, it turns various of its sides towards various standpoints. A certain correlation between certain standpoints of perceiving a thing and certain sides of its appearances proves by itself the objective reality of a bodily thing as being pregiven to its being perceived. The lawfulness of this correlation, deprived of all free will, is sufficient to contradict the subjectivity of perceiving.

To interpret the fact that things appear to us to be only one-sided as founded in the essential nature of a corporeal thing itself, as well as to assert an essential impossibility of another kind of perceiving a thing, cannot be accepted. Certainly the intellect of God as *omnipresent* must be held able to perceive beyond all particular standpoints. It is a logical consequence of this omnipresence of God's intellect that He must perceive material things completely and not always as only one-sided.

Therefore, a certain succession and synthesis of only one-sided appearances cannot be considered, either, as an ingredient of general reason necessarily regulating for everyone the perception of things.

(11) It is true that our practice and interests cause the world of our perceptions.[40] We should never discover in this world things like houses, streets, clothing, books, etc., if we were mere intellects, without bodily and practical wants. Men of former times certainly looked upon the old instruments in our museums in a way completely different from ours. Likewise it is true that the world of human per-

ceptions is always being involved in a historical change, as Hegel and his pupils (Dilthey included) have shown.

That all seems to prove Husserl's assertion that the objective world is, in truth, only caused by human subjectivity. And yet it is wrong. Why? Because subjectivity (as a function of the psychical ego) and consciousness (as a function of the perceiving intellect) are different.

The evidence for this opinion, together with an explanation of Husserl's concept of intentionality is dealt with by me in my *Psychologie*. Of the result of that work, it can be mentioned here only that human subjectivity, too, exists objectively and really for the perceiving intellect just as well as in the appearance of the environment created by the subjectivity. In the *Psychologie* I also deal with the thesis of a "realistic perspectivism"[41] which says that appearances, too, exist really and are created by subjectivity, not made by the intellect as the subject of the perceiving, but are found as objectively pregiven to the intellect, from a certain objective point of view.

(12) The most important objection against Husserl's statements is his wrong conception of reason. He describes reason as forming itself first by building up real experience, and not preceding it.[42]

Formerly Husserl was on the way to the right conception of reason when, in his **Logische Untersuchungen** he cleared away misinterpretations of the phenomenon of "ideally" existing universals. For only in the course of so-called "Platonism" (today completely misunderstood as a fable about mysterious things beyond experience) can the problem of reason be solved, namely as a phenomenon of self-evident, necessary relations among the mere *what* or *which* of existing things, whereby an abstraction is made from the particular cases which are present here and now.

Later, however, Husserl himself misinterpreted the phenomenon of "ideal" and "irreal" existence as a phenomenon forming the experience in which real single cases are approximately equally and invariantly repeated. As a phenomenon of a certain experience of a real single case, it became again a phenomenon of an experience concerning reality instead of a phenomenon concerning the experience of ideas

Let us repeat: The reality and facticity of this experience cannot be eliminated by eliminating its meaning as objectively existent beyond consciousness. Even Husserl's "transcendentally purified consciousness," preserves the facticity and reality of the "stream of consciousness," within which all phenomenological statements are made.

The self-evidence of reason is completely different from the self-evidence of all immediately and originally experienced facticity. The self-evidence of reason is a self-evidence of understanding why under the same circumstances a certain thing necessarily behaves toward another thing in the same way. The reason for this necessity, how-

ever, is seen in the *what* and *how* of things. The pure *what* and *how* of things necessarily determine their behavior toward one another. The same *what* and *how*, however, can be repeated in an infinite number of real isolated cases. This *what* and *how* as such are what so-called Platonism means when speaking about "ideas." These "ideas" are seen as indifferent concerning their realization here and now, there and then. On principle, however, it is also sensible to speak about individual ideas.[43] For ideas are intended as certain contents, and not as generalizations, in view of individual cases.

Husserl, however, bases all these analyses of generalizations upon an assumed relation of them to their realization in individual cases. He interprets the apodictic validity of generalizations as a constitution from an inductive experience by which real individual cases are only approximately repeated in an equal and invariant way.[44] In this manner the phenomenon of ideas (and thus also that of reason) becomes for him solely a problem of the facticity of real individual cases.[45]

Notes

1. Published in *Philosophia,* vol. I (1936).

2. Pages 85-6.

3. Page 84.

4. Page 141.

5. Pages 88-92.

6. Page 92.

7. Page 128.

8. Pages 108-13, 136.

9. Pages 103, 124, 125, 128.

10. Pages 103, 126, 127.

11. Pages 119, 121. Cf. my article, "Geiz als Wurzel der faustisch-dynamischen Kultur," *Philosophische Hefte,* vol. III (1931), p. 15.

12. Page 129.

13. Page 137.

14. Page 135.

15. Husserl's former analyses, especially *Ideen zu einer reinen Phänomenologie und phänomenologischen Forschung,* p. 315, are presupposed here.

16. Pages 136, 138, 139.

17. Pages 142, 143.

18. Page 141.

19. Page 162.

20. Pages 163, 171.

21. Pages 82, 83, 85.

22. Page 94; *Ideen,* pp. 43, 121, 147.

23. Pages 174, 151, 157.

24. Pages 96-7.

25. Pages 86, 92.

26. Pages 101-2.

27. Page 92.

28. Pages 90, 92, 174.

29. Page 83.

30. Pages 152-7.

31. Leiden (Netherlands), 1938. Cf. especially pp. 46ff., where § 37 of Husserl's *Ideen* is discussed.

32. Pages 91-2.

33. Page 106.

34. Page 102.

35. Page 100.

36. Pages 99, 100, 105.

37. Pages 165, 171-2, 157.

38. This, of course, must not be mistaken for what Husserl himself calls according to his theory, the individual psychical subject.

39. Cf. *Ideen,* p. 77.

40. Page 144.

41. Cf. my article, "Neue Problemlage der Erkenntnistheorie" in *Deutsche Vierteljahrsschrift für Literaturwissenschraft und Geistesgeschichte,* (1928), no. 4, p. 629 and "Ideelle Existenz" in *Philosophische Hefte,* vol. I (1929), p. 183.

42. Pages 144, 171-4.

43. It is not by chance that the separation of realistic phenomenology from Husserl started first with the rediscovery of the "individual essence" (*Individualwesen*). There seems to me to exist a necessary connection between this thesis and the strengthening of the realistic tendency concerning universals. For in this way the contents of ideas alone, and not their generality, is stressed as a decisive matter, as distinguished from their existence. If reality is no longer identical with individuality, then reality cannot be opposed either to ideality as the generalization of real individual cases.

44. Pages 100, 105, etc., 111, 115, 117, 124, 126.

45. Concerning Platonism, cf. my papers, "L'Irrationalisme actuel, sa nature, ses origines, et le moyen de le surmonter," in the *Revue de Metaphysique et de Morale,* (1934), and "Kants Ablehnung der traditionellen Ideenlehre" in *Philosophischer Anzeiger,* vol. IV (1930), no. 3, and "Ideelle Existenz."

Herbert Spiegelberg (essay date 1956)

SOURCE: "Husserl's and Peirce's Phenomenologies: Coincidence or Interaction," in *Philosophy and Phenomenological Research,* Vol. XVII, No. 1, September, 1956, pp. 164-85.

[*In the following essay, Spiegelberg compares the phenomenological philosophies of Husserl and Charles Sanders Peirce, and explores the extent of each philosopher's awareness of and influence upon the other's work.*]

Until the late thirties, phenomenology in today's sense of the term was for American philosophy a "foreign affair." To this generalization there is only one possible exception: the phenomenology of Charles Sanders Peirce.[1] True, the mere absence of the word from the works of other American philosophers does not prove the absence of the thing so designated. Thus the psychology of William James and the philosophy of George Santayana contain many phenomenological ingredients without the trademark. On the other hand, the mere presence of the name "phenomenology" in Peirce's writings constitutes no guarantee that it meant the same thing to him as it did to Edmund Husserl. The principal objective of the present paper is therefore to determine whether and to what extent there is common ground between Peirce's and Husserl's ideas, and whether this ground is sufficient to speak of their phenomenology in the singular.[2] In so far as such common ground emerges, I shall also discuss the possibility of mutual influences.

My point of departure will be the following remarkable coincidence. In 1901 the second volume of Husserl's ***Logische Untersuchungen*** appeared under the title of ***Untersuchungen zur Phanomenologie und Theorie der Erkenntnis***, a book in which Husserl used the word "Phänomenologie" prominently for the first time. The following year, 1902, seems to be the earliest certain date for Peirce's use of the term "phenomenology" as a label for a branch of his new classification of the sciences and of philosophy in particular.[3] Yet, while Husserl not only continued using it, but even made it the official label of his philosophy, Peirce, as will be shown in a later section, abandoned the term after about two years, to replace it by several neologisms, among which "phaneroscopy" is the one best known. What was behind this striking though temporary terminological parallel?

In trying to answer this question I shall begin with Husserl's phenomenology and then in this light discuss comparable features of Peirce's phenomenology. One minor reason for beginning with Husserl is that his use of the term 'phenomenology' apparently precedes Peirce's by at least one year. A more important one is that it will facilitate the subsequent comparison.

(1) THE NUCLEUS OF HUSSERL'S PHENOMENOLOGY

It would be foolhardy to attempt here a full presentation of Husserl's phenomenology, let alone of that of other phenomenologists. Besides, Husserl's conception of phenomenology was a growing and changing one, and this is not the place to trace its development. Instead I shall try (1) to point out the germinal idea of Husserl's phenomenology as it stood when Peirce was formulating his own conception of phenomenology, and (2) to indicate the later direction which it was to take.

When Husserl first used the term "phenomenology" in 1900 in a footnote close to the end of the first volume of his *Logische Untersuchungen*, which contained his celebrated refutation of psychologism in logic, he was hardly aware of a revolutionary philosophical or terminological innovation. He simply adopted a term then freely in use among various philosophical and scientific thinkers. These ranged all the way from the Hegelians to positivists like Ernst Mach, with whose use of the term in physics Husserl was demonstrably familiar. What was significant, nevertheless, was the wording of this footnote. For, after once more rejecting the "psychologistic" claims of an *empirical* psychology to supply the foundations for a pure logic, Husserl contrasted it with a "descriptive *Phänomenologie* of inner experience which forms the foundation of empirical psychology and, in a very different sense, at the same time of the critique of knowledge." This formulation[4] was the one which Husserl tried to develop and to exemplify in the decisive second volume of the *Logische Untersuchungen*, published in 1901.

The introduction to this volume contained the first systematic attempt to clarify the scope and character of such a pre-psychology and pre-epistemology, as one might call it. Among the main characteristics of this new strange science of experience were (*a*) its *purity,* (*b*) its *reflective character,* and (*c*) its analytic approach based on the pattern of so-called *intentionality.*

(*a*) *Purity* actually meant two things: Negatively, it signified independence of empirical facts; for phenomenology "makes not the slightest assertion about existence," even though most of its material may come from experience. Thus it was to study perception in its ideal structure, regardless of whether such ideal perception has ever occurred in psychological observation. Positively, purity meant exclusive concern for the general essences of the experiences in question; for phenomenology concentrated on their essential properties, while disregarding their accidental modifications in individual cases. Thus it had no interest in mere individual case studies of perception.

(*b*) *Reflectiveness* implied that phenomenology turned its attention to the way in which phenomena, for instance percepts, were given to our intuitive experience (*Anschauung*). It studied particularly the varying aspects under which these phenomena may present themselves, and the various degrees of clarity with which they were given,

(*c*) *Intentional* analysis implied that phenomenology analyzed and described the phenomena in terms of their intentional structure, that is, paying equal attention to the intending act, e.g., the perceiving, and to the intended content, e.g., the perceived. As is now commonly recognized, it was Husserl's teacher, Franz Brentano, who had first drawn attention to the phenomenon of intentional reference. But he had used it only to distinguish between psychology and the physical sciences. Husserl made it the basis for a methodical analysis of all phenomena of consciousness in which the parallel structures of the intending

acts and the intended contents were studied in their reciprocal relationships.

In the *Logische Untersuchungen* Husserl had applied this reflective analysis of consciousness in its pure structures only to the foundations of logic and mathematics. But during the first decade of the new century, he came to extend it to an ever widening range of phenomena, until he finally formulated the program of phenomenology as that of the universal foundation of science and of every philosophy that aspired to be a rigorous science (*strenge Wissenschaft*).

Up to 1906 Husserl's phenomenology was epistemologically neutral, although his doctrine of essences showed a decided tendency toward a Platonic realism. The subsequent development of his phenomenological idealism occurs in a period when Peirce had already stopped using the name "phenomenology." Nevertheless the general direction of Husserl's phenomenology should at least be indicated, if only for the sake of the record, which continues to be marred by the seemingly ineradicable legend of Husserl's epistemological realism. In 1906, in his Göttingen lectures on the *Idee der Phänomenologie*, Husserl, under the influence of Descartes' method of doubt, introduced for the first time his method of "reduction" or bracketing, which demanded the suspension of all belief in the existence of the world of our naive experience. In due course this led to the development of a phenomenological idealism, which became manifest first in the *Ideen* of 1913 and assumed even more radical form later on. While Husserl himself increasingly insisted on the fundamental importance of this step, not yet mentioned as such in the *Logische Untersuchungen*, I shall refrain from discussing this highly technical and controversial subject in this context. Yet it is important to realize that Husserl now conceived of phenomenology as a study inaccessible to the "naive" or "natural" approach. According to this later interpretation it required a fundamental reversal of this approach, which was to give access to an entirely new dimension in the world of every-day experience. It is hardly necessary to point out that this later Neo-Cartesian approach would have been utterly inacceptable to Peirce, the avowed anti-Cartesian.

(2) PEIRCE'S PHENOMENOLOGY AS SEEN FROM HUSSERL'S PERSPECTIVE

I shall not dwell upon the fundamental importance which the later Peirce attached to his new discipline of phenomenology or phaneroscopy.[5] Nor shall I attempt to duplicate accounts of Peirce's phenomenology which can be found in the comprehensive studies of such Peirce scholars as James Feibleman, Manley Thompson and Thomas A. Goudge, all based on the texts published in the *Collected Papers,* edited by Charles Hartshorne and Paul Weiss. Instead I want to utilize a still unpublished statement on phenomenology contained in one of Peirce's letters to William James, of which only a small part has been printed in Ralph Barton Perry's selection from the James-Peirce correspondence.[6] The background for this statement is briefly as follows: In an earlier letter, dated June 8, 1903, Peirce had tried vainly to convince James of the necessity of his new phenomenology as outlined in his first two Harvard Lectures on Pragmatism—those lectures which had elicited James' well-known remark about "flashes of brilliant light relieved against Cymmerian darkness;" in fact, it seems that it was precisely Peirce's doctrine of the phenomenological categories, i.e., firstness, secondness, and thirdness, which James had found so dark.[7] Now, in a second letter, dated October 3, 1904, in replying to the reprint of James' essay "Does consciousness exist?," Peirce tries to prove to James that his phenomenology is really what James himself was propounding under the new title of radical empiricism.[8] So he writes:

> As I understand you, then, the proposition you are arguing is a proposition in what I called *phenomenology,* that is just the analysis of what kind of constituents there are in our thoughts and lives (whether these be valid or invalid being quite aside from the question). It is a branch of philosophy I am most deeply interested in and which I have worked upon almost as much as I have upon logic. (*Here the letter shows an insert:* It has nothing to do with psychology.) . . . Perhaps the most important aspect of the series of papers of which the one you sent me is the first, will prove to be that phenomenology is one science and psychology a very different one. . . . Phenomenology has no right to appeal to logic, except to deductive logic. On the contrary, logic must be founded on phenomenology. Psychology, you may say, observes the same facts as phenomenology does. No. It does not *observe* the same facts. It looks upon the same world and the same world that the astronomer looks at but what it observes in that world is different. Psychology of all sciences stands most in need of the discoveries of the logician, which he makes by the aid of the phenomenologist.

There is hardly one sentence in this statement with which Husserl could not fully agree. What would have had Husserl's particular approval is the disregard for the question of validity or invalidity, the emphasis on the radical difference between phenomenology and psychology, the affirmation that phenomenology is a science, a point particularly important to Husserl, and as such the foundation not only of philosophy, but even of logic. Nor would this exhaust the list of possible agreements.

But behind the agreements of this programmatic façade of Peirce's phenomenology there remain considerable differences. Of these I shall select merely those most relevant to the proposed comparison.

A. The Phenomenology of Categories

The conception of Peirce's phenomenology had grown out of his pervading interest in a system of categories for the entire universe of knowledge. It "simply contemplates the Universal Phenomenon and discerns its ubiquitous elements, Firstness, Secondness and Thirdness, together perhaps with other series of categories." (5. 121) As such it was to exclude only the "the universal and necessary laws

of the relations of Phenomena to Ends," which Peirce reserved for *Normative Science,* and the consideration of the "Reality of Phenomena," which he left to *Metaphysics.* (5. 121) Thus, Peirce's phenomenology was primarily motivated by his intent to find a system of categories for all the ranges of being as such, an intent congenial primarily to Aristotle's science of being *qua* being, i.e., his metaphysics in the sense of ontology.

There is no direct parallel to this objective in Husserl's phenomenology, whose primary concern was epistemological. While Peirce's interest in ontological categories may not be incompatible with Husserl's philosophizing—some of it is reflected in the "formal ontology" of his Pure Logic—his phenomenology shows no particular interest in the search for and discovery of a system of categories nor any parallel to Peirce's triadic pattern.

B. The Nature of Firstness

The basic category in Peirce's phenomenology is Firstness. However, though pivotal to the whole scheme, it is far from easy to understand, since it is actually "the most elusive" of the categories.[9] Firstnesses, according to Peirce's chief characterization, consist in "Qualities" or "Qualities of Feeling." Without discussing ambiguities of this term, one had best consider its denotation which, while of "myriad-fold variety" includes such items as redness, an odor, "an infinite dead ache," and nobleness. (5. 44) Thus Firstnesses seem to coincide chiefly with what are usually called 'data,' although not only with sense data.

It would appear that in the beginning Peirce himself was far from sure that anything like a systematic study of these qualities in their chance-like flux was possible. Thus, in his *Guess at the Riddle* (1890) he wrote:

> Firstness precedes all synthesis and all differentiation; it has no unity and no parts. It cannot be articulately thought; assert it, and it has already lost its innocence; for assertion always implies the denial of something else. . . . Remember that every description of it must be false to it.

> (1. 357)

Considering such a nearly Heraclitean, or even Cratylean, picture it is not surprising that Peirce never gave any systematic development of his phenomenological program, a fact which is actually the major obstacle to a full-scale comparison between the two phenomenologies. Husserl, much as he realized that in this area precise mathematical description was essentially impossible,[10] was never that pessimistic as to the chances of phenomenological description. And while he never arrived at a final formulation of his phenomenology, he left at least an impressive array of concrete systematic studies.

Nevertheless, it would seem that even Peirce had become more hopeful as to the chances of a scientific study of Firstness by the time he had adopted the term "phenomenology" for his science of categories. Thus, when he advanced the program of phenomenology as a science in his Lectures on Pragmatism of 1903, he merely stressed the need for the student of phenomenology—in the letter to James of October 3, 1904, he called him actually the "phenomenologist"—to develop the following three qualities:

(1) "Seeing what stares one in the face, just as it presents itself, unreplaced by any interpretation, unsophisticated by any allowance for this or that modifying circumstance;"

(2) "resolute discrimination, which fastens itself like a bulldog upon the particular features that we are studying;" and

(3) "the generalizing power of the mathematician who produces the abstract formula that comprehends the very essence of the feature under examination purified from all admixture of extraneous and irrelevant accompaniments."

(C.P. 5. 42)

I can think of few, if any, passages in Husserl's writings in which the primary requirements of the phenomenological approach are stated with equal impressiveness.

But even at this stage there remained certain basic ambiguities in Peirce's conception of Firstness which make a full-scale comparison with equivalents in Husserl's phenomenology next to impossible. Thus, as far as I can make out, Peirce's Firstness occurs as a result of two basically incompatible procedures. According to the one, represented in the quotations above, it makes its first appearance once we assume a merely passive, receptive attitude and abstain from all tampering with the phenomena.[11] According to other passages, however, it would seem that Firstness is given as a result of an operation called "prescission," a type of abstraction without which it is impossible to even distinguish between the various categories. (4.235) In fact, in such contexts Firstness is even called "the most abstract of the categories," an "abstract potentality," and "a pure abstraction" (1.551); also, in his "New List of Categories" (1867) Peirce explicitly contested the view that qualities are "given in the impression." Thus there may well have been a shift in Peirce's views about the proper approach to Firstness. Nevertheless, he seems to have held at all times that "separation from all conception of reference to anything else" was characteristic of all Firstness.

Does Husserl's conception of phenomena have any equivalent of Peirce's Firstness? True, Husserl has an elaborate theory of abstractions, in which there is also room for the isolation or prescission of various features in them. But he indicates no preference for qualities as having a privileged status over other types of properties such as quantity or even of substance. In fact, from Husserl's original viewpoint there seems to be no reason for assigning priority to any particular aspect of phenomena. If at all, such priority pertains to the phenomenon as a structured and interrelated whole, which, for Husserl as well as for the gestaltists, is characterized primarily by the character of unity in the context of a horizon, or world.

There is, to be sure, in Husserl's analysis of phenomena an element, later on designated as the "hyletic datum," which one might feel tempted to relate to Pierce's Firstness. But this raw material for fully constituted phenomena is so closely linked up with Husserl's whole conception of knowledge as an "intentional" process that there would seem to be little sense in correlating it with Peirce's thought, without discussing at the same time this very conception, for which, as will be shown, there is no clear equivalent in Peirce.

c. Secondness and Thirdness

There is in Husserl's scheme no exact equivalent of Secondness, as little as there was one of Firstness. Secondness, characterized by Peirce as "the most prominent" of the three categories, is to him an "experience," which "comes out most fully in the shock of reaction between ego and non-ego," in the "double consciousness of effort and resistance."[12] Its primary character, according to Peirce, is "struggle." (5.45) It has also a "predominant" place in the idea of reality. (1.325)

Husserl reserves no peculiar status for the phenomena of interaction between ego and non-ego and for "struggle" in particular. The closest to it one might discover is the peculiar treatment he accords to the character of existence in connection with the operation of phenomenological reduction, or bracketing. For it implies that existence is presented in a way quite different from essence, which does not call, nor even allow for, a parallel operation. In passing it might be mentioned, however, that Max Scheler's conception of reality as revealed in the experience of resistance comes very close to Peirce's conception of Secondness.

Peirce's Thirdness, which, not differently from Firstness, defies any brash attempt at a definition, may be said, nevertheless, to consist in a connecting bond mediating between the other two categories. Its prime examples for Peirce are signs, meanings and general laws. Husserl, again, has no comparable status for these phenomena either. It seems legitimate, however, to suggest that his theory of intentionality, at least insofar as it deals with the structure of signs, would find its proper place under Peirce's Thirdness.

d. The Non-reflective Nature of Peirce's Phenomenology

Peirce's main injunction to the phenomenologist is to look at what is "before our minds," at "what stares one in the face." It is therefore not surprising that his findings consist primarily of such qualities as colors, rarely, if ever, of items like consciousness or acts such as seeing or hearing, but never of the "mind" itself, an entity of rather uncertain status in Peirce's whole philosophizing. Only introspection could possibly reveal it, and such introspection is for

Peirce a matter of inference (5.462, 5.244 ff.), hence not accessible to phenomenology.

From Husserl's point of view, such an approach can at best develop a phenomenology of the intended contents straight ahead (*geradeaus*), a phenomenology such as was developed particularly by some of Husserl's early students under the name of *Gegenstands-phänomenologie,* but never a phenomenology of our acts and of the structure of our consciousness. By contrast, Husserl wants us to focus as much on what is within as on what is ahead. In fact, reflection on the acts of our consciousness is for Husserl the decisive step, though only the first step, in the development of a phenomenological psychology. In Peirce's perspective there is no room for such a psychology. Actually, he seems sceptical of, if not downright hostile to, all existing psychology. Against the background of such "antipsychologism," Husserl's attitude appears to be equally removed from a certain phobia of logic in James and a similar phobia of psychology in Peirce. What Husserl's phenomenology tries to establish is, among other things, a deeper link between logic and psychology, while defending the autonomy of each.

E. THE ABSENCE OF INTENTIONALITY FROM PEIRCE'S PHENOMENOLOGY

Closely related to the preceding point is probably the most basic difference between Peirce's and Husserl's phenomenologies: the absence in Peirce of what Husserl called "intentionality."

Apparently, when Peirce speaks of Firstnesses as "qualities of feeling," he never distinguishes between the quality felt and the feeling *of* a quality. Thus it is not surprising that he lists among his Firstnesses the color of magenta side by side with the quality of emotion upon contemplating a fine mathematical demonstration, the quality of the feeling of love, etc. (1.304) In fact, in his "Objective Logic" (6.221) Peirce goes so far as to say that "a quality is a consciousness" and speaks subsequently of a "*quale*-consciousness," which he illustrates by sense-data such as redness. Here Peirce simply shares the monistic conception of phenomena, which can also be found in Ernst Mach and in the radical empiricism of the later William James.

By contrast, Husserl's conception of consciousness is fundamentally "bi-polar" (a term which seems to me more expressive than Perry's ambiguous "dualistic"). This allows Husserl not only to distinguish between acts and contents but also to pay special attention to the varying subjective appearances of the identical objective contents. It also yields a much more differentiated structure of the field of phenomena compared with Peirce's phenomenon of Firstness, which consists simply in a sequence of "seemings," without any structural depth or referential links. It is only Secondness and Thirdness that would seem to open up the possibility of phenomena comparable with Husserl's intentional patterns.

Thus, seen from Husserl's perspective, Peirce covers at best half of the world of phenomena, namely the objective or intended pole of our consciousness. The other half, the subjective or intending pole of it, remains outside its scope.[13]

The fact that Peirce's phenomenology does not include Husserl's intentionality of consciousness as the basic structure in the field of phenomena does not prevent that at least some of it is paralleled in a more limited area of Peirce's phenomenology, notably in his theory of Thirdness, in as much as it deals with the nature of signs. For the relationship between the "repraesentamen," the "object" and the "interpretant" is clearly based on some kind of reference from the sign to the object, although Peirce does not give any further description of this relationship except by words like "representation" or "signifying."

Now, Husserl too shows a considerable interest in the theory of signs. In fact, the second volume of his *Logische Untersuchungen* begins with a study of symbolism (*Ausdruck und Bedeutung*). It is here, in connection with his discussion of the structure of signs, that he introduces for the first time his doctrine of intentionality. Only in later parts of his work does he take up the intentionality of conscious acts, which also provides indirectly the foundation for the intentionality of signs. It is thus the first and more limited study which comes closest to Peirce's theory of signs as an outstanding case of Thirdness.

F. PEIRCE'S "FIRSTNESS" AND "SECONDNESS" AS PARTICULARS, NOT UNIVERSALS

Phenomenology in Husserl's sense is a study of the general essence of phenomena. Particulars may be used as stepping stones for insights into these general essences. But, at least for Husserl, there can be no phenomenology of particulars.

How far are the basic categories of Peirce's phenomenology either particulars or universals? In describing Firstnesses as qualities of feeling Peirce never makes their status plain in terms of this alternative. All he requests is the disregard of the question of reality and of connections with other phenomena. However, the fact that universals appear only under the heading of Thirdness indicates that neither Firstnesses nor Secondnesses have reached the level of universality. As to Secondness, Peirce, in denying that it can ever be conceived, asserts explicitly its essential individuality.[14]

G. INDUCTION AS THE METHOD OF PEIRCE'S PHENOMENOLOGY

The preceding section does not mean to imply that Peirce's phenomenology exhausts itself in a description of particular phenomena. For Peirce states clearly that the task of his phenomenology is to find the universal qualities of the "phenomena" by way of inductive generalization. It is, however, this very generalization which again marks an important difference from Husserl's method of determining the properties of his "phenomena." For here Husserl appeals to his characteristic intuition of essences

(*Wesensschau*). It would be beyond the scope of this account to give a full explanation of what this involves. But it certainly differs from a mere collecting generalization. For, while based on a study of examples, real and imaginary, it tries to grasp their essential character and properties in a special and unique way, very much in the manner of what W. E. Johnson in later years described under the name of intuitive induction. There is no indication that Peirce's phenomenological generalization involved a similar operation.

H. DIFFERENT ESTIMATES OF MATHEMATICS

Particularly in his criticisms of Hegel's phenomenology, Peirce, deploring his neglect of mathematics, claimed for this study the status of the fundamental science, more fundamental even than phenomenology. Despite Husserl's own indifference, if not hostility, to Hegel, this fact would also mark a sharp dividing line between Peirce and Husserl, although Husserl can certainly not be charged with a neglect of mathematics. But whereas Peirce never seems to have questioned mathematics and never seems to have been disturbed by the so-called crisis in the foundations of mathematics, as other philosophical mathematicians have been, these very difficulties were at the root of Husserl's whole turn to philosophy and ultimately to phenomenology. To him phenomenology was designed to supply not only an ultimate philosophical foundation for logic but also for a *mathematica universalis* of which mathematics proper was to be only a part. Mathematics was therefore to him anything but a pre-philosophical self-sufficient discipline. Here Husserl shares the view, proposed most effectively in Russell's and Whitehead's *Principia Mathematica,* about the derivative character of mathematics. Actually, according to Goudge's interpretation, even Peirce originally took this position.[15] I shall refrain from discussing the reasons for Peirce's reversal and for his ensuing classification of the sciences in the order mathematics-phenomenology-logic.

I. THE "ETHICS" OF THE PHENOMENOLOGICAL TERMINOLOGY

Finally, there are some aspects in the comparative histories of the term "phenomenology" in Husserl and in Peirce which throw revealing light on the different spirit of the two enterprises.

Husserl never seems to have given explicit thought to the question of the principles, let alone, the ethics, of philosophical terminology. Nor does he seem to have been guided even unconsciously by any definite policy in adopting and modifying pre-existing philosophical terms. Thus, when he took over the term "phenomenology" in 1900, which was then widely and loosely used in Germany, he seems to have felt no hesitation in assigning to it a new and more specific meaning. At that time, and even more so later on, he simply implied that he had the right to change the traditional meanings in accordance with his own evolving and deepening conception of phenomenology—a fact

which has been responsible for a good deal of confusion without and even within the so-called Phenomenological Movement.

In contrast, Peirce's scrupulous ethics of terminology not only forbade him to adopt terms which had been in use for different designata, but induced him to abandon them when they were being misused by others. Thus, quoting once more from the letter to James of October 3, 1904, Peirce, after taking James to task for his use of the term "pure experience," and recommending to him again his choice "phenomenology" states:

> It is downright bad morals so to misuse words, for it prevents philosophy from becoming a science . . . it is an indispensable requisite of science that it should have a recognized technical vocabulary composed of words so unattractive that loose thinkers are not tempted to use them, and a recognized and legitimated way of making up new words freely when a new conception is introduced, and that it is vital for science that he who introduces a new conception should be held to have a *duty* imposed upon him to invent a sufficiently disagreeable series of words to express it. I wish you would reflect seriously upon the moral aspect of terminology.[16]

It is well known how this stringent ethics made Peirce, when "finding his bantling 'pragmatism' wrongly promoted" (to wit, by James and Schiller)

> kissed his child good-by and relinquished it to its higher destiny; while, to serve the precise purpose of expressing the original definition, he begs to announce the birth of the word pragmaticism which is ugly enough to be safe from kidnappers.

(C.P. 5.414)

Apparently it has not yet been realized that the very same principles responsible for this terminological purge were also effective in both Peirce's original choice of the term "phenomenology" and its later abandonment and replacement.

It was probably in the early years of the new century that Peirce, having developed his conception of a science of categories in the nineties, also began looking for an appropriate label for it.[17] About the same time he came to think that his triadic pattern of categories was so similar to Hegel's scheme that he called his own philosophy a "variety of Hegelianism" (5.38) and a "resuscitation of Hegel, though in a strange costume" (1.42)—this despite the fact that he confessed to his original antipathy and even to his feeling of repulsion toward Hegel.[18] Thus it may well have been this new interest in Hegel which gave him the idea that Hegel's term "phenomenology" could be used without undue violence for the common doctrine of categories, although the equivalent of what Peirce interprets as Hegel's categories actually occurs in Hegel's *Encyclopedia of the Philosophical Sciences* (Part I), rather than in the *Phenomenology of the Spirit* .[19] In adopting it, he was probably guided more by the literal meaning of the term "phenomenology", as "a description or history of phenomena" (see, for instance, the *Century Dictionary and Cyclopedia* VI (1891), p. 4441), than by Hegel's much more restricted use in the third part of the *Enzyklopädie,* translated by Wallace two years later in a separate volume (*Hegel's Philosophy of Mind*).[20]

There are a number of concrete evidences for Peirce's acute interest in Hegel just during these years. The invitation which he extended to Josiah Royce to spend the summer of 1902 with him in Milford is one of them.[21] An even more concrete expression of his intensified stake in Hegel can be found in two reviews of books on Hegel for the *Nation.* Of these, the one on J. B. Baillíe's *The Origin and Significance of Hegel's Logic,* published on November 12, 1902 (Vol. 75, p. 390), contains one of the peaks of Peirce's Hegelianism, even at that clearly not without reservations:

> Hegel is a vast intellect. The properly prepared student cannot but feel that the mere contemplation of the problems he presents is good. But the student of Hegelianism tends too much toward subjectivism, and is apt to break the natural power of penetrating fallacy, which is common to all men except students of logic, especially of the German stripe.

The second review, that of J. G. Hibben's book on *Hegel's Logic* published on May 21, 1903 (Vol. 76, 419-2, 420), reveals a much severer judgment on Hegel. Thus, he states that the Logik "now condemns itself," being "anti-evolutionary," and "anti-progressive," because, as he says, "it represents thought as attaining perfect fulfilment." More pertinent to the subject of phenomenology is the following passage:

> It is evident enough that all Hegel's categories properly belong to his third grand division, the *Begriff.* What, for example, could be more monstrous than to call such a conception as that of being a primitive one, or, indeed, what more absurd than to say that the *immediate* is *abstract*? We might instance a dozen of such self-refutations. That the Hegelians should have allowed the obviously unsuccessful development of the doctrine of *Wesen* to stand all these years uncorrected, is a striking instance of the mental fossilization that results from their method of study. A powerful and original study of what the true Hegelian doctrine of *Wesen* should be according to our present lights might breathe some real life into a modified Hegelianism if anything could have any effect.

At the same time, in his Harvard Lectures on Pragmatism (March to May 1903) Peirce attacked Hegel's doctrine of *Wesen* specifically for not having properly distinguished between essence and existence, a charge which might well be based on Part I, Section 9 of Hegel's *Enzyklopädie,* were *Existenz* figures prominently in the discussion of *Wesen.* Thus Hegel, according to Pierce, dealt only with "what actually forces itself on the mind," which makes his phenomenology "pragmatoidal." (5.37) Furthermore, Hegel's catalogue of special categories as descriptions of phases of

evolution is to Peirce "utterly wrong." (5.37) Finally, he calls Hegel's phenomenology a "pitifully clubfooted affair since it does not take account of pure mathematics." (5.40)

Soon after his return from Harvard in a letter to William James of June 8, 1903, Peirce refers to Hegel's "monstrous blunders" in his interpretation of Thirdness.[22]

It is therefore not surprising that in his letter to William James of October 3, 1904, Peirce intimated that Hegel's *Phänomenologie* was "somewhat different"; and that he was in fact willing to acknowledge Hegel's prior claim to the term:

"I am not sure that Hegel ought not to have named the enterprise after his attempt": A little farther on the letter, after charging James with misusing the term "pure experience," he states by way of an afterthought, added between the lines, why he feels he has to get rid of the first part of the term "phenomenology":

"My 'phenomenon', *for which I must invent a new word,* is very near your 'pure experience' but not quite, since I do not exclude time and also speak of only *one* phenomenon."

Nine days after this letter, Peirce tells Lady Welby in his long epistle of October 12, 1904, which deals chiefly with the theory of signs, of the need of a study, named "ideoscopy," which is to consist in "describing and classifying the ideas that belong to ordinary experience or that naturally arise in connection with ordinary life, without regard to their being valid or invalid or to their psychology." He adds that the word 'phenomenology' is used in a different sense. Of this new terminological creation the second part "-scopy," had already been sanctioned previously by Peirce when his classification of the sciences in 1902 had adopted the division into "coenoscopic" and "idioscopic" (sic) ontology and divided the sciences into mathematics, philosophy, and idioscopy. (1.183) But the new *ideoscopy* had obviously nothing to do with this *idioscopy,* since the latter "embraces all the special sciences, which are principally occupied with the accumulation of new facts." (1.184) What Peirce seems to have liked in his new creation is the ending "-scopy," interpreted as "looking at," not as "observation of facts." This dates the abandonment of the term "phenomenology," as having occured between the two letters, although Peirce used it at least once more in the *Monist* of 1906 (vol. 16), where he referred in passing to "students of "phenomenology." (5.610)

The final replacement of "phenomenology" by "phaneroscopy" occurs in two paragraphs written for "Logic viewed as Semiotics, Introduction Number 2, Phaneroscopy," (1.286-287), which the editors date as "c. 1904." I submit that the first possible date for the second change is after the letter to Lady Welby of October 12, 1904, the last possible one the Adirondacks lectures of 1905, from which 1.284 is taken. Thus far no explicit statement has come to light explaining the quick abandonment of the transitional term "ideoscopy," which occurs only in the letter to Lady Welby. Quite apart from the misleading similarity of "ideoscopy" and "idioscopy," Peirce's main reason was probably that the word "idea" proved unsuited to his purposes, since, in the way it had been used by the British philosophers, it was too narrow and too loaded, as he put it, with "a psychological connotation which I am careful to exclude." (1.285) This conjecture is confirmed by Peirce's entry in the *Century Dictionary* under the heading "phaneron."[23]

The new term 'phaneron,' of which Peirce freely uses the plural form 'phanerons,' in contrast to his merely singular use of 'phenomenon,' is defined as "the collective total of all that is in any way or in any sense present to the mind, quite regardless of whether it corresponds to any real thing or not" (1.284); which is of course identical in substance with his earlier descriptions of the "phenomenon." Actually, the literal meaning of the Greek term suggests more than a mere "*phenomenon*" (which merely appears), namely something that reveals itself in its real nature; what Peirce means is described much better by the English word "seemings" or appearances.

Was "phaneroscopy" Peirce's last and final terminological choice? This might be inferred from the fact that the pertinent manuscripts were inscribed with this name, or with the Greek abbreviation '*phan*'; see, e.g., the draft for an unpublished paper in the *Monist,* written in 1905. (1.306-311; 4. 6-10; 4.539 nl; 4.553 nl) Another manuscript, dated c. 1905, bears the title "Phaneroscopy or the Natural History of Concepts." (1.332-336) Also, on November 20-22, 1906, Peirce presented to the National Academy of Sciences a communication on "Phaneroscopy, or Natural History of Signs, Relations, Categories etc. . . . ." (*Report of the National Academy of Sciences,* for the year 1906, p. 18). After this entry the chronological bibliography of Peirce's writings by Arthur W. Burks lists no further item related to the whole field.

There exists, however, one piece of evidence which may suggest some continued indecision in Peirce's mind on this score. It consists, oddly enough, of his contributions to the two new volumes of the *Century Dictionary and Cyclopedia* of 1909. The significance of this evidence would clearly depend upon the date, or dates, of their submission to the Editor, which theoretically could have occurred at any time between the first edition of 1891 and the appearance of the supplementary volumes in 1909, although circumstantial evidence would make the time after 1904 more likely for most of them. According to Miss Mary Mackey of Harvard College Library, the interleaving next to the entry "phenomenology" in Peirce's own annotated set of the *Century Dictionary* , now at the Houghton Library, shows a disappointing blank.

The most puzzling fact about these contributions is that, while there is an entry under "phaneron," (p. 990) referring specifically to Peirce as the user of this term (now defined somewhat differently as "whatever is in any sense

present to the mind, whatever its cognitive value may be, and whether it be objectified or not"), there is none under "phaneroscopy." On the other hand, there occurs an entirely new entry entitled "phenoscopy," (p. 991) which is even signed conspicuously by the name of C. S. Peirce in italics. This last neologism is defined as "that study which observes, generalizes and analyzes the elements that are always or very often present in, or along with, whatever is before the mind in any way as percept, image, experience, thought, habit, hypothesis, etc." Despite minor variations the identity with the definiens of 'phaneroscopy' is obvious.

Besides, on the very same page, there appear lengthy additions to the brief entry "phenomenology" of the original volume, presumably at least in part prepared by Peirce. They consist of two more meanings, namely Kant's, taken from *Metaphysische Anfangsgründe der Naturwissenschaft,* and Hegel's, now clearly based on his *Phänomenologie des Geistes.* These are followed by five further distinctions in small print. The first of these reads "Cenopythagorean phenomenology," described as "universal phenomenology as it is understood by those who recognize the categories of firstness, secondness, and thirdness."[24] The fifth, (which follows the distinctions of phenomenology of conscience, clearly referring to Eduard von Hartmann, phenomenology of mind, probably meaning Sir William Hamilton's conception, and phenomenology of spirit, obviously in Hegel's sense) is called "Universal Phenomenology" and characterized as "the observation, analysis, and generalization of those kinds of elements that are present in the universal phenomenon"; a cross reference to the article "phenomenon" gives the following characterization of the "universal phenomenon": "that which is in any way before the mind (as by perception, imagination, conception, emotion, desire, etc.) considered only in its most general characters." A comparison between the characterization of Universal Phenomenology and that of "phenoscopy" indicates that for all practical purposes the two enterprises are identical. Nor would it seem that "Cenopythagorean phenomenology" would differ from it except by its commitment to Peirce's doctrine of the three categories.

Thus, barring further evidence concerning the history of these entries, the provisional conclusion would seem to be that Peirce's terminological conscience was never quite at ease, even after he had coined the term 'phaneroscopy,' and that he was tending toward "phenoscopy" as the simplest and most original solution, without abandoning alternatives like "Cenopythagorean" and "Universal Phenomenology." The latter would also have protected his conception sufficiently from confusion with the Hegelian version, which seems to have been his main concern after his final rejection of Hegel's philosophy.

3. COINCIDENCE OR INTERACTION

In summary, the main characteristics which distinguish Peirce's phenomenology from Husserl's are the following:

(1) Peirce's preponderant interest in the discovery of categories;

(2) his conception of Firstness as quality of feeling;

(3) the non-reflective nature of his phenomenology;

(4) the absence of the intentional pattern from his phenomenological accounts;

(5) the status of Firstness and Secondness as particulars;

(6) the use of inductive generalization in phenomenology;

(7) the priority of mathematics to phenomenology; and

(8) the different principles governing the adoption and modification of the phenomenological terminology.

These differences appear to be important enough to demand the use of the plural in referring to Husserl's and Peirce's phenomenologies rather than the singular.

Nevertheless, apart from the temporary terminological parallel, there remain such basic agreements as:

(1) the program of a fresh approach by way of intuitive inspection and description to the immediately given, an approach free from preconceived theories.

(2) the deliberate disregard, in so doing, of questions of reality or unreality;

(3) the insistence upon the radical differences between phenomenology and psychology;

(4) the claim that such a phenomenology would be a rigorous science, basic not only for philosophy but even for logic. These agreements seem to justify the reference to the two phenomenologies by the common noun.

Under these circumstances it seems natural enough to ask whether these agreements represent mere coincidences, comparable to the conjunction in the course of two planets at their point of nearest approach, or whether there could have been one-sided or mutual influences.

An answer to this question makes it necessary first to establish how far Husserl and Peirce were even aware of one another and of their philosophical ideas.

As far as Husserl, Peirce's junior by twenty years, is concerned, there is certainly no reference to Peirce in his published writings. All one can assume is that Husserl had come across Peirce's name when his eye passed over the famous page of credit to Peirce in William James' *Pragmatism,* a book which, however, greatly disappointed Husserl, in contrast to his enthusiasm for the *Principles of Psychology.* There is also in the Husserl Archives in Louvain a letter to Husserl by Charles Hartshorne, written in October 1928, in which he reported his work on the edi-

tion of the *Collected Papers* and mentioned Peirce's phenomenology, actually suggesting the possibility of an influence from Husserl's side. However, when Dorion Cairns talked with Husserl three years later, Husserl apparently did not even recognize Peirce's name.[25]

There is, to be sure, a very different story in the case of Max Scheler. True, even Scheler knew of Peirce only through James' *Pragmatism.* But in this extended discussion of pragmatism, on which he had been working since 1910, it was Peirce who served as its main representative. In fact, he took pragmatism of the Peircean variety so much more seriously than Husserl that, in his book on epistemology and sociology[26] he devoted a lengthy chapter to an examination of its claims. Also, while rejecting pragmatism as philosophically erroneous, he defended the right of Peircean pragmatism as a correct interpretation and account of our primary relation to the world and likewise of the nature of positive science. Scheler's interest in Peirce (whose name he misspells consistently as Pierce) rather than in James would seem to be another example of Scheler's uncanny flair for what was philosophically significant, long before others had discovered it.

As to Peirce's knowledge of Husserl there is at least one piece of concrete evidence. In the course of a critique of the German logicians, which, interestingly enough, the editors found in his manuscript on "Phaneroscopy" of 1906, Peirce named as a representative example "the distinguished Husserl." However, what Husserl was supposed to exemplify was in Peirce's eyes anything but a distinguished and commendable tendency. For the context reads:

> How many writers of our generation (if I must call names, in order to direct the reader to further acquaintance with a generally described character—let it be in this case the distinguished Husserl), after underscored protestations that their discourse shall be of logic exclusively and not by any means of psychology (almost all logicians protest that on file), forthwith become intent upon those elements of the process of thinking which seem to be special to a mind like that of the human race, *as we find it,* to too great a neglect of those elements which must belong as much to any one as to any other mode of embodying the same thought. (4.7)

On the one hand, one might well wonder what gave Peirce such a surprisingly high estimate of Husserl. No English-speaking philosophical magazine had taken note of Husserl's *Logische Untersuchungen.* Of other American philosophers only W. E. Hocking and Walter Pitkin had made his acquaintance in Germany at that time. Unfortunately there seems to be no way of determining whether Peirce had owned and had worked through a copy of the *Logische Untersuchungen.* But even if he did not, there is at least the possibility that he used the copy owned by the Johns Hopkins Library since May 2, 1905.

On the other hand, Peirce's picture of Husserl's enterprise was clearly based on a grave misunderstanding. Certainly Husserl never showed the slightest interest in a study of the "thinking of the human race as we find it." What probably explains Peirce's impression was the typical surprise of those who, after reading Husserl's attack on psychologism in the first volume of the **Logische Untersuchungen,** expected from the second volume the development of a pure logic purged of all psychological infiltration. Instead they found themselves confronted with studies which, under the heading of "phenomenology," culminated in a discussion of the acts in which the logical entities and laws were given, a discussion, which Husserl in the first edition had even mistakenly called descriptive psychology. Despite Husserl's determined attempt to distinguish this phenomenology from a psychology in the current sense, the impression of a relapse into psychologism was widespread, even in Germany. This disappointment may well have prevented Peirce from reading on and finding, for instance, an important support for his "Scotist realism" which he might otherwise have discovered in Husserl's second study of the new volume ("*Ueber die ideale Einheit der Spezies*"). In any case, Peirce's reaction suggests that he was anything but sympathetic to the new kind of phenomenology which Husserl was about to develop, and simply considered it another type of psychology. This can also be gathered indirectly from the fact that Husserl's phenomenology is not listed in the extended article on "phenomenology" in the New Volume of the *Century Dictionary* of 1909.

Summing up, we may therefore say, that Husserl knew practically nothing about Peirce, and that Peirce knew about Husserl only the wrong things, at least in so far as Husserl's phenomenology was concerned. Thus I see no alternative to burying all wishful historical hypotheses about early interaction, let alone cooperation, between the European and the American branches of phenomenology. All that one might suspect—and that without concrete evidence—is that the acquaintance with Husserl's misinterpreted phenomenology confirmed Peirce in his decision to abandon the term "phenomenology" and to replace it by some new less ambiguous term. But it was chiefly Hegel who was on his mind, both when he adopted and when he dropped the phenomenological label.

Does this mean that the rapprochement between Husserl and Peirce was only a temporary affair, a "conjunction," ended perhaps less by Peirce's terminological innovation than by Husserl's shift toward phenomenological idealism? As far as the terminological aspect is concerned, the simultaneous choice of the label 'phenomenology' was clearly not more than a coincidence. There was as little connection between these choices as there was between Hegel, Peirce's source, and Brentano, the most likely inspiration for Husserl's adoption, with whom Peirce does not seem to have been acquainted at all. And there can be no question that Brentano was deadly opposed to Hegel and to all his works. The same holds true for Husserl, although in his later idealistic period he made some friendlier gestures toward the Post-Kantian Idealists collectively.

Nevertheless, there may be more than such a superficial coincidence when it comes to the *designata* behind the labels. Despite the deep-seated differences, there are enough parallels between Husserl's and Peirce's phenomenologies to justify the question about a common root for them both. This root can only be found in the very nature of the problems with which both Peirce and Husserl struggled. Both were originally mathematicians dedicated to the cause of establishing philosophy as a rigorous science. And both sought its foundation in a renewed and enriched approach to the phenomena given in experience. Thus one might look at Husserl's and Peirce's phenomenologies as two independent historical parallels. Their value is that of two experiments set up by the history of philosophy and serving as mutual controls for one another. Their outcome is all the more significant, and it does credit to both thinkers. Thus what Peirce wrote about his own relationship to Hegel could be said even more appropriately about his agreements with Husserl:

> There was no influence upon me from Hegel unless it was of so occult a kind as to entirely escape my ken; and if there was such an occult influence, it strikes me as about as good an argument for the essential truth of the doctrine, as is the coincidence that Hegel and I arrived in quite independent ways substantially to the same result. (5.38)

Notes

1. Even in this case it should be remembered at the outset that, prior to the appearance of Volume I of the edition of the *Collected Papers,* Peirce's phenomenology was practically unknown. Even the term "phenomenology" did not occur in any of his published articles and can be found only in such places as his four-page *Syllabus of Certain Topics of Logic* (Boston, Alfred Mudge & Son, 1903), an outline printed specifically for his Lowell Institute lectures of 1903, and in scattered and unidentified entries in the New Volumes of the *Century Dictionary and Cyclopedia* of 1909. Peirce's manuscripts dealing with this field were apparently inscribed "phaneroscopy," not "phenomenology." In view of the prominent place given to the term "phenomenology" in the *Collected Papers,* it seems worth pointing out that, of the two editors, Charles Hartshorne, before beginning work on the edition, had studied under Edmund Husserl at the University of Freiburg in 1923, and that Paul Weiss had likewise been in Freiburg between 1929 and 1930.

2. To my knowledge no confrontation between these two phenomenologies has as yet been undertaken, except for one suggestive page in an article by Marvin Farber on "Descriptive Philosophy and the Nature of Human Existence," in *Philosophic Thought in France and the United States* (University of Buffalo Publications, 1950), pp. 420-1.

3. "Minute Logic" (1902) in *Collected Papers* 2.120.—That "the term phenomenology appears in none of the writings of the *Collected Papers* before the Minute Logic of 1902" is also the opinion of Manley Thompson Jr. in *The Pragmatic Philosophy of C. S.*

Peirce (The University of Chicago Press, 1953), p. 157. Thomas A. Goudge, in *The Thought of C. S. Peirce* (University of Toronto Press, 1950), merely mentions the year 1900 as a *terminus post quem,* but without giving evidence that it appeared prior to 1902 (p. 76). David Savan's statement that Peirce suggested the existence of a "positive science of Phenomenology" for the first time in the early 90's ("On the Origins of Peirce's Phenomenology" in Philip P. Wiener and Frederic H. Young, editors, *Studies in the Philosophy of Charles Sanders Peirce,* Harvard University Press, 1952. p. 185) does not mean to imply that even the *term* "phenomenology" occurs in Peirce at such an early date, as Savan assures me in a recent letter.

4. In the second edition of 1913 it was slightly amended: "phenomenology understood as the pure theory of conscious acts."

5. This is confirmed by the following communication, which I owe to Professor C. I. Lewis, the first curator of the Peirce papers: "As I remember it, Peirce's Phaneroscopy was one of the few larger pieces of his manuscripts which were all together and not represented by several different and unfinished drafts."

6. *The Thought and Character of William James* (Boston, Little, Brown, and Company, 1935), Vol. II. Chapter LXXVI. I wish to thank the Library of Harvard University for the permission to include the quotations from the original letters.

7. Letter of June 3, 1903, in *The Thought and Character of William James,* II, 427.

8. To be sure this label appeared for the first time in the article "A World of Pure Experience" in the issue of the *Journal of Philosophy, Psychology and Scientific Method* of September 29; apparently Peirce had not yet seen it when he composed his letter of October 3.

9. Isabel Stearns, "Firstness, Secondness and Thirdness," in *Studies in the Philosophy of Charles Sanders Peirce* (Cambridge, Harvard University Press, 1952), p. 199. See also Ernest Nagel, "Guesses at the Riddle" in *Journal of Philosophy* XXX (1933), pp. 366 ff.

10. *Ideen zu einer reinen Phaenomenologie.* § 73.

11. See also *Collected Papers,* 1. 357: "What the world was to Adam on the day he opened his eyes to it, before he had drawn any distinctions, or had become conscious of his own existence. . . . ."

12. Letters to William James of June 8, 1903, published in R. B. Perry, *The Thought and Character of William James* Vol. II, p. 429

13. Peirce's phenomenology resembles in this respect the conception advanced in 1905 by Carl Stumpf, who preceded Husserl as student of Franz Brentano. See his "Zur Einteilung der Wissenschaften" in *Abhandlungen der preussischen Akademie der Wissenschaften.* Berlin, 1906.

14. "To conceive it is to generalize it; and to generalize it is to miss altogether the *hereness* and *nowness* which is its essence." Letter to William James of June 8, 1903 in R. B. Perry, *The Thought and Character of William James.* Vol. II, p. 429.

15. *The Thought of C. S. Peirce.* p. 57.

16. See also *Collected Papers* (5. 413), and *Nation* 76 (1903), 498.

17. This hypothesis would also fit in with Peirce's simultaneous ambitious attempts to develop a "natural classification of the sciences," including the philosophical sciences and mathematics, about which he reports to the Secretary of the Philosophical Society, S. P. Langley, in a letter of May 6, 1902 (Philip P. Wiener, "The Peirce—Langley Correspondence" in *Proceedings of the American Philosophical Society,* 91 (1947), p. 211).

18. See, E.G., Letter to Lady Welby of October 12, 1904 in *C. S. Peirce's Letters to Lady Welby,* edited by Irwin C. Lieb (New Haven, Whitlocks, Inc., 1953), p. 8; *Collected Papers* 4.2.

19. See, especially 5.43. Circumstantial evidence makes it seem very unlikely that Peirce ever studied Hegel's *Phänomenologie des Geistes,* especially since the first English translation by J. B. Baillie did not appear until 1910. His knowledge of Hegel's *Logik* and specifically of his list of the categories seems to have been based on William Wallace's translation of Part I of the *Enzyklopädie,* which appeared under the title *The Logic of Hegel* in 1892, rather than on the *Wissenschaft der Logik.* This may also be inferred from the list of the Hegelian "categories" as given in Peirce's article "Category" in the New Volumes of the *Century Dictionary and Cyclopedia* (1909), a list which differs slightly from the one in Hegel's larger work.

20. The close association between phenomenology and the doctrine of categories in Peirce's mind, which is so surprising to one familiar only with the German original, would seem to be explainable on the basis of Peirce's use of Wallace's translation of Part I. For here Wallace used the word "category" to render not only the German "*Kategorie*" but also Hegel's much more general expression *Denkbestimmung* (see his *Prolegomena to Hegel's Philosophy* (Oxford, 1894), p. 227, which results in a rather suggestive juxtaposition of the two terms in a fairly important passage of the translation (p. 58 f.), where Hegel refers back to the more comprehensive conception of his earlier phenomenology.

21. "You and I could pitch into the logical problems, and I am sure I could make it well spent time to you, while with all you should teach me of Hegel etc., I am equally sure it would tremendously benefit my own work." (Letter of May 28, 1902, published in James Harry Cotton, *Royce on the Human Self.* (Cambridge, Harvard University Press, 1954), p. 301.)

22. "The third stage" (of Hegel's thought) "is very close indeed to Thirdness, which is substantially Hegel's *Begriff*. Hegel, of course, blunders monstrously, as we shall all be seen to do; but to my mind the one fatal disease of his philosophy is that, seeing that the *Begriff* in a sense implies Secondness and Firstness, he failed to see that nevertheless they are elements of the phenomenon not to be *aufgehoben,* but as real and able to stand their ground as the *Begriff* itself." (This passage is omitted from R. B. Perry's publication of the letter).

23. "A term proposed by C. S. Peirce in order to avoid loading 'phenomenon,' 'thought,' 'idea,' etc. with multiple meanings."

24. An entry under "Cenopythagorean" identifies this kind of Neo-pythagoreanism as "pertaining to a modern doctrine which resembles Pythagoreanism in accepting universal categories that are related to and are named after numbers." A manuscript using the same adjective, entitled "Reflections upon Pluralistic Pragmatism and upon Cenopythagorean Pragmaticism," dated as c. 1906, is referred to in *Collected Papers* 5.555-5.563; see also 2.87.

25. Private communication.

26. "Der philosophische Pragmatismus" in *Die Wissensformen und die Gesellschaft* (Leipzig, Der Neue Geist, 1926), 259-323.

Aron Gurwitsch (lecture date 1959)

SOURCE: "The Kantian and Husserlian Conceptions of Consciousness," in *Studies in Phenomenology and Psychology,* Northwestern University Press, 1966, pp. 148-60.

[*In the following lecture, originally delivered in 1959, Gurwitsch distinguishes Husserl's conception of consciousness from earlier formulations by Locke, Hume, Leibnitz, and Kant.*]

A comparative study of Kant's theoretical philosophy with Husserlian phenomenology could have been attempted, indeed, should have been attempted, as early as 1913, following the publication of the first volume of Husserl's **Ideen zu einer reinen Phänomenologie und phänomenologischen Philosophie**—the only volume of the **Ideen** to appear during Husserl's lifetime. This work, in which Husserl outlines the program of constitutive phenomenology and indicates the general lines along which this program is to be realized, has a clearly Kantian inspiration. Indeed, the first generation of Husserl's students had already perceived this orientation.[1]

If one seeks a motto for the whole of Husserl's work, one could not do better than to refer to the few phrases which Kant places at the head of his *Analytic of Concepts,* when he speaks of his intention to descend into the depths of the mind to discover the notions of the understanding, which

are found therein prepared in at least a germinal form. Indeed, in the history of modern thought between Kant and Husserl one does not find a theoretician of subjectivity who is of comparable depth. Neither for Kant nor for Husserl, furthermore, is this concern for subjectivity an end in itself. They both seek to give an account of objectivity by means of the analysis of the life of consciousness, or of subjective life. Objects of every kind are viewed from the perspective of their origination and formation within the life of consciousness. To give an account of objectivity, it is necessary to bring out and make explicit the contribution of subjectivity to the constitution of objects. Husserl's intentions can be characterized, somewhat *grosso modo* certainly, in such terms as these, but they are descriptive as well, at least to a considerable extent, of the intentions of Kant. There are, in fact, some Husserlian doctines which are highly reminiscent of parallel theories advanced by Kant.

We shall choose two examples more or less at random and begin by considering the phenomenological theory of perception as established by Husserl. When we perceive an object, we perceive it from a certain point of view, and we can move from one point to another. From each of these points of view the perceived thing presents itself from a certain aspect and in a certain orientation. As we move around the thing, looking at it from different points of observation, the aspects change, the perceptual presentations of the same thing undergo variations. However, among the varying aspects there is not only a compatibility but even more a harmony and accordance. The aspects glide into one another, and, owing to this continuation and harmony, as a result of this accordance, the perspectives, the perceptual adumbrations become fitted together and form a coherent and systematized group. It is in virtue of this grouping that perceptions, perceptual acts which can be dispersed in time, are in turn organized into one process, the unity of which depends upon the relation of accord and harmony between the perceptual perspectives under which the object appears. As is known, Husserl insists emphatically on this relation of harmony and concordance. According to him, the identity and the very existence of the perceived thing depend on that relation.

These analyses remind us of Kant's formula found in the first edition of the *Transcendental Deduction of the Categories.* Posing the question concerning the relation of representations, or ideas, phenomena, sensory data, to the object, Kant gives his well-known answer: in order for the representations to be related to an object, there must exist between them this relation of concordance and conformity which is required by the very notion of objectivity.

To consider another example, let us look briefly at the theory regarding the consciousness of phenomenal time. Husserl presented this theory in his **Vorlesungen zur Phänomenologie des inneren Zeitbewusstseins** and returned to it in his posthumous work **Erfahrung und Urteil,** where he studies the phenomena in a more detailed and differentiating manner.[2] The notions of protention and particularly of retention are at the center of the Husserlian theory concerning the experience of time. At each moment of time, a certain immediately past phase of the temporal stream is still retained. This immediately past phase is not purely and simply past but is rather a "past which has just been present." This immediate past is a phase of the flowing time which was present a moment ago, which is no longer present but is still retained as having just been present.

This theory reminds us of some remarks which Kant makes concerning the synthesis of the imagination, or more exactly, the synthesis of reproduction by the imagination. Speaking of a line which is traced in thought, of a number, of a temporal interval, Kant maintains that if, for example, the segments of the line which one has just been drawing were effaced and forgotten, a whole line could never result. Therefore, the present phase of the action of drawing the line must still contain the phases which have preceded it—that is to say, those which have just been present. Here again we find another convergence of a Husserlian theory with views formulated by Kant.

However, even though encouraged by such more or less haphazardly chosen convergences, if one goes on to compare the two philosophies more systematically, a most embarrassing situation arises.

We remarked at the beginning that Kant's as well as Husserl's concern with the life of consciousness, or subjectivity, is in the service of their respective interests in objectivity. However, what is it that Kant understands by "objectivity"? And, what is its meaning for Husserl? When Kant speaks of objectivity, of an objective world, he has in mind mathematical science, the mathematical physics of his time, that is, Newtonian physics—the physics which describes the objective world. For Husserl, on the contrary, the notion of objectivity has a great many shades of meaning. When Husserl speaks of objectivity, he is not thinking exclusively or even primarily of the mathematical science of his time; he is not thinking of Einstein's physics or of quantum physics.

First and foremost there is the objectivity of a world for me, of a world with respect to which I disregard every contribution deriving from Others. It is possible—indeed, it is necessary—to effect such a reduction of the world to what pertains to me alone; thereby the first notion of objectivity is made explicit. Subsequently, there is the objectivity of our world as it is for us, the objectivity of our surrounding environment in the sense of the milieu wherein I live with my fellow-men who belong to the same social and historical group as I. This world is the world of a certain society at a certain phase of its history. A good example of such a world is perhaps that of a primitive tribe or a historical world such as that of the ancient Egyptians. On this basis a second notion of objectivity arises: that of the world as pertaining to a certain historico-social group. A third notion of objectivity relates to the Husserlian conception of the human life-world

(*Lebenswelt*) in general. The life-world understood in this sense is conceived by Husserl as an invariant with respect to the multiple socio-historical environments, between which there are often considerable differences. This life-world is the same for all human beings and for all societies. The objectivity belonging to the scientific universe as it is elaborated by the physical sciences appears only at an even higher, and perhaps the final, level.

Whereas Kant had a single notion of objectivity, Husserl develops a whole series of notions, between which there can be no other unity—we submit—than that which Aristotle called "unity by analogy."

Let us consider another example. In *Erfahrung und Urteil* and especially in his other posthumously published work, *Die Krisis der Europäischen Wissenschaften und die transzendentale Phänomenologie*,[3] Husserl advanced a theory of "pure sensibility." This phrase makes us think of Kant's "transcendental aesthetics," the goal of which is to provide the grounds for geometry. Perhaps it does not contain the whole of Kant's theory of mathematics, but it is surely a central and fundamental part of it, and especially of his theory of geometry.

When Husserl speaks of "pure sensibility," by contrast, his concern is with the role of our organism, of our own body, in perception. He describes the kinaesthesias which we experience when we move about in our perceptual field, and he studies the correlations between these kinaesthetic experiences and the unfolding of the perspectives pertaining to perceived things, which we mentioned at the beginning. This "pure sensibility" belongs to what Husserl calls "prepredicative experience," which precedes all sorts of idealizations. What characterizes the world as it presents itself to us in pre-predicative experience is that not even the most elementary logical operations, not to speak of geometrical idealizations, have yet made any contribution to it.

For Kant, perceived space is geometrical space. In his view, the axioms of geometry can, so to speak, be read off the intuition of space, which is the condition for all perception and experience. According to Husserl, to the contrary, because pre-predicative experience is at the root of every idealization and of every elaboration pertaining to a higher level, the axioms of geometry and all geometrical idealizations in general arise on the basis of perceptual space, in virtue, of course, of processes of a very specific kind whose details call for special examination.

Here is another instance in which Kant and Husserl make use of the same terminology but do not speak of precisely the same things.

Faced with such a situation, it seems advisable to forego altogether every comparison which would proceed theory by theory and doctrine by doctrine. Rather, we should attempt to go straight to the heart of things.

Let us inquire into the conception of consciousness, or understanding, which Kant has established as distinguished from that which Husserl advocates.

As regards Kant's conception, let us glance briefly—perhaps too briefly—at a certain phase of the "transcendental deduction of the categories," namely the notion of the "pure transcendental apperception," a notion which—it seems to us—is at the center not only of the deduction but also of the entire *Kritik der reinen Vernunft.*

As is known, all representations, ideas, phenomena, sensory data, and so on are for Kant subject to the condition of being mine or, as Kant more prudently expresses it, to the condition of being able to be apprehended as mine, as belonging to an identical Ego. The sensory data which form a multiplicity and which change, vary, and succeed one another stand opposed to the identical Ego, to the Ego conceived as strictly one. In order for the sensory data to be apprehended as mine, it is not enough that as regards each sensory datum I reflectively apperceive that it is given to, and experienced by, me, that it belongs to the same experiential flux as my other sensory data. Such a reflection would still not permit me to account for the strict identity of my Ego. The latter itself would in some way partake of the vicissitudes of sensory data; it would become involved in the change and variation which these data undergo; it would be dispersed along with its sensory data. In order for me to have consciousness of the identity of my Ego as opposed to the multiplicity of my sensory data, I must perform on these one single function, an identical action (*identische Handlung*), always the same. *The Ego,* asserts Kant, *cannot apperceive itself in its own identity except by apperceiving by the same token the identity of the function by means of which the multiplicity of sensory data is reunited into a context governed by certain laws.* In order for the Ego to be able to apprehend itself as an identical Ego, it must unify the sensory data.

Two kinds of unity can be distinguished from one another: on the one hand, that unity which exists between all the sensory data in virtue of their common relation to an identical Ego; on the other hand, the unification which the function or action of the identical Ego brings about between the sensory data. The originality of the Kantian thesis consists in identifying these two unities or, more exactly, in regarding each of them as a necessary and indispensable condition for the other.

It is almost trivial to state that if the sensory data did not belong to an identical Ego, this Ego could not perform any function on them. What is not trivial is to affirm that the converse is also true. In fact, Kant maintains that in order for the sensory data to belong to an identical Ego, this identical Ego must effect a unification between the sensory data. This unification is, according to Kant, an indispensable condition for the strict identity of the Ego of the pure transcendental apperception.

This pure transcendental apperception, or the transcendental Ego, is exhausted in an action or in an actual function admitting of an inner articulation, of which the categories as Kant conceives them are the conceptual fixations. Pure transcendental apperception is defined by this articulated action and by this action alone.

In order to determine the nature of the synthetic action of unification, one has to remember that the sensory data are received under the conditions of time and space. For our purposes here, however, time is more important than space. Sensory data occur either simultaneously or in succession. The operation of synthetically unifying the sensory data occurring under the condition of time consists in ratifying (or not ratifying) their temporal relations—for example, conferring a legal title upon their factual succession. If the succession of temporal data is ratified, the mere fact of this succession is legitimated and conceived as a special case of a general law. The objectification of sensory data always has the meaning, for Kant, of a ratification and legitimation of their temporal relations.

The Kantian conception of consciousness, which we have sketched rather superficially, is activistic and functionalistic. The life of the understanding consists in an action, in a single action which is always the same. The pure transcendental apperception is one with its action; it is but its articulated action.

It seems to us, though this assertion cannot be substantiated here, that Kant's notion of consciousness derives from the monadology of Leibniz. To be sure, there can be no question of a reinstatement or of a simple renewal of the Leibnizian conception of the monad. This conception has, in the hands of Kant, undergone a transformation which is fundamental, but the transformation is continuous. As a substance, the Leibnizian monad is essentially characterized by its activity. Precisely the same holds for the understanding as Kant conceives it. Although the activity of the monad is specified differently from that of the pure transcendental apperception, the latter stands to the former in a relation of filiation. The direction in which Kant has transformed the Leibnizian concept of the monad is determined by his adopting the analyses and even some of the theses of Hume, at least to a certain extent and within certain limits. It was thus unavoidable that the Leibnizian idea of the active monad should undergo a transformation.

Let us now turn to the Husserlian conception of consciousness.

It has to be emphasized at the outset that the notion of synthesis is not at all alien to Husserlian thought. Husserl's notion of synthesis exhibits a higher differentiation than that of Kant, who only knew one single synthesizing function. Husserl, however, makes a distinction between active and passive syntheses. All perceptual syntheses are passive, whereas the active syntheses come into play in the constitution of logical, mathematical, and similar entities. To simplify our exposition we are going to restrict ourselves to the passive synthesis of perceptual life.

The first question which arises concerns the materials which enter into the synthesis, the materials between which synthetic unity is established. With respect to Kant, the question is easily answered: the materials on which the pure transcendental apperception imposes unity are sensory data (conceived in more or less the same manner as by Hume). It is from this side that Hume's views have penetrated Kant's thinking. In the Husserlian theory of perception, however, the question concerning the materials which become unified by means of the passive synthesis is much more complicated.

Let us return again to the perceptual process. I perceive a house from a certain point of view, and this house (it does not matter whether it is familiar to me or not) presents itself under a certain aspect, in a certain perceptual adumbration, in a certain orientation (from far or near, in front of me or at the side, and so on). Perceived from another point of view, the same house presents itself under a different aspect, and it is between these aspects (which vary according to the points of view) that the perceptual synthesis is passively established. What, then, is this house perceived, as presenting itself under a certain aspect rather than under another? The question concerns the house *qua* perceived, precisely and strictly as it appears through a determinate perceptual act or, more briefly, the house perceived as such. Obviously, the house *qua* perceived in the above sense cannot be considered as a mere sum of sensory data in the sense in which Hume uses the term. No more can the house *qua* perceived be taken as the real house *qua* physical thing, a thing which can be perceived from diverse points of view and present itself under different aspects. For here we have to do with the house appearing under one well-determined aspect and not under another one.

Finally, one must distinguish the thing perceived as such from the perceptual act. A rather simple reflection will serve to make this clear. Suppose that we place ourselves at a certain point of observation from which we look at the house without moving, and suppose that we alternately close and open our eyes. Each time that we open our eyes, we experience an act of perception, which, once it is past, can never recur, as this generally holds for all acts of consciousness. Thus we have to distinguish the perception which we experienced before closing our eyes from the one which we are experiencing now that we have opened them again. We find, therefore, a multiplicity of perceptual acts which differ from one another (be it only because of their places in phenomenal time) and which can be enumerated. Meanwhile we perceive not only the same house *qua* physical thing but are also confronted with the same thing as presenting itself to us under the same aspect; briefly, we are faced with the same house perceived as such. The latter being neither the physical house nor an act of consciousness, we have to recognize the perceived *qua* perceived as a special and specific entity—"perceptual noema" is the technical term which Husserl uses. For this entity there was no place in traditional thought, because the only distinction admitted was that between things or physical events, on the one hand, and, on the other, acts of consciousness.

The passive synthesis which we are here considering is effected between the perceptual noemata. In the course of the perceptual process developing while we walk around the house so as to see it from all sides, the diverse aspects under which the house appears not only succeed one another in time but beyond this continuously glide and blend into one another. To borrow a phrase of Merleau-Ponty which quite adequately expresses the passivity of the perceptual synthesis, a "synthesis of transition" becomes established between the perceptual noemata. But here we must forsake embarking even upon a superficial study of the perceptual process.

These reflections have led us to the notion which is at the center of the Husserlian conception of consciousness: namely, that of *intentionality*. It has all too often been remarked that, according to this conception, every act of consciousness is a consciousness *of* something, that every act of love is a love *of* something, and so on. It is necessary, however, to analyze the phenomena more precisely instead of contenting ourselves with a formula which is almost merely verbal.

The analysis of the example taken from our perceptual experience has made us aware of both an opposition and a correlation between an identical and identifiable unity—the perceptual noema—and an indefinite multiplicity of acts of consciousness, all different from one another, if only by their respective places in phenomenal time. Acts of perception are intentional acts because, through each of them, a perceived thing appears under a certain aspect and in a certain mode of perceptual presentation—because, in one word, to each of them there corresponds a perceptual noema, and—we remember—the same noema can correspond to a multiplicity of acts. What is fundamental here is the notion of noema. According to a very telling remark made by Berger some years ago, Husserl has discovered a category which is more fundamental than that of being or of non-being: namely, the category of the object intended as such, of the object as intended through a concrete act of consciousness.[4]

What is true for perceptual life is valid quite generally, as can be shown on any example. Let us take an example from the sphere of linguistic symbols and their understanding. I can state the Pythagorean Theorem as often as I wish; or, let us suppose that I formulated it yesterday after having deduced it from other theorems, say from the very axioms of Euclidean geometry, and this morning I return to the result of my geometrical reflections in order to deduce further consequences from it. My act of yesterday evening is not this morning's act, and yet it is the same Pythagorean Theorem which I deduced yesterday and which I take as the point of departure for my thought today. Here again, it is necessary to insist on the identity of the thing intended, precisely *as* it is intended, in opposition to an indefinite multiplicity of acts through which it is intended. Incidentally, it matters but little that the Pythagorean Theorem is true. Even if I say that "three and four are nine," in order to be able to recognize this proposition as false, I must intend and apprehend it as an identifiable and identical proposition. This proposition must be intelligible, and it must have the mode of existence proper to propositions. Whenever I formulate this false proposition, it is the same falsity which I state, doing this on different occasions, i.e., through different acts.

It follows from these considerations that consciousness must not be conceived as a unidimensional series of events in the manner of traditional thought, which saw in consciousness only a series of events succeeding one another in time. To be sure, such a conception is not false, because temporality is in fact a basic law of consciousness. It is not, however, the only one. What we must say is that the traditional conception is simply incomplete, because the events in question here are events of a very particular kind. They are the events through which noemata are presented, apprehended, and actualized. As indicated by the parallel we have established between perceptual consciousness and the comprehension of linguistic expressions, noemata pertain to the same domain as meanings. One can even call them meanings, provided one understands this term in a much wider sense than is usual. *We are thus led to define consciousness by the correlation between two levels: on the one hand, the level of multiple acts, psychological events, which take place in time; on the other, the level of meanings, of significations, of noemata.* We may perhaps be permitted to refer to an article in which we sought to advance this conception of consciousness as a correlation and to show that Husserl's analyses not only agree with this interpretation of intentionality but even tend toward it as their *telos*.[5]

It is possible (by means of the example of the perception of a stable thing) to demonstrate the superiority of the Husserlian conception of consciousness as against that advocated by Kant. The problem which we have in view here is concealed in Kant because of the preeminence he gives to the relation of causality in both the *Kritik der Reinen Vernunft* and *Prolegomena*. To bring this problem out, we shall take a glance at the Kantian analysis of the relation of causality.

Suppose we have the same experience or do the same laboratory experiment on several occasions. For instance, we heat a metal rod and observe a certain elongation. It is common to speak of a repetition of the same observation, of the same experience or the same process. Let us consider this more carefully. Each time that we do the experiment in question, we measure the length of the rod; we heat it and measure its length again. Each experience furnishes us with a series of sensory data: the first one with the data a^1, a^2 . . . , a^n; the second one with the data b^1, b^2 . . . , b^n, and so on. Comparing these two series, we find that the sensory data respectively resemble one another: a^1 is similar to b^1, a^2 is similar to b^2, a^n is similar to b^n. One can go even further to say that these sensory data are totally like each other respectively, but they can never be taken as identical because the first series occurred, let us say, twenty minutes before the second. Though there may be similarity between the sensory data—even, if one wishes, perfect likeness—there can

never be identity. What is identical is the law which governs the relation between the rise of the temperature and the extent of the elongation. According to Kant, the identity of the law is guaranteed by the identity of the function pertaining to the pure transcendental apperception which, on each occasion, operates in the same manner. Properly speaking, there is no repetition of the same process; there is only an identical law which governs an entire series of processes. Furthermore, there is a similarity or likeness between the sensory data which appear each time the experience is had.

This brief analysis will help us to understand the difficulty which the Kantian theory faces when it deals with the perception of a stable thing. Let us consider the example of which Kant himself made use (without, however, sufficiently analyzing it): the perception of a house. Kant remarks that I can look at this house from top to bottom or else from the bottom to the top. Sensory data successively follow one another in each observation, but their succession is not ratified by the pure transcendental apperception, in contradistinction to the case of the causal relation where the sensory data succeed one another not only in fact but also by rights. To simplify the matter, let us suppose that we always look at the house in the same direction, say, from top to bottom, and that we do this several times. Each time we experience a sequence of sensory data: the first time, the sequence a^1, a^2 . . . , a^n; the second time, the sequence b^1, b^2 . . . , b^n, and so on. Here again, a^1 and b^1, a^2 and b^2, up to a^n and b^n, are similar to one another or are respectively alike, but they are in no way identical. Contrary to the causal relation, there is here nothing identical, not even a law. How, therefore, can we speak of the "same thing" and maintain that it is perceived on several occasions? Under these conditions, it is hard to see how the consciousness of identity could ever emerge or by what right we can say, as in fact we do at every moment and without the least hesitation, that the diverse perceptions are all, in spite of the differences between them, perceptions of the same house.

Kant's theory fails in the face of a problem which, we repeat, is concealed in the case of the causal relation. Before, we were confronted not only with different sequences of sensory data but also with different physical processes (the actual elongation of the rod each time it is heated). In the case we are now considering, however, the perceived thing stands, in its very identity, over against a multiplicity of perceptions or sensory data.

We have taken these sensory data as psychical facts, refusing to adopt the interpretation of Paton, who has suggested that Kant deliberately identified "sensory data" with "sensible qualities" as states of things.[6] If this interpretation is in keeping with Kant's intentions, the criticism which Husserl has expressed as regards Locke and the entire empiricist school also applies to Kant. This criticism consists in pointing out the confusion of sensory data (*Empfindungen*) considered as psychical facts with the sensible qualities of things which, while presenting themselves by means of sensory data, in no way coincide with these.[7] Husserl considers this confusion as an hereditary vice of modern thought, both philosophical and psychological; it is facilitated and even suggested by the fact that the sensory data and sensible qualities are expressed by the same words—such as "red," "hot," "hard."

In conclusion, we now ask where our reflection has led us. The result is certainly not a rapprochement between Husserlian and Kantian thought. Fundamentally, only the divergences have appeared.

Nevertheless the result of our considerations is not wholly negative, for this reflection does permit us to place the theory of intentionality into a historical perspective and thereby to make it appear in all its significance and importance.

In the history of modern thought three principal conceptions of consciousness have been advanced. The first is that of empiricism, the classical British school inaugurated by Locke and brought to its completion by Hume. According to this conception, consciousness is a mosaic of sensory data and images derived from these data. There is no internal connection whatever between all these facts; they merely co-exist or succeed one another. Hume has compared the mind to a kind of theatre where "perceptions" (including both what he calls "impressions" and what he calls "ideas") appear, disappear, and combine in numerous ways.[8] Hume adds that this comparison must not be pushed too far, because the stage of a theatre on which events take place has a certain stability, whereas the mind is reduced by him entirely to a heap of "perceptions" which are and remain isolated from one another.

It was against this conception of consciousness that Leibniz and Kant reacted; Leibniz to Locke, and Kant to Hume. Leibniz and Kant established the second principal conception of consciousness by insisting on the activity and spontaneity of the mind. In the Kantian theory, we recall, the understanding is conceived as function, operation, action.

The third principal conception of consciousness is established by Husserl. Although the term "intentionality" was borrowed from Brentano, who in turn took it from scholasticism, it is Husserl who gave to it a completely new and original meaning. For Husserl, the theory of intentionality is not merely one phenomenological theory among others. The idea of a fully completed phenomenology is nothing other than the idea of a theory of intentionality developed in all directions, followed out to its final ramifications.

Notes

1. Originally, this was a lecture delivered before the Société Française de Philosophie, April 25, 1959. The lecture was published in the *Bulletin de la Société Française de Philosophie* (1960).

2. The first of Husserl's works mentioned above was edited by Martin Heidegger and published in *Jahrbuch für Philosophie und phänomenologische Forschung* (Halle, 1928), Vol. IX. The second was edited by Ludwig Landgrebe (Hamburg, 1954).

3. Ed. W. Biemel (*Husserliana,* Vol. VI [The Hague, 1954]).

4. G. Berger, *Le cogito dans le philosophie de Husserl* (Paris, 1941), p. 54.

5. See above, "On the Intentionality of Consciousness."

6. H. J. Paton, *Kant's Metaphysic* of *Experience* (London, 1936), Vol. II, pp. 266ff., 306f.

7. Husserl, *Logische Untersuchungen* (Halle, 1913), II, i, pp. 128ff.; Husserl, *Die Krisis der Europäischen Wissenschaften und die transzendentale Phänomenologie,* p. 27n. As to the confusion in question in Kant, cf. H. A. Prichard, *Kant's Theory of Knowledge* (Oxford, 1909), pp. 134ff., 209n.3, 231ff., 280ff.

8. D. Hume, *A Treatise of Human Nature,* ed. L. A. Selby-Bigge (Oxford, 1951), p. 253.

Alfred Schuetz (essay date 1959)

SOURCE: "Type and Eidos in Husserl's Late Philosophy," in *Philosophy and Phenomenological Research,* Vol. XX, No. 2, December, 1959, pp. 147-65.

[*In the following essay, Schuetz explores the way Husserl uses the operative concepts of type and eidos (or essential property) in his study of perception.*]

In a brilliant paper presented to the "Colloque international de phénoménologie a Royaumont 1957"[1] Professor Eugen Fink deals with what he calls the operative concepts in Husserl's phenomenology. He distinguishes in the work of any major philosopher between thematic and operative notions. Whereas the former aim at the fixation and preservation of the fundamental concepts, the latter are used in a vague manner as tools in forming the thematic notions; they are models of thought or intellectual schemata which are not brouught to objectifying fixation, but remain opaque and thematically unclarified. According to Fink, the notions of "phenomenon," of "constitution," and "performances" (*Leistungen*), and even those of "epoché" and of "transcendental logic" are used by Husserl as operative concepts. They are not thematically clarified or remain at least operatively adumbrated, and are merely headings for groups of problems open to and requiring further analysis.

The present paper makes the attempt to show that also the notion of typicality, which, according to Husserl's later philosophy, characterizes our experiencing of the life-world in the natural attitude on both the predicative and the prepredicative level, and even the notion of ideation, (at least in the sense of eidetic generalization, that is, the grasping of the ideal genera and species of material universals) are widely used by him as mere operative schemata of a highly equivocal character and are in need of further clarification.

To start with the typicality of our experiences of the life-world so central for Husserl's late philosophy, we find that three groups of problems lead him to a closer investigation of this feature: (1) The horizontal character of our experiences in the natural attitude, and the limiting notion of "world" as the foundation of the qualities of preacquaintedness and familiarity adherent to them; (2) the problem of the genealogy of logical forms, including the constitution of universal objectivities as originating in prepredicative experience; (3) the structure of our experiences of the life-world (*Lebenswelt*), their necessary vagueness, and their determination by our interests. Although it will hardly be possible to handle separately each of the aforementioned problems in its relation to typicality, it is hoped that our analyses of the various approaches (which we propose to perform without trying to embark upon a discussion of the historical development of Husserl's pertinent thought, and without any reference to his so far unpublished writings) will show the reasons for the equivocations involved in Husserl's pertinent views. They are hardly compatible with one another and are of an operative nature. We will close with a few questions referring to the relationship between the typicality of our experiences in everyday life and the possibility of the so-called "free variations" performed in phantasy which are supposed to lead by the process of ideation to the intuition of the eidos.

I. The Preacquaintedness of the World and
its Objects; Inner and Outer Horizon

We start with a brief analysis of our experience of everyday life as described in Husserl's *Erfahrung und Urteil*.[2] As usual—and sometimes to the great disadvantage of his general theory—Husserl takes as the paradigm of our experiencing the perceiving of concrete objects of the external world given to our actual or potential sensory apperception. To the naive attitude of our everyday life objects are simply pregiven as assumedly being and being in such and such a way. They are pregiven to us in the unquestioned (although always questionable) assurance of an uncontested belief, and thus not on the ground of a particular act of positing, and still less on the ground of an existential judgment. But our experience of these given objects shows two characteristics: in the first place, all objects of our experience have from the outset the character of typical familiarity; in the second place, the process of our apperceiving these objects by originary intuition is always permeated by anticipations of not actually apperceived but cointended features. Both characteristics are closely connected with each other and with the typicality of our experiences, and this in the following way:

According to Husserl, the world and the individual objects in it are always experienced by us as having been preorganized by previous experiencing acts of the most various kinds. In any experience, even that of an objectivity apper-

ceived for the first time, a preknowledge of as yet unapperceived properties of the object is involved, a preknowledge which might be undetermined or incompletely determined as to its content, but which will never be entirely empty. In other words, any experience carries along an experiential horizon which refers to the possibility (in subjective terms: to the faculty) not merely to explicate step by step the objectivity as it is given in actual apperception, but also to obtain by additional experiencing acts ever new additional determinations of the same objectivity. This infinite open horizon of the actual experience functions in its indeterminateness from the outset as the scope of anticipated possibilities of further determination; yet in spite of their undetermined generality these anticipations are, according to Husserl, nevertheless *typically* determined by their *typical* prefamiliarity, as *typically* belonging, that is, to the total horizon of the same and identifiable objectivity, the actually apperceived properties of which show the same general *type*.

Thus, it is the horizontal anticipations which predelineate the typical preacquaintedness and familiarity of the objectivity given to our apperception. First of all the object is within that universal horizon of all horizons to which we refer in the natural attitude by the term "world." The world is the total horizon of all possible experiences. Any object is an object *within* the world which, in the natural attitude, does not become thematic itself, but is just taken for granted. For example, any single real object of the outer world is apperceived as a valid existent within the general horizon of the world, and this means, among other things, that it is apperceived as an identical and as "always the same" identifiable element of the world, and having as such its position within universal space and universal time. But the world as the unquestioned horizonal background of all possible experiences of existents within it has merely *in general* the subjective character of familiarity without being known in its *individual particularities*. Each individual existent which is apperceived as such has, in addition, its particular horizonal structure within which all further distinctions of acquaintedness and unacquaintedness originate. The object is given to the apperceiving consciousness not merely as an objectivity as such, but as an existent of a particular type: as a thing of the outer world, as a plant, an animal, a human being, a human product, and so on. Even more: it is apperceived as pertaining to further and further differentiated "genera" with their subordinated "species"—provided that we are permitted to use analogically these technical terms for the prepredicative and preconceptual forms of simple apperceptual experiences now under scrutiny. Accordingly, to Husserl structurization by preacquaintedness and unacquaintedness is a fundamental feature of our consciousness of the world. This structurization is permeated by the relative distinction between undetermined generality and determined specificity. If we call the open frame of further determinability of the apperceived object the *inner horizon* of this object, then we may say that the further determination occurs by explicating the preindicated horizonal implicata and, correlatively, the adherent open possibilities of anticipated activities of the mode "I can" (I can examine the object more closely; I can make its unseen back side visible by turning it around or by locomotions of my body, etc.). The inner horizon can thus be characterized as the empty frame of the undetermined determinability, indicating and prescribing both the particular style of any further explication and a particular typicality of the anticipated explicata so to be obtained. That is why Husserl comes to the conclusion that all particular apperceptions are fulfillments of that which has been meant in advance.

Now it has to be emphasized that the horizon is continually in flux. With any new intuitive apperception new determinations or rectifications of previous determinations modify the possible anticipations and therewith the horizon. No apperception is merely instantaneous and transient; any apperception becomes a part of habitual knowledge as a permanent result. Sometimes Husserl speaks of the "sedimentations" of preceding experiences. To be sure, these habitual possessions are latent, but this involves that they may be "wakened" or "called forth." This occurs by way of a passive synthesis of congruence (*Deckungssynthese*), based on similarity or dissimilarity, a synthesis for which Husserl uses the traditional term of "association," hastening to warn us that its meaning as used by him is a different one. To Husserl "association" designates a general form of immanent genesis inherent to consciousness. It means exclusively the purely immanent relation of "something recalls something else," "something refers to something else." Thus a *pair* is constituted, one member of which "wakens" the other. Similar experiences are called forth by similar ones and contrast with the dissimilar. It seems that Husserl changed the terminology later on[3] and handled the problem of association as a special case of "pairing" or "appresentation."

Thus the apperception of an objectivity in its horizon calls forth the recollection of other objectivities similar to or even like the former, and constitutes therewith a typicality on the ground of which by apperceptive transference (*Apperzeptive Uebertragung*) also other objectivities of a similar kind are apperceived from the outset as objectivities of the same type, that is, of a pregiven more or less specific familiarity. It can be easily seen that with any step of originary apperceiving and explicating not merely the objectivity under scrutiny becomes further determined, but that concomitantly a modification of the horizon of all possible experiences as a whole occurs. New typical determinations and familiarities are constituted and predelineate the direction of apperceptive expectations which attach themselves to the givenness of newly encountered objectivities. The extension of the typicality thus constituted might widely vary depending upon the manner in which the objectivity is anticipatorily appresented. This extension—always according to Husserl—discloses itself merely in the fulfillments of the anticipations, and can be conceptualized by particular intentional acts in hindsight only.

We shall return very soon to the problem of conceptualization, especially in its relationship to typicality. At this juncture an example of the typicality of the natural experiential apperception given by Husserl in another context[4] might be a welcome illustration of the preceding. He points out that in the natural attitude things in the factual world are from the outset experienced as types, namely, as trees, animals, snakes, birds, and in particular, as fir, maple, dog, adder, swallow, sparrow, etc. That which is apperceived as a type recalls similar things in the past and is to that extent familiar. Moreover what is typically apperceived carries along a horizon of possible further experiences in the form of a predelineation of a typicality of still unexperienced but expected characteristics of the object. If we see a dog we anticipate immediately his future behavior, his typical way of eating, playing, running, jumping, etc. Actually, we do not see his teeth, but even if we have never seen this particular dog, we know in advance what his teeth will look like—not in their individual determination, but in a typical way, since we have long ago and frequently experienced that "suchlike" animals ("dogs") have something like teeth of this and that typical kind.

But why are certain characteristics of the object paired with characteristics of other objects as typically similar, while others,—at least for the time being—are disregarded? William James and Bergson have developed their theory of the selectivity of consciousness in order to answer this question, which is directly related to the constitution of typicality. Husserl, too, acknowledges that the explicating activity by which the object is apperceived as a unity of characteristics is not evenly distributed over all the particularities which detach themselves, but that

> our glance is directed toward specifically impressive properties of the object by which the object of this particular typicality or this individual object distinguishes itself from objects of equal or similar typicality.[5]

What is, however, the factor that makes certain traits of the object "specifically impressive"? According to Husserl, it is our *interest*. He distinguishes two kinds of interest: First, the object, which is passively pregiven to us, affects our receptivity and wakens in us the more or less intense tendency to follow the stimulus emanating from and imposed upon us by the object, and to advert to it. That is why Husserl interprets receptivity as the lowest form of ego-activity. The adversion evokes an interest in the object surpassing those of its features which are merely pregiven in the mode of actuality, and striving to ever new apprehension. (This first notion of interest recalls Leibniz's definition of consciousness as the tendency to proceed to ever new experiences.) The second and broader notion of interest does not originate in the simple adversion toward the object, but in making it *thematic*. Theme (in the precise sense) and object do not always coincide, as for example in a situation in which I am occupied with a scientific work as my theme, but am "interrupted" by a noise in the street. Even then I have not dropped my theme to which I return after the interruption has passed. Acts of interest in this broader sense surpass, then, the mere being adverted to the object, say by perceiving it or even searchingly examining it: they involve "taking part" in this activity ("Dabei-sein"), an *inter-esse* in the literal sense of this word.[6]

Husserl, in the texts published so far, does not continue this analysis beyond these fugitive remarks. But it is quite clear that it is the interest, or, perhaps better, the system of interests which codetermines typicality.

So far we have spoken merely of the inner horizon of the object and its explication. But any object adverted to stands out from a background, a field, which is not adverted to, but is just "there." We may say that the object has an open, endless horizon of coexisting objects, hence a horizon of a second level which is related to the horizon of the first one. We call this horizon the *outer horizon* of coexisting objects to which I may at any time turn as to objects being either different from or typically similar to the object I am actually adverted to. In a certain sense the meaning of the latter is codetermined by its outer horizon as the totality of my potential experiences of coexistent objects, and their relations to the actually apperceived one. But this is not all: the meaning of the object which is in immediacy given to our actual intuition refers also to its—mostly hidden—relations to objects which were given to us once in the past, and might now be represented in terms of recollections of various kinds, and even to objectivities of our free phantasying, provided that a relationship of similarity between them and the actually given object prevails at all. The unity between the related elements might be experienced merely passively as pregiven in the unity of our consciousness. But—in contradistinction to the process of explicating the implicata hidden in the inner horizon—all these relations can be made thematic. The activity by which this is done is called by Husserl "relating contemplation" (*beziehendes Betrachten*). However, it has to be emphasized that a mere addition of further objects to the actually given object is as such not a relating contemplation. The latter requires a specific interest in the broader sense which makes the object taken as the point of departure the main theme. If, for example, my fountain pen is the main theme, then the table upon which it lies is not the main theme, but a theme merely with respect to the fountain pen. Which object, in such a case, becomes the main theme depends again upon the direction of the then prevailing interest, and the relating contemplation may reveal different determinations of either of the related objects such as: A B, B < A; A lies upon B, B beneath A.

It goes without saying that everything stated before in respect of the inner horizon as to the habitual sedimentation of once obtained knowledge, and as to its functions in the renewed or entirely new determination of objectivities—and therewith in the ascertainment of their typicality—is also valid for habitualities originating in relating contemplations.

II. EMPIRICAL TYPES AND UNIVERSALS

So far our analysis was restricted to the pre predicative level. We have seen how empirical types are, according to Husserl, preconstituted in passivity, which he considers as the lowest form of the constitution of universals. Of particular interest to him is now the transition from the empirical types to the predicative judgments dealing with generic concepts, and further to the constitution of universal objectivities of the highest level and the forms of all-or-none judgments. Let us first follow this development in terms of the typicality of the apperceived objects.[7] Anything apperceived in its typicality *may* lead up to the universal concept of the type under which we apprehend it. But we need not be directed in such a manner toward the generic; we need not apperceive thematically this concrete individual dog as a singularization of the general notion "dog." "*In general*" one dog is like any other dog. If, however, we remain directed toward the dog as an individual, then the passively preconstituted relation of this individual dog to the type under which he was apperceived from the outset remains unthematized. This typicality will not exhaust all similarities of the concrete object which will be revealed in the progress of our experiencing it. To the type "dog," for example, belongs a set of typical properties with an open horizon of anticipations of further typical characteristics. If we proceeded in our experiencing of this or that individual dog, we would find ever new characteristics which do not belong just to this individual dog, but to dogs in general, characteristics which are predelineated by the properties appropriated by us as typical for dogs in accordance with the incomplete and fugitive experiences we had had of them until now. This is the origin of a *presumptive idea of a universal* which surpasses the *concept* of *real* dogs as it originated in *real* experiences. Husserl calls this idea a presumptive one because we live continually in the empirical certainty—a certainty good until further notice—that what proves to be on the ground of known properties an object of a particular type will also have all the further characteristics regularly discovered in other objects of this type by regular induction, and so on. In this manner the empirical concepts undergo continual change caused by the resorption of new characteristics under the guidance of the empirical idea of an open and always rectifiable concept, an idea which is at the foundation of our empirical faith in the continuity of our real experiences.

To be sure, the prevailing assumption that always new typical moments can be grasped in the process of experiencing, may be disappointed. Immediate experience frequently distinguishes things in accordance with certain striking relations which might obfuscate factual inner relations. The appertaining of the whale (in German: *der Wallfisch*) to the class of the mammals is, for example, hidden by the exterior analogy to the way of life which this animal shares with the fishes. In such cases we speak of nonessential types (*ausserwesentliche Typen*). In the comprehensive experience of concrete Nature the individuals are more and more grouped under essential types (*wesentliche Typen*) of various degrees of universality. It is this state of affairs upon which scientific empirical research into Nature and its history is founded. By necessity it refers to prescientific and in many cases unessential types of the natural experiential apperception. Scientific concepts of species aim at the determination of essential types by systematic and methodical experiences, but they too carry along an open infinite horizon of—at the outset still unknown—typical characteristics to be determined by further research. The typical refers in this case also to causality: the causality of the "life" of the animals or plants of the particular types (species) under particular conditions, their development, procreation, etc.

III. Constitution of Universal Objectives in the Predicative Sphere[8]

Yet our presentation of the transition from the prepredicative type to the empirical presumptive idea did not deal with an important intermediary step, namely, the constitution of the typically generic and finally universal objectivities in the predicative sphere. The prepredicative receptive experience is guided by the interest in perceiving, that is, the tendency to bring the given objectivity in all its aspects and perspectives to our intuition. But this is merely a preliminary level of the interest in knowing (*Erkenntnisinteresse*) the objectivity, and in preserving the knowledge once attained. This is done by a cognitive activity of the I, the outcome of which is predication. Husserl speaks also of the predicative spontaneity as opposed to the receptive experience. It is important for the understanding of the process of predication to see that any predicative judgment includes a form of universality (*Allgemeinheitsform*), a determination of the object "*as*" being this and that. This is the counterpart of grasping from the outset an object in pure receptivity as being of a somehow familiar type. If, for example, we determine this particular perceptual object as being red and form the perceptual judgment, "S is p," then by reason of the universality of the determination "red" the relation to the universal "redness" is already implicitly contained in this "determining-as-being-red." To be sure, this relation has so far not become thematic, as it would be in the form: "this is *one* red object." But only in the latter case could we speak of conceptual thinking in the proper sense.

The simple predication "S is p" corresponds to the explication of an object perceived. But whereas the explication of a substratum S consists in a passive synthesis of congruence between S and its determinant moment *p,* the positing of S as the subject (in the logical sense) of the predicative judgment "S is p" requires a new form of activity which is motivated by the supervening interest (in the broader sense) in actively determining S as the thematic *terminus a quo* and *p* as the *terminus ad quem*. In other words, an *active* intention aims now at grasping that which was previously given in *passive* congruence. This activity is not only synthetic activity in general, but at the same time the activity of synthesizing. We become aware that S is determined by *p* in the form "S is p." This process occurs in polythetic steps.

But "S is p" is merely the archetype of predication. The determining process may go on from *p* to *q* to *r,* which

may lead to judgments of the form "S is p *and* q *and* r," if the cognitive interest is equally distributed among all members, or to (linguistically) subordinate clauses, that is, to judgments of the form "S, which is p, is q," etc. In his studies dedicated to the genesis of predicative judgments Husserl analyzed a great number of such forms, to describe which would surpass by far the limits of this paper. We turn instead immediately to his theory of the constitution of universals in productive spontaneity. It is precisely here that the notion of typicality receives a modified meaning. Husserl recalls to us that the relation of a single object to the typically general prevails already in any apperception of the individual on the ground of the horizon of familiarity. The decisive point is, however, whether or not this relation becomes thematic in a process of judging. If it does, the characters of familiarity may lead to the active, spontaneous constitution of a new kind of objectivities, namely, to *the typically generic itself,* as whose "representative" the individual object is apperceived, that is, as an *objectivity of this kind, of this type*. The universals constituted in these supervening acts of free spontaneity—the types, species, genera, etc.—may be of various levels of generality. The generality of the empirical presumptive type is merely one among them and a relatively low one; at the highest level are the pure or eidetic universals and, based upon them, judgments which no longer originate in the thematization of the relations of the objectivities to their empirical types of familiarity, but in the thematization of their relations to pure essences.

Let us very briefly illustrate the constitution of universals in productive spontaneity by an example. Suppose we found in concentration upon S the moment *p* as standing out in the form S is p. Our interest shifts now to S', S'', S''' which coaffect us because they too show the same moment *p* as *their* outstanding individual moment. In this case we have to distinguish two series of judgments: the first one in which the individual moment is predicated to each substratum: "S' is p'," "S'' is p''," "S''' is p'''"; and a second series in which everywhere the same *p* (without prime) is predicated to each substratum as the universal identical unity of the species constituted passively in the congruence of likeness of p', p'', p'''. Then we arrive at judgments such as "S' is p," "S'' is p," etc., whereby *p* is no longer a predicative individual kernel, but a general one. In the judgment "S' is p'," the *p'* designates the *individual* moment in the *individual* object S', whereby the substratum S' and its individual moment are identified. We call such a judgment an individual judgment. In the judgment "S' is p" universals appear at least on one side, since *p* designates the universal (*das Allgemeine*). We call such a judgment a generic judgment (*generelles Urteil*). This is a new form of judgments because the difference of the kernels leads to a modified form of the synthesis of identity as compared with the simple explicative synthesis which we considered to be the basic form of our categorical judgment "S is p," although the former is founded on the latter.

IV. The Enlargment of the Notion of
Typicality in Husserl's *Krisis*[9]

We would now have to study the nature of pure universals as they are revealed by the eidetic method. Before doing so, however, we want to follow the analysis of typicality which Husserl has reassumed in his last work, the *Krisis,* supplementing and, as it seems to me, considerably modifying, his theory. As usual, Husserl takes as his paradigm the apperception of concrete objects of the external world given to our actual or potential sensory experience. To the nature of the experiential givenness of such objects belongs also a typical regularity in their changeability both as to their position in space and time, and as to their qualities in form or content. None of these changes is contingent or arbitrary, but all of them, in their sensory typical mode, are empirically interdependent. These interrelations are themselves moments of the experiential intuition of everyday life; they are experienced as that which makes objects coexisting in simultaneity or succession belong together. The objects in the intuitive environment (always taken as they are given to us intuitively in the experience of everyday life, and accepted as real in the natural attitude) have, as it were, their "habits" of behaving similarly under typically similar circumstances. And even if we take the world as a whole in its fluctuant actuality ("*stroemende Jeweiligkeit*") in which it is to us simply there, this world as a whole, too, has its "habit" of continuing to be as it has been so far. Thus, our empirically intuitive environment has its empirically all-encompassing style; and this remains invariant in whatever manner we imagine this world as modified or in whatever form we represent it in the style in which we have the world now, and in which we have had it so far. Of this fact we may become conscious in reflection, and by performing free variations of these possibilities, we may make thematic the invariant general style in which this intuitive world persists in the flux of the total experience. Then we understand that, in general, things and events do not occur and take this course in a haphazard way, but that they are *a priori* bound to this style as the invariant form of the intuitive world; in other words, that by a universal causal regularity everything that coexists in the world has the character of belonging together on the ground of which the world is not merely a totality (*Allheit*) but a total unity (*Alleinheit*), a (to be sure, infinite) whole. It is this universal causal style of the intuitive environment which makes hypotheses, inductions, predictions concerning the unknown features of the present, the past, and the future possible. But in the prescientific (and, if we understand Husserl correctly, we have to add: *a fortiori* in the prepredicative) cognitive life we remain with all this in the approximation of typicality.[10]

In the *Krisis* and the related manuscripts Husserl emphasizes again and again that things in the intuitive environment and all their properties vacillate in their mere typicality; their identity with themselves and their being like

other things is just an approximation. In all these relations there prevails a gradation of perfection, the degree being dependent upon the specific practical interest to be satisfied. With a change of interest a formerly satisfactory degree of perfection might no longer satisfy the new interest.[11] In another passage of the *Krisis*[12] Husserl points out that although this typicality makes scientific description and phenomenological-transcendental truth possible, it pervades the unity of the life-world and the universe of objects in it in spite of and beyond all its relativities. It would be possible to make this typicality (without any transcendental interest, that is, in the naive attitude before performing the *epoché*) the theme of a particular science, namely, of an ontology of the life-world as the world of our actual and potential experiential intuitions. To be sure, the life-world which includes all practical objectivities, even the objectivities of the sciences as cultural facts, refers in the continual change of its relativities to subjectivity. Yet in spite of all these changes and in spite of all rectifications it follows its essential typicality, to which all life, and therewith all sciences of which it is the foundation, remain subjected. This ontology of the life-world can be revealed in pure evidence. In a supplementary text, eliminated by the editors as a mere repetition,[13] Husserl wonders why the "*Geisteswissenschaften*" have so far failed to develop such an ontology of the life-world in their search for the *a priori* peculiar to their field. It would reveal, for example, the types of sociality (family, tribe, state, etc.) or of objects of culture as well as the types of particular historical or cultural environment (of the Egyptians, the ancient Greeks, the so-called primitives, etc.). And on occasion Husserl emphasizes that this typicality of the life-world is by no means my private affair, but that of the "socialized" subjectivity (*vergemeinschaftete Subjektivitaet*): The concrete typicality of the life-world is that of the world valid for all of us. Not only my own life, but also that of each of us in the unity of its actual flux is continually surrounded by the actual horizons of our practical power (*Vermoeglichkeit*) to guide, direct, and influence actual occurrences by an interference of our Self. But although I am always certain of such a power, I am, like everyone, bound to the essential typicality which pervades all actualities and potentialities. This is so because all horizons in their modifications form one universal horizon, first my own, and then, in the general interconnectedness of all subjects, the trans-subjective universal horizon. This problem leads again to the preacquaintedness of the life-world as a whole and the concrete objects in it.

At the end of the *Krisis*[14] Husserl enlarges considerably the notion of the typicality of the life-world. Things, he says, have their particular concrete typicality, expressed by the "nouns" of the particular vernacular. But all specific typicality is encompassed by the most general one, the "regional" typicality, such as the region of inanimate and animate things, among the latter, man, etc. This typicality in its continual factual generality determines practice in everyday life; as essentially necessary it can be revealed only by an eidetic method.

V. TYPE AND EIDOS

The last part of *Erfahrung und Urteil*[15] deals with the nature of pure universals as obtained by the eidetic method. Husserl here describes this method in a similar way as in *Ideas,* I and III. An experienced or phantasied objectivity is interpreted as an example of the universal, and at the same time as a prototype (*Vorbild*) for modifications by a series of free variations in phantasy. All of these variations have concrete similarities with the same prototype, and the manifold of new images produced in phantasy is permeated by an invariant identical content in terms of which all the arbitrarily performed variations come to congruence, whereas their differences remain irrelevant. This invariant element prescribes their limits to all possible variations of the same prototype; it is that element without which an objectivity of this kind can neither be thought nor intuitively phantasied. Upon the manifold of the variants produced in the process of arbitrary variations the intuition proper of the universal as eidos is founded and can now be grasped purely as such. This intuition of the eidos consists in the active apprehension of that which was passively preconstituted: the exemplar chosen as point of departure guides us as prototype to ever new images created by association and passive phantasy or by fictitious transformation in active phantasying.

Yet there are important differences between empirical universals and eidetic ones. The former are not only contingent in the sense that their formation starts from a particular given contingently in factual experience, but also in the sense that the conceptualization proceeds on the ground of comparison with likewise contingently given similarities. In the natural attitude the experienced world is given to us as the universal persistent ground of being, and as the universal field of all of our activities, whatever interest we follow. The formation of pure concepts, however, must not depend on these contingencies of the factually given, but must be capable of prescribing rules for the experiencing of all empirical particulars. By the process of ideation we put out of play the relationship of our experience with the world, and liberate the environmental horizon of the variants from any attachment to any experiential activity. By doing so we place ourselves in a world of pure phantasy, of pure possibilities. Each of them may now become the central member of a set of possible pure variations in the mode of arbitrariness; from each of them we may arrive at an absolute pure eidos—provided that the sequences of variations can be connected to a single one. Thus we obtain a different eidos for colors and sounds; they are of different kinds with respect to that which is purely intuited in them.

Any eidetic concrete possibility permits specifications of the highest freely formed universals. Still directed toward pure possibilities, we may introduce limiting preconditions for the activities of pure phantasying, for example, by postulating that the universal "geometrical figure" should be limited by three sides. Then we may investigate the essential properties of such a formation, the eidos of the tri-angle. Of course, such a specification of eidetic universals should not be confounded with concrete concepts such as tree, dog, etc. Empirical concepts are not genuine specifications of pure universals; they mean typical generalizations, scopes of anticipations of experiences delineated by actual experiences. On the other hand, the eidetic universality can be related to appearing realities at any time. Any actually emergent color is at the same time possible in the pure sense; any one can be taken as an example or prototype and be transformed into a variant. Thus we may transpose all actualities to the level of pure possibilities, the realm of arbitrariness.

But if we do so, it turns out that even this free arbitrariness has its particular limitations. That which can be varied in arbitrary phantasying has necessarily an inner structure, an eidos, and therewith laws of necessity which determine the characteristics an objectivity must have in order to be of this or that particular kind. There is, however, another text clarifying the relationship between typicality and eidos which is of particular importance since it represents a later version than that of *Erfahrung und Urteil.* We find it in the second and fourth Cartesian Meditation[16] in connection with the description of the characteristics of intentional analysis after the performance of *epoché.* Husserl points out that the flux of intentional synthesis which noëtically and noëmatically constitutes the unity of the meaning of an objectivity is necessarily regulated in accordance with an essential typicality. (Of course, this term is here used in a new sense.) The most general typicality, which includes all specifications, is the general scheme *ego-cogito-cogitatum.* In the specifications of this typicality the intentional objectivity of the cogitatum plays the role of a transcendental clue for the disclosure of the typical manifoldness of cogitations which in possible syntheses refer to it as having the same meaning. Possible perception, retention, recollection, anticipation, signification, analogical intuition are examples of such specified types of intentionality which refer to any thinkable objectivity. These specifications may be of a formal-logical (formal-ontological) kind, such as the modes of "something in general (*Etwas ueberhaupt*)," the singular and concrete individual, the generic, the plurality, the whole, the relation, etc. It is precisely here that the radical distinction between real objects in the broadest sense and categorial objectivities becomes apparent, the latter referring to their origin in *operations* of a polythetic activity of the I, the former being the outcome of a mere passive synthesis. On the other hand, there are material-ontological specifications attached to the concept of the real individual, which is subdivided in its real regions, for example, (mere) spatial corporeal thing, animal, etc., a subdivision leading to corresponding specifications of the pertinent formal-logical modes (real quality, real plurality, real relation, etc.). If we hold fast to any objectivity in its form or category and if we continue to keep in evidence its identity subsisting in all the changes of its modes of consciousness, then we discover that the latter are by no means arbitrary ones, however fluctuant they may be. They remain always bound to a structural typicality which continues to be indestructibly the same as long as consciousness continues to grasp the objectivity as being of such and such a kind and as long as it is held in the evidence of identity through all the changes of its modes of consciousness. And Husserl adds to this important passage that it is the task of the transcendental theories to explain systematically this structural typicality and its constitution by analyzing the system of possible objectivities and their inner and outer horizon. One of the basic forms of specific transcendental methods is the eidetic intuition. Taking an empirical fact as our point of departure, we transpose the factual experiences to the realm of irrealities, of the "as if," which confronts us with the *pure* possibilities, purified, that is, of everything bound to the particular fact and any fact at all. Thus we obtain the eidos as the intuited or intuitable pure universal which, not conditioned by any fact, precedes all conceptualizations in the sense of "meanings of words"; on the contrary, all pure concepts have to be formed as adjusted to the eidos. In the *Cartesian Meditations* Husserl uses the eidetic method not only for the description of the various types of cogitations, such as perception, retention, assertion, being fond of something, etc., but also for the transformation of the factual ego into an eidos "transcendental ego," of which the former is merely a possible modification.

VI. Some Critical Remarks

At the beginning of this paper we maintained that the notion of typicality, so central in the later philosophy of Husserl, is an operative and not a thematic one. It is hoped that the preceding presentation has corroborated this statement, and has shown that this notion is fraught with manifold equivocations and used by Husserl with different meanings in different contexts. In terms of *Erfahrung und Urteil* typicality is genetically preconstituted in previous experiences which form latent habitual possessions, and are called forth or awakened by a passive synthesis of congruence if we apperceive actually a similar object. At the same time, by apperceptive transference a set of anticipations is created which attach themselves to the givenness of a newly encountered objectivity of the same type. Thus typicality is the origin of the preacquaintedness and the familiarity of the objectivities within the world. A text published by Husserl himself as Appendix 2 to *Formale und transcendentale Logik*[17] explains this process rather graphically: each mode of givenness, we read here, has a double after-effect: first, the recognition of similar objects in the congruence of a passive synthesis with objects recollected becomes possible; secondly, there is what Husserl calls in this text the "apperceptive after-effect" on the ground of which the preconstituted objectivity is apperceived in a similar situation in a similar way. These are, according to Husserl, essential intentional structures of empirical experience (although not empirical facts).

The notion of typicality as used in the *Krisis* is the form in which the objects within our intuitive environment—the *Lebenswelt*—together with their properties and their changes are given to our natural attitude. This form is that of a vacillating approximation. All regularities, even the

causal ones, belong to the typical "habit" in which things behave, as it were, under typical similar circumstances. A gradation of perfection, which, in turn, depends upon our actual practical interest to be satisfied, prevails in all these relations. On the other hand, however, this typicality, in its continual factual generality determines practice. Its essential necessity can be revealed only by the eidetic method. This essential typicality is characterized in the pertinent passages of the *Cartesian Meditations* dealing with the eidetic reduction. Here we learn that it is the flux of intentional synthesis which shows, after the performance of the *epoché,* an essential typicality; first, the most general one of *ego-cogito-cogitatum,* then more specific types of cogitations for the disclosure of which the *cogitatum* serves as transcendental clue. These specifications may be of a formal-ontological kind and then lead either to real objects as the outcome of passive synthesis or to categorial objectivities as results of operations of the I; or, they may be material-ontological specifications in accordance with the real regions. The relationship between typicality and eidos is here obviously conceived in a different way from that of the final chapters of *Erfahrung und Urteil* reported on an earlier occasion. The operative use of the notion of typicality gives rise to a series of questions which remain unclarified in Husserl's published writings.

(1) *Erfahrung und Urteil* connects the notion of typicality with a set of other operative notions which never become thematic for a philosophical analysis, and are equivocal in respect of their relation both to one another and to the notion of typicality. These are the concepts of "similarity," "synthesis by congruence," "association," "impressive aspects," "interest." Is it Husserl's view that typicality is founded upon the preconstitution of similarity by association? Or have we to assume that similarity itself presupposes an experience of typicality, namely, that of the typically similar? And what is typically similar? The "impressive" aspect of the actually perceived object. What makes this aspect impressive? Our prevailing interest in the broader or narrower sense. Moreover, what sets the passive synthesis of congruence agoing by which the actually apperceived object is paired with a recollected element that is just a latent habitual possession "called forth" as a similar or dissimilar one? Is it indeed the same passive synthesis of congruence which creates by apperceptive transference a set of anticipations that attach themselves to the givenness of a newly encountered objectivity of the same type, and thus brings about the character of preacquaintedness and familiarity of our experiencing of the life-world in the natural attitude?

(2) Does not the equivocal description Husserl gives of the awareness of similarity, of the impressive aspects of the typical due to our interest, and of the synthesis of congruence originate in the fact that he takes as his model of all his pertinent investigations the perception of an object in the outer world and, even more precisely, the visual perception of such an object? If we take as an example a musical theme with its transposition in other keys, its inver-

sion, enlargement, diminution, variations of all kinds, does then the "similarity" of all these modifications not already presuppose a similarity of specific typical characteristics? And if we turn to objectivities which are not perceptual objects of the outer world, say mathematical functions which are recognized as being "similar," does this "similarity" not refer to particular typical characteristics of these functions?

(3) Husserl develops in *Erfahrung und Urteil* the important distinction between essential and nonessential types. The question arises, however, on what level this distinction becomes visible. Are not all the types in terms of which we experience the life-world in the naive attitude equally essential? Are not all of them the outcome of similar elements paired by passive synthesis of congruence? Or does a distinction between the mere seemingly similar and similarity based on inner relations prevail even on this prepredicative level?

(4) The nature of the typicality of the life-world and the meaning of its preacquaintedness becomes especially complicated if we accept Husserl's statement that this typicality is by no means my private affair, but that of the "socialized" subjectivity. It is the concrete typicality of the world valid for all of us. This is without any doubt the case. But where is the origin or the foundation of this intersubjective or transsubjective validity? Is there such a thing as a transsubjective passive synthesis of congruence by wakening a preconstituted and latent (as an habitual possession) element of the pair? It is submitted that all the operative notions of phenomenology lead to insoluble difficulties when applied to problems of transsubjectivity.

(5) The distinction between activity and passivity of the conscious life is highly unclarified, and created many difficulties for such eminent students of phenomenology as R. Ingarden,[18] Jean Wahl,[19] and L. Landgrebe.[20] In the context of our problem we found texts in which a sharp distinction is made between passive receptivity and predicative spontaneity, and others which interpret receptivity and the "adverting" to the object as the lowest form of spontaneity. We meet the notion of an active performance of consciousness in our study of *Erfahrung und Urteil,* first in the distinction between explicating the inner horizon and the possibility of making the outer horizon thematic by the particular activity of the I which Husserl calls "relating contemplation." We then found that particular activities make the transition possible which leads from empirical types to predicative judgments dealing with generic concepts, and finally to the constitution of universals of the highest level and the form of all-or-none judgments. To be sure, according to Husserl, the type leads to the presumptive idea of a universal. A relation of a single object to the typically general prevails already in any apperception of the individual in its horizon of familiarity. But all predication presupposes a cognitive activity of the mind, an active intuition which aims at grasping thematically that which was previously given in passive congruence. The question arises, however, whether the formation of the

basic empirical type does not presuppose an activity of the I. Husserl has described in a masterful manner for the realm of predication the way in which undivided judgments of the form "S' is p'," "S" is p" . . ." are transformed into generic judgments of the form "S' is p," "S" is p . . ." which is possible on the foundation of a passive congruence of likeness of *p'*, *p"* . . . considered as instances of *p*. But does not, as we once suggested,[21] typification, even in the prepredicative sphere, consist in the "suppression of the primes" adhering to the apperceived individual object? In other words, is the distinction between passivity and activity of the conscious life indeed valid, and if valid, a suitable criterion for the determination of the "degree of generality?"

(6) Yet in spite of the texts referred to in the preceding paragraph, the whole work of Husserl shows clearly that there is a decisive difference between the formation of generic judgments of any level of generality and the intuitions of the eidos. Whereas empirical universals are contingent, ideation puts out of play the relationship of experience with the world by taking the concrete individual merely as an exemplar, a prototype, a point of departure for a series of free variations arbitrarily performed in phantasy: the empirical factuality is thus replaced by pure possibilities. (We want to speak merely of material universals arrived at by eidetic generalization, disregarding thus in this connection the formal universals arrived at by eidetic formalization.) The question of first importance which presents itself is whether the "free variations" to be performed in phantasy, starting from the individual object as example or prototype, are indeed as free as they seem, that is, whether the arbitrariness of transforming the empirically given into a special case of general possibilities does not have well-defined limits. To be sure, Husserl himself recognizes such limits, if he speaks of regional ontologies or, in a terminology used by him in earlier writings, of spheres of incompatibility (*Unvertraeglichkeitssphaeren*). The freedom of variations in phantasy will not permit us to arrive, starting from the prototype of a colored object, at the eidos of sound. It is doubtless possible to grasp eidetically material realms or regions of being, but these regions are not constituted by performances of our consciousness: they are indeed ontological regions of the world and as such given to our experience or, as we may say, imposed upon us. But we have to drive the questioning even farther. Is it possible to grasp by means of free variations in phantasy the eidos of a concrete species or genus, unless these variations are limited by the frame of the type in terms of which we have experienced in the natural attitude the object from which the process of ideation starts as a familiar one, as such and such an object within the life-world? Can these free variations in phantasy reveal anything else but the limits established by such typification? If these questions have to be answered in the negative, then there is indeed merely a difference of degree between type and eidos. Ideation can reveal nothing that was not preconstituted by the type.

It is impossible to investigate this question within the frame of this paper. But even our fugitive remarks have shown that the notion of eidetic reduction is at least partially an operative one.

Notes

1. *Actes du Colloque international de phénoménologie à Royaumont* (23-30 avril 1957), in press.

2. *Erfahrung und Urteil, Untersuchungen zur Genealogie der Logik,* redigiert und herausgegeben von Ludwig Landgrebe, 2. unveraenderte Auflage, Hamburg, 1954 (referred to as *EU*); see for the present section of this paper especially *EU*, Introduction and Part I, but also the very important sections 82 and 83.

3. *Cartesianische Meditationen und Pariser Vortraege,* herausgegeben und eingeleitet von St. Strasser, (*Husserliana* I.), Den Haag, 1950 (referred to as *CM*); cf. IV. Meditation, sections 38, 39; V. Meditation, sections 50-52.

4. *EU*, section 83.

5. *EU*, p. 139.

6. *EU*, section 20.

7. See to the following *EU* sections 82 ff., esp. 83 and 84.

8. *EU*, Parts II and III.

9. *Die Krisis der europaeischen Wissenschaften und die transzendentale Phaenomenologie, Eine Einleitung in die phaenomenologische Philosophie,* herausgegeben von Walter Biemel (*Husserliana* VI.), Den Haag, 1954 (referred to as *K*).

10. *K*, section 9b.

11. *K*, section 9a, pp. 22 f.

12. *K*, section 51, p. 176.

13. *K*, pp. 529 ff.; refers to *K*, section 51, p. 176.

14. *K*, section 63, pp. 229 f.

15. *EU*, Part III., esp. ch. II.

16. *CM*, sections 20-22, 34.

17. *Formale und Transzendentale Logik, Versuch einer Kritik der logischen Vernunft,* Halle, 1929, Beilage II, Sections 2a and b, pp. 276-279.

18. *CM*, p. 214.

19. Wahl, J., "Notes sur la première partie de Erfahrung und Urteil de Husserl," *Phénoménologie et Existence,* Paris, 1953, p. 100.

20. Lettre de L. Landgrebe sur un Article de M. Jean Wahl, ib. p. 206.

21. "Common-Sence and Scientific Interpretation of Human Action," *Philosophy and Phenomenological Research,* Vol. XIV, 1953, p. 16.

Herbert Spiegelberg (essay date 1960)

SOURCE: "Husserl's Phenomenology and Existentialism," in *The Journal of Philosophy,* Vol. LVII, No. 1, January 7, 1960, pp. 62-74.

[In the following essay, Spiegelberg discusses the relationship between phenomenology and existentialism.]

Philosophers do not seem to have had more success than other mortals in reaching centenarian age. This failure has for them the awkward consequence that between their death and the first centennial of their birth their fame has to undergo something like a probationary period during which they are no longer protected by the public's reverence for superannuity and by worshipful societies of disciples.

Outwardly Husserl's prestige has weathered this probationary period surprisingly well. At his death 21 years ago, he may well have seemed headed for total oblivion. His own University of Freiburg—to be sure, under Nazi pressure—had removed his very name from the roster of its emeriti. Moreover, philosophically he seemed deserted by most of his erstwhile students. The remarkable comeback of his fame since then is attested by such events as the foundation of the Husserl Archives at the Universities of Louvain and Cologne, by the edition of seven volumes from his unpublished writings, and by the general ascendency of phenomenology especially in France and in other Latin-speaking countries. This very occasion is living proof that at least the program committee of one Anglo-American philosophical society considers him worthy of centennial attention on a par with John Dewey.

To be sure, Husserl's new fame in this country shines largely with a reflected light. Its source is the still fashionable interest in the child of the strange alliance between Kierkegaard's "unscientific" existential thinking and Husserl's new phenomenological science that goes by the name of existentialism. In very much the same way as it happened in France in the thirties, when Heidegger was the center of interest, it is now Sartre's fame which has aroused a retroactive interest in Husserl as his supposed teacher. It was therefore highly appropriate that the Program Committee decided to use this occasion for a systematic discussion of the relations between phenomenology and existentialism. This choice can even claim Husserl's own authority. For when in 1924 Husserl gave the official address at the University of Freiburg on the occasion of the bicentennial of Kant's birth he stated that "the time for the commemoration of a great genius is an invitation for responsible self-appraisal for the living generation" and promptly proceeded to examine the relation of his phenomenology to Kant's transcendentalism.[1]

I propose to broach the subject by first bringing out some facts, not always duly noticed, about the historical connections between the two movements. Then I shall discuss in a more systematic frame the essential relations between them.

But this program presupposes at least some preliminary agreements about the Protean terms "phenomenology" and "existentialism." To make them sufficiently precise will require cutting off some marginal types. In this context there will be no time to justify the eliminations. So I shall have to be rather dogmatic, keeping my reasons in reserve.

In the case of phenomenology it would be improper to advocate here a wider conception which would include more than Husserl's version of phenomenology, as I have tried to do elsewhere.[2] Not only out of respect for Husserl, but for the purpose of sharpening the issue, it seems fitting to consider here phenomenology in its most rigorous form. To be sure, even then one has to take account of the development of his conception from a merely descriptive phenomenology to transcendental phenomenology. Yet for the sake of the present confrontation it seems defensible to condense the most important constants of his phenomenology in the following minimum list of propositions:

1. Phenomenology is a rigorous science in the sense of a coherent system of propositions; it goes even beyond positive science by aiming at absolute certainty for its foundations and at freedom from presuppositions that have not passed phenomenological scrutiny.

2. Its subject-matter is the general essences of the phenomena of consciousness; among these phenomena, the phenomenologist distinguishes between the intending acts and the intended objects in strict parallel; he pays special attention to the modes of appearance in which the intended referents present themselves; he does not impose any limitations as to the content of these phenomena.

3. Phenomenology is based on the intuitive exploration and faithful description of the phenomena within the context of the world of our lived experience (*Lebenswelt*), anxious to avoid reductionist oversimplifications and overcomplications by preconceived theoretical patterns.

4. In order to secure the fullest possible range of phenomena and at the same time doubt-proof foundations it uses a special method of reductions which suspends the beliefs associated with our naive or natural attitude and shared even by science; it also traces back the phenomena to the constituting acts in a pure subject, which itself proves to be irreducible.

5. Its ultimate objective is the examination and justification of all our beliefs, both ordinary and scientific, by the test of intuitive perception.

To perform the same kind of surgery on the much more amorphous body of beliefs and attitudes that sail under the flag of existentialism may appear as an even more foolhardy enterprise. In attempting it one does well to remember that self-confessed existentialism does not date earlier than 1944 when Sartre, having already published his major philosophical works, took the word "existentialism" out of the hands of his hostile critics and applied it retroactively to his own writings and to those of his predecessors. Any attempt to define such a sprawling phenomenon has to make incisions which may seem arbitrary. I submit, however, that there is something like a hard core of present-day existentialism based on affinities in interest and approach. It includes not only the self-confessed phenomenological existentialists such as Sartre and

Merleau-Ponty but also Gabriel Marcel, however repentant as to the term "Christian existentialism," and such unrepentant existentialists as Nicolai Berdyaev or Nicolò Abbagnano. Besides, according to their major concerns and themes, Jaspers' deliberately non-phenomenological elucidation of existence and Heidegger's phenomenological analytics of existence are inseparable from full-fledged existentialism, their vigorous protests notwithstanding. Even if their own objectives were different and ulterior, the existentialism of the forties would never have been possible without them.

Sartre has attempted to condense the cloudy essence of these existentialisms into the neat though mystifying formula that in existentialism "existence precedes essence." But this formula has been repudiated, with good reasons, by everyone but himself. For the present purposes it may be more helpful to match the preceding propositions about phenomenology by a similar set that is meant to apply to hard-core existentialism only:

1. Existentialism, unlike phenomenology, does not aspire to be scientific, though it is not essentially anti-scientific or even antisystematic. Systematic structures and absolute certainty are simply none of its primary objectives.

2. Its subject-matter is human existence or "human reality," not consciousness, as in phenomenology. It studies existence in its involvement in a situation within a world. Consciousness, however, reflective as well as pre-reflective, is part of the encompassing structure of existence.

3. Existentialism is not restricted to any particular method; Kierkegaard's existential dialectics and Jaspers' elucidation of existence have historical priority over phenomenological existentialism.

4. Phenomenological existentialism goes beyond the phenomenological description of certain highly selective phenomena by a special kind of interpretation, the so-called hermeneutic method, which aspires to decipher their meaning for existence. Phenomenological reduction as practiced by Husserl, if it is mentioned at all, is rejected; so is Husserl's concern for transcendental subjectivity as the absolute foundation of all being.

5. The ultimate objective of existentialism is not theoretical justification, but the awakening to a special way of life, usually called "authentic existence."

We are now in a position to approach the question of the historical relations between the two movements. Husserl himself during his lifetime faced only the predecessors of self-confessed existentialism: Karl Jaspers' *Existenzphilosophie* and Martin Heidegger's existential analysis of human *Dasein*. Jaspers, although he had used phenomenological description in his psychopathology, had rejected phenomenology at the very outset of his independent philosophizing because of its claims to scientific rigor. Heidegger, however, publishing his magnum opus *Sein und Zeit* in Husserl's *Yearbook for Philosophy and Phenomenological Research,* gave every indication of adhering to the phenomenological method, although he claimed at the same time the right to develop it further and, implicitly at least, to omit some of it. Such a tacit omission was, for instance, that of Husserl's cherished phenomenological reduction.

Three years later Husserl's only printed pronouncement about *Existenzphilosophie* appeared, notably in a Postscript to his **Ideen,** at the very end of the last volume of his Yearbook. It came two years after Heidegger had been appointed the successor to his chair at the University of Freiburg, an appointment which, as a matter of fact, had resulted from Husserl's own recommendation. Although this pronouncement did not mention either Jaspers or Heidegger by name, it left no doubt about the identity of the addressees. This statement rejected summarily the actual or suspected charges against Husserl's own philosophizing. It also declared *Existenzphilosophie* a relapse into the deadly sins of anthropologism and psychologism, hence not acceptable even as a specimen of genuine philosophy. Other expressions, such as lectures, letters, and especially marginal comments to his readings in Heidegger, leave no doubt about the fact that Husserl saw especially in the latter's analytics of existence a corruption of the phenomenological enterprise. These indictments led soon to a cooling off and a final ceasing of the once cordial relations between Husserl and his erstwhile assistant. From then on Heidegger practically stopped using the term "phenomenology" in his own philosophizing. As a result, phenomenology and the philosophy of existence remained two completely separate movements, as far as Germany was concerned.

It would, however, be premature to infer from this that Husserl had no appreciation for the questions raised by the philosophers of existence. Even the Postscript to the **Ideen,** while rejecting the charges that phenomenology was unable to cope with the problems of "so-called 'existence,'" implied that such problems do exist. What Husserl objected to was merely the claim to priority of the existential analytics over his own transcendental phenomenology, which Heidegger had implied. It is therefore not surprising to find Husserl himself in his last decade repeatedly resorting to existential phraseology.[3] How far the conception of the *Lebenswelt* (the world of our immediate life experience), which plays such an important part in Husserl's last work, can be traced to indirect stimulation by Heidegger's conception of *Dasein* as being-in-the-world need not be decided here. Hence there is no reason to deny the possibility of an existential philosophy within the framework of Husserl's phenomenology. There are even indications that Husserl himself conceived of his transcendental phenomenology as a distinctive existential possibility, and that in particular the transcendental reduction included for him a liberating conversion of human existence.

By contrast the French philosophers never seem to have questioned the identity of phenomenology and existentialism. One even wonders whether, when in the early thirties Sartre took up the study of phenomenology and existential

philosophy, he was at all aware of the seriousness of the break between Husserl and Heidegger. Part of the explanation for this oversight may be in the fact that Heidegger impressed the young Frenchmen interested in German philosophy much more than Husserl, and that in his writings Heidegger, ostensibly Husserl's appointed heir, gave no clear indication of serious friction between him and the master.

However, mere factual statements about the historical connection between phenomenology and existentialism, pertinent though they may be, cannot resolve the problem of their essential relation. What is required is a systematic consideration of the following questions:

> 1. Are the two movements compatible?
>
> 2. If compatible, are they necessarily connected?
>
> 3. If not necessarily connected, have they at least an affinity?
>
> 4. Can today's phenomenological existentialism be considered sound phenomenology?

1. With regard to the first question I maintain: Phenomenology and existentialism are compatible in principle. The opposite view may be argued on grounds like the following:

a. Phenomenology is outspokenly rationalistic; existential philosophy is opposed to all forms of rationalism. Now it is true that Husserl's phenomenology professes rationalism in the sense of a concerted effort to justify all human claims by rational evidence, although he opposes the uncritical rationalism of pure *a priori* metaphysics. But this does not mean that phenomenology rejects insights based on non-theoretical, notably on emotive experience. On the other hand, it is a fateful error to identify existentialism with the advocacy of "irrational man." Existentialism stresses, indeed, the practical part of human nature as expressed in choice and commitment. But "thought," though not logical thought in the technical sense, is an essential feature of Heidegger's philosophizing, and Sartre stresses the Cartesian *cogito* to the extent of seeing in the emotions primarily magic attempts to evade our situation, instead of facing it rationally.

b. It is also argued that phenomenology "brackets" all questions of existence, hence that it is essentially a philosophy of detachment in contrast to existentialism's philosophy of commitment (*engagement*). But it is a misunderstanding of the phenomenological reduction to think that bracketing our beliefs in the existence of the phenomena eliminates the phenomenon of human existence. This misunderstanding is based on an unfortunate equivocation in the meaning of the word "existence." For the existence-character in the phenomena which we bracket is something quite different from *Existenz* or *Dasein* as the structure of being-in-the-world, which is found only in human beings. As far as the latter is concerned, bracketing may well affect the belief in the reality of the world and even of the human being who is in such a world. But even this does not mean that being-in-the-world and its believed reality is totally ignored. It may be described *qua* phenomenon like any other reduced phenomenon. One may consider Husserl's treatment of this phenomenon inadequate. It may also be true that the phenomenologist's detachment implies a temporary retreat from the involvement and active participation in concrete existence. But this does not mean total neglect of the phenomena of existence. Nor must it be overlooked that the immanent residuum of consciousness which survives the ordeal of the phenomenological reduction has the character of absolute existence—an existence that can certainly rival in poignancy the existence which the existentialists attribute to the human being incarnated in the world.

c. Finally, it is alleged that phenomenology deals with universal essences, whereas existentialism is concerned with the concrete single individual. However, even though it is correct that Husserl's phenomenology is restricted to universal essences, it is an oversimplification to say that existentialism deals only with concrete individuals. Even existentialism describes its findings in universal terms and claims that its universal statements are valid for more than one single individual. Heidegger's much quoted pronouncement that "*the essence of Dasein* is existence" grants to human existence an essence. How else could this statement about an essence be substantiated except by an essential insight, a *Wesenseinsicht* in the phenomenological sense?

2. If then phenomenology and existentialism are compatible, are they dependent upon one another? My answer to this question is an unqualified "no."

That existentialism does not depend on phenomenology can be shown by the obvious examples of Kierkegaard and Jaspers. Quite apart from Jaspers' own disclaimers, the methods which they applied differ basically from those used by Husserl and even by Heidegger.

That phenomenology in turn does not depend on existentialism seems equally obvious. Yet it has been held that phenomenology entails existentialism as an essential, if not a necessary, consequence. At least implicitly this is asserted by Gilbert Varet,[4] and he is followed in this point by Wilfred Desan in his Harvard dissertation.[5] To be sure, these assertions are based on grave misconceptions of German phenomenology. It is therefore more serious that so keen an expert as Alphonse de Waelhens tries to show an essential trend from Husserl's phenomenology to existentialism.[6] De Waelhens bases his case on the fact that the emphasis in phenomenology on the importance of perspectives necessitated a consideration of the concrete existences that occupy these perspectives. But this does not seem to me compelling. Thus in the analogous case of Einstein's theory of relativity the need of considering the standpoint of the observer did not necessitate a study of the observer's personality. And even a consideration of the concrete existence of the subject at the source of a per-

spective does not justify the abandonment of the phenomenological attitude of suspension of belief. I can therefore see no valid reason for asserting a logical necessity in the historical procession from Husserlian phenomenology to Heideggerian or Sartrian existentialism.

This denial has important consequences. It cuts the ground from under Varet's and Desan's case against phenomenology based on the failure of existentialism in Sartre's supposed tragic finale. Since Sartre's existentialism is not the necessary consequent of phenomenology, denying the consequent does not affect the right of the antecedent, phenomenology.

Besides, it must not be overlooked that Husserl's phenomenology has inspired a considerable number of phenomenological enterprises other than existentialism. Specifically I have in mind the so-called Older Phenomenological Movement, as represented by such researchers as Alexander Pfänder, Moritz Geiger, or Roman Ingarden. The descriptive investigation of psychological, logical, ethical, esthetic, and religious phenomena constitutes at least equally legitimate expressions of original phenomenology. And there seems to be good reason to assert that what has been achieved in these areas does not reflect too unfavorably on Husserl's initiating enterprise.

3. While phenomenology and existentialism are essentially independent enterprises, have they at least enough affinity for fruitful coöperation? This question I shall answer affirmatively.

This answer hardly needs much substantiation. While phenomenology as such has no preference for the phenomena of human existence, it stands to gain in significance by turning its powers to a field of such vital interest. On the other hand, the pre-phenomenological insights of existentialism by means of Kierkegaard's dialectics and Jaspers' non-objectifying elucidation of existence have been provocative, but highly elusive. Once existentialism comes to grips with the epistemological problem, which it will not be able to shrug off indefinitely, it has little hope of support from the more empirical and positivist philosophies or psychologies. Its best chance is an approach which stresses and develops the faithful description of the phenomena as they present themselves, regardless of whether they fit into the framework of our more traditional methodologies. Besides, if for the existentialist, as Kierkegaard puts it, "subjectivity is the truth," a phenomenology aimed at finding the source of all consciousness in subjectivity is at least a congenial approach. Yet, before existentialism can expect substantial benefit from invoking the aid of phenomenology, it will have to accept it in its own right and undergo its discipline, instead of trying to convert it into its handmaiden.

4. How far, then, can today's existentialism be considered phenomenologically sound? Here, I am afraid, I have to make grave reservations.

Phenomenology has never been foolproof. But some of the fooling that has invoked its name need not be laid at its doorsteps. I do not want to deny that the phenomenological existentialists have made suggestive and at times even striking contributions to the fund of phenomenological insights. But most of these have to be gone over more cautiously and more critically. Thus, I submit that such brilliant pieces as Sartre's phenomenology of the social gaze are vitiated by a selective emphasis on isolated aspects of a more comprehensive phenomenon, by inadequate description, and by a hasty interpretation which ignores alternative meanings that would have deserved consideration.

However, instead of taking such sweeping exceptions I would like to present a concrete example from the very beginning of Sartre's phenomenological career which can at the same time demonstrate Husserl's still unsurpassed descriptive powers. I have in mind his discussion of the ego or the "I."

There is something strange about the relative lack of interest in the "ego" in a philosophy which professes its prime concern in personal existence. This is true particularly of Heidegger's analysis of *Dasein*. Sartre, a vigorous advocate of Husserl's descriptive phenomenology, went even farther. In his first major article, "The Transcendence of the Ego,"[7] published in 1936, he launched a frontal attack on Husserl's doctrine of the pure ego. In so doing he tried to show that this ego was not, as Husserl had maintained, the immanent source of all consciousness, but its transcendent and constituted object.

This is not the place to discuss the considerable merits and the weaknesses of Sartre's first "sketch of a phenomenological description" and its ulterior objectives. I shall focus merely on the reasoning which made Sartre repudiate one of Husserl's central tenets. For it throws light on Sartre's entire approach to phenomenology.

Sartre's primary objection to Husserl's pure ego is its superfluousness for the description of consciousness. Should such an argument carry any weight in matters of phenomenological description? It smacks more of Occam's razor, which may have its place in keeping down the number of explanatory hypotheses, but certainly not in describing the phenomena.

Phenomenologically more significant is Sartre's attempt to show that the "I" is not part of our ordinary unreflective consciousness: thus, to him, we are not aware of the "I" in reading a book or listening to a paper, but only when we reflect upon our reading or listening. Whence he infers that it is reflective consciousness which constitutes the "I" or "me" as transcendent to the immanent stream of consciousness.

Is this sound phenomenology? In what sense may reflection be said to constitute the object on which it reflects? This raises, of course, the whole question of the meaning of constitution in Husserl's phenomenology. But there is certainly no good reason for assuming *a priori* that reflec-

tion brings its object into being rather than that it merely uncovers or discovers it. In fact, when it comes to other acts of consciousness, including Sartre's original pre-reflective consciousness, Sartre himself seems to think that reflection simply illumines, but does not bring into being a consciousness which has been there all the time in pre-reflective twilight, as it were. What is more, there seems to be very good evidence for thinking that the "constitution" of the ego in reflection consists simply in its emergence from the background of consciousness rather than in its formation on its outskirts. What is constituted is its phenomenal character, not its being.

I conclude that Sartre's critique of Husserl's conception of the ego is anything but convincing, and particularly that its phenomenological basis is inadequate.[8]

How, then, does Sartre's pseudo-phenomenology of the ego compare with Husserl's research on the subject? Sartre was well aware of the fact that Husserl's views on the ego had changed between the first edition of his *Logische Untersuchungen* of 1901 and the *Ideen* of 1913. But he took it for granted that this change was a change for the worse and meant nothing but Husserl's return to the transcendental ego of Kant or rather the Neo-kantians. What Sartre and other critics of Husserl's shift seem to discount is the fact that, when, in a footnote to the second edition of his *Logische Untersuchungen,* he frankly admitted this reversal, he stated: "Since then (i.e., my earlier failure to discover the ego) I have learned to find it, or more precisely, I have learned not to be diverted from the pure grasp of the given by the excesses of the metaphysics of the ego"[9]; and in his *Ideen* he declared that he had found his earlier scepticism with regard to the ego untenable.[10] I suggest that Husserl's explanation of the reasons for his shift should be taken seriously. There must have been phenomenological evidence behind his seeming about-face. In fact, some of this evidence has become available through the recent publication of Volume II of the *Ideen,* edited by Marly Biemel.[11] For it contains the chapter on the pure ego which Husserl had promised in the first volume. It deserves the closest attention of those who think they can dispose of the pure ego as a remnant from the pre-phenomenological past. Specifically, Husserl's phenomenology of the ego makes the following points:

> 1. It is of the essence of the pure ego that it can be seized firsthand (*originäre Selbsterfassung*) by what Husserl calls self-perception (*Selbstwahrnehmung*) (§23). It is neither capable nor in need of a special constitution (§26). It forms an immanent phenomenon which does not present itself by different perspectives (*Abschattungen*).

> 2. This original perception of the self is subject to reflective modifications, for instance by recall. In these reflective modifications the identity of the persistent ego is given with self-evidence. Only its modes of appearance differ. Reflective modifications presuppose original perception to which they refer back in their very structure.

Nevertheless, Husserl denies that this intuitively self-given ego has any similarity with a Cartesian substance, much as he subscribes to the indubitableness of Descartes' "ego cogito." To him, the ego cannot occur in abstraction from his acts, just as little as the acts can be given in abstraction from the ego. Both are dependent on each other. But this does not affect their distinct existence.

The chapter on the pure ego makes other important points. Thus, it distinguishes between the pure ego as the focus of all our experiences and the empirical or "real" human ego with its factual properties, its character, its aptitudes, etc. Like Sartre, Husserl treats the latter ego as a "transcendent object" constituted by the transcendental consciousness with its focal ego.

All this does not mean that Husserl's phenomenology of the ego had reached its final form. Husserl saw well enough that, since the pure ego lives in immanent time, it is affected by the problems of constitution which are posed by the consciousness of inner time. Moreover, it cannot and must not be overlooked that, during Husserl's last period, in which he collaborated closely with Eugen Fink, his doctrine of the ego proliferated into a bewildering multiplicity of at least three egos.[12] This proliferation may well have been the cause for the increasing scepticism even among Husserl's close followers, and finally for Sartre's drastic cure. But this scepticism sacrificed the legitimate core along with the questionable outer shells.

This is not the place to pursue further the problems of Husserl's phenomenology of the ego. I introduced it merely as an instance of a case where Husserl's patient search may be shown to be more penetrating than, and still unsurpassed by, the more spectacular assertions of the existentialists who supposedly use his method. Besides, I do not mean to suggest that Husserl's claims concerning the direct perception of the ego and concerning the reflective modifications of this act are to be taken at face value. Nor should it be overlooked that Husserl withheld the volume of the *Ideen* with the chapter on the pure ego during his lifetime. All his findings will have to be examined, reexamined, and developed. But in the meantime it remains a remarkable fact that Husserl, after his initial scepticism, came out with such definitive and positive suggestions for a phenomenology of the ego. Moreover, I submit that Husserl's defense of the ego as the center of our conscious existence may be closer to the original existential conception of Kierkegaard, with his insistence on inwardness and subjectivity as the truth, than Sartre's denial of the pure ego and his ejection of the empirical ego into the outside transcendent world. Sartre's attack on the pure ego, which he replaces by a stream of impersonal consciousness, actually volatilizes existence. By denying it a center and the dimension of inwardness he deprives it at the same time of its existential weight.

Existentialism may be on the trail of more vital, more fruitful insights than pure phenomenology. But it has still to learn a few lessons from the older phenomenology, particularly from Husserl. One of these is the injunction which I heard him address to an informal group of students when he criticized Max Scheler's much more rapid but not equally solid production: "One needs bright ideas, but one must not publish them." Another lesson is his insistence on the need of making sure of the epistemological groundwork: "One must not consider oneself too good to work on the foundations." It is such lessons, lessons of philosophical solidity, integrity, and humility, which both phenomenologists and existentialists still have to learn or to relearn. It would indeed be a betrayal of the spirit of Husserl's philosophizing if phenomenology should sell its birthright for a mess of existentialist pottage.

Notes

1. See "Kant und die Idee der Transzendentalphilosophie," in *Husserliana,* Vol. VII (The Hague, Martinus Nijhoff, 1956), pp. 230 ff.

2. *The Phenomenological Movement: A Historical Introduction* (Phaenomenologica 6), The Hague, Martinus Nijhoff, 1960 (forthcoming).

3. Thus his last publication, the introduction to transcendental phenomenology entitled *The Crisis of the European Sciences and Transcendental Phenomenology,* speaks of the crisis of European "*Existenz*" which has arisen from the loss of meaning brought on by modern positivistic science, of the "existential conflict" (*existenzieller Widerspruch*) which this entails for the contemporary philosopher committed to the cause of scientific rigor, and of the responsibility of philosophers, as agents of humanity, which determines their "existential being" (*Husserliana,* Vol. VI, pp. 10, 15, ff.). How deeply, if not "existentially," Husserl himself was involved in his philosophic enterprise can be seen from some of his private diary notes ("Persönliche Aufzeichnungen," published by Walter Biemel in *Philosophy and Phenomenological Research,* Vol. XVI (1956), pp. 293 ff.).

4. *L'Ontologie de Sartre,* Paris, 1947.

5. *The Tragic Finale,* Cambridge, 1954.

6. "Les constants de l'existentialisme," *Revue internationale de philosophie,* Vol. 9 (1949), pp. 255-269.

7. "La transcendance de l'égo, Esquisse d'une description phénoménologique," *Recherches philosophiques,* Vol. VI (1936), pp. 85-123. English translation, with the misleading subtitle "An Existentialist Theory of Consciousness," by Forrest Williams and Robert Kirkpatrick (New York, Noonday Press, 1957).

8. It seems worth mentioning that in *L'Être et le néant* (Part III, Chapter I, iii, pp. 290 f.) Sartre modified his position, not to be sure as far as the "transcendence of the ego" is concerned, since he continues to consider Husserl's ego as a useless and nefarious (*néfaste*) hypothesis. But he no longer asserts that the stream of consciousness is impersonal. Instead he ascribes to it the character of "ipseity," without however making it sufficiently clear what this quality involves.

9. *Logische Untersuchungen,* 2nd edition (Halle, Max Niemeyer, 1913), Vol. II, 1, p. 361.

10. *Ideen* I (Halle, Max Niemeyer, 1913), § 57 footnote. English translation by W. R. Boyce Gibson, p. 173.

11. *Husserliana,* Vol. IV (1952), Zweiter Abschnitt, Erstes Kapitel: Das reine Ich.

12. Eugen Fink, "Die phänomenologische Philosophie Edmund Husserl's in der gegenwärtigen Kritik," *Kantstudien,* Vol. 38 (1933), 381 ff.

Maurice Merleau-Ponty (essay date 1964)

SOURCE: "The Philosopher and His Shadow," in *Signs,* edited by John Wild, translated by Richard C. McCleary, Northwestern University Press, 1964, pp. 159-81.

[*In the following tribute, Merleau-Ponty attempts to find some of the "unthought thoughts" regarding nature, consciousness, and existence which can be generated by Husserl's thought.*]

Establishing a tradition means forgetting its origins, the aging Husserl used to say. Precisely because we owe so much to tradition, we are in no position to see just what belongs to it. With regard to a philosopher whose venture has awakened so many echoes, and at such an apparent distance from the point where he himself stood, any commemoration is also a betrayal—whether we do him the highly superfluous homage of our thoughts, as if we sought to gain them a wholly unmerited warrant, or whether on the contrary, with a respect which is not lacking in distance, we reduce him too strictly to what he himself desired and said. But Husserl was well aware of these difficulties—which are problems of communication between "egos"—and he does not leave us to confront them without resources. I borrow myself from others; I create others from my own thoughts. This is no failure to perceive others; it is the perception of others. We would not overwhelm them with our importunate comments, we would not stingily reduce them to what is objectively certified of them, if they were not there for us to begin with. Not to be sure with the frontal evidence of a thing, but installed athwart our thought and, like different selves of our own, occupying a region which belongs to no one else but them. Between an "objective" history of philosophy (which would rob the great philosophers of what they have given others to think about) and a meditation disguised as a dialogue (in which we would ask the questions and give the answers) there must be a middle-ground on which the philosopher we are speaking about and the philosopher who is speaking are present together, although it is not possible even in principle to decide at any given moment just what belongs to each.

The reason why we think that interpretation is restricted to either inevitable distortion or literal reproduction is that we want the meaning of a man's works to be wholly positive and by rights susceptible to an inventory which sets forth what is and is not in those works. But this is to be deceived about works and thought. "When we are considering a man's thought," Heidegger says in effect, "the greater the work accomplished (and greatness is in no way equivalent to the extent and number of writings) the richer the unthought-of element in that work. That is, the richer is that which, through this work and through it alone, comes toward us as never yet thought of."[1] At the end of Husserl's life there is an unthought-of element in his works which is wholly his and yet opens out on something else. To think is not to possess the objects of thought; it is to use them to mark out a realm to think about which we therefore are not yet thinking about. Just as the perceived world endures only through the reflections, shadows, levels, and horizons between things (which are not things and are not nothing, but on the contrary mark out by themselves the fields of possible variation in the same thing and the same world), so the works and thought of a philosopher are also made of certain articulations between things said. There is no dilemma of objective interpretation or arbitrariness with respect to these articulations, since they are not *objects* of thought, since (like shadow and reflection) they would be destroyed by being subjected to analytic observation or taken out of context, and since we can be faithful to and find them only by thinking again.

We should like to try to evoke this unthought-of element in Husserl's thought in the margin of some old pages. This will seem foolhardy on the part of someone who has known neither Husserl's daily conversation nor his teaching. Yet this essay may have its place alongside other approaches. Because for those who have known the visible Husserl the difficulties of communicating with an author are added on to those of communicating with his works. For these men, certain memories helpfully supply an incident or a short-circuit in conversation. But other memories would tend to hide the "transcendental" Husserl, the one who is at present being solemnly installed in the history of philosophy—not because he is a fiction, but because he is Husserl disencumbered of his life, delivered up to conversation with his peers and to his omnitemporal audacity. Like all those near to us, Husserl present in person (and in addition with the genius' power to fascinate and to deceive) could not, I imagine, leave those surrounding him in peace. Their whole philosophical life must have lain for a time in that extraordinary and inhuman occupation of being present at the continuing birth of a way of thinking, and of helping it become objective or even exist as communicable thought. Afterwards, when Husserl's death and their own growth had committed them to adult solitude, how could they easily recover the full meaning of their earlier meditations, which they certainly pursued freely whether they agreed or disagreed with Husserl, but in any case pursued on the basis of his thought? They rejoin him across their past. Is this way always shorter than the way through a man's works? As a result of having put the whole of philosophy in phenomenology to begin with, do they not now risk being too hard on it at the same time they are too hard on their youth? Do they not risk reducing given phenomenological motifs to what they were in their original contingency and their empirical humility, whereas for the outside observer, these motifs retain their full relief?

Take for example the theme of phenomenological reduction, which we know never ceased to be an enigmatic possibility for Husserl, and one he always came back to. To say that he never succeeded in ensuring the bases of phenomenology would be to be mistaken about what he was looking for. The problems of reduction are not for him a prior step or preface to phenomenology; they are the beginning of inquiry. In a sense, they are inquiry, since inquiry is, as he said, a continuous beginning. We must not imagine Husserl hamstrung here by vexatious obstacles; locating obstacles is the very meaning of his inquiry. One of its "results" is the realization that the movement of return to ourselves—of "re-entering ourselves," St. Augustine said—is as if rent by an inverse movement which *it elicits*. Husserl rediscovers that identity of "re-entering self" and "going-outside self" which, for Hegel, defined the absolute. To reflect (Husserl said in *Ideen I*) is to unveil an unreflected dimension which is at a distance because we are no longer it in a naive way, yet which we cannot doubt that reflection attains, since it is through reflection itself that we have an idea of it. So it is not the unreflected which challenges reflection; it is reflection which challenges itself. For by definition its attempt to revive, possess, internalize, or make immanent has meaning only with respect to an already given terminus which withdraws into its transcendence beneath the very gaze which has set out in search of it in this attempt.

So it is not through chance or naivete that Husserl assigns contradictory characteristics to reduction. He is saying what he means here, what is imposed by the factual situation. It is up to us not to forget half the truth. Thus on the one hand reduction goes beyond the natural attitude. It is not "natural" (*natural*).[2] This means that reduced thought no longer concerns the Nature of the natural sciences but in a sense the "opposite of Nature."[3] In other words, reduced thought concerns Nature as the "ideal meaning of the acts which constitute the natural attitude"[4]—Nature become once more the noema it has always been, Nature reintegrated to the consciousness which has always constituted it through and through. In the realm of "reduction" there is no longer anything but consciousness, its acts, and their intentional object. This is why Husserl can write that Nature is relative to mind, and that Nature is relative and mind absolute.[5]

But this is not the whole truth. The fact that there is *no* Nature *without* mind, or that Nature may be *done away with* in thought *without* doing away with mind, does not mean that Nature is produced by mind, or that any combination (even a subtle one) of these two concepts suffices to give the philosophical formula of our situation in being. Mind without Nature can be thought about and Nature without mind cannot. But perhaps we do not have to think about the world and ourselves in terms of the bifurcation of Nature and mind. The fact is that phenomenology's

most famous descriptions go in a direction which is not that of "philosophy of mind." When Husserl says that reduction goes beyond the natural attitude, he immediately adds that this going beyond preserves "the whole world of the natural attitude." The very transcendence of this world must retain a meaning in the eyes of "reduced" consciousness, and transcendental immanence cannot be simply its antithesis.

From *Ideen II* on it seems clear that reflection does not install us in a closed, transparent milieu, and that it does not take us (at least not immediately) from "objective" to "subjective," but that its function is rather to unveil a third dimension in which this distinction becomes problematic. There is indeed an I which makes itself "indifferent," a pure "knower," in order to grasp all things without remainder—to spread all things out before itself—and to "objectify" and gain intellectual possession of them. This I is a purely "theoretical attitude" which seeks to "render visible the relationships which can provide knowledge of being as it comes to be."[6] But it is just this I which is not the philosopher, just this attitude which is not philosophy. It is the science of Nature, or in a deeper sense, a certain philosophy which gives birth to the natural sciences and which comes back to the pure I and to its correlative, "things simply as things" (*blosse Sachen*), stripped of every action-predicate and every value-predicate. From *Ideen II* on Husserl's reflections escape this tête-à-tête between pure subject and pure things. They look *deeper down* for the fundamental. Saying that Husserl's thought goes in another direction tells us little. His thought does not disregard the ideal correlation of subject and object; it very deliberately goes beyond it, since it presents it as relatively founded, true derivatively as a constitutive result it is committed to justifying in its proper time and place.

But what is the starting point for this new turn in Husserl's thought, and what is the deeper urgency behind it? What is false in the ontology of *blosse Sachen* is that it makes a purely theoretical or idealizing attitude absolute, neglecting or taking as understood a relation with being which founds the purely theoretical attitude and measures its value. Relative to this scientific *naturalism*, the *natural* attitude involves a higher truth that we must regain. For the natural attitude is nothing less than naturalistic. We do not live naturally in the universe of *blosse Sachen*. Prior to all reflection, in conversation and the practices of life, we maintain a "personalist attitude" that naturalism cannot account for, and here things are not nature in itself for us but "our surroundings."[7] Our most natural life as men intends an ontological milieu which is different from that of being in itself, and which consequently cannot be derived from it in the constitutive order.

Even when our knowledge of things is concerned, we know far more about them in the natural attitude than the theoretical attitude can tell us—and above all we know it in a different way. Reflection speaks of our natural relationship to the world as an "attitude," that is, as an organized totality of "acts." But this is a reflection which presupposes that it is in things and which sees no farther than itself. At the same time Husserl's reflection tries to grasp the universal essences of things, it notes that in the unreflected there are "syntheses which dwell this side of any thesis."[8] The natural attitude really becomes an attitude—a tissue of judicatory and propositional acts—only when it becomes a naturalist thesis. The natural attitude itself emerges unscathed from the complaints which can be made about naturalism, because it is "prior to any thesis," because it is the mystery of a *Weltthesis* prior to all theses. It is, Husserl says in another connection, the mystery of a primordial faith and a fundamental and original opinion (*Urglaube, Urdoxa*) which are thus not even in principle translatable in terms of clear and distinct knowledge, and which—more ancient than any "attitude" or "point of view"—give us not a representation of the world but the world itself.

Reflection cannot "go beyond" this opening to the world, except by making use of the powers it owes to the opening itself. There is a clarity, an obviousness, proper to the zone of *Weltthesis* which is not derived from that of our theses, an unveiling of the world precisely through its dissimulation in the chiaroscuro of the doxa. When Husserl insistently says that phenomenological reflection begins in the natural attitude (in **Ideen II** he repeats it in order to relate the analysis he has just made of the corporeal and intersubjective implications of the *blosse Sachen*[9] to the realm of constituted phenomena), this is not just a way of saying that we must necessarily begin with and go by way of opinion before we can attain knowledge. The doxa of the natural attitude is an Urdoxa. To what is fundamental and original in theoretical consciousness it opposes what is fundamental and original in our existence. Its rights of priority are definitive, and reduced consciousness must take them into account.

The truth is that the relationships between the natural and the transcendental attitudes are not simple, are not side by side or sequential, like the false or the apparent and the true. There is a preparation for phenomenology in the natural attitude. It is the natural attitude which, by reiterating its own procedures, seesaws in phenomenology. It is the natural attitude itself which goes beyond itself in phenomenology—and so it does not go beyond itself. Reciprocally, the transcendental attitude is still and in spite of everything "natural" (*natürlich*).[10] There is a truth of the natural attitude—there is even a secondary, derivative truth of naturalism. "The soul's reality is based upon corporeal matter, not the latter upon the soul. More generally, within the total objective world, the material world is what we call Nature, a self-contained and particular world which does not require the support of any other reality. On the contrary the existence of mental realities and a real mental world is tied to the existence of a nature in the first sense of the term, to the existence of a material nature, and it is so linked not for contingent reasons but for reasons of principle. Whereas the *res extensa,* when we examine its essence, contains neither anything which arises from mind nor anything which mediately (*über sich hinaus*) requires

connection with a real mind; we find on the contrary that a real mind, according to its essence, can only exist tied to materiality as the real mind of a body."[11] We quote these lines only to provide a counterpoise to those which affirmed the relativity of Nature and the non-relativity of mind, and demolished the sufficiency of Nature and the truth of the natural attitudes that are here reaffirmed. In the last analysis, phenomenology is neither a materialism nor a philosophy of mind. Its proper work is to unveil the pretheoretical layer on which both of these idealizations find their relative justification and are gone beyond.

How will that infrastructure, that secret of secrets this side of our theses and our theory, be able in turn to rest upon the *acts* of absolute consciousness? Does the descent into the realm of our "archeology" leave our analytical tools intact? Does it make no changes at all in our conception of noesis, noema, and intentionality—in our ontology? After we have made this descent, are we still entitled to seek in an analytics of acts what upholds our own and the world's life without appeal? We know that Husserl never made himself too clear about these questions. A few words are there like indicators pointing to the problem—signaling unthought-of elements to think about. To begin with, the element of a "pre-theoretical constitution,"[12] which is charged with accounting for "pre-givens,"[13] those kernels of meaning about which man and the world gravitate. We may with equal truth say of these pre-givens (as Husserl says of the body) either that they are always "already constituted" for us or that they are "never completely constituted"—in short, that consciousness is always behind or ahead of them, never contemporaneous. Husserl was undoubtedly thinking of these singular beings when in another connection he evoked a constitution which would not proceed by grasping a content as an exemplification of a meaning or an essence (*Auffassungsinhalt-Auffassung als . . .*), an operating or latent intentionality like that which animates time, more ancient than the intentionality of human *acts*. There must be beings for us which are not yet kept in being by the centrifugal activity of consciousness: significations it does not spontaneously confer upon contents, and contents which participate obliquely in a meaning in the sense that they indicate a meaning which remains a distant meaning and which is not yet legible in them as the monogram or stamp of thetic consciousness. In such cases we do still have a grouping of intentional threads around certain knots which govern them, but the series of retro-references (*Rückdeutungen*) which lead us ever deeper could not possibly reach completion in the intellectual possession of a noema. There is an ordered sequence of steps, but it is without end as it is without beginning. Husserl's thought is as much attracted by the haecceity of Nature as by the vortex of absolute consciousness. In the absences of explicit theses about the relationship of one to the other, we can only examine the samples of "pre-theoretical constitution" he offers us and formulate—at our own risk—the unthought-of elements we think we see there. There is undeniably something between transcendent Nature, naturalism's being in itself, and the immanence of mind, its acts, and its noema. It is into this interval that we must try to advance.

Ideen II brings to light a network of implications beneath the "objective material thing" in which we no longer sense the pulsation of constituting consciousness. The relation between my body's movements and the thing's "properties" which they reveal is that of the "I am able to" to the marvels it is within its power to give rise to. And yet my body must itself be meshed into the visible world; its power depends precisely on the fact that it has a place *from which* it sees. Thus it is a thing, but a thing I dwell in. It is, if you wish, on the side of the subject; but it is not a stranger to the locality of things. The relationship between my body and things is that of the absolute here to the there, of the source of distances to distance. My body is the field within which my perceptive powers are localized. But then what is the connection between my body and things if it is not one of objective co-variation? Suppose, Husserl says, that a consciousness were to experience satiety whenever a locomotive's boiler was full, and warmth each time its fire was lit; the locomotive would still not be its body.[14] Then what link is there between my body and me in addition to the regularities of occasional causality? There is a relation of my body to itself which makes it the *vinculum* of the self and things. When my right hand touches my left, I am aware of it as a "physical thing." But at the same moment, if I wish, an extraordinary event takes place: here is my left hand as well starting to perceive my right, *es wird Leib, es empfindet.*[15] The physical thing becomes animate. Or, more precisely, it remains what it was (the event does not enrich it), but an exploratory power comes to rest upon or dwell in it. Thus I touch myself touching; my body accomplishes "a sort of reflection." In it, through it, there is not just the unidirectional relationship of the one who perceives to what he perceives. The relationship is reversed, the touched hand becomes the touching hand, and I am obliged to say that the sense of touch here is diffused into the body—that the body is a "perceiving thing," a "subject-object."[16]

It is imperative that we recognize that this description also overturns our idea of the thing and the world, and that it results in an ontological rehabilitation of the sensible. For from now on we may literally say that space itself is known through my body. If the distinction between subject and object is blurred in my body (and no doubt the distinction between noesis and noema as well?), it is also blurred in the thing, which is the pole of my body's operations, the terminus its exploration ends up in,[17] and which is thus woven into the same intentional fabric as my body. When we say that the perceived thing is grasped "in person" or "in the flesh" (*leibhaft*), this is to be taken literally: the flesh of what is perceived, this compact particle which stops exploration, and this optimum which terminates it all reflect my own incarnation and are its counterpart. Here we have a type of being, a universe with its unparalleled "subject" and "object," the articulation of each in terms of the other, and the definitive definition of an "irrelative" of all the "relativities" of perceptual experi-

ence, which is the "legal basis" for all the constructions of understanding.[18]

All understanding and objective thought owe their life to the inaugural fact that with this color (or with whatever the sensible element in question may be) I have perceived, I have had, a singular existence which suddenly stopped my glance yet promised it an indefinite series of experiences, which was a concretion of possibles real here and now in the hidden sides of the thing, which was a lapse of duration given all at once. The intentionality that ties together the stages of my exploration, the aspects of the thing, and the two series to each other is neither the mental subject's connecting activity nor the ideal connections of the object. It is the transition that as carnal subject I effect from one phase of movement to another, a transition which as a matter of principle is always possible for me because I am that animal of perceptions and movements called a body.

Certainly there is a problem here. What will intentionality be then if it is no longer the mind's grasping of an aspect of sensible matter as the exemplification of an essence, no longer the recognition in things of what we have put there? Nor can intentionality be the functioning of a transcendent preordination or teleology we undergo, or of an "institution of nature" (in the Cartesian sense) which works in us without us. This would mean reintegrating the sensible order to the world of plans or objective projects at the moment we have just distinguished the two. It would mean forgetting that the sensible order is *being at a distance*—the fulgurating attestation here and now to an inexhaustible richness—and that things are only half-opened before us, unveiled and hidden. We give just as poor an account of all these characteristics by making the world an *aim* as we do by making it an *idea*. The solution—if there is one—can only lie in examining this layer of sensible being or in becoming accustomed to its enigmas.

We are still far from Cartesian *blosse Sachen*. The thing for my body is the "solipsist" thing; it is not yet the thing itself. It is caught up in the context of my body, which itself pertains to the order of things only through its fringes or periphery. The world has not yet closed about my body. The things it perceives would really be being only if I learned that they are seen by others, that they are presumptively visible to every viewer who warrants the name. Thus being in itself will appear only after the constitution of others. But the constitutive steps which still separate us from being in itself are of the same type as the unveiling of my body; as we shall see they make use of a universal which my body has already made appear. My right hand was present at the advent of my left hand's active sense of touch. It is in no different fashion that the other's body becomes animate before me when I shake another man's hand or just look at him.[19] In learning that my body is a "perceiving thing," that it is able to be stimulated (*reizbar*)—it, and not just my "consciousness"—I prepared myself for understanding that there are other *animalia* and possibly other men.

It is imperative to recognize that we have here neither comparison, nor analogy, nor projection or "introjection."[20] The reason why I have evidence of the other man's being-there when I shake his hand is that his hand is substituted for my left hand, and my body annexes the body of another person in that "sort of reflection" it is paradoxically the seat of. My two hands "coexist" or are "compresent" because they are one single body's hands. The other person appears through an extension of that compresence;[21] he and I are like organs of one single intercorporeality. For Husserl the experience of others is first of all "esthesiological," and must be if the other person exists effectively and not as the ideal terminus or fourth term of a proportion which supposedly would come to complete my consciousness' relationships to my objective body and his. What I perceive to begin with is a different "sensibility" (*Empfindbarkeit*), and only subsequently a different man and a different thought. "That man over there sees and hears; on the basis of his perceptions he brings such and such judgments to bear, propounds such and such evaluations and volitions, according to all the different forms possible. That an 'I think' springs forth 'within' him, in that man over there, is a natural fact (*Naturfaktum*) based upon the body and corporeal events, and determined by the causal and substantial connection of Nature. . . ."[22]

It will perhaps be asked how I am able to extend the compresence of bodies to minds, and whether I do not do so through a turning back upon myself which restores projection or introjection. Is it not within myself that I learn that an "*Empfindbarkeit*" and sensorial fields presuppose a consciousness or a mind? But in the first place this objection assumes that another person can be mind for me in exactly the same sense as I am for myself, and after all nothing is less certain—others' thought is never *wholly* a thought for us. Furthermore, this objection would imply that the problem here is to constitute a different mind, whereas the one who is constituting is as yet only animate flesh himself; nothing prevents us from reserving for the stage when he will speak and listen the advent of another person who also speaks and listens.

But above all this objection would ignore the very thing that Husserl wanted to say; that is, *that there is no constituting of a mind for a mind, but of a man for a man.* By the effect of a singular eloquence of the visible body, *Einfühlung* goes from body to mind. When a different behavior or exploring body appears to me through a first "intentional encroachment,"[23] it is the man as a whole who is given to me with all the possibilities (whatever they may be) that I have in my presence to myself in my incarnate being, the unimpeachable attestation. I shall never in all strictness be able to think the other person's thought. I can think *that* he thinks; I can construct, behind this mannequin, a presence to self modeled on my own; but it is still my self that I put in it, and it is then that there really is "introjection." On the other hand, I know unquestionably that that man over there *sees,* that my sensible world is also his, because *I am present at his seeing, it is visible* in his eyes' grasp of the scene. And when I say I see *that* he

sees, there is no longer here (as there is in "I think that he thinks") the interlocking of two propositions but the mutual unfocusing of a "main" and a "subordinate" viewing. A form that resembles me was there, but busy at secret tasks, possessed by an unknown dream. Suddenly a gleam appeared a little bit below and out in front of its eyes; its glance is raised and comes to fasten on the very things that I am seeing. Everything which for my part is based upon the animal of perceptions and movements, all that I shall ever be able to build upon it—including my "thought," but as a modalization of my presence at the world—falls all at once into the other person. I say that there is a man there and not a mannequin, as I see that the table is there and not a perspective or an appearance of the table.

It is true that I would *not* recognize him if I were *not* a man myself; and that if I did *not* have (or think I had along with myself) the absolute contact of thought, a different *cogito* would *not* spring forth before me. But these catalogues of absences do not translate what has just happened inclusively; they note down partial solidarities which stem from but do not constitute the advent of the other person. All introjection presupposes what is meant to be explained by it. If it were really my "thought" that had to be placed in the other person, I would never put it there. No appearance would ever have the power to convince me that there is a *cogito* over there, or be able to motivate the transference, since my own *cogito* owes its whole power of conviction to the fact that I am myself. If the other person is to exist for me, he must do so to begin with in an order beneath the order of thought. On this level, his existence for me is possible. For my perceptual opening to the world, which is more dispossession than possession, claims no monopoly of being and institutes no death struggle of consciousnesses. My perceived world and the half-disclosed things before me have in their thickness what it takes to supply more than one sensible subject with "states of consciousness"; they have the right to many other witnesses besides me. When a comportment is sketched out in this world which already goes beyond me, this is only one more dimension in primordial being, which comprises them all.

So from the "solipsist" layer on, the other person is not impossible, because the sensible thing is open. The other person becomes actual when a different comportment and a different gaze take possession of my things. And this articulation of a different corporeality in my world is itself effected without introjection; because my sensible existents—through their aspect, configuration, and carnal texture—were already bringing about the miracle of things which are things by the fact that they are offered to a body, and were already making my corporeality a proof of being. Man can create the alter ego which "thought" cannot create, because he is outside himself in the world and because one ek-stasis is compossible with other ek-stases. And that possibility is fulfilled in perception as *vinculum* of brute being and a body. The whole riddle of *Einfühlung* lies in its initial, "esthesiological" phase; and it is solved there because it is a perception. He who "posits" the other man is a perceiving subject, the other person's body is a perceived thing, and the other person himself is "posited" as "perceiving." It is never a matter of anything but co-perception. I see that this man over there sees, as I touch my left hand while it is touching my right.

Thus the problem of *Einfühlung*, like that of my incarnation, opens on the meditation of sensible being; or, if you prefer, it betakes itself there. The fact is that sensible being, which is announced to me in my most strictly private life, summons up within that life all other corporeality. It is the being which reaches me in my most secret parts, but which I also reach in its brute or untamed state, in an absolute of presence which holds the secret of the world, others, and what is true. There are "objects" in this absolute of presence "which are not only fundamentally and originally present to a subject but (since they are so present to one subject) can ideally be given in a fundamental and original presence to all the other subjects (as soon as they are constituted). The whole of the objects which may be fundamentally and originally present, and which constitute a common realm of fundamental and original presence for all communicating subjects, is Nature in its primary and fundamental and original sense."[24] Perhaps nowhere better than in these lines can we see the dual direction of Husserl's reflection, which is both an analytics of essences and an analytics of existences. For it is "ideally" (*idealiter*) that whatever is given to one subject is as a matter of principle given to all others, but it is from the "fundamental and original presence" of sensible being that the obviousness and universality which are conveyed by these relationships of essences come. Re-read, if you doubt it, the extraordinary pages[25] in which Husserl implies that even if we meant to posit absolute or true being as the correlative of an absolute mind, such an absolute being would not merit its name unless it had some relationship to what we men call being. We and absolute mind would have to recognize each other, as two men "can only through understanding each other recognize that the things one of them sees and those the other sees are *the same*."[26] Absolute mind would thus have to see things "through sensible appearances which can be exchanged between it and us in an act of reciprocal comprehension—or at least in a unidirectional communication—as our phenomena can be exchanged between us men." And finally, "it would also have to have a body, which would involve dependency with respect to sense organs."

There are certainly more things in the world and in us than what is perceptible in the narrow sense of the term. The other person's life itself is not given to me with his behavior. In order to have access to it, I would have to be the other person himself. Correlatively, no matter what my pretentions to grasp being itself in what I perceive, I am in the other person's eyes closed into my "representations"; I remain on this side of his sensible world and thus transcend it. But things seem this way to us because we are making use of a mutilated idea of Nature and the sensible world. Kant said Nature is "the whole of sense-objects."[27]

Husserl rediscovers sensible being as the universal form of brute being. Sensible being is not only things but also everything sketched out there, even virtually, everything which leaves its trace there, everything which figures there, even as divergence and a certain absence. "That which can be grasped through experience in the fundamental and original meaning of the term, the being which can be given in a fundamental and original presence (*das urpräsentierbare Sein*), is not the whole of being, and not even all being there is experience of, *Animalia* are realities which cannot be given in a fundamental and original presence to several subjects; they enclose subjectivities. They are the very special sorts of objects which are fundamentally and originally given in such a way that they presuppose fundamental and original presences without being able to be given in a fundamental and original presence themselves."[28] This is what *animalia* and men are: absolutely present beings who have a wake of the negative. A perceiving body that I see is also a certain absence that is hollowed out and tactfully dealt with behind that body by its behavior. But absence is itself rooted in presence; it is through his body that the other person's soul is soul in my eyes. "Negativities" also count in the sensible world, which is decidedly the universal one.

So what is the result of all this as far as constitution is concerned? By moving to the pre-theoretical, pre-thetic, or pre-objective order, Husserl has upset the relationships between the constituted and the constituting. Being in itself, being for an absolute mind, from now on draws its truth from a "layer" where there is neither absolute mind nor the immanence of intentional objects in that mind, but only incarnate minds which through their bodies "belong . . . to the same world,"[29] Of course this does not mean that we have moved from philosophy to psychology or anthropology. The relationship between logical objectivity and carnal intersubjectivity is one of those double-edged relationships of *Fundierung* Husserl spoke about in another connection. Intercorporeality culminates in (and is changed into) the advent of *blosse Sachen* without our being able to say that one of the two orders is primary in relation to the other. The pre-objective order is not primary, since it is established (and to tell the truth fully begins to exist) only by being fulfilled in the founding of logical objectivity. Yet logical objectivity is not self-sufficient; it is limited to consecrating the labors of the pre-objective layer, existing only as the outcome of the "Logos of the esthetic world" and having value only under its supervision. Between the "deeper" and the higher layers of constitution, we perceive the singular relationship of *Selbstvergessenheit* that Husserl already names in *Ideen II*,[30] and that he was to take up again later in the theory of sedimentation. Logical objectivity derives from carnal intersubjectivity on the condition that it has been forgotten as carnal intersubjectivity, and it is carnal intersubjectivity itself which produces this forgetfulness by wending its way toward logical objectivity. Thus the forces of the constitutive field do not move in one direction only; they turn back upon themselves. Intercorporeality goes beyond itself and ends up unconscious of itself as intercorporeality; it displaces and changes the situation it set out from, and the spring of constitution can no more be found in its beginning than in its terminus.

These relationships are found again at each stage of constitution. The perceived thing rests upon the body proper. This does not mean that the thing is made of kinestheses in the psychologists' sense of the term. We can just as well say that the entire functioning of the body proper hangs upon the perceived thing the circuit of behavior closes upon. The body is nothing less but nothing more than the thing's condition of possibility. When we go from body to thing, we go neither from principle to consequence nor from means to end. We are present at a kind of propagation, encroachment, or enjambment which prefigures the passage from the *solus ipse* to the other person, from the "solipsist" thing to the intersubjective thing.

For the "solipsist" thing is not *primary* for Husserl, nor is the *solus ipse*. Solipsism is a "thought-experiment";[31] the *solus ipse* a "constructed subject."[32] This isolating method of thinking is intended more to reveal than to break the links of the intentional web. If we could break them in reality or simply in thought—if we could really cut the *solus ipse* off from others and from Nature (as Husserl, we must admit, sometimes does when he imagines that first mind, then Nature is annihilated, and wonders what the consequences are for mind and Nature)—there would be fully preserved, in this fragment of the whole which alone was left, the references to the whole it is composed of. In short, we still should not have the *sclus ipse*. ". . . In reality the *solus ipse* does not merit its name. Although the abstraction we have carried out is justified intuitively, it does not give us the isolated man or the isolated human person. Furthermore, an abstraction which did succeed in doing so would not consist in preparing a mass murder of the men and animals surrounding us, a murder in which the human subject I am would alone be spared. The subject who would be left alone in this case would still be a human subject, still the intersubjective object understanding itself and still positing itself as such."[33]

This remark goes a long way. To say that the ego "prior to" the other person is alone is already to situate it in relation to a phantom of the other person, or at least to conceive of an environment in which others could be. This is not the true and transcendental solitude. True, transcendental solitude takes place only if the other person is not even conceivable, and this requires that there be no self to claim solitude either. We are truly alone only on the condition that we do not know we are; it is this very ignorance which is our solitude. The "layer" or "sphere" which is called solipsist is without ego and without ipse. The solitude from which we emerge to intersubjective life is not that of the monad. It is only the haze of an anonymous life that separates us from being; and the barrier between us and others is impalpable. If there is a break, it is not between me and the other person; it is between a primordial generality we are intermingled in and the precise system, myself-the others. What "precedes" intersubjective life

cannot be numerically distinguished from it, precisely because at this level there is neither individuation nor numerical distinction. The constitution of others does not come after that of the body; others and my body are born together from the original ecstasy. The corporeality to which the primordial thing belongs is more corporeality in general; as the child's egocentricity, the "solipsist layer" is both transitivity and confusion of self and other.

All this, it will undoubtedly be said, represents what the solipsist consciousness would think and say about itself if there could be thought and speech at this level. But whatever illusion of neutrality such a consciousness may be capable of, it is an illusion. The sensible realm is given as being for X . . . , but just the same it is I and no one else who live this color or this sound; pre-personal life itself is still one of my views of the world. The child who asks his mother to console *him* for the pains *she* is suffering is turned toward himself just the same.

At least this is the way we evaluate his conduct, we who have learned to distribute the pains and pleasures in the world among single lives. But the truth is not so simple: the child who anticipates devotion and love bears witness to the reality of that love, and to the fact that he understands it and, in his weak and passive way, plays his role in it. In the tête-à-tête of the *Füreinander* there is a linkage of egotism and love which wipes out their borders, an identification which goes beyond solipsism in the reigning as well as in the devoted one. Egotism and altruism exist against a background of belonging to the same world; and to want to construct this phenomenon beginning with a solipsist layer is to make it impossible once and for all—and perhaps to ignore the profoundest things Husserl is saying to us.

Every man reflecting upon his life does have the fundamental possibility of looking at it as a series of private states of consciousness, just as the white civilized adult does. But he can do so only if he forgets experiences which bestride this everyday and serial time, or reconstitutes them in a way which caricatures them. The fact that we die alone does not imply that we live alone; and if we consult nothing but suffering and death when we are defining subjectivity, subjective life with others and in the world will become logically impossible. On the other hand, we cannot legitimately consider ourselves instruments of a soul of the world, group, or couple. We must conceive of a primordial *We [On]* that has its own authenticity and furthermore never ceases but continues to uphold the greatest passions of our adult life and to be experienced anew in each of our perceptions. For as we have seen, communication at this level is no problem and becomes doubtful only if I forget the perceptual field in order to reduce myself to what reflection will make of me. Reduction to "egology" or the "sphere of belonging" is, like all reduction, only a test of primordial bonds, a way of following them into their final prolongations. The reason why I am able to understand the other person's body and existence "beginning with" the body proper, the reason why the compresence of my "consciousness" and my "body" is prolonged into the compresence of my self and the other person, is that the "I am able to" and the "the other person exists" belong here and now to the same world, that the body proper is a premonition of the other person, the *Einfühlung,* an echo of my incarnation, and that a flash of meaning makes them substitutable in the absolute presence of origins.

Thus all of constitution is anticipated in the fulguration of *Urempfindung.* The absolute here of my body and the "there" of the perceptible thing, the near and the distant thing, the experience I have of what is perceptible to me and that which the other person should have of what is perceptible to him—all are in the relationship of the "fundamental and original" to the "modified." Not because the "there" is a lesser or attenuated "here," and the other person an ego projected outside;[34] but because (according to the marvel of carnal existence) along with the "here," the "near," and the "self," there is set forth over there the system of their "variants." Each "here," each nearby thing, each self—lived in absolute presence—bears witness beyond itself to all the other ones which are not for me composible with it and yet, *somewhere else,* are at this same moment being lived in absolute presence. Since constitution is neither just the development of a future which is implied in its beginning, nor just the effect which an external ordering has in us, it escapes the alternative of continuous or discontinuous. It is discontinuous, since each layer is made from forgetting the preceding one. It is continuous from one end to the other because this forgetting is not simply absence (as if the beginning had not existed) but a forgetting what the beginning literally was to the profit of what it has subsequently become—internalization in the Hegelian sense, *Erinnerung.* From its position, each layer takes up the preceding ones again and encroaches upon those that follow; each is prior and posterior to the others, and thus to itself.

No doubt this is why Hesserl does not seem to be too astonished at the circularities he is led into in the course of his analysis. There is the circularity of the thing and the experience of other people. For the fully objective thing is based upon the experience of others, and the latter upon the experience of the body, which in a way is a thing itself.[35] There is another circularity between Nature and persons. For Nature in the sense of the natural sciences (but also in the sense of the *Urpräsentierbare,* which for Husserl is the truth of the first) is the whole of the world (*Weltall*)[36] to begin with, and as such it encompasses persons who, in another connection in which they are expressly made explicit, encompass Nature as the object they constitute in common.[37] No doubt this is also why Husserl, in a prophetic text in 1912, did not hesitate to speak of a reciprocal relation between Nature, body, and soul; and, as it has been well put, of their "simultaneity."[38]

These adventures of constitutive analysis—these encroachments, reboundings and circularities—do not, as we were saying, seem to disturb Husserl very much. After having shown in one place[39] that the world of Copernicus refers to

the world of lived experience, and the universe of physics to that of life, he calmly says that this view will undoubtedly seem rather excessive, and even completely mad.[40] But he adds that its only function is to enable us to examine experience better[41] and follow its intentional implications more closely. Nothing can prevail against the clarities of constitutive analysis. Does this involve asserting the claim of essences contrary to factual truths? Is it, Husserl himself wonders, "philosophical hubris"? Is it one more instance of *consciousness* assuming the right to confine itself to its thoughts against all challenges? But sometimes it is *experience* that Husserl appeals to as the ultimate basis for law. So his position would seem to be that since we *are* at the junction of Nature, body, soul, and philosophical consciousness, since we live that juncture, no problem can be conceived of whose solution is not sketched out within us and in the world's spectacle—our existence should provide means of arranging in our thought what is all of a piece in our life. If Husserl holds fast to the clarities of constitution, this is no madness of consciousness, nor does it mean that consciousness has the right to substitute what is clear to it for established natural dependencies. It means that the transcendental field has ceased to be simply the field of our thought and has become the field of the whole of experience, and that Husserl trusts the truth which we are *in* from birth and which ought to be able to contain both the truths of consciousness and the truths of Nature. The reason why the "retro-references" of constitutive analysis do not have to win out over the principle of a philosophy of consciousness is that this philosophy has been sufficiently expanded or transformed to be the match for anything, even for what challenges it.

Although it was later on that Husserl spoke of the possibility that phenomenology is a question for itself, of the existence of a "phenomenology of phenomenology" upon which the ultimate meaning of all foreseeable analyses depends, and on the continuing problematic nature of integral, self-contained, or self-supporting phenomenology, these possibilities can already be seen in a reading of ***Ideen II.*** He does not hide the fact that intentional analytics leads us conjointly in two opposite directions. On the one hand it descends toward Nature, the sphere of the *Urpräsentierbare;* whereas it is drawn on the other hand toward the world of persons and minds. "This does not necessarily mean," he continues, "and should not mean, that the two worlds have nothing to do with one another, and that their meaning does not manifest relationships of essence between them. We know of other cardinal differences between 'worlds' which are nevertheless mediated by relationships of meaning and essence. The relationship between the world of ideas and the world of experience, for example, *or that between the 'world' of pure, phenomenologically reduced consciousness and the world of transcendent unities constituted within it."*[42] Thus there are problems of mediation between the world of Nature and the world of persons—even more, between the world of constituting consciousness and the results of the labor of constitution—and the ultimate task of phenomenology as philosophy of consciousness is to understand its relationship to non-phenomenology. What resists phenomenology within us—natural being, the "barbarous" source Schelling spoke of—cannot remain outside phenomenology and should have its place within it. The philosopher must bear his shadow, which is not simply the factual absence of future light.

It is already "exceptionally" difficult, Husserl says, to not only "grasp" but "understand from within" the relationship between the "world of Nature" and the "World of mind." At least this difficulty is overcome practically in our life, since we drift constantly and without difficulty from the naturalist to the personalist attitude. It is only a question of making reflection equal to what we do with complete naturalness in going from one attitude to another—of describing alterations of intentional apprehensions, articulations of experience, and essential relationships between constituting multiplicities which give an account of differences of being among what is constituted. In this respect phenomenology can clear up what is confused and eliminate misunderstandings which are precisely the result of our going naturally and unknowingly from one attitude to the other. Yet there is no doubt that these misunderstandings and this "natural" transition exist because clearing up the connection between Nature and persons involves a fundamental difficulty. How much more difficulty will we have when we must *understand from within* the passage from the naturalist or personalist attitude to absolute consciousness, from powers which are natural to an "artificial" (*künstlich*) attitude[43]—which really should no longer be an attitude among others but the comprehension of all attitudes, being itself speaking within us? What is this "internality" which will be capable of the relationships between interior and exterior themselves? The fact that Husserl at least implicitly and *a fortiori* raises this question[44] means that he does not think that non-philosophy is included in philosophy from the outset, or that the transcendent is "constituted" in the immanence of constituting consciousness. It means that he at least glimpses, behind transcendental genesis, a world in which all is simultaneous.

Is this last problem so surprising? Had not Husserl warned from the outset that all transcendental reduction is inevitably eidetic? This meant that reflection does not coincide with what is constituted but grasps only the essence of it—that it does not take the place of intentional life in an act of pure production but only re-produces the outline of it. Husserl always presents the "return to absolute consciousness" as a title for a multitude of operations which are learned, gradually effected, and never completed. We are never wholly one with constitutive genesis; we barely manage to accompany it for short segments. What is it then which responds to our reconstitution from (if these words have a meaning) the other side of things? From our own side, there is nothing but convergent but discontinuous intentions, moments of clarity. We constitute constituting consciousness by dint of rare and difficult efforts. It is the presumptive or alleged subject of our attempts. The

author, Valéry said, is the instantaneous thinker of works which were slow and laborious—and this thinker is nowhere. As the author is for Valéry the impostor of the writer, constituting consciousness is the philosopher's professional impostor. In any case, for Husserl it is the *artifact* the teleology of intentional life ends up at—and not the Spinozist attribute of Thought.

Originally a project to gain intellectual possession of the world, constitution becomes increasingly, as Husserl's thought matures, the means of unveiling a back side of things that we have not constituted. This senseless effort to submit everything to the proprieties of "consciousness" (to the limpid play of its attitudes, intentions, and impositions of meaning) was necessary—the picture of a well-behaved world left to us by classical philosophy had to be pushed to the limit—in order to reveal all that was left over: these beings beneath our idealizations and objectifications which secretly nourish them and in which we have difficulty recognizing noema. The Earth, for example, which is not in motion like objective bodies, but not at rest either, since we cannot see what it could be "tacked on" to. It is the "soil" or "stem" of our thought as it is of our life. We shall certainly be able to move it or carry it back when we inhabit other planets, but the reason we shall is that then we shall have enlarged our native soil. We cannot do away with it. As the Earth is by definition one, all soil we tread upon becoming simultaneously a province of it, the living beings with whom the sons of the Earth will be able to communicate will simultaneously become men—or if you prefer, terrestial men will become variants of a more general human community which will remain one. The Earth is the matrix of our time as it is of our space. Every constructed notion of time presupposes our proto-history as carnal beings compresent to a single world. Every evocation of possible worlds refers to a way of seeing our own world (*Weltanschauung*). Every possibility is a variant of our reality, an effective possibility of reality (*Möglichkeit an Wirklichkeit*). These late analyses of Husserl's[45] are neither scandalous nor even disturbing if we remember everything which foretold them from the start. They make explicit that "world's thesis" prior to every thesis and theory, this side of understanding's objectifications, which Husserl has always spoken of, and which has simply become in his eyes our sole recourse in the impasse into which these objectifications have led Western knowledge.

Willy-nilly, against his plans and according to his essential audacity, Husserl awakens a wild-flowering world and mind. Things are no longer there simply according to their projective appearances and the requirements of the panorama, as in Renaissance perspective; but on the contrary upright, insistent, flaying our glance with their edges, each thing claiming an absolute presence which is not compossible with the absolute presence of the other things, and which they nevertheless have all together by virtue of a configurational meaning which is in no way indicated by its "theoretical meaning." Other persons are there too (they were already there along with the simultaneity of things). To begin with they are not there as minds, or even as "psychisms," but such for example as we face them in anger or love—faces, gestures, spoken words to which our own respond without thoughts intervening, to the point that we sometimes turn their words back upon them even before they have reached us, as surely as, more surely than, if we had understood—each one of us pregnant with the others and confirmed by them in his body. This baroque world is not a concession of mind to nature; for although meaning is everywhere figurative, it is meaning which is at issue everywhere. This renewal of the world is also mind's renewal, a rediscovery of that brute mind which, untamed by any culture, is asked to create culture anew. From then on the irrelative is not nature in itself, nor the system of absolute consciousness' apprehensions, nor man either, but that "teleology" Husserl speaks about which is written and thought about in parentheses—that jointing and framing of Being which is being realized through man.

Notes

1. "Je grösser das Denkwerk eines Denkers ist, das sich keineswegs mit dem Umfang und der Anzahl seiner Schriften deckt, um so reicher ist das in diesem Denkwerk Ungedachte, d.h. jenes, was erst und allein durch dieses Denkwerk als das Noch-nicht-Gedachte heraufkommt." *Der Satz vom Grund,* pp. 123-24.

2. *Ideen II,* Husserliana, Bd. IV, p. 180.

3. *Ibid.,* "Ein Widerspiel der Natur."

4. *Ibid.,* p. 174, "Als reiner Sinn der die natürliche Einstellung ausmachende Akte."

5. *Ibid.,* p. 297.

6. *Ibid.,* p. 26, "Zusammenhänge sichtbar zu machen, die das Wissen vom erscheinenden Sein fördern könnten."

7. *Ibid.,* p. 183, "Unsere Umgebung."

8. *Ibid.,* p. 22, "Synthesen, die vor aller Thesis liegen."

9. *Ibid.,* p. 174.

10. *Ibid.,* p. 180, "Eine Einstellung . . . die in gewissen Sinn sehr natürlich . . . ist."

11. *Ideen III,* Husserliana, Bd. V, Beilage I, p. 117.

12. *Ideen II,* p. 5, "Vortheoretische Konstituierung."

13. *Ibid.,* "Vorgegebenheiten."

14. *Ideen III,* Beilage I, p. 117.

15. *Ideen II,* p. 145.

16. *Ibid.,* p. 119, "Empfindendes Ding"; p. 124, "Das subjektive Objekt."

17. *Ibid.,* p. 60, "Die Erfahrungstendenz terminiert in ihr, erfüllt sich in ihr."

18. *Ibid.,* p. 76, "Rechtsgrund."

19. *Ideen II,* pp. 165-66.

20. *Ibid.,* p. 166, "ohne Introjektion."

21. *Ibid.,* "übertragene Kompräsenz."

22. *Ibid.,* p. 181.

23. "Intentionale überschreiten." The expression is used in the *Cartesian Meditations.*

24. *Ideen II,* p. 163.

25. *Ibid.,* p. 85.

26. *Ibid.*

27. "Der Inbegriff der Gegenstände der Sinne." (*Krit. der Urteilskraft*)

28. *Ideen II,* p. 163.

29. *Ibid.,* p. 82: "Logical objectivity is also, *eo ipso,* objectivity in the sense of intersubjectivity. What one knower knows in logical objectivity . . . any knower can also know, to the extent he fulfills the conditions any knower of such objects must satisfy. That means in this context that he must have the experience of things and of the *same* things, so that in order to be capable of recognizing that identity itself, he must be in a relationship of *Einfühlung* with the other knowers and, to this end, have a corporeality and belong to the same world. . . ." ["zur selben Welt gehören"].

30. *Ibid.,* p. 55.

31. *Ibid.,* p. 81, "Gedankenexperiment."

32. *Ibid.,* "Konstruiertes Subjekt."

33. *Ibid.,* p. 81.

34. And yet it is in this way that Eugen Fink (*Problèmes actuels de la Phénoménologie,* pp. 80-81) seems to understand the absolute priority of the perceived in Husserl's thought.

35. *Ideen II,* p. 80, "Verwickeln wir uns nicht in einen Zirkel, da doch die Menschenauffassung die Leibesauffassung, und somit die Dingauffassung, voraussetzt?"

36. *Ibid.,* p. 27.

37. *Ibid.,* p. 210, "Wir geraten hier, scheint es, in einen bösen Zirkel. Denn setzen wir zu Anfang die Natur schlechthin, in der Weise wie es jeder Naturforscher und jeder naturalistisch Eingestellte sonst tut, und fassten wir die Menschen als Realitäten, die über ihre physiche Leiblichkeit ein plus haben, so waren die Personen untergeordnete Naturobjekte, Bestandstücke der Natur. Gingen wir aber dem Wesen der Personalität nach, so stellte sich Natur als ein im intersubjektiven Verband der Personen sich Konstituierendes also ihn Voraussetzendes dar."

38. Marly Biemel: *Husserliana,* Bd IV, Einleitung des Herausgebers. Here is Husserl's text: "Nature, the body, and also, interwoven with the body, the soul are constituted all together in a reciprocal relationship with one another." *Husserliana,* Bd V, p. 124: ". . . Ist ein wichtiges Ergebnis unserer Betrachtung, dass die 'Natur' und der Leib, in ihrer Verflechtung mit dieser wieder die Seele, sich in Wechselbezogenheit aufeinander, in eins miteinander, konstituieren."

39. *Umsturz der kopernikanischen Lehre in der gewöhnlichen weltanschaulichen Interpretation. Die Ur-Arche Erde bewegt sich richt,* 7-9 May, 1934.

40. *Ibid.,* "Aber nun wird man das arg finden, geradezu toll."

41. For example, *Ideen II,* pp. 179-80. There is the same development of thought at the end of *Umsturz.*

42. *Ideen II,* p. 211 (my italics).

43. *Ibid.,* p. 180.

44. Here is the text we are commenting on: "We have in view here a new attitude which is in a certain sense completely natural (*natürlich*) but which is not natural (*natural*). 'Not natural' means that what we have experience of in this attitude is not Nature in the sense of the natural sciences, but so to speak a contrary of Nature. It goes without saying that what is exceptionally difficult is to not be satisfied with grasping the contrast between worlds but to comprehend it from within (*von innen her zu verstehen*). This difficulty does not lie in the adoption of attitudes itself. For—if we do not consider the attitude which bears on pure conciousness (*Einstellung auf das reine Bewusstsein*), this residue of different reductions which is, moreover, artificial—we slip constantly and with no trouble from one attitude to the other, from the naturalist to the personalist attitude and correlatively from the natural to the mental sciences. The difficulties begin with reflection, phenomenological comprehension of the change in intentional apprehensions and experiences, and correlates constituted through them. It is only within the framework of phenomenology and in relating the differences of being of objects which are being constituted to the essential relationships of the constituting multiplicities which correspond to them that these difficulties can be kept unembroiled (*unverwirrt*), in absolutely certain separation (*in absolut sicherer Sonderung*), freed from all the misunderstandings which arise from involuntary changes in attitude and which, in the absence of pure reflection, remain unperceived by us. It is only by returning to absolute consciousness, and to the totality of the relationships of essence we can follow in it, that we shall finally comprehend according to their meaning the relationships of dependency between objects which correspond to both attitudes, and their reciprocal relationships of essence."

45. We are summarizing *Umsturz* . . . , cited above.

Paul Ricoeur (essay date 1967)

SOURCE: "Kant and Husserl," in *Husserl: An Analysis of His Phenomenology,* Northwestern University Press, 1967, pp. 175-201.

[*In the following study of the differences between Kant and Husserl, Ricoeur endeavors to determine which elements of Husserlian phenomenology can be found in Kantian thought, and how Kant's critique of knowledge and his determination of its limits affect the Husserlian postulation of the existence of "the other."*]

The Goal of This Study is to locate the difference between Husserlian phenomenology and Kantian Criticism with some exactness. This task of differentiation follows from a study of the major works devoted to Kant during the past twenty years (to his metaphysics in particular) and from a thorough reading of the published and unpublished works of Husserl. I would like to show that this difference is not situated where the Neo-Kantians who criticized *Ideas I* think it is (cf. Natorp, Rickert, Kreis, Zocher). Their criticism remains too dependent upon an overly epistemological interpretation of Kant. The difference should be located on the level where Kant determines the ontological status of the phenomena themselves and not on the level of an exploration of the world of phenomena.

(1) To begin with, taking Husserl as our guide, we shall distinguish an implicit phenomenology behind the Kantian epistemology which Husserl might then be said to have revealed. In this respect Husserl develops something that was frustrated in Kantianism and which remained there in an embryonic state, even though necessary to its general economy.

(2) Then, in return, taking Kant as our guide and taking his ontological intention seriously, we shall inquire whether or not Husserlian phenomenology simultaneously represents the exfoliation of an implicit Kantian phenomenology and the destruction of an ontological problem-set which had found its expression in the role of limiting and founding the thing-in-itself. We can then ask whether the loss of the ontological dimension of the object *qua* phenomenon was not common to both Husserl and his turn of the century Neo-Kantian critics. If so, this would be the reason why they located their dispute in an area of secondary importance. We shall, then, be led to reinterpret the Husserlian idealism with the guidance of that sense of limits which is perhaps the soul of the Kantian philosophy.

(3) Since the process of disontologizing the object led Husserl to a crisis in his own philosophy which he himself termed "transcendental solipsism," we shall ask if it is possible to overcome this obstacle and move on to intersubjectivity without the aid of a practical philosophy in the Kantian style. Then, taking our point of departure in Husserl's difficulties with the constitution of the alter ego, we shall return a last time to Kant in order to look for the ethical and practical determination of the person.

[I] THE *CRITIQUE* AS IMPLICIT PHENOMENOLOGY

Since Husserl is going to serve us as guide in bringing an implicit phenomenology of Kantianism to light, it is necessary to state briefly those characteristics of the Husserlian phenomenology which we take to be essential for this revelatory enterprise.

(1) I must first insist forcefully on the necessity of a distinction in Husserl between the method as it was actually practiced and the philosophical interpretation which it received, above all in *Ideas I* and in the *Cartesian Meditations*. This distinction will take on its full sense when the Kantian philosophy of limits will have opened our eyes in turn to the metaphysical decision implicit in Husserlian phenomenology.

When distinguishing between the method practiced and the philosophical interpretation of this method, in no way do I mean to exclude the well-known phenomenological reduction. To do so would be to reduce phenomenology to a rhapsody of lived experiences and to baptize as "phenomenology" any concern for the curiosities of human life, as is too often the case. The reduction is the straight gate to phenomenology. But in the very act of reduction a methodological conversion and a metaphysical decision intersect, and just at that point one must distinguish between them.

In its strictly methodological intention the reduction is a conversion which causes the "for-me" to emerge from every ontic positing. Whether the being (*être*) is a thing, a state of affairs, a value, a living creature, or a person, the *epoché* "reduces" it to its appearing. A conversion is necessary here because the "for-me" is initially disguised by the positing of the particular being (*étant*). This dissimulating positing, which Husserl called the natural attitude or the general thesis of the world, is hidden from reflection. Thus, a special spiritual discipline (*ascèse*) is necessary in order to destroy its charm. Probably, one can speak only in negative terms of this "natural thesis," since its sense appears only in the movement of reducing it. Hence, it is said that this thesis is not belief in existence, and even less intuition of it, because reduction leaves this belief intact and reveals the "seeing" in all its liveliness. It is rather an operation which insinuates itself into intuition and belief and so makes the subject a captive of this seeing and believing to the degree that he overlooks himself in the ontic positing of this or that.

This is why the natural attitude is a restriction and a limitation. But in return, the reduction, despite its negative appearance, is the reconquest of the entire relationship of the ego to its world. To put it positively, the "reduction" becomes the "constitution" of the world for and in the subjective life of consciousness. The act of reduction uncovers the relativity of what appears to performing (*opérante*) consciousness. This relativity defines the phenomenon very exactly. Henceforth, for phenomenology, nothing *is* except as a sense in consciousness. Phenomenology seeks to be the science of phenomena conquered by a spiritual discipline from the positing of particular beings. We have said enough about this topic to outline the distinction between method and doctrine. The matter will not become clear until the Kantian ontology reveals a set of problems in addition to that of the reduction.

Is the whole set of problems concerning being (*être*) annulled by the reduction? In order to affirm this, it is necessary to decide whether this problem-set is entirely contained in the natural attitude, that is to say, in the positing of each particular being (*étant*) absolutely, without relation to consciousness. It must be admitted that Husserl never brought this problem directly into the open. Likewise, if the emergence of the for-me-ness of all things and if the thematization of the world as phenomenon exhaust the questions that could be raised with regard to the being of what appears, is it the case that we are then obliged to lay aside the problem of knowledge? My feeling is that the method practiced by Husserl leaves this problem intact. I will say more. The natural attitude is at once the dissimulation of the appearance for me of the world and the dissimulation of the being of the appearance. If the natural attitude loses me into the world, sticks me into the world as seen, sensed, and acted upon, its being-in-itself is the false in-itself of an existence without me. This in-itself is only the absolutization of the ontic, of the "this" and the "that," of "particular beings." "Nature exists"; this is the natural thesis. In putting an end to the omission of the subject, in uncovering the for-me-ness of the world, the "reduction" opens rather than closes the true problem-set of being. For these problems assume the conquest made by a subjectivity, and they imply the reconquest of the subject, that being to whom being opens itself.

(2) The phenomenological reduction, which made the phenomenon of the world emerge as the very sense of consciousness, is the key that opens the way to an original "experience," the experience of the "subjective process" (*vécu*) in its "flux of consciousness." This is called "immanent perception" in *Ideas I;* and in the *Cartesian Meditations* there is a "transcendental experience," which like all experience draws its validity from its intuitive character, from the degree of presence and plenitude of its object. The Jamesian sound of these words "subjective process" (*vécu*) and "flux of consciousness" should not mislead us. The accent is fundamentally Cartesian. Even though perception of the transcendent thing is always dubitable because it is produced in a flux of adumbrations or perspectival shadings which can always cease to come together into a unity of sense, the subjective process of consciousness *schattet sich nich ab*—it does not "adumbrate." It is not perceived by successive aspects or adumbrations. Hence, phenomenology is based upon an absolute perception, that is to say, upon one which is not only indubitable but also apodictic (in the sense that it is inconceivable that its object, the subjective process, should not be).

Is this to say that phenomenology is a new empiricism? A new phenomenalism? What matters here is to remember that Husserl never separated the transcendental reduction from that other reduction which he terms eidetic and which consists in grasping the fact (*Tatsache*) in its essence (*eidos*). Hence, the ego that the *epoché* reveals as the one to which all things appear should not be described in its accidental singularity but rather as eidos ego (*Cartesian Meditations*). This change of levels, obtained principally by the method of imaginative variation, converts "transcendental experience" into science.

There are two reasons why Husserl's phenomenology can serve as a guide within Kant's work. These concern (1) the reduction of the particular being to the phenomenon and (2) the descriptive experience of the subjective process in the eidetic mode. Kant himself is the authority in this matter. In the letter to Markus Herz of February 21, 1772, he announces that the great work he is projecting on the limits of sensibility and reason would include in its theoretical portion two parts: first, phenomenology in general, and second, metaphysics considered uniquely in its nature and method. Yet the *Critique of Pure Reason* is not called a phenomenology and properly speaking is not a phenomenology. Why? This question will permit us to situate the *Critique* in relation to the "reduction."

(1) Two reasons can be offered which show why the *Critique* is not a phenomenology. The first, to which we shall return in our second part, concerns the philosophy of limits which has as large a role in the *Critique* as the investigations of the domain of phenomena. In the preface of the second edition, Kant refers to the "revolution" in metaphysical method brought about by the *Critique* and declares, "It is a treatise on the method, not a system of the science itself. But at the same time it marks out the whole plan of the science, both as regards its limits and as regards its entire internal structure" (B 22-23).[1] Thus, the two intentions of the *Critique* are set forth neatly: to limit the phenomenon and to elucidate its internal structure. It is this second task that could be a phenomenological one.

This reason why the *Critique* is not a phenomenology is not the only one; in addition, the elucidation of the internal structure of phenomenality is not conducted in a phenomenological fashion. Here it is necessary to question the particularly epistemological preoccupation of the *Critique*. The fundamental question, "How are synthetic *a priori* judgments possible?" forbids a genuine description of subjective life. The problem of justification that appears in the foreground of the "Transcendental Deduction" virtually eliminates the intention of composing a genuine physiology of the mind (*Gemüt*). It seems less important to describe how the mind (*esprit*) knows than to justify the universality of knowledge by the synthetic function of the categories and ultimately by the unifying function of transcendental apperception. The three correlative notions of nature, experience, and objectivity bear the mark of this epistemological preoccupation. Nature defined (to some degree phenomenologically) as the "totality of all phenomena" in epistemological terms is "nature in general, considered in its conformity to laws (*Gesetzmässigkeit*)." And since nature is the correlate of experience, the *Gesetzmässigkeit* of nature is identical with the conditions of the possibility of experience. Regarding its epistemological task, the *Critique* searches for such a priori concepts as will render possible "the formal unity of experience" or "the form of an experience in general." It is within this framework that the problem of objectivity is presented. Objectivity is the cognitive status conferred on the empirical understanding by its *Gesetzmässigkeit*.

To be specific, the *Critique* is not limited to a purely epistemological determination of objectivity, that is, to a justification of constituted knowledge (mathematics, physics, metaphysics). The "Analytic" more than meets the needs of Newtonian physics and the "Aesthetic" those of Euclidean and even non-Euclidean geometry. It is in this marginal area where the *Critique* goes beyond a simple epistemology that there is a chance of finding the beginnings of a genuine phenomenology.

The Copernican Revolution, disengaged from the epistemological hypothesis, is nothing other than the phenomenological *epoché*. It constitutes a vast reduction which moves not merely from the constituted sciences, from successful knowledge, to their conditions of legitimacy; it also moves from the totality of appearing to its conditions of constitution. This descriptive design, usually overshadowed by the justificatory intention of the *Critique*, appears every time Kant renounces dependence on a constituted science and directly defines what he calls receptivity, spontaneity, synthesis, subsumption, production, reproduction, etc. These embryonic descriptions, quite often masked in definitions, are necessary to the epistemological enterprise itself, for the a priori which constitutes the formal determinations of all knowledge is itself rooted in the acts, operations, or functions whose description by and large gets beyond the strict domain of the sciences. Can one, then, say that the *Critique* includes a "transcendental experience"?

(2) The transcendental experience which opens up to the phenomenologist beyond the threshold of the phenomenological reduction at first glance seems totally foreign to the Kantian spirit. Is not the very notion of an "experience" of the cogito some sort of a monster for a Kantian? To examine and describe the cogito, is this not to treat it as a phenomenon, hence as an object in nature and no longer as the condition for the possibility of phenomena? Does not the combination of the transcendental and the eidetic reductions remove us still further and more decisively from Kant by the use of a suspect mixture of psychologism (the subjective process) and Platonism (the eidos ego)? Is this not the place to recall that the "I-think" of originary apperception is in no way the ego grasped in its eidos and reduced to the unifying function that supports the synthetic work of cognition? So then, how will "transcendental experience" escape from this dilemma: either I am "conscious" of the "I-think" but it is not knowledge, or I "know" the ego but it is a phenomenon in nature? It is on just these grounds that the Neo-Kantian criticisms of Husserl are founded.

It must be recognized that the *Critique* beats a difficult trail around this dilemma which lies purely on the epistemological plane, for the "I-think" and the "self phenomenon" are defined in terms of objective knowledge. In fact, however, Kant escapes from this dilemma every time he proceeds to a direct inspection of the *Gemüt* (mind). The very term *Gemüt*, so enigmatic, designates the "field of transcendental experience" which Husserl thematizes. *Gemüt* is not at all the "I-think," the epistemological guarantee for the unity of experience, but rather what Husserl calls *ego cogito cogitata.* In short, it is the theme of the Kantian phenomenology itself, the theme that the "Copernican Revolution" brings to light. When this revolution is not reduced to the *questio juris,* to the axiomatization of Newtonian physics, it is none other than the reduction of particular beings to their appearance in the *Gemüt.* With the guidance of a transcendental experience of the *Gemüt* it is possible to grasp the features of the Kantian phenomenology.

Certainly, the "Transcendental Aesthetic" is the least phenomenological part of the *Critique.* The description of the spatiality of the phenomenon—the only description that Kant undertakes, and then because it concerns mathematics—is squeezed between the epistemological preoccupation with justifying the synthetic a priori judgments of geometry[2] and the characteristic constructibility of mathematical reasoning,[3] by means of the concept of pure intuition on the one hand and on the other the ontological concern for situating exactly the being of space.[4]

Nevertheless, a phenomenology of spatiality is implied as long as space is related to the "subjective constitution of our minds" (*subjektiven Beshaffenheit unseres Gemüts*) (A 25). Only this phenomenology can establish that the purely epistemological notion of a priori intuition coincides with that of a "form situated in the subject." Kant is led to describe space as the manner in which the subject is disposed to receive something before the appearance of that something. "To render possible an external intuition" is a phenomenological determination far broader than "to render possible the synthetic a priori judgments of geometry." This possibility is no longer on the order of legitimation but is on the order of the constitution of the *Beshaffenheit unseres Gemüts.*

Nevertheless, the "Transcendental Aesthetic" is still quite deceptive, not only because of its embryonic but also because of its static character. Space and time are considered not in the movement of the entire experience but rather as forming a prior stratum, finished and inert. This too is to be understood by reference to the emphasis on epistemology. Spatiality is not a stage in the constitution of the "thing" for the geometrician. Its determination as pure intuition must be terminated within itself in order to assure the complete autonomy of mathematics.

Once Kant has placed his foot across the phenomenological threshold and relates space to the possibility of being affected by something, he is led into the actual movement of a dynamic constitution of experience and thinghood. The provisional juxtaposition of space and time is suddenly once more in question. Space must be "traversed" in temporal moments, "retained" in a total image, and "recognized" as an identical sense (A 95 ff.). The schematism accentuates even more the dynamic character of spatial constitution (A 137). This grasping of space through time ("Time is a necessary representation which founds all intuitions") marks the triumph of phenomenology over epistemology.

What is more, to the degree that we move away from the concern for axiomatizing geometry, all that appeared clear epistemologically becomes phenomenologically obscure. If space is on the level of sensibility, we still do not think anything in it; we only dispose ourselves to receive something. But then we are below all syntheses, and it is necessary to say that this (epistemological) form is a (phenomenological) manifold (A 76 f.). Kant even goes so far as to observe that space concerns the status of a being which is dependent "in its existence as well as in its intuition (and which through that intuition determines its existence in relation to the given objects)" (B 72).

At the same time, he identifies space—or the formal property of being affected by objects or receiving an immediate representation of things—with the intentionality of consciousness. This is the movement in consciousness toward something, considered as the possibility of spreading out, discriminating, or pluralizing any impression whatsoever. Thus, the more explicit phenomenology of the "Analytic" dispels the false clarity of the "Aesthetic," so feebly phenomenological.

The phenomenology of the "Analytic" stands out emphatically if one reads it in reverse order, ascending from the transcendental theory of judgment (or "Analytic of Principles") to the transcendental theory of the concept, pausing at the "Analogies of Experience" before plunging into the difficult chapter on the "Schematism" (this difficulty will be discussed below). It is to be expected that the phenomenology of Kant should be primarily a phenomenology of judging. Such a phenomenology is most apt to offer a propaedeutic to epistemology. On the other hand, it is to be expected that Husserl's phenomenology should be, preferably, a phenomenology of perception, for this is most apt to illustrate a concern for evidence, for originariness, and for presence—although, the *Logical Investigations* begins with judging, and in phenomenology the place of judging comes to be marked out in the strata of subjective life on the level of founded syntheses. (We shall see in the second part that there are other reasons which explain this difference in accent and preference in the descriptions of Kant and Husserl.) In any case no difference between them in descriptive theme hides their kinship in method of analysis.

If we begin the "Analytic" at the end, therefore, with the "Analogies of Experience," we shall see a full analysis of judging developed as the act of subsuming perceptions under the rules of intelligibility. Kant the epistemologist holds this operation to be a simple "application" of the laws of previously constituted understanding. But the tendency of the description leads the analysis in another direction as subsumption reveals itself to be an actual constitution of experience inasmuch as it is experience which is understood, judged, and expressed on the predicative level.

The "Principles," which from the epistemological point of view are the axioms of pure physics, the first synthetic judgments a priori of a science of nature, yield an admirable description of the constitution of thinghood (*Dinglichkeit*). In this regard, the intellectual character of the percept is thematized in addition to the principles of permanence, causality, and reciprocity. It is admirable that Kant linked the structures of thinghood with the structures of temporality long before Husserl. The different ways in which experience is "connected" are also the diverse ways in which time is intellectually structured. The second analogy in particular contains a veritable phenomenology of the event which answers the question: What does "to happen" signify? The phenomenologist elaborates the notion of an ordered succession upon (*sur*) the object in the world. In Husserlian language one would say that the "Analogies of Experience" develop the noematic side of the subjective process in the judgment of experience. They consider the judgment from the side of the "judged" where it connects to the object. (On the other hand, the preceding chapter on the "Schematism" yields a noetic analysis of the "event" and reflects on the operation of connecting as "the synthetic power of the imagination" [B 233]. We shall return to this matter later.)

If one considers that this second chapter of the doctrine of judgment, whose heart is the theory of the "Analogies of Experience," shows the noematic side of the judgment of experience, then one sees that this noematic analysis is completed in the "Postulates of Empirical Thought in General" (A 218 ff.). In effect, the "postulates" add no new determination to the object, but they do thematize its existence according to the modalities of the actual, the possible, and the necessary. Now, what do these postulates signify? They simply posit the fundamental correlation of the existence of things with their perceptibility: "Our knowledge of the existence of things reaches, then, only so far as perception and its advance according to empirical laws can extend" (A 226). Spatiality has furnished us with the style of intentionality as the opening to the appearing. The postulate of empirical thought determines the effectiveness of intentionality as the perceived presence of the thing which appears.

It is not by accident that Kant inserts the "refutation of Idealism" (B 274 ff.) into a corner of the second edition; it is a definition of intentionality before its time: "The mere yet empirically determined consciousness of my own existence proves the existence of objects in space outside me" (B 275). In fact, the correlation of "I am" and "something is" is intentionality itself.

If Chapter Two of the "Transcendental Doctrine of Judgment" develops the noematic side of the judgment of existence, then Chapter One, devoted to the schematism, deals with the noetic side. Hence the obscurity of Chapter One. It incessantly anticipates in a reflexive way the "Analogies of Experience" which reveal the work of judging on the object. One should always read this chapter after the one that follows and then return to Chapter One by a reflexive movement which finds "in" the *Gemüt* (mind) what was revealed "on" the object. The anticipatory char-

acter of this chapter explains Kant's brevity in elaborating the schemata. Nevertheless, these few hundred lines (A 144-47) are the subjective side of the immense noematic analysis of the following chapter.

If one considers it in this way, the theory of the schematism comes very close to being what Husserl calls autoconstitution or the constitution of the ego in temporality. We know that Kant himself was astonished at this "art concealed in the depths of the human soul whose true modes of activity nature is hardly likely ever to allow us to discover and to have open to our gaze" (A 141). Never is Kant more free with regard to his epistemological preoccupations. Likewise, he is never closer to discovering the originary time of consciousness beyond constituted time (or time as representation, according to the "Transcendental Aesthetic"). The time of the schematism is at the union of receptivity and spontaneity, of the manifold and the unitary. Time is my power of ordering, and it also offers the constant threat of escaping and defeating me. It is the indivisible, possible, rationality of order and the ever renascent irrationality of the subjective life. It looks toward affectivity, whose pure flux it is, and toward intellectuality, since the schemata mark its possible structuration in respect to "series," "content," and "order" (A 145).

Should we follow this phenomenology of the *Gemüt* to its conclusion, we would have to relate what Kant was repeatedly led to say concerning the existence of consciousness to this noetic analysis of the operation of judging. While the noematic analysis culminates in the "Postulates of Empirical Thought" that coordinate the existence of things with their perceptibility, the noetic analysis culminates in the self-determination of the I-exist. But with regard to this theme one only finds occasional notes in the *Critique*. And in effect it is here that the implicit phenomenology encounters the most formidable resistances deep within Kantianism. The whole epistemological conception of objectivity tends to make the "I-think" a function of objectivity and imposes the alternatives to which we referred at the outset. Either I am "conscious" of the I-think but do not "know" it, or I "know" the ego, but it is a phenomenon within nature. This is why Kant's phenomenological description tends toward the discovery of a concrete subject who has no tenable place in the system. However, Kant moves in the direction of this subject whenever he moves toward originary time at work in judgment by means of the schematism. Likewise, he approaches this subject when he determines the existence of the things as correlative to my existence. At this point he remarks: "I am conscious of my own existence as determined in time . . . consequently the determination of my existence in time is possible only through the existence of actual things which I perceive outside me" (B 275-76; see also the note to the preface of the second edition on B xi).

The great difficulty was in thematizing an existence which was not the category of existence, which was not, in other words, a structure of subjectivity. This difficulty is confronted for the first time in § 25 of the second edition (an existence which is not a phenomenon). The note that Kant adds here (B 158) proposes the task of grasping existence in the act of the I-think that determines this existence, hence before the temporal intuition of myself that raises my existence to the level of a psychological phenomenon (B 157). The difficulty here is great, especially if one considers that the I-think only passes into act upon the reception of a manifold which it determines logically. Above all the famous text comes to mind in the critique of "Rational Psychology," where the "I-think" is considered as an empirical proposition that includes the proposition "I-exist." Kant attempts to resolve the problem within the framework of his epistemology by linking existence to an "undetermined empirical intuition" anterior to all organized experience. This allows him to say, "Existence is not yet a category" (B 423).

Is not this extracategorial existence that very subjectivity without which the "I-think" would not merit the title of first person? Is it not in connection with this originary time that the "Analytic" stands forth from the time representation of the "Aesthetic"? In short, perhaps this is the existence of *Gemüt*, the mind, which is neither the I-think as principle of the possibility of the categories nor the self phenomenon of psychological science, but rather the mind which is offered to transcendental experience by the phenomenological reduction.

[II] The *Critique* as Envisagement of Limits

Oour first group of analyses depended on a provisional limitation. We granted that in Husserl the actually practiced method could be distinguished from the philosophical interpretation which he constantly mixed with it, especially in his published works. We made use of this actual phenomenology to reveal an implicit phenomenology in the *Critique*. Hence, the kinship of Kant and Husserl was established at the price of a legitimate but precarious abstraction applied to the total intention of the work of each man.

Now the *Critique* is something quite different from a phenomenology, not only by its epistemological preoccupation but also by its ontological intent. Only in this respect is the *Critique* more than a simple investigation of the "internal structure" of knowledge; it is also an investigation of the limits of knowledge. The rooting of the knowledge of phenomena in the thinking of being (*être*) which is not convertible into knowledge gives the Kantian *Critique* its properly ontological dimension. To destroy this tension between knowing and thinking, between the phenomenon and being, is to destroy Kantianism itself.

So then one can wonder whether the phenomenology of Husserl, which served us as guide and revealer for Kantianism's descriptive phenomenology, should not be considered in turn from the standpoint of the Kantian ontology. Perhaps the philosophical interpretation involved in the transcendental *epoché* participates in the destruction of the Kantian ontology, sanctions the loss of *Denken* in *Erkennen*, and thus thins out the philosophy into a phenomenology without ontology.

First, let us take account of the function of the positing of the thing-in-itself in relation to the inspection of phenomena as Kant sees it. There is no knowledge of being. This impossibility is somehow active and even positive. In spite of the impossibility of knowledge of being, *Denken* still posits being as that which limits the claims of the phenomena to make up ultimate reality. Thus, *Denken* confers on phenomenology its ontological dimension or status. One can trace this connection between a deception (regarding knowledge) and a positive act of limitation throughout the *Critique*.

As early as the "Transcendental Aesthetic," where the ontological intention is constantly present, Kant posits that a priori intuition is determined in contrast with a creative intuition which we do not have. Kant's very important note on *intuitus originarius*, at the end of the "Aesthetic," is clear. The *Gegen-stand* (object) holds itself up before me to the degree that it is not the *Ent-stand* (original), which would spring up from its own intuition.[5] Now, from the beginning this metaphysical deception is incorporated into the very sense of space and time and gives a negative tone to every page of the "Aesthetic." "Our whole intuition is *only* the representation of the phenomenon. The things that we intuit are not in themselves as we intuit them." In some way the phenomenon's lack of being is incorporated into it. But this shortcoming is itself the inverse of a positive act of *Denken* which in the "Aesthetic" takes the fanciful form of a supposition, the supposition of the destruction of our intuition: "If we depart from the subjective condition . . . the representation of space stands for nothing whatsoever."[6] And the same is said a bit further along with respect to time (A 37). This possible nothingness forms part of the notion of transcendental ideality since space is nothing outside of the subjective condition (A 28). This bit of fancy expresses what is positive in the negative of our lack of originary intuition. The *Denken* is the positive. It is not reducible to our being-affected and in consequence not reducible to that "dependence" of man "in his existence as well as in his intuition" (B 72) which was pointed out near the end of the "Aesthetic." The *Denken* is what imposes the limit.[7] It is not the phenomenal understanding that limits the usage of categories of experience; it is the positing of being by *Denken* that limits the claim of knowing the absolute. Knowledge, finitude, and death are thus linked by an indissoluble pact which is only recognized by the very act of *Denken* that escapes from this condition and somehow views it from without.

There should be no difficulty in showing that this supposition of the nothingness of our sensible knowledge clarifies Kant's constant affirmation that transcendental philosophy stands on the dividing line that separates the "two sides" of the phenomenon (A 38), the in-itself and the for-us. For what necessarily forces us across the limits of experience and all appearances is the unconditioned that authorizes us to speak of the things "only so far as we do not know them" (A 38).

This limiting function of the in-itself finds a striking confirmation in the "Transcendental Analytic." It touches on the sense of "nature." By indicating the empty place of an impossible science of creation, the in-itself protects knowledge of the phenomena of nature from falling into a dogmatic naturalism. This limiting function of the in-itself is given its most complete expression in the chapter on the "Distinction of all Objects into Phenomena and Noumena." The concept of the in-itself even though "problematical" (from the standpoint of knowledge; problematical, however, does not mean doubtful, but rather non-contradictory) is necessary "to prevent sensuous intuition from being extended to the things-in-themselves" (A 254). To be even clearer: "The concept of a noumenon is thus a merely limiting concept, the function of which is to limit the presumptions of sensuousness" (A 255). Hence, there would be a sort of *hubris* of sensuousness—not, correctly speaking, of sensuousness as such, but the empirical usage of the understanding, of the positive and positivistic praxis of the understanding.

This notion of the usage of categories is of first importance. Kant expressly distinguishes it from the sense of the categories (A 147, A 248). This distinction clarifies what Kant understands by the presumption of sensuousness. He says nothing else when he shows the vanity of this pretension by means of the play of transcendental illusion and the check of failure (paralogism and antinomies). It is not reason that is unsuccessful in the "Transcendental Dialectic"; it is rather sensuousness in its claim to apply to the things-in-themselves.[8]

If we believe ourselves able to use this Kantian doctrine as a guide for interpreting the implicit philosophy of Husserl, we need to be assured that Kant truly succeeded in reconciling this function of limitation with the idealism of his theory of objectivity, such as it is developed in the "Transcendental Deduction." Is not objectivity reduced to the synthesis imposed on the manifold of sensibility by apperception through the categories? If this conception of objectivity as the operation of transcendental subjectivity is truly the center of the "Transcendental Deduction," how can it be linked with another signification of the object as the in-itself? At times it seems that the word "object" can only designate "the totality of my representations" and that the intellectual structure of experience is sufficient for detaching my representations from me and opposing them to me as something over against me (there is the familiar example of the house passed through, apprehended, and recognized) (A 190-91). In this sense the object is just "appearance, in contradistinction to the representations of apprehension" (A 191). Causality consolidates the object of my representations into a counterpole to consciousness in the process of distinguishing succession *in* the object from the succession *of* representations "insofar as one is conscious of it" (A 189). And one can speak of truth, that is to say, of the agreement of the representation with its object, since by this process of objectivation of representations, there is truly "an object distinct from them," (A 191). Was it not Husserl who pointed to the constitution of the object *in* consciousness as something *over against* consciousness?

Moreover, Kant does not doubt that what radically situates the object outside is the thing-in-itself. The intending of the phenomenon beyond itself is toward the non-empirical object, the transcendental *X*. This is why Kant balances the texts where objectivity emerges from the separation between my representations and the phenomenon with others, where the phenomena remain "representations, which in turn have their object" (A 109). The transcendental object is "what can alone confer upon all of our empirical concepts in general relation to an object, that is, objective reality" (A 109).

Now, the realistic function of intentionality (the object *X* as "correlative of the unity of apperception") penetrates through and through the idealistic function of objectifying my representations. How is this possible? The key to the problem is the distinction, fundamental in Kant but totally unknown in Husserl, between *intention* and *intuition*. Kant radically separates from one another the relation to something and the intuition of something. An object = *X* is an intention without intuition. This distinction subtends that of thinking and knowing and maintains the agreement as well as the tension between them.

Rather than juxtapose the two interpretations of objectivity, Kant posits their reciprocity. It is because the relation to the object = *X* is an intention without an intuition that it refers to objectivity as unification of a manifold. From that point on, the relation to the object is nothing other than "the necessary unity of consciousness, and therefore also of the synthesis of the manifold."[9] Thus, the objectivity that issues from objectivation and the objectivity prior to this objectivation refer to each other (A 250-51). The transcendental ideality of the object turns back to the realism of the thing-in-itself, and this latter leads to the former. The preface to the second edition says nothing else when it posits the mutual implication of the conditioned and the unconditioned (B xx).

This structure in Kantianism has no parallel in Husserlian phenomenology. Like the Neo-Kantians, Husserl lost the ontological dimension of the phenomenon and simultaneously lost the possibility of a meditation on the limits and foundations of phenomenality. This is why phenomenology is not a "critique," that is to say, an envisagement of the limits of its own field of experience.

Here we have the true guide for discerning the simple methodological conversion within the phenomenological reduction, the one whose complications we saw in the first part, and also the methodological decision mixed in with it. The Second Cartesian Meditation clearly shows this clandestine shift from an act of abstention to an act of negation. In refraining (*mich enthalten*) from positing the world as absolute, I conquer it as world-perceived-in-the-reflective-life; in short, I gain it as phenomenon. Husserl can legitimately say that "the world is for me absolutely nothing else but the world existing for and being accepted by me in such a conscious cogito." Yet, notice that Husserl dogmatically posits that the world "finds in me and draws from me its sense and its being-status."[10] Ingarden has already expressed reservations regarding such expressions which, he says, anticipate the result of constitution, "for these expressions involve a metaphysical decision, a decision that one can assimilate to a categorial thesis having to do with something that is not itself an element of transcendental subjectivity."[11]

The most basic reason behind Husserl's view is that he confused the problems of being (*être*) with the naïve positing of particular beings (*étants*) in the natural attitude. Now, this naïve positing is precisely the omission of the connection of particular beings to ourselves, and it arises from that *Anmassung* (presumption) of sensuousness discussed by Kant. Furthermore, the interlacing of the significations of objectivity which we found in Kant, an objectivity constituted "in" us and a founding objectivity "of" the phenomenon, is not to be detected in Husserl. This is why this world that is "for" me in respect to its sense (and "in" me in the intentional sense of "in") is also "from" (*de*) me in respect to its *Seinsgeltung,* its "being-status." Thereupon the *epoché* is also the measure of being and cannot be measured by anything else. It can only be radicalized; it cannot be penetrated by an absolute position which, like the Good in Plato, would give the power of seeing to the subject and would give something absolute to be seen.

I would now like to show how this implicit metaphysics of the non-metaphysical explains certain traits in Husserl's own description. Certainly it does not explain the fidelity and submission of his regard for "the things themselves"; phenomenology would be ruined entirely by this reproach. But it does explain the preferences that orient the attention toward certain constitutive strata of subjective life rather than toward others.

(1) In the first place the function of reason differs profoundly in Kant and Husserl. In Kant, reason is the *Denken* itself reflecting on the "sense" of the categories beyond their empirical "usage." We know that this reflection is at once a critique of transcendental illusion and a justification of the "Ideas" of reason. Husserl employs the word reason, generally associated with the words actuality and truth, in an entirely different way. Every discernment of the claims of the subjective process to indicate something actual is a problem of reason (I, Part IV). Now this discernment of actual validity consists in measuring each type of signification (the percept as such, the imaginary, the judged, the willed, the sensed as such) by the corresponding type of originary evidence.

The problem of reason is not at all oriented toward an investigation of some sort of intention without intuition, of some intending without intuiting, that would give the phenomenon something beyond itself.[12] Quite to the contrary, reason has the task of authenticating the phenomenon itself on the basis of its own plenitude.

Henceforth, the phenomenology of reason will be entirely concerned with the notion of originary evidence, whether this evidence is perceptual, categorial, or otherwise. Thus, it is clear that phenomenology should develop a critique to replace that of Kant. In fact it does more than describe in the intuitive mode; it measures every claim by a seeing. Its virtue is no longer only descriptive, but now it is also corrective. Every empty signification (for example, a symbolic signification whose formative rule is lost), is referred back to the presence of actuality, such as it would appear if it would show itself, in its *Leiblichkeit,* in flesh and blood. Reason is this movement of referring from the "modified" to the "originary."

Thus, phenomenology has become critical, but in a way opposite to that of Kant. With Kant, intuition refers to the *Denken* that would limit it. With Husserl, "simply thinking" refers back to the evidence that fulfills it. The problem of fullness (*Fülle*) has replaced that of limitation (*Grenze*). In defining truth by evidence and actuality by the originary, Husserl no longer encounters the problem of the in-itself. While Kant was careful not to let himself be closed up in the phenomenon, Husserl is careful not to let himself be abused by inactualized thoughts. His problem is no longer one of ontological ground but is rather a problem of the authenticity of subjective life.

(2) But this critique of authenticity is to lead Husserl to reduction after reduction and first to a reduction of evidence itself. Every philosophy of seeing, of immediacy, threatens to return to naïve realism—that of Husserl more than any other, insofar as he insists on the presence of the thing itself in "flesh and blood." This is a danger which Husserl never ceased to invite. The more he insists on a return from the thought to the originarily evident, the more he has to compensate for the latent risks of this intuitionism in ever further radicalizing the idealistic interpretation of constitution.

The Third Cartesian Meditation and, likewise, the unpublished material of the last period are directed to this point. These writings try to reduce the repeatedly revived discord between the idealistic requirements of constitution—those that make the object a purely ideal unity of sense—and the intuitionistic requirements of reason. Hence, the reduction from the learned and the acquired must be practiced on evidence itself. Completely freed from old, sedimented, and suppressed evidence, evidence is reduced to the living present (*die lebendige Gegenwart*) of consciousness. Here once more is seen a new effect of the "metaphysical decision" that we have just discerned in the Husserlian reduction. Every presence remains an enigma for description because of the "addition" (*Zusatz*) that it contributes in comparison to my expectation and most exact anticipation. Husserl, crushing this last prestige of the in-itself, which might still insinuate itself into presence, decides that the presence *of* the thing itself is *my* present. The radical otherness attaching to presence is reduced to the nowness of the present; the presence of the Other is the present of myself.

Hereafter, Husserl will look on the side of temporality for the secret of the constitution of all supposed being-in-itself. Former evidences, destroying the movement of constitution where they were primally instituted (*Urstiftung*), present themselves as a mysterious transcendence. The in-itself is the past of evidence and the possibility of reactivation of it in a new present. An entire group of manuscripts, Group C, struggles at the breach opened by the Third Meditation. We find the great problem of temporality in the place of honor here. Because Husserl discerned the originary temporality, which is the advance of consciousness, beyond the time-representation of the "Transcendental Aesthetic," he can defy the most hallowed enchantment: absolute reality. The question is whether he ever saw the problem of being.

(3) The disontologizing of reality leads to a new climax: the passage from "static" to "genetic" constitution, a problem which is indicated by the intersecting role of temporality in the problems of origin and authenticity. Now, "genetic" constitution is largely "passive" genesis. *Experience and Judgment* indicates this orientation in Husserl's investigations. Every positing of sense and presence includes an abridged history which is sedimented and then suppressed. We have already seen this with regard to evidence. This history constitutes itself in the "anonymous" strata of subjective life. At the time of *Ideas I*, Husserl was not unaware of this aspect of the "passivity" of consciousness. However, he considered it rather as the obverse of consciousness (as hyle in relation to intentional form). What remained on the first level was the active anticipation of a "sense," of a unity of signification (thing, animal, person, value, or state of affairs). Above all, Husserl did not fail to emphasize that consciousness is a diversity which the phenomenologist cannot approach without the "transcendental guide of the object." In other words, it is noematic analysis which takes precedence over reflection on subjective life in the noetic perspective. Such concern to identify consciousness with synthesis, with the claiming of a unity, is basically very Kantian. But Husserl's interest moves progressively from the problem of the unity of sense to the problem of primal institution (*Urstiftung*), that is, to the problem of the rooting or founding of all sense in the evident actual subjective process. This shift of interest leads from logical reason to perceptual reason (the articulations of judgment actively seizing upon passively elaborated structures in the antepredicative sphere of perception). Likewise, it leads from perceptual reason to the sensuous impression with its mnemonic retentions and its kinesthetic protentions.

Thus, the most important unpublished writings of Groups C and D in the Louvain classification elaborate a new "Transcendental Aesthetic" which is not absorbed by a "Transcendental Deduction." According to this new "Transcendental Aesthetic," the object perceived by everyone "refers back" below intersubjectivity to the primordial world such as it would appear to the *solus ipse*. Within this primordial sphere the "external" object refers to the "immanent object"—to the *Urimpression*—by means of

the retentions and protentions of temporal constitution. In this way Husserl was called from the genius of Kant to that of Hume. Kant would found the impression on the a priori of sensibility and the entire perceived order on intellectual objectivity. In the late Husserl founding no longer signifies elevating to intellectuality, but on the contrary it signifies building up on the basis of the primordial, of the pre-given. Hume's genius is precisely that of regressing in this way from signs, symbols, and images to impressions.

(4) Owing to this identification of reason with a critique of evidence, to the reduction of evidence to the living present, and to the reference to the impression, one might say that Husserl entirely identifies phenomenology with an egology without ontology.

The most manifest purpose of the *Cartesian Meditations* leads to this identification. The Second Meditation initially contends that if every actuality is a correlate of the cogitatio, every cogitatio is a mode of the cogito. The cogito in turn is the expression of the ego. And thus phenomenology is an egological analysis (*CM*, § 13). Husserl immediately saw the formidable consequences of this view:

> Without a doubt it begins in the style of a pure egology, of a science which condemns us, it seems, to solipsism, at least transcendental solipsism. At this stage one absolutely cannot foresee how, in the attitude of reduction, it could be possible that we would have to posit the existence of other egos, not as simple mundane phenomena, but as other transcendental egos, and that thus we make them also the legitimate theme of a transcendental egology
>
> (*CM*, p. 69).

Husserl heroically accepts the difficulty and lets it be suspected that transcendental solipsism must remain a "preliminary philosophical stage" which must be assumed provisionally "in order that the problems of transcendental intersubjectivity may be stated and attacked correctly as founded problems and hence as problems belonging to a higher level" (*CM*, p. 69).

We shall see in the third part of this study whether Husserl succeeded in crossing the threshold to intersubjectivity. For the present let us note how radical a stage egology has been led to by Husserl and to what a paradox he has brought transcendental solipsism. In the Fourth Cartesian Meditation the ego itself, insofar as it is the ego of the ego cogito, is thematized: "It is continuously constituting itself as existing" (*CM*, p. 100). Thereafter, Husserl must go beyond the old thesis of *Ideas I* according to which the ego is the "identical pole of subjective processes." Henceforth, "the ego, taken in full concreteness, we propose to call by the Leibnizian name: monad" (*CM*, p. 102).

This shift from Cartesian to Leibnizian language signifies the total triumph of interiority over exteriority, of the transcendental over the transcendent: everything which exists for me is constituted in me, and this constitution is the concrete life of the ego. From here one can correctly say that all the problems of constitution are included in those of "explicating this monadic ego phenomenologically (the problem of his constitution for himself). . . . Consequently the phenomenology of this self-constitution coincides with phenomenology as a whole" (*CM,* pp. 102-3). Thus, phenomenology aspires—as a philosophical discipline—to cross the desert of solipsism. Phenomenology is the science of the only ego of which I have evidence originarily—my own.

Kantianism would never encounter such a problem. Not only because in its epistemological perspective it could encounter only a consciousness in general, the subject of true knowledge, but also because the *Gemüt* that the *Critique* presupposes as concrete subject is always tending toward "the transcendental-object = *X*" that escapes from the phenomenon and which could be the absolute existence of another person. In Husserl the disontologizing of the object virtually implies the disontologizing of the bodies of Others as well as the disontologizing of other persons. Thus, the description of the concrete subject leads, under the aegis of idealism, to a metaphysical solitude whose consequences Husserl accepted with exemplary probity.

This is why the constitution of the Other, which assures the passage to intersubjectivity, is the touchstone for the success or failure not only of phenomenology but also of the implicit philosophy of phenomenology.

[III] The "Constitution of the Other" and "Respect"

All aspects of phenomenology, therefore, converge upon the problem of the constitution of the Other. Have we, consequently, left Kant's problem behind? Are we pushing into a new area which the Kantian genius has not cleared? Not at all. The final turning point of Husserlian phenomenology, the product of what is least Kantian in Husserl's "transcendental experience," leads us in an unexpected manner to the heart of Kantianism, not, to be sure, to the *Critique of Pure Reason* but rather to the practical philosophy.

Kant has no phenomenology of the knowledge of Others. The phenomenology of *Gemüt* is too implicit and too blurred by epistemological considerations to contain even some hints of a theory of intersubjectivity. In the *Anthropology* at most the premises of such a theory might be found within the framework of the theory of the passions which in effect Kant conducts like a theory of intersubjectivity. But all this is slight in comparison with Husserl's admirable phenomenological essays on *Einfühlung* (empathy). The theory of empathy belongs to descriptive phenomenology before taking on the task of resolving the paradox of transcendental solipsism. It merges with the phenomenology of perception, the perception of Others being incorporated into the significations of the world that I perceive. It is inscribed in the constitution of the thing and determines the last stratum of objectivity. It is implied in the constitution of cultural objects, languages, and institutions. Hence, it is not on the properly descriptive level that phenomenology has something to learn from Kant. Here Husserl guides, not Kant.

On the other hand, we shall come back to Kant again in order to resolve the difficulties entailed by the philosophical interpretation of the reduction, difficulties which culminate in the paradox of transcendental solipsism. Husserl not only proposed to describe how Others appear, or in which perspective, or in which affective or practical modes the sense of "the Other" or "alter ego" are constituted; he also tried to constitute the Other "in" me and yet to constitute it as "Other."

This is the task of the Fifth Cartesian Meditation. One might say that this difficult attempt is a losing bet. The author tries to constitute the Other as a sense that forms in me, in what is most intimate to the ego, in what Husserl calls the sphere of my ownness. But at the same time that he constitutes the Other in me according to the requirements of idealism, he intends to respect the very sense that is attached to the presence of Others. This presence is that of someone different from me yet that of another me who has his world, who perceives me, addresses himself to me, and who forms relations of intersubjectivity with me out of which arise a unique world of science and the multiple worlds of culture.

Husserl wants to sacrifice neither the requirements of idealism nor compliance with the characteristic traits of *Einfühlung*. Idealism demands that the Other, like a thing, be a unity of modes of appearing which is a claimed ideal sense. The compliance with the actual requires that the Other "invade" my own sphere of experience and force an excess of presence through the boundaries of my subjective life in a fashion incompatible with the inclusion of sense into my subjective life.

The problem of the Other thus brings out the latent separation between the two tendencies of phenomenology, the dogmatic tendency and the descriptive tendency. The genius of Husserl is to have maintained his bet until the end. The descriptive care in respecting the otherness of Others and the dogmatic care for founding the Other in the ego's primordial ownness sphere find their balance in the notion of an analogical grasping of the Other. The Other is there himself, and yet I do not live in his subjective life. The Other is at best *appräsentiert* (appresented) on the basis of his body, which alone is *präsentiert* (presented) with an originary evidence in the sphere of my subjective life. "In" me a body is presented that appresents a subjective life other than my own. This life is a subjective life like mine in virtue of the *Paarung* (pairing) between my body here and the other body there. This coupled configuration founds the analogy between the subjective life *erlebt* (lived) and the subjective life *eingefühlt* (empathetically grasped).

Does Husserl succeed in constituting the outsider as outsider in one's own experiential sphere? Has he won his bet on the defeat of solipsism without the sacrifice of egology? The enigma is that the Other appresented in his body and grasped analogically by "passive synthesis" has a being-status (*Seinsgeltung*) that tears him out of my primordial sphere. Let us suppose that I do know the Other analogically. How can such an analogy have this transcendent intending when all other analogies go from one thing to another within my experience? If the Other's body is constituted "in" me, how is the subjective life belonging to him appresented "outside" me? How can a simple concordance of behavioral modes of appearing indicate (*indizieren*) an alien life and not just a more subtle thing of "my" world? Does Husserl succeed in escaping from the extraordinary temptation of the constitution of the thing as thing, of *Dinglichkeit,* in the flux of adumbrations? Is the Other more than a simple unity of concordant adumbrations?

In the third part of ***Ideas II*** Husserl does contrast the constitution of persons with the constitution of nature (things and animate bodies). In one of the appendices he even goes so far as to contrast "the unity of appearances" (*Erscheinungseinheit*) of the thing to "the unity of absolute manifestation" (*Einheit absoluter Bekundung*) of the person. Thus, the person would be much more than a display of adumbrations; he would be an absolute emergence of presence. But this opposition between the person who "announces himself" and the thing that "appears" is an opposition that description imposes and the philosophy of the reduction minimizes. It implies the complete destruction of the idealistic sense of constitution. What the person announces is precisely his own absolute existence. To constitute the person is, then, to localize the subjective modes in which this recognition of otherness, of foreignness, of other-existence is effected. Husserlian idealism is obliged to oppose this reversal of the sense of constitution.

Here we propose a return to Kant, not in the least for the purpose of perfecting a description of the appearing of the Other but rather in order to understand the sense of the existence which is announced in this appearing. It is remarkable that the philosopher most unprepared on the terrain of phenomenological description is the one who should go straight to this sense of existence. In the *Foundations of the Metaphysics of Morals,* Kant introduces the second formulation of the categorial imperative: "Act so that you treat humanity, whether in your own person or in that of another, always as an end and never as a means only."[13] One could find this brusque introduction of the Other into the Kantian formalism a shock, and one could complain that no description of the knowledge of the Other precedes this practical determination of the Other by respect. Is it not first necessary to know the Other as Other and then to respect him? But Kantianism suggests an entirely different response. The existence of the Other resides only in respect as a practical determining.

Let us examine the Kantian procedure a bit more closely. The existence in-himself of the Other is at first posited hypothetically as identical with his value:

Suppose, however, there were something whose existence has in itself an absolute value, something which as an end in itself could be a principle of determinate laws; then in it, and in it alone, would there be the principle of a possible categorical imperative—that is, of a practical law

(*K, pp. 427-28*).

In this hypothetical positing of a foundation, there appears no difference between the existential and the practical determination of the person. The contrast of person and thing is directly practicoexistential. As object of my desires, the person belongs to the order of ends in themselves: "Rational beings, on the other hand, are called *persons* because their nature already marks them out as ends in themselves . . ." (*K, pp. 428-29*).

It will be objected that respect, like sympathy, is a subjective feeling and no more has the power of attaining to an in-itself than sensuous perception or desire has. But to align respect with perception, desire, or even sympathy is an error, for respect is the practical moment that founds the transcendent intending of sympathy. Sympathy, as an affection, has no more privilege than hate or love. This is why the enlargement of the Husserlian phenomenology in the way indicated by Max Scheler, MacDougall, or by the French existentialists, although legitimate, changes nothing with respect to the problem of existence, even though it does enrich the inventory of the modes of the appearing of the Other. Respect, as a practical feeling posits a limit to my ability to act. Thus, speaking of humanity, Kant establishes that it is not a "subjective end" which my sympathy would aim at—this would mean including humanity among my inclinations "as an object which we of ourselves really make our end" (*K, p. 431*). Humanity is an "objective end," like a law of a series, which constitutes "the supreme limiting condition of subjective ends" (*K, p. 431*). Later on Kant calls it even more emphatically "the supreme limiting condition in the usage of all means" (*K, p. 438*). The same is true for the person. He is "an end that exists in himself," which I can consider only negatively "as an end against which one should never act" (*K, p. 437*).

Through respect the person is seen to be directly situated in a field of persons whose mutual otherness is founded on their irreducibility to means. Should the Other lose the ethical dimension which Kant calls his dignity (*Würde*), or his absolute price, should sympathy lose its quality of esteem, then the person becomes nothing more than a "merely natural being" (*blosses Naturwesen*) and sympathy merely an animal affect.

But, it will be said, the proposition "Rational nature exists as an end in itself" (*K, p. 429*) is only a postulate. Kant would willingly agree (see his note on p. 429). This postulate is the concept of a reign of ends, that is to say, of the systematic interconnection of reasonable beings by communal laws. The historian has no difficulty here in recognizing the Augustinian notion of the City of God and the

Leibnizian notion of the reign of grace. What is properly Kantian is compliance with this notion by a regressive movement toward the foundation of good will, that is, by radicalizing the advance toward freedom. The plurality and the communication among consciousnesses cannot be made the object of description unless they are initially posited by an act of foundation laying (*Grundlegung*). Communication among consciousnesses is, then, what renders possible the coordination of freedom and what makes each subjective will a freedom.

Doubtless, one can regret the narrow juridical turn that this mutuality of freedoms takes under the notion of an a priori legislation. But this is not the most remarkable thing in Kant. The notable thing is his not having sought a "situation" for the person other than in his "belonging" (as member or as leader) to a practical and ethical totality of persons. Outside of this, one is no longer a person. One's existence can only be a value-existence (*existence-valeur*). The affective manifestations which the other person exhibits do not of necessity get beyond the level of equipment or merchandise. Thus, the absolute existence of the Other originarily belongs to the intention of good will. Only a reflexive movement of foundation laying (*Grundlegung*) reveals that this intention includes the act of situating oneself as legislating member in an ethical community.

At the same time the determination of the person as an existent end-in-himself leads us to the problem of the thing-in-itself. In the second part we emphasized the limiting function of the thing-in-itself with respect to the claims of the phenomenon. This philosophy of limits, totally absent from phenomenology, finds its own exfoliation on the practical plane, since the Other is the one against whom I must not act. But at the same time the notion of a reign of ends brings out the positive character of the founding of the in-itself. Only the determination of the in-itself never becomes theoretical or speculative but remains practical and ethical. The only intelligible world in which I can "place" myself is the one with which I have complied through respect. By the autonomy of my will and the respect for the autonomy of the Other, "we transport ourselves into the intelligible world as members." But upon entering into this world, I can "neither see nor feel myself in it" (K, p. 458). "By thinking itself into the intelligible world, practical reason does not overstep its limits in the least: it would do so only if it sought to intuit or feel itself into that world" (K, p. 458).

Has not Kant shown in this way the limits not only of the claims of the phenomenon but also the limits of phenomenology itself? I can "see" or "sense" the appearing of things, persons, values. But the absolute existence of the Other, the model of all existences cannot be sensed. It is announced as alien to my subjective life by the very appearance of the Other in his behavior, his expression, his language, and his work. But this appearance of the Other does not suffice to announce it as a being-in-itself. His being must be posited practically as that which limits the intention of my sympathy to reduce the person to his desirable quality, and as that which founds his appearance itself.

The merit of phenomenology is to have elevated the investigation of the appearing to the dignity of a science by the "reduction." But the merit of Kantianism is to have been able to coordinate the investigation of the appearing with the limiting function of the in-itself and with the practical determination of the in-itself as freedom and as the totality of persons.

Husserl *did* phenomenology, but Kant *limited* and *founded* it.

Notes

1. [Quotations in English are based on Immanuel Kant's *Critique of Pure Reason,* trans. Norman Kemp Smith, 1st ed. (London, 1929); 2d. ed. (London, 1933). Ricoeur uses both the German edition of the *Gesammelte Schriften,* sponsored by the Royal Academy of Prussia, Vol. V, and the French translation by Tremesaygues and Pacaud (Kehrbach edition, 1909). Our citations denote the first German edition by *A* and the second by *B*.—Trans.]

2. Cf. "The Transcendental Exposition of the Concept of Space" (A 25, B 40).

3. "Transcendental Doctrine of Method" (A 712 ff., B 740 ff.).

4. The initial question is of an ontological order: "What, then, are space and time? Are they actual beings?" (Was sind nun Raum und Zeit? Sind es wirkliche Wesen?) (A 23, B 37).

5. In the letter to Markus Herz of February 21, 1772, the problem of the *Vorstellung* was presented by reference to the strange possibility of an intuition generating its own object.

6. A 26. And later on: "If without this condition of sensibility I could intuit myself, or be intuited by another being, the very same determinations which we now represent to ourselves as alterations would yield knowledge into which the representation of time, and therefore also of alteration, would in no way enter" (A 37, B 54). "If we take away from our inner intuition the peculiar condition of our sensibility, the concept of time vanishes" (A 37, B 54).

7. "But these a priori sources of knowledge, being merely conditions of our sensibility, just by this very fact determine their own limits, namely, that they apply to objects only insofar as objects are viewed as appearances and do not present things as they are in themselves" (A 39, B 56).

8. "The understanding accordingly limits sensuousness, but does not thereby extend its own sphere. In the process of warning the latter that it must not presume to claim applicability to things-in-themselves but only to appearances, it does indeed think for itself an object in itself, but only as transcendental object . . ." (A 288, B 344).

9. A 109. "But it is clear that, since we have to deal only with the manifold of our representations, and

since *X* (the object) which corresponds to them is nothing to us—being, as it is, something that has to be distinct from all of our representations—the unity which the object makes necessary can be nothing else than the formal unity of consciousness in the synthesis of the manifold of representations" (A 105).

10. *Cartesian Meditations,* p. 60; cf. also p. 65, lines 11-16.

11. *Bemerkungen von Prof. Roman Ingarden,* Appendix to *Husserliana I,* pp. 208-10.

12. At first § 128 of *Ideas* I seems to proceed in this direction. Husserl, remarking that it is the same object that incessantly gives itself differently, calls the object the "*X* of its determinations." In addition, he proposes to elucidate the way in which the noema "as meant" can have a relation to an objectivity (I, p. 315): "Every noema has a content, namely its sense, and it relates through it to its object" (I, p. 316). But after this start in the Kantian style, the analysis turns to a specifically Husserlian theme: the new intending of the noema towards its object, which seems to go out to something beyond the "sense," designates the degree of plenitude, the mode of "fulfillment" of the sense by intuition (I, §§ 135 ff.).

13. [This translation, like others from this source, is that of Lewis W. Beck found in *The Critique of Practical Reason and Other Writings in Moral Philosophy* (Chicago, 1948), p. 429. This pagination, preferred by Ricoeur, is found both in Beck and in the Cassirer edition of *Kants Werke* (Berlin, 1922). Vol. 4 contains the *Grundlegung der Metaphysik der Sitten* and Vol. 5 contains the *Kritik der praktischen vernuft.* Textual references to this work appear with the letter *K* followed by the page numbers.]

Andrea Bonomi (essay date 1970)

SOURCE: "The Problem of Language in Husserl," in *Telos: A Quarterly Journal of Critical Thought,* No. 6, Fall, 1970, pp. 184-203.

[*In the following essay, Bonomi explores the influence of Husserl's phenomenological principles and methods on the theory and practice of the grammatical analysis of language.*]

The aim of this essay is to indicate the basic orientation of Husserl's account of language. First of all, the problem is to distinguish the concept of expression from other semiological concepts such as, *e.g.,* signs. This will allow us to characterize the expression in a positive way which turns out to be founded on unities of an abstract type, *i.e.* on classes of variants. It follows that the general meaning of Husserl's attempts lies in the proposal for a formal analysis of language concerning *langue* and *parole.* This orientation can be best seen in the project of a "pure grammar" considered as a complex of an abstract and formal type.

Through this, it becomes possible to outline the concept of grammaticity of statements (which raises the problem of the autonomy of syntactics from semantics) and allows practically an infinity of possible statements with regard to the finite series of grammatical devices, among which transformation assumes a fundamental significance. The fact that the multiplicity of statements can be reduced to a limited number of elementary structures raises again the old problem of a universal grammar, *i.e.,* of a theory of possible forms of grammar. Finally, in the appendix, the procedure of eidetic variation is considered from the viewpoint of its relevance for linguistic inquiry.

In Husserl, the linguistic problem appears within a broad epistemological perspective. The question of language is approached within the framework of general phenomenological discourse concerned with the structure inherent in cognitive experience, and of the series of constitutive operations underlying this structure. The following pages will deliberately abstract from this broad perspective in order to identify some essential features of Husserl's investigations of the problem of language and some theoretical general questions pertaining to Husserlian phenomenology. It seems particularly useful to reconsider these in view of the later development of linguistic inquiry. The limits thus assigned to this discussion are due not only to the peculiarity of the adopted perspective, but to the very character of Husserl's account. Although starting out from a general epistemological frame of reference, this account seeks to outline an *intrinsic* explication of the linguistic phenomenon.

Here we are interested in emphasizing the positive element in Husserl's critique of psychologism: the proposal of a formal analysis of language outlined in the ***Logical Investigations.*** This is evident from the first pages of the *First Investigation,* where he sets the task to characterize the concept of *expression* by establishing the boundaries which distinguish it from other aspects of semiological activity. What defines the expression is, first of all, the relation between two heterogeneous terms: the physical aspect (*e.g.,* the sequence of sounds in a word) and the psychic one, *i.e.,* the "meaning", Husserl emphasizes the second term of the relation because it is precisely here that psychologistic misunderstandings have arisen. What Husserl means by meaning can be sufficiently clarified if we follow, in all its implications, the contraposition in the *First Investigation* between sign and expression. Here the concept of sign seems to include, among other things, the sphere indicated by Peirce through the concept of index and of icon. In fact, Husserl talks about signs in the case of an object which relates to another by virtue of a certain *contiguity,* both "physical" (above all in a casual sense: *e.g.,* smoke relating to fire as its origin) and perceptual (as in the case of a design which reproduces the essential features of the represented object). However, this is inadequate. We must add that for Husserl the essence of the sign lies in its relation of *indication,* and we can have a sign even without the mentioned contiguity, *i.e.,* on a merely arbitary basis, without any causal relation or perceptual isomorphism between the indication and what is indicated. What matters is that in the relation of indication, the *actual presence* of certain objects causes the apprehension of others. "If A recalls B to consciousness, not only are they simultaneously or successively present to it [consciousness]: usually there is also a *sensuous* connection according to which the one refers to the other and the latter exists as *inherent* in the first."[1]

With language, things are different. Expressions also exhibit a series of aspects which connect them with the phenomenon of indication: in particular, in its normal communicative function, every word occurrence has the task "to make known" determinate psychic contents. This means that a certain verbal manifestation which I perceive can function for me as an "index" of a certain thought or of an emotional state of the speaker: what he says informs me about his judgments, desires, etc. In this respect, expressions also function as signs: the physical fact constituted by the phonic sequence (or by the mimicry accompanying it) *indicates* another reality with which it is connected in the *concrete* and *factual* act of the sentence, and this factuality is a necessary condition for the sentence to perform its informative function since only on the basis of a determinate and empirically perceived event (the sentence) can I grasp a similarly determinate psychic content. But what is the basis of this "informative" function which connects *this* perceived reality A to *this* psychic content B? Or rather, what allows me to make this connection? Obviously, I cannot seek an answer to this question within the concrete flux of the sentence, because in this flux the two terms of the correlation are respectively subjected to a constant shifting: to reconsider De Saussure's argument, a given word, pronounced in different moments and by different speakers, undergoes some variations, both on a phonetic level (it is never pronounced exactly in the same way) as well as on a semantic level.[2] Therefore, it is necessary to abandon the ground of concrete realizations, of the actual occurrence of words, in order to attain a level of abstract elements, each of which delimits a virtually unlimited series of variables. These variables are exactly those realized in the factual performance and "recognizable" (they can perform a distinctive function) precisely by virtue of their being included in one of these classes: *i.e.*, through the mediation of an underlying abstract operator which connects each individual sentence to its "invariable" type. Once then understands Husserl's difference between *indication* (or information, in the case of language as a sign), as the constitutive act of signs, and *meaning* as the essential trait of expressions (*i.e.*, of language in its proper sense). Meaning is what is left if one abstracts from the concrete circumstantiality in which it (the meaning) is realized, *i.e.*, if one thematizes not the *given* phonic sequence and the *given* psychic content manifested in it, but what remains invariable in all possible articulations and in all possible constitutions of meaning: "The ideality of the relation between expression and meaning is immediately revealed in the fact that, if we raised the question of the meaning of any expression whatsoever (*e.g.*, *quadratic residue*) we obviously do not mean by the

term this phonetic formation pronounced *hic et nunc*, this vanishing sound which never returns in the same way. We mean the expression *in specie*. The expression *quadratic residue* remains identical to itself, independently of who pronounces it. And this will be true even if we speak of the *meaning*."[3] Thus, the initial definition of the expression as the positing of a relation between a physical and a "psychic" aspect is further defined and determined by doubly neutralizing any possible psychologistic assumptions: first, the phonic component is localized on the sensuous, material level and, what is more important, on the level constituted by a formal calculus. But from this viewpoint, it must be pointed out that in Husserl, except for some interesting remarks, the phonetic aspect of the sign is not sufficiently characterized. He recognizes in the expression a "unitary act" by virtue of which the phonetic aspect, which *per se* is meaningless, can perform its function as a vehicle of meaning. Between *phonia* and meaning there obtains no natural or intrinsic relation, *i.e.*, the second one does not determine the first and, from the viewpoint of their relation, considered in itself, there is no reason why a given concept (*e.g.*, that of "pear") should have a determinate phonetic complex ("pear" instead of, *e.g.*, "arpe"). This arbitrariness, however, is, as it were, neutralized from the point of view of language as a comprehensive *system*, where every unit is inserted in a series of relations connecting it with other units: this is why there exists for the speaker an intimate connection between *phonia* and the concept expressed, to the point that he sees in the first something that somehow "belongs" to the second.[4] In any case, we must now emphasize that Husserl is interested in the phonic aspect from the "formal" viewpoint (*i.e.*, from the viewpoint of the distinctive function that it performs) and not from the viewpoint of material and concrete sounds. The *phonia* of a given word can vary as widely as its written representation, but "what matters is only the constant recognizability of the form (*Gestalt*)."[5] Secondly, Husserl characterizes meaning so as to distinguish it (while bringing into light the possibility and the necessity of *a priori* connections with them) from extralinguistic objectivities such as perceptual formations or states of consciousness which the linguistic act "makes known". For example, if I express a judgment of a perceptual kind, the meaning of this expression does not lie properly in the state of things grasped in the actual perception to which the judgment refers. For we can have empty judgments which no intuition of a perceptual kind can adequately fulfill, and different meanings can refer to the same object or state of things while similarly the same meaning can refer to different objects. At any rate, in order to achieve expression, every extralinguistic representation must be filtered through the texture of linguistic categories. Similarly, the meaning does not lie in the "information" that the listener may derive from my sentence, *i.e.*, in the fact that at a given moment I must have performed a determinate psychic act, accomplished certain operations of collection, assigned a certain "credence" to the judgment, or simply wished it, etc. All this represents phenomena concomitant with the meaning which localize them in a determinate frame of reference, but does not constitute the meaning itself as an "ideal" and invariable unit. This assertion becomes clear if we bear in mind that what Husserl is most interested in (without, however, prejudicing the possibility of further inquiries into the whole epistemological problem) is to proceed to a characterization of the expression in its particularity, which presupposes the bracketing of the extralinguistic substances and the thematization of the expression as *form*. This will be developed in the following pages.

Therefore, what is essential to the expression and what distinguishes it from the indicative or informative function (pertaining respectively to sign and to the expression itself *qua sign, i.e.,* in its "communiticative" state) is the presence of a specific signifying intention. This act, provided with an autonomous configuration of its own, in spite of the multiplicity of the connections which correlate it to the comprehensive whole of the acts of knowledge, has precisely the task of restructuring in the peculiarity of the linguistic sphere, the extralinguistic contents derived from the external perception, the apprehension of the psychic states, etc. From this viewpoint, the difference between "external" contents and the so-called psychic lived experience vanishes. In fact, neither of the two directly constitutes the meaning. In order to be "expressed", they must be mediated by the specific linguistic act: they must be subsumed under a signifying intention which inserts them in invariable categorical units. As we have seen, this concept of invariability has nothing to do with metaphysical hypotheses and can be simply characterized in functional terms. In fact, it is called to account for the specific procedure of the linguistic component which consists, first of all, in *mediating* heterogeneous contents, such as, *e.g.,* the phonic sequence of an expression and the representation of the object or state of things to which such an expression refers. The meaning of the latter does not consist in the perceptual representation ·itself, but in an "ideal unit" which can subsume different representations of the same object or representations of other "similar" objects, in a virtually infinite range of variability. By virtue of this work of "fixation",[6] accomplished by the signifying intention, it is possible to correlate two heterogeneous elements as, *e.g.,* a phonetic complex and a perception; and to subtract them from the continuous shiftings, which, as we said, respectively characterize them if isolated from the unity of the expression. "By *expression* we mean the expression animated by all its meaning, which here is placed in a certain relation with the perception, and it is precisely because of this relation that we say that the perception is, in turn, expressed. For the very same reason, *between* the perception and the phonetic complex there is *inserted* another act (or a series of acts). . . . It is this act of mediation which must operate as a donator of sense; it belongs to the sensible expression as its essential component in such a way that the sense remains identical whether or not it is associated with a perception which confirms it."[7] We can understand why Husserl, along with De Saussure, is initially forced to rigorously criticize the conception which views "nomenclature" as the essence of language. In fact, what is a stake is the autonomy of linguistics as a disci-

pline—an autonomy which is dissolved if we reduce the linguistic phenomenon to an attribution of "names" to preformed contents as, *e.g.,* certain perceptual objects. In this sense, we can recognize both in the *Logical Investigations* and in De Saussure's *Cours* a common anti-psychologistic orientation based on the necessity to individuate the abstract categorical structure which underlies the particular manifestations of a word and which in particular, functioning as it were as a permanent skeleton, allows the correlation of the signifying with the signified in spite of all their possible fluctuations. Obviously, this anti-psychologistic orientation does not prejudice the possibility to take into consideration the problem of the relation between specifically linguistic acts and the comprehensive whole of cognitive acts. For Husserl, one of the essential questions regards the function that language performs in the wider cognitive sphere, and De Saussure, as if pre-empting all the hasty interpretations which have seen him as an unyielding supporter of the separation of linguistics from other disciplines, ultimately conceives linguistics as "a part of general psychology".[8] Thus, it is obvious that the term "anti-psychologism" here does not denote a sort of fragmentation of the inquiry, but a precise epistemological content. That is, we must direct the inquiry towards the *form* of the linguistic phenomenon, instead of preliminarily reducing it to the concrete acts in which it realizes itself. Furthermore, these concrete acts, belonging to the sphere of *parole* can be understood only on the basis of the explication of a much more abstract sphere, which is precisely that of the *langue*.[9] Husserl's discourse, however, seems to take a route other than that outlined in De Saussure's *Cours,* if we consider the problem of the arbitrariness of the sign. If, broadly speaking, we relate such a problem to that of the autonomy of linguistics, it is not difficult to see a significant convergence. The situation changes, however, if we bear in mind that the way De Saussure poses the question of the arbitrariness of the sign in the *Cours* causes him to see the work performed by language (*langue*) as the activity of articulation and structuring of thought, in so far as the latter is merely an amorphous mass. "The typical role of language, in relation to thought, is to function as an intermediary between thought and sound, under such conditions that their union necessarily brings forth reciprocal delimitations of units. Thought, *chaotic by nature,* is forced to become determinate by decomposing itself."[10] Even if it is not possible here to go further into Husserl's specific treatment of this problem, still, in regard to the general epistemological framework, we must point out that the *Logical Investigations* attempt to deal precisely with the relation correlating the linguistic act to the comprehensive legality of psychic acts. Here we must restrict ourselves to short remarks about Husserl's observations on the relation between perception and expression. At various times, he recognizes that there is no relation of reflection or of "parallelism" between thought and language. As we have seen, the signifying intention operates according to its own modalities, not necessarily identifiable with those of other cognitive functions. Simple meaning can refer to composite objects and, visa versa, composite meanings can refer to simple objects;[11] something "non-independent" (*e.g.*, a certain quality) can be subsumed (as in the case of the so-called substantiation) under an "independent" meaning, etc.[12] Rather than listing examples, we can briefly summarize all this by emphasizing one point which we have already stressed repeatedly: the meaning of the expression must not be sought *outside* of it (in this case, in the intuitive perception) but in the *expression itself*, which excludes the hypothesis of a mere "parallelism" between the perceptive contents and the linguistic units. The absence of a one to one correspondence, however, does not prejudice the possibility of their belonging to a common field of structuring. The perceptual object does not present itself to the "mediation" performed by the signifying intention in the form of a raw intuition. It has already been subjected to a process of "formation", *i.e.*, the linguistic mediation is performed on a previous mediation: the one constituted by the classifying activity. Acts of signification and of conceptualization are placed within a unitary system of laws, and this unity of the linguistic and the conceptual moment allows the expression to obtain an intuitive translation in the sphere of perception. Before being subsumed under the signifying intention, the perceptual object is inserted, by virtue of a classifying activity, in a categorical structure: ". . . to the extent that the signifying expression forms a particularly close unity with the classifying act and, in turn, as knowledge of the perceived object the latter unites itself with the perceptual act, the expression appears as if it were *imposed* on the thing, as if it were its dress."[13] Thus, the Husserlian discourse seems to develop according to a double perspective. On the one hand, the problem is to individuate the specific series of norms regulating linguistic functioning, while on the other, it is to locate the essential connection which unites this determinate structure to the comprehensive structure of cognitive acts. This verification dissolves the apparent paradox of an investigation seeking to individuate at the same time the intrinsic and formal traits of the expression, and the cognitive contents on which the expression operates. But what must be emphasized here is that this second aspect does not imply a reintroduction of extralinguistic elements in the domain of the expression. In fact, even before explicating the function of the expression within the total cognitive process, Husserl tries to shed light on the series of laws regulating the expression itself—and it is clear that this is a matter of *logical* priority. In other words, in order to grasp the function of language from an epistemological viewpoint, we must first understand what causes language to perform this function: we must explicate its formal structure. In fact, the domain of the expression exhibits its own laws which, if overlooked, can inhibit the very constitution of the expression and, consequently, its possible reference to other cognitive acts. Hence, it is understandable why the Husserlian analysis of language assumes a formal configuration and postulates, as a preliminary moment, a bracketing of the material contents concurring in the constitution of the linguistic phenomenon. As we have seen with arbitrariness, one of the essential aspects of the sign as expression consists in the fact that, unlike, *e.g.*, the icon, it lacks a "natural" motivation: "Usually the sign has

intrinsically nothing in common with what it designates. It can similarly designate both something heterogeneous and something homogeneous with it. On the contrary, the image refers to the thing by virtue of *similarity* and if this should be lacking, one could not even speak of images any longer."[14] Therefore, what matters is that signifying intention, constitutive of the expression which operates by means of distinctive procedures. The "substances" it prepares for the operations of these distinctive procedures are actually indifferent. Consequently, the inquiry must place itself within a particular perspective, which points to the formal relations regulating the expression and not to the substances (both of physical and "psychic" order) which it utilizes. Within this perspective, the phonetic matter is thus substituted by an abstract calculus which is nothing else than the whole of the distinctive properties whereby the various phonic *Gestalten* distinguish themselves from each other. On the other hand, a series of abstract norms presiding over the formation of the very meaning is substituted for the series of all possible referents to which the meaning refers. If the material contents are variable, their "recognizability" is still guaranteed by the constancy of the form. We will see later how this concept of invariable form can be interpreted not as a metaphysical platonism (as has often been claimed), but as a distributive procedure based on the method of eidetic variation. What needs to be stressed here is the very orientation of the Husserlian analysis. The need to abstract from any consideration of extralinguistic substances is motivated by the need to proceed to an individuation of the intrinsic structure of language. "We keep separate the pronounced word and the speech just delivered now, intended as a sensuous phenomenon, from the words and the proposition themselves or from a sequence of propositions constituting a longer speech. It is not accidental that when we are not understood we repeat ourselves—we speak precisely of a repetition of *the same* words and propositions. . . . The one and only linguistic structure is reproduced thousands of times."[15] We can now begin to see the meaning of the Husserlian proposal for a purely logical grammar. Actually, the critique of psychologism is the critique of any methodological assumption which, in order to account for the structure of language, finds recourse to what this structure refers to rather than to the determining formal connections. We should not be surprised if, as the following passage demonstrates, Husserl uses that Saussurian exemplification which was to be so successful in the history of linguistics, fifteen years before the publication of the *Cours* and while working within the horizon of a different discipline, in order to illustrate this epistemological orientation: "The true sense of the signs in question is revealed when we think of the well-known similarity between the operations of calculation and those performed in *games* proceeding according to rules, such as chess. The chess pieces do not function in the game as things made of ivory or of wood, having a determinate shape and colour. What constitutes them from a physical or phenomenal viewpoint is totally irrelevant and can vary freely. They become chess pieces, *i.e.*, part of the game in question, by virtue of the rules of the game which confer them their precise *game-meaning.*"[16]

According to Husserl, the apparent paradox which the grammatical theory must account for consists in the fact that a finite series of means, such as the grammatical devices of any language, produce a virtually infinite series of statements. Husserl individuates this generative capability in the recurrence of grammatical rules. The main task he assigns to the pure "morphology" of meanings consists in coagulating the series of formal rules presiding over the construction and combination of statements. Here the term "formal" must be understood in at least two senses. On the one hand, it means that the concept of grammaticity of a statement is not susceptible to a "statistical" interpretation based on the degree of acceptability that the statement may have for a greater or lesser number of speakers and on the calculation of the answers that they may give to eventual operational tests. From this viewpoint, it is important to emphasize that, for Husserl, grammatical inquiry has no normative task. It does not aim at providing "practical" rules for the actual behavior of the speaker, but it is exclusively motivated by a "theoretical" interest,[17] which directs a systematic research of the *possible* forms of statements and of the laws of their combination. On the other hand, the formal character of the inquiry implies abstraction from the semantic sphere since, as we will see, the grammaticity of a statement does not amount to the fact that it is provided with meaning (even if this constitutes its essential condition).

The starting point of the *Fourth Logical Investigation,* which Husserl devotes to the problem of "pure grammar", is the subdivision of the meanings into simple and composite.[18] If we take any statement, we can break it down into a nominal and a verbal group, and subsequently divide these two groups into other constituents, and so on, until we arrive at minimal units reducible no further on the syntactic level—units which appear precisely as simple expressions within more comprehensive composite expressions. It must be emphasized here that it is possible for the expression to combine with others in order to produce increasingly more complex yet unitary syntagms. Within composite expressions, the constituting expressions (which can in turn be complex or simple) fall into two classes of categorematic expressions (*i.e.*, independent and provided with an autonomous structure) and syncategorematic ones, which can occur only along with other expressions, *i.e.,* within a more comprehensive whole or within a wider structure.[19] Our interest here is not to go further into Husserl's discussion of the problem of the justifiability of this subdivision of expressions in categorematical and syncategorematical, but to emphasize that the central problem of this *Fourth Logical Investigation* consists precisely in the laws of composition of the expression. The fact that there exist combinatory rules in every range of the cognitive experience (*e.g.*, in perception, where determinate contents can unify only in determinate synthesis) and that we can speak of a general combinatory (in the sense of the Leib-

nizian *mathesis*) must not lead us to overlook the *specificity* of this calculus on the linguistic level: "In no field can we unify every singularity with every form: the field of the singularities *a priori* limits, on the contrary, the number of the possible forms, and determines the laws of their saturation. The generality of this fact, however, does not free us from the obligation to show its presence in each given field and to investigate the determinate laws in which it manifests itself."[20]

If we take a non-grammatical sentence such as (1) "The soundly sleeps", we see that its incongruence is not a result of the incongruence of the various terms as *specific* terms of *this* sentence, but of the form of the sentence, which means that any other sentence with the same structure but different words—*e.g.*, (2) "A fiercely infuriates"—is equally non-grammatical. In other words, if we substitute for the terms of (1) variables representing other terms belonging to the same class, we obtain the *form* of a non-grammatical sentence which remains the same in all of its possible variations. Thus, the syntactic compatibility or incompatibility consists in the possibility or impossibility of combining the terms according to a series of formal rules which have, as objects, classes of words (categories). "Every time that, in relation to given meanings, we evidently understand the impossibility of the connection, this impossibility refers to an unconditionally general law according to which the *meanings* of the corresponding categories of meaning, connected in the same order and according to the norms of the same pure forms, must necessarily be deprived of a unitary result—in one word, it is an *a priori* impossibility."[21]

It is now possible to specify what we have mentioned earlier in reference to the "formal" character of Husserl's inquiry, which reduced to three basic claims: (a) the concept of grammaticity, as defined by general combinatory principles, cannot be derived "statistically" from the concrete instances (*i.e.*, it is a concept pertaining to the *langue,* and not to the *parole*): (b) it concerns not the "substance" of sentences, but their structure, *i.e.*, the series of relations interconnecting categories (names, verbs, etc.) to which the single terms of the sentence belong; and (c) the grammaticity of the sentence is independent of its semantic congruity.[22] This last point requires further clarification. When he speaks of the independence of grammar from semantics, Husserl does not mean that it is also extraneous to it. On the contrary, he sees grammatical congruity as a prerequisite for the semantical congruity of statements. Since the whole of grammatical rules concern the very possibility of the constitution of statements, it is obvious that a deviation from one of these norms will result in the formation of anomalous statements (and, ultimately, the formation of non-statements) whose semantic incongruity is a function of grammatical deviation. If, for example, in the case of (1) and (2), we have a violation of lexical categories, we will have semantically incongruous non-statements.[23] This, however, does not mean that the grammatical and the semantical level are indistinct, as illustrated by the case of grammatical statements which are semantically anomalous, of the type (3) "A is not A" or, vice versa, in the case of semantically congruous but non-grammatical statements such as (4) "If it was dependent on me, I would leave". Husserl summarizes all of this by maintaining that while the semantic component (which in the **Formal and Transcendental Logic** he assigns to the logic of non-contradiction) has the task of preventing contradictions as in the case of statements such as (3), the grammatical component (and specifically, syntax) is bound to prevent the formation of nonsense, *i.e.*, the formation of sentences such as (1). In other words, this means that the grammatical component functions on a *preliminary* level concerning the very possibility of a sentence to function as a statement and which, therefore, defines its formal structure. If a transgression on this level implies an anomaly on the semantic level, this does not mean that the anomaly is sufficient to account for the violation itself. On the contrary, to account for the semantic interpretation it is first of all necessary to have elaborated the structural properties of the grammatical component.

For Husserl, the peculiarity of the syntax consists in the fact that it operates on a small number of primitive structures in order to produce a potentially unlimited number of statements. This is made possible by the combinatory property of the syntax, which can insert those primitive structures within more complex ones.

If we take apart a given statement, after going through a more or less long series of degrees, we will reach some final terms, which, from the syntactic viewpoint, are no longer reducible. This means that we have *minimal* combinatory units which can appear in an indefinite number of different statements while preserving their identity. Husserl calls these minimal units syntactical "matters" and tries to define their relation with syntactical "forms". In fact, the task of a syntactical form is to connect the various terms within the *totality* of the statement. Because of this structuring process, each term (or "matter") is assigned a *function,* where the term "function" serves precisely to denote the relation of that term with the total form of the statement (or with the intermediary structures connected with this form). At this point two things must be pointed out: first, syntactical matters are not individuated on the basis of their "substance" (*i.e.*, according to consideration of an extralinguistic order) but according to distributional considerations, by pointing out the possibility of their occurrence in determinate syntactical contexts: *i.e.*, the matters are elements which "emerge by abstraction from functional forms";[24] and, secondly, the process of the formation is indefinitely repeatable, which means that determinate forms can be subsumed under others of a higher order (*i.e.*, they in turn can function as matters) by means of conjunction and subordination. Thus, since they can be freely repeated and combined with each other, they can generate a virtually infinite series of statements. In the "purely logical grammar" the syntactical investigation is meant precisely to elaborate the abstract principles regulating this combinatory activity, by originally defining relations of compatibility and incompatibility.

Among the various devices utilized by the syntactical component, Husserl pays particular attention to the concept of *transformation.* The derivation from an extremely limited number of primitive structures of as many more complex statements as one likes, is made possible precisely by transformation. In this connection, the example that Husserl uses most frequently is that of the nominalization which can be summarily defined as follows: every statement can function as a member of another statement by virtue of a "modification" of its superficial form. "In the field of meanings there are *a priori* laws according to which meanings transform themselves in different ways into new meanings while preserving their essential nucleus", and it is necessary to make evident "those particularly remarkable cases in which entire propositions, by virtue of nominalization, can occupy the place of the subject as well as any other place which requires nominal members."[25] Hence, from a statement such as "the minister has arrived,"[26] we can derive a syntagm such as "the arrival of the minister" which, *e.g.*, can function as a subject in another statement.[27] In addition to nominalization, Husserl illustrates his discourse by means of other types of transformation such as the "attribution" which allows for the passage from the basic statement "S is p" to the derived statement "Sp is q" or the "conjunction" which allows for the passage from the basic statement "A is p" and "B is p" to the derived statement, "A and B are p". Generally speaking, although natural language causes modifications and re-elaborations in the underlying structures, the interpretation of derived statements is still grounded on those basic forms, and the essential problem of syntax lies precisely in the individuation of that series of rules presiding over the combination of primitive structures: "in order to grasp the idea of this pure morphology, it should have been clear that on the level of a classification of possible judgments referring to their form, we find 'fundamental forms', *i.e.*, a closed system of fundamental forms; starting from which we can always produce by constructing new and more broadly differentiated forms, by virtue of their own essential legality. . . ."[28]

These remarks serve to elucidate the Husserlian project of a "pure grammar". At the basis of this project we find the radical need for formalization. The reason of this need consists in the fact that such an investigation has as its object the *possibilities* of statement-construction, *i.e.*, a series of formal principles imposing restrictions on the speaker's combinatory choices. Precisely because they concern possibilities, these principles operate on an *abstract* level. In other words, they apply to classes or categories before they apply to actual members of these categories. Thus, their coagulation must be translated into a "systematic synopsis" of the potentially unlimited series of statements derivable by means of combination and transformation from a limited number of base-structures. Moreover, since we are dealing with forms and not with content (due to the resolution of concrete elements into variables), it is natural that this formalization veers toward an algebraization of grammar. Therefore, the formulation of laws presiding over the construction and combination of statements does not contain any reference to content, but utilizes algebraic symbols, denoting the indeterminate series of the members of the various categories (*e.g.*, of the category "adjective").[29] Precisely for this reason, such laws do *not* have a *normative* value with respect to determinate contents, but deal with mere formal possibilities. It is thus understandable why Husserl speaks of a "pure" grammar, and it is superfluous to emphasize that the latter, once defined in these terms, attains the status—not of a descriptive science of the grammar of a given language (or of more than one language)—but of a *theory of the possible forms of grammar.* It is in this sense that Husserl elaborates with explicit reservations the traditional concept of a universal grammar.[30] If descriptive linguistics starts with the facticity of the diversity of languages, and must therefore account for the particular grammatical devices which subject primitive structures to processes of construction, transformation, etc., pertaining to the various languages, the task of the "theory" meant as pure grammar is to shed light on the common structural possibilities from which those devices are selected. Hence, the reference to the problem of the "universals" which Husserl distinguishes into empirical universals (based on factual data, as, *e.g.*, the psycho-physical constitution, which determines some acoustical and articulatory properties common to all speakers in every language) and universals consisting in rules of a *formal* order, regulating the constitution of all linguistic structures (and provided with an intrinsic "logical" necessity).[31] Beneath the differences among languages, it is possible to detect a common "ideal scaffolding" whose elaboration by a general theory of language appears as a preliminary epistemological precondition: "Although determined by the factual content of historical languages, and by the grammatical forms, every language is nevertheless tied to this ideal scaffolding. Therefore, its theoretical inquiry must constitute one of the foundations of the final scientific clarification of every language."[32]

In the previous pages we have repeatedly stressed that, precisely because of its "formal" orientation, the Husserlian analysis aims preliminarily at abstracting classes and categories, instead of concrete content. Now, we have to outline briefly the methodological presuppositions of the concept of "class of variables", and to indicate its relevance for linguistic inquiry. In his essay on the *Fourth Logical Investigation,* Bar-Hillel points out that Husserl provides a significant anticipation of the concept of *commutation* as it has been developed by subsequent linguistic investigation, and indicates its limitations in terms of the exclusive recourse to the sphere of meaning, and the usage of inadequate categories of temporal linguistics.[33] We have already shown the essential validity of the first point. The same can be said of the second one. It is also necessary to add, however, that to completely grasp the linguistic significance of the concept of "type" we must go beyond Husserl's specific analyses and elaborate their general methodological implications.

By "eidetic variation" Husserl indicates a general procedure meant to individuate classes of variables. Such a pro-

cedure can be summarily described in the following terms. The starting point consists of one or more arbitrarily selected data. A device is then applied to them in order to put them through a theoretically unlimited series of variations,[34] and select equivalent results. The point of arrival is the abstract "type"[35] (eidos, essence) which includes the equivalent results. This type has therefore the peculiarity of unifying within its own range members which, from the material viewpoint, can even differ remarkably, but which nevertheless present common formal traits. Now, on the basis of eidetic variation, any two data can be included in the same type under one of two conditions:[36] when they can be freely substituted within a certain context without causing any modification in the comprehensive form of the whole; and when having essentially different contexts (and these contextual differences determine the differences between the two data in question), they present common formal traits which associate them with other traits in a systematic totality of relations. We must emphasize that every type is characterized by a "domain of variability" and that any datum falling outside of this domain automatically conflicts with any other datum belonging to it. In other words, there are two possible kinds of "differences". On the one hand, there are those which can be considered irrelevant. Husserl calls them "non-essential" because they do not refer to two different essences or types, *i.e.*, these are differences dependent on the context, or differences dependent on the variability of the situations in which the type has been realized. On the other hand, there are those concerning two types (or rather, the respective realization of these two types) which are therefore essential from the viewpoint of the whole system.[37] Thus, the procedure of eidetic variation can be interpreted as a distibutional method in a threefold sense: (a) its function consists in individuating types or classes of variables; (b) in order to do this, it must distinguish relevant differences from merely contextual ones; and (c) this distinction is possible only on the basis of a systematic consideration of the possible contexts where the data in question can occur. What follows is that the type is not a collection of concrete members, but an *abstract possibility* susceptible to many realizations and inserted in a series of formal relations with other types. As for Bar-Hillel's remark, it is now possible to develop it in this way: when he speaks of the logical priority of the abstract over the concrete,[38] Husserl anticipates the epistemological orientation which is proper to post-Saussurian linguistic inquiry and which subordinates, from the heuristic viewpoint, the *parole* to the *langue.* This epistemological similarity connects, in particular, the method of eidetic variation with the phonological analysis of the Prague School. In fact, in the latter the central problem is to individuate the relevant oppositions whereby it is possible to institute classes of variables (free or combinatory), each of which is provided, in spite of the possible differences occurring between its members, with a functional *identity.* However, from this viewpoint, a further clarification is necessary. As we know, the test of the commutation, which has performed an essential role in the inquiries of the Prague School, consists in substituting within the same context one phonic realization with another. If this substitution produces a modification on the level of meanings, then the two sounds in question are realizations of different "phonemes" (*i.e.*, "types"); otherwise we would have two free variables of the same phoneme.[39] In other words, this means that the relevant oppositions are registered on the basis of non-phonological data, *i.e.*, on the basis of differences of meaning. The method of the eidetic variation is also characterized by the fact that it proceeds to individuate the variables (and therefore the abstract "type" as a class of variables) on a purely intrinsic basis, *i.e.*, by registering the variations that the data in question undergo without recurring to levels other than that pertaining to such data. In this sense, it seems that Bar-Hillel's remark must be partially corrected and that Husserl's methodological presuppositions should be connected with a procedure of an integrally distributional kind.[40]

Notes

1. Cf. E. Husserl, *Ricerche Logiche,* Italian translation by Giovanni Piana (Milan, 1968), p. 297.

2. Cf. De Saussure's example of the *flower* of the apple tree, the *flower* of the nobility, etc., in F. De Saussure, *Corso di Linguistica Generale,* Italian translation by T. DeMauro (Bari, 1967), p. 132.

3. Husserl, *op. cit.,* p. 309.

4. *Ibid.,* p. 194.

5. *Ibid.,* p. 389.

6. This function of mediation and "fixation" performed by abstract conceptual units in regard to the manifold contents of the representation (*i.e.*, in other words, the logical priority of an abstract operator in regard to the series of representations) is a common trait of many diverse contemporary inquiries concerning the "cognitive" function of language. Thus, Cassirer claims that: "In order to be connected in the form of a *thought,* each representation needs a preliminary formation by means of which only in general they become material for logical construction." Cf. Ernst Cassirer, *Filosofia della Forme Simboliche,* Italian translation by E. Arnaud (Florence, 1961), p. 299. As we know, the function of the conceptual mediation performed by language is analyzed from a psycholinguistic perspective by L.S. Vygotskij, in *Pensiero e Linguaggio* (Florence, 1966), pp. 88 ff., particularly as far as the genesis of the concept is concerned. Vygotskij speaks of "the domination of the abstraction" which is the essential prerequisite for the formation of concepts and for the achievement of which language has a "decisive role". (*Ibid.,* p. 102). Also in Jespersen's *The Philosophy of Grammar* (London, 1924), p. 63, the problem of the cognitive function of language is connected with that of the elaboration of abstract units.

7. Husserl, *op. cit.,* pp. 316-317.

8. De Saussure, *op. cit.,* p. 26.

9. If we bear this in mind we will not be surprised by the fact that more recent developments in linguistic investigation—precisely when this investigation has reached a high degree of formalization—raise the problem of the overcoming of the separation between linguistics and other disciplines, and that of the approach to language from the viewpoint of a general "cognitive system". Cf. Noam Chomsky, *Language and Mind* (New York, 1968), pp. 1 and 4.

10. De Saussure, *op. cit.,* p. 132. Italics added. Even if, as De Mauro points out (*ibid.,* p. 439), the interpretation which sees in this part of the *Cours* an anticipation of the Whorf-Spair hypothesis concerning linguistic relativism (according to which the organization of thought derives from the linguistic structuring and, therefore, different conceptual systems correspond to different languages) is not acceptable. The problem whether thought, before being subsumed under the linguistic act, can be characterized as an "amorphous mass" still remains. De Mauro offers a solution by remarking that, for De Saussure, thought is *linguistically* amorphous, which obviously does not exclude the possibility of explicating its structure outside of linguistics, *e.g.*, in psychology. Such a solution, however, is not completely convincing, particularly if we consider the above quoted passage where De Saussure speaks of thought as something "chaotic by nature", which also stands out in the original manuscripts of the *Cours.* Cf. the Engler edition of F. De Saussure, *Cours de Linguistique Générale* (Wiesbaden, 1968), passages 1821-C and 1829-G: "Psychologiquement, que sont nos idées abstraction faite de la langue? Elles n'existent probablement pas. Ou sous une forme qu'on peut appeler amorphe. . . . La pensée, qui est de sa nature chaotique, se précise en se décomposant." It is also indicative that De Saussure confines the non-linguistic analysis of thought to a "pure psychology" which is the exact parallel of phonology. Cf. De Saussure, *Corso di Linguistica Generale, op. cit.,* p. 137. The latter studies sounds from the naturalistic viewpoint ("physiology of sounds"), *i.e.*, as raw matter with respect to the structuring obtained by language (*ibid.,* p. 45), while the former analyzes thought precisely as an "amorphous mass". That a naturalistic perspective of this sort may account for the relation between thought and language is at least problematic. The question changes if, with Chomsky (*op. cit.,* pp. 12, 24, and 62), we emphasize the need to consider the linguistic act from the viewpoint of a "cognitive system" highly abstract and characterizable as a formal series of constitutive principles. As far as De Saussure is concerned, however, we must add that in considering this problem one should take into consideration the general meaning of the Saussurian discourse which moves precisely in an anti-naturalistic direction. One should specifically re-examine, in all of its implications, the Saussian proposal for a semiology intended as the study of the "life of signs" and of the laws *regulating them* (De Saussure, *op. cit.,* p. 26)—a study which, not accidentally De Saussure places in general psychology.

11. Husserl, *Ricerche Logiche, op. cit.*, p. 89.

12. *Ibid.*, p. 104.

13. *Ibid.*, p. 324.

14. *Ibid.*, p. 353.

15. E. Husserl, *Logica Formale e Transcendentale,* Italian translation by Guido D. Neri (Bari, 1966), p. 25.

16. Husserl, *Ricerche Logiche, op. cit.*, pp. 336-337. Actually, the passage in question refers to the problem of "symbolic-arithmetic" language, *i.e.*, to the problem of the pure possibilities of combination inherent in signs which, from this viewpoint, can be considered intuitively empty. What is important here is the general epistemological orientation underlying the Husserlian discourse—an orientation which emphasizes precisely the need for a purely formal approach. At any rate, at the time of the writing of the *Logical Investigations,* the recourse to the example of chess to illustrate the combinatory value of the elements of a linguistic system was rather widespread, mainly with regard to the problem of logical languages (cf. Frege). The comparision with the Saussurian text reveals an amazing similarity: "Language is a system which knows only the order pertaining to it. A comparision of chess will help us to better understand all this. . . . If I substitute pieces of wood with pieces of ivory the change is indifferent to the system. . . ." De Saussure, *Corso di Linguistica Generale, op, cit.,* p. 33.

17. Since an investigation so defined does not have a normative task, it does not face the problem of knowing what is "right" or not. In a sense, one can say that the grammar of a language (and, therefore, the concept of grammaticity which refers to it) is something "obvious", which means that it belongs to the daily practice of every speaker of that language. But the fact that something is "obvious" does not mean that it is also transparent. By theoretically orienting itself, an investigation (as the grammatical one) excludes every evaluative task: it must not tell us what is "right" in order to subsequently allow us to draw prescriptions, but it must render explicit those *given* formal principles on which the activity of the speaker is based and which, precisely to the extent that they are acquired or "obvious", remain latent in this activity, *i.e.*, are unconscious. Concerning the problem of "obviousness", see Chomsky, *Language and Mind, op. cit.*, p. 22, and his "Explanatory Models in Linguistics", in Ernest Nagel, Patrick Suppes, and Alfred Tarski editors, *Logic, Methodology and Philosophy of Science* (Stanford, 1962), pp. 528-530, where he stresses the pertinence of an abstract model to account for linguistic operations.

18. As already indicated, by *expression* Husserl means "the unity between a phonetic complex and a whole." Cf. Husserl, *Ricerche Logiche, op. cit.*, p. 105. For him, however, the meaning is what is essential to the expression: this explains why, in the course of the *Fourth Investigation* and, in general, in all of the *Logical Investigations,* he often speaks of the meaning in order to denote the whole expression. Although Husserlian though cannot be developed in another direction, we must agree with Bar-Hillel that this restriction to the level of meaning represents a serious limitation for Husserl's *Fourth Logical Investigation.* Hence, some obvious difficulties follow. Cf. Y. Bar-Hillel, "Husserl's Conception of a Purely Logical Grammar", in *Philosophy and Phenomenological Research,* vol. XVII, no. 3, 1957, p. 366.

19. From the linguistic viewpoint, the distinction between categorematic and syncategorematic expressions is at least problematic. Husserl, in fact, bases it on the distinction between independent and nonindependent meanings, which, however, does not seem sufficiently elaborated. Here he sees a relation between what occurs at the level of "representation" (where he deals on one hand with representations as unitary and closed totalities, and on the other with partial moments in these totalities and with forms of connection among unitary representations) and what occurs at the level of meaning (where on the one hand we would have unitary and independent meanings—*e.g., the founder of ethics*—and on the other connective and non-independent parts, *e.g., of, the, and*). Now, according to Husserl, the strictly linguistic level, *i.e.*, that of the *expression* as a unity of the signifying *and* the signified, merely reflects some properties on the level of meaning (thus, it is on the latter level that the original distinction between the categorematic and the syncategorematic obtains, while the distinction which has as its object the expression is only a derivative one). In general, it seems to me that the limitations of the Husserlian analysis lie in the fact that the linguistic level is treated as a factual translation of the level of meaning: Husserl can therefore speak of a linguistic grammar as a "morphology" of the meaning, which has a prior function. Starting from this, one could conceive an interpretation of the Husserlian text markedly different from the one which is here offered, particularly concerning the relation between grammaticity and semantic congruence. One could in fact assert that what Husserl is interested in is precisely an analysis of the level of *meaning,* to which all the rest is subordinate and that according to the Husserlian text, it makes no sense to isolate a strictly grammatical moment from a semantic one, since the syntactic combinations that he discusses in the *Fourth Logical Investigation* are always combinations of meanings. The fact is that here I have pointed to the analysis that Husserl dedicates to the *possibilites* of the constitution of meaning, *i.e.*, to a level which, as we will see later, is not properly the one of meaning, but is prior to it—a level defined by certain possibilites of combination or of "calculation" (in brief, by a *syntax*). The problematic of the *Fourth Investigation* consists in the fact that Husserl, in dealing with this formal level, keeps considering it as a level that can be char-

acterized only in terms of meaning (*i.e.*, of the rules of the combination of meanings) judging irrelevant the expression *as a whole,* whose rules of combination would not be a mere duplication of those carrying the meaning (even if it is not difficult to see that actually the categories of meaning to which Husserl refers are approximately questionable linguistic categories).

20. Husserl, *Ricerche Logiche, op. cit.*, p. 107.

21. *Ibid.*, p. 108.

22. A similar position, in a more precise way, is held by Chomsky in his *Aspects of the Theory of Syntax* (Cambridge, 1965), pp. 151 ff., where he argues that the grammaticity or non-grammaticity of a statement is irrelevant to its semantic interpretation, but, on the contrary, that it is a condition of it. However, since *other* conditions also enter into the interpretation of the statement (*e.g.*, the degree of mnemonic capacity required in order to connect the various elements of a complex sentence) it is obvious that grammaticity and interpretation cannot be identified. Moreover, and this is what matters, since the "good formation" of a statement represents the necessary condition of its full comprehensibility, it is necessary to *first* study the formal rules which determine it: to study it for what it is, instead of through its effects (which, in order to be produced, require other components).

23. Here I use examples of macroscopic violations because Husserl simply distinguishes between grammaticity and non-grammaticity and he makes no reference to possible *degree* of grammaticity. Thus, *e.g.*, a sentence such as "He has a green thought" (Ziff), which violates a rule of selection, is judged as grammatical by Husserl who confines his analysis to the cases of violation of major categories (in practice, the lexical ones) without being concerned with the possibilty of further subcategories. For a further elaboration of this, see Chomsky, *op. cit.*, p. 152.

24. Husserl, *Logica Formale e Transcendentale,* op. cit., p. 373.

25. *Ibid.*, p. 114.

26. The term "statement" used here for simplicity, is actually improper since we should speak of the structure underlying the statement.

27. Husserl, *Ricerche Logiche, op. cit.*, pp. 254 ff.

28. Husserl, *Logica Formale e Transcendentale, op. cit.*, p. 62.

29. Husserl, *Ricerche Logiche, op. cit.*, p. 491.

30. It is interesting to point out that this elaboration occurs within an orientation (shared by other types of inquiry) aiming to emphasize the prior function of an "abstract" component (characterized by a series of formal restrictions) in regard to the empirical-concrete contents. In other words, the series of abstract rules characterizing language cannot be derived from a more or less wide series of "data" (*e.g.*, observed linguistic behavior). Similarly, one can account for this behavior only in view of a preliminary elaboration of this abstract component. It is only in this limited sense that one can speak of the normativity of the latter with respect to what is observed. "What is understood *in specie* as incompatible, cannot be unified and therefore rendered compatible in the individual empirical case." Cf. Husserl, *Ricerche Logiche, op. cit.*, p. 499. Thus, one can explain why Husserl refers to a logical structure underlying the various linguistic data (which is denied by Hjelmslev, *op. cit.*, p. 22). But it is significant that, in order to do this, Hjelmslev appeals to the concept of prelogical mentality introduced by Levi-Bruhl. *I.e.*, there are languages, such as those of the "primitives", which bear the mark of this mentality and which, therefore, fail from the "logical" viewpoint. However, it is known that contemporary anthropology has questioned the hypothesis of a prelogical mentality, particularly in consideration of the taxonomical capacities of so-called primitive thought. Concerning Husserl, and the problem of universal grammar, see Roman Jakobson, "Implications of Language Universals for Linguistics", in J.H. Greenberg, editor, *Universals of Language* (Cambridge, 1963), pp. 275-276.

31. This can be better understood in view of Chomsky's distinction between *substantive* and *formal* universals. The first ones are introduced by the assertion that in every language (*e.g.*, the phonetic ones), certain traits are derived from a determinate series of traits independent of every particular language. In the quoted example, this series is represented by a series of acoustical-articulatory properties. The second ones are much more "abstract" and can deal with certain formal conditions which every grammar must respect. Cf. Chomsky, *Aspects of the Theory of Syntax, op. cit.*, pp. 27 ff.

32. Husserl, *Ricerche Logiche, op. cit.*, p. 127.

33. Bar-Hillel, *op. cit.*, p. 366.

34. Obviously, a listing of all possible occurrences is an absurd task for any inquiry. What is needed are, rather, systematic considerations. From the point of view of distributional logic, this has been clarified by Harris who writes: "The analysis of a particular *corpus* achieves an interest only if it is identical to the analysis which we would have obtained be starting from any other sufficiently wide *corpus* of materials derived from the same dialect. If this is so, we can predict the relations between elements in any other *corpus* of the language on the basis of the relation found in the *corpus* we have analyzed: consequently the latter can be considered as a descriptive sample of the language." Cf. Z.S. Harris, *Structural Linguistics* (Chicago, 1960), p. 13.

35. Among Husserl's terms, I have preferred "type" to emphasize its relation with the couple *type/token*.

36. This formulation is not precise because it places on the same level what in phonology are called free

variables and the combinatory variables. Actually there is a fundamental difference between these two types of variables, consisting in the fact that the nature of the first is determined by intrinsic necessary rules (combinatory rules) while the nature of the second ones is not. In the Saussurian terminology we might say that the first ones are units of the *parole* and the second ones are units of the *langue*.

37. E. Husserl, *Esperienza e Giudizio,* Italian translation by F. Costa (Milan, 1965), p. 386.

38. This is a priority according to which the concrete realizations are "recognizable" and can therefore perform a distinctive function not because of their intrinsic material differences (which can be irrelevant and, therefore, worthless from the viewpoint of the system) but because of their belonging to abstract categories.

39. Cf. H.S. Trubeckoj, *Principles de Phonologie,* French translation by J. Cantinian (Paris, 1964), pp. 33 and 47. Similarly, the individuation of combinatory variables occurs on a merely distributional basis, *i.e.*, independently of the semantic sphere.

40. Clearly, in this essay we have dealt exclusively with the *formal* aspect of language as developed by Husserl in various writings concerning the problem of logic—particularly the *Logische Untersuchungen.* Here we have not investigated the genetic and historical theme, *i.e.*, the theme dealt with in the *Appendix III* of the *Crisis,* which, however, is closely connected with the considered approach. For an analysis of *Appendix III* of the *Crisis* see Enzo Paci, *Funzione delle Scienze e Significato dell'Uomo* (Milan, 1963), pp. 219-237.

William Leiss (essay date 1970)

SOURCE: "Husserl and The Mastery of Nature," in *Telos: A Quarterly Journal of Critical Thought,* No. 5, Spring, 1970, pp. 82-97.

[*In the following essay, Leiss discusses the relevance of Husserl's thought to the problem of how we understand science, the natural world, and the relation of the two, especially with regard to the concept of "mastery over nature."*]

> *A morality, a mode of living tried and proved by long experience and testing, at length enters consciousness as a law, as dominating—and therewith the entire group of related values and states enters into it: it becomes venerable, unassailable, holy, true; it is part of its development that its origins should be forgotten—that is a sign it has become master.*
>
> Nietzsche[1]

The idea of "mastery of nature" is a familiar theme in the intellectual history of the modern West. This and related phrases—the domination of nature, the conquest of nature, and the control of nature—will be found abundantly in social theory, philosophy, utopian literature, and most recently in theories of technological progress. Generally this idea has been used as a shorthand expression for one or more of the following historical developments: The growing scientific understanding of the "laws of nature"; the continued success in turning scientific discovery into technological innovation at an ever more rapid pace; the ability, won in the industrial revolution, to apply technological innovation to the production of commodities on a mass basis; and, most importantly, the hope that these tendencies would either entirely eliminate or significantly reduce the familiar causes of human misery and social disorder.

Although this is obviously a most complex assembly of historical events, it is possible to use the idea of mastery of nature as an analytical device in attempting to understand its ongoing dynamic.[2] In the present essay only one aspect of this investigation will be treated, namely the question concerning the role of modern science as the great human instrument for the domination of nature. This view of science has been extensively elaborated in a number of philosophical and sociological treatises, the most important of which are the writings of Max Scheler.[3] Scheler maintained that we could understand the basic difference between modern science and its predecessors primarily in terms of the vastly increased human mastery over nature made possible by the conceptual structure of the new science, and he tried to show how the conceptual revolution in science was closely related to a broader panoply of social changes which resulted in the emergence of bourgeois society.

There is thus an interesting affinity between Scheler's writings and the outstanding work of Husserl's last period, **The Crisis of the European Sciences,** despite the fact that the specific orientation and approach of the two thinkers is quite different. Scheler, in trying to relate a change in the scientific attitude toward nature to broader social changes occurring in the transition from medieval to modern society, relies most heavily on classical European sociology and philosophy of science. Husserl, who inquires in the *Crisis* about the relationship between the basic form of modern science and the *Lebenswelt* (considered as the specific social and historical framework in which that science developed), has undertaken a much narrower and strictly "phenomenological" study. Nevertheless, the two contributions complement each other.

In the present essay I would like to discuss the relevance of Husserl's *Crisis* for the general inquiry into the meaning of the mastery of nature, more specifically that aspect of mastery of nature which relates to the accomplishments of modern science and to the significance of that science for social objectives. To be sure, other writers have already drawn attention to Husserl's late work in contexts similar to this one. Ludwig Landgrebe has noted in passing that these analyses of Husserl's make clear the way in which nature can become the subject of "operative manipulation" by man and, consequently, how natural science can become "an efficient tool for the technological domination of the world." On two occasions Herbert Marcuse has pointed to this segment of Husserl's work as a valuable source for an understanding of the role and potentialities of science as they are relevant to the struggle for a liberated society. On the basis of Husserl's remarks in **Ideen III,** Paci states: "As Husserl put it very clearly, science becomes an *instrument of domination* of nature and of men." Piccone interprets the **Crisis** as follows: "Objectified science, originally a means to better control nature, turns into its opposite and, in a diabolical dialectical reversal, in freezing nature in naturalistic formulae, becomes the most effective reifier of precisely that *Lebenswelt* that it was meant to change. When man is also defined, by behavioristic psychology, as just another thing among things, the original *telos* of the new rational humanity envisaged in the Renaissance is fully betrayed and the crisis of European sciences comes into being." And in very general terms two of the best-known of Husserl's interpreters, Aron Gurwitsch and Jean Wahl, have both remarked that the central problem of Husserl's late work is the "human significance of science."[4]

The essay which Husserl published in 1936 opened with a basic question that implicitly guided the rest of the analysis. Generally stated, the essay dealt with the meaning or significance of *Wissenschaft* (exact knowledge or science) for the overall social objectives of human society as conceived by philosophy. At the very outset Husserl indicated his interest with the following question concerning science: "They [the questions concerning the meaning—or meaninglessness—of this entire human existence] concern finally men as freely determining themselves in their relations with the human and the extra-human environment, as free in their possibilities to shape themselves and their environment rationally. What does science have to say about reason and unreason, about us men as subjects of this freedom?"[5] The heading of section II of the essay (in which the above passage appears) identifies the "crisis" of science as the loss of its significance for life (*Lebensbedeutsamkeit*).

The function of Husserl's investigation, then, is to discover how this loss of significance comes about. In the latter half of the nineteenth century, the situation had been far different: The most influential trains of thought had glorified the positive sciences and their fruits, and men generally felt that "prosperity" (Husserl uses the English word) was intimately bound up with the continued success of the positive sciences in extending their domain and their methodology. In the twentieth century Husserl finds a "crisis". The exact dimensions of this crisis are never clearly stated in these writings: *i.e.,* one is never sure whether Husserl is referring basically to a profound intellectual crisis of which the social crises of that time were partial results or whether it had been the social crises which had prompted the intellectual problem. Nor does Husserl himself say just why this crisis became significant during the twentieth century.

In any case the crisis is of such a magnitude as to necessitate a re-investigation of the foundations and the origins of modern scientific philosophy. What is at stake is the very concept of science itself, for as the above quotation shows, Husserl believes that we must seriously ask at this point whether the science which we have received and which we continue to practice has anything to say about the conditions under which the relationships of men to each other and to their natural environment could be arranged in a free and rational way. When we ask about the concept of science, we immediately confront the decisive achievement of modern philosophy: The ideal of a universal science based on the model of mathematics and geometry. It is this ideal, whose chief innovators were Galileo and Descartes, which has determined the basic concept of science in modern Western history, and it is thus this science which must be investigated.

Obviously most of Husserl's analysis in the succeeding parts of this book depends for its validity upon the correctness of his starting-point. Yet there would seem to be little difficulty in accepting it. This ideal of science certainly continues to guide the natural sciences, and everyone is familiar with the persistent attempts to extend its methodology to the social sciences. But this kind of question need not detain us here, for in the contexts in which "mastery of nature" is customarily found, it is clearly the ideal of science which is supposed to achieve the objective of mastery. When "science" is used with reference to the mastery of nature, it is not very often explained in any detail, and this fact is responsible for some of the confusion attending the use of "mastery of nature." However, I think it would be safe to say that modern physics (from the seventeenth century to the present), as that field of the natural sciences in which the general laws of nature, matter, and energy have been formulated, represents the ideal of science in the body of literature in which utopian possibilities have been linked with the progress of "science." It also represents the ideal of science—as universal science—with which Husserl is concerned.

For Husserl this idea has two primary characteristics: (1) the separation of experience into subjective and objective factors—the ontological dimension; (2) the use of mathematics and geometry as the basic language of science—the methodological dimension. The ontological and methodological dimensions of the science are interdependent. This science thus creates a picture of the world in which a realm of eternally unchanging ideal objects (the objects of mathematical physics) exists "behind" the fluctuating and deceptive realm of sense-experience. The former realm is the one of true being, where a uniform matter exists as it really is, "behind" the accidental manifestations perceived by the senses.[6]

The basic point made by Husserl is that there are *two* "worlds" in the life of modern Western man, each radically different from the other; as he phrased it in an earlier manuscript, they are the discrete worlds of value-objects (*Wertobjekte*) and practical objects on the one hand, and the world of natural-scientific objects on the other. In the former we find things familiar to everyone—paintings, statues, gardens, houses, tables, clothes, tools, and so forth. In the latter is encountered another set of objects entirely, "ideal" objects which form the basis of mathematical operations.[7] Of course the two worlds are related, most immediately in the fact that the process of experimental verification to which the mathematically-formulated theories are subjected takes place in the "familiar" world.[8] But Husserl contends that the nature of this relationship is highly problematical and also most significant. He phrases the problem in the widest possible terms, a phrasing which also sets the problem in the closest affinity with the themes of this present study: The decisive question is the relationship of the truths derived from the results of the natural sciences to "scientific and extra-scientific humanity and its spiritual life."[9] In another place Husserl says that it is because of the tremendously high *valuation* which has been placed on mathematical knowledge and mathematical natural science that we must examine the origins of this science; *i.e.*, it is not primarily the theoretical foundations of this knowledge, but rather the great value which the "modern spirit" sees in it for the investigation of nature, that demands clarification.

The familiar world is called by Husserl the *Lebenswelt.*[10] It is the world of everyday experience; as used in this connection "experience" does not have a primarily epistemological connotation, but rather encompasses a sphere of the widest generality and universality, the totality of behavior comprising human life. Experience in this world takes place on the level of ordinary "intuition" (a word similarly used in a non-technical way), and it is always "pre-scientific" in the sense that it presupposes no special operations of any kind beyond the ordinary "natural" employment of human sensitivity and understanding. Husserl distinguishes simply, and without precise shading, *Lebenswelt* and *wissenschaftliche Welt;* and he boldly maintains, in order to set this distinction within a recognizable philosophical framework, that "this *Lebenswelt* is nothing but the world of traditionally so contemptuously treated, pure *doxa.*"[11] Every attempt at a scientific or exact knowledge, of whatever kind, is a departure from the *Lebenswelt*—but only and always a partial departure, because in making such an attempt we remain, as men among other men, actually existing in the everyday world. In terms of the usual terminology employed by Husserl, these realms of exact knowledge represent acts of "producing consciousness", constitutions of the world by transcendental subjectivity; but the *Lebenswelt* is also the result of productions or achievements (*Leistungen*) of a transcendental nature, *i.e.*, it also has a determinate structure,[12] the nature of which Husserl proposed to uncover by means of phenomenological investigation.

What Husserl has in mind, then, with the distinction of *Lebenswelt* and *wissenschaftliche Welt* is the traditional philosophical realms of *doxa* and *episteme.* But, in a manner strikingly akin to Nietzsche's reflections on this same pair of terms, Husserl inquires about the *gradation* implicit in the distinction, about the higher valuation assigned to *episteme,* and about the significance of the gradation (as it appears in its most characteristic modern form) for the concrete social life of man. Thus he insists, again and again, that the *Lebenswelt* is and must remain the "ground" for all exact knowledge, in the sense that all the acts and productions of *episteme* necessarily refer back to it. Scientific knowledge, no matter of how abstract a character, is knowledge attained by men who always exist in the *Lebenswelt.* Of course the theoretical coherence of any particular example of exact knowledge is in no way affected by this fact; but the human significance of every kind of exact knowledge, not its theoretical coherence, is at stake. The significance of science is determined by the fact that it arises out of human praxis in the *Lebenswelt,* which encompasses the range of sciences at first as abstract possibilities.[13] Thus when we inquire about the significance of any particular science in this context, we are not primarily judging its alleged superiority or inferiority to any other type of science, but rather its meaning for praxis in the *Lebenswelt.*

As far as the modern period is concerned, the "other" world distinguished from the *Lebenswelt,* the scientific world, is preeminently that of the natural sciences. Husserl repeatedly asserts that the sphere of the mathematical-physical natural sciences has been for centuries the "self-evident" basis or model of exact science in Western civilization. The great value which has been placed upon its results and its methodology, and the outstanding influence which it has exerted upon the the determination of the very concept of science itself, requires that the question concerning the significance of science be addressed especially to this science. This question is directed not at any specific finding or findings attributed to that science, but rather to the most fundamental operations which open the way to whatever results it might produce. In other words, what mode of abstraction guides its entire work, what principle of selectivity does it employ "on" the *Lebenswelt*?[14]

Its fundamental "method" (understood here in the widest sense), its mode of abstraction and selection, is in Husserl's words the "mathematization of nature." And accordingly the query which is formulated for the investigation of this science asks: "What is the meaning of this mathematization of nature, and how can we reconstruct the process of thought that motivates it?"[15] We can see, according to Husserl, how the science of geometry in the ancient Greek civilization emerged out of certain practical necessities, especially concerning the measurement of fields. And we can also see in the Platonic conception of a realm of ideal entities that the actually existing real world has a range of "participation" in the ideal. But if we look at the "idealization" that characterizes the field of modern theoretical physics as it is formulated by Galileo and Descartes, we confront a different situation. This modern science formulates an idealized universal structure of nature; and not only its structure, but also its process of causality (motion, interaction of physical bodies), is conceived in ideal terms, as the famous laws of motion indicate. In short, there is presented a picture of geometrical forms (the Cartesian "extension") interacting according to mathematically-expressed formulas in geometrical space, as universal conditions of nature in all its manifestations. This idealization, for Husserl, "hides" its connection with the *Lebenswelt,* unlike that of Greek geometry, where the connection with practical necessities is evident. In other words, we cannot immediately understand how this universal conception of physical nature is related to praxis.

The "significance" of the mathematization of nature, which is the central question posed by Husserl, is twofold. In the first place, the relationship between the *Lebenswelt* (common sense, intuited nature) and the *wissenschaftliche Welt* (exact knowledge, mathematized nature) remains always unclear. The *Lebenswelt* is permanently "devalued" as the realm of purely subjective experience, despite the fact that this is the world in which all human praxis occurs, and it is saved from being utterly meaningless only by the fact that it eternally carries "behind" itself another world of true being. Secondly, the abstract-universal characteristics of the science based upon the mathematization of nature make it internally impossible for that science to possess a direct relationship to specific goals formulated in human praxis; the science can only make available a certain range of new possibilities for practical use. But this entails that such a science is purely a technique (albeit a technique of a very high order).[16] As "science that has become *techne*" it could not continue to serve as a model for science itself, since at some point the purely technical level must be transcended if we are not to find ourselves in possession of ever more efficient (and deadly) means for the accomplishment of ever more obscure ends.

Out of the foregoing analysis emerge certain ideas about the meaning of "nature" as the subject of scientific investigation that illuminate critical ambiguities in the conception of the mastery of nature. One of these is that it is important to understand in what way and under what conditions nature becomes a "thematic" interest both as a general feature of human existence and as the subject of a particular form of science.[17] An aspect of experience becomes "thematic" when special and deliberate attention is focused on it or when it is viewed as having particular interest. In ordinary experience the *lebensweltliche Natur* is not thematic; rather, it subsists as the familiar background which binds together human experience on a universal scale despite all differences of culture and history. (Husserl claims that this familiar nature has become thematic only for phenomenology.) "Becoming thematic," on the other hand, always involves a process of abstraction, a deliberate focusing of interest and attention upon a particular range of experience which at the same time necessarily overshadows and devalues certain other aspects of experience. This is the case with the modern scientific conception of nature: It intentionally selects a particular class of phenomena as its thematic field and excludes certain types of evidence as purely subjective.

As a direct result of this deliberate thematic undertaking represented in the modern sciences of nature, we are faced with not one "nature," but two: *lebensweltliche Natur* and *wissenschaftliche Natur.* For the modern period these two present the sharp dichotomy between the experienced nature of everyday life (nature as intuited by the senses) and the abstract-universal, mathematized nature of the physical sciences. Nature *per se* is not the thematic interest of the natural sciences because there is no simple "nature *per se*"[18] Of course one could add others to the two mentioned above—for example, nature as conceived by European Romanticism and *Naturphilosophie;* but there is little point in trying to complete the list, for I think it is obvious that until now only the two with which Husserl is concerned have entered into the praxis of modern Western man in a concrete sense. Husserl mentions that, strictly speaking, scientific nature belongs only to the *Umwelt* of the natural scientists and of others who understand it. On the other hand, this nature has entered the mainstream of general praxis through the great influence of the scientific ideal associated with it, and most importantly, through the technological revolution accompanying it.

This situation is not exactly the same as the one described in Whitehead's phrase, "the bifurcation of nature," although it is clearly related to it. Like Whitehead, Husserl has in mind constantly the Cartesian separation of subjective and objective factors in experience. But especially insofar as human praxis is concerned there is not so much one world split into ontological gradations as two seemingly distinct worlds. In Husserl's view both worlds are productions of transcendental subjectivity, which means that both are constituted in the arena of human praxis and relate ultimately to needs arising in the course of that praxis. It is precisely because the significance of the modern scientific project with respect to this basic context has been "lost" (or remains "hidden") that Husserl undertakes his inquiry into the historical origins of that science. When he asks about the significance of the mathematization of nature, therefore, he is posing a question concerning the relationship between *two* different worlds of "nature" that result from the mathematical-scientific project.

The leading question of the *Crisis,* quoted above at the beginning of section II, sets the subsequent discussion firmly within the framework of social theory. It specifically raises the problems which have always been at the heart of the utopian tradition in social theory, namely those concerning the possibilities under which men might structure their relationships with their fellow men and with the natural environment on the basis of freedom and rationality. And it asks what "science," broadly conceived as exact knowledge, has to say about those possibilities. The analysis by Husserl which follows the posing of this question would seem to suggest an unequivocal answer: Science has nothing to say about them. By itself such an answer would be quite trivial; in trying to amplify it, however, difficulties arise because Husserl failed both to explore the implications of his own question in systematic fashion and to answer it directly in the course of his exposition.

If we were to conclude with Husserl that contemporary science has nothing to say about the possibilities for a free and rational social order, and if we were then to embark upon a search for the reasons underlying this fact, only a partial explanation (and not the most important part of the entire explanation) would be found in the historical origins of that science. Although he is occasionally aware of it, Husserl fails to keep in mind the critical difference between the state of that science at its birth and its changing social situation over the course of its development. As he recognizes at one point, the key to the problem concerns the great *valuation* of one particular ideal of science; this did not exist at its origin (except in the conception of its innovators), however, but is rather a matter of growth over centuries of time. The outlines of its supremacy, considered as a general social phenomenon, only begin to be apparent in the latter part of the nineteenth century and are still being felt today. As something "thematic" it had to compete for recognition with other thematic attitudes, such as religion, and its relative priority—which in the twentieth century has been expanding at an accelerating rate—is in reality a comparatively recent occurrence. Of course, just its present priority as a thematic concern warrants the special attention bestowed upon it.

The general valuation of a science determines the range of its significance, and this valuation is only partly a matter relating to the science itself. More important is the place which it comes to occupy in the fabric of goals and purposes fashioned in the course of human praxis. These goals and the manner of their determination in the social process express the relative situations of competing thematic attitudes and thus apportion the amount of individual energy available for their pursuit, the rewards attendant upon the expenditure of that energy, and the kinds of expectations spurring them on. For Husserl this would represent the "ground" (in a wide, non-epistemological sense) of a particular science in the *Lebenswelt*. But to say just this much is not enough: One must examine the developing and changing structure of goals and purposes in the *Lebenswelt* itself, in this particular case the history of its evolution from the seventeenth century to the present. This is especially necessary if one looks at this structure of purposes as a whole which is *contradictory* in many respects.

Husserl's contention that modern science "hides" its connection with the *Lebenswelt* would seem to contradict Scheler's viewpoint, with which we had compared it at the beginning of this essay. For Scheler the kind of relationship that Husserl is apparently seeking is precisely what is most evident about this science, since one of the prime characteristics of modern natural science is the internal and necessary connection between its theoretical structure and the range of practical goals. In concrete terms, the dynamic tie between the *Lebenswelt* and the scientific world is constituted by technology and technological progress: The development of more and more precise instrumentation is promoted by, and in turn itself promotes, continual advances both in opening up new problems and the possibility of their solution for the science and in providing new resources and techniques for the production of goods. Thus the views of Scheler and Husserl would seem to be incompatible.

The resolution of the apparent contradiction is to be found in their disparate conceptions of means and ends. Scheler consigns the positive sciences and their theoretico-practical achievements to the sphere of practical objectives and sets beside them, as parallel historical constants all of which remain distinctly separate, the spheres of metaphysical and religious knowledge, where "final" ends and causes are located. Thus the issue of the interconnection of these three strains does not arise, and Scheler can suggest that the solution for the crisis of the present is to be expected from a new elite of metaphysicians. Husserl's position is just the opposite. For him the connection between the *Lebenswelt* and the scientific world is a critical problem because the apparent relationship between the two worlds as constituted by technology or technique says nothing about the inherent *rationality* of that relationship.

The idea suggested by Scheler—that there exist three spheres as separate historical constants—is incorrect. Strictly speaking, there are no "purely" practical objectives, for every positing of such objectives and every attempt of a substantial magnitude to attain them acts as a determination, both in a positive and a negative sense, with reference to the "final" ends of man. Although we might be tempted to say that the positive sciences procure for us a panorama of means to which our chosen ends may then be superadded in accordance with our will or whim, in fact such an idea is nonsensical, for means are not posited and attained in the abstract, isolated from any ends whatever.

Of course the inner relationship between any particular set of means and ends may be partially or totally obscure as far as a definite historical period, group of thinkers, or individual thinker is concerned. And it is almost certainly true that this relationship is often obscure at the origins of a new departure in the positing of means and ends and that the relationship cannot be clarified by theoretical considerations alone. Rather, the attempt to clarify it must proceed by reflection on the actual concrete situation undertaken at the time when one can say with some degree of assurance that this actual situation has revealed a determinate relationship between means and ends. For example, Husserl quite rightly rejects what he regards as a "modish" interpretation of Cartesian philosophy, typical of the present, which represents Cartesianism as being the foundation of the modern ideal of seeking "security" for man through a growing domination of nature by means of knowledge (*Erkenntnisherrschaft über die Natur*) and a consequent infinitely expanding technical mastery over nature. He regards it as "undeniable," however, that such an ideal exists in our own time as a "mass-phenomenon."[19] The point is that this ideal represents at the outset an abstract possibility for Descartes and a real possibility for the future as a result of the achievements by him and others. The seventeenth-century historical background ought to be read in this light—namely, as an aid in understanding a project (mastery of nature) not for the purposes of interpreting seventeenth-century thought, but rather in order to analyze the nature of the contemporary situation which is in part an outcome of the acceptance of that project as a social task.

The value of these writings by Scheler and Husserl lies, as we have already mentioned, in their attempt to relate the scientific project to the general realm of ends articulated in the course of human praxis. But unlike Scheler, Husserl demands that there be an inherent rationality in that relationship. What is primarily hidden in the prevailing association of the *Lebenswelt* and the scientific world is not the connection of the two in terms of any goals at all, but rather their interrelationship in terms of a *rational* set of goals, *i.e.*, the kinds of goals implicit in an attempt by men to fashion themselves and their environment according to the dictates of freedom and rationality. Husserl's basic query concerning the "meaning of the mathematization of nature" asks about the extent to which this project makes sense from the point of view of human praxis—not any possible praxis, but one which embodies concrete potentialities for the realization of a free and rational social order. The demand and the need for a relationship between science and a rational set of ends, rather than any ends whatever, is an expression of the necessity for a set of ends in which we can have at least as much confidence as we have in our abilities to achieve them, *i.e.,* in the means at our disposal.

I shall now try to demonstrate precisely how the ambiguity with reference to the component term "nature" is an essential factor in the problematical character of "mastery of nature."[20] Husserl's analysis enables us to "prosecute" this aspect of our own inquiry much more adequately than it would otherwise be possible to do. His careful delineation of the two disparate realms of nature—the intuited, directly-apprehended nature of universal experience in everyday life (*lebensweltliche Natur*) and the idealized or mathematized nature of the modern scientific project (*wissenschaftliche Natur*)—raises a question which penetrates to the very core of the problem here under consideration: Which nature is the object of mastery in the essayed mastery of nature?

Clearly the "nature" which is experienced in everyday life has been the object of mastery in every state of human development. In general, mastery of nature with reference to the *lebensweltliche Natur* has meant control of the available natural resources of a particular region by an individual or social group and either partial or total exclusion of others from the benefits (and necessities of existence) available therein. In other words, under the conditions of the persistent social conflict that has characterized all forms of human society, the *lebensweltliche Natur* always appears either as already appropriated in the form of private property or else as subject to such appropriation. Accessibility to it is either denied or sharply restricted, actually or potentially.

Experience in the *Lebenswelt* includes, as part of the paramount reality of everyday life, conflict and struggle. The *lebensweltliche Natur* plays a vital role in that conflict: In the struggle between man and external nature the latter is the source of both grief and satisfaction. From the point of view of man as a species, external nature appears as a reluctant and recalcitrant host; she does not willingly yield all her most precious fruits, and in order to possess them man must (to use Bacon's terminology) "vex", "hound", and "torment" her. But the fruits that are won at any particular time become the subject of more or less intense conflict, for in the struggles among men control of nature's resources is obviously a decisive weapon under most circumstances.

The dominant social groups in the various historical epochs indeed have acheived a notable degree of mastery over nature in the sense just described. Yet that mastery has been neither complete nor permanent, and in some respects the struggle among men for control of nature's resources has increasingly intensified during the modern period. According to the Marxian theory of bourgeois society, the ruling class over the past few centuries managed to deprive the great majority of men of all access to the material means of existence, leaving them only their labor-power to be sold on the market under the threat of starvation; and yet—assuming for the sake of argument that this theory is correct—even this extreme form of mastery over nature did not succeed in repressing social conflict. On the contrary, such conflict steadily increased in magnitude, and gradually the social conflicts that had been formerly confined to relatively small regions became a unitary worldwide phenomenon, now occurring under the permanent threat of thermonuclear annihilation.

Such has been the fate of mastery over nature in modern times insofar as the *lebensweltliche Natur* is concerned. But the concept of mastery over nature is clearly meant to apply to the *wissenschaftliche Natur* as well. In fact, modern science and its concept of nature is supposed to express mastery over nature in a unique and highly-developed form. Thus we must ask: What is the meaning of this mastery with reference to scientific nature?

From the point of view of the scientific concept of nature, modern science expresses its mastery over nature in that it "takes off the mask and veil from natural objects, which are commonly concealed and obscured under the variety of shapes and external appearance" and deals with the "secrets" embedded in the hidden structure of nature. From the point of view of the *lebensweltliche Natur,* science expresses its mastery by creating a "veil of ideas" or "veil of symbols" over the nature experienced in everyday life.[21] Generally conceived, the conquest of nature considered as a scientific project strives for the elaboration of a theoretical system in which all the axioms implicit in its conceptual foundation (the mathematization of nature)—or, to put the point in more familiar terms, all the "laws of nature"—have been fully unfolded, tested, and unified into a coherent whole. The internal harmony, order, and regularity among the occurrences and behavior of natural phenomena, together with the universal applicability of the laws which govern them, act as heuristic principles of the intellectual disciplines that work with scientific nature: Disharmony and internal inconsistency are signs of flaws in the theoretical structure or in the experimental techniques, not in "nature" itself, which should be eliminated.

These and other elements constitute the rationality of the scientific methodology arising out of the mathematization of nature, and that rationality has proved itself decisively in practice, as is shown by the immense increase in knowledge about the behavior of natural phenomena. Mastery of nature in this sense means the increasing refinement of a theoretical schema which explains that behavior consistently; and, while that explanation certainly need not be considered as a complete "scientific" understanding of all aspects of natural phenomena, it is an enduring contribution to whatever understanding may be gained.

There is an identifiable element of mastery, then, concerning both the *lebensweltliche Natur* and the *wissenschaftliche Natur*. We have already seen that the former remains incomplete, and there is a crucial sense in which the same must be said of the latter. Many writers regard the modern natural sciences as the appropriate instrument for the realization of the human domination of nature, but they would not find the definition of mastery offered in the preceding paragraph entirely satisfying. On the contrary, they are virtually unanimous in viewing the objective of mastery as consisting in the technological applicability of scientific knowledge for the actual or potential gratification of human material needs and desires. Thus scientific nature is the object of mastery not in itself but for the sake of something else: The project for the mastery of nature sets for itself as a task and a goal (a) indirectly the refinement of the theoretical schema described above and (b) directly the relief of the inconveniences of man's estate. Since these inconveniences are experienced in the *Lebenswelt,* it seems that mastery of the *wissenschaftliche Natur* is the means by which the final objective of mastery—namely, mastery over the *lebensweltliche Natur*—is pursued.

But the question that has never been confronted adequately is why mastery in one domain should entail mastery in the other. We have seen that in a definite sense science has achieved a notable degree of mastery over nature (*i.e.,* scientific nature) and is progressively increasing its mastery. But what follows from this insofar as the nature experienced in everyday life is concerned? The question does not imply that there is no relationship at all between the two domains. The project for which scientific nature is thematic presupposes the everyday world as its basis, depends constantly on the latter for the procedure of experimental verification, and delivers its results partly as practical possibilities in the everyday world. Although Husserl may or may not be correct in contending that the *rationality* of the connection between the two realms remains hidden, neither he nor anyone else would deny that the connection itself exists in a very concrete sense. Our question

inquires about something quite different: What basis is there for assuming that mastery in the one domain can be translated into mastery in the other?

The dominant tradition in the modern West has assumed that mastery over nature considered as scientific-technological progress would be translated into mastery over nature considered as social progress, *i.e.,* a reduction in the sources of social conflict. But the two forms of mastery are quite different. The developing element of mastery in the theoretical structure of modern natural science, its progress toward greater completeness and sophistication, is the fruit of its internal rationality. But that would collapse by departing from it, because the conditions according to which that rationality first operates at all are established by the original idealization (the mathematization of nature) upon which it rests. The circumscription of the range of its application is the ransom exacted for its service. The inclusion of such rationality within the dimensions created by the acceptance of the mastery of nature as a social task, however, is not itself an expression or an outcome of that rationality. This acceptance is a fact pertaining to, or a situation occurring in, the *Lebenswelt.* "Mastery of nature" as the outcome of scientific rationality operating in the domain of scientific nature, when it is translated into the mode of an essentially different domain (*lebensweltliche Natur* as a component of everyday experience), cannot and does not preserve its character intact.

Perhaps the best illustration for this point would be an analogy drawn from the persistent attempts to understand the nature and workings of society by means of a methodology borrowed from the modern natural sciences. In the late seventeenth and eighteenth centuries the idea of a "geometry of politics" or a "social mathematics" was proposed, and in the nineteenth and twentieth centuries there have been repeated attempts on a piecemeal scale to represent aspects of the social process in the form of mathematically-expressed principles or laws. Of course the question of the validity of such principles is a complex one, and in certain areas (notably economics) this mode of analysis is increasingly favored. But the paucity of the attained results so far—especially with respect to the hope that the enlarged knowledge of social pressures would help to solve social problems—in comparison with the achievements of the natural sciences offers little encouragement for future successes along these lines. The internal rationality of the methodology cannot impose an order which is lacking in the subject-matter itself; similarly greater rationality in the exploitation of nature's resources cannot insure by itself that greater rationality will prevail in the structure of the social process within which this refined exploitation occurs.

The two senses of mastery over nature described above have had an ongoing reciprocal impact on each other. Mastery of nature, even when it is pursued via the agency of the rationality inherent in the conception of scientific nature, necessarily has its *telos* in the *Lebenswelt* (and consequently in the *lebensweltliche Natur* that is both background and component part of the *Lebenswelt*). *Thus mastery of nature considered as scientific rationality submits itself to the conditions that define mastery of nature in the prevailing socio-historical world.* To be sure, the former does not merely "submit." Its achievements, although constituting mastery of nature in a different sense, are immensely influential in setting the limits of the options available for the pursuit of mastery in the *Lebenswelt*. In turn the latter, as a result of both the attained and the promised accomplishments of scientific rationality, influences the progress of the former by gradually establishing its priority as a "thematic" concern over all other competing thematic concerns (for example, in the allocation of social resources). Mastery of nature is a dialectical unity of opposing elements whose inner tension is the source of its continued vitality.

The internal contradictions in mastery of nature are an essential part of its structure. The fact that there are decisive ambiguities both in the notion of mastery and in the notion of nature as components in the expression "mastery of nature" in no way implies the mastery of nature refers *only* to a widespread intellectual confusion; rather, it denotes at the same time a substantial historical reality. An illustration representing an extreme case might help to clarify this point, although it should be born in mind that this is an extreme case rather than a typical instance and is chosen because in such cases the contradictory features are thrown into sharp relief.

Even under relatively primitive circumstances humans wage a kind of warfare against the natural environment by way of response to the pressures of the struggle for existence: An example is the deliberate burning of great sections of forested land on the African continent for the purpose of increasing the area available for agriculture, a deed which often recoils disastrously on the unwitting perpetrators because of the resulting natural imbalance. But this kind of situation is not confined to so-called "primitive" frameworks. The persistence of the struggle for existence reproduces such contradictions even at the highest attained levels of rationality. At these levels, where the duality of *lebensweltliche Natur* and *wissenschaftliche Natur* is present, the achievements based upon the latter vastly expand human capacities to conduct warfare against the natural environment—against the *lebensweltliche Natur*—under the conditions of the intensified struggle for existence. At present one of the forms assumed by this struggle is the confrontation of guerilla operations and counterinsurgency techniques. The *lebensweltliche Natur* serves as one of the guerilla's chief allies: The cover of darkness and the cover of the jungle canopy help to offset the conventional military superiority of his opponent. And in the extreme case the counterinsurgency techniques, utilizing instruments made possible by the most advanced scientific-technological achievements, wage war against the *lebensweltliche Natur* itself in an effort to defeat the guerilla. A "defoliation" campaign simply removes vast portions of the jungle canopy, and the military proposes the orbiting

in space of gigantic reflectors which would turn night into day for an entire nation.[22]

The pursuit of the implications of the mastery of nature forces us to explore those implications in the context of the human social conflicts arising out of the struggle for existence. The paradoxical character of Husserl's late writing is that, despite its highly abstract character and its manifest lack of social analysis, it offers significant help in this effort. If the interpretation offered in the preceding pages is plausible, one can conclude that Husserl's thought breaks through its self-imposed limitations and provides a basis for understanding the historical role of scientific-technological progress in the mastery of nature.

Notes

1. *The Will to Power,* tr. W. Kaufmann (New York, 1967), sect. 514.

2. For a brief introduction to such an attempt see my article "Utopia and Technology: Reflections on the Conquest of Nature," *International Social Science Journal,* forthcoming (1971); for a more extended discussion see my unpublished Ph.D. dissertation, "The Domination of Nature" (University of California, San Diego, 1969).

3. See chapter 3 of my dissertation: "Max Scheler's Concept of Herrschaftswissen."

4. Landgrebe, *Major Problems in Contemporary European Philosophy* (New York, 1966), p. 99. Marcuse, "On Science and Phenomenology," *Boston Studies in the Philosophy of Science,* ed. R.S. Cohen and M.W. Wartofsky, II (New York, 1965), 279-290; *One-Dimensional Man* (Boston, 1964), pp. 162-165. Paci, "The Phenomenological Encyclopedia and the *Telos* of Humanity," *Telos,* I, No. 2 (1968), p. 16. Piccone, "Towards a Socio-Historical Interpretation of the Scientific Revolution," *Telos,* I, No. 1 (1968), p. 17. Gurwitsch, "The Last Work of Edmund Husserl, Part I," *Journal of Philosophy and Phenomenological Research,* XVI (1956), 383. Jean Wahl, "L'Ouvrage posthume de Husserl: La Krisis" (mimeographed, Paris, 1965), p. 4. René Toulemont's *L'Essence de la Société selon Husserl* (Paris, 1962) is disappointing and has nothing to say on this topic.

5. *Die Krisis der europäischen Wissenschaften* (ed. W. Biemel, 2nd ed., The Hague, 1962), p. 4.

6. See, e.g., *Krisis,* pp. 315, 420.

7. *Ideen II,* ed. M. Biemel (The Hague, 1952), pp. 2, 27.

8. Husserl thinks that this represents a paradoxical situation which must be clarified theoretically; it is a paradox, recognized at the outset by Descartes, which troubled Leibniz greatly. See *Krisis,* pp. 54-56. To discuss it here, however, would take us too far afield.

9. "Die heutige europäische Situation des allgemeinen Zusammenbruchs der geistigen Menschheit ändert nichts an den naturwissenschaftlichen Resultaten,

und diese in ihrer eigenständigen Wahrheit enthalten kein Motiv, Naturwissenschaft zu reformieren. Wenn da Motive bestehen, so betreffen sie die Beziehung dieser Wahrheiten zu der wissenschaftlichen und ausserwissenschaftlichen Menschheit und ihrem Geistesleben." *Krisis* p. 356; cf. p. 137. The reference in the following sentence of the text is to *ibid.*, p. 58.

10. References for the following sketch of the *Lebenswelt* will be found in *Erfahrung und Urteil* (ed. L. Landgrebe, Prague, 1939), pp. 38-59 *passim* and *Krisis,* pp. 48-54, 107, 130-138, 229, 342-343, 465-466. For another view cf. Gurwitsch, "The Last Work of Edmund Husserl, Part II," *PPR* XVII (1957), 370 ff.

11. *Krisis,* p. 465.

12. *Erfahrung,* p. 49. The use of the term "production" in phenomenological literature is clarified somewhat in the following passage by Gurwitsch: The general program of phenomenology is an attempt "to account for the world at large as well as mundane existents in particular and, for that matter, for all objective entities whatever, in terms of experiences, acts, operations, and productions (leistungen) of consciousness." "The Last Work of Edmund Husserl, Part II," p. 379.

13. *Krisis,* p. 229.

14. Cf. *Krisis,* p. 230.

15. *Krisis,* p. 20.

16. For these two points see *Krisis,* pp. 54, 57.

17. *Krisis,* pp. 308-309, 326-327.

18. In a similar vein Heisenberg has maintained that the thematic interest (to use Husserl's terminology) of science is not "nature itself" but rather "man's investigation of nature." *The Physicist's Conception of Nature* (London, 1958), pp. 24, 29.

19. *Krisis,* pp. 426-427.

20. An analysis of the ambiguity of the term "mastery" will be found in my dissertation, chapter 3, sections III-V.

21. The first quotation is from Bacon, *Preparative towards a Natural and Experimental History,* in *The Works of Francis Bacon,* ed. Spedding, Ellis, and Heath (London, 13 vols., 1857-1872), IV, 257. The phrases "veil of ideas" and "veil of symbols" are from Husserl, *Krisis,* pp. 51-52.

22. For details on the defoliation program see the report prepared for the United States Department of Defense by the Midwest Research Institute, "Assessment of Ecological Effects of Extensive or Repeated Use of Herbicides" (Washington, D.C., 1967); on the proposal for orbiting space reflectors see *The New York Times,* 29 December 1966 (page 10) and 26 May 1967 (page 4). The current status of the proposal is unknown.

Richard Schmitt (essay date 1972)

SOURCE: "Transcendental Phenomenology: Muddle or Mystery?" in *Phenomenology and Existentialism,* edited by Robert C. Solomon, Harper and Row, 1972, pp. 127-44.

[*In the following essay, Schmitt challenges the grounds of phenomenology by calling into question Husserl's distinction between the transcendental and the mundane, and, therefore, the validity of the "phenomenological reduction."*]

Phenomenology is the descriptive science of the transcendental realm. [Husserl, *Ideas III* , 141]. The realm is accessible only by way of the phenomenological reduction. No one who has not understood what this reduction consists of, who does not know how to perform it and has, in fact, performed it can understand what phenomenology is and how to work in it. The fact that the terms employed by Husserl, for instance the word "transcendental", are familiar must not mislead us as to the novelty of the phenomenological project. More than once Husserl surveyed the history of philosophy in considerable detail to show that earlier philosophers were groping for the insights embodied in the phenomenological programme but failed to achieve them. [Husserl, *Krisis* 202-203].

Commentators have, on the whole, written about Husserl as if they had found no serious difficulty in understanding the transcendental-phenomenological reduction. For myself, I have never been so fortunate. This paper is an attempt to articulate my hesitations and uncertainties about Husserl's repeated discussion of the *epoché* and reduction. I will argue that the descriptions of the *epoché* and the claims made for it presuppose the distinction between the mundane and the transcendental domain. This distinction, we shall find, cannot be made clear because it arises from a series of confusions. Husserl's great discovery is a muddle.

I

In the phenomenological *epoché* we abstain from all affirmation and negation with respect to a large range of objects. "Affirmation and negation" refers not only to explicit acts of affirming or denying but to all those mental acts in which some beliefs are ingredients. [Husserl, *Ideas I* 256ff.]

This kind of abstention is an important ingredient in the transition from straightforward thinking to reflection. Husserl's description of the *epoché* thus is a description of the transition from a non-reflective to a reflective attitude. Husserl is aware of that. The phenomenological *epoché* is the transition from non-reflective to reflective thinking of a very particular sort, namely to a universal reflection. Phenomenological reflection differs from ordinary, mundane reflection in its scope. It is not just reflecting about this or that particular subject. It is reflection about everything. [Husserl, *EP* II 154-155; *Id I* 119]

But how are we to understand this? While it seems clear that reflection, in the sense under discussion, requires a partial suspension of affirmation or negation, it would seem that a complete suspension of all such acts, past, present and future would make any reflection following this change of attitude impossible.

Reflection requires a subject matter. That subject matter must be identified and it must remain the same in the course of the reflection and unless I am at least prepared to assert that I am reflecting about . . . and that the different stages of my reflection are about one and the same subject, reflection is impossible. If the case about which I am reflecting is purely supposititious, I must at least be prepared *to assert* that I suppose to the case under consideration to have . . . features. Reflection, moreover, is a process in which I do not merely entertain disconnected propositions but I connect propositions in various ways with each other and I must be prepared to assert some logical connections between these propositions even if each of them begins with "Suppose that . . . ." In order to make such assertions about the logical connections between my suppositions, I must be prepared to make other assertions about the meanings of the propositions connected with each other and that may involve talking about truth conditions of these propositions. But these truth conditions of what I suppose to be the case are not themselves supposititious. I must be willing and able to assert them, if I am to engage in anything that could possibly be called "reflection".

Husserl is aware of this difficulty and provides a clear-cut solution. The university of the *epoché* is qualified. Specifically, it is restricted to the world of the "natural attitude" [Husserl, *Ideas* I, 67]. What is that distinction? Husserl more than once speaks of "transcendental experience" which we are enabled to have once the transcendental-phenomenological *epoché* has been performed. The subject matter of this transcendental experience is said to be "transcendental subjectivity" with "transcendental, immanent experience." This is the domain of "my pure life with all its pure, immanent experiences . . . the universe of *phenomena.*" [Husserl, *CM* 58-61] But are we as practicing phenomenologists in a position to make any affirmations or negations concerning these experiences and the ego and immanent experience etc.? It seems clear in the light of what I said before about reflection that we do make affirmations and negations in the phenomenological attitude. All we abstain from is affirming or denying anything concerning the mundane objects and their existence. It is *their* existence that is bracketed, not that of the transcendental domain and whatever is in it. It is ordinary experience and the judgments it involves that is suspended and not transcendental experience. It is clear at this point that Husserl operates with an implicit distinction between two senses of "to exist", two senses of "experience", two senses of "immanent experience", of "self" and of other concepts. For each of them we must distinguish the transcendental from the mundane sense of that term. We can understand and practice the *epoché* only if we understand that distinction. The *epoché* is legitimate only if the distinction between the mundane and the transcendental domain is legitimate.

It is clearer now what question needs to be asked and what occasions the difficulty in understanding Husserl's descriptions. The difficulties hinge on the difficulty we may have in understanding the distinction between the transcendental and the mundane. We have thereby discovered a central issue in Husserlian phenomenology: the claim that there is a transcendental domain. This claim will require a good deal of discussion.

II

An essential ingredient in Husserl's support for the existence of a transcendental realm is the argument from the possible "destruction of the world:"

> . . . the being of consciousness, of any stream of immanent experience, would of course necessarily be modified by a destruction of the world of things, but would not be affected in its existence
>
> [Husserl, *Ideas* I 115].

The expression "destruction of the world" refers to one's experience becoming chaotic. The change is not one from experience of the world to experience of an utter void, but one from ordered to disrupted experience.

At the heart of this argument to support the existence of a transcendental realm is a claim about the central feature of consciousness which Husserl, following Brentano, calls "intentionality". Conscious acts are said to be such that a true description of any act does not entail that the object of the act exists or has the properties attributed to it in the description. It follows from this that the object of any given act of consciousness cannot justifiably be asserted to exist (except in rare cases) unless there are other acts which support that assertion. Thus it is possible that acts as they follow one another fail completely to give evidential support to one another. But in that situation the individual acts, Husserl tells us here, remain intact and can be described. What thus remains, Husserl seems to suggest, is the transcendental realm. The present argument for the mundane-transcendental distinction, namely that if experience became chaotic, there would still remain the individual intentional acts, thus rests directly on Husserl's views about intentionality.

It is obvious however that this concept of intentionality will not by itself yield the distinction between the transcendental and the mundane. It does not follow from Husserl's analysis of intentional acts that intentional acts are not psychological and therefore 'mundane'. We may admit that Husserl's statements about intentional acts are not empirical psychological statements but are, instead, analyses of the concepts of intentionality and of evidence. None of this implies that the acts themselves and their concatenation in actual sequences are anything but contingent events that are properly studied by the empirical methods of the psychologist. Eidetic reflection about intentional acts and evidence may yield the analyses that Husserl provides. But this no more implies that individual intentional acts are transcendental rather than mundane occurrences which are to be studied in empirical psychology than that the possibility of making philosophic points about the concept of nature implies that there is no empirical natural science or that nature is a "transcendental" domain.

III

One question recurs, with slight variations, again and again in Husserl's writing:

> How are we to understand the fact that the 'in itself' of objectivity can become 'idea' and even be 'grasped' in knowledge and thus, ultimately, becomes subjective again . . .
>
> [*LU* II, 8].

> . . . we do not understand what sense a being can have which is in itself and nevertheless is known
>
> [*LU* 30].

> Whatever meaning it [i.e., the world] has for us . . . is meaning which is formed in our subjective genesis; every claim to existence is validated by us . . . ; that applies to the world in every respect, of course also in the self-evident one that whatever belongs to it is "in and for itself" whether I or whoever else happen to be aware of it or not
>
> [*Encyclopedia Brittanica,* 14th ed., **"Phenomenology,"** 288]

It is not terribly clear what the problem is that Husserl raises here. But the question raised seems central to any understanding of Husserl's distinction of the mundane from the transcendental. For that distinction is offered as a solution of the puzzle concerning the relation of what is "in itself" and what is "for us" pointed to in the passages cited. It is thus absolutely necessary for any more detailed understanding of Husserlian phenomenology that we try to state clearly the problem that Husserl only hints at.

Reference to a further problem, that occupied Husserl, will make it easier to throw at least some light on this one. Throughout his career, Husserl was concerned to avoid positions which he thought would lead to scepticism. In the *Logical Investigations* of 1900 he devotes a good deal of time to a position which he called "psychologism", the doctrine that logical laws depend on psychological facts. He regarded psychologism as a species of scepticism. [Husserl, *LU* I 110ff.] The problem of scepticism is raised again in a series of lectures given in 1907, ***The Idea of Phenomenology.*** In 1910 he published a long paper, **"Philosophy as Strict Science,"** in which he attacks psychologism once more but now extends the earlier polemic to the views of men like Dilthey—views which Husserl brands "historicism." The objection to these views is also that they lead to sceptical conclusions. [***PRS*** 323 ff.]. In his later writings, Husserl associates his own work closely with that of Descartes, specifically with the attempt to end sceptical doubts once and for all by means of systematic doubt and he repeatedly describes it as the goal of phenomenology to find an "Archimedean Point" [Husserl,

Krisis 82], an absolutely unshakeable starting point for the philosophical enterprise.

Does the distinction between the mundane and the transcendental realm resolve sceptical doubts once and for all or at least contribute to such a solution? If we are to answer that question we need to take a closer look at what Husserl calls "scepticism". In one fairly typical passage Husserl recognizes that Descartes uncovered the transcendental ego but criticizes him for misunderstanding that discovery. The source of the misunderstanding, Husserl thinks, is Descartes' failure to get a good grasp on the problem raised by the sceptics. There is a "frivolous" brand of scepticism which denies that we can know anything at all, on the grounds that we can never be sure that we have adequate evidence for any given knowledge claim. Such scepticism is indeed refuted by Descartes' discovery of the indubitable existence of the thinking self, for here we have at least one knowledge claim which is not open to challenge by the "frivolous" sceptic. Husserl regards this brand of scepticism as frivolous because he thinks that we are perfectly well able to discriminate true statements from those that are false [Husserl, *EP* I 54].

Descartes, however, thinking mistakenly that it needed to be shown that we can tell true from false statements, interpreted the cogito as one instance of indubitable knowledge. As a consequence, Husserl seems to suggest, he [Descartes] missed the properly transcendental nature of the thinking self. We begin to grasp this transcendental character of the ego only if we understand what Husserl thinks is the real problem raised by the sceptics, namely whether there is a distinction between "objective" and "subjective" truths and whether we are able to draw that distinction [Husserl, *EP* I 61-62].

Here we encounter again the difficulty with which this section opened, one that involves centrally the distinction between what is 'for us' or 'subjective' and what is 'in itself' or 'objective'. In some way Husserl is worrying about the concept of objectivity and about the objectivity of our knowledge.

But what shall we make of this worry? Specifically, what shall we make of his distinction between "objective truth" and "subjective truth" [*EP* I, 62]? It is not by any means unreasonable to say that the expression "subjective truth" is incoherent unless it means only "what someone (mistakenly) believes to be true." But if that is all that Husserl means by that phrase, his worry about scepticism is exactly that of Descartes.

Here is one more formulation of Husserl's question:

> Evidence, the rational insight, which gives preference to scientific judgments over the vague and blind judgments of everyday life, is itself a subjective occurrence in consciousness. What entitles us to give this subjective characteristic the status of a criterion for a truth which is valid in itself, which may claim validity independently of subjective, immanent experience? .
>
> [Husserl, *EP* I, 65]

After the refutation of psychologism was completed, that is after Husserl had argued that true propositions are objectively true, that their truth value is logically independent of the psychological or linguistic facts about the person asserting a true proposition, Husserl now feels uncertain as to whether we are justified in claiming to know such true propositions. What he seems to have in mind is something of this sort: We assert propositions either because they are immediately evident to us or because they are entailed by or supported by immediately evident propositions. Our beliefs and knowledge claims thus always rest on evident propositions and we *experience* that a proposition is evident [Husserl, *LU* I 13]. Are we entitled to take what is experienced as true to be true in itself? (The experience of truth yields, I suspect, what Husserl calls "subjective truth".) We have fairly complex criteria to separate true from false propositions. Suppose a given proposition satisfies all criteria. We shall certainly regard it as true. If it is true by our criteria, are we also entitled to call it true "in itself" that is, outside the context of human inquiry, inference and criteria? It is conceivable, is it not, that our criteria do not discriminate objective truth from objective falsity, but only discriminate what is true for us from what is false for us. The worry here is no longer whether there might not be further evidence bearing on any belief we have which would show this belief to be mistaken. The worry is not even that a corresponding mistake may have crept into the formulation of our criteria of adequate evidence. Presumably Husserl is satisfied that there are some statements which are true by our standards of truth and is also satisfied that at least some of the criteria we employ can be formulated in statements which can be shown to be valid. The worry is rather that the criteria of truth which we apply in all these cases may, although valid "for us", not be valid "in themselves."

One may object to these reflections, that they possess specious plausibility only due to misuse of language. The meaning of "true" and "false," the objection points out, is tied closely to our criteria of truth and falsity. The supposition that anything could be called "true" or "false" without conforming to our criteria for the use of these terms would therefore be incoherent. Husserl agrees. He recognizes that the words "true" and "false" can only mean what they mean for us now. Distinctions of this sort, as also the distinction between what is 'in itself' and what is 'for us' are, after all distinctions which we draw [*EP* I, 67]. All of these terms, 'true', 'false', 'in itself', 'for us' are terms in our language. The criteria employed for the use of these terms are built into our language. This however, once again, suggests to Husserl that the objectivity of what we know is compromised.

But this suggestion is the product of a confusion. On the one hand, Husserl seems prepared to recognize that words like "true" and "objective" mean what they mean in the usage of the most informed and thoughtful users of our language. On the other hand he wants to say that, therefore, our explications of these terms are valid only relative to us, i.e. that their objectivity is compromised. Such a claim implies that there is a sense to be given to "true" and to "objective" which is independent of our usage, our language and of the distinctions which we draw. But this claim is clearly inconsistent with the admission that "objective" and "true" mean what *we* mean by [them]. He seems to hold that the meaning to be given to our concepts, e.g. to the concept of objectivity, is that which we would give it after careful and exhaustive reflection and, at the same time, that these concepts have meanings independent of our usage so that we may ask whether what *we* call "objective" is objective by this other standard. But if we recognize this other standard, then the real meaning of terms is not relative to us, but only what we *think* is the meaning of terms and thus we would only be able to raise the sort of sceptical question that Husserl imputes to Descartes and calls "frivolous." As applied to statements about the meanings of concepts, this scepticism would counter all explications of concepts, however careful and exhaustive with the question whether continued reflection about any given concept would not tend to show the explication given to be mistaken. If, on the other hand, we recognize only the distinctions which we draw, then only what we call "objective" *is* objective and then the fact that we draw the distinction between what is objective and what is not does not compromise the objective validity of the explication of these two concepts.

It seems now that Husserl's worries about the relativity of our knowledge spring from using terms, particularly "objective", in two different senses, thereby generating a version of scepticism different from that of Descartes, which he [Husserl] regards as "frivolous". But like the distinction between two different versions of scepticism, [it] is confused. That distinction will therefore not do the job that Husserl claimed for it: it will not throw light on the peculiar transcendental character of the thinking subject discovered by Descartes.

We shall see, in the final section, some further considerations that tended to obscure the confusions from which spring the apparent problem of the relativity of knowledge to ourselves. But first we must draw some other distinctions, not drawn by Husserl, which lend some plausibility, however specious to the distinction between the mundane and the transcendental subject.

IV

The central claim of Husserl's transcendental phenomenology is contained in this passage:

> The objective world, which is, was or will be for me, with all its objects, derives, I said, its entire meaning and its claim to existence from me, as the transcendental ego, which first comes to light in the transcendental-phenomenological *epoché*.
>
> [Husserl, *CM* 65]

What meaning can we give to this concept of a transcendental ego and to the claim that the world is constituted by it?

One interpretation can be derived from Husserl's extensive and often extremely interesting analyses of intentional acts [See e.g., Husserl, *Ideas* I 174-375].

> 1. All acts of consciousness are intentional.

> 2. What makes an act intentional is a particular structure. Every act has a subject, an act-quality or 'noesis', and act-matter or 'noema', and an actual or merely intended object.

> 3. The objective world is constituted in complex series of intentional acts.

The sort of case that Husserl has in mind here is exemplified by seeing a material object, say, a red sphere and looking at it from different sides. The initial impression that we are seeing a red sphere may be confirmed by looking further at the thing. But it may also be disappointed. We may find out that the backside is green and concave. Our expectations are disappointed and we alter the initial description. [Cf. Husserl, *PRS* 25 ff.] There is no reason to believe that the relations between the noemata of different acts cannot be put in perfectly familiar logical terms. We may identify the noemata of different acts or recognize that they are different. In fact Husserl uses the term "*Satz* (proposition)" to describe a central core of the noema, and although this proposition is not, precisely, a linguistic entity it has all the essential characteristics of what are usually called propositions [Husserl, *Ideas* I 324]. Noemata are in a strict sense consistent or inconsistent with one another or entail each other. The relations between these noemata can thus, as far as we can tell, be formalized. The same, Husserl thinks, can be expected with respect to noeses [Husserl, *Ideas* I, 325 ff.].

On this account of constitution as the logical concatenation of noemata and noeses, we can draw an intelligible distinction between an empirical ego and a transcendental ego. In any given experience I perform a series of intentional acts. I may walk around the red sphere in different ways, or if it is small enough, pick it up etc. There are alternative sequences of acts that may yield the same result. But all of these series must, if they yield a correct result, instantiate certain general formal rules about the correct concatenations of noemata and noeses. We may say then that the term "empirical ego" refers to the actual sequence which many acts follow, a sequence which could be other than it is without affecting the outcome of the perceptual series and that the term "transcendental ego" refers to my series of acts insofar as they instantiate formal rules for doing this sort of thing correctly. There are passages to support such an interpretation. [See e.g. Husserl, *CM* 61-66]

But if the term "transcendental ego" refers to these rules, it is extremely misleading to refer to the set of them as an "ego". In the first place, this suggests, as Husserl clearly believes, that there are many egos. But there is only one set of formal rules, although many instantiations of them. Besides, egos are someone's. They belong to persons or are individual persons. But a set of formal rules does not belong to anyone, nor is it an individual person.

It would similarly be misleading to apply the word "constitution" to the way in which the formal rules determine the actual construction of knowledge and experience. The transcendental ego, in the present interpretation of that concept, no more constitutes the world (in any reasonable sense of "constitutes") than logic constitutes mathematics or, for that matter, traffic regulations constitute traffic flow.

More seriously, the conception of the transcendental ego as the formal rules instantiated in inference and other mental acts is clearly different from the transcendental ego described in the passage with which this section opens. It is simply false that "the objective world . . . derives its entire meaning and its claim to existence . . ." from a transcendental ego that is no more than a set of formal rules.

Husserl's failure to see that his account of the transcendental ego is not coherent was encouraged by further confusions.

The dependence of the world on the transcendental ego is often expressed in statements like these:

> Experience is the performance (*Leistung*) in which experienced being is there as it is, for me who has the experience . . .
>
> [Husserl, *FTL* 206].

> There is no being or being-thus-and-so, whether as actuality or possibility, unless it is as valid (*geltend*) for me
>
> [Husserl, *FTL* 207].

If we were to rewrite this and similar statements in the formal mode, it would come to this: Whatever truth claims I make about the world or about myself, the evidence I provide for these claims will contain at least some first-person statements. What is more, these first-person statements are of different sorts and appear in different contexts. The most obvious examples are statements in support of empirical claims. I support

> "There is a phenomenologist in the attic"

by detailing a series of fairly complex observations and inferences from these observations. Observation statements and inferences if challenged will be further backed up by saying "I saw . . ." and "From *p* I inferred *q*." Different first person statements will come up in the conversation if my criteria for knowing are challenged. Suppose you accept my observations and the inference but believe that the evidence I have produced does not entitle me to claim that I know that there is a phenomenologist in the attic. I may reply "I call it knowing if. . . ."

These observations are, I think, unobjectionable. This is in fact what lends considerable plausibility to Husserl's gropings, that his starting points are impeccable. Thus most epistemologists would certainly be willing to say that certain first-person statements, for instance, are the court of last resort if someone's observation statements are challenged. Usually this presents certain problems to the epistemologist, precisely because he has to make clear the nature of the transition from the report "I saw a . . ." to a valid claim of the form "There was (is) an. . . ." But it is not usually taken to imply that there is a transcendental ego on which the world and our knowledge of it are dependent. It is not too difficult to see, however, how Husserl is led to these opinions.

Husserl does not speak of first-person observation statements, he speaks, instead, of perceptual acts. [There are good reasons for using the act vocabulary in contexts of this sort, for speaking say of evidencing acts rather than of evidence statements: not all experiences, observations, sensings are put in words. But it is what we experience, observe, sense that is evidence for empirical knowledge claims, not just what we *say* we experience, observe or sense.] He also uses the act vocabulary to talk about the merely formal features of inferences. [See e.g. Husserl, *CM* 111ff.; *Ideas* I 371 & 377ff.; *FTL* 171ff.] Both the sensing which validates reports of observations as well as the formal rules that validate inferences are said to be acts. Both sorts of acts establish the validity of our beliefs. Acts, moreover, are always acts of an agent, a subject. Thus we find ourselves with a notion of a subject whose acts support both our perceptual reports and our more general claims about the world. Once we accept this notion, it is not implausible to say that the validity of our knowledge claims depend on this subject. Since the formal rules which are one of the performances of this subject are not empirical rules it is, furthermore, not implausible to speak of it as a "pure" subject, i.e., one which is not known empirically.

But, of course, Husserl ascribes quite diverse functions to the transcendental ego and its acts. He ascribes to it the rules by which we validate series of acts, rules of formal logic and rules of evidence, and he ascribes to it the first-person statements which give last ditch support to observation statements. The former are plausibly said to be nonempirical but cannot really be said to be "mine" or "yours". The latter are clearly mine or yours but cannot be plausibly be said to be nonempirical. But both serve to validate, in different ways, my empirical claims about the world. Husserl's notion of the transcendental ego seems to confuse these two very different ways of validating empirical claims because he is not clear about the very different entities, referred to by 'act'. Once we let this confusion pass, it is easy to speak of an individual that is not empirical which provides these validations.

V

One further confusion must be noted. It throws additional light on the genesis of Husserl's concept of the transcendental ego. It also helps to clarify further the earlier problem, how things can be both 'in themselves' and 'for us'.

Husserl uses the term "act" in two radically distinct senses. He tells us, on the one hand, that "act" is not to be construed as "action":

> As regards the talk about acts, on the other hand, one may, of course, not think here of the original meaning of *actus;* any idea of activity must remain completely excluded
>
> [Husserl, *LU* II 379].

A footnote to this passage makes some suggestion as to what sort of distinction Husserl has in mind when he differentiates acts from actions.

> We completely agree with Natorp (*Introduction to Psychology,* p. 21) when he objects that we must not take talk of mental acts seriously as actions of consciousness or of the ego: "Consciousness seems to be a doing and its subject a doer only because it is often or always accompanied by striving." We reject the mythology of actions, we define 'acts' not as mental activities but as intentional, immanent experiences
>
> [*ibid*].

The term 'action' refers to a doing, to the sort of thing which involves striving or trying, and thus, presumably, success or failure. Actions bring something about, if they succeed, or fail to do so. None of this is true of 'acts'.

The adoption of a second sense of act as action is quite explicit in a later passage, written in the mid 1920's:

> When we speak of producing in other contexts we have reference to the domain of the real. We mean the producing of real things or processes by doing. . . . In our case we have non-real (*irreale*) objects before us which we treat and shape by acting in this way or that, being all the while directed towards them and not towards psychological realities. . . . We may now weaken [the claim] that what takes place here is seriously a doing that shapes, an activity. . . . Indeed, judging (and in its originality, of course, in a special way judging which yields knowledge) is also a case of acting . . . in judging something non-real is constituted intentionally
>
> [Husserl, *FTL* 149].

Here the difference between acts in the psychological and the phenomenological sense is no longer a difference between action as full-fledged doing, that takes time and brings something about and an act of which neither of these is true, but is rather a difference between the objects brought about. In the psychological sphere they are real objects (i.e. spatio-temporally located objects) whereas that is not true in the phenomenological sphere. But in both cases we speak, apparently without shift of meaning or metaphorical usage, of an action, a doing, which may also be called "constituting" and thus sounds very much like making.

Husserl thus gives two quite distinct meanings to the word "act." In the sense which the term takes in the early writings, acts differ from one another as seeing differs from imagining for instance. These differences presumably can be expressed as *purely logical differences* between what is in one case seen and in the other imagined i.e., as different logical features of the contents of these acts. There is e.g., an oddity in "I saw a unicorn but unicorns do not exist" whereas there is no oddity in "I imagined a unicorn but unicorns do not exist." No more is meant by "act" than that. There is no implication of something being done, of something being produced. Yet all of this is what is meant by 'act' as Husserl uses it in *Ideas* in 1913 and later, in 1929, in *Formal and Transcendental Logic.*

Husserl never seems to notice that the word "act" is used in these utterly diverse senses. If we fail to draw this necessary distinction, it becomes easy to find the objectivity of our knowledge problematic. For if we use "act" in the sense of "action," specifically of "making," what we know and experience is made by us and is, in this way, dependent on or relative to us. That relativity extends to everything, including concepts like "objectivity". But if we then move surreptitiously to the earlier concept of act, where act differences are purely logical differences, our acts do not affect what is known and experienced and thus knowledge and experience can claim objectivity in a sense devoid of all dependence on or relativity to a subject. Using the two senses of act interchangeably further encourages use of two sorts of meaning ascribed to "objectivity" (noted previously in section III) and thus gives added support to the pressing, albeit confused, worry about the relativity of the world to ourselves as subjects.

Once this confusion has been let by, it is easier to speak of a transcendental ego as a genuinely individuated subject which, in addition, is in some sense numerically identical with the empirical ego [*EP* I 340]. For the failure to separate different senses of act goes hand in hand with failure to differentiate corresponding different senses of 'subject'. The subject of an action is, like this action itself, at least partially individuated by its position in space and time. Actions occur at particular places and times, and thus the agent must be locatable in space and time. If, on the other hand, we mean by 'act' certain formal features of actions, reference to acts does involve reference to subjects, but since acts, as purely formal features are neither in space nor in time, the corresponding subject is also not spatiotemporally located. Given the confusion of two senses of "act" we very conveniently get the notion of a subject that performs full-blooded actions—it senses, observes, believes and infers—and yet is, as subject of formal features of acts, not located in space and time. Thus we can ascribe actual mental actions to a 'pure subject'.

In this way we can understand some of the sources of Husserl's notion of the transcendental ego and of the relativity of our knowledge—a problem resolved by the discovery of the transcendental ego. Both problem and solution, we have seen, are irremediably confused. Our persistent uneasiness about the transcendental-phenomenological reduction thus turns out to be justified. That methodological move, we saw, is only intelligible if

the mundane-transcendental distinction is already available. If, as it now turns out, that distinction cannot be drawn, the transcendental-phenomenological reduction cannot be performed. This does not mean, of course, that there cannot be philosophical reflection about concepts. But it does mean that Husserl's injunction to perform universal reflection is not intelligible.

VI

If one argues for an interpretation of a given philosophic text one must make heavy use of arguments to show that alternative interpretations would make the text come out self-contradictory. On the assumption that the author of the text did not contradict himself one can reject a number of interpretations which seem plausible at first because they seem to fit specific passages. Without this appeal to the consistency of the author interpreted it is more difficult to defend a reading of a philosophic text. The interpretation which I have given in the preceding sections obviously cannot use this appeal since the claim here is precisely that Husserl's writings are shot through with inconsistencies. This makes it hard to defend this interpretation against other readers of Husserl who agree in general that Husserl is inconsistent but find the inconsistencies in different places.

But the preceding arguments have built up a strong case against those readers of Husserl who want to hold that the discussion of the transcendental-mundane distinction is intelligible and can be made clear. For the preceding arguments constitute a challenge to those readers to show that the difficulties I have found in Husserl are readily resolved and that the questions I have raised have answers. I can see no way of escaping the conclusion that Husserl's transcendental phenomenology is a big muddle. Should this conclusion be false, I have at least shown that, so far, it is a mystery.

Marx W. Wartofsky (essay date 1972)

SOURCE: "Consciousness, Praxis, and Reality: Marxism vs. Phenomenology," in *Husserl: Expositions and Appraisals,* edited by Frederick A. Elliston and Peter McCormick, University of Notre Dame Press, 1977, pp. 304-13.

[*In this comparison of Marxism and phenomenology, originally presented as a lecture in 1972, Wartofsky shows the errors of phenomenology from the Marxist point of view.*]

The beginning of phenomenology is the reassertion of subjectivity. The beginning of Marxism is the attack upon subjectivity. To contrast Marxism and phenomenology is to find, in the first place, the common point of departure for each, the common *Problematik* to which each addresses itself. Otherwise we are in the strange position of counterposing two indifferent world views or two incommensurable methodologies, without mediation. It is clear from the history of the subject that Marxism and phenomenology are not alien to each other. First, phenomenological themes lie at the heart of the origins of Marxism in Hegel and Feuerbach.[1] Second, there is a major current within Marxist theory which engages phenomenology, if it does not in fact adopt its stance. I refer here to Lukács and to an East-European Marxism, usually characterized as Marxist humanism, as well as to contemporary neo-Marxism of the Frankfurt or Italian variety.[2] Third, a major accommodation as well as critique of Marxism characterizes the problematic Marxism of the French phenomenologists, such as Sartre and Merleau-Ponty.[3]

I do not plan to enter into either a reconstruction of the Marxism of the phenomenologists or the phenomenology of the Marxists, or into the specific jargon of the schools. Just as "ordinary-language philosophy" at one point became a cottage industry in England (with branches abroad), this Marxism-phenomenology interaction has become a massive production enterprise of the word mills of Europe and America. The product is recognizable by its union labels: it is stitched with a plethora of philosophical neologisms, sometimes to the extent that the garment is hidden by the labels. These range from Hegelisms of the *pour-soi-en-soi* sort to Hellenisms of the *noema-noesis* sort to plain old Teutonisms of the *Vorhanden-Verfallen* sort. Nor do I mean to be snide with respect to philosophy's right and need to re-create language and to neologize. We pursue our human inquiry through language and in language, and the shape and forms of expression are not simply images of our thought but its structures as well. Still I will try not to ignore but to neutralize some of the divergence of expression in the service of an analysis and critique.

The question to which I address myself is the viability of phenomenology, given the Marxist critique. Its emphasis is, therefore, the reverse of the more common question: the viability of Marxism, given the phenomenological critique. I want to raise the question, first, in terms of the genesis of Marxism and of phenomenology—that is, with respect to the problem which each finds as its originating matrix; second, with respect to the sharpest (and perhaps most one-sided and abstract) form of their antithesis; and, finally, with respect to a series of what I will call mediations in which the originally formulated *Problematik* and the originally articulated stances are subjected of qualifications or determinations which each view demands of the other. However, I do not pretend to aim for a synthesis of the views for I will conclude that Marxism succeeds where phenomenology fails, at the most crucial point of difference.

So much for the schematic program of the paper; now for the substantive focus. The issues which I take to be central are almost too bald to be stated in less than a vague and general way. They are, simply, the question of how consciousness is related to reality. And where the schematic answer is that this relation is achieved by *praxis,* or by *action,* how one is to characterize this praxis or action. My conclusion will be that the phenomenologists fail to give an adequate answer to the latter question because they fail

to realize either consciousness or praxis in its historical character, and thereby fail in their attempts to give consciousness a social or nonsubjective character.

1. THE GENESIS OF MARXISM AND OF PHENOMENOLOGY

By *genesis* I do not mean the historical generation of phenomenology or Marxism in its concrete details, either as a history of ideas or in terms of the socio-historical matrix of the two philosophies. Though this is the concrete account of the origins of these two movements, I intend something more modest: an abstraction from this historical genesis in terms of a characterization of the typical *Problematik* or problem-setting in which each arose. In short, what problem or set of problems gives rise to phenomenology? What set to Marxism?

Again, abstractly, we may say that phenomenology's problem is the reappropriation of the object. In response to the kind of objectivism which puts the objects of human knowledge or of human practice beyond the subject, phenomenology strives to effect a reconstitution of the subject-object relation as an *essential* relation—but essential from the side of the subject. The classical "object" is subjectivized in a recharacterization of "subjectivity" not as mere inwardness but as a structuring and creative activity which is to be studied not simply in its products—that is, not simply in its objectification or outward form—but, rather, from the side of the subject itself. Thus the "objects" are reconstrued in terms of what is to be found "in" consciousness, either from the point of view of its necessary conditions or its structures. Within the rationalist emphasis of phenomenology these are conceived as essences; within the existentialist strain as the concrete creations of human actions or projects. But in both they are modes of subjectivity in which the ego or the knowing-acting subject is the source and repository of these structures or conditions. The objectivity thus attained is a constructed or constituted objectivity, one with which the subject finds himself inextricably bound, from which he cannot absent himself without self-destruction, and, on another emphasis, one from which he cannot escape and in which he ultimately loses himself as a unique "I." The methodology of phenomenology therefore emphasizes the construction of the "world" or of a "life," namely, of the othersidedness of the ego as itself the inevitable concomitant of ego activity. In this, phenomenology turns out to be thoroughly Fichtean. The subject-object relation is a relation of and by a subject: "of" in the sense that the object is always "for-a-subject," and even its being "in-itself" is also, at the limit, an abstraction posited by a subject; and "by" in the sense that there are no passive subjects, that subjectivity is activity and the active positing of the other is the very being of subjectivity. In this way the "other" is always a clue to the character of the subject: the object can always be "read back," so to speak, as revealing the primordial or necessary conditions or structures of subjectivity itself. The relation with this "other"—whether it is realized as nothing else than the subject in its *own* otherness (and thereby the guarantee that all consciousness is ultimately self-consciousness) or whether it is realized as an intractable and totally alien "other" which stands beyond the subject as its delimitation, as what is ultimately "not-consciousness"—yet remains a relation with respect to a subject, or a relation in consciousness. It is easy to see where alternative influences can enter here: Hegelian, Kierkegaardian, Cartesian. But this is no more than a sketch and I will not pursue these alternatives.

By contrast, the genesis of Marxism lies in the critique of subjectivity not simply as a critique of the ego or of consciousness as the bearer of objectivity but as an argument against the theory of constitution or construction. The world, or a life, is not constituted by the activity of consciousness; rather, consciousness is constituted by a life or by the world. The ego is a product, not an agent; or in more cautious dialectical terms the ego is not an agent until it has been constituted. The world is not an achievement of the ego but, rather, the ego is an achievement of the world. In turn, the ego is then capable of *re*achieving this very world which generates it by way of reflection: it can then objectify what in the first place it has interiorized; it can project an image of the world from the fact that it is a subsumption or a product of this world. The world is therefore *not* an *other* for the ego or for consciousness, except on this reconstruction. The ontological stance is therefore totally different from that of phenomenology. The notion of "otherness" or "othersidedness" demands a subject for which the "other" *is* "other": the very logic of the concept "other" demands this. But this "otherness" is not constituted by the subject except as its own reconstruction of its own origin, as a subject. The world is therefore primordial, and primordial both to the ego and to its own reconstruction as an "other." The constituted world of the phenomenologist is therefore the image of the real world. But the phenomenologist takes this image for the reality of the world itself, and thereby makes a double error: he construes the ego as primordial, since the ego is primordial *for* the ego; and then he construes the world as the construction of the ego (albeit a necessary construction, involved in the very being of the ego itself).

In less metaphysical terms, the Marxist is a materialist in that he takes the world to exist independently of any relation to consciousness and therefore to exist primordially and prior to consciousness. He takes consciousness itself as a product of the activity of non-conscious and pre-conscious matter; and he takes the biologically live organism in its manifold of interactions with an environment, which includes other organisms both like it and unlike it, to be the context in which consciousness emerges. The specific context of biological life in which consciousness emerges is an interaction of organisms capable of reproducing their own existence and that of their species by the activity of production. Here animal drives for the satisfaction of life needs become something more than desires which are consummated without residue in sheer biological satisfaction. Instead, they give rise to means, to instruments, or tools. The drive therefore embodies itself in an activity which objectifies the need or, rather, which objectifies the *way* in which the need is met; namely, it objectifies the activity of satisfying a need in a teleological object or in the tool. This activity, then, is no longer mere animal activity but becomes production.

It is out of the activity of production that consciousness arises in the first place in the Marxist view. The activity of production, as a teleological activity embodied in a means of production and in the generation of relations of production which are involved in the utilization of such means, may be characterized as *praxis*, namely, as the distinctively human mode of self-reproduction. According to Marx, this involves two forms of organization, or rather a form of organization which has two aspects: that which has to do with the production of the means of existence and that which has to do with the reproduction of the species: production relations and family relations. It is out of this context that a necessarily social being is determined and a necessarily social instrumentality is developed: language, as an instrument of communication, and with it consciousness of a distinctively human sort, that is, thought. The separation of the ego, as a self-conscious agency or distinctive entity within this "ensemble of relations," is therefore a late achievement in this process, and not its origin. The ego is in effect constituted by this process of socialization and historicization of the animal. "History" becomes the self-conscious reconstruction of this genesis and of its sequence: but that there is a history before there is "history" is to say that there is a process of coming-to-be of the ego, before the ego can reflectively reconstruct this process.

In this theory of the genesis of the ego the ego's conscious activity becomes in turn an object of the ego. Since consciousness itself then serves as an embodiment or an objectification of praxis, it becomes the characteristic "tool" of conscious teleology, id est, an instrument of production and a necessary aspect of human labor. It becomes embedded, therefore, in the very structures which labor produces. And it is, moreover, capable of rediscovering itself there: it becomes, in effect, reflexive. It comes to know itself in its own objects insofar as consciousness, or the ego, is involved in the very character of production. The products of praxis are in this sense conscious products, but not, as such, mere products of consciousness or thought. Conscious praxis (all praxis is conscious) is the totality of human activity insofar as it is human—namely, insofar as it is not mere biological reflex, mere metabolism, or mere instinct—and therefore it is "thought" or reflective consciousness only insofar as reflection is part of the process of human production itself. It is "theorized praxis," not in the sense that there is "dumb" or "blind" praxis, which then may be either "theoretical" or not, if by "theory" we mean the conscious teleology of human praxis.

Yet it becomes historically possible to separate the reflective consciousness from its role in praxis because the division of labor permits a concomitant division of the reflective component in the actual organization of production.

The division of labor and class society, in the Marxist view, permits praxis to be fragmented: first, into its sheer mechanical component—its material component as the actual power to transform natural objects into objects for human use—and, second, into its rational or reflective component: the direction and employment of this power. The fullest articulation of this division comes about when the power to produce—labor power—becomes totally divorced from its teleology, namely, the production of use-values, and thereby becomes so-called alienated labor, whose teleological character is represented only in an abstracted form, namely, in the production of commodities or exchange values. According to a Marxist view, this division is the genesis of the abstraction of consciousness from living human praxis, and it is this abstraction which makes possible the reflection of consciousness upon itself as a praxis-free or purely theoretical activity of thought.[4] Yet even in this pure reflection of a divorced consciousness, praxis lives on as an abstraction, as a reflected-upon praxis, namely, as the "praxis" of thought itself, engaged in the "production" of its own "objects." It is the image of praxis which becomes the model for consciousness of itself: it "remembers itself," so to speak, in its origins, but only in this dim way. And so consciousness takes itself to be the agency, the source, the genesis of all activity. And it takes the objects of this activity to be its own so as to reveal consciousness to itself by means of its own objectifications. "Praxis" becomes "theoretical praxis," the ghost of actual human praxis.

But Feuerbach had already unmasked this self-deception in *The Essence of Christianity* with respect to the image of man in religion and in theology, and Marx had followed Feuerbach's critique of the Holy Family with a critique of the earthly family. Feuerbach writes: "Ghosts are shadows of the past. They necessarily lead us back to the question: What was the ghost when it was still a creature of flesh and blood?"[5] The ghostly *Praxis* which appears to purely theoretical consciousness as its own (i.e., theoretical) activity is nothing but flesh-and-blood praxis of conscious production and reproduction of man divorced from its living reality and represented as merely conscious activity, that is, as the mere activity of consciousness itself.

Thus consciousness, which in its theological form takes itself to be the image of God's thought, transfers this godly creativity of itself as its own inner activity, indeed as its very nature. This is Descartes' first *cogito*. But it does so by the grace of God; it remembers its origin and appeals to it, not simply to preserve its own activity but rather to guarantee the objectivity of this activity as more than an idle dream or a thorough deception. This is Descartes' second *cogito*. Objectivity appears here in its masked form, not as the origin and object of praxis itself but as the abstract and metaphysical Being of God. For God is the origin of the activity, and thereby the guarantor of its objectivity. Thus far Feuerbach had gone in demythologizing the relation of the ego to its other, and Sartre follows him to this extent.

But even this account of the origin of the ego, remembering its birth abstractly and in this alienated form, is far from Marxism, though it has the features of a materialist genesis. What Marx adds is the historical dimension of this process in a reflection upon reflection which reveals its pre-reflective genesis. It is only in social practice that the ego becomes an ego, namely, becomes capable of the actual production of a world in its own image: not in reflection merely but in the world itself. As the *telos* of human action, the ego enters into real transformation and real reconstruction, into real subordination of the external world, or nature, to its needs. And thus the ego reconstructs this nature as an object according to its needs both in practice and in theory; its theory, the ego, becomes the reflex of its needs and, in turn, the determinant of its action. It is not simply determined but both determined and determining. Its freedom lies in its ability to meet needs by its teleological direction of action or by its intimate involvement with a socialized body, one which is already more than has made it and is the repository of skills, attitudes, social needs—in short, a human body. This ego is a historical body, one which acts in a concrete historical context and is an agent of this history, as well as a product of it. It is this dialectical two-sidedness of the humanized and socialized organism which sets the ego above nature: it transforms its past into conscious action toward a future.[6] But Marx goes further. Insofar as the ego is historical, it has no essence as such, apart from the history of its actions. And as such it is neither disembodied consciousness nor merely embodied consciousness; it is social and historical consciousness, and acts from social and historical needs which are concretely manifested in a society of a certain concrete type. Its theoretical awareness is therefore not of abstract and eternal essences but of its own historical character, which it expresses in its action. Such a consciousness or ego is therefore inevitably caught up in the web of its time and place, of its concrete situation. It transcends this parochialism only by means of historical action, id est, action which transforms this time and place into another, which changes the world. By contrast, the ego which is forever bound to its time and place and which either cannot engage in the transformation of its historical locale or (worse yet) attempts to preserve the present atemporally is bound to a theoretical consciousness which sees all praxis as its own, id est, as eternal and unchanging. It imposes this abstraction of history upon history, and becomes ahistorical. So, Marx argued, bourgeois economic theory took its present as an eternal present and read back its one-sidedness or *stasis* into the very nature of things, into theories of nature and man as fixed essences in its own image.[7] Marx explains the social dynamic of this abstracted consciousness by a historical analysis, by showing the genesis of this mode of thought in the very situation of a historical period and in the praxis of a historical class.

In summary, then, Marxism takes the genesis of thought from beyond thought, and insofar as it does it is materialist. It takes the genesis of thought from beyond the thinker as an isolated individual and traces it to his social reality—the peculiar and distinctive construction of a world in which he finds his place. Insofar as Marxism does this, it is a historical materialism. It takes thought beyond thought in its history—in its relation to other thought, and as itself a process mediated by its history, by its material, by its objects, by what it derives from, by what it attains to, by what it interacts with. And insofar as Marxism does this it is dialectical.

In such a view, the phenomenologist is seen ultimately to derive thought from itself and all else from the activity of thought.[8] Phenomenology infects history with thought, infects the body with thought and the world with thought, and sees everything in an essential relation to consciousness, from which it cannot be rescued. In general, then, on this sharp antithesis Marxism is a materialist theory of consciousness; phenomenology is only the latest and perhaps the most subtle idealist theory of consciousness.

2. THE FIRST MEDIATION

Stated in its sharpest form, the antithesis appears as one between "objective" Marxism and "subjective" phenomenology. Marx himself paid homage to idealism when, in contrasting it with mechanistic materialism, he noted that idealism had developed the notion of self-activity, of agency, by contrast to the mechanistic conception of matter as dead, inert, mere extension. But the charge may be brought—indeed *has* been brought—against Marxism—if not against Marx, then against Engels; if not against Engels, then against Lenin; and if not against Lenin, then certainly against Stalin—that Marxism itself has fallen into the trap of "objectivism": that it has overlooked at best, and at worst deliberately destroyed, the subjective, active, agential, and therefore free nature of the human and has subjected it to a determinism borrowed from that very mechanistic physics which Marx himself held in disdain as undialectical. Marxism thereafter fails to deal with subjectivity except as a reflex, and therefore as a mere epiphenomenon, incapable of a truly dialectical interaction with its object. Thus subjectivity is not seen in its activity at all, except in an objectified form, as praxis, id est, as mere externality. Subjectivity is lost in the objectification of praxis. And whereas Marx *does* see labor, production, consumption, distribution, exchange, etc., as the activity of a "subject," this subject is an empty shell, an automaton. Though it may be an active subject, it is "active" in the sense that matter is active, or even self-active. The active subject has no subjectivity, no interiority. Its only "interiority" is a reflection of its external relations, and thus simply a displaced exteriority. So the constitutive activity of consciousness becomes, in the context of praxis, nothing but a mere reflection or epiphenomenon of praxis, and ultimately redundant as an agency in the world. And so Marx's claim to the efficacy and instrumentality of consciousness vanishes in this objectivism. It is all very well to say that when an idea grips the masses, it becomes a material force. But what is this "idea" but the ghost of an idea, an un-thing? Phenomenology, on the other hand, sees structures of the world, or life, or history in essential relation to an agential praxis—the praxis of consciousness itself—whereas Marx denigrates this human praxis, this self-conscious activity, as mere *work,* as mere externality.

To the extent that phenomenologists sometimes argue that Marx has this phenomenological sense of the ego, of the self-activity and interiority of consciousness, they attempt to save Marx from the Marxists: they counterpose a voluntaristic, existential, or Hegelian Marx to the crass "positivism" of Engels in the *Dialectics of Nature,* or of Lenin in *Materialism and Empirio-Criticims.* Here the early Lukács and the Karl Korsch of 1923 become relevant to the phenomenologist, as well as to revisionist or humanist Marxism.[9] For in this critical view the "active" or "subjective" side of Marxism, its "phenomenological" side, especially as it is found in the Feuerbachian and Hegelian Marx of the *Economic-Philosophic Manuscripts,* has not yet fallen into the patterns of scientism and determinism which empty man of his subjectivity and leave him merely a historical puppet, playing out a socially fated role.

3. THE SECOND MEDIATION

The dialectical alternative to beginning from the "outside in," so to speak, is to move from the inside out. In eschewing the mere phenomenality of the self or its mere externality in the positivist tradition, phenomenology begins at the center, so to speak, with the activity of consciousness itself, or the ego, not merely "posited" but arrived at by stripping away all exteriority and all the standpoints which encumber the pure, presuppositionless activity of consciousness. Phenomenology thus begins with Descartes, with a series of "bracketings" which reduce or suspend the a priori presuppositions of one or another standpoint in order to get behind them to their constitutive genesis. In the *Krisis,* for example, Husserl subjects the mathematizing-Platonizing a priori of contemporary science to such a reduction in order to get to the life-world or world of "lived" existence, of which this scientific a priori is the idealization or reification. Once we get to the life-world, another *epoche,* a suspension of its standpoint, perhaps gets us behind it to its presuppositions, as the philosopher proceeds to peel away the layers or accretions of construction to reach the primordial constitutive activity itself. But every concrete *Lebenswelt* has its standpoint, its empirical or lived praxis; and behind them all we seek what constitutes this praxis distinctively, until at the limit we have achieved the universal or transcendental *basis* of every possible reification and of every possible praxis; and here we find the transcendental, that is to say, the presuppositionless and inexpugnable subjectivity which is the primordial ground of every constitution.

"No object without a subject." Very well. But then *human* objectivity cannot be conceived except in its dependency on human subjectivity. What is part of the world for man is nevertheless what it is *for* man. And thus we have but two choices open to us: (1) that man, in his consciousness, is merely the reflex of the world, its mirror, or spectator, and subjectivity is passivity; or (2) that the subject is at the very least an activity of engagement which modifies or reconstructs the world, so that what is *given,* so to speak, is inextricable in its givenness from the relation to a subject. At the limit, we may conceive of this givenness as ultimately brutish, impenetrable, totally opaque to the subject. But then the subject is once again faced with passivity in the face of the given, or realizes its negativity, its "nothingness," in the face of this brute existence. What it "does," so to speak, is its own affair. And so, at worst, the subject is condemned to a meaningless play *within* subjectivity, forever alienated from being-as-such. Or the subject may take this being-as-such as ultimately meaningless and create itself, in spite of this, as a self-contained activity. The subject therefore makes its own life out of itself, out of its subjectivity, its willfulness, its activity as the *only* meaning-giving activity, against a background as black as the night of matter in Leibniz' *Monadology.* The "other," as givenness, is totally other and hence beyond redemption. In effect, we arrive at the Hegelian move of the *Logic:* that being-as-such is nothing, is sheer negativity or abstract negativity—in effect, *non-existence.*[10] Existence, by contrast, is action. On the other hand, once objectivity is removed from mere brute givenness, once the activity of the subject is seen as construction or constitution of its own object, then the *nothing* is really nothing: it can be dispensed with, forgotten, ignored. The world is then not merely engaged by a subject but is constituted by it. Or more precisely, the world becomes a constitution of *subjects* which recognize each other, at least as "other" and yet not intractable. A socialized phenomenology, therefore, reintroduces otherness in an optimistic mood as the subject's otherness, not as isolated individual but as species-being or social—therefore as a *thou.* With this move, whether as *Lebenswelt* or as thou, phenomenology finally reaches the point at which Hegel and Feuerbach arrived more than a century earlier. Sheer subjectivity, in its singularity, its aloneness, ends in pessimism, despair, or in the ultimate self-reliance of the leap of faith. *Credo quia absurdum.* Socialized subjectivity finds its faith in the otherness of subjectivity, in a subjectivity suddenly rediscovered (after Kant, no less!) as intersubjectivity. It is no surprise, therefore, that Husserl's construction of a social or even historical *noema* is surprisingly like Russell's construction of physics from sense data, as the "noema" of a space of perspectives. Gurwitsch writes: "Because of the intentionality of consciousness, we are in direct contact with the world." But which world? The world which is essentially connected with the intentionality itself, of course, since *the world comes into being* out of this intentionality itself. But then we are at a dire point: the payment we have had to make for rescuing the activity of the subject from either mere passivity or reflection, or from sheer inwardness and irrelevance to the world, is in effect to ransom the world and objectivity to the sheer constitutive activity of a subject, singular, social, or transcendental. It doesn't much matter which, therefore, for the schema is the same.

But in its method phenomenology is intended to get behind this very presupposition itself, or at least to tell us where to stop because we can go no further. It has therefore transformed its very methodology into an ontology: the ontology of the theoretical philosopher or the Cartesian ego as the be-all and end-all of—of what? Of itself? For only God stands beyond it, and with the help of God the ego has surrendered, once and for all, its claim to centrality, to ultimacy, to primordiality. The ontology of this stance—if you like, the ontology of this theoretical praxis—is the ontology of pure theorizing or reflection: the dehistoricized and indeed dehumanized standpoint of speculation—timeless, static, and ultimately divorced from the very empirical praxis which it seeks to understand. For all its projecting, and acting, and constituting, it becomes a disembodied activity, and its conception of praxis is therefore a conception of a disembodied praxis. It is, in effect, a reification of theoretical praxis, but of a theory divorced from real praxis, from which theory takes its genesis in the first place and to which it returns by transcending itself as theory, or by negating its mere theoreticity.

4. THE THIRD MEDIATION

The first mediation took Marxism in its objectivist form and, from a reconstruction of the criticism of this "positivist" Marxism, argued that it lost the essential character of subjectivity and that it transformed subjectivity into a mere shell, or reflex of unconscious, or inert matter. Therefore such a Marxism violated the very dialectical character of subject and object which ostensibly lies at the sources of Marxism itself. The second mediation took phenomenology in its subjective form and argued to the ultimate enclosedness of this subjectivity as a failure to cope with the very problem of the relation of consciousness to its object, which is the origin of its *Problematik.* The third mediation is therefore obvious. It lies with an activist Marxism, that is, a Marxism in which the activity of the subject is fully realized, but not as an abstract and theorized praxis of consciousness. It seems to me that Marx offers this possibility in terms much less uncertain than one would presume from all the difficult discussions which have been generated by this question. The question is, simply, How does one get beyond the fatal egocentrism or idealism of phenomenology and yet preserve the content of real, and not merely reflected, interiority and agency? The question, rephrased, is how to put this interiority itself in touch with its own genesis, with its own transformation, and, thereby, how to avoid taking it as the ultimate and last refuge of ignorance? But this takes a metacritical, metaphilosophical move—"meta" not in the sense of yet "higher" levels of reflection but in the sense of that which dissolves the fated circularity of self-consciousness. This is to take the standpoint not of so-called "theoretical praxis"—a phrase Marx used in his dissertation to characterize philosophy[11]—but of a *theorized* praxis. It is, in essence, a very simple move; but the philosopher cannot make it. *Qua* philosopher, his praxis is *ultimately* theoretical, and no more. It cannot be more, if the philosopher is to remain a philosopher. Marx argues that the actual praxis of philosophy is the negation of philosophy: its dialectical negation, its transcendence, in political-social-human praxis; in the engagement not of theory, not of "criticism" in the theoretical sense, but of actual, practical criticism. In short, Marx's dissolution of the problem and his metacritical stance is so obvious, so absurdly plain, that only a philosopher could fail to grasp it. There is no solution for philosophy within philosophy. The attempt to get "beneath" the empirical praxis by *epoche* after *epoche,* the attempt to spin the world out of consciousness, or even to reconstruct it *in* consciousness, is doomed to failure. But here we have a paradox of a sort: the very critique of philosophy which argues for its transformation into a theorized praxis is still philosophy. But it is philosophy disabused—"disillusioned," as Marx liked to say, no longer caught in its own self-mystification. It is philosophy applied to the critique of what exists—and inevitably, therefore, a negation of its purely theoretical stance. There is no way beyond this, once Marx has done the metacritique of philosophy as *ideology,* namely, as the theorization of actual praxis, tied inevitably to its time, its place, its historical and social genesis *as* philosophy. It transcends itself only insofar as it is able to transcend its own condition, its own genesis, its own basis in a historical praxis, its own *class*-orientation, therefore. But it can do this only if it transforms its reality—not by reconstituting its world in thought but by reconstituting its world in reality by practical intervention, by the test of its validity, or of its truth. Philosophy does not measure itself against a given reality but against the very attempt to transform this given reality into something else.

The passivity and ahistoricity of phenomenology, despite its accent on the activity of the subject and on constitution, are in effect functions of its divorce from historical praxis. The divorce is not total, for historical praxis serves as a "world" for phenomenology, but a world reconstituted *in* thought, rather than constituted *by* thought as it claims. The constitution of a world, it is true, is the work of an active subject. But the subject is not a philosopher. He is a man. Moreover, his being is as a social being, as a historical being: his constituting activity is itself constituted by his history, which he transcends as he *makes* it. It is not received wisdom, and cannot be uncovered by reflection; it is achieved wisdom and therefore can only be won by practice in the world.

This presupposes a realism concerning the objectivity of existence, which is not derived from immediacy, from the *cogito,* but is rather the very condition for the structuring of a social and human consciousness. Man creates himself, certainly, but by his biological-historical activity and agency in which consciousness has both its genesis, and in turn, its agency.

Notes

1. G. W. F. Hegel, *The Phenomenology of Mind,* tr. J. B. Baillie (London: George Allen & Unwin, 1910). Baillie is the obvious work, but there is much more in Hegel, especially in the earlier works, for example, *Jenensen Schriften.* Ludwig Feuerbach's *The Essence of Christianity,* tr. Marian Evans [George Eliot] (London, 1881) is the most directly phenomenological work, but see also the newly translated *Critique of Hegelian Idealism* in *The Fiery Brook, Selected Writings of Ludwig Feuerbach,* tr. with introduction by Zawar Haufi (Garden City, N.Y.: Anchor Books, 1972), and his *Gedanken über Tod und Unsterblichkeit, Sämmtliche Werke,* vol. 1, reprinted from the Bolin and Jodl edition of 1903-11 (Stuttgard-Bad Canstatt: Frommann Verlag, Günther Holzboog, 1960).

2. Among these works available in English are Georg Lukács, *History and Class Consciousness: Studies in Marxist Dialectics,* tr. Rodney Livingstone (London: Merlin Press, 1968; Cambridge, Mass.: MIT Press, 1973); Gajo Petrović, *Marx in the Mid-Twentieth Century* (Garden City, N.Y.: Anchor, 1967); Svetozar Stojanović, *Between Ideals and Reality: A Critique of Socialism and Its Future,* tr. G. Sher (New York: Oxford University Press, 1973); Adam Schaff, *Marxism and the Human Individual* (New York: McGraw-Hill, 1970). The Frankfurt school has its contemporary expressions in such works as Jürgen Habermas, *Knowledge and Human Interests,* tr. Jeremy J. Shapiro (Boston: Beacon Press, 1971); Alfred Schmidt, *The Concept of Nature in Marx,* tr. B. Fowkes (London: New Left Books, 1971); and in the various works of Horkheimer, Adorno, and Marcuse. Enzo Paci, *The Function of the Sciences and the Meanings of Man,* tr. P. Piccone and J. Hansen (Evanston: Northwestern University Press, 1972), represents recent "phenomenological Marxism" of the Italian variety.

3. Jean-Paul Sartre, *Critique De la Raison Dialectique* précédé de *Questions de Méthodes* (Paris: Gallimard, 1960), is the crucial work; the section, *Search for a Method,* is translated into English (tr. Hazel Barnes [New York: Knopf, 1963·). See also Maurice Merleau-Ponty, *Adventures of the Dialectic,* tr. Joseph Bien (Evanston: Northwestern University Press, 1973), and *Humanism and Terror,* tr. John O'Neill (Boston: Beacon Press, 1969).

4. This is not to say that reflective consciousness—i.e. theory—arises only with commodity production. Yet the requirement for theory, as Aristotle knew in the *Metaphysics,* is a degree of detachment from workaday praxis even when that theory is a theory of this praxis itself—as it is, for example, when a priestly class is supported by a social surplus in order to intervene *theoretically* on behalf of this praxis. What is at issue here, however, is a theory of consciousness itself, taken as an abstracted object of reflection and divorced from its roots or applications in conscious praxis. Here, I think, the model of the alienated or detached commodity provides for the historical materialist the genesis of the (fetishistic) conception of consciousness itself as a detached and abstracted object of reflection, just as it is the development of a leisure class, not engaged in production, that provides the social concomitant of this abstraction. See my brief discussion of this point in *Conceptual Foundations of Scientific Thought* (New York: Macmillan, 1968). The psychological dialectic of this abstraction

and reification of consciousness is most fully analyzed as a feature of religious and philosophical consciousness by Ludwig Feuerbach in (e.g.) *The Essence of Christianity* and *Principles of the Philosophy
of the Future* (tr. Manfred Vogel [Bobbs-Merrill,
1966]), but there it is not given in any social or historical genesis.

5. Ludwig Feuerbach, *Das Wesen des Christentums,*
vol. 1, ed. Werner Schuffenhauer (Berlin: Akademie-
Verlag, 1956), p. 6. This, the critical edition, includes
all the variants in the three editions. The quotation is
from the foreword to the first edition (1841).

6. For a discussion of this see my "Telos and Tech-
nique: Models as Modes of Action," in Stanford
Anderson (ed.), *Planning for Diversity and Choice*
(Cambridge, Mass.: MIT Press, 1968), pp. 259-74.

7. See, for example, Karl Marx, *Contribution to the
Critique of Political Economy,* ed. Maurice Dobb
(New York: International Pubs. Co., 1971).

8. The change is most clearly relevant to transcendental
phenomenology. Whether Merleau-Ponty escapes it
remains, for me, an open question.

9. Georg Lukács, *History and Class Consciousness;*
Karl Korsch, *Marxism and Philosophy,* tr. F. Holli-
day (London: New Left Books, 1970).

10. *The Logic of Hegel,* tr. W. Wallace (London: Oxford
University Press, 1873), p. 161. Aron Gurwitsch,
"Husserl in Perspective," in E. N. Lee and M. Man-
delbaum (ed.), *Phenomenology and Existentialism*
(Baltimore: The Johns Hopkins Press, 1967), p. 52.

11. "Notes to the Doctoral Dissertation (1839-41)" in
*The Writings of the Young Marx on Philosophy and
Society,* ed. and tr. by Lloyd D. Easton and Kurt H.
Guddat (Garden City, N.Y.: Doubleday, 1967). p. 61.

Efraim Shmuelli (essay date 1973)

SOURCE: "Can Phenomenology Accommodate Marx-
ism?" in *Telos: A Quarterly Journal of Critical Thought,*
No. 17, Fall, 1973, pp. 169-80.

[*In the following essay, Shmuelli explores the degree to
which Husserl's phenomenology and Marx's dialectical
analysis are and are not compatible approaches to confronting alienation and establishing social change.*]

In the last decades serious attempts have been made to
bring together Edmund Husserl's phenomenology with
Marxist dialectical materialism. Although the phenomenological strain of Marxism could already be found in the
thirties, particularly in the writings of Herbert Marcuse,
this trend has become more prevalent after World War II.
In fact, the phenomenological approach became very
strong in some communist countries, particularly in Yugoslavia and Czechoslovakia. Before the Russians occupied
Prague, Karel Kosik's book, *Die Dialektik des Konkreten*

(1967), exercised considerable influence.[1] These attempts
to build a synthesis out of Husserl and Marx have broken
down barriers between two major intellectual trends which
were once considered irreconcilable. Husserl's description
of the crisis of Western civilization, and his passionate appeal to transcendental reason, intersubjective and universal, in his posthumous work, *The Crisis of European Sciences and Transcendental Phenomenology,* especially
opened some possible interconnections. Thus a host of
phenomenological Marxists or Marxist phenomenologists,
like Enzo Paci and Pier Aldo Rovatti and their associates
in *Telos,* try to discover Marxist problems, aims and methods in phenomenology, on the one hand, and a transcendental phenomenological grounding in the theory of Marx,
on the other.

One can sympathize with Piccone's statement that, "no
matter how much one tries to reformulate or strengthen
Marxism, it appears today as a set of slogans which at best
are presented with the pretenses of objective science. In
fact, they turn out to be so many categories which occlude
rather than clarify social reality."[2] This proposition, almost
a pronunciation on the bankruptcy of classical Marxian
theory, seems to describe a state of both socio-political
and theoretical affairs. Thus, neo-Marxism attempts to re-
live the Marxian heritage through phenomenology. However, great as the need of Marxism is for a phenomenological critique to make it relevant again, it is hard to
prove Piccone's thesis that "today, when Marxism is deep
in crisis, Husserl is to serious Marxists what Hegel was to
Marx."[3] I see even more difficulties in the following comparison of the same writer: "To the extent that Husserl's
Crisis can function as a starting-point for such a critique,
it can be considered the most relevant Marxist text since
Lukács' *History and Class Consciousness* and, as such, it
must be carefully studied rather than summarily dismissed."[4]

But Piccone himself is well aware of the difficulties involved in any serious effort to reconcile, or even accommodate, phenomenology with Marxism. For he admits that
"the *forced* synthesis of the two mechanically juxtaposed
frameworks (dialectic and phenomenology) is bound to
fail from the very beginning, for either phenomenology
ends up absorbed in the dialectic and ceases to be phenomenology, or the dialectic is frozen in the phenomenological foundation and ceases to be a dialectic."[5] Yet, he
believes there is a viable, i.e., scholarly and well-founded,
possibility of considering phenomenology as a "retrievable
moment of Marxism" and thus achieving a double aim, a
non-dogmatic Marxism and a socially relevant phenomenological theory.

It is the purpose of this paper to submit to a careful analysis one of the latest scholarly attempts in this direction,
namely Enzo Paci's *The Function of the Sciences and the
Meaning of Man,*[6] where he attempts to bring together
phenomenology and Marxism in a sophisticated and original way. It is the most systematic attempt yet to build a
synthesis between phenomenology and Marxism. Never-

theless, Paci himself characterizes his interpretation as a reconstruction and transformation of phenomenology.[7]

Paci's position can be stated as follows: Husserl's thought leads not only to the problem areas with which Marxism deals, but also to the same central ideas of human emancipation. Moreover, if one approaches Marxism from a phenomenological aspect, he may arrive at a critical Marxism. But generally Paci emphasizes that he is attempting to understand implications which were only hinted at by Husserl, "in a way not developed by Husserl himself."[8]

As for Marx, Paci attempts to discover "a most profound and most authentic aspect of Marx's work," namely, what Husserl calls the "transcendental foundation."[9] Marx's critique of political economy, Paci argues, has a paradigmatic character: it intends to reveal and demonstrate the root of objectification of all sciences and of the whole society. This is the historical, hermeneutical aspect of the problem.

The second aspect of the problem Paci's book poses is the systematic one, namely, the validity of arguments which claim to find in Marx's *Capital* the main thesis of transcendental phenomenology and in Husserl's *Crisis* a dominant direction towards the constitution of a new society and a new humanity as the *telos* of European civilization and its science. Distinct as these two aspects of the problem are, they cannot be isolated. Ultimately, it is the one decisive issue for determining whether an adequate understanding of Husserl and Marx can produce a valid phenomenological Marxism.

The concept of dialectic has a wide range of meanings and is, therefore, quite ambiguous. Nevertheless, at least two ideas are central:

1. Historically, dialectical method from Plotinus to Hegel and Marx held that every concept, category, or proposition implies its contradictory, contrary, or opposite. And even changes in the physical, social, or mental world are produced by contraries and oppositions and the struggle between them.

2. Therefore, dialectic ascribes a creative power to negation and the process of change becomes an advancement through rejections and conflicts towards a positive end which is the reconciliation of the struggling opposites.

However, these senses of dialectic are absent in phenomenology. For Husserl, as for Kant, the problem of the negative, e.g., the antinomies, contradictions, etc., is an embarrassment of thought which has to be removed.[10] Therefore, I agree with Piccone about the writers who, before Paci, worked on a synthesis between Marxism and phenomenology. Almost miraculously, however, Paci seems to transform Husserl into a "dialectician."

How, then, does Paci conceive Husserl's "dialectic"? Since the term is used by Paci quite loosely, it means a wide range of operations and intentions. It is a critique of experience in the direction of mediations between abstract individuals and the abstract totality. The transcendental subjectivity of the ego, which is the source and origin of world constituting is an intersubjective ego in a living society, becomes conscious of his own meaning according to a common intentionality. "The dialectic does not objectively unfold in front of other subjects as a separate, preconstituted and mechanical reality. The dialectic is inconceivable without subjects, and vice versa."[11] Dialectic, conceived as an objective process isolated from the subjects experiencing it, is a mythological construct, a mode of objectivism. Hegel's method, Paci believes, is criticized by Husserl and Marx alike as such an abstract construction.

For Husserl, Paci maintains, existence always surpasses itself in truth. Truth can never be possessed. It is a meaningful direction of being, the infinite intentionality for which the goal is always unreachable and it is in the world merely in the sense of a demand never fully realized. In this sense Husserl proclaims that "only spirit is immortal" because spirit is the movement by which the existence transcends itself towards the meaning of truth. The totalization of final truths is the infinite task of humanity.[12] Put differently: "Phenomenology aims at discovering and revealing all the ties connecting individual entities. This is what seeing the essence in the individual fact means."[13] Essence, in counter distinction to facts, is relational and not isolated, comprising the typicalities of all facts subsumed under it. The essence of the individual, for example, is his life as individuated in the progressive self-constitution, and the individual truly lives only in essential relations, that is, when the increasingly more rational social life of the community in its progressive self-constitution makes individuation possible. In this way, the essential and the factual, the general and the individual, are connected. Truths are connected to a system of universal relationships. "In this sense, Husserl denies the possibility of a science of separated individuals, the singular, or atomic, entities separate from relations."[14] Paci believes that this is the central sense of Husserl's dialectical method: the phenomenological concept of truth is essentially dialectical. So is reason in its quest for truth.

Furthermore, on the social level the world is given to every man (monad) in his modes of life, historical destiny, personal features, and finitude of all flesh. But in the human, finite vicissitudes of existence one finds a typicality, that is an eidos.[15] "There is a direction toward an agreement of ideas and a harmonious society of subjects implicit in the idea that every monad has of the world."[16] Philosophy is the science of this universality constituted in the world, and as such it is engaged in dialectic, i.e., in interconnections. Ultimately, then, the dialectical process, according to Paci's interpretation of Husserl, is aiming at the highest possible encompassment on both the cognitive and the social level. Every perception as an intentional direction implies other perceptions. Although this all-encompassing interconnection is always made possible, it can never be fully exhausted.[17] For social theory it means that "there must be a totality of meaning of the dialectic and a direction of truth of all groups and struggling communities. . . . There is no rationality coinciding with the reality of the world and history. In the dialectic, the classes and communities negated by other classes and communities tend to negate the negation. This means that subjects, groups, and communities are formed in a praxis and cannot oppose the positive meaning with their own self-destruction."[18] At the center of the dialectic is the active man who always remakes himself. Likewise, the world transforms itself in history.

One is entitled to argue that Paci uses the concept of dialectic most loosely in describing Husserl's notion of the reciprocal interpenetration of body and mind, and of the external and internal. In general, however, the concept is used by Paci for the interrelation between the part and the whole, when the part is absorbed in the whole in which it is fully realized. Paci then concludes that phenomenological reason is dialectical since it is not fragmented into theoretical, practical and ethical reason. It is a whole. Truth is the whole, and therefore dialectical, as in the philosophy of Hegel.

An analysis of any text of Husserl can easily dispel the attribution of a dialectical method in his phenomenology. Thus, we find that the either/or prevails over the mediation, reconciliation or any sort of dialectical *Aufhebung*. For example, in his paper, "**Phenomenology and Anthropology,**" Husserl insists, "It must, therefore, be possible to choose, once and for all, between anthropologism and transcendentalism without reference to any historical form of philosophy and anthropology (or psychology)."[19] By transcendentalism Husserl meant the cognitive process which aims at absolute, ultimately valid truths by grasping the changeless, essential forms of the world's intelligibility. Pure Ratio grounds cognition in order to be able to produce an explanation of fact. It is comparable to pure mathematics in its grasp of the a priori essences. Like pure mathematics which makes natural sciences possible, philosophy aims at the absolute truth, not at truth which is tied to specific historical situations, but at the ultimate truth which transcends all relativity.[20] True, the descriptive goals of phenomenology as a rigorous philosophy can only be approximated, and this only gradually. But this does not mean that they cannot be ultimately reached in apodictic insight by appealing to the eidos, i.e., to the pure a priori of any factual object or region of objects. How undialectically phenomenology discusses truth is obvious from the paper's insistence on the identification of truth with self-evidence and with intuition of absoluteness of transcendental subjectivity.

The reality of world objects cannot be naively presupposed as self-evidently existing. Therefore, Descartes grounded self-evidence in the subjectivity of consciousness. In this way, however, the foundation of all knowledge of world and of self in autonomous transcendental subjectivity became a problem in itself, in fact the central problem of phenomenology. Husserl emphasizes that transcendental subjectivity experiences "constant certitudes of

existence"[21] and ultimately asserts itself as the "apodictic ego," prior to the existence of the world. Transcendental subjectivity is not the concrete, mundane ego. It is rather the ego that brackets the existence of the world and to which the world presents itself in its phenomenal validity. Only by this reflective activity of bracketing the world and grasping it as a flow of the activities of experiencing and theoretical judgment does the transcendental field open itself. But in this change of attitude by the "phenomenological reduction," there comes to the forefront the fundamental contrast between the transcendental ego, with its apodictic absoluteness on the one hand, and the psychological ego with its historical relativity on the other hand. And Husserl assures the reader that only the consistent, although provisory, renunciation of the world through the phenomenological reduction opens the way to truly valid cognition, in the sense that transcendental subjectivity confers meaning and validity upon a world. Phenomenology is the science which elucidates the essential structures of consciousness, actual and potential, of meanings (noemata) which make the world objective, i.e., consolidate the varieties of temporal modes of consciousness in identical things. Husserl remind us that phenomenology interrogates consciousness in order to force it to betray its secrets, rather than interrogate nature as Bacon recommended.[22] In this whole discussion of transcendental subjectivity versus the psychological or anthropological ego, there is no mention of any possibility of dialectical mediation, nor is there interconnection considered dialectical. Rather, the either/or is emphasized.

Or, let us turn to Husserl's discussion of the phenomenology of reason in *Ideas* (Chapter 12). Clear distinctions are made here between assertoric and apodictic forms of evidential vision, between pure insight and impure insight, and ultimately between adequate and inadequate self-evidence. For example, Husserl maintains that in principle a thing in the real world, within its finite limits, can appear only inadequately. Many things are related to one and the same determinable X and continuously advance towards a more detailed indication of the possibilities which they present. They are filled out by a variety of aspects, strengthened or weakened, complementing each other and conflicting with each other. This is the realm of factual things in their mode of existence. But to every category of such things corresponds an essence (as explained in Chapter 1 of *Ideas*), an eidos which as a datum of essential intuition is primordially self-evident.[23] In the same chapter truth is defined as a correlate of the perfect rational character of believing certainty, that is, of that which is eidetically self-evident to an actual consciousness. In the final account, truth is identified with the self-evident position as a correlate of man's self-evidencing judging from the standpoint of the subject, "but is also a name for every kind of self-evidencing judging itself, and, lastly, for every doxic act of reason."[24] The point I wish to make clear is that Paci neglected the eidetic functions of transcendental subjectivity, which establish necessities and possibilities as an absolutely unassailable standard for the fact. The transcendental standpoint seeks out everywhere a systematic and "eidetic morphology,"[25] which cannot be found on a natural basis. It envelopes the whole natural world through the bestowal of meaning which conforms to essences. The phenomenological method consists ultimately in the elaboration of its central discovery of the importance of the intuition by which real existence can be conceived. Phenomenology aims to be the description of how essences, ideal constructs, make cognition possible, with absolute certainty. But the fact that apprehension of essences is a piecemeal operation, starting from singular essences and progressing to more comprehensive regional essences, does not make eidetic reduction dialectical.

It is clear that essence is not "individuation," as described by Paci above. The phenomenological epoche, the access to all essences, does the opposite of all individuation. It suspends any positing of reality. The real world, as it exists naturally, is neither negated nor doubted but bracketed. This assumes that the existent world is not necessary for the foundation of knowledge. Hence, the entire phenomenological method, with its techniques of bracketing, refutes the idea that an external existence can provide an absolute foundation for our knowledge of the world. We know by now that the primary, radical, apodictically-established foundation can be transcendental consciousness alone.

On this analysis, phenomenology is a non-dialectical, if not anti-dialectical, method of apprehension. Its basic techniques, e.g., the epoche, variations of the imagination, the "free fancies," eidetic and transcendental reductions show that none of this is dialectical in any accepted sense of the term. As a philosophy *qua* rigorous science, phenomenology aims at establishing a constancy of "universal humanity of reason as a binding necessity of the essence" ("Universale Vernunftmenschheit" als "verbindende Wesensnotwendigkeit").[26] Hence, truth for Husserl is not the dialectical movement toward the all-encompassing whole. We do not have to wait for the self-differentiation of the infinite self-positing consciousness and its coming back to itself before we intuit truth in a self-evidential way.

However, the problems of phenomenology, I believe, are capable of dialectical development, and indeed need such development. In special need of such development are the relations between the transcendental and the psychological subject, between essences and facts, between noesis and noema, between transcendentalism and historicism, between the primary life-world and derivative historical culture. The relations between the poles of subjectivity and objectivity are loaded with dialectical tensions and mediations. If transcendental subjectivity is indeed the absolute, it is constantly in need of mediating steps of self-realization. Paci attempted to develop some dialectical motif of Husserl's system, but since he did not realize the full anti-dialectical impact of phenomenological transcendentalism, he could hardly recognize the difficulty of his task and look for dialectics where they perhaps could be found, despite Husserl's conscous eidetic transcendentalism.

What does praxis mean for Husserl, according to Paci's interpretation? Since the totality of world experience is never actually concluded as an established reality, but is rather an infinite and teleological process, depending upon man's accomplishments, one may maintain that the meaning of all reality is constituted in human praxis. The world is a unity of meaningfulness which has to be constituted. For an object to be given means that the complexity and multiplicity of its ways of appearing come to a definiteness and unity, in virtue of bestowing upon it a definite individual meaning. This constitution is called by Paci, if I understand his interpretation correctly, praxis. Thus, theory and praxis are not opposites. Phenomenological theory is man's becoming conscious in time and in the world. It has universal validity because it rediscovers in every part, according to the principle of universal correlation, the horizon toward which this part is directed (every monad is intending) as to its final goal. Telos and praxis are correlated. Praxis seems to be the term for intentionality, constitution, and self-reflection rather than merely for acts guided by these operations of the transcendental subject. Praxis, then, for Paci, is identical with the most theoretical acts of foundation itself. The struggle against occlusion and oblivion of the subjective root of all constitutional acts, the clarifying of this genesis, and the arriving at universally valid results is for him "scientific praxis." Furthermore, phenomenology is described by Paci as the science of the life-world, as the act of becoming conscious, of man's historical situation.[27] Praxis, then, means both the theoretical foundation of phenomenological description of the world and the transformation of the world.

This is, I think, a misinterpretation of Husserl's intention. The relation between theory and praxis in Husserl's thought seems to be quite different. In what follows, therefore, I will endeavor to show how my view of this relation differs from Paci's. But let me start by underscoring that Husserl's self-reflection in the *Crisis* has obviously "bracketed" the real conflicts of the European scene on a national and international level, and thus it became a very general, reflective analysis, without providing directives for the solution of the pressing problems of socio-political practice. The ultimate aim of his critical self-understanding was only in a vague way connected with "praxis" in a socio-political sense. His main purpose was to rescue man from dispersion in scientific materialism. In this sense, it was rather abstract and academic. I would agree, then, with Marvin Farber's statement that "A philosopher who refuses or neglects to take account of the pressing practical problems of his day (the well-known ones: capital and labor, imperialism and war, etc.) incurs the cardinal error of making his reflection 'empty' in a most important respect."[28] Of course, Paci does not see Husserl's reflections this way. Paci makes the distinction "between mundane praxis and praxis free of the mundane." The former is conditioned by the various interests of the subject in his life work, the latter is disinterested, free from fetishism, and takes place in the historical world of inter-monadic rationality. This latter praxis, disinterested in partial fetishized goals but rather directed toward the whole, is the proper return to subjectivity in action, oriented toward a universal telos.[29] "The praxis free from the mundane provides the opening to the world as a universal horizon."[30] It reconstitutes the historical world as an intermonadic life with others. But this disinterested praxis was precisely called by Husserl theory, and in terms of the pressing world problems, this theory looks quite "empty," in the above sense.

What did Husserl really mean by theory and praxis? Husserl defined philosophical *theory* as the "knowledge of the totality of what is," in which no single truth may be absolutized and isolated. This function philosophy can fulfill only through phenomenology. Both the natural and the theoretical scientific attitude of modern naturalism which dominates Western civilization are naively one-sided "and constantly failed to be understood as such."[31] Both the natural attitude and scientific naturalism take it for granted that they can obtain truth in itself and do not notice that "they necessarily pre-suppose themselves in advance as communalized men and their surrounding world, in their historical time."[32]

In a passage of the Vienna lecture in which Husserl mentions *praxis* most emphatically, he stresses that his "new sort of praxis" is primarily a critique of the accepted life-goals as well as an intention to transform mankind into "a new humanity made capable of an absolute self-responsibility on the basis of absolute theoretical insights."[33] This will be the highest synthesis of theory and practice. Essentially, Husserl maintains that there are two fundamentally different kinds of praxis, derived from a theoretical framework which prescribes norms and procedures. The first kind of praxis is a set of operations in accord with the theoretical totality of hypotheses and is destined to function normatively, like logical operations. All praxis of this kind, based on science, is related to a sphere of interest, and has the practical aim of satisfying the needs implied in these interests. This interested practical activity is based on a dogmatic theory. Any theory is dogmatic where transcendental reflection is absent.

The second kind of praxis is based on transcendental reflection and is very often identified with it. This reflection considers thematically those who make judgments, and how they make normative use of the so-called laws. It is thematically directed also towards possible errors, temptations, and failures. The first type of praxis implies a naive ontology, either as suggested by the prescientific knowledge of the surrounding life-world or by objective science which transposes this prescientific, imperfect knowledge in accord with ideally determined "truths-in-themselves." The term transcendental (above) Husserl uses in the Kantian sense as "the motif of inquiring back into the ultimate source of all the formations of knowledge, the motif of the knower's reflecting upon himself and his knowing life in which all the scientific structures that are valid for him occur purposefully, are stored up in acquisitions, and have become and continue to become freely available."[34] The ultimate source in which all praxis and theory is grounded bears the title "I myself," subjectivity. The praxis of this

transcendental cognitive enterprise was described by Husserl as the most radical critique of accepted values, or the revolutionary elevation of mankind to a self-responsible humanity on the basis of absolute theoretical insights.

Logic too has to be founded transcendentally, if one wants to capture "the living intention of logicians."[35] Since the sciences have forgotten their intentional meaning by underscoring their logical procedures, this meaning has to be rediscovered and connected to time, to the constitution of the entire world by transcendental subjectivity. The sciences of the factual have a strong tendency to conceal the original meaning realized by the living experience.

For Husserl, theory is the establishment and elucidation of immutable first principles, e.g., that which lies at the base of knowledge for Aristotle, or the "Transcendentals" for Medieval philosophers. These first principles are the ultimate basis upon which the structure of our concept is built, precisely what Kant called transcendental. Theory discovers, explicates, and justifies the principles which are implicitly functioning in all cognitions, omnipresent but unrecognized.

In spite of his criticism of the metaphysical presuppositions of the classic and the modern world views as objectivistic, Husserl's concept of theory had moral implications which are very close to the classic virtues. His theory, oriented towards essential necessities, believed that contemplation of these necessities is the highest achievement of reason both in the cognitive and in the moral dimension. It leads to a life of self-understanding, that is, to human autonomy and self-responsibility. Husserl's strong emphasis, then, is on pure theory, from which he believes an enlightened, rational "conduct of life" emerges, as in the Platonic tradition. He believed that modern science, particularly modern physics, has abandoned the ideal of true theory, thereby becoming "naive and objectivistic," without insight into the connection between facts, laws, and theories of nature and the active pole of transcendental subjectivity which constitutes these facts, laws, and theories. The "inadequate" self-understanding of the natural sciences has had a devastating effect upon our whole Western civilization. The glory of modern sciences, namely their description of the world in its objective order, assisted by the mathematical model, is in fact the greatest impediment to the proper insight into the true structure of the world as regards both its subject pole and its object pole. This objectivism of the sciences neglects the transcendental basis of all possible objects of scientific analysis which are constituted in the self-evidence of a given life-world. The mathematical grasp of nature, as well as the technological control, must be retraced analytically back to transcendental subjectivity. If not, man is alienated from the sources of his selfhood. Husserl insists that this is precisely the difference between any scientific theory and his philosophical theory. Whereas all scientific theories originate out of the needs of human practice, particularly in order to secure what is given as existing, the phenomenological theory, although not losing any interests in the natural life-world, aims at clarifying the constitution of both the functioning practice and the scientific theory as well. Thus, theory, in Husserl, establishes the identification of being with intelligibility, in the sense that consciousness constitutes being, and only consciousness in its highest form as transcendental subjectivity is absolute being. It is the elucidation of the meaning of transcendental subjectivity as the absolute being and of its acts of constitution in their various modes, horizons, and regions. Such a theory is certainly not a retreat into an unworldly special field of study. On the contrary, Husserl believes that only phenomenological theory enables us to grasp in authentic knowledge both the world and human consciousness, and thus provides an all-embracing account of objectivity and subjectivity alike. But in opposition to Marx, Husserl insists that phenomenology does nothing but "interrogate just that world which is at all times the real world for us."[36] It does not change it. Ultimately, it changes us. "Phenomenology subjects this world to intentional interrogation regarding its sources of meaning and validity."[37] This is what theory discovered in Husserl's thorough interrogation of the world. Praxis, as mentioned above, leads into three directions, the third of which is identical with the totally disinterested steps of theoretical activity itself.

After this discussion of Husserl's concepts of theory and practice, let us return to Paci's interpretation. This interpretation was, from the beginning, oriented toward a reconciliation of Husserl's thought with Marxist concepts of theory and practice. A consideration of these concepts will contribute considerably toward an understanding of the scope and intention of the new phenomenological Marxism. What function does Marx attribute to theory, especially philosophical theory, and to praxis, and what are their meanings in his system? The intellectual endeavor actually to abandon philosophy by making it an effective power in the socio-political reality, in other words, to "negate" philosophy (that is, to dissolve it into its full realization and concretization), is a strong trend in dialectical materialism, deriving already from Hegel, but modified according to anti-idealistic premises. Dialectical materialism, in spite of its foundation in philosophical theory, neglected the elaboration of a theory of knowledge, of society, and of history grounded in a comprehensive ontology. It is not too difficult to find the reason for this neglect. It lies in the primacy which Marx bestowed upon praxis, which he defined as labor, the activity which produces the possible objects of experience; or, really, objectivity produced by man's activities. Labor is termed the "condition of human experience that is independent of all forms of society, the perpetual necessity of nature in order to mediate the material exchange between man and nature, in other words, human life."[38] The surrounding nature is mediated by man's process of social labor, which creates the conditions of social life. Moreover, it creates the conditions which make the very objectivity of any natural or cultural objects possible. In this sense, social labor is more than an instrumental technical process. It bestows meaning, it conditions cognition, making it possible as an instrument for grasping the very reality produced by acts of labor. It is a kind of

"transcendental" activity. Whereas praxis is active and future-oriented, theory (by which Marx meant mainly idealism) is contemplative and past-oriented, interpretative and not actively changing. Man, however, plans his future. Therefore, historical materialism must include "the energetic principle" (which Marx saw as missing in Democritus, and later in Feuerbach), in order to become an active power, and not merely a theoretical contemplation. This priority of praxis over theory does not mean that practical activity can be performed without theoretical insights. Revolutionary praxis certainly must be enlightened by the instructions of theory and follow true concepts. It is not sufficient to be practical in the sense of utilitarianism or vulgar pragmatism. Already in one of his earliest writings, Introduction to the *Critique of Hegel's Philosophy of Right,* Marx assured his reader that "you cannot abolish philosophy without realizing it," and, moreover, that this realization "can only be achieved by the negation of the previous philosophy, that is, philosophy as philosophy."[39] Against narrow-minded activists he defended philosophy, but against philosophers, that is, against contemplative quietism of theoretical abstractions and interpretations, he stressed his belief that philosophy cannot be realized without being abolished, that is, without change in form by a knowledge that leads to the realm of freedom. In this sense Ernst Bloch declares that Marx's Eleventh Thesis on Feuerbach ("The philosophers have only *interpreted* the world in various ways; the point is to *change* it") is "the greatest triumph of philosophy."[40]

However, for Marx philosophical theory could well be limited to critique, but in a sense different from the one employed by Kant. No logic, whether formal or transcendental, is Marx's point of departure for his critique, but rather the material processes of production and appropriation of products. His critique is ultimately a critique of political economy and an evaluation of the evolution of the system of social labor with its socio-political and ideological results. Although Marx acknowledges the importance of the superstructures, it is labor which conditions the configurations of consciousness and all their symbolic interactions and creations. This reduction to the modes of human labor and its history alone, limits the possibilities of Marx's philosophical interpretation to the impact of various aspects and techniques of work upon the ideological superstructure. His philosophy thus became a critique of capitalist society. Since the fundamental structures of social labor, and nothing else, are reproduced in the self-reflection of consciousness, all philosophy which does not consider the nature of man as a tool-maker and homo faber, according to the system of productive forces and relations of production which he confronts as something given, is, for Marx, merely "ideology."[41] Thus, Marx would negate Husserl's concept of theory as contemplative, interpretative, and abstract. He would compare it to Fichte's theory of the abstract subjectivity, or to the "I-idealism" and its world-abandoning praxis.

Is Husserl's philosophy complementary to Marxism in the sense of adding a new dimension—namely the emphasis upon transcendental subjectivity—for a theory of knowledge and for a comprehensive ontology? It is difficult to acknowledge that such a theory can be related to Marxism, except by a misinterpretation of both systems. Paci, as we have seen above, underestimated the significance of theory in Husserl. His point is that theory is reason, explicating the concealed telos of European civilization. The crisis of Western civilization, he believes, is a special case of the capitalist crisis in a naturalistic, objectified, i.e., sociopolitical system. The specialized, scientific worker objectifies himself in the sciences, which in their turn confront him as alien entities, often as monstrosities. The alienated reality of objects determines human beings as objects. Science controls the scientist, objective reality, the living subjects. However, the interest of reason, of truth, is active in all scientific research, "just as the whole operates in each part."[42] The fetishized division of labor—field specializations which do not acknowledge the totality—is the crisis of the sciences; and phenomenology is that theory which describes this historical situation realistically and thus demonstrates its untruths.[43]

To summarize Husserl's main points concerning theory and praxis, philosophy and the sciences: Husserl argued that modern science and technology, in capitalistic and communist systems alike, have overlooked, forgotten, and suppressed the consciousness of ordinary man in his life-world. Material and historical affairs of the surrounding world are suppressed by the very structures of these affairs, which are presented to consciousness as objective entities in themselves. Husserl saw the problem of alienation as a rising central problem of Western civilization in the post-Renaissance period when the sciences began, most likely unconsciously at first, but later intentionally, to neglect, to forget, and to suppress the ethical dimension of human existence. The history of the techno-scientific attitude over the natural and the transcendental attitude brought philosophy and science into disarray.

One may argue that Husserl is attempting to uncover the lost unity of the human purpose of Western civilization and to rescue man and society from disintegration caused by the scientific image of the world which stepped out of pace with the personal, direct understanding of ourselves and the world. The *telos* of Western civilization, namely, the integrity of self and world, of the private and public realm, of science and philosophy, must be restored. This reintegration could certainly have immense political impacts. But these are not explicated by Husserl.

Phenomenological theory is considered by Husserl not merely to be a more rigorous science, but to be the only philosophy capable of saving mankind from the greatest and most recent danger which it has encountered, namely, of being lost in a scientific image of man and world, in a communal and cumulative enterprise in which every scientist is a mere replaceable agent of an anonymous process and every man is analyzed as an object and manipulated as such. Classical philosophy exhorted men to dedicate their energies to philosophy in order to preserve themselves from being lost in a chase after property, pleasure and power. For these were the seductions of the mind in times of scarcity. In the affluent society of today, phenomenology intends to provide grounds for self-understanding as a rescue from the heteronomy of science and from technological manipulation. In this way Husserl fights alienation by theory, or, as Robert Sokolowski correctly put it, "In Husserl the human problem, the problem of preserving the self against possible heteronomy and alienation, seems to be reduced to an academic, purely speculative matter."[44]

Notes

1. Jürgen Habermas, *Knowledge and Human Interests* (Boston, 1972), pp. 32 f.; see also Appendix, pp. 301, 317, and his *Theorie und Praxis* (Frankfurt a.M., 1972). A more comprehensive review of this trend can be found in the introduction to Paci's volume, discussed below.

2. Paul Piccone, "Reading the *Crisis*," *Telos* no. 8 (Summer 1971), p. 128.

3. *Ibid.*

4. *Ibid.*

5. *Funzione delle scienze e significato dell'uomo,* translated by Paul Piccone and James E. Hansen (Evanston, 1972), p. xxxii.

6. Parts of this book were previously published in *Telos*.

7. *Op.cit.*, p. 446.

8. *Ibid.*, pp. 269, 270.

9. *Ibid.*, p. 413.

10. Immanuel Kant, *Critique of Pure Reason,* trans. F. Max Muller (Garden City, 1966), p. 246. The famous beginning sentence of the introduction to Kant's "Transcendental Logic": "We call Dialectic in general a logic of *illusion*," p. 221, illustrates sufficiently his attitude.

11. Paci, *op.cit.*, p. 281.

12. *Ibid.*, p. 88.

13. *Ibid.*, p. 120.

14. *Ibid.*, p. 124.

15. *Ibid.*, p. 218.

16. *Ibid.*, p. 280.

17. *Ibid.*, p. 271.

18. *Ibid.*, p. 279.

19. Edmund Husserl, "Phenomenology and Anthropology," in *Realism and the Background of Phenomenology,* edited by Roderick M. Chisholm (New York, 1967), p. 130.

20. *Ibid.*, pp. 131, 139, 141.

21. *Ibid.*, p. 131: "Philosophy, genuine science, aims at absolute, ultimately valid truths which transcend all relativity. . . . Although philosophy, genuine sci-

ence, can only be approximated gradually, it is reached by appealing to the *eidos,* the pure *a priori,* which anybody can grasp in apodictic insight."

22. *Ibid.,* p. 142.

23. Edmund Husserl, *Ideas,* trans. W.R. Boyce Gibson (New York, 1967), p. 357.

24. *Ibid.,* 359.

25. *Ibid.,* p. 371.

26. *Erste Philosophie,* Erster Teil: *Kristische Ideengeschichte* (1923-24). Herausgegeben von Rudolf Boehm (Husserliana, Band VII, The Hague, 1956), p. 23.

27. Paci, *op.cit.,* p. 282.

28. Marvin Farber, *Naturalism and Subjectivism* (Albany, 1959), p. 294. On the great importance of this emphasis see below.

29. Paci, *op.cit.,* p. 44.

30. *Ibid.,* p. 45.

31. *Ibid.,* p. 296.

32. *Ibid.*

33. *Ibid.,* p. 283.

34. *Ibid.,* pp. 97 f.

35. E. Husserl, *Formal and Transcendental Logic,* trans. Dorion Cairns (The Hague, 1969), p. 10.

36. E. Husserl, "Phenomenology and Anthropology," *op.cit.,* p. 140.

37. *Ibid.,* p. 142.

38. J. Habermas, *Knowledge and Human Interests,* p. 27.

39. *The Marx-Engels Reader,* edited by Robert C. Tucker (New York, 1972), p. 17.

40. Ernst Bloch, *Marx und die Menschlichkeit* (Rowohlt, 1969), p. 107.

41. Karl Marx, "German Ideology," in *The Marx-Engels Reader, op.cit.*

42. Paci, *op.cit.,* p. 322.

43. *Ibid.,* p. 323.

44. Robert Sokolowski, "Husserl's Protreptic," in *Life-World and Consciousness, Essays for Aron Gurwitsch,* edited by Lester E. Embree (Evanston, 1972), p. 61.

Francis Seeburger (essay date 1975)

SOURCE: "Heidegger and the Phenomenological Reduction," in *Philosophy and Phenomenological Research,* Vol. XXXVI, No. 2, December, 1975, pp. 212-21.

[In the following essay, Seeburger explores Heidegger's relation to the Husserlian formulation of phenomenology through an analysis of Heidegger's understanding of the "phenomenological reduction."]

> The explications of the preliminary conception of phenomenology point out that what is essential to phenomenology does not lie in its being *actual* as a philosophical "direction." Higher than actuality stands *possibility.* The understanding of phenomenology lies solely in comprehending it as possibility.[1]

Ever since the appearance of *Sein und Zeit,* the question of Martin Heidegger's relationship to the phenomenology of Edmund Husserl has remained open. Heidegger's own statements on the subject, both in *Sein und Zeit* and in his later writings, are ambiguous. Perhaps the greatest difficulty surrounds the notion of the "phenomenological reduction."

The reduction occupies a central place in Husserl's developed conception of phenomenology, and the problem of formulating the nature and consequences of the reduction as clearly as possible occupied Husserl to the end of his life. Husserl maintained that the reduction was the only way in which the "natural standpoint" could be overcome in order to reveal the intentional structures of experience. Only through the reduction, according to him, could philosophy cease to be naive.

On the other hand, references to the phenomenological reduction in Heidegger's writings are conspicuously lacking. Indeed, after *Sein und Zeit,* Heidegger rarely uses even the terms "phenomenology" and "phenomenological." Those two terms, to be sure, are used centrally in *Sein und Zeit* itself; but then there is Husserl's own judgment that *Sein und Zeit* never leaves the natural standpoint and is, therefore, still philosophically naive.

What, then, is Heidegger's relationship to Husserl's phenomenology? Is Heidegger simply not a phenomenologist, in any sense which is significantly related to Husserl's formulations of phenomenology? Has Heidegger failed to grasp the very starting point of phenomenology, the reduction? Does he, as Husserl thought, remain caught in the prephenomenological natural standpoint? Is he, therefore, a regressive influence within phenomenology?

One of the few primary sources for Heidegger's views of the phenomenological reduction is a letter which Heidegger wrote to Husserl in connection with their collaboration on the preparation of Husserl's *Encyclopedia Brittannica* article on phenomenology.[2] The issue is "transcendental consciousness" and its relationship to the world. Heidegger maintains that the phenomenological reduction is misunderstood if it is interpreted, as Husserl appears to interpret it, as being a philosophical technique which makes possible the disclosure of a pure, absolute transcendental consciousness which requires no relationship to the world in order to be. He argues that man, the being through whom the transcendental constitution of meaning occurs, is inescapably in the world, and that the truly important point for phenomenology concerns the nature of this "being-in." Man, writes Heidegger, is not "in" the world as one object present at hand among other objects, but is "in" the world precisely as that being through which the world first comes to be disclosed *as* world. Thus, the phenomenological reduction should not be interpreted to mean that the "suspension" or "bracketing" (the "reduction") of the world reveals a pure, nonworldly transcendental consciousness. The "world" as a collection of objects present at hand together is, indeed, to be suspended; but the result is not the revelation of worldless subjectivity. The phenomenological reduction is, rather, a step back from presence at hand to a more primordial, founding mode of being, through which presence at hand must first come to be "constituted" in experience. This founding mode of being is no worldless subjectivity, but is the being (*Sein*) of the world itself, as opposed to the manner of being appropriate to beings *within* the world. Thus, far from revealing a realm of transcendental consciousness wholly independent of the world, the phenomenological reduction is the philosophical operation which first makes the world itself available for phenomenological description.

It would be a mistake to conclude from Heidegger's criticism that, since Husserl's phenomenological reduction is a "suspension" of the being of the world, and since, for Heidegger, the point of phenomenology is precisely to reveal the being of the world, Heidegger cannot give the reduction any place in his own thought. In terms of such a mistaken conclusion, Husserl's characterization of phenomenology as "transcendental idealism" would be apt for his own philosophy, but totally inaccurate for Heidegger's, which would be, instead, a "phenomenological realism." In fact, this distinction between "phenomenological realism" and "phenomenological idealism" only obscures the real issues involved.

The disagreement between Heidegger and Husserl does not, at this point, concern the possibility or even the "necessity" of the phenomenological reduction, but concerns the *meaning* of the reduction. There are differences between Heidegger and Husserl here, but those differences cannot be grasped through a quick contrast of "idealism" and "realism." Heidegger's supposed "realism" is much closer to Husserl's professed "idealism" than either is close to any traditional idealism or realism. The real differences between Heidegger and Husserl appear only against a shared rejection of both traditional positions. To clarify these differences, it will be useful to discuss briefly Husserl's reduction as a "suspension" of the world.

Basically, Husserl uses the term "world" to designate the totality of the "real." Since, for him, the notion of an "*absolute* reality" is a contradiction in terms,[3] philosophers, if they are ever to clarify the sense of what is called the "real," must suspend their uncritical acceptance of the "reality" of the world and must inquire into the transcendental constitution of that meaning or sense which we designate by the term "reality." The reality of the world is not thereby either affirmed or denied. At issue is not yet whether the world *is* real, but rather the *sense* or *meaning*

of this "reality" which is to be affirmed or denied of the world and of objects within the world. That is, the sense "reality itself" must become a phenomenon available for description; and that can occur only if the phenomenologist puts his own everyday acceptance of, and dealings with, the "real" out of play. He must step back from his own involvement in the "real world," in order for that involvement and its intentional correlate (the real world itself) explicitly to emerge as phenomena.

To this point, there is no significant disagreement between Heidegger and Husserl. There is, at most, only a terminological disagreement. Husserl uses the term "world" to designate the totality of beings. Heidegger makes (at least in *Sein und Zeit*) the same use of the same term, only enclosed within quotation marks.[4] Both insist that the phenomenologist must disengage himself from his involvement with the world conceived as the totality of beings. Both insist that "reality" must be put out of play.

In *Sein und Zeit* Heidegger argues that by "reality" we have come to mean the totality of what is present at hand, and that presence at hand is not a primordial, but a founded, way of being. Accordingly, the task for phenomenology is to lay bare the more primordial manners of being upon which the being-sense "presence at hand" is founded. That is, to use Husserl's terminology, reality must be "bracketed," "suspended," "put out of play," or "reduced."

For *both* Husserl and Heidegger reality must be put out of play, precisely because the phenomenological desideratum is to reveal the phenomenal being-sense of reality itself. The disagreement, to repeat, is not about whether reality can be suspended in this way, but about the meaning and consequences of such suspension; and the point of Heidegger's criticism of Husserl's formulations is that the phenomenological reduction should not be interpreted as a philosophical operation which yields access to a pure, worldless, constituting subjectivity. Instead, according to Heidegger, the reduction is to be regarded as an attempt to interpret the relationship of man to his world from within that relationship itself. To use the language of *Sein und Zeit*, the "world" (the totality of the present at hand) must be put out of play, so that the world (i.e., the foundation for the being-sense of the "world"—what Heidegger calls "*die Weltlichkeit der Welt*," "the worldhood of the world")[5] itself can become a phenomenon available for description. If man is always "in" the world (in the sense explained above), then no reduction will ever make it possible for man to step outside his own relationship to the world, into some worldless subjectivity. To step back from reality is not to withdraw beyond the world, but to step back from one relationship to the world into another, more foundational relationship.

For these reasons, Heidegger emphasizes in *Sein und Zeit* that phenomenology should be understood as "hermeneutics." That is, phenomenology cannot be philosophy "without presuppositions," since all philosophy, as a way in which man develops his relationship to the world, "presupposes" man's definitive involvement "in" the world. Phenomenology can be only the self-explication of man's own being in the world; phenomenology can never escape the "hermeneutical circle."[6] Accordingly, insofar as Husserl claims to provide a "presuppositionless" philosophy through the phenomenological description of the "absolute being" of pure, transcendental, worldless subjectivity, Heidegger must part company with him.

For Husserl, pure transcendental consciousness is the ineluctable context for the emergence of all meaning. For Heidegger, because he rejects the possibility of basing phenomenology on any worldless subjectivity, that context must be provided by man's being in the world itself. All of Heidegger's descriptions of phenomenal structures must be understood in terms of that context.

As Heidegger argues in *Sein und Zeit,* man (*Dasein*) is that being for which its own being (*Sein*) is an issue. Correlatively, man is that being which always already has an "understanding of being" ("*Seinsverständnis*"), whether that understanding is expressly taken up as a theme, or left in the background as the foundation for the emergence of whatever else does explicitly occupy man. Therefore, phenomenology, as hermeneutics, is no more than the thematic development of an understanding which is already definitive of man himself. Furthermore, the act whereby the phenomenologist puts the totality of beings out of play, in order that the being of beings may be revealed for description (the act which Husserl calls the "phenomenological reduction"), is nothing but the making explicit of the fundamental concern of man, insofar as man is that being for whom there can first be a world and beings within the world.[7]

On this point, at least, Heidegger is very close to the position taken by Max Scheler towards the end of his life. Scheler maintained that the uniqueness of man lies in his capacity to oppose reality with "an emphatic 'No.'" Man, he held, is the being who can "de-actualize" or "de-realize" reality; and such "de-realization" is the necessary condition for the appearance of "objects" ("*Gegenstände*") which stand opposite man himself. Thus, the "de-realization" of reality is what first makes possible the emergence of objective truth, science, philosophy, culture, and whatever else is distinctively human.[8]

Viewed from such a perspective, Husserl's "phenomenological reduction" is no new philosophical "technique," but is the definitive event in the history of man. Man emerges only through the event whereby reality is "de-realized," and phenomenology is nothing but the express attempt to explicate that event. To return to Heidegger's terminology, phenomenology is the hermeneutics of being in the world.

Through man's being in the world, the context of significance which is the world itself (as "worldhood") is first disclosed; and whatever comes to be manifest in experience must occur within context. Furthermore, since man's way of being is precisely being *in the world,* the hermeneutics of man is already also the hermeneutics of the being both of the world, and of innerworldly beings. That is why Heidegger, from *Sein und Zeit* on, insists that the "question of being" ("*Seinsfrage*") is always already the question of man, that the question of man is always already the question of being, and that to talk of either being or man is always already to talk about the *relationship* of being to man, man to being. Indeed, the phenomenon proper to phenomenology, the real issue for thought (what Heidegger in some of his later writings calls "*die Sache des Denkens*") is precisely being (*Sein*) *as* this relationship, wherein the world is disclosed, providing the context of significance within which innerworldly beings come to be manifest.

A difficulty arises at this point in Heidegger's thought. It is essentially the same difficulty which Sartre mentions towards the end of *The Transcendence of the Ego.* Sartre argues that the phenomenological reduction, insofar as it is a specific *action* performed by the phenomenologist, can never be "pure." All actions occur, according to him, at the *reflective* level of experience, the only level at which it becomes possible to speak of purposive, motivated behavior. Yet the goal of phenomenology is nothing less than to reveal, through the reduction, the structures of *pre*reflective intentional experience. Insofar as the reduction is an action which the phenomenologist himself performs for complex, philosophically technical, but nevertheless specific reasons, these reasons and motives will always color and distort any phenomenological descriptions. Therefore, the reduction, as a motivated action, can never be *pure.* Sartre remarks that the reduction could be pure if it ceased to be a specific action on the phenomenologist's part and became, instead, an event which happened *to* him. The reduction could be pure only if it occurred spontaneously, absolutely without motivation.[9]

According to Heidegger, phenomenology aims at describing from within man's relationship to the world. The initial, self-conscious motivation behind such description is the desire to disclose the foundation upon which all of man's worldly activities, including, especially, those activities which constitute science and philosophy themselves, rest. To accomplish this task, the phenomenologist must disengage himself from his own worldly activities. Such disengagement, however, remains motivated by the phenomenologist's own involvement in the world; and all attempts at disengagement and description remain colored by that involvement. Thus, the phenomenologist, who sets out to provide a description of the foundation for all worldly activity, finds his descriptions always partially vitiated by his own worldly motivations.

If, however, the phenomenologist begins seriously to consider the nature and limitations of phenomenology itself, he also begins to comprehend that his own phenomenological purposes, motives, and actions rest on the very same foundation which he aims to reveal as the meaning-context for all other worldly purposes, motives, and actions. Accordingly, the phenomenological reduction and phenomenological description can stand revealed as concrete possibilities for man only insofar as something in man's contemporary being in the world calls for such phenomenological responses from man. The self-conscious attempt to perform the phenomenological reduction is founded upon, and derives its sense from, that aspect of man's relationship to the world which *elicits* such an attempt.

A phenomenological response, in turn, can be elicited only if some basic change in man's prephenomenological being in the world has already announced itself. As early as *Sein und Zeit*, Heidegger was concerned to point out that, in order for any philosophical questions even to arise, man's concernful preoccupation with his everyday affairs must somehow be broken. Some event within such everyday involvement in the world must bring man up short, casting him out of the familiar context of his concerns.[10] So, also, if philosophy is today to become phenomenology, if any *phenomenological* questions are even to arise, some event within the circuit of man's contemporary involvement in the world—an involvement inseparable from the always more or less explicit background provided in large part by philosophy itself—must break *that* circuit, again casting man into an unfamiliar context.

Heidegger himself has observed that there is a "turn" in his thought ("*eine Wendung in meinem Denken*"), but he has also insisted that this "turn" does not involve any change of "standpoint," or any rejection of his earlier thinking. Rather, he maintains, the turn in his thought is a response to a fundamental turn in the very issue (*Sache*) of thinking itself.[11] Hopefully, the sense of this remark can now be clarified, at least with regard to the phenomenological reduction and the meaning of phenomenology.

Pursuing the goal of phenomenology through the reduction, the phenomenologist eventually becomes aware of a reversal in his understanding of phenomenology and its task. Initially, the reduction appears to be a specific technique employed by the philosopher in order to lay bare, in a supposedly unadulterated fashion, an otherwise unavailable dimension for philosophical description—the dimension of pure phenomenality. However, as the meaning and the consequences of the application of this technique become clear, and as the phenomenologist becomes aware of the essentially historical determinants of his own phenomenological endeavors, it also becomes increasingly apparent that the phenomenological technique of reduction is itself a response to, and, in effect, at the service of, an already emergent change in man's relationship to the world. Accordingly, phenomenology can no longer be defined in terms of the reduction as a self-consciously applied technique, but must instead be defined in terms of the relationship of phenomenology to this change in man's being in the world, a change which is not brought about by phenomenology itself, but which precedes any explicit application of phenomenological techniques and elicits

such application in order to work *itself* out *through* phenomenology. An analogy may be helpful here.

Galileo and the other fathers of modern science certainly did not pursue their work in order to provide the foundation for contemporary technology. Nevertheless, their work did provide that foundation. The mathematical projection of nature which modern science accomplished and which first made possible the development of modern technology was the working out of a change in man's relationship to nature herself. Galileo and the other classical scientists, however, were no more aware of, and expressly aiming at, that change, that they were aware of, and aiming at, modern technology, through which that change was eventually to work itself out. Galileo and the whole of modern science and technology derive meaning from, and are at the service of, a "turn" in man's being in the world.[12]

It is of basic significance that in one of his most explicit criticisms of Husserl, Heidegger does not refer to the phenomenological reduction or even to "transcendental idealism," but takes Husserl to task for failing to recognize what is essentially *historical* in being ("*die Wesentlichkeit des Geschichtlichen im Sein*").[13] That is, Heidegger accuses Husserl of overlooking the most important consequence of Husserl's own phenomenology: the consequence that philosophy can no longer lay legitimate claim to any absolute knowledge, any "truth in itself," any "being in itself" independent of the concrete, historical disclosure of being (*Sein*) through man.

Since Husserl fails to see the importance of history (*Geschichte*) and characterizes phenomenology in terms of the discovery of absolute, constituting, transcendental subjectivity, he continues, as Heidegger sees it, to make the same fundamental mistake which has been made since the beginning of Western philosophy: He confuses being with beings, insofar as he clings to the assumption that the structures of being (*Sein*) must be grounded in some being (*Seiendes*). It is because of this that Heidegger must reject Husserl's talk of "transcendental idealism" (and not, to repeat a point made earlier, because Heidegger opts for some form of "realism"). Since Husserl attempts to ground all structures of meaning and being (*Sein*) in transcendental subjectivity, which remains, after all, *a* being (*ein Seiendes*), he does, indeed, deserve to be classified as an "idealist," for he shares the fundamental confusion which is at the root of all traditional idealism (as well as all traditional realism).

It is reasonable, therefore, for Heidegger to attempt to avoid misunderstandings by granting the legitimacy of Husserl's prior claim to the title "phenomenology" and by letting his own thought remain "nameless."[14] Heidegger does not thereby reject either phenomenology or his own phenomenological basis. Indeed, as was pointed out above, Heidegger's criticism of Husserl boils down to the claim that Husserl himself did not clearly see the consequences of his own thought, and that Heidegger's own apparent "revisions" of phenomenology are really clarifications or just those consequences. Thus, besides Husserl's obvious prior right to the term "phenomenology," there is a deeper, substantive reason for Heidegger's ceasing to use that term for his own thought: The further Heidegger pushed into phenomenological territory, the more apparent it became to him that the very meaning of phenomenology had altered. This alteration, this "turn" in the "thing itself," is the real key to Heidegger's relationship to phenomenology and, in particular to the phenomenological reduction.

To the extent that, as Husserl himself repeatedly insisted, phenomenology must be self-critical, it must come to recognize that its own meaning *as possibility* lies not in the reduction conceived as a self-consciously, purposively implemented technique, but in an event within man's being in the world, an event which is prior to, and first reveals the possibility of, any actual phenomenological activity. This event which bestows meaning on phenomenology is ultimately nothing less than the "pure," "unmotivated" reduction which Sartre mentions. Just for that reason, this event is no longer properly called a "reduction," since, as Sartre saw, this term applies to actions, which are motivated, purposive responses.

Just as, whether they were aware of it or not, Galileo and the other early modern scientists responded to an emerging change in man's relationship to the world and thereby prepared the ground for the eventual unfolding of that change, so, according to Heidegger, the phenomenologist, whether he is aware of it or not, is responding to a new emerging change, for the eventual unfolding of which he is preparing the ground. What the details or even the outlines of the world which will develop are, the phenomenologist can no more know in advance than Galileo could have known in advance that his work would help pave the way for the development of modern technology. Nor can the phenomenologist, thinking, perhaps, that he can see some of the features of the future world, decide to plan out his activities in such a way as to force events either to confirm or to negate his vision. Man may hold sway over things he encounters within the world, and he may be able to dispose of such things as he pleases; but he can never hold sway over, or dispose of, his own being in the world, since that being itself is the indisposable foundation for all human activity aimed at controlling or ordering what appears within the world. Nevertheless, the unfolding of a change in man's relationship to the world does not occur over his head, or behind his back, or at all "despite" man's activity. It works itself out *through* the activities of men, endowing those activities with meaning.

The meaning of phenomenology, for Heidegger, does not lie in the consciousness of the phenomenologist himself, but in the "thing itself": the turn in man's relationship to things, others, and himself; and, finally, this "turn" itself is nothing "new," but is, as Heidegger puts it, "the oldest of the old."[15] The turn in man's being in the world is man's return to himself, in that the definitive event through which both man and world emerge is precisely the "derealization," "suspension," or "stepping-back" which, in phenomenology, becomes an explicit concern.

Notes

1. Martin Heidegger, *Sein und Zeit.* Tübingen: Max Niemeyer, 1927, p. 38. (All translations from Heidegger are my own.)

2. This letter is published in an appendix to Edmund Husserl, *Phenomenologische Psychologie,* Husserliana Band IX. The Hague: Martinus Nijhoff, 1968, p. 600 ff.

3. See Husserl, *Ideen I,* Husserliana Band III, p. 134.

4. Heidegger, *Sein und Zeit,* p. 65.

5. *Ibid.*

6. See *Ibid.,* p. 7 f., 37 f., 310 ff.

7. See *Ibid.,* p. 32 ff., 61 f.

8. See Max Scheler, *Man's Place in Nature,* trans. Hans Meyerhoff. Boston: Beacon Press, 1961, pp. 52 ff.

9. Jean-Paul Sartre, *The Transcendence of the Ego,* trans. William Kirkpatrick and Forrest Williams. New York: Noonday Press, 1957, pp. 91 f.

10. See Heidegger, *Sein und Zeit,* p. 72 ff.

11. Heidegger, "Vorwort" to William J. Richardson, *Heidegger: Through Phenomenology to Thought.* The Hague: Martinus Nijhoff, 1963, pp. xvii ff.

12. See Heidegger, *Die Technik und die Kehre.* Pfullingen: Neske, 1962, p. 21 ff.

13. See Heidegger, *Wegmarken.* Frankfurt: Klostermann, 1967, p. 170.

14. See Heidegger, *Unterwegs zur Sprache.* Pfullingen: Neske, 1959, p. 121.

15. Heidegger, *Zur Sache des Denkens.* Tübingen: Niemeyer, 1969, p. 25.

Jacob Golomb (essay date 1976)

SOURCE: "Psychology from the Phenomenological Standpoint of Husserl," in *Philosophy and Phenomenological Research,* Vol. XXXVI, No. 4, June, 1976, pp. 451-71.

[In the following essay, Golomb explains the distinctions Husserl makes between psychology and psychologism, and between positivistic and phenomenological psychology, and analyzes the significance of these differences in the development of phenomenology and for the practice of psychology.]

A. INTRODUCTION

The title of this paper, ["Psychology from the Phenomenological Standpoint of Husserl"] which recalls the title of Brentano's major work,[1] implies an attempt to examine the relations between phenomenology and psychology from a single, consistent standpoint. Technical limitations apart, this is impossible in principle since it is difficult to find one consistent standpoint in Husserl's works. Ricoeur[2] and

Farber[3], for instance, specify four stages in Husserl's thought to which the Hegelian term *Aufhebung* can be applied. In developing his thinking, Husserl tends to eliminate some of his previous ideas, to add new elements and to retain some central motifs. In what follows I shall concentrate on the period of his phenomenological thinking in which he emphasized its descriptive aspects, thus turning phenomenology into a philosophical method free of metaphysical assumptions. This is phenomenology in its narrow sense—trying to come to grips with a field of investigation concentrating on the essential structures of intentional consciousness. But consciousness was once exclusively the province of scientific psychology so that most of Husserl's effort in this period is directed towards delineating the concerns of phenomenology as opposed to those of psychology, while establishing positive relations between the two. I shall not be dealing with the period in which he effected the transition from descriptive to transcendental phenomenology by stressing the ideal aspect of the phenomenological method and by adding the transcendental reduction, thus turning it into a metaphysics,[4] for here phenomenology (in the broad sense) is a *philosophia prima* in which all other sciences and attitudes, including empirical psychology, are anchored.[5]

The relations between phenomenology and psychology are extremely difficult and complex, as Spiegelberg has quite rightly argued.

> Even Husserl himself, during the whole of his philosophical development, did not find it easy to determine once and for all his attitude toward psychology, and to define the exact function which he assigned to it within the framework of his changing conception of phenomenology.[6]

I shall try to substantiate this claim by textual analyses, and show that these difficulties, among others, led to Husserl's ambivalent position with regard to scientific psychology. This ambivalence is expressed in his simultaneous rejection of contemporaneous psychology and attempt to outline a system of positive relations between this science and phenomenology.

In Husserl's positive attitude to psychology we encounter another problem. It seems that Husserl's attempts to give this science a special status involve a tendency to show that psychology is essentially different from the positivistic natural sciences. He makes an interesting attempt (contrary to the procedure of modern psychology which follows in the footsteps of the natural sciences) to view this scientific domain as a discipline which can legitimately determine its own subject matter and the methods appropriate to it. But a fundamental question arises here. In his threefold attempt to relate psychology to phenomenology by reforming the former and liberating it from the yoke of the natural sciences, did not Husserl absorb psychology into phenomenology, and thus put it under a new yoke, that of phenomenology? This leads to the problem I shall be dealing with below—whether psychology, as an independent science of consciousness, is possible at all from Husserl's phenomenological standpoint.

In the following discussion I shall have recourse to a distinction which may shed some light on Husserl's position: the distinction between a *meta-scientific critique* of science and a *meta-philosophical critique* of the philosophy of science. In its wider sense, the term "philosophy of science" suggests meta-scientific assumptions, which will henceforth be referred to as "scientific metaphysics," and a formal-normative system in the manner of, e.g., Carnap, which will be referred to as "logic and methodology of science." A meta-scientific critique departs from a philosophy of science which the critic accepts as valid and rejects only its distortive applications in actual scientific practice. The meta-philosophical critique arises out of an alternative philosophy of science. Here the attack is not directed at the scientific discipline per se but at that philosophy of science on which it is assumed to be based. Husserl's attacks on psychology apparently derive from the second critical position. This point is significant if Husserl's phenomenology is also taken as a philosophy of science, that is, as a philosophy which hopes to found a theoretical-scientific attitude on a primary, extrascientific basis. I am naturally assuming that my conception of phenomenological philosophy as a philosophy of science (in the wide sense) accords with Husserl's basic intentions.

B. Brentano

Husserl's attempt to grant psychology a special status as opposed to that of physics originates in the exposition of the intentional structure of consciousness. Brentano is the source of what became a leitmotif in Husserl's thought: the liberation of psychological investigation from positivist physicalism. Though Brentano's distinction between physical phenomena and the structure of psychic phenomena is still made within the ontological-natural framework, his determination of the intentional structure of the psychical enabled Husserl to reach more consistent conclusions, and to place psychology on a level of discourse essentially different from that of the natural sciences.

Husserl, following Brentano, creates a new motif—the differentiation of theoretical fields according to their special thematic structures which in turn require a specific and appropriate attitude and approach in each case. The immanence of a theoretical field and the correlation between its subject matter and the approach suited to it already appear in Brentano's distinction between descriptive psychology (psychognosy) and genetic psychology. The relationship between descriptive and genetic psychology is the same as that between anatomy and physiology. Descriptive psychology deals with "the totality of the fundamental psychological elements" and rigorously determines both the nature of the intentional relations between these elements and the derivation of all other psychical phenomena from these basic components. Exact and apodictic laws can be evolved in this field since intuition is able to disclose adequately the psychical structures which appear in inner perception. This "anatomical" description of psychical phenomena is performed by "seeing the essences" of the phenomena; these essences are revealed to us by immediate insight, without recourse to induction—as Brentano puts it, the perception is arrived at "*mit einem Schlag ohne jedwede Induktion*" (in a flash without induction). Descriptive psychology thus becomes a rigorous science, whereas "the physiology of the psychical" (that is, genetic psychology) is nothing but psychophysics, which has been the province of psychology ever since Wundt. Genetic psychology deals with the causal relations between mental phenomena and physical-physiological phenomena. From this point of view it is not a rigorous science, since it is concerned with laws of probability and induction. Husserl's later distinctions between eidetic psychology and psychophysics (in *Philosophy as Rigorous Science*) as well as between the reflective-phenomenological standpoint and the naturalistic standpoint (in his later works) evidently have their origin in Brentano.

Husserl echoes another motif in this distinction of Brentano's: the idea of founding one level of reference upon another, while determining their mutual relations. Brentano's distinctions between two kinds of procedures of psychological investigation and the nature of the laws they contain, are taken from the 'empirical' standpoint. But he nevertheless asserts (in *Psychology from the Empirical Standpoint*) the primacy of psychognosy over genetic psychology, on the grounds that the psychologist cannot fix the psycho-physical laws of the various mental phenomena without having first specified these phenomena and ascertained their boundaries and their "anatomical" structure. Hence, empirical psychology must be, first and foremost, descriptive psychology. This is an important precedent for the distinctly Husserlian aim of liberating "pure" psychology from naturalistic nonpsychological elements, like psychophysics and physiology, while repeatedly attempting to establish it on an independent basis with its original method of "seeing essence."[7] In the course of liberation the reverse occurs too: "pure" descriptive psychology is not only an autonomous discipline with its own subject matter, but also the epistemological and methodological basis of psychophysics and physiology—this in contrast to the experimental psychology of Brentano's time, practiced by Wundt, Weber, and Fechner. Actually, in Brentano, empirical psychology is placed upside down so that (from the epistemological viewpoint) the psychic occupied a primary position vis à vis psychophysics. Husserl's solution to the question of the relations between eidetic psychology and psychophysics is structurally similar to Brentano's attempt to base one field of investigation on another which is given autonomy. These similarities of attitudes in Brentano and Husserl should not blind us to their fundamental differences. In spite of the fact that Brentano gave the investigation of psychical phenomena epistemological priority over psychophysical attitude of genetic psychology, he does not, like Husserl, believe in the ontological nonreducibility of the psychical to *physis*. Like the experimental psychologists of his time, Brentano still asserts the ontic primacy of the physiological basis on which psychic phenomena are based. His adherence to the empirical level and to the world of psychic and physical things, leads Brentano to claim that the genesis of the psychical is to be

found in the empirical physis. This is where Husserl and Brentano part company. In spite of all the similarities between genetic psychology and Husserl's eidetic psychology, the latter's very act of *epoché*, indicates a nonontological attitude to the psychical. Moreover, the gap between these two thinkers becomes even wider after the transcendental reduction in Husserl's later thought, since by then for Husserl the genesis of the psychical was to be found not in the psychophysical organism but in the transcendental ego, which (in noetic acts) constitutes its physical noemata.

C. The Critique of Psychologism in the
Logische Untersuchungen[8]

I shall not here detail Husserl's critique of psychologism but confine myself to those motifs which are relevant to our discussion.

Husserl's attempts to establish an autonomous philosophical domain were also made with the objective of restricting the applicability of other methods to the data he thought belonged exclusively to his phenomenology. His opposition to the intervention of one domain in the concerns of another and to the exclusive domination of one domain becomes apparent in his critique of psychologism. Husserl attacks psychology here just as he takes a stand against the naturalization of consciousness and the prevalence of physicalism over psychology in his *Philosophy as Rigorous Science.* Psychology hinders phenomenology in its investigation of the structures of logical thinking and "psychologizes logic," that is, psychology attempts to reduce the objects of logic to mental processes and to derive its normative laws from psychological-empirical ones. However, this separation of psychology from logic does not mean that the latter becomes fully autonomous. Following his attack on psychologism (in the first part of the *Logical Investigations*), Husserl goes on (in the second part) to attack Frege's attempt to posit logic as an independent and isolated discipline. He rejects Frege's assertion that logic is based solely on normative laws and claims that it is necessary to supply this formal discipline with a theoretical basis, since a normative science needs (to be based on) a primary theoretical science. This standpoint is analogous to Husserl's attitude to scientific psychology: he both attempts to liberate it from positivistic naturalism and to found it (like logic) upon his new philosophical science. This analogy is easily understood if it is recalled that both the ideal objects of logic and the mental processes of empirical consciousness are, for the phenomenological standpoint, nothing but *noemata,* and as such become the objects of noematic analysis. From this point of view, the relation of logic to phenomenology is identical to the relation of psychology to phenomenology; logic has been liberated by phenomenology from psychology, while psychology is liberated from physics. Here I shall concentrate on psychology and try to answer the question of whether the psychology Husserl attacks and the psychology he liberates are identical, or whether we in fact have two distinct disciplines.

If the aforementioned distinction between the two kinds of critiques of science and philosophies of science is applied to the problem of psychologism, it becomes evident that there is a logical continuity in Husserl's attitude to psychology from the ***Logical Investigation*** to ***Philosophy as a Rigourous Science.*** Husserl's attack on psychologism is not directed at empirical psychology but at the philosophy of science on which it is based. Thus, for instance, Husserl claims that he looks forward to promising developments in scientific psychology, despite the fact that he does not expect it to provide any specific philosophical clarifications. In other words, Husserl already differentiates between empirical psychology (or, as Brentano would say, genetic psychology) and descriptive phenomenology (in Brentano: descriptive psychology or psychognosy) in ***Logical Investigations.*** But Husserl goes even further than this; he not only draws this distinction but, following Brentano, establishes the priority and primacy of phenomenology, which "founds empirical psychology and is described as a pure doctrine of the essence of the experience."⁹ Phenomenology, functioning as "pure logic," serves as an alternative philosophy of science to the philosophy Husserl attacks. This philosophy of science (in the sense which includes "scientific metaphysics" and "logic of science") is naturalism, also referred to in ***Philosophy as Rigorous Science*** by its modern appellation: "positivism." Hence, the psychologism attacked by Husserl is, in fact, a meta-psychological standpoint and certainly not identical with psychology as an actual-empirical science. Just as Husserl will later try to liberate psychology from naturalization and from its absorption in positivistic philosophy, so his attack on psychologism is an attempt to set logic free from this philosophy of science. Instead of naturalism Husserl gives phenomenology a constitutive role which is called "pure logic" when it functions as a foundation for logic, and "eidetic psychology" when it functions as a foundation for psychology (in ***Philosophy as Rigorous Science***).

Thus, Husserl's two aims: to release psychology from positivism and logic from psychologism are not only compatible, but actually complementary. No wonder Husserl puts the two together in ***Philosophy as Rigorous Science:***

> Characteristic of all forms of extreme and consistent naturalism . . . is on one hand the naturalizing of consciousness, . . . and on the other the naturalizing of ideas and consequently of all *absolute* ideas and *norms.*¹⁰

"Norms" refers not only to historicism but also to psychologism, which attempts to psychologize normative logic. To liberate psychology from positivistic physicalism and to liberate logic from positivistic psychologism means to liberate them from extreme naturalism, which Husserl claims in ***Philosophy as Rigorous Science*** (pp. 80-2) is self-contradictory as a philosophy of science and which also leads to extreme reductionism and relativism, as he argues in the ***Logical Investigations.*** This philosophy therefore becomes Husserl's major enemy and his aim is to establish phenomenology as the alternative to this "dangerous" relativism.

D. PHENOMENOLOGY AND PSYCHOLOGY IN
PHILOSOPHY AS RIGOROUS SCIENCE

1. Husserl's early negative attitude to psychology was due to his attempt to establish phenomenology as "rigorous science." His attempts to set psychology and phenomenology apart were not directed against experimental psychology itself (though to Husserl it too has many defects). This point is explicitly stated in ***Ideas.*** When Husserl refers to his essay **"Philosophie als strenge Wissenschaft"** (published in *Logos* in 1910):

> my criticism of the psychological method . . . which in *no* way *denied the value of modern psychology,* and in no sense depreciated the experimental work carried out by men of distinction, but *exposed* certain . . . *radical defects of method* on the removal of which . . . the raising of psychology to a higher scientific level and an extraordinary extension of its field of work must depend.¹¹

In this retrospective passage, Husserl's critique of scientific psychology is much more than a critique directed at an experimental science alone. The major consideration for Husserl is not the defects and errors within the actual psychological investigation, but the fundamental status of the science of the *psyche* as a whole. His critique is directed against the psychological method as such rather than against its faulty application in any given case. His rejection of a method which governs the whole scientific domain is an external critique of a particular philosophy of science; it starts from an alternative philosophy of science and aims to replace the other and reform the science in question. Naturally, the radical rejection of a scientific method, which is a system of norms for scientific practice requiring a theory and methodology, is meaningful only if it is performed out of another logic and methodology of science which can grant the objects of the scientific investigation a new status and formulate new principles. And, indeed, by the time this essay, ***Philosophy as Rigorous Science,*** was written the phenomenological method and its methodology¹² had been given their most consistent form—a form which had received a new impetus towards transcendental subjectivity since ***Ideas.***

2. In the conflict between the two rival philosophical methodologies the real target of Husserl's attack is easily distinguished: it is the psychologistic position which is the permanent enemy of phenomenology. Psychologism, as a meta-scientific philosophical position attempts to grant psychological investigation a primary philosophical status and claims—in Husserl's words—that:

> strict psychology is obviously the foundation for all humanistic sciences and not less even for metaphysics.¹³

It is worthwhile citing Wundt at this point in order to show how exact Husserl's formulation of the psychologistic position is:

> Just as psychology is the empirical science which completes the natural sciences and lays the foundation for

the human sciences, so it is, for that reason, the preparation for philosophy.[14]

This is a continuation of the intention encountered in the *Logical Investigations* of preventing naturalistic "imperialism" from gaining mastery over all the humanistic sciences, including philosophy and epistemology. And if Husserl there attempted to make pure logic—which was to supersede psychologism—the theoretical basis for logical discourse, here he rejects Dilthey's *Verstehen*—which was supposed to distinguish the *Geisteswissenschaften* from the natural sciences—and puts phenomenology forward as a "rigorous science." This "rigorous science," in its transcendental development, will be described as the subjective-theoretical basis of all humanistic sciences and of all other theoretical positions, like the natural sciences and psychology, which shall become mere links in the chain of intentional constitutions. From this point of view *Philosophy as Rigorous Science* is not only the logical extension of *Logical Investigations,* but also the intermediary link with the later developments of Husserl's thought to be found in the *Crisis.*

3. Thus we can see that the development of Husserl's thought is characterized by the gradual extension of his attack against naturalism. If he initially confined his attack to the attempt to psychologize logic, in his essay *Logos* he extends it to include attempts to naturalize consciousness and history. In the *Crisis* Husserl's antipositivistic stand is complete and all positivism's forms and manifestations are absolutely rejected. His growing attack on naturalism is accompanied by the development of phenomenology until it becomes a transcendental philosophy which constitutes the *noemata* of the intentional consciousness instead of a descriptive method and methodology. The final point in this development is reached when there is no longer room for an independent naturalistic standpoint governed by the rule of the "exclusiveness of the objective attitude" and it is completely superseded by the transcendental philosophy which constitutes the naturalistic standpoint itself with its naive attitude and ontological positing of its subject matter. Indeed, one of the major objectives of phenomenology, and the thrust of its development, is to disrupt the relation of positivistic philosophy to science by putting the latter upon a new meta-scientific basis, while eliminating the autonomous validity of the former by placing it within the framework of phenomenology.

4. I shall now turn to the text itself. At first Husserl attacks positivism's pretensions of basing philosophy upon science. Not only is this impossible, but, in fact, the natural sciences—physical and psychical—need a philosophic-epistemological basis to give them real meaning. Science needs philosophy since its own point of departure is "naive," that is, science posits its objects in a spatio-temporal context without considering the meaning of this act and without any attempt to justify it. Science cannot therefore be a rigorous and adequate "first philosophy," and it cannot interpret the world meaningfully. The same is true of the positivistic philosophy of science which attempts to

validate science by taking its positing of objects for granted, while inconsistently giving it priority over philosophy. Positivism's pretensions of being a basis for science are therefore completely invalidated. A valid and consistent philosophy of science is a radical and evident theory of knowledge which is free of all presuppositions;[15] it is not only the basis of science itself but also of logical norms and, finally, of all the manifestations of the spirit. Naturalism's claim, that psychology is the proper foundation for philosophy is completely erroneous for psychology in fact needs philosophy for its proper foundation and final explication.

5. This is so for Husserl because he views contemporaneous experimental psychology as a science which, like physics, posits its own objects—in this case, human consciousness: "every psychological judgment involves the existential positing of physical nature, whether expressly or not."[16] Scientific psychology deals with an object posited in the context of nature, so its distinction from the natural sciences is inessential: the psychic is granted physical meaning; it is turned into a natural object. If one is to deal with consciousness in an objective-scientific way in order to uncover its "scientific" laws—and this is, for Husserl, a legitimate objective—one must treat psychic phenomena as psychological facts in their natural context. In *Ideas,* too, Husserl's claims that "Psychology is a science of facts (*Tatsachen*) . . . it is a science of realities . . . in the one spatio-temporal world."[17] Husserl does not wish to alter the nature of science as the theoretical practice of investigating "facts" in their natural context, but to add an external meaning which depends on a specific philosophy of science. He is aware that scientific practice requires an objective and universal admission of facts to make replication, recognition, and refutation possible. Husserl must therefore admit that, if it is to be recognized as a science, psychology must deal with psychical facts and turn them into "natural" objects in the course of scientific investigation. And, indeed, he says as much:

> To eliminate the relation to nature would deprive the psychical of its character as an objectively and temporally determinable fact of nature, in short, of its character as a psychological fact.[18]

6. Husserl then does not attempt to change the nature of the "natural sciences," which include psychology defined as "the science of the facts of natural consciousness." When he speaks of a "science of consciousness" which is "nevertheless not psychology" therefore, he is evidently using the word "science" in an unconventional sense. He is referring to phenomenology which investigates the ideal essences of the intentional consciousness by a method distinct from that of science. Intentional consciousness is not posited in a natural context; it is an ideal consciousness on which the phenomenological method is performed from the point of view of the *epoché,* which encloses the "positing" in brackets. The distinction between "natural science" and "phenomenological science" also entails a distinction between their respective objects. Since Husserl says that psychology is the "natural science of the con-

sciousness" and since phenomenology is concerned with the very same object, namely consciousness, there must be a close relationship between them:

> since there will be no question here of an accidental equivocation, it is to be expected beforehand that phenomenology and psychology must stand in close relationship to each other, since both are concerned with consciousness, even though in a different way, according to a different 'orientation.'[19]

This is a very important programatic statement, but there is, unfortunately, no further explanation of the nature of the relationship between these two disciplines. A fundamental question arises here: is it meaningful to refer to the same "consciousness" as the object of investigation common to these two sciences? We have seen that these two sciences are distinct in their standpoint as well as in their attitude to their objects. I have already mentioned the important phenomenological principle concerning the correlation between the object and the subject's specific mode of knowledge. The psychologist is therefore concerned with a consciousness essentially different from that of the phenomenologist. After having suggested that we have to do with different aspects of one consciousness, Husserl himself observes that there are in fact two consciousnesses which are parallels to the two kinds of "science": psychology deals with "experimental consciousness" posited in the context of nature, whereas phenomenology is concerned with "pure consciousness" from the phenomenological standpoint in which the eidetic reduction from nature to essences is performed.

7. There are at this point two possible interpretations of Husserl's position.

I. One possible approach is that there are two kinds of consciousness essentially and immanently distinct from each other. The first type of consciousness is psychological: it is the consciousness of a person as a psychophysical being here and now; it contains factual acts and events in time, which come and go according to psychophysical causal laws. Somewhat like Kant's version of the "empirical ego," this consciousness is experimental psychology's scientific object par excellence. The second kind of consciousness is distinct from the former in essence and in content: it is the phenomenological consciousness, defined as having an intentional essence. As such, it is an aggregate of noetic-noematic correlations belonging to the phenomenological field of investigation, that attempts to discover the various intentional structures with their two components. If this is so, we must conclude that (1) the methodology and object of scientific psychology are legitimate and psychophysics is part of science in its common practice; (2) it is extremely difficult to understand Husserl's position that scientific psychology and phenomenology are closely related by virtue of their common object, in spite of the differences in their attitudes; (3) this enigma is even greater if we reflect on this problem from the point of view of two kinds of "sciences" which are supposedly closely related. As we have seen, Husserl says explicitly

that any scientific psychology must take psychological facts into account, that is, it must posit the physical in the context of nature (a view which actually strengthens this interpretation). But if so, what can he mean by asserting that:

> without taking away from the truth that psychology is not nor can be any more philosophy than the physical science of nature can—that for essential reasons psychology must be more closely related to philosophy (i.e., through the medium of phenomenology) and must in its destiny remain most intimately bound with philosophy.[20]

If psychology is only a legitimate science, why distinguish it from the other physical sciences, and what is the rationale for granting it a peculiar status and a close affinity with phenomenology? Does this suggest that Husserl is in fact referring to a new kind of psychology rather than to the scientific psychology practiced in his time which he has already said does not differ from any other naturalistic science?

II. This last question brings us to another possible explanation; that although there are two different approaches to consciousness, both the "experimental consciousness" of the positivistic-naive standpoint and the "pure consciousness" of phenomenology are only one consciousness with the same, permanent essence which sustains the intentional structure and the noetic-noematic correlation. This interpretation sounds reasonable, especially if we remember that one of Husserl's major arguments against experimental psychology (in addition to his argument against the naive positing of consciousness) is its absolute disregard of the intentional structure of consciousness without which experimental findings are meaningless.[21] In other words, there is no consciousness, either experimental or phenomenological, which is not intentional. This has far-reaching implications: (1) It follows that psychology cannot deal with consciousness except in the phenomenological manner. If it is impossible to posit the psychical and to turn it into a natural object, there can be no scientific-psychophysical psychology. This follows from the important Husserlian principle (Kantian in origin) that reflexion does not posit existence. Existence cannot be assumed on the strength of the reflexive acts necessary for the phenomenological investigation of the intentional structures of consciousness. Hence, inasmuch as it investigates its object on the "empirical" level, psychology must rely on reflexion to expose intentional structures and investigate the noetic acts which, since they take place on the nontranscendental level, are acts of the empirical ego. Psychology, therefore, attempts to classify noetic acts and to determine their intentions towards specific psychological contents which are ideal noemata rather than mental entities in their natural context. We obviously have to do with a novel kind of psychology here and Husserl does in fact mention this later on, calling it either "eidetic psychology" or "phenomenological psychology." But the question of whether the two kinds of psychology—the old, psychophysical science and a new one—are possible, remains open. (2) It is now easier to answer the question about the relationship between psychology and phenomenology, for the word 'psychology' refers not to the scientific, but to the phenomenological discipline. Husserl's argument for psychology's close affinity with phenomenology does hold with respect to phenomenological psychology because an object with the same laws and structure may serve as the mediating link between two approaches, while maintaining fruitful relations between them.

8. The obvious conclusion to be drawn from our discussion up to this point is that Husserl's attitude to psychology as manifest in his vacillation between these two approaches is distinctly ambivalent from *Philosophy as Rigorous Science* on. He does not consistently choose either, but seems committed to both at the same time. This ambivalence is also expressed in his strong criticism of psychology and of the philosophy of science on which it is based and in his attempt to grant psychology a special status over and above natural sciences. Had Husserl explicitly committed himself to the second approach, his ambivalence could have been resolved by the argument that he rejects contemporaneous empirical psychology altogether, and attempts to put phenomenological psychology in its place, relating it to his "rigorous philosophy." But there is no such resolution because Husserl goes on talking about the relations between phenomenology and experimental psychology, which he wants to preserve at all costs.

9. In what follows we shall see how Husserl continues to waver between these two approaches:

> what was said of the close affinity between psychology and philosophy, applies very little to modern exact psychology, which is as foreign to philosophy as it can possibly be. No matter how much this psychology may consider itself on the strength of the experimental method the sole scientific psychology and look down on 'armchair psychology,' I am obliged to declare its opinion that it is the psychology, psychological science in the full sense, a serious error heavy with consequences.[22]

Hence it follows that (a) when Husserl speaks of close relations between psychology and phenomenology he is not referring to scientific psychology, which posits its objects in the natural context, but to a new kind of psychology, which performs "a direct and pure analysis of consciousness" through immanent views of its contents; (b) Husserl does not reject "exact modern psychology" entirely; it is valid and may even under certain conditions determine "psychological facts and norms which may be valuable."[23] What he attacks is the philosophy of science attached to this psychology, since any reflection upon the nature of a science which views it as a whole and considers it in its relations with other sciences, is already a meta-science and should be distinguished from specific content-claims within the science itself. What Husserl is attacking, of course, is the positivistic psychologism which asserts that the experimental method alone can make psychology a real science.

This positivism attacks "armchair psychology" and, in this, as in its claim of exclusivity, rejects any possibility of a new scientific method, viz., the foundation of phenomenology. (c) Husserl rejects this philosophy of science which also constitutes the methodology of the experimental method, and attempts to establish the phenomenological method of "seeing essence" (alongside of the experimental method). But a new method requires a methodology to validate and justify it, and if the eidetic reduction and the a priori intuition of the ideal essences of psychical phenomena are accepted as a new method which establishes a new psychological science—eidetic psychology—then phenomenological philosophy necessarily becomes the "methodology" of the new approach. Phenomenology is thus turned into the philosophy of science of the new phenomenological method and its concern is with the clarification of the internal relations which obtain between epistemology and eidetic psychology, that is, between phenomenological philosophy and phenomenological psychology. However, if Husserl would also like to retain the experimental psychology of his time, beneath or side by side with eidetic psychology, he has to supply a consistent theoretical framework within which scientific psychology and phenomenological psychology can be related in a meaningful way. It is apparent that Husserl did not, up to this point, fulfill this new obligation.

10. We have seen that Husserl claims that current psychology is as foreign to phenomenological philosophy as physics because both posit the object in its spatio-temporal natural context. Nevertheless, Husserl does not reject this psychology; he rejects the philosophy of science which attempts to ascribe to it an exclusive status with regard to philosophy. But later he seems to contradict what we have been saying: "experimental psychology is related to originary psychology in the way social statistics is related to originary social science."[24] If by originary psychology Husserl means phenomenological philosophy, then his is an attempt to discover a structural system of relations between experimental psychology and philosophy in spite of his former statement that there is no relation of any sort between "exact modern psychology" and philosophy. I do not think that Husserl's ambivalent attitude to psychology can account for such a glaring contradiction between his arguments. It seems advisable, therefore, to take 'originary social sciences,' to refer not to phenomenology, but to a sort of phenomenological sociology of the kind practiced by Alfred Schütz. Hence, originary psychology is not phenomenology proper, but phenomenological psychology, that is, a novel type of psychology, whose method is that of "seeing essence." This psychology stands in close affinity to phenomenological methodology on the one hand, and to prevalent scientific psychology on the other. This is probably the origin of that mediating function Husserl later assigns phenomenological psychology, which in the *Crisis* is supposed to relate scientific psychology to transcendental phenomenology. Husserl, however, is not yet concerned with the question of the relation of "originary psychology" to phenomenological philosophy, since in this essay he was preoccupied with stressing the meaning of

the phenomenological method, with establishing its validity, and with setting phenomenology apart from psychology through a critique of the psychophysical approach.

11. We have seen that at first Husserl was concerned with
a critique of the philosophy of science; he set out from the
phenomenological philosophy of science to attack the positivistic philosophy of science, in order to establish the
phenomenological method as a legitimate method for the
new "science"—phenomenological psychology. In what
follows Husserl goes on to meta-scientific criticism, that
is, to a general analysis of the method practiced and the
mode of explanation employed in contemporaneous scientific psychology, using phenomenological methodology
which claims that the method of "a priori seeing essence"
is necessary for any a posteriori explanation. Husserl is
not very interested in an immanent scientific critique of
the actual scientific investigation, that is, in criticizing the
logical vagueness of the concepts of experimental psychology from the standpoint of this very psychology and its
system of findings and claims. His extrascientific critique
is a broad attack on the experimental procedure which he
considers incapable of providing a "truly" meaningful scientific explanation. Every scientific methodology states its
own criteria for a "true" scientific explanation. Thus, for
instance, contemporary logical positivism claims that a
true scientific explanation has to map the functions of orders and to give verifiable laws (like the nomological net
of Carnap and Feigl), which make it possible for a specific
prediction to be tested empirically. According to these criteria, Fechner and Weber's psychophysical laws (which
Husserl himself takes to be "valuable psychophysical facts
and norms")[25] constitute a full and sufficient explanation of
phenomena, since according to this methodology, "true"
scientific understanding is identical with the knowledge of
laws and predictability. Husserl does attack the obscurity
of the concepts in experimental psychology from the phenomenological standpoint, according to which laws and
predictability (that is, statistics, whether sociological or
psychological) are not criteria for a true explanation. Here
we should think back to the statement quoted earlier about
some kind of relation between empirical psychology
(statistics of natural consciousness) and "originary psychology." Now we can say that the relation Husserl was
referring to was the "meaningful explanation" and the
"more profound understanding" which the intuitive-eidetic
a priori "seeing of essence" is supposed to give the natural
facts discovered by experimental psychology. On the one
hand, therefore, Husserl upholds experimental psychology
and even gives its method of experiment and discovery of
statistical correlations relative autonomy, and, on the other
hand, he stipulates that these a posteriori findings be interpreted according to the a priori phenomenological method.
But the question arises as to whether such a procedure is
possible from the practical point of view? Is a consistent
transition from phenomenological psychology and the eidetic explanation of psychical phenomena to scientific
psychology, which is not based on intentional structuralism, possible?

12. The difficulty seems to lie in the possibility of effecting a transition from the a priori findings of the ideal *eidos*
of intentional consciousness to the a posteriori findings
reached by experimental psychology independently of the
former. For instance, how can one relate the concept of
"sensation" revealed in its ideal essence as a noematic *eidos* which the "pure" consciousness intends, to the sensation referred to by scientific psychology in its psychophysical investigations? There could be a relation only if
we were to deduce (here deduction in a wide sense of the
term) the experimental concept of "sensation" a priori
from the ideal noema of this concept, whose essence we
know through "seeing" and through the method of free
variations. And, indeed, Husserl later affirms the logical
and epistemological priority of the eidetic investigation
over the psychological investigation for meaningful findings in the phenomenological sense of the word "meaning" or "explanation":

> believing (scientific psychology—J. G.) that . . . it is
> an experimental science of the physical in fundamen-
> tally the same sense as physical science is an experi-
> mental science of the physical. It overlooks the specific
> character of certain analyses of consciousness that must
> have previously taken place, so that from naive experi-
> ences (which presuppose the existential "positing"—J.
> G.) . . . they can become experiences in a scientific
> sense.[26]

Besides the idea of the priority of the phenomenological
investigation, this paragraph once again displays Husserl's
ambivalent attitude to scientific psychology. It appears
that, if the relation of phenomenological psychology to
scientific psychology could be ascertained, this experimental psychical science would become legitimate, like the
positivistic experiments in physics. Theoretical physics
would in that case be analogous to eidetic psychology, and
experimental physics to experimental psychology. But
Husserl eliminates the possibility of any such analogy not
only by explicitly stating that experimental psychology is
not, from the point of view of its scientific status, analogous to physics, but also by using the word "empiricism"
in a sense altogether different from its usage in naturalistic
psychology:

> scientific value cannot be there from the beginning
> . . . it can in fact be obtained logically from no em-
> pirical determinations whatever (in the positivistic
> meaning of empirical and experimental—J. G.) . . .
> here is the place for phenomenological analysis of es-
> sences, which however strange and unsympathetic it
> may sound to the naturalistic psychologist, can in no
> way be but an empirical analysis.[27]

That is, Husserl uses the term "empirical analysis" for the
phenomenological investigation of intentional consciousness and for the determination of the essences of psychical
phenomena. This empirical analysis is, for him, true scientific psychology, the only psychology which is analogous
to physics. Like physics with the *physis,* this psychology
succeeds in isolating its object of investigation, the *psyche,*
from a prescientific and pretheoretical attitude and placing

it in its "pure immanency" under the methodical manipulations of "seeing essence" and the method of free variations. But the former scientific psychology thereby becomes devoid of scientific meaning and significance, and is therefore deprived of a legitimate scientific status. If this is the case, what will those positive relations (mentioned by Husserl) between phenomenology, which is the only true science of the psychical, and his contemporaneous scientific psychology actually be?

13. One of the reasons for Husserl's ambivalent attitude to scientific psychology is the fundamental difference between the sense of "science," "consciousness," and "empiricism," in the positivistic philosophy of science, and their connotations in phenomenological philosophy. The confusion, which results in the use of the same terms with different connotations without defining the framework of discourse and without laying down a univocal explication of these concepts, is rooted in Husserl's desire to maintain the science of the psychical in its positivistic sense, to place the phenomenological science of the psychical above or beside it, and, at the same time, to determine the positive relations between these two fields. There are fundamental difficulties in such an attempt: (a) we have two distinct philosophies of science here; and the concepts of one cannot be used to bridge the gap between them, since this would alter the other so that it would cease to be the discipline it was originally; (b) another complementary difficulty lies in the possibility of a transition from the ideal descriptions of intentional structures to the concrete psychical events, which constitute the facts of actual experience and with which experimental science alone can deal. In other words, there is the difficulty (not yet solved by Husserl) of the transition from the a priori, ideal and possible of philosophy, to the a posteriori, real and actual of science.[28] Husserl tried to solve this problem in the *Crisis* by arguing that science as a whole is nothing but a synthetic-theoretical attitude based on former syntheses. Thus the distance between the ideality of the contents of the intentional-transcendental consciousness and the abstractions and idealizations of empirical science is reduced. The question of whether Husserl solved all the problems involved in this attitude is outside the scope of the present paper.

14. Here, Husserl is attempting to overcome the difficulties inherent in a transition from the ideal to the empirical sphere by eliminating the experimental science of the psychical, but he also wants to uphold such a science. This ambivalence is sometimes overtly negative: scientific psychology is eliminated. Yet there are also attempts to determine the positive relations between psychology and phenomenology by ascribing meaning to psychophysics through the phenomenological method. The determination of the essence of a general-psychical object with its various components is a necessary condition, according to Husserl, for the ascription of "scientific" meaning to psychophysics; and the previous discussion makes it clear that by "scientific" meaning Husserl means phenomenological meaning, that is, "seeing essences," and not the positivistic

meaning of ascribing laws of relation and prediction. Husserl says that "it is the fundamental error of modern psychology . . . that it has not recognized and developed this phenomenological method,"[29] that is, he actually demands that scientific psychology take up the phenomenological method of "seeing essence" and that the experimental method, along with the positivistic methodology on which it is based, be replaced by the phenomenological method and methodology. But it is also possible that Husserl wants to retain the experimental method, which would commit him to fundamental reforms in scientific psychology, including new positive relations between the two "methods." And, indeed, Husserl does demand a radical reform, by which "psychology is constructed on the basis of a systematic phenomenology."[30] Husserl attempts to alter scientific psychology completely and to establish it anew on a phenomenological basis, by trying to make phenomenology the normative science for the experimental one. As a result, a new psychology would replace psychophysics: a genuine experimental psychology based on systematic phenomenological foundations. Husserl's ambivalent relation to scientific psychology can be solved temporarily in this way. Only after the appearance of the new psychological science "will we again be able to admit—what we in no way admit in regard to present-day psychology—that psychology stands in close, even the closest relation to philosophy."[31] The new scientific psychology will "stand in close relation to philosophy" through phenomenological psychology, which constitutes a specific branch of phenomenological philosophy.

15. To sum up our discussion, I shall enumerate the three kinds of psychology which emerged in it: (a) *Psychophysical scientific psychology* is eliminated, because its experiments make no reference to the results (norms) of the phenomenological investigation of the intentional *psyche,* and because of its "naturalization of consciousness." (b) *Phenomenological scientific psychology* consistently and systematically applies the results of phenomenological investigation. It is not quite clear how this scientific psychology can stay within the experimental scientific domain without "naturalizing consciousness." The only way it can do so is by referring to consciousness solely as an intentional consciousness but then it would perform phenomenological "experiments" fundamentally different from experiments which use inductive-positivistic methodology. But, if this scientific psychology is to deal with psychointentional structures, it will be extremely difficult to tell it apart from phenomenological psychology and these two psychologies will be identical. Indeed, it later becomes clear that in founding this new psychology, Husserl is actually referring to: (c) *Phenomenological psychology,* whose specific object of investigation is the psychical with all its phenomena and intentional structures, and which is part of phenomenological philosophy which, unlike phenomenological psychology, has a universal *noema* as its object.

This psychology reveals the system of structural and invariable elements in the acts of consciousness. Thus, unlike experimental psychology, this psychology is a priori and normative. Its a priori meaning is inherent in the fact that it does not deal with a posteriori actual psychological events, but with essences which belong in an a priori and necessary way to the sphere of possible acts. Thus, this psychology attains ideal and eidetic norms, to which all actual acts must conform, because these concrete acts depend on the a priori for their properties and structures though not for their actual occurrence.

Notes

1. F. Brentano, *Psychologie vom empirischen Standpoint.* Hamburg: Meiner, 1955-59. 2 vols.

2. P. Ricoeur, *Husserl: An Analysis of His Phenomenology,* Evanston: Northwestern University Press, 1967. Ch. 1.

3. M. Farber, *The Aims of Phenomenology.* New York: Harper & Row, 1966. P. 12.

4. E. Husserl, *Cartesian Meditations,* tr. D. Cairns. Hague: Martinus Nijhoff, 1960.

5. E. Husserl, *The Crisis of European Sciences and Transcendental Phenomenology,* tr. D. Carr. Evanston: Northwestern University Press, 1970. Part 3. Hereafter cited as *Crisis.*

6. H. Spiegelberg, *The Phenomenological Movement.* Hague: Martinus Nijhoff, 1960. I, p. 149.

7. The method of "seeing essence" (*Wesenschau*) intends to disclose the forms, i.e., the meanings and the essential structures of various conscious processes, as they appear immanently in one's own consciousness. By the word "seeing," Husserl wants to emphasize that we are not engaging here in a priori logical abstractions and definitions while explicating the "pure essence," but are directly "observing" and "intuiting" the cognitive contents in their self-givenness. See also: E. Husserl, *Ideas,* tr. W. R. Boyce, 2nd ed. London: Allen & Unwin, 1952. Pp. 54 ff.

8. E. Husserl, *Logische Untersuchungen.* Halle: 1900-1901. 2 vols.

9. E. Husserl, *Logical Investigations,* tr. J. N. Findlay. London: Routledge, 1970. Vol. I.

10. E. Husserl, "Philosophy as Rigorous Science," in *Phenomenology and the Crisis of Philosophy,* tr. Q. Lauer. New York: Harper & Row, 1966. P. 80 (my italics).

11. E. Husserl, *Ideas,* p. 42 (italics added).

12. For the distinction between the phenomenological method and methodology, see D. Cairns, "An Approach to Phenomenology," in *Philosophical Essays in Memory of Edmund Husserl,* ed. M. Farber. Cambridge, Mass.: Harvard University Press, 1940.

13. *Philosophy as Rigorous Science,* p. 84.

14. F. J. J. Buytendijk, "Husserl's Phenomenology and its Significance for Contemporary Psychology, in *Readings in Existential Phenomenology,* ed. N.

Lawrence and D. O'Connor. Englewood Cliffs, N. J., Prentice Hall, 1967. P. 358.

15. About Husserl's demand for a presuppositionless epistemology see M. Farber, "The Ideal of a Presuppositionless Philosophy," in *Philosophical Essays in Memory of Edmund Husserl.*

16. *Philosophy as Rigorous Science,* p. 86.

17. *Ideas,* p. 44.

18. *Philosophy as Rigorous Science,* p. 86.

19. *Ibid.,* p. 91.

20. *Ibid.,* pp. 91-92.

21. *Ibid.,* pp. 89, 92, 98.

22. *Ibid.,* p. 92.

23. *Ibid.,* p. 93.

24. *Loc. cit.* For the extension of this note through the foundation of "Phenomenological Social Science," see: Alfred Schütz, *The Phenomenology of the Social World,* tr. G. Walsh and F. Lehnert. Evanston, Illinois: Northwestern University Press, 1967.

25. *Philosophy as Rigorous Science,* p. 93.

26. *Ibid.,* pp. 97-98.

27. *Ibid.,* p. 98. Compare Husserl's concept of "empiricism" as it is stated here with his later "Principles of all Principles" which is "grounding . . . all knowledge of facts in experience" (*Ideas,* p. 93).

28. Consult: Edo Pivcevic, *Husserl and Phenomenology.* London: Hutchinson University Library, 1970.

29. *Philosophy as Rigorous Science,* p. 119.

30. *Loc. cit.*

31. *Ibid.,* p. 120.

Robert Sokolowski (essay date 1992)

SOURCE: "Husserl and Analytic Philosophy and Husserlian Intentionality and Non-Foundational Realism," in *Philosophy and Phenomenological Research,* Vol. LII, No. 3, September, 1992, pp. 725-30.

[*In the following review of two books on aspects of Husserl's thought, Sokolowski provides a comprehensive view of the state of the understanding of Husserl's thought at the end of the twentieth century.*]

The wish is often expressed for works that would bridge the gap between "continental" and "analytic" thought. The two books under review richly fulfill that wish, and they do so in different ways. Cobb-Stevens' volume [*Husserl and Analytic Philosophy*][1] is wide-ranging, Drummond's [*Husserlian Intentionality and Non-Foundational Realism*][2] concentrates on a more particular topic.

The center of Cobb-Stevens' book is an exposition of Frege's thought as seen through Husserlian categories. Cobb-Stevens observes that Frege, like Husserl, rejected psychologism, but was not able to explain the being or the origins of propositions. Frege also failed to examine the empiricist presuppositions of psychologism, which holds perception to be the mere acceptance of impressions. Both of these deficiencies, according to Cobb-Stevens, stem from the fact that Frege had an inadequate understanding of perception and could not explain how perception can lead to predication. Husserl, in contrast, developed a much more adequate understanding of perception through his concept of categorial intuition. He was able to show how propositions arise from perception through prepredicative experience and through the articulation of parts and wholes in things, an articulation that yields propositions that can be expressed in language, repeated, and subsequently quoted; as Cobb-Stevens says, it is necessary to examine "the interplay between perceptual discriminations and primitive predications" (p. 91). Husserl shows how logic and semantics can be rooted in subjective intuitions, without being dissolved into merely subjective phenomena.

Husserl's concept of categorial intuition, however, corrects more than a deficiency in Frege's thought alone. Cobb-Stevens claims that it is a corrective to a form of thinking that has characterized modern philosophy since its beginnings in thinkers like Bacon, Descartes, and Hobbes, who also had inadequate notions of perception and intuition. The epistemological problems of modern thought brought with them a deficient understanding of substance, which was taken as either something hidden and unknown behind appearances or a mere congeries of appearances. Husserl's notion of categorial intuition allows us to recover a premodern, and specifically an Aristotelian understanding of perception and knowledge, one in which species are presented through the "looks" of things. Husserl also allows us to achieve a more public understanding of mind; mind can now be taken as the part of nature which serves as the place to which the rest of nature can be displayed, and not as a Lockean "cabinet" in which ideas occur. Husserl's revision of the modern understanding of cognition also permits a revision of the modern concept of substance; we come to see that individuals are always experienced as instances of a kind, and that kinds or species are always given as embodied in individuals. This reciprocity between individual and kind (between first and second substance in Aristotle) is neither an ambiguity nor an embarrassment but a necessary structure in cognition and the display of things.

In developing his thesis, Cobb-Stevens provides an extensive commentary on the work of Frege. He examines Frege's notion of sense and reference, his concept of the True and the False as the referents of statements, his notion of assertion and the "grasping" of propositions, his interpretation of senses as modes of givenness, his treatment of concepts as functions, and his concept of number. Cobb-Stevens treats at great length the meaning of quantification, quantifiers, variables, functions, value-ranges, and the problem of substitution and reference in opaque contexts. He makes abundant use of commentators and critics such as Dummett, Baker, Hacker, Rorty, Ryle, Davidson, Rosen, Searle, Angelelli, Currie, Sluga, Quine, Furth, and others. Russell's theory of definite descriptions, and Strawson's emendations of it, are also considered, as are themes from Wittgenstein. Strawson's distinction between the recognition of sortal universals and the placing of features is interpreted as an analytical acknowledgment of prepredicative intuition. All this is done with great competence and clarity, with unity of argument and with constant reference to the basic issue of how intuition can underlie predication. It is accomplished from a point of view different from that of most commentators on Frege and thus makes a distinctive contribution to the literature on his work. Cobb-Stevens appreciates the great advances made by Frege and the influence he has had in contemporary logic, ontology, and semantics, but he is also able to situate Frege's work in a very wide historical context and to reveal some limitations in it. Frege's work is enhanced, not denigrated, by this original and insightful study.

Cobb-Stevens also discusses some other issues in analytic philosophy. He observes that its emphasis on predication as independent of intuition leads to a failure to distinguish between routine, mechanical procedures and insightful thinking; Husserl's appeal to categorial intuition corrects this weakness. He says that "facts" ought not be treated merely as true thoughts, but should be taken as confirmed displays of things in the world, achieved through categorial intuition. He observes that philosophy should treat speech and experience from a first-person point of view, since it is the first-person who speaks, predicates, and perceives; philosophy should not adopt the standpoint of an omniscient third-person observer detached from the human condition and enjoying "unproblematic access" to things in the world (pp. 34-36). Husserl's concept of the transcendental, philosophical attitude thus helps us negotiate the difficult problem of philosophical discourse. Cobb-Stevens provides interesting historical sketches concerning the origins of psychologism and historicism, and makes some valuable comparisons between Frege and Brentano. Only two chapters of the book are specifically devoted to Husserl, one on his overcoming of psychologism by means of his description of cognitive intuition, and another on his transcendental turn, which examines the nature of philosophical discourse and the distinction between propositional and philosophical reflection. A final chapter is entitled "Reason and History," and shows how a proper understanding of contextualized intuition can overcome both rationalism and historicism.

It is interesting to note that the two main currents of twentieth-century philosophy, the continental and the analytic, stem from two individuals who were contemporaries, Husserl and Frege. They are the originators of the problems treated and the perspectives adopted by the great majority of thinkers who followed them, and they—Husserl and Frege—in their turn were not beholden to any major figures immediately before them. They set the immediate context, they did not merely inhabit or adjust it. Cobb-Stevens shows what was at issue in the relationship between the two thinkers and how their relationship can be placed within the quarrel between the ancients and the moderns.

If Cobb-Stevens' book covers great distances, Drummond's is much more tightly focused, more like a dogfight than a vast sea battle. It deals with an interpretation of Husserl that has been inspired by Frege's thought: the interpretation of the Husserlian noema as a sense, as similar to Frege's *Sinn*. This interpretation was proposed in its basic form by Dagfinn Føllesdal. It was more extensively expressed in a book and some articles by David W. Smith and Ronald McIntyre, and it has been upheld by Hubert Dreyfus. It has become an established interpretation of Husserl, particularly in the United States. It has been criticized in different ways by writers such as Leonore Langsdorf, Richard Holmes, J. N. Mohanty, and the present reviewer. This Fregean reading of Husserl is the major concern of Drummond's book, but a secondary concern is the meaning of noema proposed by Aron Gurwitsch, which is different from the interpretation just mentioned. A full chapter is devoted to Gurwitsch, and his interpretation is frequently discussed in the book as a counterpiece to the Fregean reading.

Drummond rejects the interpretations of both Gurwitsch and Føllesdal. He does so after careful exposition of the two positions and their various commentaries and critiques, after a meticulous examination of the relevant texts of Husserl, and after bringing out the philosophical issues at work in this controversy. His task is formidable, because it requires that he not only present an interpretation of Husserl's writings, but also show how the alternative readings do or do not fit the texts; he must also show how and why the alternative readings have gone wrong; and he must take into account the various commentaries and critiques. Many perspectives have to be balanced and confronted. Drummond is clear and authoritative in his treatment of these tangled issues, and it seems to me that when all is said and done he clears the skies of hostile aircraft; his book invites careful study and response by those with whom he differs.

The Fregean interpretation claims that Husserl's concept of noema is an expansion of Frege's notion of sense. Frege introduced the concept of *Sinn* in connection with his treatment of the meaning of verbal expressions, but, according to this interpretation, Husserl saw that there was something like sense or *Sinn* in all forms of cognitive intentionality, even in perception. The Fregean interpretation is based primarily on texts from *Logical Investigations* and *Ideas I*. The interpretation holds furthermore that Husserl posited the noema as an abstract entity that explained how our consciousness becomes intentional, how our awareness can become related to objects and not merely enclosed in itself. It is through the noema, according to this "mediator-theory" (p. 5), that our consciousness targets an object; the contents of the noema pick out an object and make it the referent of our awareness. The noema, therefore, is ontologically distinct from the objects it helps us target. Drummond observes that while Husserl's early work, *Logical Investigations,* gives some credence to the Fregean reading, his later works do not. Especially pivotal is *Ideas I.*

The difficulty with the Fregean reading of Husserl is that it misses what is most distinctive about Husserl's philosophy. It misunderstands both the nature of intentionality and the nature of the transcendental attitude, the attitude from which philosophy is done. It reads Husserl from the point of view of Frege, and hence, as Cobb-Stevens shows, it reads him from within the epistemological dilemmas of modernity, which Frege never managed to resolve. It fails to see the breakthrough that Husserl's thought achieved. Someday the Fregean reading of Husserl will be used as a case history in hermeneutics, an example of how a fixed paradigm cannot manage to interpret something different from itself in anything except its own—the paradigm's—terms, so that it quite overlooks what is original in the new doctrine. The case is made even more interesting because there are indeed some passages in Husserl that make the Fregean reading plausible, provided they are interpreted in a certain way and provided other texts and other philosophical issues are left out of consideration. The paradigm lets the interpreter see only certain things and blinds him to others. In this instance, the paradigm in question is the epistemological set of issues that has ruled philosophy for several centuries and that is particularly powerful in what is called analytic philosophy.

For Husserl, it is not necessary to find a mediating entity that bestows intentionality upon awareness, because consciousness is intentional by its very nature: consciousness is "always already" intentional, never in need of something to make it so. No explanation is called for and it is meaningless to ask for one. If one does not begin from inside a Lockean cabinet, one does not need a key to get out of it. What Husserl discovered was the possibility of understanding philosophy in such a way that in it we examine both consciousness and the objects of consciousness in their correlation to each other. As Drummond makes clear, the noema is simply the object looked at from the philosophical point of view, i.e. from the transcendental attitude. The noema is the object phenomenologically examined, it is not a bridge-entity between us and our objects.

The philosophical attitude must be distinguished from what one could call the propositional attitude, which is another kind of reflection, one in which we reflect on what someone else has said (or how something might look to someone) and take what he has said merely as a proposal, as a proposition. This propositional reflection yields a sense and not, as such, a noema. The Fregean interpretation does not distinguish between propositional and philosophical reflection, hence it does not distinguish between sense and noema. The distinction between the two reflective attitudes is made most explicitly in Husserl's later works, such as *Formal and Transcendental Logic.* It is not distinctly made in *Ideas I,* but even in that work the noema is related to the transcendental reduction.

One of the best points in Drummond's book is his careful analysis of the text of *Ideas I.* The *experimentum crucis* in the thought experiments of this work can be found in the following point. Husserl speaks of the noematic "determinable X" as the center for all the contents we find when we reflect philosophically on objects. The Fregean interpretation of this X is to take it as something like a demonstrative pronoun (pp. 133-38). It is said to be part of the abstract entity that mediates between us and things, the part that points to the thing we intend through it. But Drummond is able to show that the determinable noematic X is indeed part of the object and not like a demonstrative pronoun pointing to the object. It is the identity that underlies all the predicates, features, and modes of givenness that belong to the object, the identity in the object's manifold of appearances.

In this and in other ways, Drummond provides a more accurate and a more comprehensive reading of the texts to which the Fregean interpretation appeals. His interpretation of the noema also allows Husserl's thought to escape the legitimate criticisms that writers like Richard Rorty have lodged against epistemological foundationalism in modern philosophy. Drummond bring out this wider issue, and it is reflected in the title of his book, which presents a Husserl who can be read as a nonfoundational realist, not one who is concerned with establishing foundationally the validity of consciousness. Drummond's Husserl is also a much more interesting and fruitful philosopher than the one presented by the Fregean interpretation; he provides philosophy with something to do, to carry out analytical descriptions of various regions of being and various forms of human intentionality. Husserl threads his way between foundationalism and its deconstructive antithesis and provides a serious speculative and cultural role for philosophy.

Drummond also criticizes Gurwitsch's reading of the noema. Gurwitsch takes the noema to be merely the sum of the appearances of an object, not as the identity distinct but never separated from the manifold of appearances. Besides providing a critique of Gurwitsch and the Fregeans on the noema, and besides his comprehensive and exact interpretation of texts and positions, Drummond also gives many philosophical analyses of his own. He discusses perception, its relation to space and motion, and its dependence on psychophysical conditions; he analyzes the issue of possible-world semantics from a Husserlian point of view, showing that for Husserl there is ultimately one world as a setting for all various possibilities; he describes three kinds of foundationalism (empiricist, rationalist, transcendental); he discusses "the realism embedded in our natural experience" (p. 258), a realism which, he observes, the Fregean interpretation cannot explain. He also speaks about the prelogical dimensions of experience and the way they yield predications, thus touching on themes found in Cobb-Stevens' work. Drummond's work is polemical, but positively and constructively so.

The two works together mark an important point in the relationship between continental and analytic philosophy, the two currents that have largely dominated Western philosophy in the twentieth century. It is appropriate, as the century draws to a close, to review these two traditions and set the stage for other configurations in our philosophical life.

Notes

1. Richard Cobb-Stevens, *Husserl and Analytic Philosophy,* Phaenomenologica 116 (Dordrecht: Kluwer Academic Publishers, 1990), pp. vii, 222.

2. John J. Drummond, *Husserlian Intentionality and Non-Foundational Realism. Noema and Object* (Dordrecht: Kluwer Academic Publishers, 1990), pp. xii, 295.

FURTHER READING

Criticism

Fuchs, Wolfgang Walter. *Phenomenology and the Metaphysics of Presence: An Essay in the Philosophy of Edmund Husserl.* The Hague: Martinus Nijhoff, 1976, 98 p.

A clearly written, comprehensible, and coherent presentation of Husserl's philosophy.

Grossmann, Reinhardt. *Phenomenology and Existentialism: An Introduction.* London: Routledge and Kegan Paul, 1984, 278 p.

Explores the influence of Descartes, Brentano, and Kierkegaard in the development of phenomenology and phenomenology's influence in turn on existentialism.

Hines, Thomas J. "Phenomenology and Poetry." In *The Later Poetry of Wallace Stevens: Phenomenological Parallels with Husserl and Heidegger,* pp. 29-58. Lewisburg, Penn.: Bucknell University Press, 1976.

Applies a phenomenological approach to the explication of Stevens's poetry.

Kockelmans, Joseph J. *Edmund Husserl's Phenomenology.* West Lafayette, Ind.: Purdue University Press, 1994, 363 p.

Includes the original text in German and English of Husserl's *Encyclopedia Britannica* article on phenomenology, as well as synopses, commentaries, and an invaluable introductory chapter.

———. *A First Introduction to Husserl's Phenomenology.* Pittsburgh, Penn.: Duquesne University Press, 1967, 372 p.

Offers an overview of the major themes of Husserl's philosophy and an outline of their development.

Levin, David Michael. "Husserl's Notion of Self-Evidence." In *Phenomenology and Philosophical Understanding,* edited by Edo Pivcevic, pp. 54-77. Cambridge: Cambridge University Press, 1975.

> An investigation of what constitutes the "self-evident" for Husserl.

Mohanty, J. N. *Edmund Husserl's Theory of Meaning.* The Hague: Martinus Nijhoff, 1969, 150 p.

> An interpretive study of Husserl's early work on logic and its effect on his theories of thinking and meaning.

Patocka, Jan. *An Introduction to Husserl's Phenomenology,* translated by Erazim Kohak, edited by James Dodd. Chicago: Open Court, 1996, 195 pp.

> Presents a survey of Husserl's development of phenomenology and an analytic discussion of its fundamental methods and problems.

Smith, F. J. "Being and Subjectivity: Heidegger and Husserl." In *Phenomenology in Perspective,* edited by F. J. Smith, pp. 122-156. The Hague: Martinus Nijhoff, 1970.

> Discusses the divergence between Husserl and Heidegger over the meaning and importance of consciousness and being.

Stapleton, Timothy J. *Husserl and Heidegger: The Question of a Phenomenological Beginning.* Albany: State University of New York Press, 1983, 148 pp.

> A study of the relation of the theories of Husserl and Heidegger that explicates the fundamental notions of phenomenology.

Additional coverage of Husserl's life and career is contained in the following source published by the Gale Group: *Contemporary Authors,* **Vols. 133, 166.**

F. O. Matthiessen
1902-1950

(Full name Francis Otto Matthiessen) American critic, essayist, and diarist.

INTRODUCTION

Matthiessen is widely considered the most significant American literary critic of the early twentieth century. A prolific reviewer and essayist, he is credited with elevating the study of American literature into a worthy academic subject that could be used as a cultural and political resource for future students and scholars. His seminal study, *American Renaissance: Art and Expression in the Age of Emerson and Whitman,* is praised as one of the most important critical works on American literature ever written.

BIOGRAPHICAL INFORMATION

Born in 1902 in Pasadena, California, Matthiessen grew up in LaSalle, Illinois. The youngest of four children, he was raised in a wealthy family. In 1919 he attended Yale University, where he became active in politics and interested in literary and religious studies. He was chosen as a Rhodes Scholar in 1923 and attended Oxford University, receiving his Bachelor of Letters degree in 1925. A year later he received his M.A. from Harvard University. He completed his Ph.D. thesis, eventually published as *Translation: An Elizabethan Art*. In 1927 Matthiessen became an instructor at Yale and then Harvard. He taught American literature at Harvard for the rest of his life, becoming an influential and distinguished member of the faculty. During his early years of teaching, he began a life-long romantic relationship with the painter Russell Cheney. In 1941 his landmark study of American literature, *American Renaissance*, was published and garnered much critical commentary. He was politically active during these years, involving himself in socialist causes and co-founding the *Monthly Review*. After Cheney's death in 1945, Matthiessen became progressively depressed and withdrawn. On April 1, 1950, he committed suicide in Boston.

MAJOR WORKS

American Renaissance is considered a classic study of American literature. Before its publication, literature written by American authors was not widely studied and was considered unworthy of serious critical attention. With *American Renaissance,* Matthiessen defined the major figures of nineteenth-century American literature—such as Herman Melville, Walt Whitman, Nathaniel Hawthorne,

Henry David Thoreau, and Ralph Waldo Emerson—and elevated the study of American authors and literature as a legitimate academic subject. His reviews and studies of later American authors such as Theodore Dreiser, Henry James, and T. S. Eliot forged a tradition of American literature that subsequent critics could use as a political and cultural resource. To do this he used the principles of New Criticism, which provided close attention to the structure and texture of language; this approach marked a departure from the work of earlier literary critics such as Vernon L. Parrington and Van Wyck Brooks. It has been asserted that Matthiessen's life-long goal of developing an American literary canon has influenced every subsequent literary critic and student of American letters.

CRITICAL RECEPTION

Matthiessen's impact on the study of American literature is invaluable, and as such the amount of critical attention his work has received is extensive. Most commentators laud his progressive, landmark studies of nineteenth-century American writers and maintain that his work helped to define a distinctive canon of American literature at a crucial time in world history. Yet a few dissenting critics deem Matthiessen's literary criticism as dated and fundamentally contradictory; furthermore, they contend that his importance as a reviewer, essayist, and critic is historical, rather than intrinsic. Recent critical studies have focused on Matthiessen's homosexuality and how it impacted his perspective and treatment of authors such as Walt Whitman, Henry James, Ralph Waldo Emerson, and Hart Crane.

PRINCIPAL WORKS

Sarah Orne Jewett (criticism) 1929
Translation: An Elizabethan Art (criticism) 1931
The Achievement of T. S. Eliot: An Essay on the Nature of Poetry (criticism) 1935
American Renaissance: Art and Expression in the Age of Emerson and Whitman (criticism) 1941
Henry James: The Major Phase (criticism) 1944
Russell Cheney, 1881-1945: A Record of His Work (letters and essays) 1947
From the Heart of Europe (journal) 1948
Theodore Dreiser (criticism) 1951
The Responsibilities of the Critic: Essays and Reviews (essays) 1952

Rat and the Devil: The Journal Letters of F. O. Matthiessen and Russell Cheney (letters) 1978

CRITICISM

R. P. Blackmur (review date 1935)

SOURCE: "A Citation of T. S. Eliot" in *The Nation* (New York), Vol. 141, No. 3668, October 23, 1935, pp. 478-80.

[*In the following review, Blackmur provides a mixed assessment of* The Achievement of T. S. Eliot.]

The great temptation in writing of T. S. Eliot's poetry is to batten upon the frequent illuminations provided for it in his critical essays; and to this temptation Mr. Matthiessen has again and again given in. His book [*The Achievement of T. S. Eliot*] is a citation rather than an examination of Eliot's work, and the circulating energy—what keeps the book going and unites its effects—is Mr. Matthiessen's felt appreciation of Eliot's governing obsessions. Thus the successive crises of interpretation and judgment tend naturally without a jar to appear as unrelieved quotation. There could be no better testimony of the scope, the consistency, and the expressive persuasiveness of Eliot's work once one gives in to it, and no clearer warning, perhaps, of the intellectual necessity of not always and never entirely giving in either to Eliot himself or, now, to Mr. Matthiessen's redaction. One gives in intellectually, emotionally, with all a reader's equipment, to find out what is there, but one draws back both to see what is not there and to situate what is. However valuable Mr. Matthiessen's book is, its very method of approach prevents it from being enough.

The advantage of the method is obvious: it keeps the discussion in terms which are actually pretty much those of Eliot's work. But the disadvantage is striking: there are no tools for detachment, for setting off, for placing Eliot, as Mr. Matthiessen attempts to do, in relation to the contemporary world and the body of poetry. It is a method which leads at its worst to the distortions of a sectary rather than the developments of a disciple or the elucidations of the genuine critic.

The trouble is, I think, that Mr. Matthiessen brings Eliot's poetry to judgment without, for the most part, having passed beyond the stage of reading it. He recites his adventure and represents its exciting details, and what he recites is an illuminating account of an immersion; but that is all he actually does, and it is not the equivalent of judgment. It is better than the application of a preconcerted formula of what poetry ought and ought not to be; and it is better, as Mr. Matthiessen himself ably argues, than judging poetry by some formula of politics or religion or of some snobbery of morals; it is better because it is at least an immersion in the poetry and not an immersion of

the poetry in something else—to see, perhaps, what color it turns—which is what most judgment comes to. There is a question whether judgment is possible and if possible whether it can stand. But if it is possible and if it is to stand, it must be the product of an experience beyond the best reading, an experience very like remaking the poetry itself. That is why Ezra Pound was right in saying that the best criticism of Flaubert was in the novels of Henry James. Since good criticism is not all in novels and poetry, we may say, perhaps, that criticism approaches valid judgment when it remakes its object, after and in consequence of the intimacy of immersion, in generalized or intellectual terms. Thus we schedule and point the consonance of art and life. These remarks would not apply to Mr. Matthiessen were it not for his declared intention: "My one aim in this essay is to evaluate Eliot's method and achievement as an artist. . . ." That aim, with his method of citation and still dripping from immersion, Mr. Matthiessen could only partly achieve.

But if we mark that limit for his book, there is yet in it plenty of material, both that which is enlightening on the way and that which directly aids a genuine evaluation of Eliot's achievement. There can be nothing but approval of the fact that Mr. Matthiessen's approach to Eliot's poetry "is through close attention to its technique," and of the assertion that "what matters is not what a poem says, but what it *is*." Especially valuable are the chapters on "The Objective Correlative" and "The Auditory Imagination"—and these because they come nearest to the positive act of remaking the poems. For the rest, especially for the unoriented reader, the book is full of instruction for reading in the light of the two phrases just quoted.

Robert E. Spiller (review date 1942)

SOURCE: "American Renaissance: Art and Expression in the Age of Emerson and Whitman," in *American Literature*, Vol. 13, No. 4, January, 1942, pp. 432-44.

[*In the following laudatory review of* American Renaissance, *Spiller considers its "importance as a contribution to American literary history and to the theory and technique of historical writing."*]

I have already reviewed Mr. Matthiessen's book elsewhere in general terms. I should like here to consider its importance as a contribution to American literary history and to the theory and technique of historical writing. Even though its method is nonchronological, **American Renaissance** seems to me to be an important piece of historical writing, and should influence our concepts of how the history of American literature might be rewritten.

First, what Mr. Matthiessen is not: He is not a passive, objective chronicler. Events pass before his review weighted by values and in interrelationships other than juxtaposition. He has conceived his problem as a whole, established his own attitude toward it, and exercised his critical judgment as well as his historical knowledge at every point in the selection and arrangement of material for discussion.

Second, he is not a social or intellectual historian in the strict uses of those terms. His interest in plan and pattern in the affairs of men is based on neither sociological nor philosophical grounds. The plane of his thought and writing is that of art and culture, and past movements in social and philosophical forces are reduced to a secondary plane to be treated, as they should be *fully* treated in literary history, as causal and consequential factors. There is not here the confusion between literary and other forms of history that one finds in those historians who evaluate literature in terms of its content of communism, agrarian democracy, Puritanism, materialistic determinism, or other borrowed ism. The central pole of reference is esthetic significance.

But he has not, on the other hand, reduced literature to pure expression by divorcing form from content and treating it in a vacuum, as belletristic critics did in an earlier day and the post-neohumanists sometimes attempt to do today. He revives from Coleridge and Emerson an organic theory of literary composition and, while keeping his emphasis upon expression, gives full and qualitative consideration to the thing expressed in its relationship to its form, developing a modern functionalism in literary criticism.

The key to his method is given in the opening sentence of his preface: "The starting point for this book was my realization of how great a number of our past masterpieces were produced in one concentrated moment of expression." This was the five years following 1850, the distillation point in our literary history for the expression of the first American man, i.e., the emotionally and intellectually mature product of the thirteen original colonies. His economic being was the result of an expanding agrarianism; his spiritual and intellectual being of the breakdown of Puritanism into cool Unitarianism and fervent Transcendentalism; his social and political being of his traditional devotion to the ideals and possibilities of democracy. Here are the three background books which Mr. Matthiessen was prepared to write, but he wrote none of them; his is a literary history. Adopting Ezra Pound's thesis that "the history of art is the history of masterwork, not of failures or mediocrity," he continues, "My aim has been to follow these books [the midnineteenth-century American masterworks] through their implications, to observe them as the culmination of their author's talents, to assess them in relationship to one another and to the drift of our literature since, and, so far as possible, to evaluate them in accordance with the enduring requirements for great art."

The statement of a theory of literary history is easier than its application to a specific problem. Mr. Matthiessen deals with his by four full-length studies of the work of Emerson, Hawthorne, Melville, and Whitman, respectively. In the first, Emerson, with the assistance of Thoreau, states the metaphysical and ethical ideals of life in America, and the organic theory of its expression. In the second, Haw-

thorne, artist and skeptic, reveals the difficulties of the artist in this situation without resolving them. His acceptance of evil in the world, even though he could not envision an evil world, opened the paths of tragedy, escape and despair and so prepared for Melville, James, and Eliot. In the third, Melville confronts the dualism in life which Emerson sought to distil to a single essence and Hawthorne, in fright, to veil thinly. Art must accept the primitive depths of nature as well as the "refined ascent of the mind." In his acceptance of the whole of experience he recalls Shakespeare, as he does in his development of original comic and tragic art forms. But he is finally an "American Hamlet," his conflict, like Hawthorne's, unresolved. In the fourth, Whitman, at his best, succeeds in bridging the void by "making the specific richly symbolic of the universal." His confident vision "led him to fulfill the most naïve and therefore most natural kind of romanticism for America, the romanticism of the future." The relationship of this vision and its expression to later American poetry (e.g., E. A. Robinson and Sandburg) and painting (e.g., Eakins and Henri) is effectively noted.

The central question of the book is adequately answered; satisfactory explanations are given for the concentration of art expression in the middle years of the last century; even though at times condensation would make the reader's progress easier and the writer's points sharper. The larger framework of the book, which involves the seventeenth-century English metaphysical poets, Coleridge and European romanticism, passages from the history of American painting, and T. S. Eliot and the modern metaphysicians, serves its purpose of high-lighting the American romantic movement, but is in itself somewhat eclectic and fortuitous, the product rather of Mr. Matthiessen's own intellectual equipment than of inevitable and organic relationship to the main study.

These are necessary weaknesses of the method, as no critic can be omniscient. They can be accepted as long as the book is merely a critical analysis of one problem in a literary history rather than an attempt to deal with that history as a whole. But a modification of the method to make it more generally applicable may well serve as a substantial platform for the reconsideration of the complete story of American letters. The emphasis upon masterworks as the primary material of literary history; the ability to remain on the plane of art and culture while giving full weight to the causal significance of social and intellectual forces; and the sense of pattern in past events provide an historical method for other special studies like this as well as for the more ambitious attack upon the whole problem, which must sooner or later be made.

Philip Rahv (review date 1945)

SOURCE: "Modernizing James," in *The Kenyon Review*, Vol. VII, No. 2 Spring, 1945, pp. 311-15.

[*In the following mixed assessment of* Henry James: The Major Phase, *Rahv perceives Matthiessen's analysis as lacking, but deems the volume a significant study of James's later novels.*]

This book [**Henry James: The Major Phase**] is an important contribution to the growing literature about Henry James. For all the talk of James as a neglected figure there is scarcely another American writer who has of late aroused so much critical ardor and discussion. Since the James number of *The Little Review* (1918) numerous appraisals of his work have appeared; and this intellectual opinion has at long last filtered down to the middlebrow public, so that now James can be said to be enjoying something of a vogue in circles heretofore indifferent to his reputation. Nevertheless one can safely predict that a good many readers, whether highbrow or middlebrow, will continue to resist the Jamesian charm. In its very nature this charm cannot but operate sporadically and superficially on those whose imagination is not caught by the historical theme of the American character in its approach to art and experience, a theme deeply problematical yet firmly grounded in the national culture. And when to the more obvious difficulties of the Jamesian prose you add insensibility to its thematic particulars, it plainly becomes very hard to be convinced of its merits.

The problematical theme referred to above is one of which the popular adulators of the national ego who have lately come to the fore with sweeping claims to the leadership of our literature are largely unaware; for to deal with America in the bulk is at once their practice and preference. Also unaware of it are the scholastic as well as the sociological critics and historians of letters; and so of course are the anti-intellectuals of all shades. The professional avantgardists, whose literary associations are narrowly confined to the memory of bohemian revolt and experiment, are for the most part blind to everything but the element of genteel snobbery in James. Thus James must run the gauntlet of these hostile groupings, impelled by different and perhaps mutually exclusive interests to reject the large claims advanced in his behalf. It seems likely that their combined influence will result in depriving him of the kind of generous and ultimate recognition so freely accorded to Melville upon the rediscovery of his work in the early nineteen-twenties.

Mr. Matthiessen's study of James's later novels is most satisfactory not only in points of scholarship and taste but also in its excellent balance of the analysis of form with that of content. He assimilates and deftly summarizes the best of the accumulated James criticism at his disposal. What is missing, however, is a sufficiently existential grasp of the works of art under examination; the unique and the odd and the unexpected in these works is too readily converted by this critic to the ideas and negotiable intellectual formulas of the age; his earnestness of temper seems to allow for too little zest or exhilaration in the reading of texts; and one is bothered, too, by his literal dependence on the characteristic assumptions and critical procedure of T. S. Eliot—a dependence quite as evident in his **American Renaissance** as in this new volume. One wishes that

he would not draw upon Eliot quite so steadily, and not with the air of a man who has just come into a fortune; the danger is that of reducing Eliot's insights to an academic system. Only in one respect does he deviate from his model, but, as I shall attempt to show further on, it is precisely in this deviation (or modification) that his thought is least substantial.

Mr. Matthiessen has had the inestimable advantage of access to James's unpublished notebooks, and the passages quoted are well used in uncovering, among other things, the origin of certain plots and the gradually unfolding intention of their author in his elaboration of them. The discussion of the last three great novels is finely sustained. One is struck by many apt particulars, such as the analogy between Impressionist painting and some of the effects in *The Ambassadors*. There is a plausible definition of James's place as a psychologist on the borderline between such older novelists as Hawthorne or George Eliot and the post-Freudians, and in the analysis of *The Wings of the Dove* we get for the first time a careful correlation of Milly Theale's character with that of her prototype in life, Minny Temple, the cousin of whom James had so much to say in *Notes of a Son and Brother*. And so far as concerns Mr. Matthiessen's general estimate of his subject, it is heartening to see him throw over the inflationary approach of the James cultists, who in their adoration of the master tend to pour into his work all the values of ideal writing.

It is in the chapter on *The Golden Bowl* that this critic's freedom from cultist attitudes is most apparent. That novel is one of the much debated items in the James canon, for in it James applied his spellbinding powers as never before to the creation of a life of illusory value for his wealthy Americans in Europe and their sponging aristocratic friends with whom they conduct a romantic historical liaison. Not a few critics have been provoked by this quality of the novel. One instance is Stephen Spender, who, flying in the face of the Jamesian specifications, describes Prince Amerigo as "an unknown, well-bred scoundrel." Some have argued, weakly I think, that the picture of the Ververs and their bought-and-paid-for Prince is to be taken in an ironical sense; Mr. Matthiessen, however, takes the story as given, and his interpretation coincides in many respects with Ferner Nuhn's mordant analysis of the story. I agree entirely with their reading of it, but I cannot go along with Mr. Matthiessen in his conclusion that this novel is "with all its magnificence . . . almost as hollow of real life as the chateaux that had risen along Fifth Avenue and that had also crowded out the old Newport world that James remembered." To say that *The Golden Bowl* is morally deficient and decadent is one thing, but to claim that for this reason it is empty of life and, by implication, an inferior work of art is something else again. To my mind, this is an example of moral overreaction at the expense of literary judgment. I can think of other novels, say Dostoevsky's *The Possessed*, which from the standpoint of any radical social morality are thoroughly distorted and even vicious but which none the less I would rate as supreme works of fiction. *The Golden Bowl* must be placed,

I believe, among the half dozen great novels of American literature; there is one section in it—the second, third, and fourth chapters of the fifth "Book"—which for vividness, directness, and splendidly alive and spacious imagery is without counterpart in the American novel. Mr. Nuhn has defined *The Golden Bowl* as a dream story. He is right of course, since the indicated position of its characters and the idea they have of themselves are not in correspondence with reality. Yet as a dream story it is far from being a mere invention. It has the enormous vitality which springs from the actual dreamlife of a social class—a dream of the "loot of empire," an imperial dream full of "real" objects and "real" life. One can object to its content on ideological grounds, and on those grounds James is indeed vulnerable; but one cannot deny that it is historically meaningful and that it has interest and artistry and a kind of meditated though cruel beauty.

And in the final passage of Mr. Matthiessen's estimate of James a point of view is expressed which seems to me unacceptable. He quotes Eliot's remark that James was "indifferent to religious dogma" but at the same time "exceptionally aware of spiritual reality," and his comment is that "it is likely that a man of James's sensibility, if his mind had been formed in our age of crisis, would have felt, as Eliot has, the ineluctable necessity of religious order." This is idle play with a very large speculative "if—an "if" much too large to swallow—a yearning and gratuitous "if" which conveniently saves James for "traditionalism" and religiosity. (It reminds me of the days when the Communist critics were busy reclaiming all sorts of classic Americans—from Daniel Boone to Emerson—on the ground that if they were alive they would surely "belong to us." Michael Gold actually wrote a piece called "Daniel Boone Belongs to Us." Thus the Communist literary tactics of the thirties are repeated by the new religionists of the forties.) Lionel Trilling has recently referred to James's indifference to religious dogma as a modern possibility. I would say that it is more than a possibility: it is a modern fact from which most of the great artists of the past hundred years are not to be divorced, for they lived this fact and their work cannot be considered significantly apart from it.

Mr. Matthiessen develops further his "traditionalist" view of James, and this is where his deviation from Eliot comes in, if it is a deviation. He would probably say that he is in fact bringing Eliot up to date:

> His [James's] intense spiritual awareness, drifting into a world without moorings, has told others beside Eliot that if religion is to persist, it must be based again in coherent dogma. At the opposite pole, the novelists of social protest can still learn much, as Robert Cantwell has incisively argued, from James's scale of values. His gradation of characters according to their degree of consciousness may be validly translated into terms of social consciousness, and thus serve as a measure in a more dynamic world than James ever conceived of. To those who believe that if both Christianity and democracy are to endure, the next synthesis must be more rigorously based in both political economy and theology, in the theology that recognizes anew man's radical

imperfection, and in the radical political economy that insists that, whether imperfect or not, men must be equal in their social opportunities, many of James's values are, oddly enough, not at all remote.

Here is as tortuous an example of the attempt to "modernize" James at all costs as we have yet seen. But why is it necessary to justify his art in terms either of a "radical political economy" or the revival of Christian dogma? The truth is that James is at bottom negatively related to both, and that we must either take him or leave him as he is. Besides, to associate the movement for a radical renewal of society with theology, as Mr. Matthiessen does, is to be guilty of an arbitrary construction. For if examined empirically, from the standpoint of concrete historical experience rather than through lax literary concepts, socialism and theology turn out to be mortal enemies. Mr. Matthiessen cannot have it both ways.

F. W. Bateson (review date 1953)

SOURCE: A review of *The Responsibilities of the Critic*, in *Modern Language Notes*, Vol. LXIII, No. 7, November, 1953, pp. 502-4.

[*In the following mixed review of* Responsibilities of the Critic, *Bateson contends that Matthiessen was an excellent reviewer, but a mediocre critic.*]

The subtitle [of *The Responsibilities of the Critic: Essays and Reviews*] is a little misleading. Of the fifty short critical pieces by Matthiessen that make up this book as many as thirty-nine are reviews, reprinted by Mr. Rackliffe, a tactful and intelligent editor, from the *Yale Review*, the *New England Quarterly*, the *New Republic* and similar journals. The "essays" presumably include everything else, from the courageous Hopwood Lecture delivered at the University of Michigan in May 1949, a liberal challenge to this iron age which gives the book its title, to some literary obituaries and unpublished fragments. It is, therefore, essentially Matthiessen the reviewer who is presented to us in this collection. Mr. Rackliffe (or perhaps his publishers) may have thought it prudent not to stress that fact. Collected reviews do not often make enthralling reading, especially when, as here, most of the reviews are comparatively short and the topics range all the way from Winslow Homer or Tocqueville to Louis MacNeice, whom Matthiessen perversely preferred to Auden, or Theodore Spencer, an old friend and colleague at Harvard. This *ought* to have been an unreadable book, or at least one to dip into merely. That it isn't, that on the whole it makes astonishingly good reading even to an Englishman who does not share Matthiessen's interest in *stellae minores Americanae*, is an indication of the exceptional quality of Matthiessen's reviewing.

One of the unpublished pieces that Mr. Rackliffe found among Matthiessen's papers boldly equates literary reviewing with literary criticism. A review is simply "a short piece of criticism." A good review, according to Matthiessen, should "at the minimum do three things. It should furnish exposition and description; it should enable you to feel concretely what is being described; and it should give you in the process an evaluation." The three things, he adds, should be interwoven, with "a few deftly foreshortened examples" worked into the exposition and the evaluation coming out in the "analytical insights."

The formula is a useful one, but I am not sure that it doesn't miss the real point. What differentiates the reviews of a Poe, who remained for Matthiessen the model reviewer, or of Matthiessen himself, from the common or garden review, those indigestible morsels of print now provided for us by the tonier Sunday newspapers on both sides of the Atlantic, isn't surely just the interweaving of exposition, illustration and evaluation. No, it is the ability to hit the nail on the head. In more formal terms, the successful review is characterized by the subordination of the particular comments to a significant central theme. Matthiessen's best reviews might each of them almost be said to say *one thing only*; each review, that is, is so organized as to establish or lead up to a single crucial *aperçu*. His review of Van Wyck Brooks's *World of Washington Irving*, for example, revolves round the dictum that "Brooks is not really a critic but a lyric poet *manqué*." And in another review, one of the best in the book, the problem of Howells, the great American novelist who never quite came off, is reduced to "a kind of nice restraint which amounts almost to complacency." The slightly vulgar headings that Mr. Rackliffe has prefixed to the separate pieces provide further evidence of Matthiessen's habit of building up his reviews, round a single proposition: "Primarily Language: John Crowe Ransom," "An Absolute Music: Hart Crane," "Selfless Devotion to the Arts: Paul Rosenfeld," "Whitman: Sanguine Confused American."

Matthiessen was an excellent reviewer, but was he a critic? Is it so certain that a review should aspire to being "a short piece of criticism?" The two disciplines seem to me, I must confess, essentially different. A review, like an article or a historical work or a scientific treatise, "wants" to be the coherent elaboration of a single proposition. Literary criticism, on the other hand, as the mirror image of imaginative writing, inevitably tends towards the synthesis of diversity rather than the analysis of unity. For the critic, therefore, there is never just one nail to hit on the head. Instead there are at least two or three opposite or discordant qualities in a condition of balance or reconciliation. This is perhaps why (i) the "practitioner" is generally such a good critic, and (ii) the best critics, like Eliot and Empson, almost always make such bad reviewers.

Matthiessen's instinct, however, was always to ignore or play down oppositions and discordances within the work of art. In consequence his discussions of the technical aspects of literature are invariably superficial. Thus he recognizes, as he could hardly fail to do, that the special quality of Ransom's verse derives from the interplay of archaisms and colloquialisms, but instead of defining and

isolating their respective contributions Matthiessen immediately blurs the essential distinction by equating the archaism with country speakers for whom the King James version of the Bible is still a living language. The archaisms, in other words, are really colloquialisms! Instead of trying to get behind the clash in Ransom's poems between the colloquial and the archaic, Matthiessen was in effect, though he did not realize it, explaining the clash away. The penalty of this instinctive anti-critical trend is that he can only *assert* that Ransom's poetry is just good minor poetry. By denying that the archaisms are primarily literary and that the colloquialisms are primarily urban vulgarisms he was in fact tearing up the very evidence which might have proved his case. The episode is an instructive example of the limitations of the good reviewer. On a larger scale it is the distinction between the critical treatise and the literary guide-book. Matthiessen's friends and pupils have sometimes tried to persuade us that *American Renaissance* and the books on Eliot and James are critical masterpieces. They are not. They are only extraordinarily useful cultural Baedekers.

Richard Ruland (essay date 1967)

SOURCE: "F. O. Matthiessen, Christian Socialist: Literature and the Repossession of Our Cultural Past," in *The Rediscovery of American Literature*, Harvard University Press, 1967, pp. 209-73.

[*In the following essay, Ruland analyzes the defining characteristics of Matthiessen's critical work and evaluates his impact on American literary theory and criticism.*]

> *The whole book is based on the proposition that what a writer believes about man, about society, and about the universe has a great deal to do with what he writes.*
> . . .
>
> —GRANVILLE HICKS on *American Renaissance* (1941)
>
> *If we are to have adequate cultural history, we must begin by respecting the texts themselves.*
>
> —F. O. MATTHIESSEN, *The Responsibilities of the Critic* (1952)

As a method, the close attention to the text insisted upon by New Criticism has had far-reaching beneficial effects. But as the sole concern of its more ordinary adherents, it has proven stultifying. The divorce of art from its cultural context must sooner or later prove sterile. By making "extra-literary" a pejorative phrase, many younger New Critics have contributed to the extreme specialization and compartmentalization of life the older Agrarians deplored in commercial civilization.

The need Brooks and Warren felt for increased sensitivity to "the poem itself" and the technique they formulated for achieving it is nowhere better described than in their lengthy "Letter to the Teacher" in *Understanding Poetry.*In revising their textbook in 1950, twelve years after its first appearance, they spoke with justifiable pride of their success: "Today the critical attitude has entered into hundreds of classrooms."[2]

But in some quarters there has apparently been misunderstanding; nothing points more eloquently to the limitations of the disciplines than the adjustments urged by the masters in their new "Postscript." In this revision, they write, "we are inclined . . . to make certain shifts of emphasis, or if not shifts of emphasis, at least certain expansions in treatment. A decade ago the chief need was for a sharp focus on the poem itself. At that time it seemed expedient to provide that focus, and to leave to implication the relation of the poem to its historical background, to its place in the context of the poet's work, and to biographical and historical study generally. The years that have followed have indicated that these relationships could not safely be left to implication."

"Some teachers," the authors continue, "have felt that *Understanding Poetry* implied a disregard for historical and biographical study." (True to my training, I cannot but read the italics as both title and the end in view.) "In this revised edition, therefore, though we continue to insist upon the need for a sharp focus upon the poem itself, we have tried . . . to view the poem in relation to its historical situation and in relation to the body of the poet's work."

Not everyone, of course, had misunderstood the early formulations of Brooks, Warren, and other first-generation New Critics. No intelligent teacher, the new preface chides, "has ever presented poetry in a vacuum. . . . On the contrary, he brings every resource he possesses to bear upon the poem . . . *to see how history, literary and general, may be related to poetic meaning.*" (The insistent italics belong to the editors.) One such intelligent teacher was F. O. Matthiessen, and though he died the year the revised textbook appeared, the work he left behind testifies to the involvement of every personal and professional resource he possessed.

I

Matthiessen understood perfectly well the historical currents which made *Understanding Poetry* necessary, and he understood—and accepted—the work of Eliot, and Richards, which supplied so much of its theoretic basis. It was because he did recognize the contribution of New Criticism that he was so pained by its misguided applications in the forties. "The little magazines," he told a University of Michigan audience in 1949, "seem now to be giving rise to the conventions and vocabulary of a new scholasticism. . . . The trouble is that the terms of the new criticism, its devices and strategies and semantic exercises, can become as pedantic as any other set of terms if they are not handled as the means to fresh discoveries but as counters in a stale game. In too many recent articles literature seems to be regarded merely as a puzzle to be solved."

Matthiessen delivered this address, **"The Responsibilities of the Critic,"** just eleven months before he died. It is

worth examining closely because, with the possible exception of the familiar "Method and Scope" preface to *American Renaissance*, it is the fullest critical credo he ever wrote. He cannot accept a situation where "textual analysis seems to be an end in itself," he says, because criticism then becomes "a kind of closed garden." Such compartmentalization leads, in Leavis' words, to a split between "mass civilization" and "minority culture," a split Matthiessen fears is extremely dangerous. He urges instead a criticism cognizant of its responsibilities. "I do not see," he insists—and here suggests his affinity with Stuart Sherman—"how the responsible intellectual in our time can avoid being concerned with politics." All his life Matthiessen believed that it is a prime function of criticism to "keep open the life-giving communications between art and society."

Matthiessen saw no need to reject New Criticism, but he felt that his contemporaries must learn from the thirties—from the Marxists and from V. L. Parrington. These men had tried, however unsuccessfully, to see life whole, to understand the role of economics and industrialism in the problems of American democracy. "Emerson held that a principle is an eye to see with, and despite all the excesses and exaggerated claims of the Marxists of the 'thirties, I still believe that the principles of Marxism . . . can have an immense value in helping us to see and comprehend our literature." What Matthiessen is insisting upon here is the tools with which the critic approaches his task. He does not accept the Marxist view of man; he wants only to broaden the base of criticism to ensure that "the analyzing mind is . . . absorbed in a wider context than the text before it."

He is also thinking of the critic's equipment when he commends the methods of cultural anthropology (history and sociology) and urges greater awareness of the popular arts of television and the movies. The important thing is that the critic must know his country—not chauvinistically and innocently, but with maturity, "by which I mean the maturity that comes from the knowledge of both good and evil." If this last is linked to Matthiessen's religious commitment ("I am not a Marxist myself but a Christian"), and indeed it is nearly as explicit as he ever was, we have seen him touch upon most of the elements in his own criticism. "In proposing an ever widening range of interests for the ideal critic," he concludes, "I have moved from his central responsibility to the text before him out to an awareness of some of the world-wide struggles of our age. We must come back to where we started, to the critic's primary function. He must judge the work of art as work of art. But knowing form and content to be inseparable, he will recognize his duty to both. Judgment of art is unavoidably both an aesthetic and a social act, and the critic's sense of social responsibility gives him a deeper thirst for meaning." Matthiessen's own application of these principles will become more clear as we examine his work. No one, I think, will deny that he followed his own call—an anticipation of Brooks' and Warren's enjoinder—to bring "everything in your life to what you read."

There was nothing doctrinaire about Matthiessen's Socialism, and so what it meant to him can only be seen in how it made him feel and what it made him do. To judge from his description in *From the Heart of Europe* (1948), his participation in the Salzburg Seminar during the summer of 1947 was one of his most rewarding experiences. He took the occasion with the utmost seriousness and regarded the gathering of students from all over Europe as a sign that a torn world could yet be made to mend. He was proud that the Seminar had been organized by his own students from Harvard, and he was proud to head the faculty and give the opening address. "Our age," he began, "has had no escape from an awareness of history. Much of that history has been hard and full of suffering. But now we have the luxury of an historical awareness of another sort, of an occasion not of anxiety but of promise." The occasion is historic, he adds—and uses a favorite phrase—because they are met "to bring man again into communication with man."

As Matthiessen said on that occasion, his address was more a speech of fraternity than of welcome. It is this same basic humanitarianism which characterized his life from his earliest awareness of the society he lived in. He later dated this awakening—or rather dramatized it—with a citizenship class he conducted at the New Haven Hungarian Club while he was a student at Yale. He was impressed by the enthusiasm with which the men regarded the education he had always taken for granted, and although most of his students were twice his age, "by the end of the lessons we had achieved something close to friendship." Matthiessen's later life was a steady effort to continue the relationship with the world he felt he had established here: "After the last session, one of the men suggested, with a sly wink, that I might like to see the rest of their building. They took me down cellar where each one had been fermenting his own cask of prohibition wine. We sampled several, with a good deal of ceremony, and the stars seemed unusually bright as I walked back to the Yale Campus. I had felt in the natural and hearty comradeship of these men a quality that I was just beginning to suspect might be bleached out of middle-class college graduates. It was a kind of comradeship I wanted never to lose." Matthiessen encountered the economic and social formulations which helped him understand his experience at about the same time. In an economics course which he hated, he was frightened into outside reading for extra credit. Quite by chance he happened upon Tawney's *The Acquisitive Society*, and "there could have been no luckier opening of the door into social theory. Tawney's ideas about equality have remained more living for me than anything else, except Shakespeare, that I read at college."

Matthiessen served as vice-president of Yale's Liberal Club, and when he reached Oxford in 1923 as a Rhodes Scholar, he joined the Oxford Labour Club. He eventually became a supporter of Debs. He read Veblen and voted for Al Smith. He came to respect Norman Thomas, and though Roosevelt seemed at first "little more than . . . a Harvard man who wanted very much to be President," once President he won Matthiessen's approval. "After he began to effect even some of the things for which Thomas had stood, I voted for him enthusiastically, though always from the left, until his death." But while abroad Matthiessen was won to the idea of a "labor party with a trade union base to which an intellectual could adhere with the realization that he could learn the first-hand facts of economic organization from this contact, and could then, in turn, be of some use in helping to provide ideas for leadership." The absence of such a party in the United States probably affected his life deeply, for he was never fully at home in any of the many political organizations he joined. He believed that "no progressive party can carry real weight unless it is solidly rooted in the labor movement," and he spoke frequently of the need the intellectual has to know "what is actually going on in the minds of the people," but as he saw, labor in this country has not been a dependable political instrument, and—what he apparently did not see, or at least did not admit to himself in print—labor has more and more become a powerfully conservative force in our society. Matthiessen did his best with the Harvard Teachers' Union (AFL), serving several times as its president. He joined the Socialist Party for a while early in the Depression, but later worked tirelessly for the Progressive Party and in 1948 delivered a speech to second the nomination of Henry Wallace for President.

Robert L. Jackson attended the 1948 Progressive Party convention, and has told me of an evening when the talk among the loyal Wallace supporters turned in question of their candidate's intellectual strength and the subtlety of his ideas. "Oh, you intellectuals," Matthiessen burst out with a sweep of his hand, and went on to defend Wallace. The story emphasizes how Matthiessen felt about the fatal split he saw between "society and solitude," between the people of the democracy on one side and the intellectual and the artist on the other. Wallace, he insisted, was "emphatically a successor in the Jeffersonian tradition, the great tradition of fearlessly introducing major principles into political discussion." If elected, the future would judge him "one of the few broad and seriously humane minds in our presidential history." As such he earned a place in Matthiessen's personal version of a viable American heritage, "the revolutionary tradition from Paine and Jefferson to the populists and progressives and Henry Wallace."

Matthiessen's ideals were focused in the Wallace candidacy, but the hopes and dreams of the man found even fuller expression in the months at Salzburg. When he bid his hosts good-bye, he thanked them "for providing the best milieu for teaching that I have ever known." The expectations of his initial speech were for him surpassed. "Here," he recalled, "was our Brook Farm, here was our ideal communistic experiment, where each . . . gave according to his abilities, and received according to his needs." Meeting in a world of Hiroshima on the depleted desert of Central Europe, the students in "our enchanted garden" had learned a new faith in "the dignity and power of the intellectual. Hardly more than a hundred men and women, some already worn beyond their years, we were nevertheless going back to our many countries with a re-newed belief in the possibility of communication. We were carrying with us too the belief that there was much we could still do, by our speaking and writing, to cut through prejudice, to destroy the barriers of ignorance and hate that otherwise will destroy us all." It is this hope and faith in the future that led to the writing of *From the Heart of Europe*. Like so much of Matthiessen's work, it moves between the individual's service to society and the kind of society which best supports a fully human life. Here Matthiessen's teaching at the Seminar is juxtaposed to a bright new Socialist world he saw foreshadowed in the Czechoslovakia of Masaryk and its promise of success in fusing the traditions of East and West. It was to see this experiment at first hand that he asked Ernest J. Simmons to arrange a term's lecturing for him at Charles University in Prague, and it was the Communist putsch of 1948 that destroyed both his hopes for a way out of the tensions of the Cold War and any unity of focus or intention his book could have. As Simmons says, it is a measure of his disappointment that he did not take the opportunity offered him to revise the optimistic tone of the work before it went to press.

The two dozen or so memoirs of Matthiessen published in the October 1950 *Monthly Review* return again and again to his intense desire for brotherhood, for the integration of himself as intellectual with his society and for a consequent satisfaction in serving it well. *From the Heart of Europe* dwells frequently on moments of comradeship, on group singing and laughter, that call up the New Haven Hungarian Club and the unusually bright stars to be seen after a trip to its cellar. In a sense, Matthiessen remained all his life a little tipsy on the Prohibition wine he tasted that night. When he urges at every opportunity his vision of a truly just and democratic society, his insistence is painful in its sincerity, but his effort to imagine how such a society might function rarely escapes a touch of sentimentality. Alfred Kazin is not the only admiring friend of Matthiessen to suggest that his Socialism was mainly emotional, that it grew from an intense dissatisfaction with the rarefied air of the Ivy League and lacked the saving critical severity which marks his literary work. But the important thing for the present study is that Matthiessen did cherish a vision of society he worked to make prevail, and that, as he himself would have been the first to insist, that vision cannot be separated from his aesthetic judgments.

It might seem that Matthiessen's political activism was the only thing to distinguish him from Stuart Sherman. There is in fact a striking similarity between the two critics' ethical and political consciousness. They shared as well a commitment to American literature and its responsibility to American life. It was Sherman's involvement with this life that attracted Matthiessen to him. How strong the attraction was and on how many points in Sherman's career it touched is revealed in Matthiessen's review of *The Life and Letters of Stuart P. Sherman* in 1929. He outlines there the essential details of Sherman's career, dwelling on his Harvard thesis ("one of the few doctoral dissertations

on record which possessed a feeling for literature") and Sherman's faith in the state university. The broadening acceptance of contemporary life which took Sherman to the *New York Herald Tribune* Matthiessen approves, but he recognizes the loosening of standards this new role demanded. In short, there is little of value in the later Sherman except the promise that he is moving "towards a greater awareness of what life actually is."

Matthiessen's idea of what life is and how literature is related to it was deeper and more subtle than Sherman's for at least two reasons, both of which are perhaps related to the twenty years separating the Americas each matured in. When Matthiessen brought his early enthusiasm for Arnold into the classroom of Irving Babbitt, he was only on the way to the influence of Van Wyck Brooks, Parrington, and—ultimately and by far most significantly—T. S. Eliot. As I hope this book has shown, no sensitive critic, after the work of Richards and Eliot, will be able to approach literature with quite the simplicity shown by the commentators who preceded them.

But more of Matthiessen's critical forebears in a moment. Unlike Sherman, Matthiessen was not pressured by the secularism of the twenties into accepting a wholly natural or human basis for morality such as Irving Babbitt's. At Yale he was vice-president of Dwight Hall (the university religious society) and chairman of the Bible Study Committee. Twenty years later he could still reject Vittorio Gabrieli's reduction of religion to an Arnoldian "morality tinctured with emotion" and oppose it with—in Gabrieli's words—"his mature unsophisticated faith in God and his dissatisfaction with a purely worldly ethics." "One hundred years ago in New England," Leo Marx has written, "he might well have been a minister . . . he spoke of taking a job at Harvard as 'accepting a call.'" J. H. Summers, another student of Matthiessen, recalls a conversation in 1943 in which Matthiessen stated his position as a Christian "in the simplest terms. He believed that love was the greatest value man could know, and he believed its power and absolute value could not be accounted for by any naturalistic or rationalistic explanation."

Matthiessen's commitment to the second great commandment is of course related to his faith in the brotherhood of Socialism, but his religious ideas are even less fully articulated than his political ones. Even so, his Christianity helped him distinguish his stand from Marxism. "Some of you are Marxists," Summers remembers him telling a group of students and friends who had met to celebrate publication of his *American Renaissance* in 1941. "I am not a Marxist. I have been influenced by Marx as has anyone who has seriously thought about political matters in the last fifty years. But Marx was often more successful in coining effective slogans for immediate political action than in arriving at statements of philosophical truth. If any of you really believe that religion is only 'the opiate of the people,' you cannot hope to understand the five figures I have tried to write about in *American Renaissance*." Matthiessen's religious views do play a large part in his major book, as we shall see, and Granville Hicks, in his searching review for the *New England Quarterly*, had good cause to complain that Matthiessen's ruling premises should be more clearly articulated.

The following passage comes closer to a definition of Matthiessen's religious position than any other I have found, and so I will quote most of it. "I am a Christian," he writes in *From the Heart of Europe*, "not from upbringing but by conviction, and I find any materialism inadequate. I make no pretense of being a theologian, but I have been influenced by the same Protestant revival that has been voiced most forcefully in America by Reinhold Niebuhr. That is to say, I have rejected the nineteenth-century belief in every man as his own Messiah, along with the other aberrations of that century's individualism; and I have accepted the doctrine of original sin, in the sense that man is fallible and limited, no matter what his social system, and is capable of finding completion only through humility before the love of God." Thus he cannot follow his radical friends who think man perfectible and blame all evil on the capitalist system. But at the same time, he adds, "I would differ from most orthodox Christians today, and particularly from the tradition represented by T. S. Eliot, in that, whatever the imperfections of man, . . . [the Commandment] to love thy neighbor as thyself, seems to me an imperative to social action. Evil is not merely external, but external evils are many, and some social systems are far more productive of them than others." "My philosophical position is of the simplest," he concludes. "It is as a Christian that I find my strongest propulsion to being a socialist. I would call myself a Christian Socialist, except for the stale and reactionary connotations that the term has acquired through its current use by European parties." The large role played by Matthiessen's Christianity in his critical work has not often been noticed, I think, because his conceptions of man and of human evil are subsumed under the term *Tragedy*. He doubtless chose his idiom from literature both to escape conventional responses to familiar ideas and to strive once again for the integration of complementary viewpoints, but his idea of tragedy is clearly as much a political and religious conception as it is an aesthetic one. "The hero of tragedy," he suggests, "is never merely an individual, he is a man in action, in conflict with other individuals in a definite social order." The writing of Hawthorne and Melville, to cite two of his favorites, approaches the heights of tragedy because it grows from a mature view of man's relation to his society.

Unlike Sherman and most earlier critics, Matthiessen's seventeenth-century Puritan was a real human being. Matthiessen was a friend of Perry Miller and he read and perhaps influenced Miller's books; he was himself a close student of the seventeenth century in England. Though persistently hopeful, he subscribed to Miller's reading of the past as closer to the truth than Parrington's rosier interpretation. The concept of original sin, which Miller explored and which Melville had pointed to for its perceptive insight into human nature, was never excluded from

Matthiessen's pleas for social solidarity and brotherly love. He always saw man as "tragic," faced with a world that was neither good nor evil but good-and-evil, complex, contradictory, and resistant to improvement. At this point Matthiessen's view is much closer to More and to Eliot than it is to Sherman. And although he could not follow Eliot all the way in his thinking, he had frequent recourse to Eliot's belief in original sin and in the psychological accuracy which gives dogma its value. Matthiessen's love of life was deepened, as he said, by "acceptance of men's constant desperate ruin, and, in the face of that, of man's heroic capacity for no less constant renewal." How this can be translated into a literary standard should become clear once we see how Matthiessen did in fact apply it. For the moment it will suffice to repeat the conviction which served as epigraph for his *Achievement of T. S. Eliot* and was later repeated in *American Renaissance*. The words are Yeats': "We begin to live when we have conceived life as tragedy."

Matthiessen reasserted in the last sentence he wrote that he was both "a Christian and a socialist." That his different commitments often failed to mesh smoothly, those who knew him repeatedly testify. "To be at once a Christian and as close to Marxism as Matty was would seem absurdly inconsistent," Leo Marx notes. "Yet perhaps the most profound and elusive lesson he taught was that a smooth and absolutely logical structure of ideas is not necessarily a sign of the greatest intellectual maturity. . . . He knew . . . that the mind, with its categories and abstractions, always trails behind life. And he felt that the value of a teacher, to borrow Henry James' criterion for the novel, depended upon the amount of life he contained." Richard Wilbur recalls that "his political convictions, his religious faith, and his love of artistic excellence led him into certain intellectual conflicts. He never resolved these for himself by dogmatism. . . . I think, to mention but one of the difficulties in his compound position, that a part of Matty wanted to believe that 'bad' beliefs make for bad art; but his taste and his honesty were too genuine to allow him any relief from doing justice." That Matthiessen failed to synthesize his disparate principles is not as much to the point as his constant effort to keep each one before his mind and operative. He strove for a total integration of the inner and outer man, of his personal and his public life. It was this that probably attracted him so forcibly to Eliot's formulation, the "dissociation of sensibility." Like the Fugitive-Agrarians, he accepted Eliot's Metaphysicals as more fortunately integrated in their emotional and intellectual lives than modern man has been given the chance to be. "Most of his friends," notes Helen Merrell Lynd, "were primarily socialists *or* Christians *or* artists *or* critics. For Matty these things were as inevitably wrought together in life."

The dramatic tension these forces brought to Matthiessen's forty-eight years of life dominates May Sarton's novel, *Faithful Are the Wounds* (1955). The book deals even more with the people around her protagonist and the impact upon them of his death, but the man who emerges must be very like her model. Edward Cavan leaves his father's home to seek a closer involvement with the world he lives in. Ashamed of his family's wealth, he develops what at one point is described as a foolish nostalgia for the workingman. Because Wallace reads his books, Cavan comes to feel that active communication between the intellectual and his government may soon develop. From various angles come criticism of his Socialism, his faith in the unions, his refusal to compromise in academic or party affairs, and the seeming incongruity of his membership in the Episcopal Church. We learn of his prickly personality, his exposed sensibilities, and his love for his friends and their love, so often tested, for him. The total picture is of a difficult but admirable man, and although the details are often etched by an uncomprehending voice, the novel moves finally to a climatic acceptance. Of his concentrated passion, one of his best students recalls, "That was the quality he had as a teacher, and I begin to think he had it partly because he had it about everything. I mean, would he have cared in the same way about literature if he hadn't been involved in human affairs themselves? That's the real question."

II

"No school that I attended went at all imaginatively into the American past," Matthiessen recalled. "Literature at Yale had still meant English literature," and (or so Matthiessen claimed) until 1930 *Moby Dick* was listed by the Yale library not under American literature but under cetology. At Oxford in 1923 he began reading American writers for the first time. "Whitman was my first big experience. . . . I took *Walden* with me . . . on a vacation trip . . . and started it on the steamer up the Rhine. I did not get to *Moby Dick* until after I was back in America." In half a dozen years he had fallen enough under the influence of Van Wyck Brooks to announce, "It is time for the history of American literature to be rewritten," and to publish a nostalgic study of a distant relation that is all but dominated by the soft shading of the later Brooks. Matthiessen's first book, **Sarah Orne Jewett** (1929), is close enough to Brooks for Bernard Bowron, one of Matthiessen's shrewdest readers, to characterize it with its author's own mature words: "By the time Brooks wrote *The Flowering of New England* he had relaxed his standards. He was no longer concerned with ideas, or with critical discriminations, but with describing the surfaces of the milieu that had produced the writing. . . . His picture is charming but sentimental . . . it has robbed the period of most of its clash and struggle."

Matthiessen was not so much relaxing his standards as finding them too slippery to grasp firmly. His own love of rural Maine and his not yet fully examined sense of the problems accompanying industrialism led him to retreat from the confrontation between the machine and the garden that Leo Marx has recently discussed. If, as Bowron suggests, the private garden of the book is seen as its central symbol, the Matthiessen who celebrates it is as yet far from the forceful denouncer of the "closed garden" that

New Criticism can make of literature. But his escape from Brooks' misty collapse into the past begins even before **Sarah Orne Jewett** comes to a close. With the sharp eye that marks all of his best work, he finally is able to place both his author and the ideas of her time, and he rejects once and for all the temptation to escape the pressure of the present through immersion in a rosy past.

In 1936, when Matthiessen reviewed *The Flowering of New England*, he objected to Brooks' failure to treat the work of Emerson, Thoreau, and Hawthorne with aesthetic subtlety, and while praising him for his rediscovery of Greenough's lectures on functional architecture, he regretted that "Mr. Brooks did not bring their doctrines into relation with Emerson's and Thoreau's conception that style in writing also must be based organically on nature." Matthiessen missed as well any discussion of tragedy in the book, a lack due, he says, to "little recognition by Mr. Brooks of any tragic factors in the actual life of the times." When we add Matthiessen's praise for Brooks' thorough grasp of his materials to his preference for Parrington's deeper penetration into ideas, we have a fairly full recipe for Matthiessen's own masterwork, **American Renaissance** (1941). That book, we are told, was ten years in the making; it seems likely that its substance was planned with reference to the work of Brooks on the one hand and Parrington on the other. In a review of *The World of Washington Irving* in 1944, Matthiessen goes even further in rejecting the loss of dramatic tension that followed Brooks' blurring of chronology, and he ultimately repudiates even the early, "wry view of our past." "Neither his earlier dejected image . . . nor his present glowing one is anything like an objective interpretation of the complex and warring forces that make up human life at any period."

There are traces of Brooks' style scattered throughout Matthiessen's work. Like Brooks, he so immersed himself in his subject that a writer's phrases flowed naturally into his own sentences, and though he always used the quotation marks that Brooks did not, he rarely identified his sources. He liked too the kind of surprise by analogy that Brooks enjoyed, the statement given that his subject could have made but did not—and so on to an illuminating similarity between seemingly different writers. These things are at best superficial, however. Brooks' idea of a usable past, on the other hand, remained central to all the teaching and writing Matthiessen did. "What makes the art of the past still so full of undiscovered wealth is that each age inevitably turns to the past for what it most wants, and thereby tends to remake the past in its own image." The word, "wants," I think, should be read "needs," for Matthiessen spoke often of the need the present has to enrich itself through assimilation of its heritage. His word was "repossession." "Today we can take no tradition for granted, we must keep repossessing the past for ourselves if we are not to lose it altogether." As Henry Nash Smith has remarked, the use the artist will make of his carefully assimilated tradition is different for Matthiessen from what it was for Brooks. Brooks sought primarily to free the writer of the teens and twenties from a suffocating society and to bring him into a productive solitude. In Matthiessen's generation the artist was undeniably free, but his freedom had proven—to Matthiessen's eyes at least—socially sterile. "He saw," notes Smith, "that the primary need was to break down the isolation that prevented the writer from participating in the life of the community, and deprived the community of the indispensible insight of the writer."

The American tradition which Matthiessen built reflects this change in emphasis, and so Brooks remained a teacher soon outgrown. Another early guide was V. L. Parrington—Matthiessen says he grew up in the "era of Van Wyck Brooks and Parrington"—but while he admired *Main Currents* and felt that even Brooks was most robust when writing in the Jeffersonian tradition, he could only see Parrington's work as incomplete. Matthiessen was from the first more interested in aesthetic questions of form and the way art works than was Parrington. Parrington shared with the New Humanists a focus on the matter of art to the neglect of its manner, and his judgment was too often betrayed by a "natural desire for a neat formulation." Matthiessen's early enthusiasm for Parrington kept him tolerant of such betrayals of taste, but he had no such sympathy for Parrington's Marxist heirs. It is precisely because Matthiessen was himself trying to evolve a socially responsible approach to literature that he could not endure the oversimplifications of Calverton and the theses he "compels to interlock with the mechanical rigidity of an intricate system of cogwheels." Granville Hicks' *Great Tradition* seemed to Matthiessen more successful because Hicks had read widely and thought his position through. And yet he too is trapped by his thesis. "For him literature is inevitably a form of action, and it has been one of the great services of Marxian criticism that it has brought to the fore the principle that 'art not only expresses something, but also does something.'" But there are different ways of defining what it does. Because Hicks finds art operative only when it grows from and speaks to man's immediate material needs, he finds no place in his American tradition for solitary craftsmen like Emily Dickinson and Henry James or humorists like Twain, Harris, and Lardner. To see literature as a weapon in the class war is ultimately to miss seeing it at all. The new historian of American literature, the young Matthiessen had already decided by 1929, "must not lose himself in his background, or forget that he is dealing primarily with literature. He must remember that his real quarry is aesthetic values, and that perhaps one does not have to master the importance of Jacksonian democracy to read intelligently 'Rappaccini's Daughter.'" The Matthiessen of *American Renaissance*, some ten years later, rarely focused for long on this particular quarry, but the remark does indicate how little he was likely to learn from what would seem to be congenial criticism by the Left.

There was a good deal to be learned, however, from the Right. "By far the most living experience in my graduate study at Harvard," Matthiessen recalled, "came through the lectures of Irving Babbitt, with whose neo-humanistic attack upon the modern world I disagreed at nearly every point. The vigor with which he objected to almost every author since the eighteenth century forced me to fight for my tastes, which grew stronger by the exercise." As we have seen, Matthiessen too rejected the isolation and elevation of the independent ego that Babbitt condemned in Romanticism. And he praised Babbitt for his fight against this "antisocial aesthetic," and for his warning "against the disasters of being either sheltered academics or shallow liberals." But the remedies proposed in a reactionary book like *Democracy and Leadership* are totally inadequate for our social complexity, while Babbitt's lack of sympathy for our common life plays into the hands of every enemy of democracy. Humanism, Matthiessen concluded in 1929, "seems increasingly arid, for it insists too blindly on what ought to be, without any view of the actual. Wise standards are the greatest need in American life and literature today, but they will never be achieved through scholars pointing them out already created for us in Plato and Aristotle. We shall have to create them for ourselves in relation not only to the literature of the past but to the demands of our own environment."

These last lines could have been phrased by Stuart Sherman, but the criticism which is in fact invoked in the next sentence as "far more fertile" than Neo-Humanism was being written by Matthiessen's lifelong master, T. S. Eliot. Eliot's remarkable impact upon his generation has yet to be analyzed. Its basis is implied in the present study, but we need to know more about his different appeal for different people, the uses made of his critical formulations and his poetry by artists on the one hand and teachers and critics on the other. Where some readers value only the young Eliot with his aesthetic emphasis and cultural pessimism, and others cherish his later social and religious concern, Matthiessen's own thinking remained close to Eliot's from first to last. He was excited by *The Waste Land* and "Tradition and the Individual Talent," and often repeated in his early work his own version of Eliot's "Honest criticism and sensitive appreciation are directed not upon the poet but upon the poetry." But very little of Matthiessen's own work adheres to this single-minded focus. Like Eliot, whom he knew at Harvard, Matthiessen had also sat at the feet of Irving Babbitt, and he too perforce developed doubts about overemphasizing the autonomy of the Individual Talent. And while Babbitt, Eliot, and Matthiessen shared distrust of the divinity of human nature and agreed that man's lot is tragic, their similar dissatisfaction with the modern world led, as we have seen, to the acceptance of three very different Traditions. Secular humanism, religious orthodoxy, and Socialism seem on the surface so totally dissimilar that we often miss the points where their negative analyses overlap.

In fact, as Matthiessen describes him in *The Achievement of T. S. Eliot* (1935, revised and enlarged in 1947), Eliot seems very much like the heir to Babbitt and More that Sherman failed to be. If, as Matthiessen says—and he often said the same thing about himself—Eliot was not primarily a profound or consistent thinker, it seems likely that Matthiessen is right to stress his debt to Arnold, Richards, Hulme, and Maurras, and to invoke frequently the name of Irving Babbitt. And though the political advisers here were uncongenial, the moral and literary guides were the same, and Matthiessen's Eliot is largely a portrait of himself. Or rather, it is his recipe for the kind of critic-in-society he wanted to be.

We have seen something of Matthiessen's disappointment with the criticism appearing during the twenties and thirties. He shows his grasp of his time by objecting, by way of preface to his Eliot essay, to the "increasing tendency to treat poetry as a social document and to forget that it is an art." The analysis which follows would serve to introduce *Understanding Poetry*; it emphasizes once again the link between Eliot and New Criticism. "The most widespread error in contemporary criticism," Matthiessen complains, "is to neglect form and to concern itself entirely with content. The romantic critic is generally not interested in the poet's work, but in finding the man behind it. The humanistic critic and the sociological critic have in common that both tend to ignore the evaluation of specific poems in their preoccupation with the ideological background from which the poems spring." Though these things all have their value, comes the by now familiar concession, it must be realized that "they are not criticism of poetry." Matthiessen's point was put neatly in a review he wrote some years later: "If we are to have adequate cultural history, we must begin by respecting the texts themselves."

Matthiessen attributes the current growing discrimination in the handling of poetic texts to Eliot's *Sacred Wood* (1920, 1928) and Richards' *Practical Criticism* (1929)—although he finds Richards guilty on occasion of "super-subtlety." He makes much of Eliot's debt to Arnold throughout the essay, but where Arnold's concern was with literature as criticism of life, "with Eliot, the emphasis is on form." Arnold makes no sustained study of aesthetic questions, while Eliot is concerned with "close technical annotation of detail"; he is preoccupied with craftsmanship. Eliot's approach, Matthiessen asserts, has been directly responsible for the modern appreciation of Donne.

From Arnold, so Matthiessen's epigraph to Chapter III would seem to suggest, came the seed of Eliot's "objective correlative," a formulation which served Matthiessen as his central critical tool. "What is *not* interesting," Arnold wrote, "is that which does not add to our knowledge of any kind; that which is vaguely conceived and loosely drawn; a representation which is general, indeterminate, and faint, instead of being particular, precise, and firm." Eliot's effort at definition aims at just this precision and firmness: "The only way of expressing emotion in the form of art is by finding an 'objective correlative'; in other words, a set of objects, a situation, a chain of events which shall be the formula of that *particular* emotion; such that when the external facts, which must terminate in sensory experience are given, the emotion is immediately evoked." Neither the label nor the phrasing is noteworthy for its fe-

licity, but as Matthiessen affirms, it was already by 1935 "a *locus classicus* of criticism." For Matthiessen, Eliot's own sensory perception—particularly his "auditory imagination"—is eminently successful in supplying his poetry with the requisite concrete external facts, and, along with the writing of Donne, Browne, Marvell, and other Metaphysicals, it gave Matthiessen the touchstone he needed for his examination of the American literary past.

Thus his approach to poetry generally would always be, as he says, "through close attention to its technique." But as he seemed to recognize himself, he would rarely be content to rest there. Although, "I agree with Mallarmé that 'poetry is not written with ideas, it is written with words,' as well as with the assertion that what matters is not what a poem says, but what it is. That does not mean that either the poem or the poet can be separated from the society that produced them, or that a work of art does not inevitably both reflect and illuminate its age." The master soon provided another *locus classicus*: "The 'greatness' of literature cannot be determined solely by literary standards." Matthiessen wrote before these words were available to him, but he was bound to be sympathetic with Eliot's earlier assessment of Edmund Gosse. Gosse, he observed, "was interested in literature for literature's sake; and I think that people whose interests are so strictly limited, people who are not gifted with any restless curiosity and not tormented by the demon of thought, somehow miss the keener emotions which literature can give." An attitude like Gosse's overlooks the fact that the true artist is immersed in his age and cannot help participating in it. "The great poet," Eliot affirms, "in writing himself, writes his time." One of Matthiessen's most interesting efforts to emphasize Eliot's breadth centers on the famous discussion of Shakespeare's levels of significance. Eliot's feeling that different groups in the audience appreciated different qualities in the plays has been frequently quoted, but by enlarging *his* citation to provide the context of Eliot's remarks, Matthiessen gives them an emphasis other commentators have rarely acknowledged. Eliot, it becomes clear, has been talking about a "social 'usefulness' for poetry," and he likes to conceive of his own work in much the same terms. "I myself should like an audience which could neither read nor write." As Matthiessen admits, little of Eliot's poetry can be described in this way, but when the ultimate test of society *or* solitude, tradition *or* the individual talent, is invoked, Eliot emerges primarily occupied not with the individual but with society.

These few remarks should suggest how Eliot furnished support for Matthiessen's efforts to integrate a sensitive approach to literary texts with the inclusive cultural awareness he believed a socially responsible criticism demanded. Furthermore, although he could not follow Eliot into the religious and political conservatism he recommended for society's ills, Matthiessen found in Eliot a full expression of man's complexity and an impressive image of the good life. If the "objective correlative" was to become the center of his critical method, the "dissociation of sensibility" Eliot saw in the modern world came equally to dominate

Matthiessen's vision of tragedy. The poets of seventeenth-century England, Eliot believed, enjoyed a fine integration of mind and body, a wholeness of soul that modern man has lost. "It is probable that men ripen best through experiences which are at once sensuous and intellectual; certainly many men will admit that their keenest ideas have come to them with the quality of a sense perception; and that their keenest sensuous experience has been 'as if the body thought.'" This "direct sensuous apprehension of thought, or a recreation of thought into feeling," that Eliot felt in the poetry of Donne's time may or may not have actually characterized that historical moment. But Eliot's formulation creates in effect a new, pre-lapsarean Eden and sets modern man to putting Humpty together again. The task is rendered all the more difficult when the second Fall is added to the first, and the dissociation of the soul's powers only aggravates the penchant for evil characterized in the dogma of original sin. Matthiessen felt the truth in Eliot's analysis, and he had no trouble linking Eliot with his own sense of what was valuable in the New England tradition, from Puritanism through Hawthorne and Melville to Emily Dickinson and Henry James.

It is only when *The Achievement of T. S. Eliot* is seen in the context of the thirties that its method and tone seem wholly defensible. As Horace Gregory complained, its treatment of Eliot is "reverent . . . the kind of tribute usually issued after a poet's death. . . . It does not quite free itself from the atmosphere of funereal idolatry." In London, *TLS* felt that Matthiessen "worries the obvious to death." And yet his central point was not obvious in the America of 1935, and this goes far to explain the intensity of his attraction to and identification with Eliot. "The poet and the political theorist, the artist and the philosopher," he says by way of summary, "though all relating integrally to the age which produces them, express that relation in different ways." Eliot emphasized the difference, and Matthiessen always followed him in trying to approach art first of all in technical, aesthetic terms. It was this side of the book which Alfred Kazin was praising when he pointed to "the best account of non-romantic diction and rhythm anyone has written since Paul Elmer More deserted to the higher mysteries." But while Matthiessen does make every effort to deal sensitively with Eliot's poetry and with the work of the writers who occupy him in his later books, his method is more a culmination of earlier cultural commentators than it is an anticipation of New Criticism. He is master of all the analytic techniques *Understanding Poetry* worked to foster, and there are passages in the later books which rival the best New Criticism has done in respecting the value and integrity of the poem itself. But Matthiessen the man-of-many-commitments, bent on being—to cite his favorite words from James—"one of the people upon whom nothing is lost," Matthiessen the Christian-Socialist could never bring himself to recognize the autonomy of art and leave it at that. He is continually being led further into the relation of the poem to its author, his life and the life of his time, and the suggested analogies to the poem from past and present. The Eliot essay, with all its talk of influences, parallels, and theoretical underpinnings, is not

so much about Eliot's poems as it is about what went into them, what made the man who has written as he has, and what made the age that made the man and that has responded to his poems. As we shall see demonstrated on a much larger scale in *American Renaissance*, once Matthiessen has shown that he can read as sensitively and perceptively as any New Critic might wish, he immediately moves outward to the role he finds more congenial and altogether more consistent with the social obligations of the scholar. He functions, in his own phrase, as a cultural historian.

III

Matthiessen's unsimplified conception of human nature, based as it was in his Christian sense of sin and his concern for its tragic implications, saved his Socialism from the naivete so notable in the manifestos of earlier decades. And stemming as it did from the best work of Van Wyck Brooks, Parrington, and Eliot (and, in the distance, A. O. Lovejoy), his reading of the American literary past was similarly more mature, less programmatic, than previous formulations. His commitments are as much in evidence, but they are shaded and qualified by the very texture of his statement, and so any summary of his usable past must make it seem more simple than it actually is. I will try to give a fuller sense of Matthiessen's position by following my summary of it with a few remarks on the contexts he built to give body to his views. For *American Renaissance,* tightly knit and massive as it is, must be taken whole. It not only represents—with a few exceptions—his American literary tradition. It is also an articulation of the total man; it *is* F. O. Matthiessen, with all his compassion and all his commitment to the wide world around him. And it moves in as many directions as he did.

By far the dominant impression today's reader must receive from Matthiessen's discussion of Emerson, Thoreau, Hawthorne, Melville, and Whitman is the familiarity of it all. As Granville Hicks predicted in his review essay, *American Renaissance* has indeed proven a "source-book for plenitude." "I have no doubt," he continued, "that at least a generation of students of American literature will draw upon it and be influenced by it." Besides the half-dozen or so major critical works which owe at least part of their impulse to issues raised in *American Renaissance*, there probably has not been a university course in American literature offered in the last twenty years which has failed to echo its conclusions or move outward from their implications. More than one colleague has confided to me that when he now picks up the book he wonders what all the excitement was about—there is very little in its pages which today seems anything more than the plainest common sense.

That Matthiessen's success in this book should be so nearly total is not due solely to the reach of his scholarship and the subtlety of his methods. As conservative critics so often complain, the dominant currents in our literary scholarship have remained Parringtonian. Matthiessen placed his study firmly and explicitly in this tradition. "In my own writing," he says in climax to his opening essay, "I have kept in mind the demands made on the scholar by Louis Sullivan. . . . 'If, as I hold,' Sullivan wrote, 'true scholarship is of the highest usefulness because it implies the possession and application of the highest type of thought, imagination, and sympathy, his works must so reflect his scholarship as to prove that it has drawn him toward his people, not away from them; that his scholarship has been used as a means toward attaining their end, hence his. That his scholarship has been applied for the good and the enlightenment of all the people, not for the pampering of a class. . . . In a democracy there can be but one fundamental test of citizenship, namely: Are you using such gifts as you possess for or against the people?'" Matthiessen's own goal, he concludes, is to measure up to these high standards.

The common denominator for his five authors, "uniting even Hawthorne and Whitman, was their devotion to the possibilities of democracy." Religion too made its social contribution "when it claimed the inalienable worth of the individual and his right to participate in whatever the community might produce." And even the taste which has determined "the best books" has been formed ultimately by "successive generations of common readers." Thus it is that Poe does not qualify for thorough study. It is not merely that he approached literature differently, but he was "bitterly hostile to democracy." (As we shall see, when Matthiessen did write of Poe, he withheld himself almost totally from critical assessment.)

Matthiessen's portrait of Emerson, running well over 125 pages, is clearly the least successful portion of *American Renaissance*. And yet Matthiessen realized its centrality. He applied to Emerson the figure Emerson had chosen for Goethe: he was the cow from which the rest drew their milk. Emerson's theories of expression were basic principles for Thoreau and Whitman, while Hawthorne and Melville developed strength by pushing against his philosophical assumptions. But Matthiessen admits that the lack of a masterpiece on which to focus has forced him to range more widely in his Emerson essay than in any other section of his book. A more basic difficulty is acknowledged in the opening sentence: it is perhaps impossible to present a unified picture of a consciousness which was itself seldom whole. Matthiessen points to Emerson's regard for Plato. "Plato had been able to bridge the gap between . . . fact and abstraction, the many and the One, society and solitude. Emerson wanted a like method for himself, but he had to confess, in words that throw a bar of light across his whole career: 'The worst feature of this double consciousness is, that the two lives, of the understanding and of the soul, which we lead, really show very little relation to each other; never meet and measure each other: one prevails now, all buzz and din; and the other prevails then, all infinitude and paradise; and, with the progress of life, the two discover no greater disposition to reconcile themselves.'" It was this same lack of integration which troubled Irving Babbitt, and it is not difficult to

trace Matthiessen's own discomfort back to Eliot's lament for the dissociated sensibility. Significantly, Matthiessen chooses his first examples from Emerson's political utterance—where he was bound to be even less consistent than usual. After praising a judgment on the principles of Bancroft and Bryant as faithful to "phenomena as they were," Matthiessen can juxtapose a "staggeringly innocent" conclusion which apparently was not based on things as they were: "Money," Emerson wrote, "is, in its effects and laws, as beautiful as roses. Property keeps the accounts of the world, and is always moral. The property will be found where the labor, the wisdom and the virtue have been in nations, in classes, and (the whole life-time considered, with the compensations) in the individual also." Matthiessen sees this as "a vicious reinforcement to the most ruthless elements in our economic life"; his exasperation foreshadows the trouble Emerson will give him, and it echoes Babbitt's earlier dismay over Emerson's saying one minute that everything is the same and the next that everything is different.

The Emerson Matthiessen wants most to remember is portrayed largely in terms of the epistemology he derived from Plato, Schelling, and Coleridge. The Emerson who resisted the authority of the senses to trust in intuition was indeed—and Matthiessen guardedly accepts Dewey's tribute—the philosopher of democracy. "In all my lectures," Emerson wrote, "I have taught one doctrine, namely, the infinitude of the private man." Taking these words as a starting point in his study of Emerson's mind, Matthiessen traces through the *Journal* his optimistic confidence in the personal "I," no matter how humble, which associated Emerson with popular democracy. And he is delighted to find that Emerson shared his fear that self-reliance might yield to self-indulgence, to romantic cultivation of the ego. "A man may say I, and never refer to himself as an individual" when he affirms that "there is One Mind, and that all the powers and privileges which lie in any, lie in all." The formula is again the harmonious relation of society and the self. "The great always introduce us to facts," Emerson insisted; "small men introduce us always to themselves."

Matthiessen finds Emerson's genius to be essentially intellectual, and while this finally leaves his own art incomplete, he has extended the meaning of the inner life in a way that is strikingly modern. And he has succeeded handsomely in analyzing his country's cultural needs and formulating remedies. Matthiessen praises Emerson's approach to the past, so like Eliot's insistence on the eternal now of what is valuable. Emerson recognized and approved the gradual extension of literature's benefits to an ever-widening public: "The human race have got possession, and it is all questions that pertain to their interest, outward or inward, that are now discussed, and many words leap out alive from bar-rooms, Lyceums, Committee Rooms, that escape out of doors and fill the world with their thunder." It would be difficult to phrase a sentiment likely to please Matthiessen more than this last or Emerson's conviction that literature was coming ever closer to the life the common man knows, to "the Necessary, the Plain, the True, the Human."

It was his desire to share in this movement that motivated Emerson's intense interest in oratory, and Matthiessen spends several pages describing the tradition of public speech during the period and pushing its claim as the supreme democratic art. Similarly, Matthiessen hymns the Emerson who urged renewed attention to words, to "the vigorous Saxon" of field hands, to "the meal in the firkin; the milk in the pan." "Poetic creation," Carlyle said, "what is this but *seeing* the thing sufficiently? The *world* that will describe the thing, follows of itself from such clear intense sight of the thing." As Emerson puts it, "Adam in the garden, I am to new-name all the beasts in the field and all the gods in the sky." Matthiessen does not focus as intently as others have done on the doctrine of correspondences implied in this intense, pristine *seeing*, but devotes a major essay to its relation to symbolism as distinct from allegory.

Matthiessen finds occasional prose passages to praise and points to "Brahma" and "Hamatreya" as "fully composed poems." Like More, he felt that "Days" was Emerson's finest achievement. But the split in Emerson's faculties with which the essay began is ultimately decisive. Emerson's belief that to transmute anything into poetry "its feet must be just lifted from the ground" was bound to prove fatal. Eliot is called to point the moral: "In one's prose reflections one may be legitimately occupied with ideals, whereas in the writing of verse one can only deal with actuality." Emerson might realize that pure thought is not enough, that the poet must reach the senses. He might insist that his words "must be pictures, his verses must be spheres and cubes, to be seen and smelled and handled." But as thinker he preferred to live in an ideal world which provided only pale reflections for his verse.

Emerson himself recognized that he failed of "that wondrous power to collect and swing his whole vital energy into one act, and leave the product there for the despair of posterity," but for Matthiessen there was yet a deeper reason why Emerson could not model for the perfect American Scholar. His liberation from his New England background was so successful that he had escaped the sense of sin and, for Matthiessen, the possibility of understanding tragedy. In his youth Emerson had been drawn to Herbert and Milton and had shared their picture of man as struggling continually against evil, depending on God for protection against the depredations of World and Self. But later his mortal man grew to potential divinity, and original sin could be dismissed as "the soul's mumps and measles." "It seemeth not to me," runs his verse, "That the high gods love tragedy." As was frequently the case when Matthiessen felt compelled to basic disagreement, he uses the voice of the best witness he can find. Charles Eliot Norton grew to feel that Emerson's work was almost totally without meaning. "His optimism becomes a bigotry, and . . . has . . . the quality of fatalism. To him this is the best of all possible worlds, and the best of all possible

times. He refuses to believe in disorder or evil. Order is the absolute law; disorder is but a phenomenon; good is absolute, evil but good in the making. . . . He is the most innocent, the most inexperienced of men who have lived in and reflected on the world." Another, far less fastidious friend was the salty Father Edward Taylor (the most likely model for Melville's Father Mapple). For Taylor, "Mr. Emerson is one of the sweetest creatures God ever made; there is a screw loose somewhere in the machinery, yet I cannot tell where it is, for I never heard it jar. He must go to heaven when he dies, for if he went to hell, the devil would not know what to do with him. But he knows no more of the religion of the New Testament than Balaam's ass did of the principles of the Hebrew grammar."

In a rare reference to Poe, Matthiessen cites by way of contrast the "intense suffering" evident in his "disjointed stanzas." But Emerson sees only the greatness of man and must ultimately impress the modern mind with his incompleteness: "Least of all do we need any suggestion of checks and measures; as if New England were anything else." As James said, Emerson found American society "too sparse for synthesis." He was, Matthiessen admits, an original genius, but "our own inevitable concern with synthesis finds his delight in the flux and his celebration of the private individual to be exaggerated, reckless, or even meaningless."

There are enough scattered references in Matthiessen's writing to prove that he knew and admired More's *Shelburne Essays*, but his discussion of Thoreau moves directly against More's belief that Thoreau was primarily a naturalist. Matthiessen sees him clearly as a poet, bent on knowing the world that he may digest it. A significant utterance, Matthiessen feels, was "Man is all in all, Nature nothing, but as she draws him out and reflects him." Another image, that of Thoreau as solitary anarchist, is more difficult to dismiss, and Matthiessen finds it "imperative" to turn at once to Thoreau's "political context." Emerson had predicted that Thoreau's example was in itself almost enough to refute the theories of Socialism. But the drift of the century in the West—as opposed to Gandhi's East—turned out in fact to be socialistic, and Thoreau is dangerously susceptible to Whitehead's dismissal: "The self-sufficing independent man . . . is a concept without any validity for modern civilization." Matthiessen sought in Thoreau the artistic and moral accomplishment of everything Emerson had called for but was unable to achieve, and so he sets to work to rescue him from any charge of social irrelevance. His famed separations of himself from his community, celebrated in *Walden* and *Civil Disobedience*, Matthiessen dismisses as imitative and without real risk. What should be emphasized is that "his contribution to our social thought lies in his thoroughgoing criticism of the narrow materialism of his day." He was the closest thing his age could produce to a proletarian writer—the phrase, Matthiessen feels, applies to Emerson, Hawthorne, Melville, and Whitman as well. We do not remember often enough that Thoreau said, "To act collectively is according to the spirit of our institutions." This remark occurs in

Walden, Matthiessen notes, "where he is maintaining that the community is responsible for providing a more adequate cultural life, good libraries, distinguished lecturers at the lyceums, encouragement for the practice of all the arts. He was as opposed to private hoarding of our spiritual resources as he was to the lust for ownership in our rapacious economy. He believed that all great values should be as public as light."

Matthiessen devotes only half the space to Thoreau that he used for Emerson, and so he feels the need to apologize for being "deflected" by "the vigorous paradoxes of his social thought." Thoreau had said, "My work is writing," and it is primarily as a fully realized artist and whole-souled human being that he has value for Matthiessen. When we turn to the central question of Thoreau's attention to words, however, we find insistence on his belief in the social foundations of speech: "What men say," Thoreau wrote, "is so sifted and obliged to approve itself as answering to a common want, that nothing absolutely frivolous obtains currency."

If Thoreau could so echo Emerson's theory and yet surpass him in practice, it was because he perceived "with my entire man," with a full play of the senses: "As I go here or there, I am tickled by this or that I come in contact with, as if I touched the wires of a battery." Matthiessen refers to Anteus and thus recalls the most pressing need of the developing national literature, a sense of place and the intimate flavor of the native soil. Thoreau drew his strength and chastened his style, so he said, by a deliberate "steady labor with the hands, which engrosses the attention also." "Emerson also advocated work in the garden as a sanative balance for the thinker," Matthiessen adds, "but neither his temperament nor muscles were geared to it, as his small son observed when he shouted, 'Papa, I am afraid you will dig your leg.'"

Matthiessen clearly feels that Emerson did in fact "dig his leg," that his inability to weld his intellectual perception to the acts and feelings of daily life represented a dissociation of sensibility. "Facts which the mind perceived, thoughts which the body thought,—with these I deal," Thoreau insisted, and thus emphasized his aspiration toward—and Matthiessen cites Eliot—a "unified sensibility." In his lengthy examination of *Walden*, Matthiessen stresses its concrete, earthy, "nutty" flavor and the densely knit tightness of its structure. Thoreau's union of thought and feeling was hard won; it had not been the birthright it would have been had he lived in the seventeenth century. But he had come to understand "that in the act of expression a man's whole being, and his natural and social background as well, function organically together." At his best he achieved the unity of self requisite for art.

Thoreau was the artist that Emerson was not, but he still fell short of Matthiessen's ideal. A unified sensibility was of course necessary, but over and above this Matthiessen demanded a mature sense of tragedy. The briefest examination of *American Renaissance* reveals where he felt

fully engaged: there are over 400 pages devoted to Hawthorne and Melville and the satellite essays which fill out their portraits. And it is *The Scarlet Letter, The House of the Seven Gables, The Marble Faun, Moby Dick,* and *Billy Budd* which call forth the fullest and most sensitive literary analysis in the book. These chapters show Matthiessen at his very best, and his obvious warming to their subjects suggests that the larger project was conceived mainly to frame them.

Matthiessen points at once to "the considerations which lie behind my entire treatment of Hawthorne and Melville," and since this is also his fullest statement of the moral and social ideas he associated with tragedy, we had best have it whole:

> The creation of tragedy demands of its author a mature understanding of the relation of the individual to society, and, more especially, of the nature of good and evil. He must have a coherent grasp of social forces, or, at least, of man as a social being; otherwise he will possess no frame of reference within which to make actual his dramatic conflicts. For the hero of tragedy is never merely an individual, he is a man in action, in conflict with other individuals in a definite social order. It is for such a reason that . . . Granville-Barker has remarked that dramatic art in its most fully developed form "is the working-out . . . not of the self-realization of the individual, but of society itself."
>
> And unless the author also has a profound comprehension of the mixed nature of life, of the fact that even the most perfect man cannot be wholly good, any conflicts that he creates will not give the illusion of human reality. Tragedy does not pose the situation of a faultless individual (or class) overwhelmed by an evil world, for it is built on the experienced realization that man is radically imperfect. Confronting this fact, tragedy must likewise contain a recognition that man, pitiful as he may be in his finite weakness, is still capable of apprehending perfection, and of becoming transfigured by that vision. But not only must the author of tragedy have accepted the inevitable co-existence of good and evil in man's nature, he must also possess the power to envisage some reconciliation between such opposites, and the control to hold an inexorable balance. He must be as far from the chaos of despair as he is from ill-founded optimism.

It would be impossible to regard this as merely a definition of literary criteria. It is as much a personal as a professional credo, and Matthiessen believed its requirements can be met, indeed were met, somewhat differently, by Hawthorne and Melville. (And later by Eliot and, in his own special way, by James.)

Matthiessen invokes More's praise for the tragic greatness of *Seven Gables*, and quotes Herbert Schneider on the basis of Hawthorne's understanding of sin. Hawthorne, Schneider wrote, "saw the empirical truth behind the Calvinist symbols. He recovered what Puritans professed but seldom practised—the spirit of piety, humility and tragedy in the face of the inscrutable ways of God." It is not so much sin as the consequences of sin which dominate Hawthorne's work, yet he understands what sin means, probably because of "the sense of personal guilt that sprang from his dread that such a detached observer as himself was failing to participate adequately in life." Whatever the basis for his insight, "his recognition of the general bond of sin brought him closest to universality."

Yet if Hawthorne were as much the detached violator of the human heart as he himself sometimes feared—and thus guilty of the unpardonable sin—he would thereby shirk the social responsibility Matthiessen required of the artist. The point is crucial, as it had been in his study of Thoreau, and Matthiessen reasons closely and carefully to demonstrate the validity of Hawthorne's democratic instincts. Unlike Emerson, Hawthorne never prized solitude as an escape from the pressure of the world. At sixteen he had anticipated, "with amazing completeness," his later position. "Man is naturally a sociable being," he had written. "It is only in society that the full energy of his mind is aroused. Perhaps life may pass more tranquilly, estranged from the pursuits and vexations of the multitude, but all the hurry and whirl of passion is preferable to the cold calmness of indifference." The stories never center merely on the individual, Matthiessen insists, but on the collective existence as well. Hawthorne kept trying, as he himself said, "to open an intercourse with the world." And finally, he was far more active in the ordinary business of life than either Emerson or Thoreau—or Whitman.

None of this denies that Hawthorne did possess "inordinate detachment" and that he did feel himself isolated and misunderstood. This draws from Matthiessen his customary denunciation for the society which must ostracize its artists and thinkers. The blame is New England's, not Hawthorne's; his lonely life was never his own choice.

Matthiessen does not rest with Hawthorne's desire for a bridge between solitude and society. In what is probably the most brilliantly controlled chapter in the book, he discovers in Hawthorne a wealth of political implication. Again More is employed as foil, and Matthiessen uses his view that Hawthorne "was singularly lacking in the political sense" to spark a subtle investigation of the novelist's paradoxical conservatism and membership in the Democratic Party. The recognition of evil and rejection of romantic belief in the infinitude of man which marked his *Blithedale Romance* was somehow wholly compatible with faith in democracy and trust in its future. It was Hawthorne's sense of history that made him too wise for the facile optimism of Transcendentalism, a wisdom he drew from the Puritan past and used to temper, but not deny, the possibilities of the present. When Matthiessen turns his avowedly "economic and social analysis" to *The House of the Seven Gables*, his treatment of the book in commercial, industrial, and class terms—complete with reference to Engels—implicitly rebukes lesser efforts to bring Marx to bear on literature. His handling of the novel's unsatisfactory close must stand as example. The suggestion that the marriage of Phoebe and Holgrave will "transcend the

old brutal separation of classes" which has produced the evil in the book is both economically and socially unrealistic. "The implications that lay ahead in the young couple's inheritance of several hundred thousand were equally beyond both Hawthorne's experience and imagination. He took for granted that in a democratic society the domineering influence of private wealth would not be able to hold the evil sway that it did in the narrowly autocratic era of Colonel Pyncheon. But the fact that he hardly cast a glance to examine what would prevail at the Holgraves' country-seat, prevented him from suggesting their participation in any definite state of existence, as, for instance, Tolstoy could suggest the Russia of which Pierre and Natasha had become part at the close of *War and Peace*." Hawthorne could simply not foresee the world of Henry Adams and *Main Street*. Eliot once remarked that Hawthorne's milieu "was not corrupt enough"; "What that means in the evidence furnished by *The Seven Gables*," Matthiessen adds, "is that Hawthorne could conceive evil in the world, but not an evil world."

Matthiessen's own response to a modern world which seemed quite evil and corrupt enough was of course Socialism. His effort to bring Hawthorne into the fold is the baldest instance of thesis-riding in his otherwise honest book. "Is, or is not, the system wrong that gives one married pair so immense a superfluity of luxurious home, and shuts out a million others from any home whatever?" Hawthorne wrote a decade after *Seven Gables*. "One day or another, safe as they deem themselves, and safe as the hereditary temper of the people really tends to make them, the gentlemen of England will be compelled to face this question." This clearly reflects, as Matthiessen says, "a deepened awareness of what he had slurred over in his novel," but it is far less clear that it contains "a faint perception of the need for collectivism."

Matthiessen does not fault Hawthorne for not envisioning whither the economic developments of his day were tending, nor does he really expect him to thump roundly for the Left. He is satisfied that Hawthorne had a fully developed sense of the artist's responsibility to his society. Similarly, he seems content with the novelist's tragic vision, his sense of man's complexity in a world of both good and evil. And yet Hawthorne fails to reach the highest rank in Matthiessen's pantheon; he is gently but firmly placed second to Melville. The reason emerges when Matthiessen turns from Hawthorne's convictions to the writing itself; here he finds two grounds for complaint.

It is not the compactness of Hawthorne's canvas that Matthiessen questions. He praises the rich humanity the novelist drew from the very lumber of the seven-gabled house and regrets the aesthetic dissipation of the *Marble Faun*. He applauds the remark of the early Van Wyck Brooks that Hawthorne was the "most deeply planted of American writers, who indicates more than any other the subterranean history of the American character." "New England is quite as large a lump of earth as my heart can really take in," Hawthorne had said. He was, then, what Donald

Davidson and the other Agrarians would call a regionalist; "within Hawthorne's provincial limitations," Matthiessen affirms, "there was a wholeness." But the "earth-smell" too often fails to penetrate Hawthorne's diction. With the close attention to language which marks all of Matthiessen's work, he judges Hawthorne's vocabulary and style as belonging at root to the eighteenth century. "Hawthorne kept a taste for . . . aspects of the age just previous to his own, for the Augustan authors who had gradually stimulated New England's enlightenment, and whom Emerson and Thoreau had joined Carlyle in dismissing as superficial to man's soul." It was not only the decorous Sophia who robbed Hawthorne's pages of the concrete immediacy both Thoreau and Matthiessen cherished. Totally unresponsive to the revolution in diction launched by Wordsworth and re-enforced by Emerson, Hawthorne depended instead "on generalized statements that no longer have the power to make us share in his sensations."

But the abstract diction condemned here is largely a symptom of a more basic weakness. In his preface to *The Scarlet Letter*, Hawthorne insisted that he wanted "to live throughout the whole range of his faculties and sensibilities." And yet, when faced with the characteristic split in his age between matter and spirit, he followed most of his contemporaries and celebrated the soul, excluding the body that alone can make soul communicable. Though he claimed to love the warm materialism of life, his failure to conceive a means of integration—as Thoreau and Melville were able to do—loosened his grasp "on the surfaces from which the realistic novelist draws his sustenance." The inevitable result for Hawthorne was romance and "what he himself deprecated as 'an inveterate love of allegory.'"

Mattiessen's occasional paragraphs on romance introduce many of the utterances and themes later developed by Richard Chase, but his greater concern is with allegory and its relation to symbolism. This subject not only permitted him to make distinctions which have proven widely influential; it also gave him the opportunity to demonstrate persuasively the means whereby Melville surpassed Hawthorne. The essay on Hawthorne is interlaced with references to Melville; by close study of the letters and marginalia available to him, Matthiessen worked out most of the story we now have of their friendship and impact on one another. Their juxtaposition served him mainly as a narrative and expository device, since he was able to elucidate Hawthorne's beliefs—and his own—by enlisting Melville as spokesman. But in the "Allegory and Symbolism" chapter Matthiessen brings the two writers more directly face to face. The confrontation makes the best possible introduction to the exploration of Melville's genius which forms the heart of the book.

"No art that sprang from American roots in this period could fail to show the marks of abstraction," Matthiessen observes. "The tendency of American idealism to see a spiritual significance in every natural fact was far more broadly diffused than transcendentalism. Loosely Platonic, it came specifically from the common background that lay behind Emerson and Hawthorne, from the Christian habit of mind that saw the hand of God in all manifestations of life, and which, in the intensity of the New England seventeenth century, had gone to the extreme of finding 'remarkable providences' even in the smallest phenomena, tokens of divine displeasure in every capsized dory or runaway cow." This common background was not of course limited to America. Matthiessen quotes Cleanth Brooks' remark that allegory "is perhaps the first attempt which man makes to unite the intellect and the emotions when they begin to fall apart. . . ." Brooks cites Spenser, but Matthiessen feels the impulse to allegory can be traced back "at least as far as St. Augustine." As an attempt at unity allegory must of course fail, because it can only exist on two infinitely parallel planes which bear a fully articulated relation to each other. The impossibility of its achieving the substantial fullness that alone can suggest the ambivalence of real life was recognized by Melville: "There is something lacking" in Hawthorne, he wrote to Duyckinck, "—a good deal lacking—to the plump sphericity of the man. What is that?—He doesn't patronize the butcher—he needs roast-beef, done rare." Matthiessen illustrates the greater richness of symbolism by contrasting Poe with the writer he so influenced, Baudelaire. "Poe always rarefied his matter, since his imagination never moved in the physical world but in the psychical. In the choice and development of his symbols, Baudelaire was more sensual, more plastic, more human."

Matthiessen translates the distinction into Coleridgean terms: "symbolism is esemplastic, since it shapes new wholes; whereas allegory deals with fixities and definites that it does not basically modify. As a result *Moby-Dick* is, in its main sweep, an example of the reconcilement of the general with the concrete, of the fusion of idea and image; whereas, even in *The Scarlet Letter*, the abstract, the idea, is often of greater interest than its concrete expression." We have learned enough of Matthiessen by now to feel the weight of words like "more human," "new wholes" and "reconcilement of the general with the concrete." The "fusion" sought clearly relates to man's soul and body and to his relations with his society as much as to the mode of his artistic expression. The long essay on allegory and symbolism, like so much else in the book, reflects the total engagement of Matthiessen the man, an engagement that extends to the chapter's conclusion with the richly apt words of D. H. Lawrence: "Symbols are organic units of consciousness with a life of their own, and you can never explain them away, because their value is dynamic, emotional, belonging to the sense-consciousness of the body and soul, and not simply mental. An allegorical image has a *meaning*. Mr. Facing-both-ways has a meaning. But I defy you to lay your finger on the full meaning of Janus, who is a symbol." Employing Eliot's conception of tradition, Matthiessen measures his five authors against the fertile achievement of the later Symbolist Movement; he finds Melville the most relevant, the most useful, and hence the greatest writer.

Hawthorne was great, Melville believed, because he sensed the "unshackled, democratic spirit of Christianity in all things." Matthiessen seems to have noticed that most of Melville's remarks about Hawthorne and other writers he happened to read often apply best to himself. By the time Matthiessen returns to this phrase, he has prepared his application of it to Melville with nearly a dozen essays on the several strands of Melville's genius.

Matthiessen traces the deepening in Melville's powers by taking his novels in the order they appeared. But he does not make the common error of dating Melville's spiritual and intellectual development wholly from his twenty-fifth year. Of all the writers he is considering, Melville had "the richest natural gifts," and Matthiessen quotes the early tattooed-queen passage from *Typee* to demonstrate "a writer fully in command of his material." This is not to deny that Melville matured in his understanding of himself and the world he inhabited. To demonstrate his progress in the single matter of style, Matthiessen quotes a lengthy passage from *Mardi*, "as an example of emotion *not* conveyed. . . . Melville's extraordinary if intermittent triumphs in *Moby-Dick* could hardly be thrown into higher relief than by realizing that only a couple of years earlier he could fall into a manner indistinguishable from that of hundreds of writers in the gift-books." The flaw, we recognize, is the same attributed to Hawthorne and Poe, "eighteenth-century generalized diction" and "loose ejaculations over natural beauty." But Melville was to learn "what Donne knew and Tennyson's day had largely forgotten: that there should be no artificial separation between the life of the mind and of the body." The first extended passage in Melville's work which reflects his fusion of inner and outer experience is the remarkable fall from the yardarm passage in *White Jacket*, and Matthiessen's analysis of it is a brilliant triumph for the critic. He concludes that Melville's mastery of the many concrete details is extraordinary, ample evidence of maturing thought and emotion won through intense living.

Matthiessen reads *Redburn* as "a study in disillusion, of innocence confronted with the world, of ideals shattered by facts." The world Redburn first encounters is the ship's brutish, insensitive crew, but the facts Matthiessen is most interested in—once the novel starts to decline from its effective opening—are economic and social. He calls it a "study of society" and points to the class structure and economic inequality which Melville has learned lies at the basis of poverty. He had come to know what Emerson never realized, that there is a "latent economic factor in tragedy." And yet his concern was never merely with studying the factory system, but "with human suffering wherever he found it." His sense of evil grew to surpass even Hawthorne's because he found its taint in both the individual and society; his essay on Hawthorne emphasizes his background in "Presbyterian orthodoxy" and the maturing to be expected from "meditations on original sin." While reading Shakespeare, Melville wrote to Duyckinck, "Ah, he's full of sermons-on-the-mount, and gentle, aye, almost as Jesus." "Such a remark," Matthiessen observes, "helps explain why Melville's tragedies are more concerned with spiritual and metaphysical issues even than with the economic and the social."

Early in *American Renaissance*, when he wanted to stress the need for what Eliot had called "objective correlative," when he wanted to instance language which was so concretely based that its emotional impact was assured, Matthiessen examined with impressive success Melville's "Loom of Time" passage from *Moby Dick*. He made use of Melville again when he wanted to illustrate the symbolic mode and distinguish it from the allegoric. To prepare us even further to appreciate the artistry Melville had available for his tragic themes, Matthiessen turns from a chronological investigation of his novels to an examination of his Homeric and biblical imagery, and to the lessons in structure and language he learned from Shakespeare. "Without the precipitant of Shakespeare, *Moby-Dick* might have been a superior *White Jacket*. With it, Melville entered into another realm, of different properties and proportions." The Melville of *White Jacket* Matthiessen associates with the narrative of the whaling voyage which provides ballast for Ahab's tragic story. But the handling of that story is more drama than narrative; its conception and management forced Melville to the peak of his powers, and the operative catalyst was Shakespeare.

Matthiessen is so struck by Melville's response to Shakespeare—he "meditated more creatively on Shakespeare's meaning than any other American has done"—that he feels the need to record the slightest verbal echoes, and even the possibility of echo, so that these pages come closer to being tedious and unreadable than any others in his huge book. But when he turns to Shakespeare's conception of tragedy, "so grown into the fibre of Melville's thought that much of his mature work became a re-creation of its themes in modern terms," he adds to our sense of Melville's deepening insight into sin and suffering. Matthiessen finds Melville's mature vision manifested in the following lines from *Battle-Pieces*, "one of the most comprehending perceptions ever made of the essence of tragedy":

> No utter surprise can come to him
>   Who reaches Shakespeare's core
> That which we seek and shun is there—
>   Man's final lore.

The essence of that lore is phrased in Melville's words earlier in *American Renaissance*: the man "who hath more of joy than sorrow in him . . . cannot be true—not true, or undeveloped." "The truest of all men was the Man of Sorrows. . . ." In probing the source of this sorrow, Melville moved into a different world from Hawthorne; this leads Matthiessen to one of his best-known formulations. "Hawthorne was concerned with depicting the good and evil within man's heart. Melville is not so concerned with individual sin as with titanic uncontrollable forces which seem to dwarf man altogether."

After his study of Melville's sensibility and the formal techniques which enabled him to embody it so successfully, Matthiessen is ready to take up once again Melville's commitment to "that unshackled, democratic spirit of Christianity in all things." Melville, no less than Hawthorne, was impressed with the terror of personal isolation. There are several Ishmaels in Melville's work, but the lesson in the relation between the narrator of *Moby Dick* and the savage Queequeg was the redemption possible through sympathy with a fellow human being. This aspect of *Moby Dick* is caught in "Knights and Squires," where Melville invokes the "great democratic God" who raised up Bunyan, Cervantes, and Andrew Jackson—"Thou who . . . ever cullest Thy selected champions from the kingly commons. . . ." With the several threads of Matthiessen's credo so neatly joined, there is no surprise in finding him passionate in his enthusiasm:

> This last paragraph-long sentence is one of the summits of Melville's rhetoric: the formal progression of its almost architecturally balanced iterations rises to an eloquence of a purity and sublimity beyond what any other American writer has been able to command. Its crescendo completes his fusion of Christianity and democracy. His unexpected linking of the three heroes would not have surprised Hawthorne, who added to his admiration for Bunyan and for Jackson a warm understanding of "the profound, pathetic humor" of Cervantes. Through such symbolical figures Melville discloses what wealth of suffering humanity he believed to be pitted in the dynamic struggle against evil. By this full-voiced affirmation of democratic dignity, even of divine equality, he reveals also with what assurance he felt that a great theme could be created from the common stuff of American life. Indeed, he lets us enter the very avenues through which he was then creating one.

And Matthiessen's paragraph, in turn, might be applied—down to its final sentence—to his own ***American Renaissance***.

This is the climax in Matthiessen's study of Melville and the climax in turn of ***American Renaissance*** and its literary tradition. But there remains, for one thing, the drama of Ahab, and Matthiessen is not blind to the tragic power generated when the redeeming contact with "the kingly commons" is rebuffed. He relates Ahab to the nineteenth-century drift from the orthodoxy of man's weak and dependent relation with God to the romantic, messianic elevation of the individual self. (His analysis here shows very clearly the influence of Irving Babbitt's intense resistance to Romanticism.) The doom of an "ungodly godlike" man is inevitable, and Matthiessen measures its "stark grandeur" on a scale with Aeschylus. He approaches Ahab's fatal flaw, as we have learned by now to expect, in terms of his dissociated sensibility. Ahab himself admits his monomania and understands how he has separated himself from a sense of common humanity that could save him; but he cannot *feel*. He is basically incomplete and inhuman. Matthiessen handles his story with a sensitivity that my brief summary belies, and yet his central value remains throughout the redeeming fellow-feeling of the crew rather than whatever dignity of classical tragedy Ahab might attain. His Ahab is more ungodly than god-like.

Though Matthiessen makes passing references to the structural flaws in the *Confidence Man* and to Israel Potter's

defeat by poverty, he looks closely only at *Pierre* and *Billy Budd* from Melville's later work. The short note on *Clarel* highlights the single point he chooses to emphasize:

> The vast reserves—the untried fields;
> These long shall keep off and delay
> The class-war, rich-and-poor man-fray
> Of history. From that alone
> Can serious trouble spring. Even that
> Itself, this good result may own—
> The first firm founding of the state.

Matthiessen refers to *Pierre* frequently to illustrate how he feels a literary critic should use biographical and Freudian analysis. When he wants to make a point about Melville that can be dramatized by reference to *Pierre* or to any of the books, he always stresses the part played by the detail in its imaginative world; he resists in every way he can a simplified reading of the author's life from his work.

Pierre, he decides, is a great failure, "a failure in an effort to express as honestly as possible what it meant to undergo the test 'of a real impassioned onset of Life and Passion.'" *Billy Budd*, on the other hand, is a successful "reassertion of the heart," a triumphant resolution of the Melvillian democratic hero's search for a father. Matthiessen sees in Budd the innocence of Christ rising to glory on the yardarm. Such a reading lets Matthiessen affirm Melville's grasp on the whole of life, a "depth of tenderness" and "boundless sympathy" which he had learned from great tragedy. "After all he had suffered Melville could endure to the end in the belief that though good goes to defeat and death, its radiance can redeem life. His career did not fall into what has been too often assumed to be the pattern for the lives of our artists: brilliant beginnings without staying power, truncated and broken by our hostile environment. Melville's endurance is a challenge for a later America."

Emerson might boast his inconsistencies, but Matthiessen found him from first to last an idealist. And in so far as Whitman simply echoed his Concord master, he was for Matthiessen not a white more successful in seeing the world or writing of it truly. But Whitman's idealism was happily not so consistent. His divergence from Emerson turns on his belief that the word can become flesh. Where Emerson would certainly transcend the flesh as quickly as possible to find the spirit manifested in the word, Whitman—at his best—honors the word as an incarnation, savors it for its very concreteness and materiality:

> We realize the soul only by you, you faithful solids
> and fluids.

His rare successes depend on moments of fused sensibility: "He is at his firmest when he says that 'imagination and actuality must be united.'" In practice, Whitman sought to achieve this fusion through diction, through experiments with words he hoped would rise to a level of true folk speech. In this he was not successful: Matthiessen contrasts his efforts with Burns' and decides that "in its curious amalgamation of homely and simple usage with half-remembered terms he read once somewhere, and with casual inventions of the moment, he often gives the impression of using a language not quite his own." There are, Matthiessen complains, far too many lines like

How plenteous! how spiritual! how resumé!

And far too few like

Out of the cradle endlessly rocking . . .

Whitman was occasionally able to escape Emerson's debilitating idealism through a success with the "meal in the firkin" dictum greater than that of its author. One reason for this success was the very laziness Babbitt had in mind when he dismissed him as a "cosmic loafer." Matthiessen felt that much of Whitman's ability to absorb the life and language around him must be traced to his Quaker-like passivity: "It hardly seems fanciful even to relate . . . [his] looseness of expression to the Friends' ecclesiastical formlessness. . . ." But, adds Matthiessen in what for him would be the crucial qualification, "what prevented this from degenerating into mere individual license was their counter-stress on social values, on sympathy and mutual helpfulness. Whitman's mystic abandon was held in check by a similar concrete humanitarianism."

Matthiessen's "concrete" is always worth noting. It was Whitman's conviction that a poet was free to express himself only after "first merging . . . in all the living flood and practicality and fervency" available to him. Such a true sense of his time separated Whitman from the sorrow, the melancholy, the egocentric reveries of European Romanticism, a distinction Babbitt and More never made.[1] Moreover, Whitman never had to "espouse" the cause of the common man; he *was* one, and "he knew how the poor really lived." Matthiessen is able to accept Whitman's humanitarianism and find it aesthetically viable when he can discern its Hebraic, biblical base, when it emphasizes "the transfiguration of common humanity through sacrifice." But when Whitman turns "to celebrating the rare individual, the poet as prophet, he could expand into the pride that annihilates all valid distinctions between the actual and the ideal." This is not only philosophically reprehensible; "it is significant that a good deal of stilted rhetoric but none of his readable poetry came from that mood." Whitman was only great, Matthiessen concludes, when he drew on "the common and humble," when he was able to maintain his hold on his central symbol, the leaf of grass.

Yeats remarked that we make rhetoric from our struggle with others, and poetry from our struggle with ourselves. To Matthiessen it seemed that both Emerson and Whitman blurred the difference. This accounts in part for the influence of American oratorical tradition on both and the soaring flights Whitman especially could venture in pursuit of eloquence. Another influence on Whitman's poetry that Matthiessen investigates with care is the poet's love of Italian opera. Whitman was confident that he had captured

its rhythms, and though his lines might not seem especially musical or singable, Matthiessen labors to show that they do indeed "have music 'at their heart.'" Third, and by far the controlling analogy for Whitman's structure—and another source for his rhythms—was the sea. Matthiessen not only finds its echoes in the verse, he also sees in Whitman's relation with the sea an illustration of the poet's confidence in the organic unity of life and hence of art. "He came to think not just of separate poems but of his whole book as an organism, and to contemplate the finished work with the hope that the whole was more than the abstract sum of its parts, a concrete entity incapable of dissection."

If I have made Matthiessen's treatment of Whitman and the others seem schematic, it was solely to show his principles playing their part in his reading of American literature. Matthiessen himself worked hard to avoid oversimplification. Thus, to begin at the broadest consideration of structure, he does not turn to his study of Whitman directly after assessing Emerson and Thoreau. "That order would . . . give a dramatic structure to my volume, since it would offset the optimistic strain from Emerson to Whitman against the reaffirmation of tragedy by Hawthorne and Melville." As we have seen, Matthiessen does make this separation and makes no effort to conceal his preference for the latter writers.

> But that white and black contrast would be too dramatic: it would tend to obscure the interrelations between the two groups, and it would make it sound as though the last word in this age lay with tragedy. Actually the pattern of the age's cultural achievement can be more accurately discerned by remembering that the impulse from Emerson was the most pervasive and far reaching, and that Whitman's extension of many of Emerson's values carried far down into the period after the Civil War. We may stay closest to the pressures of the age, as its creative imaginations responded to them, by going from the transcendental affirmation to its counterstatement by the tragic writers, and by then perceiving how Whitman rode through the years undisturbed by such deep and bitter truths as Melville had found.

As it turns out, Matthiessen does his best to strengthen the book's close by emphasizing a later, more mature Whitman in contrast to the youthful Emersonian optimist. "The Whitman who is most nearly meaningless is the one who could declare at the start of his career and repeat on occasion to the end:

> I am myself just as much evil as good, and my nation is—
>   and I say there is in fact no evil."

But the Whitman of "Lilacs" and *Drum Taps* escapes for a time such "superficial innocence of evil." As early as 1860 he could speak of the world's sorrows, of oppression and of shame, but it took the war to hold him to "a consistent tragic sense." This is the Whitman Matthiessen wants most to remember.

Similarly, Matthiessen seeks to show a maturing political awareness in Whitman, for the strength of his "democratic faith made the strength of his poetry." Here again there was persistent inconsistency: "Whitman would at no period have satisfied a strict Marxist for more than ten minutes. Indeed, not even Traubel's pertinacity could keep him pinned down to a steady commitment to socialism from one day to the next." But the early Whitman who believed that America was unique, a country where progress was inevitable and where alone "all forms of practical labor are recognized as honorable"—this Whitman learned after the war that "there was 'nothing more treacherous' than the attitude 'of nearly all the eminent persons' here towards the advance of democracy. He drafted a scheme for 'Songs of Insurrection' to warm against 'the more and more insidious grip of capital.'" He came to see "that the critical issue was the struggle for adequate distribution of wealth, since 'beneath the whole political world, what most presses and perplexes to-day, sending vastest results affecting the future, is not the abstract question of democracy, but of social and economic organization, the treatment of working-people by employers.'"

The same care which prompted Matthiessen to seek precision rather than simple drama in his structural arrangement led him to set his five writers in as rich a context as he could build. His book is actually made up of over sixty essays, which do not follow one another in any linear fashion but rather cluster about the central discussions. The interrelationships thus traced reach as often into the present as they do the past. I have already noted the careful analysis of Shakespeare's impact upon Melville. Here there is actual stylistic and thematic evidence to support Matthiessen's conclusions. There is a similar obvious link between Hawthorne and Milton, and little more than good scholarship was needed to come across Trollope's discussion and see its relevance by way of contrast with Hawthorne's kind of novel. But *American Renaissance* abounds in more imaginative flights which are almost always successful and which add a high luster to the book's critical achievement. The most impressive is probably the grouping of Hawthorne with James and Eliot, for the sequence not only helps us place the latter two writers but—as Eliot would expect—it serves to highlight the nature of Hawthorne's achievement. And when Matthiessen followed his contemporaries into intensive study of the seventeenth century, he was able to trace the influence of writers like Browne and Donne on Emerson, Thoreau, and Melville while judging the later achievement by the earlier at the same time. The literature and spirit of the eighteenth century is also called into service, and we have seen how it helps Matthiessen account for flaws in the work of Hawthorne and Whitman.

The detailed contrast of Whitman and Hopkins is perhaps his greatest gamble, for it is rhetorical strategy pure and simple, yet though its length raises the problem of digression, there is no denying its usefulness in deepening our understanding of Whitman. Whenever Matthiessen draws upon his lifelong enthusiasm for painting, the question of relevance never arises. His effort to characterize Emerson and his age through their interest in sight, in seeing, in photography and open-air painting—these moments, along with the essays linking Whitman with Mount, Millet, and Eakins, seem to me to enrich our feeling for the life of the time in precisely the way Matthiessen hoped they would. There is even less direct connection between his writers and the sculptor Horatio Greenough, and yet "what he said was so germane both to the nature of the fine arts generally and to their basis in a democratic society that it can serve to clarify the aims of our writers as well." Matthiessen takes a long, careful look at what Greenough said and manages to find most of his own fundamental principles. Thus Greenough emerges ultimately as more than an expository device; he is one of the book's heroes, second only to Melville and perhaps Hawthorne in the wisdom of his beliefs.

It is well to emphasize this agglomerated, clustered structure of *American Renaissance* because the book is so much more than a study, no matter how full and rich, of five American writers. As I have already suggested, it comes as close as one volume can to being a total expression of its author. This can be seen in the essays which radiate out from the book's ostensible focal centers—as Hicks noted, Matthiessen assumes that anything which has added to his comprehension will also increase ours—and it can be seen in so simple a thing as the wealth of footnotes, which force the discussion ever wider and deeper and which, often coming from far afield with the suggestion of afterthought, testify to their author's insistent determination to be *wholly* there in the fullness of his perception. It is clear that Matthiessen could never confine himself to either history or criticism. As his studies of Emerson and Melville progress, he is examining his own aesthetic premises, their sources and their claims upon him—so much so that parts of his book comprise in effect a manual of effective prose style. Similarly, he becomes increasingly determined to lift his discussion out of historical time and into contemporary timelessness. As his book nears its close, he becomes steadily more explicit in applying its lesson to his own age. Some two thirds of the way along we find a restrained reference to the "major problems in our culture—a culture whose greatest weakness has continued to be that our so-called educated class knows so little of the country and the people of which it is nominally part. This lack of roots helps to explain the usual selfish indifference of our university men to political or social responsibility, as well as the tendency of our artists as they became more sophisticated, from the time of James to that of Eliot, to feel less at home on our shores." Although the reflection is suggested by a remark of Emerson, it "radiates beyond my present concern." Later in the book—and perhaps deeper into the European crisis—the contemporary can occasionally all but dominate Matthiessen's critical perspective. In tracing Whitman's effort to see man achieve divinity, for instance, he seems concerned mainly with its "terrifying" consequences: "This tendency, so mildly innocent in Emerson, so confused and bombastic in Whitman, was to result in the hardness of Nietzsche."

Matthiessen examines Nietzsche's admiration for Emerson and the part Emerson's thought played in Nietzsche's Superman and his Will to Power. When it "was again transformed, or rather, brutally distorted, the voice of Hitler's megalomania was to be heard sounding through it."

The final chapter, "Man in the Open Air," moves explicitly to "where the age of Emerson may be most like our own," to the need for making the past present through myth. The following passage is interesting in several ways. It suggests what a usable past meant to Matthiessen and reflects the urgency with which he proposed his great American myth. What is more, it illustrates one of his favorite techniques, the authorities called in series to emphasize the widespread agreement with his conclusions. After quoting from Mann, Nietzsche, Emerson, Whitman, Melville, and Lawrence, Matthiessen continues:

> Twenty years ago Eliot spoke of how *The Golden Bough* "has influenced our generation profoundly." What he discovered in anthropology is what Mann has also found, the reassertion—for an age almost overwhelmed by its sense of historical tendencies—of the basic dramatic patterns in the cyclic death and rebirth of nature and of man. In the primitive and the remote Eliot first regained contact with sources of vitality deeper than his mind. But unlike Lawrence, he was not satisfied with the primitive for its own sake. The problem still remained to integrate its vitality with the complex life of the present. In the year after *The Waste Land*, Eliot wrote a short essay on *"Ulysses*, Order, and Myth"*: "In using the myth, in manipulating a continuous parallel between contemporaneity and antiquity, Mr. Joyce is pursuing a method which others must pursue after him. . . . It is simply a way of controlling, or ordering, of giving a shape and a significance to the immense panorama of futility and anarchy which is contemporary history."

To conclude his own sifting of the past, Matthiessen links his five authors as builders of the myth of the common man, of man "in his full revolutionary and democratic splendor as the base and measure of society." The type of this common man, Matthiessen suggests, is Christ, in his "union of suffering and majesty."

As we have seen, it is Melville's regard for his knights and squires which Matthiessen felt best realizes the heroic potential of democratic man. Melville did not reach the height of *Paradise Lost* or *Faust*, Matthiessen admits in his final paragraph, "for the meaning of life that could be symbolized through the struggle between Ahab and the White Whale was neither so lucid nor so universal. But he did apprehend therein the tragedy of extreme individualism, the disasters of the selfish will, the agony of a spirit so walled within itself that it seemed cut off from any possibility of salvation." Once again we find Matthiessen framing lines which might conceivably be applied to himself; the same can be said for the last sentences in the book. He is still speaking of Melville: "When the Pacific called out the response of his united body and mind, he wrote the enduring signature of his age. He gave full ex-

pression to its abundance, to its energetic desire to master history by repossessing all the resources of the hidden past in a timeless and heroic present. But he did not avoid the darkness in that past, the perpetual suffering in the heart of man, the broken are of his career which inevitably ends in death. He thus fulfilled what Coleridge held to be the major function of the artist: he brought 'the whole soul of man into activity.'"

American Renaissance, it must be recalled, is essentially a book of the thirties; its stature grows when it is compared to the contemporary efforts of Calverton, Hicks, and Bernard Smith, as well as the groundbreaking of Parrington and Brooks. As a culmination of the critical currents of a half-century and a response to the needs of its time, it would seem to move in the opposite direction from the similar culmination and response of the first *Understanding Poetry*. Matthiessen worked as he felt Melville did, to break down "the arid divisions between learning and ordinary existence." His success can be measured by his book's influence and the critical acceptance it has won.

IV

Only in recent years has a diligent student been able to learn very much about American literature while still an undergraduate. Most of today's mature scholars and critics spent the bulk of their college time in studying the British tradition: as the wag has it, "From Beowulf to Virginia Woolf." When Matthiessen began reading Whitman and Thoreau for the first time, he was twenty-one; all his work thereafter sought to place major American writers in the British context he was familiar with and into the main currents dominating the contemporary European literature he found so fascinating. What Harry Levin has called his "associative mind" persistently invokes as touchstones names like Shakespeare, Milton, Donne, Coleridge, Yeats, Joyce, Mann, Kafka, Balzac, and Flaubert. Matthiessen also subscribed to the view that the major aspects of any age can best be studied in its masterworks, that a major achievement sums up lesser efforts and renders attention to them largely unnecessary. For both these reasons Matthiessen's writing suggests the "Major American Authors" approach more than, say, the fine-tooth combing of the literary historian.

It should not surprise us then to find very little reference in *American Renaissance* and the other books to what our time—with some debt in his direction—thinks of as minor writers. By the time he put together *The Oxford Book of American Verse* (1950), he had favorites from among the poems of the bearded New England poets and could pay tribute as well to Anne Bradstreet, Philip Freneau, and Edward Taylor. Taylor's poetry came to light when *American Renaissance* was all but finished and it is not mentioned there, but Matthiessen here praises it highly as an American echo of Herbert and an authentic Metaphysical "taproot" for similar work by Eliot and other modern poets. This anthology aside, however, Matthiessen made little use of writers he could not regard as of the first rank. When we have glanced at his conception of Poe and looked into his study of James, we will have a fairly complete picture of the American tradition available to him for his final critical effort, *Theodore Dreiser*.

If his chapter on Poe in the *Literary History of the United States* were added to the several dozen citations in his other essays, Matthiessen's writing on Poe would certainly fill a small volume. Yet there are two reasons why such a volume could not be written. Poe was hostile to democracy and "ridiculed, 'among other odd ideas,' that of 'universal equality'." He was bound to seem uncongenial to Matthiessen, although this did not keep him from recognizing the genuine tragedy that Poe's unhappy life made available for his writing. The central reason why Matthiessen found it difficult to write anything deeper than the biographical chapter in *LHUS* was that he found most of Poe's work beneath criticism. And yet he valued Poe and made extensive use of him, for he saw in Poe the roots of twentieth-century literature. Most of Poe's poetry was occasional, and there are "one or two notorious stunts like 'The Bells,' which no adult reader can now face without pain." But there are about thirty pages of "viable" work, some of which "Poe, in the intensity of his suffering, transformed . . . into a dreamworld haunted with the reality of tragedy." It is with these thirty pages that "France would date the beginning of modern poetry."

Matthiessen can praise the fresh description of Sullivan's Island in "The Gold Bug" and the final room in "The Masque of the Red Death" as "a masterpiece of ballet décor for the dance of death," but he scarcely goes further in his analyses than to condemn "Poe's ghoulish extremes." After quoting Poe's insistence that his terror is not of Germany but of the soul, Matthiessen displays once again his reluctance to judge: "Upon the reader's felt acceptance or rejection of the truth of that statement seems to depend whether he regards Poe's work as mainly a meretricious fabrication or as a compellingly imaginative creation." Most critics, he grants, like "William Wilson," "Usher," and "Ligeia." The format of literary history perhaps limited his own willingness to take a stand, but his tone hints that he locates Poe's sources mainly in Germany, and not in the soul.

Matthiessen's Poe was primarily a critic. "Whatever his vagaries in taste, Poe brought to his reviews a probing intelligence such as no other American critic had shown. He made a unique stress upon 'design' and 'keeping,' 'upon a strict subordination of the parts to the whole.' He was concerned from the start with a term he found in Schlegel, 'the unity or totality of interest.' He noted Coleridge's exceptional appreciation of 'the value of *words*,' and was soon making a rigorously detailed analysis of the defects in Simms' diction." As a reviewer he insisted that criticism must limit itself to comment upon the art itself, and he followed his own principles in "a series of masterly essays." He was "magnificently fertile" in his suggestions on literary method, "one of the very few great innovators in American literature." As an innovator Poe's name is linked

with James and Eliot, and we come to see why Matthiessen found Poe so useful a theorist: he locates in Poe the roots of his favorite modern artists. "The two fundamental ways of regarding the poet, either as inspired genius or as craftsman, may divide American poetry between the descendants of Whitman and of Poe." It was Poe's "strict if brittle insistence on the principles of art that helped free Baudelaire and the French symbolists from the effluvia of romanticism, and so cleared the way in turn for the emergence of Pound and Eliot." This conception of Poe as the most thoroughly conscious American artist before Eliot is pressed into service repeatedly in every Matthiessen volume, for it is an important part of his conviction that "the dominant strain in modern art . . . leads from Hawthorne through the younger James to Proust, from Poe through the symbolists to Eliot."

Matthiessen was curiously unresponsive to Mark Twain. He praises *Huckleberry Finn* and the power of the Colonel Sherburn scene, and he occasionally mentions Twain's "broad humor" in conjunction with the frontier and the tall tale. But he seems more distressed than amused by "the heavy smartness of *The Innocents Abroad*," and he utilizes Twain for ironic effect when he wants to condemn his age: "The values of Socrates tended to be in abeyance during the era when Mark Twain, kindling to admiration of H. H. Rogers and other barons of success, could write to Whitman on his seventieth birthday that he had lived 'just the seventy years which are greatest in the world's history'." Fortunately, Matthiessen remarks elsewhere, Twain did not take his themes from "the facile myths of manifest destiny or triumphant democracy. His masterpiece was also an elegy. It gave expression to the loss of the older America of his boyhood, which . . . had been destroyed by the onrush of the industrial revolution."

Twain is thus related to Matthiessen's mature view of Sarah Jewett. The brutality of the time also forced Emily Dickinson to depend "upon the richness of her own 'crowded consciousness.'" Her poetry, Matthiessen decided, must be called Metaphysical, and he associates her with James and Eliot in affirming qualities which "have long been dominant in the American strain": renunciation, sympathy, and tenderness. But although she liked Browne and Herbert, she was not a conscious adherent to the school of Donne—she belonged ultimately to the Whitman tradition of the poet as inspired seer. More precisely, her master was Emerson. Matthiessen refers to her on several occasions for help in defining Emerson's shortcomings as a poet. To chasten Emerson's optimistic dismissal of Calvinism and "all traditional belief in the inescapable tension between good and evil," he quotes:

> Those, dying then, knew where they went,
> They went to God's right hand;
> That hand is amputated now
> And God cannot be found.
>
> The abdication of belief
> Makes the behavior small—;
> Better an *ignis fatuus*
> Than no illume at all.

The Metaphysical Poets, with their tensions of religious belief, "their struggles between doubt and acceptance," wrote poems which were dramatic where Emerson's were "simply ejaculatory." Emily Dickinson's poems, because they have similar tension, are much more authentically in the Metaphysical tradition than Emerson's are. Not, however, that many of his values were not hers also—especially where they concerned the integrity of the mind and the sufficiency of inner resources. Moreover, her ideals of language, indeed her very "tricks of phrase," are often indistinguishable from his. "She does not have any of his range as a social critic, but her best poems display an excruciated awareness of the matching of good against evil, which was foreign to Emerson's temperament." Matthiessen felt the bulk of her work required sifting. His own favorite, for its "union between metrical delicacy and philosophic discovery," was "Safe in Their Alabaster Chambers." He concludes that she was distinctly gifted in poetic thought, but not always right in her diction and meters. Still, he honors her for "her few delicate yet full-blooded marriages between spirit and form."

In *Henry James: The Major Phase* (1944), Matthiessen places James in what was for the critic the central American tradition. In *American Renaissance* he had shown James working at first within Hawthorne's conception of romance, then deserting it for his own experiments with realism. The James of the later novels, however, the James of the major phase, had returned to Hawthorne, assimilated his efforts with allegory, and forged a link with Eliot and modern art through his mastery of symbolism. Matthiessen's essay is in turn related to his volume on Eliot, for it comes nearer concentrating solely on the writing itself than Matthiessen usually could bring himself to do. The wealth of close textual criticism, as Robert Spiller later noted, led "most . . . contemporary and . . . younger students and critics of James . . . into a closer and closer (and often pedantic and repetitious) analysis of these later works." But Matthiessen himself claimed that the book was his contribution to the war effort, and a large part of his assessment of James has not been picked up by later students. For Matthiessen stresses the social relevance of James' work. Going further, he challenges Van Wyck Brooks with the assertion that this relevance is peculiarly American.

"The more one thinks of Eliot in relation to James," runs a note in the Eliot essay, "the more one realizes the extent of the similarities between them. They are similarities of content as well as of method. Both James and Eliot, no less than Hawthorne, are mainly concerned with what lies behind action and beneath appearance. And in their effort to find the exact concrete situation that will evoke an impression of the inner life, they are occupied too in expressing like states of mind and feeling." (Matthiessen sees in Densher the wholeness of the Metaphysical Poets: his thoughts, "at the moment of their coming to him had thrilled him almost like adventures.")

James' spiritual kinship with Hawthorne is apparent in later works like "The Beast in the Jungle," "The Jolly Corner," and the revised *Portrait of a Lady*, and many of James' characters are best seen against a Puritan background. When Strether wants to symbolize the illusion men have of free will, he introduces an image of life "as a tin mould, be it plain or fluted and embossed, into which the 'helpless jelly' of one's consciousness is poured by 'the great cook'." Consciousness is not limited by a Puritan God, but "by every force in the individual's background and environment"; still, there is predestination just the same. James himself was no Puritan, but he inherited from his father "the strong residue of his concern with the nature of evil." His understanding of evil never reached the depth of Hawthorne's. He had drifted too far from the insights of Christianity—its limited grasp of evil makes *The Golden Bowl* an unsatisfactory novel—but the revised *Portrait* is virtually an essay on the interplay of free will and determinism. In bringing Isabel to a kind of redemption through her suffering, James rises to close resemblance to Hawthorne and to a triumph of his art. Another triumph for James was the creation of Kate Croy. "She is by no means the nakedly brutal villainess that he had projected in his notebook. She is a much more living mixture of good and evil, a far more effective register of James' mature vision of human complexity."

In a skillful critique of Clifton Fadiman's introduction to a collection of James stories, Matthiessen rejects the idea that James was "a philosophical novelist." "James was not a thinker; his realm is consciousness and sensibility, not ideas . . . he deals with the superconscious." Nor was he religious, though, as Eliot remarked, he had an "exceptional awareness of spiritual reality." Matthiessen felt James' moral standards could be gleaned from the way he judged his own characters: "They always fell into their positions on his scale according to their degree of awareness: the good character was the one who was most sensitive, who saw the greatest variety of moral possibilities, and who wanted to give them free play in others. The bad character was obtuse or willfully blind to such possibilities; he was dead in himself, and, at his self-centered worst, tried to cause the spiritual death of others."

James set himself to watch the working of these forces. The danger in his role as bystander resembles Miles Coverdale's and Ethan Brand's, but here the risk is not the violation of the human heart so much as total irrelevance. Forces James was unaware of would make the observer created by the next generation the Tiresias of *The Waste Land*. Fated to see everything, he realized "that he fulfilled no vital rôle, that he could leave no effectual mark on his surroundings, felt his consciousness no longer a blessing, as Strether felt it to be, but a torture, since it was 'doomed to foresuffer all' that passed before him in a sequence blindly without purpose." Matthiessen saves James from Tiresias' fate by translating the basis of his character gradations from personal consciousness to social consciousness; everything in James, that is, has its social relevance if it is examined carefully enough. In response to Brooks' ire at James' expatriation, Matthiessen invokes the quiet words of Herbert Croly: "To possess much of the style and intellectual vision which one's countrymen need, and yet to be so divided from them that you cannot help them in their poverty, seems to me a high price to pay for the advantages of Mr. James' expatriation. Yet I am not bold enough to say that the price is too high. An achievement so extraordinary and so individual as that of Henry James is absolutely its own justification." Matthiessen agrees, and he tries to discover what America can learn from James' style and intellectual vision.

As will become even more apparent when we examine Matthiessen's Dreiser, James is an imperfect social photographer. Matthiessen is glad to enlist James' pictures of the vulgarity and greed of the newly monied classes; he likes the novelist's hatred for business, for the "black and merciless things that are behind the great possessions," for the American spirit of "ferocious acquisition." But James never really understood finance capitalism; unlike Dreiser, he did not have access to the kind of objective correlatives his handling of the commercial *nouveau riche* required. It is not for the verisimilitude of his social description that Matthiessen would have us read James; his cultural value is more basic and more subtle than this. In following James' life, Matthiessen comes to the pain he felt during the war, to his efforts to involve himself in the common work for community survival. "In retrospect," Matthiessen comments significantly, "it seems sad that he allowed himself to be so distracted from his proper work. Many others could have done his jobs of bolstering morale. No one else could add a sentence to his three unfinished works." Matthiessen had felt the same pain during the forties and had tried repeatedly to join the Marines (he was finally rejected for being half an inch too short). Yet when he called his *James* his "overaged contribution to the war effort," he must have seen that his function too was to serve society by pushing back the limits of its awareness.

Henry James: The Major Phase is Matthiessen's paean to art, his single most eloquent celebration of the artist as creator and conserver of value for society. James always saw imagination as a force working for preservation; his own art has fixed for us, has proven to us, the value of personal relations. In the more passionate style of his European memoir, Matthiessen tried to set down what James could mean to modern man. Several soldiers have told him they had drawn strength from James while serving in the army. "They had felt a great need, during the unrelenting outwardness of those years, for his kind of inwardness, for his kind of order as a bulwark against disorder." Matthiessen's own use for James is much the same: "In a world of breakdown such as he never conceived, we can now find in his work, not an escape, but a renewed sense of the dignity of the human spirit, however precarious this may be in our own overwhelming sense of imminent ruin." The same conclusions inform the James essay, so much so that by its close Matthiessen has succeeded in demonstrating the truth in the principle he began with: "Aesthetic criticism, if carried far enough, inevitably becomes social criticism, since the act of perception extends through the work of art to its milieu. In scrutinizing James' major novels, I

have tried also to write an essay in cultural history, by showing the kind of light that such novels throw back upon their time."

V

Dreiser has been a trial for serious readers from the moment Mrs. Doubleday exercised her version of muscular criticism. It is not easy to formulate a coherent view, as we have seen already in this book. There is first and foremost the unwieldy prose, then the curiously fuzzy materialist metaphysics delivered in weighty chunks that never seem to leave the structures of the books quite in balance. But on the other hand there is the passion and compassion, the undeniable power that often makes technical faults irrelevant. I have already referred to Irving Howe's study of Dreiser's reputation, to his suggestion that Dreiser's fame has been linked to the events we have been examining. Howe too uses Dreiser as critical barometer; his analysis runs parallel to my own, and so I will appropriate a lengthy passage:

> The decline of Dreiser's reputation has not been an isolated event. It has occurred in the context, and surely as a consequence, of the counter-revolution in American culture during the past few decades. For readers educated in these years, Dreiser often became a symbol of everything a superior intelligence was supposed to avoid. For the New Critics, to whom the very possibility of a social novel seemed disagreeable; for literary students trained in the fine but narrow school of the Jamesian sensibility; for liberals easing into a modest gentility and inclined to replace a belief in social commitment with a search for personal distinction; for intellectuals delighted with the values of ambiguity, irony, complexity and impatient with the pieties of radicalism—for all such persons Dreiser became an object of disdain. . . . He could not think: he could only fumble with the names of ideas. He could not write: he could only pile words on top of each other. He cared not for art as such, but only for the novel as a vehicle of social and "philosophical" ideas. He was uneducated, insensitive—the novelist as mastodon.

When Matthiessen's colleagues learned that he had begun using Dreiser in his classes at Harvard and that he meant to devote a book to him, they quite naturally assumed that Dreiser made a good foil, an instructive contrast to the aesthetic sensitivity of Eliot and James. But Matthiessen always valued what seemed to him true no matter where he found it. He could cherish a James because art was an important component in his vision of life, but Dreiser's failure as an artist in no way destroyed his relevance to other components in that vision. So much a New Critic in most of the James book, so much the father of the "narrow school of the Jamesian sensibility," he was yet able to find in Dreiser a major interpreter of the modern world with a much firmer grasp on things as they really are than James was able to command.

Matthiessen's enthusiasm for Dreiser stretched back at least into the thirties, for although he appears only a few times in *American Renaissance*, the context on each occasion is a significant one. Matthiessen does him the high honor, for instance, of citing him to characterize the indifferent universe of *Moby Dick*, "the 'vast skepticism and apathy' of existence, which Dreiser is always stressing." And later, during the final moments of the Whitman discussion where Matthiessen's style curves upward in oratorical summary, Dreiser is named as "the chief heir of the qualities the poet liked most to dwell on: sympathy, solidarity—obscured though these often may be by the naturalistic novelist's entanglement in clumsy and wordy despair over man's helplessness." (This relationship is pursued further in *Dreiser* where the developing novelist mirrors the mature poet in his grasp of radical politics and religious truth.)

Similarly, in *Henry James,* it is to James' discredit that he writes of factory buildings and country clubs without Dreiser's more intimate knowledge of the social forces at work behind them; this limitation, in fact, is what rendered James unable to produce a full-scale American tragedy. But no partisan of James could ever be blind to the vagaries of Dreiser's style, to his habit, as Howe says, of "crushing the English language in a leaden embrace." Matthiessen studied Dreiser's sentences not merely to pile up examples of infelicities, but to get at their very nature and determine at the same time how awkward writing succeeded in conveying such power. "Unfortunately," he writes in *Theodore Dreiser* (published posthumously in 1951), "it would be characteristic of his writing habits to the end of his life that he would always be hurrying beyond the words to develop the idea that was mastering him." Since he cared little for words, the ones which came to him were often only the "stilted usages of magazine fiction" or the artificial diction of sentimental poetry. But Matthiessen finds him far more successful in the handling of rhythms and in the accumulation of imagery. "When you start reading any of the old politician's conversation, it sounds like that of the stage Irishman; but you gradually realize that though Dreiser's words are not exact, his tune is. He has fitted the rhythm of Butler's manner and gestures to the rhythm of his speech." Matthiessen does not claim that Dreiser's use of imagery is anything more than rudimentary; when clusters occur they are probably accidental, but this does not lessen their effect. The major image is clothes, and Matthiessen indicates throughout his study how apparel and other external furnishings work to express a money culture. Another series of images helps Dreiser suggest the movement of life, his sense of flux as well as the feeling of drift which can sometimes be sustained in the midst of whirling change.

These are the things Matthiessen can point to as characterizing Dreiser's art at its most successful. He believed that the best of the novels do hold together structurally, that "the slowness with which things occur . . . is one of the ways by which he gives them weight." A meticulous analysis of *An American Tragedy* leads Matthiessen to conclude, "When one moves from smaller to larger scenes, one gets an increasing sense of the rightness of Dreiser's

over-all proportions." But as the earlier remarks in *American Renaissance* and *Henry James* suggest, it was not Dreiser's style but his view of life, of modern American life, that attracted Matthiessen to him. "Life is a tragedy," Matthiessen quotes. "The infinite suffering and deprivation of great masses of men and women upon whom existence has been thrust unasked appals me." Matthiessen clearly accepts the conclusion of Dorothy Dudley: "If genius is caring for human beings more than others know how to care, then Dreiser has genius."

"My own ambition," Dreiser remarked in an interview, "is to represent my world, to conform to the large, truthful lines of life." Matthiessen never loses sight, in any of his books, of the fact that writers have livings to earn and that their struggle will influence how and what they write. He seems as much impressed by Dreiser's early poverty as he is by the picture of poverty the novels project, and he clearly accepts the modern, urban, industrial world of these books as conforming to the "truthful lines of life." Once he had succeeded in recognizing Sarah Jewett's nostalgic local color for what it was, Matthiessen never again pictured American in the genteel, smiling image of a Howells. "No wonder Dreiser would say: 'Howells won't see American life as it is lived; he doesn't want to see it.'" Indeed, Matthiessen dwells so lengthily on Dreiser's struggle—his walk from his $1.50 a week room and desperate moment at the river's edge—and the grim lot of the poor under finance capitalism, that the book occasionally loses the focus of biography and cultural history and lapses into a socio-economic tract. The essay remains alive, however, just as the novels do, through the human feeling of the author. For his part, Matthiessen never entirely forgets that his interest is primarily in the novels and that biographical and historical material of whatever kind is only relevant when it provides illuminating context for the fiction. It is not this context which ultimately makes Matthiessen's points for him, but the art itself in its very truthfulness to life. The chief value of Dreiser's fiction thus lies "in the unflinching strength with which he recorded not the professed but the actual forces of his time."

Dreiser recognized this himself. However sympathetic he might be with social protest, he never forgot "that the greatest writers 'are not concerned with social amelioration as an end or a motive. Rather their purpose is to present life in the round, good, bad, and indifferent, alike, without thought of change and without hope of improvement. They paint the thing as it is, leaving change to nature or to others.'" In this spirit Matthiessen stresses the glittering hardness of Carrie's Chicago not as it was but as it impinges on Carrie's sensibility, and he focuses his concern with the gap between high and low in American life on Hurstwood's decline. He follows Mencken in seeing Carrie's tragedy in the opening of dreams she can never fulfill, but he decides in the end that the novel belongs not to Carrie but to Hurstwood. Matthiessen writes very well of Hurstwood's death, finding Dreiser's basic kindness the essential quality in the scene: "Even at its worst, life contains something which he, with full compassion for his beaten hero, will not reject, but will embrace with tenderness."

Like Mencken, Matthiessen preferred *Jennie Gerhardt* to *Sister Carrie*, and he is perfectly willing to grant Mencken's analogies with the tragedy of Greece. He quotes him again when he wants to pass judgment on *The "Genius"*: "As Mencken said, it is 'as gross and shapeless as Brünnhilde.'" For *The Titan*, he turns elsewhere for support. He complains that Dreiser's failure to differentiate between the many women in Cowperwood's life results in a series of stereotypes. "Here Stuart Sherman was right in his objection that the structure of this novel is 'a sort of huge club-sandwich, composed of slices of business alternating with erotic episodes.'" He finds an authentic note, however, in the suffering of Aileen and her efforts to distract herself in her unhappiness. Cowperwood himself seems to Matthiessen an accurate picture of Emersonian individualism become wildly antisocial.

With much the same care he used to place *Moby Dick* at the center of **American Renaissance**, Matthiessen draws this study to a climax with *An American Tragedy*. Although he himself treats the third volume, the 100,000 words of documentation from Clyde's trial, in a brief paragraph and centers his close analysis on the first two books, Matthiessen accepts Dreiser's own proportions as fitting. He has no trouble either with the question as to whether the novel is truly American. There is superficial support in the crime Dreiser drew upon for his plot and in a similar one ten years after it appeared, but Matthiessen finds more significant verisimilitude within the novel, in the wonder Clyde feels when confronted with affluence and the disintegrating impact American values have on the hollow character he brings with him from a childhood of poverty. He accepts both Clyde and Roberta, and their story as well, as accurately American. The question "Are such victims figures for tragedy" is not, however, so easy to answer affirmatively. Tragedy requires conflict, and Dreiser deprives Clyde of free will in his desire to emphasize the damning pressures of American life. His hero is a trapped animal, little more. "Dreiser has not shaped a tragedy in any of the traditional uses of the term, and yet he has written out of a profoundly tragic sense of man's fate. He has made us hear, with more and more cumulative power, the "disastrous beating" of the Furies' wings."

The final two chapters in the book deal with "Dreiser's Politics" and "Dreiser's Philosophy." The manuscript lay unrevised at his death, and perhaps Matthiessen would have tried to knit these discussions more tightly into his text. They are concerned with the later Dreiser, the Dreiser of strengthening leftish tendencies and increased interest in religion, the Dreiser who drew Mencken's scorn but who was bound to interest Matthiessen. This Dreiser has moved from his earlier, unfortunate interest in Herbert Spencer to Solon Barnes' "belated rediscovery of Christian love," perhaps in parallel to John Woolman, the Quaker radical. Whatever Dreiser's final religious position,

it was tinged with eastern mysticism. Matthiessen suggests that "The dawn is in the East" describes his politics as well. There is a parallel between Dreiser's faith in the Soviet Union and Matthiessen's own in the future he saw for Czechoslovakia. "He had mastered the primary truth that there could be no real political freedom without the removal of our vast economic inequalities." On his way to "a humane socialist philosophy," he came close to the Communist position, but he soon saw the loss of individuality required by the Communist concept of the masses. "He realized that equality meant the equality of individuals co-operating to create the only effective freedom." Unlike Mencken, Matthiessen regards these shifts as growth, as maturing "re-education." In his treatment of *The Bulwark*, Matthiessen almost seems to be echoing his study of *Billy Budd,* for he finds that the book brought shape and balance to Dreiser's career. "The months during which Dreiser was writing *The Bulwark* seem to have been one of the happiest periods of his life, one in which he felt a harmony between his inner and his outer worlds."

Matthiessen possibly had Sherman in mind when he insisted that Dreiser was never systematic in either his political or his philosophical thought. In **American Renaissance** he associated Dreiser and Norris with Zola, but in **Theodore Dreiser** his position resembles Mencken's in denying Dreiser Zola's pseudo-scientific detachment. Like Whitman, Dreiser was too much of the poor to join them or to study them. It is this identification which dominates Matthiessen's image of Dreiser and accounts for his insistence that Dreiser belongs in any truly American tradition. Dreiser has brought into American literature an accurate portrayal of what it means to be "on the outside looking into the brilliantly lighted windows of American wealth and power," of how America can be the cruelest place in the world in which to fail. And Dreiser's fictional truths are set in the new urban setting, a jungle not only for the poor, as Sinclair suggests, but for all those who move steadily either up or down.

In his effort to place Dreiser, Matthiessen's "associative mind" runs riot. Here again, revision might have brought pruning, but the list of authorities introduced by way of comparison or contrast is staggering. I think it is worth recording to illustrate the agility of Matthiessen's fancy. The cascade of names which in Babbitt was an effort to pack the witness stand with sympathetic testimony seems in Matthiessen rather an unceasing involvement of self that continues to probe for nuance and precision even as the sentences are framed. Here is most of the parade: Hawthorne, James, Melville, Howells, Wharton, Crane, Robinson, Sullivan, Wright, Whitman, Links, Sloan, Stieglitz, Hardy, Zola, and Gorki. About half of these are not writers, reminding us that Matthiessen was trying once again to move through art to cultural history. The weaving of Dreiser's personal life and erratic career with aesthetic analyses of the novels is nicely paced and thoroughly persuasive, Matthiessen at his best. But as I have suggested, the efforts to use Dreiser to indict finance capitalism are often more explicitly and clearly reasoned than Dreiser himself was capable of. Where Dreiser gains what success he has by *showing* us the crushing injustice of our value system, Matthiessen sacrifices much of his by an insistent spelling out of the social and economic implications of the dramatic scene in hand. Revision might have increased the book's subtlety, but as it stands **Theodore Dreiser** is less successful than either of the books with which it might be compared, *The Achievement of T. S. Eliot* or *Henry James: The Major Phase*.

VI

For Matthiessen, John Rackliffe observes, "criticism . . . was the fulfillment of a social duty, confined within the healthy limits of a craft." Many of the tools of that craft were drawn from T. S. Eliot and the critical heritage Eliot embodied. Eliot himself remained only peripherally concerned with American literature, but his formulations of the unified sensibility and objective correlative were among the tests Matthiessen used to construct his American literary tradition. When joined to the religious and social awareness he called tragedy, these formulations helped Matthiessen choose the writers he would teach during his European adventure of 1947. Emerson and Hawthorne helped place the Melville of *Moby Dick* and *Billy Budd*; Poe and Whitman defined the two major strains of American poetry; Dreiser sparked discussion of the modern novel; and Eliot contrasted with Emerson while emphasizing the continuity of Hawthorne's influence. The assumption here and in his writing was that these are major writers by any international standard. When Whitman is introduced into a paragraph with Wordsworth, Arnold, Baudelaire, and Rimbaud, there is no suggestion of apology or defense. The very massiveness of **American Renaissance** argues the worth of its subjects. It not only proclaims that the native literature should be studied: it is itself a testimony that American writing can support and reward such study. With the wide acceptance of the book, the art which it treats so seriously can also be said to have won its way. And unlike Parrington's *Main Currents*, its most notable predecessor, **American Renaissance** ensured that future study of the national letters would have to see them as richly and as fully as Matthiessen had done.

I think this is what Henry Nash Smith, one of Matthiessen's ablest commentators, had in mind when he decided that "what counts most in his probing of the American past is . . . the remarkable deepening of literary study consequent upon his determination to subject the writers he examined to ultimate tests of their value, by relating them at once to the long cultural past of western Europe, to the tensions of American society in the mid-twentieth century, and to his urgent personal need for integration. It was a gigantic task, perhaps an impossible one. But his commitment to it was heroic, and it gave to his scholarship an intensity and a dignity that are unique in our contemporary cultural life." And yet nothing less, I am sure Matthiessen would insist, will fulfill the responsibilities of the critic.

Notes

1. Though rarely explicit, Matthiessen seems to have been as much an enemy of European Romanticism as Babbitt and More, and for many of the same reasons. Note the New-Humanist catchwords in what follows.

2. For an enthusiastic account of the text's impact on the secondary school teacher, see the essay by John A. Myers, Jr. in Lewis Leary, ed., *The Teacher and American Literature*, pp. 57-63.

Kenneth S. Lynn (essay date 1976-1977)

SOURCE: "F. O. Matthiessen," in *The American Scholar*, Vol. 46, No. 1, Winter, 1976-1977, pp. 86-93.

[*In the following essay, Lynn offers personal reminiscences of Matthiessen's tenure as an American literature professor at Harvard University in the 1940s.*]

Teachers of American literature who were born, as F. O. Matthiessen was, in the first years of this century, but who are still alive today, have seen the study of their subject move through three different eras. The first, which might be called the Era of Rediscovery, began with Van Wyck Brooks and H. L. Mencken around 1908; gathered strength in the nineteen-twenties and thirties from the work of Lewis Mumford, V. L. Parrington, Granville Hicks, Constance Rourke, and Newton Arvin; reached its most concentrated moment of excitement between 1939 and 1942, when Perry Miller's *The New England Mind*, Matthiessen's **American Renaissance**, and Alfred Kazin's *On Native Grounds* appeared in rapid and dazzling succession; and was finally organized into a triumphal march past in the three-volume *Literary History of the United States* (1948) by Robert Spiller and an all-star cast of contributors.

During these forty years, the historic prejudice of college English departments against making teaching appointments and offering courses in American literature was also challenged and overcome. When Matthiessen entered Yale in the fall of 1919, *Moby Dick* was shelved under "Cetology" in the university library. "It was hardly an accident," he later recalled, "that when I graduated from college in the early nineteen-twenties, I knew very little of our own literature except some contemporary poetry that I had read with my friends." That he started to immerse himself in American literature as a graduate student at Harvard a few years later was decidedly not because he was studying with George Lyman Kittredge, Irving Babbitt, and John Livingston Lowes, but rather because he had read, and been inspired by, a new book of Lewis Mumford's, *The Golden Day* (1926). Yet by the time Matthiessen returned to Harvard as an instructor in 1929, colleges all over the country were instituting new courses in American literature, and students were flocking to them.

The men and women who taught and wrote about American literature in this period took pride in their literary heritage. At the same time, they were severely critical of American authors, and even more critical of the society that had produced them. The paradox of the Era of Rediscovery is that it was born in the polemical attacks of Brooks and Mencken on a number of American literature's most important traditions and most gifted spokesmen, and was perpetuated by a younger generation of scholar-teachers whose attitudes toward the United States were tense with contradictions. The poignant dedication page of **American Renaissance** is a case in point. In thanking two friends "who have taught me most about the possibilities of life in America," Matthiessen affirmed a faith in the land of his birth in the teeth of torturing doubts.

Such contradictions made for brilliant books and moving lectures. However, there was a considerable psychological cost in living at such a pitch of intellectual and emotional ambivalence. The nervous breakdown that Van Wyck Brooks suffered toward the end of the nineteen-twenties was the shattering climax of his love-hate relationship with the American past. (Thereafter Brooks abandoned literary criticism in favor of literary nostalgia, having discovered that nostalgia was psychologically safer.) Matthiessen also suffered some sort of breakdown in the course of writing **American Renaissance**, and nine years after the book's appearance he jumped to his death from a hotel bedroom. In the course of the next quarter of a century, other professors of American literature decided that they too would rather sink in boundless deeps than float on vulgar shoals. ("Give me, ye gods, an utter wreck," cried Melville, "if wreck I do.") One way or another, the study of American literature became the means through which a shockingly large number of gifted teachers tried—and ultimately failed—to work out an accommodation with the world around them.

The personal urgency that marked the study of American literature before World War II carried over into the nineteen-fifties and beyond. Nevertheless, the appearance of *Literary History of the United States* at the end of the forties signaled the emergence of a more impersonal, more complacent attitude. Chapter by chapter, *Literary History* recalled the troubled discernments of the Era of Rediscovery. Yet the general lavishness of the enterprise, its comprehensive scope, its impressively detailed bibliographies, and some of its contributors' unalloyed confidence that American literature was destiny's darling—all reflected a new spirit that had emerged out of the global victory of American military power and the triumphant return to health of the American economy. In literary study, as in life, we had entered the Imperialist Era.

Extravagant claims about the importance of American authors now became the order of the day. Minor writers were hailed in terms previously reserved for major writers, while major writers were treated as if their achievements ranked with Goethe's or Shakespeare's. New editions of American authors were put forth, with elaborate textual apparatus that reeked of reverence in every variant comma. Graduate students produced doctoral dissertations with such astounding titles as "Rufus W. Griswold: The Major Phase," and hack writers struck it rich with coffee-table books about Scott and Zelda, "Mr. Papa," Mark Twain, and other delightfully colorful characters. This was also the era in which the New Criticism and an unspeakably vulgar porno-criticism came into fashion—and no wonder. For the refusal of the New Critics to be bothered with social questions, and the active delight that the porno-critics took in revelations of psychosexual maladjustment and suffering, perfectly suited the deadened conscience and casual brutality of imperial America.

Like most of their fellow citizens, teachers of American literature today have a very different view of the world they live in than they did ten years ago. Yet the surprising—and depressing—fact is that this has not inspired them to take a new and harder look at the subject they teach. Perhaps it is the frightening prospect of a collapse of the social order that causes them to clutch, as at a straw, at reassuringly familiar ideas about the American past. Perhaps they are also intimidated by the more mundane thought that if they retreat from the inflated estimates of the Imperialist Era they will not be able to justify the substantive importance of their subject to budget-conscious deans. But whatever the explanation for their behavior, one fact is indisputable: unlike teachers in a number of other fields, professors of American literature have not risen to the challenge posed by the current crisis in American values.

Unwilling to go through the painful process of reexamining their cherished assumptions about American literature, some professors have simply abandoned the field and are now investing their energies in such promising growth stocks as structuralism, women's studies, and film. Most professors, however, have met the challenge of the times by falling silent. They are still giving courses in American literature, but if writing is the sign of continuing mental activity, then they are no longer thinking about what they are saying to students. In the present era, the Era of Paralysis, the senior Americanist at a leading university on the East Coast has not published so much as a book review in the last nine years; precisely the same situation obtains at a leading university on the West Coast; and across the continent that separates them there stretches a chain of extinct volcanoes, most of which do not even have the dignity of being white-topped.

The prevailing silence, it is only fair to say, is not universal. Books on individual American writers and on general themes in American literature continue to be published every month of the year. For the most part, however, the authors of the individual studies have approached their subjects as if they were going to church, while the authors of the theme books have shied away from the disturbing implications of their material. The idea that American literature is a deeply flawed body of work which nevertheless can help us to understand the innermost propulsions of the

American people does not have many genuinely serious advocates on college campuses these days.

In a time of caution and failing commitment, the need for strong models becomes acute. American scholars who want to break up the Era of Paralysis and restore our contact with our deepest sense of ourselves could do worse than to pattern their pedagogy after the whole-souled, risk-taking teaching of F. O. Matthiessen.

I first encountered Matthiessen in the fall of 1942, my sophomore year at Harvard, when I took his course in Shakespeare. I had come to college with the idea of studying English history and literature, and friends had advised me that Matthiessen's course was the best place to start. At the outset I was not impressed. A short, stocky man, largely bald-headed, and wearing rimless glasses, he looked to me like a grocer. His voice was hardly more commanding than his physical presence: it had a metallic quality, and went up and down the scale in a kind of sing-song that I found annoying. Apparently the only hand gesture in his repertoire was a sudden downward motion, thumb-side down, palm open, followed by a lateral movement in the direction toward which the palm faced. That hand gesture, however, turned out to be symbolic of what I most loved about his teaching. For the downward part of the gesture was a cutting motion, as if he were trying to force his way to the axis of reality, and the sideward part was a revelatory motion, like the pushing aside of a curtain, which was always accompanied by fresh insights into the meaning of existence.

He achieved his revelations by a variety of methods. He was as closely concerned with the specific qualities of Shakespeare's language and dramatic form as were the close readers of the New Criticism. At the same time, he always began the consideration of a play by placing it in a broad historical and cultural setting, and at the end of every analysis he turned once again from text to context—for Matthiessen agreed with Harley Granville-Barker's dictum that great dramatic art is the working out, not merely of the individual alone, but of society as a whole. He agreed, too, with Granville-Barker's conception of Shakespeare's work as plays to be acted as well as read. *Translation* was the title that Matthiessen gave to the published version of his Ph.D. thesis, and the crossing of boundaries from one realm to another was an idea that appealed to him in many ways. The translation of printed pages into living gestures was certainly one of his main goals as a teacher of Shakespeare. To that end, he required us to memorize several hundred lines of poetry, and to show our mastery of them, not by writing them down in class, but by reciting the speeches he called for in private meetings in his office. The fact that this requirement took a great deal of his time casts light on his dedication to teaching. He was absolutely determined—as he often pointed out that Coleridge was—"to reinstate the Logos as a living power, to demonstrate in poetry itself the word made flesh." Having us speak Shakespeare to him was a part of that effort.

Matthiessen also spoke to us from the plays. While he lacked the theatrical skills of his friend and fellow Shakespearean Theodore Spencer, there was a marvelous inwardness in his rendition of the lines that soon made you forget the technical deficiencies of his voice. Kent was the role that he would like to have played on the stage, but in the classroom he also made a fine Edgar and a very moving Lear. Even in parts that were obviously not suited to him, Matthiessen managed to be effective, because he always spoke from inside the character. The same thing was true of his lectures. What gave his commentaries on the plays their extraordinary emotional power was his imaginative involvement with the men and women he was talking about. It was not simply that he brought to bear upon them an exciting combination of textual criticism and historical reflection; somehow he crossed over into their lives. Matthiessen once said of Sherwood Anderson that he had tried to awaken his readers to "the fellowship in living, the fellowship in life." A sense of fellowship with the people of Shakespeare's world suffused Matthiessen's lectures.

While I realized that his course had a personal signature that was utterly lacking in other courses in English which I was taking that fall, I did not understand that he often made Shakespeare the stalking-horse of his own thoughts and feelings—not until the day he lost his temper. He was lecturing on *Hamlet*, and had not finished what he wanted to say when the bell sounded. A student sitting to Matthiessen's left at once arose and began moving toward the aisle. Suddenly Matthiessen swerved, stabbed his right index finger straight at the student, and yelled at the top of his lungs, "Will you sit down!" For approximately the next two minutes, he was out of control. He had poured his whole being into this course, he raged, and we would not even extend him the courtesy of hearing him out. Finally, he calmed down and said he was sorry for yelling, but before dismissing the class he cried out as if in pain, "Hamlet had a temper, too."

Matthiessen's identification with Hamlet was no simple narcissism. One of his most critical observations about American literature was that American authors often fell short of greatness because of their inability to transcend themselves. There was a narcissism, even a solipsism, in the poetry of Allen Tate, for example, that reduced his broodings about the tragedy of southern history to mere autobiography. Matthiessen also criticized Edna St. Vincent Millay for her failure to go beyond the personal "I" to the universal "you." In talking about the prince of Denmark, therefore, he always tried to keep Shakespeare's intentions firmly in mind. The function of a lecturer, Matthiessen believed, was to express with as much intensity as possible whatever a literary artist believed. At the same time, however, he also felt that a lecturer could never reach a really burning intensity without personal risk.

Not until after his death did I realize that in his childhood Matthiessen, like Hart Crane, had witnessed painful conflicts between his father and mother; that his mother had finally withdrawn from the situation, taking young Francis

Otto with her; that while he had dedicated a book to her, he had never once expressed a sense of indebtedness to his father; and that he had asked in his suicide note to be laid to rest beside his mother in a cemetery in Springfield, Massachusetts. If I had known or had had foreknowledge of these facts in 1942, I would have had a fuller appreciation of what *Hamlet* must have meant to him. But when he talked about himself and Shakespeare's hero in the same breath, even a naïve sophomore could sense how completely he had incarnated himself in the play. In the preface to **American Renaissance** he had asserted that the student of a work of art should not only take into account the influences that shaped it, but should also make use of what he brings to it from his own life. Clearly, what this man preached he practiced to the hilt. I walked out of the lecture hall that day with a new idea of what I wanted to study at Harvard: I wanted to study whatever Matthiessen taught.

Three years of army life intervened before I could carry out that resolve. In the spring of 1946, however, I switched from English to American history and literature, because most of Matthiessen's courses were in the American field. I also discovered that Major Perry Miller had returned to the Harvard scene. In addition to taking a number of courses from both of them, I had the great good fortune to do tutorial work with Miller in the spring of my return, and to write a thesis on Melville under Matthiessen's supervision the following year.

Some day I hope to write about my relationship with Miller, for in the long run his tough and profane intelligence meant more to me than Matthiessen's intensity. But in the stirring time at Harvard immediately after the war, when classrooms were filled to overflowing with the oldest, most experienced students the university had ever known, and cold-war disillusionments had not yet destroyed hot-war hopes, Matthiessen was the man I wanted to follow. For one thing, he made himself available to students to a degree that other professors did not. In the summer of 1946, for example, I took his course on modern American poetry. The swollen enrollment meant that it was no longer possible for Matthiessen to listen to us recite the poems he required us to memorize, and so we wrote them out in blue books. Yet he still managed to keep in touch with us. In addition to encouraging us to speak up during his lectures, he scheduled an extra, informal meeting of the class every Tuesday afternoon in his office in Grays 18. The stars of those informal sessions were two graduate students, Richard Wilbur and Laurence Holland, but undergraduates were also welcomed, and their often inchoate ideas were treated with respect. In spite of the increasing anonymity of post-war Harvard, Matthiessen created a community with his students.

Running through all his courses and tutorials in American literature was the historical conception he had taken over from the early Van Wyck Brooks and then modified for his own purposes—that American culture was split across the brow. Some Americans were the products of a tradition of learning and knowledge that went back through nineteenth-century Harvard to the Puritans, but other Americans were the children of a radical, know-nothing tradition born on the raucous and lusty frontier. Lacking the nourishment that they might have derived from one another, both traditions had eventually lost their vitality. The tradition typified by Mark Twain was filled with anxiety, a sense of dread, an exasperating inferiority complex, while the tradition typified by Henry Adams was consumed by "the Boston doubt." In our own time, the failure of belief had become the central problem of American culture. Novelists were turning in on themselves, because there was nothing else to believe in. Meter, rhyme, and other outside controls were being abandoned by poets in consequence of the view that poetry was now an end in itself, rather than a means to an end.

The question that bothered me every time I heard this analysis was why Matthiessen should have been immune to the rampant sickness he described. As he never wearied of telling audiences, he was a devout Christian and an ardent socialist. The very fact of his faith seemed to me to be a paradox, and its structure of ideas was certainly riddled with illogicalities. As a good democrat he wanted literary scholarship to be applied "for the good and enlightenment of all the people, not for the pampering of a class"; yet no elitist in all of Harvard was more scornful than Matthiessen of Granville Hicks's willingness to tailor aesthetic judgments to political measurements. As a believer in Original Sin, Matthiessen accepted the idea that man can never achieve self-realization inside history. At the same time, he hailed the Russian Revolution as "the most progressive event of our century," and worked side by side with Communists and fellow travelers in a wide variety of popular-front activities. When asked by students why a man who made common cause with Harry Bridges went around talking like T. S. Eliot, he generally said something not very helpful about being a socialist *because* he was a Christian.

Had Matthiessen's religious faith been earned, as Eliot's was, or was it merely willed, like Auden's? I have never been sure, but my guess is that Christianity was an order which had a powerful appeal to a man who hated his own disorder, but which never sustained him for very long. I also wonder about his political enthusiasms. During my undergraduate days I took his radicalism at face value and admired him for it; but afterward, in Austria, where we both spent the summer of 1947 at the inaugural session of the Salzburg Seminar in American Studies, I began to see that he could respond to ordinary people only if they played traditional roles. He wanted the good citizens of Salzburg and environs to drink the weak and watery white wine of postwar Austria, and was disturbed that they had Cokes whenever they could cadge them. He also could not understand why they tuned their radios to the popular music—"American jazz," he called it, in his nineteen-twenties vocabulary—broadcast by Armed Forces Radio. Had they forgotten that they were living in Mozart's birthplace?

Matthiessen passionately wanted a better life for the masses: there is no doubt that he had lived by this ideal ever since he had read R. H. Tawney's *Acquisitive Society* as a Yale undergraduate. But at the heart of Matthiessen's socialism was his own insatiable need for human contact. This is why the vulgarity of mass culture upset him. In his loneliness he wanted the masses to behave in ways that would make it possible for him to be at ease with them; if they refused to, he felt more alienated than ever. Thus, when he knocked on doors in Boston's West End for Henry Wallace's Progressive party or some other unpopular cause, he was most successful when he chanced upon an immigrant family that still clung to the old customs. Otherwise, the door was apt to be slammed in his face. Matthiessen did have one way of getting through to the native-born sons of the working class with whom he sometimes tried to make acquaintance in South Boston bars: by meeting their enthusiasm for the Red Sox halfway. Although he rarely went to Fenway Park, he was a fan. As soon, however, as Apeneck Sweeney switched to talking about the Bruins, Matthiessen was lost.

The multiple ambiguities in his beliefs made a number of thoughtful students suspicious of him. In fact, there were some who hated Matthiessen, as did quite a few of his colleagues on the Harvard faculty. Nevertheless, his improbable combination of ideals gave him great strength as a teacher. It was his habit in the classroom to turn questions of form and technique in American literature into larger questions about American life, and as a Christian and a socialist he was prepared to explore a wide range of social and moral problems. In Matthiessen's lectures, his sensitive readings of such works as Whitman's "Out of the Cradle," Hawthorne's *Scarlet Letter*, James's *Portrait of a Lady*, and Frost's "Death of the Hired Man" flowered into meditations on the meaning of democracy, the relationship of the artist to society, and the dignity of work, among other matters. The center of value in all his meditations was a vision of "man in his full revolutionary and democratic splendor," a phrase he had taken over from the nineteenth-century prophet of functional architecture, Horatio Greenough. When he talked about Melville or showed us Southworth and Hawes's magnificent daguerreotype of the shipbuilder Donald McKay, which he used as the frontispiece in **American Renaissance**, Matthiessen was able to make this vision come alive. But for the most part we were aware of it only as a ghost, in lectures that were full of ghosts.

Like many of his favorite American writers, Matthiessen was haunted by the feelings of loss and anguish they expressed. An almost unbearable undercurrent of personal suffering ran through his lectures at times. For example, in an analysis I heard him give of "Mr. Flood's Party" in the summer of 1946, he incorporated his own desolation within E. A. Robinson's, as he had good reason to do. Matthiessen and his most intimate friend, the painter Russell Cheney, had owned a house together in Kittery, Maine, an hour's drive or so from the Tilbury Town of Robinson's poetry. Cheney, however, had died in 1945, and in the summer of 1946 Matthiessen was trying to get used to living at Kittery without him. Listening to the sadness in Matthiessen's voice as he worked his way through the poem, I was sure that Eben Flood was not the only man who ever stood on a hilltop in the state of Maine, talking to himself, with only whiskey for company:

> "Well, Mr. Flood, we have not met like this
> In a long time; and many a change has come
> To both of us, I fear, since last it was
> We had a drop together. Welcome home!"
> Convivially returning with himself,
> Again he raised the jug up to the light;
> And with an acquiescent quaver said:
> "Well, Mr. Flood, if you insist, I might."
>
> "Only a very little, Mr. Flood—
> For auld lang syne. No more, sir; that will do."
> So, for the time, apparently it did,
> And Eben evidently thought so too;
> For soon amid the silver loneliness
> Of night he lifted up his voice and sang,
> Secure, with only two moons listening,
> Until the whole harmonious landscape rang—
>
> "For auld lang syne." The weary throat gave out,
> The last word wavered, and the song was done.
> He raised again the jug regretfully
> And shook his head, and was again alone.
> There was not much that was ahead of him,
> And there was nothing in the town below—
> Where strangers would have shut the many doors
> That many friends had opened long ago.

By bringing his own life into works of American literature, Matthiessen clarified as well as intensified their meaning. Occasionally, though, he altered their meaning—and in my judgment improved them. I had never cared for the poetry of Carl Sandburg, ever since I had attended one of his readings in my high school days. With his hair carefully combed into his eyes and his pseudofolksy voice, he had seemed to me to be an all-American fake. Matthiessen agreed that the staccato effects of his poetry were not in the same class with the magnificent flow of Whitman. Nevertheless, he asserted that Sandburg's "Happiness" was a good poem, and he made me believe it—by dint of changing the poem's point of view to fit a conflation of his own memories. As the poem told it, Sandburg had asked famous professors to tell him what happiness was, and they had shaken their heads as if he were trying to fool them. "And then one Sunday afternoon I wandered out along the Desplaines river / And I saw a crowd of Hungarians under the trees with their women and children and a keg of beer and an accordion." I felt that the poet's attitude toward this scene was marked by Sandburg's usual off-putting heartiness, but Matthiessen interpreted it differently, for personal reasons.

First of all, Matthiessen had spent part of his childhood in Sandburg country, albeit the river he remembered was not the Desplaines, but the Illinois. More important, the poem recalled for him one of the crucial experiences of his college years. Although he was deeply involved in the Elizabethan Club, the *Yale Daily News*, the *Yale Literary Magazine*, and other undergraduate activities, he had not been content, even then, to live his whole life within academic fences. Accordingly he had volunteered to teach English to a group of men at the New Haven Hungarian Club who were trying to qualify for citizenship. After the last session of the class, his students took their teacher down to the cellar, where they had been fermenting casks of Prohibition wine. Several glasses later, the stars seemed unusually bright as the young undergraduate walked back to the Yale campus. He had felt at home in the comradeship of these men. In "Happiness," Matthiessen viewed Sandburg's convivial Hungarians through the mirage of a vanished happiness of his own, thereby endowing the poem with a wistfulness that considerably enhanced its appeal.

Since there was such a strong autobiographical element in his criticism, I was struck by Matthiessen's silence, in his lectures and tutorial conversations, on the subject of homosexuality in American literature. His comments on Whitman's interest in young male beauty were singularly guarded and inadequate, while the blatant case of Hart Crane obviously made him uncomfortable. The conclusion I drew from this at the time, and have subsequently had no reason to doubt, was that Matthiessen's own sex life was a guilt-ridden horror to him. So full of revulsion was he that he could barely pronounce the word homosexuality, let alone release his feelings through candid discussions of Melville's joke about "Devil's-Tail Peak and Buggery Island" and related matters.

But if he avoided the subject of homosexual love, he seemed eager to talk about death. Vachel Lindsay's suicide, Hurstwood's suicide in *Sister Carrie*, Poe's self-destructive impulses—such things loomed large in our tutorial conversations. In the note he left when he jumped from the twelfth floor of Boston's Manger Hotel, Matthiessen said that he did not know "how much the state of the world has to do with my state of mind." There was a good deal of speculation in the following days that his death had indeed been a political act, on the model of Jan Masaryk's defenestration. I myself cannot accept this view. Not only had Matthiessen been thinking about killing himself long before Czechoslovakia fell victim to the cold war, but I am convinced that he had long since decided on the way he would do it. For a certain scene involving Clifford Pyncheon in Hawthorne's *House of the Seven Gables* held his imagination in thrall. He referred to it often during my discussions with him about my thesis on Melville (Melville, too, was fascinated by the scene), and he wrote about it—in the present tense, significantly enough—in *American Renaissance*:

> Clifford has retrogressed until he is hardly more than an idiot, a spoiled child who takes a childish pleasure in any passing attraction that can divert him from the confused memories of his terrible years of gloom. But, occasionally, deeper forces stir within him, as one day when he is watching, from the arched window at the head of the stairs, a political procession of marching men with fifes and drums. With a sudden, irrepressible

gesture, from which he is restrained just in time by Hepzibah and Phoebe, he starts forward as though to jump down into the street, in a kind of desperate effort at renewed contact with life outside himself, "but whether impelled by the species of terror that sometimes urges its victim over the very precipice which he shrinks from, or by a natural magnetism, tending towards the great centre of humanity," Hawthorne found it not easy to decide.

Nor do I find it easy to decide why Matthiessen jumped. Yet I believe that *The House of the Seven Gables* brings us closer to an explanation than does his suicide note.

Another popular theory about Matthiessen is that the golden day of his teaching was before the war. I will never agree to this. In postwar Harvard he was still the same teacher who had changed the direction of my life in 1942. Furthermore, I believe that at the Salzburg Seminar in the summer of 1947 he reached the zenith of his career. A number of distinguished professors taught at Schloss Leopoldskron that summer—Alfred Kazin, Wassily Leontief, Benjamin Wright, Margaret Mead. But Matthiessen was the acknowledged leader. He worked harder and longer at getting to know the European students than did anyone else, and he gave a lecture at the beginning of the seminar and another toward the end that framed the experience for us all.

The first lecture was a speech of welcome, delivered in the garden of the Schloss. Somewhere in Matthiessen's childhood there was a garden that had spelled security to him, because it was associated with his mother. In an act of imaginative displacement, he had evoked this placid spot in the garden imagery of his first book—a biography of Sarah Orne Jewett dedicated to the memory of his mother, Lucy Orne Matthiessen. By the end of the book, however, he had worked past his nostalgia; fenced-in gardens were for pathetic, outdated people who were afraid to face reality. Standing in the garden at Schloss Leopoldskron, he spoke of perilous journeys across boundaries, and of the chance we had to create an international community. Near the end of the seminar, he spoke to us in the library, but once again he brought a garden and a perilous journey together in our imaginations, for his text was the fifth section of *The Waste Land*: "After the torchlight red on sweaty faces. . . ." That is my best memory of Matthiessen, talking out of his American heart in the heart of Europe, just before the Era of Rediscovery began to die.

Leo Marx (essay date 1983)

SOURCE: "Double Consciousness and the Cultural Politics of F. O. Matthiessen," in *Monthly Review*, February, 1983, pp. 34-56.

[*In the following essay, Marx elucidates Matthiessen's political ideology and determines how these beliefs impacted his literary work.*]

The bulk of mankind believe in two gods. They are un-der one dominion here in the house, as friend and par-ent, in social circles, in letters, in art, in love, in reli-gion; but in mechanics, in dealing with steam and climate, in trade, in politics, they think they come un-der another; and that it would be a practical blunder to transfer the method and way of working of one sphere into the other. What good, honest, generous men at home, will be wolves and foxes on 'Change. What pi-ous men in the parlor will vote for what reprobates at the polls! To a certain point, they believe themselves in the care of a Providence. But in a steamboat, in an epi-demic, in war, they believe a malignant energy rules.

—Ralph Waldo Emerson

His given names were Francis Otto, his friends called him Matty—and still do—but on the title pages of his books and to his readers generally he is F. O. Matthiessen (1902-1950). No writer in the last half century has had a greater influence on the prevailing conception of American litera-ture and its relation to our history. He was a prolific, ac-complished literary scholar and cultural historian whose masterwork, **American Renaissance** (1941), remains an indispensable text in American studies; a Harvard teacher whose principles and passion won him a devoted student following; a committed trade unionist, member and some-time president of the Harvard Teachers' Union; a socialist, lifelong partisan of the left and, of special pertinence here, an early benefactor of this journal. "It was owing to . . . [his] interest and generosity," wrote the editors soon after his death, "that we were able to found *Monthly Review*:"[1]

But Matthiessen's desire for an explicit affiliation with a socialist movement was frustrated. For a short time in the early 1930s he was a member of the Socialist Party, but he soon lost patience with its lack of militancy and its inabil-ity to enlist working-class support. Much as he wanted to belong to an organized socialist party, he never seriously considered joining the Communist Party because, among other things (as he repeatedly explained), he was a Chris-tian, not a Marxist.

To aid a Marxist journal while declaring his differences with Marxism was characteristic of Matthiessen and his resolute heterodoxy. Doctrinal consistency was of little concern to him. What mattered most in politics were so-cial justice, peace, and civil liberty, and like many left-tending intellectuals whose allegiances were formed in the era of the Great Depression and the Spanish Civil War, he came to believe as a matter of principle in a united front, or coalition, of all left-wing parties. Before the defeat of the fascist powers that policy had been a manifest neces-sity; it was the only policy, indeed, that made sense in the presence of Hitler, Mussolini, and their potential allies within the capitalist democracies. After 1945, however, collaboration with Communists took on a very different meaning, and the fact that Matthiessen was not a Marxist did not spare him, along with many on the left, from be-coming entangled in the historical trap created by Stalin-ism.

In the fear-ridden aftermath of the Second World War he was, more than ever, convinced of the need for a united

front. The Cold War was beginning, nuclear weapons were a terrifying novelty, and the effective purge of Commu-nists from the American labor movement looked to be the first stage in a far-reaching repression of all dissent. Dur-ing the autumn of 1947, after having taught with immense satisfaction at the first session of the Salzburg Seminar, Matthiessen was a visiting professor at Charles University in Prague. At that time a Czech regime led by Eduard Benes was attempting to work out a compromise, or middle way, between East and West. After returning home, Matthiessen quickly wrote a book, **From the Heart of Eu-rope**, based on the journal he had kept while abroad. There he admiringly describes the Benes regime as an exemplary effort to mediate between Soviet collectivism and capital-ist democracy.

While the book was still in press, however—in February 1948—the Czech Communists seized power. Jan Masaryk, the foreign minister whom Matthiessen had met and liked, died under mysterious circumstances (he either jumped or was pushed from a window). These events came as a real blow to Matthiessen. Although he was invited to make last-minute revisions in his account of the situation in Czechoslovakia, he decided instead to add, as a long foot-note, most of a letter from a Czech friend explaining—and very nearly condoning—the coup. The letter suggests that Masaryk, a man "more sensitive than rational," probably had killed himself. It also argues that most Czech workers did not care about "freedom of mind," only about "eco-nomic freedom," hence their unhesitating support of the new pro-Soviet regime. His correspondent's conclusion is that this Czech "revolution" was aimed at "limiting free-dom and democracy for some, only to give it back, re-vived and strengthened, to all." (pp. 187-89) Although Matthiessen did not explicitly endorse this viewpoint, it is a good example of the kind of rationalization to which he, like many of us at the time, lent respectful attention.

In domestic politics Matthiessen also remained faithful to the waning ideal of a united, suprasectarian left. During the election of 1948 he was an active supporter of the Pro-gressive Party, and at its national convention he gave one of the speeches seconding the nomination of Henry Wal-lace for president. The Wallace candidacy was widely at-tacked as another cynical Stalinist stratagem, and Mat-thiessen's involvement in it, along with the publication of **From the Heart of Europe**, made him a conspicuous tar-get for red-baiting. By now the persecutory fever, soon to be known as McCarthyism, was rising. People on the right and the left accused Matthiessen of being a "fellow trav-eler" or "dupe" of Communists. The House Un-American Activities Committee interrogated him, *Life* magazine went after him, and Irving Howe wrote what he himself called a "very harsh and polemical" piece about him in *Partisan Review*.

These political attacks surely contributed to Matthiessen's growing sense of isolation in the period leading up to his premature and violent death. Early in the morning of April 1, 1950, he jumped to his death from a Boston hotel window. In the last of several postscripts to his suicide note he wrote: "How much the state of the world has to do with my state of mind I do not know. But as a Christian and a socialist believing in international peace, I find myself terribly oppressed by the present tensions."[2] This widely publicized statement, along with the other political circumstances surrounding his death, helps to explain the legendary character of Matthiessen's reputation. In the press, especially outside the United States, his suicide was depicted as a political act, and he was perceived by many as having been a casualty of the Cold War.

But Matthiessen knew better. However much the oppressive political atmosphere had deepened his melancholia, he knew very well that it was not the major source. In the body of his final note, with a certainty sharply contrasting with his conjectural postscript, he emphasized his state of exhaustion and the "many severe depressions" to which he recently had been subject. By now we know a lot more about his mental condition during the winter of 1949-50 than anyone knew, or cared to discuss, at the time. By his own account his state of mind then resembled the acute, suicidal depression from which he had recovered, after a brief hospitalization, twelve years earlier. (In 1938 he also had had an impulse to jump to his death from a high place.) But a vital difference between the two episodes, as Louis Hyde suggested not long ago,[3] is that in 1938 Matthiessen's closest friend and lover, the painter Russell Cheney, was standing by, ready to help him re-enter the world. They had lived together for some twenty years before Cheney's death in 1945, and all of us who knew Matty well in his own last years were aware of his desperate loneliness. What most people could not have known much about before the publication of the Matthiessen-Cheney letters in 1978 was the nature—the closeness, depth, and centrality—of the relationship between the two.

It comes as something of a shock, if also as an encouraging index of cultural change, to realize that as recently as 1950 Matthiessen's friends considered his homosexuality unmentionable—at least in print. Nowhere in the *Collective Portrait*, including John Rackliffe's otherwise astute "Notes for a Character Study," is there any forthright reference to the subject. Nor does it figure in the life of Edward Cavan, the fictive Harvard professor whose suicide, more or less undisguisedly based on Matthiessen's, is the catalytic event in May Sarton's 1955 novel, *Faithful Are the Wounds*. Perhaps this is more surprising, since homosexuality was to be a prominent theme in Sarton's later novels. The distorting effect of this inhibition is discernible in just about everything that has been written about Matthiessen, but it presumably will be corrected by George Abbott White. A Boston teacher and psychotherapist who never knew Matthiessen, White already has devoted several years to gathering material for a thoroughly documented biography.[4]

The fascination that Matthiessen continues to exercise upon new generations of scholars is unusual. Most scholarly writing is quickly superseded and most scholars are quickly forgotten—perhaps never more quickly (or deservedly) than in the United States in these days of enforced academic publication. One reason that Matthiessen is an exception, of course, is that his work occupies a unique place in the development of modern American studies. When he was a Rhodes scholar at Oxford in the early 1920s, the study of literature was still dominated by Germanic philology and a bland, documentary form of literary history. But Matthiessen responded sympathetically to two fresh, seemingly antithetical approaches to literature, and in bringing them together he developed his own critical method.

One of the new approaches was the analytic formalism identified with the early work of I. A. Richards and the essays of T. S. Eliot, soon to be known as the New Criticism. To Matthiessen this meant a liberating concern with the text itself and a belief that form, or the "how" of literary practice, is as important as the content or the "what." Close attention to the power of individual texts became an essential principle of his criticism. Almost everything he wrote was directed at the understanding and evaluation of particular works; he disliked the idea of using literature as raw material for the construction of some other kind of scholarly edifice. The critic's ultimate aim should be to redirect the reader to the text with heightened understanding. In teaching and writing he found the analytic methods developed by the "new critics" immensely useful, and he was confident that they could be detached from the reactionary mandarinism that so often accompanied their application.

Besides, the other new approach embraced by Matthiessen was, in the broadest sense of the word, political; it entailed an appreciation of the indirect ways in which the greatest American writers had lent expression to distinctive aspects of national experience. From the beginning he recognized that the significant interactions between literature and society occur well below the level of a writer's express political ideas, opinions, and institutional affiliations. Politics in this sense begins with assumptions about human nature, society, and even, for that matter, literary form and practice. In *The Rediscovery of American Literature* (1967), an examination of six scholar-critics who helped to recast the way we think about our literature, Richard Ruland credits Matthiessen with having contributed the decisive, culminating work. Following Van Wyck Brooks, Irving Babbitt, Paul Elmer More, Stuart Sherman, and H. L. Mencken, Matthiessen completed the job of liberating America's cultural past from the deadly grip of WASP Victorianism.

It is hard to remember how provincial, belletristic, and unremittingly genteel the reigning conception of our literature was before the publication of ***American Renaissance***. To be sure, the authority of that official canon had been undermined by the work of D. H. Lawrence, V. L. Parrington, and Yvor Winters (as well as those discussed by Richard Ruland). The fact remains, however, that Holmes, Longfellow, Lowell, and Whittier still occupied prominent positions in the canon, and American literature in its entirety was condescendingly regarded by American as well as British professors of English as a minor offshoot of British high culture. Rather than attack the dominion of the Brahmins, Matthiessen simply applied the method of close reading to demonstrate the clarifying power and pleasure available to readers of his five major writers: Emerson, Thoreau, Whitman, Hawthorne, and Melville. By carefully elucidating particular texts and the concepts of form behind them, he revealed for the first time just how inventive, bold, and intellectually robust the classic American writers had been. All of these writers lent expression to the egalitarian, self-assertive, well-nigh anarchic energy released by the American system, although two of them (Hawthorne and Melville) also recognized the destructive form that energy could take in our ruthless economic individualism. All of them illuminated the deep conflicts, or contradictions, in the life around them. From a classical Marxist viewpoint, to be sure, Matthiessen's conception of these conflicts—the central theme, for example, of the "individual" in conflict with "society"—is too abstract, too obscurely related, if at all, to the opposition between social classes. But of course the character and extent of class conflict in the northern American states before the Civil War remains a subject of serious historical controversy. In any case, Matthiessen's emphasis upon the contradictions rather than the harmonies of meaning, value, and purpose marks an important turning point in American studies. It signaled the virtual disappearance of the older, complacent idea of our national culture as an essentially homogeneous, unified whole.

Another reason for the continuing fascination with Matthiessen is that his work embodies a rare combination of scholarly dispassion and personal engagement. It did not occur to him that his strong convictions might skew his perceptions, partly because he tended to think of the critic's job as divided into two distinct stages. In the first stage he or she is a disinterested reader, holding off judgment, open to every possible implication of the text, with the aim of seeing the work whole, including the most serious flaws in the best-liked works. Matthiessen was impatient with ideologically bound students who tried to tailor the evidence to fit a priori schemes. In the second stage, however, the critic is permitted—indeed obligated—to bring in all his or her pertinent convictions. True criticism, like all scholarship in the humanities, is finally an act of the critic's whole being. Everything that Matthiessen wrote was part of his lifelong project of discovering what he himself believed. Unlike most academic writing, therefore, his work conveys a strong sense of passionate involvement.

It is not surprising that interest in Matthiessen and his work was renewed during the resurgence of radicalism in the Vietnam era. To many young teachers and activist intellectuals he provided an example of the engaged scholar. The editors of a volume of essays on literature and radical politics (including one on the role of ideology in Matthiessen's *American Renaissance*) dedicated the book to his memory.[5] More recently, Giles Gunn and Frederick Stern,

neither of whom knew Matthiessen, have written books about him as a critic. Both focus upon the relationships among his critical principles, his practice, and his extra-literary ideas. Gunn is chiefly concerned about the bearing of his religious ideas upon his criticism, whereas Stern is more interested in his politics.[6]

Frederick Stern's book is a sympathetic, searching examination of Matthiessen's work by a literary scholar with avowedly "radical left-wing concerns." At the outset Stern describes his excited discovery of *American Renaissance* when he was an undergraduate in the late 1940s. What impressed him was the fact that a book could be passionately devoted to a political ideal (literature for a democratic culture) yet still be a work of rigorous scholarship, "not a piece of propaganda." Later Stern wrote a doctoral dissertation, an early version of the present book, called "The Lost Cause: F. O. Matthiessen, Christian Socialist as Critic." As the title suggests, Stern interpreted Matthiessen's career as a finally unsuccessful if admirable effort to fuse his various commitments (literary, religious, political) into a logically coherent, workable whole. My impression is that Stern's earlier analysis had a sharper critical edge—a fact that presumably explains why he dropped the phrase "The Lost Cause" from the original title. What most interests Stern is Matthiessen's effort to reconcile "views of life as disparate as Christianity, socialism, and 'the tragic'." (He rightly stresses Matthiessen's belief that tragedy, as a literary kind, and the tragic view of life, are touchstones of aesthetic and intellectual profundity—of ultimate wisdom.) But Stern recognizes that Matthiessen was no system-builder, and that abstract theorizing was uncongenial to him, and he therefore touches lightly upon the alleged irreconcilability of his subject's basic commitments. In view of the "seemingly incompatible elements" in Matthiessen's thought, Stern concludes that he succeeded in developing "a remarkably unified critical structure."

But the quest for unity in Matthiessen's thought may be misleading. Even the use of "Christian Socialist" to describe him implies a greater cohesion and certitude than he ordinarily claimed for his own beliefs. "I would call myself a Christian Socialist," he wrote, "except for the stale and reactionary connotations that the term acquired through its current use by European parties."[7] Although he occasionally invoked the term, he also knew that to American ears it sounds bloodless, feeble, and foreign. The phrasing he more often used, "a Christian and a socialist," suggests the yoking together of separate, not easily combined, religious and political beliefs. The point is not merely that Matthiessen, like Emerson and Whitman, set little store by logical consistency. (He liked to quote Whitman's witty lines: "Do I contradict myself? / Very well then, I contradict myself, / (I am large, I contain multitudes.)") The more important point is that he recognized a positive, generative value in the embrace of opposed ideas. Unlike the conventional academic empiricists, the disengaged "experts" who unify their thought by narrowing its scope, he habitually tested his mental reach by widening the boundaries of his sympathies. This habit of mind is in my view a key to Matthiessen's creativity and to the close affinity he felt with the five writers who are the subjects of his most important book.

Their heroic effort to cope with powerful contrarieties of thought and feeling is a central if largely tacit theme of *American Renaissance*. In the opening sentence Matthiessen warns us that he is starting with the book's hardest problem: Emerson's habit, like Plato's, of stating things in opposites. In rejecting the formal or "linear" logic he associated with Lockean empiricism, Emerson opted for a compelling but risky way of thinking he called "double consciousness." Its worst feature, he confessed, is that we lead two lives which "really show very little relation to each other." One is a life of immediate, daily, practical experience, closely bound up with our physical existence, "all buzz and din"; the other is largely inward, less implicated in the present than in the past and the future, in memory and desire, "all infinitude and paradise." This divergence, as Matthiessen noted, is traceable to the familiar Kantian distinction between two modes of perception, understanding and reason, but he was less interested in the European sources of the idea than its characteristically American applications. In shifting the Kantian notion from the realm of learned metaphysical discourse to discourse about ordinary experience, Emerson had subtly changed it; what had been an idea chiefly concerned with two ways of knowing the world reappeared as an idea about two ways of living in the world.

Each of the writers Matthiessen focuses upon in *American Renaissance* tended, like Emerson, to construe experience as a pattern of antinomies. Even Hawthorne, who was the least sympathetic to Emersonian idealism, was obsessed by the gap between the two worlds he inhabited: the solid, beef-and-ale, mercantile world of Salem, and the disembodied, free-floating, evanescent world he created out of his ideas and imaginings. A scholar less exacting about evidence, more prone to generalization than Matthiessen, might have tried to correlate this pervasive sense of doubleness, or inner conflict, with some general theory of conflict in society. But Matthiessen characteristically held back. He had been sharply critical of earlier attempts by liberal and Marxist critics to impose a political template on literature, and he recognized the pertinence to American literature of the New Critics' emphasis upon the inner tensions—the irony, paradox, and ambiguity—embodied in literary texts. In his measured criticism of Granville Hicks, whose Marxist interpretation of American writing had elicited Matthiessen's creedal "counterstatement," he explained what he did not like about the work of most politically oriented critics. In drawing close analogies between literature and politics, he said, they invariably succeeded in blurring the essential distinctions between them. Marxist critics, like Hicks and V. F. Calverton, often invoked "fatally easy simplifications of society," and their work was marred by the crude notion that writers only can have an adequate knowledge of their age "by coming to grips with its dominant economic forces." As for a liberal critic like V. L. Parrington, Matthiessen was most put off by his dismissive attitude toward the distinctively aesthetic aspects of literature—his tendency to derogate writers like Hawthorne or James because their work was deficient in explicit political meaning.[8]

His own method of placing writers in their historical context was to recreate the network of ideas and images relating them to earlier or contemporary writers and artists working in other, often more popular, modes of thought and expression. In *American Renaissance* he ranges from folklore to ship design to political oratory to genre painting to architectural theory. One of the admirable things about the book is that Matthiessen manages to set forth this remarkably rich body of material without resorting to any general claim, or overarching thesis, about the character of the bonds between literature and the encompassing collective life we call "society." But such a thesis is latent in *American Renaissance*; it is embodied in the many correspondences that each writer's version of the double consciousness[9] enabled him to establish with the conflicting forces at work—economic, racial, political, regional, ethnic, religious—in a nation veering toward Civil War. The idea of depicting reality as a clash of opposites, whatever its ultimate validity, was immensely useful to writers attempting to see through the turbulent, opaque surface of nineteenth-century American life.

Two of their most important literary inventions may be interpreted, in Matthiessen's account, as devices for coping with the debilitating sense of disunity engendered by the double consciousness. Emerson's theory of organic form, borrowed from Coleridge and put into practice by Thoreau and Whitman, was in essence a program for achieving in art the still unachieved but ostensibly emergent coherence of American life. The three American writers were, in the philosophic sense, idealists, and they tended to regard the ability of a nation's artists to transcend conflicts or divisions in thought (or art) as evidence—a kind of optimistic forecast—of the nation's ability to resolve analogous conflicts in reality. If they were the yea-sayers of the American renaissance, Hawthorne and Melville were the skeptical naysayers. Hawthorne's method of bipolar symbolism, later adapted to his own uses by Melville, was designed to figure forth the essentially ambiguous, illusory character of the relationship between ideas and things. *The Scarlet Letter* and *Moby Dick* call into question the transcendentalist belief in a close correspondence, an "organic" relatedness, between nature and culture. Hawthorne's letter "A," officially designated to stand for "adultery," is subverted by Hester to mean "art" or "angel." And whiteness, in the world of *Moby Dick*, may be taken to represent all things pure and virtuous or, simultaneously, the most hideous morbidity and evil. Ambiguity is inherent in the nature of things. As apprehended by the aesthetically unified but tragic vision of Hawthorne and Melville, the divided consciousness Emerson had posited is an expression of an unresolvable contradiction.

To appreciate why the double consciousness had a special resonance for Matthiessen, one has only to read the

Matthiessen-Cheney letters. There we get some sense of what it was like, before the Second World War, to be a Harvard professor and a homosexual: the double life that he and Cheney felt compelled to live, and the many humiliating concealments and dissimulations it entailed. It is not surprising, then, that Matthiessen had a heightened sensitivity to the many variations in our literature on the theme of the disparity between appearance and reality. His own experience also made him particularly responsive to the inability of many of our most gifted writers to sustain a unified vision long enough to compose—fully compose—more than one book. (It is a striking fact that if we put aside the single masterpieces of Thoreau, Hawthorne, Melville, Mark Twain, or F. Scott Fitzgerald, the status of these men as "major" writers immediately comes into question.) Matthiessen was acutely aware of the insights the double consciousness allows and the precarious situation it creates—a situation that Emerson likens, in his essay on "Fate," to that of a circus rider with one foot planted on the back of one horse and the other foot planted on the back of another. To many of our artists and intellectuals, the creative life has meant just such a risk of being pulled apart by the very conflicts, conscious and unconscious, private and public, that energized their work.

. . . . .

It is revealing, in the light of Matthiessen's receptivity to dialectical modes of thought, to reconsider his ambivalent attitude toward Marxism. He made his final, most cogent statement of his views on that subject in his 1949 Hopwood Lecture, **"The Responsibilities of the Critic."** After his usual disclaimer ("I am not a Marxist myself but a Christian"), he went on to explain his belief that the principles of Marxism "can have an immense value in helping us to see and comprehend our literature."

> Marx and Engels were revolutionary in many senses of that word. They were pioneers in grasping the fact that the industrial revolution had brought about—and would continue to bring about—revolutionary changes in the whole structure of society. By cutting through political assumptions to economic realities, they revolutionized the way in which thinking men regarded the modern state. By their rigorous insistence upon the economic foundations underlying any cultural superstructure, they drove, and still drive, home the fact that unless the problems arising from the economic inequalities in our own modern industrialized society are better solved, we cannot continue to build democracy. Thus the principles of Marxism remain at the base of much of the best social and cultural thought of our century. No educated American can afford to be ignorant of them, or to be delinquent in realizing that there is much common ground between these principles and any healthily dynamic America.[10]

But he quickly followed this affirmation with a denial that Marxism contains "an adequate view of the nature of man," or that it "or any other economic theory" could provide a "substitute" for a critic's primary obligation to elucidate the interplay of form and content in specific works of art.

In 1949 Matthiessen's conception of Marxism as "an economic theory" was by no means idiosyncratic. On the contrary, it more or less accurately identified a version of Marxism in high favor during the Stalin era: a self-consciously hard, economistic, and essentially positivistic view of the world. It was positivistic in that it embraced a dichotomy between "scientific" thinking (including Marxism) and all other kinds of thinking. The scientific kind allegedly provides access, as physics does, to the underlying laws governing surface phenomena, whereas other non-scientific kinds inevitably tend to be superficial, sentimental, utopian, idealistic—in a word, unreliable. They do not yield true knowledge. From the retrospective viewpoint of the cultural historian, this Marxist-Leninist invocation of "science" belongs in part to a much wider tendency of thinkers to borrow, on behalf of any social or political theory, the impressive authority of the natural sciences as vehicles for arriving at hard, preferably quantitative, verifiable, exact knowledge.[11] This dichotomy between Marxist science and bourgeois apologetics comported with the absolutist, authoritarian political doctrines emanating from Moscow. But it would be wrong to attribute the dominion of this positivistic style of Marxism only to the power and influence of the Third International. For one thing, as Paul Sweezy reminds me, this tendency already was present in less dogmatic form in the work of such earlier followers of Marx as Kautsky and Plekhanov. For another, we should remember the incomplete state of the Marxist canon in Matthiessen's time. Even at the end of the Stalinist era such a conception of Marxism was made more plausible by the fact that several important countervailing texts, notably the *Economic-Philosophical Manuscripts of 1844* (the "Paris Manuscripts") and the *Grundrisse*, were not yet available.

What made this mid-century version of Marxism particularly objectionable to Matthiessen was the rank, seemingly ineradicable philistinism it fostered. Many Marxists of the era were Zhdanov types who tended, as Leon Trotsky put it, to "think as revolutionaries and feel as philistines."[12] They regarded religion, philosophy, art, all ideas and activities not bearing directly on the hard material facts of life, as mere derivations from those facts, and so they consigned literature to the flimsy "superstructure" that allegedly rests on society's material (economic and technological) "base." It is impossible to exaggerate the importance of this compelling architectural metaphor in disseminating the simple-minded reductionist ideas that passed for a Marxist theory of culture in that period. Even as originally invoked by Marx, the metaphor had been unfortunate—it is static and it lends itself to the mechanistic idea of a one-way, from the bottom up, interaction between the "real foundation" of society, the economic base, and the entire political, legal, and ideological superstructure. In recent years the metaphor has been the subject of extended discussion by Marxist theorists,[13] and the complicated question of its validity cannot be settled here. What remains clear, however, is that during the 1930s doctrinaire Marxists often removed the metaphor from its theoretical context and applied it so literally that it could be said to validate the undialectical notion of a direct economic determination of all ideas and, indeed, of all human behavior.

What might have given pause to Marxist critics of literature is the close resemblance between this philistine attitude and the characteristic utilitarian attitudes of bourgeois Victorians. Thus, Thomas Gradgrind, Dicken's archetypal nineteenth-century business philosopher, was a vehement exponent of a mechanistic base-and-superstructure model of reality. This was the aspect of "Marxism" that Matthiessen found most repugnant. In trying to explain himself to his Marxist friends and associates, he often recurred to their evident inability to take religious experience, even the religious experience of the past, seriously. "If any of you really believe that religion is only 'the opiate of the people,'" he said at the dinner given in his honor when *American Renaissance* was published in 1941, "you cannot hope to understand the five figures I have tried to write about in *American Renaissance*."[14]

In retrospect Matthiessen's rejection of what he took to be Marxism is doubly ironic. For one thing, some of today's practicing Marxist critics, Raymond Williams for example, would consider Matthiessen's literary theory (either as exemplified by his practice or as expressly set forth in the Hopwood Lecture) to be more acceptable—closer to their own theories—than the rigid economistic version of Marxism that Matthiessen found repugnant. This is not the place to review the remarkable development of Marxist thought since 1950, but its correlative literary theory has become a much more supple mode of analysis, far more responsive to the formal, aesthetic dimension of literature, than it was in Matthiessen's time. That is partly a result of the fact that Marxists have recovered and in some measure reinstated the work of the young (Hegelian) Marx that had been dismissed by the 1930s commissars of culture as hopelessly utopian and idealistic.[15] To recover the work of the young Marx, incidentally, is not necessarily to belittle the importance of the passage Marx had effected during the 1840s from an Hegelian to an historical materialist viewpoint. But the overall tendency of Marxist thought during the last twenty years has been to allow much greater historical efficacy to ideas and non-material culture than was allowed by the mainstream Marxism of the Stalin era. It is this development which now makes Matthiessen's thought seem less distant from Marxism than he himself believed it to be.

The striking fact is, moreover, that the ideas of the young Marx had emerged from the same body of thought that Matthiessen wrote about with so much sympathy in *American Renaissance*. In Hegel and in post-Kantian idealism generally, Marx and the American writers who were his contemporaries—especially Emerson—shared a common philosophic legacy. In Marx's essay "On the Jewish Question," written in 1843, roughly a year after Emerson's initial published formulation of the "double consciousness," the young Marx had set forth a similar distinction. Adopting terms used by Feuerbach, he distinguished between a

person's awareness as an individual, activated by the self-serving imperatives of material life in a capitalist society, and a person's awareness of being a member of the human species—or "species-consciousness." In Western culture the sense of partaking in "species-life," formerly embodied in Christianity, had been displaced to the political state. The result of this divided consciousness, for Marx as for Emerson, is that people find themselves leading two almost completely unrelated lives.

> The perfected political state is, by its nature, the *species-life* of man as *opposed* to his material life. All the presuppositions of this egoistic life continue to exist in *civil society outside* the political sphere, as qualities of civil society. Where the political state has attained to its full development, man leads, not only in thought, in consciousness, but in *reality*, in *life*, a double existence—celestial and terrestrial. He lives in the *political community*, where he regards himself as a *communal being*, and in *civil society*, where he acts simply as a *private individual*, treats other men as means, degrades himself to the role of a mere means, and becomes the play-thing of alien powers.[16]

Although Matthiessen's own work exhibits some aspects of this post-Kantian legacy (one writer has referred to his "profound grasp of humanist dialectics"[17]), he did not recognize the significance of the close affinity between the ideas of the young Marx and those of Emerson. This is surprising because Matthiessen had been a publicly avowed socialist for some ten years before the appearance of *American Renaissance*, and during that time he often had deplored the absence of a working-class socialist movement in the United States. Under the circumstances, he might have been expected to seize upon the initial conjunction and subsequent divergence of proto-Marxism and American literary thought (exemplified above all by Emerson) as a way of illuminating the vexed issue of "American exceptionalism." (Among the advanced capitalist countries of the world the United States is "exceptional" in the failure of its intelligentsia to take Marxism seriously, in the failure of socialism to gain a mass following, and in the absence of a working-class socialist party.) Unfortunately Matthiessen ignored the entire subject. This lacuna, along with his conspicuous inattention to Marx and Marxist thought in a book notable for its wide-ranging allusiveness and its highly individualized perspective, is in large measure attributable, I believe, to Matthiessen's overreaction to the shallow, mechanistic Marxism that prevailed during the 1930s.[18] Yet the lack of explicit attention to Marxism in *American Renaissance* is somewhat misleading. In his subtle treatment of the interplay between literature and society, Matthiessen in a sense anticipated the development of a more supple Marxist cultural and literary theory since its liberation from the rigid doctrinal cast of the Stalin era.

The second irony in Matthiessen's rejection of what he took to be Marxism is that he nevertheless allowed that doctrine to skew his own political thinking.[19] Some of the very formulas he repudiated within the context of literary theory informed his response to the political "line" emanating from the Soviet Union. This is not to suggest that he condoned the Stalinist repression, but rather that his opposition to it was softened by the received justification for that authoritarian regime. Like many other non-Marxists, Matthiessen was impressed by the anti-fascist policies of the USSR during the early 1930s, and his thinking about the long-term prospects in Russia followed the standard first-things-first logic inherent in the base-and-superstructure model of social reality. (Notice, incidentally, the uncritical way in which he invoked that treacherous metaphor in the passage from the Hopwood Lecture cited above.) He assumed that the aim of the Communist Party of the Soviet Union was to build the indispensable economic base for socialism, and that during the period of primitive socialist accumulation a degree of authoritarianism was a more or less unavoidable necessity. The fact that Russia had not had a bourgeois revolution, and that it was a peasant society without democratic institutions, gave added credence to this viewpoint. At bottom the cogency of the argument rests on a fundamental assumption of historical materialism—one that Matthiessen, for all his protestations about not being a Marxist, was intermittently prepared to accept: the ultimate, long-term, or "in the final analysis" primacy of a society's economic structure. Hence the need for the non-Communist left to reserve judgment or, in effect, to tolerate a hiatus between the building of the economic base and the raising of a truly socialist (hence truly democratic) superstructure.

This widely accepted latitudinarian argument was behind Matthiessen's adherence, even after 1945, to the "united front" strategy. He had long since abandoned the liberal reformism typical of American academics; he thought of himself as a radical, and did not require instruction on the systemic character of our society's problems. Then, too, he was acutely aware of the reactionary use to which anti-Communism was being put in the early years of the Cold War. "One of the most insistent clichés of the right and even of the liberal press," he wrote shortly before his death, "is that there can be no cooperation on any level between Communists and non-Communists."[20] But of course the insoluble problem was to define the extent of that cooperation. At the local level it involved the elusive issue of "Leninist" tactical duplicity, and on the global level it involved the question of limits (in duration and severity) to the allegedly temporary "dictatorship of the proletariat." But in the rush of events there was no time for Matthiessen (or anyone else) to clarify, much less resolve, these questions. Commenting on the support that Matthiessen and other non-Communists gave to Henry Wallace's presidential candidacy in 1948, Professor Stern simply notes that they were "mistaken about the possibilities and realities of Soviet life after World War II." They were listening, he says, to "their own wishes rather than to evidence and reason."[21] He might have added that Matthiessen, trapped between Stalinism and reformism, was accepting a kind of casuistry that he had identified and pointedly rejected in the interpretation of literature.

But it is doubtful, finally, whether Matthiessen's objections to Marxism would have been satisfied by the work of today's revisionists. To be sure, he would have been far more sympathetic with the "humanist" Marxism of Adorno, Fromm, and Marcuse, or the literary methods of Williams, than he was with the orthodoxy of his time. In his arguments against that doctrine, indeed, Matthiessen anticipated many of the current arguments *within* Marxism—especially those leveled by E. P. Thompson against the ideas of Louis Althusser.[22] Matthiessen charged Marxists generally, as Thompson does Althusser, with constructing their theories at too great a distance from the hard evidence—the concrete particularities—of political life. And like Thompson, Matthiessen felt that mainstream Marxism, with its bias toward economic reductionism, tends to neglect that half of culture which derives from the affective and moral consciousness. For Matthiessen, as for Thompson, a crucial shortcoming of the work of twentieth-century Marxists has been their neglect of the imaginative and utopian faculties of humanity. Unlike Thompson, however, Matthiessen did not believe that those faculties could be adequately accommodated within any form of historical materialism.

Hence Matthiessen's continuing adherence to his unfashionable, demanding, explicitly political version of Christianity. He took the commandment to love thy neighbor as thyself as "an imperative to social action." Indeed, it was "as a Christian," he said, that he found his "strongest propulsion to being a socialist." He acknowledged that this distinguished his religious views from those of "most orthodox Christians of today." It also distinguished his conception of human nature from the one he imputed to Marxism: a simplistic, psychologically shallow notion of human perfectibility; by asserting its rational, economic interests, the working class might be relied upon to achieve liberation for—eventually—all humankind. In contrast to this sanguine view, and under the influence of Freudian psychology and Nieburhian theology, Matthiessen endorsed the doctrine of original sin—the idea that human beings inescapably are "fallible and limited, no matter what . . . [the] social system."[23] At this point his belief in the tragic character of human experience impinged upon, and in a sense joined, his commitment to Christianity and to revolutionary socialism. The essence of tragedy, in his view, is the ultimate inseparability of the human capacity for destructiveness, or evil, and the capacity for nurturance, or good. In effect Matthiessen was disavowing the millennial strain that runs through Marxism and indeed the entire left tradition of political thought. This optimistic tendency of mind underestimates the psychological or, more broadly, behavioral constraints upon social amelioration. "Evil is not merely external," he wrote in distinguishing his views from both the shallow Marxism and the complacentt Christianity of his time, "but external evils are many, and some societies are far more productive of them than others."

Today the political import of Matthiessen's religious belief, with its attendant critique of Marxism, is more obvious and more telling than it was during his life. At that time, when only one nation professed a commitment to revolutionary Marxism, the shortcomings of Soviet society were relatively easy to explain away. But the coming to power of revolutionary socialist movements around the world has made it more difficult to ignore the discrepancy between political realities and the millennial expectations of Marxism. Today many of the arguments within Marxism turn upon fundamental issues raised by F. O. Matthiessen forty years ago.

Notes

1. Paul M. Sweezy and Leo Huberman, eds., *F. O. Matthiessen: A Collective Portrait* (New York: Henry Schuman, 1950), p. vii. This book originally appeared as a special issue of MR in October 1950. A list of the books about Matthiessen mentioned in this review appears on p. 55.

2. The complete text of the note appears in *A Collective Portrait*, pp. 91-2.

3. *Rat & the Devil: Journal Letters of F. O. Matthiessen and Russell Cheney*, Louis Hyde, ed., Introduction (Hamden, Connecticut: Archon Books, 1978), pp. 3-4.

4. White expresses his interest in the problem in his review of *Rat & the Devil*: "'Have I Any Right in a Community That Would So Utterly Disapprove of Me If It Knew the Facts?'" in *Harvard Magazine* (September-October, 1978), pp. 58-62. Harry Levin also discusses the problem of Matthiessen's homosexuality in a trenchant review of *Rat & the Devil*, "The Private Life of F. O. Matthiessen," *New York Review of Books* (July 20, 1978), pp. 42-46.

5. George Abbott White and Charles Newman, eds., *Literature in Revolution* (New York: Holt, Rinehart and Winston, 1972). White's contribution is "Ideology and Literature: *American Renaissance* and F. O. Matthiessen," pp. 430-500.

6. Giles B. Gunn, *F. O. Matthiessen: The Critical Achievement* (Seattle: The University of Washington Press, 1975); Frederick C. Stern, *F. O. Matthiessen: Christian Socialist as Critic* (Chapel Hill: The University of North Carolina Press, 1981).

7. *From the Heart of Europe*, p. 72.

8. "*The Great Tradition*: A Counterstatement," a review of Granville Hicks, *The Great Tradition*, in *The Responsibilities of the Critic, Essays and Reviews by F. O. Matthiessen*, John Rackliffe, ed. (New York: Oxford University Press, 1952), p. 198. Matthiessen's scathing review of V. F. Calverton's earlier effort to interpret American literature from a Marxist vantage, *The Liberation of American Literature*, is reprinted in the same collection (pp. 184-189). For Matthiessen's reservations about Parrington, see the Preface to *American Renaissance*.

9. An obvious problem, too complex to be resolved here, is whether the "double consciousness" refers to one state of mind or several states. Among the distinctions with which it is associated in *American Renaissance* are (1) Kant's "understanding" versus "reason"; (2) Emerson's "natural facts" versus "symbols"; (3) Thoreau's acting versus self-observing selves; (4) Whitman's "soul" versus "other I am"; (5) Hawthorne's daylight recording of material reality versus his moonlit vision of an imagined world; and (6) Melville's upper air of benign appearances versus an undersea realm of murderous realities.

10. *The Responsibilities of the Critic*, p. 11.

11. But this is not to suggest that all assertions of the "scientific" character of Marxism are tainted by vulgar "scientism." To resolve this complex problem it would be necessary, in each case, to consider the particular sense of "science" being invoked.

12. Quoted by Terry Eagleton, *Marxism and Literary Criticism* (Berkeley: University of California Press, 1976), p. 1.

13. Perry Anderson, *Arguments Within English Marxism* (London: Verso, 1980), pp. 71-72; G. A. Cohen, *Karl Marx's Theory of History: A Defense* (Princeton: Princeton University Press, 1978), pp. 217-248; Terry Eagleton, *Marxism and Literary Criticism*, pp. 3-16; Paul M. Sweezy, *Four Lectures on Marxism* (New York: Monthly Review Press, 1981) pp. 20-25; E. P. Thompson, *The Poverty of Theory and Other Essays* (New York: Monthly Review Press, 1978), pp. 157-62; Raymond Williams, "Base and Superstructure in Marxist Cultural Theory," *New Left Review* 82, November/December, 1973, and *Marxism and Literature* (London: Oxford University Press, 1977), pp. 75-82. If a consensus can be said to be emerging from this discussion, it is the need to preserve the indispensable premise of the Marxist theory of history, namely, the primacy of the forces of production as ultimate determinants of the limits within which any society and culture can develop and, at the same time, the need to rid the theory of the static, unidirectional implications of the base and superstructure model.

14. *A Collective Portrait*, p. 142. Here Joseph H. Summers is quoting Matthiessen's impromptu remarks from memory.

15. A particularly compelling testimonial to the intimidating effect of such an anti-utopian bias, or what he calls "the scientific/utopian antinomy," is E. P. Thompson's reconsideration of his own 1955 study of William Morris. In a "Postscript: 1976" to the reissue of the book, Thompson vividly describes how his earlier treatment of Morris had been skewed by his adherence to what he later came to reject as an excessively rigid, mechanical materialism. At issue, he believes, is the place of "moral self-consciousness" and "a vocabulary of desire" within Marxism, and its tendency to fall back, in lieu of these, upon the old utilitarian ideal of "the maximization of economic growth" (p. 792). See *William Morris, Romantic to Revolutionary* (New York: Pantheon Books, 1977), pp. 763-816. For other formulations of a less rigid Marxist literary theory, see Frederic Jameson, *Marx-

ism and Form: Twentieth-Century Dialectical Theories of Literature (Princeton: Princeton University Press, 1971), and *The Political Unconscious* (Ithaca: Cornell University Press, 1981); Raymond Williams, *Marxism and Literature* (London: Oxford University Press, 1977).

16. Karl Marx, "On the Jewish Question," in Robert C. Tucker, ed., *The Marx-Engels Reader* (New York: W. W. Norton & Company, Inc., 1978), pp. 26-52. The quotation is from pp. 34-35. Emerson's concept of the double consciousness, cited by Matthiessen in *American Renaissance*, p. 3, is from his essay, "The Transcendentalist" (1842).

17. Maynard Solomon, *Marxism and Art: Essays Classical and Contemporary* (New York: Alfred A. Knopf, 1973), p. 275; quoted in Stern, *F. O. Matthiessen*, p. 223.

18. "Over-reaction" because Matthiessen, with his aversion to theory in general, and his failure to devote himself to extra-literary problems with anything like the seriousness he devoted to literature, simply ignored the available work of Marxist or quasi-Marxist theoreticians from which he might well have profited. Among them were T. W. Adorno, Walter Benjamin, Kenneth Burke, Lucien Goldmann, Antonio Gramsci, George Lukacs, and Hans Meyer. (The fact that all but Burke were Europeans also suggests the distorting effect of Matthiessen's preoccupation with American thought.) Stern discusses the reasons for Matthiessen's failure to come to grips with Marxist cultural theory in *F. O. Matthiessen*, pp. 221-231.

19. On this subject I am relying on first-hand experience as much as on Matthiessen's published writings. Between 1945 and 1950 I spent a great deal of time with Matty in my capacity as a graduate student, a fellow tutor in the History and Literature department at Harvard, and as a friend. We had many long conversations on these issues. For corroboration I have relied on Jane Marx, my wife, who participated in many of those conversations, especially during the summer months we spent with Matty in Kittery, Maine. I also have had the benefit of criticism of this essay by former friends of Matthiessen's: Richard Schlatter, Paul Sweezy, J. C. Levenson, and G. R. Stange.

20. "Needed: Organic Connection of Theory and Practice," *Monthly Review* (May 1950), p. 11. This was one of two posthumously published fragments bearing on the problems of the left. The other, "Marxism and Literature," was a brief that Matthiessen had prepared for the defense in the trial of the leaders of the Communist Party (U.S.A.) under the Smith Act. *Monthly Review* (March 1953), pp. 398-400.

21. *F. O. Matthiessen*, p. 27.

22. Thompson's attack on Althusser is contained in "The Poverty of Theory—or an Orrery of Errors," *The Poverty of Theory and Other Essays* (New York: Monthly Review Press, 1978); for a useful interpretation of the argument, see Perry Anderson, *Arguments Within English Marxism, op. cit.*

23. His clearest statement of his creed appears in the autobiographical section of *From the Heart of Europe*, pp. 71-91, reprinted in *A Collective Portrait*, pp. 3-20.

William E. Cain (essay date 1987)

SOURCE: "Criticism and Politics: F. O. Matthiessen and the Making of Henry James," in *The New England Quarterly*, Vol. LX, No. 2, June, 1987, pp. 163-86.

[In the following essay, Cain contends that Matthiessen's ambivalent feelings about the work of Henry James provide insight into the critic's "conflicted attitudes toward the relation between literary criticism and politics."]

Probably more so than any other modern critic, F. O. Matthiessen legitimated the study of American literature. Not only did he define and develop the basic analytical method—a "close reading" of texts keyed to the articulation of central "American" myths and symbols—but he also did much to establish the canon of major authors. Matthiessen was not, of course, the first person to examine the writings of T. S. Eliot, Emerson, Thoreau, Melville, Hawthorne, Whitman, Dreiser, and others now securely a part of American literature as we know it; but in most cases, it was his critical work that proved to be crucial in bringing the author into focus and hence into the midst of scholarly debate. It comes therefore as somewhat of a surprise to discover that Henry James, the American writer to whom Matthiessen devoted perhaps the most prolonged attention, and whose novels and stories he made especially significant for students of American literature, was not, finally, a writer the critic appears to have greatly esteemed. Matthiessen seems to have remained, at best, highly ambivalent about James—and ambivalent in ways that testify not just to the writer's weaknesses but to the critic's own conflicted attitudes toward the relation between literary criticism and politics.

The revival of critical and scholarly interest in Henry James dates from the mid-1930s. Its central text, which appeared to much acclaim in 1934, was the special issue of the avant-garde little magazine *Hound and Horn*, edited by Lincoln Kirstein and including essays by Edmund Wilson, Stephen Spender, R. P. Blackmur, Francis Fergusson, and others. There had been, to be sure, a good deal published on James before 1934. Rebecca West (1916), J. W. Beach (1918), Pelham Edgar (1927), and Cornelia Kelley (1930) had written books about his work. More importantly, in 1918 Ezra Pound and T. S. Eliot had published essays in the *Little Review* which highlighted James's craftsmanship and the lessons that his unstinting devotion to art could bring to the modernist movement.

Not all agreed, however, that James's example was a positive one. The question of his artistic and cultural situation, noted by Pound and Eliot, was explored, skeptically and sometimes disdainfully, by Van Wyck Brooks (1925), V. L. Parrington (1930), and Granville Hicks (1933). Each, dwelling upon James as a case study, stressed the psychological and social limits of his craft. Parrington's indictment was especially severe:

> The spirit of Henry James marks the last refinement of the genteel tradition, the completest embodiment of its vague cultural aspirations. All his life he dwelt wistfully on the outside of the realm he wished to be a free citizen of. Did any other professed realist ever remain so persistently aloof from the homely realities of life? From the external world of action he withdrew to the inner world of questioning and probing; yet even in his subtle psychological inquiries he remained shut up within his own skull-pan. His characters are only projections of his brooding fancy, externalizations of hypothetical subtleties. He was concerned only with *nuances*. He lived in a world of fine gradations and imperceptible shades. Like modern scholarship he came to deal with less and less. It is this absorption in the stream of psychical experience that justifies one in calling Henry James a forerunner of modern expressionism. Yet how unlike he is to Sherwood Anderson, an authentic product of American consciousness.[1]

By the end of the 1930s, much of what Parrington attacked had become grounds for enthusiastic praise. James's psychological inquiries, it was now said, pointed to his sophisticated understanding of consciousness; his "projections" and "shadings" indicated an extraordinary attention to problems of artistic form and to an awareness of myth and symbolism which connected him with Joyce and Kafka. His differences from Anderson and other naturalists dramatized not so much a failure to conform to main currents in America as his invigorating tendency to heed an earlier native strain echoing in Hawthorne's stories, sketches, and romances. In those studies in which James was judged to lie outside an American context, he was praised for drawing upon the richest features of European realism, particularly those evident in the novels of Balzac, Turgenev, and Flaubert. True, James had withdrawn from the "world of action," but his decision now was taken to typify the inevitable plight of the artist in America. James's expatriation further emblematized the failure of audiences to support the best artists and interpreters of not only the American but the international scene as well.

This "James revival," as Jay Hubbell aptly notes, "is in some ways a curious thing":

> During the Great Depression when so many of our writers were denouncing the capitalist system and flirting with Russian communism, who would have expected a renewed interest in a Victorian novelist concerned not with the proletariat but with the lives of well-to-do American travelers and British aristocrats living on inherited estates? Who that had been reading the work of Thorstein Veblen, John Dos Passos, or William Faulkner could find the time or the patience to wade through James's verbose stories of the manners and minor morals of people living in country houses or vacationing in Switzerland? And what reader familiar with the theories of Sigmund Freud, the novels of Ernest Hemingway, or the plays of Eugene O'Neill could tolerate the voluminous novels of an old bachelor, who seemed both ignorant and squeamish in matters pertaining to sex?[2]

As Hubbell goes on to point out, James's expansive concern for artistic "form" made him, whatever his social and political peculiarities, a writer particularly well suited to the analytical techniques that the New Critics devised and promoted during the 1930s and 1940s. Some have even said (not always in the spirit of an accolade) that the New Criticism "chose Henry James" as its paramount author, as though he were an invention of New Criticism and a compelling instance of its power to institutionalize its values.

The New Criticism did play a formative role in heightening and complicating interest in James. Many New Critics and their students, writing often about him, produced numerous examinations of formal structure, imagery, symbolism, and metaphorical patterning. But what's striking about the James revival is that a very disparate group of critics, inside and outside the academy, helped to bring it about. Edmund Wilson, Yvor Winters, Philip Rahv, Leon Edel, W. H. Auden, F. R. Leavis, Lionel Trilling, and many others not closely affiliated, or not affiliated at all, with the New Criticism and its interpretive style made estimable contributions.

F. O. Matthiessen, a literary historian as well as a New Critical formalist, played an especially crucial role in reshaping the discussion of James. He edited and provided substantial introductory essays for two valuable collections, *Henry James: Stories of Writers and Artists* (1944) and *The American Novels and Stories of Henry James* (1947). He also assembled, in 1947, a fascinating collection of primary materials on "the James family," stitched together with his own biographical and critical commentary, and, in the same year, he coedited, with his friend and Harvard colleague Kenneth B. Murdock, *The Notebooks of Henry James*.

Henry James: The Major Phase is, however, clearly Matthiessen's most influential work on James. Matthiessen called the book—the bulk of which he presented as the Alexander Lectures at the University of Toronto in the fall of 1944—his "overaged contribution to the war effort," a remark that he meant to allude to the 1940 deal in which the United States sold outdated destroyers to Great Britain.[3] To readers of the present day, ***Henry James*** admittedly may seem superficial, a pale contrast to the monumental scope and richness of ***American Renaissance*** (1941), Matthiessen's masterpiece. But at the time it was published, ***Henry James*** was extremely significant, for it shifted critical attention to James's artistry. Deftly countering the influence of Brooks and Parrington, which still lingered in some quarters, Matthiessen argued that their criticism—"sociological" rather than "literary"—mistakenly applied itself to "content" at the expense of the artist's "form."

For Matthiessen, James, the preeminent artist, must be approached "formally," as literary art mandates.

His approach to James was always Matthiessen's favored perspective—it suggests his links to the New Criticism—but no doubt it was especially so during the war years. Though a defender of dissidents and pacifists, he was not a pacifist himself, and he had sought unsuccessfully to enlist in the Marine Corps (he was turned down because he was half an inch too short). Despite this willingness to join the armed struggle against Nazism and Fascism, Matthiessen did not lessen his commitment to the "primary values" (p. xvi) of sympathy, love, and understanding incarnated in art and transmitted in humanistic education at its best. *Henry James* is thus a statement flung against the war's horrors, a statement both of loss—the war had taken away most opportunities for intellectual and imaginative comradeship—and of hope—a saving remnant of teachers and students nevertheless labored to sustain true values.

In his book, Matthiessen views James's craftsmanship and fealty to literature as a personal and cultural enterprise. After surveying the artist's career, Matthiessen characterizes the writing of James's last three completed novels—*The Ambassadors, The Wings of the Dove, The Golden Bowl*—as the "major phase," where the art is at its greatest pitch of complexity. In a brief account of James's indebtedness to Hawthorne in *American Renaissance*, Matthiessen had already accented "the amazingly prolific sequence," the "final great series," of novels;[4] indeed, he had not even been the first to single out the late works. But it was Matthiessen, speaking as the prestigious author of *American Renaissance,* who gave the claim its special valence. Save for a few dissenting voices, notably F. R. Leavis's in *The Great Tradition* (1948), Matthiessen's judgment, bolstered by his portrait of the "late" Jamesian imagination as displayed in the notebooks, has been the accepted one. A measure of its importance is the degree to which pursuing the labyrinths of "the major phase" became a key item on the agenda of post-war criticism and pedagogy.

Henry James was also noteworthy for drawing attention to *The American Scene*, which Pound had celebrated in 1918 as the "triumph of the author's long practice," a "creation of America," a "book no 'serious American' will neglect" but which few other readers had taken seriously.[5] Matthiessen sparked an interest that burst forth in 1946, when W. H. Auden's edition of *The American Scene* and a number of reviews of it appeared. Matthiessen also heralded something of a breakthrough when he devoted a detailed chapter to James's revisions of *The Portrait of a Lady* for the New York edition, a chapter that exhibited the kind of vigilant scrutiny of differences in word choice and phrasing first evident in his 1931 study of Elizabethan translations. Dozens of essays on James's revisions followed Matthiessen's example, and they gave a new dimension to treatments of James. Not everyone, it should be added, has approved of what Matthiessen inaugurated. Hershel Parker, in a tough-minded critique, has rebuked

Matthiessen for his naive notions about the process of revision, his lack of a theoretical framework, and his "banal" and "vacuous" tributes to James's "painterly" talent in altering *Portrait*'s style and structure.[6]

For my interests, however, what's important about *Henry James* is not so much the salutary influence it had upon criticism or the errors it may have lodged in scholarship. The important—and quite curious—fact is that Matthiessen was at best, ambivalent toward James. Although he devoted much time and energy to editorial and critical tasks that concerned this author, Matthiessen does not appear to have warmed to James or to have sympathized with his preoccupations and standards. Evidence of Matthiessen's ambivalence can be found not only in the critical book but in nearly everything else he said and wrote about James.

Matthiessen taught his first course on James in the spring semester of 1943, yet he apparently was not wholeheartedly taken with James's writings. In a letter to Russell Cheney early that year, he confides that "the James course is launched, though I waver back and forth continually in the degree of my interest in him. He certainly is not someone I'm instinctively with all the way like Melville." In another letter, a month later, he seems even more dubious about James, at least as a subject for a book-length study:

> I'm up through *The Spoils of Poynton* and on the verge of the three big novels. I continue to alternate between admiration and satiety. I guess it grows even clearer that I don't want to do an extended job on James. One revealing symptom is the joy with which I rush back to Shakespeare on the alternate days.[7]

Traces of this divided response show up repeatedly and sometimes attest to a surprising hostility. In *Stories of Writers and Artists*, for instance, Matthiessen cites, and does not dispute, H. G. Wells's reply to James's famous affirmation of the primacy of art over life. "When you say," Wells had observed, that "'it is art that *makes* life, makes interest, makes importance,' I can only read sense into it by assuming that you are using 'art' for every conscious human activity: I use the word for a research and attainment that is technical and special." Matthiessen's commentary on this exchange is revealing:

> That draws the central issue between them as sharply as possible, since the emptiness or living intricacy of the figure in James's carpet depends on whether he was using "art" as a mystical abracadabra or with verifiable comprehension of the enormous value he imputes to it.

Matthiessen doesn't tender the customary interpretation here—that the lumpish sensibility of Wells was unequipped to rise to James's demands. Not only does Matthiessen refrain from siding openly with James, but he also refuses to credit James forthrightly with actually using "art" in a truly noble—and not merely self-deluded and obfuscating—sense. One could conceivably argue that Matthiessen is "balanced," intent upon leaving the case open, but it is nonetheless striking that he employs very strong language ("emptiness," "mystical abracadabra") to imply what a limiting judgment of this writer could amount to: James as more of a curiosity than a vital presence. "The value of James's figure in the carpet," Matthiessen states later in *Stories of Writers and Artists*, "may be judged, as he insisted, only if it is sought through his work as a whole. Only thus may be decided whether his scruples and renunciations are a sterile emptiness, or the guides to a peculiarly poignant suffering and inner triumph."[8] Again, the strong language of the phrase "sterile emptiness" implies that condition might indeed be the consequence of James's extraordinary obeisance to "form."

In *The James Family*, in the midst of much laudatory comment, one again finds flashes of disapproval. "Though projecting the drama of consciousness, [James] is not a philosophical novelist. By no definition of the term is he an important thinker." James, Matthiessen avers,

> was often at his flimsiest on the subject of politics. In contrast to the egalitarianism of both his father and his brother, he grew to take it for granted that democracy must inevitably level down; and on his late return to America he worried about the new aliens in a way that brought him dangerously near to a doctrine of Anglo-Saxon racial superiority. He was consistent within his own terms in that he carried his primary standard, his aesthetic perception of fitness, into all his judgments.[9]

Thus, although Matthiessen often celebrates James's astuteness and sensitivity, he chafes against James's politics and overriding passion for form: the artful observer's obsession with form sometimes distorted his view of the world.

In such comments, Matthiessen is, I believe, bearing unintentional witness to his own fissured allegiances. He is, on the one hand, a literary critic committed to examining "form," the "object as it is"; in this respect, he is attracted to James as a paradigmatic instance of the "art of fiction." Yet he is also a socialist and, by the time he was writing on James in the mid-and late 1940s, a member of the Citizens Political Action Committee and a budding supporter of Henry Wallace, who would eventually become the Progressive party candidate for president in 1948. What Matthiessen seems to expose, but not really confront, in his work on James are the tensions and contradictions between his own literary and political views. He often appears on the verge of major revelations—both about James and about himself—but he doesn't express them in a sustained fashion, doesn't rigorously follow through on them. He fails to inquire deeply into the possibility, one he gestures toward himself, that there might be a problematic relation between James's conception of his art and his shortcomings both as a writer and a political man.

I want to turn shortly to the critical book on James, where the issues I have touched upon are much in evidence, but first I think it is valuable to have some understanding of Matthiessen's own politics in 1944, the year *Henry James:*

The Major Phase was published. Matthiessen tells us in *From the Heart of Europe* that he had long searched for a party in America that, while promising some likelihood of success, would base itself upon socialist principles—"economic revolution," hatred of the "concentration of wealth" and the tyranny that accompanies it, and the rights of all "to share in the common wealth."

> In present day America, the one time when I have felt that there was a chance to share in the direct political implementation of such views was during the rise of the Citizens Political Action Committee in the presidential campaign of 1944. Here at last there seemed to be the kind of organization through which middle-class intellectuals and white-collar workers sympathetic with the labor movement could cooperate in forwarding their common aims. I had worked with many liberal groups of good will, but had come to share Lincoln Steffens' doubts of their permanent accomplishments. For without a strong ballast, such as organized labor alone can provide, these groups soon get lost in an idealistic void. By allying ourselves as closely as possible with the progressive membership of the unions, we gain the kind of discipline that has so often been lacking among American reformers—the first-hand discipline of knowing what is actually going on in the minds of the people, and of what, therefore, is feasible. Only after thorough immersion in that knowledge is any intellectual able to offer the kind of help for which his particular gifts have fitted him.[10]

These political sentiments seep into Matthiessen's criticism on James, as they invariably do not in his criticism on T. S. Eliot. (*The Achievement of T. S. Eliot* first appeared in 1935 and later in a revised edition in 1947.) Matthiessen was more successful, it seems, in cordoning off his politics in his encounters with Eliot. In my view, that restraint mars Matthiessen's work on Eliot, for it prevents him from addressing such fundamental matters as the ties between Eliot's poetry and point of view as classicist, royalist, and Anglo-Catholic. Because it's not broken and disrupted by political urgencies Matthiessen can't keep in check, the Eliot book exhibits a greater purity of argument—Matthiessen sees everything in literary and formal terms—than *Henry James* but is therefore not so cogent about Eliot and less interesting about Matthiessen. Matthiessen's religious bond and friendship with Eliot doubtless made the difference. He didn't agree with Eliot that belief in Christianity went hand-in-hand with homage to other conservative institutions of the state, but he did assent to Eliot's pained sense of man's radical imperfection and effort to place Christian values at the center of a reconstituted society. With James, Matthiessen does not have such bonds to buffer more frequent, sharper kinds of disagreement. When poring over James—"flimsy" on politics and not an "important thinker"—Matthiessen's considerable admiration for the artistry is qualified by his uneasiness about its implications.

If you read *Henry James* closely, you will detect, in the midst of Matthiessen's endorsement of the "major phase," much that intimates his reservations about James. So abundant, in fact, are these small slighting comments that they constitute a kind of second narrative which turns the book into something other than what it appears to be at first—"Matthiessen's paean to art," the "single most eloquent celebration of the artist as creator and conserver of value for society."[11] Sometimes Matthiessen frankly combines commendation and critique, as when he states in the preface that *The Bostonians* and *The Princess Casamassima* reveal "the strange mixture of perception and blindness in [James's] grasp of political issues."[12] More often, his appraisals and descriptions slant into wary or estranged phrasing. Here, for example, are sentences from Matthiessen's account of James's notebook entries and letters dealing with his life in London and Paris in the early 1880s:

> For page after page he might well be any fastidious but amiable young American with a sufficient bank account to allow him to give his time to somewhat vague cultural pursuits. . . . Nearly every glimpse of his personal life, in his letters as well, is just as decorous and mild, quite separated from the real concerns of any community. . . . The most usual topics are the marriages, the liaisons, and the divorces of the rich, and as we reconstruct the scene and envisage the dark serious man inclining his head gravely now to the right, then to the left, we can hardly fail to be struck with how far he has drifted from the social world of his inheritance. Both his father and his elder brother were militantly democratic, and both reacted strongly against such occasions as made Henry's nightly fare, and carried away a sense of the hideous and overpowering stultification of a society based upon such class distinctions. [Pp. 3, 4, 5]

Matthiessen's own sympathies are for the cause of "community" and "militant democracy," and, as an ally of Henry Sr. and William James, he keeps voicing his discontent with the novelist son-and-brother's social and political views. At one point associating James with Henry Adams, Matthiessen observes that "neither . . . could be said to have remotely understood the American world of their maturity" (p. 51). Later, in a brief treatment of *The American Scene*, he notes that

> James looked at the common man with shy friendliness, but believed that democracy inevitably levels down. Whenever he started generalizing about the America of 1905 and trusted his impressions alone to lead him to social truths, he was apt to end up with odd propositions. . . . He worried a good deal about what the new aliens from southern and central Europe would do to our Anglo-Saxon culture, and drifted dangerously close to a doctrine of racism. [P. 110]

James could be "even more misled," Matthiessen firmly adds, "when seizing upon something to praise, for positives to balance his negatives," as in his favorable treatment of "the Country Club," an institution whose "brittle glamour" Sinclair Lewis and Theodore Dreiser would crack (p. 110).

It is possible to regard such passages about James's limitations as a person and thinker as Matthiessen's inverse

measure of the greatness of the artist. When his language is reducible to "propositions," one could take Matthiessen to be saying, James is unreliable and even deplorable; therefore, how beautiful the work and how skilled a craftsman James must be, for we see not the meanness but the art, as we should. I am not sure, though, that such a formulation explains satisfactorily the intensity of Matthiessen's comments. I think he found it hard, writing as he did during a period when democracy was endangered, to speak of James only as a supreme artist. "Doctrine of racism" is a stiff sentence to pass, and it was doubtless even more so in 1944, given what was happening to the families and descendants of those "aliens from southern and central Europe" at the hands of the Nazis.[13]

Often Matthiessen does speak passionately about James's "art" in the "major phase." He is particularly eloquent about *The Wings of the Dove*, which he terms James's "masterpiece," "that single work where his characteristic emotional vibration seems deepest and where we may have the sense, therefore, that we have come to 'the very soul'" (p. 43). But even when he addresses the art on its own terms, Matthiessen is often decidedly critical, and not only in obvious places, as in his aside about "the intertness of form" in James's plays (p. 8). In his chapter on *The Ambassadors*, Matthiessen compares the imagery James employs to represent Lambert Strether's "will to live" with that which Thoreau furnishes for his own "will to live" in *Walden*. Thoreau's will was "dynamic," Matthiessen contends, "and he expressed his desire 'to suck out all the marrow of life' in a series of physical images, the energy of which was quite beyond Strether—or James" (p. 27). Matthiessen acknowledges James's fondness for Strether but maintains that the reader inevitably feels a thinness, even a "relative emptiness," in him (p. 39). What saves *The Ambassadors* is James's characterization of Madame de Vionnet: "her positive suffering and loss are far more affecting than Strether's tenuous renunciation" (p. 41). But saving the novel in this manner obliges Matthiessen to discount the depiction of Strether's growth, which for James was the novel's motive force and technical showpiece.

Also dealing severely with *The Golden Bowl*, Matthiessen stresses that James appears "to take Mr. Verver," the American billionaire, "at his own estimate" and sees his actions as springing from a wonderful naïveté. James does not succeed in handling the moral complexities implicit in a drama of good and evil that has as its protagonists the fabulously wealthy. He simply did not know what the American businessman in the late nineteenth century was like: "Mr. Verver's moral tone is far more like that of a benevolent Swedenborgian than it is like that of either John D. Rockefeller or Jay Gould" (pp. 89, 90). Nor does James seem alert to the sexually ambiguous contours of the relationship between Mr. Verver and his daughter, Maggie. The writer's psychological grasp, Matthiessen argues, is extremely limited: "What it comes down to, again and again, is that James's characters tend to live, as has often been objected, merely off the tops of their minds" (p. 93).

It is, above all, the "unsatisfactory nature of the positive values" in *The Golden Bowl* to which Matthiessen continually returns—Mr. Verver's wealth, which he innocently acquires; the father/daughter relationship, which is also innocent, in James's view, but which strikes the reader as morally and psychologically disturbing; and, finally, Maggie's own behavior, which, yet again, gives forth the luster of innocence even as she traffics in evil by immersing herself in the affair between her husband, Prince Amerigo, and her father's wife, Charlotte Stant. "James was trying," Matthiessen concludes, "to invest his triumphant Americans with qualities they could hardly possess," and, in the process, he exposes his lack of sensitivity to issues of morality, psychology, and the workings of American society. *The Golden Bowl* is, in a word, a "decadent" book (p. 102) that

> forces upon our attention too many flagrant lapses in the ways things happen both in the personal and in the wider social sphere. With all its magnificence, it is almost as hollow of real life as the chateaux that had risen along Fifth Avenue and that had also crowded out the old Newport world that James remembered. [P. 104]

Even in his chapter on *The Wings of the Dove*, Matthiessen frequently points to James's defects and limitations. He does praise James's craftsmanship in depicting Kate Croy's machinations, Morton Densher's discovery of his own complicity in Kate's plot, and Milly Theale's suffering, but throughout his chapter, and in its concluding pages in particular, Matthiessen remains skeptical about whether *The Wings of the Dove* ultimately merits the stature accorded the greatest literary works. The problem is that Milly lacks the spiritedness, active faith, and energy that James himself celebrated in her "original," his cousin Minny Temple, who had died of tuberculosis at the age of twenty-four. Milly's character—more akin to Desdemona than to Othello, Matthiessen reflects—falls short of the "substance" that tragedy requires. Her death is not truly "tragic," and her story, taken as a whole, yields only "exquisite pathos" (pp. 78, 79). Although closing his chapter positively, Matthiessen lapses into special pleading, as if to counter the adversarial tone of his insights:

> If James has shown again that the chords he could strike were minor, were those of renunciation, of resignation, of inner triumph in the face of outer defeat, he was not out of keeping with the spiritual history of his American epoch. Art often expresses society very obliquely, and it is notable that the most sensitive recorders of James's generation gave voice to themes akin to his. In the face of the overwhelming expansion, the local colorists felt compelled, like Sarah Orne Jewett, to commemorate the old landmarks before they should be entirely swept away and obliterated. Emily Dickinson discovered that the only way she could be a poet in such an age was by withdrawal, by depending, virtually like a Jamesian heroine, upon the richness of her own 'crowded consciousness.' And the least feminine, most robust talent of the age, Mark Twain, who may seem at the farthest pole from James, did not find his themes in the facile myths of manifest destiny or triumphant de-

mocracy. His masterpiece was also an elegy. It gave expression to the loss of the older America of his boyhood, which, not less than the milieu of Henry James and Minny Temple, had been destroyed by the onrush of the industrial revolution. [Pp. 79-80]

It's one thing to say that Jewett and Dickinson commemorated the past and withdrew into their own artistic consciousnesses, but this posture differs markedly from what Matthiessen has discovered about James—that he engaged social and economic aspects of life and failed to understand them. When we read James, we apprehend superbly executed forms that are ill suited to the accurate management of their subject matter. This insight, all along, has been Matthiessen's central evaluative point.

Matthiessen also forces the connection between James and Twain. One might perhaps question, first, the degree to which *Huckleberry Finn* is, at its core, an elegy and is not as much, if not more, a relentlessly satiric novel about the world of Twain's boyhood and the corruptions of life on the shore. Like many who have written about *Huckleberry Finn*, Matthiessen tends to sentimentalize it by seizing upon a relatively small part of the novel—the passages in which Huck expresses the wonder of life on the raft—to stand for the whole. It would have been interesting for Matthiessen's study of James, and especially for his effort to link James and Twain, if he had probed what *Huckleberry Finn* teaches us about "manifest destiny" and "American democracy." It's obvious that Twain didn't accept "facile myths" about America; his distinction lies in his complicated strategies for attacking those myths. In *Huckleberry Finn*, and even more in two other disorderly but provocative books, *A Connecticut Yankee in King Arthur's Court* and *Pudd'nhead Wilson*, Twain deals with issues—slavery, miscegenation, colonialism and imperialism, technology, militarism—that help us to apprehend American history as recounted through its literature. These are issues, Matthiessen has been maintaining, that James didn't care about; these are the issues that formed so much of the "world" that James, in Matthiessen's view, did not "remotely" understand.

The strength of **Henry James** is Matthiessen's critical attitude toward his subject; the book's weakness lies in his inability or unwillingness to push his criticism even further, to spell out clearly his sense of the social and political deficiencies of James's art. What's intriguing, especially to someone drawn to Matthiessen, is that he is doing something here that he could not do in his earlier book on Eliot or even in **American Renaissance**: he is beginning, if not with complete success, to bring together his literary critical skills and his politics. He is not quite "reading as a socialist"; if he were, he would undoubtedly have been even more critical of James. He is, I think, a critic in conflict with himself as he seeks and struggles to find his way in **Henry James**. Matthiessen feels the tension between his literary and political values and at moments tries to voice it, but there remains much that he does not see and cannot express.

In view of his emerging emphasis on a literary criticism that is also social and political, Matthiessen conceivably might have developed his remarks about *The American Scene*. Usually, as is the case with Matthiessen, critics locate *The American Scene* on the margins of the Jamesian canon: it is an anomaly of his oeuvre and a "curiosity" of American literature (p. 107). For purposes more general—and more subversive—one would like to have prompted Matthiessen to consider how perceptions of James might change if we saw *The American Scene* as his central book. When Matthiessen states that in it James "drifted dangerously close to a doctrine of racism" (p. 110), one wishes that he had focused this judgment in the action of James's language, perhaps in a passage like the following on life in "the Yiddish quarter":

> It was the sense, after all, of a great swarming, a swarming that had begun to thicken, infinitely, as soon as we had crossed to the East side and long before we had got to Rutgers Street. There is no swarming like that of Israel when once Israel has got a start, and the scene here bristled, at every step, with the signs and sounds, immitigable, unmistakable, of a Jewry that had burst all bounds. That it has burst all bounds in New York, almost any combination of figures or of objects taken at hazard sufficiently proclaims; but I remember how the rising waters, on this summer night, rose, to the imagination, even above the housetops and seemed to sound their murmur to the pale distant stars. It was as if we had been thus, in the crowded, hustled roadway, where multiplication of everything, was the dominant note, at the bottom of some vast sallow aquarium in which innumerable fish, of over-developed proboscis, were to bump together, for ever, amid heaped spoils of the sea.[14]

In the face of such a passage, one's moral judgment seems obvious. James proffers a fantasia of self-pleasing images that depict Jews as racially odd, rapacious creatures. What's good about these people, it seems, is the marvelous opportunity they afford for working the metaphorical transformations that James generates so readily. In a sense, then, this language is indeed "racist" and calls for our own dissent. But the extravagancies of the language make such a judgment appear at once both appropriate and simplistic, even simpleminded. As James undoubtedly knew, his verbal inventiveness, in all its brilliance, invites moral disapproval while mocking and threatening to disarm it. The capacity for simultaneously evoking and disengaging himself from moral discourse is what makes the James of *The American Scene* so difficult, and perhaps Matthiessen might have spotted this if he had toiled with the text's language: the morally right response is essential to register, but it finally doesn't characterize the stunning (and taxing) experience of reading *The American Scene*.

On a thematic level, James continually calls attention to the plight of the English language in America as it strains to be heard above the immigrants' foreign voices. The reader cannot help but be conscious, page by page, of the incredible thickness of James's own language, which is his way of being faithful to his multiplying impressions as he registers for us what a sustained and unnervingly total fidelity to language entails. James judges that the immigrants endanger his own delight in, and painstaking service to, language. The East side cafés that he visits show themselves,

> beneath their bedizenment, as torture-rooms of the living idiom; the piteous gasp of which at the portent of lacerations to come could reach me in any drop of the surrounding Accent of the Future. The accent of the very ultimate future, in the States, may be destined to become the most beautiful on the globe and the very music of humanity (here the "ethnic" synthesis shrouds itself thicker than ever); but whatever we shall know it for, certainly, we shall not know it for English—in any sense for which there is an existing literary measure. [P. 139]

James assumes that the immigrants' languages—apparently containing no "living idiom" of their own—torture the truly idiomatic speech that is the essence of the English he cherishes and has sought to honor in his novels. Here, indeed, one might be inclined once more to invoke the charge of racism that Matthiessen levels. But again such a moral response doesn't feel entirely appropriate to our reading of *The American Scene*. While it's correct to say that James dislikes the immigrants and fears the incursion of their languages, this bare statement does not, for me, get to the heart of what makes this passage, and a great many others in the book, so disconcertingly affecting. However much James may loathe the immigrants, he is nevertheless capable of envisioning some future epoch when their languages blend into a beautiful harmony quite beyond his own powers of appreciation. I like to believe, in fact, that when James refers to the "very music of humanity," he is echoing language like that which Shakespeare uses in the fifth act of *The Merchant of Venice*, where Lorenzo describes the "sweet harmony" of the "sounds of music." If the allusion is intended, the passage becomes resonant, even self-ironical, as James celebrates the immigrants by referring to a play written by the authoritative source for, and guardian of, the English idiom. *The Merchant of Venice* is a suggestive point of reference for James, for it displays the Jew, tainted with the money passion, as alien and outcast, fated, like James, never to speak like others or hear the music that they take such pleasure in.

The American Scene and the journey it records are, after all, financial as well as literary acts. Even before James sailed to America, he had contracted with George Harvey of Harper and Brothers "for the serialization of his American experiences" in *The North American Review* and "the collection of them in book form upon his return to England."[15] Writing about the trip, James realized, would be necessary to help finance it in the first place. He also hoped to make money by delivering lectures in America; as Leon Edel points out, "James became interested" in lecturing "from the moment he learned that he could command substantial fees."[16] James further planned to attend to copyright matters while in America and, above all, to undertake business arrangements for the collected edition of his works.

James's terror at seeing the immigrants becomes in part, then, a kind of self-horror and self-amazement as he recognizes his bonds with the foreigners who have displaced him. He feels deep antipathy for the exotic people he encounters, yet he himself, he knows, resembles them in striving for the best deal and in cultivating his own well-traveled, highly mannered exoticism. In returning to an America very different from the one he left twenty years earlier, he too is an outsider, an immigrant and stranger. As Ross Posnock has incisively remarked, James was both distressed by and entangled with the immigrants' situation and fate.[17] This complex attitude explains James's immense curiosity about and fascination with the scenes enacted at Ellis Island, over which he lingers for several pages (pp. 84-86). He stresses, on the one hand, his immense distance from the immigrants, each of whom epitomizes for him the changes being remorselessly driven into America's language, national identity, and cultural consciousness; yet he is also intimately in touch with the immigrants as he senses the disorientation and disturbance that the shock of "the new" creates in them.

James cannot, however, convert that sympathy into an acceptance of the ideal of American democracy. Matthiessen's term "racism" finally seems not quite to fit the strange case of *The American Scene* because the issue at the center of the problem involves race but is more political than racial in its character. "Democracy" is what bothers James. It is "monstrous" to him (p. 54), for its full realization requires the eradication of familiar kinds of privilege, distinction, difference. The aliens, to be sure, speak many different languages, but this, for James, is tantamount to saying that they speak one language massively different from English or, perhaps more accurately still, that they speak in a "hum" or "noise" that is not really language at all.

The "babel" of immigrant "tongues" forestalls communication, James emphasizes, but it is evident that his notion of "communication" obliges the communicators to perform traditional roles. To cite but one instance from *The American Scene*: in a surprisingly unguarded and unironical moment, James recounts his dismay at a thwarted communication between himself and some Italian workmen he meets one day on the New Jersey shore.

> To pause before them, for interest in their labour, was, and would have been everywhere, instinctive; but what came home to me on the spot was that whatever *more* would have been anywhere else involved had here inevitably to lapse.
>
> What lapsed, on the spot, was the element of communication with the workers, as I may call it for want of a better name; that element which, in a European country, would have operated, from side to side, as the play of mutual recognition, founded on old familiarities and heredities, and involving, for the moment, some impal-

pable exchange. The men, in the case I speak of, were Italians, of superlatively Southern type, and any impalpable exchange struck me as absent from the air to positive intensity, to mere unthinkability. It was as if contact were out of the question and the sterility of the passage between us recorded, with due dryness, in our staring silence. The impression was for one of the party a shock—a member of the party for whom, on the other side of the world, the imagination of the main furniture, as it might be called, of any rural excursion, of *the* rural in particular, had been, during years, the easy sense, for the excursionist, of a social relation with any encountered type, from whichever end of the scale proceeding. Had not that ever been, exactly, a part of the vague warmth, the intrinsic colour, of any honest man's rural walk in his England or his Italy, his Germany or his France, and was not the effect of its so suddenly dropping out, in the land of universal brotherhood—for I was to find it drop out again and again—rather a chill, straightway, for the heart, and rather a puzzle, not less, for the head? [Pp. 118-19]

Such a passage exhibits the anxious and jeopardized but finally complacent dimension of *The American Scene*.[18] Democracy cuts short the communication that a class-bound society prizes, communication that allows James to enjoy the types he greets during pastoral interludes even while resting assured that any "exchange" will be momentary, on his terms, and, in the final analysis, "impalpable," intangible, insubstantial.

One wonders how Matthiessen responded at heart to James's descriptions of immigrant language and behavior, especially when one remembers how committed he was himself to "universal brotherhood" in politics and education. As a point of contrast with *The American Scene*, one can cite a memorable passage in **From the Heart of Europe**, taken from the chapter in which Matthiessen sketches his life as a Yale undergraduate:

> I had volunteered to teach English to a group at the New Haven Hungarian Club who wanted to qualify for their citizenship papers. These men had a serious awe before the possibility of the education which I had grown up taking for granted. Most of them were double my age, but by the end of the lessons we had achieved something close to friendship. After the last session, one of the men suggested, with a sly wink, that I might like to see the rest of their building. They took me down cellar where each one had been fermenting his own cask of prohibition wine. We sampled several, with a good deal of ceremony, and the stars seemed unusually bright as I walked back to the Yale campus. I had felt in the natural and hearty comradeship of these men a quality that I was just beginning to suspect might be bleached out of middle-class college graduates. It was a kind of comradeship I wanted never to lose. [P. 73]

Like Kenneth Lynn, I think there is something forced in Matthiessen's desire to align himself with working people, as though he were determined, in a mix of moral fervor and sentimentality, to overcome the discomfort of alienation.[19] Matthiessen's embrace of "democracy," moreover, seems to depend on principles overly generalized and insufficiently examined. The celebratory rhetoric he frequently employs reveals that in his view "democracy" in America means bringing to fulfillment the opportunities for freedom and equality that the Revolution bestowed; it means capitalizing at last upon our nation's "undiminished resources."[20] Nowhere does Matthiessen make clear how this rhetoric could translate into particular kinds of social, political, and economic change. Though officially a socialist, Matthiessen was basically, judging from his writings, an American democrat in the tradition of Whitman. He characteristically defines and extols democracy in overwhelmingly literary terms, citing texts from Whitman, Emerson, Louis Sullivan, and others. Their language empowers and enriches his own, but it may also have diverted Matthiessen from addressing the political and economic consequences of a democracy truly geared toward socialism and prevented an inquiry into what a full commitment to democratic socialism might entail for his own scholarly and professional life.

This limitation to Matthiessen's understanding of democracy is important to register, but we should take care that it not cause us to miss the difference between Matthiessen, who seeks to "teach English" to immigrants seeking to become citizens, and Henry James, who defends English against the barbaric attack of foreign tongues and insinuates that English is the exclusive property of men of letters like himself. Matthiessen aspired—fiercely, unrelentingly, and at great emotional and psychological cost—toward an ideal of democratic solidarity that might bridge the differences which Henry James hankered to preserve even as he ruefully articulated the blunt truth of their disappearance.

Notes

1. Vernon Louis Parrington, *The Beginnings of Critical Realism in America, 1860-1920* (1930; reprinted, New York: Harcourt, Brace and World, 1958), pp. 240-41.

2. Jay B. Hubbell, *Who Are the Major American Writers? A Study of the Changing Literary Canon* (Durham: Duke University Press, 1972), p. 131.

3. *Rat and the Devil: Journal Letters of F. O. Matthiessen and Russell Cheney*, ed. Louis Hyde (Hamden, Conn.: Archon Books, 1978), p. 283.

4. F. O. Matthiessen, *American Renaissance: Art and Expression in the Age of Emerson and Whitman* (1941; reprinted, New York: Oxford University Press, 1972), pp. 292, 294.

5. Ezra Pound, "Henry James," collected in *Literary Essays of Ezra Pound* (New York: New Directions, 1968), p. 327.

6. Hershel Parker, *Flawed Texts and Verbal Icons: Literary Authority in American Fiction* (Evanston: Northwestern University Press, 1984), pp. 94-95.

7. Matthiessen to Cheney, 10 February and 21 March 1943, *Rat and the Devil*, pp. 274, 277.

8. Matthiessen, ed., *Henry James: Stories of Writers and Artists* (New York: New Directions, 1944), pp. 12, 17.

9. Matthiessen, ed., *The James Family: A Group Biography* (1947; reprinted, New York: Knopf, 1961), pp. 245, 646.

10. Matthiessen, *From the Heart of Europe* (New York: Oxford University Press, 1948), p. 84.

11. Richard Ruland, *The Rediscovery of American Literature: Premises of Critical Taste, 1900-1940* (Cambridge: Harvard University Press, 1967), p. 264.

12. Matthiessen, *Henry James: The Major Phase* (New York: Oxford University Press, 1944), p. xiv. Further references to this work will appear in the text.

13. Perhaps Matthiessen's judgment did not acquire the full impact I have assigned to it until the end of the war and afterwards, when Americans began finally to absorb the truth of the Holocaust. It could be argued that Matthiessen's first readers, in 1944, would not have felt the powerful rebuke in his reference to James's "doctrine of racism"; indeed, Matthiessen may have been only vaguely aware of it himself. But the evidence suggests that much about the Nazis' systematic extermination of European Jewry had become widely known in the Allied countries—if not fully comprehended in all its terrifying dimensions—by the fall of 1944, when Matthiessen gave the lectures that formed the basis for his book. See Martin Gilbert, *Auschwitz and the Allies* (New York: Holt, Rinehart, and Winston, 1981), p. 339, and David S. Wyman, *The Abandonment of the Jews: America and the Holocaust, 1941-1945* (New York: Pantheon, 1984), esp. pp. 19-58.

14. Henry James, *The American Scene* (1907; reprinted, Bloomington: Indiana University Press, 1969), p. 131. Further references will appear in the text.

15. Rosalie Hewitt, "*The American Scene*: Its Genesis and Reception, 1905-1977," *Henry James Review* 1 (1980): 179.

16. Leon Edel, *Henry James: The Master, 1901-1916* (New York: Lippincott, 1972), p. 229.

17. Ross Posnock, "Henry James, Veblen, and Adorno: The Crisis of the Modern Self," *Journal of American Studies,* forthcoming.

18. See James M. Cox, "The Memoirs of Henry James: Self-Interest as Autobiography," *Southern Review* 22 (1986): 231-51.

19. Kenneth Lynn, "F. O. Matthiessen," *Masters: Portraits of Great Teachers*, ed. Joseph Epstein (New York: Basic Books, 1981), p. 113.

20. Matthiessen, *American Renaissance*, p. xv.

Jonathan Arac (essay date 1987)

SOURCE: "F. O. Matthiessen and American Studies: Authorizing a Renaissance," in *Critical Genealogies: Histori-*

cal Situations for Postmodern Literary Studies, Columbia University Press, 1987, pp. 157-75.

[*In the following essay, Arac addresses the often contradictory nature of Matthiessen's work and assesses "the possibilities for a new literary history in the practice of American Renaissance."*]

For decades since his suicide in 1950, F. O. Matthiessen has exerted a compelling attraction. The documentation, analysis, and controversy around him bulk larger than for any other American literary scholar born in the twentieth century, and they grow.

There are at least three good reasons for this posthumous attention. First, Matthiessen played a decisive role in making possible the American academic study of American literature (for short, "American studies"). His major book, *American Renaissance* (1941), has given its name to courses taught at hundreds of institutions. More than any other single factor it enabled hundreds of Ph.D.'s in English to specialize in the American literature of the nineteenth century. Matthiessen himself, however, deplored the "barrenness" of what he termed the "now hopefully obsolescent practice of literary scholars' restricting themselves to the arbitrary confines of a single century in a single country" (*Responsibilities* 169).

Second, Matthiessen, both as a Harvard professor and as a private citizen, was widely and visibly active in left politics of the 1930s and 1940s. Although as a practicing Christian he was not a Communist and disavowed Marxism, he was considered a leading fellow-traveler. The clearest textual focus for this engagement is *From the Heart of Europe* (1948), a memoir of his time in Austria and Czechoslovakia in the months before the Czechoslovak coup of 1948.

Third, both as a teacher and friend, Matthiessen made an intense personal impression. A "collective portrait" by many hands was compiled soon after his death, but the most remarkable testimony came in *Rat and the Devil* (1978), a selection by their friend Louis Hyde from the thousands of letters exchanged by Matthiessen and the painter Russell Cheney during the twenty years they shared their lives.

The interrelations among these three aspects of Matthiessen's career do not, however, offer an occasion for the rhetoric of "wholeness," even though that rhetoric was extremely important to Matthiessen himself. As a critic, for example, he concluded *American Renaissance* (henceforth abbreviated *AR* in references) by writing of Melville that he fulfilled "what Coleridge held to be the major function of the artist: he brought the whole soul of man into activity" (656). As a politically committed man, he began the book by subscribing to the test of "true scholarship," that it be "for the good and enlightenment of all the people, not for the pampering of a class" (xv). And as early as 1925, he wrote Cheney about their love: "In these last

months I am a whole man for the first time: no more dodging or repressing for we gladly accept what we are. And sex now instead of being a nightmare is the most sacred, all embracing gift we have. Now I can see, as this morning, while riding along, a husky labouring feller asleep on a bank, one hand lying heavy across his things, and I can thrill at the deep earthiness and blood of him. For I know that I am of blood and earth too, as well as of brain and of soul, and that my whole self waits—and waits gladly—for you" (*Rat* 116).

Some problems about Matthiessen's "wholeness" emerge clearly in comparing the letters and *American Renaissance*. In the long section on Whitman, Matthiessen dispersed over sixty pages references to three topics—homosexuality (*AR* 585; cf. also 535), the "power of sex" (523), and transient "Good Moments" (541)—which are remarkably condensed in an early letter to Cheney. This letter narrated an encounter with a "workman—husky, broadshouldered, forty" at Wells cathedral. Matthiessen began with a literary reference: this man was "the perfect Chaucerian yeoman," and he concluded by explaining that he wrote so much about the event "not because it is the least bit important, but because it was so natural, so like Walt Whitman." Such cultural awareness did not conflict with but rather enhanced erotic possibilities: "He caught my eye both as a magnificently built feller, and as fitting in so perfectly to the type of fourteenth century work man." He thus embodied the permanence of the people: "He might just as well have been building the original cathederal, as repairing it centuries later." For "about a quarter of a minute" they talked, allowing Matthiessen to note the man's "unusually gentle" voice and "dark full brown" eye. Then, as the man went off, Matthiessen "deliberately let my elbow rub against his belly," for he "wanted to feel the touch of his body as a passing gesture." He acknowledged that he was sexually excited, yet also that "there was no question of not wanting to keep myself for you." The "whole self" allows marginal responses to take on their wholeness: "It thrilled me, not only with sex, but with friendliness" (*Rat* 124).

The problems of temporality here merit further attention: the mythic co-presence of the fourteenth and twentieth centuries, set against its punctual disruption, the "passing gesture," the "good moment." What stands out now, however, is the difference between the sense of reading Whitman in Matthiessen's lively letter and in his monumental book. Between these two ways of reading, and ways of writing about reading, stands a long process of transformative discipline, closely related to issues addressed in the chapter on Arnold. The modern critical practice Leavis called the "discipline of letters" required abandoning the modes of "impressionist" reading, the orientation which M. H. Abrams has called "expressive," and the rhetoric of "flash" and fragment for which the classical antecedent is Longinus on the sublime. To create the centrally authoritative critical identity of *American Renaissance*, much had to be displaced or scattered or disavowed. Loose elbows had to be tucked in. T. S. Eliot's insistence on "form" and "impersonality" in poetry chastened Matthiessen's early commitment to the "human spirit," the "man himself," and the "flash of the spark of life" that reading sets off (***Rat*** 102, 133).

Matthiessen joined his generation in sacrificing to modernist discipline a romantic theorist of the "spark," the politically and sexually revolutionary poet Shelley. Even a German left-wing modernist like Theodor Adorno (a year younger than Matthiessen) shared his derogation of Shelley, at least by the time he had emigrated to the United States. The first version of Walter Benjamin's essay on Baudelaire (the primary focus of the next chapter) cited a few lines from Shelley's "Peter Bell the Third" to contrast their "directness and harshness" (*Härte*, which may also be translated "rigor"!) to the obliquity with which Baudelaire represented Paris:

> Hell is a city much like London,
> A populous and smoky city;
> There are all sorts of people undone,
> And there is little or no fun done;
> Small justice shown, and still less pity.

(lines 147-51; Charles Baudelaire 59)

In criticizing the essay, Adorno accused Benjamin of being fooled by the "extraordinary" quality of the German translation of Shelley, for "directness and harshness are as a rule not exactly his characteristics" (Benjamin, *Gesammelte Schriften*, 1:1112). Adorno no doubt felt the odds were on his side, since the translation was by a notoriously harsh and direct German poet—Brecht. In fact the translation is lucidly literal although slightly less lapidary, and without the savage comedy of the rhyme "undone / fun done":

> Die Hölle ist eine Stadt, sehr ähnlich London—
> Eine volkreiche und eine rauchige Stadt.
> Dort gibt es alle Arten von ruinierten Leuten
> Und dort ist wenig oder gar kein Spass
> Wenig Gerechtigkeit und noch weniger Mitleid.

(Benjamin, Gesammelte Schriften, 1.2:562)

Brecht and Benjamin had been together in Denmark in 1938. While Benjamin was drafting the essay, Brecht wrote one of his several pieces against Lukács's conception of realism ("Weite"). This one translated much of Shelley's "Mask of Anarchy" (which directly precedes "Peter Bell the Third" in the Oxford Standard Authors edition to which Benjamin referred), to demonstrate that in his very different way Shelley was as important a model for realism as Lukács's Balzac. It seems likely that Brecht did the "Peter Bell" translation for Benjamin, since it is not included in the standard edition of his works, which, however, was completed before Benjamin's essay reached publication.

Matthiessen's hostility to Shelley, then, was representative, but it is especially significant because in the early letters, Matthiessen was reading Shelley with positive engagement. At one point he even archly identified himself with Shelley in their attachment to older men (***Rat*** 33, 78, 84).

By ***American Renaissance***, however, T. S. Eliot's denigration of Shelley was in full force. Some half-dozen times Shelley was evoked for predictable dismissals (*AR* 259, 311, 353, 388). Such gestures contributed to the critical authority of ***American Renaissance*** because they certified Matthiessen as emotionally "mature," and they distanced him from a figure whose philosophic, political, and literary activities can seem terribly unintegrated—in part, we have seen, because of his full commitment to both ends of polarities. Yet in the spread and energy of his own activism, Matthiessen more closely resembled Shelley than any of the antiselves he treated in ***American Renaissance***.

These analyses suggest that the problem of the whole, the indivisible, the individual, requires attention to institutional circumstances. Can we make a whole without exclusion and divisiveness? Matthiessen joined Hawthorne in abjuring the "damned mob of scribbling women" (*AR* x); students ask me why Frederick Douglass showed insufficient "devotion to the possibilities of democracy" (*AR* ix) for Matthiessen even to mention him. These are matters of institutional power: in order to be a productive unit, a field must be marked off, delimited, defined—even if your commitment is to "all the people."

This kind of discrepancy is crucial to understanding the effects of Matthiessen's career. For Matthiessen's power to authorize an American Renaissance came from his mobilizing certain figures that were then appropriated in ways contrary to his intentions. Recall the irony that his work produced specialists of a sort which he himself considered "hopefully obsolescent." No less striking is the nationalist force achieved by Matthiessen's emphatically international undertaking.

I want to explore in some detail Matthiessen's title: ***American Renaissance: Art and Expression in the Age of Emerson and Whitman***. First off, it is significant to my institutional focus that the phrase which later American literary culture most closely identifies with Matthiessen was not originally his own, but provided by a younger colleague (Levin, preface to *Power*). It was important to Matthiessen that his work be collegial, based more broadly than in the solitary individual. Matthiessen acknowledged the oddity of considering the mid-nineteenth century a cultural "rebirth." He explained that "America's way of producing a renaissance" lay in "affirming its rightful heritage in the whole expanse of art and culture" (*AR* vii). This still-cryptic clarification is better understood through a quotation from André Malraux cited a few pages later: "Every civilization is like the Renaissance, and creates its own heritage out of everything in the past that helps it to surpass itself" (xv n.). The theory of literary history adumbrated here deserves considerable attention, but for the moment note how obscure this line of intention has become; few can recall this logic for the title.

For "renaissance" has a force of its own. Ever since the historiographic notion was elaborated by Michelet and Burckhardt—in 1845 and 1860, exactly bracketing Matthiessen's period—"Renaissance" has carried a glamorous freight of secularism, progress, and preeminent individuality. All these values were in fact suspect to Matthiessen, but his title's figure translated "the Renaissance" westward to America just when the old, transatlantic Renaissance was being conservatively reevaluated in works like *The Allegory of Love* (C. S. Lewis, 1936) and *The Renaissance and English Humanism* (Douglas Bush, 1939). Matthiessen supported their claims for the medieval continuities of the Renaissance, emphasizing Christianity and traditional literary modes (cf. *AR* 246). But that was not how his figure worked.

What is the particular force of an "American" renaissance? As "American," it is new; more paradoxically, it is a repetition, a "renaissance of the Renaissance." It does for the Renaissance what the Renaissance had done for antiquity. Most important, however, it is *national*. People had long spoken of a Concord or Boston or New England "renaissance," but this was no longer local, regional, or sectional. It was shared among "all the people." Contrast Perry Miller's *The New England Mind* (1939), which not only sectionalized but also split off "mind" from the vigorous physical embodiment suggested by "Renaissance."

In emphasizing his focus on literature as "works of art" rather than as philosophical or social practice, Matthiessen imagined books that he might have written instead: *The Age of Swedenborg,* on transcendental thought; or *The Age of Fourier* on "radical movements" (*AR* vii-viii). The contrast of Emerson and Whitman with Swedenborg and Fourier strikes home. Emerson and Whitman are major, central, household words; Swedenborg and Fourier are minor, eccentric, obscure—and not even American. The literary and the American unite against the foreign, philosophical, and radical.

Matthiessen's title promoted a euphoria of America that gained power against the grain of his own methodological precepts and critical practice. From a review-essay of 1929 on the need to rewrite American literary history, to the lecture of 1949 on **"The Responsibilities of the Critic,"** Matthiessen insisted on America's relation to "Europe" (which includes England) (*Responsibilities* 181, 12). His most important books before and after *American Renaissance* addressed T. S. Eliot and Henry James, the most notoriously transatlantic of America's great writers. In *American Renaissance* itself Shakespeare occupied more lines of the index than did Thoreau! Matthiessen conceived of his subject as essentially national *and* comparative. He taught courses on world drama, Shakespeare, and an introduction to major English poets. American studies has not followed Matthiessen's precept or practice, even while drawing its warrant to exist from him. His radical energies succeeded more in reinvigorating than in remaking culturally established figures.

In speaking of a "euphoria of America," I do not mean that Matthiessen was blind to social and political problems or that he didn't care about them. *American Renaissance*

immediately proclaimed its solidarity with "those who believe now in the dynamic extension of democracy on economic as well as political levels" (4). But in writing about the social problems of America, Matthiessen failed to achieve specificity comparable to what he achieved in writing about the literary successes. Thus in Ahab he found an "ominous glimpse of what was to result when the Emersonian will to virtue became in less innocent natures the will to power and conquest." That will gave us the "empire-builders of the post-Civil War world," the "strong-willed individuals who seized the land and gutted the forests and built the railroads" (459). Matthiessen's rhetoric conflated the will with the deed, while introducing an oversharp chronological boundary. He failed to acknowledge that already in the 1850s, precisely in railroad building, not the tragic individual but the limited-liability corporation was the major agency, drawing capital from many sources, developing the techniques of bureaucratic management to organize the activities of its employees (the "hands" who executed the "will"), and even developing the ideology of free enterprise in order to get rid of existing government activities.

Matthiessen echoed the individualistic focus of Matthew Josephson's *The Robber Barons* (1934) but ignored the contrary perspective of Adolf Berle and Gardiner Means in *The Modern Corporation and Private Property* (1933), which James Burnham brought to fruit in *The Managerial Revolution* (1941). Alfred Chandler's painstaking historical work on the "Visible Hand" of the "Managerial Revolution in American Business" postdates Matthiessen, but the classic work of Matthiessen's older contemporary George Rogers Taylor bears out my emphases on the connection of prewar to postwar (Taylor 101), the prevalence of corporate over individual enterprise (240-42), and the role of giant, bureaucratic corporations in fomenting the ideology of private enterprise (383). Instead of this analytic detail, Matthiessen's approach produced an abstract division from a willed unity. That is, his theology provided the human potential for evil (*AR* 180), and his intellectual history provided the rise of "individualism" in the American 1830s (*AR* 5-6). The two combined to produce the figure of the evil individuals who obstruct the common good of an otherwise united American People.

Throughout the 1930s, the negative term of "individualism" and the positive terms of the "community" or the "people" figured in the discourse of widely different American intellectuals (Pells 118). Matthiessen's use of such terms in *American Renaissance* had an important relation to the particular political and rhetorical strategy of the Popular Front (or "People's Front"), which from 1935 was the Communist party line. In contrast to the militantly divisive rhetoric of the "Third Period," which attacked even socialists as "social fascists," the Popular Front, in belated response to Hitler's success, emphasized a defensive policy of alliance building. The situation no longer promised imminent apocalypse, requiring radical separation of sheep from goats; now, rather, from liberals to communists all were sheep together, except for that wolf out there. This policy meant a changed stance toward America. In 1933 Granville Hicks published *The Great Tradition*, on American fiction after the Civil War. In reviewing it, Matthiessen shared its concern with "the class war which is becoming increasingly the central fact of American life" (**Responsibilities** 197). In 1938, still on the staff of the *New Masses,* Hicks published his next book, *I Like America.*

Matthiessen was not a Communist party member, he did not always follow party positions, but the strategy of the Popular Front clearly appealed to him. I have already noted his rhetoric of "all the people" and noted the absence of class analysis in **American Renaissance**. As opposed to earlier Communist emphasis on independent proletarian culture, the Popular Front emphasized defending the "cultural heritage," which included the masterpieces produced by the bourgeoisie. This project defined Georg Lukács's major studies of nineteenth-century realism as well as André Malraux's brilliant speech on "The Cultural Heritage" at the second congress of the International Association of Writers for the Defense of Culture, held in London in 1936 (see further my "Struggle for the Cultural Heritage"). This was the text Matthiessen quoted for its crucial assertion that every civilization is like the Renaissance.

To locate Matthiessen's rhetoric in relation to the Popular Front helps to clarify what I find **American Renaissance**'s most extraordinary idealization: the diminishment of the Civil War. The Civil War was not even indexed, although it was not literally absent from the book. It allowed for tragic poetry by Melville and Whitman, and it was mentioned again and again—as in the passage just cited on "empire builders"—as a marker, dividing the American Renaissance from an age of rampantly destructive individualism. But the war was not integrated into any understanding of the renaissance. Matthiessen demonstrated that his object of study, the literary, functioned for writers as an evasion, though not a complete disengagement, from a political life of which they did not wholeheartedly approve (e.g., *AR* 67). But his interpretations of this compromise failed to reckon with the affirmative support compromise still gave to dubious policies. It is both more understandable and less commendable than Matthiessen suggested that Hawthorne, despite his skeptical conservatism, supported the party of Jackson. For the Democratic party's commitment to slavery made "the Democracy" include much less than "all the people," as I detail in "The Politics of *The Scarlet Letter*." Rather than facing up to divisions within the renaissance, Matthiessen divided the renaissance from the war and segregated qualities "before" and "after." His wish for wholeness led to disconnection.

By splitting off the war, Matthiessen forestalled comparisons between the 1850s and 1930s that the Depression had provoked. Edmund Wilson's "An Appeal to Progressives" (1931), for example, defined the time as "one of the turning-points in our history, our first real crisis since the Civil War" (524-25). The comparison between the 1850s and 1930s was exciting for a militant strategy but embar-

rassing for a strategy of alliance and containment. If, as Charles and Mary Beard argued in *The Rise of American Civilization* (1927), the Civil War had been "The Second American Revolution," then the analogy pointed to a class war that would make a third.

Yet to evade the analogy left a problem: what would mobilize change if "democracy" already existed and "class struggle" was forbidden? This impasse structured **American Renaissance**. Matthiessen was celebrating what he knew *must* be transformed. Renaissance yielded to Civil War, and the Popular Front too must yield to something else, but there was no acceptable image for that new state except an idealization of the present state. The result was an unhistorical freezing.

This conjunction between Matthiessen's cultural politics and those of the Popular Front has two consequences. First, it grants greater value and dignity to the cultural results of the Popular Front than they have been allowed in the most authoritative representations. Lionel Trilling devoted his career to portraying American "liberal" culture as so Stalinized as to make impossible any live or complex literary response. Such claims depend upon ignoring Matthiessen, as Trilling did, or considering his politics as unrelated to his critical accomplishments, as Irving Howe has done (*Margin* 156-58).

Lionel Trilling did not literally ignore Matthiessen. He reviewed Matthiessen's study of James, and the two appeared together on a panel (**Rat** 300, 333), yet the treatment of Matthiessen in Trilling's fundamental position paper, "Reality in America" (1950), is remarkable. The essay asserted that Parrington dominated "the college course in American literature" nationwide whenever it aimed to be "vigorous" rather than "genteel", an even stronger claim than Trilling had ventured in the essay's first version, "Parrington, Mr. Smith, and Reality" (1940). Yet according to Henry Nash Smith, also writing in 1950, Parrington's dominance in the thirties had yielded to **American Renaissance** in the forties. Trilling then spotlighted "the dark and bloody crossroads where literature and politics meet," that is, the choice between James and Dreiser. Having posed the inevitability of choice, Trilling then quoted Matthiessen's praise of Dreiser while remarking Matthiessen's admiration for James and criticism of Parrington, but he failed to notice the disruptive anomaly this introduced into his schematization (*Liberal Imagination* 1, 8, 12). Elsewhere in the volume Trilling repeated his claims for the divorce between "our liberal educated class and the best of the literary mind of our time" (94), i.e., Proust, Joyce, Lawrence, Eliot, and other modern masters. Again, Matthiessen's existence made nonsense of this claim, and he was ignored.

It is worth remarking the contrasted starting points Matthiessen and Trilling specified for their social thought about America. Matthiessen recalled the "comradeship" shared during college with older, foreign-born workers he helped to instruct in English, and he noted the self-awareness as an "American" provoked by his time in England as a Rhodes Scholar (*From the Heart* 72, 23). For Trilling, "America" only became "available" to his "imagination" through the "Jewish situation" (itself necessarily related to "social class") that he discovered working with the *Menorah Journal* in the late twenties (*Last Decade* 14-15). Matthiessen's national awakening obliterated class and ethnic divisions; Trilling's arose from them.

The second consequence of noting Matthiessen's relation to the Popular Front is to highlight the dangers of such a strategy of reconciliation, a special concern now when a renewed academic Marxism offers to embrace all other intellectual positions, a prospect to which the chapter on Jameson will return. Matthiessen's Popular Front figure of "America" suffered a sobering fate. The war (which, after all, did come) reconstellated American politics, and the figure of "America" that began as a Depression tactic of harmony became a postwar myth of empire. A mobilization intended as oppositional became incorporated hegemonically; American studies gained power by nationalistically appropriating Matthiessen.

"Reconciliation" is not only a political strategy but also a well-known operation in literary theory. Having analyzed the discrepancy between Matthiessen's internationalism and the nationalist authority his work achieved, I want now to address another area of discrepancy: Matthiessen's attempt to use the politically conservative theory of the "symbol" in a critical discourse intended to be politically progressive.

American Renaissance made a major commitment to literary theory, both as views of the 1850s and as a current activity—"our own developing conceptions of literature" (*AR* vii). Matthiessen was alert to the significance of M. H. Abrams' work, citing the dissertation version of *The Mirror and the Lamp* (*AR* 261). Matthiessen related the theory and practice of his chosen writers to his own understanding of "the nature of literature" (xiii) on such topics as mode (myth), genre (tragedy), and figurative language (allegory and symbolism). Over the four decades of American studies, such theoretical engagement has not flourished, and where it has recently begun to emerge, it appears as an imported innovation rather than as reclaiming a founding heritage. The single theoretical topic that has become institutionally part of normal procedure is nationalistic: the question of "American romance"—a topic Matthiessen briefly highlighted but also seriously limited (*AR* 264ff.). Just as comparative literature became the subfield that kept alive Matthiessen's internationalism, New Criticism after the war became less a movement than a province, the subfield into which his theoretical commitments were segregated and developed.

Matthiessen's major theoretical resource was Coleridge, as elucidated by I. A. Richards in response to T. S. Eliot, but Matthiessen understood and emphasized that Coleridge's position made larger claims than Eliot or Richards or, as we have seen, Robert Penn Warren would accept. Eliot

wished to separate poet from poem, and Richards used Coleridge in the service of utilitarian atheism, while Matthiessen proclaimed that "the transcendental theory of art is a theory of knowledge and religion as well" (*AR* 31).

The crucial passage in Coleridge has already been cited. In the fourteenth chapter of the *Biographia Literaria*, the poet, "described in *ideal* perfection, brings the whole soul of man into activity" through the "power" of "imagination," which "reveals itself in the balance or reconciliation of opposite or discordant qualities," such as general and concrete or individual and representative (*Collected Works* 7.2:15-16). From this passage, Richards in the chapter on "Imagination" in *Principles of Literary Criticism* elaborated a theory of tragedy as the most "inclusive" possible "attitude," which by contemplating the most extreme opposites—fear and pity—achieved a stable poise that he even called "invulnerable." Matthiessen drew also upon Coleridge's theory of the "symbol," which "enunciates the whole" yet "abides itself as a living part in that Unity, of which it is the representative" (*Collected Works* 6:30). Coleridge's image for this condition is "translucence," above all of "the Eternal through and in the Temporal." This exposition of the symbol appeared in *The Statesman's Manual*, a theological guide to conservative politics for post-Napoleonic, early industrial England.

Matthiessen's aesthetics agreed with Coleridge's, as did his theology, but his politics, starting from a similar romantic anticapitalism, differed widely. Matthiessen identified himself with Hazlitt (*From the Heart* 83), who remained loyal to the revolutionary cause despite its horrors, rather than like Coleridge turning away in fright or revulsion. How could Matthiessen be a trinitarian formalist radical?

He could if radicalism meant reconciliation. The Popular Front enabled Matthiessen's criticism, his politics, and his religion to interact powerfully and positively. The strategy of alliance allowed these different elements to share the same discursive space. *The Achievement of T. S. Eliot*, written just before the Popular Front, is weaker than *American Renaissance* because Matthiessen's politics found no place in it. This is not to claim Matthiessen "followed" the line; rather, the line "released" him to bring together elements previously separated. But this is not to say either that they make a perfect whole.

Each of these three components had its own particular term for the fantasied unity, the figure of wholeness, that their interaction produced as "American Renaissance." For Matthiessen the political leftist, that term would be "all the people" in the People's Front. For Matthiessen the critical formalist, the ideal term of wholeness was "literature" itself. For the Christian, in a tradition that reached back into the seventeenth century and through Jonathan Edwards, as Richard Niebuhr and Sacvan Bercovitch have demonstrated, that term would be "America." Bercovitch has analyzed the "American Jeremiad" as provoking a sense of crisis that finally produces no fundamental change but reaffirms the existing "American" way. This logic I find operates like that of Coleridge's aesthetics or Popular Front politics—in Melville's phrase, "By their very contradictions they are made to coincide." This formula offers an American translation for the "reconciliation under duress" that Theodor Adorno criticized in Georg Lukács's Stalinist Hegelian realism.

The Jeremiad position is not easy or complacent; it is anguished and sincere, but it stands in a false position. Let me explain this through Matthiessen's reading of "The Try-Works." In this chapter from *Moby-Dick*, "Ahab's tyrannic will" is "symbolized," Matthiessen argued, through the process by which "the act of burning down the blubber on the ship's deck at night becomes, in its lurid flame, 'the material counterpart of her monomaniac commander's soul.'" From the spiritual symbolized in the physical, Matthiessen went on to read the representative from the individual: "It seemed then to Ishmael, in a rare symbol for individualistic recklessness—indeed for a whole era of American development—'that whatever swift, rushing thing I stood on was not so much bound to any haven ahead as rushing from all havens astern'" (*AR* 290). Matthiessen's exposition of the "symbol" here interacted with the motifs of America and individualism that I earlier analyzed. His trinitarian aesthetic highlighted the figure of embodiment ("material counterpart"), but in emphasizing the "will," Matthiessen's reading omitted the loose elbows, the actual bodies, the "Tartarean shapes of the pagan harpooneers," and the watch with "tawny features . . . begrimed with smoke and sweat, their matted beards, and the contrasting barbaric brilliancy of their teeth." In their racist demonization, these bodies did not represent "all the people."

As earlier "America" was idealized, here the literary was idealized as "symbol." So vivid was Melville's figure that Matthiessen took it as truth, embodying all that we need to know. Ishmael, however, went on to define his vision of "rushing from all havens astern" as a double error. He mistook his object, for it referred not to the try-works scene but his backward view; and he mistook himself—as his mind wandered, his body turned: "Lo! in my brief sleep I had turned myself about, and was fronting the ship's stern. . . . In an instant I faced back, just in time to prevent the vessel from flying up into the wind, and very probably capsizing her. How glad and how grateful the relief from this unnatural hallucination of the night." Not the demonic scene, but the observer's error posed the real threat: Ishmael neglected his responsibility as helmsman. Matthiessen, then, ignored literature's own recognition that it may err: "Wrapped, for that interval, in darkness myself, I but the better saw the redness, the madness, and the ghastliness of others." Thus, even at its most passionately intelligent and concerned, the stance of American studies cultural criticism has been misplaced, through a disorienting, self-involved detachment just at the moment it believed itself most perceptively involved with the way things are. This danger threatens also the course of "detachment" Benjamin urged for historical materialism, yet despite the dangers these courses merit attention.

After treating the politics of America and of the theory of literature in Matthiessen's work, I want now to assess the possibilities for a new literary history in the practice of *American Renaissance*. These possibilities are still "new" after forty years not only because American studies failed to pick them up, but also because Matthiessen's own explicit theory of atemporal wholeness obscured his recurrent perception of transient, fragmentary moments.

I have mentioned the "freezing" of time and denial of history in Matthiessen's reading. Matthiessen used the term "structure" for the wholeness achieved by a successful symbol, a symbolic "form," when it reconciled the eternal and the temporal. His negative term for the failure of this process was "moments." Matthiessen most pointedly set these terms in opposition discussing D. H. Lawrence, that bogey of New Criticism (*AR* 313). Yet despite Lawrence's anti-Coleridgean emphases and his Shelleyan loyalties, he was quite important to Matthiessen, and Matthiessen's evaluation was more ambivalent than his theory. Indeed, when Melville himself reached the imaginative "level where both abstraction and concretion may have full play," Matthiessen did not emphasize symbolic stability; he observed instead that this was "not a level which . . . he can sustain for long—but rather, a precarious point of equilibrium between two opposed forces" (464). Melville could not "hold the wave at the crest" (408). Such evanescence resonates less with the New Critics' Coleridge than with the impressionists' Pater, who wrote: "This at least of flamelike our life has, that it is but the concurrence, renewed from moment to moment, of forces parting sooner or later" (*Renaissance* 187). Such a Paterian "tragic dividing of forces on their ways" rekindles autumnally what Emerson more buoyantly had asserted. Not an enduring "translucence" but the intermittent flare of moments proved in practice what Matthiessen found. Cleanth Brooks observed that Matthiessen's book on Eliot failed to offer a "complete, consecutive examination" of *The Waste Land* (*Modern Poetry* 136), and this remained true of *American Renaissance*. Matthiessen was typically a reader of passages, a judge of moments. The American Renaissance itself from the beginning stood as a moment: "The starting point for this book was my realization of how great a number of our past masterpieces were produced in one extraordinarily concentrated moment of expression" (*AR* vii).

As Aristotle is the exemplary structuralist, the great critic of the moment is Longinus on the sublime. Against structural unity, we have noted that the sublime is a "flash of lightning" that "scatters all before it." Longinus' discontinuous theory of influence—as the agonistic relation between two literary consciousnesses across a wide span of time, like that of Plato to Homer—offers the nearest precedent to Harold Bloom's "revisionary" theory of poetry. Bloom emphasized, however, the important precedent for his work in Emerson, and I would note that Matthiessen found it there: "Emerson knew that each age turns to particular authors of the past, not because of the authors but because of its own needs and preoccupations that those authors help make articulate" (*AR* 101-2). Thus, Melville achieved "his own full strength" through the "challenge" of Shakespeare (*AR* 424). Such a dynamic, recall, was also Malraux's claim in "The Cultural Heritage." In an italicized formulation that Matthiessen cited, "*A heritage is not transmitted, it must be conquered*" (xv n.). The energy of struggle, deflected by the Popular Front away from politics, reappears within culture.

Matthiessen understood that such claims violated established ways of conceiving and writing history, and he worried over historiographic method. He knew personally the painful struggle to possess a tradition. He wrote to Cheney in 1925: "This life of ours is entirely new—neither of us know of a parallel case. We stand in the middle of an uncharted, uninhabited country. That there have been other unions like ours is obvious, but we are unable to draw on their experience" (*Rat* 71). Against such blanking-out, Matthiessen found his own needs and preoccupations articulated in Whitman and in Proust. He accepted Richards' claim that great writing required "availability of experience" (*AR* 129).

For his own historical project Matthiessen rejected "the descriptive narrative of literary history" (*AR* vii). He was not alone in rejecting narrative. In 1929 there had appeared in England Namier's *The Structure of Politics at the Accession of George III* and in France the first issue of the great journal *Annales*. Matthiessen, however, also rejected analytic history writing. Against scientific digging "into . . . the economic, social, and religious causes" (vii), Matthiessen chose Richards' analytic of experience. His project shared this ground with Walter Benjamin's essay on "The Story-teller" (1936) and Sartre's *Nausea* (1938), both of which lamented the unavailability of "experience" and marked a crisis of narrativity. Frank Kermode's *Romantic Image* studied Anglo-American modernist alternatives to this failure of narrative discourse.

Matthiessen evaded this crisis by studying the "fusions of form and content" that defined "*what* these books were as works of art" (vii). This aesthetic ontology projected a Coleridgean, "symbolic" history like that of Joyce's *Ulysses*. There one day's happenings come into contact with as much of the human cultural past as it could possibly evoke. Likewise, Matthiessen's "moment" focused centuries of American cultural history from the Puritans through James and Eliot. This mythic rhetoric leveled history into what Matthiessen quoted Thomas Mann as calling "recurrence, timelessness, a perpetual present" (*AR* 629), a relationship of temporality that was "continuous," as Matthiessen quoted Eliot on Joyce (630).

In *American Renaissance* there also operated, however, a temporal orientation that aimed not to perpetuate but to innovate, signaled by Matthiessen's sole positive citation of Nietzsche: "Only the supreme power of the present can interpret the past," and such power required the interpreter to be "architect of the future" (*AR* 629 n.). The urgency of relationship between this particular present moment and

particular past moments contrasts both to the continuous linear sequence of traditional narrative time and to the equally continuous homogeneity of modernist myth. It produces a discontinuous, textured, historical temporality. One model for this could be found in Proust, whose correlation of moments through "involuntary memory" again highlighted Richards' problem of availability, which Matthiessen found as struggle in Malraux. During Matthiessen's work on *American Renaissance*, the critic most suggestively rethinking literary history—and working on Whitman's contemporary Baudelaire—was Walter Benjamin. (At one sole moment, Whitman occurs disruptively in Benjamin's "Central Park" notebook, 50.) It is worth noting that Malraux's original "Sur l'héritage culturel" referred to Benjamin's study of the artwork and mass reproduction (4), but that in translating and editing Malraux for the *New Republic*, Malcolm Cowley omitted that reference.

In his "Theses on the Philosophy of History," Benjamin characterized the relation between one historical moment and another as a "constellation" (*Illuminations* 263) and argued that "to articulate the past historically" meant to "seize hold of a memory as it flashes up at a moment of danger" (255)—as the French revolutionaries did with the Roman republic. This claim illuminates Matthiessen's conjunction of the 1850s and 1930s, his urgent sense that these were exactly the writers "all the people" needed at the moment of solidarity against the danger of fascism, disconnecting them from the Civil War in order to join them to "now."

Benjamin, however, opposed the Popular Front strategy. He deprecated the preservation of "cultural treasures," for they are tainted with "barbarism" (*Illuminations* 256) both in their origin and in their transmission. He urged instead "the fight for the oppressed past" (263), to redeem what was once stigmatized and suppressed as "minor" (254). Perhaps Matthiessen fulfilled this task, in rejecting the cultural treasures of Holmes, Longfellow, and Lowell to rescue once-marginal writers as Emerson, Thoreau, Hawthorne, Melville, and Whitman had been in their time. Matthiessen, however, disavowed any canon-shifting intervention, deferring to the judgment of "the successive generations of common readers" (*AR* xi) who selected the five authors. This version of the Popular Front he at once reconciled with the apparently contradictory claim by Ezra Pound that "the history of an art . . . is the history of masterwork" (xi).

Following Benjamin, I have tried both to specify the "barbarism" at work in Matthiessen's book and to "redeem" certain emphases and practices obscured through the representation of Matthiessen produced in American studies. Benjamin's concern with the cultural apparatus, his care for technical matters that relate the means chosen to the ends desired, leads me to a final question, which bears on Matthiessen's claims about his chosen writers, on his own project in his book, and on work any of us might do: can one espouse and further "all the people" by writing "masterwork"? *American Renaissance* achieved its masterful unity through the construction of figures that misrepresented Matthiessen's cherished values. Their effect was not a symbolic translucence but an allegorical alienation. He mobilized "America" on behalf of internationalism; he mobilized "renaissance" on behalf of communalism; he mobilized the theory of "structure" but actually elucidated "moments." The project of "wholeness" involved harmonizing, centralizing, normalizing, and "identifying." By tucking in elbows, Matthiessen empowered a particular self and work and nation and also rejected particular "other" identities, such as Shelley, and dispersed others, such as Whitman.

Near the end of his decade writing *American Renaissance*, Matthiessen suffered a psychic breakdown. While he was briefly hospitalized, Matthiessen posed as life-or-death choices the kind of issues that have concerned my analysis—Aristotle versus Longinus, structure versus moment. He asked, was it any reason to kill himself if his failure to accomplish this project proved to him that "I am an enthusiast trying to be a critic . . . a rhapsode trying to be an Aristotelian" (*Rat* 246)?

Matthiessen questioned the value for life of this discipline, this struggle of the will to define, formulate, mobilize, and authorize an American Renaissance. His question took its terms from a punning Latin phrase that evoked the extinction of democratic politics in ancient Rome and—as Cesare Borgia's motto—the assertion of identity in Renaissance Italy: "Must it be aut Caesar aut nullus?"—that is, is the only choice that between Caesar and utter nonentity? Only if we can define better alternatives for the intellectual career is there any chance to be of much use to "all the people."

William E. Cain (essay date 1988)

SOURCE: "F. O. Matthiessen's Labor of Translation: From Sarah Orne Jewett to T. S. Eliot," in *The South Atlantic Quarterly*, Vol. 87, No. 2, Spring, 1988, pp. 355-84.

[*In the following essay, Cain examines Matthiessen's critical writings of the late 1920s and 1930s, maintaining that with these works the critic forged his identity as a literary critic.*]

F. O. Matthiessen's *American Renaissance: Art and Expression in the Age of Emerson and Whitman* (1941) is one of the landmark texts of American literary studies, and it is the book to which critics naturally turn when they examine Matthiessen's impact and influence. As Sacvan Bercovitch has recently stated—and many others have said the same—"*American Renaissance* reset the terms for the study of American literary history; it gave us a new canon of classic texts; and it inspired the growth of American Studies in the United States and abroad."[1] But while Matthiessen's writings before and after *American Renais-*

sance are less distinguished than his masterpiece, they nevertheless remain interesting and merit scrutiny in their own right. His books on T. S. Eliot (1935), Henry James (1944), and Theodore Dreiser (1951), in particular, were extremely important in developing terms for the analysis of these writers and for consolidating their place in the literary canon. In many respects, the vocabulary we adopt when we speak about Eliot, James, and Dreiser derives from Matthiessen's seminal accounts of them.

Along with his early studies of Sarah Orne Jewett (1929) and Elizabethan translation (1931), these books also exhibit, in their different ways, the tension between literature and politics that pervades—and frequently disturbs—Matthiessen's critical enterprise. Matthiessen was a fervently political man who yearned to make his criticism "political" and who saw it as a means by which to advance the cause of democracy. Yet he was also a great admirer of Eliot and aligned himself with the formalist project that Eliot inaugurated and that the New Critics refined and institutionalized. Even as he dedicated himself to politically inspiring and benefiting the American people, he subscribed to critical views that mandated the sharp separation of literature from politics.

In this essay I intend to focus on Matthiessen's writings of the late 1920s and 1930s, where he forged his identity as a critic and made manifest his deeply felt loyalty to Eliot's literary principles. These were the writings through which Matthiessen prepared and equipped himself for *American Renaissance*, and these, too, were the writings whose foundational tenets and values Matthiessen labored, unevenly and sometimes contradictorily, to move beyond in his monographs on James and Dreiser in the 1940s.

For any assessment of Matthiessen's work, it is important to set down some biographical details. Matthiessen was born in 1902 in Pasadena, California. His father, Fredric William Matthiessen, Jr., never settled upon a career and moved his family frequently. His mother, however, often managed to stay with her four children—Francis Otto was the third son and the youngest child—in her father-in-law's home in La Salle, Illinois. This father-in-law, Frederich Wilhelm Matthiessen, an interesting figure in his own right, had arrived in America in 1850 as a poor immigrant and proceeded to become a multimillionaire factory owner. Francis Otto's youth in La Salle led him to view himself as a "small town boy" from "the mid-west."[2] Later in his life, he pointed to his lack of knowledge as a young man of Parkman's *La Salle and the Discovery of the Great West* as an "appalling" sign of what was absent from his early education. "No school that I attended," he observed, "went at all imaginatively into the American past."[3]

After spending four years at Hackley School in Tarrytown, New York, Matthiessen went on to Yale, graduating in 1923, and then studied at Oxford as a Rhodes scholar. He completed his advanced training at Harvard very quickly, receiving his M.A. in 1926 and his Ph.D. in 1927. Except for an early two-year stint at Yale as an instructor (1927-

29), he spent his entire teaching career at Harvard, serving as a member of the English department and as a tutor in history and literature. One of the numerous paradoxes of Matthiessen's career is that he led a life of privilege and distinction at major institutions yet was a radical in both political theory and practice. At Yale, when still an undergraduate, he had heard Norman Thomas and, more importantly, Eugene Debs speak. Matthiessen was inspired by their rhetoric, and felt a special admiration for Deb's capacity, as a socialist leader, "to command a mass movement."[4] Matthiessen was a leader himself at Yale, one of the "prophets" and "rebels" who in 1922 stirred up lively debates on campus by protesting against the disorganized curriculum and apathetic student body. "Short, compact, powerful," and "speaking with characteristic lunge and confidence," Matthiessen "attacked paternalism and materialism all along the line."[5]

During his student days, Matthiessen had also responded deeply to Tawney's *The Acquisitive Society*, a book he came across by accident when doing a report for an economics class. He claimed that "there could have been no luckier opening of the door into social theory": "Tawney's ideas about equality have remained more living for me than anything else, except Shakespeare, that I read at college."[6] His reading and political friendships at Yale may also have helped to sharpen his sense of the dangers of wealth which his father's life had epitomized. Matthiessen's father had been raised as a rich boy, had wasted his life, and had eventually deserted his wife and children, and this example of corruption doubtless spurred the son's highly disciplined attitude toward work and his steady movement to the left.[7] It was not until the late 1940s, near the end of his life, that Matthiessen managed a partial reconciliation with his father.

While a teacher at Harvard during the 1930s and 1940s, the intensely political Matthiessen labored vigorously for a host of radical causes. He was a key member of the Harvard Teachers' Union, serving as its vice-president when the union was founded in 1935 and as one of its representatives to the Boston Central Labor Union, the Massachusetts State Council of Teachers Union, the Massachusetts Federation of Labor, and the American Federation of Teachers. He campaigned tirelessly for the Progressive party, and presented one of the seconding speeches for Henry Wallace's nomination in 1948. There is much more that could be noted, but maybe the most cogent piece of evidence is the list of defense committees and organizations to which Matthiessen belonged. This list was published as a political smear in the *Boston Herald* just two days after Matthiessen's suicide in 1950:

> American Russian Institute, American Committee for the Protection of the Foreign Born, Artists' Front to Win the War, American Youth for Democracy, Citizens' Committee to Free Earl Browder, Civil Rights Congress, Committee for Citizenship Rights, Committee for a Democratic Far Eastern Policy, Committee for Equal Justice for Mrs. Recy Taylor, Committee to Sponsor the Daily Worker, Committee of Welcome for the

> Very Reverend Hewlett Johnson, Conference on Constitutional Liberties in America, Defense of Communist Schools, Denunciation of the Hartley Committee, Educators for Wallace, Friends of Italian Democracy, National Council of Arts Sciences and Professions, National Federation for Constitutional Liberties, New Masses, New Masses Dinner Committee, Open Letter for Closer Cooperation with the Soviet Union, Samuel Adams School for Social Studies, Schappes Defense Committee, Sleepy Lagoon Defense Committee, Supporters for Samuel Wallach, Testimonial Dinner to Carol King, Veterans of the Abraham Lincoln Brigade, Win-the-Peace Conference, Writers for Wallace.[8]

Clearly Matthiessen did what he could in his life to oppose political injustice and economic inequality. Some have judged him pathetically naive—above all in his inability or unwillingness to assail Stalinism in the 1940s—and they have remarked that his commitment to socialist solidarity may simply reflect an effort to relieve his loneliness. Some have commented, too, on the somewhat strained manner in which Matthiessen tried to be a Christian as well as a socialist. But there have been other Christian socialists besides Matthiessen. The link is not intrinsically perverse; Tawney himself, whatever his final verdict on Christianity in *Religion and the Rise of Capitalism*, maintained that Christ's lessons of love in the Gospels could empower a socialist mission. Like everybody else, Matthiessen made bad judgments in his politics, but to say this differs from impugning his motives or tallying up his activities as the manifestation of a psychological need (they could be that, but also more than that). For my purposes, what counts is that Matthiessen held certain socialist principles, acted as his conscience instructed him, and often risked much in publicly fighting for unpopular causes.

Matthiessen was also homosexual, which made him aware of another set of limits to personal choice and social freedom, and sensitive to another form of injustice and inequality.[9] He had met the painter Russell Cheney in 1924 on his return voyage to England, and these two men spent their lives together as lovers until Cheney's death in 1945. Their letters, which were published in 1978, are sometimes embarrassing to read—who would expect otherwise about love letters?—but Matthiessen's frequently reveal an admirable strength and courage. They exhibit gushes of sentiment, yet they are also tough-minded, persistent, and persevering—Matthiessen is zealously determined to carry his and Cheney's love through hard times and tensions. His fondness for Whitman's poetry also comes through in the letters; his language is akin to that found in *Leaves of Grass*, and it displays a similarly elated passion and overwhelming of boundaries. Here is one example, taken from a 1925 letter in which he expresses how his love for Cheney (nicknamed "Rat") vitalizes his consciousness of the English landscape in springtime:

> I bicycled twenty miles this morning through fallow rolling hills with an occasional glimpse of the sea. It was soft and balmy, and the rooks kept up a constant racket in the treetops. Being alone, I could feel my

heart swelling like the seeds in the ground, and I kept shouting over and over to the wind: "Rat, Rat, my God feller how I love you." I felt my life absolutely expressed in the fullness of the spring: every opportunity in the world, energy and hope abundant, and the road leading straight ahead and true with you. I realize that in these last months I am a whole man for the first time: no more dodging or repressing for we gladly accept what we are. And sex now instead of being a nightmare is the most sacred, all-embracing gift we have. Now I can see, as this morning while riding along, a husky labouring feller asleep on a bank one hand lying heavy across his thighs, and I can thrill at the deep earthiness and blood of him. For I know that I am of blood and earth too, as well as of brain and soul, and that my whole self waits—and waits gladly—for you.[10]

Matthiessen had begun to read Whitman, his "first big experience" of American literature, in 1923. The "Children of Adam" and "Calamus" poems were, he said, especially meaningful in teaching him "to trust the body," and he recalled "the excitement of starting to read the small edition [of Whitman] I had bought in London, in a dreary tearoom near the British museum."[11] The feeling, imagery, and rhythm of much of his phrasing seem to echo not only these groups of poems, but also "Song of Myself":

> I mind how once we lay such a transparent summer
>   morning,
> How you settled your head athwart my hips and gently
>   turn'd over upon me,
> And parted the shirt from my bosom-bone, and plunged
>   your tongue to my bare-stript heart,
> And reach'd till you felt my beard, and reach'd till you held
>   my feet.
>
>   . . . . .
>
> You will hardly know who I am or what I mean,
> But I shall be good health to you nevertheless,
> And filtre and fibre your blood.
> Failing to fetch me at first keep encouraged,
> Missing me one place search another,
> I stop somewhere waiting for you.[12]

Aware of it or not, Matthiessen tapped his passionate reading of Whitman to voice his love for Cheney. He communicated, and indeed sought to embody, the sexual and emotional vibrancies of the poet's words. As a sign of the manner in which institutions encroach on the personal, it is worth noting that the authorities at Harvard denied Matthiessen permission to write his dissertation on Whitman. There was nothing more to be said about Whitman, he was told.

Matthiessen spoke lovingly about Cheney in *From the Heart of Europe*, and he had earlier prepared a "record" and catalogue of Cheney's work. But despite his glad acceptance of his love for Cheney, Matthiessen seems to have been extremely uncomfortable with the fact of his homosexuality, and sometimes he even goes oddly out of

his way to speak disapprovingly about homosexual leanings expressed in literary texts. This is especially the case in the long chapter on Whitman in *American Renaissance*, which contains a number of puzzling rebukes of, and complaints about, the poet's sexuality. At one point, Matthiessen quotes the very lines from "Song of Myself" I have cited above in order to reprimand the immaturity of Whitman's attitudes. "Moreover," he adds, "in the passivity of the poet's body there is a quality vaguely pathological and homosexual."[13] Matthiessen cannot engage this aspect of Whitman's verse except to criticize it or distance himself from it, and the effect, for those who know Matthiessen's own sexual preference, is quite disorienting. His critical gestures in the public form of his book feel like expressions of self-disapproval, as though he wanted not to be what Whitman was, or else wanted readers who knew he was homosexual to see that he spurned "abnormal" homosexual attitudes in poetry.

In one sense these facts of Matthiessen's sexual and political life may seem irrelevant: what bearing do they have on his actual literary criticism? They do not, in fact, have much direct bearing at all, and that is why they are significant and warrant attention. Matthiessen always emphasizes "wholeness" and "integrity" in life and work, saying repeatedly that the teacher and critic must bring the rich range of his entire experience to his pedagogical and scholarly labors. This was the belief by which Matthiessen lived: it made him the great, if difficult and demanding, teacher and man that he unquestionably was. But part of Matthiessen seems missing from his books. In his first three books—*Sarah Orne Jewett, Translation: An Elizabethan Art*, and *The Achievement of T. S. Eliot*—Matthiessen grows as a critic but also exposes for us conspicuous absences and limitations of perspective. There is development, but also the settling in of assumptions that handicap Matthiessen, and especially curtail his attempts to engage the political. As so often when studying this critic, one ends up—unfairly but not unreasonably—wanting Matthiessen to have done his work differently. It is difficult to keep from wishing that he had not only learned lessons in new critical explication, but had also moved to relate these to social-cultural organic critique of the sort that John Crowe Ransom and the Agrarians had advocated in *I'll Take My Stand* (1930). Through Tawney and Debs, and his own experiences, Matthiessen had formed a more inclusive vision than the conservative Agrarians of what was wrong with America. Conceivably he could have angled his criticism in a radical direction and made it political as well as literary. Socialist politics would then have entered into and energized his literary criticism and scholarship.

This, obviously, is easy to say: it is to slight the Matthiessen who was, and to dream of a Matthiessen who might have been. No doubt there is much to be said for returning from visions of unrealized possibilities to an assessment of what he actually wrote early and late. Still, one might be forgiven for asking what American criticism might have been like, what alternative directions it might have taken, if Matthiessen had connected his analytical skill and historical knowledge to a broadly based literary/political/cultural enterprise. As his first two books intimate and as his third book, devoted to T. S. Eliot, confirms, Matthiessen came to define his critical work in terms that tended to disengage it from politics and precluded a general cultural address.

Matthiessen's 1929 book on Jewett—who was related to Matthiessen's mother, Lucy Orne Matthiessen—displays a type of impressionistic criticism that he would soon surpass. For understandable reasons, it has not enjoyed a good reputation. The terms regularly and rightly used about it include sentimental, soft, and self-indulgent. One commentator has accurately observed that Matthiessen yielded "to his subject, and especially to the charm of her milieu; he was writing a back-to-the womb lullaby to himself and his readers, not challenging them to exploration and judgment."[14] Matthiessen's descriptions of Jewett's life and works are thin, and he continually dabbles in atmospherics:

> Her stories caught the flavor not only of the birches, but of the salt marshes, the roadside chicory and Queen Anne's lace.
>
> . . . . .
>
> Its pages [those of *The Country of the Pointed Firs*] are as direct as the rays of the sun, and as fresh as a breeze across the water. They envelop the mingled charm and sadness of the countryside just as you feel it on the summer day that brings the first hint of autumn, when, in the midst of the wild roses along the dusty road, you are suddenly aware of the first fateful spray of goldenrod.[15]

Matthiessen does not apply his full critical intelligence to examining Jewett, preferring to speak in an evocative and deliberately unanalytical voice. But his voice keeps sounding falsified, and not only because the lucid, forthright prose in *American Renaissance* dramatizes its shortcomings. In *Sarah Orne Jewett*, Matthiessen descends into mannerism; his diction and stylistic devices (the alliterative touch and Tennysonian vowels in "first fateful spray") draw notice to themselves in a maudlin way. The reader senses that the critic is in control of the sounds, but not the substance, of his words. There are too few ideas, and too much special pleading. Later in his career, Matthiessen would sternly quarrel with the impressionism of Van Wyck Brooks's *Makers and Finders* series, and his own strictures about these volumes—elegiac, wistful, critically infirm—guide us toward the proper judgment of *Sarah Orne Jewett*.

One means by which to save *Sarah Orne Jewett* is to view it as Matthiessen's version of pastoral, as his evocation, through Jewett, of New England village settings that the Civil War and industrialism had in most cases destroyed. Such rural simplicities, one could take Matthiessen to be suggesting, remain available through Jewett's acts of imagination and the responsive reader/critic's attempts to recreate them in his prose. But though Matthies-

sen admires Jewett's writing and accords it a respectful, appreciative treatment, he does not appear to take her with real seriousness. Her stories, he implies, however adeptly they beckon us to a time gone by, cannot sustain analysis. When, in the final chapter, Matthiessen notes the limits of Jewett's art, he makes brief but pointed judgments that, if he had pressed them, would have effectively called Jewett's stature very much into question. She does not "portray passion in her books," nor does she depict what in New England countryside life is "sordid, bleak, and mean of spirit."[16] Another rendering of this second observation might be that Jewett is not articulate—to cite a chapter heading from Tawney's *The Acquisitive Society*—about "the nemesis of industrialism." What, one wonders, were Matthiessen's thoughts when he testified that in the years of Jewett's youth, at the time of the Civil War, "throughout New England the invigorating air that Emerson and Thoreau had breathed was clogged with smoke"?[17]

Sarah Orne Jewett is not a good book, but it is a labor of love and affection for another kind of life and landscape. Significantly, Matthiessen dedicated the book to his deceased mother, to whom he had been devoted, and he included in it illustrations by Cheney, with whom he had set up a household in Kittery Point, Maine, in 1927. The Jewett book was also an exercise in form, a holiday from the constraints of scholarship and teaching. Even more, it was a statement against the type of work and credentials that academic professionalism demanded, a statement—firm in the pleasures and loyalties it embraced—against the career within established institutions to which Matthiessen had decided to devote his life.

As an undergraduate at Yale, Matthiessen had already begun both to succeed within, and to resist, his home institution, and this pattern seems to thread through his life. Somewhat like F. R. Leavis, who was militantly inside and outside Cambridge University in England, Matthiessen felt himself to embody values that his institution should have endorsed but had scorned. Matthiessen loved certain features of his life at Harvard, especially his contact with students, yet he also saw himself as estranged from it and, in the postwar period, even considered resigning his professorship to take a position at Brandeis. He was, in a similar vein, a tireless, dedicated professional, one who achieved great success, yet he staunchly disliked scholarly meetings, above all those held by the Modern Language Association, where the atmosphere of "pure professionalism" struck him as totally unchallenging.[18]

In a minor chord, *Sarah Orne Jewett* shows Matthiessen's determination not to be ensnared by the folkways of professional scholarship. It hence glances backward to the dissertation on Elizabethan translation that Matthiessen had written at Harvard under J. L. Lowes in 1926-27, and forward to the revised version of it that he published in book form as *Translation: An Elizabethan Art* in 1931. *Sarah Orne Jewett* affirms personal and familial commitments that the dissertation does not, but the publishing of the dissertation makes apparent Matthiessen's ability to place the sentimental form in which he embodied them. *Translation* portrayed Matthiessen as a far more rigorous, and recognizably professional, worker, one who was intent upon getting his best scholarly discoveries quickly into print. Matthiessen's private commitments obviously continued to mean much to him, and he often spoke affectionately of the period when he wrote *Sarah Orne Jewett*, but he was surely alert to the weaknesses of the book as a piece of criticism.

Translation is lively and interesting, written with a robust conscientiousness that demonstrates Matthiessen's enthusiasm for his texts. It consists primarily of many meticulously conducted studies of passages from Hoby's translation of *The Courtier* (1561), North's translation of Plutarch's *Lives* (1579), Florio's translation of Montaigne's *Essays* (1603), and Holland's translations of Livy's *Roman History* and Suetonius's *History of Twelve Caesars* (1606). What holds together the specific analyses is Matthiessen's general argument that the Elizabethans sought to give contemporaneity to the texts they translated: "The feeling prevailed that these new books would have a direct bearing upon daily life, that they would bring new blood and vigor to the stock of England."[19] In describing translation, Matthiessen is also describing patriotism—the ways in which the literary imagination is vitally connected with the desire to rally and serve one's country. The translator does not simply "repeat" what is in the original, but reconceives the original in order to knit it to the ideals and actualities of the nation.

> Florio's greatest gift was the ability to make his book come to life for the Elizabethan imagination. Approximately the same forces surged through France and England in the Renaissance, but if Montaigne was to be fused into an integral part of the English mind and not left as a foreign classic, not only his spirit but the form of his expression had to be naturalized. And throughout his translation, sometimes consciously, more often instinctively, Florio creates a Montaigne who is an actual Elizabethan figure.
>
>   . . . . .
>
> Everything that Florio does to Montaigne is calculated to bring the Essays closer to the spirit of his time. Words and expressions of Elizabethan flavor crowd every page: "mumpes and mowes," "blockish asses," "meere bug-beares and scar-crowes, to scare birdes with all" appear in place of Montaigne's plain "grimaces," "des asniers," "vrais epouvantails de cheneviere." "I doe beware and keepe myselfe from such treasons, and cunny-catching in mine owne bosome" is the wholly characteristic version of "Je me sauve de telles trahisons en mon propre giron." Nouns are used for verbs or adjectives: "in a strange and foe country" for "en terre ennemie." Constant alterations are made in Montaigne's phrasing to introduce native idioms. "Respondirent à sa barbe" is shifted to "answered him to his teeth"; "sans suitte" is given the fullness of "without rime or reason, sans head or foot." Even more striking is the colloquial tone that Florio adopts. "God wot," "Well," "Marry, what you list" come frequently, and never with any counterpart in the original. "'Tut-tut,' said he, 'it is alreadie finished'" for the simple "Elle

est composée & preste" reveals at a glance the greatness of this change. To the same purpose is the translator's varied use of rich proverbial phrases where none had appeared in the French: "to set the foolish and the wise, us and beasts all in one ranke: no barrell better Hering."[20]

The critic who wrote passages like this about the rich colloquialism of the Elizabethans and their unified sensibility is the same one who would soon "translate" American writers of the nineteenth and twentieth centuries for contemporary audiences. Here, in *Translation*, Matthiessen is locating examples of scholarly work undertaken for more than just personal and professional purposes. Renaissance translation, he affirms, did lofty work for a particular society and culture: it was the opposite of pedantry.

Everywhere in his book Matthiessen emphasizes the concrete language that distinguishes the translators' rendering of their original texts. He states this point crisply in his introduction:

> The Elizabethan translator did not write for the learned alone, but for the whole country. He possessed a style admirably fitted to this end. Popular in the best sense, it took advantage of all the new richness of the language. His diction was racy and vivid, thronged with proverbial phrases, slang of the streets, bold compounds, robust Saxon epithets, and metaphors drawn from English ports and countryside. The structure of his sentences reveals the growing tendencies of the time—the passionate delight in fullness of expression, the free use of doublets and alliteration, the building up of parallel constructions for the sake of rhythm. Perhaps his greatest gift, that which more than any other accounts for the freshness and vigor of his work, was one which he shared with the dramatists of his day. He had an extraordinary eye for specific detail. Whenever possible he substituted a concrete image for an abstraction, a verb that carried the picture of an action for a general statement.[21]

Matthiessen's argument closely resembles one that Leavis offered several years later, in 1936, in *Revaluation*, his statement of "tradition and development in English poetry." Leavis, too, praises the suppleness and strength of Elizabethan language, noting especially the dramatic force and vivid colloquial idiom of Donne and Jonson. But the connection between *Translation* and *Revaluation* is ultimately less pertinent than the influence of T. S. Eliot that shapes both books. In speaking for the fertile bonds between language and everyday life in the Elizabethan age, both Matthiessen and Leavis root their arguments in Eliot's descriptions of metaphysical poetry, wit, and metaphor, and the later seventeenth-century dissociation of sensibility that sundered the wholeness manifest in Donne and his contemporaries. Matthiessen states his debt to Eliot explicitly:

> The most important fact in accounting for the freshness of both the poetry and prose of the early seventeenth century is that the men of that day possessed what Mr. T. S. Eliot has so accurately called "the direct sensuous

apprehension of thought." . . . Holland's thoughts came to him with the same immediacy as the odor of a rose. . . . Knowledge was fresh, language could be bent to one's will, thoughts swarmed so eagerly that they could not be separated from emotions. The language was more fully alive than it has ever been, which means that the people were also.[22]

Eliot's conception of history, particularly the lines he traces between history and language, structures Matthiessen's own account as he tells in *Translation* a story of loss roughly similar to that which he left implicit in *Sarah Orne Jewett*. In the later book, though, the crucial moment is not the industrial revolution, but is, instead, the perceptual and linguistic and cultural crisis that, according to Eliot, afflicted the England of Dryden and Milton. Modernist writers and intellectuals like Matthiessen, indebted to Eliot as a guide and authority, judged this crisis to define and delimit the twentieth century as well. In its reliance, then, on Eliot's myth of history and deployment of this myth to pattern observations about the style of the Elizabethan translations, *Translation* is a modernist text in its own right. Based in the academy, Matthiessen is supplying Eliot with formidable buttressing for the arguments advanced in *The Sacred Wood*. In these translations, Matthiessen reports, lie abundant evidence for the verdict Eliot has presented on our language and history. Here, too, is bountiful evidence for the verbal practice that Eliot, a craftsman burdened with modernity, now strives to recover.

Translation is also valuable for what it indicates about the sources for new critical "close reading." One source was the work of I. A. Richards, in *Principles of Literary Criticism* (1925) and *Practical Criticism* (1929), and his pupil, William Empson, in *Seven Types of Ambiguity* (1930). More relevantly for the American context, there were R. P. Blackmur's subtle analyses of the poetry of Eliot, Stevens, and others that appeared in *Hound and Horn* and *Direction* in the late 1920s and early 1930s. But Matthiessen's *Translation* demonstrates that Eliot's role was also a formative one. Eliot rarely engaged in close readings himself, yet in his critical prose he highlighted an understanding of language to which he gave complex form in his poetry. Matthiessen grasped what it might mean to read closely by witnessing Eliot's language in action in his early poems. It was not merely that the New Critics invented techniques for reading Eliot and his fellow modern poets. Eliot's poetry, supported by the theoretical thrust of his criticism, encouraged readers to behave in ways that altered their general response to texts. Modern poetry and modern criticism reinforced one another.

Matthiessen, for one, was superbly suited to read in this manner—and not only because Eliot's writing, with its invocations of unity and wholeness keyed to language, so appealed to him. As a scholar grounded in (and toughened by) philology and working on problems of translation, he was ready to attend analytically to language because he had been immersed in it all along. This may seem a minor point, but it reveals that New Criticism, while a new move-

ment, may not have been so radical a break from philology after all. Many philologists stayed what they were—they opposed the new generation of critics in the academy, and the New Critics in turn assailed the philologists. Other philologists, however, and graduate students schooled in this discipline, took what they had learned and fitted it to the purposes of the newer kind of close reading. The New Criticism represented a significant departure from what had been done before, but it managed its reorientation effectively because philology had furnished it with something positive: philology was more than a bad practice waiting to be corrected.

Given Matthiessen's own talents as a reader and his interest in Eliot, it seems inevitable to us that he would devote his next book to Eliot's poetry. But it is still startling that this young assistant professor at Harvard and author of a slight study of Jewett and a scholarly monograph on Elizabethan translations would dare to commit himself to defining and defending the work of a difficult modernist writer. *The Achievement of T. S. Eliot: An Essay on the Nature of Poetry*, first published in 1935, and reissued in a revised and enlarged edition in 1947, is a book that, from the vantage point of the 1980s, now appears rather uncritical. Matthiessen, who had met Eliot when the poet came to Harvard to deliver the Norton Lectures in 1932-33, never attains a detached relation to Eliot. He treats sources, influences, themes, ideas, attitudes in Eliot's own terms. He does not hone a language of his own—there is no competitive dialogue between the critic and his author. As Giles Gunn cogently puts it, *The Achievement of T. S. Eliot* "is so dependent upon Eliot's own standards for a critical evaluation of his poetry that it never quite escapes from the shadow cast by its subject."[23]

All of this is true enough, and *The Achievement of T. S. Eliot* also suffers from serious problems caused by Matthiessen's developing formalist ideology, as we shall see. But before going further, it is necessary to credit the importance of this book for audiences in the 1930s. Richards, Pound, and Conrad Aiken had resolutely backed Eliot's poetry; Edmund Wilson had devoted a chapter to Eliot's poetry and criticism in *Axel's Castle* (1931); and Blackmur had published his estimable two-part essay in *Hound and Horn* (1928). There was a scattering of other reviews and essays, and even several books. Still, no one before Matthiessen—and certainly no one with his institutional credentials—had laid out so expertly the main lines of Eliot's accomplishment in his verse. This was a great work of "translation," one tied too closely to the original, but still a translation of distinction that displayed Matthiessen's desire to teach us how to honor and approach a modern master.

Matthiessen does a number of very worthwhile things, summarizing, for instance, Eliot's view of "tradition" and bonds to Arnold, James, Dante, Donne, and Baudelaire. He also provides helpful analyses of passages, including a three-page exploration of the lines about the "typist" and "young man carbuncular" from "The Fire Sermon."[24] Curiously, if revealingly, Matthiessen places nearly all of his relatively few close readings in the footnotes; and this marginalization of the workings of Eliot's language will strike many as a disappointing aspect of *The Achievement of T. S. Eliot*. However, the real disappointment—and fault—in the book is Matthiessen's overinsistence on poetic form and refusal to come to terms with Eliot's religion and politics. In studying Eliot, Matthiessen fastens so exclusively upon questions of poetic form that he is prohibited from making the larger sociopolitical connections he often claimed he wanted to make.

In the first paragraph of his preface to the 1935 edition, Matthiessen states his intention:

> My double aim in this essay is to evaluate Eliot's method and achievement as an artist, and in so doing to emphasize certain of the fundamental elements in the nature of poetry which are in danger of being obscured by the increasing tendency to treat poetry as a social document and to forget that it is an art. The most widespread error in contemporary criticism is to neglect form and to concern itself entirely with content. The romantic critic is generally not interested in the poet's work, but in finding the man behind it. The humanistic critic and the sociological critic have in common that both tend to ignore the evaluation of specific poems in their preoccupation with the ideological background from which the poems spring.[25]

Though he refers here to new humanist and romantic critics, it is the sociological and political critics who are Matthiessen's chief foes. He respected the foremost new humanist, Irving Babbitt, noting on one occasion that "by far the most living experience in my graduate study at Harvard came through the lectures of Irving Babbitt, with whose neo-humanistic attack upon the modern world I disagreed at nearly every point. The vigor with which he objected to almost every author since the eighteenth century forced me to fight for my tastes, which grew stronger by the exercise."[26] When he attended Babbitt's lectures and read such books as *Literature and the American College* and *Rousseau and Romanticism*, Matthiessen doubtless admired this new humanist's firm point of view, the prophetic urgency of his voice, the sense of history, and, perhaps, too, the fierce isolation and identity as "outsider" within the institution. Matthiessen probably also respected Babbitt's concern for educational reform and his attack on the impersonality and mechanization of American colleges and universities. These had been Matthiessen's sturdy interests at Yale during his undergraduate days, and they remained with him all his life.

By the mid-1930s, however, new humanism was no longer an influential force. Its key text, *Humanism and America*, published in 1930, was less a declaration than a last gasp, and it was effectively demolished by the rival volume, *The Critique of Humanism,* which was published in the same year. Romantic, psychological, and psychoanalytic types of criticism, sparked by Freud's *Three Contributions to a Theory of Sexuality* (translated in 1910) and Ernest Jones's

Oedipal study of *Hamlet* (published in 1910), had also won some champions on the critical scene since the first decade of the century, but none of these were as prominent during the 1930s as Marxist, sociological, and other kinds of political approaches. It is certainly important to remember such delvings into psychoanalytic or psychological criticism as Joseph Wood Krutch's *Edgar Allan Poe: A Study in Genius* (1926), Lewis Mumford's *Herman Melville* (1929), and Ludwig Lewisohn's *Expression in America* (1932)—these books did have an impact. Yet while Matthiessen regretted this trend in criticism, he seems never to have judged it likely to endanger literary art to anything like the degree that the "sociological" did. Psychoanalyzing Shakespeare or Twain may have appeared crude and wrongheaded to Matthiessen, but it was not as subversive of literary categories as a political critique that, in his opinion, coarsely ranked art and artists according to their serviceability for the class struggle.

The motley performance of Marxist, socialist, radical, and leftist criticism during the 1930s may make most readers sympathetic to Matthiessen's complaints about the "mechanical rigidity" of V. F. Calverton's and others' books and his emphasis on literature as an art.[27] But the vehemence with which Matthiessen adheres to this principle is nettling. On the one hand, he acknowledges in his Eliot monograph that "in the last analysis content and form are inseparable" yet he does not then proceed to take their interdependence seriously.[28] He claims that "the error" that distorts criticism is the "neglect" of form and the exclusive preoccupation with content. Why then not seek a middle ground? Why not advocate a method that shows the ways in which form and content are interwoven? Why not inquire into technique *and* ideas?

These were exactly the questions Granville Hicks raised in his review of *The Achievement of T. S. Eliot*: "Mr. Matthiessen very properly regards both form and content as important. What disturbs me is that he fails to investigate the relation between the two."[29] Matthiessen at times implies that the study of this relation is indeed his goal, but his procedure is finally much more narrow. Something happens to Eliot's ideas, Matthiessen suggests, through the forms that the poet shapes for them: technique transforms ideas. Invoking Coleridge, Matthiessen identifies this process as "organic form," a perfect fusion of form and content achieved through the artistic imagination. Here, Matthiessen may have been drawing upon the work of Richards, who had begun teaching at Harvard in 1931 and whose influential book, *Coleridge on Imagination*, appeared in 1934. He was more likely, however, evoking and elaborating upon insights he had acquired through J. L. Lowes, who was not only Matthiessen's dissertation supervisor, but also the author of *The Road to Xanadu*, a 1927 study of Coleridge's "poetic imagination." Matthiessen, I suspect, interpreted and responded to Lowes's emphasis on "imaginative creation" and "controlling Form" by way of Eliot's more austere voice and views.[30] He read Lowes and Coleridge through Eliot, retaining Lowes's passion for learning but eliminating the scholar-adventurer's sometimes mystical tone and impressionism. Eliot helped to give Matthiessen's grasp of Coleridge's doctrine of "organic form" a special modernist valence and sanction, and authoritatively led Matthiessen to identify the flowering of this doctrine in the writings of the American renaissance.

"Organic form" also mattered greatly to Matthiessen because it connected the man and the work—the poet wholly at one with his art, the critic at one with his subject. But if the critic is going to praise Eliot's "wholeness," "integrity," and "authenticity," as Matthiessen does repeatedly, then should he not at some stage inquire into the nature of the content, into the substance of the ideas? Hicks appeals to Matthiessen to probe what poetic form "does" to ideas, how technique alters them, how the poet's verbal resources make them more or less palatable to readers. To be sure, Matthiessen, following Eliot, also understood organic form as a metaphor for, or representation of, the ordered society. In this respect, the form itself does signify a social content. But the difficulties that Hicks raises remain, for Eliot's notion of the ordered society differs starkly from Matthiessen's. As he made abundantly clear in *American Renaissance,* Matthiessen judged himself to be a worker for "the people"[31] who sought to further the expansive cause of democracy. Organic form figured forth for Matthiessen a social content that Eliot would never have espoused.

More generally, organic form seems conceptually geared, for Matthiessen and others, to evoke a content that cannot literally be named and detailed. To name the content would not only dramatize the conflict between an Eliot and a Matthiessen—a conflict which the generalized references to order and wholeness conceal—but would also oblige critics to articulate the varying, contested politics embedded in their apparently similar formalist views. Organic form is, in truth, a politically charged term, but an extremely variable one. It intriguingly functions to suspend political debate, forestalling particularity and implying a consensus that exists only superficially.

Matthiessen thus hardens the distinction between form and content where he might instead have tried to articulate a dialectical mode of response to texts, a mode that does not privilege technique over ideas and that strives to blend literary and sociopolitical analysis. Hicks again provides a sharp counterstatement:

> Every critic, no matter how far to the left, acknowledges, even if he sometimes appears to forget, that there is no ideological equivalent for a poem. He also knows that there is a difference between good expression and bad expression. But what some of us hold is that a thing well expressed and a thing badly expressed are two different things. . . . I think Eliot is important because he says something. That "something," I will repeat, cannot be reduced to ideas. The way he says it, I will add, is important. But the way he says his "something" is part of what he says. The form of his verse, in other words, is in large measure determined by the subtlety of his perceptions, and his artistic mastery in no small degree lies in his understanding of their demands.[32]

Throughout his career, Matthiessen sometimes says this himself, yet his practice usually reflects a different policy. This inconsistency is highly troubling: one wants the socialist Matthiessen to query the formalist Matthiessen's terms for examining Eliot and other writers. Even as he is working on, and later revising and reissuing, his book on Eliot, Matthiessen is, after all, deepening his radicalism and developing the political interests that had first stirred for him at Yale. He is an admirer of Tawney and Debs, a defender of the union leader Harry Bridges, a supporter of Harvard professors (Ray Walsh and Paul Sweezy) denied tenure because of their radical politics—the list could be easily extended. Here is Matthiessen's own account, written in the late 1940s, of his politics during the early 1930s:

> In '32, with the depression at its worst, I thought that here at last was a chance for the Socialists to regain the broad base they had developed under Debs, and I joined the party. Roosevelt's speeches during that campaign struck me as little more than the promises of a Harvard man who wanted very much to be President, and I had not gauged the sweep of middle and lower-middle class reaction against Hooverism that turned the rascals out. Roosevelt in office was something quite other than I had foreseen, and after he began to effect even some of the things for which Thomas had stood, I voted for him enthusiastically, though always from the left, until his death. . . . Whatever objective reasons compelled towards socialism in the nineteen-thirties seem even more compelling now, and it is the responsibility of the intellectual to rediscover and rearticulate that fact.[33]

When it comes to literary criticism, however, Matthiessen often sounds much more like John Crowe Ransom and Cleanth Brooks than like Granville Hicks and others on the left. Some might reply that this is all to Matthiessen's distinction, but one might answer them by saying that this allegiance tended to impel Matthiessen to work, as a literary critic, *against* his own political convictions. It lodged a limiting contradiction at the heart of Matthiessen's labors: he was an active socialist who wanted to be purely literary yet somehow still be politically engaged in his criticism. Whenever he refers to politics in his books on Eliot and other writers, his comments are invariably distancing and unspecific—they do not fulfill his organic rhetoric—and his activities in his life help make us see them as such.

Matthiessen seems never to have asked himself whether it was really desirable to keep his socialism outside—or, at best, on the margins of—his literary criticism, and this failure led to repeated dissonance in his writing and his expressed hopes for it. This is a hard charge for me to direct against Matthiessen because I concede that my first impulse is to commend his tolerance and pluralism: he is willing to take great poetry wherever he can find it, even if it does not suit his own politics. But to admit this point would imply that Matthiessen actually resolved, or at least directly faced, the ambiguities in his criticism and politics, and I don't believe that he did. With the possible exception of his work on James and Dreiser in the 1940s, he avoided the ambiguities, left them hanging.

By the 1947 edition, Matthiessen seems to have sensed that his views about Eliot contained a political problem, but he refers to it only briefly and underestimates its urgency:

> My growing divergence from his view of life is that I believe that it is possible to accept the "radical imperfection" of man, and yet to be a political radical as well, to be aware that no human society can be perfect, and yet to hold that the proposition that "all men are created equal" demands dynamic adherence from a Christian no less than from a democrat. But the scope of my book remains what it was before. I have not written about Eliot's politics or religion except as they are expressed through his poetry.[34]

Can a critic with Matthiessen's political loyalties shield himself from engaging Eliot's politics and religion? How does a committed radical manage to bracket Eliot's religious and political beliefs when he reads the poet's work? Are there not fertile opportunities and obligations for the radical, as Edmund Wilson had shown in *Axel's Castle*, when he engages and tests Eliot's and the modernists' ideas? How does such a radical detach—why should he detach?—his response to *Four Quartets* from his knowledge of Eliot's vision of "a Christian society," with its "positive distinction—however undemocratic it may sound—between the educated and the uneducated," between the elect body of Christian intellectuals and "the mob"?[35] Just how does a socialist who is also, like Matthiessen, a Christian, measure Eliot's expression of Christianity in his poetry and prose? These are some of the questions Matthiessen sidesteps in his quest for purity of method. "You begin to understand Eliot," Matthiessen insists,

> precisely as you begin to understand any other poet: by listening to the lines, by regarding their pattern as a self-enclosed whole, by listening to what is being communicated instead of looking for something that isn't. . . . One of the surest ways to fail to understand a poem is to begin by trying to tear the thought from the context in order to approve or disapprove of what it seems to express. For the important thing, as Richards has reaffirmed, is "not what a poem says, but what it *is*"; and the only way of knowing what it does express is by a sustained awareness of all the formal elements of which it is composed. Only in this way, by experiencing the poem as a whole, and then by evaluating it "from the inside," so to speak, by trusting the evidence of your senses for its effect, can you determine whether or not the poem is alive; and thus, in turn, whether or not the poet has a sense of his age, whether what he believes and imagines about human destiny springs from a direct contact with life.[36]

The New Criticism, with Matthiessen's help, has so woven these notions about poems as "self-enclosed wholes" into our readerly being that it is difficult to interrogate them. But surely it is a very risky business to profess that one knows when a poet's writing "springs from a direct contact with life" and when it does not. The ground for such a discrimination would seem all the more problematic for

Matthiessen, who presumably takes issue with Eliot's conception of what constitutes "human destiny" and what "a direct contact with life" means. Eliot doesn't believe the same things that Matthiessen does; he doesn't know the world the same way.

Matthiessen's position appears to be flexible and open, receptive above all to literature as an art and concerned to protect it from the damaging intrusions of ideology. But his position is actually quite prescriptive, and there is finally something unnatural about his ardent call—which he brands "the chief assumption of my essay"—for separating poetry and politics, art and philosophy. What follows is one of many puzzling examples, slight but significant, which he invokes to prop up his approach:

> Milton's pamphlets are read for the importance of their ideas in relation to the development of seventeenth-century political theory; but readers are drawn to *Samson Agonistes* by a quality that still enables it to be a moving experience whether or not one is a special student of the seventeenth century. For, although many of Milton's same ideas are voiced in *Samson Agonistes*, what gives the poem its life is its quality of emotional expression through its expert fusion of content and form.[37]

These are exasperatingly dogmatic claims. How does Matthiessen reply to readers who differ with him? What about readers who believe that the pamphlets Milton wrote on the eve of the Restoration are as "moving" or even more "moving" than *Samson Agonistes*? An advocate of a Christian society himself, Milton knew that the Revolution had failed, yet he endangered his life by continuing his steadfast opposition to the monarchy. Readers could propose (and have proposed) that the pamphlets possess literary value and "move" us as artistic as well as political performances. "Moving experience" is an extremely fluid category, and some readers would in fact bicker with Matthiessen's assessment of Milton's verse. This is Leavis's verdict on *Samson Agonistes* in *Revaluation*: "One can grant that it might possibly help to form taste; it certainly could not instil or foster a love of poetry. How many cultivated adults could honestly swear that they had ever read it through with enjoyment?"[38]

Like many New Critics, Matthiessen frequently seems unable to consider nonfictional prose like Milton's as more than a gloss for poems and novels. When Matthiessen does this, he is refraining from a real confrontation with the writer's ideas, the ideas that the writer seeks to express in his verse or his fiction. And the problem is especially vexed in Eliot's case, where the ideas the writer presents so often call for dissent, and particularly from people whose politics resemble Matthiessen's.

The difficulties worsen when one realizes just how selective Matthiessen's reading of Eliot's prose is. He reads it for its "literary" relevance—he sees "tradition," for instance, only in a literary sense—and he ignores explicitly social and political dimensions in the prose altogether.

This has alarming consequences, notably the fact that *After Strange Gods*, which appeared in 1933 and which even Eliot did not see fit to reprint, receives respectful mention. Matthiessen also avoids confronting many disturbing passages in Eliot's contributions to the *Criterion*, such as the following from a July 1929 piece:

> Fascism is . . . nationalistic, and communism internationalistic: yet it is conceivable that in particular circumstances fascism might make for peace, and communism for war. The objections of fascists and communists to each other are mostly quite irrational. I confess to a preference for fascism in practice, which I dare say most of my readers share; and I will not admit that this preference is itself wholly irrational. I believe that the fascist form of unreason is less remote from my own than is that of the communists.[39]

Matthiessen never comes to grips with statements like this one. In the midst of a tumultuous decade, both politically and socially, and several years before the appearance of *The World's Body, Understanding Poetry*, and *The New Criticism*, Matthiessen hews to a formalist line and celebrates a self-proclaimed classicist in literature, royalist in politics, and Anglo-Catholic in religion. This is a strange position for a socialist to find himself in. "I am not concerned," Matthiessen says at one point,

> with the direct applicability of Eliot's political ideas; indeed, he frequently confesses himself an amateur in such matters, and yet defends the valid and valuable distinction between political ideas and actual politics, a distinction particularly necessary at a time of social disruption, when practice lags behind theory, when, indeed, the only way of clarifying the chaotic jungle of events is by subjecting them to the scrutiny of an articulated theory. But what is important to understand in the present context is that the strain of thought which characterizes Eliot's conception of the ideal state also runs throughout his conception of the nature of art.[40]

Again an array of questions poses themselves. Why not inquire into what society would "look like" if it were built upon the foundation that Eliot describes in *The Idea of a Christian Society* and other writings? Why not analyze, too, what it implies about Eliot—to reverse Matthiessen's final remark—that throughout his conception of art runs his conception of the ideal state? Matthiessen shuns these questions and many others like them. One suspects that he has to do so, or else he will be forced to adjust the high valuation of Eliot he is committed to maintaining. To put this in a more general way: Matthiessen has to devote himself to preserving a methodological purity in his criticism, or else consider the full implications of his socialism for literary studies. These would be painful and disarming: he would have to give up a great deal, including, perhaps, much literature he loves.

In the Eliot book and elsewhere, Matthiessen's language frequently takes strange turns when he deals with the relation between literature, criticism, and politics. Several years after the appearance of *The Achievement of T. S. Eliot*, he reviewed Newton Arvin's book on Walt Whitman, strenuously objecting to Arvin's praise of Whitman's "optimism" in contrast to the pessimism of Poe and Melville:

> Is the availability of a poet to be made to correspond to the degree in which his opinions chime in with our hopes? Is it not rather the function of the artist to bring to concentrated expression every major phase of human experience, its doubts and anguish and tortured defeats as well as its cheerful confidence? Indeed, is not one measure of the great artist his refusal to yield us any innocent simplification, his presentation of an account of life as intricate in its harsh tragic matching of good and evil, as complex in its necessities of constant struggle as the life that we ourselves know? Will any less dense past correspond to our usages as mature human beings?[41]

This crucial passage reveals how Matthiessen's sense of the "tragic" shadows his politics. It is striking to witness the shift he makes from "our hopes" to "innocent simplification," as though the second phrase more accurately registers the essence of any desire for social change. For Matthiessen, life mixes good and evil, and this dimension of his Christian belief leads him in the final analysis to be deeply skeptical about the potential of socialism to convert our minds and reorder society and its institutions. Admittedly going somewhat beyond direct evidence, I will risk saying that Matthiessen is a courageous, earnest fighter for socialism who does not believe that his cause could ever succeed: men and women are radically imperfect, and this hard fact always colors his sense of the likely prospects for change. You must struggle against the capitalist system and for economic equality, but you cannot assume, Matthiessen seems to be maintaining, that by changing external conditions you will change human nature. Matthiessen was a Christian, not a materialist. Literature, for him, is not so much political as it is a form of expression that, especially in the tragic masterpieces of Shakespeare and Melville, exposes the limitations of the political.

Matthiessen invested much in categories he seems unable to question. In his book on Eliot and even in the later books, he circles around contradictions in his critical approach and musters defenses for views that he might have queried. It is partly true, but not wholly adequate, to say that he is admirably resisting the Marxists and the "sociologists" of the 1920s and 1930s who fail to value literature for its own sake. He is doing something for literature at the expense of a criticism that might conceivably move and mediate between literature and politics. Matthiessen makes it impossible to examine literature politically—the socialist has no option but to set aside his principles when he does literary criticism. I think we see here the self-alienating effects of Matthiessen's embrace of the New Criticism, formidably bolstered by Eliot's literary ethics. Perhaps, too, we glimpse Matthiessen's sense of the limits of the socialist cause—which might alter conditions, but not our essence—for which he fervently fought. He counsels "integrity" and "wholeness" in response, employing these very terms to commend Eliot even as, in doing so, he violates his own political allegiances.

This essay should show that I dissent from the view that Matthiessen is important because he reconciled differences and conflicts in modern criticism. Rather, he is crucially important to think about precisely because, like many literary radicals past and present in the academy, he did not achieve such an act of reconciliation, though he tried to undertake one and may have believed that he did so successfully. Frederick Stern is incorrect when he argues that Matthiessen's ability to "link" various "modes of critical thought" is perhaps his "greatest contribution." Matthiessen attempted but did not manage to "combine literary theories that seemed so totally at odds with one another that it appeared they could not be brought together into a whole."[42] At first encounter, Matthiessen admittedly does seem to profess an organic literary/sociopolitical commitment that the New Critics lacked. In 1929, more than a decade before *Understanding Poetry*, Matthiessen warned against the way that "literature has been studied in a vacuum without relation to anything but itself, a genealogy of printed works, one book begetting another."[43] And there are many similar statements in Matthiessen's later books, essays, and reviews. But his Eliot book shows ample affinities with the position to which he objects. The study of Eliot is not an isolated case: one can detect the same dedication to an intrinsic "literary" method among the very books, essays, and reviews that one would initially cite to affirm Matthiessen's divergence from the New Criticism. Before the Eliot book and after it, Matthiessen repeatedly declares that "the critic's primary task is to discern the object as it is"—which is exactly what Ransom, Brooks, and other New Critics said.[44]

A critic like Matthiessen conceivably could practice "close reading" in the service of politics, *reading as a socialist*. But a critic cannot effectively be two discrete things at once, cannot be a socialist and a formalist, a cultural historian and a critic of "self-enclosed" literary art. The costs are too high, the ambiguities too serious, the tensions too severe. Matthiessen subscribed to (and sought to keep separate) the loyalties of the political man and the literary critic. He did not work out their competing claims and labor to unify them in his practice, but, instead, tried to live with—perhaps by never really seeing—their contradictions.[45]

Notes

1. Sacvan Bercovitch, "The Problem of Ideology in American Literary History," *Critical Inquiry* 12 (1986): 631.

2. Joseph Summers and U. T. Miller Summers, "F. O. Matthiessen," *Dictionary of American Biography, Supplement 4, 1946-1950* (New York, 1974), 559.

3. F. O. Matthiessen, *From the Heart of Europe* (New York, 1948), 73-74.

4. Ibid., 76.

5. George Wilson Pierson, *Yale: The University College, 1921-1937* (New Haven, 1955), 61.

6. Matthiessen, *Heart of Europe*, 72.

7. Louis Hyde, *Rat and the Devil: Journal Letters of F. O. Matthiessen and Russell Cheney* (Hamden, 1978), 386-87.

8. Paul M. Sweezy, "Labor and Political Activities," in *F. O. Matthiessen (1902-1950): A Collective Portrait*, ed. Paul M. Sweezy and Leo Huberman (New York, 1950), 74.

9. See George Abbott White, "'Have I Any Right in a Community That Would So Utterly Disapprove of Me if It Knew the Facts?'" *Harvard Magazine* (September-October 1978): 58-62.

10. Hyde, *Rat and the Devil*, 115-16.

11. Matthiessen, *Heart of Europe*, 23.

12. Walt Whitman, "Song of Myself," lines 87-91, 1341-47.

13. F. O. Matthiessen, *American Renaissance: Art and Expression in the Age of Emerson and Whitman* (1941; rpt. New York, 1972), 535.

14. Bernard Bowron, "The Making of an American Scholar," in Sweezy and Huberman, *Collective Portrait*, 49.

15. F. O. Matthiessen, *Sarah Orne Jewett* (Boston, 1929), 64, 101-2.

16. Ibid., 144, 149.

17. Ibid., 20.

18. Quoted in Kermit Vanderbilt, *American Literature and the Academy: The Roots, Growth, and Maturity of a Profession* (Philadelphia, 1987), 475.

19. F. O. Matthiessen, *Translation: An Elizabethan Art* (Cambridge, Mass., 1931), 26.

20. Ibid., 141, 151-52.

21. Ibid., 3-4.

22. Ibid., 226, 232.

23. Giles Gunn, *F. O. Matthiessen: The Critical Achievement* (Seattle, 1975), 31.

24. F. O. Matthiessen, *The Achievement of T. S. Eliot: An Essay on the Nature of Poetry*, 3d ed., with an additional chapter by C. L. Barber (New York, 1960), 30-32. Originally published in 1935; 2d ed., 1947.

25. Ibid., vii.

26. Matthiessen, *Heart of Europe*, 74. For a description of Babbitt's style as a teacher and lecturer, see Thomas R. Nevin, *Irving Babbitt: An Intellectual Study* (Chapel Hill, 1984), 11-32.

27. "An Excited Debater," in *The Responsibilities of the Critic: Essays and Reviews by F. O. Matthiessen*, ed. John Rackliffe (New York, 1952), 185.

28. Matthiessen, *Achievement of T. S. Eliot*, vii.

29. Granville Hicks, "Eliot in Our Time," in *Granville Hicks in the New Masses*, ed. Jack Alan Robbins (Port Washington, 1974), 103.

30. J. L. Lowes, *The Road to Xanadu: A Study in the Ways of the Imagination* (1927; rpt. Boston, 1964), 395.

31. Matthiessen, *American Renaissance*, xvi.

32. Hicks, "Eliot in Our Time," 103-4.

33. Matthiessen, *Heart of Europe*, 76, 79.

34. Matthiessen, *Achievement of T. S. Eliot*, ix.

35. T. S. Eliot, *The Idea of a Christian Society* (1940; rpt. New York, n.d.), 33.

36. Matthiessen, *Achievement of T. S. Eliot*, 46, 110.

37. Ibid., 127.

38. F. R. Leavis, *Revaluation: Tradition and Development in English Poetry* (1936; rpt. London, 1969), 67.

39. Quoted in Daniel Aaron, *Writers on the Left* (New York, 1965), 265.

40. Matthiessen, *Achievement of T. S. Eliot*, 143.

41. Matthiessen, "Whitman: Sanguine Confused American," in *Responsibilities of the Critic*, 217.

42. Frederick Stern, *F. O. Matthiessen: Christian Socialist as Critic* (Chapel Hill, 1981), 31-32.

43. Matthiessen, "New Standards in American Criticism: 1929," in *Responsibilities of the Critic*, 181.

44. Matthiessen, "In the Tradition from Emerson," *New Republic* 6 (April 1938): 280. For further discussion of this tenet of the New Criticism, see my book, *The Crisis in Criticism: Theory, Literature, and Reform in English Studies* (Baltimore, 1984), 98-100.

45. I examine Matthiessen's writings on Henry James, which spring from his interest in Eliot, in "Criticism and Politics: F. O. Matthiessen and the Making of Henry James," *New England Quarterly* 60 (June 1987): 163-86. See also my forthcoming study, *F. O. Matthiessen and the Politics of Criticism*, to be published by the University of Wisconsin Press.

Eric Cheyfitz (essay date 1989)

SOURCE: "Matthiessen's American Renaissance: Circumscribing the Revolution," in *American Quarterly*, Vol. 41, No. 2, June, 1989, pp. 341-61.

[*In the following essay, Cheyfitz explicates and reconciles the contradictory images of Matthiessen in American literary critical theory.*]

In 1963, reviewing four books of criticism, including F. O. Matthiessen's posthumous *The Responsibilities of the Critic*, Leslie Fiedler marked a moment of critical exhaustion. Three of these works, including the Matthiessen, Fiedler told his audience in *The Yale Review*,

are the victims of our new canon—a brief series of literary works championed over and over in certain expected and unexciting ways. I have never been so aware how most of us, despite our differences, have become inmates of the same infernal cycle of taste; busily snapping at each other's skulls, we do not notice how we are all imprisoned from the waist down in the ice of our congealed enthusiasms. This ice, fixed at the temperature of absolute boredom, our approximate passions cannot melt. Another boost for Henry James, another good word for Melville, another cheer for T. S. Eliot—why this is hell, nor are we out of it.

And, after the allusion to Marlowe's Mephistopholes that culminates his parody of Dante, Fiedler continued: "From this circle," where, unlike the one in Dante's *Inferno*, the sinners are not completely submerged in ice, "Matthiessen himself cannot escape. . . ." For: "More than any other critic, Matthiessen was the victim of current taste. . . ."[1] Fiedler could have added here that in this case the archetypal victim (the scapegoat, shall we say?) was also the archetypal perpetrator, the crucial constructor of the infernal circle that Americanists are so busily deconstructing and reconstructing today.

In a 1958 essay that sketches the institutional development of American literature in the twentieth century, Fiedler focuses the centrality of Matthiessen: "The success of ***The American Renaissance*** [sic] has been immense; it has given a name and shape to new courses in American literature, and has had an impact outside of our own country unequalled by any other single study, except, perhaps, D. H. Lawrence's." Written over a ten year period and published in 1941, ***American Renaissance*** completed what Fiedler refers to as "the revolution in taste which dethroned the Brahmins [Longfellow, Whittier, Holmes and Lowell are typically the figureheads of this 'genteel' tradition] and elevated Twain, Whitman, and Melville [and, of course, Emerson, Thoreau, Hawthorne and James]" to canonical status.[2] In what follows I want to explore the irony or contradiction that exists between the figure of Matthiessen as the victim, or vessel, of a revolution in critical taste and the figure of him as the instigator of that revolution.

Begun in the years immediately preceding World War I, this "revolution . . . was led in the earliest stages by people outside of the universities, literary journalists like Van Wyck Brooks [who did some teaching at Stanford between 1911-1913], Lewis Mumford, H. L. Mencken, and Randolph Bourne, who thought of the 'professors' . . . as the enemies of what was most vital in contemporary art and a re-examined past." But increasingly in the twenties and thirties, this "revolutionary" labor was taken up and over in important ways by academics. It was the labor, we must remember, not only of displacing one literary canon with another, but also of simultaneously legitimizing the study of American literature as a distinct specialty within English departments. "As late as fifteen years ago," Fiedler remarked in 1958, "the graduate student who devoted himself primarily to American literature instead of, say, Renaissance drama or Medieval epic was looked on as not quite 'serious.'" But, Fiedler went on to say,

[s]ince 1928 [the year when the quarterly *American Literature* was formed] . . . the battle has been really won; and it becomes clear now that the continuing resistance of the thirties and the forties was only a desperate rear-guard action. For better or for worse, the criticism of American literature has been captured by the university departments of English; and conversely, those departments seem on the verge of being captured by the study of American literature.[3]

The twentieth century, then, has seen the increasing professionalization of American literature or, more precisely, has seen its most visible professionalization take a particular form, that of academic study. And this professionalization, it is crucial to note, has been accompanied by a simultaneous nationalization of our literature. In 1918, perpetuating the figure of the Emerson of the late 1830s, Van Wyck Brooks lamented the "virtual absence of any organic native culture" in the United States, doing so within an international context that, ironically, only intensified a nationalistic ethos. "[I]t is because our field of action has been preempted by our acquisitive instincts, because in short we have no national fabric of spiritual experience, that we are so unable today to think and feel in international terms," Brooks wrote in his essay "Letters and Leadership." There is no doubt that Brooks looks forward in this essay to an America that will be able "to think and feel in international terms. "But there is also no doubt that Brooks's international America must be grounded on a "national fabric of spiritual experience," a "'national culture,'" as he also terms it. His inverted commas are cautionary of nationalism as an end in itself or, perhaps it would be more accurate to say, of what he conceives of as a narrow, or simply materialistic, nationalism: ". . . the hope of a 'national culture' to come . . . is only in order that America may be able in the future to give something to the rest of the world that is better than what the world too generally means by 'Americanism'—'the worship of size, mass, quantity and numbers'. . . ." Yet his predication of nationalism, however spiritualized, as a precondition of internationalism leads him to ignore his own caution. Employing the kind of rhetoric that appears to equate national chauvinism with internationalism, Brooks issues a call, recognizing that "nationalities are the workshops of humanity, [and] that each nationality has . . . a special gift to contribute to the general stock of civilization," for the country to become

> a living, homogeneous entity, with its own faith and consciousness of self—could any idea more perfectly than this express the dream, the necessity, of Young America? To live creatively, to live completely, to live in behalf of some great corporate purpose,—that is its desire. A national faith we had once, a national dream, the dream of the "great American experiment."[4]

It is the "national faith," the "national dream," that centrally occupies Brooks's vision. The international dream must be postponed, both rhetorically and actually, until this nationalism is realized.

We should not confuse, then, the proclaimed internationalism of Brooks and the academic Americanists of the twen-

ties and thirties, some of whom I discuss in what follows, with an attack on an American nationalism. Quite the contrary, this internationalism was an attack not on American nationalism, which it promoted, but on the perceived provincialism, the Anglo-Saxon or New England bias, of the genteel tradition, which in the view of the critics I am and will be considering vitiated American cultural nationalism by regionalizing it, thus cutting America off from its place in the community of nations. In "America's Coming of Age," Brooks can evoke the passing of the "essentially innocent old America" of the genteel tradition for the new America of "Jews, Lithuanians, Magyars and German socialists," yet the new canon that will be based on this internationalism, indeed the writers that Brooks himself invokes as important, will remain remarkably Anglo-Saxon. This internationalism appears at times as no more than a cosmopolitanism with a decidedly Western European orientation, a call to make American literature "worldly" or "sophisticated" in relation to a particular paradigm of culture.[5]

In 1928, there appeared what was to be an exceptionally influential volume of essays entitled *The Reinterpretation of American Literature*, edited by Norman Foerster under the auspices of the American Literature Group of the MLA (a group that had been founded in 1921). This volume echoed Brooks by calling for a *national* literary history—again, within an international, or comparative, context that seems ironic because it served the post-World War I, or great-power, nationalism of the United States. On the opening page of his "Introduction," Foerster told his American audience that "our increasing awareness of our world supremacy in material force has more and more evoked a sense of need of self-knowledge," which a truly national literary history could help supply.[6] This history was to be a unified volume to replace the regional histories that had been piling up for years. The lead essay in the collection, written by Fred Lewis Pattee and entitled "A Call for a Literary Historian," declared the ethos of the group when it stated emphatically: "It is high time . . . for a history of *American* literature to be written. . . ." (*RAL*, 6). On the verge of beginning **American Renaissance**, Matthiessen reviewed the Foerster collection for the *Yale Review* in 1929, and in the first sentence of his review, paraphrasing Pattee, expressed his basic agreement with the project of the group: "It is time for the history of American literature to be rewritten,"[7] he stated, though, we note, he has dropped in his paraphrase Pattee's "high," his italicized emphasis of American, and has modified "written" to "rewritten," all of which changes mute the patriotic fervor of Pattee.

Nevertheless, in his review, Matthiessen implicitly accepted the nationalistic basis of the project for writing or rewriting an American literary history. Following to the letter the language of Foerster's own essay in the collection, which expresses the need to reorganize regional and political differences into national coherence, Matthiessen wrote of the need to reorganize American literary history around "the two interrelating factors essential to any real comprehension of our literature: the implications of American life, and the organic relation of our thought to that of Europe" (*RC*, 181). Within this circle connecting America to Europe (and the Europe intended here is decidedly Western Europe), "the political and geographical terminology" that had formerly sectioned the literary-historical space ("The Colonial Period, The Revolutionary Period, The Early National and Later National Periods. . . . The East, The West, The South, The New England Group . . . , etc., etc. . . .") (Foerster, *RAL*, 23-24) was to be erased and replaced by a simpler schema of conceptual categories, which, unifying a multitude of differences, still dominates the thinking of Americanists today, however problematic current studies have made this schema, whatever differences of race, gender and class are finally and rightly emerging within it. Foerster listed these new categories as follows: "(1) the Puritan tradition, (2) the frontier spirit, (3) romanticism, and (4) realism" (*RAL*, 26-27). Operating within this reapportioned space, Matthiessen insisted the "new historian must take into account every side of American culture: the effect of our religion and education in forming it . . .", as well as the whole range of popular culture. "In brief," Matthiessen continues,

> he must follow the impressive lead of historians like Turner, Andrews, Adams, and Beard, who have given us a new vision of the forces dominant in our political and social past. But he must not lose himself in his background, or forget that he is dealing primarily with literature. He must remember that his real quarry is aesthetic values, and that perhaps one does not have to master the importance of Jacksonian democracy to read intelligently 'Rappaccini's Daughter.' (*RC*, 181-82)

The several essays of *The Reinterpretation of American Literature* were univocal in their endorsement of the reconceptualization of American literary history along the national lines that I have been describing. And these lines are implicit in Matthiessen's formulation of such a singular and fictive notion as "*our* religion and education." Who is this unified *we*, we might ask? Nevertheless, within the circle of the univocal, there is a methodological tension in the volume between historical and literary approaches that is repeated in the passage from Matthiessen's review just cited. This tension is still central to American studies today, though now it is focused in the debate over the place of a critical theory that calls into question traditional conceptions of both literature and history, at its best strategically employing each of these disciplines to subvert the traditional autonomy and stability of the other.

In the first part of the passage, before the crucial "But," Matthiessen whole-heartedly endorses the kind of historical perspective finally most closely associated in his own mind with the seminal work of Parrington, who was a contributor to the Foerster volume, and its economic emphasis on the interpretation of American letters. Matthiessen begins his generous "Acknowledgments" to *American Renaissance* by noting: "All my reading of American literature has been done during the era of Van Wyck Brooks and Parrington."[8] In the second part of the paragraph,

however, Matthiessen makes a counter endorsement that places history ("the forces dominant in our political and social past") in the "background" and literature as "aesthetic values" in the foreground. The influences operating on him here, as we know, were those literary practices that would come to be known as the New Criticism, with its emphasis on formalist analysis. In *American Renaissance*, he acknowledges these equally formative influences under the auspices of Coleridge and Eliot, "the two critics who have helped me draw a circle of definition around my subject" (*AR*, xvii).

The language that Matthiessen employed in the second part of the passage is a paraphrase of language used by Harry Hayden Clark in the final essay of the Foerster volume (the reference to Jacksonian democracy and "Rappaccini's Daughter" comes directly from Clark [*RAL*, 196]). Indeed, the trajectory of Matthiessen's passage precisely epitomizes the strategy of Clark's essay, which begins with a strong affirmation of Parrington's historical approach, but ends by situating this approach in the "background," while foregrounding the purely literary-critical approach. The appearance of the Clark essay at the end of the collection was strategic. For in insisting on the gestalt of literary foreground and historical background, the essay repeats the emphasis of Foerster's "Introduction," which ends by exhorting professors of American literature to teach this gestalt to their graduate students (*RAL*, xv). After praising Parrington's contribution to the study of American literature, Clark wrote, in a gesture meant to establish the proper relation between literature and history,

> It remains, however, that the student of American letters is engaged primarily in interpreting American letters, and that, while one gladly admits that his field is but part of a larger whole, and has meaning only in relation to the current trend of human society, yet the literature itself remains the true subject, and the proper focal center is finally the acknowledged masterpieces. (*RAL*, 193)

With its generous acknowledgment of the "larger whole," yet its insistence that the "proper" focus of American literary study is the "acknowledged masterpieces," Clark's language, which was the language of a particular professional nexus, *is* the language of Matthiessen's methodological introduction to *American Renaissance*; and we will have the occasion, in the second part of this essay, to examine this language more closely.

In addition to adopting the methodology of the professional nexus represented by Foerster and Clark, Matthiessen continued in *American Renaissance* the project of nationalizing and professionalizing American literature, represented by the work of Brooks, in the case of nationalization, and by the work of the American Literature Group that I have been sketching. I disagree, then, with Jonathan Arac who asserts that

> Matthiessen's power to authorize an American Renaissance came from his mobilizing certain figures who

were then appropriated in ways contrary to his intentions. Recall the irony that his work produced specialists of a sort that he himself considered "hopefully obsolescent." No less striking is the nationalist force achieved by Matthiessen's emphatically international undertaking.[9]

Far from being the victim of nationalist appropriation, *American Renaissance* embraces the nationalist project at the institutional center of its academic discipline, a project carried on, as I have argued, in the name of internationalism.

The politics of this project are acutely articulated in the interplay of two figures that we have read Fiedler employing at different times to describe the development and stagnation of the study of American literature in the twentieth century: the figures of revolution (of the genteel tradition displaced by that of the moderns from Emerson to James and Eliot), and of the closed, or infernal, circle, where once revolutionary figures freeze in a homogeneous critical glare. We are reminded here by the always possible synonymity of circles and revolutions that what is apparently radical, whatever its innovations, if it does not open itself up to the participation of all members of society, particularly if it does not work for the empowerment of the disempowered, will turn out to have been another form of reaction. Whatever the potential energies released by the renaissance of Emerson, Thoreau, Hawthorne, Melville and Whitman, these energies were virtually frozen by the canonization of these figures in a transcendent realm of "acknowledged masterpieces." And it was the work of canonization, of legitimation and normalization, not the rediscovery of these writers, that *American Renaissance* performed. In 1911, George Santayana could point to "Poe, Hawthorne, and Emerson" as "[t]he three American writers whose personal endowment was perhaps the finest" and to Whitman as "perhaps . . . [t]he one American writer who has left the genteel tradition entirely behind. . . ." In 1915, Brooks could add Thoreau to this list, and Melville joined it after World War I. Matthiessen did not, then, as Arac claims, "rescue" these "once-marginal writers." Rather, he consolidated a "rescue" that had been going on throughout the century. In the Foerster volume, Paul Kaufman in his contribution on the American romantic movement expressed the wisdom of a growing establishment when he stated that "the personalities of the time which appear now as the most important [are] Emerson, Thoreau, Hawthorne, Poe, Melville, [and] Whitman. . . ." (*RAL*, 115).[10] Minus Poe—whose work Matthiessen found "factitious when contrasted with the moral depth of Hawthorne or Melville" (*AR*, xii)—*American Renaissance* established this group exclusively; and, in Fiedler's words, "gives us the sense of a passionate involvement with American letters and life and of a point of view complex enough to achieve those critical insights available to inclusiveness and reasonableness," thought "[i]t is difficult to recognize in any single passage . . . a definitive treatment of a writer or a work."[11]

In the years since his death, Matthiessen's critics, contrary to the argument that I am conducting, have consistently ar-

gued for the high originality of *American Renaissance*, and for the figure of Matthiessen as a heroic genius, working virtually in isolation. Writing in 1950, the year that Matthiessen committed suicide, Henry Nash Smith characterized Matthiessen's achievement in *American Renaissance* as, among other things, a "pionner effort" in applying the New Critical "techniques of close analysis" to the texts of classic American literature. Overall, for Smith, "The effort which Matthiessen made in *American Renaissance* to effect a synthesis of a theory of art (the organic principle), a theory of tragedy, and a thoroughgoing democratic political theory is the key to his career." And this effort was a "gigantic task, perhaps an impossible one. But his commitment to it was heroic. . . ." In *The Rediscovery of American Literature* (1967), Richard Ruland writes:

> For *American Renaissance,* tightly knit and massive as it is, must be taken whole. It not only represents—with a few exceptions—his [Matthiessen's] American literary tradition. It is also an articulation of the total man; it *is* F. O. Matthiessen, with all his compassion and all his commitment to the wide world around him. And it moves in as many directions as he did.

Within the context of the preceding statement, which personifies *American Renaissance* in a monumental way, Ruland's subsequent comment that Matthiessen's book is "a culmination of the critical currents of a half century" has the force not of emphasizing but of erasing those currents by absorbing them into the powerfully personal figure of Matthiessen's *American Renaissance* that Ruland projects. As Ruland notes, Matthiessen's book represents "*his* literary tradition," not, as I am arguing, a tradition that Matthiessen along with certain groups of literary workers helped establish at a particular historical and cultural moment. Ruland's tendency to personify American literature in the name of Matthiessen is implicitly marked in the places where he quotes the Matthiessen paraphrases of the Pattee and the Clark, which we have read, without acknowledging the sources of Matthiessen's pronouncements.[12]

More recently, book-length studies of Matthiessen by Giles B. Gunn (1975) and Frederick C. Stern (1981) continue this strain of devotional criticism by reading *American Renaissance* as a self-contained monument. Gunn terms Matthiessen's book an "astonishing achievement" and an "original discovery" that "seemed to unite the two chief strains characterizing the best American criticism of the past without falling victim either to the ideological posturing that had come to possess the one [social or historical criticism] or to the elitist formalism that had eventually captured the other." In a moment, I will address the question of this unity, which I read, contrary to Gunn, as a *contradiction* between Matthiessen's socialist politics and the politics of his aesthetics. Stern, who ends his assessment of *American Renaissance* by quoting Smith's characterization of Matthiessen's labor as "heroic," refers to the book as "Matthiessen's masterpiece" and suggests that the book transcends its particular time and place; for through it Matthiessen "seems to speak clearly to each generation, as he did to his own, and that says a great deal about his work."[13] Yet it is clear that a significant part of the audience for Stern's own book, Americanists of the present day, has not heard the Matthiessen of *American Renaissance* speak clearly, at least not in the progressive way that Stern intends. For in matters of race, gender, and class, which we will examine in *American Renaissance*, Matthiessen's book has some disturbingly repressed things to say, things that find articulation nevertheless in the conflict between Matthiessen's socialist politics and the politics of his aesthetics.

Neither Gunn nor Stern attempts to read *American Renaissance* ideologically, that is, in relation to the institutional establishment of American literature. Gunn offers us no more than an adoring paraphrase of what he sees as the major themes of Matthiessen's book. And Stern's criticism, when it occurs, is based on what he perceives as lapses in the internal logic of the book. Matthiessen's close readings, Stern argues, for example, do not take into account the problem of their own subjectivity.

In a 1983 essay on Matthiessen, Leo Marx refers to *American Renaissance* as a "masterwork" and, like Gunn, understands Matthiessen as "bringing . . . together" in the volume, unproblematically, the historical and formalist approaches to literary study. Following Ruland, Marx tells us that "Matthiessen completed the job of liberating America's cultural past from the deadly grip of WASP Victorianism," culminating the work of "Van Wyck Brooks, Irving Babbitt, Paul Elmer More, Stuart Sherman, and H. L. Mencken." Marx also acknowledges that "the authority of [the] official canon had been undermined by the work of D. H. Lawrence, V. L. Parrington, and Yvor Winters. . . ." Yet while we read Marx suggesting institutional affiliations for *American Renaissance*, though he nowhere mentions the Foerster volume, and while we have read Fiedler asserting that by 1928 "the battle" against the genteel tradition "ha[d] been really won," Marx, like the other critics I am reviewing, gives *American Renaissance* the credit for winning that battle almost singlehandedly: "It is hard to remember how provincial, belletristic, and unremittingly genteel the reigning conception of our literature was before the publication of *American Renaissance*." And in *American Renaissance*, Matthiessen "revealed *for the first time* just how inventive, bold, and intellectually robust the classic American writers had been" (my emphasis).[14] Here, in what amounts to a metaphysics of American literary history that obscures a complex cultural machinery, the end of a particular movement also becomes its origin.

For Marx, *American Renaissance* "marks an important turning point in American studies" because of "Matthiessen's emphasis upon the contradictions rather than the harmonies of meaning, value, and purpose" in the five writers he studies. And this emphasis "signaled the virtual disappearance of the older, complacent idea of our national culture as an essentially homogeneous, unified whole."[15] In what follows, I will argue something else: that *American Renaissance* composes a struggle to avoid or repress crucial conflicts in order to produce the "idea of our national culture as an essentially homogeneous, unified whole."[16] What gives the book its energy today is the possibility of reading the signs of this struggle and what they have to tell us about the possible conflicts between literary theory and political practice.

Within the literary history I am articulating, in contradistinction to the critics I have just reviewed, the force of *American Renaissance*, its immediate acceptance by its academic audience as being definitive of a whole literature, resided not in any striking originality, but in its ability to consolidate by focusing what was already the growing consensus of this largely white, male, middle-class, and Protestant-oriented audience. The book's passion was not the passion of a partisan cause that challenged or contradicted its intended audience, but a passion into which a growing majority of the professional constituents of American literature could fit a set of ideas that was emerging as the establishment platform of the discipline. Its complexity resulted not from the difficulty of an idea or feeling, but from its ability to contain or absorb the ideas of its constituency. *American Renaissance* was, in short, a classically corporate or consensual project. Representing the program of those who were establishing the new discipline of American literature, *American Renaissance* exerted a corporate power, even as, in the words of Kermit Vanderbilt, Matthiessen "disdained the MLA and therefore community with its ALG [American Literature Group] membership."[17] This corporate power, projecting its own image as canonical, substituted one group of white, Protestant, essentially middle-class male authors for another group of the same race, gender, and class. And this new group, as its predecessor had been, became within the conjoined institutions of academia and journalism the homogeneous, exclusive representative of "our" *national* literature. If *American Renaissance* helped "liberat[e] America's cultural past from the deadly grip of WASP Victorianism," it also helped place this past within the confines of WASP modernism.

These literary politics, with their emphasis on a homogeneous nationalism, contradicted in crucial ways Matthiessen's politics, the socialism to which I will turn in a moment. But then, as I am arguing, *American Renaissance* was not Matthiessen's book. For not only did he repress his politics in its production; he repressed his homosexuality, and this in a book that is centrally concerned with the question of embodiment. The social and professional danger in revealing his sexual identity or even sympathizing openly with homosexuality would have been considerable. But was it necessary to discuss Whitman's homoeroticism, when he does so in passing, within the context of the "pathological" and the "regressive" (*AR*, 535)? Such a context betrays the sustaining influence that Matthiessen's own homosexuality played in his life through his long relationship with the painter Russell Cheyney.[18] Like the radical Holgrave marrying the democrat Phoebe and thereby becoming a substantial property holder in Hawthorne's *The House of the Seven Gables*, in his scholarly writing life Matthiessen accepted the strictures that enabled him to produce a book of corporate power that his political life opposed.[19]

Throughout the thirties and forties, right up until his suicide in 1950, Matthiessen worked hard in support and defense of a variety of left wing causes.[20] He worked courageously as well, particularly in the post-World War II years, when in the growing hysteria over "reds" that marked the witch-hunting inception of the Cold War, he stood publicly by his left wing convictions and condemned the purging of individuals from American institutions because of their political views. *American Renaissance* is particularly ironic in this context because its nationalist literary politics make it absorbable by precisely the kind of liberal anti-communism that Matthiessan opposed. As Matthiessen wrote in his suicide note, he was "a Christian and a socialist."[21] And as he remarks in *From the Heart of Europe* (1948), an account of his 1947 sojourn in Salzburg and Prague that takes the form of a sustained meditation on his long commitment to socialism and that seems to me his most important, because most urgent, book, "It is as a Christian that I find my strongest propulsion to being a socialist. . . . [T]o love thy neighbor as thyself . . . seems to me an imperative to social action."[22] For Matthiessen the apotheosis of his socialism was glimpsed, briefly, in the Prague of the days immediately preceding the Communist takeover of 1948. Recalling himself listening to Hewlett Johnson, the Dean of Canterbury, give a speech in acceptance of an honorary degree, Matthiessen expressed "a faith . . . [in] a third way that a just man should accept between present-day Russia and present-day America, between—to give them their worst names—the dictator's corruptions of the communist ideal and the capitalist's corruptions of the democratic ideal. It would not be a compromise, but a more complete socialism which would do justice both to the individual and to society . . .", a socialism, as Matthiessen understood it, that would be based on the complementary relationship between political and economic freedoms (*FHE*, 111). The vision here is decidedly internationalist, as opposed to the internationalism that from Brooks to the American Literature Group to *American Renaissance* existed to buttress a decidedly nationalist vision, rather than to question it.

If Matthiessen's Christianity was the motivating force of his socialism, it was also, by his own admission, the bar to his becoming a Marxist. In his 1949 Hopwood lecture, **"The Responsibilities of the Critic,"** delivered in a time that Matthiessen recognized as one of intensifying aesthetic and political rigidities—the hegemony of formalism in the academy and of anti-communism everywhere—he "recall[ed] the atmosphere of the early 1930s, of the first years of the last depression, when the critical pendulum had swung to the opposite pole, from the formalists to the Marxists" and then identified himself as "not a Marxist myself but a Christian" (*RC*, 10). But, he went on to say,

> despite all the excesses and exaggerated claims of the Marxists of the thirties, I still believe that the principles of Marxism—so much under fire now—can have an

immense value in helping us to see and comprehend our literature. . . . No educated American can afford to be ignorant of them, or to be delinquent in realizing that there is much common ground between these principles and any healthily dynamic America.

> (*RC*, 11)

Then, characteristically, Matthiessen's thought revolves:

> This is not to say that Marxism gives what I consider an adequate view of the nature of man, or that it or any other economic theory can provide a substitute for the critic's essential painstaking discipline in the interplay between form and content in concrete works of art.

> (*RC*, 11)

The movement suggested by these quotations is one not of revolution but of continual circumscription of Marxism by Christianity or of content by form or of history by literature, in which each of these pairs is a figure of the others. This movement is exemplary of the problem in Matthiessen's thought that divides his political life from his literary work and not incidentally produces tensions in his political life as well. The problem is a conflict between each of the terms in a pair that Matthiessen reconciles in his revolving rhetoric without ever articulating the conflict as a conflict and working through it, perhaps to a new critical vocabulary that, avoiding the reductions of a purely economic Marxism, could have brought together his political, religious and aesthetic concerns. Matthiessen's contemporaries Kenneth Burke and Walter Benjamin worked in this direction.[23] Matthiessen, on the other hand, operates in the optative mood with this problem. In this mood, without contradiction, he can say at one moment that the "prime responsibility" of the critic "is to keep open the life-giving communications between art and society" and at the next that "the critic's primary function . . . must [be to] judge the work of art as work of art" (*RC*, 9, 14). He elides the contradiction, however, at the cost of a repression. This repression of his social by his aesthetic vision creates an irony in the explicitly democratic appeal of *American Renaissance* by placing this appeal in a context of formalist literary values that implicitly contradict Matthiessen's evocation of "common readers" (*AR*, xi). In his Hopwood lecture, Matthiessen spoke of a critical "point," where

> the responsible intellectual in our time can [not] avoid being concerned with politics. It is at this point [he continued] that my divergence becomes most complete from the formalists who have followed in the wake of Eliot, as well as from Eliot himself, whose reverence for the institutions of monarchy and aristocracy seems virtually meaningless for life in America.

> (*RC*, 10)

What Matthiessen believed or let himself believe in *American Renaissance* was that there was another point where a "pure" formalism and these anti-democratic values could be separated, where democracy and formalism could be reconciled. Examining some of the key theoretical terms in *American Renaissance*—"masterpiece," "organic," "symbol," and "myth"—I want to suggest in what follows how the politics of Matthiessen's aesthetics contradict the politics of the socialist vision to which he was committed.

. . . . .

In "Method and Scope," Matthiessen's methodological introduction to *American Renaissance,* the notion of "masterpieces" (*AR*, vii) of "great art" is a given. The five writers to be considered in this five year period (1850-55) all wrote masterpieces, with, in Matthiessen's judgment, the exception of Emerson who "wrote no masterpiece" but "was the cow from which the rest drew their milk" (*AR*, xii). In this manifesto, "the critic's chief responsibility" is

> to evaluate [books] in accordance with the enduring requirements for great art. . . . His obligation is to examine an author's resources of language and of genres, in a word, to be preoccupied with form . . . [which] 'was nothing else than the entire resolution of the intellectual, sentimental, and emotional material into the concrete reality of the poetic image and word, which alone has aesthetic value.'
>
> (*AR*, xi)

However, Matthiessen does not define in this manifesto what "the enduring requirements for great art" are. In one sense these requirements are simply assumed. Yet in the course of his book some concrete suggestions are given so that a conception of the great book emerges. For Matthiessen, the disciple of Coleridge, no work of art can be great unless it is "organic," a term that is synonymous with another Matthiessen favorite, "whole." Both of these terms, I want to emphasize, were central to the critical project that Matthiessen represents in *American Renaissance*. The question is, then, what kind of *values* do these figures of the organic and the whole evoke for Matthiessen within the consensual politics of his book? Primarily, they evoke what Matthiessen refers to as democratic values: "The one common denominator of my five writers . . . was their devotion to the possibilities of democracy" (*AR*, ix). The next question, then, is: how does Matthiessen define the organic in terms of the democratic?

In the first place, quoting Coleridge, Matthiessen defines the organic as a mode, the highest mode, of individualism:

> No work of true genius dares want its appropriate form, neither indeed is there any danger of this. As it must not, so genius can not, be lawless; for it is even this that constitutes it genius—the power of acting creatively under laws of its own origination. . . . The form is mechanic, when on any given material we impress a pre-determined form, not necessarily arising out of the properties of the material. . . . The organic form, on the other hand, is innate; it shapes, as it develops, itself from within, and the fulness of its development is one and the same with the perfection of its outward form. Such as the life is, such is the form.
>
> (*AR*, 133-34)

The organic is the unique, the individual, what develops naturally from within, rather than being imposed artifi-

cially from without. This is genius, an extreme and reductive opposition between the individual and society, the "within" and the "without." And as Matthiessen develops this idea of genius in the opening two sections of chapter 4, he links it "to the determination of the American writers of [Emerson's] day to speak out of a direct relationship to experience, and not through borrowed modes" (*AR*, 140), taking his text here implicitly from the opening paragraph of the "Introduction" to Emerson's *Nature*.

The notion of the organic invokes for Matthiessen the vision of an American genius free of the past, even though considerable energies will be spent in *American Renaissance* placing the five writers in the Western literary tradition (this is one way an international, or comparative, approach buttresses national authority). And in the section on Horatio Greenough, Matthiessen links this idea of the organic, of national genius, to what he refers to as the "male principle":

> Emerson recorded in his journal (1852) several passages of Greenough's extraordinarily pungent conversation, and rejoiced in him as one of the best proofs of our native capability. Emerson had probably forgotten that years before, just after he had written *Nature*, he had taken this same man as an instance of his conviction that there is "no genius in the Fine Arts in this country," that they are all feminine, with no character. To be sure, Emerson was making his standards exacting and somewhat arbitrary. . . . Nevertheless, the reasons he gave for the want of male principle in American genius were extremely cogent: the fatal imitation of Europe, and the fact that American arts "are not called out by the necessity of the people."
>
> (*AR*, 143)

As Matthiessen develops his definition of the organic, he equates it first with a certain ahistorical notion of pure Americanness, and this pure Americanness in turn becomes equated with the male, the female as "feminine" being exiled, by default if nothing else, to the realm of the inorganic, the mediocre (what has no genius or character) and the artificial.

For Matthiessen the apotheosis of the organic, what we might call the democratic sublime, is in the words of Greenough, whom he quotes enthusiastically, "'the symbolism of man's body.' That symbol gave Greenough his central clue for his interpretation of life:

> 'This stupendous form, towering as a lighthouse, commanding by its posture a wide horizon, standing in relation to the brutes where the spire stands in relation to the lowly colonnades of Greece and Egypt, touching earth with only one half the soles of its feet—it tells of majesty and dominion by that upreared spine, of duty by those unencumbered hands. Where is the ornament of this frame? It is all beauty, its motion is grace, no combination of harmony ever equalled, for expression and variety, its poised and stately gait; its voice is music. . . .'"

For Matthiessen "Greenough's rhetoric" represents "man in his full revolutionary and democratic splendor as the base and measure of society. The main source for great art lies in following the body's command to create a comparably organic structure." Yet if we look at the rhetoric that Greenough uses and that Matthiessen adopts in his own context wholeheartedly to represent the male body (and make no mistake, the phrase "man's body" with its attendant rejection of the female is not being used generically to indicate all humans), it appears not as the rhetoric of democracy, certainly not of egalitarian or socialist democracy, but with its use of words like "stupendous," "towering," "commanding," "majesty," and "dominion" as the rhetoric of manifest destiny or imperialism. Indeed, presenting us approvingly with Greenough's mistrust of the reformer—he "was even cool to the abolitionist"—with his attraction to "the savage's brute vitality," with his "welcoming acceptance of passion and belligerence, his view of social adjustment as the result of an inevitable struggle between warring forces," and with his notion of "unity" as "'the subordination of the parts to the whole'" (*AR*, 151), Matthiessen suggests an ideal figure of democracy that comes perilously close in its social Darwinist vision to the masculine cult of the worship of the state as incarnating the purest form of the natural that characterized the growing fascism of Nazi Germany, which Matthiessen opposed so vigorously through his Popular Front politics as he was writing *American Renaissance*. Indeed, the phrase "inevitable struggle between warring forces" was part of the rhetoric of the Popular Front.[24]

When at the end of his section on Greenough, Matthiessen tells us that Greenough "simply insisted that the artist must find his impulse and his completion in the community," in "'the hearts and heads of common men'" (*AR*, 152), we may feel that we have entered a realm of contradiction, where the imperial male body, the apotheosis of that commanding individualism that Matthiessen recognizes as genius, finds its culmination in the figure of the commonality of working men, of craftsmen to be exact, a figure of democratic, if strictly male, communism.

What we can begin to see is that Matthiessen's conception of great American art is founded on an unexamined contradiction between the imperial and the democratic that constitutes the doctrine of Manifest Destiny, which Matthiessen resisted vigorously in his opposition to one of its twentieth-century forms, the Truman Doctrine. In *American Renaissance* this contradiction expresses a desire to overcome the distance between the artist/intellectual/scholar and the mass of common men (there is no sense in substituting "people" for "men" here for it seems to me that Matthiessen adopted the rhetoric of "manliness," characteristic of the nineteenth century that he is projecting). This desire formed the basis for his political work, which continually looked to the American labor movement as the logical base for an American socialism.

In *American Renaissance,* this desire expresses itself most strongly in its repression of the distance between intellectual and worker and nowhere is the distance repressed more strongly than in Matthiessen's methodological intro-

duction, where he tries to argue that his choice of his five writers is not "arbitrary" but, in the century that has followed the American Renaissance, has been the choice of "the successive generations of common readers, who make the decisions" (*AR*, x, xi). To say the least, this formulation substitutes a certain myth of the unanimity of literary history for the partisan politics of that history.

Using Matthiessen's own language, but in an oppositional way, I would call the theory of canonization he articulates here the *myth* of "common readers, who make the decisions" about the hierarchy of great books. And what I want to call Matthiessen's myth of common readers, the myth that as if by magic reconciles the conflict between genius and democracy (between the imperial male body and the body of working men), finds its counterpart in what Matthiessen sees as the central myth of Emerson's age: the paradoxical myth of the hero as the mass of common men, or, as Matthiessen quotes Thoreau, "'the simplest and obscurest of men'" (*AR*, 633). The paradox is expressed in characteristically excruciating form by Emerson, whom Matthiessen also quotes: "'What is best written or done by genius in the world, was no man's work, but came by wide social labor, when a thousand wrought like one, sharing the same impulse'" (*AR*, 634). Genius, according to Emerson here, is everyman or, more precisely, no man. Matthiessen puts it without the irony in paraphrasing Whitman who "believed the worship of heroes to be poisonous" (*AR*, 633). What this suggests is that the language of democracy, if one understands it in the terms of socialism, as Matthiessen does in his explicit politics, and the language of heroism (of genius, of great art, of masterpieces—for all of these notions are synonymous) are entirely incompatible, and thus inevitably in conflict.[25] But, for example, while Matthiessen believed that "political revolution now can and must be completed by an economic revolution . . . otherwise the immense concentration of wealth in a few hands makes for a renewed form of tyranny" (*FHE*, 83), he could not bring himself to consider that the unequal distribution of wealth in the economic and the unequal distribution of talent in the artistic sphere might bear a significant relation to one another; that to endorse the idea of genius or masterpieces was one way of circumscribing the very revolution he desired. Without entertaining such considerations, he remained trapped, unconsciously, within the terms of the conflict.

For Matthiessen *myth* is a way of reconciling these terms. The idea of myth itself may appear to reconcile the conflict; for myths come from the "folk," yet are a component of all "great art." The term itself, however, as Matthiessen uses it, does nothing but repress the conflict in various ways. For myth, which carries with it the idea of the "universal" (another of the properties of "great art"), translates the powerful dissonances of race, gender, and class that compose history into the forged harmony of the *symbol* without ever bringing these dissonances into consciousness. For Matthiessen the symbol is the intended vehicle of reconciliation of the mind/body split, the split that for him is emblematic of the division of labor between the intellectual and the working class and historically is contained by the dissonances to which I have just alluded. Yet as Matthiessen continually describes it, the symbol itself is a symbol of its own powerful divisiveness. For in its Platonic, then Christian, then Puritan origin, Matthiessen's symbol, rather than democratically reconciling conflicting parties, represents the whole hierarchy of privilege that American life and politics is supposed to stand against: the privilege of Christian, white, or Western European, middle-class men from New England. Simultaneously and inseparably, the symbol privileges a particular kind of writing and a particular literary tradition, what Matthiessen refers to as "the dominant strain in modern art that leads from Hawthorne through the younger James to Proust, from Poe through the symbolists to Eliot" (*AR*, 10).

In *American Renaissance* the prime way that Matthiessen harmonizes the conflict between genius and democracy, a conflict which is itself a sublimation of class, gender, and racial conflict, is in the myth that antebellum America "was still mainly agrarian." Demographically this was certainly true. But in *American Renaissance* this statement projects a pastoral landscape, typical of a certain American nostalgia. Essentially, we can find no Indians being removed from or buried in this landscape, no slaves working it, no speculators exploiting it, no women or workers organizing in it; the farmer and the businessman have no relation to one another in it (the farmer, for example, is not seen as part of a market economy, as a businessman himself or as dependent on businessmen); country and city do not interpenetrate; cities, if seen at all, are seen as dim outlines on the very periphery of a peaceful landscape. And in a culminating group portrait of his five writers, Matthiessen places them in this landscape, "close to the soil," to the organic, which as we have seen is his way both of insisting on their genius and bringing them close to the democratic mass, who in this particular Jeffersonian myth are the farmers or country people: "All of Emerson's pictures could be those of a village parson. Melville as an old New Yorker still continued to look like a sailor, though not the 'rubicund sailor' to whom Whitman seemed akin in Eakins's canvas. Thoreau struck a surprised admirer as being indistinguishable from 'a respectable husbandman,' and Hawthorne . . . retained in his language the marks of his 'ineradicable rusticity'" (*AR*, 635).[26]

In his methodological introduction, after implying the pastoral vision of the United States that will dominate *American Renaissance*, Matthiessen immediately suggests a situation of conflict with "the last struggle of the liberal spirit of the eighteenth century in conflict with the rising forces of exploitation." But he quickly moves away from this political "background" against which his writers write to the "foreground" of "the writing itself" (*AR*, ix), a move that is typical of what I have been describing as the unconscious rhetorical strategy of *American Renaissance*, which as soon as it approaches a subject like slavery or class conflict sublimates the political issue in a "larger" or more "complex" aesthetic or metaphysical issue. More importantly, as I have tried to suggest, this movement of

foregrounding and backgrounding was the gesture of a professional program that, until recently, projected a part of American literature for the whole.

The fiction of national unanimity in the literary "revolution" that *American Renaissance* consolidated is analogous to the fiction of "We, the people," when the Constitution was first framed and revolutionary promises of equality were first circumscribed, by a group of property holding, white, Christian males, who effectively abrogated certain crucial political rights of women, blacks, American Indians, and members of the working class who did not hold property.

Today, if the fiction that the Preamble of the Constitution was in the days of its framing has been actualized in concrete ways, this actualization remains a fiction for many whom we have denied the economic freedom—freedom from poverty—upon which the actualization of political freedom rests. If the equalizing energies of the American Revolution are not to freeze permanently in a circle, and they have seemed particularly frozen in this figure over the last eight years, then the work that needs to be done rests on the articulation of the equation of political and economic freedoms, in which Matthiessen believed. The Constitution, read within its capitalist context, has not been able to produce such an equation, and that is why I am committed to reading it within the context of a contradiction in terms, *capitalist democracy*, which, as "we" have read it as a reconciliation, virtual or actual, has circumscribed the American Revolution.

At the same time that we have witnessed over the last eight years the circumscribing of potentially revolutionary energies, particularly those energies that were released by the Civil Rights, Women's, and Anti-War Movements in the time between 1954 and 1980, we have witnessed in American Studies, in part as an insistence on the necessity of these energies over and against the repression of them in the Reagan years, whet appears as a radical questioning of the homogeneous national figure of our literature that, as I have argued, was most visibly insitutionalized by Matthiessen's *American Renaissance*. Race, gender, and class are becoming the constitutive categories within which the disciplines of American literature and American Studies are re-imagining the figure of the national. And this re-imagining process is being linked to important theoretical questions about the politics of constructing canons. Yet if Americanists are not to freeze this work of constituting an authentically pluralistic American literary history, one without "masterpieces," into another infernal circle, then we must make literary history not an analogy to but a part of Constitutional history; that is, we must read it as a part of everyday politics in the United States. And we must work to direct this politics in a radically egalitarian direction. To do this we must link, in terms of extended social action, the work of empowering previously excluded texts within the academy to the work of empowering those constituencies, represented in these texts, that are now excluded from the academy and its texts—including ironically the very texts that represent them—because of poverty and the immediately attendant problem of illiteracy.

The crisis Americanists face or ignore today—and who should be more committed to the possibilities of democracy?—is the crisis of the severance of democratic theory from democratic practice. It is within the context of this crisis that the example of Matthiessen remains crucial for us. For while, as I have argued, his literary work, **American Renaissance**, circumscribes American revolutionary possibilities, his political work is in important ways an admirably committed engagement with the opening of these possibilities. This relationship between **American Renaissance** and Matthiessen's political work or, more precisely, his conscious political work, *mirrors* in a figural way the current situation in American Studies, where the best scholarly work is committed to the engagement of revolutionary possibilities, but where there is no concerted political work by the academy to extend these possibilities to the disempowered of the larger community.

Matthiessen lacked or resisted a critical vocabulary that could translate his democratic politics into the writing of literary history. Today, because of the conjunction of European theoretical concerns and an American history that is concerned with the dynamics of race, gender, and class in global ways, Americanists can imagine such a vocabulary and the literary history or, better, histories it might project. But unless we can translate these histories of social vision into social action, we will remain in a circle more tightly closed than the one Matthiessen drew with **American Renaissance**. In the memory of his marriage with Russell Cheyney and his conscious political work, Matthiessen potentially liberates himself from this circle, as we imagine him writing a book in keeping with this memory and ourselves living lives in keeping with this imagined book, which we are now able to write.

Notes

1. Leslie A. Fiedler, "Love Is Not Enough," *Yale Review* 42 (Spring 1953): 456-57.

2. Leslie A. Fiedler, "American Literature," in *Contemporary Literary Scholarship: A Critical Review*, ed. Lewis Leary (New York, 1958), 168-69, 158. The perjorative phrase "genteel tradition," which became the common currency of the literary "revolution" to which Fiedler is referring, was coined by George Santayana in 1911 in a lecture entitled "The Genteel Tradition in American Philosophy" (see: *The Genteel Tradition: Nine Essays by George Santayana*, ed. Douglas L. Wilson [Cambridge, Mass., 1967]. As Santayana employs it, the phrase is in an important way redundant; for "genteel tradition" refers to the idea of tradition itself, as a debilitating or blocking factor. Santayana, then, following the Emerson of *Nature*, is calling for American letters to take up "an original relation to the universe," and like Emerson at certain moments, he defines this relation as "the

sphere of the American man," relegating the "genteel tradition" to that "of the American woman" (*The Genteel Tradition*, 40). As we will see, Matthiessen will follow this gender division in *American Renaissance*. I have written about the rhetoric of this division in my book *The Trans-Parent: Sexual Politics in the Language of Emerson* (Baltimore, 1981). And there is by now, of course, a considerable body of literature on the sexual politics involved in the formation of the American canon. Nina Baym's essay "Melodramas of Beset Manhood: How Theories of American Fiction Exclude Woman Authors" (*American Quarterly* 33 [1981]: 123-39) remains an excellent introduction to the theoretical dynamics of the problem. And the historical dynamics of it, in relation to race as well, are ably covered by Paul Lauter in "Race and Gender in the Shaping of the American Literary Canon: A Case Study from the Twenties," *Feminist Studies* 9 (1983): 435-63. In addition to the ideology of gender that generates the notion of a "genteel tradition," there are ambiguities in the historical coordinates of the phrase. In his 1930 Nobel Prize speech, for example, Sinclair Lewis could cite William Dean Howells as an exemplar of the genteel tradition. Yet in his own time Howells was attacked by those critics who would be dubbed "genteel" by Brooks, Mencken, *et al* for his championing of the "realists." And in his seminal essay "America's Coming of Age" (1915) Brooks could group Emerson with the genteel tradition of Lowell and Holmes and yet see him as the very antithesis of that tradition as well. For a description of some of these historical problems, see: William Van O'Connor, *An Age of Criticism: 1900-1950* (Chicago, 1952); and Robert P. Falk, "The Literary Criticism of the Genteel Decades: 1870-1900," *The Development of American Literary Criticism*, ed. Floyd Stovall (Chapel Hill, 1955).

3. Fiedler, "American Literature," 158, 159. The relationship between academics and journalists in the growth of American literature is more complex, less simply oppositional, than the quotes from Fiedler allow. In the introduction to his book *The Rediscovery of American Literature: Premises of Critical Taste, 1900-1940* (Cambridge, Mass., 1967), Richard Ruland suggests the matrix of literary journalists and academics that were operative in revising the "genteel tradition." Sometimes, clearly, the effort was collaborative. For example, Fred Lewis Pattee's essay "A Call for a Literary Historian," which was a part of the influential academic collection *The Reinterpretation of American Literature: Some Contributions Toward the Understanding of its Historical Development*, ed. Norman Foerster (New York, 1928), first appeared in 1924 in Mencken's journal *The American Mercury*. Still, the trend in the field was increasingly toward academic domination, which is the *status quo* today.

4. Van Wyck Brooks, "Letters and Leadership," in *Three Essays on America* (New York, 1934), 134, 127, 129, 152-53.

5. Brooks, *Three Essays on America*, 37. What needs to be considered in relation to this internationalism is the internationalism of the American Marxist writers and critics of the early thirties, before this internationalism, as Richard Pells argues, was nationalized by the Popular Front politics of the mid and late thirties (Richard H. Pells, *Radical Visions and American Dreams: Culture and Social Thought in the Depression Years* [New York, 1973]). For example, the last chapter of Granville Hicks's *The Great Tradition* (New York, 1933) gives, in terms of gender and ethnic European origin, a more diverse group of important contemporary American writers than was being developed in the universities.

6. Foerster, *The Reinterpretation of American Literature,* vii. For the full citation of this text, see note 3, Hereafter I will cite the Foerster volume in the body of my text as *RAL*. The name of the individual who wrote a particular essay will precede the designation of the volume's title when necessary.

7. *The Responsibilities of the Critic: Essays and Reviews by F. O. Matthiessen*, selected by John Rackliffe (New York, 1952), 181. Hereafter cited as *RC* in the body of my essay.

8. F. O. Matthiessen, *American Renaissance: Art and Expression in the Age of Emerson and Whitman* (Oxford, 1941), xvii. Hereafter cited in the body of my essay as *AR*.

9. Jonathan Arac, "F. O. Matthiessen: Authorizing an American Renaissance," *The American Renaissance Reconsidered: Selected Papers from the English Institute, 1982-83*, ed. Walter Benn Michaels and Donald E. Pease (Baltimore, 1985), 93.

10. Santayana, *The Genteel Tradition*, 43, 52; Brooks, *Three Essays on America*, 39; Arac, "F. O. Matthiessen," 106. Arac appears deeply divided on the cultural power of *American Renaissance*, articulating the books reactionary strain at the same time that he tries to find a progressive strain in it.

11. Fiedler, "American Literature," 168.

12. Henry Nash Smith, "*American Renaissance*" in *F. O. Matthiessen (1902-1950): A Collective Portrait*, ed. Paul M. Sweezy and Leo Huberman (New York, 1950), 55, 59, 60; and Richard Ruland, *The Rediscovery of American Literature: Premises of Critical Taste, 1900-1940* (Cambridge, Mass., 1967), 231, 257, 222, 224.

13. Giles B. Gunn, *F. O. Matthiessen: The Critical Achievement* (Seattle, 1975), 68, 69, 70; Frederick C. Stern, *F. O. Matthiessen: Christian Socialist as Critic* (Chapel Hill, 1981), 174, 106, 173.

14. Leo Marx, "Double Consciousness and the Cultural Politics of F. O. Matthiessen," *Monthly Review* 34 (February 1983): 34, 39.

15. Marx, "Double Consciousness," 40.

16. Jonathan Arac also disagrees with Marx's assessment that *American Renaissance* expresses the contradictions of the 1850s. His essay explores cogently what he calls Matthiessen's "rhetoric of 'wholeness.'" See "F. O. Matthiessen," 91.

17. Kermit Vanderbilt, *American Literature and the Academy: The Roots, Growth, and Maturity of a Profession* (Philadelphia, 1986), 475.

18. See *Rat & the Devil: Journal Letters of F. O. Matthiessen and Russell Cheyney*, ed. Louis Hyde (Hamden, Conn., 1978).

19. While I do not have the space to develop it here, a reading of Matthiessen's reading of Hawthorne's *The House of the Seven Gables* is central to understanding the repression of Matthiessen's socialist politics that drives *American Renaissance*. Matthiessen's rationalization of Hawthorne's reprehensible stand on slavery through an appeal to an aesthetics that represents "complex actuality" rather than the "simple contrasts of black and white" (*AR*, 318) only serves, under the circumstances, to radically call into question, that is, to politicize, the idea of "complexity" itself. Within this context the socialist Holgrave's marriage to the democrat Phoebe—a "reconciliation . . . somewhat too lightly made," which "is meant finally to transcend the old brutal separation of classes" (*AR*, 332)—suggests itself as an apt figure for Matthiessen's reconciliation with consensual literary politics, precisely because both reconciliations, Holgrave's and Matthiessen's, cannot be lightly written off, cannot be ascribed, as Matthiessen does with Hawthorne's happy ending, to the essential "innocence" of a particular "milieu" (*AR*, 333, 334).

20. Stern provides a comprehensive and cogent list of Matthiessen's political activities. He also provides a sympathetic and sensitively balanced commentary on these activities and the questions they raise. See *F. O. Matthiessen: Christian Socialist as Critic*, 15-31.

21. John Rackliffe, "Notes for a Character Study," *F. O. Matthiessen (1902-1950): A Collective Portrait*, 92.

22. F. O. Matthiessen, *From the Heart of Europe* (Oxford, 1948), 82. Hereafter cited as *FHE* in the body of my essay.

23. Burke deals with the form/content (literature/politics) duality by translating this duality into the realm of rhetoric, always historically a political realm. Working from a Marxist perspective whose complex sense of culture-in-history is not reducible to the base/superstructure model, Benjamin makes the basis of his work a political critique of his *devotion* to art, of "masterpieces," something Matthiessen is unable to do. For comparison see Arac's comments on Benjamin and Matthiessen in "F. O. Matthiessen," 105-106. In his *Monthly Review* essay Leo Marx discusses the relation of Marxism and Matthiessen's literary practice in *American Renaissance* and con-

cludes that Matthiessen's "conspicuous inattention to Marx and Marxist thought in a book notable for its wide-ranging allusiveness and its highly individualized perspective . . . is in large measure attributable . . . to Matthiessen's overreaction to the shallow, mechanistic Marxism that prevailed during the 1930s" ("Double Consciousness," 49). Burke and Benjamin are counter-examples here, although Benjamin must be considered within a different social and political context. But they moved against the mainstream of both liberal and Marxist thought and were marginal figures in their own time as a result of their intellectual risks.

24. In "The Work of Art in the Age of Mechanical Reproduction," Benjamin equates the "uncontrolled . . . application" of "a number of outmoded concepts, such as creativity and genius, eternal value and mystery" with Fascism. At the end of his essay, he contrasts Fascism and Communism, noting that the former aestheticizes politics, while the latter politicizes art. In his enthusiasm for Greenough and the vocabulary of the "organic," Matthiessen is aestheticizing politics. See Walter Benjamin, *Illuminations*, ed. Hannah Arendt and trans. Harry Zohn (New York, 1969), 218, 242. See Arac, "F. O. Matthiessen," 96-97, for an interpretation of how Popular Front politics found their way into *American Renaissance*. I would like to thank Gary Kulik for calling my attention to the Popular Front context of the phrase "inevitable struggle between warring forces."

25. In "A Call for a Literary Historian," Pattee insisted that "the new historian must struggle with the unsettled question as to whether or not literature [as *art*] is really possible in a democracy" (15-16). Matthiessen never struggled with this question; he answered it simply, "yes." At the end of "F. O. Matthiessen," Arac asks: "Can one espouse and further 'all the people' by writing 'masterwork?'" (106). The answer is emphatically "no," and this answer is the beginning to any future work.

26. In *The Reinterpretation of American Literature,* Paul Kaufman, quoting the Beards, provides an antipastoral portrait for the age of Emerson (118).

James W. Tuttleton (essay date 1989)

SOURCE: "Politics and Art in the Criticism of F. O. Matthiessen," in *The New Criterion*, Vol. 7, No. 10, June, 1989, pp. 4-13.

[*In the following essay, Tuttleton perceives a discrepancy between Matthiessen's literary criticism and his political views.*]

> Down with non-partisan writers!
>
> —V. I. Lenin

At the time of his suicide in 1950, the Harvard professor F. O. Matthiessen was one of the most influential figures in the development of the academic criticism of American literature. Others—like Cleanth Brooks and Robert Penn Warren, William Empson and R. P. Blackmur, F. R. Leavis and Lionel Trilling—had greater critical authority and commanded a larger audience of intelligent and cultivated readers. But they were part of a wider cultural world. Matthiessen was pre-eminently a man of the university. Even so, his literary influence radiated from his own classroom and writing into the lectures and seminars of others, and from there to generations of students of American literature. Why is he worth remembering?

After the impressionistic study *Sarah Orne Jewett* in 1929 and Eliotic reflections on *Translation: An Elizabethan Art* in 1931, Matthiessen turned his full attention to American literature and attained great influence with *The Achievement of T. S. Eliot: An Essay on the Nature of Poetry* (1935) and *American Renaissance: Art and Expression in the Age of Emerson and Whitman* (1941). According to Lewis Leary in *American Literature: A Study and Research Guide*, *American Renaissance* was "perhaps the single most influential study of literature in America at the middle of the nineteenth century." It did "more than any other book," as Richard Brodhead has observed, "to set the [nineteenth-century] American canon as it would be taught in American universities after World War II." Widely praised for its magisterial treatment of the greatest masters of the era (Hawthorne, Melville, Emerson, Thoreau, and Whitman), *American Renaissance* shaped the thinking of Matthiessen's distinguished students (including Kenneth Lynn, Quentin Anderson, Henry Nash Smith, Leo Marx, and R. W. B. Lewis) and of many others as well. I can clearly recollect its impact on my own graduate studies in 1955; it is a book that I still recommend to students today.

Matthiessen also made other useful contributions with *Henry James: The Major Phase* (1944). This book persuasively argued the case that James's supreme accomplishment was the creation of the late novels in the complicated mandarin style. With Kenneth Murdock he edited *The Notebooks of Henry James* (1947), and in that year he compiled *The James Family: A Group Biography*, interweaving illuminating critical commentary with generous selections from the writings of Henry James, Sr., and his sons, the psychologist William and the novelist Henry. Matthiessen's autobiographical book *From the Heart of Europe* (1948) was widely reviewed. Chosen over any number of well-known living poets, he also edited *The Oxford Book of American Verse* (1950). And at his death he left a virtually completed critical study, published shortly afterward as *Theodore Dreiser* (1951). Such was Matthiessen's influence that it is perhaps only forgivable hyperbole to say—as William E. Cain does in his new book, *F. O. Matthiessen and the Politics of Criticism*[1]—that "probably more than any other modern critic, F. O. Matthiessen legitimated the study of American literature."

Cain, who is a professor of English and director of American studies at Wellesley College, is not the first to have examined the career of Matthiessen. In the year of Matthiessen's suicide, Paul M. Sweezy and Leo Huberman edited *F. O. Matthiessen (1902-1950): A Collective Portrait*, composed of laudatory reminiscences by friends and former students. But such was the numbing effect of Matthiessen's death that it took twenty-five years before a major study of the critic appeared—Giles B. Gunn's *F. O. Matthiessen: The Critical Achievement* (1975). Since then, however, the bibliography has picked up. Editor Louis Hyde has made Matthiessen's private life accessible in **Rat and the Devil: Journal Letters of F. O. Matthiessen and Russell Cheney** (1978). In *F. O. Matthiessen: Christian Socialist as Critic* (1981), Frederick C. Stern undertook to explain why Matthiessen was exemplary for "those of us who thought of ourselves as radicals in the late forties and very early fifties"; and Walter Benn Michaels and Donald E. Pease felt Matthiessen's influence important enough to have assembled a collection of new revaluations in *The American Renaissance Reconsidered* (1985).

Cain also wishes to reconsider Matthiessen's **American Renaissance** by indicating it as a case study in what, as a critic, one must not do. The arraignment comes down to this:

> As a Christian socialist, [Matthiessen] dedicated his life's work to fighting against the industrial-capitalist order and all that it had done to all aspects of life. Yet in his actual academic and critical activity, Matthiessen placed himself in a literary and political fix. Refusing to allow his politics to propel his critical agenda, he put the critical agenda first, making the formalist approach and method his central focus. He claimed to be moving beyond the disabling apolitical and ahistorical limitations set by formalism; and he made this claim even as he persistently invoked and remained obeisant to New Critical, formalist principles. . . .

In consequence, Cain believes, Matthiessen's several critical studies—especially **American Renaissance**—are vitiated by an intellectual and critical confusion.

Since Cain makes much of the contradiction between Matthiessen's criticism and his politics and has touched on this in relation to his suicide, some attention to the critic's socialist views and his disturbing death may be in order here.

Francis Otto Matthiessen was born in Pasadena, California, in 1902, one of four children in an unsettled family, and he lived, off and on, with his millionaire grandfather in LaSalle, Illinois, which he regarded as his real home. After four years at the Hackley School in Tarrytown, New York, he took his B.A. degree at Yale in 1923 and went on to Oxford as a Rhodes Scholar. With a Harvard M.A. in 1926 and a Ph.D. in 1927, he taught at Yale for two years and then returned to Harvard, where he held a faculty appointment until his death in 1950.

Troubled by the disparity between his privileged status and the spectacle of poverty, young Matthiessen, during the Depression, was converted to the views of Eugene Debs and Norman Thomas; he joined the Socialist Party in 1932. In **From the Heart of Europe**, he confessed that R. H. Tawney's defense of equality and attack on industrialism in *The Acquisitive Society* "have remained more living for me than anything else, except Shakespeare, that I read at college." Matthiessen then threw himself with enthusiasm into very nearly every public left-wing radical cause around—of which the following is a highly selective list of the organizations and defense committees he supported: the American Russian Institute, the Artists' Front to Win the War, American Youth for Democracy, Citizens' Committee to Free Earl Browder, Civil Rights Congress, Committee for Citizenship Rights, Committee for a Democratic Far East Policy, Committee to Sponsor the Daily Worker, Defense of Communist Schools, Open Letter for Closer Cooperation with the Soviet Union, Veterans of the Abraham Lincoln Brigade, and the Win-the-Peace Conference. Needless to say, many of these groups were Communist fronts. Further, as Cain remarks, Matthiessen "campaigned tirelessly for the Progressive party, and presented one of the seconding speeches for Henry Wallace's nomination in 1948"—even though the Wallace campaign had been substantially co-opted by the Communist Party.

Such was the certitude of his blind faith in socialism that Matthiessen in 1948 could still call the Russian Revolution "the most progressive event of our century, the necessary successor to the French Revolution and the American Revolution and to England's seventeenth-century Civil War." He defended the Soviet Union long after Stalin's atrocities had been revealed, and as late as 1949 could contend, in **"The Responsibilities of the Critic,"** that "the principles of Marxism remain at the base of much of the best social and cultural thought of our century."

Naturally opinions and attitudes of this kind brought Matthiessen to the attention of the authorities, for the late 1940s were a time when Communist infiltration of the universities and subversion of the government were inflamed political topics. When he was called to testify before the House Un-American Activities Committee, he proudly claimed his membership in the organizations named above. No legal action was ever brought against him. Nevertheless, in a revealing chronological juxtaposition, Cain remarks that "Matthiessen killed himself less than two months after Senator Joseph McCarthy's notorious February 1950 speech . . . in which he announced that Communists had crept into the State Department and 'thoroughly infested' it." Cain quotes a view, widely promulgated in the 1950s by the Left and here voiced by Barrows Dunham in *F. O. Matthiessen (1902-1950): A Collective Portrait*, that "when Professor Matthiessen died, the cold war made its first martyr among scholars." Was Matthiessen, in his suicide, a noble victim of right-wing McCarthyist oppression?

It may be the case, as Cain speculates, that "everything to which Matthiessen had dedicated his intellectual life . . . seemed in danger of being lost forever amid the rush to purge the nation of its political enemies." But he is candid enough to admit that Matthiessen had enemies on the Left as well as on the Right. The chief of these were former Communists and other anti-Stalinists of the Left. In particular, there was outrage on the Left at Matthiessen's distorted picture of the political situation in Czechoslovakia. He had spent 1947 teaching at the Charles University in Prague and came home to write about the sublime faith of "the majority of the people [who] are committed to the belief that socialism will work." Of course the majority of the people thought no such thing; and the Czech Communists and their Kremlin masters knew it. So in February of 1948 the Communists simply seized power in a *coup d'etat* and murdered—by defenestration—the foreign minister, Jan Masaryk. (The Czech Communists called Masaryk's death a suicide.) Matthiessen could have rewritten, in the proofs of *From the Heart of Europe* his inappropriate account of the country, but he didn't even bother to change the book. Ernest J. Simmons has remarked that Matthiessen's failure to revise the proofs seemed "a psychic symbol of defeat. It was not merely the gesture of a tired man, but of one who wished to cling to a last illusion that had seemed the only way out of an aching ideological impasse." Matthiessen had nothing to say about the brutalization of the Czechs by Stalin's henchmen. Alfred Kazin, who had counted himself as a friend, said later that he had told Matthiessen that

> some of his attachments [were] naïve and dangerous. I could never understand—or wished not to understand—how anyone who adhered so firmly to democracy, and was a Christian, could countenance the contempt of individual differences, the terror, and the suppressiveness practiced by Russia and its vassals in Eastern Europe.

Despite this criticism, Matthiessen was hostile to leftist intellectuals, particularly Granville Hicks and John Dos Passos, who in the late 1940s had retired "to a neo-liberalism which has no group adherences, a liberalism wholly of the mind." He further complained in *From the Heart of Europe* that

> when all the forces on the Left are as weak in numbers as they are in America, it seems hardly less than suicidal to waste so much of their energy in attacking one another. The Trotskyite-Stalinist struggle, when transferred to New York, has yielded, to judge by the total record of the chief writers involved, little more than sterile though heated debate, followed by a wearied disillusionment with all politics on the part of many who once believed that they stood farthest to the militant Left.

At this Irving Howe issued a blistering *Partisan Review* attack on Matthiessen's *From the Heart of Europe*. In "The Sentimental Fellow-Travelling of F. O. Matthiessen," Howe claimed that Matthiessen's support of Wallace and the Progressive Party—which he called a "completely contrived creature of Stalinism"—proved him to be a Stalinist dupe. Matthiessen was "a writer who calls himself a democratic socialist while apologizing for the regimes that have jailed, exiled, and murdered democratic socialists." In

short, he was "an apologist for a brutal totalitarian state and its agents."

What these controversies suggest is that Matthiessen's suicidal depression might just as well have come from attacks on the Left as from those on the Right. Matthiessen's death, in any case, became, as Kazin put it, a "political football" in which the radical Left claimed him as an academic martyr for his political opinions and the Right saw his suicide as positive evidence of his subversive un-Americanism, perhaps even of covert espionage. None of these explanations, however, will suffice. Another must therefore be sought.

F. O. Matthiessen, it must be said, was a homosexual and a Christian. Despite the Church's clear moral condemnation of homosexual acts, in 1924 he commenced a long homosexual affair with Russell Cheney, a painter twenty years his senior. Matthiessen's Christianity and his homosexuality, however, did not rest easily together. As he told "Rat" Cheney in one of his letters, "I don't want to mortify my flesh or deny anything for the sake of a future reward. . . . I worship Christ, but I follow him in the spirit, not in the letter." The nature of this affair is now more or less embarrassingly accessible in Lewis Hyde's edition of *Rat and the Devil: Journal Letters of F. O. Matthiessen and Russell Cheney*. But the relationship was not without its problems, partly compounded, it would seem, by Matthiessen's negative view of himself as a homosexual. In their entry on Matthiessen in the *Dictionary of American Biography*, Joseph H. and U. T. M. Summers remark that Matthiessen "was unusually hostile to homosexual colleagues [at Harvard] who mixed their academic and sexual relations." And indeed, if we look at his treatment of Whitman's sexual inversion in *American Renaissance,* Matthiessen was clearly uncomfortable with Whitman's openly avowed love of manly comrades. Matthiessen complains that "in the passivity of the poet's body there is a quality vaguely pathological and homosexual," as if conceding that the two were identical. Cain reflects that

> Matthiessen cannot engage this aspect of Whitman's verse except to criticize it or to distance himself from it, and the effect, for those who know Matthiessen's own sexual preference, is quite disorienting. His critical gestures in the public form of his book feel like expressions of self-disapproval, as though he wanted not to be what Whitman was, or else wanted readers who knew he was homosexual to see that he spurned "abnormal" homosexual attitudes in poetry.

In any case, Matthiessen became increasingly obsessed that Cheney would die, that death would deprive him of his companion, and in 1938—well before the McCarthy era—he experienced an especially acute episode of depression and committed himself to McLean's Hospital in Boston for three weeks. As Cain remarks, "His letters and journal entries from this period show him extremely tense and exhausted, self-loathing and suicidal." His obsession with suicide, as Matthiessen himself describes it in his journal, "took agonizingly vivid images of jumping out of a window during those first tortured days." He felt that he had every reason to live, yet was impelled toward death:

> Where has this fear come from to engulf one who has never even been bothered by anxiety and worry before? If I dread life without Russell, the fact is that he is alive, buoyant, rich, and I am merely hastening by my melancholy the event that might lie far in the future, for this strain is very hard for him. . . . The nub of the problem is here. When you give yourself entirely to love, you cannot demand that it last forever. For then fear intrudes, and there I am.

His psychiatrist, however, put it differently. He told him that he was turning aggression against himself, and Matthiessen "resolved to fight it."

> I cannot die because it would kill Russell. And to keep from jumping I must cast out this fear of Russell's death. Many times in these past weeks I have felt possessed with a devil. I pray now for strength of nerve and courage to resist the temptation of violent unreason.

Matthiessen succeeded for a time in suppressing his fear of Cheney's death and resumed his life as a Harvard professor. But there is no doubt that he remained a depressed personality morbidly awaiting the death of his lover. And when Cheney did die, in 1945, Matthiessen's familiar world began to fall apart. In 1948, the year Masaryk was thrown out of a window in the Czech-Communist putsch and the unrevised proofs of *From the Heart of Europe* lay on his desk, Matthiessen complained of the need of some rest that would "pull me out of a spell of oppressive melancholy over the state of the world and myself." And in his farewell letter to Lewis Hyde, written the night before his death, he said: "I can't seem to find my way out of this desperate depression. I'd try to stick it out, if I didn't think it would recur. . . . I have fought it until I'm worn out. I can no longer bear the loneliness with which I am faced." On April 1, 1950, he leaped from the window of a twelfth-floor room in the Manger Hotel in Boston. He left a note in which he said:

> I have taken this room in order to do what I have to do . . . I am exhausted. I have been subject to so many severe depressions during the past few years that I can no longer believe that I can continue to be of use to my profession and my friends . . . How much the state of the world has to do with my state of mind I do not know. But as a Christian and a socialist believing in international peace, I find myself terribly oppressed by the present tensions.

What can we conclude about the poignant fact of Matthiessen's death? In my view, the evidence is not convincing that he was so distraught over public criticism, from either the Left or the Right, that he took his own life. He was, after all, an ardent activist used to political battles. Nor, despite his comments on the state of the world in 1950, can I see his dashed hope for international peace and the triumph of worldwide socialism as the key to his death. (One is struck, however, by the parallel in the man-

ner of his own death and that of Jan Masaryk.) Matthiessen's suicidal impulse probably had its origins in an emotional state of self-loathing, confusingly and inextricably connected with his homosexuality. Yet it is probably the case that if Cheney had still been alive, Matthiessen might have pulled out of his depression, as he had earlier. But with Cheney now gone, he could not fight his depression alone. Wallace Stevens was probably right in remarking to a correspondent that "at the bottom of the whole thing there was something entirely personal," and that "when a man's trouble comes down to the final intimacy he just doesn't give anyone access to it."

It is Cain's thesis that, when F. O. Matthiessen sat down to write his criticism, he silenced his politics. Nevertheless, the increasing militancy of Matthiessen's socialism during the Depression and World War II years is clearly reflected in his changing treatment of certain American writers. In 1929, for instance, Matthiessen had written in *Sarah Orne Jewett* that "if the [literary] material is important and the technique crude, the work will continue to have historical value, such as even the clumsiest Dreiser novels will have in throwing light upon their time, but they are not works of art." But by the mid-1940s, when he launched *Theodore Dreiser*, the novelist's left-wing politics coincided with Matthiessen's and redeemed the crudity of his fictional technique. According to Lionel Trilling, Matthiessen's 1946 review of Dreiser's *The Bulwark* accepted "the liberal cliché which opposes crude experience to mind and establishes Dreiser's value by implying that the mind which Dreiser's crude experience is presumed to confront and refute is the mind of gentility." Later, in the Dreiser book, the novelist is praised for a number of reasons that have nothing to do with art; and when Matthiessen turns from the writer's compassion for the underclass to *aesthetic* considerations, we read that the lumbering and overblown *An American Tragedy* "advances magisterially from beginning to end"; that "one gets an increasing sense of the rightness of Dreiser's overall proportions"; and that "the qualifications that clog the prose are also a chief source of Dreiser's strength."

It is no wonder that in *The Liberal Imagination* Trilling called grotesque the "doctrinaire indulgence" with which Dreiser was treated by leftist critics like Matthiessen. According to Giles B. Gunn, "because of his intense concern to demonstrate Dreiser's relevance, Matthiessen was willing to dull the edge of his own critical instrument in order to make Dreiser's virtues stand out more boldly and unambiguously." To have transmogrified Dreiser's literary defects into novelistic virtues must have cost a critic with Matthiessen's aesthetic sensibility quite a great deal. In fact, Gunn cites a former friend of Matthiessen's who "suggested in private that Matthiessen's work on the Dreiser book is what finally drove him to suicide." Did he take his life because he had compromised his aesthetic standards in the service of a socialist ideology? Gunn finds the suggestion highly implausible. So does Cain. In fact, for Cain, the real problem—putting aside for the moment the ambiguous cause of his suicide—is not the compromise of Matthiessen's aesthetic standards but the compromise of his political ideology, especially in *American Renaissance*. Let us turn now to Cain's critique of the way in which the political and literary contradictions in Matthiessen's thought disabled *American Renaissance*.

By way of a preliminary, I must say that I have a great deal of sympathy with Cain's view of the current critical scene in American letters. He remarks that, to an outsider, the "poststructuralist probings of texts from *Hamlet* to *Ulysses*" looks impressive in its technical density, but he remarks that "it is incomprehensible and unrelated to the needs and interests of people who do not make their living 'doing criticism.'" Cain is sharply critical of "Derridean forays into the antics of metaphor and metonymy in Poe's poetry, or Lacanian meditations on the signifier in Melville's tales." The preoccupation in English departments with Continental theories has, in his opinion, diverted American critics from the real task:

> If we ever hope to justify teaching and writing about literature; if we seek in fact to give the humanities a marked relevance to American society; if we want our constituencies to value what we do, then we should take as a central mission a renewed commitment to informing ourselves and our students about the literature, philosophy, and history of the United States.

I, for one, am in substantial agreement with this viewpoint, as I believe F. O. Matthiessen would have been. But, as will become clearer, I cannot assent to the conclusion that Cain derives from it or the judgment he is led to pass on Matthiessen's criticism.

Despite the deplorable betrayal of his critical standards in the book on Dreiser, Matthiessen essentially, and for most of his career, saw himself as a literary critic whose function was to serve the work of art by setting it in an appropriate context, elucidating its central themes and literary techniques, and evaluating the writer in terms of his literary excellence. In accomplishing this task, Matthiessen paid close attention to the form of literary works. A founder (with Trilling and Ransom) of the Kenyon School of English, Matthiessen even assigned Brooks and Warren's *Understanding Poetry* as a classroom text. Since Eliot and the New Critics dominated Matthiessen's early critical practice, it is not surprising that his first important work should have been *The Achievement of T. S. Eliot*. For Cain, however, Matthiessen was disabled by his commitment to the principles of the New Criticism, which emphasize the literary work as a verbal artifact, not fully separable from history but understandable through attention to its formal techniques—its structure, texture, tension, paradox, irony, and ambiguity.

Cain finds it ironical that "Matthiessen, a socialist, would look to T. S. Eliot, a royalist, as a compelling authority" and that he would "dispute the narrowness of New Critical methodology and also rebuke Agrarian conservatism, yet often sound decidedly like a New Critic himself in his remarks about his own approach to literature." For Cain, the

critics "whom Matthiessen read closely" held "political assumptions [that] diverged sharply from Matthiessen's: these men were not democrats." Furthermore, how could a socialist have been so taken with mere art as to have written *Henry James: The Major Phase*, especially in view of James's aversion to radicals and reformers, as *The Bostonians* and *The Princess Casamassima* make plain? For Cain, Matthiessen's preoccupation with and appreciation for literary form produced inner contradictions that kept him from articulating, in his criticism, the socialist principles for which he stood.

American Renaissance is presented to us by Cain as a work celebrating "a literature for democracy." Matthiessen remarked that "the one common denominator of my five writers, uniting even Hawthorne and Whitman, was their devotion to the possibilities of democracy." But Cain complains that "he leaves the meaning of this 'democracy' oddly unparticularized." (Matthiessen did not, in other words, say that for him democracy meant socialism.) Further, Cain alleges that "Matthiessen's choices [of Emerson, Whitman, Thoreau, Hawthorne, and Melville] . . . were undemocratic" and unrepresentative of the taste of rank-and-file nineteenth-century readers. If we ask why, Cain enlists the support of fellow canonbuster Jane Tompkins, author of *Sensational Designs: The Cultural Work of American Fiction, 1790-1860*, to spell out Matthiessen's errors. Here is her indictment:

> Matthiessen's list is exclusive and class-bound in the extreme. If you look at it carefully, you will see that in certain fundamental ways the list does not represent what most men and women were thinking about between 1850 and 1855, but embodies the views of a very small, socially, culturally, geographically, sexually, and racially restricted elite. None of the works . . . is by an orthodox Christian. . . . None deals explicitly with the issues of abolition and temperance. . . . None . . . achieved great popular success. . . . The list includes no works by women, although women at that time dominated the literary marketplace. The list includes no works by males not of Anglo-Saxon origin, and indeed, no works by writers living south of New York, north of Boston, or west of Stockbridge, Massachusetts. . . .

Cain complains that it did not occur to Matthiessen that "by omitting [Harriet Beecher] Stowe and the women writers, he was going to end up with a list that was entirely male; and it apparently did not even enter his mind that the list was defective because it was wholly white." Looked at in retrospect, *American Renaissance* "is a book that is unfaithful to the full literary and historical actuality of the years when the 'American renaissance' bloomed." If Matthiessen "had really read and written about literature as a socialist, he would have produced a different sort of criticism."

It is worth pointing out, perhaps, that no single book could ever pretend to be faithful to the *full* literary and historical actuality of the mid-nineteenth century. Nor could any critical work of the 1930s, like *American Renaissance*, ever satisfy the 1980s orthodoxy of race-class-gender "oppression studies." The crux of Cain's objection, however, is broader than either of these points: it is that Matthiessen did not observe sexual and racial egalitarianism as a criterion for aesthetic selections. If *American Renaissance* suppressed Matthiessen's political ideology in the service of a largely formal literary analysis, Cain suggests that there is a better way for the professor to approach literature. This way is "to acknowledge one's political beliefs first, and then to make pedagogical decisions accordingly. If I claim to desire, and wish to work for, political change, then I should teach in line with my politics." Cain then confesses that "I foreground race in my teaching since, with [W. E. B.] Du Bois, I regard race 'as the central problem of the greatest of the world's democracies and so the problem of the future world.'" This is quite remarkable. I suppose that if Cain regarded the disposal of nuclear waste as our greatest political problem, then consistency would compel him to make this thesis the governing principle of his curriculum of American literature.

For Cain, Matthiessen was caught in contradictions because he insisted on literature as "a special category." Is there something wrong with distinguishing the excellent in writing as against the turbid flow of most discursive practice? There is for Cain. The reason is that our "'social thinking' keeps getting balked and deflected by our allegiance to 'literature as an art.'"

> This may be a fine loyalty, and many admirable men and women have supported it, but it is crucial to realize, as Matthiessen's scholarship confirms, how variable have been the boundaries that define "literature" and "art." It is simply historically wrong to speak as if literary art is, has always been, and will always be this or that particular thing. Matthiessen felt certain that he knew what literature was; yet when we read his books today, we notice right away the books (and constituencies) that lie outside his range of literary expertise and mission. . . . I prefer myself to begin, as I have emphasized, with present political interests and to proceed from there to choose writers and texts which I can examine with students to develop and express these interests.

The implications of this remark, for English studies, are, I must confess, appalling. No serious person in 1855 regarded the work of such female scribblers as Mrs. E. D. E. N. Southworth as art; and no one thought of the writings of Frederick Douglass or William Lloyd Garrison as literature. And no one, with any literary judgment, does now. Hence the need Cain feels to abolish literature as a special category so as to make a place for the subliterary writer whose works are politically "useful." Here is a professor of literature at a major undergraduate college, entrusted with the high obligation, indeed the very great privilege, of presenting to his students American literary art, yet baldly announcing the primacy of his political ideology, an ideology perhaps only of the moment, as the basis for his selection of literary texts. How ghastly for his students!

Given Cain's ideology of race, we cannot be in any doubt about the canon-busting to follow: "In defining my own canon, as I make choices among writers and texts, I stress four terms: dissent, struggle, vision, conflict." Dissent he illustrates by assigning the writings of Frederick Douglass and William Lloyd Garrison; struggle with C. L. R. James, Walter Rodney, Eric Williams, Frantz Fanon, and Amilcar Cabral; vision suggests to him Du Bois, Richard Wright, Martin Luther King, and Malcolm X; and finally conflict brings into the curriculum Melville, Twain, and Faulkner—although only in relation to the racial theme. I note that there are no women, black or white, on the approved list, although elsewhere he is prescriptive: "A course on the American Renaissance [unlike Matthiessen's] ought to incorporate the writings of [Frederick] Douglass and [Harriet Beecher] Stowe." Nowhere in Cain's discussion of literature do we find any interest in such literary concepts as beauty and art, style and form. Instead, Cain ends his book with a long paean to the named black writers, especially to that "premier 'man of letters,'" W. E. B. Du Bois, who has "few rivals in this century" but who suffers neglect in English classes only because "his black skin still bars him" and because of "his Communist sympathies and eventual membership in the Communist party."

None of Cain's opinions about Du Bois's merit is defended on aesthetic grounds. Cain does, however, make his case worse by quoting Du Bois's "Criteria of Negro Art" to this effect: "Viewing himself as, in everything, a writer, an artist, he [Du Bois] affirmed that 'all art is propaganda and ever must be, despite the wailing of the purists. I stand in utter shamelessness and say that whatever art I have for writing has been used always for propaganda for gaining the right for black folk to love and enjoy.'" When we contemplate the corruption of art that always occurs when it is conflated with propaganda, and when we reflect that, in fact, no one has ever denied blacks the "right" (is it a political right?) to "love and enjoy," Du Bois's imprecision of thought and language calls into question his ascribed pre-eminence. Cain himself seems a bit uneasy and evasive about his canon-busting, observing of his black writers that "one would want to call them 'great artists'" (note the conditional). But his political agenda wins out at last: "They are that." He is also uneasy that straight Marxists and radical white feminists will take him to task for his racial bias. But, good liberal that he is, he concedes that "others whose political views are similar to my own might prefer to focus upon gender and class, and on the intersections of race, class, and gender. Their choice of texts and methods will be different from, though complementary, to mine." In any case, for Cain, his black writers are really "relevant" and necessary substitutes for white American writers who subordinate race to universal human concerns.

In all of this one has a sickening sense of *déjà vu*, as if we were heading back into the vulgar Marxist sociology of literature that corrupted criticism in the 1930s, or at least back to the viewpoint of V. L. Parrington, who dismissively remarked in *Main Currents of American Thought* that "with aesthetic judgments I have not been greatly concerned. I have not wished to evaluate reputations or weigh literary merits, but rather to understand what our fathers thought." Matthiessen, for all his political confusion, at least understood what the art of literature is. He knew that it constitutes a special category of discourse. *Walden* had taught him about what Thoreau called "the select language of literature." Matthiessen understood that special techniques of literary criticism must be invoked if the art is to be understood. Matthiessen was sharply critical of Parrington, observing in the Preface to *American Renaissance* that "my concern has been the opposite [of Parrington's]." Matthiessen said that he was

> suspicious of the results of such historians as have declared that they were not discussing art, but simply using art, in a purpose of research. Both our historical writing and our criticism have been greatly enriched during the past twenty years by the breaking down of arbitrary divisions between them, by the critic's realization of the necessity to master what he could of the historical discipline, by the historian's desire to extend his domain from politics to general culture. But you cannot "use" a work of art unless you have comprehended its meaning.

One cannot comprehend the meaning of a literary work, Matthiessen felt, unless its techniques are understood; and to this end, the New Critical methods threw the clearest light on what, in its ontological reality, the work of art is. At least when he wrote *American Renaissance*, Matthiessen had seen enough of the vulgar Marxists and historical sociologists of literature (who set their radical political agenda first) to realize the extent to which their propaganda distorted, falsified, and diminished actual artworks. Matthiessen did not wish to replicate the errors of 1930s left-wing criticism, which emanated from the shallowest historical relativism. And yet here is Cain advising us, like Lenin in "Party Organization and Party Literature," that, since literary judgments are relative and culture-bound, critics and teachers should always set their political agendas first and then decide what books are "art." Matthiessen, for all his limitations, was never guilty of that folly in *American Renaissance*.

But such folly is now rampant in the academy. A decade ago, Professor Florence Howe of CCNY demanded that scholars turn "their attention to research that is needed, that will make a difference." "Let us have no more dissertations on Henry James," she wrote, "or on Melville or Hawthorne: let us remember the ladies, those hordes of 'female scribblers' that Hawthorne feared." More recently, Professor Lawrence Buell of Oberlin, in a 1987 article in *American Literature* entitled "Literary History Without Sexism," called on feminist studies to "foment reorderings in the pre-feminist canon (the demotion of Hemingway, for instance)."

To the extent that *American Renaissance* is still useful, it is precisely because Matthiessen tried to be politically non-partisan. In subordinating his politics to his literary judgment, he selected only those writers who, on the basis of style and substance, made a compelling case for our literary attention, and he made that case persuasively. He learned from Emerson that only an artistic inspiration that has found its true organic form counts in the long run. He agreed with Thoreau in *Walden* that, "having learned our letters, we should read the best that is in literature." The New Criticism made Matthiessen a close and intelligent reader whose grasp of literature's complexity forbade him, at least in *American Renaissance*, the ideological oversimplification. That Matthiessen *did* make his case for Emerson, Whitman, Thoreau, Hawthorne, and Melville as the best of their time is attested to by the ongoing influence of *American Renaissance.*

In this respect, Cain is wrong in abolishing literature as a separate category. Whatever the historian may want to explore, in literary studies Matthiessen's operating principle was the correct one: *in art, it is quality, not equality, that matters*. Aesthetic quality is what all serious students of literature have a right to demand. For these reasons, whatever may be the reigning political orthodoxy at Wellesley or in the academy at large, teachers of literature as an art have an obligation to demote not Hemingway, Hawthorne, and James but writers of marginal quality, whatever their class, race, or gender. Henry James put the matter very well in "The Lesson of Balzac": "Nothing counts, of course, in art, but the excellent; nothing exists, however briefly, for estimation, for appreciation but the superlative. . . ."

Note

1. *F. O. Matthiessen and the Politics of Criticism,* by William E. Cain; University of Wisconsin Press, 238 pages.

Paul A. Bove (essay date 1990)

SOURCE: "The Love of Reading/The Work of Criticism: F. O. Matthiessen and Lionel Trilling," in *Contemporary Literature*, Vol. 31, No. 3, Fall, 1990, pp. 373-82.

[*In the following review of William A. Cain's* F. O. Matthiessen and the Politics of Criticism, *Bove praises Cain's reading of Matthiessen's work.*]

> What magnanimity!
>
>   —Daniel O'Hara

> When the historical sense reigns *without restraint*, and all its consequences are realized, it uproots the future because it destroys illusions and robs the things that exist of the atmosphere in which alone they can live. Historical justice, even when it is genuine and practiced with the purest intentions, is therefore a dreadful virtue because it always undermines the living thing and brings it down: its judgment is always annihilating.
>
>   —Friedrich Nietzsche

It is not self-evident that contemporary critical intellectuals who are serious about their role in culture, politics, and society should devote their best energies to writing critical histories of past critics. At least from the time of Kant who, in answering the question, What is Enlightenment? turned philosophy toward the understanding of an engagement with the present; through the works of Marx and Nietzsche and their critical and poststructuralist heirs; to the present worldwide cultural and political struggles for self-determination, for affirmed "subject positions" within "postcolonialism," the critics' concern has increasingly been with the present in a struggle to understand cultural configurations of historical consequence and, often enough, as strugglers within the partisan battles of worldly conflict. Yet in this ever-increasing concern for the present, indeed, often as part of this concern, the critical study of criticism's predecessors has been an ever more important kind of work. Of course, there are many "genealogical" and "ideological" explanations for this: a concern for the career, for the shape of subjectivity; an urge to demystify and criticize, to clear intellectual political space occupied by previous figures' works; an awareness, on many different levels, of the pressing dead weight of the past on forms of production, in the forms of language; and, more cynically, a recognized way to one's own career advancement.

More interesting, perhaps, would be a thinking that would link the effort to write books about great critical predecessors to the general and important problem of writing history, especially certain forms of history themselves rooted in the metaphysics, the politics, the discursive inheritance of the rise and transformation of modernism. One thinks in this context of Michel Foucault's early and still underestimated efforts, for example, in *The Birth of the Clinic* and other books, to come to grips with the emergent awareness that somehow the "history" of "history's" link to the knowledges (*savoir* and *connaissances*) that give rise to "history" must be written and thought. Without especially privileging Foucault's efforts, one can say, I think, that his only partially successful but remarkably provocative works make inescapable not only the question of the "function" of "history," but also the theorizing of the link between its necessary dissolution into "histories" and the fragmenting of the "subject" into "subjectivities" or "subject positions." Indeed, his archaeologies make the inscription of "history" writing within liberal and dialectical political languages itself a subject of (perhaps critical) meditation—especially in regard to the power relations of emergent, dominant, and residual cultural identities in their full specificity.

Who or what is to be served by the archival, imaginative, and critical work involved in the effort to understand, to reinterpret, to reposition dead commentators on other people's works? This important question is also, however, an easy one: we know or can easily come to know the answers to it. Harder and more interesting would be the effort to know more about the relations of this kind of critical history writing to the larger formations of modernity and, if you will, "post-modernity." It would involve both scanning the archives for traces of efforts to think the relation and reading our institutions as depositories of the thought that is that relation.

William E. Cain's book, *F. O. Matthiessen and the Politics of Criticism*, is a generous, careful, and solicitous study of perhaps the most important academic critic of United States literature. Cain convincingly shows that "Matthiessen's career concerns the complicated relations between criticism and politics, scholarship and the public sphere, pedagogy and social activism" (ix) that have themselves preoccupied so many of the best minds of contemporary criticism, especially "after theory." Indeed, Cain uses Matthiessen to tell an exemplary story to young radicals among these best minds. Refreshingly, Cain does not lionize Matthiessen but seriously judges his strengths and weaknesses as just that, not as signs of tragic struggle, of heroic efforts that give his work "strength"—the word Cain uses to characterize Leo Marx's reading of Matthiessen's works. Cain reads through the works in the order of their value and complexity, aiming always to discover what of importance Matthiessen might offer us while judiciously studying the reasons for his failures both to alert us against his mistakes and to guide us toward a stronger and better critical position, particularly the one represented, in the final chapter of this book, by W. E. B. Du Bois.[1]

Cain's great virtue, I believe, is his critical generosity. Indeed, he stakes his reading of Matthiessen upon steering a difficult course between those earlier critics who have treated Matthiessen as a monument of heroic criticism and those who have denigrated especially his late works as a sign of his declining powers. Cain's generosity guides his reading so that Matthiessen comes to have more value than either of the other two typical evaluations gives us. Cain, we might say, asks questions in the right way, not coercing his subject to respond in terms inappropriate to his time and effort: "the question," Cain writes, "is not why a reading is wrong or incomplete but, instead, why Matthiessen did not undertake a particular analysis and what it might have looked like, and the consequences it might have generated, if he had" (xi). The largest part of Cain's imaginative and thoroughly scholarly effort consists in helping us know Matthiessen well enough that not only can we follow Cain's inferences, but we judge them to be right and important. Indeed, we feel the seriousness of this effort in the power of its generosity: Cain is struggling with one of his own father figures, with one part of his own critical ego, and so is dramatically coming to grips with some part of himself in the effort.

What gives this book its worth is Cain's transformation of his efforts into two positive and public values: the very critical generosity which he enacts for us and the final wisdom that generosity allows him to offer before moving on to work in other fields. This wisdom is tough, a "challenge," as Cain calls it: "My account certainly marks a limitation in Matthiessen's criticism, but it is intended, more generally, to illustrate the kind of separation of literary and political realms that has often afflicted radicals, who tend to believe that some things are not political (or to be politicized)" (xi). Cain's most important insight into Matthiessen's greatest work, *The American Renaissance,* both illustrates his general point and helps us understand why, after struggling with this critical father, Cain moves his work—and would move ours—in a direction represented by Du Bois:

> In ***American Renaissance*** . . . he tries to exhibit the social and political meanings of his five major authors, in order to demonstrate the ways in which they might vitally renew the present. Yet even as he encourages us to recognize how these authors could revivify our history, he refrains from inquiring in any significant detail into the historical contexts of the authors themselves. Emerson, Hawthorne, and the others matter crucially for our political life, Matthiessen affirms, but their own politics, it seems, do not merit scrutiny. (131)

Matthiessen's error, Cain shows us, is not methodological or scholarly. Rather, Matthiessen's mistake was to let his criticism depend upon a prior act of hope. But hope, Cain would have us understand, can lead to coercion, to neglect, to assertion, to blindness: better generosity, Cain tells us, from the pantheon of Christian virtues, for it lets us see things and see them whole. (Faith has no place here, not even for Matthiessen, who was neither a Stalinist nor an untroubled believer.) "He knew what he wanted politically, and he hoped to overcome obstacles to it through the sheer force of his hope, steadfastly reiterated, and his sincere invocations of what American writers had seen and celebrated" (131).

Not only does Cain give us Matthiessen's political context, but he ends by showing us how politics must matter in a new way for the professional academic literary critic, the kind of person who writes this sort of generous, but mournful, history. Had Cain merely substituted Du Bois for Matthiessen, his own criticism would not have progressed psychically or politically. But he ends this episode of his ongoing effort with a renewed commitment to his teaching vocation, to his generosity now fully informed by the injustice and sufferings of blacks and other repressed races throughout the world. Having attended to the history of struggles for racial equality, for an end to racism, having read and understood and admired Du Bois and others (including Faulkner), Cain leads us to change the critical question we have been too much asking:

> The question now is not, What can be done to reform departments of English and change the profession as a whole? It is, instead, What facts in the "world of practice and choice and struggle" [the quotation is from Raymond Williams, *Writing in Society*] impel me as an individual, and might lead others, toward particular kinds of literary judgment and pedagogical action? This is sounder strategy, and ultimately, I hope, it will prove more productive. (214)

As Cain returns us through generosity and conscience to hope, he leaves us with wisdom and wonder: what will this "sounder strategy" *produce*? Indeed, we might also wonder what has moved this remarkably just and amorous critic through the process of his research, his writing, and to his responsible and cogent recommendation. That Cain's book provokes such thought is the mark of its success and one illustration of how writing histories of dead critics might serve us.

It in no way diminishes Cain's achievement to suggest that in *Lionel Trilling: The Work of Liberation*, Daniel T. O'Hara gives us a way to explain psychologically and culturally some of the motivations underlying Cain's work. O'Hara adapts Freud's "Mourning and Melancholia" (1917) to offer a reading of Trilling's life and works as one single text focused on the effort of self-making and resulting in the making of a generous and tolerant critical self that struggles always to impute the noblest of motives to all the literary, cultural, and intellectual efforts of others. O'Hara stresses that Freud's lifelong influence on Trilling can be fully understood only in terms of the former's theoretical revisions of the psychoanalytic theory of mind presented originally in *The Interpretation of Dreams* (1899). In this reading of Freud's revision, the depressive, like the mourner, "has also suffered a loss but an unconscious loss of a love object with which his ego has identified. Rather than give up this expression of libido, this position of desire, the ego wholly internalizes the love object, setting it up as part of itself, against which it can begin to direct its (self-) reproaches for (its own) abandonment in a process that parodies demonically the work of mourning and its systematic disengagement from the beloved dead, the critical process by which the normal ego forms itself" (10). O'Hara argues that this demonic process has its benefits: "the work of depression, which directs the superego's severest denigrations against the internalized love object, has as its usual goal not suicide but the loosening of the ego's fixation on this particular love object, all the while preserving the ego's capacity to love" (11). O'Hara cycles this Freudian story through the imagery of Blake's poetry to express an idea about reading:

> For me, this dialectical working-through of loss, ambivalence, and regression to a renewed capacity for love, whether consciously experienced in the process of grief, acted out unconsciously in its demonic parody, neurotic depression, or reflected in the theoretical interpretation of the analytic situation, suggests a repressed (or secularized) religious allegory of reading in which there are three different kinds of readers: the tragic realist (grief), the mythic visionary (depression), and the critical theorist (analysis).

Having attended to the arguments made by Kohut, Kristeva, and other analysts about the dominance of narcissism in postmodern culture, O'Hara once more reconfigures his own previous revision to conclude that the valuable work done in mourning and depression—preserving the ego's capacity to love—has taken a form specific to criticism: "The ritual of reading stages itself as the fall of the sublime into the experience of criticism. The aim of this ritual is the legitimation of sublime transport as the loving act of attributing nobility of mind to another." He completes the theoretically explicit twists in this revision by concluding that with Freud, Trilling could "define the purpose of interpretation, the function of criticism, as this ability to imagine amidst the least fortuitous circumstances as noble a motive for the Other as one can imagine for oneself" (12).

These passages show, of course, that in this work, as in his earlier books, O'Hara remains one of our best critics within the romantic tradition refracted by psychoanalysis. They should also show, however, that *Lionel Trilling: The Work of Liberation* is paradoxically not primarily a book about Trilling, but a "work of liberation." What kind of "work" this is and whose "liberation" it involves—these are among the most likely questions asked by O'Hara's writing. The answers, I suspect, are not all that obvious.

O'Hara asserts over and again that Trilling had and must be seen again as having had a representative status not only among liberal intellectuals, "assimilated Jews," modern critics, "Americans," but also academic professionals. Most of Trilling's admirers would not agree with the idea that he belongs with the last group in that series. If I understand him correctly, Mark Krupnick, in his book, *Lionel Trilling and the Fate of Cultural Criticism*, argues that we are to admire Trilling precisely for his difference from the academic professionals, especially the theoretically inspired ones, who most easily lose sight of the struggle to preserve literature's function in propagating serious values. Most of the many recent books on the "New York Intellectuals" seem to take something like this position; indeed, Russell Jacoby, in *The Last Intellectuals*, makes the explicit argument that we no longer have public intellectuals (like Edmund Wilson), but instead have only "academic professionals"—and, therefore, no "intellectuals" at all.

O'Hara does not make a sociological, historical argument for Trilling's representative status. Rather O'Hara tells a story that positions Trilling's life and work at the cusp of a cultural shift from "modernism" to "postmodernism," from a patriarchal society to a society of the spectacle, of cultural amnesia, and, in so doing, he writes Trilling into our history as a reflexive catachresis, a space of meditation upon the liberal imagination as a form of reading, criticism, and cultural judgment. That is to say, O'Hara has written an allegory, a work that invites us to look inside it for directions as to how to read it and for evidence as to how and why it was written.

In this work, Trilling appears as a figure capable of imaginative and ethical magnanimity. Motivated in part by a putative "Jewish self-hatred"—here O'Hara relies on Sander Gilman's *Jewish Self-Hatred and the Secret Language of Jews*—Trilling, resenting particularly the figure of his father, comes to a critical position that eschews revolutionary politics for a personal ethics and aesthetics. Trilling becomes, then, a severe critic of the sublime transport that occurs in reading and depends on a relationship of identification and mastery; he develops, defends, and practices instead a certain critical ascesis: "The spirit of criticism for Trilling," O'Hara writes, "therefore, arises from the condition of a will that wills its own heroic anticlimax,

short of apocalypse of any sort." As a teacher, then, he recommits himself to the Deweyan position, the Columbia humanities courses—what O'Hara rightly calls "the Columbia University mystique of intelligence." Ethically, critically, and personally this position evolves as a defense against the "American fate of willing self-defeat," and it takes the form of that kind of high modernist aesthetics of style against which Fredric Jameson, among others, has argued for so long: "To accomplish this feat [avoiding the "American fate"], Trilling must read the moral dialectic of the individual in society aesthetically, as fundamentally a cultural matter, that is, as essentially a matter of public style" (63). Of course, as O'Hara puts it, this requires that Trilling and his followers see life as literature; this traditional gesture does new work when seen as a theory of reading: "The power of repression, that is, can become the work of liberation when dramatized, played out in the creation of a self-critical text" (66).

O'Hara writes about how Trilling develops a magnanimity of critical mind as a defensive gesture, one which imputes greatness of motive to the Other as a means of ensuring one's own and one's culture's psychic and ethical survival—on the level of style—at a time when, since everything is possible, nothing is of any particular value or importance: nothing is prohibited. Paradoxically, Trilling's defense of the Father grounds a critical ethics of generosity as much as it supports his suspicions of all "proto-postmodernisms." But as a severe critic in the tradition of Blake, Freud, and Bloom, O'Hara gives us the pride of Trilling's accomplishment as a neurotic act of melancholia: "the way this tragic doctrine of self-sacrifice can evade the charge of neurotic pathology and ideological complicity to emerge as the critical creation of a new nobility of mind" makes up the story of "Trilling's representative career as America's monumental critic of liberal culture" (66).

This very rich book contains many details, powerful readings, polemical contentions, and critical formulations that, although essential to any reading, the limits of space consign for now to the background. Two crucial aspects of the text must, however, be seen sharply, if only in outline.

First of all, the text does present a guide to its own reading; second, the book addresses itself in every way to the contemporary scene of critical work in the academy, to the personal positions, values, and stakes of individuals acting in the profession. The book repeatedly signals its readers that, in the current jargon, it is "self-referential." The New Critics would have said "autotelic." Neither term is quite right, though, for the book is directed outward toward a specific academic audience. In two ways, O'Hara uses Trilling against the current state of critical affairs: O'Hara largely ventriloquizes through Trilling about the current state of the "postmodern" profession; but more important is O'Hara's doubling enactment of "Trilling's" career: as the critic of the emergent postliberal, oppositional rhetoric, values, and performances of the academic professionals, "Trilling" proposes his ethics of critical magnanimity, located on the place of stylistic complexity, with its concerns for the individual and personal. As O'Hara produces his "Trilling," ironically this "Trillingesque" position comes to seem to us the position that itself most fully prefigures the weaknesses, especially the moral disasters, of contemporary "oppositional," that is, in O'Hara's story, "narcissistic," critics.

O'Hara, of course, does not leave himself out of the story. "Trilling," we soon discover, no more instantiates the ideal of critical love than those amnesic, antipatriarchal postmodernists he attacks. O'Hara is very good on the late Trilling. He makes *Sincerity and Authenticity* interesting, and he explains why the embarrassing late meditations on mind and culture should be taken seriously—primarily because they finally and absolutely show the consequences of "Trilling's" erotic discourse of magnanimity and style. Unable any longer to accept either a humanistic or oppositional position—despite the fact that his students continue to do so (one thinks of Norman Podhoretz)—Trilling opted for a textualized ideal. O'Hara puts it this way:

> . . . the authentic self [Trilling came to see] is the perfect worker/consumer in a postindustrial society that requires maximum flexibility for the interchangeable deployments of personnel and maximum fluidity for the transient fixations of stimulated needs. The spectral politics of the shaped self that Trilling practiced for so long have been outmoded by the global economy of the disintegrated self. Although one can say that the completion of this modernization process in our postmodern age may herald a truly world revolution, Trilling's somberer assessment sounds more realistic: a new order of disintegrated selves for the entire earth. . . .

> . . . Trilling proposes for himself alone an ideal of selfhood wholly textual in nature. (288-89)

Earlier in the text, O'Hara identifies "realism" of this sort with grief, and here we see how "Trilling's" imputed magnanimity can no longer function. What are we to make of this? Is O'Hara simply making the merely historical argument that things grew so bad Trilling needed to retreat further, away even from Arnold toward Schopenhauer, Mann, and other modern textual ironists? Would it not be more interesting to imagine rather that O'Hara's Trilling—still mourning, still trying to preserve the capacity to love—can now, explicitly, love only himself and some of the "great dead"? Do we not now see the inevitable consequences of this "magnanimous" man's representative efforts? Indeed, do we not now see them precisely because, in one sense, they were powerful enough to summon O'Hara as a reader to the point of feeling restored and reenergized (27) so that he could then imagine a Trilling as the elaborate figure of the needs of mourning and melancholia within the narcissistic profession O'Hara has helped define?

O'Hara, then, and not "Trilling" has, in this allegory, the capacities of magnanimity. He had bloodied the ghost of Trilling for his own purposes, like Cain, to make a warning—perhaps too late—to the profession as a whole (or perhaps like another Cain, himself too steeped in melancholy and grief to love his brother?). In other words, we are to read this book as the work of liberation carried out from within narcissistic postmodernism by the sorrowing or neurotic critical ego trying hard to renew the dread capacity to love. What must have motivated this struggle for liberation remains the text's secret. But, no doubt, O'Hara has made the book do the work that secret needed and offered its results, in turn, to those who do the work of reading.

In his great essay "On the Uses and Disadvantages of History for Life," Nietzsche warns of the dangers of too much history—it destroys life—and of the need for forgetting: another work of liberation in the service of life. Nietzsche warns that history is too just; it destroys illusion, especially religion; in this text, O'Hara has shown how religion remains in the unconscious of the secular modernist. But history also destroys love, for love can only live in the illusions it creates to support itself:

> historical verification always brings to light so much that is false, crude, inhuman, absurd, violent that the mood of pious illusion in which alone anything that wants to live can live necessarily crumbles away: for it is only in love, only when shaded by the illusion produced by love, that is to say in the unconditional faith of right and perfection, that man is creative. Anything that constrains a man to love less than unconditionally has severed the roots of his strength: he will wither away, that is to say become dishonest.[2]

Despite *Lionel Trilling*'s constant references to Freud, it is Nietzsche—the sentiments he expresses here, the warnings he gives here—who defines the space within which O'Hara works. The book's final warning could be cast in its terms: try as hard as he might, he cannot but love less than unconditionally. Dishonesty is what we have; the culture has destroyed the illusions of love and driven the ego inward to narcissism and outward to criticism.

Notes

1. See also William E. Cain, "Violence, Revolution, and the Cost of Freedom: John Brown and W. E. B. Du Bois," *Boundary 2: An International Journal of Literature and Culture* 17 (1990): 272-304.

2. Friedrich Nietzsche, "On the Uses and Disadvantages of History for Life," trans. R. J. Hollingdale (Cambridge: Cambridge UP, 1983) 95.

Michael Cadden (essay date 1990)

SOURCE: "Engendering F. O. M.: The Private Life of American Renaissance," in *Engendering Men: The Question of Male Feminist Criticism*, edited by Joseph A. Boone and Michael Cadden, Routledge, 1990, pp. 26-35.

[In the following essay, Cadden determines how Matthiessen's sexuality influenced his views on Walt Whitman and

discusses the incongruity of his public and private writings on the poet.]

"To work out:—The sexual bias in literary criticism. . . . What sort of person would the critic prefer to sleep with, in fact."[1]

—E. M. Forster

"'*Dosce, doce, dilige.*' 'Learn, teach, love.' For me I know no better."[2]

—F. O. Matthiessen

When I was an undergraduate at Yale, I was very aware of the ethnic and religious backgrounds of the men and (few) women who taught me literature. Complaining about the gods of the English Department who had shot down our most recent arguments, my friends and I spoke of Father Wimsatt and Father Brooks, Rabbi Bloom and Rabbi Hartman. We did so, as I recall, out of a profound sense of respect for what we saw as the connections these men had made between their various traditions and their work as critics. If we didn't agree with, say, Wimsatt in *The Verbal Icon*, "that the greater poetry will be morally right"[3] and that, consequently, *Antony and Cleopatra* is demonstrably inferior to *King Lear*, we at least knew where he was coming from. Some of us saw him at Mass on Sundays. It never occurred to us to think of criticism as a neutral enterprise in which personality is effaced; we had too many great examples to the contrary at hand.

Given our undergraduate interest in connecting at least some aspects of the critic with his or her work, it may seem surprising in retrospect that we rarely thought of our teachers as having any sexuality. We might have taken Wimsatt's comment on Shakespeare as saying as much about his heterosexual monogamy as about his Catholicism, but we simply hadn't been taught to think in those terms. The only time a professor's sexuality became an issue was when you heard a rumor or caught a pass. The mere mention of sexuality could mean only homosexuality at the all-male Yale (as it was for my first two years); the speakable variety went largely unspoken. And certainly no one ever thought about how a professor's rumored "queerness" might affect his work. Literary criticism was a thing of the mind and the soul; for the body such men had recourse, it was whispered, to vacations in Morocco with Arab boys or in Venice with the gondoliers.

There was one professor whom I might have had at Yale and who might have taught me something about embodied criticism; that is, had he lived, and had his alma mater made him the offer he longed for, and had he been an altogether different sort of man. In 1925 a young Rhodes Scholar, with a little visionary help from Walt Whitman, wrote to his physically reluctant male lover of his desire to join mind, body and soul both in his life and in his work:

You say our love is not based on the physical, but on our mutual understanding and sympathy and tenderness. And of course that is right. But we both have bodies: 'if the body is not the soul, what then is the soul?' . . . Blend together the mind, body and soul so that they are joined in a mighty symphony. The mind and the soul give an idealisation and exhaltation to the body; and the body in its turn gives an intuitive, impalpable channel of expression to the soul and mind.

(***Rat*** 86, 88)

These words from Francis Otto Matthiessen—F. O. Matthiessen on his book jackets, F. O. M. in his introductions, "Matty" to his friends, and "the Devil" to his lover.

Best known as the author of ***American Renaissance: Art and Expression in the Age of Emerson and Whitman***, F. O. Matthiessen was one of the most celebrated critics of his time. A graduate of Yale, class of 1923, he studied at Oxford on a Rhodes Scholarship before returning to the United States to do graduate work at Harvard. He taught for two years at Yale, from 1927 to 1929, before taking up a job back at Harvard. By the age of thirty-two Matthiessen had published three books—on Sarah Orne Jewett, Elizabethan translation, and the poetry of T. S. Eliot. His ***American Renaissance***, published in 1941, helped to create and legitimize the field of American Studies; college teachers throughout the country still use his title for their courses in nineteenth-century American literature. Active as a Christian Socialist, the vice-president of the Harvard Teachers' Union, and a member of the Progressive Party and innumerable leftist defense committees, Matthiessen continued to be productive until his suicide in 1950, shortly before he was to testify before the House Un-American Activities Committee about his political sympathies.

As Jonathan Arac reminds us in his book *Critical Genealogies*, there are now two F. O. Matthiessens in print—the author of the above-mentioned critical volumes *and* the author of a series of letters written over a period of twenty years to his lover, the American painter Russell Cheney. Matthiessen met Cheney in 1924 on a voyage to England prior to his second year at Oxford, and the two remained lovers until Cheney's death in 1945, corresponding daily whenever they were apart. In 1978, Matthiessen's friend and Yale classmate Louis Hyde, acting on hints in Matthiessen's will and in the letters themselves, published ***Rat and the Devil: The Journal Letters of F. O. Matthiessen and Russell Cheney***. In his chapter on Matthiessen, Arac calls attention to the extraordinary differences between Matthiessen's critical and personal voices and the ways in which such differences highlight both the "struggle of the will to define, formulate, mobilize and authorize an American Renaissance"[4] and the cost of that institutional struggle. In the process, Arac cites the difference between Matthiessen's homosexually explicit treatment of Whitman in the letters and the rather more pansexual version in his *magnum opus*; as Arac writes, to "create the centrally authoritative critical identity of ***American Renaissance***, much had to be displaced or scattered or disavowed."[5] But in concentrating on Matthiessen's *political* displacements, scatterings, and disavowals, Arac succeeds in doing to Matthiessen what Matthiessen did to Whitman in ***American Renaissance***: in both cases, politics displaces sexuality as the proper issue for scholarly investigation.

We can see this displacement at work in Arac's treatment of Matthiessen's visit to Wells Cathedral, where he had what he describes as a Whitmanesque encounter with a

> workman—husky, broad-shouldered, forty . . . the perfect Chaucerian yeoman. We stood there talking for a quarter of a minute, and as he went on I deliberately let my elbow rub against his belly. That was all: there couldn't have been anything more. I didn't want anything more. I was simply attracted by him as a simple open-hearted feller, and wanted to feel the touch of his body as a passing gesture.
>
> (*Rat* 124)

In Arac's analysis, the elbow rub becomes a figure for all that was lost in the "harmonizing, centralizing, normalizing and identifying"[6] process of writing *American Renaissance*; as Arac puts it, "Loose elbows had to be tucked in."[7] But Arac tellingly paraphrases one particular line of Matthiessen's, and this paraphrase, I would contend, works as a metaphor for the desexualization of Matthiessen that Arac's essay, like all post-*Rat and the Devil* treatments of F. O. M., eventually effects. Arac tells us that, during his encounter with the workman, Matthiessen was "sexually excited."[8] Matthiessen's own description is more colloquial: "I had a hard on." (*Rat* 124). For me, the lovely, blunt statement of the fact of the matter embodies Matthiessen—gives him a body: the body of an upper-class, gay man—in a way that his criticism rarely does. Throughout the letters to Cheney, the gay critic barely perceivable beneath his canonical drag emerges from the closet of professional and patriarchal mastery hard on in hand, thereby exposing and demystifying the "Phallus" that "disseminated" an entire Renaissance.

A Matthiessen even more decorously sober-sided than Arac's is on display in May Sarton's 1955 novel, *Faithful Are the Wounds*.[9] Like Arac, Sarton chooses to concentrate on the Matthiessen of the public witchhunt rather than the private hurt. Sarton's story focuses on the last days of Edward Cavan, an English professor at Harvard University (with a resumé closely approximating Matthiessen's) who commits suicide largely out of his sense that former political allies have abandoned him. Although Cavan's principal political involvement is with a safely liberal "Civil Liberties Union," Sarton's fictionalization reflects the usual leftist position on Matthiessen's suicide in the 1950s—that he was America's Jan Masaryck, a just man suicided by an unjust society. But as Harry Levin has observed, the publication of the Matthiessen-Cheney letters brings out "the disingenuousness of [Sarton's] effort to center a novel upon his person while ignoring the basic psychological facts,"[10] most especially Matthiessen's inability to continue his interest in life after the death of his lover.

Within the world of the novel, Sarton seems to justify her silence on the subject of Matthiessen's closet by allowing two of her characters to admit to their ignorance about Cavan's private life and then, oddly enough, to deny its relevance to his suicide:

> "But who were Edward's lovers, if he had a lover?"
>
> "I don't know."
>
> "Of course you don't. And neither do I. Don't you see? There are whole areas of Edward's life that we never touched, never could touch."
>
> "People like Edward Cavan don't commit suicide for love—a man of fifty—really, Orlando, what a romantic you are!"
>
> (*FW* 162)

Yet like Arac and, to a certain extent, Matthiessen himself, Sarton teases her readers with suggestions of a possible (homo)sexually oriented interpretation of literary life/ artifact. Of course, publishing in 1955, Sarton probably felt she could not be explicit in her references to Matthiessen's/Cavan's sexuality; no doubt even Matthiessen's friends would have considered such a breach of confidentiality an attempt to besmirch the reputation of an honorable man. Hence, although Cavan has never married and is possessed of a "personal dignity" that "almost . . . precluded intimacy" (*FW* 127), his status as an "outsider" (one of the novel's key terms) is established only in relation to his *public, overtly political* self.

But Sarton provides the occasional encoded bit of information for those who might want to speculate about why her hero remains such a *personal* cipher. When Cavan is about to depart from a friend's house, one character muses about his next destination in ways that betray a knowledge different from that possessed by the novel itself: "He would go to one of those bars in Scollay Square, she supposed, carrying his word *solidarity* like a banner which no one could see, drink with the sailors who called him Professor and treated him like a harmless drunk, walk the streets half the night, and then not sleep" (*FW* 132). It would be ten years before Sarton, herself a lesbian, published a novel dealing explicitly with gay and lesbian issues—*Mrs. Stevens Hears the Mermaids Singing*—but in passages such as this one, we can hear the content in the closet rattling around, almost begging to be let out. When a character explains that Cavan "couldn't communicate the very essence of his belief and that was his tragedy" (*FW* 209), Sarton perhaps unconsciously signals the novel's tragic inability to name at least one important part of its hero's essence. What's missing is the Whitmanesque hard on.

It was his encounter with Cheney that made Matthiessen read Whitman in a new way, "not solely because it gives me an intellectual kick . . . but because I'm living it" (*Rat* 26). The combination of his physical experience with Cheney and his intellectual experience with *The Intermediate Sex*, by Whitman's British disciple, Edward Carpenter, provided Matthiessen with a new vision of the sexual condition he had earlier assumed would be condemned to inexpressibility, the "idea that what we have is one of the divine gifts; that such as you and I are the advance guard of any hope for a spirit of brotherhood" (*Rat* 47). He saw Cheney and himself as pioneers in a new sexual landscape:

Of course this life of ours is entirely new—neither of us know [*sic*] a parallel case. We stand in the middle of an uncharted, uninhabited country. That there have been other unions like ours is obvious, but we are unable to draw on their experience. We must create everything for ourselves. And creation is never easy.

(***Rat*** 71)

As a student of American literature and culture, Matthiessen was aware that the gender territory he inhabited was not entirely unpeopled. His request to write his dissertation on Whitman, a request turned down by his Harvard mentors, suggests that he might have entertained hopes from early on in his career to profile some fellow pioneers. Indeed, at moments in ***American Renaissance*** itself, Matthiessen appears to want to make good on the observations and claims of the letters; he seems to provide a coded roster of undercover soldiers for a nascent gay political avant-garde, a map of the previously uncharted landscape of same-sex affection, and a genealogy of gay relationships.

Matthiessen's chapter on Whitman has been attacked for politically incorrect statements about Whitman's sexual identity, especially when compared to the invocations of the great gay poet in the letters where, as William E. Cain remarks, "Matthiessen tapped his passionate reading of Whitman to voice his love for Cheney."[11] Yet many of Matthiessen's comments about Whitman seem to beg for a recognition of the gay specificity of his critical analysis. Of course, it is certainly the case, as most contemporary commentators feel obliged to point out, that Matthiessen displays signs of internalized homophobia in his observation about Whitman that "in the passivity of the poet's body there is a quality vaguely pathological and homosexual."[12] But many other passages invite a more celebratory reading of the "Calamus" Whitman. He praises the earthiness of Whitman's language and its roots in "the power of sex" (***AR*** 523), and he provocatively suggests the existence of a coterie clientele for the poet's most homoerotically suggestive work:

Actually Whitman's language approximates only intermittently any customary colloquial phrasing, though the success of some of his best shorter poems, 'As I lay with my head in your lap camerado,' or, probably the most skillfully sustained of all, 'When I heard at the close of day,' is owing to their suggestion of intimate conversation. This fact raises the ambiguous problem of just who his audience was.

(***AR*** 556)

In quoting from one audience member's review of Whitman's letters to Pete Doyle (the notorious 16.4 of the poet's alphabetically encoded journals), Matthiessen implies that Henry James himself was one intimate of the Whitman reading circle. In a footnote to the James observation, Matthiessen attempts to answer "the much disputed question of what [Whitman] meant by comradeship" (***AR*** 582) by quoting at length from a steamy Whitman letter to yet another "loving comrade," the soldier Benton Wilson. He

thus wittily if elusively effects a textual four-way among James, Whitman, Doyle, and Wilson.

Two other guest appearances in the Whitman chapter indicate that Matthiessen may have been dropping hints as to the existence of a literary homintern, if not a self-conscious gay literary tradition. After documenting the fears Gerard Manley Hopkins had of appearing too Whitmanesque, the critic comments, "He must have been referring to Whitman's homosexuality and his own avoidance of this latent strain in himself" (***AR*** 585). Matthiessen sees Hopkins' own homosexuality at its most obvious in the sonnet "Harry Ploughman," where "this feeling rises closest to the surface in his pleasure in the liquid movement of the workman's body" (***AR*** 585). A reader of the Matthiessen-Cheney letters, and particularly of the Wells Cathedral episode, cannot help observing here the creation of something like a gay literary tradition, a band of scribbling brothers united by their class-determined common attraction to common workmen.

It was probably the painter Cheney who introduced Matthiessen to another kindred spirit found in the Whitman chapter of ***American Renaissance***—Thomas Eakins. Taking for his example *The Swimming Hole* (a reproduction of which appears in the book for consultation and delectation), Matthiessen seems almost coy in his fantasy about the poet's imagined response to one of the painter's most homoerotic canvases: "What would have appealed most to Whitman was the free flexible movement within the composition, and the rich physical pleasure in the outdoor scene and in the sunlight on the firmly modelled flesh" (***AR*** 610).

Like Eakins' *The Swimming Hole* and like Skull and Bones, the secret society at Yale that provided Matthiessen with his longest friendships, the critic's collection of kindred literary spirits is exclusively male. When he writes, "The one common denominator of my five writers, uniting even Hawthorne and Whitman, was their devotion to the possibilities of democracy" (***AR*** ix), he ignores another, more obvious connection: as a number of feminist critics have pointed out, Matthiessen, like many other male theorists of American literature, excluded all women authors from the national canon he created in ***American Renaissance***.[13] The man who worried that he had the "blurred and soft" voice of a "fairy" (***Rat*** 197) did everything he could to insure a manly tradition purged of the effeminate. While his discussion of Whitman's poems of psychic transvestism[14] (Section 5 of *Song of Myself*, "The Sleepers") tends to betray a certain embarrassment at the poet's "fluidity of sexual sympathy" (***AR*** 535), it is clearly Matthiessen's own fluidity of (homo)sexual sympathy that in part determines the womanless world of canonical greatness.

Nonetheless Matthiessen had no intention of becoming the Edward Carpenter of literary criticism. Neither in his work nor in his life was Matthiessen a sexual politician or rabble-rouser. Throughout his career, he remained an insider's outsider and an outsider's insider, cultivating a schizophrenic division between his relationship with Cheney and his professional mien even as he glorified the rhetoric of wholeness; dedicated as he was to consensus of all kinds, Matthiessen felt obligated to elide those personal (and political and literary) facts that challenged (and continue to challenge) the dream of a single, organic, democratic community. According to Joseph Summers and U. T. Miller Summers' entry in the *Dictionary of American Biography*, Matthiessen's homosexuality was strictly an affair of the heart; it had few consequences in the great worlds of the university or the profession: "For most of his students and younger colleagues Matthiessen's homosexuality was suggested, if at all, only by the fact that his circle was more predominantly heterosexual than was usual in Harvard literary groups at the time and that he was unusually hostile to homosexual colleagues who mixed their academic and sexual relations."[15] (*Plus ça change.*) This graphic example of Matthiessen's refusal to connect his professional and sexual lives and hence to develop any kind of sexual politics in his life or his work suggests that this refusal may have ultimately lead to his destruction every bit as much as the overt political reasons that are usually attributed to his suicide. He could begin *American Renaissance* by quoting the architect Louis Sullivan to the effect that the test of "true scholarship" is that it be "for the good and enlightenment of all the people, not for the pampering of a class" (*AR* xv), but tragically he could not see himself as part of a collective sexual identity smaller than "all of the people."

At times Matthiessen's closeted position seems to have been a source of extreme pain. He wrote to Cheney in January of 1930:

> My sex bothers me, feller, sometimes when it makes me aware of the falseness of my position in the world. And consciousness of the falseness seems to sap my confidence of power. Have I any right to live in a community that would so utterly disapprove of me if it knew the facts? . . . I hate to have to hide when what I thrive on is absolute directness.
>
> (*Rat* 200)

But directness about his sexual identity would have placed Matthiessen on the margins of the very culture he sought to center. The price of engendering an *American Renaissance* was directness about gender itself.

Given Matthiessen's total investment of his sexual identity in the person of Russell Cheney, it should come as no surprise that, when he suffered a breakdown in 1938-1939, he and his doctors connected it to his fears of Cheney's death. Cheney was twenty years older than Matthiessen and an alcoholic. At fifty-six, Cheney had good reason to believe that his health would not hold up; in a moment of desperation, after a particularly bad spree, he told Matthiessen that he wanted to die. Soon after, Matthiessen's own suicidal feelings began.

Arac and others have testified to the many political, literary critical, and sexual repressions that might have pre-cipitated both this breakdown and his later suicide. In his own journal account of the genesis of his condition, Matthiessen seems to downplay the political and professional problems he was facing, but his language suggests a critical schizophrenia with roots in his position as a gendered subject:

> Why? That is what is so baffling, so unfathomed. Because my talent is less than I thought? Because, on the first outset, I couldn't write the book I wanted? . . . Even though it should turn out that I am an enthusiast trying to be a critic, a Platonic rhapsode trying to be an Aristotelian, that means a fairly hard period of readjustment, but scarcely grounds for death for a man of thirty-six.
>
> (*Rat* 246)

It was important for Matthiessen that he tame "the enthusiast," "the Platonic rhapsode" in himself—the persona given full reign in the letters to Cheney—in order to create his "Aristotelian" masterpiece. Neither "Matty" nor "the Devil" could perform the work of authorizing an *American Renaissance*. Yet Matthiessen also acknowledges, in relation to his reaction to Cheney's death wish, that without the man who gave birth to the rhapsode in him, his own life would become meaningless:

> Having built my life so simply and wholly with Russell's, having had my eyes opened by him to so much beauty, my heart filled by such richness, my pulse beating steadily in time with his intimate daily companionship, I am shocked at the thought of life without him. How would it be possible? How go on from day to day?
>
> (*Rat* 247)

Without Russell, there would be no work for the body; the body of work might go on, but not in the vital way that it had. Without the Whitman in his life, there would be only the Whitman of *American Renaissance*, an unsexed Aristotelian version of the Platonic original and of his unsexed Aristotelian critic.

Later in this same journal entry, Matthiessen records a conversation with his doctor in language that recalls an earlier letter about his depression at being separated from Cheney ("There seems to be a film between me and everything. Nothing seems really vital: books are just a procession of words and I can't find significance in my work" [*Rat* 173]). Significantly, here Cheney is not the explicit subject; subliminally, however, he is figured as Matthiessen's connection to everything that is most important in his life and work:

> At one point in our talk I broke into tears, and said that I loved life, that I had felt myself in contact with so many sides of American society and believed there was so much work to be done, absorbing it, helping to direct it intelligently. And now I felt a film of unreality between me and everything that had seemed most real, that I had to find some way to break through it.
>
> (*Rat* 248)

Surely one of the major sides of American society that Matthiessen was most in contact with was the homosocial and homoerotic literary and social traditions. He knew it from books—through his work on Jewett, Melville, Whitman, James, and others. And he "lived it" with Cheney and the men he cruised on the streets of Boston, London, and Paris. But the connection between the tradition and the life existed only in his person, not in his book; without Cheney, the "film of unreality" would reappear, and he would be left not with a utopian sexual and political project, but with its pallid representation in *American Renaissance*.

Cheney died in 1945, six years after Matthiessen's breakdown. They had been together for over twenty years. Although Matthiessen continued to be professionally and politically active (he seconded the nomination of Henry Wallace at the Progressive Party convention in 1948), he could not sustain himself for long. In 1950, at the age of forty-seven, he fulfilled his 1938 fantasy of "jumping out of a window" (*Rat* 247) by leaping from the twelfth floor of a Boston hotel. His suicide note read: "I am exhausted. . . . I can no longer believe that I can continue to be of use to my profession and my friends" (*Rat* 367).

Twenty-five years before, Matthiessen had written Cheney from Oxford:

> I don't want to be well-informed. I want to be truly myself and by that comfortably vague statement I mean that I want to follow what I feel to be my bent to the full. I want to study the essence of the human spirit and I want to live to the full. You remember me telling you Langland's motto: '*Dosce, doce, dilige*.' 'Learn, teach, love.' For me I know no better.
>
> (*Rat* 101)

It was a harder motto to live up to than he knew. F. O. Matthiessen became the scholar and teacher; Matty the Devil lived in love. While it is true, as Eric Cheyfitz has suggested, that "Matthiessen lacked or resisted a critical vocabulary that could translate his democratic politics into the writing of literary history,"[16] it is also the case that Matthiessen lacked a sexual politics (and a resultant critical vocabulary) that could allow him to connect his many kinds of work and the life he lead with Russell Cheney.

Let me end on a fantastic and utopian note, borrowed from the imagination of Virginia Woolf.[17] Let the feminism I came of professional age with do for me what Matthiessen could not do alone—engender and legitimize the Platonic rhapsody. Let me imagine, then, since facts are so easy to come by, what would have happened had Matthiessen had a wonderfully gifted brother, called Michael, let us say. Like Francis, Michael went to Yale. Like him, he studied in England on a generous fellowship. But there their paths diverged. While in England, Michael met E. M. Forster, and one fateful day, Forster touched Michael's backside in the same way that Edward Carpenter had once touched Forster's. As if by magic, the effect was the same. In Forster's words, which Michael cherished, "It seemed to go straight through the small of my back into my ideas, without involving my thoughts."[18]

Michael found another sentence in Forster, a much shorter one, that also meant a lot to him, resonated for him in ways different from the way it did for his friends: "Only connect. . . ."[19] It seemed an invitation. To what he could not yet say. Let us now suppose that Michael returned to Yale, worked very hard, got a job at the very school that brother Francis most wanted to teach at, and fell in love with the most wonderful man in the world. Michael was nearly as productive as his now famous brother and, because he wrote the right sort of books, eventually received tenure. But he was not content with his work.

After the death of his brother, Michael reflected on their parallel lives and began to ask some very startling questions: "Could I be thinking about my work in the wrong fashion? Doesn't who and what I love affect the way I write and teach? Shouldn't who and what I love make its way into my work and into my classroom? Doesn't it do so whether I like it to or not? Isn't there a history of people who have loved as I do? Is this country as uncharted and uninhabited as Francis thought? Haven't many of our kind been writers and teachers and critics? Wouldn't it be good to tell their stories? There will be problems, of course. Who counts and who doesn't? Based on what information? And where is it in the text? But wouldn't it be worthwhile nonetheless? To at least begin the map? Yes, and with others who cannot find themselves represented there for company."

By the time I arrived at Yale in 1967, Michael Matthiessen was a legend—the great gay critic, we called him, because he seemed to like that queer word. Some felt awkward around him. I did myself at first. I'd certainly never met anyone as honest and open—in his work, in his classroom, and in his life—about something everyone else found so unspeakable. His learning, teaching, and loving were all of a piece, all connected. And, like most Yalies of the period, I had to admit that the best course I ever took was the one he cotaught with a feminist colleague based on the book they cowrote—*The Other American Renaissance*.

Notes

1. E. M. Forster, diary (25 October 1910), as quoted in introduction to *The Life to Come and Other Short Stories* (London: Edward Arnold, 1972), p. xv. This essay is a modified version of a lecture given at a conference, Lesbian/Gay Studies '87: Definitions and Explorations, at Yale University. I would like to thank Professor Ralph Hexter for his kind invitation to participate in such a lively event.

2. Quoted by F. O. Matthiessen in a letter to Russell Cheney (2 March 1925), *Rat and the Devil: Journal Letters of F. O. Matthiessen and Russell Cheney*, ed. Louis Hyde (Hamden: Archon Books, 1978), p. 101. Hereafter cited in the body of my essay as *Rat*.

3. W. K. Wimsatt, Jr., *The Verbal Icon* (Lexington: University of Kentucky Press, 1954), p. 100.

4. Jonathan Arac, *Critical Genealogies: Historical Situations for Postmodern Literary Studies* (New York: Columbia University Press, 1987), p. 175. A first version of Arac's chapter on Matthiessen appeared in *The American Renaissance Reconsidered: Selected Papers from the English Institute, 1982-83*, eds. Walter Benn Michaels and Donald E. Pease (Baltimore: Johns Hopkins University Press, 1985), pp. 90-112.

5. Arac, *Critical Genealogies*, p. 159.

6. Ibid., p. 175.

7. Ibid., p. 159.

8. Ibid.

9. May Sarton, *Faithful Are the Wounds* (New York: Norton, 1955). Hereafter cited in the body of my essay as *FW*.

10. Harry Levin, "The Private Life of F. O. Matthiessen," *The New York Review of Books*, (20 July 1978), p. 43.

11. William E. Cain, *F. O. Matthiessen and the Politics of Criticism* (Madison: University of Wisconsin Press, 1988), p. 47.

12. F. O. Matthiessen, *American Renaissance: Art and Expression in the Age of Emerson and Whitman* (Oxford: Oxford University Press, 1941), p. 535. Hereafter cited in the body of my text as *AR*.

13. On this subject, see especially Nina Baym, "Melodramas of Beset Manhood: How Theories of American Fiction Exclude Women Authors," in *The New Feminist Criticism: Essays on Women, Literature and Theory*, ed. Elaine Showalter (New York: Pantheon, 1985), pp. 63ff.

14. This formulation was suggested to me by Sandra Gilbert.

15. Joseph Summers and U. T. Miller Summers, "F. O. Matthiessen," *Dictionary of American Biography, Supplement Four: 1946-50,* eds. John A. Garraty and Edward T. James (New York: Scribner's, 1974), p. 560.

16. Eric Cheyfitz, "Matthiessen's *American Renaissance*: Circumscribing the Revolution," *American Quarterly* 41, 2 (June 1989):358.

17. Specifically, Woolf's speculations about "Shakespeare's sister" in *A Room of One's Own*.

18. E. M. Forster, "Terminal Note" to *Maurice* (New York: Norton, 1971), p. 249.

19. F. M. Forster, epigraph to *Howards End* (London: Edward Arnold, 1910, 1973), p. ii.

David Bergman (essay date 1991)

SOURCE: "F. O. Matthiessen: The Critic as Homosexual," in *Gaiety Transfigured: Gay Self-Representation in American Literature*, The University of Wisconsin Press, 1991, pp. 85-102.

[*In the following essay, Bergman considers the impact of Matthiessen's sexuality on his work.*]

Despite the publicity that attended F. O. Matthiessen's suicide in 1950, and the books that were subsequently written about him, including May Sarton's 1955 novel *Faithful are the Wounds,* it was not until a quarter of a century later that his homosexuality became public knowledge. During his life, Matthiessen had not tried to hide the fact, but neither had he made it a public issue. Friends, colleagues, and even students widely understood that Matthiessen was gay, but they felt in large measure what William E. Cain has recently said, that the "facts of Matthiessen's sexual . . . life . . . do not have much direct bearing at all" on his work (*Matthiessen*, 48).

Matthiessen would have disagreed. He kept his sexual identity and his scholarly reputation separate only because the social atmosphere in which he worked necessitated such a division. Any attempt to bring them together would have given a rare opportunity to those who wished to discredit him and his work. He understood quite clearly how dear a price he paid for his discretion and how it distorted what he said and how he spoke. "My sex bothers me," he wrote, "sometimes when it makes me aware of the falseness of my position in the world. . . . But damn it! I hate to have to hide when what I thrive on is absolute directness" (Hyde, *Rat and the Devil* [hereafter cited as *RD*], 200). Matthiessen, who prized honesty and plain speech, understood that he had to be discreet and evasive if he wished to survive.

His discretion succeeded. Today he is regarded as the most influential writer on American culture of the 1930s and 1940s. As a teacher at Harvard, he personally influenced an entire generation of students and scholars, and through his writing and especially *American Renaissance*, his masterpiece, he continues to exert an important presence. Moreover, by keeping his sexual life relatively quiet he was able to play a role in the politics of his era as president and founder of the Harvard Teachers' Union and as a campaigner for Henry Wallace, the Progressive Party's 1948 candidate for president. In these public roles he did not deny his homosexuality; he merely performed them without any reference to sexuality. No doubt, it was a difficult line to walk, and his repeated bouts of depression were likely deepened by his precarious position.

Matthiessen felt that sexuality always plays a part in a writer's work. Although he rejected crude biographical procedures, he advocated the use of psychoanalytic insights that would uncover basic structures in a writer's sensibility or development. Since Matthiessen advocated what today would be called a "holistic" approach to literary studies, an approach in which critics should "make use of what we inevitably bring from our own lives" (*Renaissance,* xiii), the absence of a careful examination of the relationship between Matthiessen's sexuality and his criticism is a gap that, despite Leo Marx's admirable attempt, cries out to be filled. Unlike most critics whose private lives remain obscure, Matthiessen's life and his sexuality were opened to our inspection through the publication of *Rat and the Devil*, a selection of the approximately three thousand letters he exchanged with his lover, Russell Cheney. We have, therefore, both the motive and the opportunity to examine Cheney's impact on Matthiessen's conception of himself as a homosexual and the impact of Matthiessen's sexuality on his writing. By examining these issues, I hope to be answering Thomas Yingling's call "to acknowledge [the] use of gay texts for gay readers and to investigate the function of writers such as Whitman, Crane and Matthiessen to the production of a homosexual culture within an American culture" (23).

F. O. Matthiessen met Russell Cheney in 1924, aboard the *Paris*, the newest, largest, and most luxurious of the French Line's fleet (Newell, 87). What began as a shipboard romance became the central emotional attachment of their lives, a relationship that ended a quarter of a century later with Cheney's death from heart disease. When they met, Cheney was a painter of some reputation, while Matthiessen was a promising student of English. Cheney came from a close-knit, old New England family who had settled one of the Connecticut valleys in colonial days. Matthiessen's family was far-flung and had relatively recently arrived, though his mother was a distant relation to Sarah Orne Jewett. While both were the children of privilege, Matthiessen had seen his father fritter away the fortune he inherited from his own father, the founder of what became Westclox. Cheney, in contrast, was part of a family that carefully husbanded its wealth through many generations and filled positions of civic and religious responsibility. In many ways, Cheney had the background that Matthiessen dreamed of having, and for all Matthiessen's belief in the goodness of the masses and the need for social justice, his writing contains more than a little of the patrician concern for social form as well as social obligation.

The most striking difference between them was their ages. When they met, Matthiessen was twenty-two, Cheney forty-two. This difference in generation affected many of the experiences that bound them together. For example, although both men were Yale graduates and were proud of their connection with their alma mater, they went to very different schools. Matthiessen was only two years old when Cheney was graduated, and consequently the faculty had largely changed by the time Matty (as he was called by his friends) was matriculated. Their attitudes toward homosexuality were also a source of occasional conflict. Born in 1881, Cheney was raised with Victorian notions of sexuality while Matthiessen, a child of the twentieth century, had studied the matter, in his words, "scientifically" and felt much freer.

Cheney entered Matthiessen's life at a time when Matthiessen was especially receptive to such a relationship. They met as Matthiessen was returning to England to complete his second and last year as a Rhodes Scholar. His mother had recently died and, with her, whatever plans he had of a home after Oxford. Having lost his own mother,

Cheney could empathize with Matthiessen, and within weeks of their meeting, he sent Matthiessen his mother's photograph. Matthiessen replied:

> How I loved that picture of your mother's birthday. Except for my quick impatience I think we must have had exactly the same sort of relationships with our mothers. And then just when it gets to the point that after I return from Oxford she is to make a home for me in New Haven and I can maybe give her some culture and some of the love she has always been denied, the poor devoted little woman dies. Never did she have anyone to look after her. When I was five, my father sent my two brothers away to boarding school. My mother, my sister, and I went to California, presumably just for the winter for my sister's health. Of course, any one with any worldliness . . . would have seen that my father never intended to give her a home again. . . . She wouldn't listen to the mention of divorce, for in spite of his being absolutely worthless—God pity her—she loved him to the end. Finally when I was thirteen he practically forced her into a divorce for he wanted to marry again. . . . How I remember the impotence of my thirteen year old rape.
>
> (*RD*, 48)

With the death of his mother, Matthiessen was without a person on whom he could bestow his love and caring attention and who might return his affection and provide a home. The letter makes clear how allied Matthiessen and his mother had been. Her unworldliness and homelessness merge with his own innocence and dispossession. He translates the imposition of his mother's divorce into a rape of his own impotent body, and the love his mother bears for her underserving husband carries with it his own unrequited affection for his father. Cheney did not so much replace Mrs. Matthiessen as fill a vaccum that her death had created.

Cheney's most immediate effect on Matthiessen was to force Matty to reconsider what it meant to be gay. Before their meeting, Matthiessen's homosexual experiences seem to have been either brief anonymous contacts or those circumscribed by boarding school. Matthiessen had bravely discussed his sexual orientation with his closest friends, telling Russell Davenport that though he "didn't want to be an alarmist," he thought he "might very likely be altogether homosexual" (*RD*, 47). At the time of his conversation with Davenport, Matthiessen saw only three possible outcomes to his predicament: (1) "morbidity" by repressing all sexual expression, (2) "self-abuse," and (3) "the old business with men," namely, anonymous sexual contacts. But by falling in love with Cheney, Matthiessen becomes aware of a fourth option—"love between men"—and he writes Cheney of the "surprise" that realization has for him: "Was it possible? I had known lust. I had prided myself that it had never touched the purity of my friendships. Was it possible for love and friendship to be blended into one? But before I had time to even ask the question it was answered" (*RD*, 48). His love for Cheney forces Matthiessen to reconsider the nature and social implications of homosexuality; it transforms an ugly truth into a glorious opportunity, "the old business with men" into "the advance guard of any hope for a spirit of brotherhood" (**RD**, 47).

Matthiessen was not, however, content to feel "this new sensitive tingling in the tips of my fingers, and on my lips" (**RD**, 48). As a firm believer in the Eliotic "unified sensibility," he had to blend an emotional apprehension of his sexuality with its intellectual comprehension. Matthiessen began to test his sexual response in the field and to research whatever was available in the library. Consequently, his letters provide one of the finest records now available of how a man formed his understanding of what it meant to be homosexual.

Some of his experiments sound boyishly comic. For example, after meeting Rudy Vallee, a fellow "son of Eli," in a London hotel, the two—at Vallee's suggestion—visit "the toughest dive in Europe." There Matthiessen "enter[s] upon a little study in the psychology of sex" by dancing with the "painted whores . . . in a way that would ordinarily land [him] in jail," but he discovers "no female physical attraction" (**RD**, 34-35). In another letter to Cheney he discusses a plan to rent a room from a "homosexual fellow . . . who ran a lodging house" and "who might have been a way to gain added sex knowledge," but he rejects the idea in deference to Cheney (**RD**, 26).

Even before they met, Matthiessen had begun to read sexual psychology, particularly Havelock Ellis's *Sexual Inversion*, which had first "brought home to me that I was what I was by *nature*" (**RD**, 47, Matthiessen's italics). But meeting Cheney accelerates the reading process. Cheney inspires him to reread Whitman, whom Matthiessen had only begun to read for "an intellectual kick" the year before (**RD**, 26). Whitman becomes a regular topic of their early letters. Then Matthiessen begins reading Edward Carpenter, first *The Intermediate Sex* and then *Days with Walt Whitman*. He takes up John Addington Symonds, Shelley, and George Barnefield's essay on Shelley as a homosexual. Cheney makes reference to Proust and Raymond Radiguet, the Rimbaud-like boy genius who had died at age twenty in 1923. Largely cut off from a gay community, Matthiessen and Cheney construct much of their sexual identities from what they read.

Matthiessen's thoughts were spurred by opposition. He claimed that he learned the most from Irving Babbitt because, by disagreeing "at nearly every point," Matthiessen was forced "to fight for [his] tastes, which grew stronger by the exercise" (Cain, *Matthiessen*, 57). Similarly, the changes in Matthiessen's attitudes toward his sexuality do not become clear until Cheney challenged them during one of his intermittent bouts of guilt, panic, and conventionality. Six months after their meeting, the relationship ripening, Matthiessen requested permission from Cheney to write his closest friends about their relationship, but the idea of exposing it to the scrutiny of outsiders drove Cheney into one of his periodic depressions. "You cannot conceive the intensity of emotion," Cheney wrote Matthiessen, "that hauled me right out of bed a couple of

times night before last." The notion of public exposure of their sexual relations was "absolutely intolerable" (**RD**, 80). Cheney believed "it absolutely impossible for two fellers to get away with the situation . . . in society . . . as it is organized" (**RD**, 80). He sums it up: "for the outside world, you are outcast" (**RD**, 81).

Cheney at times appears to approve of society's condemnation of homosexuality. He sees himself as a man driven and degraded by "two indulgences, in drink and sex" which have destroyed "the simple sweet nature that was part of me in my teens" (**RD**, 80-81). He tells Matthiessen that his "character had steadily deteriorated in will power" over the last ten to fifteen years, and the only way to return to mental health and spiritual well-being is to stop indulging in both drink and sex. "I believe, that the base of our love is not physical but intense understanding of a mutual problem," (**RD**, 80) he tells Matthiessen and invites his young lover to help him abstain from alcohol and sexual contact.

Matthiessen's lengthy response strikes me as enormously sympathetic under the circumstances even as it strongly rejects both Cheney's proposition and assumptions. The tone is notably paternal, considering their differences in age, as though Matthiessen were comforting a scared, unhappy child. At the same time, he gives Cheney hardly an inch: "I've got to tell the truth, don't I? This is the essence of our life. And the truth is that from my point of view I don't agree with anything you said" (**RD**, 86).

Matthiessen rebuts Cheney's assertion that homosexuality is an acquired trait, a bad habit that willpower alone can eradicate:

> Can you acknowledge the fact that you were born different from most people sexually and that consequently you react to different stimuli. . . .
>
> That to me is the essence of it; we are born as we are. I am no longer the least ashamed of it. What is there to be ashamed of? It simply reveals the fact that sex is not mathematical and clear-cut, something to be separated definitely into male and female; but that just as there are energetic active women and sensitive delicate men, so also there are women who appear to be feminine but have a male sex element, and men, like us, who appear to be masculine but have a female sex element. Ashamed of it? Forty years ago, perhaps, when nothing was really known about it, I would have felt myself an outcast. But now that the matter has been studied scientifically, and the facts are there in black and white?
>
> (**RD**, 87)

Matthiessen bases his argument on Havelock Ellis, Edward Carpenter, and through them on Karl Heinrich Ulrich's theory of Uranian androgyny. Though his talk about "sex elements" seems quaint today and perhaps a bit homophobic compared with the current debate on hormonal factors that might lead to sexual predispositions, Matthiessen based his assertion on the best medical and psycho-analytic theories of his time in an attempt to remain objective.

Matthiessen also refutes Cheney's notions that they should abstain from sex and keep their relationship secret from their nearest friends. At the heart of Matthiessen's argument is the importance of human "completeness" and integrity, two conditions that cannot be achieved unless the individual not only integrates the various parts of his own self, but joins his integrated self to the society at large. Sixteen years later these values, as Jonathan Arac has pointed out, will be among the most important aesthetic criteria used in *American Renaissance*. "I'm striving for . . . the realization of a fully developed character," Matthiessen writes Cheney, and that full development can only occur when sexual desires are acted on. "Before meeting you I had known love only of the mind and of the soul. I was not a fully arrived personality. I was hesitant, and partially repressed in that I had furtive sexual desires that I refused to satisfy. You changed this" (*RD*, 86). Later Matthiessen admonishes Cheney that if they "no longer lived a *complete* life of truth together, we would both be unhappy" (*RD*, 87). Matthiessen admits that "law and public opinion are clear enough" in their disdain for homosexuals, but that if gay men give in to these pressures, they will be harming only themselves. Some people will regard his decision to "follow the deepest voice of [his] nature" as "egocentric and selfish," but Matthiessen believes that by acting on his homosexual desires he realizes "a force infinitely stronger and nobler than myself," a spirit of love that binds the world. Society will be harmed if they "deny the body" (*RD*, 88-89).

While Matthiessen never fully integrated his sexual self into his public world and kept knowledge of his gay identity within the private sphere of friends and relatives, still he was perfectly aware that this secrecy damaged himself, his work, and his relationship with Cheney. During his composition of his book on Elizabethan translation, he wrote that "the falseness [of his position in the world] seems to sap my confidence of power. Have I any right in a community that would so utterly disapprove of me if it knew the facts? I ask myself that, and then I laugh; for I know I would never ask it at all if isolation from you didn't make me search into myself" (*RD*, 200). Matthiessen deeply wished to come out of the closet, but he knew that Cheney and the public, even the relatively enlightened public of Harvard University, were not ready for such truth, preferring the comforting falseness of fragmentation. As Matthiessen's political activity grew more and more controversial, he must have been aware that colleagues who wished to get rid of him on political grounds, but couldn't because he held tenure, would be ready to challenge him on moral grounds—his one vulnerable flank—were he to make his sexuality a public issue.

The extremely homophobic atmosphere in which Matthiessen lived and worked probably contributed to his suicide on the morning of 1 April 1950. The events preceding his death paint a vivid, if ugly, picture of national intolerance. On 28 February 1950, Under Secretary of State John Peurifoy testified before the Senate Appropriations Committee that most of the ninety-one employees dismissed from his department on moral grounds were homosexuals. The Republicans immediately added "sexual perverts" to the issue of communists in high government positions. In March of 1950, stories about sexual deviants in government made the front page of the *New York Times* three times, and in June, the Senate authorized an investigation into the hiring of homosexuals (D'Emilio, 41-42). Between April and September of 1950, the number of homosexuals fired by the administration rose from an average of five to sixty a month, a twelvefold increase (D'Emilio, 44). As a gay man who had made very little effort to conceal his sexual identity, Matthiessen faced a world that seemed more hostile, if anything, than it had been when he first met Cheney.

It is ironic, to say the least, that critics today, by ignoring the very realities he so painfully was forced to consider, attack Matthiessen's efforts to be scientific about homosexuality and his discretion in handling the institutional and social homophobia that surrounded him. Kenneth S. Lynn in his portrait of Matthiessen writes:

> I was struck by Matthiessen's silence, in his lectures and tutorial conversations, on the subject of homosexuality in American literature. His comments on Whitman's interest in young male beauty were singularly guarded and inadequate, while the blatant case of Hart Crane obviously made him uncomfortable. The conclusion I drew from this at the time, and have subsequently had no reason to doubt, was that Matthiessen's own sex life was a guilt-ridden horror to him. So full of revulsion was he that he could barely pronounce the word homosexuality, let alone release his feelings through candid discussions. (116)

Such a passage is a remarkable example of students' projections of "guilt-ridden horror" onto gay professors, for none of Lynn's examples of Matthiessen's "guarded" behavior warrant his extreme conclusion. Forty years after Matthiessen taught, I still find it difficult to broach such topics with students whose prejudices and misinformation are ugly, offensive, and well entrenched. One can only imagine how misunderstood Matthiessen's motives would have been had he "released his feelings" in "candid discussions" during private tutorials, as Lynn would have him do. Lynn's analysis is not merely naive, it reinforces the double-bind in which gay teachers and scholars typically find themselves: if they comment on homosexuality, they are accused of projecting their personal issues into the classroom; if they remain silent, they are accused of self-loathing. In the guise of being sympathetic, Lynn reveals the attitude that keeps gay teachers from discussing homosexuality.

Lynn's belief in Matthiessen's "guilt-ridden horror" of homosexuality appears in more recent scholarship, perpetuating the distortion. James W. Tuttleton, for example, concludes that "Matthiessen's suicidal impulse probably had its origins in an emotional state of self-loathing, confusingly and inextricably connected with his homosexuality" (9). William E. Cain finds Matthiessen's letters to Cheney "sometimes embarrassing," an embarrassment he feels in reading all love letters, yet he concedes that despite the "gushes of sentiment . . . they are also tough-minded, persistent, and persevering" and "reveal an admirable strength and courage" (46). Cain's critical language is full of masculinist coding. When Matthiessen exhibits such "feminine" traits as being gushy and "sentimental," Cain finds him embarrassing, but when he exhibits such masculine traits as "strength," "courage," and tough-mindedness, Cain declares him "admirable." Although Cain recognizes that "Matthiessen is zealously determined to carry his and Cheney's love through hard times and tensions," he also finds evidence of "self-disapproval" in *American Renaissance* when Matthiessen argues that "the passivity of [Whitman's] body" in "Song of Myself" indicates that "there is a quality vaguely pathological and homosexual" (48). I will look at Matthiessen's attitude toward Whitman, and particularly at this passage, at greater length later; here it should suffice to say that Matthiessen is only repeating what in his day was the best clinical evaluation and psychoanalytic understanding of Whitman's condition. As the entire context will reveal, he is being descriptive rather than evaluative in calling Whitman's passivity pathological, and insofar as he appears to be disapproving, he is reflecting psychiatry's general disapproval of male passivity. Cain's nonhistorical approach to Matthiessen places Matthiessen in yet another double bind. Cain criticizes him for breaking out of masculine emotional restraints in his private letters, and for being too constrained by medical opinion in his public criticism.

American Renaissance is a long and complex book, over one thousand pages in manuscript, and it was intended to serve a number of functions. Among its many interrelated themes is a sexual one. Rather than "distanc[ing] himself from" homosexuality and wanting to show that he "spurned 'abnormal' homosexual attitudes in poetry," as Cain contends (*Matthiessen*, 48), I believe Matthiessen tacitly shows that the finest strain of expression in America culture is to be found in gay works, those derived from the homosexual's "divine gifts" as "the advance guard of any hope for a spirit of brotherhood" (*RD*, 47). In short, *American Renaissance* is Matthiessen's ultimate expression of his love for Cheney and a covert celebration of the homosexual artist.

Cheney was an explicit presence in many Matthiessen books. Matthiessen wrote *Russell Cheney, 1881-1945, A Record of His Work* as a memorial. *From the Heart of Europe* includes a discussion of Cheney, and in his first book, *Sarah Orne Jewett*, Matthiessen credits Cheney, who contributed illustrations, with suggesting the subject. The Jewett book is in other respects a covert celebration of the homosexual artist, for without ever overtly calling Jewett a lesbian, Matthiessen repeatedly insists that Jewett had a great deal of the "masculine element" that might be

found even in otherwise feminine women. At one point, Matthiessen comments that "Miss Jewett could be, when she saw fit, masculine enough to equip three average male story-tellers" (95) and "had more need of a wife than a husband" since like one of her characters, she had other business than "a woman's natural work" (72-73). Moreover, by celebrating Jewett's relationship to Annie Fields, Matthiessen honors his relationship with Cheney. According to Matthiessen,

> If [Jewett] thought of marriage at all, it was as a hindrance and complication that would step between her and her dreams. But the generous warmth of her nature demanded an outlet, and she found herself sustained in her devotion to Annie Fields. They were together constantly in Boston, or in Mrs. Fields' summer home . . . and when they were separated, daily letters sped between them, hardly letters, but jotted notes of love, plans of what they would do when they met, things they wanted to talk about, books they would read together. (73)

While Matthiessen taught most of the year in Cambridge, Cheney stayed in their home in Kittery Point, Maine, not far from Jewett's house. In their divided living arrangements and in their whirlwind of correspondence, the Jewett-Fields relationship provided a model for Matthiessen and Cheney, who complained in their early letters of knowing no "parallel case" that would steer them through the "uncharted, uninhabited country" of same-sex "marriages" (*RD*, 71).

Though *American Renaissance* more explicitly discusses homosexuality, like *Sarah Orne Jewett* its larger argument about the role of the gay writer in the canon of American literature remains implicit. Such self-censorship is perfectly understandable in the 1930s and 1940s when *American Renaissance* was written, and indeed it is one of the book's subjects. For example, taking issue with Richard Henry Stoddard's contention that popular audiences, "captivated by stories of maritime life," indulged Melville's penchant for gritty realism, Matthiessen counters that Melville was "actually . . . constrained by such genteel demands." He points out that Melville, though claiming in *White Jacket* to be "withholding nothing, inventing nothing," omits the captain's epithets because, in Melville's words, he "should not like to be the first person to introduce [such language] to the public" (422). Matthiessen goes on to comment:

> His own modesty joined again with the taboos of his age when he came to probe the daily life of the men, for he skirted the subject with remote allusions to the *Oedipus* and to Shelley's *Cenci*, and with the remark that 'the sins for which the cities of the plain were overthrown still linger in some of these wooden-walled Gomorrahs of the deep.' (422)

Matthiessen's remarks on Melville should alert us to his own predicament. To get his book published, he, too, will have to skirt the subject of sexuality and especially homosexuality through remote allusions and other rhetorical diversions. In fact, in some ways, the taboos of Matthiessen's age were more difficult to skirt than those of Melville's time because Freud had made readers so much more savvy about sexual subtexts. As Matthiessen notes: "the sexual element in Claggart's ambivalence" "may have been only latent for Melville," but it is "one of the passages where a writer today would be fully aware" (506). Freud had made the public more conscious of sex without breaking down its prejudices. Consequently, Matthiessen had to be far more inventive than Melville in eluding his readers' conventional morals and avoiding their censure.

A recurring theme of *American Renaissance* is the need of mid-nineteenth-century American authors to avoid arousing the moral righteousness of their genteel and provincial readers. Matthiessen quotes Emerson's dictum, "Everything in the universe goes by indirection," (57) and he examines Whitman's belief that the American poet must be "indirect" and cannot rely on finding a "voice through any of the conventional modes" (519). He notes Henry James's practice of presenting material with "unnamed sexual implications" (476). He recalls approvingly Thoreau's belief that "Poetry *implies* the whole truth. Philosophy *expresses* a particle of it" (85, Thoreau's italics) and cites Melville's pronouncement that "All that has been said but multiplies the avenues to what remains to be said" (414). Matthiessen's close attention to the text uncovers the silences that society and the unconscious impose upon it and language's devious ways for circumventing censorship.

Structure is one way to make a point tacitly, and the structure of *American Renaissance* clearly argues for the supremacy of gay writers. The book focuses on five authors: two optimistic essayists, two tragic novelists, and a poet, in that order. Of the essayists, Emerson and Thoreau, Matthiessen prefers Thoreau; between the two novelists, Hawthorne and Melville, Matthiessen chooses Melville. But it is Whitman, the poet, who is the model writer. In each case the homosexual writer (or the one whose works reveal the strongest homoerotic tendencies) is preferred over his ostensibly heterosexual rival. Matthiessen erected in *American Renaissance* virtually a gay canon of American literature. Just how gay can be judged by the writers he admittedly excludes from the study—Poe, Longfellow, Holmes, and by stopping before the Civil War, Twain. In addition, among the subjects of Matthiessen's monographs—Jewett, James, T. S. Eliot, Dreiser—Dreiser is the sole figure whose sexual orientation has not been a serious subject of speculation. Matthiessen's elevation of gay writers rests not merely on the specific figures he chose, but on the argument he makes for these figures. If not the greatest author of the five under discussion, Whitman, nevertheless, is the one who best exemplifies Matthiessen's conception of The Great American Writer.

Matthiessen's reasons were surely personal in part. Cheney introduced Matthiessen to Whitman, and Whitman became not only the first American author Matthiessen grew to love, but the touchstone for all his notions of homosexual-

ity. Whitman's poetry voiced all Matthiessen's youthful expressions of affection and, as Cain has pointed out, Matthiessen unconsciously translated his verses into his love letters to Cheney (*Matthiessen,* 47). But such sentimental reasons alone would not have convinced Matthiessen to elevate Whitman to so honored a position as he occupies in *American Renaissance*. What fascinates Matthiessen about Whitman is that, though Whitman was no theorist, he nevertheless developed a process of writing that exemplifies for Matthiessen the ideal procedures of an American writer to achieve organic form; the procedures embody the belief that only through the acceptance of one's primordial homosexual feelings can an artist both penetrate to the deepest wellsprings of experience and fully express the democratic spirit.

Critics usually classify Matthiessen as a formalist, but as a Christian Socialist and a student of Marx and Ruskin, he refuses to split the work of art from the labor through which it came into being. He contends in *American Renaissance* that to judge a writer's contribution most adequately, one must "come to *what* he created through examining his own *process of creation*" (80, Matthiessen's italics). In his chapter "Method and Scope," Matthiessen insists that all of his authors believed "that there should be no split between art and the other functions of the community, that there should be an organic union between labor and culture" (xv). An aesthetic which attempts to split the creative process from the finished product ends up either in the fallacy of imitative form, an apology for gaseous speculation, or in an empty ornamentalism. By insisting on organic or functional formalism, Matthiessen incorporates process into considerations of form, but in so doing, he does not engage in a simplistic biographical criticism. He rejects "the vulgarization of Saint-Beuve's subtle method—the direct reading of an author's personal life into his works" (xii). Rather, through a particular sort of "cultural history," Matthiessen located larger patterns of relations "since a man can articulate only what he is, and what he has been made by the society of which he is a willing or an unwilling part" (xv). In creating this "cultural history," Matthiessen examined politics, economics, and the history of ideas, of art, of science. In particular, Matthiessen was interested in psychology, and he wrote, "What a critic can gain from Freudian theory is a very comprehensive kind of description of human norms and processes, an incalculably great asset in interpreting patterns of character and meaning" (479).

For Matthiessen, as for Freud, the creative process is directly related to specific psychic conditions which allow the individual access or propel the artist into the creative act. These psychic structures, however, are also related to social institutions which either encourage or discourage their existence. Matthiessen gains from Freudian theory an explanation of how the "cultural" environment in which a work is situated is shaped by such sociopsychological issues as the relationship between child-rearing practices and adult curiosity, daydreaming, and emotional expressiveness. As Freud had argued in his studies of Leonardo da Vinci (to which Matthiessen alludes [479]), great art emerges in cultures in which children are subjected to conditions that evoke their artistic capacities.

Throughout *American Renaissance,* Matthiessen accompanied his analysis of particularly moving passages with descriptions of the psychological state from which they arose. Whitman elicits Matthiessen's most comprehensive description and becomes the model for American authors in general:

> Readers with a distaste for loosely defined mysticism have plenty of grounds for objection in the way the poet's belief in divine inspiration is clothed in imagery that obscures all the distinctions between body and soul by portraying the soul as merely the sexual agent. Moreover, in the passivity of the poet's body there is a quality vaguely pathological and homosexual. This is in keeping with the regressive, infantile fluidity, imaginatively polyperverse, which breaks down all mature barriers, a little further on in "Song of Myself," to declare that he is "maternal as well as paternal, a child as well as a man." Nevertheless, this fluidity of sexual sympathy made possible Whitman's receptivity to life. The ability to live spontaneously on primitive levels, whose very existence was denied by the educated mind of his time, wiped out arbitrary conventions and yielded a broader experience than of any of his contemporaries. And he did not simply exhibit pathological symptoms; he created poetry. (535-36)

When William E. Cain quoted a portion of this passage to indicate Matthiessen's disapproval of homosexuality, he failed to acknowledge either the elaborate rhetorical context or the much larger and positive argument in which it occurred. Matthiessen adopts the debater's strategy of acknowledging opponents' objections, admitting that certain people would be understandably critical of Whitman for mystical vagueness, sexualizing the spiritual, and for passivity. But Matthiessen is not among those critics since, as he asserts at the end, Whitman "did not simply exhibit pathological symptoms; he created poetry." The passivity of Whitman's body is a precondition for poetic activity since "somnambulism . . . let him be swept into the currents of the unconscious mind, and so made it possible for him to plumb emotional forces far beyond the depths of most writers of his day" (574).

Matthiessen derived his notion of Whitman's creative state of mind from two sources. From Freud's essay on "Creative Writers and Daydreaming," Matthiessen learned that inspiration came from those moments when the ego could project its desires and feelings more fully into conscious life. From Edward Carpenter, Matthiessen gained the insight that these moments of revery were democratic in spirit when they derived from the desire to blur the distinctions of class and gender. Carpenter argued that the Uranian was twice as often possessed of an artistic temperament than was the general population because the Uranian's "dual nature and swift and constant interaction between its masculine and feminine elements . . . [make] it easy or natural for the Uranian man to become an artist" (*Selected,* 234).

To be sure, Matthiessen does not explicitly associate Whitman's creativity or creativity in general to a homosexual orientation. He does, however, insist that sexual fluidity and an ability "to live spontaneously on primitive levels" away from the "arbitrary conventions" of bourgeois society *are* a component of the greatest moments of art and, furthermore, that the capacity to regress and become receptive is, in turn, linked to an acceptance of homosexuality or, at the very least, bodily passivity. But this experience is not limited to homosexuals alone. Even so ostensibly a heterosexual as Hawthorne experienced the same process: "A more certain sign of his creative temperament was the tenderness mixed in with strength, an almost feminine passivity, which many of his friends noted and Alcott expressed in his own way by asking: 'Was he some damsel imprisoned in that manly form pleading alway [sic] for release?'" (230).

Matthiessen, however, carefully distinguishes between two passive psychic states that look like daydreaming: the first is a vacant daze that leads to formless woolgathering; the second is an awakening to the objective world where arbitrary distinctions have been obliterated. The vacant daze is a sign of isolation from the material world and Matthiessen associates it with Emerson's narcissism, Clifford's attempted leap from the window in *House of the Seven Gables,* and White Jacket's fall from the yard arm. In each case, the individuals lose a sense of proportion, of definition, or of the connection between things, and, quite often, their balance. In Clifford's case, Matthiessen says daydreaming is "a childish pleasure in any passing attraction that can divert him from the confused memories of his terrible years of gloom" (328). But the second state of awakened receptivity is marked by a new appreciation of the concrete, objective, and real. Because Whitman obliterates the gender distinctions at such moments, he gains an increased receptivity to things and a greater awareness of their true form. According to Matthiessen, only if writers see the world with a concreteness that transcends the conventional categories that falsify reality can they produce works whose form possesses a coherence that is more than the arbitrary imposition of an empty design.

For example, in his discussion of Whitman's language, Matthiessen points out that the relationships between sign and signified are obscured in the nineteenth century partly because of that era's "tendency to divorce education of the mind from the body and to treat language as something to be learned from a dictionary." Matthiessen goes on to argue that "such division of the individual's wholeness, intensified by the specialization of a mechanized society, has become a chief cause of the neurotic strain oppressing present-day man" (518). The organism from which organic form was to grow was the psyche reunited on a primitive level to its polymorphous sexual self. Lacan, no doubt, would insist that language as well as the desire for wholeness already are symptoms of the "division of the individual's wholeness" (40-45). But Matthiessen maintains that in his finest work Whitman returned to that primordial relationship of psychic and social wholeness in which "poetic rhythm was an organic response to the centers of ex-perience—to the internal pulsations of the body, to its ex-ternal movements in work and in making love, to such sounds as the wind and the sea" (564). No artist can sus-tain such moments, and even Whitman was reared in a culture that imposed division. Nor can there be a society in which Evil does not force such division on the psyche. Yet through art and in moments of spiritual grace, we gain glimpses of the wholeness that ordinarily eludes us, and in those glimpses that convince us of the constancy of whole-ness, we find "the strongest sign by which the Father—and he is mankind's as well as the child's—persuades that the soul endures beyond all natural phenomena" (577).

The homosexual artist and the heterosexual artist in touch with his primordial homosexual feelings are closer to such wholeness than the heterosexual who has split off his ho-mosexual feelings and no longer can retrieve them. Those, like Claggart in "Billy Budd," who split off their erotic at-tachments to persons of the same sex or seek to deny such attachments ultimately foster racial, political, and sexual oppression. But those who learn to accept such feelings gain access to the democratic impulse. As Matthiessen wrote, Melville "gave his fullest presentation of the trans-forming power of [sympathy with another human being] in the relation between Ishmael and Queequeg. When Ish-mael recognized that 'the man's a human being just as I am,' he was freed from the burden of his isolation, his heart no longer turned against society . . . he rediscovered the sense of Christian brotherhood through companionship with a tattooed pagan" (445).

I do not want to give the impression that Matthiessen's sense of organic form was merely a spasmodic emoting. He clearly "recognized that it was not enough to proclaim the radiance of the vision he had had" (28) and this vi-sionary apprehension must achieve concentrated form to be appreciated. But without the primal perception of the concrete shape of things, without the sense of the arbitrari-ness of conventional categories, writers could not create "the tension between form and liberation" (63), the hard, clear shape that Matthiessen so admired. Though Matthies-sen insisted that "the conception of art as inspiration . . . is in sharp opposition to that of art as craftsmanship," he believed with Horatio Greenough that "the normal way for an American to begin to gain that mastery [over formal principles] is by the fullest acceptance of the possibility of democracy" (*Renaissance*, 146).

Three months after their meeting, Matthiessen sent Cheney a copy of Edward Carpenter's *The Intermediate Sex*, whose concluding chapter, "The Uranian in Society," Matthiessen had annotated. Matthiessen commented that the book "doesn't tell us anything we don't know already" (*RD*, 47). In it Carpenter asserts that Uranians are predisposed to become artists (*Selected*, 234), tend to participate in "the important social work of Education" (235), and that since "true Democracy rests . . . on a sentiment which easily passes the bounds of class and caste, and unites in the closest affection the most estranged ranks in society

. . . the nobler Uranians of today may be destined . . . to be pioneers and advanced guard" of "the Comradeship on which Whitman founds a large portion of his message" (237-38). In returning to those sentiments articulated in less dramatic and simplistic form, but with some of the same passionate intensity, Matthiessen makes *American Renaissance* not only a celebration of homosexuality but of his life with Cheney. "The crucial task of the American future," Matthiessen argues in relation to Whitman, "was some reconciliation of the contradictory needs of full per-sonal development and for 'one's obligations to the State and Nation'" (591). Both the artistic and scholarly acts united these imperatives, for by "dealing with sex" Mat-thiessen was promoting a "'sanity of atmosphere'" that might heal the wounds of the world as well as Cheney's and his psychic pain. "Beyond the bright circle of man's educated consciousness lay unsuspected energies that were both magnificent and terrifying," wrote Matthiessen at the end of *American Renaissance*; it is his and our tragedy that the magnificent finally gave way to the terrifying on that midcentury night of fools, 1 April 1950, when he dove from the window of the Manger Hotel.

The Uranian, according to Carpenter, is important to soci-ety because by returning to the primal stage of gender un-differentiatedness, he can lead society beyond the duality of sexual relations. "Finding himself *different* from the great majority, sought after by some and despised by oth-ers, now an object of contumely and now an object of love and admiration," the Uranian, according to Carpenter, "was forced to *think*. His mind turned inwards on himself would be forced to tackle the problems of his own nature, and af-terwards the problem of the world and of outer nature. He would become one of the first thinkers, dreamers, discov-erers" (274). Similarly, Matthiessen's American Renais-sance was a world in which thinkers, dreamers, and dis-coverers, by turning their minds inward, were forced to reexamine the world and its outer nature. His difference was a burden not simply because it placed him at odds with "the great majority," but because it laid on him a spe-cial burden to advance society toward the democratic vista which awaited it.

Marc Dolan (essay date 1992)

SOURCE: "The 'Wholeness' of the Whale: Melville, Mat-thiessen, and the Semiotics of Critical Revisionism," in *Arizona Quarterly*, Vol. 48, No. 3, Autumn, 1992, pp. 27-58.

[*In the following essay, Dolan determines Matthiessen's important role in the critical rediscovery of the work of Herman Melville.*]

Last year we observed two important anniversaries in the history of American literature: 1991 marked both the cen-tennial of Herman Melville's death and the semicentennial of the publication of F. O. Mathiessen's *American Renais-*

sance. In the half-century between those two occurrences, Melville went from being an obscure New York writer of sea stories to his current status as one of the dozen or so American authors who cannot be ignored. In many ways, the path of his posthumous career and his consequent centrality to American literary studies is even more fascinating than the ups and downs of his career while he was alive. In what follows, I would like to re-examine the admittedly familiar story of Melville's critical rediscovery by exploring the significance of the "Melville boom" between the two world wars for the growth of American literary studies of the antebellum period. This exploration will be bracketed by a general discussion of the process of canon formation and the semiotics of critical rediscovery. Far from deploring the canonization of Melville as a "classic American author," I will suggest that this development was a structural necessity and reflects a larger movement of critical historiography, an oscillation between similarity and difference that typically proceeds by acts of critical elevation such as the "Melville boom" of the early twentieth century and the "Hurston boom" of the late twentieth century.

I

There are a number of theories of how literary reputations are built, ranging from the paranoid ("It's all an insidious conspiracy to keep out Lafcadio Hearn!") to the lackadaisical ("Things happened."). Somewhere in between lie interpretations of literary history that see critical reputations as part politics and part accident. Texts become classics not so much because they endure over time but because they prove rewarding to a varied succession of critical approaches. As Jane Tompkins notes in her survey of shifts in the critical reputation of Nathaniel Hawthorne, "*The Scarlet Letter* is a great novel in 1850, in 1876, in 1904, in 1942, and in 1966, but each time it is great for different reasons" (35).

Tompkins's work ably demonstrates the part-accident, part-politics interpretation of literary history, as does Richard Brodhead's similar examination of Hawthorne's critical "uses" in the late nineteenth and early twentieth centuries. And yet both Tompkins and Brodhead are somewhat narrow in their view of critics' overt and covert political purposes. Despite the intelligence of their reconstructions, both authors see literary history as invariably at the service of "larger" political and intellectual systems rather than as an ideological system in its own right, capable of generating its own purposes and ideological imperatives. Although it is true that literary criticism is often hostage to the partisan causes of its time, it is also, like any other discipline, just as frequently concerned with the business of self-perpetuation—with preserving the critical status quo or extending the validity of its claims purely for their own sake rather than as an extension of some other ideological agenda.

For example, in the much-cited case of Matthiessen, it is equally true that: (a) as Donald Pease and Jonathan Arac have both pointed out, Matthiessen's intellectual and critical principles were firmly grounded in the cultural poetics of the 1930s and 1940s, and (b) those underlying principles were less essential for Matthiessen's students and admirers than the "exterior" ideas presented in works such as *American Renaissance* and *Theodore Dreiser*, ideas which those original principles had generated. The number of scholars who revere Matthiessen and his work and yet do not share his distaste for domestic anti-Communism, for example, are legion, as are those whose atheism prevents them from fully appreciating the central contributions that Matthiessen's religious beliefs made to the shaping of his literary and critical tastes. After a certain point, the critical status quo becomes important *precisely because it is the status quo and for no other, underlying reason*, just as after a certain point *The Scarlet Letter* becomes important precisely because it is *The Scarlet Letter* and for no other, deeper, more cabalistic reason. As Jacques Lacan has noted (in an admittedly different context), "it is the symbolic order which is constitutive for the subject" and not the nature of the signified that lies behind it (29). Like the symptoms of a repetition compulsion, the elements of a symbolic order are often repeated more for their own sake than for the sake of whatever causes fed their pathogenesis. Why a literary canon was formed eventually becomes less important than why it is maintained.

The distinction to be drawn here is between "myths" and "sign-functions," two terms employed by Roland Barthes in his earlier writings. A myth, it will be recalled, is the form of a sign emptied of its meaning, an element in what Barthes calls "*a second-order semiological system*" ("Myth Today" 114), which transforms a first-order sign into a pre-packaged second-order signifier. The "sign-function" serves in some ways as myth's semiological precursor: sign-functions are not signs transformed into second-order signifiers but "usages" transformed into first-order signs. "*As soon as there is a society*," Barthes writes, "*every usage is converted into a sign of itself*" (*Elements of Semiology* 41). In the usual ideological reading of American literary history, novels like *The Scarlet Letter* and critical works like *American Renaissance* are seen as objects of American mythmaking. Such texts, the story goes, pass from normal, historical readings in their own time to their privileged status as classics through a process of mythologization: these texts, which begin as first-order signs of "The Democracy," say, or "Christian Socialism and the Popular Front," then pass into myth as second-order signs of "American Literature" or "American Studies."

It should be clear, however, that a text need not be mythologized to become a classic—it need only be made to signify. An alternate way of viewing the process of literary history is to see texts made classic as sign-functions rather than myths and, consequently, to see literary history as proceeding by leaps of metonymy rather than metaphor. *The Scarlet Letter* is transformed from a novel by Nathaniel Hawthorne into a sign of "American writing" rather than a sign of "American literature." Similarly,

American Renaissance becomes a sign of "American literary criticism" rather than one of "American Studies." The practical difference between myths and sign-functions is the prescriptive weight and ideological force that they carry—myths make their signifiers stand for concepts, sign-functions make them stand for uses.

While it is true that canonical works of American literature and American literary criticism have often been employed in such a way as to enforce the sort of presumption I describe here, it is equally true that, to a certain extent, any set of classics will do. Just as "needed" as an ideological justification for American culture and society is a common set of texts that will stand for "American writing" and another shared set that will stand for "American literary criticism." Simply put, we as teachers and as students need to know what we need to know, even if it is only to know what to object to. If, as has happened in the last decade or so, the standard texts in both categories have been found wanting, new texts must be found to replace them; in both cases, their "places" cannot be left vacant. The ongoing process of textual substitution in the syllabi of American literature survey courses—Rowlandson for Mather, Douglass for Thoreau, Chopin for Crane, Hurston for Hemingway (Fox-Genovese 8)—is, in its turn, both significant and "un-significant." On the level of myth, the substitution of one ideological metanarrative of "American literature" for another does signify a real change in how that symbolic field is both understood and approached. On the level of sign-functions, however, such a substitution is wholly un-significant unless the possibility of abolishing the study of American (meaning "U.S.") writing is raised.

Given the premise of the study of American writing, however, a certain number of texts must be called on to serve as signs of American writing. Thus texts like *The Scarlet Letter, The Red Badge of Courage,* and *Their Eyes Were Watching God* signify both an ideological metanarrative of American literature and a series of instances of American writing. In Barthes' terminology, they are both usages converted into signs of themselves and signs transformed into signifiers of myth. It is impossible to have one of these processes of critical signification without the other. Classic literary and critical texts inevitably serve as both mythic signifiers and as signs of Americans writing, although not necessarily at the same time. As such, however, they are dually significant.

The implications of this dual signification for the concept of the classic should be obvious. When we decide, for example, that a knowledge of Zora Neale Hurston is now essential to an understanding of twentieth-century American literature while a knowledge of Ernest Hemingway is increasingly marginal to that understanding, we are simultaneously saying that *Their Eyes Were Watching God* is more interesting to us than *A Farewell to Arms* (classic-as-sign-function) and that Hurston's novel better fits our idea of what the "real" America is like than Hemingway's does (classic-as-mythic-signifier). Using another one of Bar-

thes's distinctions, the classic novel thus functions both as "text" and as "work," as a fruitful ground for literary analysis and as an element in a linked series of such fruitful texts ("From Work to Text" 155-56ff).[1] Such sequences of works, which jointly stand for a larger understanding of the idea, mode, or context they are meant to signify, are best exemplified in course syllabi. Even the least canonically minded, most textually-oriented teachers must indulge in some "work-making" when they decide which texts belong on a syllabus and which do not. Every syllabus therefore sketches an ideological metanarrative, even if it is an oppositional one.

The act of critical rediscovery lies in the revelation that previously ignored volumes may now serve as both profitable works and profitable texts. To stick with the example of Zora Neale Hurston, a great deal of the critical attention directed toward that author's work in the last ten or fifteen years may be traced back to two pivotal instances of critical reassessment: Robert Hemenway's early essays on and groundbreaking biography of Hurston (1977) and Alice Walker's continued devotion to Hurston, exemplified in particular by her introduction to Hemenway's volume and to *I Love Myself When I Am Laughing . . . : A Zora Neale Hurston Reader* (1979). Both acts of rediscovery may be easily assimilated into our model of how classics are born: Hemenway's volume demonstrated how scholars specializing in modern American literature could find fertile ground for close reading in nearly all of Hurston's texts, while Walker, Toni Morrison, and other African-American women writers constituted a successful modern "school" or literary tradition that might be seen as springing from Hurston and her writings. To put it another way, Hemenway demonstrated the value of Hurston's writings as *texts*, and Walker and others demonstrated their value as *works*.

In both cases, however, we should note that what was most essential for the act of rediscovery was to position Hurston's works in terms of reasonably analogous intertexts, most often previously canonized texts of twentieth-century (male) African-American literature like *Cane* (Walker 86) and *Native Son* (Hemenway 6). In the case of Walker, Morrison, et al, it was the fact that *Their Eyes Were Watching God* could be profitably linked to later texts that made it suddenly not only "worth reading" but eventually "required reading." Once there was a perceived Black Women's Tradition in American literature—or even just a dozen profitable texts within the field to put on a syllabus—there could be a critical rediscovery of Zora Neale Hurston and her writings, and similar rediscoveries of Harriet Wilson, Harriet Jacobs, Mary Prince, Nella Larsen, and others could follow.

With an eye toward the Melville boom, we should also observe that before there was a generalized Hurston boom there was renewed interest in *Their Eyes Were Watching God*. Even though both Walker (Walker 86) and Hemenway (qtd. in Walker 93) considered *Mules and Men* a masterpiece too, it was *Their Eyes Were Watching God* that brought renewed attention to Hurston and that still serves as the starting-point for many studies of Hurston. Whether or not this was because it could fit in with the recently established classic texts of the ongoing feminist and colorist revisionism of the 1970s is not exactly germane to this study. First came the classic text (*Their Eyes Were Watching God*), then the classic author (Zora Neale Hurston), and then the other works that fit around it (the Black Women's Tradition in America).

Thus, to use the terminology of reader-response criticism (Eco 19-23), literary historiography proceeds as much by intertextual frames as by common frames or ideological overcoding. In order to convince people that a previously ignored novel or poem is worth taking a second look at, a critic must convince his or her peers that it is both unique (classic-as-text) and intellectually assimilable (classic-as-work)—both fresh and familiar. This labor of dual perception is almost wholly conceived in terms of intertexts, in terms of useful critical approaches and analogous primary texts. What a novel requires to be seen as great, then, is not just a new idea or a new reading but a new shelf of other books to place it on, be they critical (Derrida, Lacan, Rich, and Locke) or primary (Morrison, Marshall, Walker, and Angelou). Like Walker Benjamin in his famous essay on book collecting, it seems we are always packing, unpacking, and reshelving our books, unceasingly drawn first one way, then another, in "a dialectical tension between the poles of disorder and order" (60).

II

The story of Melville's "Burial, Disinterment, and Revival" (Parker and Hayford viii) is, in its general outlines, a familiar one. Most scholars agree that Melville was plagued by uncomprehending readers almost from the start (Parker v-vi; Stovall 240, 248). *Typee* and *Omoo* established him so clearly as a travel writer and sea writer that his readers were wholly unprepared for the murky romance and crude allegory of *Mardi*. Similarly, we are told, the more ambitious aspects of *Moby-Dick* came as something of a shock to those who had enjoyed the much "easier" *Redburn* and *White Jacket*. Both *Mardi* and *Moby-Dick* remained largely unpopular until the Melville boom came along and placed the "unreadable," more clearly "metaphysical" Melville on his pedestal.

In the eyes of Barrett Wendell, William Cranston Lawton, and other turn-of-the-century critics, Melville's minor status in American literary history was assured by means of two indices: his subject matter and his geographical location. He was seen first and foremost as a writer of "novels of maritime adventure" (Wendell 229) and somewhat secondarily as a New York writer or writer of "the Middle States," as Wendell somewhat tellingly groups such authors in his table of contents. In other words, Wendell's and Lawton's readings of Melville depend upon their employment of either one of two sets of intertexts: popular novels (like those of Robert Louis Stevenson, James Fenimore Cooper, and John Marryat) or the works of other New York writers (like Bayard Taylor, George William

Curtis, Caroline Kirkland, and Horace Greeley).[2] It is hard to say which came first here, the negative critical judgment of Melville or the intertexts applied to him, but in this early view they reinforce one another—Melville is unimportant because he is a New Yorker who wrote trash adventure books, and vice versa. He is excluded from literary greatness by a boundary of genre and by the several hundred miles of postroads that separate him from the intellectual mecca of Boston-Cambridge. This partition continues in Van Wyck Brooks' *America's Coming of Age* (1915) and Waldo Frank's *Our America* (1919), neither of which even mentions Melville's name in passing. In Brooks' book, Melville is, to modern eyes, particularly conspicuous by his absence from a grouping that features Emerson and Whitman and also includes Bryant, Longfellow, Poe, Hawthorne, Fuller, Lowell, Thoreau, Twain, and the apparently ubiquitous G. W. Curtis.[3]

At the time that Brooks was writing *America's Coming of Age*, Melville lacked Poe's and Whitman's extensive European and English followings (Stovall 40ff, 285-86ff). Nevertheless, there was at that time a small but steadily growing cult of interest in Melville's writings in England and Ireland if not in America. Just as the Hurston boom of the late twentieth century would begin with a cult of readership that centered almost exclusively on *Their Eyes Were Watching God,* the Melville boom of the early twentieth century began with this band of Anglo-Irish readers whose devotion to the author centered almost exclusively on *Moby-Dick* (Parker and Hayford 126-43). Thus, in 1921, just six years after ignoring Melville completely, Brooks was predicting that "for the next six months there is to be a Melville boom," although he also could not help observing that "next year Melville will have been forgotten again" (144). When the interest in Melville did not die in the next year, nor in the next, Brooks, not to be bested, would eventually write his own extended elegiac treatment of *Moby-Dick*. But even in the dismissive 1921 assessment he admits that *Moby-Dick* is hard to ignore, noting that in this book "Melville rises to his real height and reveals himself not as a chronicler but as a creator" (145).

Although the interest in Melville and *Moby-Dick* had been growing overseas for some time, it was the imminent publication of an American book that called forth Brooks's prediction of a "Melville boom": Raymond Weaver's *Herman Melville, Mariner and Mystic* (1921), the first full-length biography of the author. In many ways, Weaver's book served the same function in relation to Melville's critical rediscovery as Hemenway's life of Hurston has to hers. In writing his volume, Weaver, like Hemenway, had set out on a deliberate mission of rehabilitation, in which he evaluated each of the author's books in turn, assessing their strengths and weaknesses, and seeking throughout to prove his initial contention that "Melville is—as cannot be too frequently iterated—one of the chief and most unusual figures in our native literature" (24).[4]

Weaver's explicit reasons for rehabilitating Melville are a fascinating mix of the old and the new. On the one hand, he praises the author for being precisely what Wendell and Lawton despised: "the literary discoverer of the South Seas" and, with Richard Henry Dana, one of the first two authors to depict accurately the life of the common sailor (24-25). But the bulk of his opening fusillade is devoted to the magnificence of *Moby-Dick*. His initial treatment of Melville as South Seas author and documenter of shipboard life takes up just two brief paragraphs; his treatment of *Moby-Dick* as masterpiece takes up a full four pages.

This two-pronged attack on previous critical judgments like Wendell's and Lawton's—the paired suggestions that Melville was worth reading because his subject matter was important and because his greatest novel was one of America's greatest—fits the model of critical rediscovery that we have already seen in our brief examination of the Hurston boom. In recasting these old genre slurs as praise, Weaver is trying to establish Melville's worth by showing that his books can be of interest as documents of a certain type of "real life experience," and thus as a sign-function of South Sea life and life aboard a ship.

These arguments for the worth of Melville's writings as documentary texts, however, were largely unsuccessful. After all, such claims were really no different than the arguments previously advanced by isolated Melville admirers like Stevenson and John Masefield, whom Weaver quotes respectfully. Where Weaver succeeded was in arguing that *Moby-Dick* was a "masterpiece." On this score, there had been, as mentioned above, a groundswell building for at least the previous half-decade. Not only were there recent favorable comments on the book from the London *Nation*, E. L. Grant-Watson, Carl Van Doren, and Frank Jewett Mather, Jr., but articles about Melville and his leviathan had also recently appeared in the London *Bookman*, the *Dublin Review*, and the London *Atheneum*. All these articles testified to *Moby-Dick*'s status as a neglected work of genius (Parker and Hayford 126-43).

And so it was that the Melville revival was tied from the first to a rediscovery of *Moby-Dick*. In this respect, what was most emphasized in these reexaminations of Melville was the fertility of his text as a field for critical endeavor. Consequently, critics continually sought to associate that text with other great texts. Melville, these writers began asserting in the years after World War I, need not be read in light of Stevenson, Cooper, and Marryat, if they are not to your taste. Rather, he may be read in light of Shakespeare and the other masters, who are his proper peers. What this text requires, the early pro-Melville critics argued, is what all classic texts require: a sympathetic reader. "If one logically analyzes 'Moby-Dick,'" Weaver wrote in a 1919 essay that preceded his biography, "he will be disgusted, just as Dr. Johnson, who had no analysis but the logical, was disgusted with 'Lycidas.'" Thus Melville is great—or at least deserving of a second crack at greatness—because he has suffered the same fate as Milton. Later in the same essay, Weaver piles on the intertexts a bit thick, calling his subject "a gentle Smollett, a glorified Whitman, an athletic Coleridge, a dandified Rabelais, a

cynical Meredith, [and] a doubting Sir Thomas Browne," thereby establishing not only that Melville can hold his own with classic English, American, and Continental authors but that he also improves upon their presumed flaws (Smollett's harshness, Meredith's optimism, Browne's credulity, etc.) (Weaver, "[An Amazing Masterpiece]" 127).

In a way, the rediscovery of *Moby-Dick* as an isolated text in the 1910s and early 1920s makes perfect sense. As a number of critics have already suggested (Barbour 48; Poirier 144; Smith 54-55; Baym, *Novels, Readers, and Reviewers* 67, 92-93, 202), the ambiguity and loose form of the novel, as well as the insistence and willful perversity of its authorial voice, were more in keeping with the age of *Les Faux-monnayeurs*, *Tender Buttons*, and *Ulysses* than they were with the era of *The Scarlet Letter*, *The Wide, Wide World*, and *Nile Notes of a Howadji*. Yet, although Weaver's work opened up Melville's volume to the free play of Modernist exegesis and interpretation, it only suggested how Melville's myth of whaling could be connected to a larger "myth of America." After this establishment of *Moby-Dick* as a classic American *text*, it fell to D. H. Lawrence in his *Studies in Classic American Literature* to show how the novel could function as a classic American *work* that fit into a series of other classic American works which clearly implied a larger ideological metanarrative of "the real America." In this regard, Lawrence's position in relation to Melville is analogous to Walker's in relation to Hurston, just as Weaver's is analogous to Hemenway's.

It is in Lawrence's volume (published in 1923 but outlined and planned as early as 1919) that we first see not only *Moby-Dick* taking its place among canonical American texts but also the form of the canon itself. The standard American literature survey of the early national and antebellum periods is right there for all to see, laid out for nearly the first time in Lawrence's table of contents: Franklin, Crèvecoeur, Cooper, Poe, Hawthorne, Melville, and Whitman.[5] The only increasingly unfamiliar text on Lawrence's list is Dana's *Two Years Before the Mast*; the only major canonical authors that Lawrence fails to treat—Emerson and Thoreau—were getting enough play in the unreconstructed postwar incarnation of the *Seven Arts* camp to justify their omission (Blake 524). In his evocation of a peculiarly American sense of place, his emphasis on the mythopoeic/psychoanalytic dimensions of American literature, and even his invocation of Shakespeare's Caliban as a peculiarly American spirit, Lawrence prefigures the length and breadth of the midcentury American Studies movement from Henry Nash Smith and Leo Marx down to Leslie Fiedler and Richard Slotkin.

If one makes a list of all the symbolic fields that occupy Lawrence's text—White vs. Nonwhite; Orthodoxy vs. Personal Morality; Book Knowledge vs. Blood Knowledge; Civilization vs. Nature—one sees that practically the only author on Lawrence's list in whose work they all intersect is Melville. Hawthorne hardly treats race at all, at least in the two novels Lawrence focuses on; orthodoxy is not an issue for Whitman—he feels he has moved beyond it; for Cooper, there is a similar lack of conflict on book knowledge—it's purely there to make fun of; and Poe and Franklin spend most of their time in cities and hardly deal with the (external) wilderness at all. If one accepts Lawrence's postulate that these are the classic American themes, then Melville ipso-facto becomes the classic American author and *Moby-Dick* the classic American book.

Where did these themes come from? Chiefly from the general rise of *américanisme*, the explosion of interest in what made America "American" that one can see throughout the 1920s, both in the United States and abroad, in works as slick as *The Great Gatsby* and as skeptical as Gramsci's *Prison Notebooks*. Lawrence even refers to this interest in his brief Foreword to the volume, explicitly tying his studies of eighteenth- and nineteenth-century American literature to the twentieth-century vogue of interest in "the true American . . . the homunculus of the new era" (3). One can see the perceived urgency of his presentism slipping in at various points throughout the text, most notably when he compares both Benjamin Franklin and Captain Ahab to the pathetic Woodrow Wilson of the Paris Peace Conference period (26, 158).

Like most of the nascent Americanists of the post-WWI period, Lawrence was fascinated by the United States without ever really making up his mind whether he loathed the nation or adored it. Ambivalent Herman Melville was thus congenial to Lawrence's own ambivalence toward American literature and culture, which is why the critic positioned Melville at the climax of his analysis. For Lawrence's purposes, and those of many of his contemporaries, there was no question that *Moby-Dick* was primarily a book about the private tragedy of Captain Ahab, rather than Ishmael or any other member of the *Pequod*'s crew; nor was there any doubt that Ahab was a prototypically American character (Brooks 1923; Van Doren 1924; Mumford, *The Golden Day* 74-76, and *Herman Melville* 18-95; Rourke 193-200). As John Thomas has recently noted, intellectuals of the 1920s like Lawrence, and even Brooks and Lewis Mumford, were dreaming of some kind of capitalist apocalypse in America long before 1929. In *Moby-Dick*, they found a comfortable image of what that apocalypse might be: one in which the monomaniacal, Calvinist captain got his come-uppance, but only after he had first delivered two or three soliloquies fine enough to rank him with the great Shakespearean tragic heroes.

In other words, the rediscovery of *Moby-Dick* in the post WWI period offered a convenient solution to the critical and ideological problems of the moment. It gave critics a way to love American literature but still hate America, uniting an (arguably) pre-Modernist text with an (equally arguably) anti-American allegory. This was the necessary first stage of Melville's rehabilitation, but it was not altogether sufficient for his canonization.

III

As the progression of Wendell to Lawrence shows, one of the ways in which this first stage of Melville's critical re-habilitation had come about was by the successful detachment of both Melville and *Moby-Dick* from their historical and literary contexts. Both Lawrence and Weaver depended more on transtemporal intertexts (Franklin's *Autobiography*, the *Odyssey, Pilgrim's Progress*, and *Gulliver's Travels*) and intertexts contemporary with the critic (such as Lawrence's references to the doings and sayings of Woodrow Wilson) rather than on intertexts contemporaneous with the time of composition and publication. Consequently, Melville was now read as a self-consciously pre-Modernist writer and as a participant in a dehistoricized early nineteenth-century articulation of the American sense of place.[6]

In other words, Melville had escaped the stigma of popular culture by almost wholly escaping the 1850s. Even in such seminal American studies volumes as Mumford's *The Golden Day* (1926) and Constance Rourke's *American Humor* (1931), Melville was basically treated in isolation and almost solely examined in terms of his relation to *Moby-Dick*. Typical of all these etiolated judgments of the author and his work are Granville Hicks's passing observations in *The Great Tradition* (1933) on the achievement (or lack thereof) of *Moby-Dick*:

> . . . Melville's problem was real enough, but the terms in which he stated it were irrelevant [to the world he lived in]. This explains, in part, why *Moby-Dick*, with all its virtues, is not comparable to the great metaphysical epics of the past, which have made room for all the principal varieties of experience in their eras. It is impossible to suppose that Melville—or anyone else living in mid-nineteenth-century America—could have been a Lucretius or a Dante, and the mere fact that he could conceive of writing an epic is itself magnificent. There is every reason to be thankful that, in this era of intellectual expansion, there was one writer who could find terms, whatever they were, for the expression of his vision of the universe. (8)

One could hardly ask for a clearer encapsulation of all the elements of the post-Weaver-and-Lawrence Melville mystique. Hicks's comments beautifully preserve the two key components of that version of Melville's career: his genius and his isolation. The fact that an avowedly Marxist critic like Hicks apparently cannot decide whether he admires Melville for his genius or pities him for his isolation only underscores the point. It is also worth noting that, even in the two pages he devotes to Melville, Hicks, too, is almost exclusively interested in *Moby-Dick*; he notes the author's first five books and the later *Billy Budd* in passing but casts them in terms unmistakably drawn from his reading of that central novel (7-8).

Aside from any meaningful ties to the author's historical setting, what was most clearly absent in these early reexaminations of Melville was any convincing connection between him and the previously established New England version of American literature. The only treatment that might be considered a notable step in that direction was in the second volume of V. L. Parrington's *Main Currents in*

American Thought (1927). As Richard Hofstadter has noted (364-66), Parrington was influenced to some degree in his work by the personal and published example of his teacher Barrett Wendell. Even the structure of the first two volumes of *Main Currents* bears the impress of Wendell's regional segmentation of American literature. Melville, however, is part of an intriguing subsystem in Parrington's analysis that blurs these regional divisions. True, Melville is firmly placed in Parrington's Book II ("The Mind of the Middle East"), but he is only dangling off the edge of it as it blurs into Book III ("The Mind of New England"). In Parrington's conception, Melville, along with William Cullen Bryant and Horace Greeley, is grouped under the transitional heading "Some Contributions of New England."

This may seem like an odd way to close off a section on the Mid-Atlantic states, but the very ambivalence of Parrington's categorization of these three authors shows how, despite all the energy devoted to Melville in the years following World War I, critical opinion had not come all that far from Wendell's judgment of Melville as a mid-Atlantic author of sea stories who ended his life as a failure. Like most other American literary scholars of the 1920s and 1930s, Parrington bends but does not break these previously established categorizations. Melville was a New Yorker but he was also a "transcendentalist," albeit of a "different" kind from Emerson or Thoreau (255-56). Similarly, he was first and foremost a writer of sea stories but one who eventually "put the external world of experience aside" (254). Finally, although his career was still not perceived as a success, its trajectory was now described as a slow slide into "the midnight of his pessimism" (250) rather than as an inevitable descent into the wages of unjustified ambition and unfulfilled promise.

As of the late 1930s, then, Melville was still not a "classic American author," but at least now he was the author of a single piece of "classic American literature." Despite the sincere, dogged efforts of critics like Parrington, Grant-Watson, Mumford, Willard Thorp and others, it was F. O. Matthiessen's extended treatment of Melville in ***American Renaissance*** (1941) that finally established him as a "classic American author." Matthiessen's work may best be comprehended in the context of our discussion here as a conflation of Brooks's and Lawrence's analyses of American literature. He cites only the former's work overtly in his acknowledgements, but his debt to Lawrence is clear throughout. The one-hundred-and-eighty-page Book One of ***American Renaissance*** ("From Emerson to Thoreau") plays like a historicized, filled-out version of *America's Coming of Age*, while the latter three books (on Hawthorne, Melville, and Whitman) resemble a similarly concretized and more inclusive rewrite of the last half of *Studies in Classic American Literature*. The genius of Matthiessen's book lies in the connections he draws between these two parts, between the long intellectual foreground outlined in Book One and the pivotal texts examined in the rest of the volume. In a way, the overall effect of the book is to unite the reflective milieu of Emerson

and Thoreau with the juicier life experience of Hawthorne, Melville, and Whitman. By the time Matthiessen is finished with them, it is almost as if the latter group of authors has magically acquired the former's Harvard educations while the former group has annexed the latter's overactive imaginations.

That Matthiessen ultimately succeeds in yoking these two groups of authors together is undeniable. The very fact that so many recent critics have felt constrained to expose the artifice of Matthiessen's construction is proof of how well his synthesis has held for the last fifty years. The precise details of how this trick is accomplished (and the function of the book's structure in particular) is worth a book in itself, but we will need to understand how it works in general before we can focus on the specific question of how Matthiessen achieved a permanent place in the canon for Melville.

Of all the literary histories of the United States that preceded Matthiessen, most were either so diffuse as to avoid concreteness (Parrington, Wendell) or so specific that they lacked a convincing overplot (Brooks, Frank). Much of Matthiessen's rhetorical success lies in the way he blends specifics, rather than containing them in separate chapters, while still keeping those specifics distinct. In Lawrence, Hawthorne was like Melville, but he was also like Cooper, like Dana, like Whitman, and like Crèvecoeur. In Parrington, on the other hand, each of the authors was an island, a discrete career to be examined in and of itself. To put it another way, in the first model (Lawrence), authors are elements in a purely metaphorical chain; in the second (Parrington), they are elements in a purely metonymical chain. Matthiessen simply conflated the two methods, keeping his five primary authors separate but interspersing semic references to each of them throughout the passages on the others. In a way, Matthiessen's text exemplifies a sort of "critical Pointillism," in which a blob of Emerson is placed next to a tiny dot of Melville, a tiny dot of Hawthorne, a tiny dot of Whitman, etc., so that the various dots are assembled with the larger blob in the mind's eye to give a unified impression.

Similar (and similarly crucial) to this method is the way Matthiessen makes the references to mid-nineteenth-century popular culture more central to the first, philosophical section of the volume and to the final Whitman section, while the thickness of philosophical abstraction is concentrated in the middle sections of Hawthorne and Melville, the two novelists. The more traditional critical stance would be to think of the novelists as being more clearly tied to their own time while viewing the philosophers and poets from a more eternalized, transtemporal perspective. By reversing the usual order of things without pointing out that he is doing it, Matthiessen makes us believe that the connections are "really there." This trick is substained throughout the text by thousands of allusions he makes in passing, brief references to each of the other four authors in chapters on the others, so that, by the end of the volume, Whitman and Hawthorne seem to "belong" together, an idea that (in 1940) would have seemed almost wholly illogical on the face of it.

Besides blending his five principal authors together, he also ties them irrevocably to the history of world literature. As his defense of this tactic in the introduction shows, Matthiessen felt this employment of "classic" intertexts was crucial to this project, as crucial as the provision of a historical context for his authors. Just as Matthiessen ties his five authors together by semes and allusions, he also ties them to English, European, and Modernist literature by placing these two sets of texts in constant "juxtaposition" (xiii). I will leave in abeyance for the moment the question of whether this persistent rhetorical use of juxtaposition was justified or not. But, whether one reveres or despises *American Renaissance*, it is important to understand that this is the way the text works: by means of "unmotivated" (in the semiologist's sense of the word) juxtaposition.

Now that we have delineated Matthiessen's method, we may move on to the matter of Melville. As in Lawrence's volume, Melville is central to Matthiessen's project. As one of Matthiessen's biographers has observed, "[*American Renaissance*] deals as much with Melville in the 'Hawthorne' section and the 'Whitman' section as in the 'Melville' section" (Stern 106). Not only does Matthiessen go so far as to call Melville "the American with the richest natural gifts as a writer" (371), but Melville is also the only one of the three latter authors to receive extended treatment rather than just a series of passing references in Book One (119-32). This interludic discussion of *Moby-Dick* in the literal and metaphorical context of Matthiessen's disquisition on Transcendentalist ties with the Metaphysical poets is one of the two linchpins of the book. (The other is the brief but crucial discussion of Emerson's *Representative Men* embedded in the Whitman chapter, tying it to his general discussion of myth and subdividing it for easy notice [631-35]). Without these two carefully marked-off discussions, all that would separate Matthiessen's imaginative work from a heavily segmented history like Wendell's or Lawton's would be the string of semes scattered throughout the text that continually encourage the reader to connect each author with the other four. By citing *Moby-Dick* as the third panel in a metaphysical triptych that also included Thoreau's *Walden* and Emerson's Phi Beta Kappa address, Matthiessen followed up on the suggestion dropped by Parrington that Melville was as much a thinker as a novelist. But Matthiessen carried this idea farther than Parrington, Mumford, or Weaver had done, allowing Melville to mingle as much with his contemporaries as with the classics.

In a way, the subtitle to Matthiessen's book ("Art and Expression in the Age of Emerson and Whitman") is misleading, as a key passage in his initial chapter on "Method and Scope" indicates. This chapter—often read closely by latter-day critics looking for circumstantial evidence of Matthiessen's limitations (Arac 162-63; Jehlen 228)—is actually a marvelously self-effacing summary of all the

books that Matthiessen knows very well he is not writing. In particular, he singles out the treatment of social and religious feeling in the period as two topics that might have made excellent volumes in their own right. He then performs a series of (possibly unconscious) rhetorical substitutions, speaking in one paragraph of the "intellectual history" and "the economic and social forces" of the early 1850s, then in the next of *The Age of Swedenborg* and *The Age of Fourier*" as suitable titles for studies of these two subjects, and finally concluding "But the age was also that of Emerson and Melville" (viii-ix).

As Frederick Stern has demonstrated (31 and passim), down to the last moments of Matthiessen's life the two most crucial elements of his character were his religious and political beliefs, both of which he held and acted upon passionately. In this initial chain of metaphorical substitutions ([Emerson<Swedenborg<intellectual history] and [Melville<Fourier<economic and social forces]), Matthiessen shows one possible reason why he might have constructed the text as an extended play between an "Emerson-principle" and a "Melville-principle." To a great extent, we may construe his text as an attempt to unite—or at least yoke together—what he sees as the key spiritual and intellectual principles of the age (Transcendentalism and the decline of orthodoxy) with its concomitantly crucial social and economic principles (the first flowering and tragedy of American democracy). Some modern readers ignore the fact that Matthiessen does not claim these two principles were necessarily in agreement, that (Emersonian) Transcendentalism necessarily fit in with (Melvillean) Democracy. In fact, one of the major subthemes of the book is the extent to which Emerson and Melville were philosophically at odds, as evidenced in the final summary chapter, in which those two authors occupy the most space, with Emerson getting a separate section (on *Representative Men*) and Melville getting the last word (from *Moby-Dick*, of course).

But is this the only reason why Matthiessen made Melville one of the two crucial symbolic poles of his text? One suspects he did not do it solely because of the religious/political dichotomy. (He almost certainly knew that Melville did not care enough about the "great democratic experiment" even to exercise his right to vote.) One would think that *Whitman* would be the logical opposite number to Emerson, since he was just as politically active as Emerson was, but tended more toward concrete socialism than Emerson's sort of vague Unitarian-tinged brotherhood of man. In a way, Matthiessen's reading of Whitman may be perceived as a final attempt at an "integration" of his Emerson-principle and Melville-principle. He explicitly acknowledges this possibility in his introductory paragraph to Book Two, where he speaks of Book One as a chronicle of "the transcendental affirmation," Books Two and Three as the concomitant "counterstatement" to that affirmation by "the tragic writers," and Book Four as the story of "how Whitman rode through the years undisturbed by such deep and bitter truths as Melville had found." "It would be neater," Matthiessen admits, "to say that we have in Emerson and Thoreau a thesis, in Hawthorne and Melville its antithesis, and in Whitman a synthesis. But that description would distort especially the breadth and complexity of Melville" (179).

As these comments show, Matthiessen is not so much interested here in the resolution of this modal tension as he is in its full presentation. He is more concerned about "distorting" Melville than distorting Whitman, as the composition of Books Three and Four indicates; Book Three is almost wholly about Melville's career, while Book Four (like Book Two) leans as much on the work of other artists as it does on that of its ostensible subject. Melville serves as a counterbalance to Emerson in **American Renaissance** precisely because Matthiessen shows him unequivocally saying "No" when Emerson has unequivocally said "Yes." Employing both these authors rather than just one or the other saves Matthiessen from committing himself to either optimism or pessimism as a reasonable outlook on either life or the United States. In other words, the construction of such a dynamic tension between the two authors' positions allows the critic to join the chorus as a third voice whispering "Maybe" sotto voce. Unlike a great many of those who have followed in his footsteps, Matthiessen is therefore employing these five authors to impart a sense of difference rather than sameness. Suspending his text between Emerson and Melville and just leaving it to swing between those two poles allows him to, in the words of Stephen Sondheim, "know what [his] decision is / Which is not to decide."

Matthiessen's determination to depict Melville as the moral naysayer of the antebellum period results in a recasting of Melville's career. As noted above, in most previous interpretations Melville had no career—what he had were travel books, sea stories, self-indulgence, and *Moby-Dick*. Far more insistent than Parrington (who was the first to make more than a halfhearted attempt at defending the status of *Pierre* and *Clarel* in Melville's career), Matthiessen is really the first critic to place any literary or intellectual emphasis on the later works overall. He warms up with *Typee* and *Omoo*, only lingers on *Mardi* long enough to note its debt to Sir Thomas Browne and his contemporaries, and then rushes through *Redburn* and *White Jacket* to get to *Moby-Dick* and *Pierre*, the centerpieces of his analysis. The shape he delineates in Melville's career owes more to Parrington's version than it does to Mumford's, but the opening movement has been lopped off for convenience's sake and the emphasis extended a little further and later. Rather than tracing a development from *Typee* to *Pierre*, Matthiessen shows one that instead moves from *Mardi* to *Billy Budd*.

At the risk of hyperbole, I would contend that, along with the connections Matthiessen cements between Melville and his four contemporaries, this revised version of Melville's career was what guaranteed him literary immortality. The difference between Parrington's plotline for Melville's career and Matthiessen's is the difference between the former's assertion that "There is no other trag-

edy in American letters comparable to the tragedy of Herman Melville," (250) and Matthiessen's judgment that "[Melville's] career did not fall into what has been too often assumed to be the pattern for the lives of our artists: brilliant beginnings without staying power, truncated and broken by our hostile environment." "Melville's endurance," he concludes, "is a challenge for a later America" (514).

By interpreting Melville's life as a story of "endurance" rather than "tragedy," Matthiessen spared Melville the fate of the one-hit wonder. In his particular analysis of the author's accomplishments, he also pointed furture critics in the direction of the three works that have served as the focus for Melville studies since World War II: *Moby-Dick, Pierre,* and *Billy Budd.* In the Melville scholarship of the 1940s through the 1970s, one hardly sees a mention of *Typee, White Jacket,* or indeed any of the pre-1851 works that does not seek to tie it to one of the post-1851 works. The problem that nearly all the pre-Matthiessen Melville critics had kept running into was that they could not admire the works written before *Moby-Dick* and they could not understand the works written after it. Matthiessen changed all that by turning Melville's career into a journey up toward Metaphysical (with a capital M) symbolism rather than down into self-absorbed incomprehensibility.

To speculate on why Matthiessen felt constrained to reinterpret Melville's career as an enduring pessimistic counterbalance to Emerson's equally enduring optimism would be an exercise in psychoanalytic biography rather than semiotics. However, I cannot resist hazarding a concluding guess as to why the rehabilitation of Melville was so central to Matthissen's project. Without Melville, Matthissen's interpretation of the "American Renaissance" would have been far too "neat," far too perfect, far too obvious: Emerson, Thoreau, and Hawthorne were all Concordites, and Whitman was self-consciously their kinsman. Melville threw just enough tension and downright disagreement into the mix to make Matthiessen's interpretative composition "whole." He disturbed the usual New England school, and that, in Matthiessen's eyes, was good. Just so long as he didn't break anything.

IV

Since the 1940s, of course, few critics have voiced any serious doubts about Melville's proper "place" in American literature. He is now subject to the same sort of affectionate kidding regarding boredom, length, and weightiness as Milton, Tolstoy, Proust, and other canonical European authors. In the end, Melville became a "classic American author" as well as the author of a "classic American work," precisely because he was both assimilable and unique: close enough, on the one hand, to previously canonized American authors to fit with established critical views, but different enough, on the other hand, to give the post-Wendell view of American literature a much-needed shot in the arm.

There is a curious symmetry in all this, one which leads me back to the questions of critical historiography and canon formation with which I began. For the critical history traced above—the one culminating in Matthiessen's permanent elevation of Melville to canonical status by his subtle recasting of the author in **American Renaissance**—is in itself an instance of the sort of tense play between similarity and difference that Matthiessen so admired and that he constructed the text of **American Renaissance** around. He most often expressed this notion in a single, much-misunderstood word: "wholeness." Both Matthiessen's use of that word and his implied use of the concept that lies behind it have been something of a *bête noire* for recent meta-critics such as Arac, Pease, and Tompkins. Yet "wholeness" means something very different to the latter trio of critics than it did to Matthiessen. When Matthiessen discusses "wholeness" in relation to Thoreau (96), for example, his use of the word is almost oxymoronic. By "wholeness" he clearly does not mean "unity," nor bland "sameness" nor "identity" in the most artless sense of those words. Rather he suggests an accord reached by a fragile equilibrium of forces, not unlike the frequently ignored modal tension between and among the five books of **American Renaissance**. Matthiessen's rejection of mere "identity" in this sense is also clear in his discussion of what he considers to be Emerson's unfortunate experiments with "natural rhyme" (137). To be "whole" in the sense that Matthiessen believes his subjects and their Metaphysical forebears to have been "whole" is not to close off change or future growth. It is merely to fix synchronically a brief moment in which all the elements of an "integer" seem to have played productively off all the others.

When recent critics speak of Matthiessen's idea of "wholeness," however, this crucial concept of a tense play among differences is lost. Pease in particular (if I read one of his earlier essays on Matthiessen correctly) sees the critic's work as contradictory rather than complex; it is those contradictions, he believes, that allowed the American Studies movement to provide much-needed ideological reinforcement for "the Cold War consensus" ("Melville and Cultural Persuasion" 415). Similarly, when Jane Tompkins looks at Matthiessen's work, she finds it "exclusive and class-bound in the extreme." For Tompkins, Matthiessen's version of American literature in the mid-nineteenth century "does not represent what most men and women were thinking about between 1850 and 1855, but embodies the views of a very small, socially, culturally, geographically, sexually, and racially restricted elite" (199-200). For these and other present-day critics of Matthiessen, **American Renaissance** is a work of parochial sameness, not a work of revolutionary difference.[7]

These criticisms may be sustained with varying degrees of success, but if one actually sits down to re-read **American Renaissance** with an eye to the critic's possible totalizing tendencies, one finds that the evidence is scant, if it exists at all. As the *entirety* of Matthiessen's text indicates, he has both read the works of Stowe and other noncanonical contemporaries and has considered approaches more skeptical than his own. Indeed, for a man who is supposedly

nailing down a literary canon, he is remarkably critical of the work of all five of his central authors.[8] In point of fact, the literary texts of the period that Matthiessen tends to idealize and praise uncritically are most often those (like Horatio Greenough's essays) written by *non*-canonical authors whom he feels have been unduly neglected. By no stretch of the imagination can the actual text of **American Renaissance** by seen as the sort of reactionary, ancestor-worshipping, canon-shoring sort of volume it has frequently been portrayed as.

In other words, the same process that engulfed *Moby-Dick* engulfed **American Renaissance**; the same sort of critical revisionism that canonized Melville has now partially demonized Mathiessen. As I stated in my initial analysis, all critical evaluation, even meta-critical evaluation, is intertextual. If Melville gains value because his works can be connected with those of Thoreau and Whitman, then Mathiessen loses value because his works can be linked (as Tompkins indeed does link them [123] with later Americanist syntheses like R. W. B. Lewis's *The American Adam* (1955) and Richard Chase's *The American Novel and Its Tradition* (1957). Even though these two books were written little more than a decade after Mathiessen's volume was published, one can see that the earlier critic's interpretation of antebellum American literature had already been hopelessly reified, even "flattened," by the time of Lewis and Chase.[9] One might say that the "optative mood" Mathiessen cites in Emerson and Thoreau had been replaced by the mid-1950s with the indicative. While one can hardly open to a page in Mathiessen's volume where he is not hedging his bets, qualifying his praise, or drawing in other authors and tendencies from the larger world of the 1850s, these later critics see the writers of Mathiessen's Renaissance as sufficient in and of themselves. The frame of reference Mathiessen brought to his subject was not enlarged in these later volumes but restricted, narrowed to the point where, as Nina Baym put it in 1981, "the theory of American fiction has boiled down to . . . a melodrama of beset manhood" (79).

What happened was that the dynamic tension—the "wholeness"—that held Matthiessen's Renaissance together gradually vanished as interpretation after interpretation used his ideas as a jumping-off point. The differences between Whitman and Melville, between Melville and Hawthorne, between Emerson and Thoreau, and so on, were more and more downplayed or marginalized, and the similarities between these authors played up. Eventually, they all came to be seen as writing the same story over and over and were viewed as the (except for characteristic idiosyncrasies) relatively interchangeable authors of variations on a familiar theme rather than distinct intellectuals proceeding from a common and complex base. This is the difference between Matthiessen's initial assertion in 1941 of the importance of the early 1850s for American literature (vii) and Chase's initial *assumption* in 1957 that "certain books, such as *The Scarlet Letter, Moby-Dick, The Portrait of a Lady, Huckleberry Finn,* and *The Sound and the Fury,* may be expected to appear in almost any study of the American novel, and I have included these" (vii). At the time of the first statement, there clearly was no secure American canon; by the time of the second, Chase seemed to feel that there was.

As Baym notes in another essay on canon formation, this is not the first time this has happened. In the original turn-of-the-century interpretation of the six canonical New England writers heralded by William Cranston Lawton and others, each writer had his role and played off the others, just as in Matthiessen's formulation. As a group they all served as "quasi-allegorical personifications of what, even in these pre-Millerian days, was called the New England mind" ("Early Histories" 471). As long as the distinctions between these authors were preserved and they were perceived as distinct presences, that construction of American literature could claim a certain value. But once the distinctions between the authors were effaced, once "wholeness" was replaced with "identity," such an interpretation lost its value. Even before it was challenged from the outside, such an interpretation of sameness from author to author was doomed to unpersuasiveness. It simply could not sustain the very real diversity of responses that any group of readers will bring to a given set of texts.

The irony, of course, is that in hindsight all schools of interpretation are fixed for all time in their final phases of decadence rather than in their middle periods of greatest fruitfulness. Those of us who have entered the academy in the last two or three decades remember Matthiessen's Renaissance, not as the bright new idea of 1941, but as the same stale, automatic claptrap that got shoved down our throats in lecture after lecture in college or graduate school. What we remember is not Matthiessen's Renaissance but the unfortunate school of "American Romance" criticism that evolved from it. This school (represented by Chase and Lewis among others) turned Matthiessen's exploration of allegory and symbolism in Book Two of **American Renaissance** into an article of faith, and Hawthorne's preface to *The House of the Seven Gables* into a sacred text.

When we observe that reading *Moby-Dick* is a "mind-numbing" experience (Gates 36) or discover that reading *The Wide, Wide World* is a mind-expanding one (Tompkins 147), we hardly ever realize that we are being more like Matthiessen than even those critics who consider themselves his most ardent followers. The last fifty years of meta-critical revisionism have obliterated the truly radical nature of Matthiessen's interpretation, right down to his insistent presentism, comparing his authors to contemporary writers like Frost, Eliot, and Malraux in a way that some of his less perceptive acolytes would sneer at (as mere "current events") in the writings of any other critic. Just as the children and grandchildren of many European immigrants have forgotten the discrimination that their own forebears suffered just two or three generations ago, so too have many American literature and American studies scholars forgotten that as recently as 1925, the study of American literature was in much the same position as the study of African-American literature or American wom-

en's writing was a decade ago: practiced by true believers, certainly, but not taken seriously by those in authority. "It was hardly an accident," Matthiessen notes in his acknowledgments, "that when I graduated from college in the early nineteen-twenties, I knew very little of our own literature except some contemporary poetry that I had read with my friends" (xvii). This sentiment is not too far from the one with which Tompkins begins her frequently reprinted essay on *Uncle Tom's Cabin*, where she notes her own early, ignorant dismissal of the writings of Stowe and other woman novelists of the 1850s (122-23).

Ideally, of course, one should read everything. But to assert, either approvingly or disapprovingly, that "The Canon" is one big undigestible lump—that it was either handed down from God for the study of American literature and sufficient unto itself or perpetrated by F. O. Matthiessen and Co. in one brief meeting of a Harvard clique to keep us from reading Maria Cummins—is both naive and ludicrous. Canons come and canons go. In the long run, the invisible hand of the academic market supports those fresh metaphors that produce new insights and discards those ideological metanarratives that have grown stale, flat, and unprofitable. The value of such interpretations lies in these sorts of pragmatic virtues, not in whatever "wider" ideologies these interpretations may either overtly or covertly advance. If these interpretations contain an element of dynamic tension and uniqueness within an assimilable form or shape, they will continue to prove useful to our endeavors. Once these interpretations are transformed from sign-functions into myths, however, they lose their explanatory depth and cease to be of interest. Now, as always, the canon is dead. Long live the (temporary) canon.

Notes

1. I am slightly altering Barthes's concept of the work/text dichotomy here. Strictly speaking, the intent of his essay (originally published in 1971) was to proclaim the arrival of the playful Age of the Text and its victory over the tyranically exegetical Age of the Work. However, it is my contention (as will be shown below) that the "uniqueness" test applied to works alleged to be masterpieces implies a certain amount of "play" in the sense Barthes uses it here and elsewhere, as well as the polyvocal quality he imparts to the text, both in this essay and in its older, bigger brother, *S/Z*, a masterpiece in its own right. In traditional critical discourse, masterpieces are expected to be both alike and unlike earlier masterpieces. As such, the concept of the "masterpiece" or "classic text" partakes of the concepts of both the "work" and the "text" as they have been advanced by Barthes.

2. Even more telling on this score is the title of the chapter in which Lawton considers Melville: "Less Familiar Names." The rest of the chapter considers such "nonentities" as Lydia Howard Huntley Sigourney, Catherine Sedgwick, both Richard Henry Danas, Edward Everett Hale, Thomas Wentworth Higginson, William Wetmore Story, Susan and Anna Warner, and Walter [sic] Whitman.

3. The purely regional argument—that Melville is left out of these early formulations solely because of the provincial bias toward New England among the early critics of American literature (Baym, "Early Histories" 478)—is belied in Brooks' case by his admiring inclusion of Poe, Twain, and especially Whitman. Whitman, who was the most favored "classic American author" of the *Seven Arts* crowd with which Brooks is often associated, had even less claim to "New England" status than Melville, having never lived in the Berkshires, walked around the mountains with Hawthorne, or even lived north of New York for any extended period of time.

4. On this score, compare Walker's observation that "Robert Hemenway was the first critic I read who seemed indignant that Zora's life ended in poverty and obscurity" (87). More than "measured judgment," what forgotten authors seem to require in this initial stage of their revivification is the sympathy of their biographers for the neglect they have suffered.

5. Both Wendell and Lawton enforce a strict regional and temporal segmentation in the organization of their books, a practice that consigns Brown, Irving, Cooper, Bryant, Poe, and the Knickerbocker "group" or "school" to a single chapter. Both critics also create separate sections on New England that group writers by genre (history, oratory, poetry) and intellectual or political convictions (transcendentalism and abolitionism). John Macy (1913) and Van Wyck Brooks (1915) anticipate Lawrence's method of sub-chapters or chapters focused on the work of scattered authors rather than clearly defined groupings, and yet their inclusion of such vestigial figures as Bryant, Longfellow, Whittier, Holmes, Curtis, and Lowell in their surveys of the early nineteenth century make their interpretations of American literature less familiar to postmodern eyes than Lawrence's grouping of Franklin, Crèvecoeur, Cooper, Poe, Hawthorne, Dana, Melville, and Whitman.

6. The attempt to tie Melville and his writings to widely acknowledged literary masterpieces and to other American works and writers continued throughout the 1920s and 1930s. The authors invoked for comparison ranged from Rabelais (Wells) to Goethe and Milton (Van Doren, "Mr. Melville's *Moby-Dick*" and "Lucifer from Nantucket") to the inevitable Shakespeare (Hughes; Olson) and even Plato (Couch). There were also a few attempts to follow up on Lawrence's suggestion that *Moby-Dick* was an American epic (Colum; Brooks, "A Third Look"; Erskine 223-40), all of which placed more emphasis on showing how *Moby-Dick* bore a strict formal resemblance to previous epics like the *Aeneid* and *Paradise Lost* than on showing how it might be a specifically *American* epic. There were also a few attempts to connect Melville with the American culture and society of his time (Clark; Claverton 271-73; MacDonald; Gabriel), although these were usually of no more than antiquarian interest.

7. Admittedly, I am sidestepping here the most significant critique of Matthiessen's concept of "wholeness," the one advanced by Jonathan Arac, who holds that such "wholeness" implies exclusion. On the one hand, I think this critique appears more material than it may actually be because of its context; it occupies a key place in Arac's unfolding archeology of the notion of "totality" in the criticism of Coleridge, Arnold, Lukacs, and others. It would thus gain solidity from its presence in such a "work-making" series of critical instances even if Arac took note of Matthiessen's differences from these earlier critics on the notion of totality, which he does not.

On the other hand, such as observation (that what is customarily understood as interpretive "wholeness" implies exclusion) seems, to me, tautological. Meaning in criticism, as in all aspects of language and culture, is constructed through *discrimination*, in both senses of the word. It is, in Barthes's phrase, "therefore an order with chaos on either side, but this order is essentially a *division*" (*Elements of Semiology* 56). Whether the "wholeness" of a critical composition like Arac's or Matthiessen's is convincingly discriminating or merely discriminatory is, as always, left up to the reader. A single work of criticism cannot be expected to persuade every possible reader, nor can it be expected to be fully inclusive, since that would require a text of infinite length. A certain degree of "exclusion," then, is inherent in the practice of expository writing. To that extent, "the frame is thus framed . . . by part of its content; the sender . . . receives his own message backward from the receiver" (Johnson 146).

Without launching into an extended discussion of the appropriate burden of proof in critical and constitutional discrimination cases—and the parallels between Arac and Brennan on the one hand and Crews and Rehnquist on the other are admittedly tempting—suffice it to say that I think the mere fact of exclusion is not sufficient proof of Arac's charge against Matthiessen of a "totalizing" mentality. I discuss this issue at greater length below in the body of the text.

Having said all this, however, I should also explicitly state that I am not presenting my "critical genealogy" of *American Renaissance* as a denial of Arac's, merely as a separate, equally valid alternative. (In point of fact, I agree with Arac on most of his other points regarding *American Renaissance*; I really only take exception to his charge of critical exclusionism.) After all, one of the goals of the sort of Foucauldian genealogy that Arac has constructed is to *de-center* the totalism of literary historiography, a project that I am wholly in favor of and one to which this essay is intended as an additional contribution. I think Arac would agree that if we throw aside one totalistic "truth" about literary history merely to embrace another, then the only advance that we have made is on a treadmill to oblivion. Multiple centers mean multiple "truths," in the sense in which Nietzsche speaks of constructed "truth" and its "genealogy" in "On Truth and Lie in an Extra-Moral Sense" and *The Genealogy of Morals.*

Thus my delineation of Matthiessen's historiographical situation should be viewed as the delineation of a separate strand of "truth-production" running through *American Renaissance.* This strand is yet another hitherto "naturalized" process by which Nietzsche's "sum of human relations" has been "enhanced, transposed, and embellished poetically and rhetorically, and which long after [has seemed] firm, canonical, and obligatory to a people" (46-47). In other words, Arac focuses on such "truth-production" as it relates to the Coleridge-Arnold-New Criticism chain that he is tracing, whereas I have focused on a separate chain involving Raymond Weaver, D. H. Lawrence, and V. L. Parrington. There is no reason why these and any other number of parallel genealogies should not be traced to the same, undeniably seminal work. To a certain extent, what makes works like *American Renaissance* "seminal" is precisely this sort of "dissemination."

8. Particularly notable in this regard are Matthiessen's negative judgments of Emerson's poetry (53ff) and limited view of nature (158), Thoreau's alleged "wildness" (164-65), and Melville's characterizations (482-83) and dialogue (486) in *Pierre,* which he ultimately judges "a failure" albeit "a great one" (487). Most impressive of all is his extended treatment of Hawthorne's overall unreadability, which takes up most of Chapter VI.

9. Other critics have noted this historiographical simplification or "flattening" of Matthiessen's most famous work. Russell Reising, for one, has commented on the fact that the political or "historicist" aspect of Matthiessen's argument has been neglected by later critics in favor of the New Critical or "formalist" aspect of his work. It was this emphasized, New Critical aspect of *American Renaissance,* Reising theorizes, that gave rise to the postwar "romance" school of Americanist criticism of Lewis and Chase (170-73). Alternatively, Pease—in a recent essay that almost, but not quite, "contradicts" his own earlier work on Matthiessen—argues that the ideological conflicts that produced the now "classic" American Studies texts of the mid-twentieth century have been suppressed in critical memory in favor of a retrospective model of consensus. Rather tellingly, Pease displaces this over-simplification of the midcentury American Studies movement onto Frederick Crews rather than onto the so-called "New Americanists," whom Crews has attacked and whom Pease is explicitly defending in this essay by recalling Matthiessen's own meta-critical trials at the hands of Lionel Trilling ("New Americanists" 6-11).

I would like to thank Lisa Monaco for her provocative ideas on the literary historiography of Zora Neale Hurston, which have contributed to my thinking on Melville's posthumous career. I would especially like to thank Robert Paul Lamb, teacher, friend, and inspiration, for lending me both the confidence and the books necessary to write this essay. In addition, his comments on the manuscript were invaluable in revising it, as were those of my wife, Stephanie La Tour.

Works Cited

Arac, Jonathan, *Critical Genealogies: Historical Situations for Postmodern Literary Studies.* New York: Columbia University Press, 1987.

Barbour, James. "'All My Books Are Botches'": Melville's Struggle with *The Whale.*" *Writing the American Classics.* Ed. James Barbour and Tom Quirk. Chapel Hill: University of North Carolina Press, 1990. 25-52.

Barthes, Roland. *Elements of Semiology.* Tr. Annette Lavers and Colin Smith. 1967. New York: Hill & Wang, 1968.

———. "Myth Today." *Mythologies.* Tr. Annette Lavers. New York: Hill & Wang, 1972. 109-59.

———. "From Work to Text." *Image/Music/Text.* Tr. Stephen Heath. New York: Hill & Wang, 1977. 155-69.

Baym, Nina. "Melodramas of Beset Manhood: How Theories of American Fiction Exclude Women Authors." 1981. Showalter 63-80.

———. *Novels, Readers, and Reviewers: Responses to Fiction in Antebellum America.* Ithaca: Cornell University Press, 1984.

———. "Early Histories of American Literature: A Chapter in the Institution of New England." *American Literary History* 1 (1989): 459-88.

Benjamin, Walter. "Unpacking My Library: A Talk about Book Collecting." *Illuminations.* Ed. Hannah Arendt. Tr. Harry Zohn. 1968. New York: Schocken Books, 1969. 59-67.

Bercovitch, Sacvan, and Myra Jehlen, eds. *Ideology and Classic American Literature.* New York: Cambridge University Press, 1986.

Blake, Casey. "The Young Intellectuals and the Culture of Personality." *American Literary History* 1 (Fall 1989): 510-34.

Brodhead, Richard H. *The School of Hawthorne.* New York: Oxford University Press, 1986.

Brooks, Van Wyck. *America's Coming of Age.* 1915. Garden City: Doubleday, 1958.

———. "[The Melville Boom: Only a Question of Time]." 1921. Parker and Hayford 144-47.

———. "[A Third Look at Melville]." 1923. Parker and Hayford 153-58.

Claverton, V. F. *The Liberation of American Literature.* New York: Scribner's, 1932.

Chase, Richard. *The American Novel and Its Tradition.* New York: Doubleday, 1957.

Clark, Harry Hayden. "American Literary History and American Literature." *The Re-Interpretation of American Literature.* Ed. Norman Foerster. New York: Harcourt, Brace, 1928.

Colum, Padraic. "Moby-Dick as an Epic: A Note." *Measure* 13 (March 1922): 16-18.

Couch, H. N. "*Moby-Dick* and the Phaedo." *Classical Journal* 28 (February 1933): 367-68.

Eco, Umberto. *The Role of the Reader: Explorations in the Semiotics of Texts.* Bloomington: Indiana University Press, 1979.

Erskine, John. *The Delight of Great Books.* Indianapolis: Bobbs-Merrill, 1928.

Fox-Genovese, Elizabeth. "Between Individualism and Fragmentation: American Culture and the New Literary Studies of Race and Gender." *American Quarterly* 42 (1990): 7-34.

Frye, Northrop. *Anatomy of Criticism: Four Essays.* Princeton: Princeton University Press, 1957.

Gabriel, Ralph H. "Melville: Critic of Mid-Nineteenth Century Beliefs." *The Course of American Democratic Thought.* New York: Ronald, 1940. 67-77.

Gates, Henry Louis, Jr. "Canon Confidential: A Sam Slade Caper." *New York Times Book Review* 25 March 1990: 1, 36-37.

Hemenway, Robert E. *Zora Neale Hurston: A Literary Biography.* Urbana: University of Illinois Press, 1977.

Hicks, Granville. *The Great Tradition: An Interpretation of American Literature Since the Civil War.* New York: Macmillan, 1933.

Hofstadter, Richard. *The Progressive Historians: Turner, Beard, Parrington.* 1968. New York: Vintage, 1970.

Hughes, Raymond G. "Melville and Shakespeare." *Shakespeare Association Bulletin* 7 (July 1932): 103-12.

Jehlen, Myra. *American Incarnation: The Individual, the Nation, and the Continent.* Cambridge: Harvard University Press, 1986.

Johnson, Barbara. "The Frame of Reference: Poe, Lacan, and Derrida." 1978. *The Critical Difference: Essays in the Contemporary Rhetoric of Reading.* 1980. Baltimore: Johns Hopkins University Press, 1985. 110-46.

Kolodny, Annette. "A Map for Rereading: Gender and the Interpretation of Literary Texts." 1980. Showalter 46-62.

Lacan, Jacques. "Seminar on 'The Purloined Letter.'" Tr. Jeffrey Mehlman. *The Purloined Poe: Lacan, Derrida, and Psychoanalytic Reading.* Ed. John P. Muller and William J. Richardson. Baltimore: Johns Hopkins University Press, 1988. 28-54.

Lawrence, D. H. *Studies in Classic American Literature.* 1923. New York: Penguin Books, 1977.

Lawton, William Cranston. *The New England Poets: A Study of Emerson, Hawthorne, Longfellow, Whittier, Lowell, [and] Holmes.* New York: Macmillan, 1898.

———. *Introduction to the Study of American Literature.* New York: Globe School Book Co., 1902.

Lewis, R. W. B. *The American Adam: Innocence, Tragedy, and Tradition in the Nineteenth Century.* Chicago: University of Chicago Press, 1955.

MacDonald, Allan. "A Sailor among the Transcendentalists." *New England Quarterly* 8 (September 1935): 307-19.

Macy, John. *The Spirit of American Literature.* Garden City: Doubleday, 1913.

Matthiessen, F. O. *American Renaissance: Art and Expression in the Age of Emerson and Whitman.* New York: Oxford University Press, 1941.

Mumford, Lewis. *The Golden Day: A Study in American Literature and Culture.* 1926. Boston: Beacon Press, 1957.

———. *Herman Melville.* New York: Harcourt, Brace, 1929.

Nietzsche, Friedrich. "On Truth and Lie in an Extra-Moral Sense." Tr. Walter Kaufmann. In *The Portable Nietzsche.* Ed. Kaufmann. New York: Viking Press, 1954. 42-47.

Olson, Charles. "Lear and *Moby-Dick*." *Twice a Year* 1 (1938): 165-89.

Parker, Hershel, ed. *The Recognition of Herman Melville: Selected Criticism Since 1846.* Ann Arbor: University of Michigan Press, 1967.

Parker, Hershel, and Harrison Hayford, eds. *Moby-Dick As Doubloon: Essays and Extracts (1851-1970).* New York: Norton, 1970.

Parrington, Vernon L. *The Romantic Revolution in America, 1800-1860.* New York: Harcourt, Brace, & World, 1927. Vol. 2 of *Main Currents in American Thought.* 3 vols. 1927-30.

Pease, Donald E. "Melville and Cultural Persuasion." 1986. Bercovitch and Jehlen 384-417.

———. "New Americanists: Revisionist Interventions into the Canon." *Boundary 2* 17.1 (1990): 1-37.

Poirier, Richard. *A World Elsewhere: The Place of Style in American Literature.* New York: Oxford University Press, 1966.

Reising, Russell. *The Unusable Past: Theory and the Study of American Literature.* New York: Methuen, 1986.

Rourke, Constance. *American Humor: A Study of the National Character.* New York: Harcourt, Brace, 1931.

Showalter, Elaine, ed. *The New Feminist Criticism: Essays on Women, Literature, and Theory.* New York: Pantheon Books, 1985.

Smith, Henry Nash. *Democracy and the Novel: Popular Resistance to Classic American Writers.* New York: Oxford University Press, 1978.

Stern, Frederick C. *F. O. Matthiessen: Christian Socialist As Critic.* Chapel Hill: University of North Carolina Press, 1981.

Stovall, Floyd, ed. *Eight American Authors: A Review of Research and Criticism.* 1956. New York: Norton, 1963.

Thomas, John L. "The Uses of Catastrophe: Lewis Mumford, Vernon L. Parrington, Van Wyck Brooks, and the End of American Regionalism." *American Quarterly* 42 (1990): 223-51.

Tompkins, Jane. *Sensational Designs: The Cultural Work of American Fiction, 1790-1860.* New York: Oxford University Press, 1985.

Van Doren, Carl. "Mr. Melville's *Moby-Dick.*" *New York Bookman* 59 (April 1924): 154-57.

———. "Lucifer from Nantucket: An Introduction to *Moby-Dick.*" *Century* 110 (August 1925): 494-501.

Walker, Alice. *In Search of Our Mother's Gardens: Womanist Prose.* New York: Harcourt Brace Jovanovich, 1983.

Weaver, Raymond M. "[An Amazing Masterpiece]." 1919. Parker and Hayford 126-27.

———. *Herman Melville, Mariner and Mystic.* New York: George H. Doran, 1921.

Wells, W. H. "*Moby-Dick* and Rabelais." *Modern Language Notes* 38 (February 1923): 123.

Wendell, Barrett. *A Literary History of America.* New York: Charles Scribner's Sons, 1901.

Philip Horne (essay date 1995)

SOURCE: "Henry James: The Master and the 'Queer Affair' of The 'Pupil'," in *Critical Quarterly*, Vol. 37, No. 3, Autumn, 1995, pp. 75-92.

[*In the following essay, Horne discusses Matthiessen's reading of James's "The Pupil."*]

QUEER AFFAIRS

Perhaps I can best indicate some of the troubles I want to raise in this essay by quoting from a 1990 volume entitled *Engendering Men: The Question of Male Feminist Criticism.* One of the editors, Michael Cadden, has an interesting meditation on the great, homosexual critic F. O. Matthiessen—'Engendering F. O. M.: The Private Life of *American Renaissance*'—where in effect he laments the accuracy of that comma separating 'great' from 'homosexual'. Matthiessen's homosexuality only fully emerged nearly three decades after his death with the publication of his love-letters to the painter Russell Cheney; his enormously influential critical writing is extremely dis-

creet about private matters. Cadden quotes Matthiessen at the opening of ***American Renaissance*** endorsing the view that 'true scholarship' must be 'for the good and enlightenment of all the people, not for the pampering of a class'[1]—a view which seems linked to Matthiessen's Christian Socialist beliefs and activities—but he lets this drop; his emphasis falls, in contrast, despite Matthiessen's hope that he and Cheney might represent 'hope for a spirit of brotherhood', on the sense that 'tragically he could not see himself as part of a collective sexual identity smaller than "all of [sic] the people"'.[2] The essay ends with a 'fantastic and utopian' hypothesis, picking up from Virginia Woolf and her Judith Shakespeare, of an openly gay brother for Matthiessen, 'Michael', who becomes a 'great gay critic' and teaches with a feminist colleague at Yale a course 'based on the book they co-wrote—*The Other American Renaissance*' (pp. 34, 35). Cadden's purpose is perhaps clearest in a striking image he produces in response to a diary account of a 'Whitmanesque encounter' Matthiessen has with a workman in Wells Cathedral, a short conversation during which his elbow rubs the man's belly and he has an erection:

> Throughout the letters to Cheney, the gay critic barely perceivable beneath his canonical drag emerges from the closet of professional and patriarchal mastery hard on in hand, thereby exposing and demystifying the 'Phallus' that 'disseminated' an entire Renaissance. (p. 28)

The real penis of the biographically homosexual Matthiessen is brandished by Cadden as an alternative standard to the supposed 'patriarchal . . . Phallus' of the public critic; only Matthiessen's touching account is that of a gay man who is also a critic, not as quoted a 'gay critic', and Cadden's 'thereby' introduces a grand gesture that relies on its swirling camp outrageousness to carry off the idea that the knowledge of a real Matthiessen with strong homosexual feelings and an organ somehow disallows the authority of his public utterances (an authority hollowed out here by being simply attributed to the ever-ready 'Phallus', rather than earned through acuteness, accuracy, or persuasiveness). Cadden's own address here is primarily to 'a collective sexual identity smaller than "all of the people"', and indeed, alongside that sexual identity, to a collective critical identity smaller than all of the critics, let alone all the readers.

One aspect of what is going on here is the politicisation of the private: Matthiessen's troubled private life is appropriated by an attitude which knows how he should have behaved, and which, for all its apparent sympathy ('tragically'), ends by supplanting him with a preferable, liberated, unfortunately nonexistent brother. Another aspect is the privatisation of the political: Matthiessen's public utterances and his democratic aspiration to address 'all the people', presumably all genders, sexualities and classes, are regarded as a 'drag', exposed and demystified by the mere fact of his real sexuality. The critic's role is reduced to spokespersonship for his group interests, here those associated with his sexual identity.

I start with the take of 'gender studies' on the activity of literary criticism, and on the author of **Henry James: The Major Phase**, because I want to deal with questions of critical purpose and procedure which have arisen in some recent work, for instance at the Sesquicentennial Henry James conference in New York in June 1993, the first two days of which were devoted to 'Rethinking Gender and Sexual Politics: Henry James in the New Century.' Many of the speakers worked on the assumption that James was if not actively homosexual then homoerotic in his sexual orientation. As one of them, Leland S. Person Jr, said in his paper,

> Many recent James scholars (especially [Eve Kosovsky] Sedgwick and Fred Kaplan) have brought James and James studies out of the closet to the point where we can almost take James's homosexuality for granted.[3]

That 'almost' is one sticking-point to which I wish to attach my own marginal notes; another, suggested by the case of Matthiessen, is the question of what we anyway do, as literary critics, with biographical homosexuality even when established.

Before going further I want to raise a general, terminological and categorical question. There is a noticeable imbalance in the range of shadings of sexual possibility registered in most of the writings associated with 'Queer Theory', and I think certain questionable assumptions correspond to the gaps in the spectrum as currently conceived. The chain of main terms, the ones most cathected with critical charge, seems to go: homosexual, homoerotic, homosocial . . . heterosexual. I want to ask, for one thing, why we don't have, or why critics don't activate, the two missing links, heteroerotic and heterosocial. Perhaps, to attempt an answer, it is because such terms might seem to presume a homosexual identity, only for it to be complicated by either erotic feelings about persons of the opposite gender; or by an impulse to form social bonds with persons of that other gender (this might correspond to the phenomenon of the 'hag-fag', implicit in the term 'fag-hag'). These complications (let alone those that would come in with 'bierotic' and 'bisocial') would be charged with implications for the often political agendas of 'Queer Theory', for they would impinge on the questions Eve Kosovsky Sedgwick herself discusses concerning the gulf between 'essentialist' and 'behavioural' understandings of homosexuality.

A fuller range of six descriptive shadings—homosexual, homoerotic, homosocial, heterosocial, heteroerotic, heterosexual—might also cast some interesting doubt on the directional tilt that for quite intelligible polemical compensatory purposes informs the current range of four. Where the usual four suggest a dominant, monolithic heterosexuality being subverted by, desperately resisting, an overbalancing perversity, with every trace of the 'homo-' prefix indicating 'deep' predilection, the set of six might allow more helpfully and neutrally for other individual cases, less schematically predictable combinations of impulses and affects. It might be understood that much more various

permutations were possible without belonging to a grand simple narrative of conversion or repression. A homosexually identified man might experience heteroerotic feelings in relation to certain women, for instance, or take pleasure in women's company, without necessarily compromising his choice. From another angle, I would also want to enter a caveat about the assumption reflected in much current criticism, despite its lip-service to diversity, that the sexual is the basic or underlying or 'deep' realm of meaning. This assumption and its interpretative consequences seem to me to derive especially from some of Freud's less nuanced procedures. In discussions of narrative, the complex specificity of circumstances bearing on fictional characters is often neglected so that their acts and choices can be read off as direct registers of (here) sexual orientation either on the part of the character concerned or (in more abstractly sophisticated readings) on the part of the author. The risk is that all motivation can become inappropriately, a-prioristically, sexualised. As James says somewhere, it is the essence of moral energy to survey the whole field, and the whole field of human activity and relations may not be organised, or best understood, on a model where the sexual instinct is always primary.

Let me return to Leland Person and his claim that recent criticism has brought 'James and James studies out of the closet to the point where we can almost take James's homosexuality for granted'. A striking parallel to the Jamesian situation is outlined by William Shuter in a recent piece called 'The "Outing" of Walter Pater'. Shuter records that, following a forensic paper concerning Pater's relations with an undergraduate given by Billie Andrew Inman at a Pater conference in 1988, a similar consensus has taken shape in Pater studies. He quotes one Paterian:

> Intimations and innuendos have been around for over a century: Pater has finally been smoked out and uncloseted.[4]

Shuter's article addresses itself to two aspects of this development: the biographical and the critical. He does not set out to 'refute these conclusions': 'refutation' would involve producing contradictory evidence.

> I question only that the conclusions have in fact been demonstrated by the evidence and arguments thus far advanced.

('"Outing"', p. 482)

Taking up Shuter's procedural line, I also want to concentrate on 'evidence and arguments'.

Leland Person refers to Fred Kaplan's biography *Henry James: The Imagination of Genius* as having helped to bring James 'out of the closet'. But, in Shuter's words, 'a skeptic may be forgiven for preserving a state of suspended judgment' ('"Outing"', p. 491). On the biographical front, it is mostly—though not universally—acknowledged that there is no direct evidence of Henry James's having had any sexual encounters of any kind, homo- or hetero-sexual. James knew many homosexuals in the literary-artistic world, and some of his later letters to young men like the sculptor Hendrik Andersen and Jocelyn Persse contain extravagantly tactile expressions of affection;[5] while he notoriously 'never married'. Kaplan does not in fact assert active homosexuality on James's part, rather settling on the compromise formula of 'the homoerotic sensibility'. On this, however, he does lay considerable emphasis, in some strong readings of texts and events.[6] In his parallel Paterian case, Shuter suggests that gender discourse (of which Kaplan is here a popularising branch) is more convincing when it works in 'a language capable of recording even messages that frustrate the decoder's expectations' ('"Outing"', p. 501).

While repudiating certain 'heterosexist' assumptions in psychoanalysis (like the originary naturalness of the Oedipus complex), gender discourse takes over many of its sophisticated interpretative tools, like 'the resistance', as they have passed into literary criticism, but cunningly inverts them. There are different readings, but James mostly appears as what would once have been called a repressed homosexual, refusing fully to acknowledge his homosexuality to himself, but hovering round the matter, dramatising homoerotic impulses and 'possibilities', to use another of Sedgwick's favourite words, in his stories. The support of biography, in the more theoretically inflected criticism, is as a rule invoked in passing as affording strong support, only to be declared unnecessary. Textual interpretation is the crucial activity.

At this juncture I'd like to put forward what might be called a methodological misgiving about perhaps the most impressive, certainly the most influential, of 'Queer' readers of James. My misgiving concerns Eve Sedgwick's powerful and imaginative argument about 'The Beast in the Jungle' in *The Epistemology of the Closet* (1990), and that in the essay 'Is the Rectum Straight?: Identification and Identity in *The Wings of the Dove*' in *Tendencies* (1994). The point requires a remark about the history of James criticism. Readers of James are familiar with the late Jamesian practice of abstaining from specification of significant facts, names and events, creating epistemological abysses round which one warily treads—gaps one may imagine filling in a multiplicity of ways, temptations to the overconfident guesser: in *The Ambassadors* what the Newsomes manufacture in Woollett; in *The Turn of the Screw* what Miles says at school that is so bad; in *The Figure in the Carpet*, especially, what is the clue to the works of Hugh Vereker. Mysteries of reference are James's stock in trade.

Critics confronted by these abysses have tended to divide into the bravely or foolishly literal guessers, diving in after condoms or 'homoerotic sexual adventures' or 'love'; and more resignedly or elaborately sophisticated refrainers who remain peering down from the brink, trying to find a meaning for the fact of ambiguity without dissolving it. Eve Sedgwick, an ingenious reader understandably reluctant to forfeit the flexibility that comes with her hermeneutic initiations and yet seeking 'historical specificity'[7] for

Queer Theory wherever possible, does her best to keep one foot on the edge of the abyss while with the other, and most of her weight, she steps decisively into the darkness. Performing this manoeuvre in her 'Beast in the Jungle' discussion, glossing John Marcher's fate of being '*the* man, to whom nothing on earth was to have happened',[8] she makes brilliant use of a sophisticated turn on that 'nothing':

> A more frankly 'full' meaning for that unspeakable fate might come from the centuries-long historical chain of substantive uses of space-clearing negatives to void and at the same time to underline the possibility of male same-sex genitality. The rhetorical name for this figure is preterition. Unspeakable, Unmentionable, . . . 'the love that dare not speak its name'—such *were* the speakable nonmedical terms, in Christian tradition, for the homosexual possibility for men.[9]

She starts by calling the link she thus asserts between Marcher's fate and 'the love that dare not speak its name' 'an *oblique* relation' (p. 202), 'highly equivocal' (p. 203), and disavows a wish 'to pretend to say one thing' (p. 204); then for the last six pages of the essay puts forward her 'hypothesis' about Marcher's 'male homosexual panic' and the damage it does May Bartram (the concept *The Epistemology of the Closet* as a whole advances). The hypotheticalness is at first signalled formally at the head of each paragraph or the start of each new stage: 'In my hypothesis', 'In this reading', and 'I hypothesize that . . .' (pp. 206-7). 'In this reading' makes one further brief appearance, and the essay takes off into the hypothesis, which is where it resoundingly ends.

I'll quickly state my difficulties here. First on the 'preterition' move. No one would deny the ingenuity of the connection. But as *argument* we obviously can't accept the syllogism that citing it might seem to imply:

(1) James writes about the unnamable;

(2) homosexuality has often been spoken of as unnamable;

(3) James *therefore* means homosexuality when he refers to something unnamable.

Sedgwick wisely doesn't attempt to draw more than an innuendo out of this. Only a few of the things unnamable in the public world are homosexual, after all. Many other unnamable things, unnamable because of different taboos and interests, creep in under the same umbrella. And unnamability may be an effect of a particular situation or of an individual psychology.

There is a comparable question about the enlistment of 'queer' in James, one of his repertory company of terms, a matter which needs an informed, dispassionate and intelligent discussion. Partridge's *Dictionary of Historical Slang* may not be the last word but it gives a rich variety of senses for 'queer'—criminal, drunk, giddy, inauspicious, dishonest, eccentric—without specific mention of homosexuality. Of course homosexual people would have been called 'queer'—but along with many other kinds of people. I mention this because Sedgwick follows the 'preterition' argument with 'some "fuller", though still highly equivocal, lexical pointers to a homosexual meaning', in the form of quotations:

'The rest of the world of course thought him *queer.* . . .'

'She took his *gaiety* from him. . . . .'

'She traced his unhappy *perversion.* . . . .'

(*Epistemology*, p. 203)

For all her sophistication, and the hedgings about 'highly equivocal', Sedgwick, like Kaplan and others, is always quoting occurrences of 'queer' in James. The sense of 'queer' in James and much other late-nineteenth-century writing is surely extremely powerful *because* it is multiple and ambiguous. I make this point partly because my title picks up James's reference to his inspiration for 'The Pupil' as his own 'queer affair', just the sort of phrase taken as a green light by much gender discourse. As evidence for the purposes of gender discourse, I would argue, the light shed by 'queer' is amber at most.

I've already hinted at a second reservation, one which is far from applying only to gender discourse. This might be called the abuse of speculation. A crux is summarised and a hypothetical interpretation presented, explicitly as hypothetical. Building on this hypothesis, the critic reaches a second crux, another fork in the road. We get a second hypothesis, then a third and a fourth. Obviously there is nothing wrong intrinsically about hypothesis. The reader is at liberty to find a hypothesis not convincing or not useful. What can be disturbing or frustrating is when the acknowledgment of hypotheticalness functions as scaffolding, which has been put up in order to produce the argument, and then is silently removed, so that its origins in speculation disappear and it becomes more like fact. Sedgwick does this with great verve, but there remains the question of what the sceptical reader is supposed to do with these hypotheses if not convinced, how they escape arbitrariness.

The appeal of much of Sedgwick's work evidently lies in her address to 'a collective sexual identity smaller than "all [of] the people"', but she is nimble-witted enough to have a great deal to offer, if not '*all* the people', then much of the critical community at large. One of the areas of interest she is stimulatingly helping to open up, or refresh, is shame. Shame can be one obverse of Gay Pride, of course, and we could connect her new project with the recent move in homosexual politics from 'gay' to 'queer', a move which actively goes from a euphemistic label to one which takes over what has become a term of abuse, a term of shame, and revalues it as a point of pride. At any rate, in her essay 'Queer Performativity: Henry James's *The Art of the Novel*', she dwells on the 'terrifying powerlessness of gender-dissonant or otherwise stigmatized childhood', and thinks about shame as 'a form of

communication' (through blushes, etc.), as making identity, and as contagious.[10]

Sedgwick has a paragraph in her discussion of 'The Beast in the Jungle' alleging that most James criticism (including, necessarily, that of F. O. Matthiessen) has shown 'active incuriosity' and 'repressive blankness' on the subject of 'different erotic paths'. She offers some possible sympathetic (as against homophobic) reasons, considerations controlling the critical expression of a sense of James as in some way 'queer' (a word she broadens to take in many inflections of perversity): the wish to protect James, or themselves, from homophobic marginalisation; the wish to protect James from 'what they imagine as anachronistically gay readings'; a view of James as 'translating lived homosexual desires . . . into written heterosexual ones . . . so successfully that . . . the transmutation leaves no residue' (*Epistemology*, p. 197); a reluctance, even if they agree with Sedgwick that James often incompletely transmutes homosexual desires into heterosexual forms, leaving residues, to accuse him of therefore lacking candour, or of artistic failure.

This is a helpful list, and doubtless these motives have played their part in keeping silent those who believe James to have been 'queer'. Other motives, though, may have kept other, non-homophobic, critics silent: not thinking 'male-male desire' identifiably—or discussably—present in James's work; or not thinking it a centrally interesting topic, compared with many others, in appreciating James's works; or thinking the 'possibilities' interesting, but feeling the lack of firm evidence would confine discussion to ramifications of highly speculative ingenuity. Critical discussion of the matter, also, requires some reflection on, and usually some degree of subscription to, the current notions about sexuality and gender-identity, an area in which, as I've already noted, Eve Sedgwick herself identifies a persistent disagreement between 'essentialist' and 'constructed' accounts of homosexuality. There's a good deal of confusion about what it means to be 'homosexual', what 'homoerotic' involves, etc.

'THE PUPIL'

I want to use my main text, 'The Pupil' of 1890, to focus some of these current issues. For convenience of reference, I'll summarise the plot, which covers about four years, in terms as uncontroversial as possible.

A young American, Pemberton, educated at Yale and Oxford, comes to tutor a sensitive, intelligent 11-year-old boy with a weak heart, Morgan Moreen, in his family of socially pretentious but financially precarious American adventurers who live in a succession of European cities. The Moreens don't pay Pemberton, hoping that, like a former nurse, he will stay on working for nothing out of affection for Morgan. By the time Pemberton realises their attitude, he feels he cannot leave the boy, who is deeply ashamed of his shiftless, dishonest kinsfolk. Morgan knows he isn't paid; Pemberton comes to understand what the Moreens are like; Morgan proposes that they go away and live to-gether, but Pemberton has no money. Pemberton takes an-other, lucrative position in England, but returns, sacrificing it, when Mrs Moreen cables falsely that Morgan is ill. Morgan *becomes* ill when he realises what his mother has done. He recovers, and Pemberton stays on. Eventually, the Moreens' schemes collapse, and the family is humiliat-ingly detained in their hotel till they pay the bill. When the parents propose that Pemberton take Morgan away to live with him, Morgan's excitement is too much for his weak heart, and he dies.

It is perhaps not very surprising that the general 'active incuriosity' and 'repressive blankness' on the subject of 'different erotic paths' that Sedgwick alleges among James critics in the past was broken particularly early in the case of this story. It may seem more surprising that the earliest critic I have found mentioning the homosexual possibility in 'The Pupil' is the notoriously closeted F. O. Matthies-sen, in 1944; on the other hand his remarks on the subject may seem to exemplify 'active incuriosity' and 'repressive blankness'. Matthiessen praises James's treatment of the Olive-Verena relation in *The Bostonians*:

> But though he could understand Lesbianism without having to give it a name . . . he was elsewhere obliv-ious to sexual distortions which would seem an almost inevitable concomitant of the situations he posits. Take, for instance, *The Pupil*, where, in contrast with Mann's *Death in Venice*, there is no basis in homosexual attrac-tion, and a consequent vagueness, as the story is handled, in accounting for why the tutor's attachment to his charge is so strong as to make him destroy his prospects on the boy's account. What it comes down to, again and again, is that James's characters tend to live, as has often been objected, merely off the top of their minds.[11]

Matthiessen comes out, then, with a flat denial: 'there is no basis in homosexual attraction'. And his phrase 'sexual distortions' may be read as an attempt to distance himself from any imputation of homosexuality. On the other hand, Morgan Moreen is a child, and 'distortion' may denote the difference in age more than the sameness of sex; while Matthiessen's larger point is that the tale's non-conductivity of homosexual possibilities is a *weakness*, since it 'would seem an almost inevitable concomitant of the situation'. Matthiessen cites Gide deploring James's sexlessness: 'all the weight of the flesh is absent'. He is making an aesthetic judgment on 'The Pupil', based on James's failure fully to imagine his situation, on a lapse in the sphere of conscious intention and artistry: James is judged 'oblivious' because of how 'the story is handled', judged by the treatment. It at least puts a twist on the no-tion of 'repressive blankness' to have James read as *dam-agingly* blind to homosexual possibilities and thus vague about motivation (before Matthiessen goes on to praise James's 'extraordinary command of his own kind of darkness', pp. 93-4).

The following year saw Clifton Fadiman produce a more favourable judgment of the story hand-in-hand with a ho-mosexual reading stated as fact and not presented as hy-pothesis:

> The conventions of his day (which James, through his subtle logic, both obeyed and evaded) prevented him from making any more explicit the perfectly uncon-scious homosexual love—of a type that could never ripen into overt action—binding Morgan and Pember-ton.[12]

This seems a good New York Freudian reading: within the action, 'perfectly unconscious' of course here neutralises the 'homosexual love' on the one side and the fact that it's of a type that 'could never ripen into overt action' neutra-lises it on the other. Nonetheless, Fadiman is asserting this as *James's conscious intention* in the story; and it's fully in line with Sedgwick and the nature of her interest in James with its suggestion of a 'subtle logic' which allows James both to obey *and* evade 'the conventions of his day'.

There has been a minor tradition of reading the story in this way. A verbal echo strongly suggests that Fadiman's account may have prompted the inclusion of 'The Pupil' as the last and much the longest item in Stephen Wright's 1974 *Different: an Anthology of Homosexual Short Stories*. Wright's Introduction only touches briefly on the story (we may almost wonder if he has read it): '"The Pupil" is a short novel about the *perfectly unconscious homosexual love* between a precocious boy and his tutor. This deep af-fection is destined to remain without physical expression'.[13]

More recently, stronger homosexual readings have been proffered. When Edward Wagenknecht declared in 1984 that

> In days gone by, some readers were given to sniffing out homosexuality in the relations between Pemberton and his charge; this nonsense seems now to have been abandoned[14]

he seriously overplayed his hand. The story has been in-cluded, for instance, more recently as the first item in Ed-mund White's 1991 *Faber Anthology of Gay Short Fic-tion*.[15]

Fred Kaplan in his 1992 biography makes out a case for the homoerotic aspect of the story; and he is very interest-ing about the ending, which is even for James strikingly ambiguous. His claim is that 'the problematic relationship between an older man and a young boy has both auto-erotic and homoerotic resonances'; meaning by 'autoerotic' that Pemberton and Morgan both represent aspects of James himself, past and present. Kaplan uses a phrase he often applies in the biography to James's feelings about men, to evoke the 'homoerotic': Pemberton 'falls in love with' Morgan—an expression not used in the story. Ka-plan's account of the plot doesn't inspire confidence.

> From Venice, having heard that Morgan has become ill with a weak heart, Pemberton joins the Moreens in

Paris for the ostensible purpose of tutoring Morgan for his Oxford examinations.

Not quite. Pemberton is in England, tutoring another, more 'opulent youth'; he has to cross the Channel to get to Paris. 'The ostensible purpose of tutoring Morgan for his Oxford examinations' is also wrong: Pemberton crosses to Paris simply in response to Mrs Moreen's cable which announces mendaciously, 'Morgan dreadfully ill'; and it is not Morgan (who is only 15) but 'the opulent youth, who was to be taken in hand for Balliol' (p. 499).

'The Pupil' is a story in which, perhaps because of its compression—James wrote that he had 'boiled it down repeatedly'[16]—it is difficult to give due weight to all the elements. In his account of the climax, Kaplan states that in the financial and social crisis which afflicts the Moreens at the end,

> Reluctantly, they now agree, at their son's urging, that Morgan can leave with [Pemberton].
>
> (*Imagination of Genius,* p. 303)

But it is, importantly, neither altogether 'reluctantly', nor 'at their son's urging' that, as the story puts it, Mrs Moreen

> look[s] to [Pemberton] to carry a little further the influence he had so fortunately acquired with the boy—to induce his young charge to follow him into some modest retreat.[17]

Mrs Moreen's move—an active request made of Pemberton, not a passive agreement—is the culmination of a series of financially motivated insistences by her on the intimacy between Pemberton and Morgan, first to get him to stay on and tutor Morgan for nothing, and now to get both of them off the roll of expenses; though she is also anxious that Morgan should not perceive the thinness of the family's façade of respectability.

Kaplan goes on from the Moreens' offer of Morgan to Pemberton:

> Ecstatically happy, [Morgan] looks up at Pemberton's face in expectation of a moment of mutual joy. To his dismay, he sees instead hesitation, anxiety, and fear. Morgan's already weak heart breaks. Pemberton pays the ultimate penalty for his moment of homosexual panic. (pp. 303-4)

This is tendentious—in the Sedgwickian sense of filling a Jamesian gap with a strong interpretation. The passage in the story reads:

> Morgan had turned away from his father—he stood looking at Pemberton with a light in his face. His sense of shame for their common humiliated state had dropped; the case had another side—the thing was to clutch at *that*. He had a moment of boyish joy, scarcely mitigated by the reflexion that with this unexpected consecration of his hope—too sudden and too violent; the turn taken was away from a *good* boy's book—the 'escape' was left on their hands. The boyish joy was

there an instant, and Pemberton was almost scared at the rush of gratitude and affection that broke through his first abasement. When he stammered 'My dear fellow, what do you say to *that*?' how could one not say something enthusiastic? But there was more need for courage at something else that immediately followed and that made the lad sit down quickly on the nearest chair. He had turned quite livid and had raised his hand to his left side. (pp. 576-7)

Kaplan makes no mention of the 'humiliation' Morgan feels, I'll just note, what the first printed version calls the 'tears of bitter shame' he has wept (*Longman's Magazine*, p. 630), when a moment before this he enters the hotel and sees the family cases piled in the hall ready for their ignominious expulsion. But the crucial question arises about Kaplan's great leap: 'To his dismay, he sees instead hesitation, anxiety, and fear'. As we have just seen there *is* no such vision by Morgan of Pemberton described—which is why I call it a great leap—yet it contrasts with his earlier errors, in that it makes a stimulating, imaginative suggestion, picking up on Pemberton's being 'almost frightened'.

What Kaplan does, then, perhaps seeing an analogy with Winterbourne's treatment of Daisy Miller or the governess's fatal behaviour toward Miles at the end of 'The Turn of the Screw', is to make Morgan's look at Pemberton causally responsible for his death; he dies of a *broken* heart. The framework he offers us to understand this is that of 'homosexual panic', the concept reinvented from psychology and given wide currency by Eve Sedgwick. That is to say, in Kaplan's reading, Pemberton has desired Morgan homoerotically throughout—only to discover that, when the possibility of commitment, and thus self-identification as homosexual, arises, he does not have the courage to meet the boy's responsive passion. Presumably Morgan's 'stammer' is then taken to denote a terror at the uncertainty he has already discerned in Pemberton's face. If we accept this reading, incidentally, it's Morgan, not Pemberton, who 'pays the ultimate penalty for his moment of homosexual panic'. At any rate, Kaplan's implication seems to be that James consciously intends Pemberton's response in this way.

Where Kaplan's suggestion locates the 'homosexual panic' at the level of the action in the story, attributing it to a character, Pemberton, Helen Hoy, in an ebullient article called 'Homotextual Duplicity in Henry James's "The Pupil"', attributes homosexual panic to James himself. Hoy bases her argument on the idea that James creates what she calls a 'homotext' by encoding homosexual relations here and elsewhere through various displacements, mostly of gender but here of age (making Morgan too young to be a sexual partner). This metafictional interest, tracing a plot in James's construction of the story, has a thinning effect, it should be said, on the action *within* the narrative: 'Superficially, the text . . . explores . . . the growing unmasking of Moreen family pretensions'; 'The narrative ostensibly insists . . .'; the story is treated as 'a cover story' and correspondingly simplified ('Homotextual

Duplicity', pp. 36, 37). Towards the end of the tale, according to Hoy, the homoerotic subtext begins to break out and unbalance the action. As *James* sees the possibility of homoerotic fulfilment approaching *he* represses it by killing off Morgan; I take it Hoy's idea here is that James has deliberately flirted with 'coming out', while always keeping Morgan's weak heart up his sleeve so he can play it when the chips are down. (The characters are not real enough in Hoy's reading for the question of homosexual panic on *Pemberton*'s part at the last really to arise.)

I have left to last in this enumeration of readers probably the story's first reader of all, after James and perhaps a typist. Horace Scudder, the editor of the *Atlantic Monthly*, unexpectedly rejected 'The Pupil' on grounds that have long been mysterious. The exchange of letters between Scudder and James has recently been published—but still permits no final judgment as to whether this was because he detected a homoerotic strain in it. The main burden of the rejection:

> Frankly, my reluctant judgment insists upon regarding the story as lacking in interest, in precision and in effectiveness. . . . The situation seems to me too delicate to permit quick handling, and with such a family to exploit I should suppose a volume would be necessary. At any rate I find the structure of the story so weak for carrying the sentiment that I am afraid other readers will be equally dissatisfied, and say hastily—'vague'—'unformed'.

('The *Atlantic Monthly*'s Rejection of "The Pupil"', p. 79)

Scudder's impression can't be taken as evidence one way or the other, since if Scudder *has* detected a homoerotic subtext he very probably won't say so to James anyhow, and one might argue that the rather nebulous phrasing of his objection suggests some awkwardness. On the other hand, even if Scudder detected such a homoerotic subtext he may still have been mistaken, as may any number of subsequent readers getting the same impression. Questions of literary interpretation can only be answered by evidence and argument, not by votes or polls. However, an informed reading by a contemporary has interest and some evidential value, showing one response that was possible at the historical moment.

There can be no doubt that the story is centrally concerned with a relation of love between people of the same sex. When in the revised version of the story Morgan speaks sadly but stoically of his bad luck with his family, 'Pemberton held him fast, hands on his shoulders—he had never loved him so'.[18] How, though, we might ask, is our sense of the story enriched if we see Pemberton's relation to Morgan as really erotic and his frightened state at the end as 'homosexual panic'? In Kaplan's version of this reading, at least, the story becomes punitive (Pemberton 'pays the ultimate penalty'—though it's Morgan who dies), and it seems less potentially tragic. Too elaborate an interest in the boundary between heterosexual and homosexual, the grinding centrality of that axis, can elide, or usurp the interest of, other kinds of interpretation *than* the sexual.

Pemberton has some other compelling reasons for being frightened at the end: he knows of Morgan's weak heart and his extreme sensitivity about the fragile family honour, now so suddenly and publicly degraded; and, penniless again, he has no money with which he and Morgan *could* go off together. Even if Morgan does die from the shock of seeing the impossibility of escape registered on Pemberton's face—which we can hardly be sure of—blame does not necessarily attach to Pemberton for that, especially given Morgan's precocious perspicuity. James's handling of the money plot, whereby Pemberton is here paralysed and unable to help Morgan, is not *necessarily* a smokescreen for a truer homoerotic meaning. The first sentence of the whole story has Pemberton unable to 'speak of money to a person who spoke only of feelings' (p. 511); and a similar inhibition may hang over the critic wishing to attribute importance to financial constraints in the plotting of a story but faced with a critical community at large for whom 'feelings' and the sexual have such primacy that money questions are vulgarly undiscussable. Critical blindness to the evoked determinants of fictional situations has its own possibilities of 'repressive blankness'.

Eve Sedgwick's interest in shame, in the 'terrifying powerlessness of gender-dissonant or otherwise stigmatized childhood' can work for 'The Pupil'. I would like to pick up her sense of shame as making identity, and as contagious—both effects we may see in the story—only I think Morgan's shame is at being 'otherwise stigmatized' than through gender-dissonance. Morgan's shame centres on his dishonest family, which financially and morally exploits those who feel affection for him *through* their affection. Part of the point of the story's title, I think, is that Pemberton, the tutor, is progressively revealed as the true 'pupil' in the story, learning what the Moreens are like through Morgan's intelligence and correspondingly infected with this shame.

The context of James's other writings at this period, perhaps under the influence of French Naturalism and, slightly later, Ibsen, suggests a pre-occupation with questions of inheritance, of agonised young people struggling to defend compromised family honour. Tony Tanner, quoting the remark made to the small James in *A Small Boy and Others* that 'I should think you'd be too proud—!',[19] has suggested that *pride* becomes a crucial motive in James's idea of renunciation. Here Morgan shows in his anguished scorn of his own family 'the small fine passion of his pride' (p. 552). He is 'a little gentleman', cultivating 'a private ideal', cursed like Hyacinth Robinson in *The Princess Casamassima* with a mixed inheritance. Morgan may then be read as one of James's 'poor sensitive gentlemen' of the 1890s, like the overinitiated butler Brooksmith or the disablingly artistic writer Ray Limbert in 'The Next Time', doomed in a crude world to martyrdom for high values he cannot disown but cannot reconcile with his situation. Morgan's precocious intelligence, a precursor of Maisie's, expands at such a rate *through* his shame, his sensitised discovery of nuances and codes and deceptions. And this shame is linked to his sense of an honourable family tradition, valued only by himself, being first compromised and then extinguished. His attempt to escape his family doom by fleeing with Pemberton, the one person with whom he has been able to share his perceptions,[20] is itself at least to some extent infected with this doom: Mrs Moreen, manipulatively, is from the start *pushing* Pemberton towards Morgan, and friendship between Pemberton and Morgan, fostered to allow the Moreens to get Pemberton to work for nothing, keeps Morgan handily out of the family's way while they scheme for worldly advantage, and postpones (as Mrs Moreen *hopes*—wrongly) Morgan's discovery of their demoralisation and social abjectness. Morgan feels all the shame for a family otherwise lacking any 'throb of shame' (p. 554). The climax of the story is primarily the climax of *this* interest in 'his sense of shame for their common humiliated state', which is complexly worked enough in itself to be not merely a superficial 'cover story' for a 'real' subtext.

What I have said should evidently not exclude further consideration of how homoerotic possibilities might work in the story, *together with* the other considerations I've sketched. So far it seems to me a convincing case has not been presented for such dynamics.

I shall end with a reflection on Scudder's response to the story. His rejection found 'The situation . . . too delicate to permit quick handling, and with such a family to exploit I should suppose a volume would be necessary. At any rate I find the structure of the story so weak for carrying the sentiment that I am afraid other readers will be equally dissatisfied, and say hastily—"vague"—"unformed".' One might call this the insensitive reading of a busy editor under some pressure to find material which would appeal to a growing public; but James's letter to Scudder enclosing the story had emphasised how he had 'tried to make [it] as short as possible' and 'boiled it down repeatedly', and one might also suggest that James's struggles with length, as with those novels in which he misplaced his middles and had to accelerate the movement towards his conclusion, may have led him partly to lose contact with what it is possible for a reader to understand and to feel. The final pages are charged with emotional demands, on the reader as well as on Pemberton, and we have already remarked the ambiguous silence about Pemberton's response to Morgan's final appeal and whether the response is what causes his death (a silence Kaplan confidently talks away). We too, as readers, may feel called on for a response we have not been enabled wholeheartedly to supply: Morgan's heart condition, for instance, is too convenient a 'given', and Pemberton gives up a more lucrative tutorship out of his attachment to Morgan, but has no emotional ties outside the Moreen circle that would call for a sharper sacrifice. In a sense, then, perhaps Scudder is right that 'the structure of the story' is too 'weak for carrying the sentiment'; it may be that James's conception is too ambitious for the length, that our unease and Scudder's dissatisfaction correspond (at a very high level of achievement) to a failure of technique, that the impulses do not quite vividly fuse in the acute tragic balance we sometimes call 'inevitability'.

The 'vagueness' of which both Scudder and Matthiessen complain, I finally suggest, may further correspond more to an ethical than to a psychosexual reticence on James's part. Just before criticising 'The Pupil', Matthiessen remarks helpfully that 'James occupies a curious border line between the older psychologists like Hawthorne or George Eliot, whose concerns were primarily religious and ethical, and the post-Freudians' (*Henry James: The Major Phase*, p. 93). Pemberton is early in the tale described as having at Yale 'richly supposed himself to be reacting against a Puritan strain' (p. 519), and it may be that his conduct *vis-à-vis* Morgan can best be understood as manifesting a deeply ingrained, but helplessly unworldly, sense of moral duty. Henry James Sr's insistence on ethical intensity *and* hatred of what he paradoxically called 'flagrant morality' might jointly account for James's diffidence about the high-minded impulse at the heart of his story, which its action may celebrate but also shows grievously defeated. Such an awkwardness in the story, rooted in the peculiar history and moral traditions of the James family, might in turn account—as in T. S. Eliot's reading of *Hamlet*—for the sense of a missing 'objective correlative', in Eve Sedgwick's term a 'residue'—giving a cue to the psychoanalytic procedures of 'Queer Theory' and their unearthing of psychosexually loaded repressions and 'homosexual panic'.

Notes

1. F. O. Matthiessen, *American Renaissance* (New York: Oxford University Press, 1941), xv.

2. Michael Cadden, 'Engendering F. O. M.: The Private Life of *American Renaissance*', in Joseph A. Boone and Michael Cadden (eds), *Engendering Men: The Question of Male Feminist Criticism* (New York and London: Routledge, 1990), 26-35, pp. 30, 32.

3. Leland S. Person, Jr, 'James's Homo-Aesthetics: Deploying Desire in the Tales of Writers and Artists', *The Henry James Review*, 14,2 (1993), 188-203, p. 188.

4. John J. Conlon, quoted in William F. Shuter, 'The "Outing" of Walter Pater', *Nineteenth-Century Literature*, 48,2 (March 1994), 480-506; p. 482.

5. Leon Edel cites an extremely interesting discussion by James's young friend Urbain Mengin, who suggests an expressive emotional economy in which James's warm words and gestures of affection register precisely the absence of *sexual* possibility: 'Certain of his friendships, leanings, gestures, could . . . make one think he was capable of submitting himself . . . but those gestures were in themselves a signal, and I'd say a proof, that he wasn't capable of this kind of surrender. His affectionate manner of grasping your arm, or of patting you on the shoulder, or giving you a hug—he would never have done this if these gestures had, for him, the slightest suggestion

of a pursuit of physical love' (Leon Edel, *Henry James: A Life* (New York: Harper & Row, 1985), 723, 724-5).

6. An example, Kaplan on *The Aspern Papers*: 'The lust for the papers suggests for James the dangers and the attractions of a man desiring to possess another man, of the ultimate union, literary and erotic, between Henry senior and Henry junior, between father and son, between master and disciple' (*Henry James: The Imagination of Genius: A Biography*, London: John Curtis, 1992, 320).

7. Eve Kosovsky Sedgwick, *Tendencies* (London: Routledge, 1994), 13.

8. Henry James, 'The Beast in the Jungle', *The Better Sort* (London: Methuen, 1903), 139-178, p. 178.

9. Sedgwick, *The Epistemology of the Closet* (Berkeley and Los Angeles: University of California Press, 1990), 202-3. She has built on this in her discussion of *The Wings of the Dove* in *Tendencies*, where she claims that 'Lionel Croy's homosexuality is spelled out in a simple code with deep historical roots: the code of *illum crimen horribile quod non nominandum est*, of "the crime not to be named among Christian men" and "the love that dare not speak its name"'; James's locutions 'specify the homosexual secret by failing to specify anything, speak by refusing to utter' (*Tendencies*, 75).

10. Sedgwick, 'Queer Performativity: Henry James's *The Art of the Novel*', *GLO: A Journal of Lesbian and Gay Studies*, 1,1 (1993), 1-16, pp. 4, 5, 14.

11. F. O. Matthiessen, *Henry James: The Major Phase* (New York: Oxford University Press, 1944), 93.

12. Clifton Fadiman, *The Short Stories of Henry James* (New York: Random House, 1945), 272; cited in Krishna Baldev Vaid, *Technique in the Tales of Henry James* (Cambridge, Mass: Harvard University Press, 1964), 275.

13. Stephen Wright (ed.), *Different: an Anthology of Homosexual Short Stories* (New York: Bantam, 1974), xi (my emphasis).

14. Quoted in Helen Hoy, 'Homotextual Duplicity in Henry James's "The Pupil"', *The Henry James Review*, Winter 1993, vol. 14, no. 1, 34-42, p. 35.

15. Disappointingly, White's Introduction makes no specific reference to the story, and thus offers no justification for its inclusion.

16. George Monteiro, 'The *Atlantic Monthly's* Rejection of "The Pupil": An Exchange of Letters Between Henry James and Horace Scudder', *American Literary Realism, 1870-1910*, 23 (1990), 75-83, p. 78.

17. Henry James, 'The Pupil', *The New York Edition of the Novels and Tales of Henry James* (24 vols; London: Macmillan, 1907-9), vol. 11, 511-77, p. 575. All page references in the text are to this edition.

18. p. 497. The first version reads: 'Pemberton held him, his hands on his shoulders' (*Longman's Magazine*, 622).

19. Henry James, *Autobiography*, ed. F. W. Dupee (New York: Criterion Books, 1956), 130.

20. So that, like Isabel and Ralph 'looking at the truth together' towards the end of *The Portrait of a Lady*, Morgan and Pemberton 'look at the facts and keep nothing back' (p. 551).

Charles E. Morris III (essay date 1998)

SOURCE: "'The Responsibilities of the Critic': F. O. Matthiessen's Homosexual Palimpsest," in *Quarterly Journal of Speech*, Vol. 84, No. 3, August, 1998, pp. 261-82.

[*In the following essay, Morris maintains that Matthiessen's literary criticism provides insights into his attitudes toward his sexuality as well as the practice of gay historical criticism generally.*]

> "It is important to recognize that criticism creates American literature in its own image because American literature gives the American people a conception of themselves and of their history."
>
> Jane Tompkins, *Sensational Designs* (199)

> "But man, even to himself, is a palimpsest, having an ostensible writing and another beneath the lines."
>
> Thomas Hardy, *Far from the Madding Crowd* (273)

On the day reserved for foolish deeds in April 1950, an open window in Boston's Manager Hotel became an accessory to troubled legacy. Twelve floors below the "airy room" he had requested lay a dying Harvard literary critic named F. O. Matthiessen. In the days following his death, fellow socialists declared Matthiessen a casualty of the Cold War, his suicide a tragic reenactment of Czech foreign minister Jan Masaryk's defenestration two years earlier. Academic colleagues speculated instead that five years of personal loss and political disappointment had rendered Matthiessen's life meaningless. According to whispers typical of the blossoming McCarthy era, Matthiessen was just one more tortured homosexual leaving his mark, on a sidewalk.

On that sodden Boston sidewalk commenced a complicated literary, political and sexual legacy which has long survived competing theories regarding Matthiessen's demise. As author of the 1941 masterpiece **American Renaissance** and progenitor of the field we recognize today as American Studies, Matthiessen "has exerted a compelling attraction. The documentation, analysis, and controversy around him bulk larger than for any other American scholar born in the twentieth century, and they grow" (Arac 157). Donald Pease notes that Matthiessen's "work on the cultural period in which Melville wrote *Moby-Dick* would establish American literature as a discipline and America as a culture" (391). The pervasiveness and influence of **American Renaissance**—say what one will of cannos generally—is revealed in Richard Brodhead's claim that it "did more than any other book to set the American canon as it would be taught in American universities after World War II" (210).

Such literary superlatives warrant rhetorical interest insofar as *American Renaissance* has been evaluated harshly in recent decades according to a political calculus Matthiessen himself applied to criticism: "Judgment of art is unavoidably both an aesthetic and a social act, and the critic's sense of social responsibility gives him a deeper thirst for meaning" (**"Responsibilities"** 14). Many critics, expecting criticism to resemble sexual manifesto, argue with William Cain that the "facts of Matthiessen's sexual . . . life . . . do not have much direct bearing at all" on his work (48). Some have gone so far as to judge Matthiessen's most puissant text as "repressive" (Cheyfitz 349). Indeed, Jonathan Arac's comment that "To create the centrally authoritative critical identity of *American Renaissance*, much had to be displaced or scattered or disavowed" (159), offers us a rather troubled and troublesome picture of a gay man whose literary and cultural imprint is indelible.

Matthiessen's work has been contested on the grounds that his sexuality was elided from the critical act; in other words, Matthiessen's criticism was insufficiently rhetorical, failing to name, argue for, or celebrate the cause of the oppressed homosexual. The perceived absence of critical advocacy is especially objectionable because Matthiessen, an astute and vocal socialist, openly carried the banner of the Harvard Teacher's Union, yet proscribed any public expression of his private life with artist Russell Cheney. Consequently, Matthiessen's long "passing" as a straight academic, culminating in an insufficient homosexual investment in *American Renaissance*, is found to be duplicitous and cowardly. James Weldon Johnson's famous confession as an "ex-colored man" captures the objection well: ". . . I have sold my birthright for a mess of pottage" (511).

In the following essay I challenge Matthiessen's detractors, arguing that his public expression of same-sex desire, whatever its form, has yet to be adequately situated within the context of the pernicious homophobic oppression he faced. Early critics simply silenced Matthiessen's homosexuality, an omission rectified in subsequent years by academics whose critical politics have salvaged sexuality in gross measures of censure and approbation, but sacrificed Matthiessen. My own remedial historiography functions not principally to "set the record straight", as it were, but as a means of making sense of a rhetorical response to oppression in an historical moment far removed from post-Stonewall queer public discourse.[1] The reward in such a venture, I would suggest, is to enlarge the boundaries of inquiry in historical public address to include gays and lesbians, and to propose by example a critical approach to those historical texts which are not only marginal but evasive.

More specifically, I contend that passing, a mode of rhetorical action comprised of the public masking of oneself in the semiotic garb—sexual, racial, gendered, or ethnic "faces"—of dominant culture so as to "fit in", might be reconsidered as a means of resistance. I concede that passing's duplicity at times signifies self-loathing or cowardice, a marker of the closet's heavy toll. However, I do not accept the popular view that it is always "an activity whose agent is obscured, immersed in the mainstream rather than swimming against the tide . . . the sign of the victim, the practice of one already complicit with the order of things, prey to its oppressive hierarchies—if it can be seen at all" (Tyler 212). For certain individuals, passing constitutes the public expression of homosexual double-consciousness, a measured and strategic form of straight masking employed to resist, and not merely survive, homophobic oppression. Passing affords obscured agency, and immersion in the mainstream, precisely so that one might swim against the tide, undermining the homophobic order of things.

Matthiessen's own critical mandates, as I will demonstrate, invite us to consider passing more seriously than have those quick to chide his apparent political inconsistencies. Forged by more than three decades of sexual terror, Matthiessen's passing can be located not only in the public silences regarding his private life, but discerned as a form of resistance in the pages of his magnum opus. *American Renaissance* exhibits a unique version of passing, critical and transgressive in nature, that I label "homosexual palimpsest." Within the lasting parchment folds of a dominant literary history, Matthiessen inscribed the homosexual. His layered reading gave voice to the marginalized, but also subtly altered the meaning of a heterosexist literary and cultural heritage. Although Matthiessen's life may have embodied a contradiction Thomas Yingling identifies as "empowered to speak but unable to say" (26), the tensions inherent in such a contradiction arguably can be the inventional wellspring of the most creative resistance.

I begin this essay by charting the changing critical receptions of Matthiessen's sexuality in order to contextualize my own "queer" reading of Matthiessen's passing. In section two, I briefly theorize passing and palimpsest as a means of grounding the reader in the tactics that are central to Matthiessen's text and my interpretation of it. In making my case for Matthiessen's homosexual palimpsest, sections three and four offer a reading of *American Renaissance* in light of Matthiessen's address **"The Responsibilities of the Critic,"** and from within Matthiessen's particular context of homophobic oppression. Finally, I use the Matthiessen case study to ground a more generalizable approach to gay historical criticism.

AXIOMATIC ABSENCE/ERISTIC EROTICS

May Sarton's poetic tribute to Matthiessen, written in 1950, exhibits a striking prescience regarding the ineluctable imaginative gravity of his life and work: "The pieces of this death / We shall be picking up / The anguish in his cup / We drink and long shall drink / Until we clearly think / The pieces of his death" (135). Critics have long been picking up the pieces of Matthiessen's complex legacy, most recently thinking about (or avoiding) Matthiessen's sexuality with marked diligence. What I find troubling in these accounts is that the critic's rhetorical contexts (theoretical or ideological commitments and constraints) have consistently displaced Matthiessen's historical context, distorting our understanding of his public and professional expressions of homosexuality. In this section I chart these critical responses in order to contextualize my radically divergent reading of Matthiessen's passing in *American Renaissance*.

Paul Sweezy and Leo Huberman's *F. O. Matthiessen (1902-1950): A Collective Portrait*, appearing as a memorial in October of 1950 in *Monthly Review* and subsequently published as an edited volume, immediately became the first definitive word on Matthiessen. Its influence was such that a second wave of Matthiessen "criticism" would not emerge until twenty-five years later. The volume featured thirty-four essays by students, colleagues, and others who knew him well. Conspicuously, among the many biographical and critical essays constituting this "collective portrait," there is not a single explicit reference to Matthiessen's homosexuality.

Were Matthiessen's sexuality entirely invisible, even from friends and colleagues, this absence might be expected. What makes the oversight axiomatic, however, is the fact that Matthiessen, it was well known, had been "married" twenty-two years at the time of Russell Cheney's death in 1945. Paul Sweezy's sketch comes nearest to disclosing this significant biographical fact:

> The two men were immediately drawn to each other and before the boat landed in France they had agreed to join forces in traveling about Europe that summer. This was the beginning of a friendship which was to play a key part in both of their lives . . . [h]e and Russell Cheney, after renting a summer cottage in Kittery Point, Maine, in 1927, had bought a small house in Kittery which Cheney made his year-round headquarters and to which Matthiessen repaired for weekends and vacations. The two friends traveled a good deal . . . they rented an apartment at 87 Pinckney Street in Boston. . . . The death of Russell Cheney in 1945 deprived him of his closest friend and companion." (ix-xii)

Romance might easily be read into this passage, but such inferences seem meticulously policed in the volume. John Rackliffe's "Notes for a Character Study," for example, groups Cheney with Theodore Spencer and Phelps Putnam in a section on Matthiessen's friendships, only hinting at a homosexual subtext with his passing comment that Matthiessen's book on Cheney was remarkable "because its success depended so vitally on achieving exactly the right tone" (79). Only six of the thirty-four "portraits" of Matthiessen's career and private life even mention Cheney.[2]

Not until 1978, when Louis Hyde published a volume of edited letters, did the issue of sexuality become a serious consideration.[3] *Rat and the Devil*, Matthiessen and

Cheney's pet names for one another, sparked an explosion of scholarship, much of which raised and debated the question of homosexuality as a proper context in which to understand Matthiessen's criticism. Many of the first generation of critics bristled at the exposure. Harry Levin, for instance, a student of Matthiessen and one of the authors represented in *A Collective Portrait*, responded sharply in *The New York Review of Books*: "I am old-fashioned enough to believe that they [the letters of distinguished persons] should be classified when they were so clearly not intended for the eyes of outside readers, and that the secrets of lovers should be respected as such" (43).

Levin's discontent notwithstanding, scholars in the 1980s and early 1990s proceeded to wage a critical battle over the homosexual investments exhibited in Matthiessen's work, especially *American Renaissance*. Some critics agreed with Frederick Stern's rather benign speculation that "Although Matthiessen's radicalism, then, certainly derived more from intellectual than visceral sources, it was perhaps his homosexuality that provided the experimental base . . . for his wide-ranging sympathy, understanding, and support of those who lacked privilege, power, and position" (7). A majority of critics, however, characterized Matthiessen as repressing his "visceral sources," and failing to import his gay experience into a reading of nineteenth-century literature. Kenneth Lynn's comment on his mentor's silence depicts an inference drawn by many:

> Since there was such a strong autobiographical element in his criticism, I was struck by Matthiessen's silence, in his lectures and tutorial conversations, on the subject of homosexuality in American literature. . . . The conclusion I drew from this at the time, and have subsequently had no reason to doubt, was that Matthiessen's own sex life was a guilt-ridden horror to him. (116)

Lynn's reflection is significant, for he attributes Matthiessen's lack of explicit ruminations in lecture and tutorials to "a guilt-ridden horror" of his homosexuality, suggesting a total suppression of same-sex desire. As such, he forecloses the possibility of more subtle articulations of sexuality, even while acknowledging the "autobiographical element" which made Matthiessen's criticism unique.

Others more skeptical found duplicity in the discrepancy between Matthiessen's epigraph, "what [Samuel Taylor] Coleridge held to be the major function of the artist: he brought 'the whole soul of man into activity'" (*American Renaissance* 656), and the missing or disparaging sexual meditations in his work. Especially vexing for these critics is Walt Whitman, whom Matthiessen privately relished for his gay writing but whose sexuality he publicly judged with ambivalence.[4] One passage remarking on Whitman's "Song of Myself" in *American Renaissance* constitutes the single stasis point which animates the preponderance of gay critique:

> Readers with a distaste for loosely defined mysticism have plenty of grounds for objection in the way the po-

et's belief in divine inspiration is clothed in imagery that obscures all distinctions between body and soul by portraying the soul as merely the sexual agent. Moreover, in the passivity of the poet's body there is a quality vaguely pathological and homosexual. This is in keeping with the regressive, infantile fluidity, imaginatively polyperverse, which breaks down all mature barriers . . . (535).

This passage, argues Jonathan Arac, reveals "some problems about Matthiessen's 'wholeness'" (158). Arac concludes that the differences between Matthiessen's lively personal letters regarding Whitman and his treatment of Whitman's homosexuality in *American Renaissance* are suggestive of a troubling "process of transformative discipline" (159). William Cain concludes similarly: "His critical gestures in the public form of his book feel like expressions of self-disapproval, as though he wanted not to be what Whitman was, or else he wanted readers who knew he was homosexual to see that he spurned 'abnormal' homosexual attitudes in poetry" (48).

Arac and Cain's readings of the disjuncture between Matthiessen's sexuality and the "wholeness" of his criticism were largely accepted until challenged recently by Michael Cadden and David Bergman. Desiring to affirm Matthiessen in the face of a decade's worth of chiding, Cadden lavishly celebrates the openly gay Matthiessen found in *Rat and the Devil*: "Throughout the letters to Cheney, the gay critic barely perceivable beneath his canonical drag emerges from the closet of professional and patriarchal mastery hard on in hand, thereby exposing and demystifying the 'Phallus' that 'disseminated' an entire Renaissance" (28). Cadden softens earlier critique by asserting that "Matthiessen lacked a sexual politics (and a resultant critical vocabulary) that could allow him to connect his many kinds of work and the life he lead with Russell Cheney" (34).

If Cadden seems somewhat intemperate in his fantastic account of Matthiessen's phallus, David Bergman's favorable rendering of Matthiessen resembles hagiography more than criticism. Although Bergman confronts the "distortion" (93) of earlier critics by briefly exploring the ". . . very realities he so painfully was forced to consider" (92), he ultimately portrays Matthiessen as something of a gay hero. He argues, for instance, that "I believe Matthiessen tacitly shows that the finest strain of expression in American culture is to be found in gay works . . ." (94). "In short," writes Bergman, "*American Renaissance* is Matthiessen's ultimate expression of his love for Cheney and a covert celebration of the homosexual artist" (94).

The competing assessments delineated in this critical history are not troublesome for their particular verdicts regarding Matthiessen's sexuality as manifested in his criticism. To the contrary, Arac no less than Bergman has proffered plausible arguments. What makes them all problematic is that in reading his work they exhibit an insufficient balance between the critic's rhetorical context and Matthiessen's historical context of homophobic oppression, thus precluding the possibility of a more tempered but nonetheless resistive expression of homosexuality. In what follows, I attempt to account for the rhetorical tactics of resistance employed by a homosexual critic living in the second quarter of the twentieth century.

ON PASSING AND PALIMPSEST

There is a familiar scene in *Uncle Tom's Cabin* that Matthiessen likely read, and with which he might have identified deeply. A lively conversation concerning a runaway mulatto named George Harris is interrupted by the presence of a very tall man "with a dark, Spanish complexion . . . [who] walked easily in among the company" (Stowe 113). Introducing himself as Henry Butler, the man proceeded to comment on the slave advertisement, order a private apartment in the inn, and engage one Mr. Wilson in casual conversation. Later, in the privacy of the quarters, Butler disclosed to Wilson, whom he knew from the plantation, that he was, in fact, George Harris:

> "I am pretty well disguised, I fancy," said the young man, with a smile. "A little walnut bark has made my yellow skin a genteel brown, and I've dyed my hair black; so you see I don't answer to the advertisement at all."
>
> "O, George! but this is a dangerous game you are playing. I could not have advised you to it."
>
> "I can do it on my own responsibility," said George, with the same proud smile.
>
> (Stowe 113-114)

Passing, a mode of public masking precarious and yet full of potential, had been realized as a necessity by oppressed individuals long before the scourge of homosexuals in the twentieth century, and was clear to Matthiessen. "Tell it?" Matthiessen asks rhetorically about his relationship with Cheney, "Well that's difficult. For it is an anomaly the world as a whole does not understand, and if you proclaim it from the house tops you will receive a great deal of opprobrium, and will do no good" (Hyde 87). In this section, I describe passing as a rhetorical tactic, and theorize palimpsest as a unique form of resistive critical passing.

Numerous motives underlie the impulse to craft for oneself a public persona, a disguise, which differs radically from a more comfortable and more honest, if less accepted or tolerated, private self. The motive at times has been patriotic or economic, such as the gendered transformations of Deborah Sampson in order to fight for independence, and Lucy Ann Lobdell to earn a man's wages in rural New York in 1855 (San Francisco 184-5). At other moments such impersonation has meant freedom or the privileges of white culture, as was the case for educated slaves mistaken for freedmen, or light-skinned blacks perceived to be white.[5] Passing could be a transitory disguise, or a more enduring form of public improvisation vital to the maintenance of a cherished but endangered private life. Prior to 1969, most gays and lesbians were compelled to lead such double lives. As George Chauncey has written,

"They constantly moved between at least two worlds: a straight world in which they were assumed to be straight and a gay world in which they were known as gay" (273).

In order to be presumed straight, many gays and lesbians relied partially upon predictable heterosexist assumptions; but they also formed a double-consciousness which enabled them to negotiate the inherent tension in routinely camouflaging their homosexuality. African Americans have noted an analogous consciousness in living with the "two-ness" of being black in a predominantly white culture, what W. E. B. Dubois labeled "two warring ideals in one dark body, whose dogged strength alone keeps it from being torn asunder" ("Strivings" 194).[6] Homosexual double-consciousness often entailed rhetorical agility in publicly adapting mannerism, dress, and speech in conformity to that of dominant culture. "A convincing performance," observes James Scott, "may require both the suppression or control of feelings that would spoil the performance and the simulation of emotions that are necessary to the performance. . . . The performance . . . comprises not only speech acts but conformity in facial expression and gesture as well as practical obedience to commands that may be distasteful or humiliating" (28-29). Taken together, this cast of mind and rhetorical sensibility constituted for the oppressed what Socrates meant by *sophrosyne* and what many in the tradition of Aristotle have termed prudence.

Importantly, the effects of passing are not predetermined; passing is, as Eve Sedgwick notes, ". . . a performance initiated as such by the speech act of a silence—not a particular silence, but a silence that accrues particularity by fits and starts, in relation to the discourse that surrounds and differentially constitutes it" (3). Thus passing is not inherently either a progressive or a regressive response to oppression. Michelangelo Signorile's belief that "The invisibility they [closeted/passing homosexuals] perpetuate harms us more than any of their good deeds might benefit us" (364) is warranted by the examples of numerous gay and lesbian lives.

However, by providing not only safety from detection, exposure, and a host of deleterious consequences, but an opportunity for insurgency, passing also can constitute a form of resistance. Within the folds of dominant culture, the "deviant", masked as legitimate member of the masses, can potentially facilitate meaningful change. Harold Beaver's observation that "The homosexual . . . is a prodigious consumer of signs—of hidden meanings, hidden systems, hidden potentiality," (104) expresses passing's innate rhetorical capacity for resistance. Note, for instance, homosexual passing in New York in the first decades of this century:

> Gay men, in other words, used gay subcultural codes to place themselves and to see themselves in the dominant culture, to read the culture against the grain in a way that made them more visible than they were supposed to be, and to turn 'straight' spaces into gay spaces . . . they appropriated them [ads, films, songs] for the gay world and thus extended the boundaries of the gay world far beyond those officially tolerated. (Chauncey 288)

F. O. Matthiessen's passing, as I will demonstrate, is both typical of his era and extraordinary for the resistance it effects.

At the same time, recall that Matthiessen was an academic critic, rendering his particular form of passing both rhetorical and critical. In addition to the tension between passing and an open existence (or political dissent), there exists the additional dialectic between radical involvement with one's work and the professional detachment required of conscientious critics. Any desire to employ criticism for rhetorical purposes, in other words, is countered by professional and ideological constraints. If, in fact, Matthiessen's scholarship is an exemplar of resistive passing, then he necessarily struck a delicate *critical* balance: a "middle" between self-denial (professional "objectivity") and an open existence (critical advocacy).

In the crosswinds of these competing impulses surfaces the palimpsest, a curious and provocative notion supplying us with a nearly perfect metaphor for the textual resistance found deep within the pages of ***American Renaissance***. The palimpsest dates to antiquity, a term that for Plato, Cicero, and Plutarch meant literally "to scrape again," signifying a wax vellum that could be erased of inscription for re-use (Reisner 93). Monks in the middle ages, wanting to replace "heathen tragedy" with Christian legend, applied newly acquired chemicals to ancient documents in order to efface their content. Palimpsest's erasure constituted the means by which each generation could craft precious texts to suit its needs and desires. As Thomas De Quincey observed in 1845, ". . . by means of the imperfect chemistry known to the mediaeval period, the same roll has served as a conservatory for three separate generations of flowers and fruits, all perfectly different, and yet all specially adapted to the wants of the successive possessors" (142).

A new chemical process was introduced at the dawn of the nineteenth century by an Italian scholar, Cardinal Angelo Mai, proving monastic effacement to be imperfect. The monks had never completely destroyed previous inscription; like invisible ink, earlier texts could be retrieved. Through a chemical method of textual excavation, Mai and other "palimpsest editors" could recover fragments layered for centuries beneath the most recent surface of the vellum (McDonagh 210-211). The palimpsest now represented a site of both erasure and recovery, a tablet on which a text could be created in the ruins of prior texts, neither ever to be effectively destroyed nor forgotten. Historian C. W. Russell in 1867 called Mai "'the great enchanter of this world of the spirits of departed literature'" (McDonagh 212).

Palimpsest provided Thomas De Quincey with a metaphor for human consciousness: "What else than a natural and mighty palimpsest is the human brain? . . . Everlasting layers of ideas, images, feelings, have fallen upon your brain softly as light. Each succession has seemed to bury all that went before. And yet in reality not one has been extinguished" (144). This metaphor has persisted, employed variously to illustrate the woven tapestries of history, memory, and consciousness.[7] Instead of privileging either palimpsest's capacity for erasure or retrieval, however, I would like to introduce an alternative which explores the transgressive potential of embedding original, perhaps unconventional and dangerous, material into the layers of an established text.

In contrast to the radical obliteration and creation at operation in medieval cloisters, an authoritative past might be employed to camouflage freshly inscribed material on the palimpsest. Short of open rebellion, marginal individuals almost never find themselves in a position to erase an existing history, a dominant cultural text, in preparation for an insurgent inscription. Given the nature of palimpsest, however, "deviant" inscriptions could be smuggled into the "dominant transcript"; the surface of the vellum, having been but partially erased, yields to an alteration even as it cloaks its presence. For the purposes of resistance, a palimpsest is malleable enough to allow infiltration and modification while remaining virtually indistinguishable from the altered text. I have in mind Gore Vidal's use of palimpsest to characterize his memoirs: "This is pretty much what my kind of writer does anyway. Starts with life; makes a text; then a *re*-vision—literally, a second seeing, an afterthought, erasing some but not all of the original while writing something new over the first layer of the text" (6).

I suggest that palimpsest can constitute a resistive, critical form of passing because deviant material is enfolded into the dominant cultural text, narrative, or history such that it masks itself as the dominant. Once infiltrated, the dominant text unknowingly but benignly houses the "outlaw" material, and, in the case of resistant passing, is transfigured. For years F. O. Matthiessen put on the "straight" face of an Ivy League literary critic, drafting a literary history that would modify previous work to the point of revolutionizing American literature as a field of study and as a rich cultural resource. Even as he contributed to the dominant public transcript of American literary history, however, Matthiessen was smuggling into it homosexuality which could never effectively be erased.

Context of Oppression

Critics of Matthiessen's alleged inconsistencies might join him on the platform at the University of Michigan in May of 1949, and listen carefully to his comments regarding new criticism:

> But the dilemma for the serious critic in our dangerously split society is that, feeling isolated, he will become serious in the wrong sense, aloof and finally taking an inverted superiority in his isolation. At that point criticism becomes a kind of closed garden. My views are based on the conviction that the land beyond the garden's walls is more fertile, and that the responsibilities of the critic lie in making renewed contact with that soil.
>
> (**"Responsibilities"** 6)

Those claiming a disjuncture between Matthiessen's sexuality and criticism would have us believe that *American Renaissance* resembles the closed garden more than the tilled field; and Matthiessen's critical philosophy a delusion or worse. To deny these charges requires us to locate in Matthiessen's work evidence of an inscribed sexuality, proof that Matthiessen enacted his belief that "The greatest art performs its most characteristic action in more subtle ways; it 'does something' . . . by bringing its reader a new understanding or a fresh insight into the full meaning of existence. It thus acts on life by giving it release and fulfillment" ("The Great Tradition" 193).[8] Having identified Matthiessen's sexual oppression, we will discover requisite proof of inscription in a homosexual palimpsest at work in *American Renaissance.*

We might commence this counter-reading by following Matthiessen's own critical lead: "analysis itself can run to seed unless the analyzing mind is also absorbed in a wider context than the text before it" (**"Responsibilities"** 12). Matthiessen's "wider context" of homophobic oppression has been ignored or distorted by critics, at best speculatively drawn from tutorial encounters, or imaginatively assumed from the Whitman passage in *American Renaissance* and the circumstances surrounding his suicide. A deeper sense of the political/cultural/ideological forces that likely would have left some discernable mark on a gay man's sense of the world at that time ultimately eludes these critics. In response, we should take Thomas Yingling's advice: "if a gay poet seems not to write about homosexuality, one might investigate why not, what is substituted in its stead, and how the homosexual appears surreptitiously despite its apparent absence" (16).

Many of Matthiessen's contemporaries were not writing or speaking about homosexuality, or so it would seem, due to a pernicious censorship that successfully policed the boundaries of such "obscenity." During Matthiessen's life a wave of legal and extralegal censorship was at its peak. The tenacity of the Boston Watch and Ward Society, for instance, resulted in the banning of hundreds of books during the late twenties and early thirties for material deemed perverse and obscene. Prominent publishing firms found themselves in court, writes Felice Lewis, but most often "book dealers . . . paid their fines without pursuing the matter further, or were intimidated without being brought into court" (98). During the "Boston book massacre" of 1927 over sixty books were suppressed, a feat repeated in 1929 (Lewis 98-101).

Works by D. H. Lawrence, John Dos Passos, Sinclair Lewis and other "straight" authors were among those targeted, but a comprehensive assault by groups such as the Legion of Decency and the National Office for Decent Literature was waged against any material discussing homosexuality (D'Emilio *Sexual Politics* 19). In New York, the padlock bill prohibited plays "'depicting or dealing with, the subject of sex degeneracy, or sex perversion'," a ban consonant with the "anti-gay vigilance" enforced by the State Liquor Authority and Department of Licenses during the "pansy craze" of the post-Prohibition era (Chauncey 352-3). Hollywood established its own production code in 1930, which ". . . allowed the depiction of adultery, murder, and a host of other immoral practices, so long as they were shown to be wrong, but it prohibited any reference whatsoever to homosexuality, or 'sex perversion', along with a handful of other irredeemably immoral practices" (Chauncey 353).

If the conspiratorial imposition of silence attempted to erase homosexuals' representation in the public sphere, the heightened cultural and political interest in psychology, with its influence on criminology, threatened their very presence outside of a highly circumscribed closet. The wide circulation of Freudian psychosexual theory, as well as work by sexologists Richard von Krafft-Ebing, Havelock Ellis, and Magnus Hirschfeld, sparked the cultural imagination regarding sexual deviance (Freedman 204).[9] During World War II, to name but one striking example, psychiatrist Harry Stack Sullivan (who was himself a homosexual), supervised a process of psychiatric screening for the military to weed out gays and lesbians (Berube 9-22). In light of Freud's observation that homosexuality could be "cured," the American Psychiatric Association labeled same-sex desire a disease.

Significantly, psychological determinations regarding the abnormality of homosexuality played an increasing role in its criminalization. "In the fifteen years after World War II," observes John D'Emilio, "legislatures of more than half the states turned to psychiatrists for solutions to the problem of sex crimes, and they passed sexual psychopath laws that officially recognized homosexuality as a socially threatening disease" (*Sexual Politics* 17). The threat was exaggerated during two sex crime panics, 1937-1940 and 1949-1955, after a series of child murders were sensationalized by the press; panics exacerbated by that staunch public moral defender (and private drag queen) J. Edgar Hoover, who in 1937 declared "War" on the "sex fiend, most loathsome of all the vast army of crime, [who] has become a sinister threat to the safety of American childhood and womanhood" (Freedman 206). Arrests of homosexuals as a result of the hysteria became epidemic during this fifteen year period (Freedman 206).

Thus there was an easy adoption of the homosexual contagion metaphor within partisan rhetoric to warrant oppressive practices during the McCarthy era. The anticommunist purge under the Truman administration found its surest weapon in the House Un-American Activities Committee, revived in 1945, which grew as a menacing threat to a burgeoning gay and lesbian subculture: "What the Committee wanted, in the old-witch-hunt tradition, was public denunciation, public purgation, a purification of the convert by means of his public humiliation as he betrayed his old friends and comrades." (Caute *The Great Fear* 100-101). Capitalizing on Truman's lax policy regarding employment of homosexuals and the frenzy initiated in 1948 by Alfred Kinsey's *Reports*, the House Committee on Un-American Activities exposed and secured the release of more than 60 employees per month by late 1950. Even gays and lesbians not employed by the government discovered the Post Office tampering with their mail, FBI surveillance of social spaces, and intensifying harassment by urban police forces (D'Emilio *Sexual Politics* 34-36; "Homosexual Menace" 228-9).

Matthiessen, like so many of his "fellow travelers," would have been cognizant of the curtailed freedoms of expression, and the cost of radical politics. He had been investigated by various government agencies who "maintained extensive files on his 'suspicious' conduct and speech" (Cain 106), and testified before HUAC the year he died. While these facts are often conveyed in discussions of Matthiessen's socialist politics, they are never considered in relation to his sexuality. The connection between anticommunism and homosexuality would have occurred to the politically astute Matthiessen during the late 1940s, and even earlier during the highly publicized plagues of institutional harassment. Given the blatant nature of antihomosexual vigilance that had existed for twenty-five years at the time of his suicide, one could reasonably argue that the double life Matthiessen has been accused of living was more measured than tortured, an instance of *sophrosyne* and prudence rather than self-loathing.

While Matthiessen's passing undoubtedly entailed a certain degree of culturally derived homophobia, there is ample anecdotal evidence[10] to support George Chauncey's point that "Managing two lives, two personas was difficult for some men. But it did not necessarily lead them to denigrate their necessarily compartmentalized gay persona. Most men regarded the double life as a reasonable tactical response to the dangers posed by the revelation of their homosexuality to straight people" (273). Leo Marx has suggested that Matthiessen was drawn to the double-consciousness found in Emerson, Hawthorne and Melville precisely because of its consonance with "the double life he and Cheney felt compelled to live, and the many humiliating concealments and dissimulations it entailed. . . . Matthiessen had a heightened sensitivity to the many variations in our literature on the theme of the disparity between appearance and reality" (45). As early as 1925, Matthiessen had surmised the requisites and perils of passing: "We must create everything for ourselves. And creation is never easy" (Hyde 71).[11]

HOMOSEXUAL PALIMPSEST

Instead of accepting the conventional wisdom regarding Matthiessen's duplicity, consider a counter-premise embedded in John Rackliffe's comment that

> Burdened, perhaps even endowed, with these inner contradictions, Matty faced an outer world equally and fiercely full of contradictions. They insistently tore at his mind and his heart: he continued to face the world bravely. His courage was doubly rare and admirable because he carried with him always a sharp and heavy sense of his own responsibility to make that world more bearable and more livable. (76)

Recall too Kenneth Lynn's observation that "By bringing his own life into works of American literature, Matthiessen clarified as well as intensified their meaning. Occasionally, though, he altered their meaning—and in my judgment improved them" (115). From these premises, and in light of the historical context, I turn to Matthiessen's masterpiece *American Renaissance*.

Michael Cadden inadvertently identifies Matthiessen's resistant passing in claiming that "Neither in his work nor in his life was Matthiessen a sexual politician or rabble-rouser. Throughout his career, he remained an insider's outsider and an outsider's insider, cultivating a schizophrenic division between his relationship with Cheney and his professional mien even as he glorified the rhetoric of wholeness" (31-2). Perhaps Matthiessen's purported schizophrenia was instead homosexual double-consciousness, and perhaps the critical cultivation of "fertile soil" in Matthiessen's era was best achieved by "an insider's outsider and an outsider's insider," and not by a "sexual politician or rabble-rouser." As such, Matthiessen's rhetorical response to homosexual oppression is at once less heroic and more courageous than critics have determined. In the words of Marc Dolan, "It should be clear, however, that a text need not be mythologized to become a classic—it need only be made to signify" (29). A revolution is always a transformation by turns, but not necessarily a storming of the Bastille.

In his 1949 address **"Responsibilities of the Critic"** Matthiessen makes contact with the fertile soil beyond the garden wall by proposing an "ever widening range of interests for the ideal critic" (**"Responsibilities"** 14) in the form of several concise "awarenesses." "These awarenesses," declared Matthiessen, "may encompass some of the breadth and comprehensiveness which [Henry] James assumed to be the thinker's goal, and some of the feeling of being drenched with actual life, which he believed to be the thinker's best reward" (**"Responsibilities"** 6). These awarenesses constitute the method by which Matthiessen strikes a critical balance between the integrity of the academic charge and his instincts in transgression.

The first awareness is found in [T. S.] Eliot's identification of "the inescapable interplay between past and present: that the past is not what is dead, but what is already living; and that the present is continually modifying the past, as the past conditions the present" (**"Responsibilities"** 6). Because so many are "immersed wholly in the immediate," Matthiessen stresses the need for "repossessing the past for ourselves if we are not to lose it altogether. The value in this urgency is that what we manage to retain will really belong to us, and not on authority at second hand" (**"Responsibilities"** 7).

The second awareness is that the responsible critic should be concerned with politics. This not only implies being politically active—"involved in the age"—but using "political" knowledge to broaden one's critical interpretation. Matthiessen admired the work of Marxist critics of the

thirties, demonstrating the importance of ideological critique in one's interpretation of texts. "[A] concern with economics," states Matthiessen, "can surely quicken and enlarge the questions that a critic asks about the content of any new work of art with which he is faced, about the fullness to which it measures and reveals the forces that have produced both it and its author" (**"Responsibilities"** 11).

Finally, Matthiessen returns to the text, arguing that no matter what the present teaches us about the ideological forces that shaped authors in the past, we must "judge the work of art as work of art" (**"Responsibilities"** 14). Matthiessen quotes Engels, concluding that ". . . it is not the poet's duty to supply the reader in advance with the future historical solution of the conflict he describes" (**"Responsibilities"** 14). In other words, as rich as ideological critique may be for seeing the solutions to past conflicts, the richness of the text itself as a response to contextual forces is unique and equally significant. It is the text within its context that provides an "extension of our sense of living by compelling us to contemplate a broader world" (**"Responsibilities"** 17).

American Renaissance enacts these principles, for in it Matthiessen repossesses a gay past; he employs the past to refigure literary history and extend a sense of living for those attentive to the specifics of his text. Almost exclusively, critics have identified the very last section of *American Renaissance* as the only site of discussion pertaining to sexuality, inferring from the infamous Whitman passage evidence of a repressed or celebrated sexuality. I would argue that Whitman's presence overwhelms a more subtle and significant moment of resistance which occurs earlier in the text. Although the mark of the homosexual appears surreptitiously throughout the work, Matthiessen's treatment of Herman Melville is pivotal, for it constitutes his homosexual palimpsest. Critics looking for an overt sexual politics in the text have misunderstood that palimpsest is a job for "an insider's outsider and an outsider's insider" (Cadden 31-32).

The whole of *American Renaissance* is significant to our reading, for as a book it represents a history of nineteenth century literature, one that modifies and refines a dominant cultural text. Without an established surface to partially erase, a resistant critic could not imperceptibly pen a revision; could not embed a novel or transgressive interpretation in the layers of partially effaced conventional literary wisdom. The key to palimpsest is that the surface appears the same, the erased "original" version of the text still faintly visible but not discernible from the addition, the second layer of text. The success of the subversion depends upon the virtual seamlessness of the alteration.

Eric Cheyfitz, in questioning Matthiessen's influence upon literary history, unwittingly stumbles upon his palimpsest: "And it was the work of canonization, of legitimation and normalization, not the rediscovery of these writers, that *American Renaissance* performed. . . . Matthiessen's book represents '*his* literary tradition', not, as I am arguing, a tradition that Matthiessen . . . helped establish at a particular historical and cultural moment" (347-348). The fact that Matthiessen canonized, normalized, and legitimated, but did not establish, the tradition represented in **American Renaissance** is precisely how he could refigure—re-vision—that very tradition in his own image. The existing parchment enabled the palimpsest.

The canonization of Herman Melville is especially significant. Cheyfitz is correct in asserting that an existing renaissance predated **American Renaissance**, merely solidified by Matthiessen. However, as Marc Dolan suggests, it is also the case that "As of the late 1930s, then, Melville was still not a 'classic American author'. . . . Despite the sincere, dogged efforts of critics . . . it was F. O. Matthiessen's extended treatment of Melville in **American Renaissance** that finally established him as a 'classic American author'" (40). The exploration of Melville, argues Dolan, separates "Matthiessen's imaginative work" from earlier histories (43). Melville, in terms of the palimpsest, constitutes the "second layer" Matthiessen inscribes into the text of literary history.

The centrality of Melville in **American Renaissance** is apparent in Matthiessen's claim that he was "The American with the richest natural gifts" (**American Renaissance** 371), and demonstrated by his ubiquitous presence throughout the volume. As Frederick Stern observes: "it [**American Renaissance**] deals as much with Melville in the 'Hawthorne' section and the 'Whitman' section as in the 'Melville' section" (106). It was likely no accident that while Whitman constituted the final, synthetic study, Matthiessen closes the book reflecting on Melville: "He thus fulfilled what Coleridge held to be the major function of the artist: he brought 'the whole soul of man into activity'" (656). William Cain's commentary suggests the possibility that Melville's centrality also had something to do with sexuality:

> The more one reads **American Renaissance**, the more one is struck by repeated conjunctions between Melville and the other writers Matthiessen considers, always serving to dramatize where the others fall short. . . . In speaking this way about Melville's differences from his contemporaries, with the added gender-coded preference for Melville's 'vigorous thrust' and 'strength of passion', Matthiessen is exalting Melville at the expense of the rest of American literature. (177-178)

Tellingly, Cain further observes that "Matthiessen somewhat identifies with Melville, whom one might suggest Matthiessen reads through . . . his own private and public longings. What Matthiessen admires, and aspires toward, in Melville is what he reveres in Eliot . . . their virtue of 'wholeness', the 'integrity' that enables a man to treat all of his experiences as one, and that provides him with the courage and resourcefulness to confront hard truths about good and evil which other men cannot recognize or from which they flee" (176-177).

Matthiessen's affinity for Melville may have been forged by similarities in the circumstances confronting each. Cen-

sorship, for instance, was a pervasive force of oppression in Melville's life, as the "expurgations" of questionable references in *Typee* and *Redburn* illustrated (Creech, *Closet Writing* 74-75). Melville too had endured a life of passing, marrying soon after returning from his intensely homoerotic experience at sea (Creech, *Closet Writing* 74), and long hindered sexually by family attachments (See Rogin). Desiring to be unencumbered sexually, Melville lamented: "'Could I remake me! or set free / This sexless bound in sex, then plunge / Deeper than Sappho, in a lunge / Piercing Pan's paramount mystery / For nature, in no shallow surge / Against thee either sex may urge'" (Creech, *Closet Writing* 71-2). Melville's poetic yearning to live openly rings familiar as one reads Matthiessen's early reflections: "My sex bothers me, feller, sometimes when it makes me aware of the falseness of my position in the world" (Hyde 200).

Matthiessen certainly would have detected the homoerotic content "smuggled" into Melville's novels. As James Creech argues:

> Just as anything having to do with Whitman could be used as a coded marker of one's homosexuality. . . . Melville's name seems to a lesser degree to have acquired some of the same talismanic power. . . . All this suggests that . . . the homoerotic content of the sea novels surely found recognition and response at least on the part of homosexual readers who must surely have wondered whether Melville might be gay, too.
>
> (*Closet Writing* 77-78)

More than the privately admired but publicly "marked" Whitman, Melville offered Matthiessen a recognizable "homosexual wink," to use Creech's term. His insight may have resembled that of John Updike, who observed that novels like *Pierre* and *The Confidence-Man* "were written with Melville's instincts in rebellion; they are protest novels cast in a would-be popular vein, and brim with tensions the author cannot express" (105). Updike locates, as Matthiessen likely did, homosexual coding at work in Melville's writing. Arguably, Melville's writing may have precipitated Matthiessen's tactics for importing unspeakable material into one's work.

The four chapters on Melville in **American Renaissance** are laced with textual clues which express the homosexuality Matthiessen presumably admired in Melville's work; what in gay parlance of the 1940s might be called "dropping beads all over" (Chauncey 289). The emphasis and organization of Matthiessen's analysis betrays his specific focus on those novels which feature homoerotic content. Marc Dolan notes that "Matthiessen is really the first critic to place any literary or intellectual emphasis on the later works overall. He warms up with *Typee* and *Omoo*, only lingers on *Mardi* . . . and then rushes through *Redburn* and *White Jacket* to get to *Moby-Dick* and *Pierre*, the centerpieces of his analysis. . . . Rather than tracing a development from *Typee* to *Pierre*, Matthiessen shows one that instead moves from *Mardi* to *Billy Budd*" (46).[12] Shifting literary emphasis to these familiar but less celebrated texts,

Matthiessen commenced a covert process of normalization, legitimation, and ultimately canonization of homosexual literature.

As he did throughout *American Renaissance*, Matthiessen constructs a "wider context" that informs the reader of those forces—ideological, cultural, political—that animated Melville's texts. Economic forces, states Matthiessen, had ruined the aristocratic Melville family in the 1820s, contributing to the death of Melville's father and ending Melville's formal schooling. The panic of 1837, directly influencing Melville's decision to go to sea, situated him in the most overtly homosexual environment of his life. This experience inspired Melville's sea novels: "'Sad disappointments in several plans which I had sketched for my future life, the necessity of doing something for myself, united to a naturally roving disposition, had now conspired within me, to send me to sea as a sailor'" (*American Renaissance* 375).

Melville's lived and imagined maritime experiences must have inspired Matthiessen too, for in speaking of them he very nearly engages the taboo directly. Matthiessen observes that the "genteel demands" of conventional language standards hindered Melville's "aim to be a chronicler of the navy exactly as it was, of what might become obsolete, 'withholding nothing, inventing nothing'" (*American Renaissance* 422). What Melville was forced to withhold, in part, was homosexual content. "His own modesty joined again with the taboos of his age when he came to probe the daily life of the men, for he skirted the subject with remote allusions to the *Oedipus* and to Shelley's *Cenci*, and with the remark that 'the sins for which the cities of the plain were overthrown still linger in some of these wooden-walled Gomorrahs of the deep'" (*American Renaissance* 422). Matthiessen's wavering modesty here reveals the passing which veils a more candid discussion of "the subject."[13]

Most important to Matthiessen's version of Marxist ideological critique were those economic forces which circumscribed Melville's social, familia, and career choices (*American Renaissance* 186, 398-9). These forces shaped Melville's eventual tragic perspective: "The latent economic factor in tragedy," writes Matthiessen, "remained part of Melville's vision at every subsequent stage of his writing" (*American Renaissance* 400). Matthiessen's depiction of the interplay between "wider context" and a textual emphasis on tragedy foregrounds Melville's struggle and endurance, constituting the homosexual revision effected by the palimpsest.

Matthiessen's interpretation of Melville's tragic perspective counterposes two versions of tragedy, one exhibited in *Moby-Dick* and another in *Billy Budd*. Matthiessen reads Melville's Ahab as representing the tragic consequence of the unbridled optimism inherent in Emersonian transcendentalism. Ahab constitutes Melville's "most profound response to the problem of the free will *in extremis*" (*American Renaissance* 447). Ahab is the Emersonian

hero, responding to fate with sheer force of will and hubris, demonstrating "the frighteningly ironic consequences of that action: of how this puritanical sea captain, in all the mad righteousness of his hatred of evil, becomes . . . the very evil he would destroy" (Gunn 118). There is no catharsis, no "unmixed pity," in this tragedy because there is no sense of balance, no "moral recognition": "He is not caught out of himself and transfigured by sympathy" (*American Renaissance* 456). Tragedy in *Moby-Dick*, Matthiessen concludes, "is that of unregenerate will, which stifles his soul and drives his brain with an inescapable fierceness" (*American Renaissance* 457).

By contrast, Matthiessen ends with a strikingly different version of tragedy, embodied in Melville's last novel *Billy Budd*, a "reassertion of the heart" after a long hiatus in writing. "In *Billy Budd, Foretopman*," observes Matthiessen, "he gave a last, coherent statement to the issues that had plagued his mind ever since the experiences of Redburn . . . he had conceived the idea for a purer, more balanced tragedy than he had ever composed before" (*American Renaissance* 499-500). The tragic vision of Melville comported with Matthiessen's sense that "not only must the author of tragedy have accepted the inevitable co-existence of good and evil in man's nature, he must also possess the power to envisage some reconciliation between such opposites, and the control to hold an inexorable balance" (*American Renaissance* 180).

In addition to Claggart's important "mixture of attraction and repulsion . . . the sexual element in Claggart's ambivalence" (*American Renaissance* 506), such a balance is struck, Matthiessen argues, in the characters of Captain Vere and Billy. Vere, who, in keeping with the law, sentences Billy to hang for the murder of Claggart, "has the strength of mind and the earnestness of will to dominate his instincts. He believes that in man's government, 'forms, measured forms, are everything.' But his decision to fulfill the letter of the law is not won without anguish" (*American Renaissance* 509). Likewise, Billy, though he has been told by shipmates of the injustice befalling him, remains true to his "'erring sense of uninstructed honor' . . . so he remains silent, and puts himself entirely in the captain's hands" (*American Renaissance* 509). Yet, at the climax of the story, "the 'fervid heart' asserts its transcendent power" (*American Renaissance* 510) as Vere "understands the deeper reality of the spirit" and Billy "forgives him" (*American Renaissance* 511).

Billy Budd, concludes Matthiessen, demonstrates "How carefully Melville is holding the scales, how conscious he is of the delicacy of the equilibrium he has created. . . . Melville could now face incongruity; he could accept the existence of both good and evil with a calm impossible to him in *Moby-Dick*. . . . Melville's . . . is one of the most comprehending perceptions ever made of the essence of tragedy" (*American Renaissance* 511-13). Matthiessen celebrates *Billy Budd* as an exemplar of "the passionate humanity in Melville's own creation of tragedy," bearing witness to Melville's "endurance," a quality which Matthiessen calls "a challenge for later America" (*American Renaissance* 514).

I would argue that Matthiessen emphasizes Melville's later tragic vision precisely because in it he recognized Melville's personal endurance: a measured homosexual life lived in the face of incongruity, contradiction, and cruel fate. As George Abbott White has argued, "no matter how the rules are laid down, or argued, it is the constant *living out* of contradictory positions that is the hardest. . . . [This was] Matty's own special trial" (486). In other words, in turning to the texts of Melville, Matthiessen found "an extension of [his] sense of living" (**"Responsibilities"** 17): a double life full of contradictions forced by fate (ideological, cultural, and political forces) but endured by one's "ability to hold an undismayed control between the pressure of conflicting forces" (*American Renaissance* 349). "Matthiessen's particular version of tragedy," writes Frederick Stern, "was less the consequence of a thought-out ideology or critical theory than of a personal need" (147).

The "personal need" Stern describes, I would conclude, is that of passing. Melville's later tragedy reflected the balancing act required as one manages the tension between an open existence and the public mask. As Leo Marx argues "Matthiessen was acutely aware of the insights the double consciousness allows and the precarious situation it creates. . . . To many of our artists and intellectuals, the creative life has meant just such a risk of being pulled apart by the very conflicts, conscious and unconscious, private and public, that energized their work" (45). Critics longing for an explicit sexual politics or disappointed by duplicity miss the subtle point that "wholeness" for the homosexual of Matthiessen's era, like Melville's tragedy, is inclusive and tolerant of contradictions.

In practice, Matthiessen's passing exhibited rhetorical and critical manifestations. As rhetorical action, Matthiessen balanced the conservatism of disguise with a response to oppression remarkable for its resistant and transformative qualities. The homosexual palimpsest exhibited in *American Renaissance* was revolutionary insofar as "In his particular analysis of the author's accomplishments, he also pointed future critics in the direction of the three works that have served as the focus for Melville studies since World War II: *Moby-Dick, Pierre,* and *Billy Budd*" (Dolan 46). It is neither incidental nor insignificant that these three works, canonized and celebrated as exemplars of gay writing, were central to Matthiessen's establishment of "American literature as a discipline and America as a culture" (Pease 391). Matthiessen re-visioned a gay world from within the parchment folds of a dominant literary history. This "repossession of the past" enacted Matthiessen's belief that "What makes the art of the past still so full of undiscovered wealth is that each age inevitably turns to the past for what it most wants, and thereby tends to remake the past in its own image" (**"Responsibilities"** 17).

At the same time, Matthiessen's palimpsest evinces the precarious balance one negotiates between involvement and detachment in criticism. His resistance in *American Renaissance* is chastened both by homophobia and loyalty to the mandates articulated in **"The Responsibilities of the Critic."** Recognizing the "inescapable interplay between past and present," Matthiessen avoids obliterating a heterosexist literary history, choosing instead to ensconce the homosexual within the layers of the dominant text. He was "involved in his age" by importing sexuality into his criticism and adopting the methodological tools of his time (Marxist critique); but seems to have tempered an overtly political reading with his palimpsest. The text, he understood, need not be coerced to speak: "although literature reflects an age, it also illuminates it . . . books, whether of the present or the past . . . have an immediate life of their own" (*American Renaissance* x).

THE RESPONSIBILITIES OF THE CRITIC: AN APPROACH TO GAY HISTORICAL CRITICISM

On the basis of my reading of F. O. Matthiessen's homosexual palimpsest, I wish to extend a limited number of implications relevant to my critical approach. My initial motive for this essay rested with a desire to amplify the faint voice of a homosexual resisting oppression in a time less "liberated" than our own. Like David Bergman, I secretly hoped to find a gay hero, and in doing so fulfill the critical role James Klumpp and Thomas Hollihan have prescribed: ". . . a mixture of personae—the teacher, the interpreter, and the social actor—com[ing] together in the rhetorical act" (92).

Interpretation and social action, invention and judgment, I discovered instead, exist in a peculiar tension in criticism, rendering any repossession of marginal heroes a complicated business. Matthiessen may have desired to champion Melville in much more overt, even self-indulgent, critical terms, only to be chastened by homophobia. He certainly recognized, as have a diverse array of critics, the rhetorical potential inherent in criticism.[14] Involvement in one's text easily, willingly in many cases, becomes an exercise in advocacy, resistance, or ideological/theoretical affirmation. But while this essay identifies the merits in such a course of rhetorical/critical action, it also highlights potential pitfalls. My survey of shifting metacritical responses to Matthiessen demonstrates, at least, that the rhetorical can, at times, silence or distort critical judgment.

How one successfully negotiates the conflicting impulses of invention and judgment in criticism remains a provocative if daunting question in rhetorical studies. This especially confounds the gay historical critic, for whom texts, if extant at all, are almost always designed to be evasive. Torn between a desire to discover homosexual expression and the mandates of critical "objectivity," the fragile proof assembled in support of one's reading can often seem speculative even to the critic herself. In the face of authoritative readings by prominent literary critics, for instance, I could have more easily dismissed Matthiessen's sexuality than to argue for the homosexual palimpsest that articulates it. James Scott's words, however, offer encouragement: "I argue that a partly sanitized, ambiguous, and coded version of the hidden transcript is always present in the public discourse of subordinate groups. . . . Ignoring them . . . reduces us to an understanding of historical subordination that rests either on those rare moments of open rebellion or on the hidden transcript itself, which is not just evasive but often altogether inaccessible" (19).

As a practice, such a critical balance entails, in Matthiessen's terms, being both involved in the age and mindful of the historical text in its context. Such involvement assumes that ". . . our analyses and our understandings necessarily proceed from our own historically, socially and institutionally shaped vantage points; that the histories we reconstruct are the textual constructs of critics who are, ourselves, historical subjects" (Montrose 23). We should freely allow our politics, erotic impulses, ideological and theoretical assumptions and other "rhetorical contexts" to serve as directives for reading practices. Whatever constellation of factors happens to forge one's critical invention, "their significance to the critical act is undeniable" (Nothstine, Blair, and Copeland 16). For gay criticism, James Creech notes that even a visceral response can be valuable: "Proceeding from an identifactory, erotic response . . . might set us up at least to look for—and perhaps to recognize—traces of unrepresentative consciousness allied with abnormal sexual meaning" (*Closet Writing* 37).[15]

However, the rhetorical contexts that inspire and equip us for the critical act must be balanced by a willingness and ability to situate a given text within the horizon of its own historical context. Ronald Beiner, in the tradition of Kant and Arendt, labels this capacity "reflective judgment": "I must project myself, imaginatively, into a position that I do not actually occupy, in order to enlarge my perspective and thereby open up an awareness of new possibilities, to broaden the range of alternatives from which my judgment then makes its selection" (132). Matthiessen's sexual derogation and hagiography by literary critics resulted from readings that insufficiently weave *American Renaissance* within the context of a homophobic oppression specific to the second quarter of the twentieth century, shaping judgment of Matthiessen's sexuality that I would argue to be less than reflective.

Reflectively engaging one's historical text, which at times may require us to swim against the very tide of our own ideological or theoretical assumptions, seems not only judicious and responsible but valuable for the enhanced quality of critical judgment it affords. As Hannah Arendt has suggested, ". . . the better I can imagine how I would feel and think if I were in their place, the stronger will be my capacity for representative thinking and the more valid my conclusion, my opinion" (241). My own abiding trust (whatever its source) in Matthiessen's belief in his own critical mandates shaped my inquiry into the possibility of his resistance to homophobic oppression, which in turn motivated an exploration of resistive critical passing in *American Renaissance*. As a result, I can begin to answer

with a degree of specificity, as others cannot, James Creech's important question: ". . . how (despite differences in culture and time) has the queer managed to disseminate itself and to produce its culture in the very teeth of bigotry that would destroy it" ("'Forged in Crisis'" 317)?

When F. O. Matthiessen took the platform at the University of Michigan just months before he threw himself from a window in the Manger Hotel, he could not have imagined the prescience of his words. Characterizing the work of Eliot and I. A. Richards as revolutionary, Matthiessen cautioned that his choice of "revolution" may have been too violent a word in the field of arts, "where all victories fortunately are bloodless, and where what was overthrown remains undestroyed and capable of being rediscovered at the next turn of the wheel of taste" (**"Responsibilities"** 3). In a moment of tragic irony, Matthiessen described the sanguinary consequence of homosexual oppression—and expression—in McCarthy's America.

The greater irony, perhaps, is that Matthiessen was too modest in describing the potential for criticism, for his own legacy, as demonstrated by his work on Melville, belies his commentary on the impotence of the critical revolution. Matthiessen willed to us his palimpsest, the "discrete archaeological layers of a life to be excavated like the different levels of old Troy, where, at some point beneath those cities upon cities, one hopes to find Achilles and his beloved Patroclus, and all that wrath with which our world began" (Vidal 6).

Notes

1. Against the reasonable objection that such a "literary" case study falls beyond the disciplinary pale of critical practice, I submit that recognizing and understanding various and complex rhetorical responses to homophobic oppression which predate the Stonewall revolution often require critics, by necessity, to explore unorthodox texts. For F. O. Matthiessen the professional practice of literary criticism constituted a means, perhaps the sole menas, for bricolage and social action. As such, to read Matthiessen reading nineteenth-century literature is squarely within the purview and interest of the rhetorical critic.

2. Of course, it is only fair to point out that in an historical moment as treacherous for gays and lesbians as the burgeoning McCarthy era, even the "open secret" would have been dangerous knowledge for heterosexual friends. As David Caute remarks in *The Fellow Travelers,* "America in these years was neither a perceptive nor a discriminating society . . . a confession of any kind of affiliation to communist causes usually led to professional ruin and social disgrace. For sheer arbitrariness, the American notion of guilt by association was fast pursuing its Soviet counterpart" (311).

3. Critical studies did emerge in the intervening years, most notably that of Giles Gunn (1975), who per-

petuated the precedent of silence: "It is not that I lack interest in the flesh-and-blood man who did the writing, but I think Matthiessen deserves to be viewed as he endeavored to view others, by seeking the man within the work rather than the man behind it" (xviii).

4. Matthiessen, for instance, wrote to Russell Cheney in 1924, "I carried Walt Whitman in my pocket. That's another thing you've started me doing, reading Whitman. Not solely because it gives me an intellectual kick the way it did last year, but because I'm living it" (Hyde 26). The extent to which Whitman symbolized homosexuality for Matthiessen is also indicated in a long description of an erotic encounter with a "perfect Chaucerian yeoman": "I have strung this out so, feller, not because it is the least bit important, but because it was so natural, so like Walt Whitman" (Hyde 124).

5. For rich examples, see Elaine Ginsberg's recent volume, *Passing and the Fictions of Identity.*

6. The experiences of African-Americans and homosexuals are distinct (when not overlapping), of course, but there are interesting and important parallels in the use of the term. See, for example, Bruce, Jr., "W.E.B. Du Bois and the Idea of Double-Consciousness"; Adell, *Double-Consciousness/Double Bind*; and Gates, *The Signifying Monkey.*

7. Recent examples include Olmstead, "The Palimpsest of Memory: Recollection and Intertextuality in Baudelaire's 'Spleen' II," and Cagnon, "Palimpsest in the Writings of Hubert Aquin."

8. It is worth noting that Matthiessen's homosexual palimpsest is also a form of enactment insofar as in resisting he is also embodying in critical practice his literary theory/social philosophy. Importantly, Matthiessen's resistance as an enactment of his sexuality answers specifically the critical charges of inconsistency and duplicity. For a discussion of enactment, see Campbell and Jamicson, "Form and Genre in Rhetorical Criticism: An Introduction."

9. This is not to say that the theories themselves were oppressive. In fact, some were supportive of homosexuals, and liberatory for those who read them. Matthiessen attributed his own comfort with homosexuality to reading Havelock Ellis and Edward Carpenter (Hyde 47-48).

10. In addition to Chauncey's richly documented study of gay life in New York, see the case of Jeb Alexander in Russell, *Jeb and Dash: A Diary of a Gay Life, 1918-1945.*

11. Matthiessen and Cheney had, in fact, debated the merits of passing in a lively and poignant exchange. See the two letters dated February 5 and 6, 1925 (Hyde 79-84).

12. For more detailed, and convincing, arguments related to Melville's homosexual writing see Creech, *Closet Writing/Gay Reading*, Sarotte, *Like a Brother, Like a Lover*, and Martin, *Hero, Captain and Stranger.*

13. Also note a thinly veiled piece of visual evidence, a reprint of Thomas Eakins's "The Swimming Hole," which immediately precedes the discussion of homosexuality at sea, and curiously, is placed directly after a section entitled "Autobiography and Art" (398-399). The placement of the print seems strange because analysis of it is not found here, but later in the study of Whitman. Although Matthiessen notes that "Eakins errs just a little, just a little—a little—in the direction of the flesh" (604), he ultimately treats Eakins's homosexuality with compassion, and indulges in his own sexually charged reading of the painting (610). I would argue that the placement and analysis of the print is not accidental, but part of the palimpsest I describe.

14. See Brockriede, "Rhetorical Criticism as Argument"; Wander and Jenkins, "Rhetoric, Society, and the Critical Response"; Mailloux, "Misreading as a Historical Act" and *Rhetorical Power*; and Scholes "Criticism: Rhetoric and Ethics."

15. This is consonant with the curiosity prescribed in my discussion of "critical liminality." See Morris, "Contextual Twilight/Critical Liminality."

Works Cited

Adell, Sandra. *Double-Consciousness/Double Bind: Theoretical Issues in Twentieth-Century Black Literature.* Urbana: U Illinois P, 1994.

Arac, Jonathan. *Critical Genealogies: Historical Situations for Postmodern Literary Studies.* New York: Columbia UP, 1989.

Arendt, Hannah. *Between Past and Future: Eight Exercises in Political Thought.* Enlarged ed. New York: Viking, 1965.

Beaver, Harold. "Homosexual Signs (In Memory of Roland Barthes)." *Critical Inquiry* 8.1 (1981): 99-119.

Beiner, Ronald. *Political Judgment.* Chicago: U Chicago P, 1983.

Bergman, David. *Gaiety Transfigured: Gay Self-Representation in American Literature.* Madison: U Wisconsin P, 1991.

Berube, Allan. *Coming Out Under Fire: The History of Gay Men and Women in World War Two.* New York: Plume, 1991.

Brockriede, Wayne. "Rhetorical Criticism as Argument." *The Quarterly Journal of Speech* 60 (1974): 165-174.

Brodhead, Richard H. *The School of Hawthorne.* New York: Oxford UP, 1986.

Bruce, Jr., Dickson. "W. E. B. Du Bois and the Idea of Double Consciousness." *American Literature* 64 (1992): 299-309.

Cadden, Michael. "Engendering F. O. Matthiessen: The Private Life of American Renaissance." *Engendering Men:*

The Question of Male Feminist Criticism. Ed. Joseph A. Boone and Michael Cadden. New York: Routledge, 1990.

Cagnon, Maurice. "Palimpsest in the Writings of Hubert Aquin." *Modern Language Studies* 8 (1978): 80-89.

Cain, William E. *F. O. Matthiessen and the Politics of Criticism.* Madison: U Wisconsin P, 1988.

Campbell, Karlyn Kohrs and Kathleen Hall Jamieson. "Form and Genre in Rhetorical Criticism." *Form and Genre: Shaping Rhetorical Action.* Ed. Karlyn Kohrs Campbell and Kathleen Hall Jamieson. Falls Church, VA: Speech Communication Association, 1978.

Caute, David. *The Fellow-Travelers: A Postscript to the Enlightenment.* New York: Macmillan, 1975.

Caute, David. *The Great Fear: The Anti-Communist Purge Under Truman and Eisenhower.* New York: Simon and Schuster, 1978.

Chauncey, George. *Gay New York: Gender, Urban Culture, and the Making of the Gay Male World, 1890-1940.* New York: BasicBooks, 1994.

Cheyfitz, Eric. "Matthiessen's *American Renaissance*: Circumscribing the Revolution." *American Quarterly* 41.2 (1989): 341-361.

Creech, James. *Closet Writing/Gay Reading: The Case of Melville's* Pierre. Chicago: U Chicago P, 1993.

Creech, James. "'Forged in Crisis': Queer Beginnings of Modern Masculinity in a Canonical French Novel." *Studies in the Novel* 28.3 (1996): 304-318.

D'Emilio, John. "The Homosexual Menace: The Politics of Sexuality in the Cold War America." *Passion and Power: Sexuality in History.* Ed. Kathy Peiss and Christina Simmons. Philadelphia: Temple UP, 1989.

D'Emilio, John. *Sexual Politics, Sexual Communities: The Making of a Homosexual Minority in the United States, 1940-1970.* Chicago, U Chicago P, 1983.

De Quincey, Thomas. *Confessions of an Opium-Eater and Other Writings.* Ed. Grevel Lindop. Oxford: Oxford UP, 1985.

Dolan, Marc. "The 'Wholeness' of the Whale: Melville, Matthiessen, and the Semiotics of Critical Revisionism." *Arizona Quarterly* 48.3 (1992): 27-58.

Du Bois. W. E. B. "Strivings of the Negro People." *Atlantic* 80 (1897): 194.

Freedman, Estelle B. "'Uncontrolled Desires': The Response to the Sexual Psychopath, 1920-1960." *Passion and Power: Sexuality in History.* Ed. Kathy Peiss and Christina Simmons. Philadelphia: Temple UP, 1989.

Gates, Jr., Henry Louis. *The Signifying Monkey: A Theory of Afro-American Criticism.* New York: Oxford UP, 1988.

Ginsberg, Elaine K, ed. *Passing and the Fictions of Identity.* Durham: Duke UP, 1996.

Gunn, Giles. *F. O. Matthiessen: The Critical Achievement.* Seattle: U of Washington P, 1975.

Hardy, Thomas. *Far from the Madding Crowd.* London: Macmillan, 1973.

Hyde, Louis, ed. *Rat and the Devil: Journal Letters of F. O. Matthiessen and Russell Cheney.* Boston: Alyson, 1978.

Johnson, James Weldon. *The Autobiography of an Ex-Colored Man. Three Negro Classics.* New York: Avon, 1965.

Klumpp, James F. and Thomas A. Hollihan. "Rhetorical Criticism as Moral Action." *The Quarterly Journal of Speech* 75 (1989): 84-97.

Levin, Harry. "The Private Life of F. O. Matthiessen." *The New York Review of Books* 20 (1978): 42-46.

Lewis, Felice Flanery. *Literature, Obscenity, and Law.* Carbondale: Southern Illinois UP, 1976.

Lynn, Kenneth. "F. O. Matthiessen." *Masters: Portraits of Great Teachers.* Ed. Joseph Epstein. New York: Basic, 1981.

Mailloux, Stephen. "Misreading as a Historical Act: Cultural Rhetoric, Bible Politics, and Fuller's 1845 Review of Douglass's Narrative." *Readers in History: Nineteenth-Century American Literature and Contexts of Response.* Ed. James L. Machor. Baltimore: The Johns Hopkins UP, 1993.

Mailloux, Stephen. *Rhetorial Power.* Ithaca: Cornell UP, 1989.

Martin, Robert K. *Hero, Captain and Stranger: Male Friendship, Social Critique, and Literary Form in the Sea Novels of Herman Melville.* Chapel Hill: U of North Carolina P, 1986.

Marx, Leo. "Double Consciousness and the Cultural Politics of F. O. Matthiessen." *Monthly Review* 34.9 (1983): 34-56.

Matthiessen, F. O. *American Renaissance: Art and Expression in the Age of Emerson and Whitman.* New York: Oxford UP, 1941.

Matthiessen. F. O. "The Great Tradition: A Counterstatement." *The Responsibilities of the Critic: Essays and Reviews by F. O. Matthiessen.* Ed. John Rackliffe. New York: Oxford UP, 1952.

Matthiessen, F. O. "The Responsibilities of the Critic." *The Responsibilities of the Critic: Essays and Reviews by F. O. Matthiessen.* Ed. John Rackliffe. New York: Oxford UP, 1952.

McDonagh, Josephine. "Writings on the Mind: Thomas De Quincey and the Importance of the Palimpsest in Nineteenth Century Thought." *Prose Studies* 10 (1987): 207-224.

Montrose, Louis. "Professing the Renaissance: The Poetics and Politics of Culture." *The New Historicism.* Ed. H. Aram Veeser. New York: Routledge, 1989.

Morris, III, Charles E. "Contextual Twilight/Critical Liminality: J.M. Barrie's *Courage* at St. Andrews, 1922." *The Quarterly Journal of Speech* 82 (1996): 207-227.

Nothstine, William L., Carole Blair, and Gary A. Copeland, eds. *Critical Questions: Invention, Creativity, and the Criticism of Discourse and Media.* New York: St. Martin's, 1994.

Olmstead, William. "The Palimpsest of Memory: Recollection and Intertextuality in Baudelaire's 'Spleen' II." *Romantic Review* 77 (1986): 359-367.

Pease, Donald E. "Melville and Cultural Persuasion." *Ideology and Classic American Literature.* Ed. Sacvan Bercovitch and Myra Jehlen. Cambridge: Cambridge UP, 1987: 384-417.

Rackliffe, John. "Notes for a Character Study." *F. O. Matthiessen (1902-1950): A Collective Portrait.* Ed. Paul Sweezy and Leo Huberman. New York: Henry Schuman, 1950.

Reisner, Thomas A. "De Quincey's Palimpsest Reconsidered." *Modern Language Studies* 12 (1982): 93-95.

Rogin, Michael. *Subversive Genealogy: The Art and Politics of Herman Melville.* New York: Alfred A. Knopf, 1979.

Russell, Ina, ed. *Jeb and Dash: A Diary of Gay Life. 1918-1945.* Boston: Faber and Faber, 1993.

San Francisco Lesbian and Gay History Project. "'She Even Chewed Tobacco': A Pictorial Narrative of Passing Women in America." *Hidden from History: Reclaiming the Gay and Lesbian Past.* Ed. Martin Bauml Duberman, Martha Vicinus, and George Chauncey. New American Library, 1989.

Sarotte, Georges-Michel. *Like a Brother, Like a Lover: Male Homosexuality in the American Novel and Theater from Herman Melville to James Baldwin.* Garden City, New York: Anchor, 1978.

Sarton, May. "The Pieces of This Death (for F. O. M.)" *F. O. Matthiessen (1902-1950): A Collective Portrait.* Ed. Paul Sweezy and Leo Huberman. New York: Henry Schuman, 1950.

Scholes, Robert. "Criticism: Rhetoric and Ethics." *Protocols of Reading.* New Haven: Yale UP, 1989.

Scott, James C. *Domination and the Arts of Resistance: Hidden Transcripts.* New Haven: Yale UP, 1990.

Sedgwick, Eve Kosofsky. *Epistemology of the Closet.* Berkeley: U of California P, 1990.

Signorile, Michelangelo. *Queer in America: Sex, the Media, and the Closets of Power.* New York: Random House, 1993.

Stern, Frederick C. *F. O. Matthiessen: Christian Socialist as Critic.* Chapel Hill: U North Carolina P, 1981.

Stowe, Harriet Beecher. *Uncle Tom's Cabin.* New York: A.L. Burt, n.d.

Sweezy, Paul and Leo Huberman, eds. *F. O. Matthiessen (1902-1950): A Collective Portrait.* New York: Henry Schuman, 1950.

Tompkins, Jane. *Sensational Designs: The Cultural Work of American Fiction, 1790-1860.* New York: Oxford UP, 1985.

Tayler, Carole-Anne. "Passing: Narcissism, Identity, and Difference." *differences: A Journal of Feminist Cultural Studies* 6.3-4 (1994): 212-248.

Updike, John. "Melville's Withdrawal." *Hugging the Shore.* New York: Alfred A. Knopf, 1983.

Vidal, Gore. *Palimpsest: A Memoir.* New York: Random House, 1995.

Wander, Philip and Steve Jenkins. "Rhetoric, Society, and the Critical Response." *The Quarterly Journal of Speech* 58 (1992): 441-450.

White, George Abbott. "Ideology and Literature: American Renaissance and F. O. Matthiessen." *Literature in Revolution.* Ed. George Abbott White and Charles Newman. New York: Holt, Rinehart, and Winston, 1972.

Yingling, Thomas. *Hart Crane and the Homosexual Text: New Thresholds, New Anatomies.* Chicago: U Chicago P, 1990.

Jay Grossman (essay date 1998)

SOURCE: "The Canon in the Closet: Matthiessen's Whitman, Whitman's Matthiessen," in *American Literature*, Vol. 70, No. 4, December, 1998, pp. 799-832.

[*In the following essay, Grossman analyzes how Matthiessen's sexuality influenced his perception and discussion of the literary relationship between Walt Whitman and Henry David Thoreau.*]

> An artist's use of language is the most sensitive index to cultural history, since a man can articulate only what he is, and what he has been made by the society of which he is a willing or an unwilling part.
>
> —F. O. Matthiessen, ***American Renaissance***

> Family-life is not to be treated as a red flag to be flaunted in the streets, or a horn to be blown hoarsely on the housetops.
>
> —Oscar Wilde, *De Profundis*

This essay takes as its point of departure a single, perhaps startling, fact about F. O. Matthiessen's ***American Renaissance: Art and Expression in the Age of Emerson and Whitman***: the word "Calamus" does not appear anywhere in it—not in book four's extended discussion of Whitman, not even in the index. What would it have meant to include the title of this cluster of poems in 1941, or during the 1930s when Matthiessen was writing this important piece of scholarship? How shall we think through this absent word, which marks the absence in *American Renaissance* of any sustained discussion of Whitman's most overtly homoerotic lyrics, especially when considered in light of another "fact" we "know" about Matthiessen, that he was himself "homosexual" and shared more than twenty years of his life with another man, the painter Russell Cheney?[1]

In the half-century since Oxford University Press brought out *American Renaissance*, there has been relatively little sustained critical engagement with the consequences of Matthiessen's "homosexuality" for literary history and criticism, and more particularly for this book's influential configuration of nineteenth-century literary masterworks.[2] I mean this essay to begin filling in this literary-historical gap. In the opening section I review a representative revisionist essay on *American Renaissance* that delimits the range of interpretive consequences of Matthiessen's sexuality in its reading of his work and its aftermath. I then undertake a reconstruction of the assumptions that undergird Matthiessen's conceptions of sexuality and "homosexuality" as these relate to his readings of Whitman, both in his public text on the Renaissance and in private (now published) letters he exchanged with Cheney. Finally, I offer a reading of an aspect of *American Renaissance*—the literary relation between Whitman and Thoreau—that has gone underscrutinized partly as a result of the relative lack of critical attention to questions bearing upon Matthiessen's sexuality.

It is the task of this introduction to demonstrate how the heteronormativity that structures Matthiessen's own literary-critical perspective in *American Renaissance* remains a constraining feature of the perspectives of some of Matthiessen's readers even today. Criticism produced under the logic of this presumptive heteronormativity often exhibits a rhetorical or argumentative condensation around issues of sexuality and "homosexuality," such that the topic "itself" is identified and quickly shifted past, often in favor of some cumulative, contextual, or seemingly "more complex" frame. This essay, by contrast, argues that discourses of sexuality structure *American Renaissance*—particularly in its treatment of Thoreau and Whitman—even or especially at those moments when sexuality does not seem to be initially, or explicitly, present.

Leo Marx's sympathetic account of Matthiessen's dilemma can stand as a case in point in this regard.[3] For while Marx notes that "as recently as 1950 Matthiessen's friends considered his homosexuality unmentionable," and while he properly laments that "[t]he distorting effect of this inhibition is discernible in just about everything that has been written about Matthiessen" (242-43), it is also the case that his own essay turns away from offering a less "inhibited" reading just at the brink:

> To appreciate why the double consciousness had a special resonance for Matthiessen, one has only to read the Matthiessen-Cheney letters. There we get a sense of what it was like, before the Second World War, to be a Harvard professor and a homosexual: the double life

that he and Cheney felt compelled to live, and the many humiliating concealments and dissimulations it entailed. . . . Matthiessen was acutely aware of the insights the double consciousness allows and the precarious situation it creates—a situation that Emerson likens, in his essay on "Fate," to that of a circus rider with one foot planted on the back of one horse and the other foot planted on the back of another. To many of our artists and intellectuals, the creative life has meant just such a risk of being pulled apart by the very conflicts, conscious and unconscious, private and public, that energized their work. (250-51)

Marx's shift between what Eve Kosofsky Sedgwick has denominated "minoritizing" (Matthiessen "is" a homosexual) and "universalizing" ("our artists and intellectuals") paradigms has the simultaneous effect of removing homosexuality "itself" from critical analysis.[4] The historicity of Matthiessen's predicament in living a double life as a "professor and a homosexual" becomes almost at once emblematic of a national, generic predicament of "*our* artists and intellectuals," with the effect that the particularity of the "homosexual" as outsider (only ever contingently included in the space of a national "we") and the particular consequences of such a situation for the writing of Matthiessen's literary criticism fall largely outside the critical frame of the rest of the essay's nonetheless quite compelling and thoughtful analyses.[5]

Although the strictures of a certain heteronormative reading practice often displace or replace "homosexuality" as such, it is not my contention that the solution is to "restore" homosexuality to some imagined transhistorical essence. As my use of scare quotes suggests, reading the Matthiessen-Cheney letters (as Marx recommends) uncovers not consensus, nor perhaps even homology, so much as important structural differences between "homosexuality" as "we" (think we) know and recognize it, and "homosexuality" as Matthiessen and Cheney conceived it; indeed, there are even differences between the way Cheney and Matthiessen conceived "it." Putting "homosexuality" back into *American Renaissance* will be more complicated than locating where and how Matthiessen-the-gay-man (as if we know who this is) positions himself in relation to, say, Whitman or Thoreau. This is the case not only because of any contemporary critic's anachronistic position—surely one of the most significant changes that has occurred in the academy and in American culture more broadly since 1941 is the *visible* presence of gay, lesbian, and bisexual professors, students, studies, and citizens—but also because "homosexuality" cannot be granted an existence prior to its expression, "as if sexuality were not always already institutional, existing only in its historically sedimented forms and discourses."[6]

Thus, the answers to the question why *American Renaissance* is the way that it is will assuredly not (only) be "because Matthiessen made it that way"—at least not in any theoretically uncomplicated sense. If my argument is correct, much of the criticism surrounding Matthiessen ultimately overlooks the structures of homophobia/

heteronormativity within which he was imbedded and which can be said to have structured (as they still structure, however differently, even today) the comings-out and the goings-on of ("real," putatively, or perceived) "gay" men. In a word, what has fallen away from these critical accounts is the notion of heterosexism as a discursive structure prevailing across a range of cultural sites and material practices. Matthiessen's book is the way it is at least partly because it is the product of a complex interaction between "Matthiessen" and the manifold discursive practices within and through which this "professor and homosexual" learned to perceive the world, including the world of American literature between 1845 and 1855—that "one extraordinarily concentrated moment of expression"[7] This becomes particularly visible at the uniquely overdetermined site of a recent critic's reading of Matthiessen's "own" homophobia.

IT IS YOU TALKING JUST AS MUCH AS MYSELF

In "Matthiessen's *American Renaissance*: Circumscribing the Revolution," Eric Cheyfitz restores Matthiessen's volume to the context of the broad efforts to legitimate the study of American literature in the decades immediately before its publication. Cheyfitz demonstrates that Matthiessen's work is best seen as a remarkably influential consolidation of certain trends already visible in American literary study, and as evidence he points to canonical configurations of the 1910s that center upon some of the authors Matthiessen enshrined.[8] Indeed, it is part of Cheyfitz's main contention that Matthiessen's Big Five (Emerson, Thoreau, Whitman, Hawthorne, and Melville) need already to have been largely in their canonical places for the book to have performed so well its most significant work in "establish[ing] this group exclusively" (347).[9] The book's extraordinary success in this regard can be measured, of course, by innumerable university syllabi at institutions throughout the United States and abroad to the present day.

That *American Renaissance* has been, until recently, so univocally accepted is a situation Cheyfitz rather movingly laments, for the acceptance of *American Renaissance*, he argues, also signifies the ways in which Matthiessen's life-long left-wing political activism and socialism disappear in relation to what Cheyfitz calls the "classically corporate or consensual project" that is *American Renaissance*, its substitution of "one group of white, Protestant, essentially middle-class male authors for another group of the same race, gender, and class" (349-50). Cheyfitz's most significant single paragraph for our purposes begins with his appraisal of this wholesale substitution:

> These literary politics, with their emphasis on a homogeneous nationalism, contradicted in crucial ways Matthiessen's politics, the socialism to which I will turn in a moment. But then, as I am arguing, *American Renaissance* was not Matthiessen's book. For not only did he repress his politics in its production; he repressed his homosexuality, and this in a book that is centrally concerned with questions of embodiment. The social

and professional danger in revealing his sexual identity or even sympathizing openly with homosexuality would have been considerable. But was it necessary to discuss Whitman's homoeroticism, when he does so in passing, within the context of the "pathological" and the "regressive" (*American Renaissance*, 535)? Such a context betrays the sustaining influence that Matthiessen's own homosexuality played in his life through his long relationship with the painter Russell Cheyney [*sic*]. (350)

This passage is enabled by an initial separation of politics from sexuality, a gesture that, Andrew Parker argues, represents a reflex response in the practice of much Western Marxist criticism ("Unthinking Sex," 21). Under this governing assumption, repressing one's politics and repressing one's homosexuality are separate gestures, presumably because there is no political dimension to the question of sexuality or of homosexuality, its practices, or its "expression." The same gesture is redoubled in the subsequent alignment of homosexuality with questions of "embodiment," as if to posit, once again, that one's body, like one's sexuality, exists before and apart from the discursive and political constructs that contain, proscribe, prescribe, and variously make meaning of the body and its actions, somatic and sensory products, physical requirements, and physiological responses. When Cheyfitz's analysis moves next to the question of betrayal, it reinscribes a narrative that is perhaps most familiar from the Cold War, one in which homosexuals (in the government) inevitably betray; here Matthiessen is said to betray not only his "nation," or, what amounts to the same thing, his leftist democratic vision of a certain kind of United States, but also Cheney, and so his (Matthiessen's) own specifically queer nationality as well.

But wouldn't it be more accurate to say that it is Matthiessen's relationship with Cheney that sustains him rather than some abstract "orientation" called "homosexuality"? Here is Matthiessen writing to Cheney early in 1930:

> This has been a pretty bleak day, outside and within. . . . My sex bothers me, feller, sometimes when it makes me aware of the falseness of my position in the world. And consciousness of that falseness seems to sap my confidence of power. Have I any right in a community that would so utterly disapprove of me if it knew the facts? I ask myself that, and then I laugh; for I know I would never ask it at all if isolation from you didn't make me search into myself. I need you, feller; for together we can confront whatever there is.
>
> But damn it! I hate to have to hide when what I thrive on is absolute directness.[10]

This letter's description of isolation recurs often in the correspondence. Despite Matthiessen's insistence that he benefited from "more generous and devoted friends than ordinarily fall to the lot of any man" (Hyde, 254)—an appraisal he made from his bed at McLean Hospital in Waverly, Massachusetts, where, suffering from nervous exhaustion, he was briefly a patient—taken together these letters provide an opportunity to glimpse the deforming nature of homophobia across a spectrum of gay/straight interactions from before the Second World War into the Cold War.[11]

Scattered throughout the letters written during the composition of *American Renaissance* are exchanges bearing on when and in what terms Matthiessen and Cheney might explain their relationship to others—and so also, at least in part, to themselves. From the same hospital bed, Matthiessen writes to Cheney less than two years before the book's publication: "I remember that early phrase from a letter of yours from Venice, of how our gifts to each other enabled all our other relationships to share in 'largesse from our unknown wealth, untold wealth of love.' Well, it's still there even though I am your erring Spinwheel" (Hyde, 244). Given the repeated attention to the issue of disclosure, it is not merely affectionate hyperbole when Matthiessen quotes Cheney back to himself in recalling an earlier characterization of their love as "unknown" and "untold." Indeed, the circuit of exchange for these words—traveling back and forth only between the two men—might usefully serve to symbolize the closed nature of their bond. These men only intermittently felt assured enough of the devotion of their friends to disclose the nature and intensity of their commitment to each other, and Matthiessen himself, who thrived, as he said, on "absolute directness," did not always feel that such open and direct declarations were possible or wise.[12] For both these men, being homosexual recurs in their letters as a source of anguish and ambiguity that sometimes finds relief only in their mutual, loving commitment.

Thus there is another way of thinking about Matthiessen's "betrayal," another way of reconstructing whether it was "necessary" for Matthiessen to have discussed Whitman's homosexuality in pathological terms, even after we accept Cheyfitz's caveat that a sympathetic discussion of or identification with homosexuality was dangerous in the 1930s and 1940s, as it can still be today. To get at this alternative, we need to notice that there seems to be an unequal distribution of volition operating within Cheyfitz's scheme, and that what may be required is a broadening of the term *repression*. For *repression* must refer not simply to the actions of a fully conscious agent, Matthiessen, in pushing ("his own") homosexuality out of view and/or toward pathology; *repression* needs also to refer to the regime of heteronormative disciplinarity present in Matthiessen's early letters to Cheney. To ask the question again: how shall we reckon "necessity"?

Within a theoretical framework of cultural interpellation, necessity and acceptance cannot be delineated quite as plainly or as cleanly as these treatments of the issue suggest. When is Matthiessen speaking Whitman's pathology, and when is he ventriloquizing the dominant homophobic discourses of his culture? According to Cheyfitz, "Like the radical Holgrave marrying the democrat Phoebe and thereby becoming a substantial property holder in Hawthorne's *The House of the Seven Gables*, in his scholarly writing life Matthiessen accepted the strictures that en-

abled him to produce a book of corporate power that his political life opposed" (350). But Cheyfitz's argument leaves unexplained *how* Matthiessen's "betrayal" is "like" Holgrave's marriage, though, as I hope to show, it does not seem accidental that the essay should leave open at this crucial moment just how marriage, sexual orientation, and property are linked, offering instead this rather tacit analogizing.

Cheyfitz's peroration raises related issues: "In the memory of his marriage with Russell Cheyney [*sic*] and his conscious political work, Matthiessen potentially liberates himself . . . as we imagine him writing a book in keeping with this memory and ourselves living lives in keeping with this imagined book, which we are now able to write" (358). So Cheyfitz concludes his call for a new American literary studies linked inextricably to renewed social action, and there can be little doubt that he means with the term "marriage" to valorize Matthiessen and Cheney's long-standing, mutual commitment. But in adopting this term, a great deal is lost as well—and not simply because Matthiessen in one of his letters remarks upon its inapplicability. The word *marriage* obscures precisely the space of difference that Cheyfitz seeks to recover, the space of the social in which only certain relationships are granted the privileges that the term *marriage* broadly connotes.

But this misnaming would seem well-intentioned were it not for the fact that "sexual orientation" as one of the categories for reconceiving difference drops out of the essay's concluding prescriptions for revitalizing scholarly work. The final paragraphs repeat the familiar litany "race, gender, and class" with no reference to sexual orientation as an equally necessary category for the revisioning of American (literary) history (see 356, also 357 and 358). In such a context, the comparison with Holgrave and Phoebe's marriage comes to look more like a subsuming of the categories of sexual orientation by those of heterosexual marriage or by the more "traditional" Marxian categories of property, social class, and political affiliation—precisely the strategy that Cheyfitz finds most problematic in Matthiessen's writing: "The movement [in Matthiessen's analyses] . . . is one not of revolution but of continual circumscription of Marxism by Christianity or of content by form or of history by literature, in which each of these pairs is a figure of the others" (351). We might add to this list the circumscription of homosexual difference by either heterosexual "marriage" or class affiliation, and to the degree that this addition is warranted we have uncovered as well the extent to which sexual orientation and the analytical—but not only analytical—costs of heteronormativity remain beyond the bounds of some of the most important revisionist work in American literary criticism.

In Paths Untrodden

I begin my investigation of the heteronormative contexts within which Matthiessen reads the Renaissance by turning first to the readings of Whitman in the Matthiessen-Cheney correspondence, partly as a means of recovering some of the frames within which some men seem to have lived and understood their sexual attraction to other men in the first third of the twentieth century.

Soon after Cheney and Matthiessen's serendipitous meeting aboard the ocean liner *Paris* in 1924, Whitman's poetry begins to circulate in their letters. Matthiessen writes to Cheney from London in September 1924: "I carried Walt Whitman in my pocket. That's another thing you've started me doing, reading Whitman. Not solely because it gives me an intellectual kick the way it did last year, but because I'm living it" (Hyde, 26). Whitman as the governing narrative for a new mode of living signals the important place the poet occupies when Matthiessen and Cheney represent their (literally) unfolding relationship to one another. In a letter from December of the same year, Cheney incorporates ten lines from "When I Heard at the Close of the Day," a poem that, significantly, first appeared in the "Calamus" cluster in the third edition of *Leaves of Grass*:

> This is the last letter I can write you—gosh, we've earned this time together. . . . But oh, god damn, my own own Dev, you are coming and I am happy—just plain fool happy.[13]
>
> The day when I rose at dawn from the bed of perfect health—refreshed, singing, and inhaling the ripe breath of autumn;
>
> . . . . .
>
> And when I thought how my dear friend—my lover was on his way coming—O then I was happy. . . .
>
> (Hyde, 63-64, ellipsis added)

The choice of this poem is significant because it is one of the few "Calamus" poems that stresses the private dimensions of a relationship between two men to the almost total exclusion of the public or political dimensions that balance, and sometimes dominate, the series as a whole. Indeed, the poem's opening two lines—"When I heard at the close of the day how my name had been received with plaudits in the capital, still it was not a happy night for me that followed; / And else, when I caroused, or when my plans were accomplished, still I was not happy"—establish an emphatic opposition that privileges isolation over public engagement. In this way, as I have argued elsewhere, the poem is anomalous with respect to the cluster as a whole, which steadfastly refuses to confine to some isolated space apart the multivalent consequences of relationships between men.

Instead, the "Calamus" poems insist that these bonds between men have significant public consequences for the state and the body politic. Written prior to the ascension of medicalized and pathologized models that explained these relationships as an "unnatural" version of privatized, monogamous heterosexuality, and drawing upon and significantly augmenting a tradition of erotic male friendship, Whitman's "Calamus" cluster insistently straddles the binary that places sexuality in the realm of the private and the family, outside the realm of the public and the political but nonetheless subject to its scrutiny and surveillance.

"Calamus" powerfully signals its difference from modern identitarian dispensations by alternately taking as its subject the love relationships between men and the political relationships between "states," and by insistently describing, conceptualizing, and allegorizing each in terms of the other: "States! / Were you looking to be held together by the lawyers? / By an agreement on a paper? Or by arms?"[14] There is a sense, then, in which Matthiessen and Cheney are quoting Whitman against the grain when they emphasize this private dimension to the exclusion of the public arenas within which the "Calamus" poems repeatedly insist these bonds between men reveal their fullest consequences.

Matthiessen and Cheney use Whitman's poetry to endorse the public/private split that they are living, despite the fact that this use seems at least partly incompatible with the poetry. Here, for example, is Matthiessen's description of the status of their relationship, from a letter dated 23 September 1924:

> Marriage! What a strange word to be applied to two men! Can't you hear the hell-hounds of society baying full pursuit behind us? But that's just the point. We are beyond society. We've said thank you very much, and stepped outside and closed the door. In the eyes of the unknowing world we are a talented artist of wealth and position and a promising young graduate student. In the eyes of the knowing world we would be pariahs, outlaws, degenerates. This is indeed the price we pay for the unforgivable sin of being born different from the great run of mankind.
>
> (Hyde, 29)

In these lines Matthiessen allows no possibility of a public dimension to a committed loving relationship with another man. "We are beyond society," he writes, and even when he does imagine a "knowing world," it is one in which his relationship with Cheney can play no part; those who "know" would treat them as "pariahs, outlaws, degenerates." The letter depicts not simply the absence of a sympathetic, "straight" public space but the absence of any sense of community whatsoever; Matthiessen and Cheney are utterly alone, together.

When later in the same letter Matthiessen adopts the term *marriage*, it is quite overtly appropriated as the only word available to convey such emotional intensity:

> *And so* we have a marriage that was never seen on land or sea and surely not in Tennyson's poet's dream! . . . Oh it is strange enough. It has no ring, and no vows, . . . and no children. . . . It has no three hundred and sixty-five breakfasts opposite each other at the same table; and yet it desires frequent companionship, devotion, and laughter. . . . How many, when reading this, would think so? Ah there's the mockery of it: those gates of society are of iron. And when you're outside, you've got to live in yourself alone, unless—o beatissimus—you are privileged to find another wanderer in the waste land. And perhaps even you think what I have written mawkish?
>
> (Hyde, 29-30, emphasis added)

So pervasive and potentially devouring is this governing sense of isolation that, as the final, more than rhetorical question suggests, Matthiessen cannot even assume that Cheney shares his understanding of their love. He is alone and isolated outside the borders of "civil" society even when/as partnered, though he hungers for like-minded readers ("How many, when reading this, would think so?"). Taken together, such moments in the letters, when placed beside the prophecies of Whitman's "Calamus," demonstrate the full measure of the difference I mean to elucidate:

> Yet comes one, a Manhattanese, and ever at parting,
>   kisses me lightly on the lips with robust love,
> And I, in the public room, or on the crossing of the
>   street, or on the ship's deck, kiss him in return;
> We observe the salute of American comrades, land
> and sea,
> We are those two natural and nonchalant persons.

("Calamus 19," *Leaves of Grass* [1860], 364)

At a crucial juncture in the relationship, Cheney came to believe that sexual expression could no longer have any place in his interactions with Matthiessen. The terms he uses to explain this decision are particularly valuable:

> What I have to say will make you at once more happy than anything I've ever said to you, because it will prove it is true I love you and you have entered into my life as no force ever has and not so much changed me as forced me definitely to choose my path. It will hurt you perhaps because in choosing that path I definitely say that after this the relation between us has got to be that of two regular [friendly] fellers, as far as actual physical connection goes. I'm sorry, Dev, sorry, if it is true, as I believe, that the base of our love is not physical but intense understanding of a mutual problem. . . . I have dodged the issue of my character this 10 or 15 years and my character has slowly deteriorated in will power. It is lack of will power that keeps me from reaching what I want in painting. That shows mostly in the two indulgences, in drink and sex. . . . Now I imagine you are saying I am a hell of a feller to act under the pressure of opinion in this way. Well look it here, it is the pressure of opinion that has showed up what I have glimpsed off and on, but dodged—that the only possible life is one, every part of which can be acknowledged. I have been nothing but a big bluff, and it's been a hell of a wrench to admit that and say I am through—that if there is something in my life I cannot acknowledge, out it comes. Well I have sneaked drinks long enough. I have sneaked into parks and toilets long enough, and I will do neither of them any more.

(Hyde, 79-81)[15]

The most noteworthy aspect of this passage emerges in the final lines, in which a virtual equivalence (grammatical and conceptual) opens out between drink and sex; "sneaking" drinks and "sneaking" sex occupy parallel positions, though neither seems more central than the other for conferring "identity." Cheney does not seem here to be confessing his identity "as" an alcoholic or "as" a sexaholic (to name one of the twentieth century's endlessly proliferating subaddictions)[16]—and certainly not as a homosexual. Rather, what seems to trouble him is the unavoidably furtive nature of both his homosexual encounters and his drinking—and it is important to note that within these configurations furtiveness seems to be understood as an essential, defining aspect of homosexual relations *as such*. Sex in private with Matthiessen and sex in public toilets with strangers are equally suspect because equally unspeakable in public, and so both must stop, and stopping is a matter of will power.[17]

A recently published journal suggests that Cheney was not alone in his desire both to rid himself of sexual appetite and to remove the "taint" of sexual relations from an ongoing relationship. C. C. Dasham, one of the central figures in *Jeb and Dash: A Diary of Gay Life, 1918-1945*, seems to have shared Cheney's wish, much to the consteration of his sometime lover and long-time friend, Jeb Alexander.[18] Here is an excerpt from Jeb's journal account of Dash's decision to abstain, dated 30 December 1927:

> We had a delightful evening in Dash's room, desultorily reading. . . . And then when I was ready to go, he announced that he was going to have another policy, a New Year's resolution, a "Touch Me Not" policy. I was stunned. . . . I bitterly protested such folly. I urged him and asked him, "Where did you get this insane notion that our love is 'unnatural'?" He shook his head and said, "Hereafter I am not going to do it." I took bitter leave of him. It is so unnecessary. Why should we deny love, destroy happiness, suppress all natural feelings and desire?

(Russell, 111)

Jeb's account of Dash's decision as a resolution for the New Year places it firmly in the context of the temperance-inflected rhetorics we have been considering, for what is a New Year's resolution but a self-directed charge to exercise control over one's weaknesses? The same wish recurs in Cheney's desire to cease to be what he calls "a big bluff" and to recover and, importantly, to (be able to) *publicize* a restored self—one, not by any means incidentally, freed from homoerotic indulgence.

While at least some of the tension between Jeb and Dash seems to revolve around issues of fidelity, alcohol also finds its way into the debate as these new calls for abstinence are negotiated. Here is a portion of Jeb's diary for 6 January 1928:

> Dasham was washing the windows, of all things, as if it were worth the labor and the risk of standing outside six stories above the street. He had to shout from outside to be heard. "I must make a declaration of independence for my own sake—even if it kills you, Jeb. Henceforth we must be friends, and nothing more." I stood inside the window arguing helplessly. He shouted through the glass, "You make too much of this, just the way you made too much of the incident with Tony Baretto." I cried out hoarsely, "You call that an 'incident'?" "What else would I call it? I merely drank so much gin that I felt give-inney and stayed the night."

I became so frenzied mentally that the back of my head felt as if it were going to burst. I tried to calm myself. "I can't help loving you. You have come to mean everything to me." He answered determinedly, "I cannot be bound in any such way any longer. I have previously relented, but this time is final. You will have to accept it or I'll give you up entirely."

(Russell, 111)

While at one level this entry merely chronicles Dash's excuse for a one-night stand and its grudging reception, Jeb's account also stages rather brilliantly what's at stake in the exchange: Dash is (dangerously) outside, visible but separated by a pane of glass (and so untouchable); Jeb is inside, looking out but preferring the obscuring dirt on the window, which assists his production of a safe, domestic space of intimacy within. Dash's declaration repeats terms we have heard from Cheney, particularly the notion that sexual and alcoholic indulgence are linked—are perhaps even versions of each other—and consequently one often leads to the other, as the "incident with Tony Baretto" demonstrates. The phrase "I have previously relented" suggests that even in the brief span of time between these two diary entries (about two weeks), Dash has been unable to keep his pledge of abstinence with regard to Jeb as well.

Against these models of closely paired sexual and alcoholic indulgence, one finds in Jeb and in Matthiessen a stronger, identity-based conception of homosexuality's etiology. This is expressed most compellingly by the language of the "natural," which is largely absent from the accounts by Cheney and Dash. Matthiessen puts the terms of his disagreement flatly: "Can you acknowledge the fact that you were born different from most people sexually and that consequently you react to different stimuli to any but a few who will understand? That to me is the essence of it: we were born as we are" (Hyde, 87).[19]

But Matthiessen also expresses a nascent conception of the closet, in which he replaces Cheney's call for abstinence and full public disclosure with a tempered argument that Cheney's desire for complete openness is hasty at best: "You say that the only possible life is one every part of which can be acknowledged. And of course I agree, my dearest Rat. But acknowledged to whom? To the entire world, or to your [close] and understanding friends?" (Hyde, 87). For Matthiessen there is candor on the one hand and unwise self-disclosure on the other, and he seems to know well, and to desire to school Cheney in, the important differences between the two.

It's possible, then, to see in these letters and diary passages documentary evidence of an aspect of the history of sexuality that Eve Kosofsky Sedgwick has theorized: "issues of modern homo/heterosexual definition are structured, not by the supersession of one model and the consequent withering away of another, but instead by the relations enabled by the unrationalized coexistence of different models during the times they do coexist"

(*Epistemology*, 47). These texts reveal a model of sexual orientation as identity that we would recognize as determinedly modern co-existing with older, temperance-inflected models of same-sex attraction, behavior, and "acts." Within this continuum of theories about homosexuality, Matthiessen and Jeb occupy the position distinguished by the strongest sense of homosexuality as inherent in one's nature, of its being a core aspect of self-identity. But in Dash's and Cheney's framing of these "same" issues, homosexuality is rather less consistently inherent, seeming instead to be a manifestation of a characterological disposition toward "obsessive" behavior; for them there is no identitarian coherence other than a tendency to overindulge, a failure of the will to abstain.[20] The homosexual may have been a "species" since the late nineteenth century, as Foucault argues, but into the opening decades of the twentieth century at least some men seem to have experienced their attraction to other men not as the defining aspect of their "identity," and less regularly as a component of that identity that they called their "sexuality," but rather as another in a range of behaviors they tended to adopt, and which they sometimes wished they were better able to manage.[21]

In this regard—though they could hardly have known it—Cheney and Dash may be the true heirs of Walt Whitman. For, as I have argued elsewhere, Whitman too laments in his diary his inability to control his fervent emotions, especially with regard to Peter Doyle (encoded in his diary alternately as "she" or numerically as "16" or i6.4" [because *P* is the sixteenth letter of the alphabet and *D* the fourth]): "*Remember where I am most weak*, & most lacking. Yet always preserve a kind spirit & demeanor to 16. But *Pursue Her No More*. A cool, gentle (less demonstrative) *more* UNIFORM DEMEANOR."[22] A passage such as this, which has often been read as reflecting Whitman's anxiety about his "homosexuality," should rather be seen as a phrenologically inflected appraisal of his emotional "makeup" in terms broader than those we in the last years of the twentieth century generally use to configure or contain sexuality and sexual orientation. Whitman laments his propensity for hyperbole and emotional excess in the language of tendencies and general "demeanor" that is phrenology's essential diction, a translation of the shape of the skull into a pattern of correlative emotional and behavioral predispositions. In fact, language itself falls under the sway of these predispositions, for Whitman seeks to control not just his emotional and affective behavior but also his linguistic demeanor, writing later in the same notebook entry: "SAY little—make no explanations—*give no confidences*—never attempt puns, or plays upon words, or utter sarcastic comments, or (under ordinary circumstances) hold any discussions or arguments" (Holloway, 481). Whitman's call here for linguistic temperance mirrors his call for sexual/emotional temperance and includes, like Cheney's, an aversion toward and anxiety about public display—in Whitman's terms, a desire for a "(less demonstrative) . . . DEMEANOR."

We have, then, a spectrum of positions that eventually more or less coalesce into our late-twentieth-century understandings of sexual identity. For Cheney, and it seems for Dash, there is a connection between emotional and behavioral temperance, a desire to control the linked predilections toward alcoholic and sexual indulgence that recapitulates Whitman's formulations. But, quite tellingly, there seems to be no corresponding sense of the public sphere as the site for the broadest, the most politically salient consequences of these ostensibly private relationships. Cheney seems to have inherited only a negative sense of the public sphere; it is his shame at the unacknowledgeable nature of homosexuality—the impossibility of owning up to such desires and actions in public—that instigates his shift toward a "Whitmanian" temperamental balance. Matthiessen and Jeb Alexander, on the other hand, both project a sense of homosexuality as inherent in their nature, but their quasi-identitarian position brings with it a more than nascent awareness of the closet. This has important consequences, as we shall see, for Matthiessen's work as a literary scholar, not least in his treatment of Whitman in the pages of ***American Renaissance***.

For Matthiessen and Cheney, though they conceptualize their sexual attraction to men and to each other differently, Whitman remains a crucial figure throughout their correspondence. This is well demonstrated by Matthiessen's reply of 24 September 1924, after Cheney has confessed that he is "swimming" in ale and has spent the previous night cruising "the likely street" rather than "home in my bed going to sleep with my soul at peace and one with you, as I have every night before" (Hyde, 28). Matthiessen replies:

> You've got a battle on your hands. But you've got someone who is going to fight it with you. It comes down to Goethe: the secret of strength lying in the renunciation of the things that destroy the single harmony. Well, you can't have both serenity and 3 1/2 bottles of stout!
>
> We've agreed with Whitman all right that:
>
> "And if the body does not do
>   fully as much as the soul?
> And if the body were not the
>   soul, what is the soul?"
>
> But we're also agreed that there are other ways of using the body than by making it carry around a few quarts of angry liquor every day.
>
> "Was it doubted that those who
>   corrupt their own bodies
> conceal themselves?
> and if those who defile the
>   living are as they who
> defile the dead?"
> (Hyde, 31-32)

This is a remarkable excerpt not simply for its (barely) euphemistic reference to sexual pleasure ("other ways of using the body"), which Matthiessen opposes to Cheney's problem drinking, but also for the way the reference to Whitman stages consensus ("we've agreed with Whitman") and so softens the delicate situation in which the younger

Matthiessen has been called upon to adjudicate Cheney's guilt. Whitman functions as the authority Matthiessen marshals in the service of his argument in favor of the healthy possibilities of men loving men, while he deploys lines from Whitman's "I Sing the Body Electric" to bolster Cheney in his fight against alcohol.

When Matthiessen gently but explicitly rejects Cheney's call for sexual abstinence, he again quotes "Body Electric":

> You say that our love is not based on the physical, but on our mutual understanding, and sympathy, and tenderness. And of course that is right. But we both have bodies: "if the body is not the soul, what then is the soul?" . . . Perhaps just living as [intimate friends] each random thought could be shared just as freely as it has been during our life together so far. Perhaps, on the other hand, it would mean that there would no longer be the same abundant joyous *lack of restraint*, and that the dim corners of our hearts where physical desires lurked would no longer be wholly open to each other.
>
> (Hyde, 86-87, emphasis added)

Matthiessen's tender rebuttal here detaches sexual activity from either alcohol or temperance. In part this may demonstrate the generational discontinuity that underlies Matthiessen's and Cheney's relationship, the difference in their ages (Matthiessen was born in 1902, Cheny in 1881) that bespeaks as well the different positions they occupy in relation to nineteenth- and twentieth-century models of homosexual orientation and sexuality more generally: a lived example with textual evidence of the coexistence of models that Sedgwick has remarked. More than simply disconnecting sexuality from temperance, Matthiessen links it to a "joyous lack of restraint," thereby turning Cheney's categories on their heads. This lack of restraint may be the mark of "sexuality" having been split off into a separate category from other varieties of sensory and sensual experience—like drinking, say, to which sex can still be related (one can get drunk and find oneself in bed with Tony Baretto), but the relationship between alcoholic indulgence and sexual indulgence is now circumstantial rather than "essential."

Matthiessen also significantly reverses Cheney's perspective by suggesting that abstinence would have a deleterious effect on the honesty and emotional fidelity that underwrite their relationship: "the dim corners of our hearts where physical desires lurked would no longer be wholly open to each other." This language challenges not only Cheney's wish to abstain by no longer "sneaking into toilets" but also his sense that any sexual relation that cannot be publicly acknowledged must be abandoned. From Matthiessen's perspective, when sexual desire "lurks," it is because it is being squelched, because the open expression of sexual love in private—a precious, intimate intemperance—is being sacrificed. Matthiessen plainly believes that such a sacrifice is too great.

But the most significant aspect of Matthiessen's counterargument is the recurring, dual use of Whitman. Across these examples, Whitman becomes the primary proponent for both bodily restraint *and* bodily indulgence—an advocate for temperance when he claims the sanctity of the body and for open sexual expression when he insists upon the equal validity of the claims of the body and the soul. One can find only the barest remnants of this healthy, continent Whitman in the pages of *American Renaissance*. Matthiessen's private version of Whitman has no presence in the public text on the Renaissance, and the Whitman who inhabits those pages barely resembles the Whitman Matthiessen and Cheney privately exchange. To recognize this discrepancy is to restore to our appraisal of Matthiessen's best-known critical work a fuller view of the contexts within which it was produced, to inquire not simply into the American literary history that Matthiessen made but into the institutional and cultural histories that made Matthiessen. This requires that, following Matthiessen, we read Whitman together with Thoreau; in doing so, we find that Matthiessen's labeling Whitman "pathological" is only the most familiar element in a larger, emblematic network of similar inscriptions.

Do I Contradict Myself?

"Like Whitman," Matthiessen writes in the chapter of *American Renaissance* called "The Organic Principle," "Thoreau generally used the language of biology, for both held that the poet 'generates poems,' though Thoreau added, as Whitman would not have, that 'by continence he rises to creation on a higher level'" (134). Placing this assessment beside other comparisons of Thoreau and Whitman that, taken together, constitute a more significant dimension of *American Renaissance* than is generally recognized, an undertone of distaste for Whitman's "incontinence" begins to make itself heard. For example, Matthiessen presents this line of argument that subtly emphasizes Whitman's incontinence when he discusses Thoreau's emerging theories of poetry:

> In adopting the tenet that poetry consists in knowing the quality of a thing, [Thoreau] had realized by his early thirties that such knowledge could be arrived at only through the slowest unconscious process, for "at first blush a man is not capable of reporting truth; he must be drenched and saturated with it first. What was *enthusiasm* in the young man must become *temperament* in the mature man." (155)

The broad outlines of Matthiessen's argument have already begun to take shape in these two excerpts, as Thoreau comes to resemble a more mature, or more fully tempered and temperate, version of Whitman.[23]

Across a variety of contexts in *American Renaissance*, it is sometimes difficult to distinguish Whitman from Thoreau, as in these statements in which Matthiessen characterizes the sources of the best poetry the two men produced. Here is Matthiessen on Thoreau's central achievement:

> [B]y following to its uncompromising conclusion his belief that great art can grow from the center of the

simplest life, [Thoreau] was able to be universal. He had understood that in the act of expression a man's whole being, and his natural and social background as well, function organically together. (175)

In aligning "great art" and a certain unconventional simplicity, Matthiessen's explanation of Thoreau's success parallels his account of Whitman's:

> [T]he source of [Whitman's] real poetry was not in the grandiose or the orotund but in the common and humble. . . . [T]he fact is that even though Whitman did not want to be personal, but to write poems "with reference to ensemble," to make his voice that of the general bard of democracy, the evidence of the poems themselves shows that he was at his best, not when he was being sweeping, but when contemplating with delicacy and tenderness some object near at hand. (546-47)

The last phrase, "some object near at hand," emphasizes how Whitman made the quotidian the stuff of "his best" poetry, though we might also note that in rejecting "the general bard of democracy" for the poet who "contemplat[es] with delicacy and tenderness," Matthiessen's "best" Whitman closely approximates his private Whitman. Nevertheless, in Matthiessen's terms Thoreau and Whitman seem to have succeeded at the same project of expanding the boundaries of American literary expression.

The important role of the commonplace is the starting point of the passage in Matthiessen's discussion of Whitman most significant for our purposes:

> The depth and force of the imagination that could bridge the void by making the specific richly symbolic of the universal had not yet shown itself [in earlier American poetry]. Whitman's success in doing this, in such poems of his as did justice to both the parts and the whole, depended on the emotional attitude articulated near the opening of "Song of Myself." (534-35)

Here the rhetoric of equilibrium familiar from passages in Matthiessen's letters recurs: Whitman is at his best when he does "justice to both the parts and the whole." At this point Matthiessen quotes from "Song of Myself" the familiar account of the encounter that yields limitless insight for Whitman's speaker and presents for Matthiessen the "emotional attitude" upon which so much depends:

> I believe in you my soul, the other I am must not abase itself
>   to you,
> And you must not be abased to the other.
>   . . . . .
>
> I mind how once we lay such a transparent summer morning,
> How you settled your head athwart my hips and gently turn'd over
>   upon me,
> And parted the shirt from my bosom-bone, and plunged your
>   tongue to my bare-stript heart,
> And reach'd till you felt my beard, and reach'd till

you held
     my feet.

Swiftly arose and spread around me the peace and
knowledge that
     pass all the argument of the earth,
And I know that the hand of God is the promise of
my own,
And I know that the spirit of God is the brother of my
own,
And that all the men ever born are also my brothers,
and the
     women my sisters and lovers . . .

    (quoted from Matthiessen, *American Renaissance*,
                  535)

Matthiessen's extended comment on this passage begins:

> That vision is the fullest expression of the sources from
> which Whitman's poetry rose, and consequently pro-
> vides a central problem in appreciation. Readers with a
> distaste for loosely defined mysticism have plenty of
> grounds for objection in the way the poet's belief in di-
> vine inspiration is clothed in imagery that obscures all
> distinctions between the body and soul by portraying
> the soul as merely the sexual agent. (535)

Matthiessen's exegesis works adversarially along a number of different axes. While in the introductory paragraph
it seemed we would be looking in these passages to certify
the terms of "Whitman's success," in the explication that
follows we are facing instead an immediate and "central
problem in appreciation." Similarly, while Matthiessen announces his critique as proceeding from "a distaste for
loosely defined mysticism," his reading focuses upon the
physical and the material. For example, while the poetry
chronicles undressing ("And parted the shirt from my
bosom-bone"), Matthiessen describes it as *clothed* in imagery." Similarly, while the poetry depicts a state in which
distinctions between the body and soul, the physical and
the spiritual, seem to break down, Matthiessen registers
his resistance rather precisely in a language of barriers that
recalls his earlier criticisms of imbalance and incontinence; Whitman's imagery "obscures all distinctions between the body and soul." And while it is not by any
means certain that the "active" figure in the passage de-
finitively represents "the soul," that is the way Matthiessen
interprets it, chafing at the ramifications of the equation
and chastising Whitman for "portraying the soul as *merely*
the sexual agent" (emphasis added). This is in itself somewhat incongruous, given that the entire poetic excerpt *as
Matthiessen quotes it* opens out from the familiar Whitmanian assertion of equivalence and interdependence: "I believe in you my soul, the other I am must not abase itself
to you, / And you must not be abased to the other." This
last is also the Whitmanian equivalence that Matthiessen
celebrates in the letters to Cheney, and it is implicit in his
argument for continuing the free exchange of sexual love
between them.

Where Whitman collapses barriers and distinctions, Matthiessen would reinstate them, and this overarching divergence emerges vividly as the critique proceeds:

Moreover, in the passivity of the poet's body there is a
quality vaguely pathological and homosexual. This is
in keeping with the regressive, infantile fluidity, imaginatively polyperverse, which breaks down all mature
barriers, a little further on in "Song of Myself," to declare that he is "maternal as well as paternal, a child as
well as a man." (535)[24]

This is a (newly) shocking passage when we come to it
from the Matthiessen-Cheney correspondence, for these
lines seem more likely to have been written by Cheney
than by Matthiessen, who in his letters spurs Cheney on to
continued sexual exploration, arguing for a productive,
privileged fluidity over rigid "barriers." The following passage from another relevant letter to Cheney begins with a
line we have already considered:

> That to me is the essence of it: we were born as we
> are. I am no longer the least ashamed of it. What is
> there to be ashamed of? It simply reveals the fact that
> sex is not mathematical and clear-cut, something to be
> separated definitively into male and female; but that
> just as there are energetic active women and sensitive
> delicate men, so also there are women who appear to
> be feminine but have a male sex element, and men,
> like us, who appear to be masculine but have a female
> sex element. Ashamed of it? . . . No, accept it, just the
> way you accept the fact that you have two legs.

                         (Hyde, 87)

But this same letter also demonstrates Matthiessen's keen
awareness of the secrecy that must accompany such self-
acceptance:

> Tell it? Well that's difficult. For it is an anomaly the
> world as a whole does not understand, and if you pro-
> claim it from the house tops you will receive a great
> deal of uncomprehending opprobrium, and will do no
> good. But to your friends? By all means.

                         (Hyde, 87)

So here are rather precisely defined the limits of public acknowledgment, along with a possible explanation for the
public "opprobrium" Matthiessen directs against a Whitman who sounded his "barbaric yawp over the roofs of the
world." These lines trade the fluidity-of-gender model for
one that restores sharply defined boundaries between, presumably, female "passivity" and male potency, regression
and full maturity—and also between "the world as a
whole" and "friends."[25] Is crossing these boundaries the
gaff or "yawp" for which Whitman is being punished in
this reading?

David Bergman has suggested that Matthiessen's description of Whitman's behavior as "pathological" merely reflects his straightforward attempt to base his assertions in
American Renaissance "on the best medical and psychoanalytic theories of his time in an attempt to remain objective" (68). But to argue in this way is to read as if these
"medical and psychoanalytic theories" stand somehow
outside the range of Matthiessen's own cultural critique,
as though *we* should treat such formulations as "objec-

tive," or even correct, because Matthiessen seems to have done so. To do that would be to reproduce in reverse the tactical mistake that stands behind Cheyfitz's denunciation of Matthiessen's "betrayal." For the contradictions and tensions of these readings across Matthiessen's writings demonstrate the necessity of seeing an individual's perspective as inextricably—but unpredictably—linked to that of his culture, and thereby to witness a text (including the "text" and texture of the life) within frames larger than those of personal culpability (Cheyfitz) or heroism (Bergman).[26] This is to say that the distinctions between pathology and criticism cannot be so easily described. These (in)distinctions—the social pathologies that also undoubtedly *enable* Matthiessen's power and influence as a critic—leave marks in his best-known work, including the already remarked absence of the "Calamus" poems.[27] How can one decide between Matthiessen's "best" work as a critic and the silences and misperceptions that make themselves known not only as absences but also as integral parts of arguments seminal to American literary criticism?

Within the psychoanalytically inflected parameters of *American Renaissance*, Whitman is developmentally delayed, and once more Matthiessen describes the situation as the difference between "fluidity" and "barriers"; later Matthiessen notes Whitman's "ability to live spontaneously on primitive levels" (535). The primary interpretive paradigm centers upon the concept of continence, which characterizes as well the description of Whitman's poetry as possessing a "regressive, infantile fluidity . . . which breaks down all mature barriers" (535). Insofar as Whitman "respond[s] to every stimulus of his time" (547 n. 9), he demonstrates again the incontinence that Thoreau, in Matthiessen's view, seems to have been more successful in avoiding. We might conceive this view of Whitman's incontinence as an example of the contradictions put into place by the impossibility of Matthiessen's conjoining the public and the private in the writing of his own life—contradictions put into place, that is to say, by the regimes of knowing (American literature) from within the closet. Indeed, the "barriers" that Matthiessen insists Whitman constantly oversteps might well be seen as those in this gay critic's own life.

Nevertheless, my argument is not simply that Whitman is disciplined in *American Renaissance* for his public, promiscuous declarations of "homosexuality," his "proclaiming it from the house tops." Rather, Matthiessen's tome enacts a substitution of Thoreau for Whitman—replacing the poet who in the first edition of *Leaves of Grass* proclaimed the equivalence of the demands of the body and the soul with a writer who, Matthiessen insists, demonstrated a more coherent and controlled relation to these demands.[28] The substitution is the most significant interpretive crux traceable to the public/private split and to the homophobic contexts that constrain the presentation of these subjects in *American Renaissance*. In a sentence that records its own impetus, Matthiessen, at a critical point in enacting the substitution, writes that one important dimension of Thoreau's early compositions "adum-

brates *what is going to be Thoreau's particular forte*, his grasp of the close correspondence, the organic harmony between body and spirit" (84, emphasis added). The emphasized words underscore the strenuous nature of Matthiessen's interpretation insofar as he "is going to" depict Thoreau as capable of balancing the demands of body and soul better than Whitman.

But making Thoreau do the work of Whitman comes at the expense of a great deal of striking textual evidence that Matthiessen needs to ignore just as he needs to ignore "Calamus"—the verb "need" here marking the interfusion of "public" demands and "private" propensities, and, at the last, the impossibility of distinguishing one from the other. In an insightful article whose title—"Scatology and Eschatology"—confirms its relevance, Michael West discusses what he calls Thoreau's "profound ambivalence toward the body and toward those excremental processes that he explicitly undertakes to defend in 'Higher Laws.'" Tellingly, West proposes Whitman as the counter-example:

> Unlike Whitman, whose phrenological ardor begat hymns to the body electric, Thoreau could not project a convincing vision of "the bowels sweet and clean." Indeed when he first visited Whitman in Brooklyn, nothing bothered him more than being received in Walt's bedroom while the chamber pot was still clearly visible beneath the bed—a fact that Thoreau's lengthy account of their meeting stresses with unusual exasperation.[29]

West finds the question of "[h]ow to preserve an immanent divinity from pollution" a "recurring preoccupation in *Walden* and [Thoreau's] journals" (1047).[30] Through these "preoccupations," I contend, we gain some sense of the profoundly contingent nature of Matthiessen's representations in *American Renaissance*. For Matthiessen endeavors to ward off Whitman by deploying Thoreau, without apparently having seen what Henry Abelove has recently made legible: a queer sensibility and a queer nationality in Thoreau that may well get to the heart of what Matthiessen the Christian Socialist sought to hold most dear.[31]

Of course Matthiessen would not have been the first to miss these dimensions of Thoreau, for, as Abelove notes, he inherited (as have we all) a Thoreau made safe for heterosexuality through a process of reading as "reclamation," which culminated in Ralph Waldo Emerson's eulogy for Thoreau. The normative Thoreau that emerged from this process within eight years of the publication of *Walden* is a lone rebel, chaste but heterosexually inclined. Abelove unwrites Emerson's "domestication" (19) by reminding us of both the young male visitors received at Walden and the importantly collective goals of a book whose epigraph announces its author's desire "to wake [his] neighbors up" (1).

Does Matthiessen the Christian Socialist hear a queer collectivism in Thoreau that accounts for this wishful reading or misreading? There is not room here to explore this possibility fully, though it is relevant to note that in the speech he made to open the Salzburg Seminar in July 1947, Matthiessen refers to an archetypal American "mingling" that might be construed as distantly related to Thoreau's various collective commitments.[32] But with regard to Matthiessen's own queer connection to Russell Cheney, what most closely links Matthiessen and Thoreau may be a critical tradition that has usually refused to see the queer alignments in their lives, preferring instead the solitary queer utterly unimplicated in what Abelove calls "the grand narrative of connubiality, the narrative which . . . still lives most of us now" (19).[33] Among the manifold consequences of this failure of cultural imagination to acknowledge queer alternatives is a Defense of Marriage Act.

The substitution of Thoreau for Whitman preserves Whitman for Cheney and Matthiessen themselves, even as the exclusion of "Calamus" from *American Renaissance* keeps those poems safe from public scrutiny. Whitman serves as a central feature of this couple's "unknown wealth, untold wealth of love," set apart in a closet built for two. The pathologizing of Walt Whitman in *American Renaissance* is itself a defense of queer marriage—Cheney's and Matthiessen's.

It is appropriate, then, to conclude with one of the oddest, yet most telling, of Matthiessen's gestures in his substitution of Thoreau for Whitman. It occurs near the end of a largely appreciative summary of the unpretentious letters exchanged between Whitman and his longtime "boyfriend" (as Whitman called him) Peter Doyle, although it is important to note that Matthiessen treats these letters as virtual prose equivalents of the public/published *Drum-Taps*. Any sense of what Matthiessen might have read as the private nature of the relationship between Doyle and Whitman (a sense that might have suggested itself simply through the parallels with Matthiessen's own rich epistolary relation with Cheney) is omitted from the public text articulating the Renaissance. These letters possess what Matthiessen calls "the kind of flow that you feel here":

> I see in my mind the hired men and master
>   dropping the implements of their labor
>   in the field and wending their way with a
>   sober satisfaction toward the house;
> I see the well-sweep rise and fall;
> I see the preparatory ablutions and the table laden
>   with the smoking
>   meal.

Yet this is not [Matthiessen continues] from the catalogues of [Whitman's] "Salut au Monde," but is Thoreau's prose account—which I have arranged as free verse—of what had occurred to him when, during one of his rambles, he heard "a farmer's horn calling his hands in from the field to an early tea." Such dilating rhythm, suitable for the affirmation of the variety and plenitude of existence, was not limited to Whitman, but was the common property of the era which believed that, by breaking through the conventional restrictions of art, the writer could be invigorated by the elemental force of nature, "Ablutions" might give the passage away as not being Whitman's, since it is a latinate word used accurately; and yet this word also marks how hard it was, even for a man as close to the soil as

Thoreau, to throw off literary formalism and gain full realistic grasp of the commonest acts in the words that people really used for them. (583)

The rhetoric in this excerpt turns once again on the trope of boundaries, implicitly in the transposition of Thoreau's prose into Whitman's prosody, and explicitly in what Matthiessen celebrates as a "dilating rhythm" that marks a "breaking through" of "the conventional restrictions of art"—the Wordsworthian plainness of a man speaking to men.

Matthiessen's appreciation for Thoreau's "realistic grasp of the commonest acts" is disrupted, however, by the word "ablutions," which we might see as functioning as a placeholder for the absent word "Calamus" and as signaling many of the same tensions and inconsistencies. In part this is because "ablutions," like "Calamus," denominates a particularly potent intersection of the spiritual and the embodied, the individual and the institutional. "Ablutions" is a word that links not only Whitman to Thoreau but Matthiessen complexly to both, and it epitomizes and reiterates—at the sites of purity, public exhibition, private conscience, confession, and finally, perhaps, salvation—what much of the present discussion of *American Renaissance* also demonstrates.[34] For in the end Matthiessen's difficulty with Whitman is largely the same as Thoreau's: Whitman's insufficient delicacy, his inadequate sense of what should be made visible and how and when it should be displayed—his chamber-pot in full view. These are the discriminations and ultimately the deformations of what will become, ever more securely in Matthiessen's time, the closet.

Matthiessen praises a common language without "ablutions" and notes Thoreau's difficulty in keeping the "ablutions" out of the poetry, but he virtually simultaneously approves Thoreau's ability to use "ablutions" properly, even as elsewhere he favors Thoreau's continence over Whitman's enthusiasm, Thoreau's discretion over Whitman's exhibitionism. Matthiessen wants washed hands (here registered in "a latinate word used accurately"), even as he admires their rough-hewn calluses, their implication in "the elemental force of nature." Finally, then, these multiple fractures hint at another discovery: the impossibility of finding a place at the table—not only the dining table but also the writing table—cleansed of the "soils" that were the reason one washed, or in the case of Matthiessen, the reason one sat down to write in the first place.

Notes

1. Thanks to Henry Abelove, Michèle Aina Barale, Jack Cameron, Margreta de Grazia, Betsy Erkkila, Teresa Goddu, Mary Loeffelholz, Jeffrey Masten, Meredith McGill, Patrick O'Malley, Andrew Parker, and Lynn Wardley for their comments on earlier drafts, and to Lee Edelman, Paul Morrison, and the audience at Harvard's CLCS Lesbian and Gay Studies seminar.

2. I discuss below a number of essays that variously address aspects of Matthiessen's homosexuality; see

also Giles B. Gunn, *F. O. Matthiessen: The Critical Achievement* (Seattle: Univ. of Washington Press, 1975); Kenneth Lynn, "F. O. Matthiessen," *American Scholar* 46 (winter 1976): 86-93; Harry Levin, "The Private Life of F. O. Matthiessen," review of *Rat and The Devil: Journal Letters of F. O. Matthiessen and Russell Cheney,* ed. Louis Hyde, *New York Review of Books,* 20 July 1978, 42-46; George Abbott White, "'Have I Any Right in a Community That Would So Utterly Disapprove of Me If It Knew the Facts?'" *Harvard Magazine,* September-October 1978, 58-62; Paul Delany, "Varieties of Liberal Experience," review of *Rat and The Devil, Times Literary Supplement,* 5 December 1980, 1391-92; Frederick C. Stern, *F. O. Matthiessen: Christian Socialist as Critic* (Chapel Hill: Univ. of North Carolina Press, 1981); William E. Cain, *F. O. Matthiessen and the Politics of Criticism* (Madison: Univ. of Wisconsin Press, 1988); James W. Tuttleton, "Politics and Art in the Criticism of F. O. Matthiessen," *The New Criterion,* June 1989, 4-13; Michael Cadden, "Engendering F. O. M.: The Private Life of *American Renaissance,*" in *Engendering Men: The Question of Male Feminist Criticism,* ed. Joseph A. Boone and Michael Cadden (New York: Routledge, 1990), 26—35; and Robert J. Corber, *Homosexuality in Cold War America: Resistance and the Crisis of Masculinity* (Durham, N.C.: Duke Univ. Press, 1997).

3. Leo Marx, "F. O. Matthiessen" [including "The Teacher," originally published in the *Monthly Review* of October 1950, and "'Double Consciousness' and the Cultural Politics of F. O. Matthiessen"], in *The Pilot and the Passenger: Essays on Literature, Technology, and Culture in the United States* (New York: Oxford Univ. Press, 1988), 231-60. Page references for specific quotations from this essay will be cited in the text.

4. Eve Kosofsky Sedgwick, *Epistemology of the Closet* (Berkeley and Los Angeles: Univ. of California Press, 1991), 1-2. Subsequent references will be cited in the text as *Epistemology.*

5. One sees a similar tendency in Jonathan Arac's "F. O. Matthiessen and American Studies: Authorizing a Renaissance," in *Critical Genealogies: Historical Situations for Postmodern Literary Studies* (New York: Columbia Univ. Press, 1987), 157-75. Arac remarks upon the embodied and erotic metaphoricity that characterizes Matthiessen's connection to Whitman in a letter to Cheney, and contrasts this with the scholarly intensity of his appraisal of Whitman in *American Renaissance.* But Arac attributes these shifts to "a long process of transformative discipline . . . , [t]he modern critical practice Leavis called the 'discipline of letters'" (159), rather than considering how the discipline of heteronormativity might also demand the suppression of certain modes of response in public criticism. Cadden also notes "the desexualization of Matthiessen that Arac's essay . . . eventually effects" ("Engendering F. O. M.," 28).

6. Andrew Parker, "Unthinking Sex: Marx, Engels and the Scene of Writing," in *Fear of a Queer Planet: Queer Politics and Social Theory,* ed. Michael Warner (Minneapolis: Univ. of Minnesota Press, 1993), 21.

7. F. O. Matthiessen, *American Renaissance: Art and Expression in the Age of Emerson and Whitman* (1941; reprint, New York: Oxford Univ. Press, 1968), vii. Further references will be cited parenthetically.

8. Eric Cheyfitz, "Matthiessen's *American Renaissance*: Circumscribing the Revolution," *American Quarterly* 41 (June 1989): 349; further references will be cited parenthetically in the text.

9. For example, Barrett Wendell, one of the founders of Harvard's History and Literature program, where Matthiessen later served as Tutorial Board chair, in *A Literary History of America* (New York: Scribner's, 1900) brings together Emerson, Thoreau, and Hawthorne in a section on "The Renaissance of New England." Hermann [*sic*] Melville is relegated to a single sentence (229), and Whitman appears in a final section reserved for "The Rest of the Story."

10. *Rat and The Devil: Journal Letters of F. O. Matthiessen and Russell Cheney,* ed. Louis Hyde (Boston: Alyson Publications, 1988), 200. Further references to these letters will be cited in the text as Hyde.

11. George Chauncey, in *Gay New York: Gender, Urban Culture, and the Making of the Gay Male World, 1890-1940* (New York: Basic Books, 1994), especially chap. 12, sees the period through 1933 as one of relatively easy mixing between gays and straights in urban public spaces. But Marc Stein suggests that *Gay New York* may overstate "the degree of acceptance of or tolerance for gay men in New York during this period" (review in *American Historical Association Committee on Lesbian and Gay History Newsletter* [1994]: 13). Jeb Alexander's D.C. diaries (discussed at length below) record many uncomfortable interactions between gay men and straight men or straight couples; see *Jeb and Dash: A Diary of Gay Life 1918-1945,* ed. Ina Russell (Boston: Faber and Faber, 1994), 76, 82, 88; subsequent references will be cited in the text as Russell.

12. In a letter from 1925, Cheney describes a friend's advice about the closet: "[He] insists very urgently that it is not possible or desirable for either of us to tell the whole situation to more than two or three of our [closest friends], that their heads may agree but that their profound physical antagonism to the idea will make it impossible for them to see us together" (Hyde, 130). We might notice that "sympathetic" friends draw the line at the point where homosociality and homosexuality's mutual misrecognitions seem at once most coherent and least discernible: the body. This is a central tension in Matthiessen's reading of Whitman in *American Renaissance.* As this passage makes clear, however, such misrecognitions ("their

. . . antagonism to the *idea*") are at least as much a product of this culture's imaginary as of any "actual" public exhibition.

13. Matthiessen's nickname was "Devil."

14. Walt Whitman, "Calamus 5," *Leaves of Grass* (Boston: Thayer and Eldridge, 1860; reprint, Ithaca, N.Y.: Cornell Univ. Press, 1984), 349. For a more complete discussion, see my "'The Evangel-Poem of Comrades and of Love': Revising Whitman's Republicanism," *American Transcendental Quarterly* 4 (September 1990): 201-18, and my epilogue to *Breaking Bounds: Whitman and American Cultural Studies*, ed. Betsy Erkkila and Jay Grossman (New York: Oxford Univ. Press, 1996). For a contrasting view, see Michael Lynch, "'Here is Adhesiveness': From Friendship to Homosexuality," *Victorian Studies* 29 (autumn 1985): 67-96.

15. Square brackets in passages from the Matthiessen-Cheney correspondence appear in the Hyde edition.

16. See Eve Kosofsky Sedgwick, "Epidemics of the Will," in *Tendencies* (Durham, N.C.: Duke Univ. Press, 1993), 130-42.

17. Though we read many of the same texts, my account of Matthiessen differs markedly from David Bergman's in "F. O. Matthiessen: The Critic as Homosexual," *Raritan* 10 (spring 1990): 62-82; reprinted in Bergman's *Gaiety Transfigured: Gay Self-Representation in American Literature* (Madison: Univ. of Wisconsin Press, 1991). While my analysis also originates in certain identifications within twentieth-century homosexuality (broadly construed), I think it is crucial, despite the relative proximity of fifty years, to be attentive to the differences of particular rhetorics. How much precision of historical analysis is lost, for example, in Bergman's labeling himself, Matthiessen, and Melville "gay" (71-72, 75)? On the question of anachronism, see James Creech, *Closet Writing/Gay Reading: The Case of Melville's "Pierre"*; (Chicago: Univ. of Chicago Press, 1993), especially chap. 3.

18. The names are pseudonymous.

19. When Cheney does use a language of the natural, it seems not to possess the same identity-conferring logic. Here is Cheney's account of his discussion with a close friend (another part of this letter is excerpted in note 11): "I plunged in with the whole thing. He gets it absolutely. We talked till 4:30. His sympathy, his intuition, his clear reason all give him the whole situation. . . . Since I first told him the main fact of my nature at Cragmor—[he] says he had gradually made up his mind that granted I was that way, he thought it a mistake for me to be living in denial of it!! Atrophy of a part of my nature—" (Hyde, 130, my bracketed interpolation). In this excerpt "my nature" vies for definitional control with other phrases that may or may not be synonymous: "the whole thing," "the whole situation," and "it."

Clearly this "coming out"—to use an anachronistic term—is a multifaceted task, and since Cheney has already told the "main fact" sometime in the past, the new conversation must be at least in part about his new physical relation with Matthiessen. Thus the shift toward the rhetoric of the "natural" functions as shorthand for the other side of the temperance coin; now the issue is not overindulgence but its opposite, "Atrophy of a part of my nature." Once again the characterological tendency seems separate and separable rather than "inherent" or identitarian in the way Matthiessen uses it when he insists "we were born as we are."

20. Even Jeb is prone to this framing of the issue: "What an innocent boy I was, before this accursed obsession took hold of me and clouded my life" (Russell, 159); the "obsession" seems to be both his sexual desire for men generally and his specific desire for Dash.

21. Both Chauncey (*Gay New York*, 12 ff.) and David Halperin ("One Hundred Years of Homosexuality," in *One Hundred Years of Homosexuality and Other Essays on Greek Love* [New York: Routledge, 1990], 17) describe early-twentieth-century men who seem not to have recognized themselves in the binarized choice between homosexual or heterosexual.

22. Quoted in Emory Holloway, "Walt Whitman's Love Affairs," in *The Dial*, November 1920, 481; subsequent references will be cited in the text as Holloway. See also Grossman, "'The Evangel-Poem,'" 206.

23. For this reason I contest Bergman's claim that for Matthiessen, "it is Whitman, the poet, who is the model writer. . . . What fascinates Matthiessen about Whitman is that though Whitman was no theorist, he nevertheless developed a process of writing that exemplifies for Matthiessen the ideal procedures for an American writer to achieve organic form" (75-76). As my argument below will demonstrate, Matthiessen's "feelings" about Whitman (to the extent that *American Renaissance* can be properly read as a transcription of these) are more complicated than Bergman's formulation allows.

24. Michael Moon's *Disseminating Whitman: Revision and Corporeality in "Leaves of Grass"*; (Cambridge: Harvard Univ. Press, 1991) is the best account of the poetics and politics of fluidity in *Leaves of Grass*.

25. Matthiessen here adopts another late-nineteenth-century model for understanding same-sex desire-the gender inversion or "wrong soul in the wrong body" model-as a means of liberating Cheney from his shame, although this model, as many theorists have noted, prescribes proper gender behavior and so endorses gender stereotypes. This specific instance serves to remind us that the "conservative" or "radical" political potential of any model may be context specific.

26. According to Bergman. "Matthiessen makes *American Renaissance* not only a celebration of homosexuality but of his life with Cheney" ("F. O. Matthiessen," 81).

27. As Sedgwick has written, "the fact that silence is rendered as pointed and performative as speech, in relations around the closet, depends on and highlights more broadly the fact that ignorance is as potent and as multiple a thing there as is knowledge" (*Epistemology,* 4).

28. In *From The Heart of Europe* (New York: Oxford Univ. Press, 1948), Matthiessen recalls Whitman and Thoreau as the first American authors he read (23).

29. Michael West, "Scatology and Eschatology: The Heroic Dimensions of Thoreau's Wordplay," *PMLA* 89 (October 1974): 1046. Subsequent references will be cited parenthetically in the text.

30. Cf. Michael Warner in "Thoreau's Bottom" (*Raritan* 11 [winter 1992]): "insofar as Thoreau wants an ideal image of self, his actual body becomes a problem. . . . [T]he body does not cooperate with its perfection. Its materiality, its actualness, is the concrete resistance to his ideal self-recognition" (70).

31. Henry Abelove, "From Thoreau to Queer Politics" *Yale Journal of Criticism* 6 (fall 1993): 17-27; hereafter cited parenthetically in the text. See also Lauren Berlant and Elizabeth Freeman, "Queer Nationality," in *Fear of a Queer Planet* (193-229).

32. "The mingling suggested by our names is America at its best, though how far below that best it often falls we are all of us aware. Such mingling, with completely equal rights, gives the only solid basis for any truly united peoples or United Nations of the present or future" (Matthiessen, *From the Heart of Europe*, 14).

33. May Sarton has said of her 1955 *Faithful Are The Wounds* that while the novel "has quite a bit about marriage, . . . it also talks about a singular person who does live alone, the suicide, who was Matthiessen" (quoted in *Conversations with May Sarton*, ed. Earl G. Ingersoll [Jackson: Univ. Press of Mississippi, 1991], 66). Similarly, in Mark Merlis's *American Studies* (Boston: Houghton Mifflin, 1994), the protagonist—"inspired by the critic F. O. Matthiessen," as the book jacket explains—lives and dies alone. "Cadden also discusses Sarton's novel in 'Engendering F. O. M.,' 28-29."

34. In the twentieth century *ablutions* has lost some of its religious connotations, referring instead to public washrooms (1911: "The ablution places need to be located conveniently near the men's tents" [*OED*]). The word thus conjoins the communal places where men wash and the "toilets" we have heard Cheney forswear—that is, the modern tearoom.

FURTHER READING

Biography

Levin, Harry. "The Private Life of F. O. Matthiessen." In *Memories of the Moderns*, pp. 218-30. New York: New Directions, 1980.
    Brief biographical account of the events surrounding Matthiessen's suicide and his relationship with Russell Cheney.

Criticism

Aaron, Daniel. "Parrington Plus." *The Kenyon Review* IV, No. 1 (Winter 1942): 102-6.
    Positive assessment of *American Renaissance*.

Delany, Paul. "Varieties of Liberal Experience." *Times Literary Supplement* (5 December 1980): 1391-92.
    Contends that *Rat and the Devil* "may be admissible in a volume mainly concerned with illuminating Matthiessen's domestic life, but a full-scale biography would surely give quite a different sense of his place in American intellectual history."

Fiedler, Leslie A. "Love is Not Enough." *The Yale Review* (Spring 1953): 455-60.
    Asserts that *The Responsibilities of the Critic* exposes Matthiessen's "failure to close the gap between his literary allegiances and his political-ethical ones."

Trilling, Lionel. "The Head and Heart of Henry James." In *Speaking of Literature and Society, edited by Diana Trilling*, pp. 202-6. New York: Harcourt Brace Jovanovich, 1980.
    Postive assessment of *Henry James: The Major Phase*.

Additional coverage of Matthiessen's life and career is contained in the following source published by the Gale Group: *Dictionary of Literary Biography,* **Vol. 63.**

Alfred Neumann
1895-1952

German-born American novelist, dramatist, short story writer, poet, screenwriter, and biographer.

INTRODUCTION

Neumann is notable for his historical novels that focus on the abuses and danger of ambition and power. Critics maintain that he contributed to the revival of the genre by using past events to symbolize the political situations of his day, such as the rise of the Nazi party in Germany in the 1930s. Although well-respected during his lifetime, he is now often overshadowed by his contemporaries, particularly Herman Hesse, Thomas Mann, and Franz Werfel.

BIOGRAPHICAL INFORMATION

On October 15, 1895, Neumann was born into a wealthy, Jewish family in Lautenburg, West Prussia, which is now part of Poland. A few years later his family moved to Berlin. Neumann attended schools in Berlin and Rostock before traveling to Munich to study art history and German history. Wounded in 1915 while serving in World War I, he began to write poetry while recuperating from his injuries. He returned to Munich in 1917, publishing his collection of his poems, *Die Lieder vom Lächeln und der Not,* that same year. He resumed his studies in 1920, receiving a degree in romance languages and literature. In 1926, he published a few collections of short fiction and his first historical novel, *Der Teufel (The Devil),* for which he received the Kleist Prize. Neumann left Munich for Italy in 1933 to escape the Nazi regime in Germany. When Europe became untenable, he moved to the United States in 1941. Settling in Los Angeles, he worked as a screenwriter for Warner Bros. Pictures and became an American citizen in 1946. He died in Lugano, Switzerland, on October 3, 1952.

MAJOR WORKS

Neumann's major themes are the dynamics of power and guilt, in particular the abuse and corruption that can result from absolute power, and the effects of guilt on the individual. In *The Devil,* a barber named Oliver Necker rises to become a trusted advisor and confidant to King Louis XI. When Louis seduces Oliver's wife, Anne, Oliver plots against the monarch, isolating him from his staff and his friends. Eventually, Oliver becomes head of state but is executed after Louis's death. *Der Patriot* (1927; *The Patriot*) is also rooted in historical fact. A group of Russian nobles, including the honorable Count Peter von der Pahlen, conspire to overthrow the despotic rule of Tsar Paul. Paul's son, Alexander, agrees to assume the throne as long as his father's life is spared. Yet when Paul is killed, Pahlen kills himself, as he had pledged his life to Alexander that no harm would come to the Russian ruler.

CRITICAL RECEPTION

Most critics agree that Neumann's work has been surpassed by that of his better-known contemporaries. Stylistically, reviewers have found his novels wordy and dull; they have also derided his poor attention to detail and historical fact. Yet most commentators have praised his insightful and perceptive observations of the human condition, particularly his depiction of unscrupulous and ambitious individuals who eventually are corrupted by greed and insecurity.

PRINCIPAL WORKS

Die Lieder vom Lächeln und der Not (poetry) 1917

Die heiligen: Legendäre Geschichten (short stories) 1919

Neue Gedichte (short stories) 1920

Der Patriot [*The Patriot*] (novella) 1925

König Haber: Erzählung [*King Haber and Other Stories*] (short stories) 1926

Der Teufel [*The Devil*] (novel) 1926

Der Patriot: Drama in fünf Akten [*The Patriot: A Play in Three Acts;* also translated as *Such Men Are Dangerous*] (drama) 1927

Rebellen [*The Rebels*] (novel) 1927

Königsmaske (drama) 1928

Frauenschuh [*Lady's Shoe*] (drama) 1929

Guerra (novel) 1929

Der Held: Roman eines politischen Mordes [*The Hero: The Tale of a Political Murder*] (novel) 1930

Narrenspiegel [*The Mirror of Fools*] (novel) 1932

Neuer Caesar [*The New Caesar*] (novel) 1934

Königin Christine von Schweden [*The Life of Christina of Sweden*] (biography) 1935

Kaiserreich [*The Gaudy Empire*] (novel) 1937

Die Volksfreunde [*The Friends of the People*] (novel) 1940

War and Peace [with Erwin Piscator and Guntram Prüfer; adaptation of Leo Tolstoy's *War and Peace*] (drama) 1941

Es waren ihrer sechs [*There Were Six of Them*] (novel) 1944

Gesammelte Werke. 2 vols. (short stories, dramas, novels)
  1949-1950
Der Pakt [*Strange Consequences*] (novel) 1950

CRITICISM

Gilbert Gabriel (essay date 1928)

SOURCE: An introduction to *The Patriot: A Play in Three Acts,* by Alfred Neumann, Boni & Liveright, 1928, pp. v-xiv.

[*In the following essay, Gabriel provides an overview of Neumann's drama* The Patriot.]

Neumann's drama [*The Patriot*] is of intrigue and assassination at the Russian Court, St. Petersburg, in the turbulent year of 1801. It is the tragedy of poor Tsar Paul I. and of his Judas, his minister and military governor, Count Pahlen.

These two are the chief tilting posts of *The Patriot.* Against them—especially against the enigmatic, ironclad, character of Peter Pahlen—the whole of Neumann's drama jousts. A very fiend this Pahlen is depicted, a spider of most intricate cunning, weaving coldly and expertly his plot of betrayal, sedition and regicide, dragging into its strands all admirals and officers, courtiers and whole garrisons, baiting for the emperor with the body of his own mistress, binding the agonized young Tsarievitch into the unyielding center of the web. A very fiend . . . and yet—the Neumann touch—a hero of heroes.

For, in the end, his bitter task done, the foolish, ineffectual Tsar a strangled corpse, young Alexander ascended safely to the throne, Count Pahlen waits only for the tolling of the dawn before he, too, grimly contrives his own death, uncovers his chest to the bullet of an impassive soldier. A terrible, heart-breaking finale, cold with the desolation of the sallow morning, smeared with the dregs of intrigue, when the blackened, stoic minister, whom you know at last for a savior of his country, a patriot who has flung away honor itself for the sake of the Russia of his Napoleonic day, orders his body servant to shoot, to repeat the suicides of Philippae:

> "Look, Stepan, look at these hands of mine . . . they have been kissed by an emperor. And look at these lips of mine . . . they have kissed another emperor's hands. And both of them my emperors . . . my emperors . . . I am . . . But let us speak no more of that, Brother Stepan, no more of anything. Sing me a little song, Brother Stepan . . ."

> The stolid soldier, pistols in hand, begins to croon a Russian peasant song. The church bells, the song ceases. The Tsar avenged, the nation rescued. Behind the slowly fallen curtain two shots ring out.

. . . . .

So colossal does this figure of Peter Pahlen loom, you begin to wonder why his name has managed to sift through the chinks of your knowledge of history hitherto. If you know of him at all, you know him as an icy old diplomat who has been given the benefit of no more than two or three lines in the usual encyclopaedias. Even in the Russian encyclopaedias. At any rate in those which were compiled in Russia's Tsarist days, and which are the only ones the New York public libraries can yet boast. The present Russian Government, of course, is publishing a set of its own which guarantees to be franker on the subject of crazy Tsars and successful assassinations.

Until then you must be content, for instance, with the reticence of such an official account as says merely that "On the 12th of March, 1801, Paul I. was found dead" in what is tactfully designated as his "dressing room." And that "immediately thereafter Count Pahlen, in his capacity of Military Governor of St. Petersburg, reported his Imperial Majesty's death and invited all to give oaths of allegiance to Alexander I."

Of the conspiracy and Pahlen's part in it a short, sober admission. But even between the lines of Greek type it is forbidden to read any plain inference as to what all the conspiring was about. That a ruler of all Russia could have been choked to death with a common soldier's sash was something to whisper, but never to print.

Still, considering that their right hands were in peril, Russian biographers were pretty plain concerning Paul I. Perhaps his life gave them no alternative. He was a wretched Tsar, one of the unhappiest, most futile of men. He abhorred his mother. His whole "leibmotif" was one of revenge for the insults he had suffered at the bawdy, gloriously comic court of the Great Catherine. Reading his life you are somehow reading nothing but an early imprint of Emil Ludwig's recent study of the last of the Hohenzollerns. Like Wilhelm like Paul, from youth to downfall.

One idol Paul had: Prussia's Frederick the Great. So had almost all rulers of that time the same idol, but none so fiercely as poor Paul. He played the proud nationalist, the military martinet, the challenger of Western countries, the friend of the people against the nobles, all in Frederick's name and Frederick's manner. He introduced Russian titles. He refused to allow any use of the word "society," was against all class consciousness. He ordered Count Pahlen to see that more courtesy was exhibited on St. Petersburg streets.

He instituted a famous yellow box for complaints outside the Winter Palace. Anyone, everyone, was allowed to complain of his neighbor, his wife or his master. The tattling became so furious, no one was finally permitted more than two complaints per annum. In the end, when the box was found crammed every morning with foul jingles and lampoons against the Tsar himself, he had it removed. So much for good intentions.

His army despised Tsar Paul for his pains. He was forever offending and alienating his officers of the guards. He reprimanded Galitizin because his soldiers were afraid of rain. He clapped a captain into six weeks' solitary confinement for bragging that he would soon be made his Majesty's aide-de-camp. An officer of even higher rank he dismissed without court-martial for his "ignorance of his duties, his idleness to which he grew accustomed during a past reign when, instead of performing his duties, he learned only to dance and posture prettily around the lobbies."

He was as mad, you see, as Hamlet; as tragic, weak and unresolved. And, being ruler of all Muscovy, ten times more dangerous. His peevishness against England, his distrust of the new France, kept his humble servant, Count Pahlen, in a state of constant apology to the Powers. Likely as not, Neumann's play is accurate there: Paul's Minister of Foreign Policy would be among the first to realize the utter necessity of whisking him off his throne, dead or alive.

Count Peter Pahlen? A cavalryman, a soldier at the age of 15, a general in Potyomkin's army in the previous reign. An excellent tactician, both at court and on the field. He first came to the Tsar's notice when Prince Zuboff made a pompous tour of the provinces, and when an imperial edict had proclaimed that that distinguished nobleman must be treated by all with extra respect. Something went wrong. Pahlen, in charge of Riga, failed to please. He received his first letter from Paul I.:

"I was surpised to learn of all the dirty tricks you performed during the passage of Prince Zuboff through Riga. From this I draw appropriate conclusions as to your character, and I intend to treat you accordingly." Dismissed from the army, it needed the patient pleading of Pahlen's best friend in the palace to gain him reinstatement. He may have known from that moment what a vain, maniacal fool he was to deal with. And what to do about him.

At any rate, once back in favor, Pahlen climbed swiftly high. Before long he was Paul's strongest prop, his capital's military governor, his foreign minister. When English warfare threatened in 1800 Pahlen was proposed as generalissimo of Russia's troops. A year later he had the double pleasure of reporting to the Tsar that a conspiracy existed against him, and so extracted an order to arrest the Tsarievitch. It was Pahlen's way of bullying young Alexander into patricide. That much we know for certain. The next day the Tsar was dead.

But this, too, is certain: that the play is unhistorical about the final fate of Pahlen. The patriot did no such splendid thing as order his own death, that famous, blood-stained March morning. He stayed on as Alexander's counselor for some few chilly, constrained months thereafter. Then out he went, retired from all his posts on the nice excuse of ill health, a virtual exile with nobody's thanks to warm the remaining years of this life. He was not half so good a dramatist, it seems, as Alfred Neumann.

Clifton P. Fadiman (review date 1929)

SOURCE: "Pseudo-Historical Fiction," in *The Nation*, Vol. 129, No. 3349, September 11, 1929, p. 276.

[*In the following mixed review of* The Rebels, *Fadiman deems the novel "a study of the conspiratorial temperament."*]

One of the reasons for Alfred Neumann's failure to gain an American audience commensurate with his merits is that he is touted as an historical novelist when he is not one at all. By turns he is mystery-story writer and metaphysician, a sorcerer whose effects vary from the awe-inspiring to the parlor-tricky. To read his works as historical novels is simply confusing. He is never really interested in creating a background or making vivid some historical complex. The treatment in *The Rebels* of the Carbonari uprising in central Italy from 1820 to 1830 is purposely oblique and fragmentary. Actually, the reader is not supposed to know what it is all about, to have any systematic understanding of the social and economic forces which presumably lie behind the movements of the personages. A clear understanding would be murderous to the shadowy Gothic effect for which Neumann is striving. The intrigue is enveloped in a dark cloud of innuendo; tortured souls express their agonies in gnomic sentences; no one is frank or explicit; Checca, Madda, Caminer, and even Guerra himself are sinister, humorless, melodramatic. The tale is labyrinthine, a maze of dark, narrow streets in which the characters dog each other stealthily, meet but to utter a few low-voiced mysterious words, and pass on, wrapped in the black cloak of their own moral suffering.

It is a deliberate and intelligent falsification of history, just as a romantic novel by Walter Scott is a childish and uncritical one. Neumann is not interested in the Carbonari conspiracy for its own sake, but because by enmeshing his already complicated characters in a network of intrigue he can produce an effect of still greater complication. He enriches the enigma of their personalities by subjecting them to the cross-currents of a mystical patriotism. To put it a bit cheaply but not necessarily inaccurately, the political intrigue is artistically necessary because it prevents the characters from speaking openly to each other. History is like a black veil behind which their faces are nebulous and frightening, their voices muted and elusive.

Once the reader has experienced this strange terror effect, he has received most of what Neumann has to give. As a story *The Rebels* is much less interesting than *The Devil;* in fact its bare fable is banal. It reminds one of those classic "situations" dear to Corneille and Racine. The Princess Maria Corleone finds herself at once the mistress of the Grand Duke of Tuscany and of Guerra, magnetic leader of the Carbonari. By a further complication she finds herself actually involved with the Carbonari in their projected assault on the Grand Duke's life. Her vacillations and Guerra's, as they are torn between passion and duty, love and patriotism, furnish the major lines of the story's exterior movement. At bottom, however, the situation is a stock one; the plot is unimportant; the outcome is awaited by the reader with no overpowering eagerness. What one comes to look for is not the mere points which determine the tragic curves of the career of Guerra, but the half-glimpsed confrontations and dialogues, those elliptic utterances which proceed out of terrific emotional tensities, out of imagined incest and fratricide, out of loves and hates which dare not speak their names or fully unveil their chimera-faces.

In view of what has just been said it may seem a little silly to speak of *The Rebels* as a study of anything; and yet I think it is such a study, a study of the conspiratorial temperament. With the possible exception of Guerra (and then only at the end of his career) none of the characters is politically minded. Gioia, Checca, Madda, Maria Corleone might all conceivably be on the side of reaction rather than of revolution. They have no clear comprehension of the struggle in which they are pawns, nor do they in their hearts desire any such understanding. To them, intrigue and conspiracy are forms of personal salvation, not instruments of political freedom. Conspiracy is a refuge for their unhappy and unbalanced souls. In its ambiguities, its denunciations, its atmosphere of assassination, is a reflection of their own interior turmoil. In its perils and escapes they find a sort of release for their own life-despair. Real revolutions, of course, are the work of businesslike individuals, patient and practical propagandists like Lenin; but just below such leaders there is always a group of tortured romantics whose fanaticism, by reason of its very remoteness from any political aim, is sometimes all the more effective.

I may add that it needs but a touch here and there to turn *The Rebels* into a gorgeous satire on the revolutionary temperament. Neumann stops just short of extravagance; another step and his characters, with their eternal dramatizing and twilight utterances, would have been completely ridiculous. He does not take that step, affording one more proof of the oft-repeated statement that it is difficult to be at the same time a German and a humorist.

Pierre Loving (review date 1930)

SOURCE: "History as Fiction," in *The Nation*, Vol. 130, No. 3388, June 11, 1930, p. 684.

[*In the following brief review, Loving discusses Neumann's* The Rebels *as historical fiction.*]

In *The Devil*, *King Haber,* and *The Rebels* Alfred Neumann showed with what success psychological values can be applied to historical characters and events. In each one of these books we note that the author has proceeded on the assumption—an anathema, I imagine, to most professional historians—that the arcanum of facts must not be too reverently searched or worshiped. To put it another

way: history-writing and fiction meet at that focal point where both the historian and the novelist begin to revise and color the available data, which has been, of course, already tainted by the dust of time. Both go in quest, not of "ultimate truth," but of sound values. In modern philosophy these values are called percepta; nor need we think that they are themselves apprehensions of pure reality; for there are, it is conceded, many veils between our ordinary perceptions and the thing we are seeking, commonly called the truth.

Alfred Neumann in the present book takes up the revolution of the Carbonari, as in *The Rebels,* and rewrites it for us from the viewpoint of Guerra, the leader. The story begins with Guerra's release from the island of Elba. It is both effective and plausible, and the dramatic crises—of which there are many—are not at all forced. They occur naturally in the flow of the tale, which is thick with intrigue, dark plots, the scheming of prelates and aristocrats, love and lust, the shedding of blood, and the half-finished talk and action of conspirators who scarcely dare trust one another.

Guerra is in love with the Princess Maria, who is the mistress of the Grand Duke, the enemy of United Italy. He is also sinisterly attached to his own sister, who marries the head of the Radical Party. In the end he is shot when about to address his faithful followers in the piazza at Rome. From a balcony a blind man exclaims: "Why—why isn't he speaking?" The novel is full of just such dramatic touches. And it is this sort of literary device that best gives us the clue to the difference between the ordinary kind of history and the historical novel that perhaps justifies itself by the urgency of its inner truth.

Mark Van Doren (review date 1935)

SOURCE: "All Too Historical," in *The Nation*, Vol. 140, No. 3630, 1935, p. 133.

[*In the following review, Van Doren offers a negative assessment of* Another Caesar.]

Much of this novel [*Another Caesar*] sounds like the novels of Captain Mayne Reid, who never let any information escape his reader if he could help it. When Herr Neumann, for instance, has got Louis Napoleon to that point in his career at which Miss Howard, his English mistress, is about to enter it, he lets us have the following facts full in the face:

> Howard is one of the great names of England. The head of the Howard family, the Duke of Norfolk, is the first of the dukes and the hereditary Earl Marshal of England; while the Earls of Suffolk, Carlisle, Nottingham, and the Lord Howard of Glossop represent in the peerage the younger line. In this connection we think also of John Howard, the famous eighteenth-century philanthropist and reformer of prisons. Another Howard

whose name is famous was Frederick Howard, major of hussars, killed at Waterloo, immortalized by Byron (himself a relative of the Howards) in the third canto of *Childe Harold.*

Now it may seem strange, but I was not thinking also of John Howard as I approached that priceless third sentence. If I was thinking about anything it was the name Glossop. Yet I do not remember thinking about even that, though it occurs to me now that the syllables must have sounded amusing. I had long since been rendered incapable either of thought or of amusement by a historical novel which did not know how to arrange its history, so that, for example, on the three-hundredth page before this one I had been compelled to learn that:

> The election of Gregory XVI was the great challenge, the declaration of war. This took place on February 2, 1831, after the conclave had lasted sixty-four days. The revolutionary central committee fixed the central Italian rising for February 5. Modena started two days earlier, on February 3 [Yes, that would be the 3rd]; thereupon the notorious Duke of Modena, a Carbonaro, but really a Habsburg provocative agent, bombarded the house of the insurgent leader, who was his personal friend, with grape-shot; shot the place to pieces, arrested the wounded Carbonaro chief and his staff, and sent for the executioner. The news started the flames of revolution in Bologna, Parma, Reggio, Ferrara, and Ravenna, on the 5th; the movement spread like wildfire through all the States of the Church, through the Legations, the Delegations, through Romagna and Umbria.

Neumann's novel is as dull as that. Not that those facts are dull in themselves; but Neumann does nothing more with them than I have indicated. They mean nothing to the reader; they are never alluded to again; they were never needed or desired in a work presumably occupied with the story of one man, Louis Napoleon, nephew of the Emperor and one day to be Napoleon III. There are thousands of facts just like them in the book—copied, I suspect, directly from notes which the author once took with the idea that he might give them life if occasion arose; but having more the air of annotations which some assistant professor will compose in future years for a school edition; supposing the novel breathes that long, which of course it will not, since it is already dead.

Even the hero is dead. Louis Napoleon himself was never very much alive, but I can imagine something better being done with him than the thing Neumann has done. Neumann has understood the pathos of his hero's position, and has gone to enough trouble to erect a theory about his character; but he has presented him in a series of episodes and conversations, many of them prematurely and febrilely climactic, which is never more than a temporal series. The events of Louis's life and the aspects of his strange, weak, stubborn, waxy character do not compose. They remain as stringy and indigestible as Modena and Glossop, and as far apart as history is from fiction. At least bad history, which I take this to be because it is so singularly uninteresting. History is interesting and so is fiction; but Herr Neumann's kind of historical novel is as near to nothing as the human mind can come.

Catherine Radziwill (review date 1937)

SOURCE: "The Second Empire," in *The Nation*, Vol. 144, No. 23, June 5, 1937, pp. 655-56.

[In the following review, Radziwill offers a negative appraisal of The Gaudy Empire.*]*

First of all, this [*The Gaudy Empire*] is, I must hasten to say, a typical German book, with all the pathetic features which accompany every German attempt to understand foreign psychology. Once this essential fact has been grasped, it becomes easier to judge of the value of Herr Neumann's description of the brilliant days of the Second French Empire. In many points this description is an excellent one. But the book is too long; it is boring in its endless explanations of things which can only be explained by intuition; and it gets completely off the track when it launches into imaginative stories of imagined things. In order to form a just idea of such conversations as took pace at Biarritz between Napoleon III and Bismarck, one must have moved among the surroundings in which they were carried on. We live in an age when statesmen and great writers arise out of nothing, like mushrooms after a summer rain, but even writers blessed with genius cannot know all the ins and outs of the political affairs of a period like the Second Empire, when such events were kept secret and never were thrown to the man of the street for him to make his breakfast of. One who has closely followed the variations in the thought of Napoleon III as revealed by contemporary memoirs cannot quite figure to himself that the Emperor would ever have told Bismarck during those sunny afternoons when they paced together the beach at Biarritz, that "the interests of Prussia and of France were identical." This is German ignorance of foreign psychology, and it makes mincemeat of Herr Neumann's conviction that he was writing a historical work.

If his book is not that, is it a historical novel? One would read it with greater pleasure if one were sure that everybody would consider it that. But a historical novel must have more incidents and more glamor, must not fall into speculative psychological surmises; the author must remember that *The Three Musketeers* and *The Reine Margot* have survived the writer who gave them to the world because, among other reasons, they are what a novel ought to be, romantic and thrilling. There is no thrill in *Gaudy Empire;* not even in the brief description of the pathetic close of a career so illustrative of the vanity of all things as Napoleon III's.

The best pages in the book are those dealing with the plot of Orsini and the Italian policy of the Emperor. The description of both the Empress Eugénie and the famous Countess de Castiglione are so inexact as to be beneath notice. One great fault of the book is that while it is frequently so drawn out that it becomes confused, it is yet much too short when it comes to the final catastrophe which destroyed the Second Empire. The author could have expanded this with profit, for he seems to have a better knowledge of it than of French society during the reign of Napoleon III. One does not understand what has made him ascribe such importance to Rochefort, whose fiery and unscrupulous temperament only came really to the front after the fall of the empire, and who first became a popular hero during the Third Republic. Before its advent he was looked upon only as an agitator.

Gaudy Empire is decidedly a partisan book; it aims to present a period of modern history from its own point of view, the German one, and to exploit the events of that period as a justification of things which it is still too early to evaluate. It lacks conciseness, and the writer would have done better to model himself after certain French authors in his appreciation of an age still wrapped in the clouds of social and political ignorance—for example, after André Bellessort, who has recently published *French Society Under Napoleon III.* It is, as a critic said the other day, "a story of men and women of whom few people possess much definite knowledge." If Herr Neumann had possessed more, he would have given us a better book.

Gerhard F. Probst (essay date 1987)

SOURCE: "Alfred Neumann's and Erwin Piscator's Dramatization of Tolstoy's *War and Peace* and the Role of Theater as a Contribution to America's War Efforts," in *Exile and Enlightenment,* Uwe Faulhaber, Jerry Glenn, Edward P. Harris, Hans-Georg Richert eds., Wayne State University Press, 1987, pp. 265-272.

[*In the following essay, Probst chronicles the collaboration of Neumann and Piscator on the dramatization of Tolstoy's novel* War and Peace.]

It is generally known that Erwin Piscator came to the United States upon the invitation of Broadway producer Gilbert Miller to direct his and Alfred Neumann's dramatization of Tolstoy's *War and Peace.* When Miller, who had taken an option on the play after reading only a rough English translation of the original, threatened to drop the project because he did not like the finished script, particularly the second and third acts, Piscator began to look for help. One of the men he thought could be of assistance, was Harold Clurman, one of the founders and directors of the Group Theatre.

If Piscator thought that in Clurman he had a fellow-combatant for the cause of political theater who, as he himself had so often done, would produce a play on the strength of its ideas and intended effect, not so much as an esthetic object, i.e., a play that would be good theater, he was sadly disappointed. Piscator must have developed very early doubts about Gilbert Miller, who had not bothered to meet him and his wife at the New York pier, and apparently contacted Clurman almost immediately, since Clurman's answer is dated January 24, 1939. Clurman wrote:

I believe it is practically an impossible task to do *War and Peace* on the stage and so any criticism of the play that I make must be made with a sense of the great difficulty of the task assigned. I feel that your play sins not from over-simplification but from an effort to do too much, and so while the production might be scenically effective, in its varied, short and constantly moving scenes, it fails to present the characters in a way that would move an American audience and interest them in the character's [sic] problems. I think the play as written at present, would be an emotional failure because this sense of not being able to identify oneself with the characters, or to connect themselves imaginatively into their lives and milieu, which I believe is largely due to the form and structure of your dramatization, is a very serious lack, particularly from the stand-point of our American audiences, who respond much less to form and even to the excitement of stage technique than to simple characterization and situation.

Your play, I do not feel, would satisfy an audience, as it does not satisfy me from the standpoint of almost all traditional standards of current theatre. . . . I am bound in all honesty . . . to say at the moment that I do not feel that the Group Theatre would be interested in undertaking a production of the present material.[1]

Clurman, of course, had some experience with Piscator's concept of theater, since it was the Group Theatre which had presented his first dramatization of an American novel, *The Case of Clyde Griffiths* based on Theodore Dreiser's *An American Tragedy,* to New York theater-goers in 1936. The experience was not a very happy one: "reviewers generally detested the play."[2]

Moreover, the Group Theatre had moved away from the class struggle position of the early Odets, its leading dramatist since the sensational premiere of *Waiting for Lefty* in January of 1935. Only five years later, the same Cliffort Odets who had been hailed as the champion of revolutionary drama, resigned himself to the fact that there was little hope for political theater in America.[3]

Piscator kept on trying to have his *War and Peace* produced. He made a list of writers whom he apparently wanted to contact about a possible collaboration on a revision of the script. The list included such names as Sinclair Lewis, Sidney Howard, Ernest Hemingway, Walter Volmer, Stark Young, Edna St. Vincent Millay, Mrs. Norman Hapgood, Dr. Winn F. Zeller, Johann Reich, S. N. Behrman, John van Druten, and Ernest Boyd.[4]

There is a series of diary entries made between May 4 and July 14, 1939, which indicate that Piscator tried several different approaches to having *War and Peace* staged. Alfred Neumann had sent him a new version which Piscator considered producing with German exile actors who would work without pay in order to stay within the budget range of $30,000 that Gilbert Miller was still willing to invest. The last three diary entries concern contacts with two other producers.[5]

None of these attempts was successful. As late as May 1940 when the Dramatic Workshop already was in operation, Piscator tried to have John Gassner give him a hand with the play: "I am still looking for someone who could help me with the dialogues in *War and Peace.* I hesitate to ask you to do it because of your heavy schedule, naturally I would be delighted if you could. Failing this happy solution would you have anyone to suggest? What do you think of Sidney Kingsley? Do you know that Paul Muni is very much interested in the play? He suggested Maurice Samuel, the translator of Schalom Ash's latest publications. Do you know him? Let's get together soon."[6]

Less than two years later Harold L. Anderson and Maurice Kurtz, who were associated with the Dramatic Workshop, did an adaptation of *War and Peace.* By then, the United States had entered the war and, more importantly, Hitler's armies had invaded the USSR, thus giving the Tolstoy dramatization a topicality it did not have when Piscator first tried to stage it. Piscator hoped to be able to do with **War and Peace** what he had just accomplished with a similarly topical play, Lessing's *Nathan the Wise,* namely, to interest a Broadway impresario with his Studio Theatre production and to move it "uptown." This time, however, his hopes proved to be in vain. **War and Peace** opened on May 20, 1942, had its customary short, four-week run—and that was it. Piscator had to wait another thirteen years until he finally could produce *War and Peace* on a big stage with professional actors. On March 20, 1955 *Krieg und Frieden* opened at the West Berlin Schillertheater in a new version Piscator had written together with Guntram Prüfer.

This new version made use of a dramaturgical device Piscator had first employed in the stage version of Robert Penn Warren's novel *All the King's Men.* In addition to a narrator who at the same time is a character in the play, Pierre Besuchov, a commentator or interlocutor is added who informs, explains, even argues with the actors. It is interesting to note that Harold Clurman saw this 1955 production and although he still does not like this type of anti-romantic, intellectual theater, as he calls it, he is now more tolerant in his assessment of a play which he once rejected:

> This [**War and Peace**] is a schematic piece which does not attempt to dramatize the novel. It seeks only to explain it and to draw some social conclusions from it. The treatment shocks those who expect the quality of the novel to be reproduced on the stage. . . . I admired it even though it isn't 'my kind' of theatre, which I might define as reality through poetry or poetry through reality. The theatre, I believe, should not confine itself to any single type of entertainment. The theatre of emotion is fine, but there must also be a place for the 'intellectual' theatre. Nor am I averse to propaganda—and do not consider that propaganda must necessarily fail to be art. . . . Piscator's **War and Peace** . . . is a diagram of the novel. But it is handsomely and sometimes ingeniously drawn with a distinguished sense of the possibilities of the stage. That it is not conventionally stirring, that it is more lesson than epic, that it has little 'flesh and blood,' that it contains a minimum of (Russian) color or (Tolstoyan) humanity does not invalidate it for me as theatre.[7]

Alfred Neumann never saw any of the different versions of his and Piscator's Tolstoy adaptation staged. He died about two and a half years before the Berlin production, and he could not see the one at the Studio Theatre of the Dramatic Workshop because he lived in California and had a hard time making ends meet, so that a trip to New York was out of the question.

Neumann did, however, try to stay abreast of developments, gave his written approval for inclusion of Anderson and Kurtz as adaptors in the credits and commented quite favorably on their work: "Now I have read the new version; it is excellent. The first act with the prologues which lead into the present situation, and with the expansion of the relationship between the heroes I find quite outstanding. . . . The translation renders to a truly amazing degree what we wanted to say. In sum: I am hopeful again."[8]

When Neumann scolded Piscator in a letter written May 25, 1942 about his tardiness in sending him a report about the premiere of **War and Peace,** Piscator sent a telegram saying, "Great success, critics lukewarm. Letter to follow."[9]

The last correspondence between Neumann and Piscator concerning the Tolstoy play is a letter written by the former, dated May 31, 1942. Since it is such a beautiful testimony to their friendship and collaboration, it seems justifiable to reproduce it here as a coda, as it were:

> Dear Erwin, I thank you with all my heart for the enormous efforts and beautiful passion which you applied to our WAR AND PEACE, the most beautiful title of our friendship. When reading the program notes one already realizes what unbelievable things you have conjured up on this little stage and with your limited resources. That in this land without imagination, thus also without a soul, you have moved the audience, already is a victory.

After this somewhat harsh, but excusable and understandable refugee reaction to the supposed emotional make-up of the host population, Neumann continues:

> One consequence of the production seems to be that **War and Peace** is haunting the film studios and their gossip again . . . all of a sudden both MGM and Warner claim to have secured the rights to **War and Peace.** I don't quite understand this; but I don't understand most of the things that are said here.[10]

A side product, so to speak, of Piscator's unsuccessful attempts to have the Tolstoy play done on a professional stage, is a letter to Fritz Kortner, which, since it is rather long, can only be paraphrased and quoted in excerpts here.[11] Piscator reports to Kortner that Dorothy Thompson, with whom Kortner had written *Another Sun,* a refugee drama which was produced at the National Theatre in New York in February 1940, thinks the Studio Theatre should go on the road as "a kind of War Theatre" and present "a play of common political Interest and with this . . . bring new groups of people into the theatre. Now is the proper time, especially since Broadway makes very little efforts to notice the war at all, and since the one instrument of political theatre—the Federal Theatre—has completely disappeared." Piscator sees **War and Peace** as an ideal choice to strengthen the war effort of the United States and to help defeat Nazi Germany. (That the emphasis here lies on "Nazi" and not so much on "Germany" will become clear in the last part of this paper.)

The central character of the play, Pierre Besuchov, shows that pacificism is politically and morally wrong under certain conditions. And since this Pierre Besuchov is so important for the message of the play, Piscator would have liked to have Kortner play the part. But he had already offered it to the Czech actor Hugo Haas who had accepted. Therefore, Piscator could only suggest the part of Besuchov's father to Kortner who, however, was not interested and decided to stay in California. He may not have shared Piscator's vision that "with **War and Peace** we could lay the foundation stone for a new political theatre in our time." As mentioned earlier, the **War and Peace** production at the Studio Theatre did not register the expected success with the New York critics and, thus, did not move to Broadway. The Studio Theatre did not go on the road with it either and Piscator failed to make the political contribution he had hoped for. The entire plan of a war theater was abandoned.

The only contributions, then, that Piscator was able to make in the vein of the opinions expressed in the letter to Fritz Kortner, were *The Criminals* by Ferdinand Bruckner (Studio Theatre, December 1941) and *Winter Soldiers* by Dan James (Studio Theatre, November 1942). The first one was an adaptation of Bruckner's 1929 play by the same title, thematizing the view that passivity in the prevention of political crime—the rise of the NSDAP—becomes complicity. The second play consisted of ten scenes about anti-German guerrilla war activities in Czechoslovakia, Poland, Yugoslavia, and Russia. Other attempts to stage anti-nazi plays failed for reasons that have been discussed elsewhere, notably two different productions of Brecht's *Private Life of the Master Race* (1943, 1945) and an updated version of the dramatization of Hasek's *The Good Soldier Schwejk.*[12]

Toward the end of World War II Piscator began to speak and to write about the *Theatre of the Future.*[13] That he was not, as some of his detractors have said, an enemy of Germany, but an enemy of the Nazis, is shown in a correspondence with Elmer Rice. The correspondence occurred late in 1944, but clearly decided in favor of the Allied Powers. Elmer Rice's letter, dated October 13, 1944, was a response to a letter of inquiry by Piscator concerning measures to be taken against Germany:

> My dear Piscator:
>
> The only plans for Germany that seem interesting to me, at the present time, are: 1. The complete military defeat of Germany, with the greatest possible number of German casualties and an Allied march into Berlin; 2. Restitution by the Germans, as far as it is possible, of the destruction they have caused; 3. A rigid and prolonged policing of Germany, by the Allies, to check at the source any plans for another German-made war. What kind of theatre Germany has, or whether any theatre at all, seems to me unimportant. Cordially yours, Elmer Rice.

Piscator's reply dated October 15, 1944 is considerably longer, quite critical of Rice's views and toward the end rather vitriolic:

> Dear Elmer Rice:
>
> First: yes, I agree with you on the complete defeat of Hitler's Germany, but your line which reads 'with the greatest possible number of German casualties' should be amended to read 'German Nazi casualties—both in the Army and in the German civilian population.'
>
> Second: Restitution by the Germans, yes; but by all the Fascists in other countries of the world, including those who slept twenty years and didn't listen to the cries and the warnings of German Democrats, Anti-Nazis and Communists. They are the ones who warned the world, which, as you know, did not heed their pleas— and in your own country (which I hope soon to call mine) there were too many as well who paid no attention at all.
>
> Third: A rigid policing of Germany, yes; but by Germans who have proved since 1918 that they know and understand the German people—their character, psychology, economy and politics. The police force itself should be chosen from such of the Allies who have proven themselves able to police another country, and competent enough to check at its source any of the seeds of war in Germany, or in their own countries. The preparation for a war against the U.S.S.R., for instance.
>
> Fourth: All this will depend not only on the kind of a theatre which Germany has, but also on what kind of a theatre the world has—and also the art, literature, science and other fields of creative activity. It will be important to have any theatre or culture in any sense in the aftermath of the third World War. Permit me to say that I think your letter is unwise, but it is understandable in these days when we are all angry with each other and full of the malevolence which war produces. From anyone else but you (because I know you have done many good and generous things) it would be hard to accept this. Be careful that a bit of the Hitlerian influence so rampant today doesn't crush you! Sincerely, Erwin Piscator, Director.

There is no answer by Rice to Piscator's letter, because Piscator decided, for whatever reasons, not to send it.

It seems a proper conclusion for this paper on Erwin Piscator's attempts to devote his political theater to the efforts to defeat Hitler Germany, to quote passages from an essay on the post-world-war-II theater, concern about which was apparently at the core of his dialogue with Elmer Rice. As far as I have been able to ascertain, the essay has never been published.

> We know that conviction alone does not make an artist. We know, too, that an artist doesn't make the world; and that a wrong conviction is more dangerous when it is propounded with greater art. So society must protect itself from these false artists, as it would from so many gangsters.
>
> At least this fascism and this war have made the fronts clear. The fascists have ordered the theatres turned to their political service and the artists have obeyed the

order. But so far as we have heard they have not been able to produce art. The artists must feel bitter and betrayed.

The aim of art can never be the creation of a Greater Germany or the Superman, but the national and international freedom of the common man of all nations and races.

But we must start to build the great tradition anew. The Nazis will have left us nothing but dead, burned cities and even our theatres in ruins. To build anew is, we all know, for the time being a speculation. Whether it will remain only a speculation will depend upon the conditions which will follow the war. But in the last year we have come nearer than ever to these speculations, we might even call them our dreams. And no one can doubt that, even at this moment, the Nazis are losing the war. When they have lost it, everything will depend on how the social structure of Europe, especially of Germany, is worked out; on what political and psychological effect the Nazi education and the impact of the catastrophe will have had on the people.

We are in a state of war and revolution of such a scope as the world has never known. The importance of the decisions which will have to be made within the next ten years is breath-taking. But at the same time those years hold a promise for a magnificent future.

This is perhaps the only time in history that, within the space of twenty years two such total wars have engulfed the same generation—namely ours. It is by the same token, the first time that one generation will be given a second glorious chance,—to build a new life.[14]

That Piscator was given only a small part in the rebuilding of the German theater after his return from his American exile, must have been the real pain caused by the proverbial cold shoulder shown him for over ten years. When he finally did have his own theater and with it the means and the chance to do what he had written about almost twenty years before, his life was approaching its end. But he still had enough time, strength, and political sense to launch the new "Dokumentartheater" with his production of plays by Hochhut, Kipphardt, Weiss, and Kirst. It is one of the ironies of history that these documentary plays could not have been written immediately after the war, because it takes distance to see things clearly. But when they finally were written, audiences were not as open to their messages as they would have been in 1945 or 1946. But with the escalation of the war in Vietnam and the ensuing student protests in the western world, history caught up with Piscator again, and his political theater found a new audience in a new politically aware generation.

Notes

1. Letter in Collection 31, Special Collections, Morris Library, Southern Illinois University at Carbondale.

2. Harold Clurman, *The Fervent Years. The Story of the Group Theatre and the Thirties* (New York 1957), p. 163. Clurman does admit, however, that although he himself "did not care for this play," because "it was schematic in a cold way that . . . went against the American grain . . . it was nevertheless technically intriguing and capable of being fashioned into a novel type of stage production."

3. Maria Ley-Piscator, *The Piscator Experiment. The Political Theatre* (New York 1967), p. 43.

4. Undated note, Morris Library.

5. Diary in Morris Library.

6. Letter dated May 16, 1940, Morris Library.

7. Harold Clurman, *Lies Like Truth. Theatre Reviews and Essays* (New York 1958), p. 238-239.

8. Letter of March 13, 1942, Morris Library. The entire correspondence between Piscator and Neumann is in German, English translations are mine.

9. Handwritten note, possibly by Maria Ley-Piscator, on Neumann's letter of May 25, 1942.

10. Letter in Morris Library.

11. Letter dated March 11, 1942 (written in English), Morris Library.

12. E.g., John Willett, *Erwin Piscator. Die Eröffnung des politischen Zeitalters auf dem Theater* (Frankfurt/M 1982), p. 114-115. Original English edition: *The Theatre of Erwin Piscator. Half a Century of Politics in the Theatre* (London 1978).

13. Title of the essay quoted later; both essay and Rice-Piscator correspondence at Morris Library.

14. There are a German and an English version of the essay at Morris Library. There is no indication of who did the translation.

FURTHER READING

Criticism

Porter, Alan. A review of *The Hero*. *The Nation* 133, No. 3462 (1931): 524.
    Mixed assessment of *The Hero*.

Taggard, Genevieve. A review of *The Mirror of Fools*. *The Nation* 136, No. 3527 (1933): 156.
    Mixed review of *The Mirror of Fools*.

Additional coverage of Neumann's life and career is contained in the following source published by the Gale Group: *Dictionary of Literary Biography,* **Vol. 56.**

Emmeline Goulden Pankhurst
1858-1928

English autobiographer, essayist, and speechwriter.

INTRODUCTION

A feminist and activist during the suffragist movement of the late nineteenth and early twentieth centuries, Pankhurst masterminded extreme, often violent, reform protests. Despite her radical behavior, Pankhurst is remembered as an eloquent speaker and talented author who was consumed with the issue of women's rights. *My Own Story,* Pankhurst's autobiography, is considered a valuable historical document that vividly chronicles her struggle for equality.

BIOGRAPHICAL INFORMATION

Pankhurst's parents were ardent abolitionists who served as her role models for social involvement. She was born July 14, 1858, and grew up in Manchester, England. Pankhurst attended school in Paris, returning to England at age eighteen. In 1879 she married Richard Pankhurst, a lawyer of liberal leanings. Frustrated by women's inequalities, she embarked on a dual career of child rearing and social activism. The Pankhursts moved to London in 1885, where they attracted a lively group of anarchists who shared their free-thinking philosophy. When her husband died in 1889, Pankhurst became a registrar of births and deaths to support herself and her family. At the same time she and her equally radical daughters, Christabel and Sylvia, became involved in the Independent Labour Party, a left-wing political organization that appeared to support their goals of equality. But upon discovering that the party had no intention of treating men and women equally, the Pankhurst women formed the Women's Social and Political Union (WSPU). When the WSPU members learned that a bill supporting women's suffrage had been abandoned in Parliament, the women protested, first with marches and later with hunger strikes, arson, and attacks on property. In 1908 Pankhurst went to prison for the first of many times. *My Own Story* appeared in 1914. Intended to encourage support of women's rights, the candid, detailed story of Pankhurst's experiences won many admirers. Three years later Pankhurst and her daughters formed the Women's Party, a political organization devoted to women's rights. In 1918 she moved to Canada, where she toured the country as a public speaker. She returned to England in 1926. Just as she died, Parliament granted women the right to vote in England.

MAJOR WORKS

Pankhurst's primary work is *My Own Story,* an eloquently told account of her struggles and frustrations in the fight for women's suffrage. The book, published in the middle of her activist career, is a candid diary of the era. Aside from outlining her life as an activist, *My Own Story* details Pankhurst's conflict between her English middle-class upbringing and the increasingly violent and extreme protests she came to embrace. In the course of her career, Pankhurst also published several speeches and pamphlets that helped further her political causes. A captivating public speaker, Pankhurst inspired many women to seek equality aggressively.

CRITICAL RECEPTION

Since its publication, *My Own Story* has been consistently praised for its insight into women's struggles in nineteenth-century England. At the end of the twentieth century, critics still praise Pankhurst's importance as a first-hand commentator of the suffrage movement. Her efforts, which included twelve arrests and several life-threatening hunger strikes, are considered pivotal actions in the quest for equality.

PRINCIPAL WORKS

"The Importance of the Vote" (essay) 1908
My Own Story (autobiography) 1914

CRITICISM

Emmeline Pankhurst (essay date 1913)

SOURCE: "Militant Suffragists," in *The World's Greatest Speeches,* edited by Lewis Copeland, Garden City Publishing Co., Inc., 1942, pp. 196-8.

[*In the following excerpt, originally delivered as an address in Hartford, Connecticut, in 1913, Pankhurst discusses differences between the struggle for women's rights in England and America and expresses her willingness to die for her cause.*]

I do not come here as an advocate, because whatever position the suffrage movement may occupy in the United States of America, in England it has passed beyond the realm of advocacy and it has entered into the sphere of practical politics. It has become the subject of revolution and civil war, and so to-night I am not here to advocate woman suffrage. American suffragists can do that very well for themselves. I am here as a soldier who has temporarily left the field of battle in order to explain—it seems strange it should have to be explained—what civil war is like when civil war is waged by women. I am not only here as a soldier temporarily absent from the field of battle; I am here—and that, I think, is the strangest part of my coming—I am here as a person who, according to the law courts of my country, it has been decided, is of no value to the community at all; and I am adjudged because of my life to be a dangerous person, under sentence of penal servitude in a convict prison. So you see there is some special interest in hearing so unusual a person address you. I dare say, in the minds of many of you—you will perhaps forgive me this personal touch—that I do not look either very like a soldier or very like a convict, and yet I am both.

It would take too long to trace the course of militant methods as adopted by women, because it is about eight years since the word militant was first used to describe what we were doing; it is about eight years since the first militant action was taken by women. It was not militant at all, except that it provoked militancy on the part of those who were opposed to it. When women asked questions in political meetings and failed to get answers, they were not doing anything militant. To ask questions at political meetings is an acknowledged right of all people who attend public meetings; certainly in my country, men have always done it, and I hope they do it in America, because it seems to me that if you allow people to enter your legislatures without asking them any questions as to what they are going to do when they get there you are not exercising your citizen rights and your citizen duties as you ought. At any rate in Great Britain it is a custom, a time-honored one, to ask questions of candidates for Parliament and ask questions of members of the government. No man was ever put out of a public meeting for asking a question until Votes for Women came onto the political horizon. The first people who were put out of a political meeting for asking questions, were women; they were brutally ill-used; they found themselves in jail before twenty-four hours had expired. But instead of the newspapers, which are largely inspired by the politicians, putting militancy and the reproach of militancy, if reproach there is, on the people who had assaulted the women, they actually said it was the women who were militant and very much to blame.

It was not the speakers on the platform who would not answer them, who were to blame, or the ushers at the meeting; it was the poor women who had had their bruises and their knocks and scratches, and who were put into prison for doing precisely nothing but holding a protest meeting in the street after it was all over. However, we were called militant for doing that, and we were quite willing to accept the name, because militancy for us is time-honored; you have the church militant and in the sense of spiritual militancy we were very militant indeed. We were determined to press this question of the enfranchisement of the women to the point where we were no longer to be ignored by the politicians as had been the case for about fifty years, during which time women had patiently used every means open to them to win their political enfranchisement.

Experience will show you that if you really want to get anything done, it is not so much a matter of whether you alienate sympathy; sympathy is a very unsatisfactory thing if it is not practical sympathy. It does not matter to the practical suffragist whether she alienates sympathy that was never of any use to her. What she wants is to get something practical done, and whether it is done out of sympathy or whether it is done out of fear, or whether it is done because you want to be comfortable again and not be worried in this way, doesn't particularly matter so long as you get it. We had enough of sympathy for fifty years; it never brought us anything; and we would rather have an angry man going to the government and saying, my business is interfered with and I won't submit to its being interfered with any longer because you won't give women the vote, than to have a gentleman come onto our platforms year in and year out and talk about his ardent sympathy with woman suffrage.

"Put them in prison," they said; "that will stop it." But it didn't stop it. They put women in prison for long terms of imprisonment, for making a nuisance of themselves—that was the expression when they took petitions in their hands to the door of the House of Commons; and they thought that by sending them to prison, giving them a day's imprisonment, would cause them to all settle down again and there would be no further trouble. But it didn't happen so at all: instead of the women giving it up, more women did it, and more and more and more women did it until there were three hundred women at a time, who had not broken a single law, only "made a nuisance of themselves" as the politicians say.

The whole argument with the anti-suffragists, or even the critical suffragist man, is this: that you can govern human beings without their consent. They have said to us, "Government rests upon force; the women haven't force, so they must submit." Well, we are showing them that government does not rest upon force at all; it rests upon consent. As long as women consent to be unjustly governed, they can be; but directly women say: "We withhold our consent, we will not be governed any longer so long as that government is unjust," not by the forces of civil war can you govern the very weakest woman. You can kill that woman, but she escapes you then; you cannot govern her. And that is, I think, a most valuable demonstration we have been making to the world.

Now, I want to say to you who think women cannot succeed, we have brought the government of England to this position, that it has to face this alternative; either women are to be killed or women are to have the vote. I ask American men in this meeting, what would you say if in your State you were faced with that alternative, that you must either kill them or give them their citizenship,— women, many of whom you respect, women whom you know have lived useful lives, women whom you know, even if you do not know them personally, are animated with the highest motives, women who are in pursuit of liberty and the power to do useful public service? Well, there is only one answer to that alternative; there is only one way out of it, unless you are prepared to put back civilization two or three generations; you must give those women the vote. Now that is the outcome of our civil war.

You won your freedom in America when you had the Revolution, by bloodshed, by sacrificing human life. You won the Civil War by the sacrifice of human life when you decided to emancipate the negro. You have left it to the women in your land, the men of all civilized countries have left it to women, to work out their own salvation. That is the way in which we women of England are doing. Human life for us is sacred, but we say if any life is to be sacrificed it shall be ours; we won't do it ourselves, but we will put the enemy in the position where they will have to choose between giving us freedom or giving us death.

The Nation (review date 1914)

SOURCE: A review of "The Arch-Priestess of Militancy: *My Own Story*," in *The Nation*, Vol. 99, No. 2580, December 10, 1914, pp. 688-89.

[*In the following review, the critic refutes Pankhurst's arguments in* My Own Story.]

Mrs. Pankhurst begins [*My Own Story*] with the apparently unconscious admission that "those men and women are fortunate who are born at a time when a great struggle for human freedom is in progress"; no one will doubt that when a "struggle" is on she will be eager to be there. The reader who sets out to take her good-naturedly will find the story amusing and entertaining. Mrs. Pankhurst is clever and writes with a facile pen, and she flings forth charges of "duplicity," "mendacity," and "perjury," calls the judges "biassed," Asquith "treacherous," Lloyd George "slippery," and both of them "scoundrels" with a grace and ease that betray practice. The numerous illustrations, mostly of Mrs. Pankhurst at the critical points of her career, serve to demonstrate the thoughtfulness of the militant organization in matters of detail. One must suppose that she never risked an appearance in public without a photographer at her side.

The reader who proposes to take her argument seriously is likely to be exasperated by the constant evidence of a feline sophistry: to begin with, of course, the common feministic sophism, implied in the "emancipation" of women, in which she likens the present situation of women to that of the negroes before the war, and herself to Wendell Phillips. But her whole argument is characterized by a quiet ignoring of obvious considerations and by a cat-like agility in shifting ground. The main object of the book is to show that militant methods have simply followed the accepted traditions of British politics, with the implication that they are now resented because they are employed by women. Thus it is a time-honored custom to break up political meetings and embarrass the speakers by putting questions. Here she fails to note that it is also a time-honored custom, when the questioners cease to be amusing, to throw them out; and that it is no part of the accepted tradition to claim the privilege of "chivalry." In defence of the policy of "obstruction" she points to Mr. Parnell and his followers, who doubtless never expected to escape punishment for breaking the rules of the game. Of course, the "woman's revolution" and the assertion of the right to be treated as "political prisoners" are simply begging the question.

At times she becomes sweetly reasonable. If, now, Mr. Asquith had only named some other time when it would be convenient for him to receive the petition—and so forth. But Mr. Asquith had received peremptory notice that the petition would be served upon him at eight o'clock on a certain evening. Virtually, he had been ordered to be ready and had been threatened if he should be absent. As a matter of course, full use is made of the dramatic possibilities of "forcible feeding." Thus Mrs. Leigh at the door of the doctor's room: "What she saw was enough to terrify the bravest. In the centre of the room was a stout chair resting upon a cotton sheet. Against the wall, as if ready for action, stood four wardresses." Apparently, this is all that she saw. But think of it, four wardresses and a chair, where the only hope of escape lies in ordering dinner!

Says Ellen Key: "The English women have set out from the wrong notion that, because men, driven to political despair, have committed deeds of violence, women also should in cold blood conceive and organize similar outrages." Here we have a clear distinction which Mrs. Pankhurst has apparently never cared to consider. All that she thinks necessary for the justification of violence is (when she conveniently can) to find a precedent. Her justification of arson is very simple: had not arson proved a potent argument in 1832? She passes easily over the statement of Mr. C. E. H. Hobhouse that "in the case of the suffrage demand there has not been the kind of popular sentimental uprising which accounted for Nottingham Castle in 1832 or the Hyde Park railing in 1867. There has not been a great ebullition of popular feeling."

This is the point, the decisive point, which Mrs. Pankhurst keeps dexterously dark throughout her "story," and especially in her attempts to convict Mr. Herbert Gladstone of shuffling inconsistency and Mr. Asquith of treachery. No extraordinary powers of intuition are needed to see that when Mr. Gladstone advised the suffragists to create a *force majeure,* what he meant was a force, not of disorder, but of imperative popular sentiment; and it was as impudent to hold him responsible for the summons to suffragists to "rush the House of Commons" as to pretend (as seemed at first convenient) that the summons contemplated no disorder. As for Mr. Asquith, it is clear from Mrs. Pankhurst's "own story" that he never committed himself to advocacy of the cause of suffrage; but he was prepared to yield if the cause could show sufficient popular backing. There is nothing in Mrs. Pankhurst's book to show that he broke any promises in connection with the Conciliation bill. It seems clear that his promise was, not to support the bill, but only to allow it time for consideration. Nor is it evident to the reader why he was forbidden by his promise to introduce at the same session of Parliament the Government's franchise bill, which was to be open to a woman-suffrage amendment. All that looks suspicious is his failure to foresee that this amendment would be ruled out by the Speaker as irrelevant. Throughout her negotiations—or, rather, her attempts to negotiate—with the Government, Mrs. Pankhurst quietly assumed that she and her crowd were the official spokeswomen of the women of England. The fact is clear, however, from her story that, although she could furnish "demonstrations" at will, she had no warrant either from the majority of English women or from the majority of suffragists.

The truth is, however, that for moral justification of militant methods, by appeal to tradition or otherwise, Mrs. Pankhurst cares little or nothing. For her the only argument of importance is expediency. Here is her explanation of the policy of burning houses and destroying letters:

> Now our task was to show the Government that it was expedient to yield to the women's just demands. In order to do that we had to make England and every department of English life insecure and unsafe. We had to make English law a failure, and the courts farce-comedy theatres; we had to discredit the Government and Parliament in the eyes of the world; we had to spoil English sports, hurt business, destroy valuable property, demoralize the world of society, shame the churches, upset the whole orderly conduct of life—

In other words, the justification is "militant necessity." In this bland statement Mrs. Pankhurst completes a contemporary trio of distinguished moral obtusities, taking her place beside the German Foreign Secretary who politely pointed to "military necessity" as a sufficient explanation of the violation of Belgian neutrality, and the ex-President of the United States who said, "I took it."

In her foreword Mrs. Pankhurst tells us of the "noble," "generous," and "patriotic" conduct of the militants in laying down arms when war broke out with Germany, and she wonders that the Government, "mindful of their unselfish devotion," has failed to come forward with the proper reward. To take Mrs. Pankhurst seriously at this point would be an insult to her understanding. A tithe of her shrewdness was sufficient to foresee that, when Englishmen were being killed and maimed by the thousand on the field of battle, the fate of a few women who chose wilfully to starve themselves to death would pass unnoticed, and they could quietly be allowed to starve. When war broke out the militant game was over.

Nor was this all. The traditional Philistine argument against suffrage has always been that the responsibility of voting belongs to those who can back it by bearing arms. During the long period of peace the argument had grown rather thin. But the present cataclysm is sufficient to revive it in full vigor. Let the argument be good or bad, it serves to remind us that woman suffrage belongs to an advanced civilization, and presupposes a state of things in which the argument of force is ready to yield to the argument of right and reason. This is something for suffragists to remember. Mrs. Pankhurst to the contrary, women can accomplish nothing by force; all that the militant "warriors" have done has been to take advantage of masculine notions of chivalry. If suffrage is finally to win, it can only be through the appeal to reason, justice, and fair play. And this means that suffragists must not merely play the political game that men are playing, they must play a better game. If the tactics of Mrs. Pankhurst and her militants have been copied from any part of the man-made world, it has been the lowest part. That they might have succeeded, we are not now in position to deny; there can be little doubt that they have served to discredit the cause of suffrage in the eyes of many thoughtful men and women.

The Dial (review date 1915)

SOURCE: A review of *My Own Story,* in *The Dial,* Vol. LVIII, No. 686, January 16, 1915, p. 57.

[*In the following review, critic praises* My Own Story *for its vivid depiction of Pankhurst's life and the women's movement.*]

This breathing spell in the woman suffrage agitation in England is a good time to review what that agitation has effected and to consider briefly its hopes for the future. Mrs. Emmeline Pankhurst's book, **My Own Story** gives an excellent even though warmly partisan account of the movement, especially of that part in which she has been concerned, and closes with hopeful prophecies of the future. Addressing herself to American readers and appealing for their sympathies, she writes with a very telling directness of speech about the attitude and methods of the English government in seeking to withhold from women the rights to which it will be difficult for any candid reader of her book to maintain that they have no just claim. Even of the violent means for obtaining them which she so notably advocates, she makes not a bad defence—if violence is ever defensible. Certainly as material for a book, her stormy experiences of the last few years are rich in incidents of an unusual and not seldom a startling nature. And all this vehemence and hardihood, so little in harmony with accepted traditions of what is most excellent in woman and most truly characteristic of her, we find to be manifested not by one disappointed in early hopes of domestic happiness, soured by the repulse of her affection, denied the privilege of motherhood, but by a woman gently nurtured in a happy home, wedded in young womanhood to the man of her choice, with whom she enjoyed nineteen years of sympathetic and loving companionship, and to whom, as she relates, she bore five children. A most interesting and gifted personality is this that is presented so frankly in **My Own Story,** and at the same time the book is a clear and readable account of an important movement in English public life by the person most ardently devoted to the success of that movement. In closing her last chapter she feels encouraged to hope that further militancy on the part of women will be unnecessary, that past governmental mistakes in the treatment of woman suffragists will not be repeated, and that it will be recognized how impossible is the task of "crushing or even delaying the march of women towards their rightful heritage of political liberty and social and industrial freedom." The book is well illustrated, even to the point of including certain views of its writer in situations not exactly enhancing her dignity.

The Nation & Atheneum (essay date 1928)

SOURCE: "The Triumph of Mrs. Pankhurst," in *The Nation and the Athenaeum,* Vol. XLIII, No. 12, June 23, 1928, pp. 388-89.

[*In the following essay, the critic praises Pankhurst's role in the women's movement at the turn of the century*]

> Most poets are cradled into poetry by wrong,
> They learn in suffering what they teach in song.

Something of the kind might be said of Social Reformers, and it might be said of Mrs. Pankhurst. Along with her barrister husband—an expansive and generous man—she had plunged while still young into Socialism, much to the surprise of Manchester Socialists, who in the late 'eighties were unaccustomed to recruits. The newcomers quickened the pace of the local movement and led the sort of fight which in that remote age stirred the blood—a fight for free speech at Boggart Hole Clough. After victory had been won, Dr. Pankhurst, who had spent freely and neglected his worldly interests for "the cause," died.

There were four children, and very little on which to rear them. Mrs. Pankhurst, who had served on the Manchester School Board and the Board of Guardians, became a Registrar of Births and Deaths in a drab district in which many poor women came on grief. Her years in this office made upon her an impression that never faded. She heard and saw what filled her with rage and gloom. Her "piping took a troubled note." She was no longer a Socialist "sans phrase." She had realized an opposition of sexes as well as of classes. Capitalists were tyrants—so were men.

Mutterings followed in the I.L.P. What would the movement do for women? The reply that Socialism meant Universal Justice, and therefore votes for all women and all men, was not good enough. Philip Snowden, the idolized chairman of the party, saw a pistol at his head. When he said less than was demanded, the weapon was fired. The Women's Social and Political Union came to birth, to work for the immediate enfranchisement of women, and Mrs. Pankhurst and her family, "the predestined children of an implacable mother," dedicated themselves to a crusade—"To die be given us or attain." After much early hostility the development of the Union was rapid. Money was freely given. The instinct to sacrifice turned women of all ages and conditions into devotees. Mrs. Pankhurst was worshipped in the schools; she had but to beckon to induce young women to forsake pleasure and ease for the tumult and taunts of the street. She moved among these neophytes like a priestess, and conferred happiness by a look, a word, or a touch. At a hint her followers, young and old, faced insult, indignity, and risk of death. She understood her rôle and played it with conviction. She became detached, aloof, oracular. She issued her edicts.

When certain of her colleagues, groaning under her despotism, invoked the constitution of her organization, she tore up a copy of that document with the appropriate comment, "I am the constitution." A schism followed, and produced the Women's Freedom League. But the fascinated majority, "theirs but to do or die," acclaimed the action of their leader. The Dictatorship become absolute, and made the war more bitter. Over the raids on the House of Commons it was easy to laugh, but for the women who took part in them they were no laughing matter. To be the centre of a vast mob containing a large element of rowdies, to be carried off one's feet, to be thrown forward and backward as the mob helplessly heaved and receded, or lie prone as it broke before the pressure of mounted police was an experience which the hardiest might dread. But again and again women of delicacy and refinement underwent it and counted themselves repaid if their ordeal won a nod of approval from their leader.

And the leader? She would sit with the generals in Caxton House while the tumult grew and the reluctant policemen fought their way to Scotland Yard with women whose pertinacity left no alternative to arrest. Anon the scouts would report that the battle went well. Fifty, sixty, women had been taken, though the night was young. But the leader was seldom satisfied. Reserves, more reserves, would be sent into the street, until at midnight or later a new record of arrests had been created. Only then would the troops be called off and the General Staff concentrate on the possibilities of a further hullabaloo next day at the Law Courts.

The raids were the pitched battles of the campaign. But between the pitched battles went on an incessant and sometimes diverting warfare, of which the details have sunk into oblivion. Did these furies really break windows and burn churches and golf houses? Did they chain themselves to railings and seats in meeting places and in the House of Commons? Did they inject acids into pillarboxes? One remembers an attack upon Mr. Asquith on a golf course, in which he retained not only his dignity, but his putter. What was done to other political chiefs? Did they bite Mr. Churchill or try to poison Mr. Lloyd George? In a struggle so incomprehensible the defence is as fantastic as the attack. Did Mr. Asquith really believe that "Votes for Women" involved peril to men or to society? Were the views of Lord Birkenhead on the subject really pondered by the party chiefs? Did a Member of Parliament really warn his colleagues that women Ministers would bring their babies to the Treasury bench?

It is no doubt all true, but it passes understanding.

The monstrous controversy was drowned by the louder clamours of the world-war. The Suffragettes, so dreaded by the club men, hastened to attire themselves in factory overalls, to drive motor-cars, to nurse and scrub in hospitals, or maybe to distribute "white feathers." In the early stages of the struggle a hundred cameras registered a dramatic *rapprochement* of the militant leader and Mr. Lloyd George. At this point Mrs. Pankhurst, follower of John Stuart Mill, revolutionary, disruptionist, went to sleep. Someone of the same name, a strident voice in Hyde Park, imbued hate of the Germans and seemed to ridicule the thousands of suffrage speeches in which the enfranchisement of women had been urged as a guarantee of peace. When peace returned, women obtained the vote mainly, in Mr. Asquith's opinion, because of their behaviour during the war. How had he expected them to behave?

I do not like to think of Mrs. Pankhurst in these later phases. I like to think of her as I knew her long ago in Manchester before her star had mounted in the heavens. Then she came readily to talk to obscure meetings and at street-corners, and counted thousands of poor men and women as her friends. She had a gift of speech in those days that was greater than eloquence. She spoke mournfully. Her metaphors were shapes of gloom. But there was that in her voice and mien that caught and kept the mind. She would pass from a recital of some woman's hardship to an impassioned contemplation of all suffering:—

> "The whole of the world's tears,
> And all the trouble of her labouring ships,
> And all the trouble of her myriad years."

Her sombre face would glow with impersonal pity and appeal, her sad voice utter the plaint of her sex. One no longer heard a woman's voice, one heard, or one thought one heard, the voice of women.

There can be no question as to the magnitude of her achievement. The enfranchisement of women was won by Mrs. Pankhurst, not by the Serajevo pistol. Had there been no war, some minor calamity would have saved the face or changed the heart of the Prime Minister and rescued the Government from a situation repugnant to the Liberal tradition and rapidly becoming impossible. And more women are concerned than those of Great Britain. The movement towards sexual equality is now world-wide. When Mrs. Pankhurst broke windows some of the splinters fell in remote places: even the harem and the purdah were aware of them!

Hugh B. Chapman (essay date 1928)

SOURCE: "Mrs. Pankhurst," in *The English Review,* Vol. XLVII, July to December 1928, pp. 184-88.

[*In the following essay, Chapman eulogizes Pankhurst and points to her virtue and compassion for her fellow women.*]

When I received a telegram asking me to take part in Mrs. Pankhurst's funeral, I felt diffident, having endured nothing for the Suffrage Movement compared with those likely to be present. Dr. Cobb, in an eloquent address at the ceremony, pointed out how Mrs. Pankhurst, whom he eulogized in strong but unexaggerated terms, had foregone her war for the enfranchisement and the social liberty of woman in favour of the greater War, to which she and her troops nobly devoted themselves. Thus she acquired the object of her own campaign, which was more than conceded to the striking services they rendered, and the supreme fortitude they displayed.

As a public character Mrs. Pankhurst was strangely misunderstood, though, doubtless, her intimates grasped the fact not only of her gift of leadership and consummate patience, but of a certain tenderness and piety which were the marks of a saint, in its broadest meaning. Of the movement itself a more detailed account is, I understand, to be published by her daughter Christabel, who acted as her aide-de-camp throughout. Now that several years have passed, it is more possible to appraise one of the most remarkable personalities I have known, who left behind in my memory the thought of the gentlest of Spartans, and the opposite of what she was imagined to be by the world at large.

I want to speak, however, of a special trait through which I was attracted to Mrs. Pankhurst, though I have seldom heard it sufficiently appreciated. It was something far larger than the vote, or the collisions with the police which took place on behalf of Women's Rights. Mrs. Pankhurst embodied for me the word chastity, and became an inspiration through which the passionate side might be sanctified, without preaching, by the divine *élan* of public service. I can recall half a dozen times when I was carried off my feet by a figure combining both compassion and command, who, it is not saying too much, solved in her own person the vexed problem of the sex question. Why, or how eludes analysis, but anything maudlin was miraculously done away. The bare thought of uncleanness fled before this frail prophetess who seldom, if ever, referred to religion, but after hearing whom you felt you had been scorched by a flame. I reverently believe that she almost created a new type of woman, who ceased to think of man as the end-all of existence, but who heard a clarion call to use her gifts and attraction in a wholly different and higher cause. A great pathos for the woes of womanhood swept through the hall, and you left it with a vague yearning to find the Holy Grail, sensing a possible companionship without the smallest danger of soilure. For myself, at least, Mrs. Pankhurst spoke with the power of a seer, affecting me beyond truisms or tracts. Probably her silence on the point and the indirectness of her attack were more effective than unhealthy allusions to what might have defeated its own ends.

I knew nothing of her previous life, but I was certain that her own heart was concentrated on some human loyalty which made her sacrosanct to herself. This rendered her as immune as Joan of Arc, who led the armies of France and who, though brought into contact with the roughest and most turbulent of soldiery, eventually became canonized, since her fair name was never once tainted, despite the vilest treatment, which still makes us blush. Mrs. Pankhurst (and I am speaking purely of the woman herself) is bracketed in my mind with that heroine. Though, no doubt, this sublimated side of her character may have been unknown to the public who coupled her with such terms as "virago," it is by this she will be chiefly remembered among the inner circle of her friends. Whether it was the goal she aimed at or not is not for me, an outsider, to say, but probably her daughter will speak with far greater right and in far greater detail. Josephine Butler and her like have themselves become immortalized on this most delicate and difficult of adventures.

The other point with which I was impressed in Mrs. Pankhurst was her extraordinary love for womankind. I can never forget the sympathy towards woman revealed by the sadness of her face, ever, besides, illuminated with the light of victory. Of that her followers felt assured, even in their darkest moment, because their leader never once quailed. Her indignation for her sisters throughout the world was by no means sentimental, and was combined with a touch of fine sternness which braced, without weakening, those who came under her spell. If she called forth the fighting quality in women, it was on no personal account, which she treated as unimportant compared with a certain idealism and the use of their combative instincts to bring it about. She had the unique art of uniting women by the entire eclipse of herself. She made the humblest of them feel their own value, without referring to the element of beauty or sensual attraction. I fancy there was a large element of the soldier about her, and a power of encouragement sadly lacking in those of the same sex towards one another. That is why, at her funeral—which I prefer to think of as a memorial service—there was a tocsin of triumph in the air, and a standing to attention, with gratitude for a genuinely great woman who had gone on. Her spirit will surely still strive for good, for such a nature could otherwise never be truly content.

I confess to wishing there were a few more Mrs. Pankhursts at the present moment to whom I might send young women in trouble, and who would probably never refer to yesterday, but give them something hard to do today. I regard Mrs. Pankhurst as the incarnation of the spirit which has brought about Girl Guides and other bodies in which religion and athletics are blended. Therein the appeal to the heroic is, in my humble opinion, productive of a finer breed than ultra-devotional and ecclesiastical efforts which run dangerously near the sensual, and which, though they may develop their quota of saints, are, on balance, largely conducive to emasculation and eroticism. Mrs. Pankhurst's attitude towards womankind tended to a contempt of the term "the weaker sex," and was calculated to create a noble type of wife, walking on her own feet and asserting those moral and civic rights, the antithesis of a Turkish harem. It is for this cause that I rank her with Florence Nightingale; Agnes Weston; Matilda Wrede, the prisoners' friend in Finland; Mary Slessor, the Scottish lassie in Africa, and many others who have found careers worthy of their steel, and who have not regarded marriage and parentage as the *summum bonum* of existence compared to the lure of altruism.

It is the weakness of the Press that it is too often ignorant of the inner and deeper part of a personality. So it failed, to a large extent, to depict a great woman who, though exceptionally modest and retiring, became misrepresented through the publicity of her movement. Her silence for years after the victory was won had an eloquence all its own, but no one with any of the artist in him could do aught but regard her as a woman of others' sorrows and very much acquainted with their griefs. None but must be aware of a certain boldness and immodesty which are abroad. It is not within the scope of this article to trace their source, but I wish to disallow the smallest connection of such behaviour with this inspiring character, who would have been the very first to rebuke such decadence under the name of liberty, save that she was too genuinely humble to "preach a sermon." I happen to have had the honour of knowing several women such as Mrs. Despard, Mrs. Pethick Lawrence, and "Lady Connie," who actually gave her life for this emprise, all of whom have impressed me with the same admiration and respect which I have tried to express. After much meditation on the point and having to deal with an enormity of trouble due to the present non-morality which abounds, I am deeply thankful for this voice which nobly went out into the wilderness so long and will continue to speak with an eloquence of its own, though she has passed from this life.

It is by no means an easy task which I have faultily tried to fulfil in laying these flowers upon her grave, in strange contrast to the violence, anger, and rebellious things done, all of which are not only wiped out, but palliated in the eyes of those who have the wit to look beyond the letter into the spirit. In fine, she achieved a winsome holiness and self-eclipse which will always be woman's strongest power. It is by such that we men are eventually dominated vastly more than by what is termed individualism, or force-fulness, whereas it is women of her type who move men to undertake forlorn hopes, by becoming their staunch and strengthening comrades. Quite lately, before she passed, Mrs. Pankhurst joined the forces of law and order without, I trust, losing her wings, though where or how she learned the lesson of personal discipline I have no knowledge. Possibly private sorrow and pain had done their blessed work. My earnest prayer is that similar women may be raised up to guide the new liberties which have come to women in the political world, whether wisely or unwisely, in their suddenness it is not for me to say. I felt at that celebration of her Easter a mystical longing for a further loan of this exquisite soul, nor do I doubt that many a woman in high places, whether in politics, or on the stage, or young beginners in the finest of all services, that of rescue in any direction, must have echoed my desire. The three words which Mrs. Pankhurst has burned into my mind are Chastity, Courage, and Compassion, without the barest sense of caste or class, so that she will ever rank amongst the benefactors of her age, and hand down a school which she never strove to form, but which she formed by being herself. It will never die.

Rebecca West (essay date 1933)

SOURCE: "Mrs. Pankhurst," in *The Post-Victorians,* Ivor Nicholson & Watson, LTD., September, 1933, pp. 477-500.

[*In the following essay, West offers a detailed overview of Pankhurst's life and her role as a suffragette.*]

There has been no other woman like Emmeline Pankhurst. She was beautiful; her pale face, with its delicate square

jaw and rounded temples, recalled the pansy by its shape and a kind of velvety bloom on the expression. She dressed her taut little body with a cross between the elegance of a Frenchwoman and the neatness of a nun. She was courageous; small and fragile and no longer young, she put herself in the way of horses' hooves, she stood up on platforms under a rain of missiles, she sat in the darkness of underground jails and hunger-struck, and when they let her out because she had starved herself within touching distance of death, she rested for only a day or two and then clambered back on to the platforms, she staggered back under the horses' hooves. She did this against the grain. What she would have preferred, could her social conscience have been quieted, was to live in a pleasant suburban house, and give her cronies tea with very thin bread and butter, and sit about in the garden in a deck-chair.

Mrs. Pankhurst came to these cruel and prodigious events not as some who have attained fame in middle life. She had not lived in ease all her youth and dammed up her forces, so that there was a flood to rush forth when the dam was broken. She had borne five children, she had been distracted by the loss of a beloved husband, she had laboured long at earning a livelihood and at public work. Enough had happened to her to draw off all her natural forces. That she was not so depleted can be partly explained by the passion for the oppressed which burned in her as a form of genius; and she drew, no doubt, refreshment from the effect she had on her fellow creatures, the response they made to her peculiar quality, which was apart from her beauty, her courage, her pity. She was vibrant. One felt, as she lifted up her hoarse, sweet voice on the platform, that she was trembling like a reed. Only the reed was of steel, and it was tremendous.

On an Atlantic liner during a great storm passengers will feel in their bones the quiver that runs through the ship's backbone as her stern rests on a wave and her prow hangs in mid-air over the trough till she finds the next wave to carry her. Something of the same sort was the disturbance, the perturbation, the suspense at the core of Mrs. Pankhurst's being. She was not a particularly clever woman. One could name scores of women who were intellectually her superior. She was constitutionally naïve, she could swallow fairy stories, she had only an imperfect grasp of the map of the universe man has drawn with his thought. She was one of those people who appear now and then in history against whom it would be frivolous to lay a complaint on these grounds, since they are part of that map. She was the embodiment of an idea. Her personality was possessed by one of man's chief theories about life, which it put to the test, and which it worked out in terms of material fact. She went forward, precariously balanced on what there was of old certainty, hanging in mid-air till she could attain a new certainty, her strength vibrating as if it were going to shatter into pieces like glass, maintaining itself because it was steel.

She was born in Manchester on July 14, 1858, of North-country stock with character. Her grandfather, a master cotton-spinner, had in his youth been cruelly used by the State. One day he was carried off to sea by the Press Gang, and did not manage to make his return for many years, by which time his family had completely disappeared. Later he fled before the soldiers at the Battle of Peterloo, and with his wife, a fustian cutter of sturdy disposition, took part in the Cobdenite agitations of the Hungry Forties. His son, Robert Goulden, was brilliant and versatile. He began as an errand boy and ended as a manufacturer, he was an amateur actor who made a great impression in the heavier Shakespearean parts; he ran a theatre in Salford as a hobby, and he was a romantic Liberal. He took a leading part in that altruistic movement by which Lancashire, brought to beggary by the American Civil War and constrained by every economic reason to side with the South, solidly upheld Lincoln and the North. He had by that time married a Manxwoman, who bore him five sons and five daughters. His eldest girl, little Emmeline, rattled a collecting box for the poor Negroes and learned to weep over *Uncle Tom's Cabin*, though, with an entirely characteristic refusal to restrict herself to logical categories, she gave the most fervent loyalty of her imagination to Charles the First.

When she was thirteen Robert Goulden took her to school in Paris. He left her at the Ecole Normale at Neuilly, a green and spacious suburb which must have been a pleasing contrast to Manchester. In any case, Emmeline's love of beauty would have made her a friend to France; but owing to an accident, Neuilly offered a seduction even more specially appealing to her temperament. Because Mr. Goulden had to make the expedition fit in with business engagements, he left her at the school during the holidays, when there was but one other pupil. This was a fascinating little girl called Noémie, who had no home to go to, because her mother was dead, and her father, Henri de Rochefort, was in prison in New Caledonia for the part he had played in the Commune. The two girls became instantly welded in a friendship that lasted till the end of their lives, and Emmeline learned to adore Henri de Rochefort in his daughter's talk, as later she was to adore him in his own person. He was something for a romantic little Radical to adore, a splendid, spitting cat of a man, who spoke his mind in the face of any danger, who, though Napoleon III sat on the throne, began his leader on the shooting of Victor Noir by Prince Pierre-Napoleon Bonaparte with the words, *"J'ai eu la faiblesse de croire qu'un Bonaparte pouvait être autre qu'un assassin. J'ai osé m'imaginer qu'un duel loyal était possible dans cette famille où le meutre et le guet-apenus sont de tradition et de l'usage . . ."*; who fought duel after duel, suffered arrest again and again, and endured exile and imprisonment with like fiery fortitude.

Emmeline was, owing to a real or maldiagnosed weakness of health, forbidden to take part seriously in the school work; she never then or later knew any form of study stricter than desultory reading, or appreciated its uses. But she was receiving, from Noémie and her absent father and her guardian, Edmond Adam, a thorough education in a certain department of French life, in the passionate and picturesque conduct of politics. There the prizes went to the daring. There it was no shame to act violently and fight one's enemies as if they were enemies. And in this atmosphere she spent those very formative years between thirteen and twenty; for she loved Paris so much that, when her own school-days were over, she coaxed her father to let her stay on as companion to a younger sister.

She tried her best to stay in France for ever; and that, alas, led to her smarting and tearful removal back to Lancashire. There was a curious event which, for the first time, revealed that Emmeline was an odd fish who was not going to take life as she found it. Noémie married, and thought it would be delightful if Emmeline found a French husband and settled down as her neighbour. Such a husband could be obtained, of course, only by a bride with a *dot*. But Emmeline knew that her father was well-to-do, and she found nothing abhorrent in the *dot* system. She had disliked the scenes that her father had made when her mother brought him bills, and had seen with her clear eyes that, in a masculinist and capitalist social system, where women have not economic freedom and wives are not paid, the dowry is the only way by which a woman can be given self-respecting security and independence. Romantic Liberalism could go and hang itself. She was a realist. But unfortunately her father was still a romantic Liberal. When Emmeline found a pleasing suitor and asked for her *dot,* Robert Goulden stormed the house down at the idea of buying a husband for his daughter, and immediately made her leave Paris and come home. She obeyed with the worst possible grace; and suddenly looked up through her sulks and saw someone as spectacular as Rochefort, Dr. Richard Marsden Pankhurst, and fell in love with him.

It was, on the surface, an astounding match. He was twice her age, a scholar with many academic honours, a distinguished jurist, whose studies filled all his leisure hours. He was dedicated to public work, of a laborious and unrewarded sort; he achieved great things in the promotion of popular education, he was a Republican, and an indefatigable enemy of Disraeli's Imperialism. He had a great position in the North. When he arrived at a meeting thousands waited cheering and waving their handkerchiefs. Though he had what would have been a crushing handicap for most politicians, an extremely unpleasant, shrill, edgy voice, the force of his mind and the transparent beauty of his nature was such that an audience never remained conscious of this defect for more than the first few minutes. He was a saint who had put all weaknesses behind him and wore himself out in acts of benevolence. Such works of art were these private good deeds that they had something of that immortality: a visitor to Manchester more than a decade after his death thought that he must have been dead only a month or so, so vividly had some whom he had helped spoken of him.

But Emmeline was just a wicked little thing, fond of pretty clothes and French novels. It happened, however, to be a perfectly right and wise marriage. Emmeline committed herself gravely and honestly to her love for him. Her mother was deeply shocked, and tried to inspire her to the proper female monkey-tricks by telling her of the coldness with which she herself had received her prospective husband's wooings, and was shocked still more when her daughter suggested to her betrothed as a protest against the then legal disabilities of married women, that they should form a free union. (Noémie's mother had married Henri de Rochefort only on her death-bed to give her children a legal protector.) Dr. Pankhurst would not consent, however, partly because he feared to expose her to disrespect, partly because he knew that those who challenged the marriage-laws were usually prevented from challenging any other abuses. So they married, and were happy ever after. Not the bitterest critic of Mrs. Pankhurst ever suggested that her husband did not find her, from beginning to end of the nineteen years of their marriage, a perfect wife.

They had five children: Christabel, who was born when her mother was twenty-two, Sylvia, born two years later, Frank, born two years later, Adela, born a year later, and Harry, born four years later. Theirs was not a home in which parents exerted themselves to keep their children's lives a thing apart, a pool of quietness in which they could develop until they were mature. Mrs. Pankhurst was a young woman, full of appetite for life, and wildly in love with her husband, so that she was delighted to stand by him in his public work. She did not neglect her children, but the stream of affairs flowed through her home, and the children bobbed like corks on the tide of adult life. One of them hated it. Sylvia Pankhurst's *The Suffragette Movement* stands beside Gordon Craig's *Memories of My Mother* as an expression of the burning resentment that the child of a brilliant mother may feel at having to share her brilliance with the world. But the other children liked it, and revelled in the dramas that followed one after another. First, there was the famous Manchester by-election, at which Dr. Pankhurst stood as an Independent candidate on a platform including Adult Suffrage, Republicanism, Secular Education, the payment of Members of Parliament, Disestablishment, Home Rule, Disarmament, and a kind of League of Nations. The year was 1883. He was not elected; but a quarter of the electorate supported him—an incredible proportion at that time—and his expenses were £500 as against his opponents' £5,000. It was a triumphant piece of propaganda work; but it ended in personal bitterness, in the first display by Mrs. Pankhurst of that ruthlessness which she shared with the armed prophets. Till then she and her family had lived in her father's home, a patriarchal dwelling where the Manx mistress of the house carried on all the domestic arts, even to bread-baking and butter-making. But though Robert Goulden had stood by Dr. Pankhurst during the by-election, he rebuked him afterwards for his Socialist extremism, and to mark a dissociation of political interests Dr. Pankhurst and his family left the Goulden home, accompanied by Mrs. Pankhurst's sister Mary. On this separation Mrs. Pankhurst reminded her father that he had promised her some property on her marriage. He denied ever having made such a promise. They never spoke to each other again.

This deep feeling over a matter of property was odd to find in a woman who all her life long regarded money chiefly as something to give away. But it was a consequence of the simple, surgical directness of her mind. If Robert Goulden wanted to accept the masculinist and capitalist world, then he ought to be logical about it, and protect her in the only way that a woman can be protected in a masculinist and capitalist world. The only reason he could have for failing to do so must be that he did not love her. But it must also be remembered that her childhood hero had been Charles I, the King who lost his crown and his head, and that she attached an importance to Henri de Rochefort's refusal to use his marquisate which was, since the renunciation had actually been made by a previous generation of the family, historically undue. The men she specially admired were those who had power and renounced it. It is an indication that in her there was an element of sex-antagonism, that neurosis which revolts against the difference of the sexes, which calls on the one to which the neurotic does not belong to sacrifice its special advantage so that the one to which the neurotic does belong may show superior. But neuroses often engender the dynamic power by which the sane part of the mind carries on its business. Mrs. Pankhurst sublimated her sex-antagonism. She was in no way a man-hater, loving her sons as deeply as her daughters, and she completely converted her desire to offend the other sex into a desire to defend her own.

Dr. Pankhurst stood for Parliament again at Rotherhithe, and was again defeated. There followed a painful libel action. A Conservative speaker had told a lying story which put into Dr. Pankhurst's mouth a coarse declaration of atheism. He was in fact an agnostic of the gentlest type, full of reverence and love for the person of Christ. He brought action, not so much for his own sake, as to bring a test case which would show how far Socialist candidates could find remedy in the new libel law for the flood of slanderous abuse that was turned on them at every election. There were aspects of this libel action which were calculated to remove certain comfortable illusions about human nature from the minds of the least critical. Dr. Pankhurst, never worldly-wise, appealed to Mr. A. J. Balfour as a brother agnostic, on the indisputable evidence of certain passages in *A Defence of Philosophic Doubt*. Mr. Balfour received the appeal without brotherly enthusiasm, and practised the arts of evasion to avoid associating himself with this crude imbroglio. The trial itself was conducted with what might have seemed shameless prejudice to those who did not know that British justice is above suspicion. Mrs. Pankhurst ran the risk of prosecution for contempt of court by sending a cutting letter to the judge who tried the case.

The Pankhursts went to live in London. There Mrs. Pankhurst was extremely happy. It is true that shortly after she settled there her son Frank died and her grief was terrible. But she had a gay time establishing herself as a political hostess with tea-urns in Russell Square for the Socialist London that was humbly proliferating in the Fabian

Society, the Social Democratic Federation, the Independent Labour Party, and half a dozen other obscure organisations; a naïve and ludicrous parody it must have seemed to those who really knew the world, of the real social functions of power, where great ladies shining with diamonds received at the head of wide staircases under magnificent chandeliers. She worked hard for all feminist causes, for all issues which promised man more liberty, although always she regarded herself not as an independent worker, but as her husband's helpmate. She had much amusement, too, trying to support herself by running Emerson's, a kind of amateurish Liberty's. The French influence came back into her life at full strength, for Henri de Rochefort was an exile living in London, and he constantly visited her.

It had to come to an end soon. Both Mrs. Pankhurst and her husband were children about money. They spent it, not like drunken sailors, but like drunken saints. They gave it away with both hands. Emerson's, owing to bad costing, was an expensive toy. They had taken the Russell Square house on the fag-end of a lease without reflecting that at the end they would have to pay dilapidations. In bad order they retreated to Lancashire, first to Southport, and then to Manchester, where they got on a sounder financial footing, and Mrs. Pankhurst came to her proper form as a social worker. She helped to organise the unemployed in the slump of 1894, and did much to popularise her husband's views on productive public works as a means of relieving unemployment. She was elected to the Chorlton Board of Guardians, and blazed with rage because she found the little girls in the workhouse still wearing eighteenth-century dress, with low necks and no sleeves. For some obscure reason they had no nightdresses, and they had no drawers or knickers, even in winter time—a fact which infuriated her beyond bearing—because the matron and a couple of refined female guardians had been too modest to mention such garments to the male members of the Board. This was the kind of tomfoolery which Mrs. Pankhurst could not stand, and which her Movement did much to end. These, and many other abuses, she reformed.

There was a fight, too, against an attempt by the City Council to deny the I.L.P., now newly become formidable, the right of meeting in the public places of Manchester. Mrs. Pankhurst acted as chairman to the speakers at the test meeting, sticking the ferrule of her open umbrella in the ground so that the faithful could throw their pennies into it. With eight others she was arrested, and stood calmly in the dock, dressed her prettiest, wearing a little pink straw bonnet. The case against her was dismissed, though she announced that she would repeat her offence so long as she was at liberty. This she did, although she was summoned again and again. She always wore her pink straw bonnet, and it became the signal round which the rebels gathered. This was a real fight, and it took a long time to win. She lived therefore for many months under the expectation of prison. She was willing then, had the need arisen, to prove the point she proved later.

There was an election, too, at Gorton, Lancashire, where Dr. Pankhurst stood as I.L.P. candidate. The I.L.P. had the scantiest funds, and had to use cheap methods of campaign, such as chalking announcements of meetings on the pavements. For £343 of election expenses against the Conservative candidate's £1,375, Dr. Pankhurst gained 4,261 votes against the Conservative's 5,865. The Pankhurst children helped in the campaign, and it was no minor part of their education, which was indeed unconventional.

Mrs. Pankhurst as a mother offers certain surprises to those who would expect her to have the same views as the kind of woman who has followed in her steps regarding feminism. She was thoroughly of her time. She believed in corporal punishment for children as mothers did in the 'eighties, and in making them finish their porridge even if their stomachs revolted against it. She had some of the prejudices of her Manx country-bred mother. She had no such great opinion of fresh air as a nursery remedy, and she strongly disapproved of spectacles, causing her younger son, who had weak eyes, great inconvenience thereby. And in one respect she was almost behind her times. She attached no importance to ordinary education for her daughters. They were often put in the care of governesses who gave them no lessons whatsoever, but trained them in such unusual subjects as the appreciation of Egyptian art; and when they did attend schools she connived shamelessly at their truancy. This was due in part, perhaps, to her knowledge that schools were so much part of the capitalist system that her family could have no comfortable welcome there, and it is true that at least one headmistress persecuted and humiliated the children because their father was a Socialist. In those days political rancours went deeper than we care to imagine today. When Mrs. Pankhurst was on the Manchester Education Committee she had to intervene to protect a woman teacher who had been dismissed by the owner of a school because it had leaked out that she was a daughter of Ernest Jones, the Chartist, who had been dead for over thirty years.

But there was also a deeper reason for Mrs. Pankhurst's unconcern about education. It is said that the only occasion on which she showed overwhelming grief about a personal matter other than over the death of her husband and her sons and her final alienation from one of her family, was when her daughter Christabel decided that she would not become a professional dancer. The child had shown great promise at her dancing classes, and it had been her mother's dream that she should become a great ballerina, who should practise her art all over the world. This anecdote has been repeated querulously, as if it were a proof of Mrs. Pankhurst's light-mindedness. But it surely gives a clue to the secret of her greatness as a leader. She knew that no culture can evolve values which wholly negate primitive ones. She would have understood that Sir Walter Scott's boy spoke better sense than the learned when, brought up in ignorance of *Waverley* and its fame, he accounted for the fuss people made of his father by saying, "It's commonly him that sees the hare sitting." She had not lost touch with primitive wisdom; she knew that man's first necessity is to be a good animal, that rhythm can prove as much as many arguments, that the mind is only one of the instruments of human power.

Dr. Pankhurst died. His widow was heartbroken. For a time she was too distracted to attend to any public work. But she could not be idle, for she was without means. Her husband had been splendidly careless about money. His last months had been spent in successfully organising opposition to a dirty and dangerous scheme by which the Manchester Corporation intended to pollute the Mersey with the town sewage by diverting it through a new culvert, designed to dump it in a part of the river outside the scope of sanitary jurisdiction. Had he not opposed the construction of the culvert he would have been instructed to act as Counsel for the scheme, and might have made over £8,000 by it. With poverty earned thus his family were well content, but Mrs. Pankhurst had to work. She became Registrar of Births and Deaths in Chorlton, and opened another Emerson's, which lingered on for some time and then had to be abandoned. She came back to public life for a little in 1900, in the Pro-Boer agitation. Then she began to feel a special interest in Woman Suffrage, perhaps because her daughter Christabel had suddenly, and for the first time, become keenly interested in feminism, and was studying for a law degree at Victoria University. It also happened that about this time she was stung to fury by an incident connected with a memorial to her dead husband. Though she had accepted some funds raised by his wealthier friends, she had refused to touch the subscriptions gathered from the predominantly working-class readers of Robert Blatchford's *The Clarion,* on the grounds that she did not wish them to give her children an education which they could not have afforded for their own; and she suggested that the money should be spent on building a Pankhurst Memorial Hall for the use of Socialist societies. When it was finished she found that the branch of the Independent Labour Party which was to use it as headquarters refused to admit women. This led her to review the attitude of the I.L.P. and the Socialist Movement generally towards feminism. She found that it was no more than lukewarm; and therefore on October 10, 1903, in her drawing-room at 62 Nelson Street, she held the inaugural meeting of a society called the Women's Social and Political Union.

For the first two years the proceedings of this society were limited to humdrum harrying of the Socialist societies. But the result of this routine was to force up to explosion point Mrs. Pankhurst's realisation of the wrongs inflicted on women by their status, and the indifference on this subject which was felt by even the most progressive societies dominated by men. It was becoming every day more clear, too, that a certain condition she found necessary if she was to act effectively was about to be abundantly fulfilled. Oddly enough, she never did anything important alone. She had to work with an ally. For that purpose Dr. Pankhurst had been perfect; but the development of her daughter Christabel made her see that he might not be irreplaceable. Though Christabel had never studied anything

but dancing at all seriously until her middle teens, she was taking her law studies well, and when she went up to London to apply for admission to the Benchers of Lincoln's Inn she conducted the proceedings with a strange, cool, high-handed mastery that was remarkable in a girl in her early twenties.

In 1905 Mrs. Pankhurst came to London to find a private member who would give his place in the ballot to a measure giving votes for women. There was then, as for many years before, a majority of members in the House pledged to support Woman Suffrage, but this meant nothing more than a polite bow and smile to their more earnest female helpers in their constitutencies. Hardly any of them meant to lift a little finger to make Woman Suffrage an accomplished fact.

Mrs. Pankhurst had the greatest difficulty in finding a sincere Suffragist among the small number of members who had been fortunate in the ballot that gave them the right to introduce a Bill on one or other of the Friday afternoons during the Session; but on May 12, Mr. Bamford Slack brought in a Suffrage Bill. Mrs. Pankhurst brought with her to the House of Commons an immense number of women, which was swelled by members of the more old-fashioned and conservative Suffrage societies, who had been excited by the agitation of the new movement. There were so many that they filled the Lobby, the passages, and the Terrace. When it became obvious that the Bill was, as usual, going to be obstructed and talked out, Mrs. Pankhurst looked round her at the great crowd of women. Much more than the future of the feminist movement was decided in that second. Then she scribbled a note to be taken in to the Prime Minister, in which, with the arrogance of a leader writing to a leader, she told him that unless he gave facilities for the further discussion of this Bill her Union would work against his Government. She was a little woman in her late forties, without a penny, without a powerful friend. The threat was comic. As soon as the Bill was talked out, there was an impromptu meeting outside the House which would have been stopped had not Keir Hardie intervened.

Mrs. Pankhurst went home. There were some new recruits in the North, a mill girl called Annie Kenney, an Irish school-teacher called Teresa Billington. All that summer Mrs. Pankhurst with these girls and Christabel and Sylvia went from wake to wake in the Lancashire and Yorkshire mill-towns, and stood on I.L.P. and Trade Union platforms. In the autumn Sir Edward Grey came to speak at Manchester, and failed to reply to a letter from the Women's Social and Political Union asking him to receive a deputation. They attended his meeting and asked questions regarding the attitude of the coming Liberal Government. But these were not answered, so they interrupted the subsequent proceedings, and were ejected. Outside the hall they addressed a meeting and were arrested on a charge of having assaulted the police, and were sent to prison for seven and three days in the third division. It is hardly necessary to say that the balance of the assaults committed on this occasion were committed by the stewards and police-men on the Suffragists; but the Suffragists would them-selves hardly have troubled to raise that point. They candidly admitted they had meant to be arrested. For it was their intention to maintain that in a democratic State government rests on the consent of the governed, and that until they were granted the franchise on the same terms as men they were going to withhold that consent; and that they were going to mark the withholding of their consent by disturbing the peace, to the precise degree which the resistance of the Government made necessary; and that they would not take it that the Government had yielded unless whatever party was in power itself passed an Act for the enfranchisement of women.

For nine years this policy was carried into effect by innumerable women under the leadership of Mrs. Pankhurst. For nine years no politician of any importance could address a meeting without fear of interruption. There was never any lack of women volunteers for this purpose, even though the stewards nearly always ejected them with great physical violence, sometimes of a sort that led to grave internal injuries. One of the most brilliant Suffragists, or Suffragettes, as *The Daily Mail* started people calling them, May Gawthorpe, was an invalid for many years as a result of a blow received in this way. When the harried political organisers tried to solve the problem by excluding all women from the meetings, interruptions were made through windows and skylights, even if this involved perilous climbing over roofs and gutters, and evading police search by concealment in neighbouring attics for two or three days. There were also constant disturbances at the House of Commons. When a Private Member's Bill for Woman Suffrage was being talked out in 1906, Mrs. Pankhurst and some friends created a riot in the Ladies' Gallery. From that time repeated raids were made on the House of Commons by women seeking interviews with Cabinet Ministers, and these became in time vast riots which it taxed the power of Scotland Yard to keep within bounds. All the area round Whitehall and St. Stephen's Square was packed with people, watching while women threw themselves against a cordon of police, and withstood massed charges of mounted men. The spectators divided themselves as the night went on into supporters and opponents, and there would be dashes made to rescue individual women or to manhandle them. The police were ordered to make as few arrests as possible, so some of the women would find themselves thrown about like so many footballs.

Participation in these interruptions and in these riots meant imprisonment. Very soon the women were getting sentences of six weeks' imprisonment. They rose soon to three months, to nine months, to two years. To put the Government in an impossible position, they hunger-struck, abstaining from food, and sometimes even from water. At first they were released. Then the Government employed surgical methods of forcible feeding. The prisoners resisted that, but this meant that their gums were hacked to pieces with steel gags, and the tubes were apt to injure the internal organs, and the food was often vomited, so they frequently had to be released all the same. Then the Government passed the Cat-and-Mouse Act, which enabled them to release the hunger-striking prisoners when they were within touching distance of death, wait till they had recovered their health, and then arrest them again, and bring them back to death once more, and so on. It was one of the most unlovely expedients that the English legislature has ever invented, and it is ironical that it should have been the work of a Liberal Government. And it had the further disgrace of being ineffectual, for it entirely failed to quench the Movement. That spread like wild-fire over the country. It had hundreds of thousands of supporters, its income rose to nearly £38,000 a year, its weekly newspaper had a circulation of 40,000. It held enthusiastic meetings all over the country, though its militancy evoked attack, and Suffragist speakers were not protected as Cabinet Ministers. Many suffered grave physical injury. But for the most part these meetings were passionate acclamations of the rightness of the Cause and its leaders. London saw long, long processions, longer than it had ever known follow any other than Mrs. Pankhurst.

The Press was overwhelmingly against them; which was one of the first proofs that the modern sensational newspaper has no real influence, that its readers buy it for its news and not for its opinions. There were, of course, certain noble supporters among journalists, such as Mr. Nevinson, Mr. Brailsford, and the late Mr. H. W. Massingham; but for the rest the Press loved to represent the Movement with contempt and derision. Mrs. Pankhurst and her daughters were crazy hooligans, their followers were shrieking hysterics, their policy was wild delirium. Nothing could be further from the truth. The Movement contained some of the *détraqués* who follow any drum that is beaten, but these were weeded out, for the Cat-and-Mouse Act was something of a test for the solider qualities.

But the Movement was neither crazy nor hysterical nor delirious. It was stone-cold in its realism. Mrs. Pankhurst was not a clever woman, but when she experienced something she incorporated it in her mind and used it as a basis for action. When she started the Women's Social and Political Union she was sure of two things: that the ideas of freedom and justice which had been slowly developing in England during the eighteenth and nineteenth centuries had grown to such maturity that there existed an army of women resentful of being handicapped by artificial disadvantages imposed simply on the grounds of their sex, and that sex antagonism was so strong among men that it produced an attitude which, if it were provoked to candid expression, would make every self-respecting woman want to fight it. In both of these suppositions she was entirely correct. The real force that made the Suffrage Movement was the quality of the Opposition. Women, listening to Anti-Suffrage speeches, for the first time knew what many men really thought of them. One such speech that brought many into the Movement had for its climax a jocular description of a future female Lord Chancellor being seized with labour pains on the Woolsack; and left no doubt that the speaker considered labour pains as in themselves, apart from the setting, a funny subject. The allegation, constantly made, that all women became insane at the age of forty-five also roused much resentment. But apart from general principles, the wicked frivolity of the attitude adopted towards the women by the Liberal Government was the real recruiting serjeant for the Movement.

It must be remembered that the majority of the Liberal Members of Parliament, and indeed the majority of the Cabinet, were pledged to support Woman Suffrage. There was therefore every logical and every moral reason why they should have granted it; and they did not need to fear the ignominy of seeming to yield to force, for Christabel, with her fine political mind, frequently declared truces and gave them every opportunity to save their bacon. The explanation commonly accepted—and it is the only one that appears possible—was that the opposition to votes for women was insisted on by one important member of the Cabinet, influenced by the views of his wife who has since published book after book of almost incredible silliness. That the protection women can expect from men is highly limited and personal in its scope many Suffragists learned, as they noticed that the stewards of Liberal meetings not only ejected them, but thoroughly enjoyed inflicting as much physical injury on them as possible. They were to learn that even more poignantly in the next few years, as they hid in cellars from bombs dropped by the protective sex; but the previous lesson was even more disgusting, because it was completely gratuitous. The matter could have been settled in ten minutes. But it was not, and the Cabinet Ministers who might have settled it saw nothing to limit their stewards to the task of ejection and often even encouraged them to exceed it; and outside the halls they showed even less adherence to the standards to which, one had believed, our governors adhered.

Was justice, even British justice, blind? The case of Lady Constance Lytton suggested it was not. She, chivalrous soul, suspected that some of the Suffrage prisoners were roughly treated because they were persons of no social importance. She herself had been sentenced to six weeks' imprisonment, and had been instantly dismissed as medically unfit. She went to jail again, not as Lord Lytton's sister, but as Jane Warton, a seamstress, and although on the second occasion as on the first she had mitral disease of the heart, she was forcibly fed within an inch of her life.

Mrs. Pankhurst had said that she would go on applying pressure to the Government till it yielded. She continued to do so. She seemed made of steel, although she had suffered a most crushing bereavement in the death of her son Harry in distressing circumstances. He had contracted infantile paralysis, and to pay for his nursing-home expenses, which seemed likely to continue indefinitely, she had to leave him to go on a lecture tour in America, since for all the tens of thousands of pounds that were coming into the Union she drew no more than £200 a year. Shortly after her return he died, and this inflicted a blow from which

she never recovered. But she went on inflexibly along the road she had planned. She thought of new ways of making the Government's existence intolerable every day. The plateglass windows of the West End of London went down one night in a few minutes to answer the challenge of a member of the Government who had reproached the Suffragists for having committed no act of violence comparable to the pulling up of Hyde Park Railings by the Reform rioters of 1867. Christabel fled to France so that the Movement could be sure of one leader to dictate the policy. Mrs. Pankhurst and the two other chief officials of the Union, Frederick and Emmeline Pethick Lawrence, were tried for conspiracy and sentenced to nine months' imprisonment, in spite of the jury's plea that they should be treated with the utmost leniency. They hunger-struck and were released.

But a new side of her implacability then showed itself. Her policy had meant a ruthless renunciation of old ties. She had cut herself off entirely from the Labour Party; she was even prepared, in these later years, to attack it as a component part of the Liberal Party's majority. She had silenced her youngest daughter, Adela, as a speaker because of her frank Socialist bias, and her second daughter Sylvia afterwards left the Union to form societies that were as much Labour as Suffragist in the East End. She had been merciless in her preservation of party discipline. There was no nonsense about democracy in the Women's Social and Political Union. Teresa Billington had long been driven out for raising the topic. Mrs. Pankhurst, Christabel, and the Lawrences exercised an absolute dictatorship. But now the Lawrences had to go. They opposed the further prosecution of militancy, and Christabel and Mrs. Pankhurst quietly told them to relinquish their positions in the Union. There was more than appears to be said for the Pankhursts' position from their point of view. They knew that the Government intended to strip the Pethick Lawrences of their fortune by recovering from them (as the only moneyed officials of the Union) the cost of all the damage done by the militants; and as they knew that in actual fact Christabel settled the policy of the Union, they saw no reason why the Pethick Lawrences should stay on to the embarrassment of all persons concerned. But the Pethick Lawrences were heartbroken. Not for a moment did the crisis appall Mrs. Pankhurst. Letters were burned in pillarboxes; houses—but only empty ones—went up in flames; riot was everywhere. Mrs. Pankhurst was again tried for conspiracy, and this time received a sentence of three years' imprisonment, though again the jury fervently recommended her to mercy. She was then dragged in and out of prison under the Cat-and-Mouse Act, while militancy rose to a pitch that had never been imagined by its most fervent supporters, and acquired a strange, new character of ultimate desperation. Emily Wilding Davidson tried to stop the Derby by throwing herself under the horses' hooves, and, as she had anticipated, was killed. A vast silent cortège of women followed her coffin through the streets. Mrs. Pankhurst, rising from her bed in a nursing home to attend the funeral, was re-arrested. But they were careful never quite to break her body. Both the Government and the Suffragettes knew what was bound to happen if Mrs. Pankhurst should be killed.

Suddenly war came, and in the sight of the world her star darkened. Immediately the pacifism she had learned from Dr. Pankhurst vanished and left no trace. In an instant she stopped all militancy, all Suffrage work; with perfect discipline her army disbanded. She then declared herself a fierce Jingo, her paper *The Suffragette* became *Britannia*, and Christabel wrote leaders that grew into more crudely Chauvinist attacks on certain members of the Government, such as Lord Grey of Fallodon, for insufficiently vigorous prosecution of the War. But this did not represent nearly such a fundamental reversal as might be supposed. She had, after all, been brought up in France just after the Franco-Prussian War, and she had then conceived a life-long hatred of Germany; and there was nothing surprising if *Britannia* translated it into French. "*J'ai eu la faiblesse de croire qu'un Bonaparte pouvait être autre chose qu'un assassin. . . .*" Rochefort would have thought himself failing in an obvious duty if he had let a day pass without announcing that somebody, somewhere, was betraying France. This astonishing trace of the influence of French politics on Mrs. Pankhurst, so little modified by time, makes us realise that the Suffrage Movement had been the copy of a French model executed with North-country persistence. We had been watching a female General Boulanger with *nous.*

Besides these patriotic successes and some propaganda for women's war service, Mrs. Pankhurst and her daughter did little, and they did not undertake any important administrative duties. They were both of them trained and temperamentally adapted for political organisation, for which there was now no place; and the older woman, who was now fifty-six, and had been leading a campaign life in and out of prison for eleven years, was too exhausted for any first-rate work. It is said that Christabel Pankhurst did much good work, much better than her writings would suggest, in an advisory capacity to a certain politician. But this was not ostentatiously done, and it must have seemed to many of their followers that Mrs. Pankhurst and her daughter had passed into obscurity. Yet it was then that she did perhaps the most decisive Suffrage work of her life. She persuaded a certain important politician that when peace came again she could reassemble her party and begin militancy where it had left off. There were many other causes which united to contribute to the triumph of the Suffrage cause at that time. Parallel to the militant movement had developed a nonmilitant movement, also immensely powerful, which had caused a dangerous discontent among the female members of the older political parties. But if the threat of Mrs. Pankhurst's existence had not been there women might not have been given the vote on the same terms as men in 1917, ostensibly as a reward for their war services.

After that victory, Mrs. Pankhurst wellnigh vanished from the eyes of her followers. The rebellious glory was departed. She repudiated utterly now everything she had fought for in her youth, besides her husband, and came out of the War a high Tory. She seemed a little puzzled what to do, for her ally had left her. Christabel, the quality of whose mind remains a profound mystery, had taken one look at the map of Europe, spread out in the sunshine of peace, and had grown pale with horror. Her gift for fore-seeing political events had often amounted to clairvoyance, and there is reason to suppose that it did not desert her then. Her realisation had the effect, curious in Dr. Pankhurst's daughter, bred in agnosticism, of making her announce that here were the signs and portents that herald the Second Coming of the Lord Jesus Christ. She went to America and led a frugal life as an evangelist of a sober and unsensational kind, devoting her leisure to the care of an adopted daughter. For a time Mrs. Pankhurst lived in Canada, delivering lectures to women's societies on such subjects as the legal protection of women and children, public health, the blessings of the British Empire, and the contempt of liberty she had seen during a visit to Russia. But finally she returned to England and accepted the post of nursing the unpromising constituency of Whitechapel as a Tory candidate, a duty which she fulfilled conscientiously. She secured no financial advantage by this conservatism, for she was paid only a pittance and lived over a baker's shop; she could have attained a much higher standard of living by remaining an unattached feminist writer and lecturer. Now she enjoyed life in little, gentle, old-ladyish ways. She loved window-shopping, and sometimes bought a dress at the sales and remodelled it herself. She liked dropping in on her old friends, the Marshalls, where "she had her own chair," and talking about the old days in France, about her husband, about her dead boys. There were letters from Christabel and Adela, who, though long alienated from her mother by her Communist views, was ultimately reconciled to her. But Mrs. Pankhurst had never wanted to be old, and her body had been hideously mal-treated. As a result of injuries received in forcible feedings, she still suffered from a recurrent form of jaundice. In 1928, shortly after women had received full adult suffrage, she went to church on Easter Monday in the country, was driven home to White-chapel, took to her bed, and, for no particular medical reason, died. She left £72.

It is all forgotten. We forget everything now. We have forgotten what came before the War. We have forgotten the War. There are so many newspapers so full of so much news, so many motor-cars, so many films, that image is superimposed on image, and nothing is clearly seen. In an emptier age, which left more room for the essential, it would be remembered that Emmeline Pankhurst with all her limitations was glorious. Somehow, in her terse, austere way she was as physically glorious as Ellen Terry or Sarah Bernhardt. She was glorious in her physical courage, in her obstinacy, in her integrity. Her achievements have suffered in repute owing to the fashion of jeering at the Parliamentary system. Women novelists who want to strike out a line as being specially broadminded declare they think we are no better for the vote; if they spent half an hour turning over pre-War newspapers and looking out references to women's employment and legal and social status, they might come to a different opinion. Women who do not like working in offices and cannot get married write letters to the papers ascribing their plight to feminism. But even before women got the vote they had to work in offices, with the only difference that they received less money and worked under worse conditions; and then as now there existed no machinery to compel men to marry women they did not want. Few intelligent women in a position to compare the past with the present will deny that the vote brought with it substantial benefits of both a material and spiritual kind.

There were also incidental benefits arising out of the Movement. The Suffragettes' indignant denunciation of the insanitary conditions in the jails meant an immense advance of public opinion regarding penal reform. In 1913 it suddenly came into Christabel Pankhurst's head to write a series of articles regarding the prevalence of venereal disease. These were ill-informed and badly written, but they scattered like wind an age-long conspiracy of prudishness, and enabled society to own the existence of these diseases and set about exterminating them as had never been possible before. But Mrs. Pankhurst's most valuable indirect contribution to her time was made in May 1905; a dusty and obscure provincial, she sent in a threatening note to the Prime Minister, and spent the next years proving that that threat had thunder and lightning behind it. She thereby broke down the assumption of English politicians, which till then no legislative actions, no extensions of the franchise had been able to touch, that the only people who were politically important were those who were socially important; and all the democratic movements of her day shared in the benefits. It would be absurd to deny that the ultimate reason for the rise of the Labour Party was the devoted work of its adherents, but it would be equally absurd to deny that between 1905 and 1914 it found its path smoothed by an increasingly respectful attitude on the part of St. Stephen's, the Press, and the public.

But Mrs. Pankhurst's chief and most poignant value to the historian will be her demonstration of what happens to a great human being of action in a transition period. She was the last popular leader to act on inspiration derived from the principles of the French Revolution; she put her body and soul at the service of Liberty, Equality, and Fraternity, and earned a triumph for them. Then doubt seized her, as it was to seize a generation. In the midst of her battle for democracy she was obliged, lest that battle should be lost, to become a dictator. Later we were all to debate whether that sacrifice of principle could be justified in the case of Russia. She trembled under the strain of the conflict, and perhaps she trembled also because she foresaw that she was to gain a victory, and then confront a mystery. She had always said and felt she wanted the vote to feed the hungry. Enfranchised, she found herself aware that economic revolution was infinitely more difficult and drastic than the fiercest political revolution. With her childlike honesty, her hate of pretentiousness, she failed to put up a good show to cover her perplexity. She spoke the truth—she owned she saw it better to camp among the ru-

ins of capitalism than push out into the uncharted desert. With her whole personality she enacted our perplexity, as earlier she had enacted our revolt, a priestess of the people.

Piers Brendon (essay date 1980)

SOURCE: "Mrs. Pankhurst," in *Eminent Edwardians*, Houghton Mifflin Company, 1980, pp. 131-94.

[*In the following essay, Brendon offers a historical overview of Pankhurst's life and discusses the role of violence in her life and work.*]

I

Mrs Emmeline Pankhurst became the most famous and the most notorious woman of her day by means of violence. Violence, after all, was a male prerogative. Its employment by this new Joan of Arc and her Suffragette minions was at once a castrating threat to the lords of humankind and a vile outrage against all notions of feminine propriety. But Mrs Pankhurst's own violence was less striking as a form of political agitation than as a mode of personal dominance. With clenched fists and a fierce tilt of her chin she confessed to a group of intimates, 'I *love* fighting!' The moral force and the evangelistic power of her oratory stemmed from a harnessed Niagara of passion. Her leadership of the militant movement was won by a combination of overwhelming charisma and histrionic dare-devilry. It was maintained by a sectarian ruthlessness and a disposition to 'smash' those who challenged her autocracy. It was sealed by a turbulent determination to secure her place in the temple of fame not just by crusading for the women's vote but by embracing martyrdom. As she said, 'If men will not do us justice, they shall do us violence.' Nowhere was Mrs Pankhurst's maenadic fury so unconstrained as in prison. A fellow-gaolbird described her confrontation with two visiting officials,

> the men apparently embarrassed and explanatory, the slight form, clad in a long cloak, her head enwrapped in chiffon, rigid with anger. From time to time the arm is raised in a short sharp gesture of incredible violence, to fall again quickly; the whole figure silhouetted against the prison wall reminds one . . . of a strange archaic relief from the fallen Selinonte temple,—Dian urging on her hounds to devour Actaeon. The voice rises like an angry sea—a terrible cadence in it never heard from a platform—then dies down to a still stranger sonority, the very essence of contempt and defiance. And yet her back shows dolphin-like above her anger, and from such a contest she will emerge as a giant refreshed with wine.

Mrs Pankhurst's friend, the composer Ethel Smyth, sought in many ways to account for the absolute sovereignty of the Suffragette queen. Was it her unscrupulous single-mindedness, her sacred indignation, her magical personality, her 'crystal purity of spirit', her bewitching voice? The composer of *The Wreckers* concluded that one element in

Mrs Pankhurst dominated all the rest, 'the sublime and ter-rific violence of her soul'.

Yet what most intrigued Edwardians about Mrs Pankhurst was the extraordinary contrast between her 'she-male' ag-gressiveness and her lady-like looks. For it was notorious that feminists were vinegary harridans like those great women's leaders of the previous generation, the mannish Susan B. Anthony and the forbidding Lydia Becker. The stereotype was perpetuated in hackneyed epigrams, trite slogans and cheap jibes: 'Women who wanted women's rights also wanted women's charms'; 'Women's Rights are Men's Lefts'; 'There are three sexes, masculine, femi-nine and Miss Becker.' The desire for equal rights was ob-viously a symptom of deep-seated female neurosis. Lord Northcliffe was typical in imagining that he had probed to the root of the matter by describing Suffragettes, in Max Beerbohm's phrase, as 'the unenjoyed'. But Mrs Pankhurst was beautiful. She had the face, it was often said, of a weary saint. A mother and widow, she resembled a virgin rather than a virago. With her svelte pre-Raphaelite figure borne majestically erect, with her clear, olive complexion and full, rosy cheeks, with her raven-black hair, with her delicately pencilled eyebrows and deep violet-blue eyes, above all with her entrancingly melodious voice, she was the very antithesis of the frustrated spinster and the soured old maid of popular mythology. Americans especially were transfixed by her. They expected a bloomered revolution-ary with a cropped head, blue spectacles and a billycock hat. They received a slender, cultivated, soft-toned, fash-ionably garbed gentlewoman whose visage 'recalled the pansy by its shape and a kind of velvety bloom on the expression'. One newspaper exclaimed, 'Can this pale, frail woman have terrified Mr Asquith and created an up-roar in the Commons? Why she looks more like a quiet housewife going shopping.' Paradoxically enough, the out-ward appearance expressed much of the inner reality. It was not just that Mrs Pankhurst actually did adore shop-ping, the drama of a sale and the excitement of employing sharp wits and sharper elbows to secure a bargain—'With your perpetual *Come* on! *Come* on!' she once scolded Ethel Smyth in Regent Street, 'You are as bad as a husband.' Nor was it simply that Mrs Pankhurst revelled in the pretty clothes she bought and in adorning herself with a coquettish grace which was all the more artful for seeming to be artless. No, the truth was that Mrs Pankhurst not only looked like a perfect Edwardian lady, in essen-tials she was a perfect Edwardian lady.

Her manner was so modest, so dignified, so proper, that one Suffragette described her as 'the best bred human be-ing I ever met'. Mrs Pankhurst had worshipped her hus-band with all the ardour of a romantic and all the abase-ment of a domestic. Glorying in the matrimonial bond, she had seemed to acknowledge that her place was in the home, and she had expended energy and ingenuity on (what Ruskin had defined as the wife's cardinal task) its 'sweet ordering'. She had brought up her children in the familiar bourgeois way, imposing strict discipline, insisting that they finish their lumpy porridge, forbidding her astig-

matic son to wear spectacles, chastising recalcitrance, and once instructing the servants to tie her second daughter Sylvia to a bed all day long for refusing to take her cod liver oil. Never a scholar herself, Mrs Pankhurst had set less store by education than by 'accomplishments'—her eldest daughter Christabel was 'too highly strung' to ben-efit from school, though she was permitted to take classes in logic as well as French and dressmaking. A domestic ornament which any man would have been proud to pos-sess, Mrs Pankhurst disapproved of ugly feminist breaches of decorum, Helen Taylor's trousers, for example, or the short skirts and shorter hair affected by Annie Besant. She was intensely fastidious, once insisting that her family should leave a Socialist meeting because she had found a bug on her glove. Her main worry in prison seems to have been the vermin and the stained underclothes which she was obliged to wear. Being so 'meticulously dainty' in her personal habits Mrs Pankhurst could never have realized, so Ethel Smyth reckoned, that during and after hunger-and-thirst strikes, her body, feeding off its own tissue, emitted a 'strange, pervasive, sweetish odour of corruption'. Mrs Pankhurst was as much of a Puritan as was consistent with being a Francophile—she found it 'odd how what is quite ordinary in French immediately becomes coarse and improper in English'. She was dis-turbed by the subject of sex and never instructed her chil-dren in its mysteries. When she sent the young Suffragette, Annie Kenney, to 'rouse' London for the cause in 1906, Mrs Pankhurst warned her to speak publicly to no one of the opposite sex except policemen. (Christabel mimicked her mother's prudery, even going so far as to ban the use of 'coarse screen blocks' for printing *The Suffragette*—'A woman's paper ought to be a finished and almost dainty production however robust the point of view expressed in it.') In short, then, Mrs Pankhurst was very much an or-thodox woman of her age and class. She created the Suf-fragette Movement in her own image.

This may seem a contentious claim, for the traditional view of the militant Edwardian feminist is that she was a stark reaction against the docile Victorian female. The Suf-fragette Movement is generally seen as an expression of the pent-up rage of middle-class matrons who had for too long been inhibited by feminine gentility and patronized by masculine chivalry. Their campaign is usually pre-sented as a violent protest against being treated as children and idiots politically, as angels and slaves domestically, against the whole gamut of ideas embodied in the patriar-chal maxim, 'My wife and I are one and I am he.' It is ex-plained as an explosive revolt against nineteenth century stereotypes which represented women as nymphs of supe-rior intuition and rarefied emotion who should neverthe-less honour and obey, suffer and be still. These depicted women as weaker vessels, their creative power drained by the menstrual flow and their intellects porous from an early evolutionary arrest 'necessitated', in Herbert Spen-cer's opinion, 'by the reservation of vital power to meet the cost of reproduction', who should nevertheless be para-gons of high-minded purity. The Suffragettes themselves asserted that their rebellion signalled, in the words of Mrs

Pethick-Lawrence, 'the discovery of woman by herself, the realization of her own powers, the overthrow by herself of traditions and conventions that were the real bondage. . . . The world and the press cried "unladylike" and forthwith women themselves turned down the word "lady".' Christabel, it has been said, 'lit a fire which consumed the past'. The historian George Dangerfield maintained that Pankhurstian militancy, combined, at the end of the Edwardian era, with assaults on the body politic by subversive strikers, pugnacious peers and belligerent Irish Unionists, contributed to 'the strange death of Liberal England'. In fact the Suffragette Movement was more notable as a manifestation of the strange survival of Conservative England. It was not the first blast of the trumpet of Women's Liberation so much as the last trump of Victorian religious revivalism. It did not so much herald the birth of the New Woman as proclaim the vitality of the Old Lady.

Charles Dickens defined a lady as one who was doubtful about the propriety of attending a christening, considering the implications of human birth. But the Victorian lady was less of a helpless, insipid prig than she has been painted. Many women were prepared, in the tradition of Florence Nightingale and Josephine Butler, to renounce a degree of respectability in order to uphold a higher ideal of morality. Suffragette self-mortification, what Mrs Pankhurst called the 'heroic sacrifice by which alone the soul of civilization is saved', was an intensified form of the Victorian lady's spirit of self-denying service. Suffragette militancy was more extreme in England than elsewhere precisely because Mrs Pankhurst and her fellows were so confident of their superior social status and their elevated moral role.

On the other hand, there were limits. 'Rise up, women!' cried Mrs Pankhurst—but so far and no further. In order to vindicate their policy and to preserve their caste the Suffragettes needed to conform slavishly, when out of the fray, to the dictates of convention. Even when engaged in hostilities the rebels liked to pretend that they were victims. Christabel went to great lengths to explain that spitting at a policeman was the only form of assault she could commit with her arms pinioned and that in any case it had been nothing more than a lady-like '"pout", a perfectly dry purse of the mouth'. Nothing distressed Mrs Pankhurst more than the stiff collars, trilby hats and other masculine trappings sported by a few of her adherents. And she would have been horrified by American feminists who had questioned accepted sexual ethics, by Elizabeth Cady Stanton, for example, who denounced 'hypocritical prating about purity' as 'one of man's most effective engines for our division and subjugation'. Shocked beyond words at her daughter Sylvia's unmarried motherhood (itself a deliberate, socialistic flouting of gentlewomanly standards) Mrs Pankhurst would have been outraged still further had she known that a revolution in feminine sensibility of more profound significance than the suffrage insurrection was being engendered almost on her doorstep.

It was conceived in a Bloomsbury drawing-room on 11 August 1908 at about five o'clock in the afternoon. Vanessa Bell and her sister Virginia, shortly to be Mrs Woolf, were having tea.

> Suddenly the door opened and the long and sinister figure of Mr Lytton Strachey stood on the threshold. He pointed his finger at a stain on Vanessa's white dress. 'Semen?' he said. Can one really say it? I thought and we burst out laughing. With that one word all barriers of reticence and reserve went down. A flood of the sacred fluid seemed to overwhelm us. Sex permeated our conversation. The word bugger was never far from our lips. We discussed copulation with the same excitement and openness that we had discussed the nature of good.

Too much can be made of a symbolic moment; too much has been made of a narcissistic group. Nevertheless, in Bloomsbury, to quote the well-worn witticism, all the couples were triangles and lived in squares, whereas even to speak of sexual freedom for women (though not, of course, for men) had been taboo under the Victorian dispensation. Mrs Pankhurst proposed to sustain and refine that dispensation. Enfranchised women could enforce virtue by law. With her obsessive concern for purity Mrs Pankhurst stiffened the sinews of Mrs Grundy and summoned up blood-curdling images of her own about the incipient degeneration of the race. Her message was that chastity belts must be tightened up all round. Moreover she connived at the customary subjection of her sex in other spheres, education, employment and, especially, in the home. For she aimed exclusively to win 'Votes for Women', or as radical opponents more accurately described it, referring to her willingness to see only a higher class of females enfranchised, 'Votes for Ladies'. (It was no accident that the Women's Liberation Movement of the 1960s began in America where female emancipation had never been understood solely in narrow terms of the vote and where women were traditionally more independent—it would have been difficult, if not impossible, to find an English feminist rebuking her sisters, as Emma Goldman did, for keeping their mouths shut and their wombs open.) By exercising despotic control over the movement Mrs Pankhurst even denied Suffragettes the experience of democratic participation, the achievement of which was its object. By fostering a quasi-religious hero-worship of herself and of Christabel Mrs Pankhurst imposed on her disciples, in the disillusioned words of one of their number, 'a thousand servitudes in order to win one small symbol of liberty. . . . A slave woman with a vote will still be essentially a slave.' However vigorous their evangelism, Suffragette ladies in the missionary position were still essentially supine.

All the same, it must be acknowledged that Mrs Pankhurst was a missionary of consummate brilliance. She was the messianic leader of a 'moral crusade'. She was the inspired prophetess of a 'spiritual awakening'. She was the courageous general of a secular salvation army engaged in a 'Holy War for the emancipation of our sex'. She was a hot-gospeller conducting 'the greatest mission the world has ever known . . . to free half the human race, and through that freedom to save the rest'. She was a preacher against vice, and its consequential 'loathsome disease', whose sermons were inspired by the vision of a new apocalypse.

> The fire of suffering whose flame is upon our sisters in prison is burning us also. For we suffer with them, we partake of their affliction, and we shall share their victory by-and-by. This fire will breathe into the ear of many a sleeper the one word 'Awake', and she will arise to slumber no more. It will descend with the gift of tongues upon many who have hitherto been dumb, and they will go forth to preach the news of deliverance. Its light will be seen afar off by many who suffer and are sorrowful and oppressed, and will irradiate their lives with a new hope. . . . For the spirit which is in women to-day cannot be quenched; it is stronger than all earthly potentates and powers; it is stronger than all tyranny, cruelty and oppression; it is stronger even than death itself.

The more violent their movement became, the more Mrs Pankhurst and Christabel stressed its sacred and moral character, its 'supernatural quality which, as it were, raises the hair and freezes the blood of those grosser beings', men. *The Suffragette*'s comment on the campaign of arson reflected its belief that no mortal incendiary was at work: 'The people that walk in darkness shall see a great light.' Mrs Pankhurst was hailed as the 'Illuminator of women'. On platform, podium, or plinth, her eyes now smouldering with pathos, now flashing with excitement, she seemed transfigured. On the demonstration or in the mêlée she was possessed by a divine fury, a fury which she compared to Christ's when he cast the money-changers out of the temple and destroyed the Gadarene swine. She was never more vibrant than when enjoying the limelight (what compensated those poor Suffragettes who languished in obscurity? she wondered pityingly). She was never more thrilled than when taking part in some act of militancy. On the first skirmish in the House of Commons, in 1906, a Suffragette, observing her leader prostrate on the marble floor under two large policemen, rushed to her aid. She was greeted by a fearless and amused glance from a pair of sparkling amethyst eyes. Mrs Pankhurst was having the time of her life. She had seized the time. The hour was surely at hand which would vindicate her faith in the feminist millennium and realize her hope of personal glory.

II

With a theatrical flair which was never to desert her Mrs Pankhurst, *née* Emmeline Goulden, entered the world on the anniversary of the storming of the Bastille, 14 July 1858. At the time, the happy event was regarded as a sad anti-climax. Victorian parents were wont to describe the birth of a girl as 'our fiasco', and Robert Goulden, though otherwise enlightened and progressive, was no exception. Emmeline later overheard her father lamenting the fact that she 'wasn't born a lad'. Her mother, a pretty farmer's daughter from the Isle of Man, shared her husband's belief in women's rights. But despite the availability of contra-

ceptives she allowed herself to become a breeding-machine. And she considered that her girls should devote themselves to dusting, arranging flowers and fetching their brothers' slippers. Emmeline inherited her father's thespian talents—as well as having worked himself up from errand boy to owner of a cotton printing business, Goulden was Manchester's foremost amateur actor—and she created emotional scenes over the inconsistency between her mother's principles and practice. Emmeline was conscious of being stronger, brighter, bolder than her brothers. They knew her as 'the dictionary' because she read so much, her favourite books being *Uncle Tom's Cabin,* Carlyle's *French Revolution* and Bunyan's *Holy War.* She was early inclined towards rebellion by stories of her paternal grandfather who had narrowly escaped with his life at the 'Peterloo' Massacre of 1819 and had been press-ganged, returning after years in the navy to find no trace of his family or friends. Imbued with the romance of action and adventure, Emmeline demonstrated her juvenile support for radicalism by staging a daring tableau. At a meeting of rough Mancunian factory workers, during the election of 1868, she and a younger sister paraded the Liberal colours by hoisting their green dresses to reveal red petticoats. An outraged nursery maid whisked them home and the disgraced exhibitionists were confined to bed. There, perhaps, Emmeline consoled herself by sating her imagination once again in the drama of the true 'hero of her heart', King Charles the Martyr.

Emmeline engaged in few other youthful pranks for, being the eldest girl in a large family, she was forced to mature quickly. At the age of fourteen she attended her first suffrage meeting, addressed by Lydia Becker. Miss Becker was subsequently to utter in Emmeline's presence the bitter cry of outcast spinsterdom: 'Married women have all the plums of life!' But in 1872 she merely confirmed the young novice's faith in the gospel of votes for women. Later that year Emmeline was sent from Manchester dame school to the Ecole Normale in Paris where her 'bosom friendship' with a dashing fellow pupil, Noémie de Rochefort, daughter of an exiled Communard nobleman, strengthened her liberal ideas and her taste for excitement. The much-vaunted moral discipline and intellectual training of the Ecole Normale affected her hardly at all. She enjoyed the course on embroidery and learnt to sew with skill and enthusiasm. As for chemistry and book-keeping . . . a knowledge of such dismal subjects could only cramp a smart young lady's style. But Paris—gay, republican, sophisticated, fashionable Paris—captivated her. She wanted to stay for ever. But for this plum, and for all the other plums of life, to fall into her lap, she needed a husband. Noémie produced a suitor who was complaisant in everything but the question of a dowry. This Emmeline's father indignantly refused to pay. Hard-headed Englishmen tended to regard marriage as a matter of purchase just as prostitution was a matter of hire, and Robert Goulden was determined not to make a rich present of his daughter to an improvident and licentious Frenchman. Emmeline, in a state of rage and humiliation, was recalled to grimy, provincial Manchester. Its only compensation was that there she attracted everyone's attention. From the top of her head, crowned with a fetching little bonnet or a scarlet ribbon knotted with elaborate carelessness, to the tips of her minute, elegantly-shod feet, she was every inch the 'finished' young lady. Inwardly still a diffident girl, Emmeline, aged twenty, had all the outward self-possession of a woman.

If a husband was the 'Open Sesame' to ecstasy in Paris how much more was this so in Manchester, where Emmeline had no function and no duty but to adorn her parents' home. Such service was perfect serfdom. Her spirit yearned to harness itself to the yoke of some liberating idealism . . . or idealist. She was determined 'only to give herself to an important man'. Of course, she would not flirt; that was 'degrading'. A lady revealed her want of a mate with refined circumspection; as one contemporary journal wrote, 'Half the art of the woman of the world consists in doing disgusting things delicately.' However, when she found her prospective spouse she kindled his ardour so directly that Mrs Goulden accused Emmeline of 'throwing herself' at him. Richard Marsden Pankhurst, Ll.D., with his carroty beard and a piping treble voice which often caused him to be mistaken for a woman, seemed an improbable key to bliss. He was twice Emmeline's age. He had always lived with his Baptist parents and never left the house for an hour without telling them where he was going. A scholarly barrister, he was small, unprepossessing and so physically incompetent that his wife always had to do the carving. Still, he had beautiful hands. And in other respects the 'Red Doctor' was a distinctly glamorous figure. He was the most prominent and the most flaming radical in 'Cottonopolis'. He was a pioneer of every advanced faith and a 'standard-bearer of every forlorn hope'. He was a democrat, a republican, a communist, a Home Ruler, a pacifist, an internationalist, an agnostic. He was an opponent of imperialism and the House of Lords—it was 'a public abattoir' in which human rights were butchered. He was a proponent of free secular education and women's rights—clawing the air with his long, curved finger-nails, he once exclaimed, 'Why are women so patient? Why don't you force us to give you the vote? Why don't you scratch our eyes out?' In short, Dr Pankhurst was an extremist and he courted Emmeline with an impetuosity that matched her own. On 8 September 1879 he wrote to 'Dear Miss Goulden' trying to interest her, 'one of the party of progress', in the movement for female higher education. On 23 September he addressed her as 'Dearest Treasure', assured her that 'Every struggling cause shall be ours' and rejoiced at the prospect 'of two lives made one by that love which seeks more the other than self'. Emmeline was so transported by the eloquence and devotion of this glorious revolutionary that she proposed they should enter into a 'free union'. The Doctor quickly explained that to violate sexual orthodoxy was to invite social damnation and thus to miss their chance of reforming the world. Emmeline learnt the lesson well and reconciled herself to defying convention in a brown velvet wedding-dress. Discovering too late that a superfluous row

of brass buttons down the front made her look 'like a little page boy', she burst into tears.

On the eve of the marriage Mrs Goulden embarked on an explanation of what were euphemistically known as the duties of a bride: 'I want to talk to you.' Emmeline replied, 'I do not want to listen.' Maybe she knew already. Or perhaps she preferred to be instructed by the mildmannered fire-eater whose helpmate she was to be. If so she proved a quick pupil. In the space of five years she gave birth to four children, Christabel (1880), Sylvia (1882), Henry Francis (1884) and Adela (1885). Christabel alone she nursed and the bond established between the feline daughter and the passionate mother was preternaturally strong. Other Pankhurstian ties were to dissolve like cobwebs; Adela was to be exiled to Australia for denying Christabel's infallibility and for the same sin Sylvia was to be excommunicated amidst her mother's public regrets that she was entitled to bear the family name. Whereas, talking to a friend in Holloway Prison, Mrs Pankhurst 'dwelt upon the name of her daughter "Christabel the Anointed One", the young deliverer who was to emancipate the new generation of women'. Despite a professed atheism Mrs Pankhurst had a profound, if misty, religious sense. And whatever the psychological explanation for her adoration of Christabel, who bore a marked physical resemblance to her earthly father, Mrs Pankhurst was to deem her firstborn the Saviour of womankind—though at this early stage she was ambitious for Christabel to become a dancer. Unlike many of her contemporaries, Mrs Pankhurst never pretended to believe that babies were made by a species of remote control. But Christabel she conceived to be immaculate.

Meanwhile the domestic scene absorbed Mrs Pankhurst's attention. She was an indifferent manager. She spent too little on mutton and too much on bon-bons. She complained of sick headaches and languished in bed for days with hot water bottles, a prey to boredom and irritation. Though unable to finish the stiff course of reading which the Doctor, at her insistence, had prescribed, she was a compulsive skimmer of light novels. Luckily the 'devoted service' of their Welsh nurse freed her from mundane chores, including the care of the children. Mrs Pankhurst's role was to beautify the home. Though most of the Doctor's legal work was in Manchester, she persuaded him in 1886 to move to London, 'where everybody wants to be'. She decorated their Bloomsbury house in her favourite colour, yellow. And, loving 'comfort and the pretty things of life', she furnished it with more than oriental splendour, with Japanese blinds, embroidery and coloured beads, with Chinese teapots, Persian plates, Indian brasses, Turkish rugs. The expense was to be met by starting a fancy goods shop—in all she embarked on three such artistic missions to the housewife, each one called Emersons, each one opening with radiant expectations, each one closing in dismal failure. The children learnt to live plainly. Their mother would tolerate 'no likes and dislikes'. They ate milk puddings and wore blue serge knickers. The régime may have taken its toll on the delicate son, who died of diphtheria in 1888. Mrs Pankhurst was prostrated with grief. The following year she bore, with great difficulty and some danger, a substitute, another son, also delicate. Though known as Harry, he was given his deceased brother's names, Henry Francis. He was also to die prematurely, the victim, Sylvia thought, of his mother's neglect. By contrast the Pankhurst women were all blessed with a vigorous longevity—the female of the species was more vital than the male.

Mrs Pankhurst did not trick out her Bloomsbury house to provide an elegant domestic setting so much as a spectacular political set, an ornate backcloth to the radical salon over which she dreamt of presiding. The Pankhurst 'At Home' was to be a splendid stage, draped with arabesques of white gauze and garlands of purple heliotrope, on which she could play the leading lady while the vanguard of the march of mind acted as supporting cast. She did perform as hostess to many progressive writers and politicians. And at her house in 1889 Mrs Pankhurst, Josephine Butler, Elizabeth Cady Stanton and others founded the Women's Franchise League. It was a protest against the timid constitutional methods of what they called the 'Spinster Suffrage Party' led by Lydia Becker and Millicent Fawcett. The Franchise League soon dissolved for lack of funds, the very circumstance which was to mar and then to close Mrs Pankhurst's salon and to send the family back to Manchester in 1893. But straitened means never checked Mrs Pankhurst's quicksilver ways. She broke with her father forever when her husband abandoned the Liberal party for socialism in the first of his three unsuccessful attempts to enter Parliament. And when the Doctor became involved in a libel case, a result of describing the Holy Ghost as 'the foggy member of the Trinity' whose credentials he would like to examine in the witness-box, Mrs Pankhurst attacked the judge. She accused him of being part of

> a conspiracy to crush the public life of an honourable public man. It is to be regretted that there should be found on the English Bench a judge who will lend his aid to a disreputable section of the Tory Party in doing their dirty work; but for what other reason were you ever placed where you are?

Recognizing a member of the 'shrieking sisterhood' when he heard one, his lordship wisely disregarded this act of provocation. Nothing exasperated Mrs Pankhurst more than indifference. It was death in life, doom of her hopes for immortal renown. She exclaimed fiercely, 'I want to go to prison for contempt of court!'

Whatever the cost, Mrs Pankhurst would not be ignored. Back in Manchester she gained in confidence and competence as a speaker on behalf of suffragism and socialism. In 1894 she was elected to the Chorlton Board of Poor Law Guardians, controllers of the workhouse. There she discovered destitute waifs shivering for want of undergarments because the matron had been too modest to discuss their provision with the authorities. Scorning the false delicacy of the socially insecure, Mrs Pankhurst, called 'My Lady' by the paupers, saw that the need was supplied.

Employing her 'passionate and persuasive' oratory, she helped to ease the lot of the unemployed and to effect other workhouse reforms. Unfortunately her stormy rhetoric was apt to cloud her philanthropic perspicacity. She insisted that the bread of the poor should be 'buttered with margarine'. And by 1897, considering the Chorlton workhouse so improved that children were worse off in the average working-class home, she proposed to increase the authority of the Guardinas in order 'to cancel parental power' and assume direct wardship of children whose welfare was jeopardized by their parents' 'inability' or 'evil conduct'. Understandably, one of her opponents on the board inscribed on his blotting paper this injunction to himself: 'Keep your temper!' The Manchester magistrates must have written themselves a similar rubric, for they refused in 1896 to bestow on Mrs Pankhurst the public martyrdom she craved over the affair of Boggart Hole Clough. This was a natural amphitheatre in one of the city's parks where the Independent Labor Party (ILP) held open-air meetings, illegally in the view of the Council. Mrs Pankhurst and other socialist leaders defied the ban. At rally after rally Mrs Pankhurst, in her pink straw bonnet, 'her mellow, effortless tones carrying far beyond the shouts of excited men', challenged the magistrates to convict her. She promised to pay no fine and 'put upon the bench the full responsibility' of committing her to Strangeways Gaol. They sensibly denied her that seductive accolade. After a complex legal wrangle the City Council was defeated and what was, in effect, the dress rehearsal for the Suffragette drama ended in triumph. It was quickly followed by disaster. In 1898, exhausted by tempestuous political involvements and drained by his efforts to support the family, Dr Pankhurst paid his last debt to nature. Summoned home from the Continent, where she had been taking Christabel to visit Noémie, Mrs Pankhurst read the news of his death in a passenger's evening paper on the train from London. She shrieked aloud in her anguish. So stricken by misery and loneliness was she that Sylvia had to sleep with her in the matrimonial bed. On her husband's headstone Mrs Pankhurst had carved Walt Whitman's words, 'Faithful and true—my loving comrade.' The Pankhurst Memorial Hall was so named in the Red Doctor's honour. To his widow's incredulous fury the branch of the ILP, whose headquarters it was, barred the entry of women.

III

Mrs Pankhurst was thus obliged, at the age of forty, to become an employed lady (a state fast ceasing to be a contradiction in terms) and from this novel experience she was to draw powder and shot enough to fill the militant woman's magazine. The Doctor's possessions were sold to pay his debts. The family moved from a select Crescent to a prosaic Street (though the smaller house was carefully chosen for its 'air of distinction'). And Mrs Pankhurst resigned as an unpaid Poor Law Guardian and became a salaried Registrar of Births and Deaths. Her duties brought her into close contact with the squalid wretchedness of working-class life and she was quick to diagnose the worst ills as moral ones. Sweated labour, rape, incest, illegitimacy, prostitution, the white slave traffic—such wicked forms of social and sexual exploitation could only be eradicated by enfranchised womanhood. Until the vote was won these evils were to afford a justification for Suffragette violence, which had the merit of being directed against property, not persons. Everywhere Mrs Pankhurst looked it was apparent that the chief victims of injustice were females. Behind every poor man, she observed, stood a still poorer woman. Elected in 1900 as an ILP candidate to the Manchester School Board, she discovered that there was little or no technical training provided for girls, even in the baking and confectionery trades. Females were a fettered sub-proletariat, 'a servant class'. Christabel agreed, but she lacked her mother's faith in, and preoccupation with, Labour. Now assisting the radical suffragist Eva Gore-Booth, whose blonde neuralgic head she would massage for hours, much to the jealous annoyance of Mrs Pankhurst, Christabel accused socialists and trade unionists of wanting 'beef-steaks and butter for working men; tea and bread for working women'. By 1903 mother and daughter were together belabouring friends in the ILP on behalf of the women's cause. The response of Bruce Glasier, who regarded female suffrage as a bourgeois diversion from the socialist highway, was typical.

> At last get roused and speak with something like scorn of their miserable individualist sexism, and virtually tell them that the ILP will not stir a finger more than it has done for all the women suffragists in creation. Really the pair are not seeking democratic freedom but self-importance . . . Christabel paints her eyebrows grossly and looks selfish, lazy and wilful. They want to be ladies and lack the humility of real heroinism.

Certainly Mrs Pankhurst was arrogant. Courage alone would scarcely have sustained her had she not felt herself to be pregnant with a world-important message. Its delivery would be marked by signs, wonders and vociferations for she was, as Lloyd George said, 'a big woman, but narrow'. There was, indeed, to be a frenetic quality about her actions, a hysterical note to her rhetoric. Christabel claimed that her mother's voices were of God. Prejudiced persons found it all too easy to disparage Mrs Pankhurst's procedures as . . . essentially feminine.

It was obvious to Mrs Pankhurst that all males, whatever their political persuasion, were locked in a vicious conspiracy against those whom they were wont to call, in that revealing metonymy, 'the Sex'. Was it not clear that women were kept down so that men could more conveniently get up to no good? Women were a recumbent indication of men's rampant inclinations. Lust, said Bernard Shaw, was the greatest single obstacle to female emancipation, just as 'the cry for the vote is often really the cry for the key to one's bedroom'. Of course, men disguised their desire to maintain political power, for it was really the power to consort with prostitutes, the power to assault children, the power to infect their wives with syphilis. They concealed their desires behind arguments of impeccable respectability. For example, it was obvious that females could not become aldermen because there was no such word as 'alderwomen', let alone 'alderpersons'.

Women should be excluded from Parliament for it would not do to have Lord Chancellors eloping or Prime Ministers in an interesting condition—why, there might be knitting on the Woolsack and *accouchements* on the front bench. Then again, canvassing was surely a form of licensed soliciting. Domestic happiness could hardly be sustained, said Labouchere, Parliamentary leader of the Anti-Suffragists, 'if a man is perpetually leaving his own wife and visiting another man's wife on the plea that he wanted to be a town councillor'.

The 'Antis' had axioms to meet every occasion. Proper women, emotional and illogical, did not want the vote; militant, masculine-minded suffragists demonstrated their unworthiness to exercise it. Females would not use the vote; female voters would neglect their families. Women would vote with their husbands or priests; women would cause domestic or religious dissension by voting against their husbands or priests. Women did not understand politics; women would outnumber men, vote *en bloc,* change the laws and impose 'a crushing tax on bachelors'. Women did not defend the state or earn its wealth and therefore had no title to vote; women fighters and workers were so unladylike as to be disqualified from the franchise. Women were essentially domestic creatures; women were better off working as volunteers for one of the big political parties. The vote would mean nothing to women; the vote accorded with the dignity of man. In short, men were men and women were women and never the twain should meet inside a polling-booth—where who knew what indescribable indecencies might take place.

Mrs Pankhurst was not deceived. It did not require a Freud to see the ballot box, with its suggestive orifice, as a symbol of man's sovereign promiscuity. As Ethel Smyth later wrote to Mrs Pankhurst, all men, from bishops down, were 'tainted by the brothel ideas of the sanctity of women's bodies and hence fail to be horrified at venereal disease'. Only a moral crusade could free women from captivity and men from iniquity. 'Women,' proclaimed Mrs Pankhurst to her friends, 'We must have an independent woman's movement. Come to my house tomorrow and we will arrange it.' So, imperiously, on 10 October 1903, the Women's Social and Political Union (WSPU) was formed. Its ends were 'Votes for Women and Chastity for Men.' Its means, in a motto endlessly reiterated, were 'Deeds not Words.'

At first the WSPU seemed little more than an ambitious 'family party'. Mrs Pankhurst maintained a rigid matriarchal discipline. Christabel, now training as a barrister though excluded by her sex from the bar, exercised her celebrated skill as an organizer. Sylvia, Adela and even Harry also served. However, the Pankhursts were joined by the purposeful Mrs Flora Drummond whose life had been blighted by the fact that she was under regulation height to become a post-mistress. She was nicknamed 'Bluebell', 'the Precocious Piglet', and finally, because she so loved to command Suffragette parades, 'the General'. Another early ally was the intellectual Teresa Billington—

unfortunately her sexual habits were somewhat natural and she was soon to break with the movement because it was 'socially exclusive, punctiliously correct, gracefully fashionable, ultra-respectable and narrowly religious'. Hannah Mitchell, renegade from a Labour Church where they sang hymns like 'The Red Flag', was a useful recruit until she succumbed to a nervous breakdown—none of the Pankhurst family showed the slightest sympathy. Most valuable of all was the tractable, attractive Lancashire mill-hand (she had lost the finger of one hand in a mill), Annie Kenney. Called by her 'still small voice', she became the most winning of 'Mrs Pankhurst's suffrage missionaries,' as they were termed, preaching of her conviction that the vote would end poverty, bring Paradise and do the washing. It was Annie Kenney who advised the WSPU to conduct its propaganda at the Lancashire Wakes, or travelling fairs. Soon its members were competing for the attention of the public with merry-go-rounds and Aunt Sallies, and exptying the booths of tooth drawers, vendors of quack medicines, fortune tellers and religious revivalists of other persuasions.

Her crusade lifted Mrs Pankhurst to a condition of almost permanent effervescence. She was determined that 'Votes for Women' would be achieved now. The millennium was imminent—or would be if exhortation could make it so. She lived 'in a frenzy of suspense; all the woes of the world, all the sorrows of women hung, one would say, in the balance'. By 1905 Sylvia was quite worried about her mother's state.

> Far into the night she railed against the treachery of men and bemoaned the impotence of women! 'Poor women!' The overburdened mothers, the sweated workers, the outcasts of the streets, the orphan children of the workhouse mingled in the imagery of her discourse. She appeared so greatly to distress herself that I feared for her health and her reason. On some later occasion, when, after a night of these agonies . . . she began again to declaim, I gazed at her in sorrowful concern. . . . Suddenly turning on me with a smile, she struck me lightly on the arm: 'Don't look at me like that! Bless you, your old mother likes it. This is what I call life!'

It was in this spirit that Mrs Pankhurst embarked on her first act of militancy. When, in May 1905, a Private Member's Bill for woman's suffrage was talked out by Labouchere and his friends with porcine jokes about 'the Sex', she organized a demonstration of protest. The police jostled and then expelled her from the precincts of Parliament. So, outside Westminster Abbey, she addressed the crowd. At last she was in her element, a petticoated Parnell, a Savonarola in silk stockings. Her body taut, her eyes alight, her tones tremulous with anger, she was no longer just a woman speaker. She was the voice of womanhood, 'maternity pleading for the race'. Mrs Pankhurst would accomplish the downfall of Labouchere morally, by harsh words, and not physically, as she had planned, by a fine trip-wire.

After this convulsion there was an anticlimactic pause in the progress of the movement. As his government drifted towards dissolution Balfour rightly assured the WSPU that women's suffrage was not 'in the swim'. Street-corner meetings in Lancashire, even those summoned by Christabel's muffin bell, caused only insignificant ripples. The movement needed to make a mighty national splash. All Mrs Pankhurst's instincts cried out for martyrdom. The women's cause must become an issue of blood. But at the moment, for the sake of her registrarship, Mrs Pankhurst could not afford to spill her own. She would send her beloved daughter. Christabel should make the sacrifice and win the glory. On 13 October 1905 Sir Edward Grey was to address supporters at Manchester's Free Trade Hall. Christabel announced, 'I shall sleep in prison tonight.' When Grey refused to pledge a future Liberal government to 'Votes for Women', she and Annie Kenney created a disturbance. They were expelled from the meeting, a steward covering Annie's pretty face with his hat, and arrested amidst further struggles outside, when Christabel spat at her policeman. On refusing to pay the fines, they were sentenced to short terms of imprisonment. At this stage Mrs Pankhurst succumbed to a moment of panic. Perhaps she was intimidated by the police; later she had such a dread of the inspector who regularly arrested her that she would turn pale at the mention of his name—the Suffragettes tried to kidnap him but unhappily they attacked the wrong man. Anyway the mother offered to dash the cup of suffering from her daughter's lips. Christabel knew it must be drained to the lees if womankind were to be saved: 'Mother, if you pay my fine I will never go home.' She went to gaol, where, Annie Kenney reported, she looked 'very coy and pretty in her prison cap. She took my hand and held it tenderly as though I were a lost child being guided home.'

Christable's act was hailed as a piece of arrant, impertinent, unmaidenly folly which should have been punished by 'the discipline of the nursery': the bad publicity was the best publicity that the WSPU had ever enjoyed. The *Daily Mail* coined for its members the insulting diminutive 'Suffragette', a nickname they eagerly embraced. According to the press Mrs Pankhurst and her daughters were 'crazy hooligans, their followers were shrieking hysterics, their policy was wild delirium'. But all over the country female hearts responded to the call to sacrifice. The Suffragette creed, though written as a *jeu d'esprit* (in 1908), expressed genuine feelings of reverence for Mrs Pankhurst and a real sense that the movement owed its soul to the intercession of Christabel.

> I believe in Emmeline Pankhurst—founder of the Women's Social and Political Union. And in Christabel Pankhurst, her eldest daughter, our Lady, who was inspired by the passion for Liberty, born to be a leader of women. She descended into prison; the seventh day she returned again to the world. She was entertained to breakfast, and sat on the right hand of her mother, our glorious Leader. From thence she went forth to judge both the Government and the Antis. I believe in Votes for Women on the same terms as men, the policy of the Women's Social and Political Union, the equality of the sexes, Representation for Taxation, the necessity for militant tactics, and Freedom Everlasting.

Mrs Pankhurst was not amused—her sense of humour was, indeed, about as rudimentary as that of the great Queen. But the Suffragette sovereign did not spurn less blasphemous forms of idolatry. Her own newspaper was to proclaim her 'a creative genius whose deeds and words are her masterpieces'. Personal adulation helped to swell the ranks of the militants and to establish their *esprit de corps*. It was understandable that a Lancashire Suffragette, homeward bound after a London rally, should ask directions for a railway station called St Pankhurst.

Mrs Pankhurst demanded crescendo. During the general election of 1906 the campaign was still being conducted on a relatively small scale. Ministers were heckled by 'vixens in velvet'. Churchill was 'hen-pecked' in Manchester. Balfour's sister, close to tears, begged the Suffragettes not to interrupt Arthur's meetings: 'He could not stand it.' The priorities of the victorious Liberals were clearly not those of Mrs Pankhurst and it became essential to concert all Suffragette efforts in London. A 'Women's Parliament' met on 16 February 1906 at Caxton Hall, near what Mrs Pankhurst contemptuously called the 'Men's Parliament'. Wearing regal black and 'the dignity of a mother who has known great sorrow', Mrs Pankhurst played on the feelings of her hearers, exercising what H. N. Brailsford called 'her almost intolerable power to move'. She spoke quietly, in an accent still marked by the Lancastrian twang ('Join uzz!') which she had wanted her children to lose. Her phrases were plain. Her theme was almost a cliché. She made hardly a gesture with her lorgnette. But her bearing was an exclamation mark. Her eyes blazed as though she nursed some secret fire. Her personality was charged with magnetic force, all the more palpable for seeming to be suppressed. Her voice thrilled with emotion, poignant, mournful, edged with terrible menace. That voice was, said Ethel Smyth, 'a stringed instrument in the hands of a great artist'—though the composer noted with surprise that in church, where Mrs Pankhurst joined 'loudly, fervently and even gloatingly in the hymns', she 'sang flatter than I should have thought it possible to sing'. Anyway, such was her performance that many women 'silently pledged their faith to her for life'. And the Caxton Hall audience rose in a body to follow Mrs Pankhurst as she marched on the Parliament of men. Soaked by torrential rain, they were at first denied entry and then admitted in small batches. Nothing was achieved. Only one MP, Keir Hardie, veteran leader of the ILP, showed any real sympathy for the Suffragettes. And his compassion for women in general was a symptom of his passion for the Pankhurst women in particular. Rumour-mongers scented hanky-panky, hinted that Hardie knew Emmeline better than he should have done—'Verily,' said Bruce Glasier, 'Mrs Pankhurst has been the Delilah that has cut our Samson's locks.' And he undoubtedly did have carnal knowledge of Sylvia. Despite a gallant struggle Hardie was virtually impotent in Parliament—as Christabel complained, 'the Private Member is a very rudimentary organ.' Mrs Pankhurst wept, raged and implored him to do more for the women's cause. Instead, in April 1906, he combined with Sylvia to stop her, for sound tactical reasons, making a disturbance

in the Ladies' Gallery of the House of Commons. 'You have baulked me—both of you!' cried Mrs Pankhurst, in one of those *prima donna* paroxysms that punctuated her life, 'I thought there would have been one little niche in the temple of fame for me!'

Later that month Mrs Pankhurst achieved her purpose, if entry to the temple of fame may indeed be secured via expulsion from the senate of Albion. Crying, 'Divide, divide!' over a suffragist resolution being moved by Keir Hardie, she and her acolytes were bundled from the Ladies' Gallery amid uproar. What a ravishing adventure! The glare of publicity quite made Mrs Pankhurst's skin glow. More than ever she had faith in the cause she served. Such drama, such *éclat,* such idealism—here was fulfilment of which she had scarcely dared dream. The movement was the fount of her seething emotions, the focus of her 'desperate heart-hunger'. Mrs Pankhurst instinctively knew, as Mrs Pethick-Lawrence wrote, that she had been 'cast for a great role. . . . She could have been a queen on the stage or in the salon. Circumstances had baulked her.' Now Mrs Pankhurst's 'daemon' drove her on to realize her destiny. She was uniquely well qualified to be proselytizer-in-chief, an aloof high priestess with 'a witch's charm' (Suffragettes often told her that had she 'lived in earlier days she would have been burnt as a witch'). Nothing should thwart Mrs Pankhurst now. With ever-increasing urgency she heckled, agitated, led processions and deputations, campaigned in by-elections, addressed meetings, was ejected from meetings and created disgraceful scenes. But other Suffragettes were being arrested and imprisoned. Mrs Pankhurst would not be outdone in self-abnegation. In March 1907 she gave up her registrarship, packed all her belongings and embarked on the glory trail for good, travelling the country with a repertoire of speeches which kept her bathed in limelight. She did not scruple to sacrifice even her frail adolescent son Harry. With disastrous consequences to his health, she apprenticed him to a Buddhist builder of slums in Glasgow who shortly went bankrupt.

Mrs Pankhurst herself was better off as a full-time evangelist. Her expensive clothes and extravagant ways could be justified as professional necessities and the access of so many silked and satined ladies to the cause, though it occasioned some internal dissent, filled the war chest. The support of the affluent Pethick-Lawrences was especially valuable. Believing themselves to be, as Mrs Pethick-Lawrence later said, 'agents of unseen forces that are guiding the evolution of the world', husband and wife worked so busily that they had to make appointments even to see each other. Fred Pethick-Lawrence was a clever, altruistic lawyer who helped Christabel to manage the efficient WSPU organization and edited the newspaper, *Votes for Women.* Elegant and well-born ('All our family go to Heaven'), Emmeline Pethick-Lawrence became treasurer of the WSPU. Like other Suffragettes she had previously been engaged in a bizarre form of Edwardian philanthropy, the endeavour to restore to the brutalized urban masses their lost sense of the pulsating joy of Merrie England by means of folk songs and Morris dances. Now she invested her eurhythmic exuberance in 'the greatest spiritual and moral awakening that has taken place for centuries'. With the rapt expression of a visionary or a somnambulist, she roused well-bred young ladies to yield up their money or their lives to the movement: 'Come with us! Come! Come! You will come!' But like Mrs Pankhurst, who rejoiced that her daughter was a political genius limited by none of her mother's human weaknesses, Mrs Pethick-Lawrence always deferred to Christabel. As for Mr Pethick-Lawrence, he found the eldest Miss Pankhurst 'quite irresistible'. Indeed, the Pethick-Lawrences and Christabel all lived at Clement's Inn, above the expanding offices of the WSPU. There they formed an intimate group from which Mrs Pankhurst was, as she complained to Sylvia with scalding tears of jealousy, virtually excluded.

However, Mrs Pankhurst was invariably on hand during crises and she was always summoned from the 'preaching platform' to conduct 'executions'. There was, for example, the sad case of Mrs Montefiore who sucked cocaine lozenges, had been involved in some 'scandal' and lacked that humble 'delicacy of heart' so vital to ladies 'who work in this cause'. A Suffragette reported, 'Mrs Pankhurst was heated and spoke plainly—as she can!—in the interview with her which was practically a dismissal; she seems to have been overheard speaking to her daughter even more plainly, a most unfortunate thing.' Another woman was formally censured by a packed committee of paid Suffragette organizers under Mrs Pankhurst's direction, without a hearing or even a notification that she was being tried. In 1907 disaffected Suffragettes, led by Teresa Billington ('a wrecker' in Mrs Pankhurst's view) and that gallant old sandal-wearing, fruit-juice-drinking, theosophizing suffragist Mrs Despard, protested about the WSPU's severing its links with the Independent Labour Party. They criticized the gradual exclusion of working-class women from the Suffragette ranks and the policy of 'Votes for Ladies'.

What might have been a revolution in the female condition seemed to have become a charade of rebellion mounted for the self-aggrandizement of its star mummers. According to Teresa Billington-Greig, the Suffragettes' poverty of spirit was summed up in such remarks as, '"I do interrupt meetings but I am a perfect lady,"' and '"I knocked off a policeman's helmet, but I only want a little thing, a quite respectable thing—a vote."' The dissidents tried to use constitutional means to destroy the power of the ruling clique. With a dramatic gesture Mrs Pankhurst declared, 'I shall tear up the constitution!' So she did, causing the first great schism in the Suffragette body—the secessionists formed a new sect, the Women's Freedom League. Mrs Pankhurst never seemed to grasp the incongruity of her new position, autocrat of a movement dedicated to the extension of democracy. But then an uncultivated mind was as much the attribute of an Edwardian lady as was a 'cultured' mien. Christabel said proudly that her mother was feminine to a degree 'in her ability to "jump", as it is called, to a conclusion'. A woman thinking was like a dog standing on its hind legs . . . Mrs

Pankhurst had no pretensions to mannish intellectual subtlety: as she told Ethel Smyth, 'I am simply an agitator.'

Agitation brought its due recompense. Early in 1908 Mrs Pankhurst was assaulted by a gang of roughs during a Devon by-election. In a fainting state, convinced that they intended to roll her around Newton Abbot in a barrel, she was rescued by the police. Still white, weak and shaken, she determined now to graduate into the noble company of Suffragette martyrs, to attain her 'Holloway degree'. Taking as her cue the adoring cries from Caxton Hall—'Mrs Pankhurst must not go! We cannot spare her!'—she limped, with a band of twelve disciples, towards the men's Parliament. On the way she was arrested as 'a common brawler', a charge she indignantly rebutted. Found guilty, she would neither pay a fine nor be bound over to keep the peace. So, in her fiftieth year (Mrs Pankhurst would never give her age in court), she was sentenced to her first term of imprisonment—six weeks in the Second (unprivileged) Division. It was, she recollected later, like being buried alive. The Black Maria was 'a hearse of many coffins', each one enclosing a blasted female soul. Holloway was an underworld of the debased, the despairing and the depraved—one of the subterranean cells in which Mrs Pankhurst was entombed was made intolerable to her not so much by the plank bed, the damp, the cockroaches, the disgusting sanitary conditions, as by obscene graffiti carved on the door. The public disrobing ('Unfasten your chests', instructed the wardress), the ritual search, the filthy bath, all these were dehumanizing indignities. But nothing affronted and demoralized Mrs Pankhurst more than the prison uniform. The clumsy, mis-mated shoes, the coarse brown woollen stockings with red stripes, (lack of garters made her feel naked) the 'hideous prison dress stamped all over with the broad arrow of disgrace', the 'small Dutch cap' which, as Lady Constance Lytton noted, had to be treated with 'the utmost reverence' because it was 'white and starched'—these were grave clothes indeed. Most sinister of all were the nether garments, old, patched and discoloured in 'a revolting and suggestive manner'; the Suffragette actress Kitty Marion described these 'undies' as 'ugly reflections' of the authorities' minds. Christabel said that prison itself was emblematic of women's political bondage. But to Mrs Pankhurst confinement was purgatory. The lack of reading matter (the Bible was only good for summoning up fits of feminist rage) troubled a mind not given to repose. The loneliness tormented a spirit incapable of serenity. Mrs Pankhurst's migraines recurred and she was transferred to the prison hospital. There the enforced inactivity so galled her that she pleaded for something to sew.

Unprompted, the government released Mrs Pankhurst before the end of her sentence. She was thus able to achieve a sensational apotheosis on the stage of the Albert Hall, where Suffragettes had gathered to celebrate the culmination of a 'self-denial week' which raised over £7,000 for the cause. Her skin was almost transparent. Her face shone with an unearthly pallor. Her eyes were deep-sunken, yet irradiated with a zealot's light. Her voice rose again to its wonted pitch. 'The old cry was "you will never rouse women." We have done what they thought, and what they hoped was impossible; we women are roused!' Wave upon wave of emotion broke over Mrs Pankhurst. The huge audience hurrahed; women sprang from their seats, stretching their hands towards her. One Suffragette later wrote that Mrs Pankhurst held out a light to the world, led the crusade with supreme inspiration.

> She was . . . a mighty spirit in a fragile frame, endowed with superb courage, mental and physical, an indomitable will, great natural dignity at all times and the keenest sense of duty. Her wonderful eloquence and beautiful voice appealed to all, and stirred all hearts with a desire to help her carry on the fight. She had an indescribably gracious personality, and her courteous manner carried with it such straightness of purpose.
> . . .
>
> Mrs Pankhurst was unique, because to know her was to love her and to love her was to follow her.

To be sure, her 'feelings on sex problems' were 'rigid and wanting in elasticity', but she was so 'plucky', such 'a perfect brick', that no act of self-surrender was too extravagant to perform in her name. Suffragettes 'raided' the House of Commons in furniture vans. They harangued MPs from the river. They distributed leaflets by balloon. They chained themselves to railings. They insinuated themselves into meetings by forging tickets, by hiding in organ lofts, by squirming under platforms. They permeated Society: one Suffragette reportedly entered a reception 'disguised as a lady'. They even made so bold as to invade the sanctuary of the golf course and on one lamentable occasion they caused Mr Asquith to foozle his drive. Above all they processed, with marshals, bands, pageantry, insignia and colours—green for hope, purple for dignity, white for purity. They consciously modelled themselves on the Salvation Army, which had counted it all honour to be a 'jail-bird for Jesus'. But even though the Suffragettes mounted the largest political demonstration ever seen in Britain—perhaps half a million people, many drawn by curiosity, rallied at Hyde Park in June 1908—the vote seemed as distant as ever. Mrs Pankhurst had marched under a huge banner inscribed with the word RECTITUDE. But it was apparent to her that Asquith's morally flaccid government could neither aspire to rectitude itself nor respond to that quality in others. Feverishly Mrs Pankhurst searched round for some new expedient, perhaps an Irish rather than a Salvationist one. 'I want to be tried for sedition,' she cried.

In the summer of 1908 Mrs Pankhurst condoned, though she did not initiate, the first deliberate Suffragette attack on property, the dispatch of two 'flinty messages', as she called them, through the windows of 10 Downing Street. In October, having issued a handbill urging the populace to help Suffragettes '*RUSH the House of Commons*', Mrs Pankhurst, Christabel and 'General' Drummond were arrested. Lady Constance Lytton, a strict vegetarian won over to the cause by perceiving in the maltreatment of a sheep on its way to the slaughterhouse a revelation of 'the

position of women throughout the world', visited the Bow Street cells and was struck by the 'splendour of defiance and indignation' which pervaded Mrs Pankhurst's countenance. The prisoner complained of the cold—the blankets were 'almost certainly verminous'. A friendly MP hastened to the Savoy hotel which quickly provided comfortable beds and a table set with damask cloths, 'silver, flowers, tall wax candles, gaily coloured fruit'. Three waiters served an elaborate meal while the gaolers looked on with respectful awe. At the trial Mrs Pankhurst was keen that Christabel should demonstrate her legal expertise. And Christabel did, indeed, achieve the great coup of summoning two members of the government, Lloyd George and Herbert Gladstone, as witnesses of the incitement to breach the peace. The Suffragettes and the press made much of Christabel's clever cross-examination and more of her fresh white muslin dress with the broad band of purple, white and green stripes around her lissome waist, of the silky curls with just a hint of gold in them clustering demurely about her neck, of her alabaster skin and rose-petal cheeks, more exquisitely flushed than usual. But though she was 'bright and dainty as a newly opened flower' and though she up-staged both magistrate and ministers, Christabel could not steal the scene from so experienced a tragedienne as her mother. With 'mournful melody' Mrs Pankhurst expatiated on the 'difficulty which women have in throwing off their natural diffidence', on their patience, self-restraint and lack of hysteria. She concluded with a flourish, 'We are here, not because we are law-breakers; we are here in our efforts to become law-makers.' Even the police were moved to tears. The magistrate, who had been accused of presiding over 'the Star Chamber of the twentieth century', sentenced her to three months in Holloway. This time she would not submit to being stripped and searched. And after a week she broke the soul-searing silence. As they tramped, in single file, round the prison yard she cried out, 'Christabel, stand still till I come to you!' Trembling, she linked arms with her daughter and began talking to her in low, vibrant tones. A wardress rushed up: 'I shall listen to everything you say!' 'You are welcome to do that, but I shall insist on my right to speak to my daughter!' Pandemonium broke loose, whistles were blown, more wardresses arrived and the Suffragette leader was marched off to solitary confinement amid the excited shouts of her supporters, 'Three cheers for Mrs Pankhurst!'

How could that applause be prolonged? How could Mrs Pankhurst sustain the Suffragettes' spirit and the movement's momentum? Her own early 'cerebral excitement', noticed by the Holloway authorities, was soon deadened by protracted incarceration. And no new tactic, certainly not the systematic defiance of prison rules which Mrs Pankhurst pronounced official policy at her release breakfast, seemed capable of moving the government. Admittedly Suffragette morale was still buoyed up by the rapture of self-denial and, what Lady Constance Lytton experienced at Cannon Row Police Station after her first arrest, 'the delights of that full, unfettered companionship' with those who worked for the cause. Many of Lady Con's fellows lived on that high emotional level (though none of them followed her example in prison—in an ecstasy of self-laceration she attempted to inscribe the motto 'Votes for Women' on her chest with a needle) and their hero-worship was not confined to Mrs Pankhurst. One Suffragette appealed to Helen Ogston, who had flogged the male curs attacking her at a political meeting, 'Let me touch the hand that used the dog-whip!' Other Suffragettes were ravished by the actor Forbes-Robertson's speech which ended with this invocation:

> Mary Wollstonecraft! John Stuart Mill! May your spirits, your beautiful, noble and generous spirits, look down upon us, and assist and encourage us to soften the hearts of those opposed to us! And when the hour of our victory comes—as most certainly it will—may the Master of all convey to you the joyous news, that you may rejoice greatly with us.

For some reason Mr Asquith remained unaffected by the intercession of the feminist saints. Perhaps Mrs Pankhurst and Christabel sensed what really stirred him—the fear that Suffragettes might tear off all his clothes. At any rate, by the autumn of 1909 the WSPU leaders adopted more forceful measures. These, spontaneously developed by the rank and file, were the hustling of Cabinet Ministers wherever possible, the hunger strike and the destruction of private property. The last particularly offended public feeling. Mrs Pankhurst proclaimed that to stop it would be 'folly, weakness and wickedness' and a betrayal of her 'sacred trust'.

The appeal for greater self-sacrifice was ever Mrs Pankhurst's recipe for success. 'Just as it is in the hottest furnace that steel is most finely tempered, so it is in this hour of fiercest trial that the great spirit of women is being called forth . . . every successive act of repression brings new recruits to the corps for active service.' As the Suffragettes mortified their flesh they sanctified the soul of the movement. Neither stone walls nor iron bars could contain such spiritual force, and Christabel claimed that only now, as emaciated women burst their bonds, was it possible to understand 'the true manner and meaning of the miracles of old times'. The suffering of the hunger strikers was made that much more sublime when the authorities resorted to forcible feeding. The politicians called it 'hospital treatment'. The Suffragettes knew it as a 'violation' of their starved bodies, a kind of oral, nasal or rectal rape symbolizing the base treatment to which women had been subjected by men throughout the ages. Mrs Pankhurst denounced this 'torture' unsparingly, but she found it difficult to disguise the elements of artifice and illogic in her impeachment. Wearing the aspect of violent rebels her Suffragettes provoked the government, but when it duly retaliated they took on the air of blameless victims. Mrs Pankhurst was both a militant who courted martyrdom as a means of inspiring women to cast off their shackles and a lady who condemned persecution as an outrage against the privileges of her sex. She brazened out the incongruity, nowhere with greater panache than on her first visit to the United States in October 1909. An Amazon of 'genteel feminine appearance', Boadicea attired in a violet

chiffon velvet gown lined with dull green silk, she won 'wild hurrahs' from a Carnegie Hall audience with her first words, 'I am what you call a hooligan!' Her triumphal tour not only raised money for the Suffragettes, it gave 'a distinct fillip' to the suffragist movement in the United States, though Mrs Pankhurst found the 'definite opposition' of the English male more manageable than the 'half-amused indifference which I see in the men of America'. This transatlantic trip involved Mrs Pankhurst in a supreme sacrifice of her own. She had gone in the knowledge that her son Harry, having been sent (against doctor's advice) to work on the land after the failure of the Buddhist builder, was seriously ill with infantile paralysis. Others could nurse him, she thought; only she could fulfil her mission. On her return she was greeted with a giant banner announcing 'No Surrender. Welcome Mrs Pankhurst, Liberator of Women', and the news that Harry would never walk again. In despair she exclaimed, 'He would be better dead!' He soon was, his mother's anguish being aggravated by the presence of a rival, Harry's sweetheart, at his deathbed. After the funeral, Sylvia recalled, Mrs Pankhurst 'was broken as I had never seen her; huddled together without a care for her appearance, she seemed an old, plain, cheerless woman. Her utter dejection moved me more than her vanished charm.'

Despite this bereavement Mrs Pankhurst remained an old woman in a hurry. She was 'unscrupulous', as Teresa Billington-Greig wrote, in never counting the cost of her acts but 'human and appealing' in paying the price with a pang and sorrowing over it. Still, after campaigning against Asquith in forty constituencies during the first election of 1910, Mrs Pankhurst unwillingly agreed to a suspension of what Christabel called 'mild militancy'. The hope was that the new Parliament would pass an all-party 'Conciliation Bill' giving votes to about a million female property-owners, ladies to the last woman. Asquith opposed it on principle. Of course, he held the traditional view that women's 'natural sphere is not the turmoil and dust of politics, but the circle of social and domestic life'. And he enjoyed the caressing company of frivolous women of his own circle too much to risk their being metamorphosed into prickly seekers after notoriety, certainly dangerous and probably demented, like Mrs Pankhurst. She would scarcely have permitted the Prime Minister to take her hand, as he took that of Viscount Esher's daughter when she sat beside him on a sofa at Garsington, and cause it (in Lytton Strachey's words) to 'feel his erected instrument under his trousers'. However, Asquith had sound, political reasons for regarding the Suffragettes as 'Toryettes' and for resisting the enfranchisement of women who would be predominantly Conservative. Seeing the proposed voters in terms of their class as much as their sex, he resisted the Conciliation Bill as undemocratic. Thus on 18 November 1910, 'Black Friday', Mrs Pankhurst resumed hostilities.

She led a huge phalanx of Suffragettes on Parliament. When the police (unfortunately a rough contingent from the East End unaccustomed to the ways of ladies) barred their progress, a violent and prolonged struggle ensued. Its sexual overtones were shockingly pronounced. The women described many cases of brutal and indecent assault, the most frequent complaint being that their breasts were twisted, pinched, screwed, nipped and wrung. One policeman clutched a Suffragette by the thigh: 'Unhand it, sir!' 'My old dear, I can grip you where I like today.' Another policeman accompanied his 'consciously sensual' actions by a remark which exposed their psychological root: 'You have been wanting this for a long time, haven't you?' Mrs Pankhurst was horrified. 'Is there not a man in the House of Commons who will stand up for us?' she expostulated. The new Home Secretary, Winston Churchill, obliged by releasing about a hundred arrested women, those who had not broken windows. Their detention and trial, with another election pending, was not to the 'public advantage'. The following day Mrs Pankhurst announced to the Women's Parliament, 'I am going to Downing Street: come along all of you!' The police were taken by surprise. Asquith and Augustine Birrell incautiously showed their faces and they were mobbed in what came to be known as the Battle of Downing Street. The Prime Minister, looking white and frightened, like a fascinated rabbit, had some broken glass stuffed down his neck before effecting his escape in a taxi. The Chief Secretary for Ireland became the victim of what he indignantly termed 'a brutal, outrageous and unprovoked assault . . . it may have lamed me for life.' The

> hags . . . pulled me about and hustled me, 'stroked' my face, knocked off my hat and kicked it about, and one whose unpleasant features yet dwell in my memory harangued me with 'Oh! you wicked man; you must be a wicked man not to help us.'

Mrs Pankhurst and her myrmidons were arrested, but again the charges were dropped. With the prospect of reviving the Conciliation Bill and in an access of loyalty summoned up by the approaching coronation of George V, the widow of the Red Republican Doctor resumed the truce.

She did so reluctantly. Mrs Pankhurst came not to bring peace but the sword. By now danger was her element. Excitement was her salamander's fire. Drama was her drug. Unresting, unceasing, she continued the campaign by other means. She organized resistance to the national census—women did not count so they should not be numbered. (*Punch* inevitably remarked that the ladies had taken leave of their census.) She inveighed more frequently against the white slave traffic and sexual assaults upon children, flaying her male auditors unmercifully. 'Men! . . . men! . . . I know what shame is in your hearts!' she cried at one meeting. Masculine heads bowed. Such contrition! 'What DEARS men are!' she enthused to Ethel Smyth afterwards, her 'wonderful light-holding eyes shining like stars'. In her fast motor, the present of an American admirer, Mrs Pankhurst toured the country impressing audiences by her 'absolute sincerity, her freedom from all cant, pose and artificiality'. She rode like an empress, not even getting out of the car when it was stopped by punctures, leaving everything to her young chauffeuse—whose parents considered that in serving such a 'dreadful woman' their

daughter was being embraced by 'the dark arms of Hell'. On one occasion, though, Mrs Pankhurst did alight. Driving to a rally at the Albert Hall the car struck a member of the booing, jeering crowd. Hatred and menace were in the air as Mrs Pankhurst leapt out to succour 'the blowzy victim of Suffragette brutality'. Like one born to command Mrs Pankhurst ordered a policeman to fetch an ambulance. Her obvious distress, her sincere regret that because of the meeting she could not take the injured woman to hospital, transformed the bystanders' mood. Soon they were solacing her, taking a collection for her, urging her not to be late. Her face, 'soft with pity, radiant with love, was the face of an angel'. Safely back in the motor Mrs Pankhurst could be heard fulminating in a furious undertone, 'Drunken old beast. I wish we'd run her over.'

While the armistice lasted at home Mrs Pankhurst felt constrained to make two more sorties to the United States, in 1910 and 1911. The challenge of new audiences made the blood sing in her veins. Americans welcomed her as 'the fourteen-inch gun of the militant suffrage party'. Americans were amused by her accounts of how Mr Asquith had been forced to slide through a mail chute to evade the Suffragettes. Americans did not scoff at her claim that Californian women owed their enfranchisement, won in 1911, 'very largely to the impetus given to the movement by the agitation in England'. Above all Americans were susceptible to her brand of genteel revivalism. When she addressed a suffrage convention in Louisville the *Lexington Herald* reported,

> The moment she appeared on the platform one realized by what power of personality she has become the best loved and best hated woman in England. We have seen William Jennings Bryan capture a convention. We have seen those we account greater than Bryan dominate men. We have never seen any personality that instantly impressed itself more than does Mrs Pankhurst. A gentlewoman she is, evidently, in all that sweet word implies; but a leader with a courage to stake all on the cast of a die.

Better than Britain, the United States, later home of Elmer Gantry and Aimée Semple Macpherson, recognized Mrs Pankhurst for what she was, an old-fashioned Holiness preacher. Americans realized that she was primarily 'out for purity'. After an address at Milwaukee the audience crowded eagerly round her at the rostrum ejaculating, 'You are a God-send!' 'God give you health!' 'You've converted me!' Shortly afterwards Mrs Pankhurst heard that the government had finally 'torpedoed' (the word was Lloyd George's) the Conciliation Bill. 'Protest imperative,' she cabled. By January 1912 she had returned to England. Her new watchwords were 'Sedition' and 'The Women's Revolution'.

The Suffragette agitation reached its climax just at a time when Mrs Pankhurst was experiencing what Sylvia called 'the flood-tide of the last great energies of her personality'. In this period, immediately before the First World War, the most full-blooded Suffragette violence coincided with the most consummate Suffragette puritanism. The harshness of male retaliation and the extremism of Mrs Pankhurst and her eldest daughter drove their forces underground, replaced open demonstration by secret arson. 'Militancy,' wrote Christabel, 'is doing the work of purification'. By winning women the power to outlaw vice, Suffragette violence aimed to end all violence, especially that done to white slaves, assaulted children and the like. But as the subversives dwelt upon the evils of the opposite sex, as they embraced the 'scientific' doctrine that 'life is feminine' and that the male element is 'primarily an excrescence, a superfluity, a waste product of nature', as they consorted furtively together, so their feminist impulses quickened. Homosexuality is the ultimate expression of male or female chauvinism, just as incest is the ultimate expression of social snobbery. And some of Mrs Pankhurst's followers prosecuted the sex war with such vehemence that it is impossible to discount some kind of sapphic incentive—one Suffragette advocated the segregation of married women on the grounds that they were 'contaminated'. Other evidence confirms the supposition. Mrs Pethick-Lawrence and Annie Kenney paraded their attraction for one another so openly that Teresa Billington-Greig 'saw it as something unbalanced and primitive and possibly dangerous to the movement'. Christabel sent hothouse missives to the WSPU secretary, Mrs Tuke: 'My dear and darling Pansy . . . with very very much love'. And Ethel Smyth, with her mannish hats, her tweed jackets and her green, purple and white ties, fell passionately in love with Mrs Pankhurst (who forgave her sartorial eccentricity). Dame Ethel was later to develop a similar infatuation for Virginia Woolf, who described her wooing as 'hideous and horrid and melancholy sad. It is like being caught by a giant crab.'

Mrs Pankhurst did not spurn this novel attachment. True, her deepest feelings were always bound up with Christabel ('my fellow—a born bachelor', said Ethel Smyth). And, wholly engaged in her mission, Mrs Pankhurst had held aloof from other emotional entanglements. But, as Ethel Smyth wrote to her 'darling Em',

> I am the glorious exception for you—and I think it is the crowning achievement of my life to have made you love me. And proof of your cleverness to have found me—and found a new gift in yourself—the friendship you give me. Yes, I also am getting more and more 'off' men.

Ethel Smyth was a powerful woman and her advances were difficult to resist. Mrs Pankhurst did not try. At this fraught stage of her career, the fabric of her slight body wasted by repeated hunger strikes, the wings of her swift spirit clipped by constant imprisonments, this intimacy seemed to satisfy her most profound psychological needs. Mrs Pankhurst had always accepted the traditional view that woman's moral nature was infinitely superior to man's. Ladies were the better half, though, of course, the sexes should be absolutely equal in terms of civil rights. She had invariably exalted chastity as the female virtue to which males should aspire. But by 1913 she endorsed Christabel's assertion that most of women's ailments and disabilities stemmed from diseases contracted from those seventy-five per cent of males suffering from gonorrhoea and syphilis. Men seemed incapable of following the Pankhursts' admonition to conserve 'the complex seminal fluid, with its wonderfully invigorating influence', despite

Christabel's warning that 'the secretion of the testicles . . . if wrongfully used . . . is so potent that it may figuratively be classed with the secretions of the poison fangs of venomous reptiles.' Thus women should avoid their embraces altogether. Mrs Pankhurst positively advised against marriage 'unless you care so much that you cannot help it'. Not, of course, that she favoured Lesbianism. But she found much needed comfort in the bosom of Ethel Smyth, who wrote to 'my treasure and my pride',

> I lie awake at night sometimes and see you like Atlas, bearing up the world of women on your head. I can't tell you what I think of you. . . . If you were to come in now all I could do would be to hold you in my arms . . . and be silent.

Mrs Pankhurst responded as warmly to Ethel Smyth's endearments as she did to her music. She also found the composer an able tutor in the *recherché* art of breaking windows. Together they went to practise on Hook Heath. Mrs Pankhurst's first stone shot backwards, narrowly missing Ethel Smyth's dog. Wearing a scowl of ferocious concentration, Mrs Pankhurst tried and tried again. Finally she hit the target and 'a smile of such beatitude—the smile of a baby that has blown a watch open—stole across her countenance'.

In fact 'the argument of the stone', as deployed by Mrs Pankhurst, proved singularly ineffective; for, leading an assault by some of 'our bad, bold ones' on 10 Downing Street in March 1912, both her missiles flew wide of the mark. And although the Prime Minister's windows were smashed, and although the main shopping streets of London resounded to the tinkle of glass as cohorts of fashionably dressed women produced hammers from handbags and flints from muffs, the effect was to enrage the public not to coerce the politicians. Mrs Pankhurst's indisputably great achievement had been to make women's suffrage a major national issue, something forty years of constitutional agitation had failed to do. Now her sight was dimmed by floods of dazzling limelight, her vision was obscured by cataracts of sectarian enthusiasm. She talked grandiosely of destroying governments but she failed to perceive that her violence was back-firing, that it was chiefly, like her stone-throwing, a danger to her own followers. The 'madness of the militants' was universally condemned. They were fanatics, hysterics, unfit to vote. No less a person than Sir Almroth Wright said so, in a letter to *The Times*. More, the eminent bacteriologist indicted women in general as tending to become morally warped and mentally sick in response to 'the reverberations of their physiological emergencies'—ion, menstrual tension, menopausal disorder and Lesbian perversion. This was somewhat strong for contemporary taste and the letter was denounced as pornography. But militant behaviour certainly seemed to confirm Leo Maxse's view that 'female suffrage would be worse than a German invasion in the way of a national calamity.' Lloyd George was not alone in thinking that Christabel had lost all sense of reality: 'It's just like going to a lunatic asylum and talking to a man who thinks he's God Almighty.' Even the Anti-Suffragist movement was temporarily able to mask the fundamental absurdity of its position—for the more successfully its female members conducted their campaign the more decisively they demonstrated women's fitness to participate in politics. Mrs Pankhurst ignored 'the priceless Antis'. Back in 'that horrible Holloway' she kept up her spirits by joining in the Suffragette sing-song, her 'queer cracked voice' rising tunelessly to the strains of the 'March of the Women' as its composer, Ethel Smyth, conducted from a cell window 'in almost Bacchic frenzy with a toothbrush'.

Suffering from bronchitis, she was soon released to face a much more serious charge than stone-throwing. With the Pethick-Lawrences (Christabel escaped to concert future operations from the safety and comfort of Paris) Mrs Pankhurst was accused of conspiracy to damage property. The trial was notable both for its revelation that the Suffragettes kept a code-book in which Cabinet Ministers were identified by the names of 'the commonest weeds' and for Mrs Pankhurst's spirited defence. 'Swifter and more impassioned than a tigress', she was 'by turns petulant, imperious and appealing'. Her hottest denial was reserved for the allegation that the WSPU was a collection of 'unimportant wild women'. It contained ladies like herself (indeed, she owed her leadership to her superior social standing) ladies who would not dream of biting, kicking or wielding hatpins. 'We have always put up an honourable fight.' The jury were impressed by the purity of her motives, but they found her guilty and she was sentenced to nine months' imprisonment. With her fellows she went on hunger strike. Holloway became a Gehenna, as all around her Suffragettes endured the agony of being stuffed like Christmas turkeys. Eventually a deputation of doctors and nurses proposed to subject Mrs Pankhurst to the same revolting treatment. 'If any of you dare take a step inside this cell, I shall defend myself!' she threatened, seizing a heavy earthenware chamber-pot. They withdrew in disarray. The government apparently feared the lengths to which Mrs Pankhurst would go if they fed her by force. So, a wraith, she was freed. She journeyed to Paris to recuperate amid an orgy of shopping.

Now Mrs Pankhurst and her daughter began to talk in terms of guerilla tactics, civil war. The Pethick-Lawrences demurred and in one of 'her summer-storms of anger' Mrs Pankhurst blazed, 'If you do not support Christabel's policy we shall smash you!' The Pethick-Lawrences departed for Canada unperturbed. On their return, in October 1912, they discovered what an 'extreme and violent person' Mrs Pankhurst was, how 'ruthless', how 'insensitive to ordinary human considerations', 'like some irresistible force of nature—a tidal wave, or a river in full flood'. The Pethick-Lawrences were treated like pariahs, no one would talk to them, their offices had vanished. Finally Mrs Pankhurst (gladdened by regaining spiritual possession of Christabel) announced their expulsion from the WSPU. Having supported her dictatorship in 1907, they could only challenge it now at the expense of the cause 'to which we have contributed our life-blood'. So they accepted the *coup,* continued to edit *Votes for Women* (Christabel began a rival paper, *The Suffragette*) and allowed Mrs Pankhurst to veil the rift, to plead for union and to foment bolder militancy. Like some accomplished high-wire artist, she gave a dizzying performance (Fred Pethick-Lawrence ad-

mired it as a means of winning sympathy and condemned it as an exercise in 'playacting') which inspired the Albert Hall audience with the vertigo of her own self-sacrifice. She lamented the sorrows of women who had 'exposed themselves to the indecent violence' of the mob. She mourned the fate of outraged and diseased young girls. She concluded, 'Be militant each in your own way. . . . I incite this meeting to rebellion. I say to the Government: You have not dared to take the leaders of Ulster for their incitement to rebellion. Take me if you dare.' The 'Panks' thus triumphed over the 'Peths', but the loss of its less extreme wing left the movement sadly unbalanced. Having excommunicated the Pethick-Lawrences, Mrs Pankhurst never communicated with them again.

The Suffragettes burned to vote. Public buildings and private houses went up in flames. Letter-boxes were assaulted, railway stations were attacked, telephone wires were cut, orchids were destroyed, putting greens were damaged with acid, works of art were defaced, churches were gutted, bombs were planted. One exploded, destroying Lloyd George's new house at Walton, the 'Bombazines' or 'Outragettes' leaving as sinister evidence of their guilt 'two broken hat-pins, a hairpin, and a golosh indisputably feminine'. Old ladies bought gun licences to terrify the authorities. Envelopes containing red pepper and snuff were sent to all Cabinet Ministers. Mrs Pankhurst took full responsibility for everything. But in April 1913 she pleaded innocent to the charge of inciting to commit a felony on the grounds that she had not done so 'wickedly and maliciously'. From the bench the 'red-robed mumbler, cruel, hard' (as a Suffragette called him) dismissed Mrs Pankhurst's plea and her justification—it included a tale about a judge being found dead in a brothel which his lordship found both irrelevant and improper. The rest of her defence consisted of a searing condemnation of London's 'regulated traffic . . . in little children . . . [who are] being trained to minister to the vicious pleasures of persons who ought to know better in their positions in life'. From the dock Mrs Pankhurst breathed fiery defiance:

> I feel I have done my duty. I look upon myself as a prisoner of war. I am under no moral obligation to conform to, or in any way accept, the sentence imposed upon me. . . . I shall fight, I shall fight, I shall fight, from the moment I enter prison.

She was condemned to three years' penal servitude. The 'Cat and Mouse' Act, recently passed, ensured that released hunger-strikers could be re-arrested at will to continue their sentences. Nevertheless starvation was the limbo through which she must pass to attain even temporary freedom. For ten days Mrs Pankhurst endured its pains, depressed, miserable, spurning the delicacies thoughtfully placed in her cell. Only once was she roused, when the prison governor, smelling strongly of drink, offered to fetch her a minister. Her conscience was clear!

Finally Mrs Pankhurst was liberated 'on licence', a document which, with a mummer's flourish, she tore up in front of the governor as her valedictory act: 'I have no intention of obeying this infamous law.' The 'Queen' then dragged her macerated carcase through the prison gates, to be greeted rapturously by her 'subjects', who had been keeping long vigil outside. Soon she was recovering, revelling in the 'sportingness' of the struggle, eating fish and drinking champagne, complaining that to have her movements spied on by the police was an 'intolerable insult'. 'All the old Adam (or, Eve, which is better) is coming back, and I begin to realize the glorious fight ahead of me.' The fight consisted of rhythmic rounds of detentions and releases (ten of each in the fifteen months before the armistice of August 1914) interspersed by moments of high excitement as she addressed meetings or evaded capture. At this she became adept, with the help of veiled decoys dressed in her clothes. She had only to cry, 'Women, they are arresting me!' for her specially trained bodyguard of athletic young women to leap to the rescue, wielding Indian clubs. After one escape she exulted, 'The girl who had her head cut open would not have it stitched as she wanted to keep the scar as big as possible! The real warrior spirit!' Mrs Pankhurst paid for the drama with pounds of flesh. By refusing to rest or to drink, she made her fasts quick indeed, but deathly. That her periods of liberty were purchased at a fearful price can be seen in her description of the effects of hunger, thirst and sleep strikes.

> The body cannot endure the loss of moisture. It cries out in protest with every nerve. The muscles waste, the skin becomes shrunken and flabby, the facial appearance alters horribly. . . . Every natural function is, of course, suspended. . . . The body becomes cold and shivery, there is constant headache and nausea, and sometimes there is fever. The mouth and tongue become coated and swollen, the throat thickens and the voice sinks to a thready whisper.

Having refused to let the prison doctor examine her ('I gave him one of my storms. . . ."You are a Government torturer."') Mrs Pankhurst would emerge, desiccated, skeletal, the yellow parchment skin so tightly drawn over her face that it seemed the bones must break through, to be kept in 'cotton wool' until she was sufficiently recovered to endure the hell once more. This cycle of suffering touched the wardresses themselves, over whom she had established a social ascendancy—'All the women officers are now devoted to me . . . perfect angels.' The Suffragettes interrupted church services, chanting their own litany:

> Save Emmeline Pankhurst
> Spare her! Spare her!
> Give her light and set her free
> Save her! Save her!
> Hear us while we pray to thee.

Among the fascinated observers of Mrs Pankhurst's terrible waxing and waning only Christabel seemed to endure her mother's progressive mummification with unmoved fortitude. Ethel Smyth commented that in allowing her aged parent to act as scapegoat for womankind Christabel 'goes one better than God who sacrified his son—a young person!!' It was a remark which Mrs Pankhurst neither forgot nor forgave.

No one actually liked Mrs Pankhurst and Christabel: the Suffragette leaders were either abominated or worshipped.

Mrs Pankhurst's evident fanaticism offended the many. Her nobly borne torments inspired the few to emulate, even to outdo her in eccentric feats of chivalry. Some, though prohibited from taking life, attempted personal violence—Philip Snowden found it necessary to protect one of his political meetings by employing as stewards wardresses from a lunatic asylum. Others made vain and embarrassing appeals to the Archbishop of Canterbury and to the yet more sacred person of the sovereign. Emily Wilding Davison, writhing with desire to make the ultimate surrender, to achieve what she called 'the supreme consummation of sacrifice', committed suicide by throwing herself in front of the monarch's horse as it raced in the Derby. (For the Suffragettes it was a sensation; for the British public it was 'such bad manners to the King'.) A specific protest against the 'slow murder' of Mrs Pankhurst by 'Iscariot politicians' was the slashing of Velasquez's 'Rokeby' Venus by Mary Richardson, a radical Suffragette who later attempted to start a communist nunnery. With the tortured logic that is the first refuge of fanatics everywhere, she argued that justice was an element of beauty as much as colour and form. 'I have tried to destroy the picture of the most beautiful woman in mythological history as a protest against the government for destroying Mrs Pankhurst, who is the most beautiful character in modern history.' At a safe distance Mrs Pankhurst attracted more than she repelled. Admittedly the United States Immigration authorities attempted to bar her entry in October 1913, detaining her on Ellis Island as a person suspected, ironically enough, of 'moral turpitude'. But the chorus of scorn and execration which greeted this affront to 'the best known of living women', claimed by some Americans to be a 'spiritual giantess' and a 'revolutionary hero' in the same class as Washington, Jefferson and Lincoln (not to mention Mrs Pankhurst's threat to go on hunger strike) secured her quick release. The headlines blazed, 'Mrs Pankhurst beats Uncle Sam.' For Mrs Pankhurst it was another 'thrilling adventure' which swelled her audiences and her takings in the United States—as Suffragette numbers dwindled she became obsessed with increasing 'monied' support. For Alice Paul and those who were to form the American Women's Party, it was a further call to employ the methods of their transatlantic sisters. Alice Paul, schooled in the Suffragette struggle, possessed an indomitable will and seems in certain respects to have modelled herself on Mrs Pankhurst, most notably in a commitment to militancy which no ridicule, no failure and no argument could shake. Ethel Smyth's judgement of Mrs Pankhurst might equally have applied to her American counterpart: as well try to hold up an avalanche with a child's spade as persuade her out of an idea that had once taken root in her mind.

Could nothing check Mrs Pankhurst's inexorable course? Among others, Sylvia attempted to divert her mother into more democratic and pacific ways, but she was ignominiously swept aside. Now Mrs Pankhurst carried on the fight for its own sake, sought martyrdom as an end in itself. For it was clear that militant tactics were actually postponing victory and that Suffragettes could never compete with, say, Irish Unionists (who were anyway monopolizing the government's attention) when it came to coercion. The inconsistency between Mrs Pankhurst's avowed aims and the means she employed to realize them was not due simply to a lady-like lack of logic. As Dr Mary Gordon, the psychiatrist at Holloway who had taken a professional interest in the Suffragette leader, explained, the WSPU had 'fire not form'. It

> leapt into being like a flame. . . . It released vast stores of unconscious energy. . . . It cohered fiercely, ignoring thinking . . . and good order. . . . It swept where it listed, and when its work was done died down and out. . . . Such spiritual upheavals are always irrational, and irrational human types are swept into them as high priests.

By 1914 Mrs Pankhurst was the focus of a small, intense, chiliastic cult. Its satisfactions lay in immediate emotional climaxes, 'the exaltation, the rapture of battle,' rather than in final fulfilment, when, as Christabel prophesied, joy would mingle with 'regret that the most glorious chapter in women's history is closed'. Countrywide conversion would deprive the chief evangelist of her *raison d'être.* Only an earth-shaking event could stop Mrs Pankhurst's agitation, could afford a more sublime afflatus, could demand a more heroic sacrifice. It was provided by the outbreak of the Great War. At first Mrs Pankhurst and Christabel saw this as God's vengeance upon men for subjecting women through the ages to their lusts. After a few days, however, they were vouchsafed a new revelation: this was another holy war and the enemy was not man but German. Sexual chauvinism submitted to the paramount claims of racial jingoism.

Armageddon provided a fitting new part for an experienced old trouper. It involved Mrs Pankhurst in nothing less than acting as the chief preserver of English civilization. Naturally the war must be won, at whatever cost in blood and money. Mrs Pankhurst became the flail of slackers, shirkers and strikers. She exhorted men to join the colours. She encouraged ladies to distribute white feathers. She rampaged for conscription. She led a huge procession of women demanding 'The Right to Serve'. They would strike or riot, she warned, if they were not permitted to fill male jobs and so free men for the trenches. But perhaps even more important than military success was spiritual victory. Mrs Pankhurst expressed delight that Lord Kitchener had impressed on his soldiers 'the duty to keep themselves clean and pure'. However, there were more insidious perils than germs—Germans! They were everywhere; not just in obvious places, such as Belgian nunneries and British pacifist organizations. They infested the Stock Exchange, the Churches, Westminster, the War Office, even the WSPU itself. Mrs Pankhurst called for their elimination from the government with such vehemence that her remarks verged on treason, and in 1915 she was arrested (though at once released) during a rally in Trafalgar Square. For the same reason *Britannia*, as *The Suffragette* had been re-christened, was often raided by the police. The *Daily Mail* was fairly outdone and Lord Northcliffe revised his hostile opinion of Mrs Pankhurst. They vied with one another in patriotic proscription. Ethel Smyth recorded that, on the day Asquith resigned, Mrs Pankhurst found Lord Northcliffe bouncing up and down in his chair crying:

> '*I* did it. . . . *I* did it'; and timing the 'I' on the down bounce. Mrs Pankhurst, much astonished, said something about the worst of the lot, the Foreign Office, being still in the saddle. Whereupon he leapt up, patted her on the back, and said: 'Don't you worry, my dear girl, we'll get 'em all out.'

Lord Northcliffe might have been less cordial, and less familiar, had he known that Mrs Pankhurst reckoned the root of all Germany's evil lay in its being 'a male nation', which had violated Belgium and was attempting to repeat the outrage on the 'feminine' state of France. He might also have nursed doubts about the explanation, which Mrs Pankhurst's bellicose new role had afforded her, of a puzzling pre-war phenomenon: the stewards who had ejected Suffragettes from political meetings most brutally all spoke with thick, guttural accents. They were, of course, Huns.

Mrs Pankhurst attempted to foster British civilization in other ways. When her scheme to start a home for illegitimate war babies foundered, owing to a 'lamentable lack of public spirit', she adopted four little girls herself, setting up house in London with the formidable Sister Pine, who had nursed her so diligently after hunger strikes. Perhaps Mrs Pankhurst sought recompense for the loss of Harry (whom she still mourned in moods of dejection) or even of Sylvia and Adela (whom she publicly disowned for their pacifism). Unfortunately, though, her maternal instincts remained erratic. She taught the girls to curtsy but she neglected their education. She promised, 'If you're very good you'll get the name of Pankhurst', but it was not to be—after a decade or so the children proved too expensive and three of them were handed over to rich guardians, while Christabel adopted the fourth. Meanwhile the girls had, and were, attractive properties; Mrs Pankhurst carefully rehearsed them in the business of hugging and kissing her for the benefit of photographers. Her flair for publicity never failed. Even the King had advised Lloyd George 'to make use of Mrs Pankhurst'. In 1916 she went on another tour of North America, interspersing propagandist speeches on the war with lectures on 'social hygiene'—the prevention of venereal disease. In 1917 she travelled to Russia, under official auspices, in a vain attempt to instil fighting spirit into Kerensky's armies by appeals to the soldiers' wives. She was thrilled by the female 'Battalions of Death' who paraded before her, but they proved to be aptly named, at first derided by the Russian troops they were supposed to inspire and then well-nigh exterminated by the Germans they were supposed to kill. The mind of the Russian masses had clearly been poisoned by Hun agents and Kerensky himself was obviously sick in body and weak in will. As Mrs Pankhurst departed, the Provisional Government was teetering towards its downfall and she received a sinister warning that the new World Enemy was to be Bolshevism. It had actually been suggested that her safety could not be assured in the streets of Petrograd unless she wore hideous 'proletarian' clothes.

The purifying fire of Mrs Pankhurst's present convictions seemed to devour her past. She never paused, never hesitated, never looked back. She despised 'potterers', waverers, compromisers, reminiscers. Perhaps the crowning irony of Mrs Pankhurst's career was her vitriolic attack on Asquith when, in 1916, he announced his conversion to female suffrage. It was more important, she asserted, for all servicemen to be enfranchised. Votes for women could take second place. Asquith was guilty of using women as 'catspaws' to 'dish' the defenders of the realm 'while any and every crank, coward or traitor, is to be free to vote as usual'. However, her sex had patently earned the ballot. In 1918 Lloyd George, anxious to avoid a renewal of Suffragette militancy, at last did justice to women—to those, at least, over thirty. The triumph of enfranchisement was marred for Mrs Pankhurst by the fact that Christabel, standing as a candidate at Smethwick on the ticket of a man she had so often denounced as 'Oily' George, was defeated by a Socialist. Bernard Shaw's acid comments on the general election were understandable. Instead of elevating politics to a nobler plane

> Women voted for hanging the Kaiser; rallied hysterically round the worst male candidates; threw out all the women candidates of tried ability, integrity and devotion; and elected just one titled lady of great wealth and singular demagogic fascination.

Of course this proved nothing, except perhaps the soundness of Mrs Poyser's celebrated judgement that women were fools, God having made them to match men. Mrs Pankhurst, at any rate, had no time to consider the effects of women's suffrage. To do so might have involved her in that untimeliest of fates—anticlimax. In 1918, and once more in 1919, she toured North America at Lloyd George's behest. Again she was the inspired preacher, uttering fiery comminations, speaking with tongue of flame, bearing the torch for her new mission. Its practical aim was the abolition of the proletariat by assimilating its members into the bourgeoisie. Its spiritual purpose was to cleanse the world of the pestilence of Bolshevism. Spawned by a German Jew, the germ of Bolshevism had spread a mental infection akin to venereal disease. The sores on the body politic should be cauterized. The public mind should be purged. 'It would be an excellent thing,' wrote Mrs Pankhurst in the *New York Tribune*, 'if all the books written before the war, and many that have been written since 1914, could be burned in one great conflagration.'

In her declining years Mrs Pankhurst was obliged to orate less from fullness of soul than from emptiness of purse. Ever optimistic, capable of earning $500 a speech, she believed that 'financial Nirvana was imminent', but she was tormented in practice by abysmal penury. The flood of Suffragette cash had evaporated, her testimonial fund had produced only a disappointing trickle and she remained habitually improvident. 'I cannot reduce my standard to one of constant pinch and save.' Was it not economy to buy the best? How could she take the stage without a suitable costume? Anyway, she could not resist dashing feathered hats, elegant velvet gowns, finely wrought lace, soft leather gloves, delicate kid shoes. But when Ethel Smyth offered her money Mrs Pankhurst's pride was wounded

and they were permanently estranged. So between 1920 and '24, sponsored by the National Council for Combating Venereal Disease, Mrs Pankhurst spent most of her time lecturing in Canada on 'social hygiene'. With her accustomed panache she insisted that her meetings should be advertised as 'public health demonstrations' and she filled theatres, halls and churches all over the country. Branding sexual misconduct as 'moral Bolshevism', advocating the exclusion of all but eugenically sound Anglo-Saxon immigrants, she lifted the whole question of VD, as the *Toronto Globe* said, 'from the purely medical to the realm of the spiritual'. She had a sharply temporal riposte, though, for the Mayor of Bathurst, New Brunswick, who showed her his new Home for Fallen Women: 'And where, pray, is your Home for Fallen Men?' Mrs Pankhurst liked Toronto, a 'city of churches, trees and kind hearts', and she so favoured the dominion as a bastion of the British Empire that she became a Canadian citizen. But by 1925 the winters had become intolerable. After a long recuperative spell in Bermuda, where frequent 'At Homes' failed to alleviate her boredom, she travelled to Juan-les-Pins on the French Riviera. There, with Christabel and 'Pansy' Tuke, she embarked on an enterprise which, had it succeeded, would have brought her career to a truly bizarre conclusion. Among the expatriate community, cosy and secluded, she opened 'The English Teashop of Good Hope'.

It was a hopeless venture, doomed from the start and quickly abandoned. Yet some found it less astonishing than Mrs Pankhurst's final apotheosis as a Conservative *grande dame*, which was considered 'a denial of her whole life's work'. She returned to London. She expressed horror at the socialistic distemper which was the General Strike. She impressed Mr Baldwin by disdaining the proffered microphone and transmitting the faintest vibrations of that extraordinary voice from the past to the farthest corners of the Albert Hall. She was adopted as Tory candidate for the forlorn seat of Whitechapel. She descended into the abyss of the East End to live among her constituents, some of whom had been infected with the communist virus spread by her daughter Sylvia. Frail and withered, Mrs Pankhurst still managed on the platform to transfigure herself into the radiant prophetess of former times. True, the purport of her message had altered: now the extension of the suffrage to irresponsible 'flappers' did not find favour in her sight. But she still campaigned for righteousness: now she was agonized by the fear that growing sexual equality involved men's dragging women down to their own base level. What with short skirts, lipstick, jazz, cigarettes, contraceptives, a new age of immorality seemed to be dawning—unless Mr Baldwin intervened. To cap it all, Sylvia was 'carrying on' with an Italian socialist! The news of her illegitimate baby brought down Mrs Pankhurst's exquisitely coiffured silver hairs with sorrow to the grave. For hours she wept. She would be stigmatized with her daughter's shame, would never be able to speak in public again. From Stygian despair she rallied gamely for a while. Then she relapsed and Christabel removed her to the polite privacy of a Hampstead nursing home. There, at the end of her seventieth year and at the height of the London season, on 14 June 1928, Mrs Pankhurst's tempestuous spirit at last forsook her ravaged body. Her dramatic instinct was impeccable. After lying in state, surrounded by bouquets of flowers and a Suffragette guard of honour, all arrayed in purple, green and white, after scenes of great public emotion—women sobbed, kissed the funeral pall, knelt on the pavements as the cortège passed—her mortal remains were laid to rest at Brompton Cemetery. In the same hour the House of Lords passed the measure giving all adult women the vote.

Two years later a statue of Mrs Pankhurst was erected near the Houses of Parliament. There she poses still, a refined, feminine figure clad in a long coat with a fur collar, her outstretched hand clasping a lorgnette. In bronze, as in flesh, she is every inch the lady on her pedestal.

At the unveiling ceremony traffic was diverted around Parliament Square, Mr Baldwin delivered a speech of unparalleled banality and the music, conducted by Ethel Smyth, was provided by the band of the Metropolitan Police. A heretic, duly qualified for sainthood by apostasy and death, had been canonized—so, at least, went the popular myth. In fact, Mrs Pankhurst had been a bigot for orthodoxy, a martyr for morality. Her nonconformity consisted of nothing but uncompromising dedication to strait-laced dogmas and obdurate scorn for the constitutional suffragists' maxim that the last infirmity of noble minds was to do ill that good might come. Mrs Pankhurst conveyed her invincible sense of rectitude to her daughters, as their remarkable careers demonstrate. Adela, having been a militant Suffragette, an extreme radical and an active trade unionist, became a fervent imperialist just in time to effect a last reconciliation with her mother. Following the rightward path, Adela condemned criticism of Hitler and Mussolini during the 1930s, deplored the outbreak of war and was interned in Australia in 1943 for expressing pro-Japanese sentiments. Mrs Pankhurst was implacable towards her second daughter. Sylvia crusaded for everything from Esperanto to vegetarianism and was by turns a socialist, a pacifist, a Bolshevist (she was imprisoned in 1920 for inciting the British fleet to mutiny), a free-lance revolutionary, an anti-Fascist. She became so obsessed by Italy's rape of Ethiopia that she spent her last twenty-five years championing the feudal theocracy of the Emperor Haile Selassie, Elect of God, Lion of Judah, King of Zion. Having for so long prophesied the feminist millennium, Dame Christabel (as she became in 1936) devoted the rest of her life to predicting the Millennium *tout court.* She became a travelling evangelist of the Second Advent. This would be ushered in by a 'season of tribulation and world-purification' and might be foretold by any number of auguries, from the return of the Jews to Jerusalem to an earth tremor in New York. As Mrs Pethick-Lawrence once ruefully observed, 'The Pankhursts did nothing by halves.' At the infernal centre of the daughers' causes chafed the mother's violent spirit. That spirit has never been laid. It is the spirit of zealotry, it haunts the modern world and its manifestations are legion.

FURTHER READING

Biographies

Mitchell, David. *The Fighting Pankhursts: A Study in Tenacity.* New York: The MacMillan Company, 1967, 352 p.
    A biography of the Pankhurst family.

Noble, Iris. *Emmeline and Her Daughters: The Pankhurst Suffragettes.* Folkestone: Bailey Brothers and Swinfen Ltd., 1974, 190 p.
    A detailed study of the Pankhurst women.

Pankhurst, E. Sylvia. *The Life of Emmeline Pankhurst: The Suffragette Struggle for Women's Citizenship.* Boston and New York: Houghton Mifflin Company, 1936, 180 p.
    The story of Pankhurst's life as told by her daughter.

Criticism

Morrison, Sylvia. "*My Own Story*: An Autobiography of Emmeline Pankhurst." *Books and Bookmen* 24, No. 8 (May 1979): 64.
    A retrospective analysis of *My Own Story.*

Spacks, Patricia Meyer. "The Selves in Hiding." In *Women's Autobiography: Essays in Criticism,* edited by Estelle C. Jelenek, pp. 112-32. Bloomington: Indiana University Press, 1980.
    Places Pankhurst's autobiography in the realm of submerged personas.

Additional coverage of Pankhurst's life and career is contained in the following source published by the Gale Group: *Contemporary Authors,* **Vol. 116.**

How to Use This Index

Literary Criticism Series
Cumulative Author Index

Andersen, Hans Christian
1805-1875 .... **NCLC 7, 79; DA; DAB; DAC; DAM MST, POP; SSC 6; WLC**
See also CLR 6; DA3; MAICYA; SATA 100; YABC 1

Anderson, C. Farley
See Mencken, H(enry) L(ouis); Nathan, George Jean

Anderson, Jessica (Margaret) Queale
1916- .... **CLC 37**
See also CA 9-12R; CANR 4, 62

Anderson, Jon (Victor) 1940- . **CLC 9; DAM POET**
See also CA 25-28R; CANR 20

Anderson, Lindsay (Gordon)
1923-1994 .... **CLC 20**
See also CA 125; 128; 146; CANR 77

Anderson, Maxwell 1888-1959 .... **TCLC 2; DAM DRAM**
See also CA 105; 152; DLB 7, 228; MTCW 2

Anderson, Poul (William) 1926- .... **CLC 15**
See also AAYA 5, 34; CA 1-4R, 181; CAAE 181; CAAS 2; CANR 2, 15, 34, 64; CLR 58; DLB 8; INT CANR-15; MTCW 1, 2; SATA 90; SATA-Brief 39; SATA-Essay 106

Anderson, Robert (Woodruff)
1917- .... **CLC 23; DAM DRAM**
See also AITN 1; CA 21-24R; CANR 32; DLB 7

Anderson, Sherwood 1876-1941 ..... **TCLC 1, 10, 24; DA; DAB; DAC; DAM MST, NOV; SSC 1; WLC**
See also AAYA 30; CA 104; 121; CANR 61; CDALB 1917-1929; DA3; DLB 4, 9, 86; DLBD 1; MTCW 1, 2

Andier, Pierre
See Desnos, Robert

Andouard
See Giraudoux, (Hippolyte) Jean

Andrade, Carlos Drummond de **CLC 18**
See also Drummond de Andrade, Carlos

Andrade, Mario de 1893-1945 .... **TCLC 43**

Andreae, Johann V(alentin)
1586-1654 .... **LC 32**
See also DLB 164

Andreas-Salome, Lou 1861-1937 ... **TCLC 56**
See also CA 178; DLB 66

Andress, Lesley
See Sanders, Lawrence

Andrewes, Lancelot 1555-1626 .... **LC 5**
See also DLB 151, 172

Andrews, Cicily Fairfield
See West, Rebecca

Andrews, Elton V.
See Pohl, Frederik

Andreyev, Leonid (Nikolaevich)
1871-1919 .... **TCLC 3**
See also CA 104; 185

Andric, Ivo 1892-1975 .... **CLC 8; SSC 36**
See also CA 81-84; 57-60; CANR 43, 60; DLB 147; MTCW 1

Androvar
See Prado (Calvo), Pedro

Angelique, Pierre
See Bataille, Georges

Angell, Roger 1920- .... **CLC 26**
See also CA 57-60; CANR 13, 44, 70; DLB 171, 185

Angelou, Maya 1928- .... **CLC 12, 35, 64, 77; BLC 1; DA; DAB; DAC; DAM MST, MULT, POET, POP; WLCS**
See also AAYA 7, 20; BW 2, 3; CA 65-68; CANR 19, 42, 65; CDALBS; CLR 53; DA3; DLB 38; MTCW 1, 2; SATA 49

Anna Comnena 1083-1153 .... **CMLC 25**

Annensky, Innokenty (Fyodorovich)
1856-1909 .... **TCLC 14**
See also CA 110; 155

Annunzio, Gabriele d'
See D'Annunzio, Gabriele

Anodos
See Coleridge, Mary E(lizabeth)

Anon, Charles Robert
See Pessoa, Fernando (Antonio Nogueira)

Anouilh, Jean (Marie Lucien Pierre)
1910-1987 .... **CLC 1, 3, 8, 13, 40, 50; DAM DRAM; DC 8**
See also CA 17-20R; 123; CANR 32; MTCW 1, 2

Anthony, Florence
See Ai

Anthony, John
See Ciardi, John (Anthony)

Anthony, Peter
See Shaffer, Anthony (Joshua); Shaffer, Peter (Levin)

Anthony, Piers 1934- .... **CLC 35; DAM POP**
See also AAYA 11; CA 21-24R; CANR 28, 56, 73; DLB 8; MTCW 1, 2; SAAS 22; SATA 84

Anthony, Susan B(rownell)
1916-1991 .... **TCLC 84**
See also CA 89-92; 134

Antoine, Marc
See Proust, (Valentin-Louis-George-Eugene-) Marcel

Antoninus, Brother
See Everson, William (Oliver)

Antonioni, Michelangelo 1912- .... **CLC 20**
See also CA 73-76; CANR 45, 77

Antschel, Paul 1920-1970
See Celan, Paul
See also CA 85-88; CANR 33, 61; MTCW 1

Anwar, Chairil 1922-1949 .... **TCLC 22**
See also CA 121

Anzaldua, Gloria 1942-
See also CA 175; DLB 122; HLCS 1

Apess, William 1798-1839(?) .... **NCLC 73; DAM MULT**
See also DLB 175; NNAL

Apollinaire, Guillaume 1880-1918 .. **TCLC 3, 8, 51; DAM POET; PC 7**
See also Kostrowitzki, Wilhelm Apollinaris de
See also CA 152; MTCW 1

Appelfeld, Aharon 1932- .... **CLC 23, 47**
See also CA 112; 133; CANR 86

Apple, Max (Isaac) 1941- .... **CLC 9, 33**
See also CA 81-84; CANR 19, 54; DLB 130

Appleman, Philip (Dean) 1926- .... **CLC 51**
See also CA 13-16R; CAAS 18; CANR 6, 29, 56

Appleton, Lawrence
See Lovecraft, H(oward) P(hillips)

Apteryx
See Eliot, T(homas) S(tearns)

Apuleius, (Lucius Madaurensis)
125(?)-175(?) .... **CMLC 1**
See also DLB 211

Aquin, Hubert 1929-1977 .... **CLC 15**
See also CA 105; DLB 53

Aquinas, Thomas 1224(?)-1274 ..... **CMLC 33**
See also DLB 115

Aragon, Louis 1897-1982 .. **CLC 3, 22; DAM NOV, POET**
See also CA 69-72; 108; CANR 28, 71; DLB 72; MTCW 1, 2

Arany, Janos 1817-1882 .... **NCLC 34**

Aranyos, Kakay
See Mikszath, Kalman

Arbuthnot, John 1667-1735 .... **LC 1**
See also DLB 101

Archer, Herbert Winslow
See Mencken, H(enry) L(ouis)

Archer, Jeffrey (Howard) 1940- ...... **CLC 28; DAM POP**
See also AAYA 16; BEST 89:3; CA 77-80; CANR 22, 52; DA3; INT CANR-22

Archer, Jules 1915- .... **CLC 12**
See also CA 9-12R; CANR 6, 69; SAAS 5; SATA 4, 85

Archer, Lee
See Ellison, Harlan (Jay)

Arden, John 1930- .... **CLC 6, 13, 15; DAM DRAM**
See also CA 13-16R; CAAS 4; CANR 31, 65, 67; DLB 13; MTCW 1

Arenas, Reinaldo 1943-1990 . **CLC 41; DAM MULT; HLC 1**
See also CA 124; 128; 133; CANR 73; DLB 145; HW 1; MTCW 1

Arendt, Hannah 1906-1975 .... **CLC 66, 98**
See also CA 17-20R; 61-64; CANR 26, 60; MTCW 1, 2

Aretino, Pietro 1492-1556 .... **LC 12**

Arghezi, Tudor 1880-1967 .... **CLC 80**
See also Theodorescu, Ion N.
See also CA 167

Arguedas, Jose Maria 1911-1969 .... **CLC 10, 18; HLCS 1**
See also CA 89-92; CANR 73; DLB 113; HW 1

Argueta, Manlio 1936- .... **CLC 31**
See also CA 131; CANR 73; DLB 145; HW 1

Arias, Ron(ald Francis) 1941-
See also CA 131; CANR 81; DAM MULT; DLB 82; HLC 1; HW 1, 2; MTCW 2

Ariosto, Ludovico 1474-1533 .... **LC 6**

Aristides
See Epstein, Joseph

Aristophanes 450B.C.-385B.C. .... **CMLC 4; DA; DAB; DAC; DAM DRAM, MST; DC 2; WLCS**
See also DA3; DLB 176

Aristotle 384B.C.-322B.C. .... **CMLC 31; DA; DAB; DAC; DAM MST; WLCS**
See also DA3; DLB 176

Arlt, Roberto (Godofredo Christophersen)
1900-1942 .... **TCLC 29; DAM MULT; HLC 1**
See also CA 123; 131; CANR 67; HW 1, 2

Armah, Ayi Kwei 1939- . **CLC 5, 33; BLC 1; DAM MULT, POET**
See also BW 1; CA 61-64; CANR 21, 64; DLB 117; MTCW 1

Armatrading, Joan 1950- .... **CLC 17**
See also CA 114; 186

Arnette, Robert
See Silverberg, Robert

Arnim, Achim von (Ludwig Joachim von Arnim) 1781-1831 ..... **NCLC 5; SSC 29**
See also DLB 90

Arnim, Bettina von 1785-1859 .... **NCLC 38**
See also DLB 90

Arnold, Matthew 1822-1888 ..... **NCLC 6, 29, 89; DA; DAB; DAC; DAM MST, POET; PC 5; WLC**
See also CDBLB 1832-1890; DLB 32, 57

Arnold, Thomas 1795-1842 .... **NCLC 18**
See also DLB 55

Arnow, Harriette (Louisa) Simpson
1908-1986 .... **CLC 2, 7, 18**
See also CA 9-12R; 118; CANR 14; DLB 6; MTCW 1, 2; SATA 42; SATA-Obit 47

Arouet, Francois-Marie
See Voltaire

Arp, Hans
See Arp, Jean

Baker, Nicholson 1957- .... **CLC 61; DAM POP**
See also CA 135; CANR 63; DA3; DLB 227

Baker, Ray Stannard 1870-1946 .... **TCLC 47**
See also CA 118

Baker, Russell (Wayne) 1925- .... **CLC 31**
See also BEST 89:4; CA 57-60; CANR 11, 41, 59; MTCW 1, 2

Bakhtin, M.
See Bakhtin, Mikhail Mikhailovich

Bakhtin, M. M.
See Bakhtin, Mikhail Mikhailovich

Bakhtin, Mikhail
See Bakhtin, Mikhail Mikhailovich

Bakhtin, Mikhail Mikhailovich
1895-1975 .... **CLC 83**
See also CA 128; 113

Bakshi, Ralph 1938(?)- .... **CLC 26**
See also CA 112; 138

Bakunin, Mikhail (Alexandrovich)
1814-1876 .... **NCLC 25, 58**

Baldwin, James (Arthur) 1924-1987 . **CLC 1, 2, 3, 4, 5, 8, 13, 15, 17, 42, 50, 67, 90, 127; BLC 1; DA; DAB; DAC; DAM MST, MULT, NOV, POP; DC 1; SSC 10, 33; WLC**
See also AAYA 4, 34; BW 1; CA 1-4R; 124; CABS 1; CANR 3, 24; CDALB 1941-1968; DA3; DLB 2, 7, 33; DLBY 87; MTCW 1, 2; SATA 9; SATA-Obit 54

Ballard, J(ames) G(raham)
1930-1964 .... **CLC 3, 6, 14, 36; DAM NOV, POP; SSC 1**
See also AAYA 3; CA 5-8R; CANR 15, 39, 65; DA3; DLB 14, 207; MTCW 1, 2; SATA 93

Balmont, Konstantin (Dmitriyevich)
1867-1943 .... **TCLC 11**
See also CA 109; 155

Baltausis, Vincas
See Mikszath, Kalman

Balzac, Honore de 1799-1850 ... **NCLC 5, 35, 53; DA; DAB; DAC; DAM MST, NOV; SSC 5; WLC**
See also DA3; DLB 119

Bambara, Toni Cade 1939-1995 ...... **CLC 19, 88; BLC 1; DA; DAC; DAM MST, MULT; SSC 35; WLCS**
See also AAYA 5; BW 2, 3; CA 29-32R; 150; CANR 24, 49, 81; CDALBS; DA3; DLB 38; MTCW 1, 2; SATA 112

Bamdad, A.
See Shamlu, Ahmad

Banat, D. R.
See Bradbury, Ray (Douglas)

Bancroft, Laura
See Baum, L(yman) Frank

Banim, John 1798-1842 .... **NCLC 13**
See also DLB 116, 158, 159

Banim, Michael 1796-1874 .... **NCLC 13**
See also DLB 158, 159

Banjo, The
See Paterson, A(ndrew) B(arton)

Banks, Iain
See Banks, Iain M(enzies)

Banks, Iain M(enzies) 1954- .... **CLC 34**
See also CA 123; 128; CANR 61; DLB 194; INT 128

Banks, Lynne Reid CLC 23
See also Reid Banks, Lynne
See also AAYA 6

Banks, Russell 1940- .... **CLC 37, 72**
See also CA 65-68; CAAS 15; CANR 19, 52, 73; DLB 130

Banville, John 1945- .... **CLC 46, 118**
See also CA 117; 128; DLB 14; INT 128

Banville, Theodore (Faullain) de
1832-1891 .... **NCLC 9**

Baraka, Amiri 1934- . **CLC 1, 2, 3, 5, 10, 14, 33, 115; BLC 1; DA; DAC; DAM MST, MULT, POET, POP; DC 6; PC 4; WLCS**
See also Jones, LeRoi
See also BW 2, 3; CA 21-24R; CABS 3; CANR 27, 38, 61; CDALB 1941-1968; DA3; DLB 5, 7, 16, 38; DLBD 8; MTCW 1, 2

Barbauld, Anna Laetitia
1743-1825 .... **NCLC 50**
See also DLB 107, 109, 142, 158

Barbellion, W. N. P. TCLC 24
See also Cummings, Bruce F(rederick)

Barbera, Jack (Vincent) 1945- .... **CLC 44**
See also CA 110; CANR 45

Barbey d'Aurevilly, Jules Amedee
1808-1889 .... **NCLC 1; SSC 17**
See also DLB 119

Barbour, John c. 1316-1395 .... **CMLC 33**
See also DLB 146

Barbusse, Henri 1873-1935 .... **TCLC 5**
See also CA 105; 154; DLB 65

Barclay, Bill
See Moorcock, Michael (John)

Barclay, William Ewert
See Moorcock, Michael (John)

Barea, Arturo 1897-1957 .... **TCLC 14**
See also CA 111

Barfoot, Joan 1946- .... **CLC 18**
See also CA 105

Barham, Richard Harris
1788-1845 .... **NCLC 77**
See also DLB 159

Baring, Maurice 1874-1945 .... **TCLC 8**
See also CA 105; 168; DLB 34

Baring-Gould, Sabine 1834-1924 ... **TCLC 88**
See also DLB 156, 190

Barker, Clive 1952- ...... **CLC 52; DAM POP**
See also AAYA 10; BEST 90:3; CA 121; 129; CANR 71; DA3; INT 129; MTCW 1, 2

Barker, George Granville
1913-1991 .... **CLC 8, 48; DAM POET**
See also CA 9-12R; 135; CANR 7, 38; DLB 20; MTCW 1

Barker, Harley Granville
See Granville-Barker, Harley
See also DLB 10

Barker, Howard 1946- .... **CLC 37**
See also CA 102; DLB 13

Barker, Jane 1652-1732 .... **LC 42**

Barker, Pat(ricia) 1943- .... **CLC 32, 94**
See also CA 117; 122; CANR 50; INT 122

Barlach, Ernst (Heinrich)
1870-1938 .... **TCLC 84**
See also CA 178; DLB 56, 118

Barlow, Joel 1754-1812 .... **NCLC 23**
See also DLB 37

Barnard, Mary (Ethel) 1909- .... **CLC 48**
See also CA 21-22; CAP 2

Barnes, Djuna 1892-1982 .... **CLC 3, 4, 8, 11, 29, 127; SSC 3**
See also CA 9-12R; 107; CANR 16, 55; DLB 4, 9, 45; MTCW 1, 2

Barnes, Julian (Patrick) 1946- .... **CLC 42; DAB**
See also CA 102; CANR 19, 54; DLB 194; DLBY 93; MTCW 1

Barnes, Peter 1931- .... **CLC 5, 56**
See also CA 65-68; CAAS 12; CANR 33, 34, 64; DLB 13; MTCW 1

Barnes, William 1801-1886 .... **NCLC 75**
See also DLB 32

Baroja (y Nessi), Pio 1872-1956 ..... **TCLC 8; HLC 1**
See also CA 104

Baron, David
See Pinter, Harold

Baron Corvo
See Rolfe, Frederick (William Serafino Austin Lewis Mary)

Barondess, Sue K(aufman)
1926-1977 .... **CLC 8**
See also Kaufman, Sue
See also CA 1-4R; 69-72; CANR 1

Baron de Teive
See Pessoa, Fernando (Antonio Nogueira)

Baroness Von S.
See Zangwill, Israel

Barres, (Auguste-) Maurice
1862-1923 .... **TCLC 47**
See also CA 164; DLB 123

Barreto, Afonso Henrique de Lima
See Lima Barreto, Afonso Henrique de

Barrett, (Roger) Syd 1946- .... **CLC 35**

Barrett, William (Christopher)
1913-1992 .... **CLC 27**
See also CA 13-16R; 139; CANR 11, 67; INT CANR-11

Barrie, J(ames) M(atthew)
1860-1937 .... **TCLC 2; DAB; DAM DRAM**
See also CA 104; 136; CANR 77; CDBLB 1890-1914; CLR 16; DA3; DLB 10, 141, 156; MAICYA; MTCW 1; SATA 100; YABC 1

Barrington, Michael
See Moorcock, Michael (John)

Barrol, Grady
See Bograd, Larry

Barry, Mike
See Malzberg, Barry N(athaniel)

Barry, Philip 1896-1949 .... **TCLC 11**
See also CA 109; DLB 7, 228

Bart, Andre Schwarz
See Schwarz-Bart, Andre

Barth, John (Simmons) 1930- ... **CLC 1, 2, 3, 5, 7, 9, 10, 14, 27, 51, 89; DAM NOV; SSC 10**
See also AITN 1, 2; CA 1-4R; CABS 1; CANR 5, 23, 49, 64; DLB 2, 227; MTCW 1

Barthelme, Donald 1931-1989 ... **CLC 1, 2, 3, 5, 6, 8, 13, 23, 46, 59, 115; DAM NOV; SSC 2**
See also CA 21-24R; 129; CANR 20, 58; DA3; DLB 2; DLBY 80, 89; MTCW 1, 2; SATA 7; SATA-Obit 62

Barthelme, Frederick 1943- ...... **CLC 36, 117**
See also CA 114; 122; CANR 77; DLBY 85; INT 122

Barthes, Roland (Gerard)
1915-1980 .... **CLC 24, 83**
See also CA 130; 97-100; CANR 66; MTCW 1, 2

Barzun, Jacques (Martin) 1907- ...... **CLC 51**
See also CA 61-64; CANR 22

Bashevis, Isaac
See Singer, Isaac Bashevis

Bashkirtseff, Marie 1859-1884 .... **NCLC 27**

Basho
See Matsuo Basho

Basil of Caesaria c. 330-379 .... **CMLC 35**

Bass, Kingsley B., Jr.
See Bullins, Ed

Bass, Rick 1958- .... **CLC 79**
See also CA 126; CANR 53; DLB 212

Bassani, Giorgio 1916- .... **CLC 9**
See also CA 65-68; CANR 33; DLB 128, 177; MTCW 1

Bastos, Augusto (Antonio) Roa
See Roa Bastos, Augusto (Antonio)

Bataille, Georges 1897-1962 .... **CLC 29**
See also CA 101; 89-92

Borowski, Tadeusz 1922-1951 .... **TCLC 9**
See also CA 106; 154

Borrow, George (Henry)
1803-1881 .... **NCLC 9**
See also DLB 21, 55, 166

Bosch (Gavino), Juan 1909-
See also CA 151; **DAM MST, MULT;** DLB
145; HLCS 1; HW 1, 2

Bosman, Herman Charles
1905-1951 .... **TCLC 49**
See also Malan, Herman
See also CA 160; DLB 225

Bosschere, Jean de 1878(?)-1953 ... **TCLC 19**
See also CA 115; 186

Boswell, James 1740-1795 ...... **LC 4, 50; DA;**
DAB; DAC; DAM MST; WLC
See also CDBLB 1660-1789; DLB 104, 142

Bottoms, David 1949- .... **CLC 53**
See also CA 105; CANR 22; DLB 120;
DLBY 83

Boucicault, Dion 1820-1890 .... **NCLC 41**

Bourget, Paul (Charles Joseph)
1852-1935 .... **TCLC 12**
See also CA 107; DLB 123

Bourjaily, Vance (Nye) 1922- .... **CLC 8, 62**
See also CA 1-4R; CAAS 1; CANR 2, 72;
DLB 2, 143

Bourne, Randolph S(illiman)
1886-1918 .... **TCLC 16**
See also CA 117; 155; DLB 63

Bova, Ben(jamin William) 1932- ...... **CLC 45**
See also AAYA 16; CA 5-8R; CAAS 18;
CANR 11, 56; CLR 3; DLBY 81; INT
CANR-11; MAICYA; MTCW 1; SATA 6,
68

Bowen, Elizabeth (Dorothea Cole)
1899-1973 . **CLC 1, 3, 6, 11, 15, 22, 118;**
DAM NOV; SSC 3, 28
See also CA 17-18; 41-44R; CANR 35;
CAP 2; CDBLB 1945-1960; DA3; DLB
15, 162; MTCW 1, 2

Bowering, George 1935- .... **CLC 15, 47**
See also CA 21-24R; CAAS 16; CANR 10;
DLB 53

Bowering, Marilyn R(uthe) 1949- .... **CLC 32**
See also CA 101; CANR 49

Bowers, Edgar 1924-2000 .... **CLC 9**
See also CA 5-8R; CANR 24; DLB 5

Bowie, David CLC 17
See also Jones, David Robert

Bowles, Jane (Sydney) 1917-1973 ..... **CLC 3,**
68
See also CA 19-20; 41-44R; CAP 2

Bowles, Paul (Frederick) 1910-1999 . **CLC 1,**
2, 19, 53; SSC 3
See also CA 1-4R; 186; CAAS 1; CANR 1,
19, 50, 75; DA3; DLB 5, 6; MTCW 1, 2

Box, Edgar
See Vidal, Gore

Boyd, Nancy
See Millay, Edna St. Vincent

Boyd, William 1952- .... **CLC 28, 53, 70**
See also CA 114; 120; CANR 51, 71

Boyle, Kay 1902-1992 .... **CLC 1, 5, 19, 58,**
121; SSC 5
See also CA 13-16R; 140; CAAS 1; CANR
29, 61; DLB 4, 9, 48, 86; DLBY 93;
MTCW 1, 2

Boyle, Mark
See Kienzle, William X(avier)

Boyle, Patrick 1905-1982 .... **CLC 19**
See also CA 127

Boyle, T. C. 1948-
See Boyle, T(homas) Coraghessan

Boyle, T(homas) Coraghessan
1948- .... **CLC 36, 55, 90; DAM POP;**
SSC 16
See also BEST 90:4; CA 120; CANR 44,
76, 89; DA3; DLBY 86; MTCW 2

Boz
See Dickens, Charles (John Huffam)

Brackenridge, Hugh Henry
1748-1816 .... **NCLC 7**
See also DLB 11, 37

Bradbury, Edward P.
See Moorcock, Michael (John)
See also MTCW 2

Bradbury, Malcolm (Stanley)
1932- .... **CLC 32, 61; DAM NOV**
See also CA 1-4R; CANR 1, 33, 91; DA3;
DLB 14, 207; MTCW 1, 2

Bradbury, Ray (Douglas) 1920- .... **CLC 1, 3,**
10, 15, 42, 98; DA; DAB; DAC; DAM
MST, NOV, POP; SSC 29; WLC
See also AAYA 15; AITN 1, 2; CA 1-4R;
CANR 2, 30, 75; CDALB 1968-1988;
DA3; DLB 2, 8; MTCW 1, 2; SATA 11,
64

Bradford, Gamaliel 1863-1932 .... **TCLC 36**
See also CA 160; DLB 17

Bradley, David (Henry), Jr. 1950- ... **CLC 23,**
118; BLC 1; DAM MULT
See also BW 1, 3; CA 104; CANR 26, 81;
DLB 33

Bradley, John Ed(mund, Jr.) 1958- . **CLC 55**
See also CA 139

Bradley, Marion Zimmer
1930-1999 .... **CLC 30; DAM POP**
See also AAYA 9; CA 57-60; 185; CAAS
10; CANR 7, 31, 51, 75; DA3; DLB 8;
MTCW 1, 2; SATA 90; SATA-Obit 116

Bradstreet, Anne 1612(?)-1672 ...... **LC 4, 30;**
DA; DAC; DAM MST, POET; PC 10
See also CDALB 1640-1865; DA3; DLB
24

Brady, Joan 1939- .... **CLC 86**
See also CA 141

Bragg, Melvyn 1939- .... **CLC 10**
See also BEST 89:3; CA 57-60; CANR 10,
48, 89; DLB 14

Brahe, Tycho 1546-1601 .... **LC 45**

Braine, John (Gerard) 1922-1986 . **CLC 1, 3,**
41
See also CA 1-4R; 120; CANR 1, 33; CD-
BLB 1945-1960; DLB 15; DLBY 86;
MTCW 1

Bramah, Ernest 1868-1942 .... **TCLC 72**
See also CA 156; DLB 70

Brammer, William 1930(?)-1978 ...... **CLC 31**
See also CA 77-80

Brancati, Vitaliano 1907-1954 .... **TCLC 12**
See also CA 109

Brancato, Robin F(idler) 1936- .... **CLC 35**
See also AAYA 9; CA 69-72; CANR 11,
45; CLR 32; JRDA; SAAS 9; SATA 97

Brand, Max
See Faust, Frederick (Schiller)

Brand, Millen 1906-1980 .... **CLC 7**
See also CA 21-24R; 97-100; CANR 72

Branden, Barbara CLC 44
See also CA 148

Brandes, Georg (Morris Cohen)
1842-1927 .... **TCLC 10**
See also CA 105

Brandys, Kazimierz 1916- .... **CLC 62**

Branley, Franklyn M(ansfield)
1915- .... **CLC 21**
See also CA 33-36R; CANR 14, 39; CLR
13; MAICYA; SAAS 16; SATA 4, 68

Brathwaite, Edward (Kamau)
1930- ...... **CLC 11; BLCS; DAM POET**
See also BW 2, 3; CA 25-28R; CANR 11,
26, 47; DLB 125

Brautigan, Richard (Gary)
1935-1984 .... **CLC 1, 3, 5, 9, 12, 34, 42;**
DAM NOV
See also CA 53-56; 113; CANR 34; DA3;
DLB 2, 5, 206; DLBY 80, 84; MTCW 1;
SATA 56

Brave Bird, Mary 1953-
See Crow Dog, Mary (Ellen)
See also NNAL

Braverman, Kate 1950- .... **CLC 67**
See also CA 89-92

Brecht, (Eugen) Bertolt (Friedrich)
1898-1956 .... **TCLC 1, 6, 13, 35; DA;**
DAB; DAC; DAM DRAM, MST; DC
3; WLC
See also CA 104; 133; CANR 62; DA3;
DLB 56, 124; MTCW 1, 2

Brecht, Eugen Berthold Friedrich
See Brecht, (Eugen) Bertolt (Friedrich)

Bremer, Fredrika 1801-1865 .... **NCLC 11**

Brennan, Christopher John
1870-1932 .... **TCLC 17**
See also CA 117

Brennan, Maeve 1917-1993 .... **CLC 5**
See also CA 81-84; CANR 72

Brent, Linda
See Jacobs, Harriet A(nn)

Brentano, Clemens (Maria)
1778-1842 .... **NCLC 1**
See also DLB 90

Brent of Bin Bin
See Franklin, (Stella Maria Sarah) Miles
(Lampe)

Brenton, Howard 1942- .... **CLC 31**
See also CA 69-72; CANR 33, 67; DLB 13;
MTCW 1

Breslin, James 1930-
See Breslin, Jimmy
See also CA 73-76; CANR 31, 75; **DAM**
NOV; MTCW 1, 2

Breslin, Jimmy CLC 4, 43
See also Breslin, James
See also AITN 1; DLB 185; MTCW 2

Bresson, Robert 1901- .... **CLC 16**
See also CA 110; CANR 49

Breton, Andre 1896-1966 .. **CLC 2, 9, 15, 54;**
PC 15
See also CA 19-20; 25-28R; CANR 40, 60;
CAP 2; DLB 65; MTCW 1, 2

Breytenbach, Breyten 1939(?)- .. **CLC 23, 37,**
126; DAM POET
See also CA 113; 129; CANR 61; DLB 225

Bridgers, Sue Ellen 1942- .... **CLC 26**
See also AAYA 8; CA 65-68; CANR 11,
36; CLR 18; DLB 52; JRDA; MAICYA;
SAAS 1; SATA 22, 90; SATA-Essay 109

Bridges, Robert (Seymour)
1844-1930 ... **TCLC 1; DAM POET; PC**
28
See also CA 104; 152; CDBLB 1890-1914;
DLB 19, 98

Bridie, James TCLC 3
See also Mavor, Osborne Henry
See also DLB 10

Brin, David 1950- .... **CLC 34**
See also AAYA 21; CA 102; CANR 24, 70;
INT CANR-24; SATA 65

Brink, Andre (Philippus) 1935- . **CLC 18, 36,**
106
See also CA 104; CANR 39, 62; DLB 225;
INT 103; MTCW 1, 2

Brinsmead, H(esba) F(ay) 1922- ...... **CLC 21**
See also CA 21-24R; CANR 10; CLR 47;
MAICYA; SAAS 5; SATA 18, 78

Brittain, Vera (Mary) 1893(?)-1970 . **CLC 23**
See also CA 13-16; 25-28R; CANR 58;
CAP 1; DLB 191; MTCW 1, 2

Broch, Hermann 1886-1951 .... **TCLC 20**
See also CA 117; DLB 85, 124

Buero Vallejo, Antonio 1916-2000 ... **CLC 15, 46**
    See also CA 106; CANR 24, 49, 75; HW 1; MTCW 1, 2
Bufalino, Gesualdo 1920(?)- .... **CLC 74**
    See also DLB 196
Bugayev, Boris Nikolayevich
    1880-1934 .... **TCLC 7; PC 11**
    See also Bely, Andrey
    See also CA 104; 165; MTCW 1
Bukowski, Charles 1920-1994 ... **CLC 2, 5, 9, 41, 82, 108; DAM NOV, POET; PC 18**
    See also CA 17-20R; 144; CANR 40, 62; DA3; DLB 5, 130, 169; MTCW 1, 2
Bulgakov, Mikhail (Afanas'evich)
    1891-1940 . **TCLC 2, 16; DAM DRAM, NOV; SSC 18**
    See also CA 105; 152
Bulgya, Alexander Alexandrovich
    1901-1956 .... **TCLC 53**
    See also Fadeyev, Alexander
    See also CA 117; 181
Bullins, Ed 1935- .... **CLC 1, 5, 7; BLC 1; DAM DRAM, MULT; DC 6**
    See also BW 2, 3; CA 49-52; CAAS 16; CANR 24, 46, 73; DLB 7, 38; MTCW 1, 2
Bulwer-Lytton, Edward (George Earle Lytton) 1803-1873 .... **NCLC 1, 45**
    See also DLB 21
Bunin, Ivan Alexeyevich
    1870-1953 .... **TCLC 6; SSC 5**
    See also CA 104
Bunting, Basil 1900-1985 ..... **CLC 10, 39, 47; DAM POET**
    See also CA 53-56; 115; CANR 7; DLB 20
Bunuel, Luis 1900-1983 .. **CLC 16, 80; DAM MULT; HLC 1**
    See also CA 101; 110; CANR 32, 77; HW 1
Bunyan, John 1628-1688 ... **LC 4; DA; DAB; DAC; DAM MST; WLC**
    See also CDBLB 1660-1789; DLB 39
Burckhardt, Jacob (Christoph)
    1818-1897 .... **NCLC 49**
Burford, Eleanor
    See Hibbert, Eleanor Alice Burford
Burgess, Anthony -1993 .... **CLC 1, 2, 4, 5, 8, 10, 13, 15, 22, 40, 62, 81, 94; DAB**
    See also Wilson, John (Anthony) Burgess
    See also AAYA 25; AITN 1; CDBLB 1960 to Present; DLB 14, 194; DLBY 98; MTCW 1
Burke, Edmund 1729(?)-1797 .... **LC 7, 36; DA; DAB; DAC; DAM MST; WLC**
    See also DA3; DLB 104
Burke, Kenneth (Duva) 1897-1993 ... **CLC 2, 24**
    See also CA 5-8R; 143; CANR 39, 74; DLB 45, 63; MTCW 1, 2
Burke, Leda
    See Garnett, David
Burke, Ralph
    See Silverberg, Robert
Burke, Thomas 1886-1945 .... **TCLC 63**
    See also CA 113; 155; DLB 197
Burney, Fanny 1752-1840 .... **NCLC 12, 54**
    See also DLB 39
Burns, Robert 1759-1796 . **LC 3, 29, 40; DA; DAB; DAC; DAM MST, POET; PC 6; WLC**
    See also CDBLB 1789-1832; DA3; DLB 109
Burns, Tex
    See L'Amour, Louis (Dearborn)
Burnshaw, Stanley 1906- .... **CLC 3, 13, 44**
    See also CA 9-12R; DLB 48; DLBY 97
Burr, Anne 1937- .... **CLC 6**
    See also CA 25-28R

Burroughs, Edgar Rice 1875-1950 . **TCLC 2, 32; DAM NOV**
    See also AAYA 11; CA 104; 132; DA3; DLB 8; MTCW 1, 2; SATA 41
Burroughs, William S(eward)
    1914-1997 .. **CLC 1, 2, 5, 15, 22, 42, 75, 109; DA; DAB; DAC; DAM MST, NOV, POP; WLC**
    See also AITN 2; CA 9-12R; 160; CANR 20, 52; DA3; DLB 2, 8, 16, 152; DLBY 81, 97; MTCW 1, 2
Burton, SirRichard F(rancis)
    1821-1890 .... **NCLC 42**
    See also DLB 55, 166, 184
Busch, Frederick 1941- .... **CLC 7, 10, 18, 47**
    See also CA 33-36R; CAAS 1; CANR 45, 73, 92; DLB 6
Bush, Ronald 1946- .... **CLC 34**
    See also CA 136
Bustos, F(rancisco)
    See Borges, Jorge Luis
Bustos Domecq, H(onorio)
    See Bioy Casares, Adolfo; Borges, Jorge Luis
Butler, Octavia E(stelle) 1947- .... **CLC 38, 121; BLCS; DAM MULT, POP**
    See also AAYA 18; BW 2, 3; CA 73-76; CANR 12, 24, 38, 73; CLR 65; DA3; DLB 33; MTCW 1, 2; SATA 84
Butler, Robert Olen (Jr.) 1945- .... **CLC 81; DAM POP**
    See also CA 112; CANR 66; DLB 173; INT 112; MTCW 1
Butler, Samuel 1612-1680 .... **LC 16, 43**
    See also DLB 101, 126
Butler, Samuel 1835-1902 . **TCLC 1, 33; DA; DAB; DAC; DAM MST, NOV; WLC**
    See also CA 143; CDBLB 1890-1914; DA3; DLB 18, 57, 174
Butler, Walter C.
    See Faust, Frederick (Schiller)
Butor, Michel (Marie Francois)
    1926- .... **CLC 1, 3, 8, 11, 15**
    See also CA 9-12R; CANR 33, 66; DLB 83; MTCW 1, 2
Butts, Mary 1892(?)-1937 .... **TCLC 77**
    See also CA 148
Buzo, Alexander (John) 1944- .... **CLC 61**
    See also CA 97-100; CANR 17, 39, 69
Buzzati, Dino 1906-1972 .... **CLC 36**
    See also CA 160; 33-36R; DLB 177
Byars, Betsy (Cromer) 1928- .... **CLC 35**
    See also AAYA 19; CA 33-36R, 183; CAAE 183; CANR 18, 36, 57; CLR 1, 16; DLB 52; INT CANR-18; JRDA; MAICYA; MTCW 1; SAAS 1; SATA 4, 46, 80; SATA-Essay 108
Byatt, A(ntonia) S(usan Drabble)
    1936- ..... **CLC 19, 65; DAM NOV, POP**
    See also CA 13-16R; CANR 13, 33, 50, 75; DA3; DLB 14, 194; MTCW 1, 2
Byrne, David 1952- .... **CLC 26**
    See also CA 127
Byrne, John Keyes 1926-
    See Leonard, Hugh
    See also CA 102; CANR 78; INT 102
Byron, George Gordon (Noel)
    1788-1824 .... **NCLC 2, 12; DA; DAB; DAC; DAM MST, POET; PC 16; WLC**
    See also CDBLB 1789-1832; DA3; DLB 96, 110
Byron, Robert 1905-1941 .... **TCLC 67**
    See also CA 160; DLB 195
C. 3. 3.
    See Wilde, Oscar (Fingal O'Flahertie Wills)
Caballero, Fernan 1796-1877 .... **NCLC 10**
Cabell, Branch
    See Cabell, James Branch

Cabell, James Branch 1879-1958 .... **TCLC 6**
    See also CA 105; 152; DLB 9, 78; MTCW 1
Cable, George Washington
    1844-1925 .... **TCLC 4; SSC 4**
    See also CA 104; 155; DLB 12, 74; DLBD 13
Cabral de Melo Neto, Joao 1920- ... **CLC 76; DAM MULT**
    See also CA 151
Cabrera Infante, G(uillermo) 1929- . **CLC 5, 25, 45, 120; DAM MULT; HLC 1; SSC 39**
    See also CA 85-88; CANR 29, 65; DA3; DLB 113; HW 1, 2; MTCW 1, 2
Cade, Toni
    See Bambara, Toni Cade
Cadmus and Harmonia
    See Buchan, John
Caedmon fl. 658-680 .... **CMLC 7**
    See also DLB 146
Caeiro, Alberto
    See Pessoa, Fernando (Antonio Nogueira)
Cage, John (Milton, Jr.) 1912-1992 . **CLC 41**
    See also CA 13-16R; 169; CANR 9, 78; DLB 193; INT CANR-9
Cahan, Abraham 1860-1951 .... **TCLC 71**
    See also CA 108; 154; DLB 9, 25, 28
Cain, G.
    See Cabrera Infante, G(uillermo)
Cain, Guillermo
    See Cabrera Infante, G(uillermo)
Cain, James M(allahan) 1892-1977 .. **CLC 3, 11, 28**
    See also AITN 1; CA 17-20R; 73-76; CANR 8, 34, 61; DLB 226; MTCW 1
Caine, Hall 1853-1931 .... **TCLC 97**
Caine, Mark
    See Raphael, Frederic (Michael)
Calasso, Roberto 1941- .... **CLC 81**
    See also CA 143; CANR 89
Calderon de la Barca, Pedro
    1600-1681 .... **LC 23; DC 3; HLCS 1**
Caldwell, Erskine (Preston)
    1903-1987 .. **CLC 1, 8, 14, 50, 60; DAM NOV; SSC 19**
    See also AITN 1; CA 1-4R; 121; CAAS 1; CANR 2, 33; DA3; DLB 9, 86; MTCW 1, 2
Caldwell, (Janet Miriam) Taylor (Holland)
    1900-1985 .. **CLC 2, 28, 39; DAM NOV, POP**
    See also CA 5-8R; 116; CANR 5; DA3; DLBD 17
Calhoun, John Caldwell
    1782-1850 .... **NCLC 15**
    See also DLB 3
Calisher, Hortense 1911- ..... **CLC 2, 4, 8, 38, 134; DAM NOV; SSC 15**
    See also CA 1-4R; CANR 1, 22, 67; DA3; DLB 2; INT CANR-22; MTCW 1, 2
Callaghan, Morley Edward
    1903-1990 ...... **CLC 3, 14, 41, 65; DAC; DAM MST**
    See also CA 9-12R; 132; CANR 33, 73; DLB 68; MTCW 1, 2
Callimachus c. 305B.C.-c. 240B.C. .... **CMLC 18**
    See also DLB 176
Calvin, John 1509-1564 .... **LC 37**
Calvino, Italo 1923-1985 .... **CLC 5, 8, 11, 22, 33, 39, 73; DAM NOV; SSC 3**
    See also CA 85-88; 116; CANR 23, 61; DLB 196; MTCW 1, 2
Cameron, Carey 1952- .... **CLC 59**
    See also CA 135
Cameron, Peter 1959- .... **CLC 44**
    See also CA 125; CANR 50

Castro, Guillen de 1569-1631 .... **LC 19**

Castro, Rosalia de 1837-1885 ... **NCLC 3, 78; DAM MULT**

Cather, Willa -1947
See Cather, Willa Sibert

Cather, Willa Sibert 1873-1947 ...... **TCLC 1, 11, 31, 99; DA; DAB; DAC; DAM MST, NOV; SSC 2; WLC**
See also Cather, Willa
See also AAYA 24; CA 104; 128; CDALB 1865-1917; DA3; DLB 9, 54, 78; DLBD 1; MTCW 1, 2; SATA 30

Catherine, Saint 1347-1380 .... **CMLC 27**

Cato, Marcus Porcius 234B.C.-149B.C. .... **CMLC 21**
See also DLB 211

Catton, (Charles) Bruce 1899-1978 . **CLC 35**
See also AITN 1; CA 5-8R; 81-84; CANR 7, 74; DLB 17; SATA 2; SATA-Obit 24

Catullus c. 84B.C.-c. 54B.C. .... **CMLC 18**
See also DLB 211

Cauldwell, Frank
See King, Francis (Henry)

Caunitz, William J. 1933-1996 .... **CLC 34**
See also BEST 89:3; CA 125; 130; 152; CANR 73; INT 130

Causley, Charles (Stanley) 1917- .... **CLC 7**
See also CA 9-12R; CANR 5, 35; CLR 30; DLB 27; MTCW 1; SATA 3, 66

Caute, (John) David 1936- .... **CLC 29; DAM NOV**
See also CA 1-4R; CAAS 4; CANR 1, 33, 64; DLB 14

Cavafy, C(onstantine) P(eter) 1863-1933 ...... **TCLC 2, 7; DAM POET**
See also Kavafis, Konstantinos Petrou
See also CA 148; DA3; MTCW 1

Cavallo, Evelyn
See Spark, Muriel (Sarah)

Cavanna, Betty **CLC 12**
See also Harrison, Elizabeth Cavanna
See also JRDA; MAICYA; SAAS 4; SATA 1, 30

Cavendish, Margaret Lucas 1623-1673 .... **LC 30**
See also DLB 131

Caxton, William 1421(?)-1491(?) .... **LC 17**
See also DLB 170

Cayer, D. M.
See Duffy, Maureen

Cayrol, Jean 1911- .... **CLC 11**
See also CA 89-92; DLB 83

Cela, Camilo Jose 1916- .... **CLC 4, 13, 59, 122; DAM MULT; HLC 1**
See also BEST 90:2; CA 21-24R; CAAS 10; CANR 21, 32, 76; DLBY 89; HW 1; MTCW 1, 2

Celan, Paul **CLC 10, 19, 53, 82; PC 10**
See also Antschel, Paul
See also DLB 69

Celine, Louis-Ferdinand **CLC 1, 3, 4, 7, 9, 15, 47, 124**
See also Destouches, Louis-Ferdinand
See also DLB 72

Cellini, Benvenuto 1500-1571 .... **LC 7**

Cendrars, Blaise 1887-1961 ...... **CLC 18, 106**
See also Sauser-Hall, Frederic

Cernuda (y Bidon), Luis 1902-1963 .... **CLC 54; DAM POET**
See also CA 131; 89-92; DLB 134; HW 1

Cervantes, Lorna Dee 1954-
See also CA 131; CANR 80; DLB 82; HLCS 1; HW 1

Cervantes (Saavedra), Miguel de 1547-1616 .. **LC 6, 23; DA; DAB; DAC; DAM MST, NOV; SSC 12; WLC**

Cesaire, Aime (Fernand) 1913- . **CLC 19, 32, 112; BLC 1; DAM MULT, POET; PC 25**
See also BW 2, 3; CA 65-68; CANR 24, 43, 81; DA3; MTCW 1, 2

Chabon, Michael 1963- .... **CLC 55**
See also CA 139; CANR 57

Chabrol, Claude 1930- .... **CLC 16**
See also CA 110

Challans, Mary 1905-1983
See Renault, Mary
See also CA 81-84; 111; CANR 74; DA3; MTCW 2; SATA 23; SATA-Obit 36

Challis, George
See Faust, Frederick (Schiller)

Chambers, Aidan 1934- .... **CLC 35**
See also AAYA 27; CA 25-28R; CANR 12, 31, 58; JRDA; MAICYA; SAAS 12; SATA 1, 69, 108

Chambers, James 1948-
See Cliff, Jimmy
See also CA 124

Chambers, Jessie
See Lawrence, D(avid) H(erbert Richards)

Chambers, Robert W(illiam) 1865-1933 .... **TCLC 41**
See also CA 165; DLB 202; SATA 107

Chamisso, Adelbert von 1781-1838 .... **NCLC 82**
See also DLB 90

Chandler, Raymond (Thornton) 1888-1959 .... **TCLC 1, 7; SSC 23**
See also AAYA 25; CA 104; 129; CANR 60; CDALB 1929-1941; DA3; DLB 226; DLBD 6; MTCW 1, 2

Chang, Eileen 1920-1995 .... **SSC 28**
See also CA 166

Chang, Jung 1952- .... **CLC 71**
See also CA 142

Chang Ai-Ling
See Chang, Eileen

Channing, William Ellery 1780-1842 .... **NCLC 17**
See also DLB 1, 59

Chao, Patricia 1955- .... **CLC 119**
See also CA 163

Chaplin, Charles Spencer 1889-1977 .... **CLC 16**
See also Chaplin, Charlie
See also CA 81-84; 73-76

Chaplin, Charlie
See Chaplin, Charles Spencer
See also DLB 44

Chapman, George 1559(?)-1634 .... **LC 22; DAM DRAM**
See also DLB 62, 121

Chapman, Graham 1941-1989 .... **CLC 21**
See also Monty Python
See also CA 116; 129; CANR 35

Chapman, John Jay 1862-1933 .... **TCLC 7**
See also CA 104

Chapman, Lee
See Bradley, Marion Zimmer

Chapman, Walker
See Silverberg, Robert

Chappell, Fred (Davis) 1936- ..... **CLC 40, 78**
See also CA 5-8R; CAAS 4; CANR 8, 33, 67; DLB 6, 105

Char, Rene(-Emile) 1907-1988 .... **CLC 9, 11, 14, 55; DAM POET**
See also CA 13-16R; 124; CANR 32; MTCW 1, 2

Charby, Jay
See Ellison, Harlan (Jay)

Chardin, Pierre Teilhard de
See Teilhard de Chardin, (Marie Joseph) Pierre

Charlemagne 742-814 .... **CMLC 37**

Charles I 1600-1649 .... **LC 13**

Charriere, Isabelle de 1740-1805 .. **NCLC 66**

Charyn, Jerome 1937- .... **CLC 5, 8, 18**
See also CA 5-8R; CAAS 1; CANR 7, 61; DLBY 83; MTCW 1

Chase, Mary (Coyle) 1907-1981 .... **DC 1**
See also CA 77-80; 105; DLB 228; SATA 17; SATA-Obit 29

Chase, Mary Ellen 1887-1973 .... **CLC 2**
See also CA 13-16; 41-44R; CAP 1; SATA 10

Chase, Nicholas
See Hyde, Anthony

Chateaubriand, Francois Rene de 1768-1848 .... **NCLC 3**
See also DLB 119

Chatterje, Sarat Chandra 1876-1936(?)
See Chatterji, Saratchandra
See also CA 109

Chatterji, Bankim Chandra 1838-1894 .... **NCLC 19**

Chatterji, Saratchandra -1938 .... **TCLC 13**
See also Chatterje, Sarat Chandra
See also CA 186

Chatterton, Thomas 1752-1770 ..... **LC 3, 54; DAM POET**
See also DLB 109

Chatwin, (Charles) Bruce 1940-1989 . **CLC 28, 57, 59; DAM POP**
See also AAYA 4; BEST 90:1; CA 85-88; 127; DLB 194, 204

Chaucer, Daniel -1939
See Ford, Ford Madox

Chaucer, Geoffrey 1340(?)-1400 .. **LC 17, 56; DA; DAB; DAC; DAM MST, POET; PC 19; WLCS**
See also CDBLB Before 1660; DA3; DLB 146

Chavez, Denise (Elia) 1948-
See also CA 131; CANR 56, 81; DAM MULT; DLB 122; HLC 1; HW 1, 2; MTCW 2

Chaviaras, Strates 1935-
See Haviaras, Stratis
See also CA 105

Chayefsky, Paddy **CLC 23**
See also Chayefsky, Sidney
See also DLB 7, 44; DLBY 81

Chayefsky, Sidney 1923-1981
See Chayefsky, Paddy
See also CA 9-12R; 104; CANR 18; DAM DRAM

Chedid, Andree 1920- .... **CLC 47**
See also CA 145

Cheever, John 1912-1982 ..... **CLC 3, 7, 8, 11, 15, 25, 64; DA; DAB; DAC; DAM MST, NOV, POP; SSC 1, 38; WLC**
See also CA 5-8R; 106; CABS 1; CANR 5, 27, 76; CDALB 1941-1968; DA3; DLB 2, 102, 227; DLBY 80, 82; INT CANR-5; MTCW 1, 2

Cheever, Susan 1943- .... **CLC 18, 48**
See also CA 103; CANR 27, 51, 92; DLBY 82; INT CANR-27

Chekhonte, Antosha
See Chekhov, Anton (Pavlovich)

Chekhov, Anton (Pavlovich) 1860-1904 .... **TCLC 3, 10, 31, 55, 96; DA; DAB; DAC; DAM DRAM, MST; DC 9; SSC 2, 28, 41; WLC**
See also CA 104; 124; DA3; SATA 90

Chernyshevsky, Nikolay Gavrilovich
1828-1889 .... NCLC 1

Cherry, Carolyn Janice 1942-
See Cherryh, C. J.
See also CA 65-68; CANR 10

Cherryh, C. J. CLC 35
See also Cherry, Carolyn Janice
See also AAYA 24; DLBY 80; SATA 93

Chesnutt, Charles W(addell)
1858-1932 .. TCLC 5, 39; BLC 1; DAM
MULT; SSC 7
See also BW 1, 3; CA 106; 125; CANR 76;
DLB 12, 50, 78; MTCW 1, 2

Chester, Alfred 1929(?)-1971 .... CLC 49
See also CA 33-36R; DLB 130

Chesterton, G(ilbert) K(eith)
1874-1936 . TCLC 1, 6, 64; DAM NOV,
POET; PC 28; SSC 1
See also CA 104; 132; CANR 73; CDBLB
1914-1945; DLB 10, 19, 34, 70, 98, 149,
178; MTCW 1, 2; SATA 27

Chiang, Pin-chin 1904-1986
See Ding Ling
See also CA 118

Ch'ien Chung-shu 1910- .... CLC 22
See also CA 130; CANR 73; MTCW 1, 2

Child, L. Maria
See Child, Lydia Maria

Child, Lydia Maria 1802-1880 .. NCLC 6, 73
See also DLB 1, 74; SATA 67

Child, Mrs.
See Child, Lydia Maria

Child, Philip 1898-1978 .... CLC 19, 68
See also CA 13-14; CAP 1; SATA 47

Childers, (Robert) Erskine
1870-1922 .... TCLC 65
See also CA 113; 153; DLB 70

Childress, Alice 1920-1994 .. CLC 12, 15, 86,
96; BLC 1; DAM DRAM, MULT,
NOV; DC 4
See also AAYA 8; BW 2, 3; CA 45-48; 146;
CANR 3, 27, 50, 74; CLR 14; DA3; DLB
7, 38; JRDA; MAICYA; MTCW 1, 2;
SATA 7, 48, 81

Chin, Frank (Chew, Jr.) 1940- ...... CLC 135;
DAM MULT; DC 7
See also CA 33-36R; CANR 71; DLB 206

Chislett, (Margaret) Anne 1943- ...... CLC 34
See also CA 151

Chitty, Thomas Willes 1926- .... CLC 11
See Hinde, Thomas
See also CA 5-8R

Chivers, Thomas Holley
1809-1858 .... NCLC 49
See also DLB 3

Choi, Susan CLC 119

Chomette, Rene Lucien 1898-1981
See Clair, Rene
See also CA 103

Chomsky, (Avram) Noam 1928- ..... CLC 132
See also CA 17-20R; CANR 28, 62; DA3;
MTCW 1, 2

Chopin, Kate TCLC 5, 14; DA; DAB; SSC
8; WLCS
See also Chopin, Katherine
See also AAYA 33; CDALB 1865-1917;
DLB 12, 78

Chopin, Katherine 1851-1904
See Chopin, Kate
See also CA 104; 122; DAC; DAM MST,
NOV; DA3

Chretien de Troyes c. 12th cent. - . CMLC 10
See also DLB 208

Christie
See Ichikawa, Kon

Christie, Agatha (Mary Clarissa)
1890-1976 .... CLC 1, 6, 8, 12, 39, 48,
110; DAB; DAC; DAM NOV
See also AAYA 9; AITN 1, 2; CA 17-20R;
61-64; CANR 10, 37; CDBLB 1914-1945;
DA3; DLB 13, 77; MTCW 1, 2; SATA 36

Christie, (Ann) Philippa
See Pearce, Philippa
See also CA 5-8R; CANR 4

Christine de Pizan 1365(?)-1431(?) .... LC 9
See also DLB 208

Chubb, Elmer
See Masters, Edgar Lee

Chulkov, Mikhail Dmitrievich
1743-1792 .... LC 2
See also DLB 150

Churchill, Caryl 1938- .... CLC 31, 55; DC 5
See also CA 102; CANR 22, 46; DLB 13;
MTCW 1

Churchill, Charles 1731-1764 .... LC 3
See also DLB 109

Chute, Carolyn 1947- .... CLC 39
See also CA 123

Ciardi, John (Anthony) 1916-1986 . CLC 10,
40, 44, 129; DAM POET
See also CA 5-8R; 118; CAAS 2; CANR 5,
33; CLR 19; DLB 5; DLBY 86; INT
CANR-5; MAICYA; MTCW 1, 2; SAAS
26; SATA 1, 65; SATA-Obit 46

Cicero, Marcus Tullius
106B.C.-43B.C. .... CMLC 3
See also DLB 211

Cimino, Michael 1943- .... CLC 16
See also CA 105

Cioran, E(mil) M. 1911-1995 .... CLC 64
See also CA 25-28R; 149; CANR 91; DLB
220

Cisneros, Sandra 1954- . CLC 69, 118; DAM
MULT; HLC 1; SSC 32
See also AAYA 9; CA 131; CANR 64; DA3;
DLB 122, 152; HW 1, 2; MTCW 2

Cixous, Helene 1937- .... CLC 92
See also CA 126; CANR 55; DLB 83;
MTCW 1, 2

Clair, Rene CLC 20
See also Chomette, Rene Lucien

Clampitt, Amy 1920-1994 .... CLC 32; PC 19
See also CA 110; 146; CANR 29, 79; DLB
105

Clancy, Thomas L., Jr. 1947-
See Clancy, Tom
See also CA 125; 131; CANR 62; DA3;
DLB 227; INT 131; MTCW 1, 2

Clancy, Tom CLC 45, 112; DAM NOV, POP
See also Clancy, Thomas L., Jr.
See also AAYA 9; BEST 89:1, 90:1; MTCW
2

Clare, John 1793-1864 ... NCLC 9, 86; DAB;
DAM POET; PC 23
See also DLB 55, 96

Clarin
See Alas (y Urena), Leopoldo (Enrique
Garcia)

Clark, Al C.
See Goines, Donald

Clark, (Robert) Brian 1932- .... CLC 29
See also CA 41-44R; CANR 67

Clark, Curt
See Westlake, Donald E(dwin)

Clark, Eleanor 1913-1996 .... CLC 5, 19
See also CA 9-12R; 151; CANR 41; DLB 6

Clark, J. P.
See Clark Bekedermo, J(ohnson) P(epper)
See also DLB 117

Clark, John Pepper
See Clark Bekedermo, J(ohnson) P(epper)

Clark, M. R.
See Clark, Mavis Thorpe

Clark, Mavis Thorpe 1909- .... CLC 12
See also CA 57-60; CANR 8, 37; CLR 30;
MAICYA; SAAS 5; SATA 8, 74

Clark, Walter Van Tilburg
1909-1971 .... CLC 28
See also CA 9-12R; 33-36R; CANR 63;
DLB 9, 206; SATA 8

Clark Bekedermo, J(ohnson) P(epper)
1935- .. CLC 38; BLC 1; DAM DRAM,
MULT; DC 5
See also Clark, J. P.; Clark, John Pepper
See also BW 1; CA 65-68; CANR 16, 72;
MTCW 1

Clarke, Arthur C(harles) 1917- .... CLC 1, 4,
13, 18, 35; DAM POP; SSC 3
See also AAYA 4, 33; CA 1-4R; CANR 2,
28, 55, 74; DA3; JRDA; MAICYA;
MTCW 1, 2; SATA 13, 70, 115

Clarke, Austin 1896-1974 ... CLC 6, 9; DAM
POET
See also CA 29-32; 49-52; CAP 2; DLB 10,
20

Clarke, Austin C(hesterfield) 1934- .. CLC 8,
53; BLC 1; DAC; DAM MULT
See also BW 1; CA 25-28R; CAAS 16;
CANR 14, 32, 68; DLB 53, 125

Clarke, Gillian 1937- .... CLC 61
See also CA 106; DLB 40

Clarke, Marcus (Andrew Hislop)
1846-1881 .... NCLC 19

Clarke, Shirley 1925- .... CLC 16

Clash, The
See Headon, (Nicky) Topper; Jones, Mick;
Simonon, Paul; Strummer, Joe

Claudel, Paul (Louis Charles Marie)
1868-1955 .... TCLC 2, 10
See also CA 104; 165; DLB 192

Claudius, Matthias 1740-1815 .... NCLC 75
See also DLB 97

Clavell, James (duMaresq)
1925-1994 .. CLC 6, 25, 87; DAM NOV,
POP
See also CA 25-28R; 146; CANR 26, 48;
DA3; MTCW 1, 2

Cleaver, (Leroy) Eldridge
1935-1998 . CLC 30, 119; BLC 1; DAM
MULT
See also BW 1, 3; CA 21-24R; 167; CANR
16, 75; DA3; MTCW 2

Cleese, John (Marwood) 1939- .... CLC 21
See also Monty Python
See also CA 112; 116; CANR 35; MTCW 1

Cleishbotham, Jebediah
See Scott, Walter

Cleland, John 1710-1789 .... LC 2, 48
See also DLB 39

Clemens, Samuel Langhorne 1835-1910
See Twain, Mark
See also CA 104; 135; CDALB 1865-1917;
DA; DAB; DAC; DAM MST, NOV; DA3;
DLB 11, 12, 23, 64, 74, 186, 189; JRDA;
MAICYA; SATA 100; YABC 2

Clement of Alexandria
150(?)-215(?) .... CMLC 41

Cleophil
See Congreve, William

Clerihew, E.
See Bentley, E(dmund) C(lerihew)

Clerk, N. W.
See Lewis, C(live) S(taples)

Cliff, Jimmy CLC 21
See also Chambers, James

Cliff, Michelle 1946- .... CLC 120; BLCS
See also BW 2; CA 116; CANR 39, 72;
DLB 157

Clifton, (Thelma) Lucille 1936- .... **CLC 19, 66; BLC 1; DAM MULT, POET; PC 17**
See also BW 2, 3; CA 49-52; CANR 2, 24, 42, 76; CLR 5; DA3; DLB 5, 41; MAI-CYA; MTCW 1, 2; SATA 20, 69

Clinton, Dirk
See Silverberg, Robert

Clough, Arthur Hugh 1819-1861 ... **NCLC 27**
See also DLB 32

Clutha, Janet Paterson Frame 1924-
See Frame, Janet
See also CA 1-4R; CANR 2, 36, 76; MTCW 1, 2

Clyne, Terence
See Blatty, William Peter

Cobalt, Martin
See Mayne, William (James Carter)

Cobb, Irvin S(hrewsbury)
1876-1944 .... **TCLC 77**
See also CA 175; DLB 11, 25, 86

Cobbett, William 1763-1835 .... **NCLC 49**
See also DLB 43, 107, 158

Coburn, D(onald) L(ee) 1938- .... **CLC 10**
See also CA 89-92

Cocteau, Jean (Maurice Eugene Clement)
1889-1963 .... **CLC 1, 8, 15, 16, 43; DA; DAB; DAC; DAM DRAM, MST, NOV; WLC**
See also CA 25-28; CANR 40; CAP 2; DA3; DLB 65; MTCW 1, 2

Codrescu, Andrei 1946- .... **CLC 46, 121; DAM POET**
See also CA 33-36R; CAAS 19; CANR 13, 34, 53, 76; DA3; MTCW 2

Coe, Max
See Bourne, Randolph S(illiman)

Coe, Tucker
See Westlake, Donald E(dwin)

Coen, Ethan 1958- .... **CLC 108**
See also CA 126; CANR 85

Coen, Joel 1955- .... **CLC 108**
See also CA 126

The Coen Brothers
See Coen, Ethan; Coen, Joel

Coetzee, J(ohn) M(ichael) 1940- ...... **CLC 23, 33, 66, 117; DAM NOV**
See also CA 77-80; CANR 41, 54, 74; DA3; DLB 225; MTCW 1, 2

Coffey, Brian
See Koontz, Dean R(ay)

Coffin, Robert P(eter) Tristram
1892-1955 .... **TCLC 95**
See also CA 123; 169; DLB 45

Cohan, George M(ichael)
1878-1942 .... **TCLC 60**
See also CA 157

Cohen, Arthur A(llen) 1928-1986 ...... **CLC 7, 31**
See also CA 1-4R; 120; CANR 1, 17, 42; DLB 28

Cohen, Leonard (Norman) 1934- ...... **CLC 3, 38; DAC; DAM MST**
See also CA 21-24R; CANR 14, 69; DLB 53; MTCW 1

Cohen, Matt 1942-1999 .... **CLC 19; DAC**
See also CA 61-64; CAAS 18; CANR 40; DLB 53

Cohen-Solal, Annie 19(?)- .... **CLC 50**

Colegate, Isabel 1931- .... **CLC 36**
See also CA 17-20R; CANR 8, 22, 74; DLB 14; INT CANR-22; MTCW 1

Coleman, Emmett
See Reed, Ishmael

Coleridge, Hartley 1796-1849 .... **NCLC 90**
See also DLB 96

Coleridge, M. E.
See Coleridge, Mary E(lizabeth)

Coleridge, Mary E(lizabeth)
1861-1907 .... **TCLC 73**
See also CA 116; 166; DLB 19, 98

Coleridge, Samuel Taylor
1772-1834 .... **NCLC 9, 54; DA; DAB; DAC; DAM MST, POET; PC 11; WLC**
See also CDBLB 1789-1832; DA3; DLB 93, 107

Coleridge, Sara 1802-1852 .... **NCLC 31**
See also DLB 199

Coles, Don 1928- .... **CLC 46**
See also CA 115; CANR 38

Coles, Robert (Martin) 1929- .... **CLC 108**
See also CA 45-48; CANR 3, 32, 66, 70; INT CANR-32; SATA 23

Colette, (Sidonie-Gabrielle)
1873-1954 . **TCLC 1, 5, 16; DAM NOV; SSC 10**
See also CA 104; 131; DA3; DLB 65; MTCW 1, 2

Collett, (Jacobine) Camilla (Wergeland)
1813-1895 .... **NCLC 22**

Collier, Christopher 1930- .... **CLC 30**
See also AAYA 13; CA 33-36R; CANR 13, 33; JRDA; MAICYA; SATA 16, 70

Collier, James L(incoln) 1928- .... **CLC 30; DAM POP**
See also AAYA 13; CA 9-12R; CANR 4, 33, 60; CLR 3; JRDA; MAICYA; SAAS 21; SATA 8, 70

Collier, Jeremy 1650-1726 .... **LC 6**

Collier, John 1901-1980 .... **SSC 19**
See also CA 65-68; 97-100; CANR 10; DLB 77

Collingwood, R(obin) G(eorge)
1889(?)-1943 .... **TCLC 67**
See also CA 117; 155

Collins, Hunt
See Hunter, Evan

Collins, Linda 1931- .... **CLC 44**
See also CA 125

Collins, (William) Wilkie
1824-1889 .... **NCLC 1, 18**
See also CDBLB 1832-1890; DLB 18, 70, 159

Collins, William 1721-1759 . **LC 4, 40; DAM POET**
See also DLB 109

Collodi, Carlo 1826-1890 .... **NCLC 54**
See also Lorenzini, Carlo
See also CLR 5

Colman, George 1732-1794
See Glassco, John

Colt, Winchester Remington
See Hubbard, L(afayette) Ron(ald)

Colter, Cyrus 1910- .... **CLC 58**
See also BW 1; CA 65-68; CANR 10, 66; DLB 33

Colton, James
See Hansen, Joseph

Colum, Padraic 1881-1972 .... **CLC 28**
See also CA 73-76; 33-36R; CANR 35; CLR 36; MAICYA; MTCW 1; SATA 15

Colvin, James
See Moorcock, Michael (John)

Colwin, Laurie (E.) 1944-1992 .... **CLC 5, 13, 23, 84**
See also CA 89-92; 139; CANR 20, 46; DLBY 80; MTCW 1

Comfort, Alex(ander) 1920- .... **CLC 7; DAM POP**
See also CA 1-4R; CANR 1, 45; MTCW 1

Comfort, Montgomery
See Campbell, (John) Ramsey

Compton-Burnett, I(vy)
1884(?)-1969 .... **CLC 1, 3, 10, 15, 34; DAM NOV**
See also CA 1-4R; 25-28R; CANR 4; DLB 36; MTCW 1

Comstock, Anthony 1844-1915 ...... **TCLC 13**
See also CA 110; 169

Comte, Auguste 1798-1857 .... **NCLC 54**

Conan Doyle, Arthur
See Doyle, Arthur Conan

Conde (Abellan), Carmen 1901-
See also CA 177; DLB 108; HLCS 1; HW 2

Conde, Maryse 1937- .... **CLC 52, 92; BLCS; DAM MULT**
See also BW 2, 3; CA 110; CANR 30, 53, 76; MTCW 1

Condillac, Etienne Bonnot de
1714-1780 .... **LC 26**

Condon, Richard (Thomas)
1915-1996 ...... **CLC 4, 6, 8, 10, 45, 100; DAM NOV**
See also BEST 90:3; CA 1-4R; 151; CAAS 1; CANR 2, 23; INT CANR-23; MTCW 1, 2

Confucius 551B.C.-479B.C. .. **CMLC 19; DA; DAB; DAC; DAM MST; WLCS**
See also DA3

Congreve, William 1670-1729 .... **LC 5, 21; DA; DAB; DAC; DAM DRAM, MST, POET; DC 2; WLC**
See also CDBLB 1660-1789; DLB 39, 84

Connell, Evan S(helby), Jr. 1924- . **CLC 4, 6, 45; DAM NOV**
See also AAYA 7; CA 1-4R; CAAS 2; CANR 2, 39, 76; DLB 2; DLBY 81; MTCW 1, 2

Connelly, Marc(us Cook) 1890-1980 . **CLC 7**
See also CA 85-88; 102; CANR 30; DLB 7; DLBY 80; SATA-Obit 25

Connor, Ralph **TCLC 31**
See also Gordon, Charles William
See also DLB 92

Conrad, Joseph 1857-1924 .... **TCLC 1, 6, 13, 25, 43, 57; DA; DAB; DAC; DAM MST, NOV; SSC 9; WLC**
See also AAYA 26; CA 104; 131; CANR 60; CDBLB 1890-1914; DA3; DLB 10, 34, 98, 156; MTCW 1, 2; SATA 27

Conrad, Robert Arnold
See Hart, Moss

Conroy, Pat
See Conroy, (Donald) Pat(rick)
See also MTCW 2

Conroy, (Donald) Pat(rick) 1945- ... **CLC 30, 74; DAM NOV, POP**
See also Conroy, Pat
See also AAYA 8; AITN 1; CA 85-88; CANR 24, 53; DA3; DLB 6; MTCW 1

Constant (de Rebecque), (Henri) Benjamin
1767-1830 .... **NCLC 6**
See also DLB 119

Conybeare, Charles Augustus
See Eliot, T(homas) S(tearns)

Cook, Michael 1933- .... **CLC 58**
See also CA 93-96; CANR 68; DLB 53

Cook, Robin 1940- .... **CLC 14; DAM POP**
See also AAYA 32; BEST 90:2; CA 108; 111; CANR 41, 90; DA3; INT 111

Cook, Roy
See Silverberg, Robert

Cooke, Elizabeth 1948- .... **CLC 55**
See also CA 129

Cooke, John Esten 1830-1886 .... **NCLC 5**
See also DLB 3

Cooke, John Estes
See Baum, L(yman) Frank

Cooke, M. E.
See Creasey, John

Cooke, Margaret
See Creasey, John

Crow Dog, Mary (Ellen) (?)- .... **CLC 93**
See also Brave Bird, Mary
See also CA 154
Crowfield, Christopher
See Stowe, Harriet (Elizabeth) Beecher
Crowley, Aleister TCLC 7
See also Crowley, Edward Alexander
Crowley, Edward Alexander 1875-1947
See Crowley, Aleister
See also CA 104
Crowley, John 1942- .... **CLC 57**
See also CA 61-64; CANR 43; DLBY 82;
SATA 65
Crud
See Crumb, R(obert)
Crumarums
See Crumb, R(obert)
Crumb, R(obert) 1943- .... **CLC 17**
See also CA 106
Crumbum
See Crumb, R(obert)
Crumski
See Crumb, R(obert)
Crum the Bum
See Crumb, R(obert)
Crunk
See Crumb, R(obert)
Crustt
See Crumb, R(obert)
Cruz, Victor Hernandez 1949-
See also BW 2; CA 65-68; CAAS 17;
CANR 14, 32, 74; DAM MULT, POET;
DLB 41; HLC 1; HW 1, 2; MTCW 1
Cryer, Gretchen (Kiger) 1935- .... **CLC 21**
See also CA 114; 123
Csath, Geza 1887-1919 .... **TCLC 13**
See also CA 111
Cudlip, David R(ockwell) 1933- .... **CLC 34**
See also CA 177
Cullen, Countee 1903-1946 .... **TCLC 4, 37;**
BLC 1; DA; DAC; DAM MST, MULT,
POET; PC 20; WLCS
See also BW 1; CA 108; 124; CDALB
1917-1929; DA3; DLB 4, 48, 51; MTCW
1, 2; SATA 18
Cum, R.
See Crumb, R(obert)
Cummings, Bruce F(rederick) 1889-1919
See Barbellion, W. N. P.
See also CA 123
Cummings, E(dward) E(stlin)
1894-1962 .... **CLC 1, 3, 8, 12, 15, 68;**
DA; DAB; DAC; DAM MST, POET;
PC 5; WLC
See also CA 73-76; CANR 31; CDALB
1929-1941; DA3; DLB 4, 48; MTCW 1,
2
Cunha, Euclides (Rodrigues Pimenta) da
1866-1909 .... **TCLC 24**
See also CA 123
Cunningham, E. V.
See Fast, Howard (Melvin)
Cunningham, J(ames) V(incent)
1911-1985 .... **CLC 3, 31**
See also CA 1-4R; 115; CANR 1, 72; DLB
5
Cunningham, Julia (Woolfolk)
1916- .... **CLC 12**
See also CA 9-12R; CANR 4, 19, 36;
JRDA; MAICYA; SAAS 2; SATA 1, 26
Cunningham, Michael 1952- .... **CLC 34**
See also CA 136
Cunninghame Graham, R. B.
See Cunninghame Graham, Robert
(Gallnigad) Bontine

Cunninghame Graham, Robert (Gallnigad)
Bontine 1852-1936 .... **TCLC 19**
See also Graham, R(obert) B(ontine) Cun-
ninghame
See also CA 119; 184; DLB 98
Currie, Ellen 19(?)- .... **CLC 44**
Curtin, Philip
See Lowndes, Marie Adelaide (Belloc)
Curtis, Price
See Ellison, Harlan (Jay)
Cutrate, Joe
See Spiegelman, Art
Cynewulf c. 770-c. 840 .... **CMLC 23**
Czaczkes, Shmuel Yosef
See Agnon, S(hmuel) Y(osef Halevi)
Dabrowska, Maria (Szumska)
1889-1965 .... **CLC 15**
See also CA 106
Dabydeen, David 1955- .... **CLC 34**
See also BW 1; CA 125; CANR 56, 92
Dacey, Philip 1939- .... **CLC 51**
See also CA 37-40R; CAAS 17; CANR 14,
32, 64; DLB 105
Dagerman, Stig (Halvard)
1923-1954 .... **TCLC 17**
See also CA 117; 155
Dahl, Roald 1916-1990 ...... **CLC 1, 6, 18, 79;**
DAB; DAC; DAM MST, NOV, POP
See also AAYA 15; CA 1-4R; 133; CANR
6, 32, 37, 62; CLR 1, 7, 41; DA3; DLB
139; JRDA; MAICYA; MTCW 1, 2;
SATA 1, 26, 73; SATA-Obit 65
Dahlberg, Edward 1900-1977 .. CLC 1, 7, 14
See also CA 9-12R; 69-72; CANR 31, 62;
DLB 48; MTCW 1
Daitch, Susan 1954- .... **CLC 103**
See also CA 161
Dale, Colin TCLC 18
See also Lawrence, T(homas) E(dward)
Dale, George E.
See Asimov, Isaac
Dalton, Roque 1935-1975
See also HLCS 1; HW 2
Daly, Elizabeth 1878-1967 .... **CLC 52**
See also CA 23-24; 25-28R; CANR 60;
CAP 2
Daly, Maureen 1921-1983 .... **CLC 17**
See also AAYA 5; CANR 37, 83; JRDA;
MAICYA; SAAS 1; SATA 2
Damas, Leon-Gontran 1912-1978 .... **CLC 84**
See also BW 1; CA 125; 73-76
Dana, Richard Henry Sr.
1787-1879 .... **NCLC 53**
Daniel, Samuel 1562(?)-1619 .... **LC 24**
See also DLB 62
Daniels, Brett
See Adler, Renata
Dannay, Frederic 1905-1982 . CLC 11; DAM
POP
See also Queen, Ellery
See also CA 1-4R; 107; CANR 1, 39; DLB
137; MTCW 1
D'Annunzio, Gabriele 1863-1938 ... TCLC 6,
40
See also CA 104; 155
Danois, N. le
See Gourmont, Remy (-Marie-Charles) de
Dante 1265-1321 .... **CMLC 3, 18, 39; DA;**
DAB; DAC; DAM MST, POET; PC
21; WLCS
See also Alighieri, Dante
See also DA3
d'Antibes, Germain
See Simenon, Georges (Jacques Christian)
Danticat, Edwidge 1969- .... **CLC 94**
See also AAYA 29; CA 152; CANR 73;
MTCW 1

Danvers, Dennis 1947- .... **CLC 70**
Danziger, Paula 1944- .... **CLC 21**
See also AAYA 4; CA 112; 115; CANR 37;
CLR 20; JRDA; MAICYA; SATA 36, 63,
102; SATA-Brief 30
Da Ponte, Lorenzo 1749-1838 .... **NCLC 50**
Dario, Ruben 1867-1916 .... **TCLC 4; DAM**
MULT; HLC 1; PC 15
See also CA 131; CANR 81; HW 1, 2;
MTCW 1, 2
Darley, George 1795-1846 .... **NCLC 2**
See also DLB 96
Darrow, Clarence (Seward)
1857-1938 .... **TCLC 81**
See also CA 164
Darwin, Charles 1809-1882 .... **NCLC 57**
See also DLB 57, 166
Daryush, Elizabeth 1887-1977 ...... **CLC 6, 19**
See also CA 49-52; CANR 3, 81; DLB 20
Dasgupta, Surendranath
1887-1952 .... **TCLC 81**
See also CA 157
Dashwood, Edmee Elizabeth Monica de la
Pasture 1890-1943
See Delafield, E. M.
See also CA 119; 154
Daudet, (Louis Marie) Alphonse
1840-1897 .... **NCLC 1**
See also DLB 123
Daumal, Rene 1908-1944 .... **TCLC 14**
See also CA 114
Davenant, William 1606-1668 .... **LC 13**
See also DLB 58, 126
Davenport, Guy (Mattison, Jr.)
1927- .... **CLC 6, 14, 38; SSC 16**
See also CA 33-36R; CANR 23, 73; DLB
130
Davidson, Avram (James) 1923-1993
See Queen, Ellery
See also CA 101; 171; CANR 26; DLB 8
Davidson, Donald (Grady)
1893-1968 .... **CLC 2, 13, 19**
See also CA 5-8R; 25-28R; CANR 4, 84;
DLB 45
Davidson, Hugh
See Hamilton, Edmond
Davidson, John 1857-1909 .... **TCLC 24**
See also CA 118; DLB 19
Davidson, Sara 1943- .... **CLC 9**
See also CA 81-84; CANR 44, 68; DLB
185
Davie, Donald (Alfred) 1922-1995 .... **CLC 5,**
8, 10, 31; PC 29
See also CA 1-4R; 149; CAAS 3; CANR 1,
44; DLB 27; MTCW 1
Davies, Ray(mond Douglas) 1944- ... **CLC 21**
See also CA 116; 146; CANR 92
Davies, Rhys 1901-1978 .... **CLC 23**
See also CA 9-12R; 81-84; CANR 4; DLB
139, 191
Davies, (William) Robertson
1913-1995 .... **CLC 2, 7, 13, 25, 42, 75,**
91; DA; DAB; DAC; DAM MST, NOV,
POP; WLC
See also BEST 89:2; CA 33-36R; 150;
CANR 17, 42; DA3; DLB 68; INT
CANR-17; MTCW 1, 2
Davies, Walter C.
See Kornbluth, C(yril) M.
Davies, William Henry 1871-1940 ... TCLC 5
See also CA 104; 179; DLB 19, 174
Da Vinci, Leonardo 1452-1519 ..... LC 12, 57,
60
Davis, Angela (Yvonne) 1944- .... **CLC 77;**
DAM MULT
See also BW 2, 3; CA 57-60; CANR 10,
81; DA3

Desnos, Robert 1900-1945 .... **TCLC 22**
See also CA 121; 151

de Stael, Germaine 1766-1817 .... **NCLC 91**
See also Stael-Holstein, Anne Louise Germaine Necker Baronn
See also DLB 119

Destouches, Louis-Ferdinand
1894-1961 .... **CLC 9, 15**
See also Celine, Louis-Ferdinand
See also CA 85-88; CANR 28; MTCW 1

de Tolignac, Gaston
See Griffith, D(avid Lewelyn) W(ark)

Deutsch, Babette 1895-1982 .... **CLC 18**
See also CA 1-4R; 108; CANR 4, 79; DLB 45; SATA 1; SATA-Obit 33

Devenant, William 1606-1649 .... **LC 13**

Devkota, Laxmiprasad 1909-1959 . **TCLC 23**
See also CA 123

De Voto, Bernard (Augustine)
1897-1955 .... **TCLC 29**
See also CA 113; 160; DLB 9

De Vries, Peter 1910-1993 ..... **CLC 1, 2, 3, 7, 10, 28, 46; DAM NOV**
See also CA 17-20R; 142; CANR 41; DLB 6; DLBY 82; MTCW 1, 2

Dewey, John 1859-1952 .... **TCLC 95**
See also CA 114; 170

Dexter, John
See Bradley, Marion Zimmer

Dexter, Martin
See Faust, Frederick (Schiller)

Dexter, Pete 1943- .. **CLC 34, 55; DAM POP**
See also BEST 89:2; CA 127; 131; INT 131; MTCW 1

Diamano, Silmang
See Senghor, Leopold Sedar

Diamond, Neil 1941- .... **CLC 30**
See also CA 108

Diaz del Castillo, Bernal 1496-1584 .. **LC 31; HLCS 1**

di Bassetto, Corno
See Shaw, George Bernard

Dick, Philip K(indred) 1928-1982 ... **CLC 10, 30, 72; DAM NOV, POP**
See also AAYA 24; CA 49-52; 106; CANR 2, 16; DA3; DLB 8; MTCW 1, 2

Dickens, Charles (John Huffam)
1812-1870 .... **NCLC 3, 8, 18, 26, 37, 50, 86; DA; DAB; DAC; DAM MST, NOV; SSC 17; WLC**
See also AAYA 23; CDBLB 1832-1890; DA3; DLB 21, 55, 70, 159, 166; JRDA; MAICYA; SATA 15

Dickey, James (Lafayette)
1923-1997 .... **CLC 1, 2, 4, 7, 10, 15, 47, 109; DAM NOV, POET, POP**
See also AITN 1, 2; CA 9-12R; 156; CABS 2; CANR 10, 48, 61; CDALB 1968-1988; DA3; DLB 5, 193; DLBD 7; DLBY 82, 93, 96, 97, 98; INT CANR-10; MTCW 1, 2

Dickey, William 1928-1994 .... **CLC 3, 28**
See also CA 9-12R; 145; CANR 24, 79; DLB 5

Dickinson, Charles 1951- .... **CLC 49**
See also CA 128

Dickinson, Emily (Elizabeth)
1830-1886 ..... **NCLC 21, 77; DA; DAB; DAC; DAM MST, POET; PC 1; WLC**
See also AAYA 22; CDALB 1865-1917; DA3; DLB 1; SATA 29

Dickinson, Peter (Malcolm) 1927- .. **CLC 12, 35**
See also AAYA 9; CA 41-44R; CANR 31, 58, 88; CLR 29; DLB 87, 161; JRDA; MAICYA; SATA 5, 62, 95

Dickson, Carr
See Carr, John Dickson

Dickson, Carter
See Carr, John Dickson

Diderot, Denis 1713-1784 .... **LC 26**

Didion, Joan 1934- .... **CLC 1, 3, 8, 14, 32, 129; DAM NOV**
See also AITN 1; CA 5-8R; CANR 14, 52, 76; CDALB 1968-1988; DA3; DLB 2, 173, 185; DLBY 81, 86; MTCW 1, 2

Dietrich, Robert
See Hunt, E(verette) Howard, (Jr.)

Difusa, Pati
See Almodovar, Pedro

Dillard, Annie 1945- .. **CLC 9, 60, 115; DAM NOV**
See also AAYA 6; CA 49-52; CANR 3, 43, 62, 90; DA3; DLBY 80; MTCW 1, 2; SATA 10

Dillard, R(ichard) H(enry) W(ilde)
1937- .... **CLC 5**
See also CA 21-24R; CAAS 7; CANR 10; DLB 5

Dillon, Eilis 1920-1994 .... **CLC 17**
See also CA 9-12R, 182; 147; CAAE 182; CAAS 3; CANR 4, 38, 78; CLR 26; MAICYA; SATA 2, 74; SATA-Essay 105; SATA-Obit 83

Dimont, Penelope
See Mortimer, Penelope (Ruth)

Dinesen, Isak -1962 .. **CLC 10, 29, 95; SSC 7**
See also Blixen, Karen (Christentze Dinesen)
See also MTCW 1

Ding Ling **CLC 68**
See also Chiang, Pin-chin

Diphusa, Patty
See Almodovar, Pedro

Disch, Thomas M(ichael) 1940- ... **CLC 7, 36**
See also AAYA 17; CA 21-24R; CAAS 4; CANR 17, 36, 54, 89; CLR 18; DA3; DLB 8; MAICYA; MTCW 1, 2; SAAS 15; SATA 92

Disch, Tom
See Disch, Thomas M(ichael)

d'Isly, Georges
See Simenon, Georges (Jacques Christian)

Disraeli, Benjamin 1804-1881 ... **NCLC 2, 39, 79**
See also DLB 21, 55

Ditcum, Steve
See Crumb, R(obert)

Dixon, Paige
See Corcoran, Barbara

Dixon, Stephen 1936- .... **CLC 52; SSC 16**
See also CA 89-92; CANR 17, 40, 54, 91; DLB 130

Doak, Annie
See Dillard, Annie

Dobell, Sydney Thompson
1824-1874 .... **NCLC 43**
See also DLB 32

Doblin, Alfred **TCLC 13**
See also Doeblin, Alfred

Dobrolyubov, Nikolai Alexandrovich
1836-1861 .... **NCLC 5**

Dobson, Austin 1840-1921 .... **TCLC 79**
See also DLB 35; 144

Dobyns, Stephen 1941- .... **CLC 37**
See also CA 45-48; CANR 2, 18

Doctorow, E(dgar) L(aurence)
1931- .... **CLC 6, 11, 15, 18, 37, 44, 65, 113; DAM NOV, POP**
See also AAYA 22; AITN 2; BEST 89:3; CA 45-48; CANR 2, 33, 51, 76; CDALB 1968-1988; DA3; DLB 2, 28, 173; DLBY 80; MTCW 1, 2

Dodgson, Charles Lutwidge 1832-1898
See Carroll, Lewis
See also CLR 2; DA; DAB; DAC; DAM MST, NOV, POET; DA3; MAICYA; SATA 100; YABC 2

Dodson, Owen (Vincent)
1914-1983 .... **CLC 79; BLC 1; DAM MULT**
See also BW 1; CA 65-68; 110; CANR 24; DLB 76

Doeblin, Alfred 1878-1957 .... **TCLC 13**
See also Doblin, Alfred
See also CA 110; 141; DLB 66

Doerr, Harriet 1910- .... **CLC 34**
See also CA 117; 122; CANR 47; INT 122

Domecq, H(onorio Bustos)
See Bioy Casares, Adolfo

Domecq, H(onorio) Bustos
See Bioy Casares, Adolfo; Borges, Jorge Luis

Domini, Rey
See Lorde, Audre (Geraldine)

Dominique
See Proust, (Valentin-Louis-George-Eugene-) Marcel

Don, A
See Stephen, SirLeslie

Donaldson, Stephen R. 1947- .... **CLC 46; DAM POP**
See also CA 89-92; CANR 13, 55; INT CANR-13

Donleavy, J(ames) P(atrick) 1926- .... **CLC 1, 4, 6, 10, 45**
See also AITN 2; CA 9-12R; CANR 24, 49, 62, 80; DLB 6, 173; INT CANR-24; MTCW 1, 2

Donne, John 1572-1631 .... **LC 10, 24; DA; DAB; DAC; DAM MST, POET; PC 1; WLC**
See also CDBLB Before 1660; DLB 121, 151

Donnell, David 1939(?)- .... **CLC 34**

Donoghue, P. S.
See Hunt, E(verette) Howard, (Jr.)

Donoso (Yanez), Jose 1924-1996 .... **CLC 4, 8, 11, 32, 99; DAM MULT; HLC 1; SSC 34**
See also CA 81-84; 155; CANR 32, 73; DLB 113; HW 1, 2; MTCW 1, 2

Donovan, John 1928-1992 .... **CLC 35**
See also AAYA 20; CA 97-100; 137; CLR 3; MAICYA; SATA 72; SATA-Brief 29

Don Roberto
See Cunninghame Graham, Robert (Gallnigad) Bontine

Doolittle, Hilda 1886-1961 . **CLC 3, 8, 14, 31, 34, 73; DA; DAC; DAM MST, POET; PC 5; WLC**
See also H. D.
See also CA 97-100; CANR 35; DLB 4, 45; MTCW 1, 2

Dorfman, Ariel 1942- ...... **CLC 48, 77; DAM MULT; HLC 1**
See also CA 124; 130; CANR 67, 70; HW 1, 2; INT 130

Dorn, Edward (Merton)
1929-1999 .... **CLC 10, 18**
See also CA 93-96; CANR 42, 79; DLB 5; INT 93-96

Dorris, Michael (Anthony)
1945-1997 .... **CLC 109; DAM MULT, NOV**
See also AAYA 20; BEST 90:1; CA 102; 157; CANR 19, 46, 75; CLR 58; DA3; DLB 175; MTCW 2; NNAL; SATA 75; SATA-Obit 94

Dorris, Michael A.
See Dorris, Michael (Anthony)

Dunn, Katherine (Karen) 1945- .... **CLC 71**
See also CA 33-36R; CANR 72; MTCW 1
Dunn, Stephen 1939- .... **CLC 36**
See also CA 33-36R; CANR 12, 48, 53;
DLB 105
Dunne, Finley Peter 1867-1936 ...... **TCLC 28**
See also CA 108; 178; DLB 11, 23
Dunne, John Gregory 1932- .... **CLC 28**
See also CA 25-28R; CANR 14, 50; DLBY
80
**Dunsany, Edward John Moreton Drax
Plunkett** 1878-1957
See Dunsany, Lord
See also CA 104; 148; DLB 10; MTCW 1
Dunsany, Lord -1957 .... **TCLC 2, 59**
See also Dunsany, Edward John Moreton
Drax Plunkett
See also DLB 77, 153, 156
du Perry, Jean
See Simenon, Georges (Jacques Christian)
Durang, Christopher (Ferdinand)
1949- .... **CLC 27, 38**
See also CA 105; CANR 50, 76; MTCW 1
Duras, Marguerite 1914-1996 . **CLC 3, 6, 11,
20, 34, 40, 68, 100; SSC 40**
See also CA 25-28R; 151; CANR 50; DLB
83; MTCW 1, 2
Durban, (Rosa) Pam 1947- .... **CLC 39**
See also CA 123
Durcan, Paul 1944- .... **CLC 43, 70; DAM
POET**
See also CA 134
Durkheim, Emile 1858-1917 .... **TCLC 55**
Durrell, Lawrence (George)
1912-1990 .... **CLC 1, 4, 6, 8, 13, 27, 41;
DAM NOV**
See also CA 9-12R; 132; CANR 40, 77;
CDBLB 1945-1960; DLB 15, 27, 204;
DLBY 90; MTCW 1, 2
Durrenmatt, Friedrich
See Duerrenmatt, Friedrich
Dutt, Toru 1856-1877 .... **NCLC 29**
Dwight, Timothy 1752-1817 .... **NCLC 13**
See also DLB 37
Dworkin, Andrea 1946- .... **CLC 43, 123**
See also CA 77-80; CAAS 21; CANR 16,
39, 76; INT CANR-16; MTCW 1, 2
Dwyer, Deanna
See Koontz, Dean R(ay)
Dwyer, K. R.
See Koontz, Dean R(ay)
Dwyer, Thomas A. 1923- .... **CLC 114**
See also CA 115
Dye, Richard
See De Voto, Bernard (Augustine)
Dylan, Bob 1941- .... **CLC 3, 4, 6, 12, 77**
See also CA 41-44R; DLB 16
E. V. L.
See Lucas, E(dward) V(errall)
Eagleton, Terence (Francis) 1943- .. **CLC 63,
132**
See also CA 57-60; CANR 7, 23, 68;
MTCW 1, 2
Eagleton, Terry
See Eagleton, Terence (Francis)
Early, Jack
See Scoppettone, Sandra
East, Michael
See West, Morris L(anglo)
Eastaway, Edward
See Thomas, (Philip) Edward
Eastlake, William (Derry)
1917-1997 .... **CLC 8**
See also CA 5-8R; 158; CAAS 1; CANR 5,
63; DLB 6, 206; INT CANR-5

Eastman, Charles A(lexander)
1858-1939 .... **TCLC 55; DAM MULT**
See also CA 179; CANR 91; DLB 175;
NNAL; YABC 1
Eberhart, Richard (Ghormley)
1904- .. **CLC 3, 11, 19, 56; DAM POET**
See also CA 1-4R; CANR 2; CDALB 1941-
1968; DLB 48; MTCW 1
Eberstadt, Fernanda 1960- .... **CLC 39**
See also CA 136; CANR 69
**Echegaray (y Eizaguirre), Jose (Maria
Waldo)** 1832-1916 .... **TCLC 4; HLCS 1**
See also CA 104; CANR 32; HW 1; MTCW
1
Echeverria, (Jose) Esteban (Antonino)
1805-1851 .... **NCLC 18**
Echo
See Proust, (Valentin-Louis-George-
Eugene-) Marcel
Eckert, Allan W. 1931- .... **CLC 17**
See also AAYA 18; CA 13-16R; CANR 14,
45; INT CANR-14; SAAS 21; SATA 29,
91; SATA-Brief 27
Eckhart, Meister 1260(?)-1328(?) ... **CMLC 9**
See also DLB 115
Eckmar, F. R.
See de Hartog, Jan
Eco, Umberto 1932- .... **CLC 28, 60; DAM
NOV, POP**
See also BEST 90:1; CA 77-80; CANR 12,
33, 55; DA3; DLB 196; MTCW 1, 2
Eddison, E(ric) R(ucker)
1882-1945 .... **TCLC 15**
See also CA 109; 156
Eddy, Mary (Ann Morse) Baker
1821-1910 .... **TCLC 71**
See also CA 113; 174
Edel, (Joseph) Leon 1907-1997 .. **CLC 29, 34**
See also CA 1-4R; 161; CANR 1, 22; DLB
103; INT CANR-22
Eden, Emily 1797-1869 .... **NCLC 10**
Edgar, David 1948- .. **CLC 42; DAM DRAM**
See also CA 57-60; CANR 12, 61; DLB 13;
MTCW 1
Edgerton, Clyde (Carlyle) 1944- ...... **CLC 39**
See also AAYA 17; CA 118; 134; CANR
64; INT 134
Edgeworth, Maria 1768-1849 .... **NCLC 1, 51**
See also DLB 116, 159, 163; SATA 21
Edmonds, Paul
See Kuttner, Henry
Edmonds, Walter D(umaux)
1903-1998 .... **CLC 35**
See also CA 5-8R; CANR 2; DLB 9; MAI-
CYA; SAAS 4; SATA 1, 27; SATA-Obit
99
Edmondson, Wallace
See Ellison, Harlan (Jay)
Edson, Russell CLC 13
See also CA 33-36R
Edwards, Bronwen Elizabeth
See Rose, Wendy
Edwards, G(erald) B(asil)
1899-1976 .... **CLC 25**
See also CA 110
Edwards, Gus 1939- .... **CLC 43**
See also CA 108; INT 108
Edwards, Jonathan 1703-1758 .... **LC 7, 54;
DA; DAC; DAM MST**
See also DLB 24
Efron, Marina Ivanovna Tsvetaeva
See Tsvetaeva (Efron), Marina (Ivanovna)
Ehle, John (Marsden, Jr.) 1925- ...... **CLC 27**
See also CA 9-12R
Ehrenbourg, Ilya (Grigoryevich)
See Ehrenburg, Ilya (Grigoryevich)
Ehrenburg, Ilya (Grigoryevich)
1891-1967 .... **CLC 18, 34, 62**
See also CA 102; 25-28R

Ehrenburg, Ilyo (Grigoryevich)
See Ehrenburg, Ilya (Grigoryevich)
Ehrenreich, Barbara 1941- .... **CLC 110**
See also BEST 90:4; CA 73-76; CANR 16,
37, 62; MTCW 1, 2
Eich, Guenter 1907-1972 .... **CLC 15**
See also CA 111; 93-96; DLB 69, 124
Eichendorff, Joseph Freiherr von
1788-1857 .... **NCLC 8**
See also DLB 90
Eigner, Larry CLC 9
See also Eigner, Laurence (Joel)
See also CAAS 23; DLB 5
Eigner, Laurence (Joel) 1927-1996
See Eigner, Larry
See also CA 9-12R; 151; CANR 6, 84; DLB
193
Einstein, Albert 1879-1955 .... **TCLC 65**
See also CA 121; 133; MTCW 1, 2
Eiseley, Loren Corey 1907-1977 .... **CLC 7**
See also AAYA 5; CA 1-4R; 73-76; CANR
6; DLBD 17
Eisenstadt, Jill 1963- .... **CLC 50**
See also CA 140
Eisenstein, Sergei (Mikhailovich)
1898-1948 .... **TCLC 57**
See also CA 114; 149
Eisner, Simon
See Kornbluth, C(yril) M.
Ekeloef, (Bengt) Gunnar
1907-1968 ... **CLC 27; DAM POET; PC
23**
See also CA 123; 25-28R
Ekelof, (Bengt) Gunnar
See Ekeloef, (Bengt) Gunnar
Ekelund, Vilhelm 1880-1949 .... **TCLC 75**
Ekwensi, C. O. D.
See Ekwensi, Cyprian (Odiatu Duaka)
Ekwensi, Cyprian (Odiatu Duaka)
1921- ...... **CLC 4; BLC 1; DAM MULT**
See also BW 2, 3; CA 29-32R; CANR 18,
42, 74; DLB 117; MTCW 1, 2; SATA 66
Elaine TCLC 18
See also Leverson, Ada
El Crummo
See Crumb, R(obert)
Elder, Lonne III 1931-1996 .... **DC 8**
See also BLC 1; BW 1, 3; CA 81-84; 152;
CANR 25; DAM MULT; DLB 7, 38, 44
Eleanor of Aquitaine 1122-1204 ... **CMLC 39**
Elia
See Lamb, Charles
Eliade, Mircea 1907-1986 .... **CLC 19**
See also CA 65-68; 119; CANR 30, 62;
DLB 220; MTCW 1
Eliot, A. D.
See Jewett, (Theodora) Sarah Orne
Eliot, Alice
See Jewett, (Theodora) Sarah Orne
Eliot, Dan
See Silverberg, Robert
Eliot, George 1819- . **NCLC 4, 13, 23, 41, 49,
89; DA; DAB; DAC; DAM MST, NOV;
PC 20; WLC**
See also CDBLB 1832-1890; DA3; DLB
21, 35, 55
Eliot, John 1604-1690 .... **LC 5**
See also DLB 24
Eliot, T(homas) S(tearns)
1888-1965 ...... **CLC 1, 2, 3, 6, 9, 10, 13,
15, 24, 34, 41, 55, 57, 113; DA; DAB;
DAC; DAM DRAM, MST, POET; PC
5, 31; WLC**
See also AAYA 28; CA 5-8R; 25-28R;
CANR 41; CDALB 1929-1941; DA3;
DLB 7, 10, 45, 63; DLBY 88; MTCW 1,
2

Elizabeth 1866-1941 .... **TCLC 41**

Elkin, Stanley L(awrence)
1930-1995 .. **CLC 4, 6, 9, 14, 27, 51, 91; DAM NOV, POP; SSC 12**
See also CA 9-12R; 148; CANR 8, 46; DLB 2, 28; DLBY 80; INT CANR-8; MTCW 1, 2

Elledge, Scott **CLC 34**

Elliot, Don
See Silverberg, Robert

Elliott, Don
See Silverberg, Robert

Elliott, George P(aul) 1918-1980 .... **CLC 2**
See also CA 1-4R; 97-100; CANR 2

Elliott, Janice 1931- .... **CLC 47**
See also CA 13-16R; CANR 8, 29, 84; DLB 14

Elliott, Sumner Locke 1917-1991 ..... **CLC 38**
See also CA 5-8R; 134; CANR 2, 21

Elliott, William
See Bradbury, Ray (Douglas)

Ellis, A. E. **CLC 7**

Ellis, Alice Thomas **CLC 40**
See also Haycraft, Anna (Margaret)
See also DLB 194; MTCW 1

Ellis, Bret Easton 1964- ..... **CLC 39, 71, 117; DAM POP**
See also AAYA 2; CA 118; 123; CANR 51, 74; DA3; INT 123; MTCW 1

Ellis, (Henry) Havelock
1859-1939 .... **TCLC 14**
See also CA 109; 169; DLB 190

Ellis, Landon
See Ellison, Harlan (Jay)

Ellis, Trey 1962- .... **CLC 55**
See also CA 146; CANR 92

Ellison, Harlan (Jay) 1934- ... **CLC 1, 13, 42; DAM POP; SSC 14**
See also AAYA 29; CA 5-8R; CANR 5, 46; DLB 8; INT CANR-5; MTCW 1, 2

Ellison, Ralph (Waldo) 1914-1994 .... **CLC 1, 3, 11, 54, 86, 114; BLC 1; DA; DAB; DAC; DAM MST, MULT, NOV; SSC 26; WLC**
See also AAYA 19; BW 1, 3; CA 9-12R; 145; CANR 24, 53; CDALB 1941-1968; DA3; DLB 2, 76, 227; DLBY 94; MTCW 1, 2

Ellmann, Lucy (Elizabeth) 1956- ..... **CLC 61**
See also CA 128

Ellmann, Richard (David)
1918-1987 .... **CLC 50**
See also BEST 89:2; CA 1-4R; 122; CANR 2, 28, 61; DLB 103; DLBY 87; MTCW 1, 2

Elman, Richard (Martin)
1934-1997 .... **CLC 19**
See also CA 17-20R; 163; CAAS 3; CANR 47

Elron
See Hubbard, L(afayette) Ron(ald)

Eluard, Paul **TCLC 7, 41**
See also Grindel, Eugene

Elyot, Sir Thomas 1490(?)-1546 .... **LC 11**

Elytis, Odysseus 1911-1996 .... **CLC 15, 49, 100; DAM POET; PC 21**
See also CA 102; 151; MTCW 1, 2

Emecheta, (Florence Onye) Buchi
1944- .. **CLC 14, 48, 128; BLC 2; DAM MULT**
See also BW 2, 3; CA 81-84; CANR 27, 81; DA3; DLB 117; MTCW 1, 2; SATA 66

Emerson, Mary Moody
1774-1863 .... **NCLC 66**

Emerson, Ralph Waldo 1803-1882 . **NCLC 1, 38; DA; DAB; DAC; DAM MST, POET; PC 18; WLC**
See also CDALB 1640-1865; DA3; DLB 1, 59, 73, 223

Eminescu, Mihail 1850-1889 .... **NCLC 33**

Empson, William 1906-1984 ... **CLC 3, 8, 19, 33, 34**
See also CA 17-20R; 112; CANR 31, 61; DLB 20; MTCW 1, 2

Enchi, Fumiko (Ueda) 1905-1986 ..... **CLC 31**
See also CA 129; 121; DLB 182

Ende, Michael (Andreas Helmuth)
1929-1995 .... **CLC 31**
See also CA 118; 124; 149; CANR 36; CLR 14; DLB 75; MAICYA; SATA 61; SATA-Brief 42; SATA-Obit 86

Endo, Shusaku 1923-1996 ..... **CLC 7, 14, 19, 54, 99; DAM NOV**
See also CA 29-32R; 153; CANR 21, 54; DA3; DLB 182; MTCW 1, 2

Engel, Marian 1933-1985 .... **CLC 36**
See also CA 25-28R; CANR 12; DLB 53; INT CANR-12

Engelhardt, Frederick
See Hubbard, L(afayette) Ron(ald)

Engels, Friedrich 1820-1895 .... **NCLC 85**
See also DLB 129

Enright, D(ennis) J(oseph) 1920- .. **CLC 4, 8, 31**
See also CA 1-4R; CANR 1, 42, 83; DLB 27; SATA 25

Enzensberger, Hans Magnus
1929- .... **CLC 43; PC 28**
See also CA 116; 119

Ephron, Nora 1941- .... **CLC 17, 31**
See also AITN 2; CA 65-68; CANR 12, 39, 83

Epicurus 341B.C.-270B.C. .... **CMLC 21**
See also DLB 176

Epsilon
See Betjeman, John

Epstein, Daniel Mark 1948- .... **CLC 7**
See also CA 49-52; CANR 2, 53, 90

Epstein, Jacob 1956- .... **CLC 19**
See also CA 114

Epstein, Jean 1897-1953 .... **TCLC 92**

Epstein, Joseph 1937- .... **CLC 39**
See also CA 112; 119; CANR 50, 65

Epstein, Leslie 1938- .... **CLC 27**
See also CA 73-76; CAAS 12; CANR 23, 69

Equiano, Olaudah 1745(?)-1797 .... **LC 16; BLC 2; DAM MULT**
See also DLB 37, 50

ER **TCLC 33**
See also CA 160; DLB 85

Erasmus, Desiderius 1469(?)-1536 ...... **LC 16**

Erdman, Paul E(mil) 1932- .... **CLC 25**
See also AITN 1; CA 61-64; CANR 13, 43, 84

Erdrich, Louise 1954- .... **CLC 39, 54, 120; DAM MULT, NOV, POP**
See also AAYA 10; BEST 89:1; CA 114; CANR 41, 62; CDALBS; DA3; DLB 152, 175, 206; MTCW 1; NNAL; SATA 94

Erenburg, Ilya (Grigoryevich)
See Ehrenburg, Ilya (Grigoryevich)

Erickson, Stephen Michael 1950-
See Erickson, Steve
See also CA 129

Erickson, Steve 1950- .... **CLC 64**
See also Erickson, Stephen Michael
See also CANR 60, 68

Ericson, Walter
See Fast, Howard (Melvin)

Eriksson, Buntel
See Bergman, (Ernst) Ingmar

Ernaux, Annie 1940- .... **CLC 88**
See also CA 147

Erskine, John 1879-1951 .... **TCLC 84**
See also CA 112; 159; DLB 9, 102

Eschenbach, Wolfram von
See Wolfram von Eschenbach

Eseki, Bruno
See Mphahlele, Ezekiel

Esenin, Sergei (Alexandrovich)
1895-1925 .... **TCLC 4**
See also CA 104

Eshleman, Clayton 1935- .... **CLC 7**
See also CA 33-36R; CAAS 6; DLB 5

Espriella, Don Manuel Alvarez
See Southey, Robert

Espriu, Salvador 1913-1985 .... **CLC 9**
See also CA 154; 115; DLB 134

Espronceda, Jose de 1808-1842 ..... **NCLC 39**

Esquivel, Laura 1951(?)-
See also AAYA 29; CA 143; CANR 68; DA3; HLCS 1; MTCW 1

Esse, James
See Stephens, James

Esterbrook, Tom
See Hubbard, L(afayette) Ron(ald)

Estleman, Loren D. 1952- ..... **CLC 48; DAM NOV, POP**
See also AAYA 27; CA 85-88; CANR 27, 74; DA3; DLB 226; INT CANR-27; MTCW 1, 2

Euclid 306B.C.-283B.C. .... **CMLC 25**

Eugenides, Jeffrey 1960(?)- .... **CLC 81**
See also CA 144

Euripides c. 485B.C.-406B.C. .... **CMLC 23; DA; DAB; DAC; DAM DRAM, MST; DC 4; WLCS**
See also DA3; DLB 176

Evan, Evin
See Faust, Frederick (Schiller)

Evans, Caradoc 1878-1945 .... **TCLC 85**

Evans, Evan
See Faust, Frederick (Schiller)

Evans, Marian
See Eliot, George

Evans, Mary Ann
See Eliot, George

Evarts, Esther
See Benson, Sally

Everett, Percival L. 1956- .... **CLC 57**
See also BW 2; CA 129

Everson, R(onald) G(ilmour) 1903- . **CLC 27**
See also CA 17-20R; DLB 88

Everson, William (Oliver)
1912-1994 .... **CLC 1, 5, 14**
See also CA 9-12R; 145; CANR 20; DLB 212; MTCW 1

Evtushenko, Evgenii Aleksandrovich
See Yevtushenko, Yevgeny (Alexandrovich)

Ewart, Gavin (Buchanan)
1916-1995 .... **CLC 13, 46**
See also CA 89-92; 150; CANR 17, 46; DLB 40; MTCW 1

Ewers, Hanns Heinz 1871-1943 ..... **TCLC 12**
See also CA 109; 149

Ewing, Frederick R.
See Sturgeon, Theodore (Hamilton)

Exley, Frederick (Earl) 1929-1992 .... **CLC 6, 11**
See also AITN 2; CA 81-84; 138; DLB 143; DLBY 81

Eynhardt, Guillermo
See Quiroga, Horacio (Sylvestre)

Ezekiel, Nissim 1924- .... **CLC 61**
See also CA 61-64

Ezekiel, Tish O'Dowd 1943- .... **CLC 34**
See also CA 129

Fadeyev, A.
See Bulgya, Alexander Alexandrovich

Fadeyev, Alexander **TCLC 53**
See also Bulgya, Alexander Alexandrovich

Fagen, Donald 1948- .... **CLC 26**

Fainzilberg, Ilya Arnoldovich 1897-1937
See Ilf, Ilya
See also CA 120; 165

Fair, Ronald L. 1932- .... **CLC 18**
See also BW 1; CA 69-72; CANR 25; DLB 33

Fairbairn, Roger
See Carr, John Dickson

Fairbairns, Zoe (Ann) 1948- .... **CLC 32**
See also CA 103; CANR 21, 85

Falco, Gian
See Papini, Giovanni

Falconer, James
See Kirkup, James

Falconer, Kenneth
See Kornbluth, C(yril) M.

Falkland, Samuel
See Heijermans, Herman

Fallaci, Oriana 1930- .... **CLC 11, 110**
See also CA 77-80; CANR 15, 58; MTCW 1

Faludy, George 1913- .... **CLC 42**
See also CA 21-24R

Faludy, Gyoergy
See Faludy, George

Fanon, Frantz 1925-1961 ... **CLC 74; BLC 2; DAM MULT**
See also BW 1; CA 116; 89-92

Fanshawe, Ann 1625-1680 .... **LC 11**

Fante, John (Thomas) 1911-1983 ..... **CLC 60**
See also CA 69-72; 109; CANR 23; DLB 130; DLBY 83

Farah, Nuruddin 1945- ...... **CLC 53; BLC 2; DAM MULT**
See also BW 2, 3; CA 106; CANR 81; DLB 125

Fargue, Leon-Paul 1876(?)-1947 .... **TCLC 11**
See also CA 109

Farigoule, Louis
See Romains, Jules

Farina, Richard 1936(?)-1966 .... **CLC 9**
See also CA 81-84; 25-28R

Farley, Walter (Lorimer)
1915-1989 .... **CLC 17**
See also CA 17-20R; CANR 8, 29, 84; DLB 22; JRDA; MAICYA; SATA 2, 43

Farmer, Philip Jose 1918- .... **CLC 1, 19**
See also AAYA 28; CA 1-4R; CANR 4, 35; DLB 8; MTCW 1; SATA 93

Farquhar, George 1677-1707 ... **LC 21; DAM DRAM**
See also DLB 84

Farrell, J(ames) G(ordon)
1935-1979 .... **CLC 6**
See also CA 73-76; 89-92; CANR 36; DLB 14; MTCW 1

Farrell, James T(homas) 1904-1979 . **CLC 1, 4, 8, 11, 66; SSC 28**
See also CA 5-8R; 89-92; CANR 9, 61; DLB 4, 9, 86; DLBD 2; MTCW 1, 2

Farren, Richard J.
See Betjeman, John

Farren, Richard M.
See Betjeman, John

Fassbinder, Rainer Werner
1946-1982 .... **CLC 20**
See also CA 93-96; 106; CANR 31

Fast, Howard (Melvin) 1914- .. **CLC 23, 131; DAM NOV**
See also AAYA 16; CA 1-4R, 181; CAAE 181; CAAS 18; CANR 1, 33, 54, 75; DLB 9; INT CANR-33; MTCW 1; SATA 7; SATA-Essay 107

Faulcon, Robert
See Holdstock, Robert P.

Faulkner, William (Cuthbert)
1897-1962 .... **CLC 1, 3, 6, 8, 9, 11, 14, 18, 28, 52, 68; DA; DAB; DAC; DAM MST, NOV; SSC 1, 35; WLC**
See also AAYA 7; CA 81-84; CANR 33; CDALB 1929-1941; DA3; DLB 9, 11, 44, 102; DLBD 2; DLBY 86, 97; MTCW 1, 2

Fauset, Jessie Redmon
1884(?)-1961 .... **CLC 19, 54; BLC 2; DAM MULT**
See also BW 1; CA 109; CANR 83; DLB 51

Faust, Frederick (Schiller)
1892-1944(?) .... **TCLC 49; DAM POP**
See also CA 108; 152

Faust, Irvin 1924- .... **CLC 8**
See also CA 33-36R; CANR 28, 67; DLB 2, 28; DLBY 80

Fawkes, Guy
See Benchley, Robert (Charles)

Fearing, Kenneth (Flexner)
1902-1961 .... **CLC 51**
See also CA 93-96; CANR 59; DLB 9

Fecamps, Elise
See Creasey, John

Federman, Raymond 1928- .... **CLC 6, 47**
See also CA 17-20R; CAAS 8; CANR 10, 43, 83; DLBY 80

Federspiel, J(uerg) F. 1931- .... **CLC 42**
See also CA 146

Feiffer, Jules (Ralph) 1929- ..... **CLC 2, 8, 64; DAM DRAM**
See also AAYA 3; CA 17-20R; CANR 30, 59; DLB 7, 44; INT CANR-30; MTCW 1; SATA 8, 61, 111

Feige, Hermann Albert Otto Maximilian
See Traven, B.

Feinberg, David B. 1956-1994 .... **CLC 59**
See also CA 135; 147

Feinstein, Elaine 1930- .... **CLC 36**
See also CA 69-72; CAAS 1; CANR 31, 68; DLB 14, 40; MTCW 1

Feldman, Irving (Mordecai) 1928- ..... **CLC 7**
See also CA 1-4R; CANR 1; DLB 169

Felix-Tchicaya, Gerald
See Tchicaya, Gerald Felix

Fellini, Federico 1920-1993 .... **CLC 16, 85**
See also CA 65-68; 143; CANR 33

Felsen, Henry Gregor 1916-1995 ..... **CLC 17**
See also CA 1-4R; 180; CANR 1; SAAS 2; SATA 1

Fenno, Jack
See Calisher, Hortense

Fenollosa, Ernest (Francisco)
1853-1908 .... **TCLC 91**

Fenton, James Martin 1949- .... **CLC 32**
See also CA 102; DLB 40

Ferber, Edna 1887-1968 .... **CLC 18, 93**
See also AITN 1; CA 5-8R; 25-28R; CANR 68; DLB 9, 28, 86; MTCW 1, 2; SATA 7

Ferguson, Helen
See Kavan, Anna

Ferguson, Niall 1967- .... **CLC 134**

Ferguson, Samuel 1810-1886 .... **NCLC 33**
See also DLB 32

Fergusson, Robert 1750-1774 .... **LC 29**
See also DLB 109

Ferling, Lawrence
See Ferlinghetti, Lawrence (Monsanto)

Ferlinghetti, Lawrence (Monsanto)
1919(?)- .... **CLC 2, 6, 10, 27, 111; DAM POET; PC 1**
See also CA 5-8R; CANR 3, 41, 73; CDALB 1941-1968; DA3; DLB 5, 16; MTCW 1, 2

Fern, Fanny 1811-1872
See Parton, Sara Payson Willis

Fernandez, Vicente Garcia Huidobro
See Huidobro Fernandez, Vicente Garcia

Ferre, Rosario 1942- .... **SSC 36; HLCS 1**
See also CA 131; CANR 55, 81; DLB 145; HW 1, 2; MTCW 1

Ferrer, Gabriel (Francisco Victor) Miro
See Miro (Ferrer), Gabriel (Francisco Victor)

Ferrier, Susan (Edmonstone)
1782-1854 .... **NCLC 8**
See also DLB 116

Ferrigno, Robert 1948(?)- .... **CLC 65**
See also CA 140

Ferron, Jacques 1921-1985 .... **CLC 94; DAC**
See also CA 117; 129; DLB 60

Feuchtwanger, Lion 1884-1958 .... **TCLC 3**
See also CA 104; DLB 66

Feuillet, Octave 1821-1890 .... **NCLC 45**
See also DLB 192

Feydeau, Georges (Leon Jules Marie)
1862-1921 .... **TCLC 22; DAM DRAM**
See also CA 113; 152; CANR 84; DLB 192

Fichte, Johann Gottlieb
1762-1814 .... **NCLC 62**
See also DLB 90

Ficino, Marsilio 1433-1499 .... **LC 12**

Fiedeler, Hans
See Doeblin, Alfred

Fiedler, Leslie A(aron) 1917- .. **CLC 4, 13, 24**
See also CA 9-12R; CANR 7, 63; DLB 28, 67; MTCW 1, 2

Field, Andrew 1938- .... **CLC 44**
See also CA 97-100; CANR 25

Field, Eugene 1850-1895 .... **NCLC 3**
See also DLB 23, 42, 140; DLBD 13; MAI-CYA; SATA 16

Field, Gans T.
See Wellman, Manly Wade

Field, Michael 1915-1971 .... **TCLC 43**
See also CA 29-32R

Field, Peter
See Hobson, Laura Z(ametkin)

Fielding, Henry 1707-1754 ..... **LC 1, 46; DA; DAB; DAC; DAM DRAM, MST, NOV; WLC**
See also CDBLB 1660-1789; DA3; DLB 39, 84, 101

Fielding, Sarah 1710-1768 .... **LC 1, 44**
See also DLB 39

Fields, W. C. 1880-1946 .... **TCLC 80**
See also DLB 44

Fierstein, Harvey (Forbes) 1954- .... **CLC 33; DAM DRAM, POP**
See also CA 123; 129; DA3

Figes, Eva 1932- .... **CLC 31**
See also CA 53-56; CANR 4, 44, 83; DLB 14

Finch, Anne 1661-1720 .... **LC 3; PC 21**
See also DLB 95

Finch, Robert (Duer Claydon)
1900- .... **CLC 18**
See also CA 57-60; CANR 9, 24, 49; DLB 88

Findley, Timothy 1930- . **CLC 27, 102; DAC; DAM MST**
See also CA 25-28R; CANR 12, 42, 69; DLB 53

Fink, William
See Mencken, H(enry) L(ouis)

Firbank, Louis 1942-
See Reed, Lou
See also CA 117

Firbank, (Arthur Annesley) Ronald
1886-1926 .... **TCLC 1**
See also CA 104; 177; DLB 36

Fisher, Dorothy (Frances) Canfield
1879-1958 .... **TCLC 87**
See also CA 114; 136; CANR 80; DLB 9, 102; MAICYA; YABC 1

Fraser, (Lady) Antonia (Pakenham)
1932- .... **CLC 32, 107**
See also CA 85-88; CANR 44, 65; MTCW
1, 2; SATA-Brief 32

Fraser, George MacDonald 1925- ...... **CLC 7**
See also CA 45-48, 180; CAAE 180; CANR
2, 48, 74; MTCW 1

Fraser, Sylvia 1935- .... **CLC 64**
See also CA 45-48; CANR 1, 16, 60

Frayn, Michael 1933- .... **CLC 3, 7, 31, 47;**
DAM DRAM, NOV
See also CA 5-8R; CANR 30, 69; DLB 13,
14, 194; MTCW 1, 2

Fraze, Candida (Merrill) 1945- .... **CLC 50**
See also CA 126

Frazer, J(ames) G(eorge)
1854-1941 .... **TCLC 32**
See also CA 118

Frazer, Robert Caine
See Creasey, John

Frazer, Sir James George
See Frazer, J(ames) G(eorge)

Frazier, Charles 1950- .... **CLC 109**
See also AAYA 34; CA 161

Frazier, Ian 1951- .... **CLC 46**
See also CA 130; CANR 54

Frederic, Harold 1856-1898 .... **NCLC 10**
See also DLB 12, 23; DLBD 13

Frederick, John
See Faust, Frederick (Schiller)

Frederick the Great 1712-1786 .... **LC 14**

Fredro, Aleksander 1793-1876 .... **NCLC 8**

Freeling, Nicolas 1927- .... **CLC 38**
See also CA 49-52; CAAS 12; CANR 1,
17, 50, 84; DLB 87

Freeman, Douglas Southall
1886-1953 .... **TCLC 11**
See also CA 109; DLB 17; DLBD 17

Freeman, Judith 1946- .... **CLC 55**
See also CA 148

Freeman, Mary E(leanor) Wilkins
1852-1930 .... **TCLC 9; SSC 1**
See also CA 106; 177; DLB 12, 78, 221

Freeman, R(ichard) Austin
1862-1943 .... **TCLC 21**
See also CA 113; CANR 84; DLB 70

French, Albert 1943- .... **CLC 86**
See also BW 3; CA 167

French, Marilyn 1929- .... **CLC 10, 18, 60;**
DAM DRAM, NOV, POP
See also CA 69-72; CANR 3, 31; INT
CANR-31; MTCW 1, 2

French, Paul
See Asimov, Isaac

Freneau, Philip Morin 1752-1832 ... **NCLC 1**
See also DLB 37, 43

Freud, Sigmund 1856-1939 .... **TCLC 52**
See also CA 115; 133; CANR 69; MTCW
1, 2

Friedan, Betty (Naomi) 1921- .... **CLC 74**
See also CA 65-68; CANR 18, 45, 74;
MTCW 1, 2

Friedlander, Saul 1932- .... **CLC 90**
See also CA 117; 130; CANR 72

Friedman, B(ernard) H(arper)
1926- .... **CLC 7**
See also CA 1-4R; CANR 3, 48

Friedman, Bruce Jay 1930- ...... **CLC 3, 5, 56**
See also CA 9-12R; CANR 25, 52; DLB 2,
28; INT CANR-25

Friel, Brian 1929- .... **CLC 5, 42, 59, 115; DC**
8
See also CA 21-24R; CANR 33, 69; DLB
13; MTCW 1

Friis-Baastad, Babbis Ellinor
1921-1970 .... **CLC 12**
See also CA 17-20R; 134; SATA 7

Frisch, Max (Rudolf) 1911-1991 ... **CLC 3, 9,**
14, 18, 32, 44; DAM DRAM, NOV
See also CA 85-88; 134; CANR 32, 74;
DLB 69, 124; MTCW 1, 2

Fromentin, Eugene (Samuel Auguste)
1820-1876 .... **NCLC 10**
See also DLB 123

Frost, Frederick
See Faust, Frederick (Schiller)

Frost, Robert (Lee) 1874-1963 .. **CLC 1, 3, 4,**
9, 10, 13, 15, 26, 34, 44; DA; DAB;
DAC; DAM MST, POET; PC 1; WLC
See also AAYA 21; CA 89-92; CANR 33;
CDALB 1917-1929; DA3; DLB 54;
DLBD 7; MTCW 1, 2; SATA 14

Froude, James Anthony
1818-1894 .... **NCLC 43**
See also DLB 18, 57, 144

Froy, Herald
See Waterhouse, Keith (Spencer)

Fry, Christopher 1907- .... **CLC 2, 10, 14;**
DAM DRAM
See also CA 17-20R; CAAS 23; CANR 9,
30, 74; DLB 13; MTCW 1, 2; SATA 66

Frye, (Herman) Northrop
1912-1991 .... **CLC 24, 70**
See also CA 5-8R; 133; CANR 8, 37; DLB
67, 68; MTCW 1, 2

Fuchs, Daniel 1909-1993 .... **CLC 8, 22**
See also CA 81-84; 142; CAAS 5; CANR
40; DLB 9, 26, 28; DLBY 93

Fuchs, Daniel 1934- .... **CLC 34**
See also CA 37-40R; CANR 14, 48

Fuentes, Carlos 1928- .. **CLC 3, 8, 10, 13, 22,**
41, 60, 113; DA; DAB; DAC; DAM
MST, MULT, NOV; HLC 1; SSC 24;
WLC
See also AAYA 4; AITN 2; CA 69-72;
CANR 10, 32, 68; DA3; DLB 113; HW
1, 2; MTCW 1, 2

Fuentes, Gregorio Lopez y
See Lopez y Fuentes, Gregorio

Fuertes, Gloria 1918- .... **PC 27**
See also CA 178, 180; DLB 108; HW 2;
SATA 115

Fugard, (Harold) Athol 1932- . **CLC 5, 9, 14,**
25, 40, 80; DAM DRAM; DC 3
See also AAYA 17; CA 85-88; CANR 32,
54; DLB 225; MTCW 1

Fugard, Sheila 1932- .... **CLC 48**
See also CA 125

Fukuyama, Francis 1952- .... **CLC 131**
See also CA 140; CANR 72

Fuller, Charles (H., Jr.) 1939- .... **CLC 25;**
BLC 2; DAM DRAM, MULT; DC 1
See also BW 2; CA 108; 112; CANR 87;
DLB 38; INT 112; MTCW 1

Fuller, John (Leopold) 1937- .... **CLC 62**
See also CA 21-24R; CANR 9, 44; DLB 40

Fuller, Margaret
See Ossoli, Sarah Margaret (Fuller marchesa
d')

Fuller, Roy (Broadbent) 1912-1991 ... **CLC 4,**
28
See also CA 5-8R; 135; CAAS 10; CANR
53, 83; DLB 15, 20; SATA 87

Fuller, Sarah Margaret 1810-1850
See Ossoli, Sarah Margaret (Fuller marchesa
d')

Fulton, Alice 1952- .... **CLC 52**
See also CA 116; CANR 57, 88; DLB 193

Furphy, Joseph 1843-1912 .... **TCLC 25**
See also CA 163

Fussell, Paul 1924- .... **CLC 74**
See also BEST 90:1; CA 17-20R; CANR 8,
21, 35, 69; INT CANR-21; MTCW 1, 2

Futabatei, Shimei 1864-1909 .... **TCLC 44**
See also CA 162; DLB 180

Futrelle, Jacques 1875-1912 .... **TCLC 19**
See also CA 113; 155

Gaboriau, Emile 1835-1873 .... **NCLC 14**

Gadda, Carlo Emilio 1893-1973 .... **CLC 11**
See also CA 89-92; DLB 177

Gaddis, William 1922-1998 ... **CLC 1, 3, 6, 8,**
10, 19, 43, 86
See also CA 17-20R; 172; CANR 21, 48;
DLB 2; MTCW 1, 2

Gage, Walter
See Inge, William (Motter)

Gaines, Ernest J(ames) 1933- ...... **CLC 3, 11,**
18, 86; BLC 2; DAM MULT
See also AAYA 18; AITN 1; BW 2, 3; CA
9-12R; CANR 6, 24, 42, 75; CDALB
1968-1988; CLR 62; DA3; DLB 2, 33,
152; DLBY 80; MTCW 1, 2; SATA 86

Gaitskill, Mary 1954- .... **CLC 69**
See also CA 128; CANR 61

Galdos, Benito Perez
See Perez Galdos, Benito

Gale, Zona 1874-1938 .... **TCLC 7; DAM**
DRAM
See also CA 105; 153; CANR 84; DLB 9,
78, 228

Galeano, Eduardo (Hughes) 1940- . **CLC 72;**
HLCS 1
See also CA 29-32R; CANR 13, 32; HW 1

Galiano, Juan Valera y Alcala
See Valera y Alcala-Galiano, Juan

Galilei, Galileo 1546-1642 .... **LC 45**

Gallagher, Tess 1943- ...... **CLC 18, 63; DAM**
POET; PC 9
See also CA 106; DLB 212

Gallant, Mavis 1922- .. **CLC 7, 18, 38; DAC;**
DAM MST; SSC 5
See also CA 69-72; CANR 29, 69; DLB 53;
MTCW 1, 2

Gallant, Roy A(rthur) 1924- .... **CLC 17**
See also CA 5-8R; CANR 4, 29, 54; CLR
30; MAICYA; SATA 4, 68, 110

Gallico, Paul (William) 1897-1976 ..... **CLC 2**
See also AITN 1; CA 5-8R; 69-72; CANR
23; DLB 9, 171; MAICYA; SATA 13

Gallo, Max Louis 1932- .... **CLC 95**
See also CA 85-88

Gallois, Lucien
See Desnos, Robert

Gallup, Ralph
See Whitemore, Hugh (John)

Galsworthy, John 1867-1933 .... **TCLC 1, 45;**
DA; DAB; DAC; DAM DRAM, MST,
NOV; SSC 22; WLC
See also CA 104; 141; CANR 75; CDBLB
1890-1914; DA3; DLB 10, 34, 98, 162;
DLBD 16; MTCW 1

Galt, John 1779-1839 .... **NCLC 1**
See also DLB 99, 116, 159

Galvin, James 1951- .... **CLC 38**
See also CA 108; CANR 26

Gamboa, Federico 1864-1939 .... **TCLC 36**
See also CA 167; HW 2

Gandhi, M. K.
See Gandhi, Mohandas Karamchand

Gandhi, Mahatma
See Gandhi, Mohandas Karamchand

Gandhi, Mohandas Karamchand
1869-1948 .... **TCLC 59; DAM MULT**
See also CA 121; 132; DA3; MTCW 1, 2

Gann, Ernest Kellogg 1910-1991 ..... **CLC 23**
See also AITN 1; CA 1-4R; 136; CANR 1,
83

Garber, Eric 1943(?)-
See Holleran, Andrew
See also CANR 89

Garcia, Cristina 1958- .... **CLC 76**
See also CA 141; CANR 73; HW 2

Gilliam, Terry (Vance) 1940- .... **CLC 21**
See also Monty Python
See also AAYA 19; CA 108; 113; CANR
35; INT 113

Gillian, Jerry
See Gilliam, Terry (Vance)

Gilliatt, Penelope (Ann Douglass)
1932-1993 .... **CLC 2, 10, 13, 53**
See also AITN 2; CA 13-16R; 141; CANR
49; DLB 14

Gilman, Charlotte (Anna) Perkins (Stetson)
1860-1935 .... **TCLC 9, 37; SSC 13**
See also CA 106; 150; DLB 221; MTCW 1

Gilmour, David 1949- .... **CLC 35**
See also CA 138, 147

Gilpin, William 1724-1804 .... **NCLC 30**

Gilray, J. D.
See Mencken, H(enry) L(ouis)

Gilroy, Frank D(aniel) 1925- .... **CLC 2**
See also CA 81-84; CANR 32, 64, 86; DLB
7

Gilstrap, John 1957(?)- .... **CLC 99**
See also CA 160

Ginsberg, Allen 1926-1997 .... **CLC 1, 2, 3, 4,**
6, 13, 36, 69, 109; DA; DAB; DAC;
DAM MST, POET; PC 4; WLC
See also AAYA 33; AITN 1; CA 1-4R; 157;
CANR 2, 41, 63; CDALB 1941-1968;
DA3; DLB 5, 16, 169; MTCW 1, 2

Ginzburg, Natalia 1916-1991 .... **CLC 5, 11,**
54, 70
See also CA 85-88; 135; CANR 33; DLB
177; MTCW 1, 2

Giono, Jean 1895-1970 .... **CLC 4, 11**
See also CA 45-48; 29-32R; CANR 2, 35;
DLB 72; MTCW 1

Giovanni, Nikki 1943- .... **CLC 2, 4, 19, 64,**
117; BLC 2; DA; DAB; DAC; DAM
MST, MULT, POET; PC 19; WLCS
See also AAYA 22; AITN 1; BW 2, 3; CA
29-32R; CAAS 6; CANR 18, 41, 60, 91;
CDALBS; CLR 6; DA3; DLB 5, 41; INT
CANR-18; MAICYA; MTCW 1, 2; SATA
24, 107

Giovene, Andrea 1904- .... **CLC 7**
See also CA 85-88

Gippius, Zinaida (Nikolayevna) 1869-1945
See Hippius, Zinaida
See also CA 106

Giraudoux, (Hippolyte) Jean
1882-1944 .... **TCLC 2, 7; DAM DRAM**
See also CA 104; DLB 65

Gironella, Jose Maria 1917- .... **CLC 11**
See also CA 101

Gissing, George (Robert)
1857-1903 .... **TCLC 3, 24, 47; SSC 37**
See also CA 105; 167; DLB 18, 135, 184

Giurlani, Aldo
See Palazzeschi, Aldo

Gladkov, Fyodor (Vasilyevich)
1883-1958 .... **TCLC 27**
See also CA 170

Glanville, Brian (Lester) 1931- .... **CLC 6**
See also CA 5-8R; CAAS 9; CANR 3, 70;
DLB 15, 139; SATA 42

Glasgow, Ellen (Anderson Gholson)
1873-1945 .... **TCLC 2, 7; SSC 34**
See also CA 104; 164; DLB 9, 12; MTCW
2

Glaspell, Susan 1882(?)-1948 . **TCLC 55; DC**
10; SSC 41
See also CA 110; 154; DLB 7, 9, 78, 228;
YABC 2

Glassco, John 1909-1981 .... **CLC 9**
See also CA 13-16R; 102; CANR 15; DLB
68

Glasscock, Amnesia
See Steinbeck, John (Ernst)

Glasser, Ronald J. 1940(?)- .... **CLC 37**

Glassman, Joyce
See Johnson, Joyce

Glendinning, Victoria 1937- .... **CLC 50**
See also CA 120; 127; CANR 59, 89; DLB
155

Glissant, Edouard 1928- . **CLC 10, 68; DAM**
MULT
See also CA 153

Gloag, Julian 1930- .... **CLC 40**
See also AITN 1; CA 65-68; CANR 10, 70

Glowacki, Aleksander
See Prus, Boleslaw

Gluck, Louise (Elisabeth) 1943- .. **CLC 7, 22,**
44, 81; DAM POET; PC 16
See also CA 33-36R; CANR 40, 69; DA3;
DLB 5; MTCW 2

Glyn, Elinor 1864-1943 .... **TCLC 72**
See also DLB 153

Gobineau, Joseph Arthur (Comte) de
1816-1882 .... **NCLC 17**
See also DLB 123

Godard, Jean-Luc 1930- .... **CLC 20**
See also CA 93-96

Godden, (Margaret) Rumer
1907-1998 .... **CLC 53**
See also AAYA 6; CA 5-8R; 172; CANR 4,
27, 36, 55, 80; CLR 20; DLB 161; MAI-
CYA; SAAS 12; SATA 3, 36; SATA-Obit
109

Godoy Alcayaga, Lucila 1889-1957
See Mistral, Gabriela
See also BW 2; CA 104; 131; CANR 81;
DAM MULT; HW 1, 2; MTCW 1, 2

Godwin, Gail (Kathleen) 1937- ..... **CLC 5, 8,**
22, 31, 69, 125; DAM POP
See also CA 29-32R; CANR 15, 43, 69;
DA3; DLB 6; INT CANR-15; MTCW 1,
2

Godwin, William 1756-1836 .... **NCLC 14**
See also CDBLB 1789-1832; DLB 39, 104,
142, 158, 163

Goebbels, Josef
See Goebbels, (Paul) Joseph

Goebbels, (Paul) Joseph
1897-1945 .... **TCLC 68**
See also CA 115; 148

Goebbels, Joseph Paul
See Goebbels, (Paul) Joseph

Goethe, Johann Wolfgang von
1749-1832 ...... **NCLC 4, 22, 34, 90; DA;**
DAB; DAC; DAM DRAM, MST,
POET; PC 5; SSC 38; WLC
See also DA3; DLB 94

Gogarty, Oliver St. John
1878-1957 .... **TCLC 15**
See also CA 109; 150; DLB 15, 19

Gogol, Nikolai (Vasilyevich)
1809-1852 . **NCLC 5, 15, 31; DA; DAB;**
DAC; DAM DRAM, MST; DC 1; SSC
4, 29; WLC
See also DLB 198

Goines, Donald 1937(?)-1974 . **CLC 80; BLC**
2; DAM MULT, POP
See also AITN 1; BW 1, 3; CA 124; 114;
CANR 82; DA3; DLB 33

Gold, Herbert 1924- .... **CLC 4, 7, 14, 42**
See also CA 9-12R; CANR 17, 45; DLB 2;
DLBY 81

Goldbarth, Albert 1948- .... **CLC 5, 38**
See also CA 53-56; CANR 6, 40; DLB 120

Goldberg, Anatol 1910-1982 .... **CLC 34**
See also CA 131; 117

Goldemberg, Isaac 1945- .... **CLC 52**
See also CA 69-72; CAAS 12; CANR 11,
32; HW 1

Golding, William (Gerald)
1911-1993 ..... **CLC 1, 2, 3, 8, 10, 17, 27,**
58, 81; DA; DAB; DAC; DAM MST,
NOV; WLC
See also AAYA 5; CA 5-8R; 141; CANR
13, 33, 54; CDBLB 1945-1960; DA3;
DLB 15, 100; MTCW 1, 2

Goldman, Emma 1869-1940 .... **TCLC 13**
See also CA 110; 150; DLB 221

Goldman, Francisco 1954- .... **CLC 76**
See also CA 162

Goldman, William (W.) 1931- ...... **CLC 1, 48**
See also CA 9-12R; CANR 29, 69; DLB 44

Goldmann, Lucien 1913-1970 .... **CLC 24**
See also CA 25-28; CAP 2

Goldoni, Carlo 1707-1793 .... **LC 4; DAM**
DRAM

Goldsberry, Steven 1949- .... **CLC 34**
See also CA 131

Goldsmith, Oliver 1728-1774 . **LC 2, 48; DA;**
DAB; DAC; DAM DRAM, MST, NOV,
POET; DC 8; WLC
See also CDBLB 1660-1789; DLB 39, 89,
104, 109, 142; SATA 26

Goldsmith, Peter
See Priestley, J(ohn) B(oynton)

Gombrowicz, Witold 1904-1969 .... **CLC 4, 7,**
11, 49; DAM DRAM
See also CA 19-20; 25-28R; CAP 2

Gomez de la Serna, Ramon
1888-1963 .... **CLC 9**
See also CA 153; 116; CANR 79; HW 1, 2

Goncharov, Ivan Alexandrovich
1812-1891 .... **NCLC 1, 63**

Goncourt, Edmond (Louis Antoine Huot) de
1822-1896 .... **NCLC 7**
See also DLB 123

Goncourt, Jules (Alfred Huot) de
1830-1870 .... **NCLC 7**
See also DLB 123

Gontier, Fernande 19(?)- .... **CLC 50**

Gonzalez Martinez, Enrique
1871-1952 .... **TCLC 72**
See also CA 166; CANR 81; HW 1, 2

Goodman, Paul 1911-1972 ... **CLC 1, 2, 4, 7**
See also CA 19-20; 37-40R; CANR 34;
CAP 2; DLB 130; MTCW 1

Gordimer, Nadine 1923- ...... **CLC 3, 5, 7, 10,**
18, 33, 51, 70, 123; DA; DAB; DAC;
DAM MST, NOV; SSC 17; WLCS
See also CA 5-8R; CANR 3, 28, 56, 88;
DA3; DLB 225; INT CANR-28; MTCW
1, 2

Gordon, Adam Lindsay
1833-1870 .... **NCLC 21**

Gordon, Caroline 1895-1981 . **CLC 6, 13, 29,**
83; SSC 15
See also CA 11-12; 103; CANR 36; CAP 1;
DLB 4, 9, 102; DLBD 17; DLBY 81;
MTCW 1, 2

Gordon, Charles William 1860-1937
See Connor, Ralph
See also CA 109

Gordon, Mary (Catherine) 1949- .... **CLC 13,**
22, 128
See also CA 102; CANR 44, 92; DLB 6;
DLBY 81; INT 102; MTCW 1

Gordon, N. J.
See Bosman, Herman Charles

Gordon, Sol 1923- .... **CLC 26**
See also CA 53-56; CANR 4; SATA 11

Gordone, Charles 1925-1995 .... **CLC 1, 4;**
DAM DRAM; DC 8
See also BW 1, 3; CA 93-96, 180; 150;
CAAE 180; CANR 55; DLB 7; INT 93-
96; MTCW 1

Gore, Catherine 1800-1861 .... **NCLC 65**
See also DLB 116

Griffith, D(avid Lewelyn) W(ark)
　　1875(?)-1948 .... **TCLC 68**
　　See also CA 119; 150; CANR 80
Griffith, Lawrence
　　See Griffith, D(avid Lewelyn) W(ark)
Griffiths, Trevor 1935- .... **CLC 13, 52**
　　See also CA 97-100; CANR 45; DLB 13
Griggs, Sutton (Elbert)
　　1872-1930 .... **TCLC 77**
　　See also CA 123; 186; DLB 50
Grigson, Geoffrey (Edward Harvey)
　　1905-1985 .... **CLC 7, 39**
　　See also CA 25-28R; 118; CANR 20, 33;
　　DLB 27; MTCW 1, 2
Grillparzer, Franz 1791-1872 .... **NCLC 1;**
　　SSC 37
　　See also DLB 133
Grimble, Reverend Charles James
　　See Eliot, T(homas) S(tearns)
Grimke, Charlotte L(ottie) Forten
　　1837(?)-1914
　　See Forten, Charlotte L.
　　See also BW 1; CA 117; 124; DAM MULT,
　　POET
Grimm, Jacob Ludwig Karl
　　1785-1863 .... **NCLC 3, 77; SSC 36**
　　See also DLB 90; MAICYA; SATA 22
Grimm, Wilhelm Karl 1786-1859 .. **NCLC 3,**
　　77; SSC 36
　　See also DLB 90; MAICYA; SATA 22
Grimmelshausen, Johann Jakob Christoffel
　　von 1621-1676 .... **LC 6**
　　See also DLB 168
Grindel, Eugene 1895-1952
　　See Eluard, Paul
　　See also CA 104
Grisham, John 1955- .... **CLC 84; DAM POP**
　　See also AAYA 14; CA 138; CANR 47, 69;
　　DA3; MTCW 2
Grossman, David 1954- .... **CLC 67**
　　See also CA 138
Grossman, Vasily (Semenovich)
　　1905-1964 .... **CLC 41**
　　See also CA 124; 130; MTCW 1
Grove, Frederick Philip TCLC 4
　　See also Greve, Felix Paul (Berthold
　　Friedrich)
　　See also DLB 92
Grubb
　　See Crumb, R(obert)
Grumbach, Doris (Isaac) 1918- . **CLC 13, 22,**
　　64
　　See also CA 5-8R; CAAS 2; CANR 9, 42,
　　70; INT CANR-9; MTCW 2
Grundtvig, Nicolai Frederik Severin
　　1783-1872 .... **NCLC 1**
Grunge
　　See Crumb, R(obert)
Grunwald, Lisa 1959- .... **CLC 44**
　　See also CA 120
Guare, John 1938- .... **CLC 8, 14, 29, 67;**
　　DAM DRAM
　　See also CA 73-76; CANR 21, 69; DLB 7;
　　MTCW 1, 2
Gudjonsson, Halldor Kiljan 1902-1998
　　See Laxness, Halldor
　　See also CA 103; 164
Guenter, Erich
　　See Eich, Guenter
Guest, Barbara 1920- .... **CLC 34**
　　See also CA 25-28R; CANR 11, 44, 84;
　　DLB 5, 193
Guest, Edgar A(lbert) 1881-1959 ... **TCLC 95**
　　See also CA 112; 168
Guest, Judith (Ann) 1936- .... **CLC 8, 30;**
　　DAM NOV, POP
　　See also AAYA 7; CA 77-80; CANR 15,
　　75; DA3; INT CANR-15; MTCW 1, 2

Guevara, Che CLC 87; HLC 1
　　See also Guevara (Serna), Ernesto
Guevara (Serna), Ernesto
　　1928-1967 .... **CLC 87; DAM MULT;**
　　HLC 1
　　See also Guevara, Che
　　See also CA 127; 111; CANR 56; HW 1
Guicciardini, Francesco 1483-1540 ..... **LC 49**
Guild, Nicholas M. 1944- .... **CLC 33**
　　See also CA 93-96
Guillemin, Jacques
　　See Sartre, Jean-Paul
Guillen, Jorge 1893-1984 .... **CLC 11; DAM**
　　MULT, POET; HLCS 1
　　See also CA 89-92; 112; DLB 108; HW 1
Guillen, Nicolas (Cristobal)
　　1902-1989 ... **CLC 48, 79; BLC 2; DAM**
　　MST, MULT, POET; HLC 1; PC 23
　　See also BW 2; CA 116; 125; 129; CANR
　　84; HW 1
Guillevic, (Eugene) 1907- .... **CLC 33**
　　See also CA 93-96
Guillois
　　See Desnos, Robert
Guillois, Valentin
　　See Desnos, Robert
Guimaraes Rosa, Joao 1908-1967
　　See also CA 175; HLCS 2
Guiney, Louise Imogen
　　1861-1920 .... **TCLC 41**
　　See also CA 160; DLB 54
Guiraldes, Ricardo (Guillermo)
　　1886-1927 .... **TCLC 39**
　　See also CA 131; HW 1; MTCW 1
Gumilev, Nikolai (Stepanovich)
　　1886-1921 .... **TCLC 60**
　　See also CA 165
Gunesekera, Romesh 1954- .... **CLC 91**
　　See also CA 159
Gunn, Bill CLC 5
　　See also Gunn, William Harrison
　　See also DLB 38
Gunn, Thom(son William) 1929- .. **CLC 3, 6,**
　　18, 32, 81; DAM POET; PC 26
　　See also CA 17-20R; CANR 9, 33; CDBLB
　　1960 to Present; DLB 27; INT CANR-33;
　　MTCW 1
Gunn, William Harrison 1934(?)-1989
　　See Gunn, Bill
　　See also AITN 1; BW 1, 3; CA 13-16R;
　　128; CANR 12, 25, 76
Gunnars, Kristjana 1948- .... **CLC 69**
　　See also CA 113; DLB 60
Gurdjieff, G(eorgei) I(vanovich)
　　1877(?)-1949 .... **TCLC 71**
　　See also CA 157
Gurganus, Allan 1947- . **CLC 70; DAM POP**
　　See also BEST 90:1; CA 135
Gurney, A(lbert) R(amsdell), Jr.
　　1930- ..... **CLC 32, 50, 54; DAM DRAM**
　　See also CA 77-80; CANR 32, 64
Gurney, Ivor (Bertie) 1890-1937 ... **TCLC 33**
　　See also CA 167
Gurney, Peter
　　See Gurney, A(lbert) R(amsdell), Jr.
Guro, Elena 1877-1913 .... **TCLC 56**
Gustafson, James M(oody) 1925- ... **CLC 100**
　　See also CA 25-28R; CANR 37
Gustafson, Ralph (Barker) 1909- ..... **CLC 36**
　　See also CA 21-24R; CANR 8, 45, 84; DLB
　　88
Gut, Gom
　　See Simenon, Georges (Jacques Christian)
Guterson, David 1956- .... **CLC 91**
　　See also CA 132; CANR 73; MTCW 2

Guthrie, A(lfred) B(ertram), Jr.
　　1901-1991 .... **CLC 23**
　　See also CA 57-60; 134; CANR 24; DLB
　　212; SATA 62; SATA-Obit 67
Guthrie, Isobel
　　See Grieve, C(hristopher) M(urray)
Guthrie, Woodrow Wilson 1912-1967
　　See Guthrie, Woody
　　See also CA 113; 93-96
Guthrie, Woody CLC 35
　　See also Guthrie, Woodrow Wilson
Gutierrez Najera, Manuel 1859-1895
　　See also HLCS 2
Guy, Rosa (Cuthbert) 1928- .... **CLC 26**
　　See also AAYA 4; BW 2; CA 17-20R;
　　CANR 14, 34, 83; CLR 13; DLB 33;
　　JRDA; MAICYA; SATA 14, 62
Gwendolyn
　　See Bennett, (Enoch) Arnold
H. D. CLC 3, 8, 14, 31, 34, 73; PC 5
　　See also Doolittle, Hilda
H. de V.
　　See Buchan, John
Haavikko, Paavo Juhani 1931- .. **CLC 18, 34**
　　See also CA 106
Habbema, Koos
　　See Heijermans, Herman
Habermas, Juergen 1929- .... **CLC 104**
　　See also CA 109; CANR 85
Habermas, Jurgen
　　See Habermas, Juergen
Hacker, Marilyn 1942- ...... **CLC 5, 9, 23, 72,**
　　91; DAM POET
　　See also CA 77-80; CANR 68; DLB 120
Haeckel, Ernst Heinrich (Philipp August)
　　1834-1919 .... **TCLC 83**
　　See also CA 157
Hafiz c. 1326-1389 .... **CMLC 34**
Hafiz c. 1326-1389(?) .... **CMLC 34**
Haggard, H(enry) Rider
　　1856-1925 .... **TCLC 11**
　　See also CA 108; 148; DLB 70, 156, 174,
　　178; MTCW 2; SATA 16
Hagiosy, L.
　　See Larbaud, Valery (Nicolas)
Hagiwara Sakutaro 1886-1942 ..... **TCLC 60;**
　　PC 18
Haig, Fenil
　　See Ford, Ford Madox
Haig-Brown, Roderick (Langmere)
　　1908-1976 .... **CLC 21**
　　See also CA 5-8R; 69-72; CANR 4, 38, 83;
　　CLR 31; DLB 88; MAICYA; SATA 12
Hailey, Arthur 1920- ..... **CLC 5; DAM NOV,**
　　POP
　　See also AITN 2; BEST 90:3; CA 1-4R;
　　CANR 2, 36, 75; DLB 88; DLBY 82;
　　MTCW 1, 2
Hailey, Elizabeth Forsythe 1938- ..... **CLC 40**
　　See also CA 93-96; CAAS 1; CANR 15,
　　48; INT CANR-15
Haines, John (Meade) 1924- .... **CLC 58**
　　See also CA 17-20R; CANR 13, 34; DLB
　　212
Hakluyt, Richard 1552-1616 .... **LC 31**
Haldeman, Joe (William) 1943- .... **CLC 61**
　　See also Graham, Robert
　　See also CA 53-56, 179; CAAE 179; CAAS
　　25; CANR 6, 70, 72; DLB 8; INT
　　CANR-6
Hale, Sarah Josepha (Buell)
　　1788-1879 .... **NCLC 75**
　　See also DLB 1, 42, 73
Haley, Alex(ander Murray Palmer)
　　1921-1992 . **CLC 8, 12, 76; BLC 2; DA;**
　　DAB; DAC; DAM MST, MULT, POP
　　See also AAYA 26; BW 2, 3; CA 77-80;
　　136; CANR 61; CDALBS; DA3; DLB 38;
　　MTCW 1, 2

Hasek, Jaroslav (Matej Frantisek)
    1883-1923 .... **TCLC 4**
    See also CA 104; 129; MTCW 1, 2
Hass, Robert 1941- ... **CLC 18, 39, 99; PC 16**
    See also CA 111; CANR 30, 50, 71; DLB
    105, 206; SATA 94
Hastings, Hudson
    See Kuttner, Henry
Hastings, Selina CLC 44
Hathorne, John 1641-1717 .... **LC 38**
Hatteras, Amelia
    See Mencken, H(enry) L(ouis)
Hatteras, Owen TCLC 18
    See also Mencken, H(enry) L(ouis); Nathan,
    George Jean
Hauptmann, Gerhart (Johann Robert)
    1862-1946 .... **TCLC 4; DAM DRAM;**
    SSC 37
    See also CA 104; 153; DLB 66, 118
Havel, Vaclav 1936- ..... **CLC 25, 58, 65, 123;**
    DAM DRAM; DC 6
    See also CA 104; CANR 36, 63; DA3;
    MTCW 1, 2
Haviaras, Stratis CLC 33
    See also Chaviaras, Strates
Hawes, Stephen 1475(?)-1523(?) .... **LC 17**
    See also DLB 132
Hawkes, John (Clendennin Burne, Jr.)
    1925-1998 .. **CLC 1, 2, 3, 4, 7, 9, 14, 15,**
    27, 49
    See also CA 1-4R; 167; CANR 2, 47, 64;
    DLB 2, 7, 227; DLBY 80, 98; MTCW 1,
    2
Hawking, S. W.
    See Hawking, Stephen W(illiam)
Hawking, Stephen W(illiam) 1942- . **CLC 63,**
    105
    See also AAYA 13; BEST 89:1; CA 126;
    129; CANR 48; DA3; MTCW 2
Hawkins, Anthony Hope
    See Hope, Anthony
Hawthorne, Julian 1846-1934 .... **TCLC 25**
    See also CA 165
Hawthorne, Nathaniel 1804-1864 . **NCLC 39;**
    DA; DAB; DAC; DAM MST, NOV;
    SSC 3, 29, 39; WLC
    See also AAYA 18; CDALB 1640-1865;
    DA3; DLB 1, 74, 223; YABC 2
Haxton, Josephine Ayres 1921-
    See Douglas, Ellen
    See also CA 115; CANR 41, 83
Hayaseca y Eizaguirre, Jorge
    See Echegaray (y Eizaguirre), Jose (Maria
    Waldo)
Hayashi, Fumiko 1904-1951 .... **TCLC 27**
    See also CA 161; DLB 180
Haycraft, Anna (Margaret) 1932-
    See Ellis, Alice Thomas
    See also CA 122; CANR 85, 90; MTCW 2
Hayden, Robert E(arl) 1913-1980 . **CLC 5, 9,**
    14, 37; BLC 2; DA; DAC; DAM MST,
    MULT, POET; PC 6
    See also BW 1, 3; CA 69-72; 97-100; CABS
    2; CANR 24, 75, 82; CDALB 1941-1968;
    DLB 5, 76; MTCW 1, 2; SATA 19; SATA-
    Obit 26
Hayford, J(oseph) E(phraim) Casely
    See Casely-Hayford, J(oseph) E(phraim)
Hayman, Ronald 1932- .... **CLC 44**
    See also CA 25-28R; CANR 18, 50, 88;
    DLB 155
Haywood, Eliza (Fowler)
    1693(?)-1756 .... **LC 1, 44**
    See also DLB 39
Hazlitt, William 1778-1830 ...... **NCLC 29, 82**
    See also DLB 110, 158
Hazzard, Shirley 1931- .... **CLC 18**
    See also CA 9-12R; CANR 4, 70; DLBY
    82; MTCW 1

Head, Bessie 1937-1986 .... **CLC 25, 67; BLC**
    2; DAM MULT
    See also BW 2, 3; CA 29-32R; 119; CANR
    25, 82; DA3; DLB 117, 225; MTCW 1, 2
Headon, (Nicky) Topper 1956(?)- ..... **CLC 30**
Heaney, Seamus (Justin) 1939- ..... **CLC 5, 7,**
    14, 25, 37, 74, 91; DAB; DAM POET;
    PC 18; WLCS
    See also CA 85-88; CANR 25, 48, 75, 91;
    CDBLB 1960 to Present; DA3; DLB 40;
    DLBY 95; MTCW 1, 2
Hearn, (Patricio) Lafcadio (Tessima Carlos)
    1850-1904 .... **TCLC 9**
    See also CA 105; 166; DLB 12, 78, 189
Hearne, Vicki 1946- .... **CLC 56**
    See also CA 139
Hearon, Shelby 1931- .... **CLC 63**
    See also AITN 2; CA 25-28R; CANR 18,
    48
Heat-Moon, William Least CLC 29
    See also Trogdon, William (Lewis)
    See also AAYA 9
Hebbel, Friedrich 1813-1863 .... **NCLC 43;**
    DAM DRAM
    See also DLB 129
Hebert, Anne 1916-2000 .... **CLC 4, 13, 29;**
    DAC; DAM MST, POET
    See also CA 85-88; CANR 69; DA3; DLB
    68; MTCW 1, 2
Hecht, Anthony (Evan) 1923- ...... **CLC 8, 13,**
    19; DAM POET
    See also CA 9-12R; CANR 6; DLB 5, 169
Hecht, Ben 1894-1964 .... **CLC 8**
    See also CA 85-88; DLB 7, 9, 25, 26, 28,
    86; TCLC 101
Hedayat, Sadeq 1903-1951 .... **TCLC 21**
    See also CA 120
Hegel, Georg Wilhelm Friedrich
    1770-1831 .... **NCLC 46**
    See also DLB 90
Heidegger, Martin 1889-1976 .... **CLC 24**
    See also CA 81-84; 65-68; CANR 34;
    MTCW 1, 2
Heidenstam, (Carl Gustaf) Verner von
    1859-1940 .... **TCLC 5**
    See also CA 104
Heifner, Jack 1946- .... **CLC 11**
    See also CA 105; CANR 47
Heijermans, Herman 1864-1924 .... **TCLC 24**
    See also CA 123
Heilbrun, Carolyn G(old) 1926- .... **CLC 25**
    See also CA 45-48; CANR 1, 28, 58
Heine, Heinrich 1797-1856 .... **NCLC 4, 54;**
    PC 25
    See also DLB 90
Heinemann, Larry (Curtiss) 1944- .. **CLC 50**
    See also CA 110; CAAS 21; CANR 31, 81;
    DLBD 9; INT CANR-31
Heiney, Donald (William) 1921-1993
    See Harris, MacDonald
    See also CA 1-4R; 142; CANR 3, 58
Heinlein, Robert A(nson) 1907-1988 . **CLC 1,**
    3, 8, 14, 26, 55; DAM POP
    See also AAYA 17; CA 1-4R; 125; CANR
    1, 20, 53; DA3; DLB 8; JRDA; MAICYA;
    MTCW 1, 2; SATA 9, 69; SATA-Obit 56
Helforth, John
    See Doolittle, Hilda
Hellenhofferu, Vojtech Kapristian z
    See Hasek, Jaroslav (Matej Frantisek)
Heller, Joseph 1923-1999 . **CLC 1, 3, 5, 8, 11,**
    36, 63; DA; DAB; DAC; DAM MST,
    NOV, POP; WLC
    See also AAYA 24; AITN 1; CA 5-8R;
    CABS 1; CANR 8, 42, 66; DA3; DLB 2,
    28, 227; DLBY 80; INT CANR-8; MTCW
    1, 2

Hellman, Lillian (Florence)
    1906-1984 .. **CLC 2, 4, 8, 14, 18, 34, 44,**
    52; DAM DRAM; DC 1
    See also AITN 1, 2; CA 13-16R; 112;
    CANR 33; DA3; DLB 7, 228; DLBY 84;
    MTCW 1, 2
Helprin, Mark 1947- .... **CLC 7, 10, 22, 32;**
    DAM NOV, POP
    See also CA 81-84; CANR 47, 64;
    CDALBS; DA3; DLBY 85; MTCW 1, 2
Helvetius, Claude-Adrien 1715-1771 .. **LC 26**
Helyar, Jane Penelope Josephine 1933-
    See Poole, Josephine
    See also CA 21-24R; CANR 10, 26; SATA
    82
Hemans, Felicia 1793-1835 .... **NCLC 71**
    See also DLB 96
Hemingway, Ernest (Miller)
    1899-1961 .... **CLC 1, 3, 6, 8, 10, 13, 19,**
    30, 34, 39, 41, 44, 50, 61, 80; DA;
    DAB; DAC; DAM MST, NOV; SSC 1,
    25, 36, 40; WLC
    See also AAYA 19; CA 77-80; CANR 34;
    CDALB 1917-1929; DA3; DLB 4, 9, 102,
    210; DLBD 1, 15, 16; DLBY 81, 87, 96,
    98; MTCW 1, 2
Hempel, Amy 1951- .... **CLC 39**
    See also CA 118; 137; CANR 70; DA3;
    MTCW 2
Henderson, F. C.
    See Mencken, H(enry) L(ouis)
Henderson, Sylvia
    See Ashton-Warner, Sylvia (Constance)
Henderson, Zenna (Chlarson)
    1917-1983 .... **SSC 29**
    See also CA 1-4R; 133; CANR 1, 84; DLB
    8; SATA 5
Henkin, Joshua CLC 119
    See also CA 161
Henley, Beth CLC 23; DC 6
    See also Henley, Elizabeth Becker
    See also CABS 3; DLBY 86
Henley, Elizabeth Becker 1952-
    See Henley, Beth
    See also CA 107; CANR 32, 73; DAM
    DRAM, MST; DA3; MTCW 1, 2
Henley, William Ernest 1849-1903 .. **TCLC 8**
    See also CA 105; DLB 19
Hennissart, Martha
    See Lathen, Emma
    See also CA 85-88; CANR 64
Henry, O. TCLC 1, 19; SSC 5; WLC
    See also Porter, William Sydney
Henry, Patrick 1736-1799 .... **LC 25**
Henryson, Robert 1430(?)-1506(?) ...... **LC 20**
    See also DLB 146
Henry VIII 1491-1547 .... **LC 10**
    See also DLB 132
Henschke, Alfred
    See Klabund
Hentoff, Nat(han Irving) 1925- .... **CLC 26**
    See also AAYA 4; CA 1-4R; CAAS 6;
    CANR 5, 25, 77; CLR 1, 52; INT CANR-
    25; JRDA; MAICYA; SATA 42, 69;
    SATA-Brief 27
Heppenstall, (John) Rayner
    1911-1981 .... **CLC 10**
    See also CA 1-4R; 103; CANR 29
Heraclitus c. 540B.C.-c. 450B.C. ... **CMLC 22**
    See also DLB 176
Herbert, Frank (Patrick)
    1920-1986 .... **CLC 12, 23, 35, 44, 85;**
    DAM POP
    See also AAYA 21; CA 53-56; 118; CANR
    5, 43; CDALBS; DLB 8; INT CANR-5;
    MTCW 1, 2; SATA 9, 37; SATA-Obit 47
Herbert, George 1593-1633 ..... **LC 24; DAB;**
    DAM POET; PC 4
    See also CDBLB Before 1660; DLB 126

Herbert, Zbigniew 1924-1998 ..... **CLC 9, 43;**
DAM POET
See also CA 89-92; 169; CANR 36, 74;
MTCW 1
Herbst, Josephine (Frey)
1897-1969 .... **CLC 34**
See also CA 5-8R; 25-28R; DLB 9
Heredia, Jose Maria 1803-1839
See also HLCS 2
Hergesheimer, Joseph 1880-1954 ... **TCLC 11**
See also CA 109; DLB 102, 9
Herlihy, James Leo 1927-1993 .... **CLC 6**
See also CA 1-4R; 143; CANR 2
Hermogenes fl. c. 175- .... **CMLC 6**
Hernandez, Jose 1834-1886 .... **NCLC 17**
Herodotus c. 484B.C.-429B.C. .... **CMLC 17**
See also DLB 176
Herrick, Robert 1591-1674 .... **LC 13; DA;**
DAB; DAC; DAM MST, POP; PC 9
See also DLB 126
Herring, Guilles
See Somerville, Edith
Herriot, James 1916-1995 ..... **CLC 12; DAM**
POP
See also Wight, James Alfred
See also AAYA 1; CA 148; CANR 40;
MTCW 2; SATA 86
Herris, Violet
See Hunt, Violet
Herrmann, Dorothy 1941- .... **CLC 44**
See also CA 107
Herrmann, Taffy
See Herrmann, Dorothy
Hersey, John (Richard) 1914-1993 .... **CLC 1,**
2, 7, 9, 40, 81, 97; DAM POP
See also AAYA 29; CA 17-20R; 140; CANR
33; CDALBS; DLB 6, 185; MTCW 1, 2;
SATA 25; SATA-Obit 76
Herzen, Aleksandr Ivanovich
1812-1870 .... **NCLC 10, 61**
Herzl, Theodor 1860-1904 .... **TCLC 36**
See also CA 168
Herzog, Werner 1942- .... **CLC 16**
See also CA 89-92
Hesiod c. 8th cent. B.C.- .... **CMLC 5**
See also DLB 176
Hesse, Hermann 1877-1962 ... **CLC 1, 2, 3, 6,**
11, 17, 25, 69; DA; DAB; DAC; DAM
MST, NOV; SSC 9; WLC
See also CA 17-18; CAP 2; DA3; DLB 66;
MTCW 1, 2; SATA 50
Hewes, Cady
See De Voto, Bernard (Augustine)
Heyen, William 1940- .... **CLC 13, 18**
See also CA 33-36R; CAAS 9; DLB 5
Heyerdahl, Thor 1914- .... **CLC 26**
See also CA 5-8R; CANR 5, 22, 66, 73;
MTCW 1, 2; SATA 2, 52
Heym, Georg (Theodor Franz Arthur)
1887-1912 .... **TCLC 9**
See also CA 106; 181
Heym, Stefan 1913- .... **CLC 41**
See also CA 9-12R; CANR 4; DLB 69
Heyse, Paul (Johann Ludwig von)
1830-1914 .... **TCLC 8**
See also CA 104; DLB 129
Heyward, (Edwin) DuBose
1885-1940 .... **TCLC 59**
See also CA 108; 157; DLB 7, 9, 45; SATA
21
Hibbert, Eleanor Alice Burford
1906-1993 .... **CLC 7; DAM POP**
See also BEST 90:4; CA 17-20R; 140;
CANR 9, 28, 59; MTCW 2; SATA 2;
SATA-Obit 74
Hichens, Robert (Smythe)
1864-1950 .... **TCLC 64**
See also CA 162; DLB 153

Higgins, George V(incent)
1939-1999 .... **CLC 4, 7, 10, 18**
See also CA 77-80; 186; CAAS 5; CANR
17, 51, 89; DLB 2; DLBY 81, 98; INT
CANR-17; MTCW 1
Higginson, Thomas Wentworth
1823-1911 .... **TCLC 36**
See also CA 162; DLB 1, 64
Highet, Helen
See MacInnes, Helen (Clark)
Highsmith, (Mary) Patricia
1921-1995 .... **CLC 2, 4, 14, 42, 102;**
DAM NOV, POP
See also CA 1-4R; 147; CANR 1, 20, 48,
62; DA3; MTCW 1, 2
Highwater, Jamake (Mamake)
1942(?)- .... **CLC 12**
See also AAYA 7; CA 65-68; CAAS 7;
CANR 10, 34, 84; CLR 17; DLB 52;
DLBY 85; JRDA; MAICYA; SATA 32,
69; SATA-Brief 30
Highway, Tomson 1951- .... **CLC 92; DAC;**
DAM MULT
See also CA 151; CANR 75; MTCW 2;
NNAL
Higuchi, Ichiyo 1872-1896 .... **NCLC 49**
Hijuelos, Oscar 1951- .... **CLC 65; DAM**
MULT, POP; HLC 1
See also BEST 90:1; CA 123;
CANR 50, 75; DA3; DLB 145; HW 1, 2;
MTCW 2
Hikmet, Nazim 1902(?)-1963 .... **CLC 40**
See also CA 141; 93-96
Hildegard von Bingen 1098-1179 . **CMLC 20**
See also DLB 148
Hildesheimer, Wolfgang 1916-1991 .. **CLC 49**
See also CA 101; 135; DLB 69, 124
Hill, Geoffrey (William) 1932- ...... **CLC 5, 8,**
18, 45; DAM POET
See also CA 81-84; CANR 21, 89; CDBLB
1960 to Present; DLB 40; MTCW 1
Hill, George Roy 1921- .... **CLC 26**
See also CA 110; 122
Hill, John
See Koontz, Dean R(ay)
Hill, Susan (Elizabeth) 1942- .... **CLC 4, 113;**
DAB; DAM MST, NOV
See also CA 33-36R; CANR 29, 69; DLB
14, 139; MTCW 1
Hillerman, Tony 1925- . **CLC 62; DAM POP**
See also AAYA 6; BEST 89:1; CA 29-32R;
CANR 21, 42, 65; DA3; DLB 206; SATA
6
Hillesum, Etty 1914-1943 .... **TCLC 49**
See also CA 137
Hilliard, Noel (Harvey) 1929- .... **CLC 15**
See also CA 9-12R; CANR 7, 69
Hillis, Rick 1956- .... **CLC 66**
See also CA 134
Hilton, James 1900-1954 .... **TCLC 21**
See also CA 108; 169; DLB 34, 77; SATA
34
Himes, Chester (Bomar) 1909-1984 .. **CLC 2,**
4, 7, 18, 58, 108; BLC 2; DAM MULT
See also BW 2; CA 25-28R; 114; CANR
22, 89; DLB 2, 76, 143, 226; MTCW 1, 2
Hinde, Thomas **CLC 6, 11**
See also Chitty, Thomas Willes
Hine, (William) Daryl 1936- .... **CLC 15**
See also CA 1-4R; CAAS 15; CANR 1, 20;
DLB 60
Hinkson, Katharine Tynan
See Tynan, Katharine
Hinojosa(-Smith), Rolando (R.) 1929-
See also CA 131; CAAS 16; CANR 62;
DAM MULT; DLB 82; HLC 1; HW 1, 2;
MTCW 2

Hinton, S(usan) E(loise) 1950- .... **CLC 30,**
111; DA; DAB; DAC; DAM MST,
NOV
See also AAYA 2, 33; CA 81-84; CANR
32, 62, 92; CDALBS; CLR 3, 23; DA3;
JRDA; MAICYA; MTCW 1, 2; SATA 19,
58, 115
Hippius, Zinaida **TCLC 9**
See also Gippius, Zinaida (Nikolayevna)
Hiraoka, Kimitake 1925-1970
See Mishima, Yukio
See also CA 97-100; 29-32R; DAM DRAM;
DA3; MTCW 1, 2
Hirsch, E(ric) D(onald), Jr. 1928- .... **CLC 79**
See also CA 25-28R; CANR 27, 51; DLB
67; INT CANR-27; MTCW 1
Hirsch, Edward 1950- .... **CLC 31, 50**
See also CA 104; CANR 20, 42; DLB 120
Hitchcock, Alfred (Joseph)
1899-1980 .... **CLC 16**
See also AAYA 22; CA 159; 97-100; SATA
27; SATA-Obit 24
Hitler, Adolf 1889-1945 .... **TCLC 53**
See also CA 117; 147
Hoagland, Edward 1932- .... **CLC 28**
See also CA 1-4R; CANR 2, 31, 57; DLB
6; SATA 51
Hoban, Russell (Conwell) 1925- . **CLC 7, 25;**
DAM NOV
See also CA 5-8R; CANR 23, 37, 66; CLR
3; DLB 52; MAICYA; MTCW 1, 2; SATA
1, 40, 78
Hobbes, Thomas 1588-1679 .... **LC 36**
See also DLB 151
Hobbs, Perry
See Blackmur, R(ichard) P(almer)
Hobson, Laura Z(ametkin)
1900-1986 .... **CLC 7, 25**
See also CA 17-20R; 118; CANR 55; DLB
28; SATA 52
Hoch, Edward D(entinger) 1930-
See Queen, Ellery
See also CA 29-32R; CANR 11, 27, 51
Hochhuth, Rolf 1931- .. **CLC 4, 11, 18; DAM**
DRAM
See also CA 5-8R; CANR 33, 75; DLB 124;
MTCW 1, 2
Hochman, Sandra 1936- .... **CLC 3, 8**
See also CA 5-8R; DLB 5
Hochwaelder, Fritz 1911-1986 .... **CLC 36;**
DAM DRAM
See also CA 29-32R; 120; CANR 42;
MTCW 1
Hochwalder, Fritz
See Hochwaelder, Fritz
Hocking, Mary (Eunice) 1921- .... **CLC 13**
See also CA 101; CANR 18, 40
Hodgins, Jack 1938- .... **CLC 23**
See also CA 93-96; DLB 60
Hodgson, William Hope
1877(?)-1918 .... **TCLC 13**
See also CA 111; 164; DLB 70, 153, 156,
178; MTCW 2
Hoeg, Peter 1957- .... **CLC 95**
See also CA 151; CANR 75; DA3; MTCW
2
Hoffman, Alice 1952- ... **CLC 51; DAM NOV**
See also CA 77-80; CANR 34, 66; MTCW
1, 2
Hoffman, Daniel (Gerard) 1923- . **CLC 6, 13,**
23
See also CA 1-4R; CANR 4; DLB 5
Hoffman, Stanley 1944- .... **CLC 5**
See also CA 77-80
Hoffman, William M(oses) 1939- ..... **CLC 40**
See also CA 57-60; CANR 11, 71
Hoffmann, E(rnst) T(heodor) A(madeus)
1776-1822 .... **NCLC 2; SSC 13**
See also DLB 90; SATA 27

Hofmann, Gert 1931- .... CLC 54
    See also CA 128
Hofmannsthal, Hugo von
    1874-1929 ...... TCLC 11; DAM DRAM;
    DC 4
    See also CA 106; 153; DLB 81, 118
Hogan, Linda 1947- .. CLC 73; DAM MULT
    See also CA 120; CANR 45, 73; DLB 175;
    NNAL
Hogarth, Charles
    See Creasey, John
Hogarth, Emmett
    See Polonsky, Abraham (Lincoln)
Hogg, James 1770-1835 .... NCLC 4
    See also DLB 93, 116, 159
Holbach, Paul Henri Thiry Baron
    1723-1789 .... LC 14
Holberg, Ludvig 1684-1754 .... LC 6
Holcroft, Thomas 1745-1809 .... NCLC 85
    See also DLB 39, 89, 158
Holden, Ursula 1921- .... CLC 18
    See also CA 101; CAAS 8; CANR 22
Holderlin, (Johann Christian) Friedrich
    1770-1843 .... NCLC 16; PC 4
Holdstock, Robert
    See Holdstock, Robert P.
Holdstock, Robert P. 1948- .... CLC 39
    See also CA 131; CANR 81
Holland, Isabelle 1920- .... CLC 21
    See also AAYA 11; CA 21-24R, 181; CAAE
    181; CANR 10, 25, 47; CLR 57; JRDA;
    MAICYA; SATA 8, 70; SATA-Essay 103
Holland, Marcus
    See Caldwell, (Janet Miriam) Taylor
    (Holland)
Hollander, John 1929- .... CLC 2, 5, 8, 14
    See also CA 1-4R; CANR 1, 52; DLB 5;
    SATA 13
Hollander, Paul
    See Silverberg, Robert
Holleran, Andrew 1943(?)- .... CLC 38
    See also Garber, Eric
    See also CA 144
Holley, Marietta 1836(?)-1926 .... TCLC 99
    See also CA 118; DLB 11
Hollinghurst, Alan 1954- .... CLC 55, 91
    See also CA 114; DLB 207
Hollis, Jim
    See Summers, Hollis (Spurgeon, Jr.)
Holly, Buddy 1936-1959 .... TCLC 65
Holmes, Gordon
    See Shiel, M(atthew) P(hipps)
Holmes, John
    See Souster, (Holmes) Raymond
Holmes, John Clellon 1926-1988 ...... CLC 56
    See also CA 9-12R; 125; CANR 4; DLB 16
Holmes, Oliver Wendell, Jr.
    1841-1935 .... TCLC 77
    See also CA 114; 186
Holmes, Oliver Wendell
    1809-1894 .... NCLC 14, 81
    See also CDALB 1640-1865; DLB 1, 189;
    SATA 34
Holmes, Raymond
    See Souster, (Holmes) Raymond
Holt, Victoria
    See Hibbert, Eleanor Alice Burford
Holub, Miroslav 1923-1998 .... CLC 4
    See also CA 21-24R; 169; CANR 10
Homer c. 8th cent. B.C.- .. CMLC 1, 16; DA;
    DAB; DAC; DAM MST, POET; PC
    23; WLCS
    See also DA3; DLB 176
Hongo, Garrett Kaoru 1951- .... PC 23
    See also CA 133; CAAS 22; DLB 120
Honig, Edwin 1919- .... CLC 33
    See also CA 5-8R; CAAS 8; CANR 4, 45;
    DLB 5

Hood, Hugh (John Blagdon) 1928- . CLC 15,
    28
    See also CA 49-52; CAAS 17; CANR 1,
    33, 87; DLB 53
Hood, Thomas 1799-1845 .... NCLC 16
    See also DLB 96
Hooker, (Peter) Jeremy 1941- .... CLC 43
    See also CA 77-80; CANR 22; DLB 40
hooks, bell CLC 94; BLCS
    See also Watkins, Gloria Jean
    See also MTCW 2
Hope, A(lec) D(erwent) 1907- .... CLC 3, 51
    See also CA 21-24R; CANR 33, 74; MTCW
    1, 2
Hope, Anthony 1863-1933 .... TCLC 83
    See also CA 157; DLB 153, 156
Hope, Brian
    See Creasey, John
Hope, Christopher (David Tully)
    1944- .... CLC 52
    See also CA 106; CANR 47; DLB 225;
    SATA 62
Hopkins, Gerard Manley
    1844-1889 .... NCLC 17; DA; DAB;
    DAC; DAM MST, POET; PC 15; WLC
    See also CDBLB 1890-1914; DA3; DLB
    35, 57
Hopkins, John (Richard) 1931-1998 .. CLC 4
    See also CA 85-88; 169
Hopkins, Pauline Elizabeth
    1859-1930 ...... TCLC 28; BLC 2; DAM
    MULT
    See also BW 2, 3; CA 141; CANR 82; DLB
    50
Hopkinson, Francis 1737-1791 .... LC 25
    See also DLB 31
Hopley-Woolrich, Cornell George 1903-1968
    See Woolrich, Cornell
    See also CA 13-14; CANR 58; CAP 1; DLB
    226; MTCW 2
Horace 65B.C.-8B.C. .... CMLC 39
    See also DLB 211
Horatio
    See Proust, (Valentin-Louis-George-
    Eugene-) Marcel
Horgan, Paul (George Vincent
    O'Shaughnessy) 1903-1995 . CLC 9, 53;
    DAM NOV
    See also CA 13-16R; 147; CANR 9, 35;
    DLB 212; DLBY 85; INT CANR-9;
    MTCW 1, 2; SATA 13; SATA-Obit 84
Horn, Peter
    See Kuttner, Henry
Hornem, Horace Esq.
    See Byron, George Gordon (Noel)
Horney, Karen (Clementine Theodore
    Danielsen) 1885-1952 .... TCLC 71
    See also CA 114; 165
Hornung, E(rnest) W(illiam)
    1866-1921 .... TCLC 59
    See also CA 108; 160; DLB 70
Horovitz, Israel (Arthur) 1939- ...... CLC 56;
    DAM DRAM
    See also CA 33-36R; CANR 46, 59; DLB 7
Horton, George Moses
    1797(?)-1883(?) .... NCLC 87
    See also DLB 50
Horvath, Odon von
    See Horvath, Oedoen von
    See also DLB 85, 124
Horvath, Oedoen von 1901-1938 ... TCLC 45
    See also Horvath, Odon von; von Horvath,
    Oedoen
    See also CA 118
Horwitz, Julius 1920-1986 .... CLC 14
    See also CA 9-12R; 119; CANR 12
Hospital, Janette Turner 1942- .... CLC 42
    See also CA 108; CANR 48

Hostos, E. M. de
    See Hostos (y Bonilla), Eugenio Maria de
Hostos, Eugenio M. de
    See Hostos (y Bonilla), Eugenio Maria de
Hostos, Eugenio Maria
    See Hostos (y Bonilla), Eugenio Maria de
Hostos (y Bonilla), Eugenio Maria de
    1839-1903 .... TCLC 24
    See also CA 123; 131; HW 1
Houdini
    See Lovecraft, H(oward) P(hillips)
Hougan, Carolyn 1943- .... CLC 34
    See also CA 139
Household, Geoffrey (Edward West)
    1900-1988 .... CLC 11
    See also CA 77-80; 126; CANR 58; DLB
    87; SATA 14; SATA-Obit 59
Housman, A(lfred) E(dward)
    1859-1936 ...... TCLC 1, 10; DA; DAB;
    DAC; DAM MST, POET; PC 2;
    WLCS
    See also CA 104; 125; DA3; DLB 19;
    MTCW 1, 2
Housman, Laurence 1865-1959 .... TCLC 7
    See also CA 106; 155; DLB 10; SATA 25
Howard, Elizabeth Jane 1923- ..... CLC 7, 29
    See also CA 5-8R; CANR 8, 62
Howard, Maureen 1930- ...... CLC 5, 14, 46
    See also CA 53-56; CANR 31, 75; DLBY
    83; INT CANR-31; MTCW 1, 2
Howard, Richard 1929- .... CLC 7, 10, 47
    See also AITN 1; CA 85-88; CANR 25, 80;
    DLB 5; INT CANR-25
Howard, Robert E(rvin)
    1906-1936 .... TCLC 8
    See also CA 105; 157
Howard, Warren F.
    See Pohl, Frederik
Howe, Fanny (Quincy) 1940- .... CLC 47
    See also CA 117; CAAS 27; CANR 70;
    SATA-Brief 52
Howe, Irving 1920-1993 .... CLC 85
    See also CA 9-12R; 141; CANR 21, 50;
    DLB 67; MTCW 1, 2
Howe, Julia Ward 1819-1910 .... TCLC 21
    See also CA 117; DLB 1, 189
Howe, Susan 1937- .... CLC 72
    See also CA 160; DLB 120
Howe, Tina 1937- .... CLC 48
    See also CA 109
Howell, James 1594(?)-1666 .... LC 13
    See also DLB 151
Howells, W. D.
    See Howells, William Dean
Howells, William D.
    See Howells, William Dean
Howells, William Dean 1837-1920 .. TCLC 7,
    17, 41; SSC 36
    See also CA 104; 134; CDALB 1865-1917;
    DLB 12, 64, 74, 79, 189; MTCW 2
Howes, Barbara 1914-1996 .... CLC 15
    See also CA 9-12R; 151; CAAS 3; CANR
    53; SATA 5
Hrabal, Bohumil 1914-1997 .... CLC 13, 67
    See also CA 106; 156; CAAS 12; CANR
    57
Hroswitha of Gandersheim c. 935-c.
    1002 .... CMLC 29
    See also DLB 148
Hsun, Lu
    See Lu Hsun
Hubbard, L(afayette) Ron(ald)
    1911-1986 .... CLC 43; DAM POP
    See also CA 77-80; 118; CANR 52; DA3;
    MTCW 2
Huch, Ricarda (Octavia)
    1864-1947 .... TCLC 13
    See also CA 111; DLB 66

Isaacs, Jorge Ricardo 1837-1895 ... **NCLC 70**
Isaacs, Susan 1943- .... **CLC 32; DAM POP**
See also BEST 89:1; CA 89-92; CANR 20,
41, 65; DA3; INT CANR-20; MTCW 1, 2
Isherwood, Christopher (William Bradshaw)
1904-1986 .. **CLC 1, 9, 11, 14, 44; DAM
DRAM, NOV**
See also CA 13-16R; 117; CANR 35; DA3;
DLB 15, 195; DLBY 86; MTCW 1, 2
Ishiguro, Kazuo 1954- . **CLC 27, 56, 59, 110;
DAM NOV**
See also BEST 90:2; CA 120; CANR 49;
DA3; DLB 194; MTCW 1, 2
Ishikawa, Hakuhin
See Ishikawa, Takuboku
Ishikawa, Takuboku
1886(?)-1912 ... **TCLC 15; DAM POET;
PC 10**
See also CA 113; 153
Iskander, Fazil 1929- .... **CLC 47**
See also CA 102
Isler, Alan (David) 1934- .... **CLC 91**
See also CA 156
Ivan IV 1530-1584 .... **LC 17**
Ivanov, Vyacheslav Ivanovich
1866-1949 .... **TCLC 33**
See also CA 122
Ivask, Ivar Vidrik 1927-1992 .... **CLC 14**
See also CA 37-40R; 139; CANR 24
Ives, Morgan
See Bradley, Marion Zimmer
Izumi Shikibu c. 973-c. 1034 .... **CMLC 33**
J. R. S.
See Gogarty, Oliver St. John
Jabran, Kahlil
See Gibran, Kahlil
Jabran, Khalil
See Gibran, Kahlil
Jackson, Daniel
See Wingrove, David (John)
Jackson, Helen Hunt 1830-1885 .... **NCLC 90**
See also DLB 42, 47, 186, 189
Jackson, Jesse 1908-1983 .... **CLC 12**
See also BW 1; CA 25-28R; 109; CANR
27; CLR 28; MAICYA; SATA 2, 29;
SATA-Obit 48
Jackson, Laura (Riding) 1901-1991
See Riding, Laura
See also CA 65-68; 135; CANR 28, 89;
DLB 48
Jackson, Sam
See Trumbo, Dalton
Jackson, Sara
See Wingrove, David (John)
Jackson, Shirley 1919-1965 . **CLC 11, 60, 87;
DA; DAC; DAM MST; SSC 9, 39;
WLC**
See also AAYA 9; CA 1-4R; 25-28R; CANR
4, 52; CDALB 1941-1968; DA3; DLB 6;
MTCW 2; SATA 2
Jacob, (Cyprien-)Max 1876-1944 .... **TCLC 6**
See also CA 104
Jacobs, Harriet A(nn)
1813(?)-1897 .... **NCLC 67**
Jacobs, Jim 1942- .... **CLC 12**
See also CA 97-100; INT 97-100
Jacobs, W(illiam) W(ymark)
1863-1943 .... **TCLC 22**
See also CA 121; 167; DLB 135
Jacobsen, Jens Peter 1847-1885 .... **NCLC 34**
Jacobsen, Josephine 1908- .... **CLC 48, 102**
See also CA 33-36R; CAAS 18; CANR 23,
48
Jacobson, Dan 1929- .... **CLC 4, 14**
See also CA 1-4R; CANR 2, 25, 66; DLB
14, 207, 225; MTCW 1
Jacqueline
See Carpentier (y Valmont), Alejo

Jagger, Mick 1944- .... **CLC 17**
Jahiz, al- c. 780-c. 869 .... **CMLC 25**
Jakes, John (William) 1932- . **CLC 29; DAM
NOV, POP**
See also AAYA 32; BEST 89:4; CA 57-60;
CANR 10, 43, 66; DA3; DLBY 83; INT
CANR-10; MTCW 1, 2; SATA 62
James, Andrew
See Kirkup, James
James, C(yril) L(ionel) R(obert)
1901-1989 .... **CLC 33; BLCS**
See also BW 2; CA 117; 125; 128; CANR
62; DLB 125; MTCW 1
James, Daniel (Lewis) 1911-1988
See Santiago, Danny
See also CA 174; 125
James, Dynely
See Mayne, William (James Carter)
James, Henry Sr. 1811-1882 .... **NCLC 53**
James, Henry 1843-1916 ..... **TCLC 2, 11, 24,
40, 47, 64; DA; DAB; DAC; DAM
MST, NOV; SSC 8, 32; WLC**
See also CA 104; 132; CDALB 1865-1917;
DA3; DLB 12, 71, 74, 189; DLBD 13;
MTCW 1, 2
James, M. R.
See James, Montague (Rhodes)
See also DLB 156
James, Montague (Rhodes)
1862-1936 .... **TCLC 6; SSC 16**
See also CA 104; DLB 201
James, P. D. 1920- .... **CLC 18, 46, 122**
See also White, Phyllis Dorothy James
See also BEST 90:2; CDBLB 1960 to
Present; DLB 87; DLBD 17
James, Philip
See Moorcock, Michael (John)
James, William 1842-1910 .... **TCLC 15, 32**
See also CA 109
James I 1394-1437 .... **LC 20**
Jameson, Anna 1794-1860 .... **NCLC 43**
See also DLB 99, 166
Jami, Nur al-Din 'Abd al-Rahman
1414-1492 .... **LC 9**
Jammes, Francis 1868-1938 .... **TCLC 75**
Jandl, Ernst 1925- .... **CLC 34**
Janowitz, Tama 1957- .. **CLC 43; DAM POP**
See also CA 106; CANR 52, 89
Japrisot, Sebastien 1931- .... **CLC 90**
Jarrell, Randall 1914-1965 .... **CLC 1, 2, 6, 9,
13, 49; DAM POET**
See also CA 5-8R; 25-28R; CABS 2; CANR
6, 34; CDALB 1941-1968; CLR 6; DLB
48, 52; MAICYA; MTCW 1, 2; SATA 7
Jarry, Alfred 1873-1907 . **TCLC 2, 14; DAM
DRAM; SSC 20**
See also CA 104; 153; DA3; DLB 192
Jawien, Andrzej
See John Paul II, Pope
Jaynes, Roderick
See Coen, Ethan
Jeake, Samuel, Jr.
See Aiken, Conrad (Potter)
Jean Paul 1763-1825 .... **NCLC 7**
Jefferies, (John) Richard
1848-1887 .... **NCLC 47**
See also DLB 98, 141; SATA 16
Jeffers, (John) Robinson 1887-1962 .. **CLC 2,
3, 11, 15, 54; DA; DAC; DAM MST,
POET; PC 17; WLC**
See also CA 85-88; CANR 35; CDALB
1917-1929; DLB 45, 212; MTCW 1, 2
Jefferson, Janet
See Mencken, H(enry) L(ouis)
Jefferson, Thomas 1743-1826 .... **NCLC 11**
See also CDALB 1640-1865; DA3; DLB
31

Jeffrey, Francis 1773-1850 .... **NCLC 33**
See also DLB 107
Jelakowitch, Ivan
See Heijermans, Herman
Jellicoe, (Patricia) Ann 1927- .... **CLC 27**
See also CA 85-88; DLB 13
Jemyma
See Holley, Marietta
Jen, Gish **CLC 70**
See also Jen, Lillian
Jen, Lillian 1956(?)-
See Jen, Gish
See also CA 135; CANR 89
Jenkins, (John) Robin 1912- .... **CLC 52**
See also CA 1-4R; CANR 1; DLB 14
Jennings, Elizabeth (Joan) 1926- ...... **CLC 5,
14, 131**
See also CA 61-64; CAAS 5; CANR 8, 39,
66; DLB 27; MTCW 1; SATA 66
Jennings, Waylon 1937- .... **CLC 21**
Jensen, Johannes V. 1873-1950 ...... **TCLC 41**
See also CA 170
Jensen, Laura (Linnea) 1948- .... **CLC 37**
See also CA 103
Jerome, Jerome K(lapka)
1859-1927 .... **TCLC 23**
See also CA 119; 177; DLB 10, 34, 135
Jerrold, Douglas William
1803-1857 .... **NCLC 2**
See also DLB 158, 159
Jewett, (Theodora) Sarah Orne
1849-1909 .... **TCLC 1, 22; SSC 6**
See also CA 108; 127; CANR 71; DLB 12,
74, 221; SATA 15
Jewsbury, Geraldine (Endsor)
1812-1880 .... **NCLC 22**
See also DLB 21
Jhabvala, Ruth Prawer 1927- . **CLC 4, 8, 29,
94; DAB; DAM NOV**
See also CA 1-4R; CANR 2, 29, 51, 74, 91;
DLB 139, 194; INT CANR-29; MTCW 1,
2
Jibran, Kahlil
See Gibran, Kahlil
Jibran, Khalil
See Gibran, Kahlil
Jiles, Paulette 1943- .... **CLC 13, 58**
See also CA 101; CANR 70
Jimenez (Mantecon), Juan Ramon
1881-1958 .... **TCLC 4; DAM MULT,
POET; HLC 1; PC 7**
See also CA 104; 131; CANR 74; DLB 134;
HW 1; MTCW 1, 2
Jimenez, Ramon
See Jimenez (Mantecon), Juan Ramon
Jimenez Mantecon, Juan
See Jimenez (Mantecon), Juan Ramon
Jin, Ha
See Jin, Xuefei
Jin, Xuefei 1956- .... **CLC 109**
See also CA 152; CANR 91
Joel, Billy **CLC 26**
See also Joel, William Martin
Joel, William Martin 1949-
See Joel, Billy
See also CA 108
John, Saint 7th cent. - .... **CMLC 27**
John of the Cross, St. 1542-1591 .... **LC 18**
John Paul II, Pope 1920- .... **CLC 128**
See also CA 106; 133
Johnson, B(ryan) S(tanley William)
1933-1973 .... **CLC 6, 9**
See also CA 9-12R; 53-56; CANR 9; DLB
14, 40
Johnson, Benj. F. of Boo
See Riley, James Whitcomb
Johnson, Benjamin F. of Boo
See Riley, James Whitcomb

Korzybski, Alfred (Habdank Skarbek)
1879-1950 .... **TCLC 61**
See also CA 123; 160

Kosinski, Jerzy (Nikodem)
1933-1991 .... **CLC 1, 2, 3, 6, 10, 15, 53, 70; DAM NOV**
See also CA 17-20R; 134; CANR 9, 46; DA3; DLB 2; DLBY 82; MTCW 1, 2

Kostelanetz, Richard (Cory) 1940- .. **CLC 28**
See also CA 13-16R; CAAS 8; CANR 38, 77

Kostrowitzki, Wilhelm Apollinaris de
1880-1918
See Apollinaire, Guillaume
See also CA 104

Kotlowitz, Robert 1924- .... **CLC 4**
See also CA 33-36R; CANR 36

Kotzebue, August (Friedrich Ferdinand) von
1761-1819 .... **NCLC 25**
See also DLB 94

Kotzwinkle, William 1938- ..... **CLC 5, 14, 35**
See also CA 45-48; CANR 3, 44, 84; CLR 6; DLB 173; MAICYA; SATA 24, 70

Kowna, Stancy
See Szymborska, Wislawa

Kozol, Jonathan 1936- .... **CLC 17**
See also CA 61-64; CANR 16, 45

Kozoll, Michael 1940(?)- .... **CLC 35**

Kramer, Kathryn 19(?)- .... **CLC 34**

Kramer, Larry 1935- .. **CLC 42; DAM POP; DC 8**
See also CA 124; 126; CANR 60

Krasicki, Ignacy 1735-1801 .... **NCLC 8**

Krasinski, Zygmunt 1812-1859 .... **NCLC 4**

Kraus, Karl 1874-1936 .... **TCLC 5**
See also CA 104; DLB 118

Kreve (Mickevicius), Vincas
1882-1954 .... **TCLC 27**
See also CA 170; DLB 220

Kristeva, Julia 1941- .... **CLC 77**
See also CA 154

Kristofferson, Kris 1936- .... **CLC 26**
See also CA 104

Krizanc, John 1956- .... **CLC 57**

Krleza, Miroslav 1893-1981 .... **CLC 8, 114**
See also CA 97-100; 105; CANR 50; DLB 147

Kroetsch, Robert 1927- . **CLC 5, 23, 57, 132; DAC; DAM POET**
See also CA 17-20R; CANR 8, 38; DLB 53; MTCW 1

Kroetz, Franz
See Kroetz, Franz Xaver

Kroetz, Franz Xaver 1946- .... **CLC 41**
See also CA 130

Kroker, Arthur (W.) 1945- .... **CLC 77**
See also CA 161

Kropotkin, Peter (Aleksieevich)
1842-1921 .... **TCLC 36**
See also CA 119

Krotkov, Yuri 1917- .... **CLC 19**
See also CA 102

Krumb
See Crumb, R(obert)

Krumgold, Joseph (Quincy)
1908-1980 .... **CLC 12**
See also CA 9-12R; 101; CANR 7; MAICYA; SATA 1, 48; SATA-Obit 23

Krumwitz
See Crumb, R(obert)

Krutch, Joseph Wood 1893-1970 ..... **CLC 24**
See also CA 1-4R; 25-28R; CANR 4; DLB 63, 206

Krutzch, Gus
See Eliot, T(homas) S(tearns)

Krylov, Ivan Andreevich
1768(?)-1844 .... **NCLC 1**
See also DLB 150

Kubin, Alfred (Leopold Isidor)
1877-1959 .... **TCLC 23**
See also CA 112; 149; DLB 81

Kubrick, Stanley 1928-1999 .... **CLC 16**
See also AAYA 30; CA 81-84; 177; CANR 33; DLB 26

Kueng, Hans 1928-
See Kung, Hans
See also CA 53-56; CANR 66; MTCW 1, 2

Kumin, Maxine (Winokur) 1925- ..... **CLC 5, 13, 28; DAM POET; PC 15**
See also AITN 2; CA 1-4R; CAAS 8; CANR 1, 21, 69; DA3; DLB 5; MTCW 1, 2; SATA 12

Kundera, Milan 1929- . **CLC 4, 9, 19, 32, 68, 115, 135; DAM NOV; SSC 24**
See also AAYA 2; CA 85-88; CANR 19, 52, 74; DA3; MTCW 1, 2

Kunene, Mazisi (Raymond) 1930- ... **CLC 85**
See also BW 1, 3; CA 125; CANR 81; DLB 117

Kung, Hans 1928- .... **CLC 130**
See also Kueng, Hans

Kunikida Doppo 1869-1908 .... **TCLC 99**
See also DLB 180

Kunitz, Stanley (Jasspon) 1905- .. **CLC 6, 11, 14; PC 19**
See also CA 41-44R; CANR 26, 57; DA3; DLB 48; INT CANR-26; MTCW 1, 2

Kunze, Reiner 1933- .... **CLC 10**
See also CA 93-96; DLB 75

Kuprin, Aleksander Ivanovich
1870-1938 .... **TCLC 5**
See also CA 104; 182

Kureishi, Hanif 1954(?)- .... **CLC 64, 135**
See also CA 139; DLB 194

Kurosawa, Akira 1910-1998 .... **CLC 16, 119; DAM MULT**
See also AAYA 11; CA 101; 170; CANR 46

Kushner, Tony 1957(?)- .... **CLC 81; DAM DRAM; DC 10**
See also CA 144; CANR 74; DA3; DLB 228; MTCW 2

Kuttner, Henry 1915-1958 .... **TCLC 10**
See also CA 107; 157; DLB 8

Kuzma, Greg 1944- .... **CLC 7**
See also CA 33-36R; CANR 70

Kuzmin, Mikhail 1872(?)-1936 ...... **TCLC 40**
See also CA 170

Kyd, Thomas 1558-1594 .... **LC 22; DAM DRAM; DC 3**
See also DLB 62

Kyprianos, Iossif
See Samarakis, Antonis

La Bruyere, Jean de 1645-1696 .... **LC 17**

Lacan, Jacques (Marie Emile)
1901-1981 .... **CLC 75**
See also CA 121; 104

Laclos, Pierre Ambroise Francois Choderlos de 1741-1803 .... **NCLC 4, 87**

Lacolere, Francois
See Aragon, Louis

La Colere, Francois
See Aragon, Louis

La Deshabilleuse
See Simenon, Georges (Jacques Christian)

Lady Gregory
See Gregory, Isabella Augusta (Persse)

Lady of Quality, A
See Bagnold, Enid

La Fayette, Marie (Madelaine Pioche de la Vergne Comtes 1634-1693 .... **LC 2**

Lafayette, Rene
See Hubbard, L(afayette) Ron(ald)

La Fontaine, Jean de 1621-1695 .... **LC 50**
See also MAICYA; SATA 18

Laforgue, Jules 1860-1887 . **NCLC 5, 53; PC 14; SSC 20**

Lagerkvist, Paer (Fabian)
1891-1974 ...... **CLC 7, 10, 13, 54; DAM DRAM, NOV**
See also Lagerkvist, Par
See also CA 85-88; 49-52; DA3; MTCW 1, 2

Lagerkvist, Par SSC 12
See also Lagerkvist, Paer (Fabian)
See also MTCW 2

Lagerloef, Selma (Ottiliana Lovisa)
1858-1940 .... **TCLC 4, 36**
See also Lagerlof, Selma (Ottiliana Lovisa)
See also CA 108; MTCW 2; SATA 15

Lagerlof, Selma (Ottiliana Lovisa)
See Lagerloef, Selma (Ottiliana Lovisa)
See also CLR 7; SATA 15

La Guma, (Justin) Alex(ander)
1925-1985 .... **CLC 19; BLCS; DAM NOV**
See also BW 1, 3; CA 49-52; 118; CANR 25, 81; DLB 117, 225; MTCW 1, 2

Laidlaw, A. K.
See Grieve, C(hristopher) M(urray)

Lainez, Manuel Mujica
See Mujica Lainez, Manuel
See also HW 1

Laing, R(onald) D(avid) 1927-1989 . **CLC 95**
See also CA 107; 129; CANR 34; MTCW 1

Lamartine, Alphonse (Marie Louis Prat) de
1790-1869 . **NCLC 11; DAM POET; PC 16**

Lamb, Charles 1775-1834 ..... **NCLC 10; DA; DAB; DAC; DAM MST; WLC**
See also CDBLB 1789-1832; DLB 93, 107, 163; SATA 17

Lamb, Lady Caroline 1785-1828 ... **NCLC 38**
See also DLB 116

Lamming, George (William) 1927- ... **CLC 2, 4, 66; BLC 2; DAM MULT**
See also BW 2, 3; CA 85-88; CANR 26, 76; DLB 125; MTCW 1, 2

L'Amour, Louis (Dearborn)
1908-1988 ...... **CLC 25, 55; DAM NOV, POP**
See also AAYA 16; AITN 2; BEST 89:2; CA 1-4R; 125; CANR 3, 25, 40; DA3; DLB 206; DLBY 80; MTCW 1, 2

Lampedusa, Giuseppe (Tomasi) di
1896-1957 .... **TCLC 13**
See also Tomasi di Lampedusa, Giuseppe
See also CA 164; DLB 177; MTCW 2

Lampman, Archibald 1861-1899 ... **NCLC 25**
See also DLB 92

Lancaster, Bruce 1896-1963 .... **CLC 36**
See also CA 9-10; CANR 70; CAP 1; SATA 9

Lanchester, John CLC 99

Landau, Mark Alexandrovich
See Aldanov, Mark (Alexandrovich)

Landau-Aldanov, Mark Alexandrovich
See Aldanov, Mark (Alexandrovich)

Landis, Jerry
See Simon, Paul (Frederick)

Landis, John 1950- .... **CLC 26**
See also CA 112; 122

Landolfi, Tommaso 1908-1979 .... **CLC 11, 49**
See also CA 127; 117; DLB 177

Landon, Letitia Elizabeth
1802-1838 .... **NCLC 15**
See also DLB 96

Landor, Walter Savage
1775-1864 .... **NCLC 14**
See also DLB 93, 107

Landwirth, Heinz 1927-
See Lind, Jakov
See also CA 9-12R; CANR 7

Lee, Tanith 1947- .... **CLC 46**
See also AAYA 15; CA 37-40R; CANR 53;
SATA 8, 88

Lee, Vernon TCLC 5; SSC 33
See also Paget, Violet
See also DLB 57, 153, 156, 174, 178

Lee, William
See Burroughs, William S(eward)

Lee, Willy
See Burroughs, William S(eward)

Lee-Hamilton, Eugene (Jacob)
1845-1907 .... **TCLC 22**
See also CA 117

Leet, Judith 1935- .... **CLC 11**

Le Fanu, Joseph Sheridan
1814-1873 ..... **NCLC 9, 58; DAM POP;
SSC 14**
See also DA3; DLB 21, 70, 159, 178

Leffland, Ella 1931- .... **CLC 19**
See also CA 29-32R; CANR 35, 78, 82;
DLBY 84; INT CANR-35; SATA 65

Leger, Alexis
See Leger, (Marie-Rene Auguste) Alexis
Saint-Leger

**Leger, (Marie-Rene Auguste) Alexis
Saint-Leger** 1887-1975 .. **CLC 4, 11, 46;
DAM POET; PC 23**
See also CA 13-16R; 61-64; CANR 43;
MTCW 1

Leger, Saintleger
See Leger, (Marie-Rene Auguste) Alexis
Saint-Leger

Le Guin, Ursula K(roeber) 1929- ..... **CLC 8,
13, 22, 45, 71; DAB; DAC; DAM MST,
POP; SSC 12**
See also AAYA 9, 27; AITN 1; CA 21-24R;
CANR 9, 32, 52, 74; CDALB 1968-1988;
CLR 3, 28; DA3; DLB 8, 52; INT CANR-
32; JRDA; MAICYA; MTCW 1, 2; SATA
4, 52, 99

Lehmann, Rosamond (Nina)
1901-1990 .... **CLC 5**
See also CA 77-80; 131; CANR 8, 73; DLB
15; MTCW 2

Leiber, Fritz (Reuter, Jr.)
1910-1992 .... **CLC 25**
See also CA 45-48; 139; CANR 2, 40, 86;
DLB 8; MTCW 1, 2; SATA 45; SATA-
Obit 73

Leibniz, Gottfried Wilhelm von
1646-1716 .... **LC 35**
See also DLB 168

Leimbach, Martha 1963-
See Leimbach, Marti
See also CA 130

Leimbach, Marti CLC 65
See also Leimbach, Martha

Leino, Eino TCLC 24
See also Loennbohm, Armas Eino Leopold

Leiris, Michel (Julien) 1901-1990 ..... **CLC 61**
See also CA 119; 128; 132

Leithauser, Brad 1953- .... **CLC 27**
See also CA 107; CANR 27, 81; DLB 120

Lelchuk, Alan 1938- .... **CLC 5**
See also CA 45-48; CAAS 20; CANR 1, 70

Lem, Stanislaw 1921- .... **CLC 8, 15, 40**
See also CA 105; CAAS 1; CANR 32;
MTCW 1

Lemann, Nancy 1956- .... **CLC 39**
See also CA 118; 136

Lemonnier, (Antoine Louis) Camille
1844-1913 .... **TCLC 22**
See also CA 121

Lenau, Nikolaus 1802-1850 .... **NCLC 16**

L'Engle, Madeleine (Camp Franklin)
1918- .... **CLC 12; DAM POP**
See also AAYA 28; AITN 2; CA 1-4R;
CANR 3, 21, 39, 66; CLR 1, 14, 57; DA3;

DLB 52; JRDA; MAICYA; MTCW 1, 2;
SAAS 15; SATA 1, 27, 75

Lengyel, Jozsef 1896-1975 .... **CLC 7**
See also CA 85-88; 57-60; CANR 71

Lenin 1870-1924
See Lenin, V. I.
See also CA 121; 168

Lenin, V. I. TCLC 67
See also Lenin

Lennon, John (Ono) 1940-1980 .. **CLC 12, 35**
See also CA 102; SATA 114

Lennox, Charlotte Ramsay
1729(?)-1804 .... **NCLC 23**
See also DLB 39

Lentricchia, Frank (Jr.) 1940- .... **CLC 34**
See also CA 25-28R; CANR 19

Lenz, Siegfried 1926- .... **CLC 27; SSC 33**
See also CA 89-92; CANR 80; DLB 75

Leonard, Elmore (John, Jr.) 1925- . **CLC 28,
34, 71, 120; DAM POP**
See also AAYA 22; AITN 1; BEST 89:1,
90:4; CA 81-84; CANR 12, 28, 53, 76;
DA3; DLB 173, 226; INT CANR-28;
MTCW 1, 2

Leonard, Hugh CLC 19
See also Byrne, John Keyes
See also DLB 13

Leonov, Leonid (Maximovich)
1899-1994 .... **CLC 92; DAM NOV**
See also CA 129; CANR 74, 76; MTCW 1,
2

Leopardi, (Conte) Giacomo
1798-1837 .... **NCLC 22**

Le Reveler
See Artaud, Antonin (Marie Joseph)

Lerman, Eleanor 1952- .... **CLC 9**
See also CA 85-88; CANR 69

Lerman, Rhoda 1936- .... **CLC 56**
See also CA 49-52; CANR 70

Lermontov, Mikhail Yuryevich
1814-1841 .... **NCLC 47; PC 18**
See also DLB 205

Leroux, Gaston 1868-1927 .... **TCLC 25**
See also CA 108; 136; CANR 69; SATA 65

Lesage, Alain-Rene 1668-1747 .... **LC 2, 28**

Leskov, Nikolai (Semyonovich)
1831-1895 .... **NCLC 25; SSC 34**

Lessing, Doris (May) 1919- ... **CLC 1, 2, 3, 6,
10, 15, 22, 40, 94; DA; DAB; DAC;
DAM MST, NOV; SSC 6; WLCS**
See also CA 9-12R; CAAS 14; CANR 33,
54, 76; CDBLB 1960 to Present; DA3;
DLB 15, 139; DLBY 85; MTCW 1, 2

Lessing, Gotthold Ephraim 1729-1781 . **LC 8**
See also DLB 97

Lester, Richard 1932- .... **CLC 20**

Lever, Charles (James)
1806-1872 .... **NCLC 23**
See also DLB 21

Leverson, Ada 1865(?)-1936(?) .... **TCLC 18**
See also Elaine
See also CA 117; DLB 153

Levertov, Denise 1923-1997 .. **CLC 1, 2, 3, 5,
8, 15, 28, 66; DAM POET; PC 11**
See also CA 1-4R, 178; 163; CAAE 178;
CAAS 19; CANR 3, 29, 50; CDALBS;
DLB 5, 165; INT CANR-29; MTCW 1, 2

Levi, Jonathan CLC 76

Levi, Peter (Chad Tigar) 1931- .... **CLC 41**
See also CA 5-8R; CANR 34, 80; DLB 40

Levi, Primo 1919-1987 . **CLC 37, 50; SSC 12**
See also CA 13-16R; 122; CANR 12, 33,
61, 70; DLB 177; MTCW 1, 2

Levin, Ira 1929- .... **CLC 3, 6; DAM POP**
See also CA 21-24R; CANR 17, 44, 74;
DA3; MTCW 1, 2; SATA 66

Levin, Meyer 1905-1981 .... **CLC 7; DAM
POP**
See also AITN 1; CA 9-12R; 104; CANR
15; DLB 9, 28; DLBY 81; SATA 21;
SATA-Obit 27

Levine, Norman 1924- .... **CLC 54**
See also CA 73-76; CAAS 23; CANR 14,
70; DLB 88

Levine, Philip 1928- .. **CLC 2, 4, 5, 9, 14, 33,
118; DAM POET; PC 22**
See also CA 9-12R; CANR 9, 37, 52; DLB
5

Levinson, Deirdre 1931- .... **CLC 49**
See also CA 73-76; CANR 70

Levi-Strauss, Claude 1908- .... **CLC 38**
See also CA 1-4R; CANR 6, 32, 57; MTCW
1, 2

Levitin, Sonia (Wolff) 1934- .... **CLC 17**
See also AAYA 13; CA 29-32R; CANR 14,
32, 79; CLR 53; JRDA; MAICYA; SAAS
2; SATA 4, 68

Levon, O. U.
See Kesey, Ken (Elton)

Levy, Amy 1861-1889 .... **NCLC 59**
See also DLB 156

Lewes, George Henry 1817-1878 ... **NCLC 25**
See also DLB 55, 144

Lewis, Alun 1915-1944 .... **TCLC 3; SSC 40**
See also CA 104; DLB 20, 162

Lewis, C. Day
See Day Lewis, C(ecil)

Lewis, C(live) S(taples) 1898-1963 .... **CLC 1,
3, 6, 14, 27, 124; DA; DAB; DAC;
DAM MST, NOV, POP; WLC**
See also AAYA 3; CA 81-84; CANR 33,
71; CDBLB 1945-1960; CLR 3, 27; DA3;
DLB 15, 100, 160; JRDA; MAICYA;
MTCW 1, 2; SATA 13, 100

Lewis, Janet 1899-1998 .... **CLC 41**
See also Winters, Janet Lewis
See also CA 9-12R; 172; CANR 29, 63;
CAP 1; DLBY 87

Lewis, Matthew Gregory
1775-1818 .... **NCLC 11, 62**
See also DLB 39, 158, 178

Lewis, (Harry) Sinclair 1885-1951 . **TCLC 4,
13, 23, 39; DA; DAB; DAC; DAM
MST, NOV; WLC**
See also CA 104; 133; CDALB 1917-1929;
DA3; DLB 9, 102; DLBD 1; MTCW 1, 2

Lewis, (Percy) Wyndham
1882(?)-1957 .... **TCLC 2, 9; SSC 34**
See also CA 104; 157; DLB 15; MTCW 2

Lewisohn, Ludwig 1883-1955 .... **TCLC 19**
See also CA 107; DLB 4, 9, 28, 102

Lewton, Val 1904-1951 .... **TCLC 76**

Leyner, Mark 1956- .... **CLC 92**
See also CA 110; CANR 28, 53; DA3;
MTCW 2

Lezama Lima, Jose 1910-1976 .... **CLC 4, 10,
101; DAM MULT; HLCS 2**
See also CA 77-80; CANR 71; DLB 113;
HW 1, 2

L'Heureux, John (Clarke) 1934- ...... **CLC 52**
See also CA 13-16R; CANR 23, 45, 88

Liddell, C. H.
See Kuttner, Henry

Lie, Jonas (Lauritz Idemil)
1833-1908(?) .... **TCLC 5**
See also CA 115

Lieber, Joel 1937-1971 .... **CLC 6**
See also CA 73-76; 29-32R

Lieber, Stanley Martin
See Lee, Stan

Lieberman, Laurence (James)
1935- .... **CLC 4, 36**
See also CA 17-20R; CANR 8, 36, 89

Lowell, Robert (Traill Spence, Jr.)
1917-1977 .... CLC 1, 2, 3, 4, 5, 8, 9, 11, 15, 37, 124; DA; DAB; DAC; DAM MST, NOV; PC 3; WLC
See also CA 9-12R; 73-76; CABS 2; CANR 26, 60; CDALBS; DA3; DLB 5, 169; MTCW 1, 2

Lowenthal, Michael (Francis)
1969- .... CLC 119
See also CA 150

Lowndes, Marie Adelaide (Belloc)
1868-1947 .... TCLC 12
See also CA 107; DLB 70

Lowry, (Clarence) Malcolm
1909-1957 .... TCLC 6, 40; SSC 31
See also CA 105; 131; CANR 62; CDBLB 1945-1960; DLB 15; MTCW 1, 2

Lowry, Mina Gertrude 1882-1966
See Loy, Mina
See also CA 113

Loxsmith, John
See Brunner, John (Kilian Houston)

Loy, Mina CLC 28; DAM POET; PC 16
See also Lowry, Mina Gertrude
See also DLB 4, 54

Loyson-Bridet
See Schwob, Marcel (Mayer Andre)

Lucan 39-65 .... CMLC 33
See also DLB 211

Lucas, Craig 1951- .... CLC 64
See also CA 137; CANR 71

Lucas, E(dward) V(errall)
1868-1938 .... TCLC 73
See also CA 176; DLB 98, 149, 153; SATA 20

Lucas, George 1944- .... CLC 16
See also AAYA 1, 23; CA 77-80; CANR 30; SATA 56

Lucas, Hans
See Godard, Jean-Luc

Lucas, Victoria
See Plath, Sylvia

Lucian c. 120-c. 180 .... CMLC 32
See also DLB 176

Ludlam, Charles 1943-1987 .... CLC 46, 50
See also CA 85-88; 122; CANR 72, 86

Ludlum, Robert 1927- .... CLC 22, 43; DAM NOV, POP
See also AAYA 10; BEST 89:1, 90:3; CA 33-36R; CANR 25, 41, 68; DA3; DLBY 82; MTCW 1, 2

Ludwig, Ken CLC 60

Ludwig, Otto 1813-1865 .... NCLC 4
See also DLB 129

Lugones, Leopoldo 1874-1938 ...... TCLC 15; HLCS 2
See also CA 116; 131; HW 1

Lu Hsun 1881-1936 .... TCLC 3; SSC 20
See also Shu-Jen, Chou

Lukacs, George CLC 24
See also Lukacs, Gyorgy (Szegeny von)

Lukacs, Gyorgy (Szegeny von) 1885-1971
See Lukacs, George
See also CA 101; 29-32R; CANR 62; MTCW 2

Luke, Peter (Ambrose Cyprian)
1919-1995 .... CLC 38
See also CA 81-84; 147; CANR 72; DLB 13

Lunar, Dennis
See Mungo, Raymond

Lurie, Alison 1926- .... CLC 4, 5, 18, 39
See also CA 1-4R; CANR 2, 17, 50, 88; DLB 2; MTCW 1; SATA 46, 112

Lustig, Arnost 1926- .... CLC 56
See also AAYA 3; CA 69-72; CANR 47; SATA 56

Luther, Martin 1483-1546 .... LC 9, 37
See also DLB 179

Luxemburg, Rosa 1870(?)-1919 ..... TCLC 63
See also CA 118

Luzi, Mario 1914- .... CLC 13
See also CA 61-64; CANR 9, 70; DLB 128

Lyly, John 1554(?)-1606 .... LC 41; DAM DRAM; DC 7
See also DLB 62, 167

L'Ymagier
See Gourmont, Remy (-Marie-Charles) de

Lynch, B. Suarez
See Bioy Casares, Adolfo; Borges, Jorge Luis

Lynch, B. Suarez
See Bioy Casares, Adolfo

Lynch, David (K.) 1946- .... CLC 66
See also CA 124; 129

Lynch, James
See Andreyev, Leonid (Nikolaevich)

Lynch Davis, B.
See Bioy Casares, Adolfo; Borges, Jorge Luis

Lyndsay, Sir David 1490-1555 .... LC 20

Lynn, Kenneth S(chuyler) 1923- ...... CLC 50
See also CA 1-4R; CANR 3, 27, 65

Lynx
See West, Rebecca

Lyons, Marcus
See Blish, James (Benjamin)

Lyre, Pinchbeck
See Sassoon, Siegfried (Lorraine)

Lytle, Andrew (Nelson) 1902-1995 ... CLC 22
See also CA 9-12R; 150; CANR 70; DLB 6; DLBY 95

Lyttelton, George 1709-1773 .... LC 10

Maas, Peter 1929- .... CLC 29
See also CA 93-96; INT 93-96; MTCW 2

Macaulay, Rose 1881-1958 .... TCLC 7, 44
See also CA 104; DLB 36

Macaulay, Thomas Babington
1800-1859 .... NCLC 42
See also CDBLB 1832-1890; DLB 32, 55

MacBeth, George (Mann)
1932-1992 .... CLC 2, 5, 9
See also CA 25-28R; 136; CANR 61, 66; DLB 40; MTCW 1; SATA 4; SATA-Obit 70

MacCaig, Norman (Alexander)
1910- .... CLC 36; DAB; DAM POET
See also CA 9-12R; CANR 3, 34; DLB 27

MacCarthy, Sir(Charles Otto) Desmond
1877-1952 .... TCLC 36
See also CA 167

MacDiarmid, Hugh CLC 2, 4, 11, 19, 63; PC 9
See also Grieve, C(hristopher) M(urray)
See also CDBLB 1945-1960; DLB 20

MacDonald, Anson
See Heinlein, Robert A(nson)

Macdonald, Cynthia 1928- .... CLC 13, 19
See also CA 49-52; CANR 4, 44; DLB 105

MacDonald, George 1824-1905 .... TCLC 9
See also CA 106; 137; CANR 80; DLB 18, 163, 178; MAICYA; SATA 33, 100

Macdonald, John
See Millar, Kenneth

MacDonald, John D(ann)
1916-1986 .. CLC 3, 27, 44; DAM NOV, POP
See also CA 1-4R; 121; CANR 1, 19, 60; DLB 8; DLBY 86; MTCW 1, 2

Macdonald, John Ross
See Millar, Kenneth

Macdonald, Ross CLC 1, 2, 3, 14, 34, 41
See also Millar, Kenneth
See also DLBD 6

MacDougal, John
See Blish, James (Benjamin)

MacDougal, John
See Blish, James (Benjamin)

MacEwen, Gwendolyn (Margaret)
1941-1987 .... CLC 13, 55
See also CA 9-12R; 124; CANR 7, 22; DLB 53; SATA 50; SATA-Obit 55

Macha, Karel Hynek 1810-1846 .... NCLC 46

Machado (y Ruiz), Antonio
1875-1939 .... TCLC 3
See also CA 104; 174; DLB 108; HW 2

Machado de Assis, Joaquim Maria
1839-1908 ..... TCLC 10; BLC 2; HLCS 2; SSC 24
See also CA 107; 153; CANR 91

Machen, Arthur TCLC 4; SSC 20
See also Jones, Arthur Llewellyn
See also CA 179; DLB 36, 156, 178

Machiavelli, Niccolo 1469-1527 ..... LC 8, 36; DA; DAB; DAC; DAM MST; WLCS

MacInnes, Colin 1914-1976 .... CLC 4, 23
See also CA 69-72; 65-68; CANR 21; DLB 14; MTCW 1, 2

MacInnes, Helen (Clark)
1907-1985 .... CLC 27, 39; DAM POP
See also CA 1-4R; 117; CANR 1, 28, 58; DLB 87; MTCW 1, 2; SATA 22; SATA-Obit 44

Mackenzie, Compton (Edward Montague)
1883-1972 .... CLC 18
See also CA 21-22; 37-40R; CAP 2; DLB 34, 100

Mackenzie, Henry 1745-1831 .... NCLC 41
See also DLB 39

Mackintosh, Elizabeth 1896(?)-1952
See Tey, Josephine
See also CA 110

MacLaren, James
See Grieve, C(hristopher) M(urray)

Mac Laverty, Bernard 1942- .... CLC 31
See also CA 116; 118; CANR 43, 88; INT 118

MacLean, Alistair (Stuart)
1922(?)-1987 .. CLC 3, 13, 50, 63; DAM POP
See also CA 57-60; 121; CANR 28, 61; MTCW 1; SATA 23; SATA-Obit 50

Maclean, Norman (Fitzroy)
1902-1990 .... CLC 78; DAM POP; SSC 13
See also CA 102; 132; CANR 49; DLB 206

MacLeish, Archibald 1892-1982 ... CLC 3, 8, 14, 68; DAM POET
See also CA 9-12R; 106; CANR 33, 63; CDALBS; DLB 4, 7, 45; DLBY 82; MTCW 1, 2

MacLennan, (John) Hugh
1907-1990 . CLC 2, 14, 92; DAC; DAM MST
See also CA 5-8R; 142; CANR 33; DLB 68; MTCW 1, 2

MacLeod, Alistair 1936- .... CLC 56; DAC; DAM MST
See also CA 123; DLB 60; MTCW 2

Macleod, Fiona
See Sharp, William

MacNeice, (Frederick) Louis
1907-1963 .... CLC 1, 4, 10, 53; DAB; DAM POET
See also CA 85-88; CANR 61; DLB 10, 20; MTCW 1, 2

MacNeill, Dand
See Fraser, George MacDonald

Macpherson, James 1736-1796 .... LC 29
See also Ossian
See also DLB 109

Macpherson, (Jean) Jay 1931- .... CLC 14
See also CA 5-8R; CANR 90; DLB 53

Marlowe, Christopher 1564-1593 ...... **LC 22, 47; DA; DAB; DAC; DAM DRAM, MST; DC 1; WLC**
See also CDBLB Before 1660; DA3; DLB 62

Marlowe, Stephen 1928-
See Queen, Ellery
See also CA 13-16R; CANR 6, 55

Marmontel, Jean-Francois 1723-1799 .. **LC 2**

Marquand, John P(hillips)
1893-1960 .... **CLC 2, 10**
See also CA 85-88; CANR 73; DLB 9, 102; MTCW 2

Marques, Rene 1919-1979 ..... **CLC 96; DAM MULT; HLC 2**
See also CA 97-100; 85-88; CANR 78; DLB 113; HW 1, 2

Marquez, Gabriel (Jose) Garcia
See Garcia Marquez, Gabriel (Jose)

Marquis, Don(ald Robert Perry)
1878-1937 .... **TCLC 7**
See also CA 104; 166; DLB 11, 25

Marric, J. J.
See Creasey, John

Marryat, Frederick 1792-1848 .... **NCLC 3**
See also DLB 21, 163

Marsden, James
See Creasey, John

Marsh, Edward 1872-1953 .... **TCLC 99**

Marsh, (Edith) Ngaio 1899-1982 .... **CLC 7, 53; DAM POP**
See also CA 9-12R; CANR 6, 58; DLB 77; MTCW 1, 2

Marshall, Garry 1934- .... **CLC 17**
See also AAYA 3; CA 111; SATA 60

Marshall, Paule 1929- .. **CLC 27, 72; BLC 3; DAM MULT; SSC 3**
See also BW 2, 3; CA 77-80; CANR 25, 73; DA3; DLB 33, 157, 227; MTCW 1, 2

Marshallik
See Zangwill, Israel

Marsten, Richard
See Hunter, Evan

Marston, John 1576-1634 .... **LC 33; DAM DRAM**
See also DLB 58, 172

Martha, Henry
See Harris, Mark

Marti (y Perez), Jose (Julian)
1853-1895 ...... **NCLC 63; DAM MULT; HLC 2**
See also HW 2

Martial c. 40-c. 104 .... **CMLC 35; PC 10**
See also DLB 211

Martin, Ken
See Hubbard, L(afayette) Ron(ald)

Martin, Richard
See Creasey, John

Martin, Steve 1945- .... **CLC 30**
See also CA 97-100; CANR 30; MTCW 1

Martin, Valerie 1948- .... **CLC 89**
See also BEST 90:2; CA 85-88; CANR 49, 89

Martin, Violet Florence
1862-1915 .... **TCLC 51**

Martin, Webber
See Silverberg, Robert

Martindale, Patrick Victor
See White, Patrick (Victor Martindale)

Martin du Gard, Roger
1881-1958 .... **TCLC 24**
See also CA 118; DLB 65

Martineau, Harriet 1802-1876 .... **NCLC 26**
See also DLB 21, 55, 159, 163, 166, 190; YABC 2

Martines, Julia
See O'Faolain, Julia

Martinez, Enrique Gonzalez
See Gonzalez Martinez, Enrique

Martinez, Jacinto Benavente y
See Benavente (y Martinez), Jacinto

Martinez Ruiz, Jose 1873-1967
See Azorin; Ruiz, Jose Martinez
See also CA 93-96; HW 1

Martinez Sierra, Gregorio
1881-1947 .... **TCLC 6**
See also CA 115

Martinez Sierra, Maria (de la O'LeJarraga)
1874-1974 .... **TCLC 6**
See also CA 115

Martinsen, Martin
See Follett, Ken(neth Martin)

Martinson, Harry (Edmund)
1904-1978 .... **CLC 14**
See also CA 77-80; CANR 34

Marut, Ret
See Traven, B.

Marut, Robert
See Traven, B.

Marvell, Andrew 1621-1678 .. **LC 4, 43; DA; DAB; DAC; DAM MST, POET; PC 10; WLC**
See also CDBLB 1660-1789; DLB 131

Marx, Karl (Heinrich) 1818-1883 . **NCLC 17**
See also DLB 129

Masaoka Shiki TCLC 18
See also Masaoka Tsunenori

Masaoka Tsunenori 1867-1902
See Masaoka Shiki
See also CA 117

Masefield, John (Edward)
1878-1967 ..... **CLC 11, 47; DAM POET**
See also CA 19-20; 25-28R; CANR 33; CAP 2; CDBLB 1890-1914; DLB 10, 19, 153, 160; MTCW 1, 2; SATA 19

Maso, Carole 19(?)- .... **CLC 44**
See also CA 170

Mason, Bobbie Ann 1940- ... **CLC 28, 43, 82; SSC 4**
See also AAYA 5; CA 53-56; CANR 11, 31, 58, 83; CDALBS; DA3; DLB 173; DLBY 87; INT CANR-31; MTCW 1, 2

Mason, Ernst
See Pohl, Frederik

Mason, Lee W.
See Malzberg, Barry N(athaniel)

Mason, Nick 1945- .... **CLC 35**

Mason, Tally
See Derleth, August (William)

Mass, William
See Gibson, William

Master Lao
See Lao Tzu

Masters, Edgar Lee 1868-1950 .... **TCLC 2, 25; DA; DAC; DAM MST, POET; PC 1; WLCS**
See also CA 104; 133; CDALB 1865-1917; DLB 54; MTCW 1, 2

Masters, Hilary 1928- .... **CLC 48**
See also CA 25-28R; CANR 13, 47

Mastrosimone, William 19(?)- .... **CLC 36**
See also CA 186

Mathe, Albert
See Camus, Albert

Mather, Cotton 1663-1728 .... **LC 38**
See also CDALB 1640-1865; DLB 24, 30, 140

Mather, Increase 1639-1723 .... **LC 38**
See also DLB 24

Matheson, Richard Burton 1926- .... **CLC 37**
See also AAYA 31; CA 97-100; CANR 88; DLB 8, 44; INT 97-100

Mathews, Harry 1930- .... **CLC 6, 52**
See also CA 21-24R; CAAS 6; CANR 18, 40

Mathews, John Joseph 1894-1979 .. **CLC 84; DAM MULT**
See also CA 19-20; 142; CANR 45; CAP 2; DLB 175; NNAL

Mathias, Roland (Glyn) 1915- .... **CLC 45**
See also CA 97-100; CANR 19, 41; DLB 27

Matsuo Basho 1644-1694 .... **PC 3**
See also DAM POET

Mattheson, Rodney
See Creasey, John

Matthews, (James) Brander
1852-1929 .... **TCLC 95**
See also DLB 71, 78; DLBD 13

Matthews, Greg 1949- .... **CLC 45**
See also CA 135

Matthews, William (Procter, III)
1942-1997 .... **CLC 40**
See also CA 29-32R; 162; CAAS 18; CANR 12, 57; DLB 5

Matthias, John (Edward) 1941- .... **CLC 9**
See also CA 33-36R; CANR 56

Matthiessen, F(rancis) O(tto)
1902-1950 .... **TCLC 100**
See also CA 185; DLB 63

Matthiessen, Peter 1927- ... **CLC 5, 7, 11, 32, 64; DAM NOV**
See also AAYA 6; BEST 90:4; CA 9-12R; CANR 21, 50, 73; DA3; DLB 6, 173; MTCW 1, 2; SATA 27

Maturin, Charles Robert
1780(?)-1824 .... **NCLC 6**
See also DLB 178

Matute (Ausejo), Ana Maria 1925- .. **CLC 11**
See also CA 89-92; MTCW 1

Maugham, W. S.
See Maugham, W(illiam) Somerset

Maugham, W(illiam) Somerset
1874-1965 ... **CLC 1, 11, 15, 67, 93; DA; DAB; DAC; DAM DRAM, MST, NOV; SSC 8; WLC**
See also CA 5-8R; 25-28R; CANR 40; CDBLB 1914-1945; DA3; DLB 10, 36, 77, 100, 162, 195; MTCW 1, 2; SATA 54

Maugham, William Somerset
See Maugham, W(illiam) Somerset

Maupassant, (Henri Rene Albert) Guy de
1850-1893 . **NCLC 1, 42, 83; DA; DAB; DAC; DAM MST; SSC 1; WLC**
See also DA3; DLB 123

Maupin, Armistead 1944- ..... **CLC 95; DAM POP**
See also CA 125; 130; CANR 58; DA3; INT 130; MTCW 2

Maurhut, Richard
See Traven, B.

Mauriac, Claude 1914-1996 .... **CLC 9**
See also CA 89-92; 152; DLB 83

Mauriac, Francois (Charles)
1885-1970 .... **CLC 4, 9, 56; SSC 24**
See also CA 25-28; CAP 2; DLB 65; MTCW 1, 2

Mavor, Osborne Henry 1888-1951
See Bridie, James
See also CA 104

Maxwell, William (Keepers, Jr.)
1908- .... **CLC 19**
See also CA 93-96; CANR 54; DLBY 80; INT 93-96

May, Elaine 1932- .... **CLC 16**
See also CA 124; 142; DLB 44

Mayakovski, Vladimir (Vladimirovich)
1893-1930 .... **TCLC 4, 18**
See also CA 104; 158; MTCW 2

Mayhew, Henry 1812-1887 .... **NCLC 31**
See also DLB 18, 55, 190

Mayle, Peter 1939(?)- .... **CLC 89**
See also CA 139; CANR 64

Melville, Herman 1819-1891 ..... **NCLC 3, 12, 29, 45, 49, 91; DA; DAB; DAC; DAM MST, NOV; SSC 1, 17; WLC**
See also AAYA 25; CDALB 1640-1865; DA3; DLB 3, 74; SATA 59

Menander c. 342B.C.-c. 292B.C. ... **CMLC 9; DAM DRAM; DC 3**
See also DLB 176

Menchu, Rigoberta 1959-
See also HLCS 2

Menchu, Rigoberta 1959-
See also CA 175; HLCS 2

Mencken, H(enry) L(ouis)
1880-1956 .... **TCLC 13**
See also CA 105; 125; CDALB 1917-1929; DLB 11, 29, 63, 137; MTCW 1, 2

Mendelsohn, Jane 1965(?)- .... **CLC 99**
See also CA 154

Mercer, David 1928-1980 .... **CLC 5; DAM DRAM**
See also CA 9-12R; 102; CANR 23; DLB 13; MTCW 1

Merchant, Paul
See Ellison, Harlan (Jay)

Meredith, George 1828-1909 .. **TCLC 17, 43; DAM POET**
See also CA 117; 153; CANR 80; CDBLB 1832-1890; DLB 18, 35, 57, 159

Meredith, William (Morris) 1919- .... **CLC 4, 13, 22, 55; DAM POET; PC 28**
See also CA 9-12R; CAAS 14; CANR 6, 40; DLB 5

Merezhkovsky, Dmitry Sergeyevich
1865-1941 .... **TCLC 29**
See also CA 169

Merimee, Prosper 1803-1870 ... **NCLC 6, 65; SSC 7**
See also DLB 119, 192

Merkin, Daphne 1954- .... **CLC 44**
See also CA 123

Merlin, Arthur
See Blish, James (Benjamin)

Merrill, James (Ingram) 1926-1995 .. **CLC 2, 3, 6, 8, 13, 18, 34, 91; DAM POET; PC 28**
See also CA 13-16R; 147; CANR 10, 49, 63; DA3; DLB 5, 165; DLBY 85; INT CANR-10; MTCW 1, 2

Merriman, Alex
See Silverberg, Robert

Merriman, Brian 1747-1805 .... **NCLC 70**

Merritt, E. B.
See Waddington, Miriam

Merton, Thomas 1915-1968 ..... **CLC 1, 3, 11, 34, 83; PC 10**
See also CA 5-8R; 25-28R; CANR 22, 53; DA3; DLB 48; DLBY 81; MTCW 1, 2

Merwin, W(illiam) S(tanley) 1927- ... **CLC 1, 2, 3, 5, 8, 13, 18, 45, 88; DAM POET**
See also CA 13-16R; CANR 15, 51; DA3; DLB 5, 169; INT CANR-15; MTCW 1, 2

Metcalf, John 1938- .... **CLC 37**
See also CA 113; DLB 60

Metcalf, Suzanne
See Baum, L(yman) Frank

Mew, Charlotte (Mary) 1870-1928 .. **TCLC 8**
See also CA 105; DLB 19, 135

Mewshaw, Michael 1943- .... **CLC 9**
See also CA 53-56; CANR 7, 47; DLBY 80

Meyer, Conrad Ferdinand
1825-1905 .... **NCLC 81**
See also DLB 129

Meyer, June
See Jordan, June

Meyer, Lynn
See Slavitt, David R(ytman)

Meyer-Meyrink, Gustav 1868-1932
See Meyrink, Gustav
See also CA 117

Meyers, Jeffrey 1939- .... **CLC 39**
See also CA 73-76; CAAE 186; CANR 54; DLB 111

Meynell, Alice (Christina Gertrude Thompson) 1847-1922 .... **TCLC 6**
See also CA 104; 177; DLB 19, 98

Meyrink, Gustav .... **TCLC 21**
See also Meyer-Meyrink, Gustav
See also DLB 81

Michaels, Leonard 1933- .... **CLC 6, 25; SSC 16**
See also CA 61-64; CANR 21, 62; DLB 130; MTCW 1

Michaux, Henri 1899-1984 .... **CLC 8, 19**
See also CA 85-88; 114

Micheaux, Oscar (Devereaux)
1884-1951 .... **TCLC 76**
See also BW 3; CA 174; DLB 50

Michelangelo 1475-1564 .... **LC 12**

Michelet, Jules 1798-1874 .... **NCLC 31**

Michels, Robert 1876-1936 .... **TCLC 88**

Michener, James A(lbert)
1907(?)-1997 .... **CLC 1, 5, 11, 29, 60, 109; DAM NOV, POP**
See also AAYA 27; AITN 1; BEST 90:1; CA 5-8R; 161; CANR 21, 45, 68; DA3; DLB 6; MTCW 1, 2

Mickiewicz, Adam 1798-1855 .... **NCLC 3**

Middleton, Christopher 1926- .... **CLC 13**
See also CA 13-16R; CANR 29, 54; DLB 40

Middleton, Richard (Barham)
1882-1911 .... **TCLC 56**
See also DLB 156

Middleton, Stanley 1919- .... **CLC 7, 38**
See also CA 25-28R; CAAS 23; CANR 21, 46, 81; DLB 14

Middleton, Thomas 1580-1627 .... **LC 33; DAM DRAM, MST; DC 5**
See also DLB 58

Migueis, Jose Rodrigues 1901- .... **CLC 10**

Mikszath, Kalman 1847-1910 .... **TCLC 31**
See also CA 170

Miles, Jack .... **CLC 100**

Miles, Josephine (Louise)
1911-1985 .. **CLC 1, 2, 14, 34, 39; DAM POET**
See also CA 1-4R; 116; CANR 2, 55; DLB 48

Militant
See Sandburg, Carl (August)

Mill, John Stuart 1806-1873 .... **NCLC 11, 58**
See also CDBLB 1832-1890; DLB 55, 190

Millar, Kenneth 1915-1983 ... **CLC 14; DAM POP**
See also Macdonald, Ross
See also CA 9-12R; 110; CANR 16, 63; DA3; DLB 2, 226; DLBD 6; DLBY 83; MTCW 1, 2

Millay, E. Vincent
See Millay, Edna St. Vincent

Millay, Edna St. Vincent
1892-1950 .... **TCLC 4, 49; DA; DAB; DAC; DAM MST, POET; PC 6; WLCS**
See also CA 104; 130; CDALB 1917-1929; DA3; DLB 45; MTCW 1, 2

Miller, Arthur 1915- ...... **CLC 1, 2, 6, 10, 15, 26, 47, 78; DA; DAB; DAC; DAM DRAM, MST; DC 1; WLC**
See also AAYA 15; AITN 1; CA 1-4R; CABS 3; CANR 2, 30, 54, 76; CDALB 1941-1968; DA3; DLB 7; MTCW 1, 2

Miller, Henry (Valentine)
1891-1980 .... **CLC 1, 2, 4, 9, 14, 43, 84; DA; DAB; DAC; DAM MST, NOV; WLC**
See also CA 9-12R; 97-100; CANR 33, 64; CDALB 1929-1941; DA3; DLB 4, 9; DLBY 80; MTCW 1, 2

Miller, Jason 1939(?)- .... **CLC 2**
See also AITN 1; CA 73-76; DLB 7

Miller, Sue 1943- .... **CLC 44; DAM POP**
See also BEST 90:3; CA 139; CANR 59, 91; DA3; DLB 143

Miller, Walter M(ichael, Jr.) 1923- ... **CLC 4, 30**
See also CA 85-88; DLB 8

Millett, Kate 1934- .... **CLC 67**
See also AITN 1; CA 73-76; CANR 32, 53, 76; DA3; MTCW 1, 2

Millhauser, Steven (Lewis) 1943- .... **CLC 21, 54, 109**
See also CA 110; 111; CANR 63; DA3; DLB 2; INT 111; MTCW 2

Millin, Sarah Gertrude 1889-1968 ... **CLC 49**
See also CA 102; 93-96; DLB 225

Milne, A(lan) A(lexander)
1882-1956 ..... **TCLC 6, 88; DAB; DAC; DAM MST**
See also CA 104; 133; CLR 1, 26; DA3; DLB 10, 77, 100, 160; MAICYA; MTCW 1, 2; SATA 100; YABC 1

Milner, Ron(ald) 1938- .... **CLC 56; BLC 3; DAM MULT**
See also AITN 1; BW 1; CA 73-76; CANR 24, 81; DLB 38; MTCW 1

Milnes, Richard Monckton
1809-1885 .... **NCLC 61**
See also DLB 32, 184

Milosz, Czeslaw 1911- ...... **CLC 5, 11, 22, 31, 56, 82; DAM MST, POET; PC 8; WLCS**
See also CA 81-84; CANR 23, 51, 91; DA3; MTCW 1, 2

Milton, John 1608-1674 .... **LC 9, 43; DA; DAB; DAC; DAM MST, POET; PC 19, 29; WLC**
See also CDBLB 1660-1789; DA3; DLB 131, 151

Min, Anchee 1957- .... **CLC 86**
See also CA 146

Minehaha, Cornelius
See Wedekind, (Benjamin) Frank(lin)

Miner, Valerie 1947- .... **CLC 40**
See also CA 97-100; CANR 59

Minimo, Duca
See D'Annunzio, Gabriele

Minot, Susan 1956- .... **CLC 44**
See also CA 134

Minus, Ed 1938- .... **CLC 39**
See also CA 185

Miranda, Javier
See Bioy Casares, Adolfo

Miranda, Javier
See Bioy Casares, Adolfo

Mirbeau, Octave 1848-1917 .... **TCLC 55**
See also DLB 123, 192

Miro (Ferrer), Gabriel (Francisco Victor)
1879-1930 .... **TCLC 5**
See also CA 104; 185

Mishima, Yukio 1925-1970 .... **CLC 2, 4, 6, 9, 27; DC 1; SSC 4**
See also Hiraoka, Kimitake
See also DLB 182; MTCW 2

Mistral, Frederic 1830-1914 .... **TCLC 51**
See also CA 122

Mistral, Gabriela .... **TCLC 2; HLC 2**
See also Godoy Alcayaga, Lucila
See also MTCW 2

Mistry, Rohinton 1952- .... **CLC 71; DAC**
See also CA 141; CANR 86

Mitchell, Clyde
See Ellison, Harlan (Jay); Silverberg, Robert

Mitchell, James Leslie 1901-1935
See Gibbon, Lewis Grassic
See also CA 104; DLB 15

Mitchell, Joni 1943- .... CLC 12
See also CA 112
Mitchell, Joseph (Quincy)
1908-1996 .... CLC 98
See also CA 77-80; 152; CANR 69; DLB
185; DLBY 96
Mitchell, Margaret (Munnerlyn)
1900-1949 . TCLC 11; DAM NOV, POP
See also AAYA 23; CA 109; 125; CANR
55; CDALBS; DA3; DLB 9; MTCW 1, 2
Mitchell, Peggy
See Mitchell, Margaret (Munnerlyn)
Mitchell, S(ilas) Weir 1829-1914 .... TCLC 36
See also CA 165; DLB 202
Mitchell, W(illiam) O(rmond)
1914-1998 .. CLC 25; DAC; DAM MST
See also CA 77-80; 165; CANR 15, 43;
DLB 88
Mitchell, William 1879-1936 .... TCLC 81
Mitford, Mary Russell 1787-1855 ... NCLC 4
See also DLB 110, 116
Mitford, Nancy 1904-1973 .... CLC 44
See also CA 9-12R; DLB 191
Miyamoto, (Chujo) Yuriko
1899-1951 .... TCLC 37
See also CA 170, 174; DLB 180
Miyazawa, Kenji 1896-1933 .... TCLC 76
See also CA 157
Mizoguchi, Kenji 1898-1956 .... TCLC 72
See also CA 167
Mo, Timothy (Peter) 1950(?)- ... CLC 46, 134
See also CA 117; DLB 194; MTCW 1
Modarressi, Taghi (M.) 1931- .... CLC 44
See also CA 121; 134; INT 134
Modiano, Patrick (Jean) 1945- .... CLC 18
See also CA 85-88; CANR 17, 40; DLB 83
Moerck, Paal
See Roelvaag, O(le) E(dvart)
Mofolo, Thomas (Mokopu)
1875(?)-1948 .. TCLC 22; BLC 3; DAM
MULT
See also CA 121; 153; CANR 83; DLB 225;
MTCW 2
Mohr, Nicholasa 1938- .... CLC 12; DAM
MULT; HLC 2
See also AAYA 8; CA 49-52; CANR 1, 32,
64; CLR 22; DLB 145; HW 1; JRDA;
SAAS 8; SATA 8, 97; SATA-Essay 113
Mojtabai, A(nn) G(race) 1938- ..... CLC 5, 9,
15, 29
See also CA 85-88; CANR 88
Moliere 1622-1673 ..... LC 10, 28; DA; DAB;
DAC; DAM DRAM, MST; DC 13;
WLC
See also DA3
Molin, Charles
See Mayne, William (James Carter)
Molnar, Ferenc 1878-1952 .. TCLC 20; DAM
DRAM
See also CA 109; 153; CANR 83
Momaday, N(avarre) Scott 1934- ...... CLC 2,
19, 85, 95; DA; DAB; DAC; DAM
MST, MULT, NOV, POP; PC 25;
WLCS
See also AAYA 11; CA 25-28R; CANR 14,
34, 68; CDALBS; DA3; DLB 143, 175;
INT CANR-14; MTCW 1, 2; NNAL;
SATA 48; SATA-Brief 30
Monette, Paul 1945-1995 .... CLC 82
See also CA 139; 147
Monroe, Harriet 1860-1936 .... TCLC 12
See also CA 109; DLB 54, 91
Monroe, Lyle
See Heinlein, Robert A(nson)
Montagu, Elizabeth 1720-1800 .... NCLC 7
Montagu, Elizabeth 1917- .... NCLC 7
See also CA 9-12R

Montagu, Mary (Pierrepont) Wortley
1689-1762 .... LC 9, 57; PC 16
See also DLB 95, 101
Montagu, W. H.
See Coleridge, Samuel Taylor
Montague, John (Patrick) 1929- ..... CLC 13,
46
See also CA 9-12R; CANR 9, 69; DLB 40;
MTCW 1
Montaigne, Michel (Eyquem) de
1533-1592 .... LC 8; DA; DAB; DAC;
DAM MST; WLC
Montale, Eugenio 1896-1981 ... CLC 7, 9, 18;
PC 13
See also CA 17-20R; 104; CANR 30; DLB
114; MTCW 1
Montesquieu, Charles-Louis de Secondat
1689-1755 .... LC 7
Montgomery, (Robert) Bruce 1921(?)-1978
See Crispin, Edmund
See also CA 179; 104
Montgomery, L(ucy) M(aud)
1874-1942 .... TCLC 51; DAC; DAM
MST
See also AAYA 12; CA 108; 137; CLR 8;
DA3; DLB 92; DLBD 14; JRDA; MAI-
CYA; MTCW 2; SATA 100; YABC 1
Montgomery, Marion H., Jr. 1925- .... CLC 7
See also AITN 1; CA 1-4R; CANR 3, 48;
DLB 6
Montgomery, Max
See Davenport, Guy (Mattison, Jr.)
Montherlant, Henry (Milon) de
1896-1972 ..... CLC 8, 19; DAM DRAM
See also CA 85-88; 37-40R; DLB 72;
MTCW 1
Monty Python
See Chapman, Graham; Cleese, John
(Marwood); Gilliam, Terry (Vance); Idle,
Eric; Jones, Terence Graham Parry; Palin,
Michael (Edward)
See also AAYA 7
Moodie, Susanna (Strickland)
1803-1885 .... NCLC 14
See also DLB 99
Mooney, Edward 1951-
See Mooney, Ted
See also CA 130
Mooney, Ted CLC 25
See also Mooney, Edward
Moorcock, Michael (John) 1939- ...... CLC 5,
27, 58
See also Bradbury, Edward P.
See also AAYA 26; CA 45-48; CAAS 5;
CANR 2, 17, 38, 64; DLB 14; MTCW 1,
2; SATA 93
Moore, Brian 1921-1999 ... CLC 1, 3, 5, 7, 8,
19, 32, 90; DAB; DAC; DAM MST
See also CA 1-4R; 174; CANR 1, 25, 42,
63; MTCW 1, 2
Moore, Edward
See Muir, Edwin
Moore, G. E. 1873-1958 .... TCLC 89
Moore, George Augustus
1852-1933 .... TCLC 7; SSC 19
See also CA 104; 177; DLB 10, 18, 57, 135
Moore, Lorrie CLC 39, 45, 68
See also Moore, Marie Lorena
Moore, Marianne (Craig)
1887-1972 .... CLC 1, 2, 4, 8, 10, 13, 19,
47; DA; DAB; DAC; DAM MST,
POET; PC 4; WLCS
See also CA 1-4R; 33-36R; CANR 3, 61;
CDALB 1929-1941; DA3; DLB 45;
DLBD 7; MTCW 1, 2; SATA 20
Moore, Marie Lorena 1957-
See Moore, Lorrie
See also CA 116; CANR 39, 83

Moore, Thomas 1779-1852 .... NCLC 6
See also DLB 96, 144
Moorhouse, Frank 1938- .... SSC 40
See also CA 118; CANR 92
Mora, Pat(ricia) 1942-
See also CA 129; CANR 57, 81; CLR 58;
DAM MULT; DLB 209; HLC 2; HW 1,
2; SATA 92
Moraga, Cherrie 1952- .... CLC 126; DAM
MULT
See also CA 131; CANR 66; DLB 82; HW
1, 2
Morand, Paul 1888-1976 .... CLC 41; SSC 22
See also CA 184; 69-72; DLB 65
Morante, Elsa 1918-1985 .... CLC 8, 47
See also CA 85-88; 117; CANR 35; DLB
177; MTCW 1, 2
Moravia, Alberto 1907-1990 .... CLC 2, 7, 11,
27, 46; SSC 26
See also Pincherle, Alberto
See also DLB 177; MTCW 2
More, Hannah 1745-1833 .... NCLC 27
See also DLB 107, 109, 116, 158
More, Henry 1614-1687 .... LC 9
See also DLB 126
More, Sir Thomas 1478-1535 .... LC 10, 32
Moreas, Jean TCLC 18
See also Papadiamantopoulos, Johannes
Morgan, Berry 1919- .... CLC 6
See also CA 49-52; DLB 6
Morgan, Claire
See Highsmith, (Mary) Patricia
Morgan, Edwin (George) 1920- .... CLC 31
See also CA 5-8R; CANR 3, 43, 90; DLB
27
Morgan, (George) Frederick 1922- .. CLC 23
See also CA 17-20R; CANR 21
Morgan, Harriet
See Mencken, H(enry) L(ouis)
Morgan, Jane
See Cooper, James Fenimore
Morgan, Janet 1945- .... CLC 39
See also CA 65-68
Morgan, Lady 1776(?)-1859 .... NCLC 29
See also DLB 116, 158
Morgan, Robin (Evonne) 1941- .... CLC 2
See also CA 69-72; CANR 29, 68; MTCW
1; SATA 80
Morgan, Scott
See Kuttner, Henry
Morgan, Seth 1949(?)-1990 .... CLC 65
See also CA 185; 132
Morgenstern, Christian 1871-1914 .. TCLC 8
See also CA 105
Morgenstern, S.
See Goldman, William (W.)
Moricz, Zsigmond 1879-1942 .... TCLC 33
See also CA 165
Morike, Eduard (Friedrich)
1804-1875 .... NCLC 10
See also DLB 133
Moritz, Karl Philipp 1756-1793 .... LC 2
See also DLB 94
Morland, Peter Henry
See Faust, Frederick (Schiller)
Morley, Christopher (Darlington)
1890-1957 .... TCLC 87
See also CA 112; DLB 9
Morren, Theophil
See Hofmannsthal, Hugo von
Morris, Bill 1952- .... CLC 76
Morris, Julian
See West, Morris L(anglo)
Morris, Steveland Judkins 1950(?)-
See Wonder, Stevie
See also CA 111

Morris, William 1834-1896 .... **NCLC 4**
  See also CDBLB 1832-1890; DLB 18, 35, 57, 156, 178, 184

Morris, Wright 1910-1998 .. **CLC 1, 3, 7, 18, 37**
  See also CA 9-12R; 167; CANR 21, 81; DLB 2, 206; DLBY 81; MTCW 1, 2

Morrison, Arthur 1863-1945 .... **TCLC 72; SSC 40**
  See also CA 120; 157; DLB 70, 135, 197

Morrison, Chloe Anthony Wofford
  See Morrison, Toni

Morrison, James Douglas 1943-1971
  See Morrison, Jim
  See also CA 73-76; CANR 40

Morrison, Jim **CLC 17**
  See also Morrison, James Douglas

Morrison, Toni 1931- . **CLC 4, 10, 22, 55, 81, 87; BLC 3; DA; DAB; DAC; DAM MST, MULT, NOV, POP**
  See also AAYA 1, 22; BW 2, 3; CA 29-32R; CANR 27, 42, 67; CDALB 1968-1988; DA3; DLB 6, 33, 143; DLBY 81; MTCW 1, 2; SATA 57

Morrison, Van 1945- .... **CLC 21**
  See also CA 116; 168

Morrissy, Mary 1958- .... **CLC 99**

Mortimer, John (Clifford) 1923- ..... **CLC 28, 43; DAM DRAM, POP**
  See also CA 13-16R; CANR 21, 69; CD-BLB 1960 to Present; DA3; DLB 13; INT CANR-21; MTCW 1, 2

Mortimer, Penelope (Ruth)
  1918-1999 .... **CLC 5**
  See also CA 57-60; CANR 45, 88

Morton, Anthony
  See Creasey, John

Mosca, Gaetano 1858-1941 .... **TCLC 75**

Mosher, Howard Frank 1943- .... **CLC 62**
  See also CA 139; CANR 65

Mosley, Nicholas 1923- .... **CLC 43, 70**
  See also CA 69-72; CANR 41, 60; DLB 14, 207

Mosley, Walter 1952- .... **CLC 97; BLCS; DAM MULT, POP**
  See also AAYA 17; BW 2; CA 142; CANR 57, 92; DA3; MTCW 2

Moss, Howard 1922-1987 ...... **CLC 7, 14, 45, 50; DAM POET**
  See also CA 1-4R; 123; CANR 1, 44; DLB 5

Mossgiel, Rab
  See Burns, Robert

Motion, Andrew (Peter) 1952- .... **CLC 47**
  See also CA 146; CANR 90; DLB 40

Motley, Willard (Francis)
  1909-1965 .... **CLC 18**
  See also BW 1; CA 117; 106; CANR 88; DLB 76, 143

Motoori, Norinaga 1730-1801 .... **NCLC 45**

Mott, Michael (Charles Alston)
  1930- .... **CLC 15, 34**
  See also CA 5-8R; CAAS 7; CANR 7, 29

Mountain Wolf Woman 1884-1960 .. **CLC 92**
  See also CA 144; CANR 90; NNAL

Moure, Erin 1955- .... **CLC 88**
  See also CA 113; DLB 60

Mowat, Farley (McGill) 1921- .... **CLC 26; DAC; DAM MST**
  See also AAYA 1; CA 1-4R; CANR 4, 24, 42, 68; CLR 20; DLB 68; INT CANR-24; JRDA; MAICYA; MTCW 1, 2; SATA 3, 55

Mowatt, Anna Cora 1819-1870 ..... **NCLC 74**

Moyers, Bill 1934- .... **CLC 74**
  See also AITN 2; CA 61-64; CANR 31, 52

Mphahlele, Es'kia
  See Mphahlele, Ezekiel
  See also DLB 125

Mphahlele, Ezekiel 1919- .... **CLC 25, 133; BLC 3; DAM MULT**
  See also Mphahlele, Es'kia
  See also BW 2, 3; CA 81-84; CANR 26, 76; DA3; DLB 225; MTCW 2

Mqhayi, S(amuel) E(dward) K(rune Loliwe) 1875-1945 ...... **TCLC 25; BLC 3; DAM MULT**
  See also CA 153; CANR 87

Mrozek, Slawomir 1930- .... **CLC 3, 13**
  See also CA 13-16R; CAAS 10; CANR 29; MTCW 1

Mrs. Belloc-Lowndes
  See Lowndes, Marie Adelaide (Belloc)

Mtwa, Percy (?)- .... **CLC 47**

Mueller, Lisel 1924- .... **CLC 13, 51; PC 31**
  See also CA 93-96; DLB 105

Muir, Edwin 1887-1959 .... **TCLC 2, 87**
  See also CA 104; DLB 20, 100, 191

Muir, John 1838-1914 .... **TCLC 28**
  See also CA 165; DLB 186

Mujica Lainez, Manuel 1910-1984 ... **CLC 31**
  See also Lainez, Manuel Mujica
  See also CA 81-84; 112; CANR 32; HW 1

Mukherjee, Bharati 1940- .... **CLC 53, 115; DAM NOV; SSC 38**
  See also BEST 89:2; CA 107; CANR 45, 72; DLB 60; MTCW 1, 2

Muldoon, Paul 1951- .... **CLC 32, 72; DAM POET**
  See also CA 113; 129; CANR 52, 91; DLB 40; INT 129

Mulisch, Harry 1927- .... **CLC 42**
  See also CA 9-12R; CANR 6, 26, 56

Mull, Martin 1943- .... **CLC 17**
  See also CA 105

Muller, Wilhelm **NCLC 73**

Mulock, Dinah Maria
  See Craik, Dinah Maria (Mulock)

Munford, Robert 1737(?)-1783 .... **LC 5**
  See also DLB 31

Mungo, Raymond 1946- .... **CLC 72**
  See also CA 49-52; CANR 2

Munro, Alice 1931- .... **CLC 6, 10, 19, 50, 95; DAC; DAM MST, NOV; SSC 3; WLCS**
  See also AITN 2; CA 33-36R; CANR 33, 53, 75; DA3; DLB 53; MTCW 1, 2; SATA 29

Munro, H(ector) H(ugh) 1870-1916
  See Saki
  See also CA 104; 130; CDBLB 1890-1914; DA; DAB; DAC; DAM MST, NOV; DA3; DLB 34, 162; MTCW 1, 2; WLC

Murdoch, (Jean) Iris 1919-1999 ... **CLC 1, 2, 3, 4, 6, 8, 11, 15, 22, 31, 51; DAB; DAC; DAM MST, NOV**
  See also CA 13-16R; 179; CANR 8, 43, 68; CDBLB 1960 to Present; DA3; DLB 14, 194; INT CANR-8; MTCW 1, 2

Murfree, Mary Noailles 1850-1922 ... **SSC 22**
  See also CA 122; 176; DLB 12, 74

Murnau, Friedrich Wilhelm
  See Plumpe, Friedrich Wilhelm

Murphy, Richard 1927- .... **CLC 41**
  See also CA 29-32R; DLB 40

Murphy, Sylvia 1937- .... **CLC 34**
  See also CA 121

Murphy, Thomas (Bernard) 1935- ... **CLC 51**
  See also CA 101

Murray, Albert L. 1916- .... **CLC 73**
  See also BW 2; CA 49-52; CANR 26, 52, 78; DLB 38

Murray, Judith Sargent
  1751-1820 .... **NCLC 63**
  See also DLB 37, 200

Murray, Les(lie) A(llan) 1938- .... **CLC 40; DAM POET**
  See also CA 21-24R; CANR 11, 27, 56

Murry, J. Middleton
  See Murry, John Middleton

Murry, John Middleton
  1889-1957 .... **TCLC 16**
  See also CA 118; DLB 149

Musgrave, Susan 1951- .... **CLC 13, 54**
  See also CA 69-72; CANR 45, 84

Musil, Robert (Edler von)
  1880-1942 .... **TCLC 12, 68; SSC 18**
  See also CA 109; CANR 55, 84; DLB 81, 124; MTCW 2

Muske, Carol 1945- .... **CLC 90**
  See also Muske-Dukes, Carol (Anne)

Muske-Dukes, Carol (Anne) 1945-
  See Muske, Carol
  See also CA 65-68; CANR 32, 70

Musset, (Louis Charles) Alfred de
  1810-1857 .... **NCLC 7**
  See also DLB 192

Mussolini, Benito (Amilcare Andrea)
  1883-1945 .... **TCLC 96**
  See also CA 116

My Brother's Brother
  See Chekhov, Anton (Pavlovich)

Myers, L(eopold) H(amilton)
  1881-1944 .... **TCLC 59**
  See also CA 157; DLB 15

Myers, Walter Dean 1937- ..... **CLC 35; BLC 3; DAM MULT, NOV**
  See also AAYA 4, 23; BW 2; CA 33-36R; CANR 20, 42, 67; CLR 4, 16, 35; DLB 33; INT CANR-20; JRDA; MAICYA; MTCW 2; SAAS 2; SATA 41, 71, 109; SATA-Brief 27

Myers, Walter M.
  See Myers, Walter Dean

Myles, Symon
  See Follett, Ken(neth Martin)

Nabokov, Vladimir (Vladimirovich)
  1899-1977 .... **CLC 1, 2, 3, 6, 8, 11, 15, 23, 44, 46, 64; DA; DAB; DAC; DAM MST, NOV; SSC 11; WLC**
  See also CA 5-8R; 69-72; CANR 20; CDALB 1941-1968; DA3; DLB 2; DLBD 3; DLBY 80, 91; MTCW 1, 2

Naevius c. 265B.C.-201B.C. .... **CMLC 37**
  See also DLB 211

Nagai Kafu 1879-1959 .... **TCLC 51**
  See also Nagai Sokichi
  See also DLB 180

Nagai Sokichi 1879-1959
  See Nagai Kafu
  See also CA 117

Nagy, Laszlo 1925-1978 .... **CLC 7**
  See also CA 129; 112

Naidu, Sarojini 1879-1943 .... **TCLC 80**

Naipaul, Shiva(dhar Srinivasa)
  1945-1985 .... **CLC 32, 39; DAM NOV**
  See also CA 110; 112; 116; CANR 33; DA3; DLB 157; DLBY 85; MTCW 1, 2

Naipaul, V(idiadhar) S(urajprasad)
  1932- .... **CLC 4, 7, 9, 13, 18, 37, 105; DAB; DAC; DAM MST, NOV; SSC 38**
  See also CA 1-4R; CANR 1, 33, 51, 91; CDBLB 1960 to Present; DA3; DLB 125, 204, 206; DLBY 85; MTCW 1, 2

Nakos, Lilika 1899(?)- .... **CLC 29**

Narayan, R(asipuram) K(rishnaswami)
  1906- . **CLC 7, 28, 47, 121; DAM NOV; SSC 25**
  See also CA 81-84; CANR 33, 61; DA3; MTCW 1, 2; SATA 62

Nash, (Frediric) Ogden 1902-1971 . **CLC 23; DAM POET; PC 21**
  See also CA 13-14; 29-32R; CANR 34, 61; CAP 1; DLB 11; MAICYA; MTCW 1, 2; SATA 2, 46

Nashe, Thomas 1567-1601(?) .... **LC 41**
  See also DLB 167

Nwapa, Flora 1931- .... **CLC 133; BLCS**
See also BW 2; CA 143; CANR 83; DLB 125

Nye, Robert 1939- . **CLC 13, 42; DAM NOV**
See also CA 33-36R; CANR 29, 67; DLB 14; MTCW 1; SATA 6

Nyro, Laura 1947- .... **CLC 17**

Oates, Joyce Carol 1938- .. **CLC 1, 2, 3, 6, 9, 11, 15, 19, 33, 52, 108, 134; DA; DAB; DAC; DAM MST, NOV, POP; SSC 6; WLC**
See also AAYA 15; AITN 1; BEST 89:2; CA 5-8R; CANR 25, 45, 74; CDALB 1968-1988; DA3; DLB 2, 5, 130; DLBY 81; INT CANR-25; MTCW 1, 2

O'Brien, Darcy 1939-1998 .... **CLC 11**
See also CA 21-24R; 167; CANR 8, 59

O'Brien, E. G.
See Clarke, Arthur C(harles)

O'Brien, Edna 1936- ..... **CLC 3, 5, 8, 13, 36, 65, 116; DAM NOV; SSC 10**
See also CA 1-4R; CANR 6, 41, 65; CD-BLB 1960 to Present; DA3; DLB 14; MTCW 1, 2

O'Brien, Fitz-James 1828-1862 ..... **NCLC 21**
See also DLB 74

O'Brien, Flann CLC 1, 4, 5, 7, 10, 47
See also O Nuallain, Brian

O'Brien, Richard 1942- .... **CLC 17**
See also CA 124

O'Brien, (William) Tim(othy) 1946- . **CLC 7, 19, 40, 103; DAM POP**
See also AAYA 16; CA 85-88; CANR 40, 58; CDALBS; DA3; DLB 152; DLBD 9; DLBY 80; MTCW 2

Obstfelder, Sigbjoern 1866-1900 .... **TCLC 23**
See also CA 123

O'Casey, Sean 1880-1964 .... **CLC 1, 5, 9, 11, 15, 88; DAB; DAC; DAM DRAM, MST; DC 12; WLCS**
See also CA 89-92; CANR 62; CDBLB 1914-1945; DA3; DLB 10; MTCW 1, 2

O'Cathasaigh, Sean
See O'Casey, Sean

Occom, Samson 1723-1792 .... **LC 60**
See also DLB 175; NNAL

Ochs, Phil(ip David) 1940-1976 .... **CLC 17**
See also CA 185; 65-68

O'Connor, Edwin (Greene)
1918-1968 .... **CLC 14**
See also CA 93-96; 25-28R

O'Connor, (Mary) Flannery
1925-1964 .... **CLC 1, 2, 3, 6, 10, 13, 15, 21, 66, 104; DA; DAB; DAC; DAM MST, NOV; SSC 1, 23; WLC**
See also AAYA 7; CA 1-4R; CANR 3, 41; CDALB 1941-1968; DA3; DLB 2, 152; DLBD 12; DLBY 80; MTCW 1, 2

O'Connor, Frank CLC 23; SSC 5
See also O'Donovan, Michael John
See also DLB 162

O'Dell, Scott 1898-1989 .... **CLC 30**
See also AAYA 3; CA 61-64; 129; CANR 12, 30; CLR 1, 16; DLB 52; JRDA; MAI-CYA; SATA 12, 60

Odets, Clifford 1906-1963 ..... **CLC 2, 28, 98; DAM DRAM; DC 6**
See also CA 85-88; CANR 62; DLB 7, 26; MTCW 1, 2

O'Doherty, Brian 1934- .... **CLC 76**
See also CA 105

O'Donnell, K. M.
See Malzberg, Barry N(athaniel)

O'Donnell, Lawrence
See Kuttner, Henry

O'Donovan, Michael John
1903-1966 .... **CLC 14**
See also O'Connor, Frank
See also CA 93-96; CANR 84

Oe, Kenzaburo 1935- .... **CLC 10, 36, 86; DAM NOV; SSC 20**
See also CA 97-100; CANR 36, 50, 74; DA3; DLB 182; DLBY 94; MTCW 1, 2

O'Faolain, Julia 1932- .... **CLC 6, 19, 47, 108**
See also CA 81-84; CAAS 2; CANR 12, 61; DLB 14; MTCW 1

O'Faolain, Sean 1900-1991 ...... **CLC 1, 7, 14, 32, 70; SSC 13**
See also CA 61-64; 134; CANR 12, 66; DLB 15, 162; MTCW 1, 2

O'Flaherty, Liam 1896-1984 .... **CLC 5, 34; SSC 6**
See also CA 101; 113; CANR 35; DLB 36, 162; DLBY 84; MTCW 1, 2

Ogilvy, Gavin
See Barrie, J(ames) M(atthew)

O'Grady, Standish (James)
1846-1928 .... **TCLC 5**
See also CA 104; 157

O'Grady, Timothy 1951- .... **CLC 59**
See also CA 138

O'Hara, Frank 1926-1966 .... **CLC 2, 5, 13, 78; DAM POET**
See also CA 9-12R; 25-28R; CANR 33; DA3; DLB 5, 16, 193; MTCW 1, 2

O'Hara, John (Henry) 1905-1970 . **CLC 1, 2, 3, 6, 11, 42; DAM NOV; SSC 15**
See also CA 5-8R; 25-28R; CANR 31, 60; CDALB 1929-1941; DLB 9, 86; DLBD 2; MTCW 1, 2

O Hehir, Diana 1922- .... **CLC 41**
See also CA 93-96

Ohiyesa
See Eastman, Charles A(lexander)

Okigbo, Christopher (Ifenayichukwu)
1932-1967 ... **CLC 25, 84; BLC 3; DAM MULT, POET; PC 7**
See also BW 1, 3; CA 77-80; CANR 74; DLB 125; MTCW 1, 2

Okri, Ben 1959- .... **CLC 87**
See also BW 2, 3; CA 130; 138; CANR 65; DLB 157; INT 138; MTCW 2

Olds, Sharon 1942- ... **CLC 32, 39, 85; DAM POET; PC 22**
See also CA 101; CANR 18, 41, 66; DLB 120; MTCW 2

Oldstyle, Jonathan
See Irving, Washington

Olesha, Yuri (Karlovich) 1899-1960 .. **CLC 8**
See also CA 85-88

Oliphant, Laurence 1829(?)-1888 .. **NCLC 47**
See also DLB 18, 166

Oliphant, Margaret (Oliphant Wilson)
1828-1897 .... **NCLC 11, 61; SSC 25**
See also DLB 18, 159, 190

Oliver, Mary 1935- .... **CLC 19, 34, 98**
See also CA 21-24R; CANR 9, 43, 84, 92; DLB 5, 193

Olivier, Laurence (Kerr) 1907-1989 . **CLC 20**
See also CA 111; 150; 129

Olsen, Tillie 1912- .... **CLC 4, 13, 114; DA; DAB; DAC; DAM MST; SSC 11**
See also CA 1-4R; CANR 1, 43, 74; CDALBS; DA3; DLB 28, 206; DLBY 80; MTCW 1, 2

Olson, Charles (John) 1910-1970 .. **CLC 1, 2, 5, 6, 9, 11, 29; DAM POET; PC 19**
See also CA 13-16; 25-28R; CABS 2; CANR 35, 61; CAP 1; DLB 5, 16, 193; MTCW 1, 2

Olson, Toby 1937- .... **CLC 28**
See also CA 65-68; CANR 9, 31, 84

Olyesha, Yuri
See Olesha, Yuri (Karlovich)

Ondaatje, (Philip) Michael 1943- .... **CLC 14, 29, 51, 76; DAB; DAC; DAM MST; PC 28**
See also CA 77-80; CANR 42, 74; DA3; DLB 60; MTCW 2

Oneal, Elizabeth 1934-
See Oneal, Zibby
See also CA 106; CANR 28, 84; MAICYA; SATA 30, 82

Oneal, Zibby CLC 30
See also Oneal, Elizabeth
See also AAYA 5; CLR 13; JRDA

O'Neill, Eugene (Gladstone)
1888-1953 .... **TCLC 1, 6, 27, 49; DA; DAB; DAC; DAM DRAM, MST; WLC**
See also AITN 1; CA 110; 132; CDALB 1929-1941; DA3; DLB 7; MTCW 1, 2

Onetti, Juan Carlos 1909-1994 ... **CLC 7, 10; DAM MULT, NOV; HLCS 2; SSC 23**
See also CA 85-88; 145; CANR 32, 63; DLB 113; HW 1, 2; MTCW 1, 2

O Nuallain, Brian 1911-1966
See O'Brien, Flann
See also CA 21-22; 25-28R; CAP 2

Ophuls, Max 1902-1957 .... **TCLC 79**
See also CA 113

Opie, Amelia 1769-1853 .... **NCLC 65**
See also DLB 116, 159

Oppen, George 1908-1984 ...... **CLC 7, 13, 34**
See also CA 13-16R; 113; CANR 8, 82; DLB 5, 165

Oppenheim, E(dward) Phillips
1866-1946 .... **TCLC 45**
See also CA 111; DLB 70

Opuls, Max
See Ophuls, Max

Origen c. 185-c. 254 .... **CMLC 19**

Orlovitz, Gil 1918-1973 .... **CLC 22**
See also CA 77-80; 45-48; DLB 2, 5

Orris
See Ingelow, Jean

Ortega y Gasset, Jose 1883-1955 ... **TCLC 9; DAM MULT; HLC 2**
See also CA 106; 130; HW 1, 2; MTCW 1, 2

Ortese, Anna Maria 1914- .... **CLC 89**
See also DLB 177

Ortiz, Simon J(oseph) 1941- . **CLC 45; DAM MULT, POET; PC 17**
See also CA 134; CANR 69; DLB 120, 175; NNAL

Orton, Joe CLC 4, 13, 43; DC 3
See also Orton, John Kingsley
See also CDBLB 1960 to Present; DLB 13; MTCW 2

Orton, John Kingsley 1933-1967
See Orton, Joe
See also CA 85-88; CANR 35, 66; DAM DRAM; MTCW 1, 2

Orwell, George -1950 ...... **TCLC 2, 6, 15, 31, 51; DAB; WLC**
See also Blair, Eric (Arthur)
See also CDBLB 1945-1960; DLB 15, 98, 195

Osborne, David
See Silverberg, Robert

Osborne, George
See Silverberg, Robert

Osborne, John (James) 1929-1994 .... **CLC 1, 2, 5, 11, 45; DA; DAB; DAC; DAM DRAM, MST; WLC**
See also CA 13-16R; 147; CANR 21, 56; CDBLB 1945-1960; DLB 13; MTCW 1, 2

Osborne, Lawrence 1958- .... **CLC 50**

Osbourne, Lloyd 1868-1947 .... **TCLC 93**

Oshima, Nagisa 1932- .... **CLC 20**
See also CA 116; 121; CANR 78

Oskison, John Milton 1874-1947 .. **TCLC 35; DAM MULT**
See also CA 144; CANR 84; DLB 175; NNAL

Ossian c. 3rd cent. - .... **CMLC 28**
See also Macpherson, James

Ossoli, Sarah Margaret (Fuller marchesa d') 1810-1850 .... **NCLC 5, 50**
See also Fuller, Margaret; Fuller, Sarah Margaret
See also CDALB 1640-1865; DLB 1, 59, 73, 83, 223; SATA 25

Ostriker, Alicia (Suskin) 1937- .... **CLC 132**
See also CA 25-28R; CAAS 24; CANR 10, 30, 62; DLB 120

Ostrovsky, Alexander 1823-1886 .. **NCLC 30, 57**

Otero, Blas de 1916-1979 .... **CLC 11**
See also CA 89-92; DLB 134

Otto, Rudolf 1869-1937 .... **TCLC 85**

Otto, Whitney 1955- .... **CLC 70**
See also CA 140

Ouida TCLC 43
See also De La Ramee, (Marie) Louise
See also DLB 18, 156

Ousmane, Sembene 1923- ... **CLC 66; BLC 3**
See also BW 1, 3; CA 117; 125; CANR 81; MTCW 1

Ovid 43B.C.-17 . **CMLC 7; DAM POET; PC 2**
See also DA3; DLB 211

Owen, Hugh
See Faust, Frederick (Schiller)

Owen, Wilfred (Edward Salter) 1893-1918 .... **TCLC 5, 27; DA; DAB; DAC; DAM MST, POET; PC 19; WLC**
See also CA 104; 141; CDBLB 1914-1945; DLB 20; MTCW 2

Owens, Rochelle 1936- .... **CLC 8**
See also CA 17-20R; CAAS 2; CANR 39

Oz, Amos 1939- ..... **CLC 5, 8, 11, 27, 33, 54; DAM NOV**
See also CA 53-56; CANR 27, 47, 65; MTCW 1, 2

Ozick, Cynthia 1928- .... **CLC 3, 7, 28, 62; DAM NOV, POP; SSC 15**
See also BEST 90:1; CA 17-20R; CANR 23, 58; DA3; DLB 28, 152; DLBY 82; INT CANR-23; MTCW 1, 2

Ozu, Yasujiro 1903-1963 .... **CLC 16**
See also CA 112

Pacheco, C.
See Pessoa, Fernando (Antonio Nogueira)

Pacheco, Jose Emilio 1939-
See also CA 111; 131; CANR 65; DAM MULT; HLC 2; HW 1, 2

Pa Chin CLC 18
See also Li Fei-kan

Pack, Robert 1929- .... **CLC 13**
See also CA 1-4R; CANR 3, 44, 82; DLB 5

Padgett, Lewis
See Kuttner, Henry

Padilla (Lorenzo), Heberto 1932- ..... **CLC 38**
See also AITN 1; CA 123; 131; HW 1

Page, Jimmy 1944- .... **CLC 12**

Page, Louise 1955- .... **CLC 40**
See also CA 140; CANR 76

Page, P(atricia) K(athleen) 1916- ...... **CLC 7, 18; DAC; DAM MST; PC 12**
See also CA 53-56; CANR 4, 22, 65; DLB 68; MTCW 1

Page, Thomas Nelson 1853-1922 .... **SSC 23**
See also CA 118; 177; DLB 12, 78; DLBD 13

Pagels, Elaine Hiesey 1943- .... **CLC 104**
See also CA 45-48; CANR 2, 24, 51

Paget, Violet 1856-1935
See Lee, Vernon
See also CA 104; 166

Paget-Lowe, Henry
See Lovecraft, H(oward) P(hillips)

Paglia, Camille (Anna) 1947- .... **CLC 68**
See also CA 140; CANR 72; MTCW 2

Paige, Richard
See Koontz, Dean R(ay)

Paine, Thomas 1737-1809 .... **NCLC 62**
See also CDALB 1640-1865; DLB 31, 43, 73, 158

Pakenham, Antonia
See Fraser, (Lady) Antonia (Pakenham)

Palamas, Kostes 1859-1943 .... **TCLC 5**
See also CA 105

Palazzeschi, Aldo 1885-1974 .... **CLC 11**
See also CA 89-92; 53-56; DLB 114

Pales Matos, Luis 1898-1959
See also HLCS 2; HW 1

Paley, Grace 1922- .... **CLC 4, 6, 37; DAM POP; SSC 8**
See also CA 25-28R; CANR 13, 46, 74; DA3; DLB 28; INT CANR-13; MTCW 1, 2

Palin, Michael (Edward) 1943- .... **CLC 21**
See also Monty Python
See also CA 107; CANR 35; SATA 67

Palliser, Charles 1947- .... **CLC 65**
See also CA 136; CANR 76

Palma, Ricardo 1833-1919 .... **TCLC 29**
See also CA 168

Pancake, Breece Dexter 1952-1979
See Pancake, Breece D'J
See also CA 123; 109

Pancake, Breece D'J CLC 29
See also Pancake, Breece Dexter
See also DLB 130

Pankhurst, Emmeline (Goulden) 1858-1928 .... **TCLC 100**
See also CA 116

Panko, Rudy
See Gogol, Nikolai (Vasilyevich)

Papadiamantis, Alexandros 1851-1911 .... **TCLC 29**
See also CA 168

Papadiamantopoulos, Johannes 1856-1910
See Moreas, Jean
See also CA 117

Papini, Giovanni 1881-1956 .... **TCLC 22**
See also CA 121; 180

Paracelsus 1493-1541 .... **LC 14**
See also DLB 179

Parasol, Peter
See Stevens, Wallace

Pardo Bazan, Emilia 1851-1921 .... **SSC 30**

Pareto, Vilfredo 1848-1923 .... **TCLC 69**
See also CA 175

Paretsky, Sara 1947- .. **CLC 135; DAM POP**
See also AAYA 30; BEST 90:3; CA 125; 129; CANR 59; DA3; INT 129

Parfenie, Maria
See Codrescu, Andrei

Parini, Jay (Lee) 1948- .... **CLC 54, 133**
See also CA 97-100; CAAS 16; CANR 32, 87

Park, Jordan
See Kornbluth, C(yril) M.; Pohl, Frederik

Park, Robert E(zra) 1864-1944 ..... **TCLC 73**
See also CA 122; 165

Parker, Bert
See Ellison, Harlan (Jay)

Parker, Dorothy (Rothschild) 1893-1967 .... **CLC 15, 68; DAM POET; PC 28; SSC 2**
See also CA 19-20; 25-28R; CAP 2; DA3; DLB 11, 45, 86; MTCW 1, 2

Parker, Robert B(rown) 1932- .... **CLC 27; DAM NOV, POP**
See also AAYA 28; BEST 89:4; CA 49-52; CANR 1, 26, 52, 89; INT CANR-26; MTCW 1

Parkin, Frank 1940- .... **CLC 43**
See also CA 147

Parkman, Francis Jr., Jr. 1823-1893 .... **NCLC 12**
See also DLB 1, 30, 186

Parks, Gordon (Alexander Buchanan) 1912- .... **CLC 1, 16; BLC 3; DAM MULT**
See also AITN 2; BW 2, 3; CA 41-44R; CANR 26, 66; DA3; DLB 33; MTCW 2; SATA 8, 108

Parmenides c. 515B.C.-c. 450B.C. .... **CMLC 22**
See also DLB 176

Parnell, Thomas 1679-1718 .... **LC 3**
See also DLB 94

Parra, Nicanor 1914- ...... **CLC 2, 102; DAM MULT; HLC 2**
See also CA 85-88; CANR 32; HW 1; MTCW 1

Parra Sanojo, Ana Teresa de la 1890-1936
See also HLCS 2

Parrish, Mary Frances
See Fisher, M(ary) F(rances) K(ennedy)

Parson
See Coleridge, Samuel Taylor

Parson Lot
See Kingsley, Charles

Parton, Sara Payson Willis 1811-1872 .... **NCLC 86**
See also DLB 43, 74

Partridge, Anthony
See Oppenheim, E(dward) Phillips

Pascal, Blaise 1623-1662 .... **LC 35**

Pascoli, Giovanni 1855-1912 .... **TCLC 45**
See also CA 170

Pasolini, Pier Paolo 1922-1975 .. **CLC 20, 37, 106; PC 17**
See also CA 93-96; 61-64; CANR 63; DLB 128, 177; MTCW 1

Pasquini
See Silone, Ignazio

Pastan, Linda (Olenik) 1932- .... **CLC 27; DAM POET**
See also CA 61-64; CANR 18, 40, 61; DLB 5

Pasternak, Boris (Leonidovich) 1890-1960 .... **CLC 7, 10, 18, 63; DA; DAB; DAC; DAM MST, NOV, POET; PC 6; SSC 31; WLC**
See also CA 127; 116; DA3; MTCW 1, 2

Patchen, Kenneth 1911-1972 .. **CLC 1, 2, 18; DAM POET**
See also CA 1-4R; 33-36R; CANR 3, 35; DLB 16, 48; MTCW 1

Pater, Walter (Horatio) 1839-1894 . **NCLC 7, 90**
See also CDBLB 1832-1890; DLB 57, 156

Paterson, A(ndrew) B(arton) 1864-1941 .... **TCLC 32**
See also CA 155; SATA 97

Paterson, Katherine (Womeldorf) 1932- .... **CLC 12, 30**
See also AAYA 1, 31; CA 21-24R; CANR 28, 59; CLR 7, 50; DLB 52; JRDA; MAI-CYA; MTCW 1; SATA 13, 53, 92

Patmore, Coventry Kersey Dighton 1823-1896 .... **NCLC 9**
See also DLB 35, 98

Powell, Adam Clayton, Jr.
1908-1972 .... **CLC 89; BLC 3; DAM MULT**
See also BW 1, 3; CA 102; 33-36R; CANR 86

Powell, Anthony (Dymoke) 1905- . **CLC 1, 3, 7, 9, 10, 31**
See also CA 1-4R; CANR 1, 32, 62; CD-BLB 1945-1960; DLB 15; MTCW 1, 2

Powell, Dawn 1897-1965 .... **CLC 66**
See also CA 5-8R; DLBY 97

Powell, Padgett 1952- .... **CLC 34**
See also CA 126; CANR 63

Powell, Talmage 1920-
See Queen, Ellery
See also CA 5-8R; CANR 2, 80

Power, Susan 1961- .... **CLC 91**
See also CA 145

Powers, J(ames) F(arl) 1917-1999 ..... **CLC 1, 4, 8, 57; SSC 4**
See also CA 1-4R; 181; CANR 2, 61; DLB 130; MTCW 1

Powers, John J(ames) 1945-
See Powers, John R.
See also CA 69-72

Powers, John R. CLC 66
See also Powers, John J(ames)

Powers, Richard (S.) 1957- .... **CLC 93**
See also CA 148; CANR 80

Pownall, David 1938- .... **CLC 10**
See also CA 89-92, 180; CAAS 18; CANR 49; DLB 14

Powys, John Cowper 1872-1963 ... **CLC 7, 9, 15, 46, 125**
See also CA 85-88; DLB 15; MTCW 1, 2

Powys, T(heodore) F(rancis)
1875-1953 .... **TCLC 9**
See also CA 106; DLB 36, 162

Prado (Calvo), Pedro 1886-1952 ... **TCLC 75**
See also CA 131; HW 1

Prager, Emily 1952- .... **CLC 56**

Pratt, E(dwin) J(ohn)
1883(?)-1964 .... **CLC 19; DAC; DAM POET**
See also CA 141; 93-96; CANR 77; DLB 92

Premchand TCLC 21
See also Srivastava, Dhanpat Rai

Preussler, Otfried 1923- .... **CLC 17**
See also CA 77-80; SATA 24

Prevert, Jacques (Henri Marie)
1900-1977 .... **CLC 15**
See also CA 77-80; 69-72; CANR 29, 61; MTCW 1; SATA-Obit 30

Prevost, Abbe (Antoine Francois)
1697-1763 .... **LC 1**

Price, (Edward) Reynolds 1933- ... **CLC 3, 6, 13, 43, 50, 63; DAM NOV; SSC 22**
See also CA 1-4R; CANR 1, 37, 57, 87; DLB 2; INT CANR-37

Price, Richard 1949- .... **CLC 6, 12**
See also CA 49-52; CANR 3; DLBY 81

Prichard, Katharine Susannah
1883-1969 .... **CLC 46**
See also CA 11-12; CANR 33; CAP 1; MTCW 1; SATA 66

Priestley, J(ohn) B(oynton)
1894-1984 .... **CLC 2, 5, 9, 34; DAM DRAM, NOV**
See also CA 9-12R; 113; CANR 33; CD-BLB 1914-1945; DA3; DLB 10, 34, 77, 100, 139; DLBY 84; MTCW 1, 2

Prince 1958(?)- .... **CLC 35**

Prince, F(rank) T(empleton) 1912- .. **CLC 22**
See also CA 101; CANR 43, 79; DLB 20

Prince Kropotkin
See Kropotkin, Peter (Alekseievich)

Prior, Matthew 1664-1721 .... **LC 4**
See also DLB 95

Prishvin, Mikhail 1873-1954 .... **TCLC 75**

Pritchard, William H(arrison)
1932- .... **CLC 34**
See also CA 65-68; CANR 23; DLB 111

Pritchett, V(ictor) S(awdon)
1900-1997 ...... **CLC 5, 13, 15, 41; DAM NOV; SSC 14**
See also CA 61-64; 157; CANR 31, 63; DA3; DLB 15, 139; MTCW 1, 2

Private 19022
See Manning, Frederic

Probst, Mark 1925- .... **CLC 59**
See also CA 130

Prokosch, Frederic 1908-1989 ...... **CLC 4, 48**
See also CA 73-76; 128; CANR 82; DLB 48; MTCW 2

Propertius, Sextus c. 50B.C.-c. 16B.C. .... **CMLC 32**
See also DLB 211

Prophet, The
See Dreiser, Theodore (Herman Albert)

Prose, Francine 1947- .... **CLC 45**
See also CA 109; 112; CANR 46; SATA 101

Proudhon
See Cunha, Euclides (Rodrigues Pimenta) da

Proulx, Annie
See Proulx, E(dna) Annie

Proulx, E(dna) Annie 1935- .. **CLC 81; DAM POP**
See also CA 145; CANR 65; DA3; MTCW 2

Proust, (Valentin-Louis-George-Eugene-)
Marcel 1871-1922 .... **TCLC 7, 13, 33; DA; DAB; DAC; DAM MST, NOV; WLC**
See also CA 104; 120; DA3; DLB 65; MTCW 1, 2

Prowler, Harley
See Masters, Edgar Lee

Prus, Boleslaw 1845-1912 .... **TCLC 48**

Pryor, Richard (Franklin Lenox Thomas)
1940- .... **CLC 26**
See also CA 122; 152

Przybyszewski, Stanislaw
1868-1927 .... **TCLC 36**
See also CA 160; DLB 66

Pteleon
See Grieve, C(hristopher) M(urray)
See also DAM POET

Puckett, Lute
See Masters, Edgar Lee

Puig, Manuel 1932-1990 .... **CLC 3, 5, 10, 28, 65, 133; DAM MULT; HLC 2**
See also CA 45-48; CANR 2, 32, 63; DA3; DLB 113; HW 1, 2; MTCW 1, 2

Pulitzer, Joseph 1847-1911 .... **TCLC 76**
See also CA 114; DLB 23

Purdy, A(lfred) W(ellington) 1918- ... **CLC 3, 6, 14, 50; DAC; DAM MST, POET**
See also CA 81-84; CAAS 17; CANR 42, 66; DLB 88

Purdy, James (Amos) 1923- .... **CLC 2, 4, 10, 28, 52**
See also CA 33-36R; CAAS 1; CANR 19, 51; DLB 2; INT CANR-19; MTCW 1

Pure, Simon
See Swinnerton, Frank Arthur

Pushkin, Alexander (Sergeyevich)
1799-1837 . **NCLC 3, 27, 83; DA; DAB; DAC; DAM DRAM, MST, POET; PC 10; SSC 27; WLC**
See also DA3; DLB 205; SATA 61

P'u Sung-ling 1640-1715 .... **LC 49; SSC 31**

Putnam, Arthur Lee
See Alger, Horatio Jr., Jr.

Puzo, Mario 1920-1999 .... **CLC 1, 2, 6, 36, 107; DAM NOV, POP**
See also CA 65-68; 185; CANR 4, 42, 65; DA3; DLB 6; MTCW 1, 2

Pygge, Edward
See Barnes, Julian (Patrick)

Pyle, Ernest Taylor 1900-1945
See Pyle, Ernie
See also CA 115; 160

Pyle, Ernie 1900-1945 .... **TCLC 75**
See also Pyle, Ernest Taylor
See also DLB 29; MTCW 2

Pyle, Howard 1853-1911 .... **TCLC 81**
See also CA 109; 137; CLR 22; DLB 42, 188; DLBD 13; MAICYA; SATA 16, 100

Pym, Barbara (Mary Crampton)
1913-1980 .... **CLC 13, 19, 37, 111**
See also CA 13-14; 97-100; CANR 13, 34; CAP 1; DLB 14, 207; DLBY 87; MTCW 1, 2

Pynchon, Thomas (Ruggles, Jr.)
1937- ...... **CLC 2, 3, 6, 9, 11, 18, 33, 62, 72, 123; DA; DAB; DAC; DAM MST, NOV, POP; SSC 14; WLC**
See also BEST 90:2; CA 17-20R; CANR 22, 46, 73; DA3; DLB 2, 173; MTCW 1, 2

Pythagoras c. 570B.C.-c. 500B.C. . **CMLC 22**
See also DLB 176

Q
See Quiller-Couch, SirArthur (Thomas)

Qian Zhongshu
See Ch'ien Chung-shu

Qroll
See Dagerman, Stig (Halvard)

Quarrington, Paul (Lewis) 1953- ..... **CLC 65**
See also CA 129; CANR 62

Quasimodo, Salvatore 1901-1968 ..... **CLC 10**
See also CA 13-16; 25-28R; CAP 1; DLB 114; MTCW 1

Quay, Stephen 1947- .... **CLC 95**

Quay, Timothy 1947- .... **CLC 95**

Queen, Ellery CLC 3, 11
See also Dannay, Frederic; Davidson, Avram (James); Hoch, Edward D(entinger); Lee, Manfred B(ennington); Marlowe, Stephen; Powell, Talmage; Sturgeon, Theodore (Hamilton); Vance, John Holbrook

Queen, Ellery, Jr.
See Dannay, Frederic; Lee, Manfred B(ennington)

Queneau, Raymond 1903-1976 ..... **CLC 2, 5, 10, 42**
See also CA 77-80; 69-72; CANR 32; DLB 72; MTCW 1, 2

Quevedo, Francisco de 1580-1645 .... **LC 23**

Quiller-Couch, SirArthur (Thomas)
1863-1944 .... **TCLC 53**
See also CA 118; 166; DLB 135, 153, 190

Quin, Ann (Marie) 1936-1973 .... **CLC 6**
See also CA 9-12R; 45-48; DLB 14

Quinn, Martin
See Smith, Martin Cruz

Quinn, Peter 1947- .... **CLC 91**

Quinn, Simon
See Smith, Martin Cruz

Quintana, Leroy V. 1944-
See also CA 131; CANR 65; DAM MULT; DLB 82; HLC 2; HW 1, 2

Quiroga, Horacio (Sylvestre)
1878-1937 .... **TCLC 20; DAM MULT; HLC 2**
See also CA 117; 131; HW 1; MTCW 1

Quoirez, Francoise 1935- .... **CLC 9**
See also Sagan, Francoise
See also CA 49-52; CANR 6, 39, 73; MTCW 1, 2

Reymont, Wladyslaw (Stanislaw)
1868(?)-1925 .... **TCLC 5**
See also CA 104

Reynolds, Jonathan 1942- .... **CLC 6, 38**
See also CA 65-68; CANR 28

Reynolds, Joshua 1723-1792 .... **LC 15**
See also DLB 104

Reynolds, Michael S(hane) 1937- ..... **CLC 44**
See also CA 65-68; CANR 9, 89

Reznikoff, Charles 1894-1976 .... **CLC 9**
See also CA 33-36; 61-64; CAP 2; DLB 28, 45

Rezzori (d'Arezzo), Gregor von
1914-1998 .... **CLC 25**
See also CA 122; 136; 167

Rhine, Richard
See Silverstein, Alvin

Rhodes, Eugene Manlove
1869-1934 .... **TCLC 53**

Rhodius, Apollonius c. 3rd cent.
B.C.- .... **CMLC 28**
See also DLB 176

R'hoone
See Balzac, Honore de

Rhys, Jean 1890(?)-1979 ...... **CLC 2, 4, 6, 14, 19, 51, 124; DAM NOV; SSC 21**
See also CA 25-28R; 85-88; CANR 35, 62; CDBLB 1945-1960; DA3; DLB 36, 117, 162; MTCW 1, 2

Ribeiro, Darcy 1922-1997 .... **CLC 34**
See also CA 33-36R; 156

Ribeiro, Joao Ubaldo (Osorio Pimentel)
1941- .... **CLC 10, 67**
See also CA 81-84

Ribman, Ronald (Burt) 1932- .... **CLC 7**
See also CA 21-24R; CANR 46, 80

Ricci, Nino 1959- .... **CLC 70**
See also CA 137

Rice, Anne 1941- .. **CLC 41, 128; DAM POP**
See also AAYA 9; BEST 89:2; CA 65-68; CANR 12, 36, 53, 74; DA3; MTCW 2

Rice, Elmer (Leopold) 1892-1967 ...... **CLC 7, 49; DAM DRAM**
See also CA 21-22; 25-28R; CAP 2; DLB 4, 7; MTCW 1, 2

Rice, Tim(othy Miles Bindon)
1944- .... **CLC 21**
See also CA 103; CANR 46

Rich, Adrienne (Cecile) 1929- ... **CLC 3, 6, 7, 11, 18, 36, 73, 76, 125; DAM POET; PC 5**
See also CA 9-12R; CANR 20, 53, 74; CDALBS; DA3; DLB 5, 67; MTCW 1, 2

Rich, Barbara
See Graves, Robert (von Ranke)

Rich, Robert
See Trumbo, Dalton

Richard, Keith CLC 17
See also Richards, Keith

Richards, David Adams 1950- .... **CLC 59; DAC**
See also CA 93-96; CANR 60; DLB 53

Richards, I(vor) A(rmstrong)
1893-1979 .... **CLC 14, 24**
See also CA 41-44R; 89-92; CANR 34, 74; DLB 27; MTCW 2

Richards, Keith 1943-
See Richard, Keith
See also CA 107; CANR 77

Richardson, Anne
See Roiphe, Anne (Richardson)

Richardson, Dorothy Miller
1873-1957 .... **TCLC 3**
See also CA 104; DLB 36

Richardson, Ethel Florence (Lindesay)
1870-1946
See Richardson, Henry Handel
See also CA 105

Richardson, Henry Handel TCLC 4
See also Richardson, Ethel Florence (Lindesay)
See also DLB 197

Richardson, John 1796-1852 .... **NCLC 55; DAC**
See also DLB 99

Richardson, Samuel 1689-1761 ...... **LC 1, 44; DA; DAB; DAC; DAM MST, NOV; WLC**
See also CDBLB 1660-1789; DLB 39

Richler, Mordecai 1931- ...... **CLC 3, 5, 9, 13, 18, 46, 70; DAC; DAM MST, NOV**
See also AITN 1; CA 65-68; CANR 31, 62; CLR 17; DLB 53; MAICYA; MTCW 1, 2; SATA 44, 98; SATA-Brief 27

Richter, Conrad (Michael)
1890-1968 .... **CLC 30**
See also AAYA 21; CA 5-8R; 25-28R; CANR 23; DLB 9, 212; MTCW 1, 2; SATA 3

Ricostranza, Tom
See Ellis, Trey

Riddell, Charlotte 1832-1906 .... **TCLC 40**
See also CA 165; DLB 156

Ridge, John Rollin 1827-1867 ...... **NCLC 82; DAM MULT**
See also CA 144; DLB 175; NNAL

Ridgway, Keith 1965- .... **CLC 119**
See also CA 172

Riding, Laura CLC 3, 7
See also Jackson, Laura (Riding)

Riefenstahl, Berta Helene Amalia 1902-
See Riefenstahl, Leni
See also CA 108

Riefenstahl, Leni CLC 16
See also Riefenstahl, Berta Helene Amalia

Riffe, Ernest
See Bergman, (Ernst) Ingmar

Riggs, (Rolla) Lynn 1899-1954 ..... **TCLC 56; DAM MULT**
See also CA 144; DLB 175; NNAL

Riis, Jacob A(ugust) 1849-1914 ..... **TCLC 80**
See also CA 113; 168; DLB 23

Riley, James Whitcomb
1849-1916 .... **TCLC 51; DAM POET**
See also CA 118; 137; MAICYA; SATA 17

Riley, Tex
See Creasey, John

Rilke, Rainer Maria 1875-1926 .. **TCLC 1, 6, 19; DAM POET; PC 2**
See also CA 104; 132; CANR 62; DA3; DLB 81; MTCW 1, 2

Rimbaud, (Jean Nicolas) Arthur
1854-1891 . **NCLC 4, 35, 82; DA; DAB; DAC; DAM MST, POET; PC 3; WLC**
See also DA3

Rinehart, Mary Roberts
1876-1958 .... **TCLC 52**
See also CA 108; 166

Ringmaster, The
See Mencken, H(enry) L(ouis)

Ringwood, Gwen(dolyn Margaret) Pharis
1910-1984 .... **CLC 48**
See also CA 148; 112; DLB 88

Rio, Michel 19(?)- .... **CLC 43**

Ritsos, Giannes
See Ritsos, Yannis

Ritsos, Yannis 1909-1990 .... **CLC 6, 13, 31**
See also CA 77-80; 133; CANR 39, 61; MTCW 1

Ritter, Erika 1948(?)- .... **CLC 52**

Rivera, Jose Eustasio 1889-1928 ... **TCLC 35**
See also CA 162; HW 1, 2

Rivera, Tomas 1935-1984
See also CA 49-52; CANR 32; DLB 82; HLCS 2; HW 1

Rivers, Conrad Kent 1933-1968 .... **CLC 1**
See also BW 1; CA 85-88; DLB 41

Rivers, Elfrida
See Bradley, Marion Zimmer

Riverside, John
See Heinlein, Robert A(nson)

Rizal, Jose 1861-1896 .... **NCLC 27**

Roa Bastos, Augusto (Antonio)
1917- .... **CLC 45; DAM MULT; HLC 2**
See also CA 131; DLB 113; HW 1

Robbe-Grillet, Alain 1922- .... **CLC 1, 2, 4, 6, 8, 10, 14, 43, 128**
See also CA 9-12R; CANR 33, 65; DLB 83; MTCW 1, 2

Robbins, Harold 1916-1997 .... **CLC 5; DAM NOV**
See also CA 73-76; 162; CANR 26, 54; DA3; MTCW 1, 2

Robbins, Thomas Eugene 1936-
See Robbins, Tom
See also CA 81-84; CANR 29, 59; DAM NOV, POP; DA3; MTCW 1, 2

Robbins, Tom CLC 9, 32, 64
See also Robbins, Thomas Eugene
See also AAYA 32; BEST 90:3; DLBY 80; MTCW 2

Robbins, Trina 1938- .... **CLC 21**
See also CA 128

Roberts, Charles G(eorge) D(ouglas)
1860-1943 .... **TCLC 8**
See also CA 105; CLR 33; DLB 92; SATA 88; SATA-Brief 29

Roberts, Elizabeth Madox
1886-1941 .... **TCLC 68**
See also CA 111; 166; DLB 9, 54, 102; SATA 33; SATA-Brief 27

Roberts, Kate 1891-1985 .... **CLC 15**
See also CA 107; 116

Roberts, Keith (John Kingston)
1935- .... **CLC 14**
See also CA 25-28R; CANR 46

Roberts, Kenneth (Lewis)
1885-1957 .... **TCLC 23**
See also CA 109; DLB 9

Roberts, Michele (B.) 1949- .... **CLC 48**
See also CA 115; CANR 58

Robertson, Ellis
See Ellison, Harlan (Jay); Silverberg, Robert

Robertson, Thomas William
1829-1871 .... **NCLC 35; DAM DRAM**

Robeson, Kenneth
See Dent, Lester

Robinson, Edwin Arlington
1869-1935 ..... **TCLC 5, 101; DA; DAC; DAM MST, POET; PC 1**
See also CA 104; 133; CDALB 1865-1917; DLB 54; MTCW 1, 2

Robinson, Henry Crabb
1775-1867 .... **NCLC 15**
See also DLB 107

Robinson, Jill 1936- .... **CLC 10**
See also CA 102; INT 102

Robinson, Kim Stanley 1952- .... **CLC 34**
See also AAYA 26; CA 126; SATA 109

Robinson, Lloyd
See Silverberg, Robert

Robinson, Marilynne 1944- .... **CLC 25**
See also CA 116; CANR 80; DLB 206

Robinson, Smokey CLC 21
See also Robinson, William, Jr.

Robinson, William, Jr. 1940-
See Robinson, Smokey
See also CA 116

Robison, Mary 1949- .... **CLC 42, 98**
See also CA 113; 116; CANR 87; DLB 130; INT 116

Rod, Edouard 1857-1910 .... **TCLC 52**
Roddenberry, Eugene Wesley 1921-1991
  See Roddenberry, Gene
  See also CA 110; 135; CANR 37; SATA 45;
  SATA-Obit 69
Roddenberry, Gene CLC 17
  See also Roddenberry, Eugene Wesley
  See also AAYA 5; SATA-Obit 69
Rodgers, Mary 1931- .... **CLC 12**
  See also CA 49-52; CANR 8, 55, 90; CLR
  20; INT CANR-8; JRDA; MAICYA;
  SATA 8
Rodgers, W(illiam) R(obert)
  1909-1969 .... **CLC 7**
  See also CA 85-88; DLB 20
Rodman, Eric
  See Silverberg, Robert
Rodman, Howard 1920(?)-1985 .... **CLC 65**
  See also CA 118
Rodman, Maia
  See Wojciechowska, Maia (Teresa)
Rodo, Jose Enrique 1872(?)-1917
  See also CA 178; HLCS 2; HW 2
Rodriguez, Claudio 1934- .... **CLC 10**
  See also DLB 134
Rodriguez, Richard 1944-
  See also CA 110; CANR 66; DAM MULT;
  DLB 82; HLC 2; HW 1, 2
Roelvaag, O(le) E(dvart)
  1876-1931 .... **TCLC 17**
  See Rolvaag, O(le) E(dvart)
  See also CA 117; 171; DLB 9
Roethke, Theodore (Huebner)
  1908-1963 .... **CLC 1, 3, 8, 11, 19, 46,**
  101; DAM POET; PC 15
  See also CA 81-84; CABS 2; CDALB 1941-
  1968; DA3; DLB 5, 206; MTCW 1, 2
Rogers, Samuel 1763-1855 .... **NCLC 69**
  See also DLB 93
Rogers, Thomas Hunton 1927- .... **CLC 57**
  See also CA 89-92; INT 89-92
Rogers, Will(iam Penn Adair)
  1879-1935 ... **TCLC 8, 71; DAM MULT**
  See also CA 105; 144; DA3; DLB 11;
  MTCW 2; NNAL
Rogin, Gilbert 1929- .... **CLC 18**
  See also CA 65-68; CANR 15
Rohan, Koda
  See Koda Shigeyuki
Rohlfs, Anna Katharine Green
  See Green, Anna Katharine
Rohmer, Eric CLC 16
  See also Scherer, Jean-Marie Maurice
Rohmer, Sax TCLC 28
  See also Ward, Arthur Henry Sarsfield
  See also DLB 70
Roiphe, Anne (Richardson) 1935- .. **CLC 3, 9**
  See also CA 89-92; CANR 45, 73; DLBY
  80; INT 89-92
Rojas, Fernando de 1465-1541 .... **LC 23;**
  HLCS 1
Rojas, Gonzalo 1917-
  See also HLCS 2; HW 2
Rojas, Gonzalo 1917-
  See also CA 178; HLCS 2
Rolfe, Frederick (William Serafino Austin
  Lewis Mary) 1860-1913 .... **TCLC 12**
  See also CA 107; DLB 34, 156
Rolland, Romain 1866-1944 .... **TCLC 23**
  See also CA 118; DLB 65
Rolle, Richard c. 1300-c. 1349 ...... **CMLC 21**
  See also DLB 146
Rolvaag, O(le) E(dvart)
  See Roelvaag, O(le) E(dvart)
Romain Arnaud, Saint
  See Aragon, Louis

Romains, Jules 1885-1972 .... **CLC 7**
  See also CA 85-88; CANR 34; DLB 65;
  MTCW 1
Romero, Jose Ruben 1890-1952 .... **TCLC 14**
  See also CA 114; 131; HW 1
Ronsard, Pierre de 1524-1585 . **LC 6, 54; PC**
  11
Rooke, Leon 1934- . **CLC 25, 34; DAM POP**
  See also CA 25-28R; CANR 23, 53
Roosevelt, Franklin Delano
  1882-1945 .... **TCLC 93**
  See also CA 116; 173
Roosevelt, Theodore 1858-1919 ..... **TCLC 69**
  See also CA 115; 170; DLB 47, 186
Roper, William 1498-1578 .... **LC 10**
Roquelaure, A. N.
  See Rice, Anne
Rosa, Joao Guimaraes 1908-1967 ... **CLC 23;**
  HLCS 1
  See also CA 89-92; DLB 113
Rose, Wendy 1948- .. **CLC 85; DAM MULT;**
  PC 13
  See also CA 53-56; CANR 5, 51; DLB 175;
  NNAL; SATA 12
Rosen, R. D.
  See Rosen, Richard (Dean)
Rosen, Richard (Dean) 1949- .... **CLC 39**
  See also CA 77-80; CANR 62; INT
  CANR-30
Rosenberg, Isaac 1890-1918 .... **TCLC 12**
  See also CA 107; DLB 20
Rosenblatt, Joe CLC 15
  See also Rosenblatt, Joseph
Rosenblatt, Joseph 1933-
  See Rosenblatt, Joe
  See also CA 89-92; INT 89-92
Rosenfeld, Samuel
  See Tzara, Tristan
Rosenstock, Sami
  See Tzara, Tristan
Rosenstock, Samuel
  See Tzara, Tristan
Rosenthal, M(acha) L(ouis)
  1917-1996 .... **CLC 28**
  See also CA 1-4R; 152; CAAS 6; CANR 4,
  51; DLB 5; SATA 59
Ross, Barnaby
  See Dannay, Frederic
Ross, Bernard L.
  See Follett, Ken(neth Martin)
Ross, J. H.
  See Lawrence, T(homas) E(dward)
Ross, John Hume
  See Lawrence, T(homas) E(dward)
Ross, Martin
  See Martin, Violet Florence
  See also DLB 135
Ross, (James) Sinclair 1908-1996 ... **CLC 13;**
  DAC; DAM MST; SSC 24
  See also CA 73-76; CANR 81; DLB 88
Rossetti, Christina (Georgina)
  1830-1894 . **NCLC 2, 50, 66; DA; DAB;**
  DAC; DAM MST, POET; PC 7; WLC
  See also DA3; DLB 35, 163; MAICYA;
  SATA 20
Rossetti, Dante Gabriel 1828-1882 . **NCLC 4,**
  77; DA; DAB; DAC; DAM MST,
  POET; WLC
  See also CDBLB 1832-1890; DLB 35
Rossner, Judith (Perelman) 1935- . **CLC 6, 9,**
  29
  See also AITN 2; BEST 90:3; CA 17-20R;
  CANR 18, 51, 73; DLB 6; INT CANR-
  18; MTCW 1, 2
Rostand, Edmond (Eugene Alexis)
  1868-1918 .... **TCLC 6, 37; DA; DAB;**
  DAC; DAM DRAM, MST; DC 10
  See also CA 104; 126; DA3; DLB 192;
  MTCW 1

Roth, Henry 1906-1995 ..... **CLC 2, 6, 11, 104**
  See also CA 11-12; 149; CANR 38, 63;
  CAP 1; DA3; DLB 28; MTCW 1, 2
Roth, Philip (Milton) 1933- ... **CLC 1, 2, 3, 4,**
  6, 9, 15, 22, 31, 47, 66, 86, 119; DA;
  DAB; DAC; DAM MST, NOV, POP;
  SSC 26; WLC
  See also BEST 90:3; CA 1-4R; CANR 1,
  22, 36, 55, 89; CDALB 1968-1988; DA3;
  DLB 2, 28, 173; DLBY 82; MTCW 1, 2
Rothenberg, Jerome 1931- .... **CLC 6, 57**
  See also CA 45-48; CANR 1; DLB 5, 193
Roumain, Jacques (Jean Baptiste)
  1907-1944 ...... **TCLC 19; BLC 3; DAM**
  MULT
  See also BW 1; CA 117; 125
Rourke, Constance (Mayfield)
  1885-1941 .... **TCLC 12**
  See also CA 107; YABC 1
Rousseau, Jean-Baptiste 1671-1741 ...... **LC 9**
Rousseau, Jean-Jacques 1712-1778 .... **LC 14,**
  36; DA; DAB; DAC; DAM MST; WLC
  See also DA3
Roussel, Raymond 1877-1933 .... **TCLC 20**
  See also CA 117
Rovit, Earl (Herbert) 1927- .... **CLC 7**
  See also CA 5-8R; CANR 12
Rowe, Elizabeth Singer 1674-1737 ..... **LC 44**
  See also DLB 39, 95
Rowe, Nicholas 1674-1718 .... **LC 8**
  See also DLB 84
Rowley, Ames Dorrance
  See Lovecraft, H(oward) P(hillips)
Rowson, Susanna Haswell
  1762(?)-1824 .... **NCLC 5, 69**
  See also DLB 37, 200
Roy, Arundhati 1960(?)- .... **CLC 109**
  See also CA 163; CANR 90; DLBY 97
Roy, Gabrielle 1909-1983 .... **CLC 10, 14;**
  DAB; DAC; DAM MST
  See also CA 53-56; 110; CANR 5, 61; DLB
  68; MTCW 1; SATA 104
Royko, Mike 1932-1997 .... **CLC 109**
  See also CA 89-92; 157; CANR 26
Rozewicz, Tadeusz 1921- .. **CLC 9, 23; DAM**
  POET
  See also CA 108; CANR 36, 66; DA3;
  MTCW 1, 2
Ruark, Gibbons 1941- .... **CLC 3**
  See also CA 33-36R; CAAS 23; CANR 14,
  31, 57; DLB 120
Rubens, Bernice (Ruth) 1923- .... **CLC 19, 31**
  See also CA 25-28R; CANR 33, 65; DLB
  14, 207; MTCW 1
Rubin, Harold
  See Robbins, Harold
Rudkin, (James) David 1936- .... **CLC 14**
  See also CA 89-92; DLB 13
Rudnik, Raphael 1933- .... **CLC 7**
  See also CA 29-32R
Ruffian, M.
  See Hasek, Jaroslav (Matej Frantisek)
Ruiz, Jose Martinez CLC 11
  See also Martinez Ruiz, Jose
Rukeyser, Muriel 1913-1980 . **CLC 6, 10, 15,**
  27; DAM POET; PC 12
  See also CA 5-8R; 93-96; CANR 26, 60;
  DA3; DLB 48; MTCW 1, 2; SATA-Obit
  22
Rule, Jane (Vance) 1931- .... **CLC 27**
  See also CA 25-28R; CAAS 18; CANR 12,
  87; DLB 60
Rulfo, Juan 1918-1986 ...... **CLC 8, 80; DAM**
  MULT; HLC 2; SSC 25
  See also CA 85-88; 118; CANR 26; DLB
  113; HW 1, 2; MTCW 1, 2

Rumi, Jalal al-Din 1297-1373 .... **CMLC 20**
Runeberg, Johan 1804-1877 .... **NCLC 41**
Runyon, (Alfred) Damon
    1884(?)-1946 .... **TCLC 10**
    See also CA 107; 165; DLB 11, 86, 171;
    MTCW 2
Rush, Norman 1933- .... **CLC 44**
    See also CA 121; 126; INT 126
Rushdie, (Ahmed) Salman 1947- .... **CLC 23,**
    31, 55, 100; DAB; DAC; DAM MST,
    NOV, POP; WLCS
    See also BEST 89:3; CA 108; 111; CANR
    33, 56; DA3; DLB 194; INT 111; MTCW
    1, 2
Rushforth, Peter (Scott) 1945- .... **CLC 19**
    See also CA 101
Ruskin, John 1819-1900 .... **TCLC 63**
    See also CA 114; 129; CDBLB 1832-1890;
    DLB 55, 163, 190; SATA 24
Russ, Joanna 1937- .... **CLC 15**
    See also CA 5-28R; CANR 11, 31, 65; DLB
    8; MTCW 1
Russell, George William 1867-1935
    See Baker, Jean H.
    See also CA 104; 153; CDBLB 1890-1914;
    DAM POET
Russell, (Henry) Ken(neth Alfred)
    1927- .... **CLC 16**
    See also CA 105
Russell, William Martin 1947- .... **CLC 60**
    See also CA 164
Rutherford, Mark **TCLC 25**
    See also White, William Hale
    See also DLB 18
Ruyslinck, Ward 1929- .... **CLC 14**
    See also Belser, Reimond Karel Maria de
Ryan, Cornelius (John) 1920-1974 ..... **CLC 7**
    See also CA 69-72; 53-56; CANR 38
Ryan, Michael 1946- .... **CLC 65**
    See also CA 49-52; DLBY 82
Ryan, Tim
    See Dent, Lester
Rybakov, Anatoli (Naumovich)
    1911-1998 .... **CLC 23, 53**
    See also CA 126; 135; 172; SATA 79;
    SATA-Obit 108
Ryder, Jonathan
    See Ludlum, Robert
Ryga, George 1932-1987 .... **CLC 14; DAC;**
    DAM MST
    See also CA 101; 124; CANR 43, 90; DLB
    60
S. H.
    See Hartmann, Sadakichi
S. S.
    See Sassoon, Siegfried (Lorraine)
Saba, Umberto 1883-1957 .... **TCLC 33**
    See also CA 144; CANR 79; DLB 114
Sabatini, Rafael 1875-1950 .... **TCLC 47**
    See also CA 162
Sabato, Ernesto (R.) 1911- .... **CLC 10, 23;**
    DAM MULT; HLC 2
    See also CA 97-100; CANR 32, 65; DLB
    145; HW 1, 2; MTCW 1, 2
Sa-Carniero, Mario de 1890-1916 . **TCLC 83**
Sacastru, Martin
    See Bioy Casares, Adolfo
Sacastru, Martin
    See Bioy Casares, Adolfo
Sacher-Masoch, Leopold von
    1836(?)-1895 .... **NCLC 31**
Sachs, Marilyn (Stickle) 1927- .... **CLC 35**
    See also AAYA 2; CA 17-20R; CANR 13,
    47; CLR 2; JRDA; MAICYA; SAAS 2;
    SATA 3, 68; SATA-Essay 110
Sachs, Nelly 1891-1970 .... **CLC 14, 98**
    See also CA 17-18; 25-28R; CANR 87;
    CAP 2; MTCW 2

Sackler, Howard (Oliver)
    1929-1982 .... **CLC 14**
    See also CA 61-64; 108; CANR 30; DLB 7
Sacks, Oliver (Wolf) 1933- .... **CLC 67**
    See also CA 53-56; CANR 28, 50, 76; DA3;
    INT CANR-28; MTCW 1, 2
Sadakichi
    See Hartmann, Sadakichi
Sade, Donatien Alphonse Francois, Comte
    de 1740-1814 .... **NCLC 47**
Sadoff, Ira 1945- .... **CLC 9**
    See also CA 53-56; CANR 5, 21; DLB 120
Saetone
    See Camus, Albert
Safire, William 1929- .... **CLC 10**
    See also CA 17-20R; CANR 31, 54, 91
Sagan, Carl (Edward) 1934-1996 .... **CLC 30,**
    112
    See also AAYA 2; CA 25-28R; 155; CANR
    11, 36, 74; DA3; MTCW 1, 2; SATA 58;
    SATA-Obit 94
Sagan, Francoise **CLC 3, 6, 9, 17, 36**
    See also Quoirez, Francoise
    See also DLB 83; MTCW 2
Sahgal, Nayantara (Pandit) 1927- .... **CLC 41**
    See also CA 9-12R; CANR 11, 88
Said, Edward W. 1935- .... **CLC 123**
    See also CA 21-24R; CANR 45, 74; DLB
    67; MTCW 2
Saint, H(arry) F. 1941- .... **CLC 50**
    See also CA 127
St. Aubin de Teran, Lisa 1953-
    See Teran, Lisa St. Aubin de
    See also CA 118; 126; INT 126
Saint Birgitta of Sweden c.
    1303-1373 .... **CMLC 24**
Sainte-Beuve, Charles Augustin
    1804-1869 .... **NCLC 5**
Saint-Exupery, Antoine (Jean Baptiste
    Marie Roger) de 1900-1944 .... **TCLC 2,**
    56; DAM NOV; WLC
    See also CA 108; 132; CLR 10; DA3; DLB
    72; MAICYA; MTCW 1, 2; SATA 20
St. John, David
    See Hunt, E(verette) Howard, (Jr.)
Saint-John Perse
    See Leger, (Marie-Rene Auguste) Alexis
    Saint-Leger
Saintsbury, George (Edward Bateman)
    1845-1933 .... **TCLC 31**
    See also CA 160; DLB 57, 149
Sait Faik **TCLC 23**
    See also Abasiyanik, Sait Faik
Saki **TCLC 3; SSC 12**
    See also Munro, H(ector) H(ugh)
    See also MTCW 2
Sala, George Augustus **NCLC 46**
Saladin 1138-1193 .... **CMLC 38**
Salama, Hannu 1936- .... **CLC 18**
Salamanca, J(ack) R(ichard) 1922- .. **CLC 4,**
    15
    See also CA 25-28R
Salas, Floyd Francis 1931-
    See also CA 119; CAAS 27; CANR 44, 75;
    DAM MULT; DLB 82; HLC 2; HW 1, 2;
    MTCW 2
Sale, J. Kirkpatrick
    See Sale, Kirkpatrick
Sale, Kirkpatrick 1937- .... **CLC 68**
    See also CA 13-16R; CANR 10
Salinas, Luis Omar 1937- ..... **CLC 90; DAM**
    MULT; HLC 2
    See also CA 131; CANR 81; DLB 82; HW
    1, 2
Salinas (y Serrano), Pedro
    1891(?)-1951 .... **TCLC 17**
    See also CA 117; DLB 134

Salinger, J(erome) D(avid) 1919- .. **CLC 1, 3,**
    8, 12, 55, 56; DA; DAB; DAC; DAM
    MST, NOV, POP; SSC 2, 28; WLC
    See also AAYA 2; CA 5-8R; CANR 39;
    CDALB 1941-1968; CLR 18; DA3; DLB
    2, 102, 173; MAICYA; MTCW 1, 2;
    SATA 67
Salisbury, John
    See Caute, (John) David
Salter, James 1925- .... **CLC 7, 52, 59**
    See also CA 73-76; DLB 130
Saltus, Edgar (Everton) 1855-1921 . **TCLC 8**
    See also CA 105; DLB 202
Saltykov, Mikhail Evgrafovich
    1826-1889 .... **NCLC 16**
Samarakis, Antonis 1919- .... **CLC 5**
    See also CA 25-28R; CAAS 16; CANR 36
Sanchez, Florencio 1875-1910 .... **TCLC 37**
    See also CA 153; HW 1
Sanchez, Luis Rafael 1936- .... **CLC 23**
    See also CA 128; DLB 145; HW 1
Sanchez, Sonia 1934- .... **CLC 5, 116; BLC 3;**
    DAM MULT; PC 9
    See also BW 2, 3; CA 33-36R; CANR 24,
    49, 74; CLR 18; DA3; DLB 41; DLBD 8;
    MAICYA; MTCW 1, 2; SATA 22
Sand, George 1804-1876 ..... **NCLC 2, 42, 57;**
    DA; DAB; DAC; DAM MST, NOV;
    WLC
    See also DA3; DLB 119, 192
Sandburg, Carl (August) 1878-1967 . **CLC 1,**
    4, 10, 15, 35; DA; DAB; DAC; DAM
    MST, POET; PC 2; WLC
    See also AAYA 24; CA 5-8R; 25-28R;
    CANR 35; CDALB 1865-1917; DA3;
    DLB 17, 54; MAICYA; MTCW 1, 2;
    SATA 8
Sandburg, Charles
    See Sandburg, Carl (August)
Sandburg, Charles A.
    See Sandburg, Carl (August)
Sanders, (James) Ed(ward) 1939- ... **CLC 53;**
    DAM POET
    See also CA 13-16R; CAAS 21; CANR 13,
    44, 78; DLB 16
Sanders, Lawrence 1920-1998 .... **CLC 41;**
    DAM POP
    See also BEST 89:4; CA 81-84; 165; CANR
    33, 62; DA3; MTCW 1
Sanders, Noah
    See Blount, Roy (Alton), Jr.
Sanders, Winston P.
    See Anderson, Poul (William)
Sandoz, Mari(e Susette) 1896-1966 .. **CLC 28**
    See also CA 1-4R; 25-28R; CANR 17, 64;
    DLB 9, 212; MTCW 1, 2; SATA 5
Saner, Reg(inald Anthony) 1931- .... **CLC 9**
    See also CA 65-68
Sankara 788-820 .... **CMLC 32**
Sannazaro, Jacopo 1456(?)-1530 .... **LC 8**
Sansom, William 1912-1976 .... **CLC 2, 6;**
    DAM NOV; SSC 21
    See also CA 5-8R; 65-68; CANR 42; DLB
    139; MTCW 1
Santayana, George 1863-1952 .... **TCLC 40**
    See also CA 115; DLB 54, 71; DLBD 13
Santiago, Danny **CLC 33**
    See also James, Daniel (Lewis)
    See also DLB 122
Santmyer, Helen Hoover 1895-1986 . **CLC 33**
    See also CA 1-4R; 118; CANR 15, 33;
    DLBY 84; MTCW 1
Santoka, Taneda 1882-1940 .... **TCLC 72**
Santos, Bienvenido N(uqui)
    1911-1996 .... **CLC 22; DAM MULT**
    See also CA 101; 151; CANR 19, 46
Sapper **TCLC 44**
    See also McNeile, Herman Cyril

Scudery, Madeleine de 1607-1701 .. **LC 2, 58**
Scum
See Crumb, R(obert)
Scumbag, Little Bobby
See Crumb, R(obert)
Seabrook, John
See Hubbard, L(afayette) Ron(ald)
Sealy, I(rwin) Allan 1951- .... **CLC 55**
See also CA 136
Search, Alexander
See Pessoa, Fernando (Antonio Nogueira)
Sebastian, Lee
See Silverberg, Robert
Sebastian Owl
See Thompson, Hunter S(tockton)
Sebestyen, Ouida 1924- .... **CLC 30**
See also AAYA 8; CA 107; CANR 40; CLR
17; JRDA; MAICYA; SAAS 10; SATA
39
Secundus, H. Scriblerus
See Fielding, Henry
Sedges, John
See Buck, Pearl S(ydenstricker)
Sedgwick, Catharine Maria
1789-1867 .... **NCLC 19**
See also DLB 1, 74
Seelye, John (Douglas) 1931- .... **CLC 7**
See also CA 97-100; CANR 70; INT 97-
100
Seferiades, Giorgos Stylianou 1900-1971
See Seferis, George
See also CA 5-8R; 33-36R; CANR 5, 36;
MTCW 1
Seferis, George **CLC 5, 11**
See also Seferiades, Giorgos Stylianou
Segal, Erich (Wolf) 1937- . **CLC 3, 10; DAM
POP**
See also BEST 89:1; CA 25-28R; CANR
20, 36, 65; DLBY 86; INT CANR-20;
MTCW 1
Seger, Bob 1945- .... **CLC 35**
Seghers, Anna **CLC 7**
See also Radvanyi, Netty
See also DLB 69
Seidel, Frederick (Lewis) 1936- .... **CLC 18**
See also CA 13-16R; CANR 8; DLBY 84
Seifert, Jaroslav 1901-1986 .. **CLC 34, 44, 93**
See also CA 127; MTCW 1, 2
Sei Shonagon c. 966-1017(?) .... **CMLC 6**
Séjour, Victor 1817-1874 .... **DC 10**
See also DLB 50
Selby, Hubert, Jr. 1928- .... **CLC 1, 2, 4, 8;
SSC 20**
See also CA 13-16R; CANR 33, 85; DLB
2, 227
Selzer, Richard 1928- .... **CLC 74**
See also CA 65-68; CANR 14
Sembene, Ousmane
See Ousmane, Sembene
Senancour, Etienne Pivert de
1770-1846 .... **NCLC 16**
See also DLB 119
Sender, Ramon (Jose) 1902-1982 ...... **CLC 8;
DAM MULT; HLC 2**
See also CA 5-8R; 105; CANR 8; HW 1;
MTCW 1
Seneca, Lucius Annaeus c. 1-c.
65 .... **CMLC 6; DAM DRAM; DC 5**
See also DLB 211
Senghor, Leopold Sedar 1906- .... **CLC 54,
130; BLC 3; DAM MULT, POET; PC
25**
See also BW 2; CA 116; 125; CANR 47,
74; MTCW 1, 2
Senna, Danzy 1970- .... **CLC 119**
See also CA 169

Serling, (Edward) Rod(man)
1924-1975 .... **CLC 30**
See also AAYA 14; AITN 1; CA 162; 57-
60; DLB 26
Serna, Ramon Gomez de la
See Gomez de la Serna, Ramon
Serpieres
See Guillevic, (Eugene)
Service, Robert
See Service, Robert W(illiam)
See also DAB; DLB 92
Service, Robert W(illiam)
1874(?)-1958 .... **TCLC 15; DA; DAC;
DAM MST, POET; WLC**
See also Service, Robert
See also CA 115; 140; CANR 84; SATA 20
Seth, Vikram 1952- .... **CLC 43, 90; DAM
MULT**
See also CA 121; 127; CANR 50, 74; DA3;
DLB 120; INT 127; MTCW 2
Seton, Cynthia Propper 1926-1982 .. **CLC 27**
See also CA 5-8R; 108; CANR 7
Seton, Ernest (Evan) Thompson
1860-1946 .... **TCLC 31**
See also CA 109; CLR 59; DLB 92; DLBD
13; JRDA; SATA 18
Seton-Thompson, Ernest
See Seton, Ernest (Evan) Thompson
Settle, Mary Lee 1918- .... **CLC 19, 61**
See also CA 89-92; CAAS 1; CANR 44,
87; DLB 6; INT 89-92
Seuphor, Michel
See Arp, Jean
Sevigne, Marie (de Rabutin-Chantal)
Marquise de 1626-1696 .... **LC 11**
Sewall, Samuel 1652-1730 .... **LC 38**
See also DLB 24
Sexton, Anne (Harvey) 1928-1974 ..... **CLC 2,
4, 6, 8, 10, 15, 53, 123; DA; DAB;
DAC; DAM MST, POET; PC 2; WLC**
See also CA 1-4R; 53-56; CABS 2; CANR
3, 36; CDALB 1941-1968; DA3; DLB 5,
169; MTCW 1, 2; SATA 10
Shaara, Jeff 1952- .... **CLC 119**
See also CA 163
Shaara, Michael (Joseph, Jr.)
1929-1988 .... **CLC 15; DAM POP**
See also AITN 1; CA 102; 125; CANR 52,
85; DLBY 83
Shackleton, C. C.
See Aldiss, Brian W(ilson)
Shacochis, Bob **CLC 39**
See also Shacochis, Robert G.
Shacochis, Robert G. 1951-
See Shacochis, Bob
See also CA 119; 124; INT 124
Shaffer, Anthony (Joshua) 1926- ..... **CLC 19;
DAM DRAM**
See also CA 110; 116; DLB 13
Shaffer, Peter (Levin) 1926- .. **CLC 5, 14, 18,
37, 60; DAB; DAM DRAM, MST; DC
7**
See also CA 25-28R; CANR 25, 47, 74;
CDBLB 1960 to Present; DA3; DLB 13;
MTCW 1, 2
Shakey, Bernard
See Young, Neil
Shalamov, Varlam (Tikhonovich)
1907(?)-1982 .... **CLC 18**
See also CA 129; 105
Shamlu, Ahmad 1925- .... **CLC 10**
Shammas, Anton 1951- .... **CLC 55**
Shandling, Arline
See Berriault, Gina

Shange, Ntozake 1948- .... **CLC 8, 25, 38, 74,
126; BLC 3; DAM DRAM, MULT; DC
3**
See also AAYA 9; BW 2; CA 85-88; CABS
3; CANR 27, 48, 74; DA3; DLB 38;
MTCW 1, 2
Shanley, John Patrick 1950- .... **CLC 75**
See also CA 128; 133; CANR 83
Shapcott, Thomas W(illiam) 1935- .. **CLC 38**
See also CA 69-72; CANR 49, 83
Shapiro, Jane **CLC 76**
Shapiro, Karl (Jay) 1913- . **CLC 4, 8, 15, 53;
PC 25**
See also CA 1-4R; CAAS 6; CANR 1, 36,
66; DLB 48; MTCW 1, 2
Sharp, William 1855-1905 .... **TCLC 39**
See also CA 160; DLB 156
Sharpe, Thomas Ridley 1928-
See Sharpe, Tom
See also CA 114; 122; CANR 85; INT 122
Sharpe, Tom **CLC 36**
See also Sharpe, Thomas Ridley
See also DLB 14
Shaw, Bernard
See Shaw, George Bernard
See also BW 1; MTCW 2
Shaw, G. Bernard
See Shaw, George Bernard
Shaw, George Bernard 1856-1950 .. **TCLC 3,
9, 21, 45; DA; DAB; DAC; DAM
DRAM, MST; WLC**
See also Shaw, Bernard
See also CA 104; 128; CDBLB 1914-1945;
DA3; DLB 10, 57, 190; MTCW 1, 2
Shaw, Henry Wheeler 1818-1885 .. **NCLC 15**
See also DLB 11
Shaw, Irwin 1913-1984 .... **CLC 7, 23, 34;
DAM DRAM, POP**
See also AITN 1; CA 13-16R; 112; CANR
21; CDALB 1941-1968; DLB 6, 102;
DLBY 84; MTCW 1, 21
Shaw, Robert 1927-1978 .... **CLC 5**
See also AITN 1; CA 1-4R; 81-84; CANR
4; DLB 13, 14
Shaw, T. E.
See Lawrence, T(homas) E(dward)
Shawn, Wallace 1943- .... **CLC 41**
See also CA 112
Shea, Lisa 1953- .... **CLC 86**
See also CA 147
Sheed, Wilfrid (John Joseph) 1930- . **CLC 2,
4, 10, 53**
See also CA 65-68; CANR 30, 66; DLB 6;
MTCW 1, 2
Sheldon, Alice Hastings Bradley
1915(?)-1987
See Tiptree, James, Jr.
See also CA 108; 122; CANR 34; INT 108;
MTCW 1
Sheldon, John
See Bloch, Robert (Albert)
Shelley, Mary Wollstonecraft (Godwin)
1797-1851 ..... **NCLC 14, 59; DA; DAB;
DAC; DAM MST, NOV; WLC**
See also AAYA 20; CDBLB 1789-1832;
DA3; DLB 110, 116, 159, 178; SATA 29
Shelley, Percy Bysshe 1792-1822 .. **NCLC 18;
DA; DAB; DAC; DAM MST, POET;
PC 14; WLC**
See also CDBLB 1789-1832; DA3; DLB
96, 110, 158
Shepard, Jim 1956- .... **CLC 36**
See also CA 137; CANR 59; SATA 90
Shepard, Lucius 1947- .... **CLC 34**
See also CA 128; 141; CANR 81

Sinjohn, John
See Galsworthy, John
Sinyavsky, Andrei (Donatevich)
1925-1997 .... **CLC 8**
See also CA 85-88; 159
Sirin, V.
See Nabokov, Vladimir (Vladimirovich)
Sissman, L(ouis) E(dward)
1928-1976 .... **CLC 9, 18**
See also CA 21-24R; 65-68; CANR 13;
DLB 5
Sisson, C(harles) H(ubert) 1914- .... **CLC 8**
See also CA 1-4R; CAAS 3; CANR 3, 48,
84; DLB 27
Sitwell, Dame Edith 1887-1964 ..... **CLC 2, 9,
67; DAM POET; PC 3**
See also CA 9-12R; CANR 35; CDBLB
1945-1960; DLB 20; MTCW 1, 2
Siwaarmill, H. P.
See Sharp, William
Sjoewall, Maj 1935- .... **CLC 7**
See also Sjowall, Maj
See also CA 65-68; CANR 73
Sjowall, Maj
See Sjoewall, Maj
Skelton, John 1463-1529 .... **PC 25**
Skelton, Robin 1925-1997 .... **CLC 13**
See also AITN 2; CA 5-8R; 160; CAAS 5;
CANR 28, 89; DLB 27, 53
Skolimowski, Jerzy 1938- .... **CLC 20**
See also CA 128
Skram, Amalie (Bertha)
1847-1905 .... **TCLC 25**
See also CA 165
Skvorecky, Josef (Vaclav) 1924- ...... **CLC 15,
39, 69; DAC; DAM NOV**
See also CA 61-64; CAAS 1; CANR 10,
34, 63; DA3; MTCW 1, 2
Slade, Bernard CLC 11, 46
See also Newbound, Bernard Slade
See also CAAS 9; DLB 53
Slaughter, Carolyn 1946- .... **CLC 56**
See also CA 85-88; CANR 85
Slaughter, Frank G(ill) 1908- .... **CLC 29**
See also AITN 2; CA 5-8R; CANR 5, 85;
INT CANR-5
Slavitt, David R(ytman) 1935- ..... **CLC 5, 14**
See also CA 21-24R; CAAS 3; CANR 41,
83; DLB 5, 6
Slesinger, Tess 1905-1945 .... **TCLC 10**
See also CA 107; DLB 102
Slessor, Kenneth 1901-1971 .... **CLC 14**
See also CA 102; 89-92
Slowacki, Juliusz 1809-1849 .... **NCLC 15**
Smart, Christopher 1722-1771 .. **LC 3; DAM
POET; PC 13**
See also DLB 109
Smart, Elizabeth 1913-1986 .... **CLC 54**
See also CA 81-84; 118; DLB 88
Smiley, Jane (Graves) 1949- ...... **CLC 53, 76;
DAM POP**
See also CA 104; CANR 30, 50, 74; DA3;
DLB 227; INT CANR-30
Smith, A(rthur) J(ames) M(arshall)
1902-1980 .... **CLC 15; DAC**
See also CA 1-4R; 102; CANR 4; DLB 88
Smith, Adam 1723-1790 .... **LC 36**
See also DLB 104
Smith, Alexander 1829-1867 .... **NCLC 59**
See also DLB 32, 55
Smith, Anna Deavere 1950- .... **CLC 86**
See also CA 133
Smith, Betty (Wehner) 1896-1972 .... **CLC 19**
See also CA 5-8R; 33-36R; DLBY 82;
SATA 6
Smith, Charlotte (Turner)
1749-1806 .... **NCLC 23**
See also DLB 39, 109

Smith, Clark Ashton 1893-1961 .... **CLC 43**
See also CA 143; CANR 81; MTCW 2
Smith, Dave CLC 22, 42
See also Smith, David (Jeddie)
See also CAAS 7; DLB 5
Smith, David (Jeddie) 1942-
See Smith, Dave
See also CA 49-52; CANR 1, 59; DAM
POET
Smith, Florence Margaret 1902-1971
See Smith, Stevie
See also CA 17-18; 29-32R; CANR 35;
CAP 2; DAM POET; MTCW 1, 2
Smith, Iain Crichton 1928-1998 .... **CLC 64**
See also CA 21-24R; 171; DLB 40, 139
Smith, John 1580(?)-1631 .... **LC 9**
See also DLB 24, 30
Smith, Johnston
See Crane, Stephen (Townley)
Smith, Joseph, Jr. 1805-1844 .... **NCLC 53**
Smith, Lee 1944- .... **CLC 25, 73**
See also CA 114; 119; CANR 46; DLB 143;
DLBY 83; INT 119
Smith, Martin
See Smith, Martin Cruz
Smith, Martin Cruz 1942- .... **CLC 25; DAM
MULT, POP**
See also BEST 89:4; CA 85-88; CANR 6,
23, 43, 65; INT CANR-23; MTCW 2;
NNAL
Smith, Mary-Ann Tirone 1944- .... **CLC 39**
See also CA 118; 136
Smith, Patti 1946- .... **CLC 12**
See also CA 93-96; CANR 63
Smith, Pauline (Urmson)
1882-1959 .... **TCLC 25**
See also DLB 225
Smith, Rosamond
See Oates, Joyce Carol
Smith, Sheila Kaye
See Kaye-Smith, Sheila
Smith, Stevie CLC 3, 8, 25, 44; PC 12
See also Smith, Florence Margaret
See also DLB 20; MTCW 2
Smith, Wilbur (Addison) 1933- .... **CLC 33**
See also CA 13-16R; CANR 7, 46, 66;
MTCW 1, 2
Smith, William Jay 1918- .... **CLC 6**
See also CA 5-8R; CANR 44; DLB 5; MAI-
CYA; SAAS 22; SATA 2, 68
Smith, Woodrow Wilson
See Kuttner, Henry
Smolenskin, Peretz 1842-1885 .... **NCLC 30**
Smollett, Tobias (George) 1721-1771 ... **LC 2,
46**
See also CDBLB 1660-1789; DLB 39, 104
Snodgrass, W(illiam) D(e Witt)
1926- .... **CLC 2, 6, 10, 18, 68; DAM
POET**
See also CA 1-4R; CANR 6, 36, 65, 85;
DLB 5; MTCW 1, 2
Snow, C(harles) P(ercy) 1905-1980 ... **CLC 1,
4, 6, 9, 13, 19; DAM NOV**
See also CA 5-8R; 101; CANR 28; CDBLB
1945-1960; DLB 15, 77; DLBD 17;
MTCW 1, 2
Snow, Frances Compton
See Adams, Henry (Brooks)
Snyder, Gary (Sherman) 1930- . **CLC 1, 2, 5,
9, 32, 120; DAM POET; PC 21**
See also CA 17-20R; CANR 30, 60; DA3;
DLB 5, 16, 165, 212; MTCW 2
Snyder, Zilpha Keatley 1927- .... **CLC 17**
See also AAYA 15; CA 9-12R; CANR 38;
CLR 31; JRDA; MAICYA; SAAS 2;
SATA 1, 28, 75, 110; SATA-Essay 112
Soares, Bernardo
See Pessoa, Fernando (Antonio Nogueira)

Sobh, A.
See Shamlu, Ahmad
Sobol, Joshua CLC 60
Socrates 469B.C.-399B.C. .... **CMLC 27**
Soderberg, Hjalmar 1869-1941 ...... **TCLC 39**
Sodergran, Edith (Irene)
See Soedergran, Edith (Irene)
Soedergran, Edith (Irene)
1892-1923 .... **TCLC 31**
Softly, Edgar
See Lovecraft, H(oward) P(hillips)
Softly, Edward
See Lovecraft, H(oward) P(hillips)
Sokolov, Raymond 1941- .... **CLC 7**
See also CA 85-88
Solo, Jay
See Ellison, Harlan (Jay)
Sologub, Fyodor TCLC 9
See also Teternikov, Fyodor Kuzmich
Solomons, Ikey Esquir
See Thackeray, William Makepeace
Solomos, Dionysios 1798-1857 .... **NCLC 15**
Solwoska, Mara
See French, Marilyn
Solzhenitsyn, Aleksandr I(sayevich)
1918- .. **CLC 1, 2, 4, 7, 9, 10, 18, 26, 34,
78, 134; DA; DAB; DAC; DAM MST,
NOV; SSC 32; WLC**
See also AITN 1; CA 69-72; CANR 40, 65;
DA3; MTCW 1, 2
Somers, Jane
See Lessing, Doris (May)
Somerville, Edith 1858-1949 .... **TCLC 51**
See also DLB 135
Somerville & Ross
See Martin, Violet Florence; Somerville,
Edith
Sommer, Scott 1951- .... **CLC 25**
See also CA 106
Sondheim, Stephen (Joshua) 1930- . **CLC 30,
39; DAM DRAM**
See also AAYA 11; CA 103; CANR 47, 68
Song, Cathy 1955- .... **PC 21**
See also CA 154; DLB 169
Sontag, Susan 1933- .... **CLC 1, 2, 10, 13, 31,
105; DAM POP**
See also CA 17-20R; CANR 25, 51, 74;
DA3; DLB 2, 67; MTCW 1, 2
Sophocles 496(?)B.C.-406(?)B.C. .... **CMLC 2;
DA; DAB; DAC; DAM DRAM, MST;
DC 1; WLCS**
See also DA3; DLB 176
Sordello 1189-1269 .... **CMLC 15**
Sorel, Georges 1847-1922 .... **TCLC 91**
See also CA 118
Sorel, Julia
See Drexler, Rosalyn
Sorrentino, Gilbert 1929- .. **CLC 3, 7, 14, 22,
40**
See also CA 77-80; CANR 14, 33; DLB 5,
173; DLBY 80; INT CANR-14
Soto, Gary 1952- .... **CLC 32, 80; DAM
MULT; HLC 2; PC 28**
See also AAYA 10; CA 119; 125; CANR
50, 74; CLR 38; DLB 82; HW 1, 2; INT
125; JRDA; MTCW 2; SATA 80
Soupault, Philippe 1897-1990 .... **CLC 68**
See also CA 116; 147; 131
Souster, (Holmes) Raymond 1921- .... **CLC 5,
14; DAC; DAM POET**
See also CA 13-16R; CAAS 14; CANR 13,
29, 53; DA3; DLB 88; SATA 63
Southern, Terry 1924(?)-1995 .... **CLC 7**
See also CA 1-4R; 150; CANR 1, 55; DLB
2
Southey, Robert 1774-1843 .... **NCLC 8**
See also DLB 93, 107, 142; SATA 54

Theroux, Paul (Edward) 1941- ..... **CLC 5, 8, 11, 15, 28, 46; DAM POP**
See also AAYA 28; BEST 89:4; CA 33-36R; CANR 20, 45, 74; CDALBS; DA3; DLB 2; MTCW 1, 2; SATA 44, 109

Thesen, Sharon 1946- .... **CLC 56**
See also CA 163

Thevenin, Denis
See Duhamel, Georges

Thibault, Jacques Anatole Francois 1844-1924
See France, Anatole
See also CA 106; 127; DAM NOV; DA3; MTCW 1, 2

Thiele, Colin (Milton) 1920- .... **CLC 17**
See also CA 29-32R; CANR 12, 28, 53; CLR 27; MAICYA; SAAS 2; SATA 14, 72

Thomas, Audrey (Callahan) 1935- .... **CLC 7, 13, 37, 107; SSC 20**
See also AITN 2; CA 21-24R; CAAS 19; CANR 36, 58; DLB 60; MTCW 1

Thomas, Augustus 1857-1934 .... **TCLC 97**

Thomas, D(onald) M(ichael) 1935- . **CLC 13, 22, 31, 132**
See also CA 61-64; CAAS 11; CANR 17, 45, 75; CDBLB 1960 to Present; DA3; DLB 40, 207; INT CANR-17; MTCW 1, 2

Thomas, Dylan (Marlais) 1914-1953 ... **TCLC 1, 8, 45; DA; DAB; DAC; DAM DRAM, MST, POET; PC 2; SSC 3; WLC**
See also CA 104; 120; CANR 65; CDBLB 1945-1960; DA3; DLB 13, 20, 139; MTCW 1, 2; SATA 60

Thomas, (Philip) Edward 1878-1917 .... **TCLC 10; DAM POET**
See also CA 106; 153; DLB 98

Thomas, Joyce Carol 1938- .... **CLC 35**
See also AAYA 12; BW 2; CA 113; 116; CANR 48; CLR 19; DLB 33; INT 116; JRDA; MAICYA; MTCW 1, 2; SAAS 7; SATA 40, 78

Thomas, Lewis 1913-1993 .... **CLC 35**
See also CA 85-88; 143; CANR 38, 60; MTCW 1, 2

Thomas, M. Carey 1857-1935 .... **TCLC 89**

Thomas, Paul
See Mann, (Paul) Thomas

Thomas, Piri 1928- .... **CLC 17; HLCS 2**
See also CA 73-76; HW 1

Thomas, R(onald) S(tuart) 1913- ...... **CLC 6, 13, 48; DAB; DAM POET**
See also CA 89-92; CAAS 4; CANR 30; CDBLB 1960 to Present; DLB 27; MTCW 1

Thomas, Ross (Elmore) 1926-1995 .. **CLC 39**
See also CA 33-36R; 150; CANR 22, 63

Thompson, Francis Clegg
See Mencken, H(enry) L(ouis)

Thompson, Francis Joseph 1859-1907 .... **TCLC 4**
See also CA 104; CDBLB 1890-1914; DLB 19

Thompson, Hunter S(tockton) 1939- ... **CLC 9, 17, 40, 104; DAM POP**
See also BEST 89:1; CA 17-20R; CANR 23, 46, 74, 77; DA3; DLB 185; MTCW 1, 2

Thompson, James Myers
See Thompson, Jim (Myers)

Thompson, Jim (Myers) 1906-1977(?) .... **CLC 69**
See also CA 140; DLB 226

Thompson, Judith **CLC 39**

Thomson, James 1700-1748 ... **LC 16, 29, 40; DAM POET**
See also DLB 95

Thomson, James 1834-1882 .... **NCLC 18; DAM POET**
See also DLB 35

Thoreau, Henry David 1817-1862 .. **NCLC 7, 21, 61; DA; DAB; DAC; DAM MST; PC 30; WLC**
See also CDALB 1640-1865; DA3; DLB 1, 223

Thornton, Hall
See Silverberg, Robert

Thucydides c. 455B.C.-399B.C. ..... **CMLC 17**
See also DLB 176

Thumboo, Edwin 1933- .... **PC 30**

Thurber, James (Grover) 1894-1961 .... **CLC 5, 11, 25, 125; DA; DAB; DAC; DAM DRAM, MST, NOV; SSC 1**
See also CA 73-76; CANR 17, 39; CDALB 1929-1941; DA3; DLB 4, 11, 22, 102; MAICYA; MTCW 1, 2; SATA 13

Thurman, Wallace (Henry) 1902-1934 .... **TCLC 6; BLC 3; DAM MULT**
See also BW 1, 3; CA 104; 124; CANR 81; DLB 51

Tibullus, Albius c. 54B.C.-c. 19B.C. .... **CMLC 36**
See also DLB 211

Ticheburn, Cheviot
See Ainsworth, William Harrison

Tieck, (Johann) Ludwig 1773-1853 .... **NCLC 5, 46; SSC 31**
See also DLB 90

Tiger, Derry
See Ellison, Harlan (Jay)

Tilghman, Christopher 1948(?)- .... **CLC 65**
See also CA 159

Tillich, Paul (Johannes) 1886-1965 .... **CLC 131**
See also CA 5-8R; 25-28R; CANR 33; MTCW 1, 2

Tillinghast, Richard (Williford) 1940- .... **CLC 29**
See also CA 29-32R; CAAS 23; CANR 26, 51

Timrod, Henry 1828-1867 .... **NCLC 25**
See also DLB 3

Tindall, Gillian (Elizabeth) 1938- ...... **CLC 7**
See also CA 21-24R; CANR 11, 65

Tiptree, James, Jr. **CLC 48, 50**
See also Sheldon, Alice Hastings Bradley
See also DLB 8

Titmarsh, Michael Angelo
See Thackeray, William Makepeace

Tocqueville, Alexis (Charles Henri Maurice Clerel, Comte) de 1805-1859 . **NCLC 7, 63**

Tolkien, J(ohn) R(onald) R(euel) 1892-1973 .. **CLC 1, 2, 3, 8, 12, 38; DA; DAB; DAC; DAM MST, NOV, POP; WLC**
See also AAYA 10; AITN 1; CA 17-18; 45-48; CANR 36; CAP 2; CDBLB 1914-1945; CLR 56; DA3; DLB 15, 160; JRDA; MAICYA; MTCW 1, 2; SATA 2, 32, 100; SATA-Obit 24

Toller, Ernst 1893-1939 .... **TCLC 10**
See also CA 107; 186; DLB 124

Tolson, M. B.
See Tolson, Melvin B(eaunorus)

Tolson, Melvin B(eaunorus) 1898(?)-1966 .... **CLC 36, 105; BLC 3; DAM MULT, POET**
See also BW 1, 3; CA 124; 89-92; CANR 80; DLB 48, 76

Tolstoi, Aleksei Nikolaevich
See Tolstoy, Alexey Nikolaevich

Tolstoy, Alexey Nikolaevich 1882-1945 .... **TCLC 18**
See also CA 107; 158

Tolstoy, Count Leo
See Tolstoy, Leo (Nikolaevich)

Tolstoy, Leo (Nikolaevich) 1828-1910 .. **TCLC 4, 11, 17, 28, 44, 79; DA; DAB; DAC; DAM MST, NOV; SSC 9, 30; WLC**
See also CA 104; 123; DA3; SATA 26

Tomasi di Lampedusa, Giuseppe 1896-1957
See Lampedusa, Giuseppe (Tomasi) di
See also CA 111

Tomlin, Lily **CLC 17**
See also Tomlin, Mary Jean

Tomlin, Mary Jean 1939(?)-
See Tomlin, Lily
See also CA 117

Tomlinson, (Alfred) Charles 1927- .... **CLC 2, 4, 6, 13, 45; DAM POET; PC 17**
See also CA 5-8R; CANR 33; DLB 40

Tomlinson, H(enry) M(ajor) 1873-1958 .... **TCLC 71**
See also CA 118; 161; DLB 36, 100, 195

Tonson, Jacob
See Bennett, (Enoch) Arnold

Toole, John Kennedy 1937-1969 ..... **CLC 19, 64**
See also CA 104; DLBY 81; MTCW 2

Toomer, Jean 1894-1967 .... **CLC 1, 4, 13, 22; BLC 3; DAM MULT; PC 7; SSC 1; WLCS**
See also Pinchback, Eugene; Toomer, Eugene; Toomer, Eugene Pinchback; Toomer, Nathan Jean; Toomer, Nathan Pinchback
See also BW 1; CA 85-88; CDALB 1917-1929; DA3; DLB 45, 51; MTCW 1, 2

Torley, Luke
See Blish, James (Benjamin)

Tornimparte, Alessandra
See Ginzburg, Natalia

Torre, Raoul della
See Mencken, H(enry) L(ouis)

Torrence, Ridgely 1874-1950 .... **TCLC 97**
See also DLB 54

Torrey, E(dwin) Fuller 1937- .... **CLC 34**
See also CA 119; CANR 71

Torsvan, Ben Traven
See Traven, B.

Torsvan, Benno Traven
See Traven, B.

Torsvan, Berick Traven
See Traven, B.

Torsvan, Berwick Traven
See Traven, B.

Torsvan, Bruno Traven
See Traven, B.

Torsvan, Traven
See Traven, B.

Tournier, Michel (Edouard) 1924- .... **CLC 6, 23, 36, 95**
See also CA 49-52; CANR 3, 36, 74; DLB 83; MTCW 1, 2; SATA 23

Tournimparte, Alessandra
See Ginzburg, Natalia

Towers, Ivar
See Kornbluth, C(yril) M.

Towne, Robert (Burton) 1936(?)- ..... **CLC 87**
See also CA 108; DLB 44

Townsend, Sue **CLC 61**
See also Townsend, Susan Elaine
See also AAYA 28; SATA 55, 93; SATA-Brief 48

Townsend, Susan Elaine 1946-
See Townsend, Sue
See also CA 119; 127; CANR 65; DAB; DAC; DAM MST

Vaihinger, Hans 1852-1933 .... **TCLC 71**
See also CA 116; 166

Valdez, Luis (Miguel) 1940- .. **CLC 84; DAM MULT; DC 10; HLC 2**
See also CA 101; CANR 32, 81; DLB 122; HW 1

Valenzuela, Luisa 1938- .... **CLC 31, 104; DAM MULT; HLCS 2; SSC 14**
See also CA 101; CANR 32, 65; DLB 113; HW 1, 2

Valera y Alcala-Galiano, Juan 1824-1905 .... **TCLC 10**
See also CA 106

Valery, (Ambroise) Paul (Toussaint Jules) 1871-1945 ... **TCLC 4, 15; DAM POET; PC 9**
See also CA 104; 122; DA3; MTCW 1, 2

Valle-Inclan, Ramon (Maria) del 1866-1936 .... **TCLC 5; DAM MULT; HLC 2**
See also CA 106; 153; CANR 80; DLB 134; HW 2

Vallejo, Antonio Buero
See Buero Vallejo, Antonio

Vallejo, Cesar (Abraham) 1892-1938 .. **TCLC 3, 56; DAM MULT; HLC 2**
See also CA 105; 153; HW 1

Valles, Jules 1832-1885 .... **NCLC 71**
See also DLB 123

Vallette, Marguerite Eymery 1860-1953 .... **TCLC 67**
See also CA 182; DLB 123, 192

Valle Y Pena, Ramon del
See Valle-Inclan, Ramon (Maria) del

Van Ash, Cay 1918- .... **CLC 34**

Vanbrugh, Sir John 1664-1726 .... **LC 21; DAM DRAM**
See also DLB 80

Van Campen, Karl
See Campbell, John W(ood, Jr.)

Vance, Gerald
See Silverberg, Robert

Vance, Jack CLC 35
See also Vance, John Holbrook
See also DLB 8

Vance, John Holbrook 1916-
See Queen, Ellery; Vance, Jack
See also CA 29-32R; CANR 17, 65; MTCW 1

Van Den Bogarde, Derek Jules Gaspard Ulric Niven 1921-1999 .... **CLC 14**
See also CA 77-80; 179; DLB 19

Vandenburgh, Jane CLC 59
See also CA 168

Vanderhaeghe, Guy 1951- .... **CLC 41**
See also CA 113; CANR 72

van der Post, Laurens (Jan) 1906-1996 .... **CLC 5**
See also CA 5-8R; 155; CANR 35; DLB 204

van de Wetering, Janwillem 1931- ... **CLC 47**
See also CA 49-52; CANR 4, 62, 90

Van Dine, S. S. TCLC 23
See also Wright, Willard Huntington

Van Doren, Carl (Clinton) 1885-1950 .... **TCLC 18**
See also CA 111; 168

Van Doren, Mark 1894-1972 .... **CLC 6, 10**
See also CA 1-4R; 37-40R; CANR 3; DLB 45; MTCW 1, 2

Van Druten, John (William) 1901-1957 .... **TCLC 2**
See also CA 104; 161; DLB 10

Van Duyn, Mona (Jane) 1921- ...... **CLC 3, 7, 63, 116; DAM POET**
See also CA 9-12R; CANR 7, 38, 60; DLB 5

Van Dyne, Edith
See Baum, L(yman) Frank

van Itallie, Jean-Claude 1936- .... **CLC 3**
See also CA 45-48; CAAS 2; CANR 1, 48; DLB 7

van Ostaijen, Paul 1896-1928 .... **TCLC 33**
See also CA 163

Van Peebles, Melvin 1932- .... **CLC 2, 20; DAM MULT**
See also BW 2, 3; CA 85-88; CANR 27, 67, 82

Vansittart, Peter 1920- .... **CLC 42**
See also CA 1-4R; CANR 3, 49, 90

Van Vechten, Carl 1880-1964 .... **CLC 33**
See also CA 183; 89-92; DLB 4, 9, 51

Van Vogt, A(lfred) E(lton) 1912-2000 .... **CLC 1**
See also CA 21-24R; CANR 28; DLB 8; SATA 14

Varda, Agnes 1928- .... **CLC 16**
See also CA 116; 122

Vargas Llosa, (Jorge) Mario (Pedro) 1936- .... **CLC 3, 6, 9, 10, 15, 31, 42, 85; DA; DAB; DAC; DAM MST, MULT, NOV; HLC 2**
See also CA 73-76; CANR 18, 32, 42, 67; DA3; DLB 145; HW 1, 2; MTCW 1, 2

Vasiliu, Gheorghe 1881-1957
See Bacovia, George
See also CA 123; DLB 220

Vassa, Gustavus
See Equiano, Olaudah

Vassilikos, Vassilis 1933- .... **CLC 4, 8**
See also CA 81-84; CANR 75

Vaughan, Henry 1621-1695 .... **LC 27**
See also DLB 131

Vaughn, Stephanie CLC 62

Vazov, Ivan (Minchov) 1850-1921 . **TCLC 25**
See also CA 121; 167; DLB 147

Veblen, Thorstein B(unde) 1857-1929 .... **TCLC 31**
See also CA 115; 165

Vega, Lope de 1562-1635 .... **LC 23; HLCS 2**

Venison, Alfred
See Pound, Ezra (Weston Loomis)

Verdi, Marie de
See Mencken, H(enry) L(ouis)

Verdu, Matilde
See Cela, Camilo Jose

Verga, Giovanni (Carmelo) 1840-1922 .... **TCLC 3; SSC 21**
See also CA 104; 123

Vergil 70B.C.-19B.C. .... **CMLC 9, 40; DA; DAB; DAC; DAM MST, POET; PC 12; WLCS**
See also Virgil
See also DA3; DLB 211

Verhaeren, Emile (Adolphe Gustave) 1855-1916 .... **TCLC 12**
See also CA 109

Verlaine, Paul (Marie) 1844-1896 .. **NCLC 2, 51; DAM POET; PC 2**

Verne, Jules (Gabriel) 1828-1905 ... **TCLC 6, 52**
See also AAYA 16; CA 110; 131; DA3; DLB 123; JRDA; MAICYA; SATA 21

Very, Jones 1813-1880 .... **NCLC 9**
See also DLB 1

Vesaas, Tarjei 1897-1970 .... **CLC 48**
See also CA 29-32R

Vialis, Gaston
See Simenon, Georges (Jacques Christian)

Vian, Boris 1920-1959 .... **TCLC 9**
See also CA 106; 164; DLB 72; MTCW 2

Viaud, (Louis Marie) Julien 1850-1923
See Loti, Pierre
See also CA 107

Vicar, Henry
See Felsen, Henry Gregor

Vicker, Angus
See Felsen, Henry Gregor

Vidal, Gore 1925- ...... **CLC 2, 4, 6, 8, 10, 22, 33, 72; DAM NOV, POP**
See also AITN 1; BEST 90:2; CA 5-8R; CANR 13, 45, 65; CDALBS; DA3; DLB 6, 152; INT CANR-13; MTCW 1, 2

Viereck, Peter (Robert Edwin) 1916- .... **CLC 4; PC 27**
See also CA 1-4R; CANR 1, 47; DLB 5

Vigny, Alfred (Victor) de 1797-1863 .. **NCLC 7; DAM POET; PC 26**
See also DLB 119, 192

Vilakazi, Benedict Wallet 1906-1947 .... **TCLC 37**
See also CA 168

Villa, Jose Garcia 1904-1997 .... **PC 22**
See also CA 25-28R; CANR 12

Villarreal, Jose Antonio 1924-
See also CA 133; DAM MULT; DLB 82; HLC 2; HW 1

Villaurrutia, Xavier 1903-1950 ...... **TCLC 80**
See also HW 1

Villehardouin 1150(?)-1218(?) .... **CMLC 38**

Villiers de l'Isle Adam, Jean Marie Mathias Philippe Auguste, Comte de 1838-1889 .... **NCLC 3; SSC 14**
See also DLB 123

Villon, Francois 1431-1463(?) .... **PC 13**
See also DLB 208

Vine, Barbara CLC 50
See also Rendell, Ruth (Barbara)
See also BEST 90:4

Vinge, Joan (Carol) D(ennison) 1948- .... **CLC 30; SSC 24**
See also AAYA 32; CA 93-96; CANR 72; SATA 36, 113

Violis, G.
See Simenon, Georges (Jacques Christian)

Viramontes, Helena Maria 1954-
See also CA 159; DLB 122; HLCS 2; HW 2

Virgil 70B.C.-19B.C.
See Vergil

Visconti, Luchino 1906-1976 .... **CLC 16**
See also CA 81-84; 65-68; CANR 39

Vittorini, Elio 1908-1966 .... **CLC 6, 9, 14**
See also CA 133; 25-28R

Vivekananda, Swami 1863-1902 .... **TCLC 88**

Vizenor, Gerald Robert 1934- .... **CLC 103; DAM MULT**
See also CA 13-16R; CAAS 22; CANR 5, 21, 44, 67; DLB 175, 227; MTCW 2; NNAL

Vizinczey, Stephen 1933- .... **CLC 40**
See also CA 128; INT 128

Vliet, R(ussell) G(ordon) 1929-1984 .... **CLC 22**
See also CA 37-40R; 112; CANR 18

Vogau, Boris Andreyevich 1894-1937(?)
See Pilnyak, Boris
See also CA 123

Vogel, Paula A(nne) 1951- .... **CLC 76**
See also CA 108

Voigt, Cynthia 1942- .... **CLC 30**
See also AAYA 3, 30; CA 106; CANR 18, 37, 40; CLR 13, 48; INT CANR-18; JRDA; MAICYA; SATA 48, 79, 116; SATA-Brief 33

Voigt, Ellen Bryant 1943- .... **CLC 54**
See also CA 69-72; CANR 11, 29, 55; DLB 120

Voinovich, Vladimir (Nikolaevich) 1932- .... **CLC 10, 49**
See also CA 81-84; CAAS 12; CANR 33, 67; MTCW 1

Washington, Alex
See Harris, Mark

Washington, Booker T(aliaferro)
 1856-1915 ...... **TCLC 10; BLC 3; DAM MULT**
 See also BW 1; CA 114; 125; DA3; SATA 28

Washington, George 1732-1799 .... **LC 25**
 See also DLB 31

Wassermann, (Karl) Jakob
 1873-1934 .... **TCLC 6**
 See also CA 104; 163, DLB 66

Wasserstein, Wendy 1950- .. **CLC 32, 59, 90; DAM DRAM; DC 4**
 See also CA 121; 129; CABS 3; CANR 53, 75; DA3; DLB 228; INT 129; MTCW 2; SATA 94

Waterhouse, Keith (Spencer) 1929- . **CLC 47**
 See also CA 5-8R; CANR 38, 67; DLB 13, 15; MTCW 1, 2

Waters, Frank (Joseph) 1902-1995 .. **CLC 88**
 See also CA 5-8R; 149; CAAS 13; CANR 3, 18, 63; DLB 212; DLBY 86

Waters, Roger 1944- .... **CLC 35**

Watkins, Frances Ellen
See Harper, Frances Ellen Watkins

Watkins, Gerrold
See Malzberg, Barry N(athaniel)

Watkins, Gloria Jean 1952(?)-
See hooks, bell
 See also BW 2; CA 143; CANR 87; MTCW 2; SATA 115

Watkins, Paul 1964- .... **CLC 55**
 See also CA 132; CANR 62

Watkins, Vernon Phillips
 1906-1967 .... **CLC 43**
 See also CA 9-10; 25-28R; CAP 1; DLB 20

Watson, Irving S.
See Mencken, H(enry) L(ouis)

Watson, John H.
See Farmer, Philip Jose

Watson, Richard F.
See Silverberg, Robert

Waugh, Auberon (Alexander) 1939- .. **CLC 7**
 See also CA 45-48; CANR 6, 22, 92; DLB 14, 194

Waugh, Evelyn (Arthur St. John)
 1903-1966 .. **CLC 1, 3, 8, 13, 19, 27, 44, 107; DA; DAB; DAC; DAM MST, NOV, POP; SSC 41; WLC**
 See also CA 85-88; 25-28R; CANR 22; CD-BLB 1914-1945; DA3; DLB 15, 162, 195; MTCW 1, 2

Waugh, Harriet 1944- .... **CLC 6**
 See also CA 85-88; CANR 22

Ways, C. R.
See Blount, Roy (Alton), Jr.

Waystaff, Simon
See Swift, Jonathan

Webb, Beatrice (Martha Potter)
 1858-1943 .... **TCLC 22**
 See also CA 117; 162; DLB 190

Webb, Charles (Richard) 1939- .... **CLC 7**
 See also CA 25-28R

Webb, James H(enry), Jr. 1946- ...... **CLC 22**
 See also CA 81-84

Webb, Mary Gladys (Meredith)
 1881-1927 .... **TCLC 24**
 See also CA 182; 123; DLB 34

Webb, Mrs. Sidney
See Webb, Beatrice (Martha Potter)

Webb, Phyllis 1927- .... **CLC 18**
 See also CA 104; CANR 23; DLB 53

Webb, Sidney (James) 1859-1947 .. **TCLC 22**
 See also CA 117; 163; DLB 190

Webber, Andrew Lloyd CLC 21
 See also Lloyd Webber, Andrew

Weber, Lenora Mattingly
 1895-1971 .... **CLC 12**
 See also CA 19-20; 29-32R; CAP 1; SATA 2; SATA-Obit 26

Weber, Max 1864-1920 .... **TCLC 69**
 See also CA 109

Webster, John 1579(?)-1634(?) ... **LC 33; DA; DAB; DAC; DAM DRAM, MST; DC 2; WLC**
 See also CDBLB Before 1660; DLB 58

Webster, Noah 1758-1843 .... **NCLC 30**
 See also DLB 1, 37, 42, 43, 73

Wedekind, (Benjamin) Frank(lin)
 1864-1918 .... **TCLC 7; DAM DRAM**
 See also CA 104; 153; DLB 118

Weidman, Jerome 1913-1998 .... **CLC 7**
 See also AITN 2; CA 1-4R; 171; CANR 1; DLB 28

Weil, Simone (Adolphine)
 1909-1943 .... **TCLC 23**
 See also CA 117; 159; MTCW 2

Weininger, Otto 1880-1903 .... **TCLC 84**

Weinstein, Nathan
See West, Nathanael

Weinstein, Nathan von Wallenstein
See West, Nathanael

Weir, Peter (Lindsay) 1944- .... **CLC 20**
 See also CA 113; 123

Weiss, Peter (Ulrich) 1916-1982 .. **CLC 3, 15, 51; DAM DRAM**
 See also CA 45-48; 106; CANR 3; DLB 69, 124

Weiss, Theodore (Russell) 1916- ... **CLC 3, 8, 14**
 See also CA 9-12R; CAAS 2; CANR 46; DLB 5

Welch, (Maurice) Denton
 1915-1948 .... **TCLC 22**
 See also CA 121; 148

Welch, James 1940- ..... **CLC 6, 14, 52; DAM MULT, POP**
 See also CA 85-88; CANR 42, 66; DLB 175; NNAL

Weldon, Fay 1931- . **CLC 6, 9, 11, 19, 36, 59, 122; DAM POP**
 See also CA 21-24R; CANR 16, 46, 63; CDBLB 1960 to Present; DLB 14, 194; INT CANR-16; MTCW 1, 2

Wellek, Rene 1903-1995 .... **CLC 28**
 See also CA 5-8R; 150; CAAS 7; CANR 8; DLB 63; INT CANR-8

Weller, Michael 1942- .... **CLC 10, 53**
 See also CA 85-88

Weller, Paul 1958- .... **CLC 26**

Wellershoff, Dieter 1925- .... **CLC 46**
 See also CA 89-92; CANR 16, 37

Welles, (George) Orson 1915-1985 .. **CLC 20, 80**
 See also CA 93-96; 117

Wellman, John McDowell 1945-
See Wellman, Mac
 See also CA 166

Wellman, Mac 1945- .... **CLC 65**
 See also Wellman, John McDowell; Wellman, John McDowell

Wellman, Manly Wade 1903-1986 ... **CLC 49**
 See also CA 1-4R; 118; CANR 6, 16, 44; SATA 6; SATA-Obit 47

Wells, Carolyn 1869(?)-1942 .... **TCLC 35**
 See also CA 113; 185; DLB 11

Wells, H(erbert) G(eorge)
 1866-1946 . **TCLC 6, 12, 19; DA; DAB; DAC; DAM MST, NOV; SSC 6; WLC**
 See also AAYA 18; CA 110; 121; CDBLB 1914-1945; CLR 64; DA3; DLB 34, 70, 156, 178; MTCW 1, 2; SATA 20

Wells, Rosemary 1943- .... **CLC 12**
 See also AAYA 13; CA 85-88; CANR 48; CLR 16; MAICYA; SAAS 1; SATA 18, 69, 114

Welty, Eudora 1909- ...... **CLC 1, 2, 5, 14, 22, 33, 105; DA; DAB; DAC; DAM MST, NOV; SSC 1, 27; WLC**
 See also CA 9-12R; CABS 1; CANR 32, 65; CDALB 1941-1968; DA3; DLB 2, 102, 143; DLBD 12; DLBY 87; MTCW 1, 2

Wen I-to 1899-1946 .... **TCLC 28**

Wentworth, Robert
See Hamilton, Edmond

Werfel, Franz (Viktor) 1890-1945 ... **TCLC 8**
 See also CA 104; 161; DLB 81, 124

Wergeland, Henrik Arnold
 1808-1845 .... **NCLC 5**

Wersba, Barbara 1932- .... **CLC 30**
 See also AAYA 2, 30; CA 29-32R; 182; CAAE 182; CANR 16, 38; CLR 3; DLB 52; JRDA; MAICYA; SAAS 2; SATA 1, 58; SATA-Essay 103

Wertmueller, Lina 1928- .... **CLC 16**
 See also CA 97-100; CANR 39, 78

Wescott, Glenway 1901-1987 .. **CLC 13; SSC 35**
 See also CA 13-16R; 121; CANR 23, 70; DLB 4, 9, 102

Wesker, Arnold 1932- ... **CLC 3, 5, 42; DAB; DAM DRAM**
 See also CA 1-4R; CAAS 7; CANR 1, 33; CDBLB 1960 to Present; DLB 13; MTCW 1

Wesley, Richard (Errol) 1945- .... **CLC 7**
 See also BW 1; CA 57-60; CANR 27; DLB 38

Wessel, Johan Herman 1742-1785 .... **LC 7**

West, Anthony (Panther)
 1914-1987 .... **CLC 50**
 See also CA 45-48; 124; CANR 3, 19; DLB 15

West, C. P.
See Wodehouse, P(elham) G(renville)

West, Cornel (Ronald) 1953- .... **CLC 134; BLCS**
 See also CA 144; CANR 91

West, (Mary) Jessamyn 1902-1984 ... **CLC 7, 17**
 See also CA 9-12R; 112; CANR 27; DLB 6; DLBY 84; MTCW 1, 2; SATA-Obit 37

West, Morris L(anglo) 1916-1999 ..... **CLC 6, 33**
 See also CA 5-8R; CANR 24, 49, 64; MTCW 1, 2

West, Nathanael 1903-1940 .... **TCLC 1, 14, 44; SSC 16**
 See also CA 104; 125; CDALB 1929-1941; DA3; DLB 4, 9, 28; MTCW 1, 2

West, Owen
See Koontz, Dean R(ay)

West, Paul 1930- .... **CLC 7, 14, 96**
 See also CA 13-16R; CAAS 7; CANR 22, 53, 76, 89; DLB 14; INT CANR-22; MTCW 2

West, Rebecca 1892-1983 ... **CLC 7, 9, 31, 50**
 See also CA 5-8R; 109; CANR 19; DLB 36; DLBY 83; MTCW 1, 2

Westall, Robert (Atkinson)
 1929-1993 .... **CLC 17**
 See also AAYA 12; CA 69-72; 141; CANR 18, 68; CLR 13; JRDA; MAICYA; SAAS 2; SATA 23, 69; SATA-Obit 75

Westermarck, Edward 1862-1939 . **TCLC 87**

Westlake, Donald E(dwin) 1933- .... **CLC 7, 33; DAM POP**
 See also CA 17-20R; CAAS 13; CANR 16, 44, 65; INT CANR-16; MTCW 2

Williams, William Carlos
1883-1963 .... **CLC 1, 2, 5, 9, 13, 22, 42, 67; DA; DAB; DAC; DAM MST, POET; PC 7; SSC 31**
See also CA 89-92; CANR 34; CDALB 1917-1929; DA3; DLB 4, 16, 54, 86; MTCW 1, 2

Williamson, David (Keith) 1942- ..... **CLC 56**
See also CA 103; CANR 41

Williamson, Ellen Douglas 1905-1984
See Douglas, Ellen
See also CA 17-20R; 114; CANR 39

Williamson, Jack CLC 29
See also Williamson, John Stewart
See also CAAS 8; DLB 8

Williamson, John Stewart 1908-
See Williamson, Jack
See also CA 17-20R; CANR 23, 70

Willie, Frederick
See Lovecraft, H(oward) P(hillips)

Willingham, Calder (Baynard, Jr.)
1922-1995 .... **CLC 5, 51**
See also CA 5-8R; 147; CANR 3; DLB 2, 44; MTCW 1

Willis, Charles
See Clarke, Arthur C(harles)

Willy
See Colette, (Sidonie-Gabrielle)

Willy, Colette
See Colette, (Sidonie-Gabrielle)

Wilson, A(ndrew) N(orman) 1950- .. **CLC 33**
See also CA 112; 122; DLB 14, 155, 194; MTCW 2

Wilson, Angus (Frank Johnstone)
1913-1991 . **CLC 2, 3, 5, 25, 34; SSC 21**
See also CA 5-8R; 134; CANR 21; DLB 15, 139, 155; MTCW 1, 2

Wilson, August 1945- ... **CLC 39, 50, 63, 118; BLC 3; DA; DAB; DAC; DAM DRAM, MST, MULT; DC 2; WLCS**
See also AAYA 16; BW 2, 3; CA 115; 122; CANR 42, 54, 76; DA3; DLB 228; MTCW 1, 2

Wilson, Brian 1942- .... **CLC 12**

Wilson, Colin 1931- .... **CLC 3, 14**
See also CA 1-4R; CAAS 5; CANR 1, 22, 33, 77; DLB 14, 194; MTCW 1

Wilson, Dirk
See Pohl, Frederik

Wilson, Edmund 1895-1972 .. **CLC 1, 2, 3, 8, 24**
See also CA 1-4R; 37-40R; CANR 1, 46; DLB 63; MTCW 1, 2

Wilson, Ethel Davis (Bryant)
1888(?)-1980 .... **CLC 13; DAC; DAM POET**
See also CA 102; DLB 68; MTCW 1

Wilson, John 1785-1854 .... **NCLC 5**

Wilson, John (Anthony) Burgess 1917-1993
See Burgess, Anthony
See also CA 1-4R; 143; CANR 2, 46; DAC; DAM NOV; DA3; MTCW 1, 2

Wilson, Lanford 1937- .... **CLC 7, 14, 36; DAM DRAM**
See also CA 17-20R; CABS 3; CANR 45; DLB 7

Wilson, Robert M. 1944- .... **CLC 7, 9**
See also CA 49-52; CANR 2, 41; MTCW 1

Wilson, Robert McLiam 1964- .... **CLC 59**
See also CA 132

Wilson, Sloan 1920- .... **CLC 32**
See also CA 1-4R; CANR 1, 44

Wilson, Snoo 1948- .... **CLC 33**
See also CA 69-72

Wilson, William S(mith) 1932- .... **CLC 49**
See also CA 81-84

Wilson, (Thomas) Woodrow
1856-1924 .... **TCLC 79**
See also CA 166; DLB 47

Winchilsea, Anne (Kingsmill) Finch Counte
1661-1720
See Finch, Anne

Windham, Basil
See Wodehouse, P(elham) G(renville)

Wingrove, David (John) 1954- .... **CLC 68**
See also CA 133

Winnemucca, Sarah 1844-1891 ..... **NCLC 79**

Winstanley, Gerrard 1609-1676 .... **LC 52**

Wintergreen, Jane
See Duncan, Sara Jeannette

Winters, Janet Lewis CLC 41
See Lewis, Janet
See also DLBY 87

Winters, (Arthur) Yvor 1900-1968 .... **CLC 4, 8, 32**
See also CA 11-12; 25-28R; CAP 1; DLB 48; MTCW 1

Winterson, Jeanette 1959- .... **CLC 64; DAM POP**
See also CA 136; CANR 58; DA3; DLB 207; MTCW 2

Winthrop, John 1588-1649 .... **LC 31**
See also DLB 24, 30

Wirth, Louis 1897-1952 .... **TCLC 92**

Wiseman, Frederick 1930- .... **CLC 20**
See also CA 159

Wister, Owen 1860-1938 .... **TCLC 21**
See also CA 108; 162; DLB 9, 78, 186; SATA 62

Witkacy
See Witkiewicz, Stanislaw Ignacy

Witkiewicz, Stanislaw Ignacy
1885-1939 .... **TCLC 8**
See also CA 105; 162

Wittgenstein, Ludwig (Josef Johann)
1889-1951 .... **TCLC 59**
See also CA 113; 164; MTCW 2

Wittig, Monique 1935(?)- .... **CLC 22**
See also CA 116; 135; DLB 83

Wittlin, Jozef 1896-1976 .... **CLC 25**
See also CA 49-52; 65-68; CANR 3

Wodehouse, P(elham) G(renville)
1881-1975 .... **CLC 1, 2, 5, 10, 22; DAB; DAC; DAM NOV; SSC 2**
See also AITN 2; CA 45-48; 57-60; CANR 3, 33; CDBLB 1914-1945; DA3; DLB 34, 162; MTCW 1, 2; SATA 22

Woiwode, L.
See Woiwode, Larry (Alfred)

Woiwode, Larry (Alfred) 1941- ... **CLC 6, 10**
See also CA 73-76; CANR 16; DLB 6; INT CANR-16

Wojciechowska, Maia (Teresa)
1927- .... **CLC 26**
See also AAYA 8; CA 9-12R; 183; CAAE 183; CANR 4, 41; CLR 1; JRDA; MAICYA; SAAS 1; SATA 1, 28, 83; SATA-Essay 104

Wojtyla, Karol
See John Paul II, Pope

Wolf, Christa 1929- .... **CLC 14, 29, 58**
See also CA 85-88; CANR 45; DLB 75; MTCW 1

Wolfe, Gene (Rodman) 1931- .... **CLC 25; DAM POP**
See also CA 57-60; CAAS 9; CANR 6, 32, 60; DLB 8; MTCW 2

Wolfe, George C. 1954- .... **CLC 49; BLCS**
See also CA 149

Wolfe, Thomas (Clayton)
1900-1938 ...... **TCLC 4, 13, 29, 61; DA; DAB; DAC; DAM MST, NOV; SSC 33; WLC**
See also CA 104; 132; CDALB 1929-1941; DA3; DLB 9, 102; DLBD 2, 16; DLBY 85, 97; MTCW 1, 2

Wolfe, Thomas Kennerly, Jr. 1930-
See Wolfe, Tom
See also CA 13-16R; CANR 9, 33, 70; DAM POP; DA3; DLB 185; INT CANR-9; MTCW 1, 2

Wolfe, Tom CLC 1, 2, 9, 15, 35, 51
See also Wolfe, Thomas Kennerly, Jr.
See also AAYA 8; AITN 2; BEST 89:1; DLB 152

Wolff, Geoffrey (Ansell) 1937- .... **CLC 41**
See also CA 29-32R; CANR 29, 43, 78

Wolff, Sonia
See Levitin, Sonia (Wolff)

Wolff, Tobias (Jonathan Ansell)
1945- .... **CLC 39, 64**
See also AAYA 16; BEST 90:2; CA 114; 117; CAAS 22; CANR 54, 76; DA3; DLB 130; INT 117; MTCW 2

Wolfram von Eschenbach c. 1170-c.
1220 .... **CMLC 5**
See also DLB 138

Wolitzer, Hilma 1930- .... **CLC 17**
See also CA 65-68; CANR 18, 40; INT CANR-18; SATA 31

Wollstonecraft, Mary 1759-1797 ..... **LC 5, 50**
See also CDBLB 1789-1832; DLB 39, 104, 158

Wonder, Stevie CLC 12
See also Morris, Steveland Judkins

Wong, Jade Snow 1922- .... **CLC 17**
See also CA 109; CANR 91; SATA 112

Woodberry, George Edward
1855-1930 .... **TCLC 73**
See also CA 165; DLB 71, 103

Woodcott, Keith
See Brunner, John (Kilian Houston)

Woodruff, Robert W.
See Mencken, H(enry) L(ouis)

Woolf, (Adeline) Virginia
1882-1941 .. **TCLC 1, 5, 20, 43, 56, 101; DA; DAB; DAC; DAM MST, NOV; SSC 7; WLC**
See also Woolf, Virginia Adeline
See also CA 104; 130; CANR 64; CDBLB 1914-1945; DA3; DLB 36, 100, 162; DLBD 10; MTCW 1

Woolf, Virginia Adeline
See Woolf, (Adeline) Virginia
See also MTCW 2

Woollcott, Alexander (Humphreys)
1887-1943 .... **TCLC 5**
See also CA 105; 161; DLB 29

Woolrich, Cornell 1903-1968 .... **CLC 77**
See also Hopley-Woolrich, Cornell George

Woolson, Constance Fenimore
1840-1894 .... **NCLC 82**
See also DLB 12, 74, 189, 221

Wordsworth, Dorothy 1771-1855 .. **NCLC 25**
See also DLB 107

Wordsworth, William 1770-1850 .. **NCLC 12, 38; DA; DAB; DAC; DAM MST, POET; PC 4; WLC**
See also CDBLB 1789-1832; DA3; DLB 93, 107

Wouk, Herman 1915- ... **CLC 1, 9, 38; DAM NOV, POP**
See also CA 5-8R; CANR 6, 33, 67; CDALBS; DA3; DLBY 82; INT CANR-6; MTCW 1, 2

Wright, Charles (Penzel, Jr.) 1935- .. **CLC 6, 13, 28, 119**
See also CA 29-32R; CAAS 7; CANR 23, 36, 62, 88; DLB 165; DLBY 82; MTCW 1, 2

Wright, Charles Stevenson 1932- ... **CLC 49; BLC 3; DAM MULT, POET**
See also BW 1; CA 9-12R; CANR 26; DLB 33

Wright, Frances 1795-1852 .... NCLC 74
See also DLB 73
Wright, Frank Lloyd 1867-1959 .... TCLC 95
See also AAYA 33; CA 174
Wright, Jack R.
See Harris, Mark
Wright, James (Arlington)
1927-1980 .... CLC 3, 5, 10, 28; DAM
POET
See also AITN 2; CA 49-52; 97-100; CANR
4, 34, 64; CDALBS; DLB 5, 169; MTCW
1, 2
Wright, Judith (Arundell)
1915-2000 .... CLC 11, 53; PC 14
See also CA 13-16R; CANR 31, 76; MTCW
1, 2; SATA 14
Wright, L(aurali) R. 1939- .... CLC 44
See also CA 138
Wright, Richard (Nathaniel)
1908-1960 .... CLC 1, 3, 4, 9, 14, 21, 48,
74; BLC 3; DA; DAB; DAC; DAM
MST, MULT, NOV; SSC 2; WLC
See also AAYA 5; BW 1; CA 108; CANR
64; CDALB 1929-1941; DA3; DLB 76,
102; DLBD 2; MTCW 1, 2
Wright, Richard B(ruce) 1937- .... CLC 6
See also CA 85-88; DLB 53
Wright, Rick 1945- .... CLC 35
Wright, Rowland
See Wells, Carolyn
Wright, Stephen 1946- .... CLC 33
Wright, Willard Huntington 1888-1939
See Van Dine, S. S.
See also CA 115; DLBD 16
Wright, William 1930- .... CLC 44
See also CA 53-56; CANR 7, 23
Wroth, LadyMary 1587-1653(?) .... LC 30
See also DLB 121
Wu Ch'eng-en 1500(?)-1582(?) .... LC 7
Wu Ching-tzu 1701-1754 .... LC 2
Wurlitzer, Rudolph 1938(?)- .... CLC 2, 4, 15
See also CA 85-88; DLB 173
Wyatt, Thomas c. 1503-1542 .... PC 27
See also DLB 132
Wycherley, William 1641-1715 ...... LC 8, 21;
DAM DRAM
See also CDBLB 1660-1789; DLB 80
Wylie, Elinor (Morton Hoyt)
1885-1928 .... TCLC 8; PC 23
See also CA 105; 162; DLB 9, 45
Wylie, Philip (Gordon) 1902-1971 ... CLC 43
See also CA 21-22; 33-36R; CAP 2; DLB 9
Wyndham, John CLC 19
See also Harris, John (Wyndham Parkes
Lucas) Beynon
Wyss, Johann David Von
1743-1818 .... NCLC 10
See also JRDA; MAICYA; SATA 29; SATA-
Brief 27
Xenophon c. 430B.C.-c. 354B.C. ... CMLC 17
See also DLB 176
Yakumo Koizumi
See Hearn, (Patricio) Lafcadio (Tessima
Carlos)
Yamamoto, Hisaye 1921- .... SSC 34; DAM
MULT
Yanez, Jose Donoso
See Donoso (Yanez), Jose
Yanovsky, Basile S.
See Yanovsky, V(assily) S(emenovich)
Yanovsky, V(assily) S(emenovich)
1906-1989 .... CLC 2, 18
See also CA 97-100; 129
Yates, Richard 1926-1992 .... CLC 7, 8, 23
See also CA 5-8R; 139; CANR 10, 43; DLB
2; DLBY 81, 92; INT CANR-10
Yeats, W. B.
See Yeats, William Butler

Yeats, William Butler 1865-1939 .... TCLC 1,
11, 18, 31, 93; DA; DAB; DAC; DAM
DRAM, MST, POET; PC 20; WLC
See also CA 104; 127; CANR 45; CDBLB
1890-1914; DA3; DLB 10, 19, 98, 156;
MTCW 1, 2
Yehoshua, A(braham) B. 1936- .. CLC 13, 31
See also CA 33-36R; CANR 43, 90
Yellow Bird
See Ridge, John Rollin
Yep, Laurence Michael 1948- .... CLC 35
See also AAYA 5, 31; CA 49-52; CANR 1,
46, 92; CLR 3, 17, 54; DLB 52; JRDA;
MAICYA; SATA 7, 69
Yerby, Frank G(arvin) 1916-1991 . CLC 1, 7,
22; BLC 3; DAM MULT
See also BW 1, 3; CA 9-12R; 136; CANR
16, 52; DLB 76; INT CANR-16; MTCW
1
Yesenin, Sergei Alexandrovich
See Esenin, Sergei (Alexandrovich)
Yevtushenko, Yevgeny (Alexandrovich)
1933- .. CLC 1, 3, 13, 26, 51, 126; DAM
POET
See also CA 81-84; CANR 33, 54; MTCW
1
Yezierska, Anzia 1885(?)-1970 .... CLC 46
See also CA 126; 89-92; DLB 28, 221;
MTCW 1
Yglesias, Helen 1915- .... CLC 7, 22
See also CA 37-40R; CAAS 20; CANR 15,
65; INT CANR-15; MTCW 1
Yokomitsu, Riichi 1898-1947 .... TCLC 47
See also CA 170
Yonge, Charlotte (Mary)
1823-1901 .... TCLC 48
See also CA 109; 163; DLB 18, 163; SATA
17
York, Jeremy
See Creasey, John
York, Simon
See Heinlein, Robert A(nson)
Yorke, Henry Vincent 1905-1974 ..... CLC 13
See also Green, Henry
See also CA 85-88; 49-52
Yosano Akiko 1878-1942 .... TCLC 59; PC 11
See also CA 161
Yoshimoto, Banana CLC 84
See also Yoshimoto, Mahoko
Yoshimoto, Mahoko 1964-
See Yoshimoto, Banana
See also CA 144
Young, Al(bert James) 1939- . CLC 19; BLC
3; DAM MULT
See also BW 2, 3; CA 29-32R; CANR 26,
65; DLB 33
Young, Andrew (John) 1885-1971 ...... CLC 5
See also CA 5-8R; CANR 7, 29
Young, Collier
See Bloch, Robert (Albert)
Young, Edward 1683-1765 .... LC 3, 40
See also DLB 95
Young, Marguerite (Vivian)
1909-1995 .... CLC 82
See also CA 13-16; 150; CAP 1
Young, Neil 1945- .... CLC 17
See also CA 110
Young Bear, Ray A. 1950- ..... CLC 94; DAM
MULT
See also CA 146; DLB 175; NNAL
Yourcenar, Marguerite 1903-1987 ... CLC 19,
38, 50, 87; DAM NOV
See also CA 69-72; CANR 23, 60; DLB 72;
DLBY 88; MTCW 1, 2
Yuan, Chu 340(?)B.C.-278(?)B.C. . CMLC 36
Yurick, Sol 1925- .... CLC 6
See also CA 13-16R; CANR 25

Zabolotsky, Nikolai Alekseevich
1903-1958 .... TCLC 52
See also CA 116; 164
Zagajewski, Adam 1945- .... PC 27
See also CA 186
Zamiatin, Yevgenii
See Zamyatin, Evgeny Ivanovich
Zamora, Bernice (B. Ortiz) 1938- .. CLC 89;
DAM MULT; HLC 2
See also CA 151; CANR 80; DLB 82; HW
1, 2
Zamyatin, Evgeny Ivanovich
1884-1937 .... TCLC 8, 37
See also CA 105; 166
Zangwill, Israel 1864-1926 .... TCLC 16
See also CA 109; 167; DLB 10, 135, 197
Zappa, Francis Vincent, Jr. 1940-1993
See Zappa, Frank
See also CA 108; 143; CANR 57
Zappa, Frank CLC 17
See also Zappa, Francis Vincent, Jr.
Zaturenska, Marya 1902-1982 ...... CLC 6, 11
See also CA 13-16R; 105; CANR 22
Zeami 1363-1443 .... DC 7
Zelazny, Roger (Joseph) 1937-1995 . CLC 21
See also AAYA 7; CA 21-24R; 148; CANR
26, 60; DLB 8; MTCW 1, 2; SATA 57;
SATA-Brief 39
Zhdanov, Andrei Alexandrovich
1896-1948 .... TCLC 18
See also CA 117; 167
Zhukovsky, Vasily (Andreevich)
1783-1852 .... NCLC 35
See also DLB 205
Ziegenhagen, Eric CLC 55
Zimmer, Jill Schary
See Robinson, Jill
Zimmerman, Robert
See Dylan, Bob
Zindel, Paul 1936- ..... CLC 6, 26; DA; DAB;
DAC; DAM DRAM, MST, NOV; DC 5
See also AAYA 2; CA 73-76; CANR 31,
65; CDALBS; CLR 3, 45; DA3; DLB 7,
52; JRDA; MAICYA; MTCW 1, 2; SATA
16, 58, 102
Zinov'Ev, A. A.
See Zinoviev, Alexander (Aleksandrovich)
Zinoviev, Alexander (Aleksandrovich)
1922- .... CLC 19
See also CA 116; 133; CAAS 10
Zoilus
See Lovecraft, H(oward) P(hillips)
Zola, Emile (Edouard Charles Antoine)
1840-1902 .... TCLC 1, 6, 21, 41; DA;
DAB; DAC; DAM MST, NOV; WLC
See also CA 104; 138; DA3; DLB 123
Zoline, Pamela 1941- .... CLC 62
See also CA 161
Zoroaster 628(?)B.C.-551(?)B.C. ... CMLC 40
Zorrilla y Moral, Jose 1817-1893 .... NCLC 6
Zoshchenko, Mikhail (Mikhailovich)
1895-1958 .... TCLC 15; SSC 15
See also CA 115; 160
Zuckmayer, Carl 1896-1977 .... CLC 18
See also CA 69-72; DLB 56, 124
Zuk, Georges
See Skelton, Robin
Zukofsky, Louis 1904-1978 ... CLC 1, 2, 4, 7,
11, 18; DAM POET; PC 11
See also CA 9-12R; 77-80; CANR 39; DLB
5, 165; MTCW 1
Zweig, Paul 1935-1984 .... CLC 34, 42
See also CA 85-88; 113
Zweig, Stefan 1881-1942 .... TCLC 17
See also CA 112; 170; DLB 81, 118
Zwingli, Huldreich 1484-1531 .... LC 37
See also DLB 179

Literary Criticism Series
Cumulative Topic Index

This index lists all topic entries in Gale's *Classical and Medieval Literature Criticism, Contemporary Literary Criticism, Literature Criticism from 1400 to 1800, Nineteenth-Century Literature Criticism,* and *Twentieth-Century Literary Criticism.*

TCLC Cumulative Nationality Index

Prishvin, Mikhail　**75**
Remizov, Aleksei (Mikhailovich)　**27**
Shestov, Lev　**56**
Sologub, Fyodor　**9**
Stalin, Joseph　**92**
Tolstoy, Alexey Nikolaevich　**18**
Tolstoy, Leo (Nikolaevich)　**4, 11, 17, 28, 44, 79**
Trotsky, Leon　**22**
Tsvetaeva (Efron), Marina (Ivanovna)　**7, 35**
Zabolotsky, Nikolai Alekseevich　**52**
Zamyatin, Evgeny Ivanovich　**8, 37**
Zhdanov, Andrei Alexandrovich　**18**
Zoshchenko, Mikhail (Mikhailovich)　**15**

SCOTTISH

Barrie, J(ames) M(atthew)　**2**
Bridie, James　**3**
Brown, George Douglas　**28**
Buchan, John　**41**
Cunninghame Graham, Robert (Gallnigad) Bontine　**19**
Davidson, John　**24**
Frazer, J(ames) G(eorge)　**32**
Gibbon, Lewis Grassic　**4**
Lang, Andrew　**16**
MacDonald, George　**9**
Muir, Edwin　**2, 87**
Sharp, William　**39**
Tey, Josephine　**14**

SOUTH AFRICAN

Bosman, Herman Charles　**49**
Campbell, (Ignatius) Roy (Dunnachie)　**5**
Mqhayi, S(amuel) E(dward) K(rune Loliwe)　**25**

Plaatje, Sol(omon) T(shekisho)　**73**
Schreiner, Olive (Emilie Albertina)　**9**
Smith, Pauline (Urmson)　**25**
Vilakazi, Benedict Wallet　**37**

SPANISH

Alas (y Urena), Leopoldo (Enrique Garcia)　**29**
Barea, Arturo　**14**
Baroja (y Nessi), Pio　**8**
Benavente (y Martinez), Jacinto　**3**
Blasco Ibanez, Vicente　**12**
Echegaray (y Eizaguirre), Jose (Maria Waldo)　**4**
Garcia Lorca, Federico　**1, 7, 49**
Jimenez (Mantecon), Juan Ramon　**4**
Machado (y Ruiz), Antonio　**3**
Martinez Sierra, Gregorio　**6**
Martinez Sierra, Maria (de la O'LeJarraga)　**6**
Miro (Ferrer), Gabriel (Francisco Victor)　**5**
Ortega y Gasset, Jose　**9**
Pereda (y Sanchez de Porrua), Jose Maria de　**16**
Perez Galdos, Benito　**27**
Ramoacn y Cajal, Santiago　**93**
Salinas (y Serrano), Pedro　**17**
Unamuno (y Jugo), Miguel de　**2, 9**
Valera y Alcala-Galiano, Juan　**10**
Valle-Inclan, Ramon (Maria) del　**5**

SWEDISH

Bengtsson, Frans (Gunnar)　**48**
Dagerman, Stig (Halvard)　**17**
Ekelund, Vilhelm　**75**
Heidenstam, (Carl Gustaf) Verner von　**5**

Key, Ellen　**65**
Lagerloef, Selma (Ottiliana Lovisa)　**4, 36**
Soderberg, Hjalmar　**39**
Strindberg, (Johan) August　**1, 8, 21, 47**

SWISS

Ramuz, Charles-Ferdinand　**33**
Rod, Edouard　**52**
Saussure, Ferdinand de　**49**
Spitteler, Carl (Friedrich Georg)　**12**
Walser, Robert　**18**

SYRIAN

Gibran, Kahlil　**1, 9**

TURKISH

Sait Faik　**23**

UKRAINIAN

Aleichem, Sholom　**1, 35**
Bialik, Chaim Nachman　**25**

URUGUAYAN

Quiroga, Horacio (Sylvestre)　**20**
Sanchez, Florencio　**37**

WELSH

Davies, William Henry　**5**
Evans, Caradoc　**85**
Lewis, Alun　**3**
Machen, Arthur　**4**
Thomas, Dylan (Marlais)　**1, 8, 45**

Nationality Index

TCLC-100 Title Index